Churchill's Cold War

Churchill's Cold War

The Politics of Personal Diplomacy

Klaus Larres

Yale University Press
New Haven and London

For information about this and other Yale University Press publications, please contact:
U.S. Office: sales.press@yale.edu
Europe Office: sales@yaleup.co.uk

Set in Minion by Northern Phototypesetting Co. Ltd, Bolton, Lancs
Printed in Great Britain by St Edmundsbury Press, Suffolk

Library of Congress Cataloging-in-Publication Data

Larres, Klaus
  Churchill's Cold War: the politics of personal diplomacy / Klaus Larres.
    p. cm.
Includes bibliographical references and index.
  ISBN 0-300-09438-8 (alk. paper)
  1. Churchill, Winston, Sir, 1874–1965—Contributions in diplomacy. 2.
Great Britain—Foreign relations—1945–1964. 3. Great Britain—Foreign
relations—1936–1945. 4. World politics—1945–1955. 5. World
politics—1900–1945. 6. Cold War. I. Title.
DA588 .L364 .2002
327 .41'0092—dc21   2002000830

A catalogue record for this book is available from the British Library

10   9   8   7   6   5   4   3   2   1

For Patricia

Contents

Preface

There is no lack of literature on Churchill. In the year 2001 alone two major biographies – stimulating volumes by Geoffrey Best and Roy Jenkins – appeared; in addition a number of more specialized studies were published. Nevertheless, with the exception of a few scholarly accounts, in particular John W. Young's learned 1996 book, a good earlier study by Steven Lambakis, and a few other works as well as my own writing on Churchill (listed in the bibliography including a 1995 book published in German under the auspices of the German Historical Institute in London), Churchill's 'summitry' and his personal diplomacy have not received the attention they deserve. Yet both were typical of and fundamental to his policies throughout his long political life and, in particular, during his last decade in politics, the early Cold War years.

Churchill's personal diplomacy from 1908 to 1955, including his thinking and pronouncements on European integration during and after the Second World War, warrant a much more intensive treatment than they have received so far. In particular his attempts to use summit policy to achieve a détente in East-West relations, decrease the risk of a nuclear third world war and, not least, maintain Britain's great power status offer fascinating insights into Churchill's political thinking. After all, his ambition to defuse East-West tension developed long before the inauguration of the era of superpower détente which characterized the 1970s and the second half of the 1980s and eventually led to the end of the Cold War in 1989/90. This book argues that Churchill's Cold War policies need to be taken much more seriously, to be seen as imaginative and constructive proposals to overcome the East-West conflict and prevent its escalation.

Churchill is a most fascinating, stimulating and indeed controversial person to think and write about, and I have never regretted devoting a considerable period of time to studying and analysing his policies. With this presentation of

my thinking on Churchill, as it has developed and evolved over the years, I hope
to contribute to modifying and altering the still widespread perception of
Churchill as a simplistic cold warrior. He never was such a person. His thinking
on the East-West conflict and his controversial proposals on how to overcome
the Cold War often stubbornly ignored the fact that power relations had
changed, in particular that the USA and the Soviet Union were dominant influences in the post-war world and that Britain's role had diminished to that of a
mere junior partner to America. But Churchill's thinking and political activities
as Leader of the Opposition after 1945 and as Prime Minister in the early to
mid-1950s certainly displayed a much more sophisticated understanding of the
necessity to negotiate and enter into compromise solutions with the ideological
and military enemy than his 'cold warrior' image allows for.

Any author involved in a major research project is indebted to a plethora of
archivists and librarians kind enough to support his work by providing
valuable information and making research resources available. It is impossible
to thank everyone. But special thanks are due to the archivists at the Public
Record Office in Kew, London; the National Archives in Washington, DC; the
Truman and Eisenhower Presidential Libraries in Independence, Missouri
and Abilene, Kansas; Princeton University Archive; Birmingham University
Library; Churchill College, Cambridge; Trinity College, Cambridge; the House
of Lords Records Office; King's College, London; and the Bodleian Library,
Oxford. Without the resources of the excellent library of the London School of
Economics and Political Science, the British Library, the Library of Congress
(including their manuscript division), the very good library of the German
Historical Institute in London, the Institute of Historical Research in London
and, not least, the main library of Queen's University Belfast, this work could
not have been undertaken.

At Queen's University I wish to thank in particular Prof. Bob Eccleshall
and Elizabeth Childs of the School of Politics and assistant librarian Norma
Menabney for their valuable support. I am also most grateful for having
received several travel grants from Queen's University Belfast, the British
Academy, the German Historical Institute in Washington, DC, and its former
director Prof. Detlef Junker of the University of Heidelberg.

Friends and relatives have had to endure my preoccupation with Churchill's
policies for rather longer than expected. I wish to thank everyone, and, in
particular, my wife Patricia for her patience, love and unflagging support. My
parents Ännie and Albert (†) Larres have also been a constant source of great
encouragement and understanding for which I am genuinely grateful.

A heartfelt thank you is also due to George Radcliffe for his very helpful
advice; and also to Prof. Mick Cox of the University of Wales at Aberystwyth,

Prof. Hans-Jürgen Schröder of the University of Giessen, Prof. Rolf Steininger of the University of Innsbruck, Prof. Ronald Pruessen of the University of Toronto, Prof. Mark Kramer of Harvard University, Prof. Lothar Kettenacker of the German Historical Institute in London, and, not least Prof. John Young of the University of Nottingham for their long-standing support and advice. Of particular help to my thinking on Churchill's role in international history and politics were the many discussions with senior and junior colleagues and the papers I gave and attended at the annual conferences of that most inspiring and active scholarly organization, the Society of Historians of American Foreign Relations (SHAFR) in the United States.

I also wish to use the opportunity to express a word of heartfelt gratitude to Prof. Donald Cameron Watt, my old teacher at the LSE in the early 1990s, to Prof. Peter Alter of the University of Duisberg and to Prof. Fraser Harbutt of Emory University whose support and advice over the years have been invaluable. I would also like to thank Prof. Hermann Wellenreuther of the University of Göttingen and Prof. Erich Angermann (†) who first introduced me to the joys (and labours) of history at Cologne University in the 1980s. I am also much obliged to the anonymous referees for their constructive recommendations on the first draft of the manuscript. Last but not least I am most grateful for the support and wise words of Robert Baldock, Candida Brazil and Diana Yeh at Yale University Press in London who did their best to help this work come to fruition. Naturally responsibility for any remaining mistakes and flaws is mine.

Klaus Larres
Belfast, January 2002

Introduction

This book deals with one of the central aspects of Churchill's political career: his belief in the power of personal diplomacy. From the time of his first tentative involvement in international politics in 1908 until his retirement as Prime Minister and one of the world's foremost statesmen in 1955, Churchill was fascinated by personal summit diplomacy. He always wished to be personally involved in dramatic high-level negotiations. Throughout his long political life Winston Churchill was inclined to personalize international politics: he believed that relations between nation states could be positively influenced by 'individual sentiment and human affection'.[1] In the years after 1945, this became his credo.

Churchill's lifelong beliefs in the value of personal diplomacy can be traced back to his early political career in the years before the First World War. These beliefs would also play a dominant role in his 'Big Three' diplomacy during the Second World War. While this book includes an analysis of the main aspects of Churchill's pre-First World War and Second World War summit diplomacy, particular attention has been paid to his Cold War policies. Churchill's often overlooked penchant for negotiations and personal diplomacy during the Cold War was a prominent feature of his policies both as Leader of the Opposition (1945–51) and Prime Minister (1951–55). Even his famous 'iron curtain' speech in Fulton, Missouri, was characterized not only by a call for the build-up of western strength in the face of an aggressive Soviet Union but by the simultaneous call for negotiations with the Soviet dictator Stalin. In subsequent years, until and indeed even beyond his retirement just before the Geneva four-power summit conference in 1955, Churchill's inclination to favour negotiation and mediation over the martial rhetoric and nuclear diplomacy of the Cold War found an increasingly favourable response among western public opinion. The American President and many other western heads of government, however, remained sceptical of Churchill's proposals.

Churchill was confident of his own powers of persuasion. He strongly believed in his ability to persuade people of the correctness of his ideas by the mere force of his arguments. Convincing proof of this assumption can be found in his comprehensive and often passionately argued correspondence with Franklin D. Roosevelt during the Second World War,[2] and his equally forceful and robust exchange of letters with President Eisenhower in the 1950s.[3]

Already Churchill's political career before May 1940, when he became wartime Prime Minister, had confirmed his firmly held belief in the correctness of his own reasoning and the value of his personal intervention. In 1915 as First Lord of the Admiralty, for example, Churchill was able to get his own way with the controversial proposal for the Gallipoli landing as part of the Dardanelles expedition.[4] He also succeeded when as Chancellor of the Exchequer, in spite of fierce opposition from John Maynard Keynes among others, he argued for the reintroduction of the Gold Standard in the 1925 budget.[5] Both of these measures failed miserably.

Defeats, however, did nothing fundamentally to alter Churchill's conviction that at least the attempt to implement his plans had been good politics. His belief had been strengthened even more by the agreement of his Cabinet colleagues, who apparently also had faith in his proposals. Churchill therefore came to the conclusion that the failure of his suggested initiatives could not have been predicted.[6] Churchill had earned his first spurs as a war reporter and active soldier before he entered politics in February 1901 at the age of twenty-six when he became a Conservative Member of Parliament.[7] Throughout his entire political career, he was almost always of the opinion that whatever position he occupied or whatever task he had been entrusted with, 'owing to my experience as a soldier and politician I can do it better than anyone else.'[8]

Churchill usually failed to appreciate that when people agreed with him in Cabinet, Parliament or in private circles, they had not necessarily accepted the correctness of his arguments. He did not realize that their agreement often had more to do with the fact that friends and opponents alike could not compete with the energy and imagination that he was able to draw upon to support his standpoint and therefore gave in, due to fatigue and impatience. Lord Snow's characterization of Churchill is particularly apt and also applies to Churchill's controversial penchant for personal summit diplomacy:

Churchill had a very powerful mind, but a romantic and unquantitative one. If he thought about a course of action long enough, if he conceived it alone in his own inner consciousness and desired it passionately, he convinced himself that it must be possible. Then, with incomparable invention, eloquence, and high spirits, he set out to convince everyone else that it was not only possible, but the only course of action open to man. Unfortunately the brute facts of life were not always so malleable as his listeners.[9]

While Churchill greatly enjoyed the tremendous fun of being in the thick of events, he never overlooked the benefits he could obtain for his personal career. Yet as an old-fashioned British patriot and imperialist he also always had the good of his country in mind. 'Cause and Self served each other.'[10] At a very early stage, as a young politician in the first decade of the twentieth century, Churchill realized that Britain faced an increasing number of very serious external and domestic challenges which threatened the country's wellbeing and long-standing role as a world power. In the course of the Second World War, and in particular during the early years of the Cold War, he recognized once again the enormous challenges facing the continuation of Britain's global influence. Churchill deeply resented the fact that Britain appeared to be in the process of being relegated to a 'tame and minor role in the world'.[11]

At every stage of his career Churchill attempted to address this challenge and contribute to the resolution of the crises that threatened Britain's world power status through the use of personal negotiations and international summit diplomacy. Thus, early in the twentieth century, as a rising politician with increasingly important ministerial responsibilities, Churchill attempted to negotiate with the German Kaiser and the formidable Admiral Tirpitz to de-escalate the Anglo-German naval race before the First World War. The rivalry with the German Reich threatened Britain's superiority on the high seas and forced the country to invest much more in its defence policy to maintain its naval supremacy, the foundation of Britain's global importance, than was economically sound.

During the Second World War personal summit diplomacy was Churchill's preferred method of managing the 'Grand Coalition' with the United States and the Soviet Union. This was his solution for bringing about the defeat of Hitler without, as he hoped, undermining the health and vitality of the British Empire and Commonwealth and thus Britain's status as a world power. However, in the course of the war Churchill also proposed the creation of a 'United States of Europe' backed up and guided from the outside by Britain. Although for a time he believed that Britain's global role could best be maintained as the leader of a regional European organization and a closely integrated Europe, he soon abandoned this concept. Ultimately, he relied on his beloved summit diplomacy and the Anglo-American 'special relationship' to stabilize and enhance Britain's international position and deal with the changing balance of power in the post-war world whose contours had already begun to emerge by the time of the first 'Big Three' conference in Tehran in late 1943.

Churchill's personal diplomacy achieved its greatest successes in 1940–41, when the war-time Prime Minister managed to commit the United States to the material and then physical support of Britain's lonely but resolute fight against Hitler. His most persistent efforts to employ this method to bring about a more peaceful and less violent world occurred, however, during the Cold War. By the 1950s, Churchill recognized that in the increasingly hostile and aggressively conducted Cold War, Britain was less and less able to compete with the two superpowers. Britain's role as a world power was rapidly diminishing and Churchill feared that this decline would soon be irreversible. He saw continental Europe, his country's backyard, as dangerously exposed to a Soviet invasion and thought Britain itself would soon became vulnerable to a Soviet nuclear attack. He also knew that his country would remain entirely dependent on American economic and military aid unless an early end to the Cold War could be achieved. Only then would Britain be able to relax its frantic rearmament efforts and dedicate its rapidly diminishing industrial resources to economic and social reconstruction at home. In an ever more competitive world, with the Empire quickly dissolving and the European continent recovering from the war, the United Kingdom urgently needed to focus on its technological and industrial development instead of dissipating its energies and resources in fighting the Cold War.

Thus, as soon as he returned to office as Prime Minister in October 1951 at the age of almost 77, Churchill attempted to overcome the Cold War by means of high-level negotiations with US President Truman and Stalin. But neither of them was interested in a revival of a 'Big Three' summit meeting. Only when Stalin's death was announced in early March 1953 did Churchill once again become hopeful that he might be able to negotiate an end to the East-West conflict. In fact, Churchill became the first practitioner of détente in the post-war world.[12] He began dedicating all his remaining energy to organizing a 'parley at the summit' with new American President Dwight D. Eisenhower, his war-time comrade-in-arms, and Stalin's successors in the Kremlin. After Stalin, the Soviet Union was ruled by a new collective leadership apparently headed by Georgi Malenkov. Yet, Vyacheslav Molotov and Lavrenti Beria as well as Nikita Khrushchev were hovering in the background attempting to prevent the emergence of a sole successor to the dead dictator. They too were distrustful of Churchill, whom they regarded, not without justification, as an arch-imperialist and strong anti-Communist.

As in his attempts in the years leading up to the First World War and in the course of the Second World War, during the Cold War Churchill also hoped to employ international summit diplomacy to create a better, more peaceful world. European statesman Jean Monnet asked himself, 'Did he [Churchill] see beyond the interests of Great Britain? I think not.'[13] In fact, Churchill had a more global and holistic vision for the Cold War era than Monnet recognized. However, his immediate concern was also retaining Britain's standing as a great power. Churchill would not have agreed with the scientist Sir Henry Tizard who, in 1949, said, 'We persist in regarding ourselves as a Great Power capable of everything and only temporarily handicapped by economic difficulties. We are not a Great Power and never will be again.'[14]

All his life Churchill viewed his country as one of the world's foremost powers and he never gave up hope that Britain's political and economic decline after 1945 could be reversed by negotiating a peaceful settlement of the East–West conflict. During his entire political career Churchill believed in his long-standing remedy for international problems: 'that the leading men of the various nations ought to be able to meet together without trying to cut attitudes before excitable publics or using regiments of experts to marshal all the difficulties and objections.' He proposed, 'let us try to see whether there is not something better for us all than tearing and blasting each other to pieces, which we can certainly do.' In the last resort Churchill was convinced that much could be achieved 'with the help of friendly acquaintance and goodwill instead of impersonal diplomacy and propaganda'. He was unable to see 'how this could make things worse'.[15]

Churchill's visions of how to resolve prolonged international crisis situations and enable his country to survive as a world power were often highly unrealistic. He always tended to overestimate greatly his own importance and powers of persuasion as well as his country's ability to influence international developments. Yet throughout his long political life Churchill displayed an enormous persistence and consistency in pursuing his objectives by means of vigorous and imaginative policies.[16] Although Churchill ultimately failed, his efforts should not be dismissed out of hand. Churchill did his best to find solutions to highly dangerous conflict situations to avoid major catastrophes and create a more stable and peaceful world.

In the literature, Churchill's attempts at summit diplomacy prior to the First World War have often been ignored; they certainly have not induced a lively debate. Instead, his controversial role as Home Secretary in 1910–11 has been much scrutinized. In particular, attention has been focused on his encounters with the Suffragette movement in 1910 and his attempt to root out a Latvian anarchist cell in London in the first few days of 1911, the so-called siege of Sidney

Street, when Churchill deployed troops and, to everyone's surprise, proceeded to command them himself. His role in the events surrounding Tonypandy, outside the Glamorgan Colliery in Wales, in early November 1910 was even more damaging to his reputation. Although initially Churchill gave orders to employ in the region of a thousand Metropolitan police officers to clamp down on the rioting miners, eventually he agreed to the deployment of soldiers to restore order. Moreover, in the summer of 1911 he repeatedly used soldiers against striking dock-workers, railway-workers and indeed once again against miners to uphold public order and undermine any potential left-wing revolutionary activities.[17] Churchill's even more controversial role, fatal for many British and Allied soldiers, in the failed offensives of the poorly planned Gallipoli campaign of 1915 has also attracted much attention and indeed condemnation. His unwise return to the Gold Standard as Chancellor of the Exchequer in 1925 and his activities on behalf of the Baldwin government in helping to break up the General Strike of 1926 continue to arouse the suspicions of many commentators. During his wilderness years between 1929 and 1939, when Churchill was a Member of Parliament but held no ministerial office, his dogmatic positions as revealed in the heated parliamentary debates about the future of India and the Abdication Crisis of 1936 gave him the still lingering reputation of being a die-hard imperialist who was opposed to the forces of modernity.[18]

A critical appraisal of his towering personal role and his policies and strategies during the Second World War has emerged comparatively recently. For at least the first two decades after the end of the Second World War Churchill himself greatly influenced the perception of the war with the publication of his six-volume memoirs, *The Second World War*, which began to appear as early as 1948. With the help of hindsight, the revelation of hitherto secret documents and his impressive writing skills, Churchill was able to make a very persuasive case for the correctness of most of his major strategic and political decisions during the war. Thus Churchill greatly influenced the way his contemporaries and a whole generation of later historians viewed the Second World War and his role in it. Not without reason had Churchill quipped that 'History will bear me out particularly as I shall write that history myself.' Only fairly recently have historians been able to overcome Churchill's clever historical manipulations and develop a more detached consideration of his activities and his by no means always brilliant or infallible policies; for example, some authors have argued that his wartime decisions with regard to the Far East were very questionable and probably undermined Britain's long-term future in the entire region.[19]

Despite all justified criticism, in the late 1980s and 1990s Churchill revisionism assumed rather extreme positions; the pendulum had swung from the naïve and uninhibited hero worship of the aftermath of the Second World War to the wholesale debunking of his achievements. Good cases in point are the books by the left-of-centre Clive Ponting and by John Charmley, whom the American historian Arthur M. Schlesinger Jr has described as 'unabashedly a right-wing Thatcherite'.[20] Although they come from very different ideological starting points, both authors paint an overly harsh and unfair picture of Churchill. Charmley's work has caused particular controversy, due above all to an exaggerated, almost emotional review of the book by the Conservative politician and historian, the late Alan Clarke.[21] Yet other historians had paved the way for this kind of drastic revisionism. The pioneers were the historian Maurice Cowling in the mid-1970s and the Nazi apologist David Irving in the mid-1980s.[22] Subsequently a handful of other authors has also put a considerable portion of the blame for Britain's decline as a great power and for the country's economically precarious post-1945 existence on Churchill and his conduct of the war.

The revisionists from the right of the political spectrum essentially argue that Churchill's decision to commit all of Britain's available resources to fighting the Second World War was a major mistake, possibly taken by Churchill for careerist reasons to establish himself as a successful Prime Minister and remain in power. It led to the sacrifice of Britain's Empire and to the country's post-war economic and social problems. Instead of aligning Britain closely with the United States, which openly advocated the abolition of the Empire and the sterling area, Churchill should have sought a compromise peace with Germany in 1940–41, at a very early stage in the war. Charmley believes that an 'honourable peace' could have been negotiated if Churchill had been prepared to appease Hitler, which would have been quite feasible. According to Charmley, peace could have been made. This, it is assumed, would have prevented the electoral victory of the Labour Party in 1945 and the Attlee government's establishment of the welfare state, which Charmley sees as having done great damage to the country. Above all, an early peace agreement would have enabled Churchill and Hitler to divide up the world into German and British spheres of influences; this would have preserved the Empire and Britain's world power status and would not have made Britain dependent on the goodwill of a United States led by a cunning and manipulative Roosevelt and his equally shrewd successors. Moreover, Charmley argues, later in the war it was not Churchill but the indefatigable Eden who realized the importance of avoiding too close a relationship with the US and of maintaining a genuinely independent British world role.[23]

This kind of far-fetched scenario, which is essentially based on the optimistic and unrealistic assumption that a victorious Hitler would have been happy with the future existence of the Empire and the continuation of an independent British sphere of influence as a third global player alongside the US and a continental Europe dominated by Hitler, has led to considerable debate. However, as early as 28 May 1940 the newly appointed Prime Minister had managed to convince his Cabinet that 'in his judgement the prospect of Nazi rule throughout the Continent was intolerable, and that its protracted existence would become a steadily increasing threat to Britain itself and to British imperial rule overseas'.[24] Most scholars have agreed with this reasoning and dismissed the exaggerations of the late twentieth-century Churchill revisionists. Moreover, while 'individuals do make a difference in history',[25] there were many economic and socio-cultural developments which were outside the control of any British government but had a decisive impact on the country's position as a great power. For instance, even without Churchill's pro-American policy, it can safely be assumed that the movement towards global de-colonization would have occurred, making the survival of the British Empire for any length of time untenable. Recently a more level-headed approach has emerged which avoids both hero worship and vilification. After all, as, for example, Paul Addison has persuasively argued, although Churchill made many strategic and political mistakes that may well have obliged the British to pay a higher price for winning the war than would otherwise have been the case, without Churchill's leadership Britain might never have come even close to victory.[26]

With regard to Churchill's Cold War summit diplomacy, and in particular his efforts at détente after Stalin's death, no revisionism was necessary. Ever since the documents of the early 1950s became available in the mid-1980s in the British Public Record Office, the Churchill College archive in Cambridge, the American National Archives and the Truman and Eisenhower presidential libraries, scholars have been divided about Churchill's Cold War and Churchill's Cold War policies have been viewed with great scepticism.[27] Indeed, Churchill's contemporaries had been in two minds about his unconventional personal summit diplomacy in the 1950s. They wondered whether it represented a wise and visionary strategy or was merely a great nuisance that undermined the coherence of the western alliance.

Not surprisingly, among subsequent historians and analysts there have also been many positive and negative evaluations of Churchill's Cold War policy. An astute assessment was arrived at by Henry Kissinger when considering Churchill's 1953–54 détente initiatives for overcoming the Cold War; he concluded that 'Churchill, as so often before, had the right insight even if, for once, he did not have the appropriate remedy.'[28] Some authors go far beyond this cautious judgement and believe perhaps somewhat too generously that Churchill's summit diplomacy was wise and far-sighted,[29] constituting a sensible 'grand strategy' as well as a 'sweeping vision' and a 'refreshing departure from the arid tensions of Cold War' and previous attempts at conflict resolution.[30] Yet there are also writers who view his 'summitry' much more negatively. Although it is claimed that Churchill 'could still manage the big occasion' and 'display great energy and imagination at times',[31] his efforts are also often described as consisting of a hopelessly unrealistic policy which does not deserve to be taken seriously.[32]

Moreover, almost all writers express their doubts about the seriousness and appropriateness of Churchill's underlying motives. In general, they cite not his wish to prevent a nuclear holocaust and create a more peaceful and stable world but much more selfish intentions. These include Churchill's desire to postpone his imminent retirement from politics, his undiminished hope once again to play a dominant and decisive role on the world stage, and to win the Nobel Peace Prize to add to the Nobel Literature Prize which he was awarded in 1953 for his war memoirs. Sometimes, and not entirely without justification, his well-known 'arrogance, over-confidence, and imperviousness to argument' are mentioned as the reasons for his Cold War summit diplomacy.[33] It is also claimed by David Carlton that Churchill's increasing senility and deafness were behind his Cold War summit diplomacy. The aged Churchill is depicted as a misguided, idealistic and tearfully emotional politician with illusionary dreams of détente in a merciless world dominated by the East–West conflict which, above all, required realistic Cold Warriors.[34]

While the present author does not deny that some of these factors influenced Churchill's actions, Churchill's personal diplomacy is interpreted in this book as an imaginative and perhaps even visionary policy through which he attempted to reverse his country's declining fortunes and prevent or undo major catastrophes before the First World War, in the course of the Second World War and during the Cold War years.

During the Cold War his personal summit diplomacy was certainly too quickly dismissed by many of his contemporaries in influential political positions in Washington, London, Bonn, Paris and Moscow. An analysis of Churchill's personal 'summitry' throughout his political career and in particular during his Cold War years not only sheds light on Churchill's attempts to preserve global peace but provides a greater understanding of Churchill's political beliefs and convictions. It may also contribute to a better comprehension of his and his contemporaries' perception of Britain's role in the world in the first six decades of the twentieth century, when his country was in fierce competition with the Kaiser's and then Hitler's Germany, Stalin's Soviet Union and not least the United States in the eras of Franklin D. Roosevelt, Harry S. Truman and Dwight D. Eisenhower.

After all, the world Churchill inhabited was very different to the world of the early twenty-first century. In many respects it was a simpler and less complex world still largely based on the power of the nation state, including the dominating influence of the leading personalities. It was also a world where it was frequently still possible to conduct interstate relations with the help of a traditional alliance system and often within a bilateral or trilateral framework. Churchill's political vision tended to be based on the assumption that this would continue to be the case. His lukewarm if not entirely negative attitude to the European Defence Community showed that he was not fond of supra-national schemes. However, the challenges which plague the world of the early twenty-first century, such as environmental disasters, ethnically deeply divided societies and elusive cross-border international terrorism conducted by diverse networks of highly organized individuals and groups rather than nation states, were not entirely unknown. Yet the seriousness of these problems remained largely unrecognized; they were not regarded as major threats to the survival of western and indeed global civilization. Equally, the requirement of a broad multilateral and cross-cultural approach to solve or at least defuse these problems was hardly understood, while the influence of the only fairly limited number of Non-Governmental Organizations was still very much in its infancy.

But Churchill's world was of course not an age of innocence. His world had come of age during a period of enormous suffering, destruction and huge loss of life, encompassing – to list only a few of the most horrendous events – the slaughter of Armenians in Turkey, the Russian civil war, Stalin's Gulags and of course the two world wars and the wholesale elimination of Jews, gypsies and many others in the Holocaust. Moreover, Churchill was well aware of the bloody upheavals on the Indian continent and in Palestine when Britain gave up its responsibilities in the aftermath of the end of the Second World War. In particular during the two world wars Churchill personally, both as a politician and military leader, was confronted with the violent forces of aggressive nationalism and unsurpassed ideological hatred. In the course of the Cold War, during the last ten years of his political career, the dangers of nuclear annihilation, emerging religious fanaticism in some parts of the world, inter-national economic turmoil giving rise to huge waves of refugees and widespread political destablization appeared as very real dangers on the horizon. Soon the beginning of political and economic globalization and simultaneous economic and cultural fragmentation in combination with the proliferation of weapons of mass destruction would be recognized as severe threats to global stability.[35]

While Churchill had little understanding of the problems created by the forces of cultural dislocation and the intricacies of western capitalism and socialist economic planning, he was immensely worried about the East–West conflict in its political, military and ideological confrontation. He greatly feared a violent outburst of the forces of neo-nationalism in Eastern Europe and divided Germany and the imminence of a nuclear disaster whether brought about intentionally or by default. Churchill's solution for overcoming the Cold War and thus the arms race, neo-nationalism and the manifold other conflicts which threatened western civilization and therefore, as he saw it, the return to an orderly and stable world, was essentially his dictum that 'to jaw-jaw is always better than to war-war'.[36]

This dictum is by no means out of date. Indeed, it still may be the only way forward to overcome some of the most dangerous cross-border and indeed cross-cultural conflicts and global challenges of the contemporary world. Thus, not only Churchill's activities as a military leader during the Second World War but perhaps even more his political strategy to overcome international conflict situations by negotiation may be his lasting legacy.[37] In 1984 for instance, in the midst of American considerations to enter into talks with the Soviet Union which would lead to the end of the Cold War a few years later, even the hard-line anti-Communist Reagan administration remembered Churchill's earlier efforts. In a foreign policy speech Secretary of State George Shultz approvingly quoted Churchill's belief that despite the existence of severe political conflicts and disagreements among the world's major powers informal talks and formal negotiations could do no harm. Quoting Churchill, Shultz believed that it would be unwise to wait too long before being prepared to enter into talks: 'it would be a mistake to assume that nothing can be settled … unless or until everything is settled.'[38]

CHAPTER 1

Churchill's Personal Diplomacy before the First World War

Anglo-German Antagonism and Attempts to Negotiate with the Kaiser and Admiral Tirpitz

The importance Churchill attributed to personal diplomacy of the written or spoken kind not only with friendly states but also with Britain's potential enemies can be observed during his first years in public office before the First World War. Together with his friend David Lloyd George, Churchill attempted several times to initiate talks between Britain and the German Reich between 1908 and 1911.[1] He had come to fear that the Anglo–German naval race might lead to war between the two great powers which undoubtedly would do irreversible damage to both countries' political and economic health.

The Development of the Anglo-German Naval Race

In the late nineteenth and early twentieth centuries successive British governments had observed with great concern the Kaiser's rapid naval build-up. The Naval Laws of 1898 and 1902 were introduced to the Reichstag by Admiral Alfred von Tirpitz, the increasingly influential German Navy Minister. In 1902, Lord Selborne, the First Lord of the Admiralty, was 'convinced that the great new German navy is being carefully built up from the point of war with us'.[2] The German programme, which was greatly stimulated by the writing of American naval expert Alfred Mahan and largely originated with the Kaiser himself, was considerably expanded with the Naval Laws of 1906 and 1908.[3]

German intervention in Morocco (1905/6), Austria's annexation of Bosnia (1908/9), and the dispatch of German guns out to Agadir in 1911 confirmed British fears that an ambitious and restless Germany had embarked on an aggressive push for continental hegemony at the expense of France and Russia.[4] It was believed that such a disturbance of the European balance of power would seriously endanger Britain's military security. The country's economic well-being, including its food supplies, was also at risk, since a hegemonic Germany could be expected to successfully challenge Britain's industrial and trading position on a global scale.[5] After all, from the 1890s Germany had emerged as Britain's main economic rival and replaced it as Europe's foremost manufacturing country.[6] A rapidly industrializing, colonizing and demographically growing Germany seemed to have instituted a plan to dominate the European continent with the aim of eventually reversing Britain's global supremacy on the seas. With Sir Edward Grey's appointment as Foreign Secretary on the formation of Henry Campbell-Bannerman's Liberal government in late 1905, there was an increasing tendency in Britain to view Germany as the major potential enemy, a foe who could not be permitted to win the naval race Berlin seemed to have embarked upon.[7]

Repeated attempts by the German government to seek a declaration of neutrality from London in return for the promise to end the expansion of the German fleet gave credence to the widespread belief in Britain that Kaiser Wilhelm II was planning to attack France and possibly the Low Countries, including neutral Belgium, if the opportunity presented itself. And indeed this was the essence of Germany's top secret Schlieffen Plan, developed in 1905 and initially entitled 'War of attack against France'. It was assumed in London that once this aim had been achieved the Germans would then turn against Britain to complete their global ambitions.[8]

After 1909 the preparedness of the British Army's Expeditionary Force for a campaign on the continent had been considerably improved,[9] but British strategists still gave priority to the Navy. With hindsight, they exaggerated the naval threat from Germany and to some extent began preparing for the wrong war.[10] Britain's political elite, including Churchill, appear to have reacted from a sense of weakness and vulnerability by taking the numbers game about ships and battle cruisers too seriously. Most politicians overestimated Germany's ability to cope with the financial and political problems caused by the naval race, which threatened to undermine further the strained internal fabric of the Reich. In fact, the danger of a social revolution in Germany was one of Berlin's motives for embarking on naval rearmament, which would defuse internal dissatisfaction by demonstrating a successful foreign policy.[11]

Most British politicians, underestimating Britain's naval superiority, were convinced that Admiral Tirpitz would be well able to close the naval gap between London and Berlin within a short time unless Britain also launched a rapid rearmament programme. The country's naval strength was severely underrated. Perhaps even more important than the real threat was the perceived threat to Britain's global status and Empire. Across all party and class lines there was a firm conviction that the fleet was still of utmost symbolic and military importance if Britain wished to retain global supremacy and be able to compete successfully with Germany or any other rising power. The whole issue became very emotional. Moreover, there were many interest groups that did not overlook the economic benefits of a rapid rearmament programme.[12]

In order to continue dominating the seas, Britain decided in 1909 to sustain a 60 per cent (or 3:2) superiority over the German navy, replacing the traditional but increasingly over-ambitious Two-Power Standard (or 2:1 superiority).[13] To maintain even this reduced level of superiority it soon became apparent that the global activities of the Royal Navy had to be whittled down and the fleet brought closer to home, and simultaneously qualitatively better and prohibitively expensive ships, the so-called Dreadnoughts, had to be built at an ever-increasing pace.[14] Thus the British Empire withdrew most of its major battleships from the Atlantic and the Pacific, a process begun gradually in 1904 by Admiral Sir John Fisher, the First Sea Lord. This course of action was later speeded up and extended to the Mediterranean by Churchill as First Lord of the Admiralty. Formal and informal alliances were concluded with the United States towards the end of the nineteenth century and with Japan in 1902 (renewed in 1905 and 1911). Closer to home, *ententes cordiales* were entered into with Britain's old enemy France in 1904 and, in 1907, and with Russia (complementing the Franco-Russian alliance of 1894). This meant that the task of safeguarding Britain's trading routes with the Empire could be shared with other nations without endangering British access and presence.

The Foreign Secretary, Sir Edward Grey, was convinced that the existence of two European power blocs, the Triple Alliance consisting of Germany, Austria-Hungary and Italy and the less formal Triple Entente of Britain, France and Russia would guarantee peace in Europe. However, once the Triple Entente had been formed and had led to the effective termination of England's 'splendid isolation' from the European continent, Germany felt increasingly encircled and isolated.[15] The unexpected establishment of a network of alliances by London caused a severe shock in Berlin, not least as by 1902 Italy was about to leave the Triple Alliance when it concluded a secret neutrality treaty with France. By 1907/8 Germany found itself left with Austria-Hungary as its only reliable ally. Although Berlin had effectively started the naval race to challenge Britain's global dominance, Germany could now conveniently blame other powers, and particularly Britain, for its predicament. Yet it had clearly been Germany that had effectively pushed Britain into a policy of lavishing much greater attention on the European continent and rapidly improving its relations with France and Russia.

In July 1908 Captain Dumas, the British naval attaché to the embassy in Berlin, wrote in his final report before leaving his post that he had come to believe that his country was increasingly hated in Germany and that 'Germany means to fight England the moment she feels strong enough'. The Captain continued,

> Moreover, I dare not finish without recording that I believe that at the bottom of every German's heart today is rising a vain and wildly exhilarating hope that a glorious day is approaching when by a grave breaking through of the lines which he feels are encircling him he might even wrest the command of the seas from England and thus become a member of the greatest Power by land or sea that the world has ever seen. It is possible that he realizes that he must suppress this feeling for the present, but he hopes . . .[16]

Churchill's First Involvement in International Politics

Churchill was not yet influenced by such sentiments. In the first decade of the twentieth century his attitude to Germany was in principle quite positive.[17] Churchill's admiration for Britain's royalty may even have led him to view 'Germans as rustic Continental cousins'. He certainly greatly admired the Kaiser's personal glamour when at the age of sixteen he first saw him at an exhibition at Crystal Palace in London in 1891.[18] A decade later, Churchill was elected to Parliament as a Conservative MP on the strength of his reputation as a war correspondent during the Boer War. In 1904 he crossed the floor to join the Liberals on the issue of Free Trade, and after their landslide victory in the general election of December 1905 he was rewarded with the post of Under-Secretary for the Colonies (two and a half years later he obtained his first Cabinet post).[19] In 1906 and 1909 Churchill met Wilhelm II again, when in his ministerial capacity he was invited to attend army manoeuvres in Silesia and Württemberg.[20] On the latter occasion Churchill was greatly impressed by the strength of the German army. Although he may have begun 'reluctantly to admit to himself that war with Germany was not as completely unlikely as he had thought',[21] before the Agadir crisis of 1911 Churchill did not believe that Germany was seriously threatening Britain's global position. He was convinced that the English Channel and the might of the British navy protected his country from any serious challenges to its hegemonic position. Yet in 1907 and 1908 he gradually began to see the necessity for talks to settle rising Anglo-German tensions.[22]

Churchill and a number of other 'radical' members of the Liberal government notably David Lloyd George, John Burns, Lewis Harcourt and Lord Morley, sometimes supported by Lord Crewe, thought that negotiations to achieve an Anglo-German rapprochement were imperative. Only negotiations between London and Berlin could avoid the dangers of ever-increasing mistrust and an uncontrollable arms race. Moreover, the realization of the government's programme of domestic reform required a drastic reduction in military expenditure on both the army and the navy.[23] Already in March 1898 and January 1901 British Colonial Secretary Joseph Chamberlain had attempted to obtain a binding agreement between Britain and the Triple Alliance, but this had been politely rejected by Berlin. The German government insisted on the pursuit of its naval policy; Berlin was convinced moreover that British-Russian antagonism in the Far East and the Middle East would continue and could eventually be exploited by Germany.[24]

Another attempt to improve Anglo-German relations was made by the British in the course of the peace conference at The Hague from June to October 1907. This initiative was also unsuccessful. London and Berlin were unable to arrive at an understanding regarding the delay – let alone the reduction – of German naval construction.[25] In February 1908, however, this did not stop some of the radical reformers in the Cabinet led by Lloyd George, the President of the Board of Trade, from continuing to battle for a lowering of the fairly moderate estimates for new naval ships for that year. It had just been announced that Britain would build one new Dreadnought annually compared to Germany's four. An uneasy compromise among the various factions in the government was eventually achieved.[26]

As an Under-Secretary at the Colonial Office Churchill was not a member of the Cabinet and was therefore too junior to have been involved in these activities. However, in April 1908 Herbert Henry Asquith succeeded Sir Henry Campbell-Bannerman as Prime Minister and Lloyd George became Chancellor of the Exchequer and Churchill found himself as President of the Board of Trade. Lloyd George and Churchill were close friends at the time and generally regarded as 'radicals' and pro-German 'economists', committed to improving social legislation and to cutting military expenditure. Both believed passionately in détente with Germany to reduce the burdensome navy estimates. The Board of the Admiralty had recommended that the 1909 budget should provide the money for building four new Dreadnoughts annually, and if need be for as many as six ships, to maintain the 2:1 power standard with Germany. Lloyd George, however, hoped to use the money for covering the looming bill for Old Age Pensions, which had been introduced in 1908; he also wanted to be able to introduce an employment insurance scheme without having to increase taxation.[27]

Thus in the summer of 1908 the 'radicals' made another attempt to achieve an Anglo-German rapprochement.[28] With their customary energy and enthusiasm and much to the displeasure of Foreign Secretary Grey, Lloyd George and Churchill began a crusade to improve Anglo-German relations by attempting to embark on renewed negotiations. To persuade the 'radicals' that the Foreign Office (FO) was doing everything possible to arrive at a rapprochement with Germany, Lloyd George was asked to attend Grey's interview on 14 July with the German ambassador, the amicable Count Paul von Wolff-Metternich zur Gracht who was no friend of Tirpitz's naval policy.[29]

However, the Chancellor of the Exchequer remained unconvinced of the merit of Grey's cautious policy. On 28 July Lloyd George made a passionate speech at Queen's Hall calling for a speedy Anglo-German understanding, blaming Britain for having started the naval race and saying that it was understandable that Germany felt encircled and threatened.[30] During a three-week visit to Germany in August 1908, principally to investigate the German welfare system, Lloyd George emphasized in interviews with the press the need to overcome the senseless naval race and build an entente between London and Berlin. This caused much concern in France and, not surprisingly, the Prime Minister immediately asked Lloyd George to be more circumspect and not to tread on Foreign Office territory. Lloyd George resented this admonition. After all, an attempt to facilitate Anglo-German naval discussions by talking to the Kaiser and Chancellor Bernhard von Bülow may have been Lloyd George's main reason for travelling to Germany. However, neither showed any interest in receiving him and Lloyd George had to be content with talking to the upright Theobald von Bethmann Hollweg, the Minister of the Interior.[31]

In Swansea on 15 August Churchill expressed sentiments similar to those of Lloyd George. He described Germany as among Britain's 'very best customers' and observed that there was 'no real cause of difference between' the two nations. In addition, he had 'a high and prevailing faith in the essential goodness of a great people'. His audience were mostly Welsh miners and Churchill used the opportunity to display his somewhat surprising socialist credentials. He referred to the 'common interests' of the 'working classes all over the world' and expressed himself convinced that 'the international solidarity of labour' also applied to the peoples of Germany and Britain. Churchill's pronouncements were much praised by Lloyd George and the Germans but condemned by the Foreign Office and the British conservative press. His speech seemed to confirm his 'radical' and pro-German reputation. An increasing number of people within and without the government regarded Churchill as 'thoroughly untrustworthy'. Prime Minister Asquith was deeply disappointed about the young politician on whom he had set very high hopes.[32]

A meeting between the Kaiser and King Edward VII in Cronberg on 11 and 12 August proved to be largely unsuccessful.[33] Foreign Secretary Grey cancelled his tentative plans for Anglo-German naval negotiations. The preliminary approaches to Berlin had been instigated by Albert Ballin, the German managing director of the Hamburg-American line, who was close to the Kaiser, and Sir Ernest Cassel, a London-based but German-born banker who was a friend of both King Edward VII and Churchill. Despite his aggressive expansionism in commercial shipping, which caused international resentment,[34] Ballin believed that the German Reich 'cannot afford a race in Dreadnoughts against the much wealthier British'. However, the Kaiser gave a belligerent interview with the *Daily Telegraph* in October 1908, at the height of the Bosnian crisis, worsening Anglo-German relations further.[35]

Thus, by the autumn of 1908 Grey's half-hearted efforts and Lloyd George's and Churchill's enthusiastic though unusual attempts to bring about a British-German rapprochement had largely ended in failure. By the end of 1908 an uneasy Anglo-German détente prevailed while tension within the Liberal government over the naval race and other questions had considerably increased. Charles Hobhouse, the Financial Secretary to the Treasury, noted that 'Winston Churchill's introduction into the cabinet has been followed by the disappearance of that harmony which its members all tell me has been its marked feature.'[36]

In a climate of hostile media agitation, with rumours of German invasion plans and the secret construction of ever bigger German warships, Lloyd George and Churchill continued their campaign in early 1909. They were still very sceptical 'about the danger of the European situation and not convinced by the Admiralty case' to start immediately on the construction of six instead of four new Dreadnoughts so that they would be available by the 'danger year' 1912. This was the year when Berlin was expected to have more Dreadnoughts than Britain and thus be in a position to challenge the British navy successfully if London did not increase its construction programme.[37] Lloyd George and Churchill, supported by some of the other 'radicals', led an increasingly acrimonious division of opinion in the Liberal government, and at one point the 'radical' ministers threatened resignation. In March 1909 Grey himself made it clear that he would only remain in the Cabinet if the new naval estimates were accepted.[38]

Throughout the summer of 1909 Grey considered proposing Anglo-German talks to appease the 'radicals'. However, in the end Grey and Prime Minister Asquith – who was particularly irritated by Lloyd George and

Churchill – and Reginald McKenna, the new First Lord of the Admiralty, had their way. In view of the rapid German shipbuilding programme as well as reports of Austrian and Italian construction of Dreadnoughts and the general hysteria over the naval scare in the country and the press, McKenna was victorious. In late July 1909 he could announce that the Cabinet had decided to approve the construction of eight new Dreadnoughts, four immediately and four additional ones during the next year. The 'economists' had been out-manoeuvred. Churchill wrote: 'In the end a curious and characteristic solution was reached. The Admiralty had demanded six ships: the economists offered four: and we finally compromised on eight.'[39]

In the same month that the British Cabinet decided in favour of greatly increasing the country's naval strength, Bethmann Hollweg became German Chancellor. He was no friend of Tirpitz and he realized the dangerous tension in Anglo-German relations brought about by the naval race. Albeit a Prussian Conservative and loyal supporter of the Kaiser's personal rule, Bethmann appears to have been genuinely interested in working for a rapprochement with London.[40]

On 21 August 1909 the new Chancellor proposed Anglo-German talks to arrive at a naval and political agreement, expressing his 'earnest desire' to negotiate in secret 'a scheme for a good general understanding'.[41] With the Kaiser's approval, the preparatory work was again conducted by Cassel and Ballin. At first they attempted to persuade Wilhelm II to initiate a meeting between Admiral Tirpitz and Admiral Fisher, the First Lord, but this was unsuccessful.[42] Soon the German government took the negotiations out of the hands of the inexperienced Ballin and Cassel and conducted them on a more official level. Grey received Bethmann Hollweg's approaches 'in the most friendly spirit', not least to appease Churchill, Lloyd George and the 'radicals' on the Liberal backbenches, but, on the whole he found Bethmann's proposals somewhat disappointing. Churchill himself embarked on personal diplomacy by holding various talks with the German ambassador in London behind the back of the Foreign Office to establish 'a spirit of real trust and confidence between the two countries'.[43] However, both the official talks and Churchill's semi-official meetings proved very difficult.

In October 1909, in the course of top-secret Anglo-German negotiations, it became clear once again that Germany was only prepared to offer a limited naval agreement restricted to slowing German naval construction during the next three years. Berlin did not appear to envisage any reduction in the overall number of ships to be built. In return, the Kaiser insisted on a comprehensive political settlement to ensure that Britain would not be on the side of Germany's opponents if war broke out. Such an agreement, however, was unacceptable to London. It would have meant either the outright alliance with Germany Wilhelm II hoped for or, at least, a British pledge of full neutrality, which would have constituted Britain's approval of Germany's domination of the European continent and its pursuit of *Weltpolitik*.[44]

Bethmann deluded himself by believing he might be able to obtain 'a treaty of neutrality in which England promises to remain neutral if we are attacked by France or Russia, singly or together, or if we are forced by our alliance to help Austria'. Grey recognized that such a neutrality clause and indirect alliance with Berlin would go 'beyond anything we have with France or Russia'; it was therefore unacceptable.[45] The Germans tried to put pressure on London by raising the unlikely spectre of a German-Russian rapprochement, but this did not succeed. By April 1910 the negotiations were deadlocked. They already had been interrupted by the heavily anti-German rhetoric of the British general election in January, necessitated by the House of Lords' opposition to Lloyd George's reforming budget of 1909. The election result enabled Asquith to remain in power but with a very slim majority largely based on the support of the Irish Nationalists.

Bethmann Hollweg had not managed to escape the ambitious framework of Germany's foreign policy. He had been able to achieve no more than a tentative Anglo-German agreement regarding an exchange of naval information and even this had proved very difficult.[46] Churchill did not expect war with Germany at this stage, but his suspicions regarding German intentions were seriously aroused. In a memorandum to the Cabinet on 3 November 1909 he explained that the naval programme was putting ever-increasing pressure on the difficult financial situation of the Reich. He believed that 'the overflowing expenditure of the German Empire strains and threatens every dyke by which the social and political unity of Germany is maintained'. He asked rhetorically: 'Will the tension be relieved by moderation or snapped by calculated violence?'[47] Churchill's increasingly gloomy outlook was confirmed by the reports from the Berlin embassy. The British naval attaché Captain Heath believed that Tirpitz was without doubt 'one of the foremost men in Germany' and had the 'whole navy under his thumb'. But he was of an 'excitable position' and entirely 'devoted to the carrying out of the Navy Law'.[48]

In May 1910, Churchill, who had become Home Secretary in February and was hardly responsible for negotiations with foreign powers, managed to become involved again. He once again embarked on his beloved personal diplomacy and began discussing Austria's building of Dreadnoughts with the Anglophile German ambassador, Count von Metternich. Grey did not favour such unofficial contacts, fearing that the Germans would receive the mistaken impression that London was scared and would eventually resign itself to

accepting Berlin's naval build-up. Moreover, France might easily misunderstand such contacts between a British minister and a representative of the
German government.[49] Although Anglo-German exchanges of view, including
Churchill's talks, continued in a haphazard way into the autumn, they were
effectively brought to an end by the dissolution of Parliament on 28 November
1910 and the second general election within a year. The December election
once again enabled Asquith's Liberal government to stay in Downing Street,
with the Irish Nationalists continuing to hold the balance of power in
Parliament.[50]

In January 1911, pressure from Lloyd George and the other 'economists' in
the Cabinet, Churchill among them, was largely responsible for reviving the
idea of negotiations to avoid a costly rearmament programme. Thus talks to
arrive at a 'friendly understanding with Germany' were soon entered into.
While the officials in the Foreign Office continued to believe that Foreign
Secretary Grey was 'perfectly sound on the whole matter', they feared that
Churchill, Lloyd George and the other 'radicals' in the Cabinet were ready for
an Anglo-German accommodation 'at almost any cost'.[51] A document about
how to achieve an Anglo-German rapprochement, drawn up by a new Cabinet
committee on foreign affairs set up in January to handle the talks, was handed
to Berlin in early March 1911.[52] However, by May it had become clear that
Anglo-German relations remained deadlocked. Grey still favoured the
conclusion of a political agreement prior to a naval agreement, but he was now
willing to enter into a compromise with his 'radical' colleagues by accepting
the simultaneous conclusion of such agreements if they gave no offence to
France. In his answer of 9 May 1911 the Kaiser did not seem to be prepared to
compromise, though London intended to continue the negotiations.[53]

On the main issues the two countries were as far apart as ever. While
London wished above all to obtain an agreement to contain the naval race,
Berlin insisted on a British promise of full neutrality. This would have
irreparably damaged the Triple Entente with France and Russia, isolating
France and leaving the door open for German hegemony in Europe; it would
also have threatened Britain's role as a world power, for in such circumstances
a rapprochement between London's entente partners and Germany would
occur.[54]

The sudden appearance of the German gunboat *Panther* in Agadir on 1 July
to oppose French colonial ambitions in Morocco confirmed these fears in
London. The French occupation of the Moroccan city of Fez had violated the
understanding on the neutrality of Morocco achieved at an international
conference in 1905, and the Kaiser now wished to demonstrate German
colonial ambitions and commercial interests in Morocco and in other parts of

French colonial Africa. In Germany colonial venture was 'a valve to release some of the domestic pressure' on the Reich's political system, which was under severe financial and social strain.[55] Above all it seemed to be an attempt by Berlin to demonstrate that France could not rely on British support despite the entente. The Agadir crisis almost provoked a war between Britain and Germany, as London remained firmly in support of the French position in Morocco whilst deciding against sending a British gunboat. It led to the termination of the Anglo-German negotiations and the consolidation of Franco-British relations. It also accelerated the international armaments race and weakened Bethmann Hollweg's domestic position.[56] Churchill told his wife that the government 'decided to use pretty plain language to Germany and to tell her if she thinks that Morocco can be divided up without John Bull, she is jolly well mistaken'.[57]

The Agadir crisis made Churchill increasingly suspicious of the Kaiser's intentions and led to the reversal of his moderate if not pro-German position. He began to emphasize, even exaggerate, the German danger. For example, when he was made aware in late July 1911 that the London Metropolitan Police were responsible for guarding the magazines with the country's naval cordite reserves, he immediately raised an alarm that insufficient protection was available and concluded that any invading German forces could easily get hold of the reserves, entirely ignoring the fact that any such troops would still find it extremely difficult to cross the Channel barrier, overcome the British navy and to sneak into the country unobserved. Dramatically, Churchill ordered better protection of the magazines and admitted that once he 'had begun to view the situation in this light, it became impossible to think of anything else'. As Home Secretary, he also instructed Britain's young secret service to intercept suspicious letters from Germany.[58] Churchill's description of Lord Rosebery – 'He was unduly attracted by the dramatic, and by the pleasure of making a fine gesture'[59] – could certainly be applied to himself in times of crisis.

Lloyd George had also begun to view Germany with increasing mistrust. As agreed by Asquith and Grey, he used his Mansion House speech on 21 July 1911 to warn Germany not to rush into war with its irrational and unilateral activities and its intention to dictate a Moroccan settlement which excluded Britain altogether although 'her interests were vitally affected'. This speech by a known pro-German cabinet minister made a deep impact on the German government and reassured the French.[60] Churchill commented to his wife: 'They sent their Panther to Agadir & we sent our little Panther to the Mansion House: with the best results.'[61]

Thus in the second half of 1911 the former rebels Churchill and Lloyd George had become convinced that it was Britain's duty to support the French, to insist on upholding British naval superiority under all circumstances and to maintain the status quo on the continent.[62] In late December 1911 Churchill wrote that 'The union of a Navy of such great power with the largest Army in Europe will be a most sinister and disquieting fact, especially when we consider these gigantic engines of destruction will not be wielded by a ... democratic Government ... but by a military and bureaucratic oligarchy supported by a powerful Junker landlord class'.[63]

Indeed, the issue of a quick preventive war before the realignment against Germany had been completed gained increasing currency in Berlin after Agadir; it also contributed to the domestic instability of the Kaiser's Reich.[64] Germany's hot-headed brinkmanship in the Agadir crisis led to an intensification of Anglo-French cooperation; in the middle of the crisis the British and French army commands had agreed for the first time on a joint strategy to be prepared in case of war with Germany. In Britain the Agadir crisis also resulted in an important domestic political realignment between Grey, Asquith and other Liberal imperialists and the former 'economists' and leading members of the so-called pro-German 'Potsdam Party', Lloyd George and Churchill.[65]

In the aftermath of the Moroccan crisis, the anti-German voices within the British government became louder. Britain's strategic experts were more than ever in agreement that London would support France if it was attacked by Germany; the precarious nature of Anglo-German relations had become 'the dominant element of the international situation'.[66] Paradoxically, with the real possibility of the outbreak of a European war, a climate of mutual goodwill developed between London and Berlin in their negotiations regarding the future of the Portuguese colonies in Africa and the Baghdad Railway project.[67] In December 1911 Grey had embarked on talks with the German ambassador about a relaxation of tension with the help of Anglo-German agreements over extra-European issues.[68] The talks went so well that Count Metternich was able to report to Germany in a moment of optimism that Grey had hinted in Parliament that in return for the end of the naval race, Germany might be able to obtain London's support for establishing a huge colonial empire in Central Africa. This helped Bethmann in late 1911 to persuade the Kaiser to overrule Tirpitz for the time being and postpone the envisaged submission of a new supplementary Naval Law to the Reichstag until the spring of 1912.[69]

Much to his satisfaction, Churchill was appointed First Lord of the Admiralty in October 1911 and quickly turned from a strong economist into an ardent navalist. With the energy of the recently converted and much to the dismay of Tirpitz, whose so-called 'risk theory' was thus undermined,[70] Churchill was responsible for implementing the Royal Navy's new naval strategy. It effectively hastened the end of 'Pax Britannica' and the country's 'splendid isolation' from the European continent. Britain started concentrating its ships in the North Sea to be prepared for an attack from Germany and left only token forces in the Mediterranean; this was highly controversial within the Admiralty, the Navy League, the Colonial Service and the conservative press. However, Churchill strongly defended his strategy of concentrating the fleet in the North Sea and advocated concluding a formal alliance with France, as he thought that 'Britain had the obligations of an alliance without its advantages and above all without precise definitions'. France assumed the main responsibility for the Mediterranean towards the end of 1912.[71]

Despite the British government's insistence on maintaining its flexibility and independence from binding alliances, Britain had become morally obligated to come to the help of France if the latter were attacked.[72] Churchill, like many others, believed that 'if we win the big battle in the decisive theatre we can put everything straight afterwards'; after all 'it would be very foolish to lose England in safeguarding Egypt'.[73] The new First Lord also began to create a naval staff for joint planning with the army which had been much neglected until then.[74] Churchill was determined to prepare the navy for a possible Anglo-German conflict. In his Guildhall speech on 9 November 1911 he spelled out his intention to maintain Britain's present naval superiority and introduce higher naval estimates if Germany increased its navy programme as was gloomily anticipated.[75] In a memorandum and a speech to the Committee of Imperial Defence in July 1912, Churchill explained that the 'whole character of the German Fleet . . . is designed for aggressive and offensive action'. He added carefully that he did not wish 'to make any suggestion that the Germans would deliver any surprise or sudden attack upon us', but he concluded that 'we at the Admiralty have got to see, not that that they will not do it, but that they cannot do it'.[76]

Nevertheless, at the same time as preparations to defend Britain against a German naval attack were advancing, ministers were still hopeful that a conflict could be avoided by means of Anglo-German negotiations. The Foreign Office, however, was hostile to any further talks and continued to view negotiations as 'indecisive, vacillating and highly dangerous'. As the Foreign Office saw it, a 'radical' campaign of 'amateur diplomatists, peace mongers and meddlesome busybodies' was seeking to undermine the Foreign Secretary's policy.[77] But after Agadir, dissatisfaction with Grey's seemingly inflexible and stubborn policy had grown: in the press, among the British public, and among Liberal ministers there was a desire for Anglo-German negotiations and a rapid rapprochement between these two great powers to avoid a European war.[78]

The years 1908–11 had witnessed Churchill's growing interest in international politics and his increasing tendency to advocate and, if possible, participate in high-level negotiations with foreign powers, although he still had to be content with a relatively minor role. The years 1912–14 saw the last efforts to regulate Anglo-German naval competition and arrive at a European détente. Churchill was to play a major role in these final attempts to avoid the catastrophe of war between the world's predominant powers. The true origins of Churchill's beloved personal summit diplomacy as pursued during the Second World War and his peace-time government in the 1950s go back to the years of global crisis between 1912 and 1914.

Churchill's Attempts to Negotiate with the German Empire

Early in 1912 Churchill began to develop a firm belief in informal personal summit diplomacy. Referring to the early months of 1912 in the first volume of his war memoir, *The World Crisis*, published in 1923, Churchill wrote that despite the forthcoming German supplementary Naval Law of 1912 he had been hopeful that a realistic possibility existed of coming to a mutually satisfactory settlement. The British government had been aware 'that a formidable new [German] Navy Law was in preparation and would shortly be declared. If Germany had definitely made up her mind to antagonize Great Britain, we must take up the challenge; but it might be possible by friendly, sincere and intimate conversation to avert this perilous development.'[79]

This was not a position developed with hindsight. In January 1912 Churchill wrote to his friend Sir Ernest Cassel explaining that he 'deeply deplore[d] the situation' which had developed in Anglo-German relations. He expressed his concern about the increasingly hostile perception of Germany in his country, 'for as you know I have never had any but friendly feelings towards that great nation & her illustrious Sovereign & I regard the antagonism wh[ich] has developed as insensate. Anything in my power to terminate it, I w[oul]d gladly do.'[80] In early 1912 Churchill hoped he might be able to embark on high-level negotiations that would result in an Anglo-German accommodation and a rapid termination of the naval race.

Churchill's tendency towards informal personal diplomacy meant, however, that he kept his cards very close to his chest. He did not hesitate to side-step the official channels and Foreign Office experts in favour of conducting his personal foreign policy. As Prime Minister during the Second World War and between 1951 and 1955 Churchill was also to ignore the Foreign Secretary and the Foreign Office whenever it suited him. This inclination can already be detected in his early political career. In 1912 he tended to inform the Foreign Secretary only after considerable delay about the informal negotiations he was involved in.[81]

Initially, Churchill, as First Lord of the Admiralty, hesitated to go to Berlin to discuss the Anglo-German naval race with Admiral Tirpitz – the risk of failure seemed too great – but, he soon reversed this view. Early in January 1912 Albert Ballin had taken the initiative and had told Cassel that he was planning to arrange private talks between Churchill and Tirpitz if on his next visit to Germany (planned for March) Cassel would bring Churchill with him.[82] Cassel was enthusiastic about Ballin's proposal and wrote to the First Lord as he believed Churchill would be interested. After all, as he told Ballin, Churchill genuinely looked 'upon the estrangement existing between the two countries as senseless', and Cassel was sure that 'he would do anything in his power to establish friendly relations' with Germany. Churchill had many 'friendly sentiments towards Germany' and great 'admiration of the Kaiser and of the German people'.[83]

On 7 January Churchill replied to Cassel that he was flattered but that 'the occasion w[oul]d have to arise naturally & I sh[oul]d have to be empowered by Grey & the Prime Minister'. He therefore felt he had to decline the offer. However, if Wilhelm II invited the new King, his cousin George V, to Berlin this would be a different matter. If the Cabinet agreed Churchill would like to accompany the King and would 'be honoured' to talk with Tirpitz. The Germans should however be aware that only if 'Germany dropped the naval challenge' would 'an immediate détente with much good will from all England' be possible.[84]

Cassel reported this to Ballin, adding that Churchill's present position as First Lord 'ties him down to some special limitations'. Thus the opportunity to discuss the naval question with the German government had to come about 'spontaneously'.[85] On 13 January Ballin repeated his proposal to Churchill via Cassel.[86] Churchill asked Cassel to interrupt his holiday in the south of France and return to London as the matter was becoming increasingly important, though he did not immediately inform Grey of this most recent approach. Churchill only told Lloyd George and other friends in the Cabinet, but the Foreign Office may well have heard of the German approaches from other quarters.[87]

Two weeks later, on 27 January, Churchill convened a meeting with Grey, Lloyd George and Cassel at his house in London to discuss Ballin's proposals; there were no Foreign Office officials present. Regarding the question of sending a British minister to Berlin, Grey was 'willing but not hopeful'. He could not overlook the fact that the proposal had not been put to him 'but had reached members of the Cabinet who were likely to be most favourable to it'. Moreover, Grey was doubtful whether the German Emperor really wished to receive a member of the British Cabinet.[88] A brief paper summarizing the British position was drawn up and, presumably with the agreement of the Prime Minister, Cassel was asked to hand it to Chancellor Bethmann Hollweg and find out whether Ballin's idea had the support of the Kaiser and the German government.[89]

The following day Cassel travelled to Berlin. He was received by the Chancellor on the morning of 29 January and in the afternoon he had a meeting with the Emperor; also present were Bethmann Hollweg and Ballin but, tellingly, not Tirpitz. Cassel explained that the British government continued to insist on its naval superiority and on its demand that the German naval programme had to be 'retarded and reduced'. He believed, however, that London was ready to accept not only an enlargement of the German colonial empire in Africa but was even prepared to sign a 'neutrality' agreement. According to Churchill's letter to Grey reporting on the events as explained to him by Cassel, the Germans were all 'deeply pleased' and the Emperor was even 'enchanted' by the initiative.[90]

However, Wilhelm II did not seem to be aware that the initiative had originated with Ballin. Instead he mistakenly assumed this was an official British approach, which confirmed him in his belief that his policy of naval strength was showing results.[91] During his audience with the Kaiser Cassel submitted the British paper and in reply a memorandum was drawn up in English which Cassel was asked to deliver to the government in London. The memorandum included an invitation to Foreign Secretary Grey himself or, if he was unable to come, any other suitable British Cabinet minister like the First Lord to travel to Berlin for private talks. Bethmann Hollweg appeared to expect both Grey and Churchill to come to Berlin for negotiations.[92] Cassel was given a 'fairly full' and 'invaluable' summary of the forthcoming new German supplementary Naval Law to pass on to London.[93]

This document was 'devoured' all night by Churchill and his advisers on Cassel's return to London on 30 January.[94] While the Germans did not seem to be overly keen on colonial expansion, they intended to create a third battle squadron and raise the personnel necessary to man the ships, which Churchill regarded as 'a serious and formidable provision'. Moreover, the Kaiser was also planning to increase the number of his capital ships substantially in the next six years.[95] On 31 January 1912, Cassel, Churchill, Lloyd George and Lord Haldane, the Secretary of State for War, discussed the whole matter over breakfast at Cassel's London house. Grey, much to his later annoyance, was not told of the meeting – perhaps because it was known that he was not in favour of yet another round of negotiations with Germany.[96]

Eventually, on 3 February 1912, almost exactly a month after the first contacts had been made, the issue was discussed by the Cabinet. Grey was adamant that he did not want to travel to Berlin himself: his appearance would give the talks too much weight, give rise to considerable mistrust in Paris and might thus endanger the Triple Entente. Asquith also regarded a visit by Grey as 'premature'. Grey therefore proposed that Haldane, one of Asquith's and Grey's closest personal friends in the Cabinet, should once again (as in 1906) go to Germany 'to feel the way in the direction of a more definite under-standing'. Moreover, Haldane seemed to be the one who could travel to Berlin most inconspicuously as he was a fluent German speaker, greatly interested in German culture and philosophy and had many learned contacts in Germany.[97] This proposal was accepted.

Although the French were told of the mission and Haldane made sure to pay a visit to the French ambassador when he was in Berlin, Grey was subse-quently anxious to reassure Paris of Britain's loyalty to the entente. The Foreign Secretary also ensured that the Foreign Office was properly consulted. The British ambassador to Germany, Sir Edward Goschen, was asked to return to London to brief Haldane on the situation in Germany prior to his departure for Berlin. Goschen, however, was less than enthusiastic about Haldane's mission.[98] In his memoirs Grey explains that he 'agreed without demur and with good-will to Haldane's visit'; however, it appears, as Keith Robbins writes, that Grey had 'mixed feelings' about it. Most Foreign Office officials regarded the visit as a grave mistake and even as a 'foolish move'. It was widely believed that the 'absurd' mission only went ahead to appease the increasing number of 'Grey-must-go radicals' among the Liberals both within and without the government who wished to replace the Foreign Secretary with a man less keen on spending ever greater amounts on Britain's armaments industry.[99]

Indeed, the strong pressure from the remaining 'economists' in the Cabinet and the 'radical' backbenchers was one of the main reasons for the Cabinet's decision that Lord Haldane ought to go to Berlin for informal, unofficial and non-binding negotiations. He would be accompanied by his brother, the scholar John Haldane, and Ernest Cassel. To the general disbelief of the British and German press it was announced that Haldane would undertake a journey to Berlin to investigate the German university system. In a letter to the British ambassador to Paris Grey summarized the events as follows:

Last month a communication reached one of my colleagues [Churchill] from the German Emperor through Ballin and Cassel. It was brought to me, and some further communications passed through the same channel. The

Emperor expressed a strong wish that I should go to Berlin, and he sent me an invitation . . . It happens to be convenient for Haldane to go to Berlin about the business of a University Committee . . . He is to see Bethmann-Hollweg, and have a very frank exchange of views about naval expenditure.[100]

In his memoirs the Kaiser claimed that there was a battle for power in London about who should go to Berlin and be able to claim the glory for success in negotiating an Anglo-German agreement. Churchill wrote in his *World Crisis*: 'there never was any question of my going to Berlin to negotiate about the Navy; nor did I at this time wish to go.'[101] Cassel, however, was convinced that Churchill was keen on travelling to Berlin. Once it had transpired that Haldane would conduct the preliminary talks there, Cassel believed that both Grey and Churchill would eventually journey to the German capital to conduct the main negotiations and sign an agreement. British newspaper articles at the time also alleged that there was a conflict between Grey and Churchill in the matter, but there is no clear evidence that this was indeed the case.[102]

There is, however, some circumstantial evidence available to indicate that Churchill would have liked to travel to Berlin and was put out that Grey had not given him permission to go. Churchill may well have been trying to spoil Haldane's negotiations in Berlin (and thus be given a chance to negotiate himself) in a speech in Glasgow on 9 February 1912, the second day of Haldane's mission, when he claimed that the German fleet really represented 'something in the nature of a luxury'. This remark caused much offence and indignation in Germany and in the Liberal press in Britain, but Churchill later claimed that his speech did not have any negative impact on Haldane's mission.[103] Even if Churchill genuinely misjudged the storm of outrage which would result from his use of the derogatory term 'luxury fleet', it is difficult to believe that he would not have realized the negative consequences of attacking the German naval build-up while one of his colleagues was conducting difficult negotiations in Germany, which required an amicable atmosphere to arrive at a mutually satisfactory *modus vivendi*. Thus Churchill's ill-judged remark and his earlier attempt to omit Grey from the initial negotiations in the matter lend some credibility to the ex-Kaiser's statement in his memoirs and the rumours circulating in the British press of a power struggle in London over who should negotiate with Berlin.

On the whole, it appears safe to assume that Churchill was much less averse to travelling to Berlin in early 1912 to bring about a rapprochement with Germany – and reap the glory of such a success – than he later professed. His disquiet since Agadir regarding the naval race and his intensive endeavours to arrange a personal meeting with Tirpitz in the spring of 1914 also point to his deep concern about the poor state of Anglo-German relations and the resulting danger to world peace. His efforts in 1912–14 (and throughout his subsequent career) confirm his strong interest in personal high-level diplomacy to further his own ambitions.

However, this should not be taken too far. Clive Ponting's allegation that in 1912 Churchill 'did his best to sabotage any chances of an [Anglo-German] agreement being reached' is based on a misunderstanding. Ponting's assumption that when Churchill refused to accompany Cassel to Berlin in early January 1912, the First Lord 'ensured that Grey . . . did not go either' also seems to be a misinterpretation.[104] There is no evidence whatsoever that Churchill was opposed to an Anglo-German agreement or made sure that Grey did not travel to Germany, an assertion that exaggerates Churchill's importance within the Cabinet at the time. Furthermore, Churchill was strongly in favour of an Anglo-German rapprochement to preserve peace with or without his personal involvement. However, quite understandably, if at all possible he wished to bring about such a settlement himself to reap the glory and thereby further his political influence. The origins of Churchill's consuming interest in being personally involved in international summit diplomacy can be traced back to January/February 1912.

Prince Lichnowsky, the new German ambassador to London, summarized Churchill's political position succinctly when he warned his Foreign Ministry not to exaggerate Churchill's influence on Grey and Asquith. The latter two regarded Churchill as 'impulsive and flighty'. The ambassador was also convinced that Churchill was a 'very vain' man and above all 'bent, come what may, on playing a brilliant part'.[105] Prince Lichnowsky appears to have gained a fairly clear idea of Churchill's personality at this stage of his career, when the up-and-coming politician was very keen to make an impact and a name for himself both in Britain and in the international arena.

Although Haldane would not be in a position to offer an Anglo-German alliance or the neutrality pledge which the German government was bound to press for,[106] the British government hoped that his mission to Berlin might succeed in reducing the speed of the German naval build-up. Before Lord Haldane embarked on his journey on 7 February 1912 it was made clear to Berlin that negotiations could only be fruitful 'on the understanding that the point of naval expenditure is open to discussion and that there is a fair prospect of settling it favourably'.[107] As Churchill explained in his letter to Grey on 31 January 1912, short of the unlikely event of Berlin abruptly terminating its naval build-up, the only possible way to improve Anglo-German relations appeared to be if the Germans were prepared 'to slow down the "tempo" so that their Fleet Law is accomplished in twelve and not in six years'. Then, 'friendly relations would ensue, and we, though I should be reluctant to bargain about it, could slow down too'.[108] Grey agreed with this reasoning but also insisted that 'we must keep our hands free' to uphold the ententes with France and Russia. However, he conceded his willingness to satisfy the Germans 'that we have no intention of attacking them or supporting [an] aggressive policy against them'.[109]

As soon became apparent, the Kaiser had not yet entirely closed his mind to a compromise in the naval race on the basis of a prior political settlement. The rising strength of pacifist opinion in Germany, reflected in the impressive victory of the Social Democrats in the general election of January 1912, when they emerged as the largest party in the Reichstag, could not be ignored.[110] Nor could the strong domestic German opposition to further expansion of the fleet at the expense of investments in social programmes be disregarded. The immense efforts to expand both the navy and the army put a severe burden on the German taxpayer.[111] As early as late 1910 there was a growing realization within the German government and naval establishment that due to Britain's much larger industrial and colonial resources it would be very difficult if not impossible for the German navy to attain naval superiority.[112]

The decisive stumbling-block preventing an Anglo-German compromise remained the absence of a political settlement regarding the future European balance of power. Germany continued to insist on obtaining a neutrality pledge from London prior to a naval arrangement, while understandably Grey was not prepared to sign a blank cheque for German hegemony on the continent.[113] Within the Foreign Office it was generally and quite correctly believed that 'The Germans have no use for an agreement with Great Britain which would not alienate us from our present friends.'[114]

This is not the place to analyse in detail the Haldane Mission of 7–11 February 1912 and the subsequent Anglo-German negotiations in March and April.[115] Suffice it to say that Haldane himself believed initially that his talks with the Emperor, Chancellor Bethmann Hollweg and Tirpitz had been successful and that an Anglo-German rapprochement had been brought much closer. However, Haldane was outmanoeuvred on several occasions during his mission and unintentionally may have given the wrong impression of the position of the British government regarding Germany's naval programme. Moreover, Berlin does not seem to have understood how tentative and unofficial Haldane's mission was and that any assurances given by Haldane about the naval race or colonial questions required subsequent Cabinet approval.[116]

During the talks in Berlin, the Kaiser indicated his readiness to reduce (and not merely delay) the naval build-up – something he referred to as a 'substantial concession' – in return for a major political agreement.[117] Moreover, much to London's surprise, after his mission to Berlin Haldane was told by the German embassy in London on 12 March 1912 that the German government would withdraw the new Naval Law in return for a British promise not to combine against Germany with aggressive intentions.[118] However, as soon became clear, a mutual misunderstanding had occurred. Berlin still insisted on a promise of unconditional and absolute neutrality as the basis for any compromise solution and London still refused to offer such a substantial concession. Instead of reducing friction, in the long run the Haldane Mission contributed to a further increase in tension between the two countries. The whole mission was surrounded by confusion, misunderstandings and also hurt pride regarding the main issues and in respect to matters such as who had initiated the conversations and which channels had been used.[119]

To make matters even more complex, the day before Haldane's visit the final version of the new German supplementary Naval Law had been published (a detailed copy was given to Haldane to take back to London) and proved to be much more expansionist than had been expected. It caused 'genuine shock' within Whitehall.[120] What worried the British most was not so much the creation of a third battle squadron and the intention to build three additional Dreadnoughts but the large increase in destroyers and submarines (72 new ones were to be built) and a more than 20 per cent increase in active naval personnel to 15,000 instead of an increase to 4,000 as had been expected in London. This effectively meant that the German navy could be on active war strength throughout the year.[121] Moreover, the new Novelle severely curtailed the negotiating position of the German Chancellor, who was deeply interested in an accommodation with London but was fighting a losing battle against the expansionist plans of Admiral Tirpitz and Wilhelm II. The arrogant and not very bright Kaiser frequently changed his mind but in the last resort almost always supported his navy minister, and the failed Haldane mission had weakened Bethmann further. It has been rightly said that due to 'growing domestic polarisation, German foreign policy in the last years of peace witnessed a struggle between the reactionary navalist and moderate imperialist quest for the *fata morgana* of world power'.[122]

Chancellor Bethmann Hollweg continued to believe that only a political agreement in which London promised 'benevolent neutrality' in case 'either of the high contracting parties become entangled in a war with one or more other Powers' would allow him to delay or even reduce the German naval build-up against the opposition of Tirpitz and Wilhelm II.[123] The German Chancellor still hoped that via a policy of gradual rapprochement he would eventually obtain an agreement with Britain. Yet such a neutrality clause remained unacceptable to Grey and Asquith. Still, despite all opposition in Berlin, Bethmann Hollweg managed to continue the negotiations with Britain after Haldane had returned to London. The German Chancellor threatened to resign if he did not obtain the Emperor's agreement for another postponement of the introduction to the Reichstag of the supplementary Naval Law and the planned new Army Law until a further attempt had been made to arrive at a political agreement with Britain. Reluctantly, the Kaiser gave in after his initial anger over the differing interpretations of Haldane's mission in the two countries and his talk of mobilizing for war with Britain had subsided.[124]

While the official Anglo-German negotiations continued haphazardly, Ballin and Cassel attempted to be helpful. On 14 or 15 March they held discussions in London with Churchill and probably Haldane. The First Lord sounded optimistic regarding the possibility of a political settlement. It is not clear whether Churchill misinformed Ballin and misinterpreted the situation or whether Ballin misunderstood or deliberately misinterpreted him. In any event Ballin, who still had an exaggerated notion of Churchill's influence in the Cabinet,[125] believed at the end of the meeting that a declaration of absolute neutrality would be forthcoming soon. When he returned to Berlin on 17 March he presented himself to the Kaiser with the words, 'Your Majesty, I bring the alliance with England.'[126] One must agree with Richard Langhorne that in this situation Grey's compromise offer submitted on the afternoon of 17 March was a severe anti-climax, though it seems to have been received with glee in some quarters in Berlin.[127] Despite the willingness of Haldane and some other Cabinet members to offer a promise of unconditional neutrality, Grey's final offer only consisted of the formula that 'England declares that she will neither make nor join in any unprovoked attack upon Germany and pursue no aggressive policy towards her'.[128] On 18 March this draft was rejected by Berlin and a day later Grey was told by the German ambassador that his formula was 'so elastic as to be valueless'.[129]

However, Grey was still not willing to compromise on the question of a political agreement. After all, he did not merely wish to contain Germany's naval power and maintain the superiority of the British fleet; his main aim was to uphold the existing European balance of power.[130] On 22 March 1912 the new supplementary Naval Law was introduced to the Reichstag. For the time being, Anglo-German negotiations continued half-heartedly into April.[131]

On 18 March, when London believed that the possibility of an Anglo-German accommodation still existed, Churchill delivered his first naval estimates to parliament and included his first proposal for a 'naval holiday' – a plan to freeze the armaments race on the basis of the status quo.[132] Churchill was utterly convinced of its potential to overcome Anglo-German tension.[133] His proposal had the added advantage of convincing his colleagues in the Liberal government as well as the 'radical' Liberal backbenchers that the First Lord, who had crossed over from the Tories in 1904, was indeed a true Liberal. After all, already in 1904 the magazine *Vanity Fair* had written about him: 'He is ambitious; he means to get on, and he loves his country. But he can hardly be regarded as the slave of any Party.'[134] Moreover, in the face of growing domestic opposition to the huge sums allocated to the navy, Churchill's proposal had the potential to unite the 'economists' and the 'navalists' within the Cabinet and appease the Liberal Party's 'radical' backbenchers by demonstrating that every effort had been made to avoid an increase in the estimates. The Foreign Office, however, was opposed to the proposal.[135]

In the House of Commons, Churchill explained that in 1913 'Germany will build three capital ships, and it will be necessary for us to build five in consequence'.[136] Thus, Churchill threatened Germany with the prospect of further strenuous British rearmament efforts if the German government did not become more reasonable. Churchill made clear that Britain would adhere to its aim of maintaining a 60 per cent naval superiority under all circumstances. His robust declaration of a 'policy of strength' was, however, accompanied by an offer to compromise and to find a mutually satisfactory accommodation.[137] He declared that any 'retardation or reduction in German construction will, within certain limits, be promptly followed here'. To achieve this Churchill proposed that both countries should 'take a holiday for that year . . . The three ships that she [Germany] did not build would therefore automatically wipe out no fewer than five British potential super-Dreadnoughts, and that is more than I expect them to hope to do in a brilliant naval action.'[138]

The First Lord's imaginative proposal was not well received in Germany. In fact, according to Ballin, it made a 'very bad impression' in Berlin (though much less so in the German press). The German government greatly feared the negative consequences of the cancellation of large shipping orders on Germany's shipyards; it was bound to lead to a considerable rise in unemployment and, perhaps, to social unrest.[139] Thus the Kaiser believed, as he expressed it in a 'courteous message' to Churchill via Cassel, that the proposed arrangement 'would only be possible between allies'.[140]

On 10 April the German government announced that it intended to proceed with the supplementary Navy Law and the law was passed by the Reichstag in May 1912. For the time being this effectively ended all discussions about a naval agreement and the British press soon lost interest in the naval race. The sinking of the *Titanic* on the night of 14–15 April 1912 overshadowed all other issues in the media. Instead of pursuing a genuine Anglo-German rapprochement in the course of 1912, both parties merely managed to achieve an uneasy détente by once again concentrating on colonial matters and avoiding any substantial discussions of the mutual limitation of armaments.[141]

This state of affairs seemed threatened by the outbreak of war in the Balkans in October. In December Haldane, with Grey's authorization, told Prince Lichnowsky, the German ambassador, in no uncertain terms that Britain would not be able to remain neutral if Austria invaded Serbia. The balance of power on the European continent should be maintained; power must not be concentrated in the hands of one nation. London would intervene on behalf of Paris if Germany should ever attempt to fight an unprovoked war against the militarily inferior France or if Berlin supported Austrian aggression in the Balkans. This caused much resentment in Berlin and an outburst of anger from the Kaiser. It was clear that the uneasy détente in British-German relations was very fragile indeed. However, subsequently Bethmann Hollweg successfully managed to work for a Balkan settlement in cooperation with Britain. He also achieved an Anglo-German agreement of outstanding questions in the Middle East, such as disputes over the construction of the Baghdad railway line.[142]

In early 1913 both countries announced new navy estimates. Tirpitz used the opportunity to make a conciliatory speech in the Reichstag in early February and even accepted Britain's superiority ratio of 8:5 in terms of battle squadrons. Grey had no difficulty in realizing that the reason for Tirpitz's restraint was not 'the love of our beautiful eyes, but the extra 50 million required for the German army', which made Tirpitz's domestic position increasingly precarious.[143] Churchill, however, felt encouraged to repeat his holiday proposal on 26 March, when he presented the new naval estimates to the House of Commons and announced the need for a further increase in naval spending.[144] Again the 'holiday proposal' was much resented in Berlin. The German government feared that the growing domestic opposition to further spending on the army and navy might well find Churchill's proposal attractive.[145]

Thus, while the government in Berlin publicly declared, as for example did Bethmann Hollweg in a speech in April 1913, that they were looking forward to disarmament proposals from London, privately the British government was told by the German ambassador and even by the Kaiser himself that Berlin would not welcome such diplomatic approaches.[146] Although Bethmann was regarded as 'intelligent, hard-working, conscientious, and, above all, honest and straightforward' in British diplomatic circles,[147] this annoyed the politicians in London. It also put them on the defensive as far as British public opinion and the radical Liberal press were concerned. Churchill in particular resented this hypocrisy. Therefore, he let it be known in June that he would repeat his holiday proposal in the autumn. He explained to Grey in early July 1913 that in case the Cabinet decided that he should not do so, he 'ought to be at liberty to state that we have received representations from the German government to the effect that they do not desire to discuss any such proposals'.[148] This strategy seemed to be rather risky and Grey hesitated. Eventually, however, the Foreign Secretary agreed that in view of German duplicity in the matter 'it was absolutely necessary that some reference should be made to it in public'.[149]

Keeping in mind the planned increases in the British naval estimates for 1914, which were bound to shock the nation and the radical wing of his party, Churchill explained his renewed proposal for a one-year 'naval holiday' at length in a speech in Manchester in October 1913. It provoked a storm of protest in Germany and also in Britain; his proposal was viewed with deep mistrust in both countries, albeit for different reasons. While Churchill's good intentions were generally accepted, the British public resented the enormous amounts to be spent on rearmament. In Germany, his proposal was regarded as highly unrealistic. Editorials in the German press asked Churchill to refrain from meddling in Germany's internal affairs and encouraged him to take a holiday from making speeches. The Kaiser told his Chancellor that he was not prepared to embark yet again on the 'endless, dangerous chapter on the limitation of armaments'.[150]

Officials in the British Foreign Office continued to be deeply worried about Churchill's idea. They viewed with horror the opportunity handed to Germany to drive a wedge between Britain and its entente partners. Unlike Churchill, they could not ignore the fact that for the holiday proposal to be successful, other countries would also have to freeze their naval construction. Any diplomatic pressure exerted by London on Russia and France to freeze their naval build-up would cause great resentment in these countries and might turn both countries away from their ententes with Britain.[151] However, the Germans missed this opportunity to divide the ententes. They 'were too suspicious of Churchill, and too wedded to their own construction schedule, to attempt to do so'.[152] Instead, Tirpitz continued his 'hide-and-seek' strategy of proclaiming that the German government was keenly awaiting British proposals on how to end the naval race while indicating in private that such approaches were highly unwelcome.

Eventually, on 3 February 1914, during a speech in Manchester, Grey indicated what was going on behind the scenes; he said that it was useless to make proposals which were not welcome and which the German government was not prepared to receive.[153] In the face of rising domestic opposition to the

growing spending on the British navy and the armaments race which seemed
to be spiralling out of control (even Lloyd George turned against the First
Lord),[154] Churchill had managed to display his willingness to compromise by
engaging in talks with the help of his holiday proposals without sacrificing
Britain's security as he viewed it. He thus avoided the accusation of being
either a warmonger or an appeaser. In early 1914 Churchill achieved an
increase of the naval estimates by another £3 million to the staggering amount
of almost £53 million for 1914–15; this was announced in Churchill's estimates
speech on 17 March 1914.[155]

In an atmosphere of financial and political doom and gloom which accompanied the continuation of the naval race, in May 1914 Churchill made one
further dramatic attempt to improve Anglo-German relations and halt the
rearmament process before the outbreak of the First World War. Thus it is not
correct to assume that after the collapse of Haldane's mission in mid-1912 'the
British no longer entertained the possibility of a rapprochement with
Germany'.[156] Churchill at least was still hopeful of arriving at an Anglo-
German détente by means of personal diplomacy.

May 1914: Last Attempts to Negotiate with Tirpitz

Initially it was again Ballin and Cassel who attempted to re-convene Anglo-
German naval negotiations. In late April 1914 Ballin suggested to Cassel that it
might be a good idea if the First Lord attended the forthcoming Kiel week in
June, the annual celebratory review display of the German fleet. He would then
be able to meet Tirpitz personally and discuss all outstanding Anglo-German
differences. A British squadron was expected to participate in the review.
According to Churchill's later account, Ballin wrote to Cassel: 'How I wish that
I could get Churchill here during the Kiel week. Tirpitz will never allow the
Chancellor to settle any naval questions, but I know he would like to have a talk
with his English colleague on naval matters, and I am sure that if the subject of
limiting naval armaments were ever approached in a businesslike way, some
agreement would be reached.'[157] Churchill was 'enthusiastic' about Ballin's idea
when he heard about it from Cassel and he asked his friend 'to find out whether
Tirpitz really wanted to see me and have a talk'.[158] As he was reassured that 'this
is so', Churchill believed it might be sensible to make an official visit to the
Russian Kronstadt on board a British Dreadnought to reassure the entente
partners of Britain's loyalty and then join the British squadron in Kiel. This
would provide an opportunity to talk to Tirpitz. The German ambassador was
convinced that Churchill had made up his mind to travel to Kiel.[159]

However, neither Tirpitz nor anyone else in Berlin was interested in conducting negotiations with Churchill. Only the Kaiser initially seemed to be keen on making the Kiel week event more glamorous with the help of the presence of a British Cabinet minister. Grey (and presumably Churchill) were informed by the German ambassador on 18 May 'that the Emperor wishes it to be understood that he has invited the First Lord of the Admiralty and the Sea Lord to Kiel officially'.[160]

Encouraged by this, on 20 May 1914 Churchill took the initiative by writing to the Prime Minister and the Foreign Secretary. In his memorandum he informed them that the naval race between the British and German Empires was no more than a misunderstanding. A friendly *tête-à-tête* between Admiral Tirpitz and himself would enable the differences to be put aside. He therefore hoped that, if the opportunity arose, he would be able to set off on a trip to Germany.[161] With the exception of his rather more tentative and much more cautious endeavour to arrange a visit to Berlin in January/February 1912, this was Churchill's first open attempt at active personal summit diplomacy. Churchill informed Asquith and Grey:

> I have heard verbally from Cassel that he knows for a fact through Ballin that Tirpitz would like to see me . . . Personally I should like to meet Tirpitz, and I think a non-committal, friendly conversation, if it arose naturally and freely, might do good, and could not possibly do any harm. Indeed, after all I have said about a Naval holiday, it would be difficult for me to repulse any genuine desire on his part for such a conversation. . . . I do not expect any agreement on these, but I would like to strip the subject of the misrepresentation and misunderstanding with which it has been surrounded, and put it on a clear basis in case circumstances should ever render it admissible. . . . I hope . . . my wish to put these points to Admiral Tirpitz if a good opportunity arises . . . may not be dismissed.[162]

Churchill's suggestion of a visit to Berlin in 1914 bears a close resemblance to his plans to visit Moscow in the years 1953 and 1954.[163] In the 1950s Churchill also spoke about misunderstandings that could easily be brushed aside by an informal conference with Britain's main adversary. At the same time he added that it could not be expected that the discussions would immediately lead to concrete results. The objective of stabilizing the general political situation and reducing defence burdens that would result from talking and negotiating with a potential enemy and thus enable his country to maintain its world power status played a major role in Churchill's argumentation both in 1914 and three decades later.

In this respect the views and ambitions of the 40-year-old First Lord of the Admiralty in 1914 did not differ much from those of the almost 80-year-old Prime Minister in 1953. Contrary to the often-expressed opinion in the scholarly literature, Churchill did not suddenly develop his ideas on summit diplomacy during his search for a major political theme in the period of opposition between 1945 and 1951 or after Stalin's death in March 1953. Nor can his views on how a summit meeting should be conducted be attributed to his age or his increasing senility.[164] Already in 1912–14 (and later during the bi- and multilateral conferences of the Second World War), he held very similar views: Churchill sought to set up informal conferences without any strict agenda but with himself at the centre of attention to further world peace and, above all, ensure Britain's continued status as a great power.

In 1914 Churchill was, however, less impatient than four decades later. Despite being rightly described as a 'young man in a hurry',[165] he had more time in hand than in the 1950s, when his health was declining and his colleagues were increasingly attempting to push him into retirement. Thus Churchill had made it clear in his letter to Asquith and Grey that he would not journey to the German capital under any circumstances. The Germans were not to receive the impression of Great Britain being so alarmed by their competition as to necessitate a Minister of the Crown having to travel to Berlin in person. 'I do not wish to go to Germany for the purpose of initiating such a discussion. I would rather go for some other reason satisfactory in itself and let the discussion of these serious questions come about only if it is clearly appropriate.' Aware of Grey's and the Foreign Office's lack of enthusiasm for his proposal, Churchill thus wished to keep open a way of saving face should a visit to Germany not be possible after all: he suggested that 'For the present ... nothing should be done until the Emperor's invitation arrives; and, secondly, until we hear what Tirpitz's real wish is.'[166]

This was a wise strategy. In late May 1914 Grey and Asquith turned down Churchill's proposal to meet Tirpitz at the end of June. By 25 May an official written invitation had not yet arrived and Grey recalled that 'hitherto all efforts on our part to get naval expenditure discussed have been resented by Tirpitz even when welcomed by Bethmann Hollweg'; furthermore, it had been intimated to him several times that he should not even 'mention naval expenditure' to the German ambassador.[167] Sir Edward Grey was therefore 'apprehensive that more harm than good might result from such a discussion' between Churchill and Tirpitz.[168] Moreover, if Tirpitz really wished to enter into talks, he could just let the British embassy in Berlin know and discussions could easily be arranged. Thus, displaying an attitude quite similar to the views of Foreign Secretary Anthony Eden and the Foreign Office in 1953–54, Grey believed that informal and unofficial discussions with the main potential enemy 'may not only be futile but may cause resentment'.[169]

Grey also resented the attempts made between May and July 1914 by Colonel House, American President Woodrow Wilson's confidant, to mediate in European affairs during his visit to Europe. House's personal ambition was to 'bring about the naval holiday which W. Churchill has proposed'. He hoped that this would eventually result in 'a sympathetic understanding between England, Germany and America' and preserve world peace.[170] After House had talked to most of the influential politicians in Berlin, including the Kaiser, in the last week of May, he travelled to London via Paris to persuade the entente partners of his grand design. In Britain, House proposed that Grey, the Kaiser and himself should meet in Kiel to discuss his plan. Although not many people among the British elite were impressed by this, the government did everything to be as polite as possible to the American. House and Permanent Under-Secretary Sir William Tyrell, Grey's trusted senior adviser, began working on the development of House's vague ideas. The American was also given the opportunity on various occasions to meet Britain's leading politicians such as the Prime Minister, Lord Haldane, Lloyd George and Lord Crewe.[171]

However, Grey himself was too busy to see House for any length of time though they met in the course of several luncheons. In view of the reservations regarding personal diplomacy with the German government which Grey had expressed to Churchill, it was not surprising that House's plan of involving the Foreign Secretary personally in summit diplomacy with the Kaiser proved unacceptable. Grey still feared it would lead to the rise of suspicion and mistrust in Paris and St Petersburg and would put Britain's alliances unneces-sarily at risk. After all, by June 1914 Britain was in the middle of conducting secret negotiations with Russia, which included an agreement about joint naval operations in case of war with Germany. Although these negotiations were subsequently denied by Grey in the House of Commons, their revelation contributed to a worsening of Anglo-German relations which House was unable to avoid. Bethmann Hollweg believed that the Anglo-French negotia-tions constituted a severe breach of faith; he felt that the rug was being pulled from under his careful policy of obtaining a rapprochement with London.[172]

Moreover, President Wilson's emissary seemed to be quite ill-informed and largely unaware of the difficulties inherent in Britain's carefully nurtured system of alliances. House's diplomatic inexperience with respect to European affairs and lack of understanding of Britain's domestic political situation may also explain why he appears to have failed to consult Churchill at any length, although Churchill was more or less the only influential British politician who might have supported his initiative with enthusiasm. Thus House sailed back to the United States without having achieved anything; his 'great adventure', as he called it, had failed.[173]

In the summer of 1914 Churchill had to resign himself to the fact that he had been refused permission to pursue his personal diplomacy with Tirpitz. He had no choice but to accept the Foreign Secretary's decision of late May. He remained convinced, however, that it was a mistake to dismiss a chance to engage in personal diplomacy with Tirpitz which could possibly resolve a major conflict and preserve world peace. He also took it almost for granted that Tirpitz would be interested in Anglo-German naval discussions – as in the 1950s when he would not doubt the Soviet Union's great interest in negotiating with him. In 1914 this view was utterly mistaken but it was strengthened by the Kaiser's apparent expectation 'up to the last moment' that Churchill would come to Kiel, where a berth remained reserved for Churchill's official ship, the *Enchantress*, during the naval festivities in the city.[174]

Churchill continued to believe that he was ideally suited to conduct such informal talks at this dangerous juncture in international politics. He explained in a memorandum to the Foreign Secretary:

> I am convinced that no discussion other than by me and Tirpitz personally w[ou]ld be useful on the points mentioned. These sort of questions become much too crude and formal when treated through routine channels. Every kind of guarding condition to meet all possible contingencies w[ou]ld have to be hammered out; and there w[ou]ld not be much confidence or good-will left at the end.[175]

This remained his view of informal personal 'summit' diplomacy until his retirement from politics more than four decades later. In the same week Churchill had hoped to speak to Tirpitz to overcome Anglo-German rivalries, the shots in Sarajevo heralded the outbreak of war. Churchill continued to believe that an opportunity to settle Anglo-German antagonism had been thrown away. He remained convinced that his powers of persuasion should have been used to bring about a more peaceful world.

Churchill maintained his conviction of the value of personal diplomacy, first shaped in the years 1908–14, when after the Gallipoli disaster, which led to his dismissal as First Lord of the Admiralty in 1915, and his subsequent voluntary military service in the trenches in France, Lloyd George, now Prime Minister, was courageous enough to give him another chance in politics. Although Lloyd George had become increasingly suspicious of Churchill's wide-ranging political ambitions, he appointed the disgraced politician Minister of Munitions (1917–19) and subsequently to Secretary of State for War and Air

(1919–21) and Colonial Secretary (1921–22). In 1921, after some hesitation, Churchill was strongly in favour of talks to achieve a settlement of the Irish question and prevent the shedding of further blood in Ireland. He partici-pated actively in the ensuing negotiations in London. Shortly before his assas-sination, Michael Collins, the leader of the Irish negotiating team, passed on a message to Churchill with regard to the successful conclusion of the Anglo-Irish negotiations for Irish Home Rule and Dominion status (as well as the partition of the country): 'Tell Winston we could never have done anything without him.'[176]

During Churchill's long spell as Chancellor of the Exchequer (1924–29), he had little involvement in international diplomacy. In the 'wilderness years' between 1929 and 1939, when Churchill was out of office and forced to focus on his writing career, his opportunities were even more constrained. In January 1931 he left the Conservative shadow cabinet over violent disagreements with the Tory leadership with regard to India. Subsequently he fell out with the leadership of his party over his support for King Edward VIII in the abdication crisis of 1936; his repeated calls for a vigorous British rearmament effort were also resented. By that time many of his 'countrymen generally regarded him', as Arthur M. Schlesinger Jr has said, as 'unreliable, reactionary and reckless, a brilliant man who had thrown away what might have been a brilliant political career'.[177]

Not surprisingly, during most of the 1930s Churchill found himself largely side-lined with little opportunity for being involved in high politics and meeting the important political personalities of other countries. He never met Hitler although in 1932 there had nearly been an opportunity. In late August and early September of that year, Churchill, accompanied by his family and a few friends, visited Germany to research his *Life of Marlborough*, the biography of his famous ancestor. His son Randolph had alerted Ernst Hanfstaengl (nicknamed 'Putzi'), one of his German acquaintances, asking him to join them for dinner at their Munich hotel and bring Hitler along.[178] Hanfstaengl was at that time a close associate and financial supporter of Hitler who in early August had for the first time demanded to be appointed German Chancellor.[179] According to Churchill's memoirs, he met Hanfstaengl by chance at the Munich hotel and as the German, a Harvard history graduate, spoke fluent English and was 'a lively and talkative fellow', they had dinner together. In the course of the conversation Hanfstaengl offered to arrange a meeting with Hitler; this, he said, could easily be done as every day Hitler came to the hotel at 5 p.m. Churchill was interested but, according to his memoirs, after he had expressed his distaste for Hitler's anti-Semitism in the course of the conver-sation, the meeting was cancelled as 'the Führer would not be coming to the hotel that afternoon'. Churchill did not see Hanfstaengl again although he and his 'family expedition' stayed several more days at the hotel.[180]

Hanfstaengl's memoirs, published in 1957, vary a little from Churchill's account. According to him, Randolph Churchill asked him to join Churchill and his entourage for dinner; he 'hoped that I would be able to bring Hitler along to meet his father'. However, Hitler refused the invitation. He told Hanfstaengl that he was busy, had to get up early the next morning and 'produced a thousand excuses ... as he always did when he was afraid of meeting someone'. Hanfstaengl believed that Hitler had realized that Churchill was 'a figure whom he knew to be his equal in political ability'. Although Hanfstaengl attempted to convince Hitler to join them for coffee, remarking that Churchill was 'the easiest man to talk to in the world – art, politics, architecture, anything you choose', the Führer remained unconvinced.[181]

Hanfstaengl left to have dinner with the British visitors. In the course of the dinner conversation Churchill allegedly said, 'Tell me ... how does your chief feel about an alliance between your country, France and England?' Although this remark by a controversial ex-minister who had no immediate chances of again becoming a Cabinet member was of no particular consequence, Churchill seems indeed to have made a remark to this effect; in his own memoirs he writes that 'I always wanted England, Germany, and France to be friends.'[182] Hanfstaengl, however, regarded it as a most serious statement. He became excited and excused himself in order to find Hitler to convince him to meet Churchill after all. Much to his surprise he bumped into the Führer in the hotel hall and again attempted to persuade him to come and meet Churchill in the restaurant just down the corridor. Hitler, however, said that he was unshaven (which was true) and had too much to do and made his excuses. Although Hanfstaengl had been unable to pass on either Churchill's remark about a tripartite alliance or his aversion to Hitler's anti-Semitism, Hitler 'had made up his mind not to expose himself to anyone with the capacity to steal his thunder'. Apparently, Hitler was apprehensive of meeting Churchill and deliberately 'kept away' until the Briton and his entourage had left Munich.[183]

Subsequently, Hitler appears to have regretted his timidity, as in the course of the 1930s he twice invited Churchill to come and see him. But unlike Lloyd George, who visited Hitler in September 1936 in Berchtesgaden and was 'completely misled' (according to Churchill's memoirs),[184] Churchill apparently believed that the discrepancy in influence and power between the German Führer and himself – at the time a mere parliamentarian without public office – would not be conducive to constructive talks. Churchill reasoned that if he agreed with the man in conversation he would mislead him; if he disagreed with him he would be 'accused of spoiling Anglo-German relations' in Britain.[185] Yet, as Hanfstaengl's memoirs seem to indicate, in 1932 Churchill was, quite naturally, curious to meet Hitler. After all, Hitler was the controversial, but rising man in German politics; at the time Churchill 'had no special prejudices' and he 'knew little of his doctrine or record and nothing of his character'.[186] A few years later, in 1935, Churchill was still able to write that 'Those who have met Herr Hitler face to face in public business or on social terms have found a highly competent, cool, well-informed functionary with an agreeable manner, a disarming smile, and few have been unaffected by a subtle personal magnetism.'[187] Although Churchill narrowly missed meeting Hitler in 1932, he had several private meetings with various German and Czech politicians in 1938 and paid a visit to French politician Paul Reynaud in Paris in the same year. Naturally, after the German invasion of Poland on 1 September 1939 and the outbreak of the Second World War a meeting with Hitler became very difficult if not impossible.

On 3 September 1939, the day when Britain and France declared war on Nazi Germany, Prime Minister Chamberlain again offered him the position of First Lord of the Admiralty, the post from which he had been dismissed in 1915, and a seat in the War Cabinet. Churchill's ever louder calls for British rearmament, the introduction of conscription, the setting up of a coalition system including above all an alliance with the Soviet Union to protect the world from Hitler's expansionist policies, and his increasing popularity with the British people and the press had left Chamberlain little choice.[188] Churchill would lose little time in embarking on personal diplomacy once again. He focused on the important attempt to exploit his personal charisma in his relations with both American President Franklin D. Roosevelt and, despite his visceral anti-Communism, with Soviet dictator Joseph Stalin. During as well as after the war Churchill's first concern was to maintain the great power position of the British Empire. His personal summit diplomacy was meant to facilitate the achievement of this goal while also allowing him personally to remain at the centre of international attention.

CHAPTER 2

The Politics of War
Summit Diplomacy with Roosevelt and Stalin

During the Second World War Churchill became convinced of his powers of persuasion and the usefulness of personal diplomacy. After he became Prime Minister in May 1940, his strong belief in his ability to influence international developments through personal diplomacy was shown in his enthusiasm to undertake the many bilateral negotiations and the 'Big Three' conferences of the war. Churchill knew that the very survival of his country would depend on his ability to negotiate with American President Roosevelt to elicit much needed military support from the United States and to forge an alliance with the Soviet dictator Stalin. Churchill would not, however, contemplate the idea of a compromise peace with Hitler, though some of his cabinet colleagues were tempted. In the War Cabinet on 26 and 28 May 1940 and the following month after the fall of France, Churchill prevailed against Lord Halifax's inclination to start immediate peace negotiations.[1] With regard to peace feelers from Nazi Germany, and in stark contrast to his penchant for personal diplomacy, Churchill generally believed in 'absolute silence'; he remained 'absolutely opposed to the slightest contact'.[2]

The War Unfolds: Bilateral Summit Diplomacy with Roosevelt and Stalin

The high point of Churchill's personal diplomacy was achieved in the course of the Second World War. In 1940–41 his influence and powers of persuasion were decisive in securing Washington's assistance for a beleaguered Britain. Hitler's invasion of the Soviet Union in June 1941 and his declaration of war on the United States on 11 December gave rise to the 'Big Three' anti-Hitler coalition. Prior to these events, Churchill had done his best to induce both Roosevelt and Stalin to join the war against Nazi Germany and his personal diplomacy contributed decisively to the formation of the 'Grand Alliance'. Churchill had even managed to overcome his powerful anti-Communism and loathing of the Bolsheviks, which went back to the revolution of 1917. As John Lewis Gaddis has written, he realized that 'geopolitics was more important than ideology'.[3] Yet Churchill's relations with both Roosevelt and Stalin proved to be much less harmonious than he liked to admit in public and in his subsequent war memoirs.

On 11 September 1939 only eight days after the declaration of war on 3 September and nine days after Churchill had again been appointed First Lord of the Admiralty, President Roosevelt suggested to him that they engage in an occasional correspondence. Roosevelt had realized Churchill's potential as future Prime Minister. The President was always inclined to ignore the State Department and correspond personally with foreign leaders and American ambassadors. Like Churchill Roosevelt believed deeply in personal diplomacy and his own powers of persuasion. Churchill accepted Roosevelt's offer immediately.[4] Churchill had spotted the opportunity to cultivate a personal contact important both for his country and his own career. He believed too much in himself to worry about the fact that he was virtually ignoring the Foreign Office as well as the British and American ambassadors in his high-level diplomacy with Roosevelt.[5]

In his war memoirs, Churchill expressed a high regard for Roosevelt's suggestion in early 1938 that a high-level international conference should be convened at the White House to discuss the arms race and economic matters; he believed it might well have prevented the outbreak of war. The Prime Minister Neville Chamberlain had viewed Roosevelt's initiative as 'preposterous' and an example of economic imperialism designed to usurp British markets. According to Churchill, Chamberlain had thus rejected negotiations to explore 'this last frail chance to save the world from tyranny otherwise than by war'.[6] Churchill did not intend to make the same mistake; if anything this missed opportunity made him even more determined to use his cherished personal summit diplomacy to obtain America's assistance for Britain's war effort.

When Churchill became Prime Minister on 10 May 1940 and following the rapid and entirely unexpected German defeat of France and the entry of Italy into the war in June, the personal contact between the British and American heads of government became ever closer.[7] Although the United States was still officially neutral, in September 1940 Roosevelt placed fifty destroyers at the disposal of the British government for the fight against the Axis powers.[8] FDR's third consecutive election victory in November 1940 facilitated even more cooperation. The President was now able to pay less attention to the anti-war opinions that were expressed in many isolationist circles in the United States.[9] Moreover, due to the fierce resistance during the Battle of Britain in August and October 1940,[10] the British gained a tremendous degree of admiration and respect from the American public. Roosevelt ordered a gradual increase in the output of the American armaments industry. In January 1941 he presented the Lend-Lease Act to Congress. This would enable the British government, now desperately low on dollar reserves, to receive goods and weapons of all kinds from Washington without having to worry, for the time being, as to how the shipments would be financed.[11] However, Britain became increasingly dependent on American goodwill. In January 1941, Roosevelt's confidant Harry Hopkins flew to London to make Churchill's acquaintance; ambassador Averell Harriman and Under Secretary of State Sumner Welles paid a visit to Churchill in March. Churchill was very keen to gain their trust and did every-thing possible to establish a close relationship with all three.[12]

In August 1941 the first meeting between Churchill and Roosevelt took place aboard the *Prince of Wales* in Placentia Bay near Argentia in Newfoundland. It led to the signing of the Atlantic Charter, a vague Anglo-American statement on common war aims which expressed the two leaders' 'hopes for a better future for the world'.[13] However, Anglo-American differences on self-determi-nation, anti-colonialism, the future system of global trade and the post-war order had already come out in the open to some extent. In the long run these disagreements would seriously affect the war-time alliance as well as Churchill's personal relations with Roosevelt.[14]

On 21 December 1941, two weeks after the Japanese attack on Pearl Harbor, Churchill met Roosevelt in Washington for prolonged discussions. The Prime Minister had more or less invited himself and could not be dissuaded by a report from Lord Halifax, the British ambassador, that the President had expressed reservations about the planned meeting; Roosevelt had, however, succeeded in persuading Churchill not to rush to Washington immediately after Pearl Harbor.[15] With his first visit to Washington as Prime Minister, Churchill was able to give significant impetus to the formation of the 'Grand Alliance' of the Second World War and thereby lay the basis for victory over the Axis powers.[16] He would never forget his success between mid-1940 to the end of 1941 in binding the United States more closely to his country and obtaining American support for the British war effort and, as he believed, for the preservation of both Britain and the Empire. After the Japanese attack on Pearl Harbor Churchill exulted: 'I knew the United States was in the war, up to the neck and in to the death. So we had won after all! . . . England would live;

Britain would live; the Commonwealth of Nations and the Empire would live.'[17] Churchill's emotional outburst ignored the very real threat that the US might focus on the war in the Pacific rather than on the European theatre of war, but it soon became clear that he was essentially right. Only a month before, Roosevelt had doubted whether he would get a declaration of war from Congress if he asked for it; after Pearl Harbor this was no problem.[18] According to Lord Halifax the Roosevelt administration was 'terribly shaken' by the Japanese assault, and 'fully realize that they have been caught napping. I think they realise too what it means.'[19]

Close Anglo-American relations would indeed prove to be decisive for the further course of the war and the Prime Minister believed that it was above all his personal diplomacy, including the correspondence he conducted with Roosevelt, frequently outflanking the Foreign Office, that was the key to his success.[20] Churchill's attempts at summit diplomacy during and after the war were to a large extent based on his successful policy in the years 1940–41. The early expression of American support was complemented by many subsequent examples of Washington's generosity which he secured through personal negotiation. For example, in June 1942 Churchill was in Washington for his third visit as Prime Minister when news of the devastating loss of the British garrison in Tobruk arrived; he was able to persuade Roosevelt to offer immediate replacements for the lost tanks and guns.[21]

During 1942–43 Churchill managed to obtain Roosevelt's support for the North African campaign and his Mediterranean strategy (invasions of Sicily and Italy), which necessitated a postponement of the opening of a Second Front in France until 1943 and ultimately even 1944. Although this was strongly opposed by the American Chiefs of Staff, including Army Chief of Staff General Marshall, who favoured a rapid attack on Germany through France, the President gave in to Churchill's powers of persuasion.[22]

Throughout the war Churchill continued to seek to arrange meetings with Roosevelt on a regular basis and took care not to neglect his correspondence with the President. In total, Churchill and Roosevelt met eleven times without Stalin, usually every four to five months.[23] Prior to the war summit conferences of the 'Big Three' at Tehran, Yalta and Potsdam, the Prime Minister suggested meetings with Roosevelt so as to establish a joint position *vis-à-vis* the USSR and increase the chance of impressing the British point of view on Roosevelt. He was however not always successful with this strategy.[24]

Before the Tehran conference in November/December 1943 Churchill was the only one of the 'Big Three' who had maintained personal, direct contact with the other two. He was extremely pleased with this arrangement and did not care for the prospect of Roosevelt and Stalin establishing closer contact.

Churchill deeply mistrusted the Soviet dictator, whom he frequently suspected of considering a separate peace treaty with Hitler in 1942 and 1943.[25] Nor could he entirely trust Roosevelt: he tremendously disliked the President's tendency to ignore Britain when attempting to obtain Stalin's cooperation for his internationalist design for the post-war world.[26] Churchill suspected both Roosevelt and Stalin of intending to place Britain's far-flung colonial interests on the negotiating table and, in particular during the last two years of the war, to ignore many of his country's strategic concerns and preferences for the shape of the post-war world.[27]

Despite those difficulties, the Prime Minister was always convinced that the 'fraternal association' with the United States, brought about by the common language and a similar democratic culture, was of a very different quality from the alliance with the Soviet Union.[28] Nonetheless, the latter was no less important to Britain's survival and future role; thus whilst Churchill maintained close contacts with the American President, he was also greatly interested in pursuing a close relationship with Stalin. He sought to correspond with and meet the dictator as often as possible.[29]

Stalin, however, remained deeply distrustful of Churchill and his long standing anti-Communist reputation.[30] In 1944, he told the Yugoslav communist Djilas: 'Perhaps you think that just because we are the allies of the English we have forgotten who they are and who Churchill is ... Churchill is the kind of man who will pick your pocket of a kopeck if you don't watch him.'[31] Since early 1942 Stalin had known of the secret Anglo-American research programme to develop an atomic bomb which he was not told about;[32] together with the issue of the Second Front it confirmed his continued suspicion of the Anglo-Americans.

The Bolshevik Danger and Churchill's Anti-Communism

Ever since the Bolshevik revolution of 1917 Churchill had been one of the Soviet Union's most outspoken enemies and had done his best 'to strangle Bolshevism at its birth'.[33] He had been strongly in favour of the Allied intervention in the Russian civil war, after the signing of the Russo-German Brest-Litovsk peace treaty in March 1918.[34] In the summer of 1918, a force numbering some 30,000 soldiers (half of them British), was dispatched to northern Russia, the Caucasus and Siberia to create a new eastern front against the German Reich and prevent the substantial military equipment stored in Murmansk and Archangel falling into Germany's hands. There were also almost 70,000 anti-Bolshevik Czech troops in Siberia.[35] Churchill was outraged that the new leaders of Russia had refused to continue hostilities against the Kaiser, thereby endangering the Allied victory over Germany. Furthermore, the Bolsheviks had brought about the downfall (and execution) of the Romanov dynasty. For a dedicated royalist like Churchill this constituted sacrilege, as well as an insult to his sense of the importance of upholding established authority and the traditional social order.[36]

Churchill often compared Bolshevism to a cancer and called it a 'monstrous growth swelling and thriving upon the emaciated body of its victim'.[37] According to Philip Kerr (later Lord Lothian), Lloyd George's private secretary, Churchill believed that 'the Bolsheviks are the enemies of the human race and must be put down at any cost'.[38] Only a day before the armistice with the German Reich in November 1918, Churchill advocated strengthening the defeated German army as a protective wall against the communist threat.[39]

In February 1919, he warned of the danger that Germany and the Soviet Union might enter into an alliance directed against Great Britain.[40] Two months later he advocated more lenient economic peace conditions for Germany, arguing that otherwise the country might well 'be swept into the Bolshevik camp'. Fighting the Bolsheviks could be 'a way of atonement' for the Germans; it would be their 'first step toward ultimate reunion with the civilised world'. Remembering his early admiration for Germany, he regarded the country suddenly once again as 'a dyke of peaceful, lawful, patient strength and virtue against the flood of red barbarism from the East'.[41] Increasingly, at least until the Soviet-German treaty at Rapallo in 1922, his motto became: 'Kill the Bolshie, Kiss the Hun'.[42] Churchill also did his best to commit Britain to the vigorous support of the anti-Bolshevik forces in the Russian civil war.

As Minister for Munitions Churchill was not directly involved in planning the Russian campaign,[43] but in public speeches, in the press and during many heated Cabinet sessions, Churchill opposed the Prime Minister and the majority of the Cabinet by demanding a great expansion of the Allied intervention in the Russian civil war. Moreover, the signing of the armistice between Russia and Germany and its allies in mid-December 1917 raised the awkward question whether continued intervention in Russia's internal affairs was legally justified. Churchill invoked the protection of India and the Near East and the negative impact of Bolshevism on Britain's working class, endangering the entire stability of British society, as reasons for continuing the campaigns in Russia. However, the cost of the intervention, the generally anarchic situation in Russia and not least pressure from public opinion to restore peaceful conditions ensured that the Cabinet became increasingly doubtful about the enterprise.[44]

Churchill's appointment as Secretary of State for War and Air in January 1919 for reasons unrelated to the Russian civil war meant that he became responsible for directing the British involvement in Russia although he was not a member of Prime Minister Lloyd George's small War Cabinet. Churchill soon dedicated most of his time and energy to overseeing his 'private war' in Russia, as the British media called it.[45] In February 1919, he expressed the hope that the Allies would declare 'war on the Bolsheviks' and 'send huge forces there'. In the summer of 1919 he did not hesitate to authorize the use of newly developed chemical weapons against the Red Army.[46]

Lloyd George and the majority of the Cabinet were not persuaded by Churchill's arguments in favour of expanding Britain's support for the White armies in Russia. The Prime Minister described Churchill's campaign as 'a purely mad enterprise out of hatred of Bolshevik principles'; Lloyd George urged him to 'throw off this obsession which ... is upsetting your balance'.[47] In view of the lack of success of the Allied forces in Russia it increasingly appeared to be a highly unrealistic endeavour, and in the general climate of exhaustion and weariness following the war, the Allied powers and the British people were in no mood to sanction an 'expensive war of aggression against Russia'. Lloyd George believed that Churchill's plans to fight a major war against the Red Army would cause revolution in Britain and put the country on 'the road to bankruptcy and Bolshevism'.[48] The Prime Minister thought Churchill under-estimated the support the Communists enjoyed in Russia and tended to overlook the Russian counter-revolutionaries' dubious and reactionary nature. A great number of the generals commanding the White armies were regarded by the officials in the Foreign Office as 'most unreliable and crooked' characters. They seemed prepared to recreate the corrupt czarist empire, reverse all land reforms, reintegrate the newly independent states like Finland and the Baltic nations into Russia and thus create all kinds of political complications.[49]

Churchill also failed in his desperate attempt during the Versailles peace conference to use personal summit diplomacy (with Lloyd George's hesitant permission) to get his way. In Paris, on the evening of 14 February 1919, Churchill attempted to persuade American President Woodrow Wilson to approve intensified joint Anglo-American military cooperation in Russia and even a full-scale war against the Bolsheviks. Wilson was not impressed; instead he proclaimed his view that all Allied forces should leave Russia.[50] At the Supreme War Council meetings in Paris Churchill's ideas on how to defeat the Bolsheviks led to very acrimonious discussions (particularly on 17 February) and were totally rejected although Wilson had already left for America. Churchill's far-reaching proposals, which had not received Cabinet approval, deeply annoyed Lloyd George.[51]

Throughout 1919, despite strong opposition in the Cabinet, Churchill managed to sustain Britain's naval blockade of the Baltic and the Black Sea as well as the country's half-hearted military involvement in Russia by convincing the Cabinet to continue supplying arms to the White Russian generals. While this enabled the Whites to prolong the civil war, it was not enough to overpower Lenin's and Trotsky's forces. The defeat of General Denikin in early November showed the strength and fervour of the Red Army. Advancing from the south with a force of almost 30,000 men, Denikin had been generously supplied by Churchill with British arms, ammunition and other military provisions. In April 1919 Churchill once again suggested that German troops should be used to fight the Red Army. He even considered joining a victorious Denikin in Moscow as a kind of roving ambassador to help him draw up a new Russian constitution. Denikin had almost managed to reach Moscow before he was decisively beaten.[52]

By the time of Denikin's defeat, the British Cabinet had already insisted on the withdrawal of most British troops from Russia and in November/ December 1919 it became clear that the Russian civil war was coming to a rapid end. In his Guildhall speech on 8 November Lloyd George effectively announced the termination of the British intervention. Despite all the many clever and emotional arguments Churchill had presented in favour of continuing the enterprise, the Prime Minister had finally decided that the country had neither the will nor the resources to prevent the victory of the Bolsheviks in Russia. After all, Churchill had already spent more than £100 million without any noticeable successes.[53]

Although Churchill continued to hope for a reversal of the fortunes of the White Russian armies, by February/March 1920 the Russian civil war had come to an end. The British government realized that it would soon have to enter into an arrangement with Lenin's new government in Moscow. Negotiations for an Anglo-Soviet trade agreement began in mid-1920 and were concluded in March 1921. This agreement effectively extended de facto recognition to the Soviet Union.[54]

Churchill remained unconvinced of the new policy and was deeply opposed to the trade negotiations. In late January 1920 he wrote in the *Illustrated Sunday Herald* that in his view Communism must be regarded as 'a pestilence more destructive of life than the Black Death or the Spotted Typhus'.[55] Although Churchill was free of anti-Semitism, his hatred of Communism was great enough to make him adopt common parlance and refer to Bolshevism as the 'rabble of Eastern European ghettos'.[56] Throughout the 1920s and most of the 1930s he continued to believe this and adhered to the view he expressed in the London *Times* in November 1920: 'I will always advocate ... the overthrow and destruction of that criminal regime.' It was not only the military threat which western civilization had to fear but also the Bolsheviks' dangerous ideology and propaganda.[57] In May 1920 Churchill had made a particularly violent attack in the House of Commons, declaring that 'Bolshevism is not a policy; it is a disease. It is not a creed; it is a pestilence. It presents all the characteristics of a pestilence. It breaks out with great suddenness; it is violently contagious; it throws people into a frenzy of excitement; it spreads with extraordinary rapidity; the mortality is terrible; so that after a while, like other pestilences, the disease tends to wear itself out.'[58] (This of course left the question unanswered why Churchill was so concerned about the Bolsheviks if in the end Communism would collapse from within and disappear altogether.)

Since 1917, Churchill had regarded the communist regime in Russia as one of Britain's greatest enemies and, increasingly, the United States, which had courageously joined the fight against the Kaiser (and to a limited degree against the Red Army), as the natural and closest friend of the British Empire.[59] During a visit to America in 1931, he had announced confidently that 'the two great opposing forces of the future will be the English speaking peoples and Communism'.[60] Churchill's loathing for Communism had, on occasion, even led him to praise Mussolini and Hitler for their anti-Communism.[61] Between 1933 and 1936, however, Churchill became convinced that the greatest danger to world peace came not from the Soviet Union but from Hitler's Germany. Thus he gradually began to dampen his criticism of Stalin and to differentiate between Stalin as a person and international Communism as such. Whilst he continued to regard the communist ideology as an enemy which had to be resisted, he expressed increasing admiration for Stalin.[62] Churchill remained true to his convictions and would always be repelled by the egalitarian, anti-monarchical, anti-democratic and atheistic nature of Communism.

Churchill was fully aware, however, that Stalin had offered London and Paris a tripartite alliance in May 1939 which against his strong advice had been rejected by Chamberlain and Halifax. In his memoirs, Churchill described the Soviet proposal as 'a fair offer' and even referred to Stalin's subsequent treaty with Hitler as a 'realistic' decision.[63] Nonetheless, Churchill was never able to overcome his resentment at the fact that the USSR had concluded a neutrality pact with Nazi Germany in 1939. Only Hitler's invasion of the Soviet Union in June 1941 had brought Stalin onto the side of the western democracies. Churchill was firmly convinced that if Britain 'had been invaded and destroyed in July 1940 or August 1940 ... they [the Soviets] would have remained entirely indifferent'.[64] Churchill's attitude towards cooperation with the Soviet Union is well expressed in his famous statement: 'I have only one purpose, the destruction of Hitler ... If Hitler invaded Hell I would make at least a favourable reference to the Devil in the House of Commons.'[65] Thus, whilst he remained ideologically deeply hostile to Communism, he was very much alive to the fact that Britain needed Stalin to defeat Hitler. Naturally, despite Churchill's changing rhetoric, Stalin and his lieutenants were fully aware of Churchill's feelings about their regime.

In July 1940, Churchill highlighted the common threat that the possible domination of Nazi Germany would pose to the European continent. He sent a personal letter to Stalin and suggested Anglo-Soviet consultations. The dictator did not respond favourably.[66] In April 1941, using information derived from Britain's breaking the Enigma code of the encrypted secret German radio messages, Churchill warned Stalin about the imminent German invasion. However, Stalin refused to believe an invasion of the Soviet Union was possible. He entirely misjudged Hitler and ignored the warnings of Churchill and the British ambassador Stafford Cripps together with the numerous other indications from his intelligence agents of an impending German invasion.[67] Stalin even assumed that these were British ploys to provoke Moscow into fighting Germany. Soviet mistrust was further aroused by the flight of Rudolf Hess to Scotland in May 1941, which was regarded in Moscow as the prelude to British–German peace talks. This episode encouraged the Soviets to discard all British information about Hitler's imminent invasion of the Soviet Union.[68] In accordance with the Marxist interpretation of the immanent forces of history, Stalin continued to believe that the capitalists and western imperialists would fight it out among themselves and that, contrary to all the available evidence, Hitler intended to defeat Britain first before turning towards the East. Stalin was convinced that Germany wanted to avoid a war on two fronts and therefore assumed that Hitler would negotiate or at least send an ultimatum before embarking on a war against the Soviet Union.[69]

When on 22 June 1941 Hitler invaded the Soviet Union, Churchill publicly welcomed the Soviet Union as a new ally and promised immediate British help to the Russian nation.[70] On July 8 and 10 two more messages from Churchill were delivered to Stalin. They resulted in Anglo-Soviet negotiations and the eventual signing of an Anglo-Soviet Declaration in Moscow and the mutual promise not to enter into separate peace agreements with Hitler.[71] Soon, however, Churchill's refusal to give a commitment on the date for a Second Front in France to relieve the pressure of the invading German forces on the Red Army aroused Stalin's anger and increased his great suspicion of British motives.[72] The Prime Minister believed that 'there was no point in opening another front or shedding blood just to please the Russians'. After all, Stalin himself had only entered the war 'to protect their own interests'.[73] Churchill was therefore not moved by Stalin's anger; he realized that the dictator was attempting to imbue him with a sense of guilt by repeatedly emphasizing the heavy toll of casualties the Soviet army (and indeed the civilian population) was suffering. The Prime Minister informed the British ambassador in Moscow that the Soviets appeared to assume 'that they were conferring a great favour on us by fighting in their own country for their own lives. The more they fought the heavier our debt became.' Churchill concluded that this 'was not a balanced view'.[74]

In July and September 1941 Stalin asked Britain for military aid. In view of the German armies' push towards Moscow, he hinted in his message to Churchill of 8 November at his readiness to participate in an agreement on war objectives and the organization of the post-war world.[75] Although the Prime Minister resented the tone of Stalin's letter, in December he eventually sent Foreign Secretary Anthony Eden to the Soviet capital. Eden too believed strongly in his ability to overcome difficult situations by means of personal diplomacy,[76] but, due to disagreements regarding the future frontiers of the post-war world and Soviet insistence on the recognition of its borders as negotiated with Hitler in 1939, the draft twenty-year Anglo-Soviet Treaty of Alliance could not be sealed.[77] The treaty was finally signed with Soviet Foreign Minister Molotov in London in late May 1942 and it was emphasized that annexations and interference in the internal affairs of other states were not acceptable.[78]

In August 1942, Churchill travelled to Moscow with Averell Harriman, Roosevelt's confidant, to inform Stalin in person that the Second Front in northern France could still not be opened by the end of the year.[79] Churchill and Stalin met four times and in spite of one very difficult and vociferous session with the dictator, Churchill felt 'encouraged' by his visit. Stalin had after all told him that 'we like a downright enemy better than a pretending friend'.[80] The Prime Minister reported to Roosevelt later that the atmosphere in the Kremlin was generally very 'easy and friendly' and that he had been able to build up a 'personal relationship' with Stalin: 'the disappointing news I brought could not have been imparted except by me personally without leading to really serious drifting apart.'[81]

Throughout the war, Churchill was not prepared to leave discussions with Stalin or Roosevelt in the hands of the British Foreign Office. Although his officials were mostly quite competent, in Churchill's view they lacked imagination and flair. Even Foreign Secretary Eden would only be sent on reconnaissance missions if the Prime Minister was unable to go himself or if it was inappropriate for the head of government to negotiate in person; thus Eden, not Churchill, attended the foreign ministers' conference in Moscow in October 1943.[82] This strategy showed a great similarity with Churchill's methods in the 1950s and indeed in the period before the First World War. Then as during the Second World War Churchill was convinced that his country would benefit most if he conducted his summit diplomacy personally; in addition, he tremendously enjoyed this style of politics and this had been his inclination ever since he had first become greatly interested in international politics between 1908 and 1914. He wanted to be in continuous demand, cope with challenging situations and be the centrepoint of all action. Churchill had to be in the thick of things.[83]

The drawback of this kind of diplomacy lay in the fact that Churchill's sentimental and romantic personality and his very subjective and often idiosyncratic preferences and dislikes became more important than they would have been had he relied to a greater degree on the sober advice and restrained judgement of his official advisers. It may well be correct that in his 1942 meetings with Stalin in Moscow, as with Roosevelt at Placentia Bay the year before, 'Churchill probably persuaded himself more effectively than he did his interlocutor' of the correctness of his opinions.[84] Conversely, in the course of his meetings and correspondence with Stalin, Churchill found it increasingly difficult to escape the dictator's charisma.[85]

Churchill (like Roosevelt) was therefore not immune to the myth which developed during the war that Stalin himself was a quite benign person with a common-sense approach but that he was directed by evil men in the background, perhaps members of the military or the security services overseen by the evil Beria. Thus it was concluded in many quarters in both Britain and the United States that Stalin could not act as he would have liked.[86] This was of course mere wishful thinking, but it lingered on into the post-war period.[87] During the war conferences of the 'Big Three' from Tehran to Potsdam, as well as during his bilateral talks with Stalin in 1942 and in October 1944, and in the course of casual conversations during the war conferences, the Prime Minister was convinced that he alone could obtain concessions from Stalin and move the dictator towards a more compromising mode of cooperation with the Anglo-Saxon powers.

Anglo-American Competition for Stalin's Favour

Churchill's personal diplomacy met with fierce competition from Roosevelt who had first entered into diplomatic relations with the USSR in 1933.[88] As early as July 1941, well before America's entry into the war and five months before Eden's first wartime journey to Moscow, Roosevelt had sent his confidant Harry Hopkins to Moscow to begin consultations over extending the Lend-Lease programme to the Soviet Union.[89] Roosevelt strongly believed, as he informed Churchill in 'brutally frank' terms in February 1942, that he himself was able to 'handle Stalin better than either your Foreign Office or my State Department. Stalin hates the guts of all your top people. He thinks he likes me better, and I hope he will continue to do so.'[90]

In May 1943 the President's special ambassador, the pro-Soviet Joseph Davies, travelled to Russia to convey proposals for a secret round of talks between Stalin and Roosevelt. The President planned to use such a meeting to discuss the question of a Second Front whose constant postponement aroused greater mistrust in Stalin regarding the intentions of the Anglo-Saxon powers than any other issue. It appeared to Roosevelt that only a personal clarification of the situation could bring about long-term trustful cooperation with the USSR.[91] Roosevelt mentioned nothing of his plans to Churchill, who still regarded a Second Front in France as premature. The Prime Minister preferred to focus on the Mediterranean theatre to secure the lines of communication with Britain's colonial possessions and protect the British Empire. In his correspondence with Churchill, Roosevelt denied his intention to meet Stalin alone, thereby deliberately deceiving the Prime Minister. The American President did not believe that he needed Churchill to mediate between Washington and Moscow.[92] Much to the annoyance of the British Foreign Office, Roosevelt had begun corresponding with Stalin unilaterally in February 1942. The President believed this would help him to obtain a better deal with Stalin regarding the future of the Baltic States, but to London it looked as if Washington did not seem to treat Britain as an equal partner. Contrary to the British practice, Washington hardly ever informed London about the bilateral exchanges with the Soviets, although these conversations dealt with the Second Front and other questions of vital interest to Britain.[93]

The President also avoided meeting the Prime Minister before the Tehran conference in late November 1943, when Roosevelt was to see Stalin for the first time. He did not wish to create the impression that the Anglo-Saxon powers were 'ganging up' on Stalin. During the Tehran meeting Roosevelt repeatedly turned down invitations from Churchill for a personal chat. While refusing to talk in a more intimate way to his British friend, the President did not hesitate to have three confidential talks with Stalin in the course of the conference.[94]

It is clear that Churchill and Roosevelt were highly competitive, and even jealous of each other in their mutual attempts to win Stalin's favour. While

Roosevelt did not entirely trust the British and their war aims and also felt that the predominant western power should not have to wait for permission from its much smaller ally before entering into contact with Stalin, Churchill realized that he was battling for Britain's survival as a great power. Thus under all circumstances the Prime Minister intended to avoid being excluded from negotiations between Washington and Moscow. Just as was the case in his later strategy towards Presidents Truman and Eisenhower, the British Prime Minister constantly sought to check even the remotest tendency in Washington to call a bilateral American-Soviet summit conference which excluded Britain and might result in important decisions being made without British influence. Churchill was adamant in his determination to remain an equal partner of the 'Big Three'. He wished to be regarded as such not only by the other two powers but also in the public perception.[95] It was only in the summer of 1943, when he was at his wits' end and when Britain's relations with Stalin had reached rock bottom, that Churchill spoke in support of Roosevelt arranging to meet 'Uncle Joe' alone.[96] Yet such a meeting was never to take place.

During 1943 the Prime Minister realized that his country had increasingly less influence on the planning and execution of Allied war strategy. In the spring of 1943 British–Soviet relations over yet another postponement of the Second Front had become very tense. After Stalingrad, when in late 1942 and early 1943 in one of the most ruthless battles of the war the Red Army managed to repulse the German onslaught on the USSR and thus effectively demonstrated that Hitler was no longer able to win the Second World War, Soviet confidence was in the ascendant and Stalin needed the help of Britain much less than hitherto. Even the Second Front was not regarded as quite as urgent as before. Furthermore, British support for ensuring the continued flow of provisions to the Soviet Union was no longer quite so vital, as American goods were now able to reach Russia through Persia.[97]

Churchill hoped that with a joint Anglo-American policy towards Stalin he would be able to improve his country's precarious position. He believed 'that we should do much better with the Russians if we first got on to intimate terms with the United States'. It certainly was 'important not [to] allow the Russians to try to play the United States and the United Kingdom off against each other'.[98] Roosevelt, antagonized by Churchill's apparent imperialist ambitions, was fully aware of Britain's weakness and the Soviet Union's increasing strength, and had little desire to form a united front with the British. Instead, in late 1943 Roosevelt posted the influential ambassador Harriman from London to Moscow, a move which is often interpreted as a rearrangement of priorities by the American government.[99]

In addition to his concerns about the declining British influence on war strategy, Churchill also became seriously worried about the long-term economic consequences of the domination of the anti-Hitler coalition by the other two powers. Churchill intended to use all his influence to prevent the unilateral supremacy of either the Soviet Union or the United States in the post-war world and, above all, in post-war Europe. The Prime Minister developed an imaginative concept for a 'United States of Europe' overseen by Britain to prevent such a possibility; his vision as it emerged between 1940 and 1943 is analysed in chapters three and four.

Britain's waning influence on war strategy became particularly obvious to Churchill during the Tehran conference in November/December 1943, arguably one of the most important meetings of the war.[100] During this somewhat chaotic and ill-prepared first 'Big Three' conference, important deliberations took place regarding the timing of Operation OVERLORD (the new name for the Second Front strategy) during which the British preferences were largely ignored. Churchill also had to give in with regard to his post-war plans; instead, the nature and frontiers of the post-war world were almost entirely decided by Roosevelt and Stalin.[101]

At Tehran Roosevelt and Stalin effectively entered into an implicit, almost Faustian pact largely at the expense of their British ally. Stalin agreed to commit the USSR to participation in the American President's envisaged United Nations Organization, which was to be organized on a global rather than a regional basis as Churchill desired. Roosevelt did not wish to antagonize American public opinion by being seen to accept any long-lasting entangling commitments in Europe. The Soviet dictator also promised to join the war against Japan in the Pacific once Hitler had been defeated. Both objectives were very dear to Roosevelt's heart. In return, the President appeared to offer Stalin the promise of American support for Moscow's envisaged territorial policy in Eastern Europe, in particular with regard to the Baltic countries and Poland. Much to Churchill's displeasure, Roosevelt confirmed the American intention to commence Operation OVERLORD as quickly as possible in 1944. He thus effectively agreed to reject Churchill's preferred strategy of an assault on Germany from the Mediterranean, the encouragement of Turkey to enter into the fight against Hitler, and increased resources for the war in Italy. On the contrary, the President even wanted to begin with supporting operations for OVERLORD in the south of France (ANVIL), which would have led to the almost immediate termination of the Italian campaign.[102]

Churchill, it has been argued, was unwise in continuing to focus on military rather than strategic issues at the Tehran conference. It became increasingly clear that with Roosevelt's and Stalin's collusion, he became more and more isolated.[103] To add insult to injury, Britain's role as a full member of the 'Big Three' club was also increasingly questioned by Stalin's and Roosevelt's dismissive attitude: Churchill found it difficult to overlook the condescension with which he was treated. Although a few months before the conference he had proclaimed that he was 'always prepared to be snubbed for his country',[104] enduring the experience at the Tehran conference was a very different matter. Churchill was most disconcerted by the unexpected and hurtful developments in the course of the conference. Moreover, during the conference his health was rather fragile.[105]

On the whole, the Tehran meeting proved to be a disaster for Churchill and his country. The Prime Minister realized that after Tehran the major decisions concerning the remainder of the war and the post-war world would effectively be taken by the much more powerful Americans and Russians.[106] He later remarked in despair that he noticed 'at Tehran for the first time what a small nation we are'.[107] Yet in characteristic fashion Churchill remained deeply convinced of the superiority of his personal strategy for both Germany's ultimate defeat and post-war security. The Prime Minister succinctly summarized the situation at Tehran: 'There I sat with the great Russian bear on one side of me with paws outstretched, and, on the other side, the great American buffalo. Between the two sat the poor little English donkey, who was the only one who knew the right way home.'[108]

Churchill was deeply depressed by this state of affairs and attempted everything in his power to rectify the situation in the following months by intensifying his personal relations with Stalin and, above all, with Roosevelt. However, after Tehran the American President and his close associates became more aloof in their dealings with Churchill while making increasingly demanding requests on Britain's financial and economic resources; they also were less restrained in attempting to restrict Britain's political and military independence of action. Indeed, as Fraser Harbutt has observed, 'Britain was being nudged, gently but firmly, toward second-rank status.'[109]

Churchill was not prepared to accept this. He hoped that with the help of his personal charisma he would eventually be able to move Roosevelt and even Stalin towards a war strategy and a post-war world more conducive to the interests of Great Britain and its empire. Churchill certainly had no intention of abandoning Britain's claim to great power status after Tehran. After all, fundamentally he was and remained one of Britain's most imperialistically orientated defenders of 'power politics'; he believed deeply in the continued importance of Britain and its empire for the creation of a peaceful world. He could never really accept the strong stirrings for independence in India and Egypt which became obvious during the war. His fierce opposition to offering

Dominion status to India had made him resign from the Conservative shadow cabinet in January 1931, a decision which had cost him dearly. 'The loss of India,' he believed, not altogether wrongly, 'would mark and consummate the downfall of the British Empire.'[110] On the whole, during the Second World War he clung to his stubborn belief that 'I have not become the King's First Minister in order to preside over the liquidation of the British Empire.'[111]

Churchill possessed 'a romantic devotion to British greatness' and 'a pugnacious determination to maintain the greatness of the British Empire'.[112] It was his desire to maintain Britain's position as a global power as well as his wish to play a significant personal role on the global stage which inspired Churchill to insist on Britain's inclusion as one of the 'Big Three' and oppose vehemently Roosevelt's and Stalin's tendency to dismiss the Empire as a useless relic of the past, downgrade Britain's international importance and move towards a 'Big Two' alliance. Churchill was not prepared to accept as permanent the diminishing significance of his country in global politics.

Once his preferred strategies for the continuation of the war and his vision for the post-war world had been rejected by Roosevelt and Stalin at Tehran, Churchill attempted to fall back on summit diplomacy and use this to prevent the further marginalization of Britain by the overwhelming power of the United States and the Soviet Union. The Prime Minister had realized that Britain, as by far the weakest member of the 'grand alliance', needed to reassert its continued membership of the 'Big Three' by all means possible. For this reason Churchill deployed his formidable reputation, his long political experience and his great powers of persuasion to his utmost ability at the war conferences and bilateral summit meetings to emphasize his country's view. He attempted to employ the whole force of his personality to Britain's advantage. In the same way as before 1914 he had sought to use personal diplomacy, 'to mitigate asperity between the German and British Empires',[113] he attempted during 1940–42 and then again in 1944–45 to use this strategy to maintain Britain's place in the sun.

In the last two years of the war and in view of American aloofness from Europe, Churchill became increasingly uneasy about Stalin's territorial ambitions, some of which might well be at the expense of the British Empire. In October 1942 he had warned his Foreign Secretary that it would be a 'measureless disaster if Russian barbarism overlaid the culture and independence of the ancient states of Europe'.[114] A year later Churchill returned to his idea, first ventilated after the 1917 revolution, of building up Germany as a buffer state between the Soviet Union and continental Europe. He told the British Cabinet in 1943 that we 'mustn't weaken Germany too much – we may need her against

Russia'.[115] Even in December 1940 he had stressed the necessity of differentiating between the Nazi regime and the German people. He hoped that the victorious powers would succeed in ensuring that 'Germany was going to remain in the European family ... there should be no Pariahs'. After all, 'Germany existed before the Gestapo.'[116] In November 1943, on the way to the Tehran conference, he explained to Harold Macmillan that 'Germany is finished ... The real problem now is Russia. I can't get the Americans to see it.'[117]

By July 1944 the British Chiefs of Staff (COS) firmly supported this view. Ever since the German defeat at Stalingrad in early 1943 the COS had begun to express the opinion that the maintenance of amicable Anglo-Soviet relations rather than the remote likelihood of renewed German aggression would be crucial for the post-war period. The British military were increasingly suspicious of Stalin's intentions. Soon, their anti-Russian views became widely known and, at this stage, clashed with the somewhat more optimistic Foreign Office.[118] Churchill, however, considered the COS's scepticism fully justified. In August 1944 Lord Moran, his personal physician, jotted in his diary: 'Winston never talks of Hitler these days; he is always harping on the dangers of Communism. He dreams of the Red Army spreading like a cancer from one country to another. It has become an obsession, and he seems to think of little else.'[119]

However, as happened quite frequently, Moran was too impressed by one of Churchill's dramatic outbursts. Even in 1944–45 Churchill tended to be torn between deep mistrust about the territorial strategy of the Soviet dictator in Central Europe and elsewhere and wishful thinking about Stalin's personality and the possibility of friendly cooperation with Moscow in the post-war years.[120] In January 1944, for example, recovering from his first heart attack, Churchill spoke to Foreign Secretary Eden of 'the new confidence which has grown in our hearts towards Stalin'.[121] Yet in the spring of 1944 he became deeply concerned about the advance of the Red Army into the Baltic states and northern Romania and Poland which he had consented to at Tehran. The Prime Minister increasingly feared not only the 'communizing' of these countries and the whole of Eastern Europe but also the possibility, if not the likelihood, of Stalin intending to conquer the Balkans and the entire Mediterranean including Greece, Italy and perhaps even France. Only together with the USA would Britain be able to resist Stalin's territorial and ideological drive.[122] Churchill's confidence in Stalin was also temporarily shattered by the Warsaw Uprising in August and September 1944. The Prime Minister was horrified by Stalin's refusal to order the Soviet troops outside the city to intervene and thus prevent the wholesale slaughter of 200,000 Polish civilians by the German army; he was also shocked by Roosevelt's coolness regarding the whole terrible situation.[123]

However, by late 1944, after the so-called 'Tolstoy' meetings with Stalin in Moscow, during which Churchill entered into the notorious percentage deal to contain Moscow's expansionist ambitions by means of an Anglo-Soviet pact to divide up South-East Europe, Churchill told Roosevelt of the 'extraordinary atmosphere of goodwill' he had encountered in Moscow. To Eden he spoke of Stalin as a 'great and good man'.[124] And the Foreign Secretary agreed with this assessment. In conversation with the by then much more pessimistic Czecho-slovakian President Beneš, Eden explained that 'despite occasional irritants' on the whole he was convinced that 'the Russians genuinely wished to work' with Britain.[125] After the Yalta conference in February 1945, during which decisions were taken regarding the war against Japan, the four-power occupation of Germany, the new Russo-Polish border and the westward shift of Poland at the expense of Germany as well as the composition of the new Polish government, Churchill was still optimistic. He told the British people that he knew 'of no Government which stands to its obligations ... more solidly than the Russian Soviet Government'. Churchill was convinced 'that Marshal Stalin and the Soviet leaders wish to live in honourable friendship and equality with the Western democracies'.[126] On 17 July 1945, during the Potsdam conference, the Prime Minister told Eden, 'I like that man'.[127]

Despite his increasing geopolitical and ideological fears regarding Soviet intentions, it appears that as late as the spring and summer of 1945, Churchill, like Roosevelt and his successor Harry Truman, 'still had some hope of friendship with Stalin, even if it was a badly battered hope'.[128] Indicative of Churchill's attitude in the closing months of the war was the message he sent Stalin in late April 1945 regarding Moscow's apparent intention to impose a communist government on Poland, annex the Baltic states, extend the Kremlin's dominance across most of Central Europe and ignore altogether the Yalta agreements and his promise to hold free elections in Poland. Churchill asked Stalin: 'But do not, I beg you, my friend Stalin, underrate the divergences which are opening about matters which you may think are small to us, but which are symbolic of the way the English-speaking democracies look at life.'[129] However, Stalin was not overly impressed.

Churchill was never willing to accept that after the war Europe might become subservient to Moscow or that Britain would be put in an inferior position to the United States. He took the stance, as he wrote to Roosevelt in March 1944, 'that Great Britain seeks no advantage, territorial or otherwise, as the result of the war. On the other hand she will not be deprived of anything which rightly belongs to her after having given her best services to the good cause.'[130]

While the Prime Minister greatly resented American anti-colonialism and Washington's insistence on free trade and the post-war removal of all tariff barriers including the abolition of Britain's imperial preference system, which would effectively lead to the dismantling of the sterling area, he came to fear even more Stalin's apparent territorial ambitions in Eastern and Central Europe. Churchill intended to maintain the independence of Britain with the European continent in its backyard and restore, as he saw it, Europe's strong and beneficial role in world politics. As is outlined in the two following chapters, between 1940 and 1943 the British Prime Minister had already devised concepts for a new European order by means of the development of a European Council and several European confederations that were to be overseen by Britain. This was Churchill's imaginative as well as desperate attempt to design an alternative concept of a new international order for the post-war world to preserve global peace and, not least, maintain his country's status as a great power.

CHAPTER 3

Churchill and 'the United States of Europe' during the Second World War
Attempts to Preserve Britain's Status as a World Power

In Churchill's view, the new order required for a peaceful post-war world had to include an important role for Britain and the Empire. In essence the Prime Minister hoped that his ideas for a vaguely defined 'Council of Europe' and a 'United States of Europe' would enable the three great powers to maintain their peaceful cooperation and turn Europe – led from the outside by a strong Britain – once again into a crucial player on the world stage. At the heart of this concept was Churchill's quest for a stable and peaceful post-war Europe and the revival of Britain as a European power to enable Britain and its Empire to continue playing an important global role. Yet President Roosevelt was adamant that 'when we've won the war, I will work with all my might and main to see to it' that the USA would not be 'wheedled into a position' that would 'aid or abet the British Empire and its imperial ambitions'.[1] This, together with Stalin's ruthless plans for Eastern and Central Europe, meant that the implementation of Churchill's post-war vision faced almost insurmountable difficulties. Moreover, even Churchill's own Foreign Office was not entirely convinced of the Prime Minister's rather muddled ideas on European unity.

Churchill and European Integration

Churchill's repeated calls for the creation of a United States of Europe during the Second World War and the early post-war years must be seen as part of his strategy to ensure the survival of the Empire and the British way of life. Churchill's aim was the re-creation of a strong and independent Europe overseen and guided by Britain from the outside. Only then, he believed, would Britain be able to maintain its role as a world power. Overcoming the fragmentation of the European continent for federalist reasons, however, was never Churchill's objective. He was always strongly opposed to Britain becoming part of an integrated federal Europe.[2]

Churchill expressed his attitude to European integration as early as February 1930. He had been impressed by French Foreign Minister Aristide Briand's idealistic proposal in September 1929 for the development of a 'confederal bond' ('une sorte de lien fédéral') among European countries to make another world war impossible,[3] and Churchill's views echoed Briand's ideas. After all, the Frenchman's vision apparently entailed no loss of sovereignty for the participating nation states and his aim, as Briand indicated in his speech to the League of Nations Assembly in Geneva, was to focus mainly on economic aspects. It was soon recognized that Briand's proposal was not a scheme for a genuinely federal or united Europe[4] and Churchill found it easy to agree with his ideas. In an article for the *Saturday Evening Post*, published on 15 February 1930, he declared that Britain saw 'nothing but good and hope in a richer, freer, more contented European communality. But we have our own dream and our own task. We are with Europe, but not of it. We are linked but not compromised. We are interested and associated but not absorbed.'[5]

During the 1930s, Churchill, like many others, was influenced by the popularity of the ideas for the creation of a stable and more united Europe. Since the rise of the Round Table Movement, founded in 1910, and the activities of formidable intellectuals such as Lord Lothian (Lloyd George's former private secretary), Lionel Curtis and Lionel Robbins, the British federalist movement held an influential position within certain circles in Britain. The Federal Union, set up in the autumn of 1938, could build on this. It advocated a united Europe by means of establishing supranational institutions with the power to make unanimous decisions, and appealed to a wider public with its pragmatic ideas for resolving the world crisis brought about by the war.[6]

Federal ideas were much popularized by the hugely successful publication of American journalist Clarence Streits's book *Union Now*, emphasizing Atlantic union, in the spring of 1939 as well as a plethora of books by writers such as Curtis, Curry, Robbins, R.G.W. MacKay, Ivor Jennings, Channing Pearce, Barbara Wooton, and Sir William (later Lord) Beveridge mostly focusing on Europe. Essentially these works argued that the outmoded concept of national sovereignty, whose flaws were made responsible for the collapse of the interwar system and the League of Nations, needed to be replaced by a world government with federalist structures and sound and unanimous decision-making procedures.[7] Churchill was particularly inspired by Count Richard Coudenhove-Kalergi's influential Pan-European Union, established in 1923 and propagated by the Count's tireless campaigning, although a British section was only founded in June 1939.[8] The New Commonwealth Society, set up as early as 1923 by Lord Davies, initially attracted more attention in Britain. Influenced by Davies's 1940 book, *A Federated Europe*, the organization became an advocate of federalism and was in favour of the creation of a 'United States of Europe' including a joint foreign and defence policy under the aegis of the League of Nations.[9] Still, despite his interest in these developments, Churchill never fully warmed to federalist concepts. In 1940 he served as President of the New Commonwealth Society[10] but he nevertheless believed that with regard to the new post-war order which needed to be established, Britain ought to maintain a certain benevolent distance from European affairs: 'we have no right to meddle too closely in Europe'.[11]

This view of Great Britain's relationship with continental Europe remained Churchill's policy on European integration throughout his political career. He would hardly ever waver in his conviction. Like his summit diplomacy, his belief in Britain as a world power and the importance he attached to the Anglo-American 'special relationship', Churchill's European policy was consistent both before and after 1945. At the heart of his thinking about the future of Europe was his aim to maintain Britain's status as a fully independent global power and his belief in a world that was divided into clear geographic spheres of interest and that rested on a balance of power. During the war Churchill frequently referred to the fact that he had 'only one aim, to destroy Hitler'.[12] He was careful not to endanger the unity of the anti-Hitler coalition by publicly pronouncing controversial ideas for the future of the European continent. Yet, as will be seen, this did not stop him developing plans in the early 1940s for a more integrated and united Europe. As far as Europe was concerned he believed that a new international order should be based on several regional confederations overseen from the outside by Great Britain as one of the 'Big Three'.[13]

It was Churchill's dogged determination to defeat Hitler that led to his offer of an Anglo-French union in June 1940, an idea suggested by Jean Monnet, an influential member of Paul Reynaud's government, which had earlier been discussed by the Chamberlain government.[14] Within the envisaged union, France and Britain would cease to be two separate states, and would merge their respective parliaments and embark upon a common policy for defence, and foreign and economic matters. In view of the popularity of the various federal movements in Britain during the 1930s, Altiero Spinelli among others has claimed that by 1940, 'The idea of federation was, so to speak, in the air, and Churchill only had to reach for it.'[15] Churchill's proposal is also sometimes viewed as the 'high mark of British federalism' and 'a prototype of total integration' which had never before been suggested in the history of European integration.[16] Indeed, if the dramatic British offer had been accepted by the French government before it had to surrender to Hitler's invading army, it would have led to an integrated Franco-British war effort.[17] However, Churchill's proposal was only a desperate attempt to overcome a seemingly hopeless situation by preventing the French from signing a separate peace treaty with Hitler. The new Prime Minister did not have 'any wider perspective' than to keep the struggle against Hitler going.[18] The offer of a Franco-British union was certainly not part of a more detailed and comprehensive plan for the future of Europe; Churchill never had any such precise formula.[19] In the event, the collapse of France and the German occupation of Belgium, the Netherlands, Denmark and Norway in the summer of 1940 undermined any support, limited at the best of times, in Westminster for a post-war European continent organized along federal lines.

In 1940–41 the predominant issue in British governmental circles was national survival, which was to be achieved by committing the United States to the war effort and, after June 1941, aiding the Soviet Union in its fight against Hitler. This largely explains why after Pearl Harbor the Prime Minister did not take the initiative to hold discussions on the shape of post-war Europe with Britain's new allies, the United States and soon also the Soviet Union.[20] Moreover, in the long run the national experience of holding together to withstand Hitler's onslaught strengthened rather than weakened the government and the British people's confidence in their own political and military strength and national identity.[21]

Nevertheless, the 1940 proposal of a Franco-British union led some Resistance leaders in Eastern and Western Europe into the mistaken belief that they had the support of the British government for their imaginative post-war plans. Some were convinced that only federalist ideas were powerful enough to overcome national pride and old-fashioned political concepts based on national sovereignty and traditional state boundaries. Many of the foreign leaders exiled in London were thinking of incorporating at least some elements of supranationalism into their designs for a new post-war order based on regional federations. Such confederations would also offer some protection against Stalin's expected expansionist ambitions, which were greatly feared by most Eastern European politicians.[22]

Thus the ultimate aim of many of the various non-communist Resistance groups based in London, Switzerland and, clandestinely, in the countries under German occupation, was a strong federal and supranational European government with a single foreign, defence and economic policy which, in due course, was to encompass the whole or a large part of Europe. With the failure of the League of Nations and the second major war provoked by Germany within a few decades, a united Europe and a common market, including a fully integrated (or dismembered) Germany, were seen as the only way to preserve peace and economic prosperity on the European continent.[23] More traditional alliance systems had not been able to provide protection from aggressive warfare.[24]

The Foreign Office did very little to correct the perceptions of the exiled leaders who credited the British government with pro-federal views. Instead, London signalled strong support for the old idea of the creation of Eastern and Central European confederations, albeit in the form of intergovernmental organizations. In 1940 General Sikorski, the Polish Prime Minister in exile, proposed a Polish–Czech federation and gained the support of Czechoslovak President Beneš despite the latter's suspicions of Poland's authoritarian past and much larger territory. Beneš also remained uneasy about the attitude off the western powers, who had sacrificed his country at Munich. Nevertheless, a joint Czech–Polish communiqué of intent was published in November 1940 and an agreement to establish a Polish–Czech union after the end of the war was officially concluded in early December 1941. Although there were suspicions in Whitehall (mostly well concealed) regarding Sikorski's ambitions, he was encouraged to proceed with his plan; moreover, at this stage the Foreign Office still hoped that the Soviet Union would regard itself mainly as 'an Asiatic Power and will not consider herself threatened by the Polish–Czech Federation'.[25]

Similarly, a far-reaching Greek–Yugoslav federation, involving the merger of foreign, defence and economic policies, was agreed in January 1942. Although the Greeks were much less enthusiastic than the Yugoslavs about a genuine confederate state, the Foreign Office expressed its strong support and eventually persuaded the Greek ministers to compromise.[26] Throughout 1942, talks among the leaders of the exiled governments in London took place for the establishment of a partially supranational 'European Community'; here the Foreign Office view was much more circumspect.[27] British officials were, however, supportive of the plans for some sort of western European union on the model of the 1922 economic and monetary union between Belgium and Luxembourg put forward mostly by exiled statesmen from Luxembourg and, in particular, by Belgian politicians like Paul-Henri Spaak and Paul van Zeeland; these ideas eventually culminated in the agreement for the post-war Benelux customs union of 1948 as agreed in a customs convention signed in 1944.[28]

In general, it was hoped in London that the economic and political harm done by the break-up of the old empires in Eastern Europe could be reversed to some extent by the development of intergovernmental federations for Eastern Europe, Central Europe, the Balkans and perhaps Southern Europe.

The Foreign Office expected that overcoming the post-First World War fragmentation of Eastern Europe would stabilize the whole area and balance the power of the individual nations. Thus it was concluded that the various proposals for bi- and multilateral federations on the continent might be able to fill the power vacuum in Europe after the defeat of Germany and could well serve as a buffer zone against renewed German militarism and a victorious and much-strengthened Soviet Union.[29]

During the war Churchill was not particularly interested in post-war planning; he had more pressing problems and left post-war planning largely to Foreign Secretary Anthony Eden and the civil servants in the Foreign Office. However, the Prime Minister often delayed and hindered any wider discussion and implementation of the ideas explored by his officials. Although in August 1940 he approved the convening of a Cabinet committee on war aims,[30] he feared that the formulation of clear war objectives and firm post-war plans would encourage disunity in the anti-Hitler coalition as well as within the British Cabinet, thus weakening the war effort and therefore the likelihood of defeating Hitler. In September 1941 Churchill told the House of Commons that he had 'consistently deprecated the formulation of peace aims or war aims' and intended to continue doing so 'at this time when the end of the war is not in sight and when conditions and associations at the end of the war are unforeseeable'. In early December he explained to Eden that 'All these attempts to settle the world while we are still struggling with the enemy seem to me most injurious.'[31] Throughout the war Churchill believed that dealing with 'remote post-war problems' might well 'absorb energy ... required ... for the prosecution of the war'.[32]

Despite some tentative thinking on the future of Europe and a western European bloc in the corridors of Whitehall, until mid- to late 1942 neither the British government as a whole nor the Foreign Office as the responsible agency had developed any well-considered concepts regarding the post-war fate of Eastern and Central Europe, including Germany.[33] This contrasted sharply with the practice in Washington, where the consideration of long-term and post-war problems began shortly after Hitler's invasion of Poland and before Washington had even become involved in the war against Germany. In 1941, with the establishment of the President's Advisory Committee on Postwar Foreign Policy, chaired by Secretary of State Cordell Hull, American post-war planning assumed a much more formal character.[34] Nothing comparable had been achieved in London; no concrete war aims and post-war plans had yet been formulated.[35]

Although Hitler's invasion of the Soviet Union in June 1941 and his declaration of war on the United States in December introduced two new players crucial for the future of Europe and whose importance for the shaping of the post-war world was obvious, the Foreign Office had neither the resources nor the time and energy to develop more than very vague post-war plans. Equally, Hitler's first decisive setback in the East, his failure to conquer Moscow in late 1941, did not result in strenuous British efforts to prepare a well-considered plan for the post-war world. When Stalin complained to Churchill in November 1941 about the absence of any agreement on Allied war aims, the Foreign Office had to admit to themselves that indeed 'we have not made up our own minds on the questions of the economic and political settlement'.[36]

By late 1941 there existed only the vague commitments and tentative war aims outlined in the Atlantic Charter of August 1941 and the even less concrete Anglo-American Declaration of the United Nations of December 1941.[37] Throughout 1941 and 1942 Churchill still held the opinion that 'all this talk about war aims was absurd at the present time'.[38] Indeed, he often expressed puzzlement over the fact that there were people in the Foreign Office and in other 'influential circles' who seemed to have sufficient leisure to spend a considerable period of time reflecting on these matters.[39]

To no small degree, the lack of post-war planning was due to Churchill's vacillations and his lack of encouragement for a structured and coordinated approach. The Prime Minister still feared that the drawing up of any specific post-war plans might well divide his government, undermine the crucial support of the US for Britain's war effort and commit the Prime Minister to a course of action which might subsequently be revealed as inadvisable. Churchill resented the fact that the Foreign Office had made a few tentative attempts at post-war planning. In fact, he appeared to be 'quite allergic to any proposals for post-war action which he had not himself engendered, or at least discussed personally with the President of the United States'.[40] However, despite his dislike of some of his officials' penchant for post-war planning, on occasion the Prime Minister did not hesitate to voice his views regarding the post-war order in Europe. His interventions were not quite as rare as is sometimes claimed in the secondary literature.[41]

Churchill's ideas were, however, rather imprecise and often uttered on the spur of the moment without having been given much careful consideration and planning.[42] Throughout most of the war his reasoning about the post-war European order remained vague and ambiguous. The Prime Minister's thoughts, as randomly expressed between 1940 and 1943, consisted largely of a compilation of the plans which were circulating in Resistance circles in London and among British and American intellectuals,[43] merged with his own deeply held convictions regarding the shape of post-war Europe. Despite the vagueness and ambiguity of Churchill's conception for the future of Europe, these views were the closest the Prime Minister came to formulating his thinking on the role of European integration in the post-war world.

When summarizing Churchill's vague thoughts on these issues, the impression could easily be conveyed that Churchill had developed a systemic scheme for post-war Europe. This would be an exaggeration. The British Prime Minister was much too preoccupied with planning and fighting the war to have the time and the inclination to attempt this. Nevertheless, some of Churchill's ideas on the future of Europe are highly interesting. They illuminate Churchill's thoughts on Britain's post-war prospects and his plans for maintaining, stabilizing and perhaps increasing his country's global status and influence, although much of this was wishful thinking.

In the dark months of 1940, reacting to a speech by Walter Funk, the Nazi Minister for Economic Affairs, Churchill indicated his views on a united Europe to John Colville, one of his private secretaries. Funk's speech had promised the peoples of Europe that the Nazis would construct a widely beneficial new economic order on the European continent after the war. In London, Funk's speech was regarded as a serious attempt to undermine resistance to Nazi Germany in occupied Europe; the Foreign Office was sufficiently alarmed to ask the economist John Maynard Keynes to draw up a paper to counter Funk's arguments.[44]

On 10 August, shortly after the Nazi minister's speech, Churchill told Colville that 'much constructive thinking' needed to be done after the war to build up something similar to the League of Nations. Based on some earlier thoughts in his pre-war essays,[45] Churchill explained that the creation of a 'United States of Europe' was very desirable, with Britain as 'the link connecting this federation with the new world and able to hold the balance between the two'; the Prime Minister believed this would be a 'balance of virtue'.[46]

Almost two weeks later, at a meeting of the War Cabinet on 23 August, Churchill referred to his belief that after the war there would remain a handful of European great powers and in addition 'there should be three groups of smaller States – in Northern Europe, in Middle Europe, and in the Balkans'. These 'three confederations' and 'the five great nations', he continued, should be 'linked together in some kind of Council of Europe'. In addition he believed there ought to be 'a Court to which all justiciable disputes should be referred, with an international air force. There must be a scheme for a fair distribution of raw materials.' Churchill emphasized, as he frequently did thereafter, that it was 'important that there should be no attempt at a vindictive settlement after the war'.[47]

The Prime Minister became a little more concrete later in the year, when suddenly, after dinner with friends on 13 December 1940, he began to give a more detailed outline of his 'noble and lofty' 'grand design' for the post-war era.[48] Although his ideas shifted a little over time, not least to accommodate opposition to his plans in the US and elsewhere, the core elements of his concept remained largely the same throughout the war. On 13 December, and similarly on a few subsequent occasions, the Prime Minister elaborated on his vision and expressed the belief that once Britain had won the war, five great European nations (England, France, Italy, Spain and Prussia) as well as four (rather than three as initially envisaged) regional confederations would regularly discuss the main directions of European policy within a Council of Europe. The regional confederations would consist of a Northern Bloc (Scandinavia, the Netherlands), a Middle European Confederation (Czecho-slovakia, Poland), the important Danubian Confederation (Bavaria, Württemberg, Austria, Hungary) and a Turkish-led Balkan Confederation. He also saw the partial dismemberment of Germany by separating the Austrians and the Southern Germans from the Prussians as crucial for future harmony in Europe.[49]

According to Churchill the Council of Europe, consisting of nine or ten powers, would be established at the end of the war and 'would have a supreme judiciary and a Supreme Economic Council to settle currency questions, etc.' Whilst 'all air forces, military and civil, would be internationalised', every state would continue to have its own army with the exception of Prussia, which he believed ought to be demilitarized for a hundred years apart from an air contingent. 'The Council would be unrestricted in its methods of dealing with a Power condemned by the remainder in Council.[50]

Although his plan seemed to indicate the inclusion of some supranational elements, this was misleading. Churchill was thinking of a Council of Europe organized along strictly intergovernmental lines and overseen from outside by Great Britain. In the course of his remarks he referred somewhat enigmatically to the fact that Britain would be both 'part of Europe' and would 'also be part of the English-speaking world'. However, his thinking clearly focused on the predominant role a victorious Britain would assume as the strongest and most distinguished country in Europe. Britain, like the USA, could not be expected to become directly involved in the proposed scheme for Europe: 'the English speaking world would be apart from this, but closely connected with it, and it alone would control the seas, as the reward of victory.'[51]

Churchill believed that the Russians ought to be part of an Eastern Confed-eration while 'the whole problem of Asia would have to be faced'. However, 'as far as Europe was concerned', he was convinced that 'a system of confederation was necessary to allow the small powers to continue to exist and to avoid balkanisation'. Having learnt from the Versailles Peace Treaty, which he had always criticized as deeply flawed, Churchill was firmly convinced that 'There must be no war debts, no reparations and no demands on Prussia.' While he thought that Germany would have to give up 'certain territories' and 'exchanges of population would have to take place', he believed deeply that 'there must be no pariahs, and Prussia, though unarmed, should be secured by the guarantee of the Council of Europe.'[52]

Churchill entirely neglected to work out any procedural details of his scheme. Many years later he would make the same mistake when proposing a grand scheme for overcoming the Cold War without paying any attention to devising procedures for implementing his vision.[53] Moreover, as for example Clive Ponting has pointed out, Churchill did not pay any attention to the potential ethnic, nationalist and religious conflicts among the various groups and nations to be thrown together in his confederations. Nor did he address the question whether or not these nations would be prepared to sacrifice their independence as sovereign states and, if not, who was to impose the confederate structures on them.[54] He also tended to shroud in ambiguity the position of his own country within his grand European scheme.

Churchill clarified his thoughts on Britain's role within a united Europe a month later, in January 1941. According to John Colville, the Prime Minister told him at Ditchley, Churchill's grand weekend retreat near Oxford, that 'there must be a United States of Europe and that he believed that it should be built by the English: if the Russians built it there would be Communism and squalor; if the Germans built it there would be tyranny and brute force.' The Prime Minister believed that 'while Britain might be the builder and Britain might live in the house, she would always preserve her liberty of choice and would be the natural, undisputed link with the Americas and the Commonwealth'.[55]

It is difficult to avoid the conclusion that the Prime Minister's concept for the future role of Britain and Europe was rather muddled; his ideas were ambivalent and potentially contradictory. On the one hand he seemed to think of Britain as a kind of benign hegemonic power in Europe, a position which might well result in a competitive relationship with the USA. On the other hand, the Prime Minister liked to view his country as Washington's closest ally and thus as the disinterested mediator between Europe, the colonial world and the Americans. At this stage, both the establishment of a Council of Europe, guided if not dominated by his own country, and the continuation of the Anglo-American alliance were the most important pillars of Churchill's post-war vision.[56]

Reconciling these alternative visions through a happy compromise that neither antagonized the Americans nor endangered Britain's post-war importance was to remain a problem whose solution would ultimately escape him. Eventually, as will be seen, the dilemma would convince him to give up the pursuit of his vision for post-war Europe and make him once again concentrate solely on summit diplomacy and the 'special relationship' to restore and maintain Britain's great power status. The ultimate aim of all of Churchill's post-war aspirations remained his intention to salvage 'as much of Britain's influence, wealth, and power as circumstances would permit'.[57] As is explained in greater detail in the next chapter, once he realized that his European vision was unable to support this aim, he fell back on his beloved summit diplomacy. Churchill's goals for the future of Europe had, after all, met with little enthusiasm in Moscow and Washington.

Opposition to Churchill's Plans in Moscow, Washington and London

In late 1941 Stalin expressed his strong opposition to European confederations, whether pan-European or regional. In particular, he was opposed to the creation of Eastern European federations as envisaged by many leaders of the governments in exile.[58] Moscow clearly feared the development of anti-Soviet buffer states. Instead, the Kremlin desired the creation of small independent states between its territory and a dismembered and partitioned Germany.[59] Confederations reminded the Kremlin of the *cordon sanitaire* of post-First World War days when the western powers had attempted to contain the Bolsheviks.[60]

When Anthony Eden visited Moscow in December 1941, Stalin told him he favoured the restoration of an independent Austria, the expansion westwards of Poland, and the break-up of Germany. He was considering the creation of separate and autonomous countries like Bavaria, a Rhenish state and possibly a northern German state. The USSR also insisted on retaining the borders agreed with Germany in the 1939 Hitler–Stalin Pact.[61] American diplomat Charles Bohlen later concluded that if Stalin's scheme was realized, 'the Soviet Union would be the only important military and political force on the continent of Europe. The rest of Europe would be reduced to military and political impotence.'[62]

Stalin believed that once the war was over Germany would recover relatively quickly, perhaps in 15–20 years. Germany would thus soon dominate Churchill's European confederation and be in a position to threaten the Soviet

Union once again.[63] The Soviet embassy in London repeatedly pointed out to the leaders of the various Resistance movements that their policy was contradictory and would not gain public support: they were fighting to regain their countries' freedom from Nazi domination, but they seemed to be happy to give up their independence to post-war federations.[64]

So long as the Soviet Union desperately needed Britain's assistance in the war against Hitler, Stalin's opposition to the establishment of European federations remained comparatively muted. In December 1941, during Eden's visit to Moscow, Stalin seemed prepared to tolerate a degree of European federalism, although he refused to include in the draft Anglo-Soviet friendship treaty a clause explicitly expressing the Soviet Union's backing for European confederations.[65] Similarly, during the talks in London in May 1942 which eventually led to the conclusion of the Anglo-Soviet treaty, the Soviet Foreign Minister Molotov expressed no strong reservations. However, once the Soviet Union's military victory at Stalingrad had bolstered the Kremlin's confidence, Moscow again voiced its strong opposition to the establishment of Eastern European federations.[66]

Even before these events the Soviets had indicated their opposition to Eastern European confederations in a more circumspect way. In February 1942 the Czech ambassador was informed of Moscow's strong antipathy to the proposed Czech–Polish federation, and during his visit to London Molotov told Czechoslovakian President Beneš of Stalin's strong opposition to the idea. A month later, in June 1942, Moscow effectively vetoed it when the Soviet ambassador made Stalin's position clear. Thus, towards the end of the year Beneš began to waver and let it be known that he regarded a Polish–Czech federation as premature. Six months later, in May 1943, he finally fell in line. Moscow had broken off diplomatic relations with the Polish government in exile in London due to Stalin's resentment that the Poles (quite rightly) held Moscow responsible for the Katyn massacre. As a result, Beneš decided not to continue the negotiations about a future federation with Poland; instead, on 12 December 1943 he entered into an alliance with the Soviet Union, hoping this would provide his country with greater security.[67]

Polish Prime Minister in exile Sikorski's sudden death in an air accident in July 1943 had already led to the termination of the talks begun in 1942 regarding the establishment of a 'European Community' among the exiled governments in London. The Greek–Yugoslav union also soon fell foul of Moscow's disfavour.[68] In view of these developments the persistent efforts by Resistance leaders, in particular Norwegian and Dutch politicians, to persuade the Foreign Office to remain committed to at least some degree of European regionalism had little chance of success.[69]

At this stage in the war, the Foreign Office was much more interested in the development of an Atlantic security system for post-war defence. Eden argued that if Washington accepted offers from Britain and some of the smaller European countries to hand over control of some of their military bases after the war, 'it would represent a definite undertaking by the United States to bear a share of responsibility for the maintenance of peace in post-war Europe'.[70] In view of the escalating role of the USSR and the USA in the war during 1943, the officials were concerned not to undermine further Britain's increasingly weak position among the 'Big Three'.[71] The Foreign Office believed that the confederation plans as promulgated by Churchill and some of the Resistance groups and exiled governments in London might have been an important factor in Stalin's decision to encourage intensive contacts with the German embassy in Stockholm in the first half of 1943. The threat of a separate Soviet peace with Hitler seemed to loom on the horizon, coming so soon after the German counter-offensive in March 1943, only weeks after the Soviet victory at Stalingrad.[72]

Both Washington and London were ready to do everything in their power to persuade Stalin not to make a separate peace with Germany, particularly when in early September 1943 Stalin's approach to Hitler seemed to indicate the very real possibility of a Soviet-German arrangement.[73] The western Allies were fully aware of Stalin's anger that the Second Front would not materialize in 1943 despite the promises made after its first postponement the year before. Stalin had been told in May 1943 that he would have to wait until the spring of 1944 before preparations for the Normandy invasion could begin.[74] Great efforts were made to reassure the Soviets that the Second Front had been postponed due to issues of military strategy and not for other devious reasons, as Stalin suspected. Roosevelt and Churchill were therefore prepared to offer Stalin other incentives, like territorial compromises and a willingness not to insist on the creation of Eastern European confederations, to ensure the continuation of the anti-Hitler alliance.[75]

Thus, Stalin's determined opposition to the establishment of European confederations, as well as the need to appease him in regard to the Second Front, decisively undermined the likelihood that Churchill's plan to base the post-war world on confederate schemes would be realized. Furthermore, not only Stalin but also the Americans were unimpressed by Churchill's concepts for the future of Europe and his apparent intention to restore spheres of influence and the balance of power as the basis of international relations in the post-war world.

Although in the last resort the American administration too pursued a spheres of influence policy, Washington's rhetoric sounded very different. Churchill's grandiose and woolly rhetoric could not hide the fact that the Prime Minister was above all interested in preserving Britain's Empire and re-establishing a world based on a conventional view of the balance of power. The United States had a much more lofty vision. FDR and Secretary of State Cordell Hull were thinking of a 'one world' concept and publicly proclaimed their belief in Wilsonian principles. In effect this meant the institutionalization of something approaching a world government, including the abandonment of all divisive empires, spheres of influence ideas and protective tariffs.[76] The American President was strongly convinced that after the end of the war supreme world power ought to be managed by the great powers, consisting of the 'Big Three' and China, as global trustees. Roosevelt believed that these four powers should be largely responsible for the preservation of world peace.[77]

In August 1941, at their first meeting at Placentia Bay, Roosevelt had told Churchill that Britain and the USA ought to police the world until a world organization had been created.[78] In early 1942 Roosevelt hinted at his 'four policemen' concept in a general way. The President became more precise in May 1942, when he told Soviet Foreign Minister Molotov that 'the United States, England and Russia and perhaps China should police the world and enforce disarmament by inspection'. He also outlined his trusteeship idea and his thoughts on economic reconstruction.[79] Roosevelt elaborated on these thoughts during a confidential conversation in November, when he spoke of Russia's responsibility for preserving peace in the western hemisphere; he believed that the USA and China had the same task in the Far East.[80] The American President repeated this belief to the Canadian Prime Minister in December. Three months later, in March 1943, Roosevelt told visiting British Foreign Secretary Eden that the future United Nations Organization ought to consist of three organs, including a general assembly of all nations which would only meet once a year 'to blow off steam'. The important instrument was to be an executive committee of the four great powers responsible for taking the really important decisions and policing the globe. There would also be an advisory council consisting of the four great powers and representatives of some six or eight other countries, which would meet occasionally to settle international questions.[81]

Initially, Roosevelt as well as other leading politicians in Washington, like Under-Secretary of State Sumner Welles and many of the experts in the State Department's Advisory Committee on post-war planning, were not opposed to European unity and a measure of regionalism based on the model of the USA's own federal structure.[82] The President hoped that it would be possible to manage world affairs through the personal diplomacy of the leaders of the four great powers. Thus at first Roosevelt largely agreed with Churchill's suggestion that regional councils and separate economic agencies should be responsible for the day-to-day administration of international affairs; the hegemonic 'four policemen' were to concentrate on the really essential security issues.[83] As Robin Edmonds has pointed out, that solution for the new post-war global order had the advantage of avoiding the pitfalls of the League of Nations, obtaining the support of Congress, and maintaining the cooperation of the 'Big Three' plus China.[84]

Yet, as always, Roosevelt's personal opinions fluctuated and he often appeared to express differing views to different people. His advisers as well as his British ally found it difficult to comprehend and interpret the President's position. Moreover, Roosevelt often played cynical 'board games' with European boundaries, perhaps because he, like his Secretary of State, viewed European identity and frontier squabbles as 'piddling little things', the phrase Cordell Hull once used to refer to the Polish border question.[85] In contrast to Churchill's and Stalin's deep concerns about developments in Europe, it seems reasonable to describe FDR's attitude towards the frontiers of Europe as 'aloof'.[86] Anthony Eden certainly harboured serious doubts about Roosevelt's plans to change European borders by, for example, carving out a new state of Wallonia from parts of France, Belgium and Luxembourg.[87]

Both Roosevelt and his Secretary of State saw the primary aim as the attempt to co-opt Stalin into an international system of cooperation. For Roosevelt, the preservation of world peace demanded continued cooperation with the Soviet Union, which was about to become the largest and strongest power on the European continent. The more Stalin opposed the establishment of European confederations, the clearer it became that the USA would not support these schemes either. Hull hoped that instead of antagonizing Moscow, he would be able to inspire 'international cooperative action to set up the mechanisms which can thus ensure peace'.[88] His primary goal was to bring about the creation of an 'international agency' to 'keep the peace among nations in the future', if necessary by means of force. Hull believed that this would be the precondition for constructing a peaceful and prosperous post-war world. Once such a global structure had been created an atmosphere more conducive to the solution of border questions and other controversial issues would exist.[89]

Strongly influenced by his Secretary of State, FDR gradually changed his mind and began to oppose Churchill's confederate structure for Europe. Hull managed to convince the President of the great advantages of a 'universal international organization' and persuaded him to dismiss the creation of any regional confederate institutions which were on a par with the world organization and would perhaps even begin to compete with it.

Although Hull was well aware that the establishment of a few regional organizations might be useful as they could act as a kind of buffer between the individual nations and the world organization, he believed that any regional councils should be clearly subordinate to the global organization. Hull and Roosevelt were only prepared to accept regional federations which had a clearly defined role inferior to that of the envisaged world organization and would thus not be in a position to absorb the global responsibilities of the world organization.

Churchill's post-war vision, in Hull's view, would lead to the creation of powerful and competitive regional federations, a development that would reintroduce the old balance of power concept into the management of the post-war world. If the federal concept was pursued, Hull believed that conflicts would arise not between individual countries but between mighty regions and 'groups of nations' and the new 'universal organization might find itself incapable of dealing with such conflicts. It would be easier for the proposed United Nations organization to deal with a nation alone than with a nation tied into and supported by a region.'[90] Hull aimed to create a truly global organization that would ensure the participation of the smaller states as individual actors; this would make the creation of regional organizations superfluous and indeed disadvantageous.

One of Hull's strongest arguments in favour of a world organization was his belief that American public opinion would not support Washington's participation in regional councils concerned only with Europe or Asia. In such a case, the American public would insist on limiting US activities to the western hemisphere in the spirit of the Monroe Doctrine. This would force Washington to accept a new kind of regional isolationism and decisively undermine the creation of any effective world organization.[91] There was, moreover, the difficult question whether or not the regional power ought to represent the smaller nations in its primary region when it acted as a member of the board of other regional councils. The Latin American nations, for example, might well resent the likelihood that the USA would represent them on a European Council.[92]

In general, the American Secretary of State and the progressive wing of the Democratic Party remained very suspicious of Churchill's imperial frame of mind and, quite correctly, viewed the Prime Minister's hankering after regional organizations as part of his desire to preserve the British Empire and Britain's world power status. Not least, Hull was greatly concerned that Churchill's regionalist approach to the post-war world would result in continued protectionism and 'closed trade areas' like the sterling bloc which, he believed, were bound to lead to the creation or consolidation of harmful spheres of influence. Such a development might well disadvantage American businesses; the world market ought to be freely accessible, the Secretary of State believed.[93]

Impressed by Hull's reasoning, Roosevelt in the spring and summer of 1943 felt less and less sympathy for Churchill's divisive regionalist proposals and moved towards his Secretary of State's more global approach.[94] Hull successfully convinced Roosevelt to agree to his Four-Nation Declaration, his 'pride and joy' according to Warren Kimball,[95] which was meant to facilitate post-war cooperation with the Soviet Union.[96] Churchill did not object to this fairly vague and general declaration.[97] Eden was given the document during the first Quebec conference in August 1943 and it was adopted and signed at the allied foreign ministers' conference in Moscow on 30 October 1943. While the declaration was a very general statement, Hull explained his underlying thinking in his address to a joint session of Congress in November 1943 on the occasion of the signing of the Four-Nation Declaration on General Security. He asserted that in the post-war world he envisaged there would no longer be any necessity 'for spheres of influence, for alliances, for balance of power or any other of the special arrangements through which, in the unhappy past, the nations strove to safeguard their security or to promote their interests'.[98]

The idealistic global structure Hull aspired to was, in the words of William Hardy McNeill, the creation of 'a world composed of liberal, independent, and democratic states' which would 'exhibit a natural harmony of interests'.[99] Undoubtedly, the world's strongest power would benefit particularly from such a scenario, both in political and economic terms. Throughout the war Hull never tired of advocating the importance of a genuinely internationalist policy for reasons of free trade and world peace, and he constantly warned against the invention of a regionalist 'European control body'. By managing to obtain Roosevelt's endorsement of his alternative 'one world' and 'free trade' scheme, Hull decisively undermined Churchill's vision for the creation of a European Council and a group of European confederations.[100]

The Foreign Office Plans for Post-war Europe

Not only were Washington and Moscow opposed to Churchill's plans for the future of Europe: the Foreign Office and the Foreign Secretary Anthony Eden were not enthusiastic either. The officials regarded Churchill's proposals as unrealistic, and resented the fact that the Prime Minister had managed to antagonize Britain's allies with his vague ideas. While Eden was much more interested in post-war planning than Churchill, his aims for post-war Europe were also vague and ambiguous. In 1939 Eden had spoken of the establishment of 'some form of European federation' and in a December 1940 memorandum he had suggested that European reconstruction after the war would require that all 'nations must be prepared to surrender *some of their sovereign rights* in the cause of greater unity', but his enthusiasm for the reconstruction of Europe along genuinely federalist lines was very short-lived.[101] As David Dutton has commented with some understatement, after 1940 Eden, and indeed almost the entire British political establishment, displayed a 'cautious scepticism on the European issue'.[102]

Moreover, the Foreign Secretary was often at a loss when attempting to evaluate Stalin's post-war intentions. Like Churchill, he was frequently torn between great optimism and utter pessimism when reflecting on the future relationship with the Soviet Union. But Eden also viewed the potential dependence of Europe on the military and economic aid of the United States with great concern. He wished to see Britain continue as a global power and the domination of the European continent by the USA or any other country prevented, and to this extent Eden's thinking about the future of the European continent closely resembled Churchill's concept.[103]

However, there were also significant differences between Eden's and Churchill's ideas for the future of Europe. Initially, Eden's solution to Britain's expected security dilemma in post-war Europe consisted largely of his vigorous attempts, pursued since mid-1941, to convince both Churchill and Roosevelt that France needed to be restored as a European great power; eventually Churchill adopted this view.[104] Eden believed that a strong France and the establishment of good Franco-British relations would help Britain to remain the predominant European country despite Soviet expansionist designs and the expected resurgence of Germany after the war. At times the Foreign Secretary even contemplated that Britain's relations with France might well need to be closer than his country's relationship with the USA. Eden firmly believed that 'FDR does NOT want us to take the lead in Europe' but he had 'equally no doubt that we should'.[105]

Churchill would have agreed, although in general the Prime Minister was much better disposed towards Roosevelt than his Foreign Secretary and tended to downplay or ignore the President's activities which were damaging to Britain's interests. While Eden looked with amazement at the apparent chaos in FDR's governmental organization and was dismayed at the President's often contradictory and opaque statements of policy,[106] Churchill was more tolerant in these matters. Perhaps he felt reminded of his own way of governing.

In contrast to Churchill, Eden and his advisers were largely prepared to go along with Roosevelt's 'four policemen' scheme. The Foreign Secretary was convinced that the Prime Minister's emphasis on the formation of regional blocs would only lead to great power competition and dangerous rivalries; instead of preserving world peace it might well lead to another war. Together with the majority of his senior officials, Eden believed that regional groups should be integrated into Roosevelt's proposed world organization so that the 'four policemen' would not only be interested in the well-being of their respective primary regional blocs but also in the global maintenance of peace.[107] Despite his great concerns about Russia's territorial ambitions and Britain becoming subservient to the United States, the Foreign Secretary could not see 'how anything European could work unless we and Russia and also to some extent America took a continuous part in it'.[108]

Eden and his officials were not moved by Churchill's plea that they ought 'to have a little confidence' in the Prime Minister's 'insight into Europe'.[109] Instead, the Foreign Office began to develop its own plans for post-war Europe. The visit of two officials to Washington in August 1942 resulted in intensive discussions in the Foreign Office and the establishment of a think-tank, the Economic and Reconstruction Department, to develop a British vision for the post-war world.[110] Institutionalizing a more formal approach to post-war planning was a response to the general discontent about the lack of governmental thinking which had been voiced from within the House of Commons, the House of Lords, the Foreign Office and even the Cabinet. More immediately, the Foreign Office plan was a reaction to Hitler's faltering war in the East and the increasing likelihood that Germany would ultimately be defeated. The perceived danger that the Soviet Union and indeed the United States might intend to fill the power vacuum in Europe after the eventual collapse of Hitler's Reich increasingly worried Whitehall.[111]

By mid-1942 the Foreign Office had also become concerned about Britain's post-war standing in the world. It was realized that any abdication of the country's post-war responsibilities, as advocated by some in London, and any unwillingness to 'fulfil our world-wide mission' would lead to the UK becoming a mere 'second-class Power'. Such 'an agonising collapse' from Britain's traditional world power status would undoubtedly make the country 'emerge as a European Soviet state, the penurious outpost of an American pluto-democracy, or a German *Gau*, as forces might dictate'.[112] In order to prevent the realization of such a depressing eventuality after the end of the war, it was concluded that Britain needed to restore its export trade, maintain the strength of its armed forces, uphold its influence throughout the Empire and contribute to an international system for restricting the power of Germany and Japan, while also maintaining global peace and the sterling area.[113]

Most importantly, the Foreign Office hoped to be able to shape and influence American post-war planning by formulating its own ideas before it was too late. It was concluded, however, that if Whitehall wished for its vision to be taken seriously in Washington, the British concept ought not to diverge too much from the American plans.[114] Although the Foreign Office rejected as impracticable Roosevelt's idea that only the Great Powers should possess major arms,[115] the British officials' general sympathy for the President's 'four policemen' scheme did not seem to make it an impossible task to move closer to Washington's scheme. Much to the relief of the officials, Churchill and the Cabinet were too preoccupied with the fall of Tobruk and Singapore and Germany's dangerous submarine warfare to be able to interfere much in the drafting of the Foreign Office plan for a post-war settlement.[116]

Eventually, in late 1942, Foreign Office official Gladwyn Jebb, the head of the new Economic and Reconstruction Unit, submitted the so-called Four-Power Plan to the Secretary of State. It was the Foreign Office's first substantial attempt to influence allied post-war planning.[117] The name of the scheme reflected the Foreign Office's insight into 'the desirability of some post-war international organization' which was 'based on co-operation between all the Allied Great Powers'.[118] Although the officials were convinced that the 'simplest' and 'perhaps the most desirable solution' was the joint leadership of the united nations by the US and Britain, it was assumed that the Soviet Union and the European countries, and probably the US itself, were unlikely to accept such 'Anglo-Saxon hegemony'. Therefore, London should aim for four-power co-operation.[119]

In view of American preferences for a non-regionalist concept for the post-war world, the Four-Power Plan was essentially an attempt to overcome differences between British and American thinking.[120] Jebb expressed the belief 'that we should willingly accept the underlying conception of the Roosevelt Administration and seek to render it more practicable by an admixture of our own political sense, standing absolutely fast on the Four-Power idea with possible extension to provide for France'.[121] Not surprisingly, the plan was therefore strongly influenced by American ideas; in fact, the Foreign Office scheme largely rested on Roosevelt's 'Four World Policemen' scheme.[122] The officials had realized much earlier than the Prime Minister that it was the revival of the old European spheres of influence approach which the Americans most strongly opposed; Washington's fears needed to be alleviated. The Foreign Office believed that Jebb's Four-Power Plan was the best scheme available and should be 'put into operation' as soon as possible. Britain's foreign policy experts were agreed, however, that this could not be done 'until and unless the Americans were definitely committed'.[123]

The Foreign Office primarily intended to achieve two aims with the Four-Power Plan: to dilute Churchill's emphasis on regionalism, particularly European regionalism, and, most importantly, to amalgamate Washington's focus on four-power cooperation with Foreign Office thinking and even with some of the Prime Minister's vague ideas. The Foreign Office thus hoped to placate Churchill and, much more importantly, ensure that Washington would feel committed to Europe after the war.

Thus the Four-Power Plan emphasized that regionalism did not mean 'the establishment of the power of any one great power in any particular region'. Instead, regionalism 'should connote districts in which one of the great Powers should have primary responsibility for defence against Germany or Japan'.[124] Although this still smacked of a spheres of influence approach, albeit a somewhat diluted one, what the Foreign Office had in mind was the creation of 'a real world balance of power' as well as a large degree of influence and autonomy for Britain, its Empire and its European primary region.[125] Yet while the officials believed that 'regional groupings should be encouraged', a 'limited liability system, whereby one Great Power is solely responsible for keeping the peace in a given area' was eventually rejected. This would only lead to rivalries between the various groupings. Instead, like the Roosevelt administration, the officials in London came to believe that 'in principle' the four great powers should be 'equally interested in maintaining the peace everywhere in the world' and should speak and act together whenever peace was under threat.[126] It was, however, recognized that in practice all the great powers would predominate in at least one of the respective regions and thus be in charge of one of the four regional councils which were meant to coordinate the individual regions' defence and economic policies. It was expected that the US would dominate the Far East region while Britain and Russia would oversee the European countries.[127]

While the potential conflict between Britain and Russia over predominance in Europe was not discussed, the future division of the continent was already contemplated in the British plan. It was assumed that Britain would exercise 'effective regional control in north-west Europe' and 'the greatest responsibility for the restoration of this western European area would rest with us'. At this stage in the war, the Foreign Office also still hoped to be able 'to amalgamate the smaller Powers into confederations' and expected the development of Polish–Czech and Greek–Yugoslav federations.[128] It was hoped that these confederations would 'achieve a common military, economic and political system, and act in collaboration with the U.S.S.R.' and thus 'might form a real buttress against German penetration'.[129]

On 8 November 1942 the Four-Power Plan was circulated to the Cabinet.[130] Eden had already given Churchill a summary of the scheme in early October, though he subsequently revised it. The Foreign Secretary attempted to undermine the Prime Minister's expected objection to this kind of elaborate thinking on the post-war world by expressing the view that Britain's lack of a clear post-war policy had already had a detrimental effect on negotiations with the United States. In late October Roosevelt had indeed indicated that he wished to discuss the broad outlines of a post-war settlement and put pressure on London to develop its own concept.[131] The Four-Power Plan was eventually discussed by the Cabinet on 27 November together with two other memoranda: a paper by Churchill's rival Stafford Cripps, the Minister for Aircraft Production and former ambassador to Moscow, and one by the Secretary of State for India, Leo Amery, whom Jebb aptly characterized in his memoirs as an 'isolationist – a sort of English Luce'.[132]

Cripps's paper proposed the establishment of five regional councils or, as he called them world councils, including a British Commonwealth Council. In particular he believed that the creation of a Council of Europe with British, Soviet and American participation was necessary, a scheme not unlike Churchill's idea. Cripps was worried about future German predominance in Europe and therefore believed that his Council of Europe ought to have power to deal with all political, economic and social issues that could endanger future peace. He also proposed the development of an international world police system and the establishment of a 'Supreme World Council' on which all the regional councils would be represented.[133]

Amery's memorandum expressed great pessimism about the likelihood that the anti-Hitler coalition would survive for any length of time after the war. Amery advocated the creation of a European union (without British participation) which would not be overseen by any of the great powers; Germany should be kept under control by France and an Eastern European confederation. The 'Big Three' would only deal with their own hemispheres and major areas of interest (Asia for the USSR, the Americas and part of the Far East for the US, and the Empire and Commonwealth countries for the UK). Amery saw no contradiction between a united European continent which did not include his own country and Britain's continued world power status, which rested exclusively on its Empire. He entirely neglected the fact that Britain had an essential interest in influencing developments on the continent and failed to recognize that Moscow would hardly be content with being relegated to Asia; he also seemed to ignore entirely that Stalin might insist on marching westward to dominate most or all of continental Europe.[134] Eden was not impressed by Amery's paper and it disappeared without much trace.[135] Cripps's memorandum, however, was taken much more seriously.

The Foreign Secretary was asked by the Cabinet to prepare a third paper integrating Cripps's ideas. There was growing concern among British politicians and diplomats that the anti-Hitler coalition had still not worked out any agreed post-war policies, and that the events in Stalingrad might bring about the end of the war rather more quickly than expected.[136] Eden's revised plan, now called the United Nations Plan although it still closely resembled the original Four-Power Plan, was eventually submitted to the War Cabinet on 16 January 1943, though it was not discussed.[137]

After the Foreign Office draft had gone through a number of revisions, including a change of name to Suggestions for a Peace Settlement in early March, and after a discussion of the scheme by the War Cabinet in mid-June, the plan was finally completed in early July and renamed The United Nations Plan for Organising Peace. As almost all of the various drafts as well as the final version had been largely authored by Gladwyn Jebb, the UN Plan for Organising Peace was 'basically, the old Four-Power Plan'. It remained fundamentally based on American ideas for a new world organization while incorporating some of Churchill's ideas.[138]

However, a few features were given much greater prominence in the final draft. Above all, the paper incorporated some of Cripps's ideas and proposed the establishment of a World Council of the great powers including China; the World Council was seen as a kind of directorate for the future United Nations.[139] As a concession to the Prime Minister's European Council idea and as a result of pressure from Eden, who had insisted on incorporating a European dimension, the establishment of a 'Reconstruction Commission' or a 'United Nations Commission for Europe' was recommended. Eden frequently reiterated that 'We shall never turn our backs on Europe'.[140] It was believed that this new element could develop into a Council of Europe of all European states if none became dominant. The Council of Europe might also possibly include the participation of the UK, Russia, and the USA.[141]

Roosevelt soon began to suspect that the UN Commission for Europe would develop into 'a kind of super-government for Europe' and thus threaten the prospects for making his beloved world organization a success. So, in the course of the Moscow foreign ministers' conference in October 1943 Eden's grand 'United Nations Commission for Europe' evolved into the European Advisory Commission, located in London with a very restricted brief. It was confirmed at the 'Big Three' meeting at Tehran that the remit of the EAC should be largely limited to discussions of German and Austrian issues; the Commission became the main instrument of allied planning for post-war

Germany. Moreover, the EAC was closely watched by Cordell Hull, who wished to keep its tasks as restricted as possible. On the whole, Washington did not differentiate between Eden's constructive approach and Churchill's much more sweeping regionalist strategy.[142]

There was some awareness in the Foreign Office that both the British and American concepts for the post-war world were based on fruitful cooperation among the great powers and their full agreement on either the firm control of Germany or its dismemberment. If the 'Big Three' fell out with each other or, as was more likely, if cooperation with the Soviet Union proved unsuccessful, it was realized that eventual cooperation with a revived and democratized Germany might well become necessary.[143] Thus the officials in Whitehall fully understood that they 'could not be sure that a four-Power plan would work. The uncertainties of American policy, the suspicions of the U.S.S.R., dislike of Great-Power tyranny among the smaller Powers and the Dominions would be difficult obstacles.' However, from the Foreign Office's point of view 'there was no satisfactory alternative'; Churchill's vague notions about European councils and confederations were certainly not regarded as sensible substitutes.[144]

Despite the development of the Four-Power Plan and its successor, the United Nations Plan for Organising Peace, it is fair to say that by early 1943 British post-war planning was still in a very fluid and undecided state. In view of the rapidly changing military developments of the war, the Foreign Office and the Foreign Secretary had not really been able to come to terms with the unenviable task of drawing up plans for the organization of post-war Europe. Churchill's lack of interest in post-war planning, combined with his occasional interference by advancing his own grand but vague post-war schemes, had clearly hampered the Foreign Office.

Moreover, Washington was becoming increasingly exasperated. When Churchill appeared to indicate in a speech in the House of Commons in late November 1942 that allied discussions about a post-war settlement should only take place after an armistice, the Americans were flabbergasted. With reference to Russian intentions, Roosevelt's adviser Sumner Welles told the British ambassador in late 1942 'that he could not emphasise too strongly how disastrous he thought it would be' if the war ended 'without having achieved complete agreement between our two Governments as to what we meant to do'.[145] Churchill chose to ignore this advice. Despite Washington's dislike of his ideas, during the year 1943 the Prime Minister continued to proclaim his intention to insist on the revival of a strong and autonomous European concert of nations in the post-war world.

CHAPTER 4

The Emergence of the Post-war World
European Regionalism, Big Three 'Summitry',
and Anglo-American Difficulties

Throughout 1943 Churchill remained convinced of his vision for post-war Europe. He still wished to create a 'United States of Europe' and establish a European Council and various regional confederations overseen by Britain. The British Prime Minister expected that such a scheme would enable his country to uphold its great power status in competition with Washington and Moscow in the post-war world. However, the Four-Power Plan and its successor the United Nations Plan, devised by the Foreign Office, reflected American preferences and were very different from what the Prime Minister had in mind. The Foreign Office had begun to realize the necessity of going along with American ideas, but Churchill stubbornly refused to follow. His proposals antagonized the Roosevelt administration, angered Stalin and drove the Foreign Office to despair. Only when Washington and Moscow put increasing pressure on Churchill did he reluctantly acquiesce in Roosevelt's universalist scheme for the post-war world. Instead of pursuing his European ideas further, he once again began to focus on his personal diplomacy to uphold Britain's status in the post-war world.

Churchill Insists on his Vision for Post-war Europe

In early 1943 Churchill still believed in the value of European regionalism and the continued need for something like a European concert of nations. He was strongly opposed to making Europe's ancient civilizations and traditional nation states subservient to a world organization dominated by the Big Four. Fraser Harbutt has noted that while Churchill always expressed support for the League of Nations, he largely did this to pacify domestic opinion; he 'was not an instinctive protagonist of the world organization'.[1] After all, a United Nations Organization based on the hegemonic power of a few great powers might well discriminate against British imperialism. In October 1942, when Churchill had first listened to a more detailed account of FDR's 'Four Policemen' scheme, he dismissed it as a 'very simple' concept. Then as later Churchill remained unimpressed by Roosevelt's fanciful notions about world government; he argued that Europe ought to be Britain's 'prime care'.[2]

On 21 October 1942 Churchill had explained the core ideas of his concept to Eden. He elaborated on his European vision as described in December 1940 and on a few subsequent occasions.[3] Churchill's minute to Eden outlined the major elements of his thinking on the distribution of power in the post-war world as they had developed half-way through the war. The memorandum clearly revealed the Prime Minister's fundamental beliefs and his differences with Washington. Churchill's thoughts as expressed to Eden would remain characteristic of his thinking on a post-war settlement in Europe throughout the war and in the immediate aftermath. The paper is therefore quoted at length.

It sounds very simple to pick out these four Big Powers. We cannot however tell what sort of a Russia and what kind of Russian demands we shall have to face. A little later on it may be possible. ... I must admit that my thoughts rest primarily in Europe – the revival of the glory of Europe, the parent continent of the modern nations and of civilisation. It would be a measureless disaster if Russian barbarism overlaid the culture and independence of the ancient States of Europe. Hard as it is to say now, I trust that the European family may act unitedly as one under a Council of Europe. I look forward to a United States of Europe in which the barriers between the nations will be greatly minimised and unrestricted travel will be possible. I hope to see the economy of Europe studied as a whole. I hope to see a Council consisting of perhaps ten units, including the former Great Powers, with several confederations – Scandinavian, Danubian, Balkan, etc. – which would possess an international police and be charged with keeping Prussia disarmed. Of course we shall have to work with the Americans in many ways, and in the greatest ways, but Europe is our prime care, and we certainly do not wish to be shut up with the Russians and the Chinese when Swedes, Norwegians, Danes, Dutch, Belgians, Frenchmen, Spaniards, Poles, Czechs, and Turks will have their burning questions, their desire for our aid, and their very great power of making their voices heard. It would be easy to dilate upon these themes. Unhappily the war has prior claims on your attention and mine.[4]

In late January 1943, during a visit to Turkey shortly after he had announced the need for Germany's unconditional surrender at the Casablanca conference, the Prime Minister dictated his controversial 'Morning Thoughts'.[5] Among other matters he dwelt on the idea of a Council of Europe as an 'instrument of European government' which would 'embody the spirit' but not the weaknesses of the League of Nations and include the old European and Asian nations and several confederations 'formed among the smaller states'. In a concession to Washington, he stated the intention to integrate this future European government in a 'world organisation for the preservation of peace' which would be established by 'the Chiefs of the United Nations'. He hoped that the United States would cooperate with Britain 'to organise a coalition resistance to any act of aggression committed by any Power' and perhaps even 'take the lead of the world'. He expected that the post-war era would for many years be dominated by 'economic reconstruction and rehabilitation' and hoped that the mistakes made in connection with the reparation payments decided upon at the Versailles peace conference could be avoided.[6]

Despite a slight shift towards the American point of view, Churchill thus continued to emphasize the necessity of European regionalism. It was certainly not his intention to exclude the United States from European affairs; on the contrary, he aspired to include Washington. However, Churchill was convinced that he needed to avoid American domination of Europe after the war if Britain was to survive as a great power. Although the Foreign Office had realized that since the United States only seemed to be interested in participating in a global and not a merely regional organization, the post-war world should be organized by great power collaboration within a world organization, Churchill had perhaps a more realistic view of the danger of Britain becoming a secondary power in a world dominated by the 'Big Two'.

The Prime Minister was aware that Britain would only be able to continue playing a leading role in the world if placed in charge of overseeing a European regional organization. Despite the Empire and Commonwealth, which in any case might well witness popular demands for independence after the war, it was unlikely that Britain would remain an important international player as a member of a global organization where it would have to compete with the USA and the Soviet Union and was bound to lose out eventually. Thus, as Avi Shlaim has observed, Churchill was greatly concerned 'with re-establishing the importance of Europe in the balance of world power'. The Prime Minister believed that only a more united Europe, led by Britain from the outside, would help his country 'to deal on equal terms with the continental resources of Russia and the United States'. Indeed, Churchill 'subordinated everything ... to the pursuit of the British national interest as he understood it'.[7]

Despite Churchill's personal friendship with Roosevelt and his strong belief in the Anglo-American 'special relationship', he did not intend to sit back while Washington began to dominate Europe and Britain. Churchill wished to maintain Britain's independence. In fact, the goals Churchill pursued with both his European regional strategy and his personal summit diplomacy were essentially identical, both during and after the war: the maintenance and, if necessary, the restoration of Britain's great power role. His European regionalism and personal diplomacy were different strategies for achieving the same result.

While Lord Halifax believed that Churchill's 'Morning Thoughts' of January 1943 'could not have been better',[8] the officials in the Foreign Office, however, were appalled. In a cheeky counter-memorandum entitled 'Early Morning Thoughts', written by Gladwyn Jebb, the Foreign Office dismissed Churchill's idea of an all-European government as impractical and 'romantic'. The officials deplored Churchill's 'rapid approach and equally rapid conclusions' as 'irrational' and overly adventurous. The 'only hopeful feature' appeared to be the Prime Minister's vagueness, which suggested the possibility of developing his ideas in a more realistic direction.[9] Jebb's counter-memorandum was a vastly 'exaggerated vision of a Churchillian future', depicting the post-war world as ruled by Anglo-America and 'divided up into exactly equal "confederations"'. The Foreign Office paper also contained the proposal for 'a really workable *Cordon Sanitaire*' and the declaration that 'if the Russians did not agree to all this they would be boycotted by the combined Chiefs-of-Staff', which were to be 'preserve[d] indefinitely'.[10]

This most unusual outburst of cynicism among the officials can be explained by the Foreign Office's concern that in the event that Europe organized itself along Churchill's lines, the Americans were likely to withdraw into isolation; while the Soviets might withdraw cooperation.[11] Thus Churchill's plans would only achieve the worst of all worlds: American isolationism, Soviet antagonism, and a Britain that would be left on its own, burdened with a destroyed and weak Europe in its backyard.

Neither Stalin nor Roosevelt was impressed by Churchill's 'Morning Thoughts'; the Prime Minister had sent them his memorandum in early February.[12] In particular Churchill's suggestion for the creation of 'an instrument of European government' was received badly in Washington. In the President's view, the Prime Minister's ideas once again smacked of a spheres of influence solution; Churchill still appeared to think in terms of the old-fashioned concept of the balance of power.[13]

Similar fears were expressed with respect to Churchill's broadcast, powerful in rhetoric but vague in substance, on 21 March 1943 at the opening of the

Pan-European Congress in New York, organized by Count Coudenhove-Kalergi.[14] In the course of his broadcast from London, Churchill announced publicly for the first time his preference for the creation of a Council of Europe (as well as a Council of Asia) after the end of the war.[15] However, to many of his American listeners it appeared that he was advocating a Council of Europe that excluded the USA. It reminded Americans of the stereotype of the devious, secretive and exclusive European diplomacy of pre-war days; not surprisingly, it met with fierce criticism in Washington. Nor was Roosevelt impressed by the fact that Coudenhove-Kalergi's Pan-European convention in New York had proclaimed that one of the Allied war aims ought to be the creation of a 'federal organisation for Europe'.[16]

Furthermore, Churchill had rather neglected to pay much attention to the establishment of a world organization, even though he knew that this was Washington's primary interest. Foreign Secretary Eden, who was visiting the United States at the time of Churchill's broadcast for the 'first review of war aims',[17] was told by Harry Hopkins, Summer Welles and other members of the US government that the Prime Minister seemed to be intent on resuscitating a world divided into spheres of influence. Such sentiments would be opposed by the American people and would strengthen the isolationists in the US, who were still a force to be reckoned with and would use an American regional Council as a pretext for renouncing Washington's global commitments.[18]

Eden was also informed in no uncertain terms that the American people and the American government were extremely reluctant to become involved in a Council of Europe, as the US would then have to deal with political and economic matters which only concerned the European continent. Washington, however, would not be opposed to contributing to the policing of the world and participation in a World Council dealing with global political matters. It was also explained to Eden that the British and Americans ought to avoid creating the impression that London and Washington intended to 'settle the future of the world'. The Soviet Union and China, with the latter being a useful counter force to Moscow, needed to feel involved.[19]

Roosevelt himself was particularly unhappy about the fact that in his broadcast Churchill had not mentioned the participation of the Soviet Union and China in the running of the post-war world. While the President was thinking more than ever in terms of the creation of a world organization, free trade and his 'four policemen concept', the British Prime Minister still appeared to believe that the post-war order should once again concentrate primarily on Europe and be the exclusive business of the Anglo-Americans, possibly in order to uphold the British Empire.[20] As Warren Kimball has pointed out, Roosevelt and his advisers still perceived Britain as a formidable potential rival in the post-war world and even feared that the protectionist British Empire with its high tariff walls might unite against the United States after the end of the war.[21]

During his visit to Washington in late May 1943, which mainly served the purpose of discussing military matters, Churchill elaborated on his ideas. He spoke of the necessity of establishing a Supreme World Council (the 'Big Three' plus China if Roosevelt desired this) which ought to incorporate three subordinate regional councils (Europe, American hemisphere, Pacific).[22] Churchill's thoughts were expressed particularly clearly in a memorandum dated 28 May, written by Lord Halifax and subsequently approved by Churchill. The paper referred to a luncheon at the British embassy on 22 May with members of Roosevelt's government; the President himself had been unable to attend.[23]

According to the memorandum, Churchill had made it clear in the course of the meeting that he believed that the new world organization should consist of the 'Big Three', who would be in overall charge (with the African and Asian nations remaining European colonies), and the three regional councils. He now envisaged that the European regional council would consist of up to twelve states or confederations led by a strong France. In the Prime Minister's view, 'each of the dozen or so of the European countries should appoint a representative to the European Regional Council thus creating a form of United States of Europe'. Churchill thought that 'Count Coudenhove-Kalergi's ideas on this subject had much to recommend them'.[24] In particular, Churchill emphasized the importance of the re-establishment of a powerful French nation as he did not think that the United States would be prepared to leave a large number of troops on the European continent for any length of time. He also believed that it would be sensible to separate Prussia from Germany as forty million Prussians were 'a manageable European unit'.[25]

During his visit to Washington, the Prime Minister also put forward his view that the 'members of the World Council should sit on the Regional Councils in which they were directly interested'. He believed that the United States should be the only power which would be represented on all the councils, no doubt hoping that this would ensure Washington's further involvement in world affairs. Canada ought to be a member of the regional council of the Americas and would thus represent the British Common-wealth. Russia could participate in the regional council for the Pacific; Churchill expected that Moscow would soon begin to pay great attention to the Far East. He also argued that a few other powers should be represented on the World Council 'by election in rotation from the Regional Councils'. The Prime Minister explained that the 'central idea of the structure was that of a three-legged stool – the World Council resting on three Regional Councils'. Such a system would be capable of preventing renewed aggression from Germany, Japan or any other potential enemy.[26] Churchill repeatedly emphasized his belief that the 'regional principle' was of the utmost importance; he explained that after all 'only the countries whose interests were directly affected by a dispute could be expected to apply themselves with sufficient vigour to secure a settlement'.[27]

With reference to Anglo-American relations, he said that a world organization did not exclude 'special friendships devoid of sinister purpose against others'. This of course aroused the suspicion of Moscow, as the Foreign Office had anticipated, while Washington became convinced that it was another one of Churchill's endeavours to persuade the USA to join Britain in an attempt 'to boss the world' and combine against the USSR.[28] After all, the Prime Minister had even mentioned that he was thinking of a 'fraternal association' between the Anglo-Americans: common Anglo-American citizenship, a common foreign policy and the joint use of military assets.[29] In a speech at Harvard University in early September 1943, Churchill repeated his appeal for 'Anglo-American Unity' and the continuation of the Anglo-American combined staff organization 'for a considerable time' after the war.[30]

The American political establishment liked Churchill's emphasis on Anglo-American friendship and Lord Halifax felt 'in his bones' that the Prime Minister's visit had 'done immense good, and will bear growing fruit in the days ahead of us'.[31] However, this was a huge exaggeration. Despite some polite remarks to the contrary, most American politicians were not enamoured by the details of Churchill's scheme; in particular his continued emphasis on European regionalism and independence was greatly resented. Peter Stirk has expressed it succinctly: 'With Cordell Hull there to pounce upon anything which strayed from a global approach, European integration was increasingly excluded from the decision-making agenda'.[32]

Eden and the Foreign Office were also unhappy with some of the proposals Churchill advanced during his American visit. They still criticized many aspects of his European scheme and were convinced that joint American-British citizenship would smack of an 'Anglo-Saxon dictatorship'. Moreover, like the Roosevelt administration, Eden believed that Churchill tended to neglect the issue of British-American-Soviet post-war cooperation, which was of crucial importance and ought to be emphasized in any statements referring to the organization of the post-war world. Above all, the Foreign Office was convinced that the development of a mechanism to iron out any future difficulties among the three or four great powers within the World Council was long overdue and ought to attract the attention of the Prime Minister.[33]

Thus neither the British Foreign Office nor Washington nor Moscow saw much value in Churchill's ideas. Moreover, in the meantime, and perhaps not without some pressure from Moscow, US Secretary of State Hull had become rather impatient with the President's Advisory Committee on Post-war Foreign Policy and its recently founded Subcommittee on Problems of European Organization. In August 1943 he discarded the Committee's 'Draft Constitution of International Organization', drawn up in mid-July, which foresaw an Executive Committee of the four great powers with a subordinate Council of five confederations spanning all continents. Eventually Hull dissolved the committee and instead established a new advisory committee within the State Department.[34]

In accord with the President, the Secretary of State instructed the new body to work on a draft that focused on a world organization dominated by the 'four policemen'; it was not meant to include any regional sub-organizations which might conceivably be in a position to compete with the 'Big Four' and impede international free trade. The Roosevelt administration also rejected the various other plans for closer European integration proposed by the President's Advisory Committee and the manifold groups of experts within the American Churches and the Council on Foreign Relations.[35] In effect, by August/September 1943 the United States had decided to repudiate Churchill's grand European vision and similar schemes once and for all. This meant that in effect Washington and Moscow shared the view that it was inadvisable to give the European continent any particular importance in the post-war settlement.[36]

The British Prime Minister became aware of this in the course of his meeting with Roosevelt in Quebec in August 1943. At Quebec, Churchill had effectively no choice but to agree to the American proposal to begin planning for a world organization without any special European dimension; the Prime Minister attempted, however, to avoid any decision by referring to the need to consult his Cabinet.[37] Roosevelt showed no interest whatsoever in the development of European confederations. Instead, he feared that the British desire to set up a 'United Nations Commission for Europe' was a perfidious attempt to establish a Council of Europe prior to a world organization.[38] Gladwyn Jebb had not helped Churchill's case by reassuring Cordell Hull's advisers Norman Davis and Jimmy Dunn that the British government by no means intended to establish a European Council in preference to a World Council. In fact, as Jebb admits in his memoirs, he 'consciously' argued 'against the views of my own PM'.[39]

The Soviets followed suit during the first allied foreign ministers' meeting in Moscow in October 1943. They accepted Washington's 'four policemen' concept as a transitional solution until the creation of a genuine world organization had been achieved. Foreign Minister Molotov was not inclined to explore Churchill's federation concepts or Eden's proposal for joint British–Soviet responsibilities in Central and South-eastern Europe including a Danubian federation. The British suggestion for an agreement on certain designated spheres of influence in the region was also turned down. When Molotov promised to participate in the European Advisory Commission, whose importance Eden clearly overestimated in view of Washington's lack of interest in it, the British Foreign Secretary did not press the confederation issue any further.[40]

Molotov, however, agreed to Hull's 'Four-Power Declaration' and the importance of free trade. Hull hoped this would pave the way for Roosevelt's cherished post-war world organization. Shortly afterwards he gave his well-known address to Congress during which he mentioned the American objective of the abolition of all spheres of interest and 'special arrangements' in the post-war era.[41] Soviet–American concurrence on the general organization of the post-war world may well have been one of the reasons why Stalin agreed to the first 'Big Three' conference in Tehran a month later, where the settlement reached at the Moscow foreign ministers' conference in October could be officially ratified.[42] After all, during the foreign ministers' meeting in Moscow the Soviets had also obtained Anglo-American agreement that the Normandy invasion would finally take place in May 1944.

Despite these setbacks in Quebec and Moscow, Churchill attempted to resuscitate his ideas during the Tehran conference in November/December 1943. He again attempted to persuade Stalin to agree to a Danubian confederation, that would include southern Germany, and the creation of a separate Prussian state to keep Germany under control and prevent a power vacuum in the middle of Europe.[43] But it was to no avail. Stalin himself had initially raised the issue by suggesting the establishment of European and Far Eastern councils with Soviet and American membership but Roosevelt stalled, referring to the lack of support from the Congress and American public opinion. The President was adamant about not being 'roped into accepting any European sphere of influence'. Roosevelt and his Secretary of State feared that this might result in the prolonged deployment of American troops in Europe and the development of a European economic federation which might undermine the American principle of free global trade.[44] While Stalin was not opposed to the establishment of a western European Council provided there was Soviet participation, he firmly rebuffed the creation of eastern, south-eastern and central European confederations.[45]

Eventually Stalin and Roosevelt agreed to reject Churchill's proposals. Neither the Soviet dictator nor the American democrat had any desire to strengthen European autonomy and Britain's status in the post-war world. Thus, Stalin accepted Roosevelt's world organization dominated by the great powers while insisting on the inclusion of a veto clause to prevent the hegemony of any one of them. He also agreed in principle to Soviet participation in the Pacific war. In return, the American President largely accepted the Soviet Union's borders as laid down in the 1939 Hitler–Stalin Pact, including the westward shift of Poland.[46]

It is paradoxical that despite Roosevelt's and Hull's emphasis on a genuinely integrative and global approach to post-war security, the Tehran conference led in fact to the development of a new balance of power and a division of the world into spheres of interest. If one cuts through the rhetorical verbiage, it becomes clear that several features of Churchill's approach to power politics were adopted by Roosevelt. Eventually a spheres of influence solution in all but name was seen by both Washington and Moscow as the best method of securing political and economic stability and maintaining their respective spheres of political and economic influence. Although it has been argued that tactically and strategically a 'sphere of influence meant something very different to each of the Big Three',[47] genuine conceptual rather than rhetorical differences were soon hardly noticeable between London's and Washington's approaches; in practice, the main substance of the British and American ideas appeared to be very similar. However, during the remainder of the war as well as during the Cold War, this realist policy would continue to be clouded by American references to the value of democracy, self-determination, and, above all, free trade and a 'commitment to abundance'.[48]

Thus, as regards Churchill's vision for the future of Europe, the turning point came in the late summer and autumn of 1943, when Roosevelt and Stalin effectively joined forces against the establishment of regional confederations and expressed themselves in favour of a 'Big Three' solution. The decisions taken during the 1943 conferences in Quebec, Moscow and Tehran reflected this.[49] The Tehran conference of course was also a turning point with regard to Britain's rapidly declining strategic and military contribution to the defeat of Hitler, and thus for Churchill's ability to be regarded as a full member of the 'Big Three'.[50]

Churchill Abandons the Pursuit of his European Vision

In view of Roosevelt's and Stalin's strong opposition to his European regionalism and the distinct lack of enthusiasm on the part of his own Foreign Office, Churchill reluctantly decided to let the issue rest. The officials in the Foreign Office continued to work on plans for a world organization that largely corresponded with American ideas and only superficially integrated Churchill's European vision. Both the FO and the War Cabinet's Armistice and Post-War Committee, which in this form emerged in April 1944, continued to argue that Churchill's scheme for a Council of Europe and a 'United States of Europe' was 'not practicable'. The Russians were unlikely to agree to any scheme that implied the restoration of Germany's power, while if the US participated in the Council of Europe, as the Prime Minister desired, this body would be almost identical with the World Council.[51]

The Foreign Office's arguments were not without influence on the Prime Minister, who gradually began to distance himself from his earlier European ideas and became ever more adamant that Britain, like the Soviet Union and the United States, could not be party to any future European organization. Instead, the great powers would need to oversee and guide matters from without as the leaders of the United Nations.[52] Churchill's thinking became increasingly less influenced by the movement for a federal Europe, which still had an impressive, though perhaps declining, number of supporters among the members of exiled governments and Resistance leaders in London. The Prime Minister was soon distinctly cool about the plans worked out by General Sikorski (until his death in July 1943), President Beneš, the Belgian Foreign Minister in exile Paul-Henri Spaak, former Belgian Prime Minister Paul van Zeeland, the former Italian foreign minister Carlo Sforza, Altiero Spinelli and Jean Monnet. In July 1944 this led, for example, to the issue of a 'Draft Declaration of the European Resistance' for a federally united Europe.[53]

Finally, in May 1944 the Dominion Prime Ministers decisively rejected Churchill's plan for regional councils as part of a new global structure. In reply to a memorandum by Eden on the 'Future World Organization', Churchill had submitted a memorandum to the meeting of Commonwealth Prime Ministers in London.[54] His paper focused on the establishment of two new organizations: the United States of Europe dominated by Britain and an Anglo-American fraternal association. Both organs were meant to become part of the new world organization. He explained that the former 'would arise naturally out of the European Regional Council and might well take as its model the British Empire and Dominions, with all the additional intimacy which would come from geographical proximity'. Churchill believed that 'In this way only can the glory of Europe rise again and its ancient nations dwell together in peace and mutual goodwill instead of tearing themselves and the world to pieces in their frightful and recurring quarrels.'[55]

Churchill expressed his desire that Britain should speak on behalf of the entire Empire and Commonwealth. However, all his proposals were rejected on the grounds that regional councils would hinder cooperation among

Commonwealth countries. It was also felt that if the Commonwealth countries were to be confined to a single regional council, it would preclude their representation in geographical areas which might have an important impact on their economic and political well-being. Only the idea of a regional council for Europe (which was to include the three great powers) survived as a 'special case though within the world organisation'.[56] In view of Moscow's and Washington's lack of interest, however, it was unlikely that such a European instrument would ever be established.

Churchill did not give up immediately. When he slyly attempted to leave the emphasis on the creation of regional organizations for Europe, Asia and the western hemisphere in the revised paper despite the 'strong objections of principle' by the Dominions Prime Ministers during the meeting in London, he was faced with forceful written protests from New Zealand and other Commonwealth countries. In particular, it was felt most unwise for the UK to 'enter negotiations with settled aims which we know in advance the U.S.A. will not share'. The fact that the UK still desired to speak on behalf of all Commonwealth members in the future world organization was also strongly resented.[57] Eden took the side of the Dominion Prime Ministers and was 'inclined' to agree that the revised document rested on a misrepresentation of their views as expressed during the meeting with the Prime Minister.[58]

Churchill did his best to defend his version and thus his intention to 'rescue' the concept of 'The United States of Europe'. He explained that the Supreme World Council consisting of the 'Big Three' or 'Big Four' would 'be the trustees or steering committee' to prevent 'the outbreak of more wars' but the great powers did not intend 'to rule the nations'. He declared poignantly: 'We should certainly not be prepared ourselves to submit to an economic, financial and monetary system laid down by, say, Russia, or the United States with her faggot vote China.'[59] Whilst Churchill had once again made clear that Britain did not wish to be dominated by either the United States or the Soviet Union, the Dominion Prime Ministers had no wish to prolong their semi-colonial domination by the UK. Thus, ultimately Churchill had to withdraw his revised paper and his vision for an independent and united Europe overseen by Britain.

The rejection of Churchill's plan for the future of Europe by the Dominion Prime Ministers appears to have been the last straw. The Prime Minister lost all motivation to continue battling for his thinking on regional councils and federations, including a powerful European Council, as a way to organize the post-war world. In late November 1944 he told Stalin that any 'European arrangements for better comradeship' would only be made 'after and subordinate to any such world-structure'.[60] Finally, the decision agreed upon at the Yalta conference in early 1945, which had been foreshadowed since the Tehran conference, that all three allied powers would participate in the occupation and administration of Germany meant in fact that Churchill's conception of the establishment of an autonomous European grouping could no longer be realized, even if he had wanted this.[61]

In the last resort, however, it had not been the ideal of European unity or the fate of the European continent as such that had appealed to Churchill but the idea of employing the help of federalist schemes to shore up Britain's declining power *vis-à-vis* the 'Big Two'. After the defeat of his plans, Churchill increasingly focused on the importance of maintaining the unity of the 'Big Three' and Britain's continued global significance by means of personal summit diplomacy.[62] He felt that he had no other way to strengthen British influence *vis-à-vis* the two stronger powers.

Yet, from mid-1943 and certainly after the Tehran conference in November/December of that year, Churchill's summit diplomacy also faced increasing difficulties and became less successful as Britain's dwindling resources and the country's much smaller manpower base rapidly turned it into the 'Big Two's' junior partner.[63] Churchill fully appreciated Britain's financial and military weakness and was aware that the 'Big Three' had become merely the 'Big Two and a Half'.[64] Still, Churchill's summit diplomacy, especially in 1940–41, had not been without success. His negotiations with Roosevelt, Stalin and their ministers and advisers had decisively contributed to strengthening Britain's position in the war and thus helped to bring about the very survival of Britain as a liberal democracy.[65] It was thus not surprising that after the defeat of his European vision and notwithstanding his negative experiences during the Tehran conference, Churchill turned to his summit diplomacy to strengthen his country's post-war importance.

After Tehran, Churchill also gradually began to subscribe to the widely shared British illusion that the Empire and Commonwealth together with the Anglo-American 'special relationship' (all under the umbrella of the US-dominated world organization), rather than some kind of united Europe or western European bloc, would serve as a power base for the country's influence in the post-war world.[66] Britain needed, in Denis Healey's words, 'new sources of power, not new sources of responsibility'.[67] Thus Churchill decided to reject proposals for the development of a Western European bloc, the importance of which the Foreign Office now began to emphasize.

Thus towards the end of the war Churchill no longer believed that his idea of a 'United States of Europe' and a regional Council for the European continent was feasible. Both he and the British Chiefs of Staff became strongly opposed to the creation of a Western European security bloc, which they did not believe could possibly be strong enough, either militarily or politically, to serve as a bulwark against Soviet expansionist designs. By 1944 the Prime Minister viewed most of the European countries as 'liabilities' and saw 'nothing but hopeless weakness'.[68] Furthermore, the establishment of a western European bloc could well undermine what was left of Stalin's willingness to maintain 'Big Three' cooperation after the war, which would make life even more difficult for a weakened Britain. In late November 1944 he therefore wrote to Stalin that he had 'not yet considered' proposals for a western bloc.[69] A few days later he again emphasized in a telegram to the Soviet dictator that 'As regards a Western Bloc, so far I am scantily informed on the subject and the Press reports are conflicting.'[70]

Nevertheless, in the last years of the war Churchill could not avoid being drawn into the lengthy deliberations within the Foreign Office regarding the establishment of a Western European security bloc. Such a scheme had played a certain role in post-war planning discussions in the Foreign Office since 1942. Duff Cooper, the francophile British representative to De Gaulle's government in exile, played a prominent role in advocating an alliance with France.[71] Cooper was deeply influenced by deliberations which had taken place from late 1943 within the French government in Algiers about the potentially dominant role of post-war Germany in Europe. Ideas of an economic federation between France, Belgium, Holland and the German Rhineland and Ruhr valley, which De Gaulle wished to separate from Germany, were frequently discussed in Algiers. De Gaulle and his economic adviser Jean Monnet envisaged a pact encompassing most European countries and leading to the integration of the individual members' economic and military policies to protect Europe from yet another German onslaught. The organization was also seen as a defensive mechanism against potential Soviet expansionism.[72]

Influenced by these debates Duff Cooper warned his government that relying on 'Big Three' cooperation, great power summit diplomacy and a yet-to-be-established new world organization to preserve peace and stability was a less than impressive strategy for the post-war world. Instead, he recommended that Britain should take the initiative to set up a Western European organization and ignore Soviet and American displeasure. 'The leadership of Europe will await us, but we may miss the opportunity of acquiring it if we hesitate to adopt a positive foreign policy through fear of incurring the suspicion of Russia on the one hand, or the disappointment of America on the other.'[73]

Discussions within the British government with regard to the creation and membership of a Western European bloc came to a head in mid-1944. In response to an initiative by the Belgian Foreign Minister in exile, Paul-Henri

Spaak, Gladwyn Jebb was asked to draw up further proposals for Britain's policy towards Europe. Eventually a so-called 'combined memorandum' entitled 'Western Europe' was submitted to the Foreign Secretary on 20 June 1944.[74]

The paper was in favour of working towards some form of regional European system which would include security matters to prevent renewed German aggression. Like Duff Cooper, Jebb emphasized that this grouping was not intended to divide Europe into a Russian bloc and a British one but was meant to be part of the world organization favoured by Roosevelt and had as its first aim the prevention of renewed German aggression. Whilst at first it might be necessary for Britain to shoulder a heavier defence burden than the other European countries, the British government ought to assist the rapid economic recovery of France and the smaller European nations to enable them to take part in this plan. The paper expressed the opinion that within a 'United Nations Commission for Europe', a body Eden had long advocated, Britain should be prepared to work towards a system of mutual defence agreements between London and Paris that would eventually lead to the participation of other Western European countries.[75]

Jebb was careful to point out that his scheme would not involve any continental commitment for Britain but would merely lead to the standardization of equipment, the maintenance of a considerable amount of armament in Britain and France, and the planning of common defence schemes. He was optimistic enough to believe (somewhat naively) that the Soviet Union could be convinced that the new grouping was directed against Germany, not the USSR. Jebb stressed that his scheme had the advantage of providing a line of defence against both Germany and, should it prove necessary, against the Soviet Union. To offer Stalin something in return, Duff Cooper favoured giving Moscow a free hand to develop a similar defence plan for Eastern Europe.[76]

Jebb's paper was given considerable attention within the Foreign Office. In particular, the officials were concerned with the important question whether linking Britain to a western European bloc would strengthen the UK by providing a 'defence in depth' or weaken the country by tying it to the defence of the European continent at the expense of its overseas commitments. Britain might well find itself dependent on the land armies of the weak continental nations. It was concluded that it did not yet seem possible to give any final answers to these considerations.[77]

In view of the rebuff Churchill's grand European designs had suffered in 1943 and 1944, and due to the dramatic developments in the war which dominated everything in 1944, the Prime Minister had neither the time for nor much interest in dealing with the Foreign Office's latest post-war plans. Eden, however, became more interested.[78] He asked the Chiefs of Staff to comment on the 'combined memorandum'. Due to Operation OVERLORD and the Normandy invasion, they were only able to do so at the end of July 1944. Even then the COS were too pressed for time to be able to analyse the document properly. However, they spelled out that in the long run it was not so much renewed German aggression but the UK's relationship with the Soviet Union that would be crucial. Unless a world organization could successfully balance the concerns of the great powers, the COS expected a clash of interests between Britain and the Soviet Union on the European continent in which the potential of Germany would play an important role. It was therefore unlikely, they concluded presciently, that a western European bloc would be effective without the inclusion of 'the whole or at least part of Germany' at a later stage.[79]

When this discussion took place Churchill had already abandoned his earlier European vision. His move away from a regionalist solution to focus once again on 'Big Three' summit diplomacy had brought the difficult relationship with the Soviet Union even more to the forefront of British policy.[80] In any case, since the Tehran conference Churchill had had increasing premonitions about the dire consequences of future Soviet influence on Europe; he had also finally appreciated Roosevelt's strong opposition to his plans. The Prime Minister therefore became openly hostile towards any discussions regarding the formation of a British-led western European security bloc. Instead, he hoped that Washington would remain sufficiently committed to European affairs to make the establishment of a European bloc superfluous. He feared increasingly that the formation of a western European bloc would not only antagonize Stalin but also convince the USA that its aid was no longer needed as a result and the new world organization would be undermined. It now appeared to Churchill that only the creation of Roosevelt's cherished world organization would prevent the United States from withdrawing into isolation and leaving Britain and Europe exposed to the Soviet Union's overwhelming military power.[81]

Churchill himself had originally only been thinking in terms of a loose European unity based on intergovernmental links. The Prime Minister had certainly no liking for a close military federation with the feeble and weakened European countries which had recently been overrun by Hitler's armies. Such a scheme, as he would explain in the 1950s when he opposed the development of the European Defence Community, would be militarily inefficient, a 'sludgy amalgam' which would give the soldiers enlisted in a European army no incentives to fight for a deeply felt national cause.[82]

In particular, Churchill was apprehensive that a western European bloc might weaken Britain by making it responsible for the defence of the war-ravished European nations at the expense of Britain's responsibilities for and commitments to the Empire and Commonwealth. Churchill and Eden decided in mid-July 1944 that Britain was at this stage not prepared to enter into any detailed considerations of a western European pact.[83] On 25 July 1944, Churchill told the War Cabinet that he had decided to reject the idea of a military alliance of the western democracies as a precautionary measure against the domination of the continent by Moscow, as had been advocated by Duff Cooper and others. Any leakage of these discussions regarding the division of the world into blocs would antagonize Stalin, and this in turn would endanger the chance of 'Big Three' collaboration and European recovery in the post-war world.[84]

However, in early October 1944, Spaak took the initiative once again and on 20 October another meeting was held in the Foreign Office to discuss the western bloc idea. The Foreign Office decided against attempting to reach a formal agreement at this stage. The officials believed however that France and the Benelux countries and, as soon as possible, Denmark and Norway ought to begin discussing military and technical arrangements for a western European association aimed at security against Germany. The COS accepted this in principle on 8 November. Churchill objected. He instructed Eden not to initiate discussions among the western European countries which might lead to Britain being drawn into the negotiations. The Prime Minister was still convinced that France and the Benelux countries were so weak that an agreement to defend them would not be in Britain's interest; it might also antagonize both Washington and Moscow.[85] When Spaak visited London in early November, discussions were confined to a general exchange of views. Churchill and Eden were also vague about the formation of a western European bloc when they visited France in November 1944: they told Georges Bidault, President of the Conseil National de la Résistance, that the British government had not yet got round to considering the Spaak memorandum.[86]

It was therefore not surprising that a memorandum produced by the British interdepartmental Post-Hostilities Planning Staff (PHPS) in November 1944 was also given short shrift.[87] The paper had suggested that due to Britain's changing strategic situation it was vital to obtain 'powerful allies' by forming a western European security group consisting of France, the Benelux and the Scandinavian countries and one day maybe even Germany. The paper recommended that this group should cooperate closely with both the Commonwealth and the United States in order to eventually create something like a North Atlantic organization, which appeared to be necessary to avoid Soviet domination of Western Europe.[88]

Once again Churchill and to some extent Eden were very sceptical as to whether the European nations would have the necessary resources to participate in a North Atlantic alliance in the aftermath of the war. The scheme, Churchill believed, would exclude Britain from the 'Big Three' club in the long run and put it on a par with the defeated European nations.[89] Both the Prime Minister and his Foreign Secretary were also still greatly worried about antagonizing the Soviet Union and jeopardizing post-war cooperation among the three great powers. The best policy seemed to be to build up the European nations 'one by one', starting with France and continuing with the smaller countries. These nations and Britain could eventually attempt to draw up a common plan for their mutual defence. 'I do not know', Churchill wrote to Eden, 'how these ideas of what is called a "Western bloc" got around in Foreign Office and other influential circles'.[90]

The Prime Minister clearly disapproved of the discussions. Nonetheless, Eden and the Foreign Office, though not Churchill, gradually became more interested in the idea of some kind of defensive agreement with Western Europe. They also recognized that in the long run it would necessitate a British military commitment to the continent.[91] This kind of thinking, which was later incorporated in Labour Foreign Secretary Ernest Bevin's short lived 'third force' idea, would eventually lead to the Franco-British Dunkirk Treaty of 1946 and the Brussels Treaty Organization (BTO) of 1948, the forerunner of NATO.[92]

Transition to the Post-war World

However, by the summer of 1945, no long-term strategic decisions had been taken regarding Britain's western European policy. To no small degree this was due to Churchill's outright opposition to a western European bloc that included Britain but not the United States. Churchill had therefore not taken any initiative to make progress with his earlier idea of an intergovernmental European Council 'of lesser powers'. Such a scheme was still opposed by the USA, which continued to insist that the creation of any new sphere of influence solution for the post-war world was unacceptable.[93] Consequently, the Allied negotiations regarding the establishment of the United Nations in 1945 were dominated by the consideration of the more global powers of the General Assembly and the Security Council with its five permanent members. Although initially it had been intended to emphasize some regional aspects of the new world organization, as for example Eden had strongly favoured, this did not happen.[94]

Thus, by the end of the war Churchill had clearly lost interest in his imaginative though always rather vague plan for a 'United States of Europe' involving European councils and federations. Instead, his major concern became the continuation of the 'fraternal association' with the United States; which, as he had announced somewhat over-enthusiastically in mid-1943, might even result in common citizenship. By 1945 he was convinced that only on the basis of the 'special relationship' with the United States could Britain continue to be regarded as one of the 'Big Three'. It was also Churchill's intention to use the coherence, strength and resolution of the western world led by the Anglo-American 'special relationship' to impress upon Stalin the dangers of his expansionist policies. Thus, towards the end of the war, Churchill was not so much occupied with working out grand concepts for the future of Europe as with practical policies to prevent another situation which might precipitate a major military conflict. The best way to react to Stalin's expansionist policies in Eastern Europe and elsewhere was foremost in his mind. However, his attempt to contain Stalin's ambitions by entering into an agreement with Moscow on a spheres of influence policy in the Balkans by means of the famous 'percentage deal' of October 1944 did not have the desired effect. In the countries conquered by the Red Army, a new post-war reality dictated by Stalin was already emerging.[95]

Although in early 1945 Churchill once again advocated the creation of a Balkan confederation, he failed again to make any headway with his idea. His only successful attempt to restrict Stalin's expansionist policies was the elevation of France to one of the occupying powers in Germany.[96] Like a number of other politicians in France, Germany and the United States, Churchill had begun to realize that the future peace of Europe did not depend so much on the establishment of European councils and federations as on a rapprochement between France and Germany and a more integrated European continent which, he felt, did not require British participation.[97] Twenty years earlier, reflecting on the origins of the First World War, he had speculated whether prior to 1914 the British 'by some effort, some compulsive gesture, at once of friendship and command [could] have reconciled France and Germany in time and forced that grand association on which alone the peace and glory of Europe would be safe?'[98] At the end of the Second World War he was thinking along the same lines. Churchill had come to believe that 'The whole purpose of a united democratic Europe is to give decisive guarantees against aggression'.[99] He therefore hoped that Britain would be able to develop a 'new association with Europe without in the slightest degree weakening the sacred ties which unite Britain with her daughter States across the oceans'.[100] This had of course been Churchill's objective during the early years of the war. In the post-war era, as then, Britain would ultimately find it impossible to reconcile the demands of this policy with the perception of itself as a sovereign state and a great power.

Franklin Roosevelt, Churchill's friend, rival and nemesis, died shortly after the Yalta conference in early 1945. His successor, Vice-President Harry Truman assumed office on 12 April. The new President was inclined to endorse the State Department's revised assessment of the need for a more hard-line position towards Stalin on the future of Central and Eastern Europe. However, despite increasing dissatisfaction with Moscow's policy, the new President's strategy towards the USSR during his first six to eight months in office was somewhat inconsistent, particularly because the new Secretary of State, James Byrnes, had not yet given up hope that amicable relations with Stalin might be possible.[101]

With regard to the United Kingdom, Truman showed greater consistency. On the recommendation of his advisers, the new President began to insist on a less personal and more businesslike style in his dealings with the British Prime Minister. Churchill later regretted that due to his preoccupation with the war he did not immediately fly to Washington to attend Roosevelt's funeral and establish cordial relations with Truman. After all, there was still great suspicion in many influential circles in Washington that Churchill intended to use the difficulties with the Soviet Union as an opportunity to prop up the old British Empire with American support. As early as April 1945 it was feared in Washington that Britain's catastrophic economic situation 'threatened to leave them clinging upon us for existence'. The influential American financier Bernard Baruch, although a close friend of Churchill's, recommended that the United States should 'resolutely resist British pleas for special consideration'.[102]

This line of thinking undermined one of Churchill's few remaining assets in his dealings with the now overpoweringly dominant United States. Churchill was not informed about Harry Hopkins' journey to meet Stalin in May 1945, which resulted in a joint paper on Poland. Churchill was not pleased; he feared that the new President trusted Stalin too much and ignored Russian expansionist designs in Europe. On 12 May the Prime Minister sent a telegram to Truman warning him that an 'iron curtain' had been 'drawn down upon' the Russian front. 'We do not know what is going on behind. There seems to be little doubt that the whole of the regions east of the line Lübeck–Trieste–Corfu will soon be completely in their hands.' He also feared that the 'enormous area' between Eisenach and the Elbe would be occupied by Stalin 'when the Americans retreat'. The Russians would soon be advancing towards the 'waters of the North Sea and the Atlantic'.[103] A settlement with Stalin had to be achieved while British and American war mobilizations were still formidable and had not yet 'melted' away, as he expected would happen within a year or two. Churchill explained:

Surely it is vital now to come to an understanding with Russia, or see where we are with her, before we weaken our armies mortally or retire to the zones of occupation. This can only be done by a personal meeting. ... Of course we can take the view that Russia will behave impeccably, and no doubt that offers the most convenient solution. To sum up, this issue of a settlement with Russia before our strength has gone seems to dwarf all others.[104]

Thus, as early as May 1945 Churchill raised the issue of a negotiated settlement with the Soviet Union to preserve world peace. It was the theme which was to dominate the last ten years of his political life: the attempt to overcome the East–West conflict would overshadow all other issues during Churchill's last term as Prime Minister between 1951 and 1955.

In view of Churchill's pleading, Truman agreed to a conference with the Russians. Yet, even before the Potsdam conference was convened, Churchill felt that he needed to employ all his powers of persuasion to prevent a bilateral meeting between Truman and Stalin which the new President, continuing Roosevelt's strategy, was apparently planning. Truman had declined a bilateral meeting with the British Prime Minister; like Roosevelt, he did not want to 'gang up' on the Soviets.[105] At this stage the new President tended to believe that 'difficulties with Churchill are very nearly as exasperating as they are with the Russians'.[106] Thus Churchill faced great problems in his attempts to ensure that Britain would be regarded by Washington as an equal member of the 'Big Three' at the Potsdam conference. He had to accept that this major conference would not commence in mid-June as had been planned but in the middle of July, as Truman preferred. This meant that the meeting would take place in the midst of the election campaign in Britain.[107]

By mid-1945 a clear downturn in Anglo-American relations had occurred. This resulted in the sudden and very painful abandonment of American lend-lease deliveries to Britain (and Russia) after the termination of the war in Europe. Towards the end of the year the British had great difficulties in obtaining a generous American loan to replace the lend-lease programme. American mistrust of Great Britain also led to the abrupt and, as far as London was concerned, entirely unexpected and unjustified end of atomic collaboration between the two countries by means of the McMahon Act introduced to Congress in December 1945.[108]

However, by this time Churchill had to observe developments from the opposition benches in the House of Commons. His election defeat in July 1945 and his enforced departure from the political limelight caused a bout of prolonged depression and political apathy which for a period of time even endangered his survival as leader of the Conservative Party. It was only in early

1946 that Churchill once again began to involve himself more actively in international politics, though as Leader of the Opposition rather than Prime Minister he was hardly able to participate in a more direct way.

Throughout the second half of the 1940s Churchill was therefore restricted to making speeches in the House of Commons and before international fora. He no longer occupied a political position which would have allowed him to take the political initiative himself. He could merely advise his successor, the Labour leader Clement Attlee, and public opinion about the importance of a negotiated East–West settlement by means of 'Big Three' summit diplomacy to preserve global peace and Britain's world power status. During his years in opposition Churchill would also once again resort to his European vision and advocate a more integrated European continent.[109]

CHAPTER 5

Early Cold War Years
Churchill's Survival as Leader of the Conservative Party and Attlee's Interest in Negotiating with Stalin

In the middle of the Potsdam conference the British Conservative Party lost power. Churchill and Eden were replaced by Clement Attlee and Ernest Bevin. While the latter soon assumed a strongly anti-Communist position, Prime Minister Attlee was much more open-minded. Like Churchill, Attlee was confident that it would be possible to overcome the unfolding East–West conflict by means of negotiations with Moscow; the new Prime Minister did not believe that conflict with the Soviet Union was inevitable. However, unlike Churchill, Attlee was prepared to embark on a major overhaul of Britain's foreign policy and a decisive reduction in the country's global obligations, and was thinking of withdrawing entirely from the Middle East and the eastern Mediterranean. While a heated debate took place within the Labour government over the future of Britain's world role, Churchill had to be content with a seat on the opposition benches. It would be the better part of a year before he returned to the international limelight with his 'iron curtain' speech of early 1946. In view of rising discontent with his absentee leadership of the Conservative Party, Churchill had no choice but to focus his depleted energies on remaining Leader of the Opposition and avoiding being pushed into retirement from active politics by his 'well meaning' colleagues on the Conservative front bench.

Churchill's Survival as Leader of the Conservative Party

Churchill took the massive electoral defeat in July 1945, when the younger generation deserted the Tories,[1] very personally.[2] Deeply disappointed, he concentrated on dictating his memoirs and took long vacations; occasionally, he also gave spectacular speeches before international fora.[3] As Leader of the Opposition in the House of Commons, the 70-year-old Churchill was rather passive; he generally appeared to be 'semi-detached'.[4] Only sporadically did he take part in parliamentary meetings and debates. He entirely neglected to define a political strategy to counter the activities of the Labour government. Churchill was exhausted and did not find it very stimulating to draw up an alternative programme of domestic policies.[5] John Ramsden aptly characterizes Churchill's recipe for leading the opposition as a 'combination of masterly inactivity and generalised criticism'.[6] However, Ramsden thinks Churchill's 'lack of leadership as such has perhaps been exaggerated' and that some aspects of his 'semi-retirement' benefited the Conservative Party. Above all, 'he was allowed a much-needed rest' and was able to preserve 'his reputation as a leader above and beyond British politics'.[7]

Indeed, his inactivity in domestic politics largely prevented Churchill from committing embarrassing political gaffes in an increasingly complex and bewildering environment which required detailed economic and socio-political knowledge. During the war, and indeed also after 1945, Churchill regarded such issues as tiresome and of minor importance. Similar disinterest and exhaustion were also evident in the conduct of Anthony Eden, Churchill's deputy and heir apparent as party leader since 1942, who even pondered on whether or not to withdraw from domestic politics altogether.[8]

As early as November 1945 Churchill and Eden faced critical questions from the 1922 Committee of Conservative backbenchers; they promised to attend the debates in the House of Commons more regularly and to perform their duties as leaders of the opposition more vigorously.[9] This, however, did not stop Churchill spending the next few months in the United States when he had just returned from a five-week holiday in Italy. He also dedicated a considerable part of his time to painting and to enjoying life in the south of France.[10]

For all practical purposes, by early 1946 Eden and 'Rab' Butler, the wartime Minister of Education, were in charge of H.M.'s Opposition. Although Eden popularized the phrase 'property-owning democracy' to explain what the new Conservatism was all about, he never developed a liking or much talent for domestic politics. It fell to Butler in particular but also to rising Conservative politicians such as Harold Macmillan, David Maxwell-Fyfe and David Eccles to work out plans for a coherent economic programme and the modernization of the Conservative Party. They established the Industrial Policy Committee, revived the defunct Central Research Department (both chaired by Butler), and eventually attempted to draw up several new and relatively progressive political programmes, the major ones being the *Industrial Charter* of May 1947 and *The Right Road for Britain* in 1949. In particular the *Industrial Charter* was an important and ground-breaking document. It endorsed the 'mixed economy' and the government's leading role in a corporatist economy; the charter also recognized the value of a 'welfare state' and the necessity for a future Conservative government to cater for both industrialists and trade unions to keep unemployment down.[11] To some extent, future American Secretary of State Dean Acheson was right when he quipped that after the end of the war 'even the Conservatives would be socialists'.[12] In addition, the party's organization was gradually re-activated, streamlined and made more efficient at local, regional and central level. Central Office was fundamentally reorganized and the Junior Imperial League was replaced with the more modern Young Conservatives. Responsible for this was above all Lord Woolton, the new Party Chairman who had been Minister for Reconstruction during the war. Woolton also succeeded in increasing considerably the party's membership and fund-raising activities.[13]

Initially, the devastating electoral defeat in 1945 and the generally perceived lack of political direction which continued to linger,[14] led to suggestions in Conservative circles that the party's name should be changed. It was argued that this would be helpful in bringing together an anti-socialist bloc by enabling the National Liberals and perhaps even the Liberal Party to consider merging fully with the Conservatives to form a centrist, truly national party. Macmillan talked about a 'New Democratic Party' and Churchill himself and also Lord Woolton were in favour of calling it 'the Union Party'.

Churchill and the Conservative Party continued to view each other with a good deal of scepticism. It was apparent that the former Prime Minister regarded his role as leader of the Tory Party merely as a tiresome necessity in the sense that 'the horse is essential to the rider'.[15] Moreover, it was not forgotten that in 1904, in times of great difficulties, Churchill had joined the Liberal Party only to return to the Tories twenty years later. As early as 1905/6 the historian H.W. Lucy had commented that Churchill 'will always be handicapped by the aversion that always pertains to a man who, in whatsoever honourable circumstances, has turned his coat'.[16] Above all, Churchill regarded himself not so much as leader of the Conservatives but as 'elder statesman' and wise leader of the entire nation; he viewed himself as a national rather than a Conservative politician and hankered after the re-creation of a national government.[17] There appears to be a good deal of truth in the statement that 'Churchill was a profoundly egocentric statesman for whom parties were vehicles of ambition rather than causes to be served'.[18]

While many historians continue to argue that the Conservative Party embarked upon 'a sustained effort after 1946 to regain the initiative and political power', this appears to apply only to the organizational restructuring of the party.[19] Recent research has challenged the view that the great impact of the 1945 defeat contributed decisively to shaking 'the Conservative party out of its lethargy and impelled it to rethink its philosophy ... with a thoroughness unmatched for a century'.[20] First Paul Addison and then an increasing number of other historians have shown that the development of the so-called Attlee or post-war consensus ('Butskellism') had already begun in the pre-war era, was much accelerated during the Second World War, and continued to flourish after 1945.[21] Furthermore, some scholars question the notion of a post-war consensus.[22] Serious disagreements between Britain's major parties still occurred, though it is clear that these disagreements 'took place within a broad set of shared assumptions about the goals – and the mechanics – of government action'.[23] These included the gradual Conservative acceptance of the necessity of social reforms and the establishment of a welfare state as well as the need to aspire to full employment and a more economically active government. At the same time the Conservative Party cautiously began opening its ranks to a much more broadly based social spectrum. Thus, as far as political substance was concerned, during the opposition years not so much radical departures from the evolution of domestic policies during the Second World War but 'major elements of continuity alongside cumulative and gradual change' could be observed within the Conservative Party.[24]

Churchill eventually supported these developments and the new policy programmes like the *Industrial Charter*, though he did not like them much. He also endorsed Woolton's organizational reforms. However, the Leader of the Opposition himself played hardly any role in the attempts to revive the long-term fortunes of the Conservatives, either in terms of organization or policy. On the whole, Churchill believed that 'his own popularity and the mistakes of the Socialist Government are sufficient to win the [next] Election, and that it is unwise to produce a policy in such difficult times'.[25]

To a certain extent, with respect to the British people's great 'disaffection with austerity, rationing and controls' in the late 1940s, Churchill may have been correct.[26] But it is unlikely that his passive approach towards revitalizing the party would have been sufficient to regain power. The recovery of the Conservatives as a party with a viable and more modern image, which required the re-emergence of the party's perceived competence in domestic and economic politics, largely occurred 'despite Winston Churchill rather than because of him'.[27] American politician and businessman Averell Harriman came to the conclusion that 'the marked increased strength of the Conservatives came in the first place from the far better organization of the party under the direction of Woolton'; it had very little to do with Churchill.[28]

Moreover, the enthusiasm for Europe Churchill was to display during the first four years in opposition displeased many of his parliamentary colleagues, including Eden. Churchill appeared not only to be absent most of the time but also keen on exploiting his position as elder statesman by once again focusing on bringing about a united Europe while leaving Britain's role unspecified and ambiguous. This implied the danger of Britain becoming a member of a federal Europe and neglecting her precious links with the Empire and Commonwealth. Anti-Americanism also played a role in the Conservative Party's scepticism with regard to the establishment of a European federation, which the Truman administration favoured. There was considerable suspicion of American economic imperialism, as expressed in the 1945 loan, the Bretton Woods system and even the Marshall Plan, among many party activists and indeed in the country at large. Not least, the 'imperialists' in the Conservative Party resented being pushed into a more European policy by Washington; it implied that the USA merely viewed Britain as a European country and not as a global world power in its own right.[29]

In view of the growing discontent with Churchill's dire domestic performance and his overly enthusiastic European policy, it was little wonder that senior members of the Conservative Party and many backbenchers began to question whether it would be better if Churchill were to resign as party leader and hand over his responsibilities to Eden.[30] According to David Carlton, early in 1946 Eden appears to have participated in such intrigues behind Churchill's back, but Eden was not involved in similar and equally unsuccessful mini-revolts in 1947 and again in 1949.[31]

While there remained an 'anti-Churchill rump' in the Conservative Party, 'Churchill and his supporters had ruthlessly weeded out party opponents' during the war and many former supporters of Chamberlain had failed to re-enter Parliament in 1945.[32] Furthermore, Churchill would not allow himself to be pressured into resigning. After the 1945 defeat he was obsessed with the idea of once more regaining power – this time through the votes of the British electorate. Although Churchill was partially blamed for the electoral defeat by many Conservative Members of Parliament, his following within the rank-and-file of the party, and more importantly among the British people, was still significant; he was almost 'worshipped'.[33]

Eden and other leading Tory politicians were thus in no position to drive the party leader from office without his consent; they even hushed up his first mild stroke in late August 1949. Unbeknown to him and his entourage, Churchill had begun to suffer from atherosclerotic vascular disease, a progressive narrowing and hardening of the arteries supplying the brain with blood.[34] However, in 1949 Churchill recovered very quickly. In mid-November Averell

Harriman, now Truman's Secretary of Commerce, was surprised to find him 'in such good health and vigor' and, when in conversation Churchill recalled previous meetings as far back as 1927 and 1929, marvelled at his 'extraordinary memory'.[35]

Furthermore, Churchill himself was not deterred from remaining as leader by claims that he had become a liability for the electoral fortunes of the Conservatives.[36] From early 1946, when he had conquered his initial depression and ceased talking about resigning from politics, Churchill was not to be moved to consider retirement. Although he would occasionally mention the issue to Eden and others in the party, this was for largely tactical reasons: he wished to 'string Eden along' and avoid facing the retirement issue directly.[37] On the whole, both as Leader of the Opposition and as Prime Minister during 1951–55, when the resignation question arose with considerably more urgency and justification, his view remained the same as in April 1946: 'All my most intimate friends recommend retirement and I will fight the lot till the bitter end and challenge them to sack me.'[38]

From the beginning of 1948, Churchill gradually revived his interest in detailed policy-making. For Labour, the year 1947 had been a time of 'almost unrelieved [economic] disaster' and it appeared quite possible that the government's difficulties and in-fighting within the Cabinet might lead to an early election.[39] In the course of 1949, with the next general election looming on the horizon, Churchill even spoke occasionally on such issues as the health service and British industry.[40] However, in general he continued to neglect the domestic scene. His weak performance as party leader and his lack of inspiration regarding the Conservatives' domestic programme were blamed for the loss of the important South Hammersmith by-election in February 1949. In view of the great popular dissatisfaction with Labour's austerity programme and 'a world of queuing and rationing',[41] a victory here and the gain of a marginal seat would have sent out the right signals to the electorate. Traditionally the constituency had had a Conservative majority and was only lost in 1945.[42]

After the by-election defeat Churchill attempted to placate the critics of his leadership in the party, but on the whole he remained detached from practical 'bread and butter' politics. When he did become involved, he concentrated almost exclusively on his beloved foreign policy. Alongside his vague but very popular comments on a united Europe, which were however taken much too seriously abroad,[43] he showed above all strong interest in the East–West conflict.

In the middle of 1945, at a time when the British people were war-weary and longing for continued cooperation with 'Uncle Joe' and when many were convinced that 'Left could talk to Left' to obtain much better political results,[44]

Churchill's perceived enthusiasm for war had been deeply unpopular. His exaggeration of the 'red peril' and his accusation in a broadcast during the election campaign in June 1945 that if Labour came to power it would establish a Gestapo organization in Britain appeared to confirm his aggressive and reactionary image. The Labour Party's depiction of Churchill as a belligerent bulldog, a fierce anti-Communist and a statesman only good for war may well have contributed to the electoral defeat of the Tories.[45]

Soon, however, in view of the increasingly dangerous development of the Cold War, Churchill's anti-Communist convictions came to be more widely shared. It seemed that his early warnings about Stalin's intentions had been proved right once again, as he would maintain at length in the last volume of his memoirs.[46] Influential speeches depicting the shifting mood of the times, such as the powerful 'iron curtain' address of March 1946, convinced people to listen to Churchill with renewed attention. Yet, as John Ramsden has persuasively argued, when Churchill delivered his 'iron curtain' speech in Fulton, Missouri, and called for close Anglo-American relations, negotiations with Stalin, and for forceful resistance to the encroachments of Soviet Communism, 'he took a very great gamble'.[47] His speech was condemned both in Britain and in the United States as the pronouncements of a warmonger. Only in mid to late 1946, months after the delivery of the speech, would public opinion in both countries shift towards a more hostile anti-Stalin mood.[48]

Naturally Churchill was quick to claim the credit for making the western world aware of the looming threat from the East; he appeared to have been more visionary and clear-sighted than his contemporaries. Moreover, his prophecy regarding the unfolding Cold War tied in nicely with his reputation of having repeatedly warned about the rise of Hitler and the lack of military preparation in the 1930s; both reinforced each other in the public mind and turned Churchill into an even more pre-eminent statesman.[49] His whole post-war career greatly benefited from this general perception. It also helped tremendously to ensure his political survival in domestic British politics. Churchill became almost unassailable, despite his increasingly fragile health and his continued failure to lead the Conservatives on domestic issues.

The unfolding Cold War and Churchill's role in characterizing it helped the party strategists, Oliver Poole, the deputy chairman of the Conservative Party, and Harold Macmillan, who had lost his seat in 1945, to identify an election strategy to get the party back into power: 'to define clearly the sort of state which is the Western answer to Communism. This is something quite new, but based on experience and the character of the people.'[50] Macmillan even believed it necessary to embark upon a 'battle against Anti-Christ'. Dramatically he explained to Butler in mid-January 1949, that 'Britain is in danger; the Empire is in danger; Europe is in danger; the whole world is in danger from the Communist menace.' Macmillan claimed that this situation would give the Conservative Party the opportunity to respond with 'a new crusade, spiritual as well as material'.[51]

The historian Bill Schwarz believes that 'it was the shifting order of foreign relations which generated the dynamic underpinning of the Conservative recovery, providing Tory strategists with the cutting-edge as putative defenders of the West and the Empire.'[52] However, this overlooks the fact that there was not merely a post-war consensus regarding Britain's economic and social policy (however fragile it may have been), but also a precarious foreign policy consensus (particularly on East–West issues) between the front bench of the two major parties. The senior members of the Labour government and the Conservative opposition shared a strongly anti-Communist world view.[53]

Moreover, all of the country's major parties partook in the firm conviction that Britain's great power role was natural and right. This shared view was largely responsible for fusing together Labour's radical domestic programme and 'the strong, belligerent foreign policy which Foreign Secretary Bevin was allowed to conduct' and which the Conservatives approved of.[54] As far as external policy was concerned, the belief Attlee had expressed in a 1937 publication, that there was 'a deep difference of opinion between the Labour Party and the capitalist parties on foreign as well as home policy', had long been discarded.[55]

Nevertheless, under the surface there were some fundamental differences between the government and the opposition. There were also numerous dissenting views within the ranks of the parliamentary Labour Party. Churchill's preferred method of summit diplomacy differed fundamentally from the Labour government's official 'hard-line' policy towards Moscow, but, in 1945–46 the paradoxical situation arose that Prime Minister Attlee disliked the official policy of his own government: he preferred to deal with the Soviet Union by means of personal diplomacy. Thus Attlee's approach was temporarily similar to Churchill's and stood in stark contrast to the ideas of Bevin and the Foreign Office about how to manage the Soviet threat. It is interesting to note that the strategies the Foreign Office adopted to undermine Attlee's policy of negotiation with Moscow in 1946 and early 1947 were not dissimilar to the situation in 1953–54, when Churchill's summit diplomacy was strongly opposed by Foreign Secretary Eden and Britain's foreign policy elite.

Although in 1946–47 Attlee took the same line as Churchill on the need to negotiate with Moscow, there were also major differences of opinion between them. While Churchill would always be firmly in favour of upholding the global power and influence of Britain and its Empire, Attlee did not share Churchill's imperialist attitude. In the mid-1940s, given Britain's diminished economic and financial resources, Attlee regarded this as an unrealistic political course, though not many among Britain's politicians and officials shared his sober view.

In principle, Britain's foreign affairs elite shared a strong belief in the importance of upholding the country's great power position and independent role in world affairs. Foreign Secretary Bevin was as adamant as Churchill and Eden had been since the spring of 1944 in his attempts to limit Soviet influence in the Mediterranean and the Middle East.[56] Bevin often consulted Eden and Churchill on relations with the Soviet Union, and in August 1945 warned the House of Commons that in Bulgaria, Romania and Hungary 'one kind of totalitarianism' was 'being replaced by another'.[57] A month later, in the course of the first Council of Foreign Ministers meeting in London, Bevin told the assembled plenum that Soviet Foreign Minister Molotov's attitude towards the countries of Eastern Europe was 'reminiscent of Hitler'.[58] Yet in view of the pro-Soviet feeling on the left of the Labour Party, Washington's still uncertain commitment to Europe and the new American Secretary of State James Byrnes's ambiguous policy towards Stalin, Bevin was careful to avoid 'a complete break with Russia'.[59]

It was only in December 1945 and January 1946, after the failure of the Council of Foreign Ministers' conference in New York, that the Truman administration began to take a stronger line towards the Soviet Union. The increasingly disconcerting Soviet behaviour in the oil-rich 'northern tier' countries of the Near East (above all in Iran but also in Turkey and Greece), combined with what appeared to be Stalin's expansionist policy in the Baltic states, Poland and other Soviet-dominated Eastern European countries, decisively influenced this change of policy.[60] Stalin's hostile anti-western speech in early February 1946 and George F. Kennan's 'long telegram' from the Moscow embassy to the State Department on 22 February warning of the Soviet Union's potentially aggressive intentions were also milestones in this development.[61] But it was Churchill's 'iron curtain' speech in Fulton, Missouri, in early March 1946 that significantly influenced American public opinion and the White House to accept that there were irreconcilable differences of view with Moscow.

In early 1946 American public opinion still seemed very unsure about the need to break with 'Uncle Joe'. In fact, Churchill's speech was used by Washington as a 'trial balloon' to evaluate whether the American public and the Congress were ready to stand up to Stalin so soon after the Grand Alliance's joint victory over Hitler. Bevin's tough line towards the Soviet Union was not yet the prevalent strategy in Washington, where the situation was still very much in flux.[62] Churchill's speech helped to alter the balance in favour of Truman's evolving 'strategy of containment'. According to Lord Halifax, Britain's ambassador in Washington, the speech gave 'the sharpest jolt to American thinking of any utterance since the end of the war'.[63] Thus, Truman's outburst in January 1946 – 'Unless Russia is faced with an iron fist and strong language another war is in the making ... I'm tired of babying the Soviets' – gradually became the official American view of how to deal with Stalin.[64] The American Joint Chiefs of Staff recommended the 'adoption of a firm and friendly attitude' towards the Soviet Union. Yet they intended to put 'the emphasis upon firmness' and generally believed that it was of great importance that the USA had 'the ability to back with force the policies and commitments undertaken'.[65]

After the abrupt cooling of Anglo-American relations towards the end of the war in Europe, the beginning of the East–West conflict led to renewed Anglo-American collaboration. In his 'iron curtain' speech, as well as in other speeches made during his visit to America in early 1946, Churchill passionately argued for the renewal of the Anglo-American 'fraternal association'. Compared with the Communist threat from behind the 'iron curtain', American suspicion of the dubious character of the Labour government ('too damned much Socialism at home and too much damned Imperialism abroad') suddenly became rather unimportant.[66] The British Foreign Secretary was no longer ignored and excluded by Washington, as had happened during the London Council of Foreign Ministers' conference in September/October 1945; instead, his anti-Communist views were attentively listened to. Indeed, the lack of Anglo-American consultation which could be observed during the various international conferences in the immediate post-war period was gradually reversed.

Still, Bevin proceeded cautiously. Although he had no illusions about Moscow's pursuit of an aggressive and expansionist policy which threatened Britain's continued great power position and the lifeline of the Empire and the sterling area,[67] in public Bevin adopted a much more circumspect approach. He had no desire to upset Labour's left wing. Moreover, the Prime Minister himself was doubtful about Bevin's hard-line policy towards Moscow. Attlee largely shared Churchill's belief in the value of personal negotiations with Moscow; he also had a less pessimistic view of Moscow's political objectives than his Foreign Secretary.

Attlee's Interest in Negotiating with Moscow

In the summer of 1945 and during 1946, Prime Minister Attlee wondered whether Stalin's policy was really as expansionist as it was perceived to be in the West. Perhaps Stalin merely intended to erect defensive buffers around his country as he felt threatened by the western world's policy and only wished to have uninhibited access to the oceans. Attlee thought that this was not 'unnatural'; one ought 'to look at the matter from the Russian angle'.[68]

The Prime Minister was convinced that Britain did not have the resources to support countries such as Greece, Turkey, Iran and Iraq and build them up into democratic and militarily efficient barriers against the USSR.[69] This would only be possible with the financial aid of the USA. But in late 1945 and early 1946 it still appeared that Washington favoured a policy of isolationism. The Prime Minister therefore believed that ultimately these problems could only be solved with the help of the new 'general world organisation for peace'.[70] During a meeting of the Cabinet in September 1945, Attlee argued that Britain should not base its policy 'on outworn conceptions'; the British Empire could 'only be defended by its membership of the United Nations Organisation'. Once the UN had become a reality, 'it does not matter who holds Cyrenaica or Somalia or controls the Suez Canal'.[71]

Above all, Attlee was convinced that with the invention of the atomic bomb and the new developments in air power, which 'transcends all frontiers and menaces all home lands', there were no longer strategic reasons for Britain to be in control of the eastern Mediterranean and the Middle East. Currently, the country seemed to have 'an obsolete conception of imperial defence derived from the naval era' and ought to withdraw from the Middle East and the eastern Mediterranean.[72] The Prime Minister's belief may have been influenced by the top-secret decision taken between late 1946 and January 1947 to develop a British atomic bomb.[73] This would enable the country to defend itself and its territories without the necessity of the physical control of the Mediterranean and the Middle East.

Attlee strongly believed that Britain could not afford to meet the requirements of the new era of air power. In a Cabinet memorandum he argued that 'The advent of air power means that instead, as in the era of navalism, of being able to maintain the [Middle Eastern and Mediterranean] route by the possession of Malta and Gibraltar and by a friendly attitude on the part of Egypt, we must now provide very large air forces in North Africa, large military forces in Egypt and Palestine and also large sums of money for the deficit areas, such as Cyrenaica and Libya, if we wish to occupy them as air forces.'[74] However, Attlee's unconventional proposals were neither shared by Bevin and the Foreign Office nor by Churchill and the Conservative opposition; all of them continued to view Britain's post-war options within an imperialist framework.

Unperturbed, Attlee adhered to his views throughout 1946. In January, both Attlee and Hugh Dalton, the Chancellor of the Exchequer, questioned the necessity for the large number of British troops based overseas; in view of Britain's growing financial difficulties, this appeared to be a luxury the country could not afford.[75] A month later, Attlee once again wondered about the importance of the Mediterranean for upholding Empire communication lines in the era of far-reaching air power. Since neither the Mediterranean sea routes nor the Middle Eastern oil fields could be defended against any serious Soviet aggression, Britain ought to withdraw from the entire region. He assumed that once India had become independent as planned, the importance of Egypt and the Suez Canal would rapidly decline: communications between Africa and the Far East and to Commonwealth countries like Australia and New Zealand could equally well be maintained by way of the Panama Canal, the Cape and the re-location of the strategic reserve from the Middle East to Kenya.[76] Attlee also believed that 'Western Europe cannot live by itself as an economic unit'; it needed the 'wider integration' with Africa and other British overseas terri-tories. The Prime Minister thus attempted to obtain the support of the many within the Labour Party who opposed closer ties with continental Europe. Churchill's repeated calls for a more united Europe, which often dominated the international political agenda in the immediate post-war years, were much resented by the Labour government and the Labour Party.[77]

Like Churchill, the Prime Minister had realized that not Britain and the Empire but the USA was now the focal point of the western world. But Attlee was one of the very few British politicians at the time who seemed prepared to accept what he saw as the unfortunate but inevitable results of the Second World War. Very much unlike Churchill, Attlee argued that 'We must not, for sentimental reasons based on the past, give hostages to fortune. It may be we shall have to consider the British Isles as an easterly extension of a strategic area, the centre of which is the American continent, rather than as a power looking eastwards through the Mediterranean to India and the East'.[78] Moreover, perhaps in view of the American refusal to share atomic secrets with Britain, he believed that Washington regarded Britain and its Empire as an expendable outpost of America and thus 'an outpost that they will not have to defend'. For Attlee this was another reason to withdraw.[79]

Attlee's thinking was summarized by Hugh Dalton after a conversation with the Prime Minister in late March 1946:

The P.M. ... is indeed pressing on the Chiefs of Staff and the Defence Committee a large view of his own, which aims at considerable disen-gagement from areas where there is a risk of us clashing with the Russians. This would mean giving up any attempt to keep open the passage through the Mediterranean in war-time, and to pull out from all the Middle East,

including Egypt, and, of course, from Greece. ... We should face the
prospect of going round the Cape in war-time and we should concentrate a
great part of the Commonwealth defence, including many industries, in
Australia. We should thus put a wide glacis of desert and Arabs between
ourselves and the Russians. This is a very bold and interesting idea and I am
inclined to favour it.[80]

Bevin, the Foreign Office and the British military deeply resented and firmly
rejected the Prime Minister's interference, which seemed to endanger Britain's
security, economic recovery and world role. Bevin and almost the entire British
foreign policy elite, including Churchill and the Conservative opposition,
remained convinced that 'the Middle East [was] an area of cardinal importance
to the U.K., second only to the U.K. itself'. They all believed that there were
strong strategic, military and economic reasons for holding on to the region.
'Strategically the Middle East is a focal point of communications, a source of
oil, a shield to Africa and the Indian Ocean, and an irreplaceable offensive base.
Economically it is, owing to oil and cotton, essential to United Kingdom
recovery.'[81] The Foreign Secretary and his advisers were aware, however, that
with respect to Arab nationalism Britain only had 'a short time to influence the
development of the M.E. and to push ideas towards evolution rather than
revolution.'[82] The anti-British nationalists who seemed to spread like wildfire
throughout the entire region needed to be appeased, Bevin reasoned. Thus,
Britain's approach to Empire had to undergo a dramatic transformation if the
country was to maintain its influence in the Middle East and elsewhere. British
imperialism should be given a more positive and beneficial direction; after all,
colonial 'economic development on the basis of independent states' was 'part of
the ethos of the Labour era'.[83]

Bevin developed a 'grand design' to stabilize and improve Britain's relations
with the countries of the Middle East. The proper development of the Empire
territories in a visionary socialist way would result in a mutually satisfactory
economic relationship based on respect and political equality, which would
ensure the future prosperity of the individual colonies and dependencies. It
would also greatly benefit the Empire at large and the economic and political
well-being of the UK. It was part of Bevin's plan 'to develop the Middle East as
a producing area to help our own economy and take the place of India, which
henceforth will absorb her own produce'.[84] Whilst Britain could not compete
with American economic and military might, Labour's election victory offered
the peoples of the world the unique chance of a social-democratic alternative
between America's ruthless capitalism and the Soviet Union's Communist
dictatorship.[85] The Labour Party shared the assumption that Britain was in

charge of the moral leadership of the world: 'Britain stands today at the summit of her power and glory, and we hold that position because today, following the election, we have something unique to offer.'[86]

Bevin's grand plans possessed a certain inner logic and coherence, but they were also characterized by a good deal of unwarranted optimism, if not naivety, which did not escape the attention of the Prime Minister. Above all, Bevin's strategy did not pay sufficient attention to the anti-British nationalist resentments which had been building up over the last six decades. British reoccupation of the Middle East was unlikely to be acceptable to nationalists in the region. Moreover, London had no choice but to continue cooperating with the governments in the area whether or not they were corrupt and disliked by their own people. Often only the old elites were prepared to negotiate with Britain while the younger nationalists refused any dealings with the colonial power.[87] And most importantly, Britain simply did not have the financial and manpower resources to aid substantially the countries of the region so that they would be able to reform their economies and social structures and make the continuation of Britain's strategic and military regional dominance acceptable to their peoples.[88]

This was perhaps the most fundamental flaw in Bevin's reasoning. On the one hand, Bevin believed that Britain would be able to contribute decisively to the progressive economic development of the Middle East; on the other, he was aware of Britain's economic weakness and even wished to assist the UK's financial recovery with the help of the Middle East and other Empire territories. Bevin and the Foreign Office do not seem to have grasped this fundamental contradiction in the 'grand design' for maintaining Britain's position in the Middle East and the Mediterranean. Bevin did realize that although his plans might improve matters in the medium to long run, in the short term Britain needed to maintain its traditional imperial prestige in the Middle East and the Mediterranean to defend its great power position until his 'grand design' had taken effect. Britain's position was threatened not only by Middle Eastern nationalism but in the short term perhaps even more by the Soviet Union. At least that is what Bevin concluded when analysing Soviet territorial demands during the meetings of the Council of Foreign Ministers and the Paris Peace conference in 1946.[89] Moscow appeared to be keen on establishing itself in North Africa and obtaining a foothold in the Mediterranean and in the Middle East. This would threaten the very lifeline of the British Empire and the economic prosperity and the safety of the UK.[90]

In view of what Bevin, the Foreign Office and the Chiefs of Staff perceived as Soviet expansionist ambitions, Attlee's admonition not to adopt a worst-case scenario when interpreting Moscow's policy was not regarded as a credible option. Without a strong military position it would be impossible 'to retain the necessary diplomatic strength' in the region and Stalin appeared to take seriously only countries 'which had the power to command respect'.[91] Bevin and the British Chiefs of Staff were agreed that 'control of the area Egypt-Palestine would provide the Russians with a ready-made base area which could be built up by short sea route from Russia itself and which would enable them to extend their influence both westward and southward into Africa'.[92] With the imminent loss of India, the increasingly untenable British position in Palestine and the difficult treaty negotiations with Egypt, Africa had become one of the last safe bastions of the British Empire. The continent was regarded as of prime importance not only for strategic reasons but also as an invaluable source for Britain's access to inexpensive natural resources and a potentially huge market for British goods.

Therefore, Bevin and the British Chiefs of Staff were strongly convinced that British control of the Middle East, the eastern Mediterranean and Africa had to be maintained under all circumstances. Indeed, Bevin even wished to expand and strengthen the Empire by attempting to obtain Cyrenaica and perhaps other former Italian colonies like Tripolitana or Somalia in trusteeship from the United Nations.[93] Attlee regarded these territories as 'deficit areas' Britain could not afford to support.[94] The Foreign Secretary, however, was thinking of developing Britain's East and West African possessions by creating a major base in Mombasa, establishing a strategic centre in the Sudan and a trans-African trunk road from Lagos to Cairo, with a branch leading south to Mombasa. These could serve as fallback positions for the maintenance of Empire communication lines to make up for the loss of India and possibly the withdrawal from Palestine and a reduction of the British presence in Egypt and other Middle Eastern countries.

These ideas were largely based on the strategic thinking of military theorist Basil Liddell Hart, one of Churchill's close friends, who hoped that his plans would help to avoid a confrontation between Britain and the Soviet Union. They would also bring Britain's declining economic resources into line with the imperial policy the country was still able to afford.[95] While Liddell Hart was prepared to give up the Middle East in favour of a strengthened imperial position in Africa, a strategy which Attlee gradually adopted despite his doubts about the plans' financial viability,[96] Bevin and the Foreign Office had a very different vision. They intended to expand the British Empire in Africa in order to prop up the British presence in the Middle East and the eastern Mediterranean. Withdrawal seemed to imply decline and defeat and would undoubtedly be interpreted by the Soviet Union (and Middle Eastern nationalism) in this vein. Moscow was bound to fill the vacuum created by Britain's departure. 'If we move out in peacetime, Russia will move in, pursuing her policy of extending her influence by all means short of major war to further strategic areas.' It would 'bring Russia to the Congo and the Victoria Falls'.[97]

William Roger Louis and John Kent, among others, have persuasively demonstrated that behind the reasoning of Bevin and the Foreign Office was not merely the maintenance of Britain's strategic and economic influence in the region but also the conviction that without her dominance in the Mediterranean and the Middle East, Britain's position as a global power would be decisively undermined and could not be defended. In this respect Bevin's thinking coincided with the views of Churchill and the Conservative opposition.[98] Most Foreign Office officials also accepted that there were 'far weightier reasons than the route to India argument for making sacrifices to hold the Mediterranean [and the Middle East]'. The Foreign Office was convinced that, for example, the Mediterranean was 'the area through which we bring influence to bear on the soft underbelly of France, Italy, Yugoslavia, Greece, Turkey and southern Europe. Without our physical presence these states would fall, like Eastern Europe, under the totalitarian yoke. The Mediterranean would become a second Black Sea and Russian influence would spread into Africa'.[99]

Thus, much to Churchill's delight, Bevin's 'grand design' and his rhetoric about equality and partnership were meant to uphold the British Empire and safeguard Britain's ability to intervene by more appropriate modern means. It seemed to be more than obvious that British withdrawal from Empire would lead to a drastic decline in Britain's influence in the world, in particular *vis-à-vis* the Soviet Union and the United States. A senior Foreign Office official, Orme Sargent, expressed his pessimistic belief:

> If we no longer have the political and military strength to maintain our position, the world will draw its own conclusion with inevitable consequences. We shall thereafter only be able to play a subordinate part in the affairs of Europe and a still smaller one in the affairs of other continents. We shall not be able to convince either our friends or our enemies that we are merely retreating owing to the changes of modern warfare from an indefensible position to a stronger and shorter line in the politico-strategic front.[100]

The running battle between Attlee and Bevin about Britain's future as a global power gained urgency towards the end of 1946. The country's foreign currency reserves were rapidly diminishing in view of Britain's responsibilities in Palestine, Germany, India, Burma, Egypt, Malaya and many other countries. The harsh winter of 1946–7, possibly the worst of the twentieth century, with the accompanying power cuts and a severe decline in industrial production in the UK, contributed to an increasingly difficult economic and financial situation. Thus, the Cabinet was greatly concerned about the high level of expenditure on defence.[101]

With hindsight, Attlee had a much more realistic perception of the financial and political limitations of Britain's role as a great power than Bevin and the military. (Churchill shared this realism, but, as will be seen, he drew entirely different conclusions from it.) In contrast to the Foreign Office and most senior British politicians, including Churchill, Attlee was much less concerned about the loss of prestige that would accompany a withdrawal from the Middle East. The factors that the British foreign policy establishment regarded as important strategic necessities to prevent the Soviet Union from replacing Britain as the dominant power in the Mediterranean and the Middle East were regarded by the Prime Minister as outdated.

Throughout 1946 Attlee continued to argue that Soviet air power would make it impossible to defend the Mediterranean and Middle Eastern sea routes or protect the Middle Eastern oilfields and Britain's territories in Africa from Soviet aggression. Even the argument that the Middle East was in effect a strategic and military barrier preventing or at least reducing the effectiveness of a Soviet attack on Britain itself cut little ice with the Prime Minister. Attlee wished to pursue a financially and politically much more affordable imperial strategy. However, he modified his policy somewhat in the course of 1946. He began to base his strategy on strengthening Britain's position in Africa, though as a replacement for the Middle East, not as an attempt to hold on to it as Bevin envisaged.[102] Attlee expressed the view that if Britain had Cyrenaica, 'there would be no need to stay in either Egypt or Palestine'.[103]

Like the Leader of the Conservative Opposition, the Prime Minister continued to believe that confrontation with the Soviet Union was not inevitable.[104] And also like Churchill, Attlee objected both to the Foreign Office's image of the Soviet Union as an inevitable enemy and to the preparation of contingency plans to bomb the Soviet Union from the British bases in the Middle East. Attlee did not believe that Britain should use the Middle East to prepare for war against the Soviet Union. He regarded this as 'a strategy of despair' which might well lead to the outbreak of a major conflict.[105] It could well be the case, 'fantastic as this is', that the West's current defensive policies might be viewed by Stalin as the 'preparations for an attack'.[106] Attlee expected that once the Soviet Union's economic situation had improved, Stalin was bound to embark on a more restrained foreign policy and would abandon the Communist dream of world revolution. Thus, Attlee wondered whether it might not be more realistic 'to reach an agreement with Russia' on turning the eastern Mediterranean and the Middle East into a 'neutral zone', thereby diminishing Stalin's fear of a western attack.[107]

At heart Attlee, Bevin and Churchill were disciples of the classic realist school of international relations but despite viewing East–West politics through a very similar interpretative framework, they arrived at very different political conclusions. While Bevin was convinced that Stalin followed an aggressive plan for world revolution dictated by an expansionist ideology and short-term political advantages and opportunism,[108] Attlee and Churchill believed that Stalin was a common-sense politician who had above all the national interest of his country at heart. They concluded that it must be possible to convince Stalin of the peaceful intentions of the UK and the USA by deeds and words and arrive at a satisfactory accommodation. Thus, both the Prime Minister and the Leader of the Opposition were in favour of entering into negotiations with Stalin to achieve a settlement of the many outstanding East–West problems and stabilize the post-war world in the process.

In 1946 and early 1947 Attlee expressed sentiments similar to those Churchill voiced between 1945 and 1951 and was to reiterate after Stalin's death in 1953.[109] On 12 April 1946 Attlee publicly proclaimed his belief that there were 'no suspicions that cannot in time be removed by goodwill, no clash of national interests in the world to-day that cannot be resolved, if there is willingness on all sides, to state honestly and clearly what the difficulties are, and to agree to settle them by negotiation'.[110] In a memorandum to Bevin on 5 January 1947 Attlee made it once again clear that he wished to enter into talks with Stalin; he still did not believe that Moscow had to be regarded as an inevitable and irreversible enemy.[111] Attlee reminded Bevin that Britain's past conflicts with France 'all over the world' had been resolved in a comparatively short period of time. Moreover, in earlier decades Britain was frequently at loggerheads with Russia over Afghanistan and other matters and it had been possible to overcome these problems. Though he realized that it had only been the rise of Hitler which had brought Russia and Britain closer together in the 1930s and again after 1941, Attlee argued that 'to-day there is a common fear of what another world war may bring to us all'. On the whole the Prime Minister was cautiously optimistic that it would not be 'too difficult to deal with points of friction' between London and Moscow.[112]

Yet, Attlee showed a certain lack of realism. In 1946/7 it was unrealistic to imagine that a *modus vivendi* could be worked out between London and Moscow which did not involve the United States. This was reminiscent of Churchill's brave but also somewhat illusory attempts at bilateral personal diplomacy during the Second World War and later. The early Cold War had to be viewed as at least a trilateral if not a multilateral affair which could hardly be solved on the basis of a bilateral Anglo-Soviet rapprochement.

Bevin and the Foreign Office disputed Attlee's contention that Britain's Middle Eastern policy could appear to be offensive to Moscow; after all, the UK was reducing its troops in Egypt and elsewhere. Borrowing some of the arguments employed by American politicians, it was held that 'to attempt an agreement [with Stalin] now would be bidding from weakness. The time to attempt to conclude an agreement is when we can bid from strength.' Currently the chances of negotiating a successful deal were 'practically nil'.[113] If an agreement with Stalin would result in the Middle East being regarded as a neutral zone where neither the Russians nor the British exerted a predominant influence, 'this is Alice in Wonderland, since Russia would infiltrate into the vacuum'.[114]

Other arguments were that an agreement with Stalin would have a disastrous effect on Britain's relations with the US, the Europeans, the Dominions and the countries bordering on the Middle East. Even if Britain's primary line of defence were to focus on Central Africa, it would be impossible in the age of the atomic bomb 'to dispense with a first line of defence'. Furthermore, it was clear that for the next 10–15 years, until the realization of Bevin's 'grand design' had been achieved, 'our central African main defence exists only on paper'.[115] It seemed to be obvious that the Soviets believed in 'natural conflict between the capitalist and communist world'. A British withdrawal and surrender without any reciprocal action from the Russians in the Balkans or Eastern Europe 'would only encourage the Russian leaders to believe that they could get their ends without war'. This would 'lead them into the same error that Hitler made of thinking that he could get away with anything by bluff and bullying'.[116]

The parallel with Hitler was frequently drawn by the Foreign Office. Bevin compared Attlee's intentions with Neville Chamberlain's policy of appeasement in the late 1930s: 'It would be Munich over again, only on a world scale, with Greece, Turkey and Persia as the first victims in place of Czechoslovakia. . . . If we speak to Stalin as you propose, he is as likely to respect their independence as Hitler was to respect Czechoslovakia's and we should get as much of Stalin's goodwill as we got of Hitler after Munich.' Similarly, in the early 1950s the Foreign Office did not hesitate to refute Churchill's inclination to find a negotiated East–West agreement by referring to 'Munich' and appeasement.

Most importantly, Bevin repeatedly emphasized that 'a retreat from the Middle East would appear to the world as the abdication of our position as a world power'. The realization of Attlee's suggested strategy would involve 'leading from weakness'. In contradiction to the Chancellor of the Exchequer's gloomy views of the country's financial position, Bevin thought

Britain's economic situation was bound to improve in the near future. There was thus no reason for a hasty withdrawal from Empire and the abandonment of such areas as the Middle East. Instead, Bevin proposed to adopt a 'wait and see' strategy.

> When we have consolidated our economy, when the economic revival of Europe ... has made progress, when it has become finally clear to the Russians that they cannot drive a wedge between the Americans and ourselves, we shall be in a position to negotiate with Stalin from strength. There is no hurry. Everything suggests that the Russians are now drawing in their horns and have no immediate aggressive intentions. Let us wait until our strength is restored, and let us meanwhile, with American help as necessary, hold on to essential positions and concentrate on building up U.N.O.[117]

On 9 January 1947 Attlee and Bevin discussed the situation privately. They agreed a compromise that for the time being no new withdrawals of British forces from the Middle East would be considered. Attlee was 'still not satisfied' that the present Middle Eastern defence policy ought to be sustained, and insisted on continuing the discussions with the British military.[118] However, on 13 January 1947, the Prime Minister suddenly gave in to Bevin, the Foreign Office mandarins and the Chiefs of Staff; he ceased arguing for the wholesale British withdrawal from the Middle East and the eastern Mediterranean. The COS had threatened to resign *en masse* if the Middle East was abandoned; this might well have brought down the government.[119] Thus, Attlee's 'bid to reorient British policy' was defeated.[120]

It may not have been only the opposition of the COS that convinced the Prime Minister to change course, as is generally argued in the literature. Although Anglo-Egyptian negotiations had collapsed by mid-December 1946,[121] there were some indications that cooperation might be possible with more moderate Arab leaders like King Abdullah of Transjordan.[122] Above all, the United States appeared to be showing an increasing interest in cautiously supporting the huge British Suez Canal base in Egypt and especially Britain's dominant role as a 'protector' of the 'northern tier' countries (Iran, Turkey, and above all Greece). While this was a double-edged sword – as would become clear in the next few years when the USA gradually replaced Britain as the preponderant power in, for example, Iran and Egypt – in 1946–47 Attlee welcomed American involvement enthusiastically. In February 1946 Attlee had said 'the whole thing would look different' if Washington 'were to become interested in Middle Eastern oil' and thus in participating in the defence of the whole region.[123]

Throughout 1946 he was also deeply worried about the political and economic situation in Greece, which was rapidly disintegrating into civil war. It made Attlee wonder 'whether the Greek game is worth the candle'.[124] Whilst the positions in Egypt and other Middle Eastern countries were perhaps strategically, economically and also emotionally of particular importance for Britain, Greece appeared to be much less crucial. Attlee therefore was not prepared to tolerate the Chiefs of Staff's view that British forces needed to stay in Greece 'for at least another year'.[125] This time, Bevin largely shared Attlee's sentiments. By the middle of 1946 Bevin was speaking of a 'bottomless well', an 'irremediably corrupt' system run by terrorists and of the necessity to get the British troops out of the Greek civil war.[126] Not surprisingly Dalton, the Chancellor, also viewed the Greeks 'as a very poor investment for the British taxpayer'.[127] Gradually Bevin became convinced that Moscow might respect Greece as falling within the western sphere of influence and might be less tempted to get involved. Moreover, by mid-October 1946 the British had fairly firm indications that the USA was developing a new policy for Greece, the only non-Communist country in the Balkans; Washington appeared to feel very strongly that Greece needed to be kept in the western camp.[128]

Indeed, in the course of 1946 Washington had grudgingly begun to accept the continued existence of the British Empire. The American Joint Chiefs of Staff (JCOS) had come to the conclusion that 'The U.S. should ... explore its relationship with Great Britain and give all feasible political, economic, and if necessary military support ... to the United Kingdom and the communications of the British Commonwealth.' Although the JCOS believed that it should be made clear that this 'does not imply a blank check of American support throughout the world for every interest of the British Empire', in fact this came close to underwriting British imperialism. Almost all the areas and interests which were 'vital to the maintenance of the United Kingdom and the British Commonwealth of nations as a great power' would soon be regarded as deserving American support in the unfolding global struggle with the Soviet Union.[129] After all, it appeared that 'If Soviet Russia is to be denied the hegemony of Europe, the United Kingdom must continue in existence as the principal power in Western Europe economically and militarily'.[130] And the British seemed to need their Empire resources to overcome their economic and financial problems. In the early post-war era both Washington and London viewed Britain's problems as largely temporary and reversible.[131] The unfolding conflict with the Soviet Union, however, appeared to be of a longer-lasting nature. Thus by mid- to late 1946 the trilateral Grand Alliance of the Second World War was being replaced by renewed bilateral Anglo-American cooperation, albeit still largely on an ad hoc basis.

For London this development was a relief. By late January 1947 even the Foreign Office had to admit that maintaining the British position in the Middle East was 'in fact impossible ... owing to the commitment in manpower and finance which it involves'. By then it was clear that Washington realized the importance of the region for the western world; the Foreign Office expected them 'increasingly to share the burden'.[132] On 21 February the British informed the Americans that they would stop economic aid to Greece and Turkey at the end of March, the end of Britain's fiscal year. Thus, notice was given to the Americans that Britain would in effect withdraw from involvement in Greece and Turkey, a decision which led to the announcement of the Truman Doctrine in March 1947, promising that America would support 'free peoples who are resisting attempted subjugation by armed minorities or by outside pressures'.[133]

From the British point of view, the American assumption of responsibility for Greece and Turkey would enable London to concentrate on maintaining and rebuilding Britain's position in the Middle East by means of Bevin's 'grand design' and the development of Britain's African Empire. Thus, the Truman Doctrine meant that America had clearly come out in favour of the British Empire in the Middle East.[134] Churchill expressed his admiration for the American initiative in a very courteous letter to Truman.[135] Ultimately, Britain appeared to benefit from the withdrawal from Greece. This contributed to Attlee's change of mind with regard to his agreement not to abandon the British Empire in the Middle East.

It therefore appears to be an exaggeration to claim that the Prime Minister was 'defeated' by Bevin and the Chiefs of Staff. After all, when the British did decide to terminate their military and financial support for Greece, the Americans came out in support of the British Empire in the Middle East. Thus, the rationale for the Prime Minister's injunction 'to consider our commitments very carefully lest we try to do more than we can' was at least partially vindicated.[136] Attlee believed that a solution had been found by means of partial withdrawal and the obtaining of American support; this made a radical overhaul of Britain's imperial policy much less urgent and perhaps even unnecessary.

Attlee's belief that the British ought to attempt negotiations with Stalin, however, was buried for good by the events of early 1947. Passing responsibility for Greece and Turkey to Washington appeared to make the development of a position of strength feasible. In the following months, Attlee moved closer to Bevin's point of view and came to doubt the wisdom of entering into negotiations with Moscow. Attlee's hopes for imperial 'disengagement and large economies in defence spending' were soon 'much toned down'.[137]

Churchill became the only major British politician who continued to be in favour of negotiating with the Soviets. Bevin's policy that negotiations with the Soviet Union concerning the Middle East and other areas of conflict ought to be postponed until a western position of strength had been achieved would remain the Labour government's view throughout its years in office. It corresponded with the attitude of the United States. But neither Bevin nor the White House and the State Department ever attempted to define what they actually meant by a 'position of strength'. In a world rapidly separating into two major spheres of influence and two irreconcilably opposed hostile camps, it was deliberately left unclear when the conditions for such a situation would be met. It appears, however, that until the breakdown of the Council of Foreign Ministers meeting in London in November/December 1947 Bevin (like Churchill) had not entirely given up hope of better relations with Moscow. Perhaps, as has been suggested, Bevin was even 'more reluctant to abandon hope of an agreement with Russia than either the United States or his own officials'.[138]

Be this as it may, after 1947/8 the main difference between the Labour government's stance and the warnings of the Conservative opposition about Stalin's expansionist policies was that Downing Street spoke out against negotiations with Moscow at this stage. Churchill, however, continued to push for speedy and early talks and managed to drag along a more hesitant Eden. Bevin and by now Attlee left it to Churchill to advocate a policy of strength in combination with an offer to start immediate negotiations with Stalin. The Labour government focused on advocating the development of a position of military and economic firmness. After 1946/7 it would take Attlee seven years to endorse East-West negotiations and a three-power summit conference: only in March 1954, when he became seriously worried about the escalating nuclear arms race, did he advocate summit negotiations in the House of Commons.[139]

Thus, throughout the years 1945–51 when Labour was in power, Churchill was repeatedly to exploit the opportunity to emphasize the dire necessity of embarking upon his proposed dual-track strategy: the build-up of the western military and economic positions and the pursuit of simultaneous summit negotiations with the Kremlin. This was a policy which was to remain very unpopular with the foreign policy elites in Britain and other western countries but, as the following years were to show, it captured the imagination of British and western public opinion.[140]

CHAPTER 6

Waiting in the Wings
Churchill's Foreign Policy as Leader of the Opposition

The more hostile and dangerous the Cold War became with the rapid development and refinement of nuclear weapons in West and East, the more apprehensive was Churchill at the prospect of war with the Soviet Union. His concern to preserve world peace, combined with his abiding aim of upholding Britain's great power status and maintaining the Empire, led him to advocate summit diplomacy to arrive at an early settlement of the Cold War. He was convinced that 'Big Three' negotiations on the Yalta and Potsdam model were essential to achieve a general relaxation of international tension and make another major war, which might well be a nuclear war, much less likely.

After 1945, Churchill and the vast majority of the British people continued to view their country as the third world power, which alongside its numerous colonial and Commonwealth responsibilities had the role of mediator between the United States, the USSR and the downtrodden continental European nations.[1] Churchill believed that securing Britains's traditional status as a great power could best be achieved through an intensification of the 'special relationship' with the United States and the historical ties with the Dominions and colonies, together with British support for a Franco-German rapprochement on the basis of a 'Europe of Fatherlands'. This would enable a unified West to negotiate with the Soviet Union from a position of strength and enable Britain to continue playing a global role.

The key to a proper understanding of Churchill's summit diplomacy after the Second World War is his desire to maintain the power and influence of Great Britain. His interventions cannot be explained by senility, the occasional inspirational flash, nor the attempt to postpone his resignation. These factors played a part, but essentially Churchill's summit diplomacy after 1945 represents the continuation of the methods he had always advocated to preserve peace, guarantee Britain a significant role in the world and restore this position after setbacks. These enduring factors in Churchill's thinking were often unrecognized both by Churchill's contemporaries and by later historians. Yet, a look at the immediate post-war period confirms this interpretation and clarifies further the roots of Churchill's foreign policy.

The 'Iron Curtain' Speech and Negotiations with Moscow

One of Churchill's first initiatives calling for negotiations with Moscow came during his 'iron curtain' speech in Fulton, Missouri, in March 1946. This address attracted great attention and may have been decisive in persuading American public opinion of the hostile intentions of the Soviet Union. It was generally perceived as strongly anti-Communist and led to the image of Churchill as the Cold Warrior *par excellence* in East and West. However, this view rested on a major misunderstanding of the speech.

A closer look at Churchill's Fulton address, officially entitled 'The Sinews of Peace', indicates that he not only warned the world about the Kremlin's expansionist policies but also called for peaceful reconciliation with Moscow. In fact, the 'iron curtain' address was Churchill's first major attempt after the war to call for summit negotiations with Moscow. Outlining his grand strategy for the post-war world, Churchill called for both an international settlement and a policy of strength. At Fulton, he first publicly proposed his twin-track approach for dealing with the Soviet Union. He had already hoped during the war that it might be possible to continue cooperation with Stalin in peacetime and, like Prime Minister Attlee, he did not consider war with the Soviet Union inevitable. Churchill declared:

> I repulse the idea that a new war is inevitable; still more that it is imminent. … I do not believe that Soviet Russia desires war. What they desire is the fruits of war and the indefinite expansion of their power and doctrines. . . . Our difficulties and dangers will not be removed by closing our eyes to them. They will not be removed by mere waiting to see what happens; nor will they be removed by a policy of appeasement. *What is needed is a settlement, and the longer this is delayed the more difficult it will be and the greater our dangers will be.*[2]

These and other passages in which Churchill called for a 'good understanding on all points with Russia',[3] however, were disregarded. Alongside the slogan 'iron curtain', which was not that new anyway,[4] immediate attention was focused on the call for the West to increase its military power *vis-à-vis* the

Soviet Union. Churchill had pronounced that he was 'convinced that there is nothing they [the USSR] admire so much as strength, and there is nothing for which they have less respect than for weakness, especially military weakness'.[5] By stressing both the significance of military strength alongside the importance of reconciliation through discussion, Churchill had called for 'negotiations from strength' for the first time. At this early stage of the Cold War, however, the two elements of Churchill's policy – strength and negotiations – were not perceived as belonging together. In the aftermath of the speech, confrontation rather than negotiation with Moscow dominated western public opinion. With the announcement of the Truman Doctrine in March 1947, Stalin's creation of the COMINFORM in September 1947 for spreading Communist propaganda, the Communist coup in Czechoslovakia of February 1948 and the Berlin blockade of 1948/9, the lasting impression of Churchill's 'iron-curtain' address was not its call for negotiations but its call for resistance to Communism.

Thus Churchill came to be regarded as the outstanding western statesman who was not afraid to confront the Soviet Union, and who, perhaps, even enjoyed doing so.[6] And frequently Churchill did nothing to refute these views. In a parliamentary debate on 5 June 1946, he declared it was no longer Germany that represented a threat to the future peace of Europe; instead, the main enemy was 'the confusion and degeneration into which all of Europe ... [was] rapidly sinking' due to Stalin's activities. Churchill recommended 'the adoption of clear and firm policies'.[7] In March 1950, three months before the outbreak of the Korean War, he stimulated a bitter debate in Britain by arguing for the necessity of rearming the Federal Republic of Germany and the formation of a European army.[8] However, the increasing division of the world into two political and economic blocs still failed to convince Churchill that East and West had to confront each other aggressively. If this occurred, he argued, a new global war could not be prevented. Thus along with promoting rapprochement between Germany and France, he advocated a speedy 'settlement' with Moscow.[9] He believed this was feasible despite all appearances to the contrary: hostile comments by the Soviet Union, he observed, should not be given too much significance. Although he lacked any firm evidence, Churchill was convinced these remarks were made mainly for domestic consumption in the USSR.[10]

Thus within five years of the end of the war Churchill had become the chief proponent of two controversial policies: the proposal for the defence of the European continent with the help of German soldiers and an international summit meeting with the Soviet Union. In the event, his contentious views on German rearmament overshadowed the call for East–West negotiations, which initially failed to make an impact upon the course of the political debate. Nobody took the proposal seriously at the time, and neither Churchill's contemporaries nor later historians have paid much attention to them.[11] Churchill's reputation as a dedicated anti-Communist was too firmly established.

To the British public Churchill's statements often appeared contradictory. Whereas on the one hand he drew attention to the Soviet threat, calling for military strength and warning against too conciliatory a policy towards Moscow, on the other hand he recommended seeking a peaceful arrangement with Stalin. For Churchill (and also for Attlee in 1946/7), this was quite a logical course of action in order to prevent an escalation of the conflict and the outbreak of a third world war. However, as far as public opinion in Britain was concerned, Churchill's viewpoints appeared to be confused. And indeed, on superficial examination Churchill's views would more often than not appear contradictory, and so his ideas on how a 'settlement' with Moscow could be reached were simply ignored. So soon after the war few people were prepared to write off the esteemed statesman as an over-excited visionary; this would not happen before 1954/5.

Although Churchill's public comments showed a degree of ambiguity, he was in fact merely reiterating the double-track policy outlined in his 'iron curtain' speech in 1946, when he called for both firmness and negotiation. In a parliamentary speech on foreign affairs in January 1948, he supported the Labour Party's 'tough' policy towards the USSR while re-emphasizing the need for serious negotiations with Moscow: only such negotiations could bring about an end to the Cold War and prevent the outbreak of another world war.[12] The timing of a call for negotiation was hardly likely to succeed when the last of a series of conferences of the Council of Foreign Ministers between September 1945 and December 1947 had just failed miserably.[13] The day before, Foreign Secretary Bevin, disillusioned by the failure of the meeting of the Council of Allied Foreign Ministers in London in late 1947, had stated that 'His Majesty's Government cannot agree to Four-Power co-operation while one of the four Powers proceeds to impose its political and economic system on the smaller states.'[14] In his reply, Churchill stressed the common ground between himself and the government. He was very pleased 'to see that not only the British, but the American government, have adopted to a very large extent the views which I expressed at Fulton nearly two years ago, and have, indeed, in many ways gone far beyond them'.[15] Nevertheless, he believed that the speeches by senior members of the government 'about Soviet Russia, and about the dangers of a new war, far exceed in gravity and menace anything which I ... have ever said on this subject since the war.'[16] International relations had undoubtedly worsened in the last six months and the renewed danger of war could not be ignored. However, instead of abandoning all communication and cooperation, this was the precise reason why a negotiated 'settlement' between the western world and the Soviet Union was long overdue:

> There seems to me very real danger in going on drifting too long. I believe that the best chance of preventing war is to bring matters to a head and come to a settlement with the Soviet Government before it is too late. This would imply that the Western democracies ... would take the initiative in asking the Soviets for a settlement ... and, by formal diplomatic processes, with all their privacy and gravity, to arrive at a lasting settlement.[17]

He did not go into any detail about how this 'settlement' with the Soviet Union might be reached, but he recommended that the West grasp the initiative and avail itself of 'formal diplomatic processes'. He repeated his belief that the time for negotiations with the Soviet Union had come; in fact it was already two years overdue. With regard to the development of the American atomic bomb, Churchill had declared to Parliament as early as August 1945: 'there are at least three, and perhaps four, years before the concrete progress made in the United States can be overtaken'. In this period of time the relationships of nations with one another had to be newly defined and an international control organization should be formed: 'There is not an hour to be wasted; there is not a day to be lost.'[18] Churchill was convinced that since the dropping of the atomic bombs on Hiroshima and Nagasaki the relationship between the western world and Moscow had changed fundamentally if only temporarily in favour of the West.[19] This situation needed to be exploited – but by means of negotiations not by embarking on a preventive war, as was sometimes advocated in the United States.

Churchill's belief in negotiations with Moscow was not shared in Washington. Following the American presidential election in late 1948, which confirmed Truman in office,[20] the Democratic administration became more convinced than ever that the military strength of the West was significantly inferior to that of the Soviet Union. In January 1949, Under-Secretary of State Dean Acheson was appointed Secretary of State and in early 1950 he began to use the phrase 'negotiations from strength'. However, what he had in mind were not so much negotiations with Moscow as the build-up of the western world's economic and military position.[21] Acheson believed that due to the USSR's superiority in manpower and conventional weaponry, the West needed to build up its armaments before 'negotiations from strength' would be possible.[22]

Churchill disagreed with this view. For him the West was still in a dominant position because of the atomic monopoly of the United States, and discussions over a 'settlement' with Moscow should therefore take place as soon as possible. It would be only a matter of time before the USSR would wipe out the West's superiority with the production of its own atomic bombs, and that time must be used to negotiate:

> When this Parliament first assembled, I said that the possession of the atomic bomb would give three or four years' breathing space. ... But more than two of those years have already gone. I cannot think that any serious discussion which it may be necessary to have with the Soviet government would be more likely to reach a favourable conclusion, if we wait until they have got it, too.'[23]

Even after the Soviet Union had successfully exploded its first atomic bomb on 29 August 1949, a fact which western scientists had ascertained by mid-September, Churchill believed that the military lead of the West would still be secure for a short time, since Moscow would hardly be able to match immediately the increasing American nuclear arsenal.[24] Thus the chance for a satisfactory settlement still remained, but every passing month would make an agreement less likely. Moreover, the West would be less and less able to dictate the terms of such a 'settlement'. There was still a 'breathing space' when Britain and the United States could negotiate from a position of relative strength and thereby prevent the outbreak of another war.[25] Churchill thought the American policy of postponing discussions until the West had achieved absolute supremacy in both nuclear and conventional weapons was dangerous. 'It is said that we are getting stronger, but to get stronger does not necessarily mean that we are getting safer. It is only when we are strong enough that safety is achieved; and the period of the most acute danger might well arise just before we were strong enough.'[26]

Churchill was not aware that the Soviet Union's explosion of an atomic fission bomb had led to the acceleration of the American attempt to develop an even more powerful thermonuclear device and begin production of such a weapon: in January 1950 Truman had ordered the Atomic Energy Commission to embark on developing an H-bomb.[27] During the next two decades, the United States remained convinced of the conventional military supremacy of the East and, on occasion, even predicted an imminent 'missile gap'. According to successive American governments, discussions could not be risked until parity in military capacity had been achieved.[28]

During these immediate post-war years, Churchill was not always optimistic about the possibility of talks with the Kremlin. In April 1948, in a letter to Averell Harriman, then Secretary of Commerce, he had spoken of the danger the world was facing and expressed satisfaction about the increasing air power of the United States.[29] He told the Conservative Party conference in October

1948 of the 'abyss which now yawns across Europe and the world' and warned of the 'false hopes of a speedy friendly settlement with Soviet Russia'; even if a compromise solution were to be found, 'the fundamental danger and antagonism will still remain'.[30] He was even tempted to advocate a show-down with Moscow since Stalin was not yet in possession of the atomic bomb, though it is questionable whether he really meant this.[31]

Other developments had also made Churchill gloomy about the global situation and Britain's capacity to influence events. He was particularly depressed about the apparent readiness of the United States to begin bilateral talks with Moscow without British participation and consultation, as evidenced by an American proposal in May 1948.[32] He was also deeply worried by the Berlin blockade, which began on 24 June 1948 and threatened to lead to global military conflict. The blockade was Stalin's response to the introduction of a new German currency and western preparations for setting up a separate West German state. Cutting off West Berlin by land and sea from western Germany did not only increase political tension between East and West, it also meant that the city could only be kept alive by a large-scale airlift through three air corridors. The western and in particular the American resolve to stand by its new West German ally was at stake.[33] Unsuccessful talks in Moscow in August 1948 between Stalin and Molotov and western representatives contributed to Churchill's sombre outlook.[34]

Furthermore, Churchill was displeased by Truman's first and only serious attempt to embark on personal summit diplomacy à la Roosevelt. The President revealed his plan to negotiate with the Soviets in a speech to the American Legion in October 1948, after the story had already been leaked to a hostile newspaper which condemned it as 'appeasement'. On the model of Roosevelt's use of Harry Hopkins, Truman had intended to send Supreme Chief Justice Fred Vinson to Moscow to convince Stalin of the US administration's 'peaceful intentions' and 'genuine desire to co-operate'. In the middle of the Berlin crisis and the American election campaign, Truman was trailing Republican presidential candidate Thomas Dewey and believed it would be a good idea to show his dedication to world peace. Displaying an unusual degree of naivety, Truman hoped that Vinson would be able to 'get Stalin to unburden himself to someone on our side he felt he could trust fully'; the Chief Justice should see if Stalin would not 'open up'.[35] The State Department was prompt in preventing the mission, which aroused such hostility that there was even talk of Secretary of State George Marshall threatening to resign.[36] Churchill as well as the Attlee government in London deplored the lack of any consultation or even information, but as Truman had intended to circumvent the State Department it was hardly surprising that the western allies would only have been informed of the Vinson mission at the last moment.

By late 1948 Churchill was considerably more depressed. 'Nothing stands between Europe today and complete subjugation to Communist tyranny but the atomic bomb in American possession,' he told Parliament.[37] In March 1949 he dramatically declared at the Massachusetts Institute of Technology: 'It is certain that Europe would have been communized and London under bombardment some time ago but for the deterrent of the atomic bomb in the hands of the United States.'[38] Despite these words, which caused a great deal of excitement in America, Churchill still believed in discussions with Moscow, although from late 1948 he expressed himself more cautiously. In December 1948 he told the House of Commons:

> I have frequently advised that we should endeavour to reach a settlement with Russia on fundamental, outstanding questions before they have the atomic bomb as well as the Americans. I believe that in this resided the best hope of avoiding a third world war. I wish to make it clear … that I have never attempted to suggest the timing of such a solemn and grave negotiation.[39]

Despite these qualifications, it still sounded as if he was quite prepared to embark upon East–West negotiations as a matter of urgency. But what did Churchill believe could be gained from discussions with the Soviet Union in the icy atmosphere of the Berlin blockade? He seems to have found solace in his long-held belief that personal contact was valuable in itself. He was convinced that this was the only way to improve relations with a potential enemy. Churchill was adhering to the sentiments he had expressed in October 1944:

> [It] is so much easier to enter into arrangements by conversation than by telegram and diplomatic correspondence, however carefully phrased and however lengthily expressed, or however patiently the discussion may be conducted. Face to face, difficulties which appear really insuperable at a distance are very often removed altogether from one's path.[40]

He remained true to that belief when he told Parliament in March 1950:

> The first stage is to create a friendly atmosphere and feelings of mutual confidence and respect. Then difficulties at present insuperable may simply become irrelevant.[41]

'A Parley at the Summit'

In 1949 it briefly appeared as if negotiations among the world's major powers were likely to materialize, although possibly without Britain. For the first time since the Potsdam conference, a meeting between Truman and Stalin became a topic of serious discussion in the international media in early 1949.[42] On 2 February 1949 Radio Moscow transmitted Stalin's answers to four written questions submitted by the American journalist Kingsbury Smith, Stalin hinting at his readiness to meet Truman for the conclusion of a global peace pact. It soon emerged, however, that neither Washington nor Moscow had any interest in a meeting.[43] Nonetheless, the idea of personal summit diplomacy between the heads of government of the superpowers, as they were soon called, had come to stay. From now on, proposals for a 'Big Two' or occasionally a 'Big Three' summit meeting appeared quite frequently in the media and during parliamentary debates, and 'high-level talks' came to be regarded as the panacea for East–West conflicts. Churchill's forceful rhetoric may have had some influence on this development.[44]

Although Washington and Moscow showed no interest in a bilateral summit conference, Stalin's replies via Radio Moscow led to talks about an end to the Berlin blockade between the American and Soviet UN ambassadors, Philip Jessup and Yakov Malik.[45] During their confidential talks in New York between 15 March and 4 May 1949, agreement over a peaceful end to the Berlin blockade was reached, to take effect on 12 May.[46] To Acheson's distaste, the United States was compelled to declare its support for another meeting of the Allied Council of Foreign Ministers. This would allow the Soviet Union to save face and agree to the termination of the blockade without having achieved any of its aims.[47]

Compared with the last foreign ministers' conference in London in November/December 1947, the Paris Four-Power conference of May/June 1949 was something of a success. Allied relations did not worsen and it seemed that a first step had been taken to reduce tension in Europe.[48] At least the great powers were once more talking with one another and for the time being the imminent danger of war seemed to have disappeared.[49] Churchill thought that the value of personal summit diplomacy had been confirmed by the Jessup–Malik talks and the Paris conference, although Britain's exclusion from participation in the resolution of the Berlin crisis worried him. During the British election campaign in February 1950, Churchill again took up the topic of talks with Moscow, mainly in reaction to disparaging comments by American Secretary of State Acheson, which he found particularly annoying.

As part of a general review of American foreign policy in 1950,[50] Acheson gave a press conference on 8 February setting out the reasons for a policy of strength towards the Soviet Union. He said that agreements with Moscow would only be constructive if they dealt specifically with existing situations and were put down in writing. The policy of the United States was to bring about such understandings, 'by creating situations so strong that they can be recognized and out of them can grow agreement'.[51] Addressing a group of company directors on 16 February, Acheson again spoke of the need 'to create situations of strength'.[52] Regarding discussions with Moscow, 'No good would come from our taking the initiative in calling for conversations at this point.' It seemed to him that Moscow had no interest in a speedy resolution of East–West conflicts.[53] Stalin and the other politicians in the Kremlin, Acheson believed, were still convinced that they could use the uneasy international situation to their advantage; only when this was no longer the case would Moscow be prepared to conclude satisfactory agreements with the West. Until then, only limited agreements in certain clearly defined troublespots where the West was in a strong position (as in Berlin) seemed possible.[54]

Acheson's position was largely shared by the British Chiefs of Staff and the Labour government. In their major assessment of Britain's Defence Policy and Global Strategy, submitted to the Cabinet's Defence Committee in June 1950, the Chiefs of Staff suggested that the country 'make all the sacrifices necessary to build up and maintain our military strength'. Only then would the Russians gradually realize that 'modern war would be mass mutual suicide. And in time a political settlement might evolve from that realisation.' Like Washington, Britain's military considered that the West would only gain a 'conclusive victory' in the Cold War if the current 'indefinite uneasy armistice on the Iron Curtain frontier' was replaced 'by the restoration of freedom to Eastern Europe and Russia's withdrawal behind her own frontiers'. Instead of calling for East–West negotiations, the COS argued that 'we should not be unduly anxious about provoking the Russians ... even now the Allies could afford to adopt a more forward strategy in the cold war, and should be making all possible plans and preparations to be more and more offensive as their military strength grows.'[55] On the whole, the COS did not think that Russia would 'attack Western Europe' in the near future.[56]

The Labour administration too still regarded discussions with Moscow as premature. This became evident on 10 February 1950 with the publication of an exchange of letters between Attlee and leading Quakers, who had attempted to convince the Prime Minister that he should take the initiative in supporting an atomic non-proliferation treaty and convene a conference of the great powers. Preferring not to remember his own support for negotiations with Stalin in

1946, the Prime Minister replied that 'it would be presumptuous to suppose that personal contact ... would do anything but raise hopes unduly.'[57] He specifically declined to sponsor high-level discussions with Moscow. Churchill very much disliked the comments of Attlee and Acheson. He responded in a speech in Edinburgh on 14 February and for the first time introduced foreign policy into an election campaign hitherto entirely dominated by domestic policy.[58] He called for discussions with Moscow, reiterating views he had held since 1945/6. For the first time he used the phrase 'a parley at the summit' as the appropriate method of negotiation. Real progress in East–West relations no longer appeared possible merely by way of vague 'diplomatic processes' as he had said in January 1948. He was now convinced that success could only be achieved by convening a meeting of the heads of government; he was thinking of a Second-World-War style 'Big Three' summit. For the first time since the war he explicitly called for a summit meeting of the heads of government of the USA, the USSR and Britain – the policy he would attempt to realize as Prime Minister in 1953/4. In 1950 Churchill expressed his ideas much more precisely and energetically than before:

> I look back to 1945 when I was last in relation with Mr. Stalin and his colleagues ... still, I cannot help coming back to this idea of another talk with Soviet Russia upon the highest level. The idea appeals to me of a supreme effort to bridge the gulf between the two worlds, so that each can live their life if not in friendship, at least without the hatreds and manoeuvres of the cold war. ... It is not easy to see how things could be worsened by a parley at the summit if such a thing were possible.[59]

Churchill's public support for summit diplomacy at the highest level was the way he sought to prevent a global conflict. Of course there was also an election strategy here, with Churchill wanting to remind the British electorate of his long experience of negotiating with heads of government.[60] In addition, the rumours about an impending meeting between Stalin and Truman the year before had not failed to make an impression upon Churchill. The suspicious Churchill believed that Truman intended to ignore Britain's role in international diplomacy with Moscow as Roosevelt had attempted to do during the war. Therefore, Churchill used his speech in Edinburgh to play the patriotic card and reassert Great Britain's right to a place at the table of the 'Big Three'.

The Labour government regarded Churchill's arguments as cheap electioneering, the Prime Minister declaring that conducting negotiations with Moscow did not lie within the responsibility of the British government, but 'rests with the United Nations'.[61] Although Churchill's ideas were fairly popular with the general public in the United States, few politicians in

Washington, apart from the influential Senator Tydell, were ready to lend him their support. During a speech in Virginia on 22 February, Truman hinted that he preferred Attlee's viewpoint to Churchill's.[62] However, on 17 February, a week before the election, when Churchill was making a radio broadcast defending his remarks in Edinburgh,[63] Trygve Lie, the General Secretary of the United Nations, spoke out in support of 'negotiations among the Great Powers': 'I am for it at all times and on all levels, both inside and outside the United Nations. The world would be a lot better today if there had been more real negotiations among the Great Powers during the past three years.'[64] Churchill was much encouraged.

Churchill's Edinburgh speech had set out his political goals if the British electorate were to open the door of Number 10 Downing Street to him again. At the election of 20 February 1950, however, Labour was returned with a majority of only five seats. This slim victory made another general election likely in the immediate future and thus, despite a groundswell against him, Churchill was able to stay on as Leader of the Opposition.[65]

By 1950, most Labour ministers had been continuously involved with the responsibilities of government since the formation of the national government in 1940, and many key figures were close to physical and mental exhaustion: indeed, Bevin and Stafford Cripps, Chancellor of the Exchequer since November 1947, would die within the year. The new Foreign Secretary was Herbert Morrison, who took over in mid-March 1950 but largely disappointed in the post. After its initial years of constructive reform, the Labour government was now confronted with increasingly complex problems in both domestic and foreign policy.[66] Britain's mounting economic and financial problems presented the government with serious difficulties, which undermined the Labour Party's internal cohesion; increasingly, the party's left and right wing were at each other's throat. When the Korean War began on 25 June 1950, infighting over the financing of the rearmament programme provoked a major crisis; the government's proposal to scale back expenditure on the welfare state led to the resignation of two cabinet members (Nye Bevan and Harold Wilson) and a junior minister (John Freeman) in April 1951.[67]

Thus the Attlee government was increasingly preoccupied with its own survival, and the Conservative opposition could concentrate on making life for the weakened Cabinet as difficult as possible to provoke a government defeat in the House of Commons.[68] Churchill found this situation of uncertainty difficult. He later admitted to President Truman that '[it] was a great strain when an election could be called at any time. It was like walking under a tree with a jaguar on the limb waiting to pounce.'[69] For the greater part of 1950–51, neither the government nor the opposition was inclined to suggest major initiatives in domestic or foreign policy.

The only exception appeared to be Churchill, who continued to persist in the pursuit of his summit plans. In March 1950, during the first foreign policy debate of the new Parliament, he repeated his conviction that talks with Moscow 'upon the highest level' were necessary.[70] But apart from the Conservative MP Julian Amery, delivering his maiden speech, and the Labour MP Raymond Blackburn, hardly anyone in the House of Commons was ready to support the call 'for a further effort for a lasting and peaceful settlement' with Moscow.[71]

During the same debate, Anthony Eden mentioned only at the very end of his speech that 'it should be possible to negotiate with Moscow on a basis of strength' once the non-Communist states had stabilized and strengthened their economies. Then, at an unspecified time in the future, 'no method of negotiation ought to be excluded'. This hardly indicated much enthusiasm for Churchill's summit diplomacy.[72] Eden shared the belief that Acheson was to express again in a speech on 8 October 1950: 'Building the strength of the free nations is not by itself a method of settling differences with the Soviet leaders. It is a way – and the only way – to prevent those differences from being settled by default.'[73] Eden and Acheson agreed that negotiations with the Soviet Union should take place at some time in the future, but unlike Churchill they were not convinced that time was running out for the West.

Although there were some senior Conservatives, like Lord Woolton and Lord Beaverbrook, who felt that Churchill's proposal for negotiations with Stalin was 'desirable, particularly to offset the warmonger attack levelled against him' and 'to retrieve' Britain's position as a world power, hardly anyone on the Conservative front bench shared this view.[74] In mid-March 1950 Averell Harriman told Churchill that in view of the position of both the President and the Secretary of State 'it would not help his personal relations [with them] if he went any further at this time in proposing tripartite talks with Stalin'. In a letter to Truman, Harriman attempted to explain Churchill's grave misjudgement in the matter: he told him that the British, 'particularly Churchill, recall a certain flexibility in Stalin during the wartime conferences. They appear to overlook that at that time Stalin was afraid we would make a separate peace with Germany and of course he then wanted our material assistance – conditions that do not exist today.' Since Churchill and Eden had no access to Foreign Office information they appeared to have no understanding of the attitude of the Kremlin 'as it had developed since 1945'.[75] Churchill, whom Harriman found 'in high spirits and remarkably vigorous' during a short visit to the UK in early 1950, responded to his old friend's warning not to endanger relations with Washington by proposing a summit meeting that 'he had no intention of doing so'. However, this did not stop him from returning to his beloved theme in his speech in the House of Commons just over two weeks later.[76]

This did not go down well in Washington. Acheson and Truman were firmly convinced of the futility of attempting to negotiate with Stalin at this stage. The Secretary of State did not believe in the value of summit negotiations on principle, neither with enemies nor with allies. When Attlee visited Washington in December 1950, to restrain Truman from considering the use of atomic bombs in Korea and discuss the dangerous war situation on the peninsula, where Chinese and North Korean Communist troops had succeeded in pushing back the western UN forces deep into South Korea and were about to recapture Seoul, Acheson was not impressed. The meetings with the British delegation left him with 'a deep dislike and distrust' of 'summitry' as a 'diplomatic instrument'. He even came to regard it as a 'dangerous diplomatic method' as the participants were often ill-prepared and unreliable which tended to lead to 'nerve-racking' and 'unsatisfactory' results. At the end of the conference with the British delegation, which in fact was Acheson's first summit conference ever, the Secretary of State uttered 'an ungranted prayer that [he] might be spared another'.[77]

Churchill's advocacy of summit negotiations with Moscow was therefore most unlikely to succeed while the Truman administration was in office, particularly since the British Labour government continued to disapprove of East–West negotiations. In the foreign policy debate in March 1950, Minister of State Kenneth Younger had declared that in view of Moscow's 'withdrawal from co-operation' and 'scarcely veiled hostility to everything that we are trying to do', the Cabinet did not see any possibility of beginning negotiations with the Kremlin; such discussions needed 'adequate preparations' which required time.[78]

Churchill was therefore isolated, but he was not to be dissuaded. Even the Korean War had not made him change his view, although it led to outbursts of panic in western capitals, particularly in Bonn.[79] On 14 July 1950, when the military situation in Korea was anything but stable, Churchill told the Conservative party conference in Plymouth that although the situation was reminiscent of 1940, 'I do not mean that war is imminent. But I must not lead you to suppose that time is on our side.' A 'supreme effort to bridge the gulf between the two worlds' was necessary.[80] On 27 July 1950 he told Parliament: 'We must never abandon the hope that a peaceful settlement may be reached with the Soviet government if a resolute effort is made.'[81] He still believed in the necessity of strengthening the military potential of the West, but his response was to advocate minimizing the delay in building a 'position of strength' and beginning early negotiations with the Soviet Union. Two years should be long enough for the West to build up its defence capabilities; negotiations with the Kremlin should begin after this period at the very latest, but ideally both processes ought to take place simultaneously.

Churchill was unrelenting in his pressure for a reorientation of western policy and in accusing the Labour government of wasting precious time – 'Several years have been wasted and frittered away' – though he also warned of over-optimism with respect to the likelihood of an East–West rapprochement, telling Parliament that he was 'strongly in favour of every effort being made by every means to secure a fair and reasonable settlement with Russia. I should, however, be failing in frankness ... if I did not make it clear at this stage that we must not place undue hopes upon the success of any negotiations.'[82]

Churchill's Methods, Aims and Motives

It is interesting that although Churchill had called for a 'settlement' with Moscow since the beginning of 1946 and had advocated a summit meeting of the 'Big Three' since February 1950, he never explained how such negotiations would lead to a relaxation in tension and perhaps even to an end of the Cold War. He remained silent on the question of which topics were to be raised at a summit and in what sequence they were to be discussed. He never pronounced a view on whether, during the meetings of the Council of Foreign Ministers and the failed pre-conference of four-power foreign ministers in the Palais Marbre Rose in Paris in early 1950,[83] it was a mistake to restrict the discussions to the almost insurmountable German question. Would it perhaps have been better to attempt to find solutions to the Austrian question or to the numerous other apparently less significant conflicts of the Cold War? Thus, had he drawn any lessons from the fiascos of the recent past?

Important issues such as these, decisive for the success or failure of any summit conference, were never addressed by Churchill. Indeed, compared with the great issues of the time he regarded such considerations with a certain disdain. He seems to have believed that questions of detail were the task of the Foreign Office, while he could simply repeat his assertions that a third world war could be prevented so long as the West was able to negotiate from a position of relative strength.

Churchill's most valuable contribution to international relations during this time was that from the very first months of the Cold War he had begun to warn of a possible catastrophe and a nuclear holocaust. He had introduced the topic of East–West détente as a subject for discussion as early as 1946, but he failed to present a methodology to make his general theory more tangible in the practical world. This lack of detail decisively contributed to the mistrust with which he was increasingly regarded in political circles in both Britain and the United States.[84] He thus undermined his own vision. Public opinion in the

West might view his general calls for active negotiations with sympathy, but politicians remained much more sceptical of their usefulness.

Alongside the preservation of world peace, Churchill's constant theme was the strengthening of Britain's position in the world. This is nowhere more clearly expressed than in the so-called 'Three Circles' speech of 9 October 1948. After once again pointing to the gulf between East and West and proposing a 'settlement' with Moscow, he explained that Great Britain was at the interface of three circles which encompassed the British Empire and Commonwealth, the English-speaking world and a united Europe. The British people had the opportunity of 'joining them all together'. 'If we rise to the occasion in the years that are to come it may be found that once again we hold the key to opening a safe and happy future to humanity, and will gain for ourselves gratitude and fame.'[85]

Churchill was not only interested in a relaxation of the East–West conflict *per se*. He was utterly convinced of Britain's crucial role in initiating such a policy, if possible under his leadership: 'Our influence in the world is not what it was in bygone days. I could wish indeed that it was greater, because I am sure it would be used as it always has been used to the utmost to prevent a life and death struggle between the great nations.'[86] Churchill believed deeply in a missionary role for Britain and its Empire.'[87] In a radio broadcast on 17 February 1951 he declared: 'What a reflection it would be on our national dignity and moral elevation, and indeed upon the whole status of British democracy, if at this time of choice we find nothing to talk about but material issues and calculations about personal gain or loss. What a humiliation it would be if proud Britain ... were found completely absorbed in party and domestic strife.'[88] In a speech to 50,000 people in Wolverhampton's football stadium on 22 July 1949, he proclaimed that 'The main aim of all Conservative policy is to restore the greatness of Britain.'[89]

For Churchill, agreement with the Soviet Union and closer unity among European states including European rearmament only served his primary objective: the well-being, power and reputation of Great Britain. He planned to achieve this by continuing 'an ever closer and more effective' 'fraternal association' with the United States,[90] but he realized that 'a continuance of the present arms race can only cause increasing danger, increasing military expense, and diminishing supplies to the homes'.[91] Churchill was fully aware of Britain's precarious economic situation. He believed that in the event of a continuing Soviet and American military build-up, Britain would have to follow suit. Consequently his country's global economic position would deteriorate further and Britain would become increasingly reliant on the economic and also military power of the United States. Only a period of détente, which would give Great Britain an economic breathing space, along with an increased concentration on harnessing imperial resources, could prevent, let alone reverse, this process.[92]

During the election campaign of autumn 1951 Churchill insisted on the necessity of talks with Moscow. He explained for example in a radio broadcast: 'I do not hold that we should rearm in order to fight. I hold that we should rearm in order to parley. I hope and believe that there may be a parley.'[93] He was much offended by Labour's accusation that he was a 'warmonger', unqualified to conduct the affairs of government in times of peace. He was greatly hurt by the headline in the *Daily Mirror* which compared him with the sober and peace-loving Attlee and depicted him as an emotional promoter of war. In the context of the dangerous developments in Iran, where the assumption of political power by the strongly anti-British nationalist Dr Mussadiq appeared to endanger the British-controlled oil installations at Abadan and, perhaps, Britain's position in the whole of the Middle East, the newspaper coined the headline: 'Whose Finger on the Trigger?'[94]

Churchill attempted to turn the situation to his advantage by playing on his long experience in world affairs. In a speech in Plymouth on 23 October 1951 he reaffirmed his peace-loving intentions, explaining that he aimed to become Prime Minister again because he wished to pursue summit diplomacy to prevent a global war and to bring about a 'lasting peace settlement'.[95] Two days later Churchill gained a narrow victory in the general election. Much to his satisfaction, albeit to the horror of his wife, he had been voted back into office. Churchill proudly went to Buckingham Palace to be formally appointed Prime Minister by King George VI.

CHAPTER 7

Ever Closer Union?
Churchill and European Integration in the Post-war Years

Churchill's repeated calls for European unity and even for the creation of a 'United States of Europe' as Leader of the Opposition between 1945 and 1951 were one aspect of his strategy to impress upon Stalin the coherence, strength and resolution of the western world led by the Anglo-American 'fraternal association'. He believed that 'The whole purpose of a united democratic Europe is to give decisive guarantees against aggression.'[1] The development of a Franco-German rapprochement, Germany's re-integration into the civilized world, economic stability in Europe, and a certain willingness to bow to American pressure on the question of European integration, were also important considerations in his calls for a united Europe.[2] The main impetus, however, was Churchill's grand design for the post-war world to reach an amicable settlement with the Soviet Union, which would in turn reduce Britain's financial and military burden and lead to economic stability and her future as a world power. European integration for its own sake was not one of Churchill's primary objectives. His 'ultimate aim' was the end of the Cold War and with it 'the unity and freedom of the whole of Europe'.[3]

Churchill's Europe, the 'Iron Curtain' Speech and the 1946 Zurich Speech

Like the twin-track policy of negotiations from strength and the aim to improve relations with the United States, Churchill's views on European unity made an appearance in his 'iron curtain' speech of March 1946. In this speech, made at Fulton, Missouri, Churchill declared that 'the world requires a new unity in Europe from which no nation should be permanently outcast', thus hinting at the necessity of integrating Germany into such a scheme. He partially resurrected his wartime ideas on the future of Europe by emphasizing that 'we should work with conscious purpose for a grand pacification of Europe, within the structure of the United Nations ... one cannot imagine a regenerated Europe without a strong France'. It was obvious to Churchill, however, that a united Europe led by France would hardly be able to deal with the world's post-war problems. American support was needed. He therefore referred to the importance of the Anglo-American special relationship for achieving peaceful relations with Moscow under the umbrella of a world organization. He well remembered the importance the Roosevelt administration had attached to the creation of a universalist rather than a regionalist United Nations.[4] Thus, Churchill affirmed at Fulton that 'a good understanding with Russia' and its maintenance 'through many peaceful years' could only be reached with the help of 'the general authority of the United Nations Organisation' and, above all, with the support of 'the whole strength of the English-speaking world and all its connections'. He did not fail to emphasize the importance of his own country by declaring that nobody should 'underrate the abiding power of the British Empire and Commonwealth':

> If the population of the English-speaking Commonwealths be added to that of the United States with all that such co-operation implies in the air, on the sea, all over the globe and in science and in industry, and in moral force, there will be no quivering, precarious balance of power to offer its temptation to ambition or adventure. On the contrary, there will be an overwhelming assurance of security.[5]

Churchill was not thinking of Britain as part of a united Europe. Instead, the USA and the UK, supported by its Empire and Commonwealth, would together safeguard the security as well as the democratic spirit of the world.[6] Already at Fulton in March 1946 Churchill was thinking of Britain at the centre of three interlocking circles with his country having a stake and a decisive role in all three: the Empire, the USA, Europe.[7]

Six months later, at Zurich University on 19 September 1946, Churchill gave another speech that attracted great attention. During this address he discussed more fully his vision for a united Europe, reiterating his conception of Britain as a benevolent but detached supporter of European unity, but he managed to remain fairly ambiguous regarding what he meant by European union, European federation, European integration or a 'United States of Europe'.

The Zurich address was influenced by a speech given by Leo Amery at London University in mid-1946. Amery in turn was impressed by the thinking of Count Coudenhove-Kalergi, who was still influential in the European unity movement on the continent.[8] Churchill's own speech was partially written by Duncan Sandys, his strongly pro-European son-in-law. Churchill tended to lose interest in the European integration question once he had made yet another ringing speech on this theme, but Sandys was responsible for 'maintaining the momentum unleashed by Churchill' on European issues during the opposition years.[9]

In his Zurich speech, Churchill called for the rebuilding of the 'European family in a regional structure' by establishing 'a kind of United States of Europe' to restore the material and spiritual wealth and happiness of the people on the continent. Such a 'regional organisation of Europe' would not conflict with the United Nations; on the contrary, it was essential to the global organization: 'the larger synthesis will only survive if it is founded upon coherent natural groupings'. Such a 'natural grouping', already existed: 'We British have our own Commonwealth of Nations. These do not weaken, on the contrary they strengthen, the world organisation. They are in fact its main support.' To save Europe from 'infinite misery' and 'final doom', an 'act of faith in the European family and an act of oblivion against all the crimes and follies of the past' were required.[10]

Churchill outlined a vision of a strong and energetic Europe based on an idea 'that will astonish you' – a policy of close Franco-German cooperation.[11] However, to close followers of his speeches Churchill's suggestion was not quite so surprising. In June 1946 he had told the House of Commons that the main threat to post-war European stability came not from a devastated Germany but resulted from the chaos, economic dislocation and accompanying social misery on the continent, a situation that could easily be exploited by the forces of international Communism.[12] In Zurich, he proposed that 'France and Germany must take the lead together':

> The first step in the re-creation of the European family must be a partnership between France and Germany. In this way only can France recover the moral leadership of Europe. There can be no revival of Europe without a spiritually great France and a spiritually great Germany. The structure of the United States of Europe, if well and truly built, will be such as to make the material strength of a single state less important. Small nations will count as much as large ones and gain their honour by their contribution to the common cause.[13]

Churchill's prescription for dealing with the defeated German nation was based on the hope that the western world would manage 'over a period of years to redeem and reincorporate' Germany into the free world. The Germans had to be fully integrated into a united Western Europe,[14] a view soon supported in influential circles in the United States.[15] However, events had persuaded him that integration would be delayed; he had told the House of Commons in June 1946 that the world had

> to face the fact that, as we are going on at present, two Germanys are coming into being ... I say it with much regret, but without any hesitancy – that, when all has been tried and tried in vain ... It is better to have a world united than a world divided; but it is also better to have a world divided than a world destroyed.[16]

In Zurich in September 1946 Churchill was realistic enough to appreciate that he could only talk about the unity of Western Europe. He explained that he envisaged the United States of Europe as a 'federal system' and expected the formation of a long overdue 'Council of Europe', which he had already advocated stubbornly but quite unsuccessfully during the war. With a view to developments in Eastern Europe, he realized that not all European states were prepared to join this system immediately.[17]

Time was running out since the protective shield of the atomic bomb would not last long. 'If we are to form the United States of Europe or whatever name or form it may take, we must begin now.' In a few years' time 'this awful agency of destruction will be widespread' and any war 'will not only bring to an end all that we call civilisation, but may possibly disintegrate the globe itself'. At the very end of the speech, to the disappointment of some, Churchill stated unambiguously that Britain would remain outside such a united Europe. 'Great Britain, the British Commonwealth of Nations, mighty America, and I trust Soviet Russia – for then indeed all would be well – must be the friends and sponsors of the new Europe and must champion its right to live and shine.'[18] Britain would merely be a mediator or at best a 'facilitator' of the unity of Europe.[19]

Despite the rousing phrases he used in Zurich and Fulton, Churchill's concept of a united Europe was still rather vague and did not go beyond the sentiments he had expressed during the war. The considerable opposition to these ideas in 1943–44 from leading politicians in the USA, the USSR and the Dominions had not affected his beliefs.[20] He held to his vision of a united Europe as a regional organization closely associated with the 'Big Three' who, as the leaders of the United Nations, would oversee European developments in a peaceful and cooperative way. For Churchill Britain was still 'with' Europe but 'not of' it, as he had expressed it as early as 1930. In Zurich in September 1946 he still held this view when he referred to Britain's 'benevolent associ-ation' with a united Europe.[21] Count Coudenhove-Kalergi's belief that now that Churchill had 'raised the European question' the British government could 'no longer ignore it' proved to be mistaken.[22] The Labour government continued to be rather lukewarm if not hostile to British participation in the movements for a more integrated Europe.

Churchill's European Image and the Congress at The Hague

In the aftermath of his Zurich speech, Churchill's support for the European unity movement was taken for granted. Due to his popularity and prestige, the entire Tory Party was often regarded as pro-European, although according to Sue Onslow, out of a total of 228 Conservative MPs there were never more than approximately 60 'hard core' pro-Europeans in the parliamentary Tory Party.[23] Churchill's larger-than-life presence on the political stage helped to give the Conservative Party a pro-European image, and he did nothing to correct the impression.

Under pressure from Duncan Sandys, Churchill agreed to become chairman of the all-party and largely non-federalist United Europe Committee, officially founded in January 1947 to promote the development of a more united continent.[24] At the inaugural meeting of the United Europe Movement (UEM) at the Royal Albert Hall in May 1947, Churchill was carried away by the enthusiastic reception prior to his address and described Britain as a full and active member of the European family; he expected that the Dominions and the Commonwealth would support this.[25]

It was not surprising that Churchill's audiences were often confused by his contradictory positions. Listeners frequently misunderstood his words, which often, but not always, clearly distanced Britain from participation in the European project. They preferred not to listen too carefully to these statements, hoped that Churchill did not really mean what he said and focused instead on his (relatively few) outspoken statements supporting Britain's joining a united Europe. His references to Britain's role in Europe were often couched in deliberately cryptic terms, since Churchill frequently made use of his high-profile addresses on European unity to embarrass the Labour government, enhance his own profile and score electioneering points for the Conservatives.[26] As Hugo Young has commented, Churchill 'encouraged Europe to misunderstand Britain, and Britain to misunderstand herself'.[27] Some authors, like Geoffrey Warner or Miriam Camps, go further and view Churchill's and the Conservative Party's strategy in the mid to late 1940s as 'irresponsible' and 'hypocritical'. Churchill was in fact no more willing than the Labour Party 'to surrender British sovereignty to the kind of federalist authority advocated at The Hague'.[28]

Yet to the British public and to most politicians on the continent, Churchill seemed far more pro-European than the Labour government, with its cautious attitude to the increasingly popular movement far European unity.[29] The Labour Party forbade its members to join Churchill's bipartisan 'United Europe Committee' and initially ordered its MPs to boycott the first Congress of Europe held in The Hague in May 1948, though in the end a delegation of 41 Labour MPs, led by Herbert Morrison, did attend the meeting.[30] In the event, the first Congress of Europe was a huge success: it was attended by over 700 delegates, including a handful of former Prime Ministers, 29 former Foreign Ministers and several active government ministers. The British Conservative Party was represented by fewer than 40 delegates.[31]

Churchill, whose influence and ideas dominated the Congress, had agreed to give the keynote speech at The Hague.[32] He received an enthusiastic reception and the applause became thunderous when he made his famous V sign which, according to one observer, made him look 'like a Giant Panda with a bamboo shoot'.[33] Although he enjoyed the attention lavished on him tremendously, he also wished to get his message across. Taking heed of the Communist coup in Prague three months earlier, Churchill was keen to use the opportunity to call upon the delegates in The Hague to start working for a more democratic and a more united Europe, though in private he had already declared that 'Nothing will induce me to be a federalist.'[34] A few days later Churchill asked the delegates at The Hague not to be content with inter-governmental organs like the Brussels Treaty Organization or the Organization for European Economic Cooperation (OEEC), which was responsible for the distribution of Marshall Plan aid, but to go further and 'resolve that in one form or another a European Assembly shall be constituted'.[35] Ultimately, Churchill's strong support and the prodigious energy of Duncan Sandys led to the establishment of the Council of Europe in May 1949, consisting of a Council of Ministers and a Consultative Assembly as Churchill had proposed.[36]

While the Labour government would have been much happier to stop with the formation of a Council of Ministers and other intergovernmental European organs, it had no choice but to show support, however lukewarm, for a European Assembly. Public enthusiasm and pressure from France and Belgium made it very difficult for Attlee and Bevin to refuse to endorse the establishment of a Consultative Parliamentary Assembly.[37] Churchill was indeed 'running a powerful "unofficial" foreign policy' and his 'vision and enthusiasm continued to exceed what Bevin and the Foreign Office considered desirable or practicable politics.'[38]

Churchill's Proposal for a European Army

A few months later, addressing the inaugural meeting of the Consultative Assembly in Strasbourg on 11 August 1949, Churchill made a dramatic proposal for the 'immediate creation of a unified European Army', including a German contingent.[39] This controversial suggestion was fiercely opposed not only in France and Britain but also in West Germany, where the violent militarism of the Hitler years had been replaced by widespread pacifist sentiments. American planners in the Pentagon, however, had already begun to develop a German rearmament policy similar to that proposed by Churchill.[40]

In early June 1950 the British Chiefs of Staff (COS) also took the same view. In a top-secret strategy paper, they recognized the need for 'some form of German armed forces', though they suggested that the build-up of French and other Western European troops should take precedence for political reasons. The COS believed that 'the formation of a German contingent within the forces of Western Europe' should be the 'ultimate aim',[41] a suggestion later revived to secure West Germany's integration into NATO. This strategy, however, would not be embarked upon until the attempts to set up a supranational European army between 1951/2 and August 1954 had failed.[42]

In late 1950, Churchill's proposal for a European army encouraged French senior civil servant Jean Monnet and his Prime Minister René Pleven to devise a scheme for a supranational European Defence Community (EDC). With the outbreak of the Korean War having demonstrated the military threats to the western world, the European Army proposal was meant to allow France to subscribe to German rearmament while avoiding the creation of an independent German army and a German general staff.

The EDC was a French compromise proposal which was eventually accepted by Washington to advance West German rearmament, and was supported by the NATO Allied Supreme Commander, and Second-World-War hero Dwight D. Eisenhower, who persuaded the Truman administration that the EDC project was a sensible way of obtaining West German rearmament without antagonizing the other European countries too much. At a western foreign ministers' conference in September 1950 the Truman administration firmly insisted on the necessity of enlisting West German soldiers in the defence of the western world. Washington was not swayed by concerns of the French and British governments about re-creating the German *Wehrmacht* and the effect that would have on public opinion.[43] Despite strong pressure from France and the US, the British government was unwilling to join a supranational European defence scheme.[44] Indeed, in June 1951 Eisenhower wrote in exasperation that there was 'a definite feeling on the Continent that Britain has failed to produce any leadership ... I think it is a general conclusion that Britain has been rather flat and colorless in the whole [European] business.'[45] This was a fair assessment.

The Labour government was equally unenthusiastic about participating in the talks on the establishment of a European Coal and Steel Community (ECSC), which was eventually instituted on 18 April 1951 without British participation. The ECSC proposal for a new organization of the European core countries, structured by industrial sectors, was first announced by French Foreign Minister Robert Schuman in May 1950. It was based on a concept drawn up by Jean Monnet and aimed above all at integrating the French and German coal and steel industries. In Paris, it was hoped that this would not only lead to economic recovery of the French coal and steel industries, prevent the predominance in Europe of their German counterparts and ensure the early detection of any secret German rearmament schemes but also lead to a more general Franco-German rapprochement.[46] The ECSC soon served as the model for the supranational structure of the planned EDC, which did not help to endear it to British politicians.

Churchill strongly criticized the Labour government's refusal to participate in the ECSC project. On 27 June 1950 he was so carried away that in the House of Commons he proclaimed that 'the whole movement of the world is towards an inter-dependence of nations'. He expressed his newly discovered conviction that 'national sovereignty is not inviolable' and should be 'resolutely diminished' for the sake of the nations concerned.[47] As he would soon demonstrate, he did not even himself believe these words. While he was in opposition, and had no need to translate his sweeping statements on European unity into practical politics, Churchill frequently advocated policies he would entirely ignore once he had returned to office. But during his years as Leader of the Opposition many continental politicians regarded Churchill as possibly the only genuine pro-European British statesman. Even the shrewd Eisenhower appears to have believed that Churchill's return to power 'would mean more emphasis on political union',[48] while Averell Harriman expected 'to see a change' in the British attitude towards European unity if Churchill came to power again.[49]

At times, the American government even worried that Churchill meant to employ 'European unity as a means for "liberating" [the] peoples of Eastern Europe', which, according to Washington, came dangerously close to implying 'offensive action' against the Soviet empire on the part of the western world.[50] However, this was not what Churchill had in mind; in fact, when considering the prolonged disagreements between Churchill and President Eisenhower in the mid 1950s about the latter's aggressive psychological warfare policy to undermine the Soviet Union, the American fears were quite paradoxical.[51] Yet,

Belgium Prime Minister Spaak was also concerned about 'Churchill's aggressive attitude'; he believed that 'it would be impossible to inspire and unify [the] peoples of Western Europe on [the] basis of a crusade against [the] Communist governments of Eastern Europe' which the author of the 'iron curtain' speech might well have in mind.[52]

However, they were all profoundly misled by Churchill's powerful rhetoric. Churchill was not contemplating an anti-Communist crusade. Moreover, despite his manifold activities on behalf of a united Europe, he continued to believe firmly in his three circles, with the United Kingdom at the centre of the British Empire and Commonwealth, the English-speaking world, and a united Europe.[53] Thus he remained convinced that his country was a special case. Politicians of all major parties in Britain and the vast majority of the British general public genuinely believed that the UK had a unique and ultimately beneficial global role and could not join the continental European nations in a federation. Together with the United States, Britain was the leader of the free world, with the additional task of guiding the inexperienced and at times somewhat brash politicians in Washington towards a responsible policy. In general, Churchill, and indeed most politicians in the UK at the time, would have agreed with Harold Macmillan's analogy describing the British as the clever and sophisticated Greeks to the more powerful but also much more vulgar and impertinent Americans, the modern-day Romans.[54]

Despite the party political rhetoric, Churchill's views on Europe hardly differed from those of Attlee and Bevin. 'Cooperation with Europe was desirable; integration with Europe was not.'[55] The main reason Churchill spoke out in favour of a united Europe during his years in opposition was his insight that the creation of a long-term friendly relationship between France and Germany was absolutely indispensable for preserving peace on the European continent. He was prepared to support this strongly since bringing this about did not require that Britain join an integrated Europe. He still held on to the traditional belief that it was Britain's task to maintain the balance of power on the continent, particularly between France and Germany.[56] This would prevent Moscow from being able to exploit any political instability in Europe.

Thus, Churchill and other post-war British leaders were 'prepared to work for a united Europe, seeing that as the only way in which Western Europe could survive in the long run as a narrow fringe on the west of the great Communist empire of Eurasia'. However, they did not intend to participate in that venture themselves. According to Denis Healey, a Labour Defence Minister in the 1960s and Chancellor of the Exchequer in the 1970s, politicians from all major parties had a 'nasty feeling' that if Britain 'went off into Europe and left the Americans outside, they would reduce their own commitment'. Securing the American commitment and thus US military and economic aid to Western Europe was the 'prime concern' which united the vast majority of politicians in Westminster.[57] The concerns Churchill expressed when towards the end of the war he declined to participate in the creation of a purely Western European bloc under British leadership were still widely shared.[58] It was still believed that setting up a Western European political organization could easily be misinterpreted in Washington as an attempt to exclude the United States from Europe at a time when protection from the Soviet Union required American commitment.

The Prime Objective: Committing the USA to Europe

The early interest of both the Labour government and the Conservative opposition in close cooperation with the states on the European continent between 1945 and 1948 has to be regarded as no more than contingency planning. The creation of an Anglo-French military alliance in March 1946 (the Dunkirk Treaty), along with Bevin's initial enthusiasm for a customs union with some of the continental European states were aspects of this policy. Similarly, the formation of a Western European Union, as envisaged in Bevin's famous speech to Parliament on 22 January 1948 and implemented with the creation of the Brussels Treaty Organization three months later, was also part of this strategy.[59] Although these schemes largely avoided supranational elements and concentrated on intergovernmental cooperation, they initially represented attempts to develop an independent British-led 'third force' in world affairs based on cooperation with the European continent.[60]

Until the beginning of the successful implementation of the Marshall Plan with the help of the OEEC in early 1948 and the subsequent negotiations that led to the creation of NATO in April 1949, Britain could not be sure of an active and benevolent American involvement in Western Europe. Bevin's policy of British–European cooperation was always regarded as a compromise solution, an alternative to an American commitment to Europe should this not materialize.[61] For both the Labour government and the Conservative opposition, American involvement in European affairs was the ultimate aim. Essentially, the European strategy of Britain's two main parties consisted of merely attempting to oversee developments on the continent in close consultation and cooperation with the United States.[62]

The chasm between the attitude prevalent in London and the view of the 'federalists' on the continent became clear to the French and others in the course of 1948–49, when the government in Paris began to propose the creation of a genuine 'European parliament'. While Bevin and Churchill were thinking in terms of a pragmatic and evolutionary 'step-by-step' approach to European cooperation, France, Italy, the Benelux countries and soon also the newly created West German state favoured a speedy formal federation to advance economic and political reconstruction. European unity was also sometimes seen as a way to neutralize Europe in the Cold War; some continental politicians continued talking about the development of a genuine European 'third force' between the two superpowers after Bevin had already abandoned the idea, but the notion also soon lost its impetus on the continent.[63]

From the announcement of the Marshall Plan in June 1947, the United States began to favour the creation of a supranational Europe where majority decision-making would apply.[64] There were several reasons behind American pressure for the speedy creation of an integrated Europe: the perception of an ever-increasing threat from the Soviet Union; a view in Congress which seemed to be inclined to make further Marshall aid dependent on progress with European integration; a worsening of the general atmosphere in Europe; and not least a lack of identity and feeling of inferiority in the new Federal Republic of Germany. Washington hoped that a revival of German nationalism and the ensuing international instability could be prevented if the West Germans were firmly and irreversibly integrated into a federally organized Western Europe.[65]

Underlying America's post-war vision was the assumption that only a fully integrated, stable and economically viable Europe would develop into a peaceful and democratic region. The achievement of prosperity in Western Europe appeared to depend on the creation of a unified single market, and the lessons from America's past as well as her federalist structure could serve as the model to achieve such a European market. Integration would prevent economic nationalism and lead to a truly free and multilateral transatlantic economic system, a strategy which would in due course make American economic aid to Western Europe unnecessary. Economic stability would close the dollar gap, permit the convertibility of European currencies, allow Europeans to export to the USA, and create a huge market for American exporters. On the whole, it was hoped that in time European integration would enable the 'self-healing' forces of the free market to take over: active American governmental support and interference were always regarded as limited and temporary.[66]

In the heady days of the late 1940s and throughout the 1950s, it appeared to Washington that the eventual unification of Europe (or at least of Western Europe) would not only ensure permanent peace and well-being on the continent but also America's long-term economic prosperity. Thus, Washington's reasons for supporting European integration were hardly altruistic.[67] In fact, European integration was the means by which the Truman administration hoped to square the circle and solve the daunting economic and military problems of the post-war world. Both Truman and his successor Dwight D. Eisenhower expected that an economically healthy Europe would be able to build up strong military forces and follow a policy of strength towards the Soviet Union. Both hoped that a prosperous Europe would allow Washington to reduce the number of troops based there, and this was important since Congress had to approve America's expensive Western European and Cold War policies.[68]

It was also expected that the creation and development of NATO and the successful implementation of George Kennan's 'strategy of containment' would help foster a sense of security and stability in Europe.[69] This would prevent any internal challenges to the NATO framework, the security roof which Washington superimposed on western political and economic integration. The system was expected to become mutually reinforcing, as it would give considerable advantages both to the United States and to Western Europe.[70] The US would be able 'to sit back and relax somewhat', while 'each and every one' of the Western Europeans 'would profit by the union of them all and none would lose'.[71]

Politicians in London, however, were not impressed by American enthusiasm for closer European union. Both Churchill and Attlee were highly suspicious of Washington's increasingly impatient demands that Britain should shoulder the responsibility of leading Western Europe into a supranational federation. Even less to their liking were American ideas that Britain should participate in such a union. President Roosevelt's declaration at the end of the war that the United States would withdraw from Europe within a short time was fresh in the minds of British politicians. The different approach of the British and continental governments and of the Americans became clear for example in disputes over whether the OEEC should adopt an integrationist or intergovernmental approach for the successful administration of Marshall Plan aid.[72]

As a result of these difficulties it was hardly surprising that the Council of Europe soon proved to be a bad compromise, as it represented the combination of a 'federal' with a 'functional' solution.[73] Although the Council included a Consultative Parliamentary Assembly, it was not a proper European parliament with legislative powers. Instead, it was merely a debating chamber ('an irresponsible talking-shop', Churchill called it), largely controlled by the Committee of Ministers – an organ based on traditional intergovernmental cooperation.[74] Indeed, Churchill was in full agreement with the Labour government when he came out strongly against attempting to turn the Council into a supranational body by changing 'the powers which belong to the duly constituted national parliaments'. Ignoring the sentiments expressed in some of his European speeches, like his Zurich address of 1946, in August

1949 he pronounced that 'such a course would be premature ... [and] detrimental to our long-term interests'.[75]

As soon became clear, the most positive feature of the Council of Europe was its very existence as a symbol of some kind of Western European cooperation and West German participation which, it was hoped, would be useful in facilitating Franco-German rapprochement.[76] The widespread belief on the continent in Churchill's enthusiasm for European integration received a cold douche from his sceptical attitude to the Council of Europe.

Churchill's European Policy as Peacetime Prime Minister

When Churchill returned to No. 10 Downing Street in late 1951, he was still widely associated with his calls for a 'united Europe' in Zurich, The Hague, Strasbourg and elsewhere. This misperception of Churchill's views led to unfounded expectations among continental politicians that Britain's European policy was about to change. This was wishful thinking. In a climate of increasing enthusiasm for European unity as an instrument to overcome the continent's post-war problems, Churchill's careful differentiation between a policy of increasing unity for continental countries and a very different policy of full independence for Britain had been either ignored or greatly misunderstood. Most American diplomats were also misled.[77] It was therefore predictable that after his return to office in October 1951 a considerable number of continental and American politicians, as well as some of the so-called pro-European members of his government, would be deeply disappointed by the European policy of the new Conservative administration.[78]

The Churchill government in turn resented the international pressure on Britain to participate in supranational institutions. Even Eisenhower's more flexible attitude was not welcomed in London. The General proposed in late 1951 that as Britain was not willing to join a European Defence Force and other integrationist schemes like the Schuman Plan, which he hoped would be 'a stepping stone toward developing political union', the Churchill government should at least 'minimize' its doubts and 'emphasize British moral, political, and military support' as a nonparticipant, if only to benefit from public opinion.[79]

Churchill very reluctantly agreed to do this. He no longer needed the issue of Europe as a means to embarrass the Labour Party or gain global attention, and once he had become Prime Minister again he had lost almost all interest in the question of European unity. Jean Monnet had discovered this early on, much to his disappointment. In late 1951, Monnet talked to the new Prime Minister until two o'clock in the morning about the necessity of establishing a surpranational European army rather than continuing with separate national armies, but was unable to sway him. Although Churchill admitted that Monnet put forward a 'powerful argument' when he reasoned that a European army might be able to prevent the old national rivalries coming to the forefront again, he remained entirely unconvinced of the military value of a European army.[80] Despite the sentiments he had voiced at Strasbourg and elsewhere, Churchill had not become a proponent of a European defence identity.[81]

Contrary to general expectations, Churchill's post-war administration did not embark upon a more open-minded policy towards the European continent. In fact, it was extremely difficult to discern any difference between his European policy and that of the previous Labour government.[82] Churchill left unaltered Labour's decision not to participate in the Schuman Plan. In 1952 Eden put forward a plan to re-design the High Authority of the ECSC and turn both the ECSC and the EDC into non-supranational bodies, linking them closely to the Council of Europe. This plan was eventually rejected by most European states.[83] Subsequently, Eden was at pains to demonstrate Britain's support for the EDC by proposing military links between the British armed forces and the European army, without however offering any substantial concessions regarding British membership of the EDC.[84]

Churchill had taken no active interest in the ill-fated Eden Plan and he remained reluctant to support any of the various initiatives between 1952 and 1954 to link Britain more closely with the EDC. His almost complete lack of interest in European integration after October 1951 would remain characteristic of his entire term as peacetime Prime Minister. In late November 1951, referring to his Zurich speech of 1946 in a cabinet paper entitled 'United Europe', Churchill made it clear that he had 'never thought that Britain ... should become an integral part of a European Federation'.[85] His government's attitude towards the EDC treaty, signed in May 1952 by France, West Germany, Italy and the Benelux countries, was never more than lukewarm. The EDC was the dominant issue during his peacetime government as far as European integration was concerned, but Churchill attempted to ignore the matter as far as possible.

However, the EDC was not only the instrument to achieve Western European rearmament on a supranational basis but also the means to integrate West Germany irreversibly with the West, giving the Federal Republic its sovereignty in return. On the insistence of the French, the validity of the so-called contractual agreements for West German sovereignty signed in May 1952 between the western allies and the West German government led by Chancellor Konrad Adenauer was linked to the successful ratification of the EDC. Thus, the realization of the EDC had important repercussions for the development of the western alliance. Although everything seemed to depend on the ratification of the EDC by its six member states,[86] Churchill saw the EDC only as a stumbling block, delaying the progress of his summit diplomacy.[87]

Despite the importance of the issues involved, the problems over ratifying the EDC did not much impress Churchill. European matters were largely left to the Foreign Secretary Anthony Eden, who was not particularly pro-Europe, and neither Churchill not his senior cabinet colleagues recognized the need to draw closer to continental Europe.[88] They were unable to see that the movement for European unity and the building of supranational European institutions could be successful and might contribute to improving Britain's economic and industrial performance.[89] Most British politicians were not prepared to dedicate time and resources to embarking on close cooperation with the weakened European states. In their eyes, Britain was still one of the 'Big Three' and had to look after its global obligations and its 'special relationship' with the United States; the United Kingdom was not merely a European state.[90] In March 1952, the former French Prime Minister Paul Reynaud summed up his frustration: 'the trouble is … that in England the statesmen are pro-European when they belong to the Opposition, and anti-European when they are in power.'[91]

Churchill would have been surprised at the suggestion that he was inconsistent. His views on European integration had not changed. The issue had never been at the heart of Churchill's policy and, with the exception of a few emotional occasions, he never saw Britain as part of a federal Europe. Foremost in his mind at all times was Britain's survival as a world power, which seemed to depend on negotiations with Moscow to bring about an early end to the Cold War. Although this aspiration might at times be linked to some loose association with Britain's European neighbours, Churchill regarded the need to overcome the East–West conflict and prevent the outbreak of a third world war as infinitely more important. Churchill's last years as Prime Minister between 1951 and 1955 therefore were not characterized by a policy of European integration but by intensive advocacy of personal summit diplomacy to overcome the Cold War and maintain Britain's perceived world power status. In his final election address in 1951 Churchill made his aims clear. He hoped that Stalin would be willing to participate in 'a friendly talk with the leaders of the free world [to] see if something could not be arranged which enabled us all to live together quietly':

> If I remain in public life at this juncture it is because, rightly or wrongly, but sincerely, I believe that I may be able to make an important contribution to the prevention of a third world war and to bring nearer that lasting peace settlement which the masses of the people … fervently desire. I pray indeed that I may have this opportunity. It is the last prize I seek to win.[92]

CHAPTER 8

Against All Odds

Return to Power and a Visit to Harry Truman

In October 1951 Churchill returned to office, though his government's majority was only 17 seats.[1] The Prime Minister was almost 77 years old and his health had been precarious for some time. In early 1952 he suffered from a period of aphasia entailing temporary confusion in his speech; he began to deteriorate more rapidly after his second stroke in July 1952.[2] Roy Jenkins aptly assesses Churchill's peacetime government as 'too much characterized by its chief's stubborn battle for [political and physical] survival to be a splendid affair'.[3]

Churchill's age and health no longer allowed him to give more or less equal consideration to all areas of government. With the exception of Egyptian affairs and the attempt to maintain Britain's role in the Middle East, Churchill concentrated almost exclusively on summit diplomacy and related issues. He neglected nearly all other external and domestic matters.[4] Increasingly it appeared to observers that he had developed a tendency 'to live completely in the past and to forget or underestimate the enormous changes which have occurred since the war in the rest of the world'.[5] But, as will be seen, this assessment was not entirely correct.

Apart from his controversial summit diplomacy, Churchill's government in the 1950s was largely a consensual affair aiming at domestic consolidation rather than radical change. He reversed only a few of the Labour government's legislative measures (notably the nationalization of iron and steel) and largely continued the policies pursued by Attlee's two administrations at home and abroad. He believed that after the socialist upheavals of the Attlee era, the 'deeply and painfully divided' British nation needed 'several years of quiet, steady administration'.[6]

As we have seen, he also abided by Attlee's sceptical approach to European integration.[7] European issues would only attract his attention when they were directly connected to his policy as a global peacemaker. Churchill was not so much concerned with the successful integration of the Federal Republic of Germany (FRG) into the West by means of the European Defence Community (EDC) as with the creation of an international détente and an end to the Cold War, thus rendering the EDC unnecessary, and negotiating an end to the division of Europe.

After becoming Prime Minister once more, Churchill concentrated his energies almost exclusively on seeking to uphold Britain's great power status by attempting to relax and perhaps even end the Cold War through an informal Anglo-American summit conference with the Soviet Union. He pursued his aims with an ever greater sense of purpose since he felt his increasing age and knew his time was running out. This would be his final chance to make a lasting contribution to world peace. Churchill's primary aim during 1951–55 was to maintain Britain's global role and ensure his reputation as a peacetime Prime Minister and the harbinger of a *modus vivendi* with Moscow. He wished to go down in history as the politician who had enabled his nation to survive during the Second World War and had then managed to preserve Britain as a great power by creating a less dangerous world.

Churchill's New Caution and Eden's Informal Diplomacy

Before commencing his attempt, Churchill felt it necessary to 'utter a word of caution'. On 6 November he told the House of Commons, 'We must be careful not to swing on a wave of emotion from despondency to over-confidence.'[8] A few days later he replied to a parliamentary question regarding his summit plans by saying that 'if circumstances are favourable' a summit conference 'should not be excluded', but currently there were no plans for such a meeting.[9]

Statements like these were music to the ears of Konrad Adenauer, who had become the first Chancellor of the newly created West German state in September 1949. Adenauer and Churchill had much in common: both were of a similar age (born in 1874, Adenauer was two years younger) and both led large but not very homogeneous Conservative parties which were likely to make trouble for their leaders. Adenauer was largely unknown outside West Germany and had yet to prove his reliability to the western allies, but as the East–West divide became more pronounced, his role as the head of government of the country at the front line of the Cold War became crucial.[10]

Although Adenauer would soon become one of the western allies' most trusted friends, he always managed to retain his independent spirit and was inclined to view critically the policy emanating from Washington, London and Paris. On the whole, it was clear that the USA stood 'well above the UK and French in German estimation'. Washington's powerful position as leader of the western alliance and Marshall aid for German reconstruction were highly appreciated.[11] Adenauer viewed the British with particular distrust. Ever since Churchill's speech in Edinburgh in February 1950, the Chancellor had regarded his comments on summit diplomacy with Moscow with suspicion,[12] and in the months and years after Stalin's death Adenauer, together with his close political friend John Foster Dulles, was to become one of Churchill's severest critics. Even during Adenauer's state visit to London on 3–8 December 1951, the first by a German Chancellor since 1931, Anthony Eden became aware of his mistrust and informed Churchill accordingly.[13]

The Chancellor seemed to fear that the British government 'might be brought to do a deal with Russia behind the back of the German government'. The Prime Minister reassured Adenauer that he 'ardently desired to restore a tolerable relationship with Russia' but that this would not be done at the expense of Germany: 'He would not do such a thing even to avoid a war.' Adenauer indicated his gratitude for Churchill's assurance 'in regard to the firm resolve of the British government not to embark on any transactions with the Russians to the detriment of German interests',[14] but he did not entirely trust Churchill's pledge. When talking to other politicians and to the British press, he repeatedly stressed that the creation of a neutral Germany would be disadvantageous to the western world. A return to Potsdam, and thus to 'Big Three' cooperation and to the treatment of Germany as a powerless object of international politics, would entail great dangers for the whole of Europe. Churchill was again quick to promise Adenauer that he would not sacrifice German interests for a rapprochement with Moscow.[15]

Within a few weeks of taking office, the Prime Minister had become generally rather pessimistic about the prospects for 'Big Three' summit diplomacy. He had sent Stalin a telegram of greetings as soon as he resumed power, but Stalin's somewhat restrained response left little room for hope. Instead of congratulating him on his election victory, Stalin curtly replied 'Thank you for greetings'. Although Churchill attempted a positive twist – 'Apparently we are again on speaking terms which is about as much as I expected at this stage' – he could not have failed to notice Stalin's lack of interest in more intensive lines of communication with Britain. The Soviet dictator certainly did not seem to be interested in a personal meeting.[16]

A further disappointment came with Foreign Secretary Eden's unsuccessful attempts to resume diplomatic contact with Moscow between November 1951 and January 1952. In the late 1940s, before the Conservatives were returned to power, Eden had largely agreed with Dean Acheson and had expressed considerable scepticism about negotiations with the Soviet Union.[17] But in 1950, in the context of the outbreak of the Korean War and the heated discussions in the western world about German rearmament, Eden changed his mind and became convinced of the necessity of negotiations with Moscow. Unlike Churchill, however, he insisted on a firm agenda for such talks. In February 1951 he told the House of Commons that on 'the question of conversations with Russia' he had 'always believed that if the Soviets were prepared to take part in discussions which gave even modest hopes of relieving the tension, which is not confined to Germany alone, we ought to make the attempt'. Eden thought there was 'not the slightest use going back to the kind of slanging match as has taken place at previous Foreign Ministers' Conferences ... We ought to try to draw up an agenda for this meeting with the Soviets, which is wider than covering Germany alone.'[18]

After the failure of the lengthy Palais Marbre Rose conference in June 1950 after 74 unsuccessful meetings,[19] Eden came to believe that informal talks with the Soviet Union might be more productive after all. In view of the fact that international tension was increasing, he saw an urgent need to embark upon some kind of dialogue with the East as contact had effectively ceased since the start of the Korean War. Eden decided that in the past East–West negotiations had been too ambitious, as these talks had tried to solve all East–West problems at once. Instead of beginning with 'package proposals', Eden now thought both sides 'should drop ambitious plans and meetings' to handle the problems of the Cold War. He now began to advocate choosing 'detailed topics and working them out one by one'.[20]

Unlike Churchill, Eden was convinced of the correctness of the Foreign Office view, as expressed by Deputy Under-Secretary Roger Makins, that there was 'no short cut to peace through a high level meeting'. However, it seemed eminently sensible that the West attempt 'to solve outstanding problems individually by discussion and negotiation' and seek to improve East–West relations gradually by means of a 'step-by-step approach'.[21] In his memoirs, Eden described his dismay at the situation he found when he became Foreign Secretary again in October 1951: 'The relations between Russia and the Western powers were vituperative and bad. Meetings of the United Nations were often the occasion of slanging matches, never of negotiation. This was not only a disagreeable state of affairs, it was also dangerous. ... I thought I must make an immediate effort to try to put a stop to name-calling.'[22]

An opportunity arose in early November, when the meeting of the sixth General Assembly of the United Nations was due to begin in Paris.[23] Shortly before polling day, Eden had been informed that the Polish ambassador had expressed the view that 'a change at the Foreign Office could improve East–West relations',[24] and a few days after becoming Foreign Secretary (for the third time), Eden gained the impression in the course of a conversation with the ambassador that 'the Soviet countries might not be averse to some informal discussions arising at Paris'.[25] The United Nations secretariat had also informed Selwyn Lloyd, Minister of State and, in Eden's absence, leader of the British UN delegation, that Moscow appeared to be interested in talks with Eden in Paris.[26] Both Eden and Churchill took this to be a most encouraging signal, particularly since in the aftermath of the Conservative election victory Moscow had been quite restrained in its anti-British pronouncements.

Thus, almost immediately after returning to the Foreign Office Eden sent Soviet Foreign Minister Vyshinsky a note in which he emphasized his willingness to embark on informal talks. He dropped similar hints in two public statements but he was not prepared to go any further without some positive reaction from Moscow.[27] However, Vyshinsky's speech to the Paris meeting of the General Assembly of the United Nations on 8 November 1951 was characterized by 'terrifying violence'. Nevertheless, in front of hundreds of journalists, Eden and Vyshinsky had 'quite a friendly looking encounter'; a more private chat had not been possible and, in view of the tenor of the Soviet Foreign Minister's speech, Eden's officials from the Foreign Office had advised strongly against it.[28] (The ever-suspicious West German Chancellor was told by his adviser Herbert Blankenhorn, who observed Eden's brief chat with Vyshinsky, that the British Foreign Secretary greeted the Soviet politician 'heartily'.[29]) Despite this unhelpful episode, UN Secretary General Trygve Lie felt able to confirm shortly afterwards that Moscow appeared to be looking for an informal exchange of views with the British government. Lie said that he would inform the Soviet UN ambassador Zinchenko of Eden's willingness to enter into informal talks.[30] During a subsequent conversation with Eden in London, Georgi Zaroubin, the Soviet ambassador, confirmed Moscow's general interest in a meeting between Eden and Vyshinsky in the course of the UN conference in Paris.[31]

Eden liked what the ambassador told him; the Foreign Secretary was still rather keen on informal talks with the Soviet government. He intended to make an official visit to Paris, so he would be able to talk to Vyshinsky without attracting too much public interest. In view of the touchiness of both the United States and West Germany, Eden wished to avoid undue attention.[32] He told the Soviet ambassador that he 'did not wish such an informal discussion to become an earth-shaking event, and therefore ... hoped that no indication would be given that the meeting might take place. The meeting must be informal, and, while the Prime Minister knew about it, no-body else should know even of the possibility of such a meeting at this time.' Eden went on to say that he 'shared' the Soviet ambassador's view 'on the understanding that in whatever we discussed we would, of course, stand loyal to our obligations and do nothing behind the backs of our friends, but even so we had a responsibility to meet and try to make progress.'[33]

On 31 December Eden accompanied Churchill on an extended visit to the USA and Canada.[34] Within the week, the fall of the French government led by Prime Minister René Pleven robbed Eden of his official reason for visiting Paris, which he regarded as 'essential if my meeting with Vyshinsky was to be kept informal and secret'.[35] It took almost two weeks before the socialist Edgar Faure succeeded in forming a new government on 20 January; the Christian Democrat Robert Schuman was again appointed Foreign Minister. The day after the new government was installed, Eden asked Schuman to invite him to Paris for 1 February. However, Vyshinsky had already told the press that he intended to return to Moscow on 22 January. Eden was annoyed. He assumed that Vyshinsky had known about his willingness to meet since his conversation with Soviet ambassador Zaroubin on 28 December and would postpone his departure from Paris until after Eden's arrival. The Foreign Secretary concluded that 'we have not to reproach ourselves'. It appeared that the Soviet government was no longer interested in embarking on informal talks, though the initiative for such meetings had come from Moscow.[36]

Although Eden's biographer Victor Rothwell agrees that Vyshinsky 'did not wish to meet Eden',[37] it appears that Eden's reaction was somewhat exaggerated. The Soviet government may well have received a similar impression of disinterest on the part of the British government. After all, Eden had not managed to travel to Paris to meet Vyshinsky though he had found the time to go to Washington. The British Foreign Office had not considered it necessary to approach the Soviet embassy in Paris or Moscow's UN delegation and officially request a delay of Vyshinsky's departure for Moscow. Rothwell's conclusion that Eden 'gained rather than lost by not seeing him in 1952' is understandable in view of the Soviet politician's involvement in Stalin's gruesome purges in the 1930s,[38] but in regard to improving East–West relations a talk between Eden and Vyshinsky could have done no harm. Eden himself certainly thought along these lines and believed that a meeting with the man, whose death in 1954 he was unable to regret, would have been desirable.

Thus at the beginning of 1951, Eden was not opposed to high-level talks with Moscow. As in mid-1955, when he was Prime Minister, this can largely be explained by the fact that he was involved personally. Contrary to the view widely expressed in the literature,[39] and in contrast to his attitude in 1953–54, in late 1951 Eden agreed with Churchill on the merits of engaging in a dialogue with the Kremlin. Churchill was therefore able to declare quite truthfully in the House of Commons in November 1951 that he and his Foreign Secretary acted 'in the closest, spontaneous accord' as far as East–West relations were concerned.[40] A year later, referring to the UN meeting in Paris in November 1951, Eden told Selwyn Lloyd:

> The main problems that confronted us when we took over were to try to bring some reduction of tension between the East and the West, hence our appeals and our practice to refrain from slanging matches at international assemblies, and try to get the temperature down and tackle any minor points where agreement might be possible.[41]

In early 1952 the only difference of opinion between Eden and Churchill on summit diplomacy was that the Prime Minister preferred the public dynamic of a meeting of the 'Big Three' while Eden thought it wiser to engage, at least initially, in informal talks away from the gaze of the media. The public was, therefore, kept in ignorance of the Foreign Secretary's unsuccessful summit initiatives. Selwyn Lloyd referred briefly to the British attempts in the House of Commons on 5 February 1952, when he said that the government had 'made great efforts to impress the Soviet *bloc* with the peaceful intentions of this country and to establish some kind of common ground with them, in spite of their constant and abusive rebuffs'.[42] Both Eden and Churchill felt let down by Moscow in their quest for an improvement of East–West relations. They encountered similar difficulties in the course of their visit to Washington.

Uneasy Partners: Churchill Visits President Truman

When Churchill visited Truman in January 1952, the main topics of discussion were problems in the Far East, the Middle East and South-east Asia as well as atomic, strategic and intelligence matters. Britain's economic difficulties, the lack of progress with the EDC[43] and the organization of NATO (Churchill adamantly refused to accept an American as head of NATO's Atlantic Command) were also given high priority.[44] Discussion of how to achieve an East–West détente took up very little time. Churchill and Truman only talked about it twice. The topic was mentioned indirectly during their first informal conversations on board the presidential yacht on the evening of 5 January, and was not considered extensively until the final round of British–American conversations almost two weeks later. When Churchill addressed a joint session of Congress on 17 January, he avoided the issue of détente, merely indicating at the end of his speech that there might be a possibility 'that presently a new mood will reign behind the Iron

Curtain'. If there were new developments in the Kremlin, it would be 'easy for them to show it but the democracies must be on their guard against being deceived by a false dawn'.[45]

Churchill was aware that East–West détente was a touchy subject for both Congress and the Truman administration. Perhaps, as has been suggested, he merely intended to use his visit to the US to concentrate on reviving the 'special relationship' in the hope that a strong bond with Truman would be the basis of a later détente.[46] While Churchill undoubtedly saw the urgent need to 're-establish relations' and to demonstrate that there existed a 'real partnership' between London and Washington,[47] he was also keen to gain direct and immediate support for his summit diplomacy, but he had decided to move carefully and to avoid any open clashes with the Truman administration.

The Americans were unsure whether he would raise the issue. They expected the 'informal introduction' of the subject and this was in fact the way Churchill intended to raise the topic of summit diplomacy.[48] Washington had already indicated its opposition to a high-level conference. In October 1951 the State Department had decided that 'Churchill should be warned not to proceed hastily or publicly',[49] and the American ambassador, Walter Gifford, was instructed to let the new Prime Minister know that the United States had 'grave doubts as to the desirability of any such meeting, as there has been no indication of any change in the Soviet attitude which would imply the Soviets would be prepared to reach realistic accommodations on any of the issues creating tensions today'.[50]

In case Churchill were to press the matter during his visit to Washington, the State Department had prepared a speaking note for Truman outlining that the US had 'not abandoned ... the idea of negotiation as a way of handling our differences with the Soviet Union'. However, the 'best form of contact' did not seem yet another high-level meeting at foreign ministers' level but to 'maintain contacts with Soviet officials' without 'all the fanfare' and 'through regular diplomatic levels'. Churchill should be told that this was the reason why Truman had decided to send George Kennan as ambassador to Moscow. Kennan was 'very well suited to this type of informal contact and discussion with Soviet officials if he is given the chance'. The failure of yet another top-level meeting would only 'plunge world opinion into the deepest gloom'. Washington was not convinced that the western world could 'hope to bring about any miraculous changes in Soviet policy' by means of negotiations. Churchill should be informed that the President sincerely hoped that he 'would not make a public proposal for a meeting with Stalin' as it would put Truman 'in the embarrassing position of having to say' that while he was always 'glad to see Stalin in Washington', he did 'not desire to pay him a visit in his capital'.[51]

However, there was more at stake than a divergence over the level at which contacts with Moscow should be pursued. The Truman administration recognized the fundamental difference of approach between London and Washington regarding relations with the Soviet Union: due to Britain's geographical proximity to the USSR and its vulnerability to attack from the air, the UK was 'apt to put great weight on the narrow objective of reducing tensions'.[52] As the US was still invulnerable from such attacks, explained Charles Bohlen, one of the State Department's foremost Soviet experts, a war would be 'much more catastrophic for the UK than for the US'. He believed that this had led to 'a greater degree of caution', even 'timidity' on the part of the British. According to Bohlen, this had already resulted in a predisposition in London 'to play down the extent of the Soviet menace and an accompanying tendency, its natural corollary, to play up the possibilities of settlements through diplomatic means'.[53] State Department official H. Freeman Matthews believed that matters were made even more complicated by the fact that Churchill still held the mistaken view 'that the meetings with Stalin during the war produced good results. He likes the face-to-face method of approach.'[54]

Indeed, while Churchill thought that the danger of war was decreasing and that the West ought to attempt to find a more or less permanent settlement with the Soviet Union and thus bring the Cold War to an end,[55] Washington had a very different strategy in mind. The Truman administration believed that the best course of action was to continue building the strength of the western world 'so that we will be in a position to continue the cold war on terms increasingly advantageous to the West'. Although it was not the policy of the USA to force 'a showdown with the U.S.S.R.', 'opportunities for poisoning the relations between the Kremlin and its satellites and [thus for] weakening the hold of the communist regimes over the people' should be exploited.[56] The American government believed that the West ought to 'put greater emphasis on working toward that degree of strength and solidarity in the free world that will permit us to look forward to a retraction of the U.S.S.R. and a modification of the Soviet system'. According to Acheson's understanding of the 'doctrine of containment', which had little in common with George Kennan's original much more restrained thinking,[57] the US needed to build up American strength. It would be 'dangerous to freeze an unsatisfactory situation'.[58]

There was little understanding in British political circles of American long-term objectives, which were intended to bring about a drastic change in the Soviet system and, perhaps, the roll-back of Soviet power. In London, this strategy was viewed as provocative. American officials were fully aware, as a top secret document makes clear, that the British questioned 'the necessity or desirability of political warfare operations' and favoured instead the acceptance of the status quo.[59]

Washington's position was not without contradictions. The American political warfare paper of 6 January 1952 emphasized that 'In no sense, however, do we propose to foment premature and useless large-scale sabotage or armed revolt in the USSR or the satellite area'. But it also proposed that in view of the Soviet Union's 'massive' psychological warfare attack on the 'free world', the West 'must counter-attack by political warfare activities directed against the USSR itself and against the Soviet satellites of Eastern Europe with the objective of increasing the discontent, tensions and divisions known to exist in the Soviet orbit'. The authors of the paper considered that 'on balance, this positive activity will operate to deter rather than to provoke the Soviet Union to military aggression'. They realized that the Soviet leaders were 'extremely sensitive to any activity designed to undermine Moscow's domination', but they believed that 'the risk must be taken and that political warfare measures will serve to augment the difficulties of the Kremlin in Sovietizing this area and, in case of armed conflict, reduce Soviet military capabilities'.[60]

London was not quite as averse to considering psychological warfare activities as the Americans believed. In December 1951, Roger Makins, who the following month took up his new post as British ambassador to Washington, had recommended a 'controlled and phased counter-attack against the Soviet empire' to cause 'trouble and disturbance' among the satellite countries. Makins believed that 'intensified psychological warfare operations' combined with 'firm and patient negotiations from strength' might 'eventually lead to fundamental changes in the nature of the Soviet system'. This should be the western world's 'ultimate objective' and would make possible a 'genuine settlement' with the Kremlin.[61]

This approach was the basis of a paper forwarded to the Truman administration by the British embassy in Washington on 7 January 1952, when Churchill was already conferring with the President. Entitled 'Future Policy Towards Soviet Russia', the paper stopped short of recommending the forceful liberation and incitement to mass revolt of the Soviet satellite states, but spoke of 'useful' measures which could be taken to provoke major difficulties in the satellite countries. It suggested that 'subversive operations' ought to be part 'of a wide-scale psychological attack on the political structure of the Soviet orbit' and would constitute a 'controlled and phased counter-attack against the Soviet empire' to win the Cold War. The Foreign Office emphasized, however, that 'intensified psychological warfare operations' should go hand in hand with the policy of attempting to reach a *modus vivendi* with the Soviet Union, to be achieved 'by negotiating settlements, each one probably local and limited in character, which would improve the Western position and which might be expected to lead cumulatively to a general stabilization' of the East–West conflict. Although the Foreign Office did not entirely rule out political warfare, the aim of the British policy appeared no longer to be a 'conclusive victory' in the Cold War, as the Chiefs of Staff had advocated in June 1950.[62] Instead, the British were prepared to accept the Soviet Union's sphere of influence and the division of the world into East and West and were in favour of creating situations of peaceful co-existence. As the Foreign Office paper of January 1952 made clear, 'A long period of peace is essential if the British economic position is to be restored'.[63] Churchill had long since recognized this; in fact, it was one of the driving forces behind his summit diplomacy. How could Britain rally its political and economic forces to revive and maintain its world power position if the country became embroiled in a potentially even more devastating conflict than the Second World War?[64]

The American Policy Planning Staff, however, were not impressed by the British paper. It was regarded as a rather 'feeble effort' compared with 'the brilliant presentation contained in NSC 68', the notoriously aggressive American policy paper of April 1950 which called for an all-out western push to combat international Communism with all direct and indirect means available.[65] In Washington, Britain's position was viewed as defeatist; the British seemed to be prepared to 'avoid irritating the USSR on its "sore spots" world-wide' and be ready 'to give ground in fields which are not considered by the British to be of vital sensitivity to them'.[66] While it was recognized that London had at least made an effort to contemplate proposals for psychological warfare activities, the Foreign Office paper was dismissed as too soft. Reading between the lines, the American officials perceived indications of 'a distinct weariness about the feasibility of such measures' on the part of the British.[67] The Foreign Office paper was seen as an 'extreme' position; to the Americans the document appeared to call for a distasteful programme of 'accommodation' with the Soviet Union 'which might border on appeasement'.[68] Yet the British paper had not even mentioned a high-level meeting with Stalin. The document had merely attempted to outline how to arrive at a peaceful settlement with Moscow while also indicating the potential usefulness of some political warfare activities. The American perception, however, was entirely different:

The [Foreign Office] document recommends reaching an accommodation with the USSR through negotiations and without the use of armed force anywhere, even in its recommendations regarding what is termed a 'counterattack against the Soviet Empire.' This counterattack, as envisaged by the British, in the Conclusions to this paper, apparently would be limited to psychological and possibly economic warfare operations coupled with 'patient negotiations.'[69]

Instead of improving the coordination of Anglo-American strategy during Churchill's talks with Truman, the Foreign Office paper contributed to persuading the State Department and the Policy Planning Staff that their British allies lacked the stamina to fight the Cold War.[70] Washington whole-heartedly dismissed the British approach.

What worried Bohlen and the American foreign policy establishment was not only Churchill's tendency, as witnessed during the Second World War, to embark on personal diplomacy. This was bad enough. However, they also found confirmation of their fears regarding the Prime Minister's dangerous inclination to think in terms of spheres of influence solutions. Churchill's 1944 agreement with Stalin was well remembered in Washington. The State Department and the American military were sure that Churchill was still convinced 'that the world can be divided up in such a way that Stalin will agree to stay here and we will agree to stay there'.[71] The Foreign Office paper received from the British embassy in January 1952 seemed to confirm this position. Although eventually this would become more or less the unofficial *modus vivendi* entered into by Washington and Moscow after the 1962 Cuban Missile Crisis, in the early 1950s such a view was regarded as a dangerous misper-ception of the inherent aggressive tendencies in Soviet Communism which needed to be actively opposed. As John Charmley puts it, 'the Americans were attempting to construct a global strategy of containment', whilst 'the British still seemed obsessed with their old-fashioned notions of spheres of influence'.[72] However, Charmley's implied criticism of London's strategy is unfair; it ignores the fact that ultimately Washington's globalism failed. Eventually, President Kennedy and his successors had no choice but to accept the division of the world into an eastern and a western sphere of influence, abandon the American dream of political warfare, and embark on a policy of détente, as had been long advocated by Churchill and others.

In late 1951 and early 1952 the US deplored the fact that there was no tendency in Britain, 'and certainly not in Mr Churchill', to indicate a 'moral recoil' from the method 'of settling big-power differences' by means of summit diplomacy and uneasy compromises. Bohlen believed that due to 'generations of experience' and a certain habit of working within the context of 'expediency' and 'power realism', British politicians seemed to be 'less sensitive' to the accusation of 'appeasement' than their American counterparts.[73] Bohlen thought that spheres of influence solutions were 'for moral reasons ... quite unacceptable to the American people'.[74] In fact, he was less concerned with the morality of the American people than with the forces of McCarthyism. A vicious onslaught on the administration from Senator Joe McCarthy and his followers could be expected if Truman were to show any inclination to enter into summit diplomacy with Moscow. The American public, whipped up by McCarthy's anti-Communist crusade since the Senator's notorious speech in Wheeling, Virginia, in February 1950, would not tolerate any indication that the administration was ready to leave the 'captive peoples' in Eastern Europe to their fate and allow Stalin to dominate them forever. The administration's rhetoric, though not necessarily its practical policy, had to demonstrate firm anti-Communist convictions. Moreover, even if an uneasy spheres of influence deal were entered into with Moscow as the best way to prevent a war – the solution favoured by the British – western politicians could still have no confidence in Stalin actually keeping his word and observing its terms.[75]

With regard to practical policy-making, however, the State Department was quite prepared to adopt a piecemeal approach to solving specific East–West problems with Moscow. It was Churchill's preference for organizing a major 'Big Three' event to solve all or at least most major East–West problems that was regarded as grossly unrealistic.[76] The administration could pursue a relatively low-level step-by-step strategy without raising the suspicions of the American public and the right wing of the Republican Party, but a big event like a three-or four-power conference could not easily be explained away while fighting in Korea continued.

After the outbreak of the war in late June 1950 General Douglas MacArthur's counter-offensive had initially led to the capture of the North Korean capital Pyongyang; the Communist forces were even driven back as far as the Yalu river on the Chinese border. However, in late November 1950 Chinese and North Korean troops staged a counter-attack; they pushed far into South Korea, eventually capturing Seoul, the capital, in January 1951. By mid-March 1951 the western UN forces had managed to free Seoul and repulsed a Chinese offensive in April. From then on the war developed into a stalemate concentrating on the 38th parallel, the old line of division between the two Koreas as drawn up at the end of the Second World War. MacArthur's repeated criticism of Truman's decision not to attempt another invasion of North Korea and run the risk of further Chinese involvement or even the use of atomic weapons led to his dismissal and replacement by General Ridgeway in early April 1951. While protracted truce negotiations broke down repeatedly small scale military action with heavy casualties on both sides continued without either side making any substantial territorial gains. Naturally the unresolved and potentially highly dangerous situation in Korea contributed much to Cold War tension in the early 1950s. An armistice in Korea had to be achieved before East–West negotiations would be remotely feasible.[77]

The Personal Factor, the 'Special Relationship', and 'Summit Diplomacy'

As well as seeking to overcome American opposition to a summit meeting, Churchill faced an additional problem during this visit: Truman was determined not to be taken in by his personal charm. The President insisted on a formal agenda and spurned Churchill's attempts to hold impromptu meetings without a specific agenda. As always, the Prime Minister would have preferred to deal with the many problems which needed to be discussed by means of a personalized 'broad-sweep approach'.[78] Truman, however, wished to have his advisers present during the meetings with the British delegation; in general, he ignored Churchill's and Eden's request for the attendance of 'a very limited number of advisors only'.[79] After all, according to the American ambassador to London, Churchill was 'definitely aging' and was 'no longer able to retain his full clarity and energy for extended periods'. He also seemed to be 'increasingly living in the past and talking in terms of conditions no longer existing'. It therefore seemed to be wise to ensure the presence of senior advisers during the talks with the 'notoriously unpredictable' Prime Minister.[80]

The Americans also doubted that Churchill had a clear understanding of Britain's economic predicament and the country's deterioration in world affairs. It was assumed that the Prime Minister probably believed that persuading Washington to support his policies was the main problem. However, Truman's officials agreed that the 'deep and complex' issues of 'Britain's decline' had to be confronted. The UK's global power was disintegrating and when it eventually collapsed the US would once again be expected to pick up the pieces.[81] In general, the Americans thought Britain was not making sufficient effort to improve its economy. They did not hesitate to voice their criticism, which the British strongly repudiated, pointing to their extraordinary military effort in keeping international Communism at bay and contributing to the defence of the western world.[82] Clashes of opinion on these and other issues meant that Churchill's visit was regarded with mixed feelings in the American capital.

In his memoirs, Truman referred to 'a welcome reunion with an old friend' and his 'distinct pleasure' at seeing Churchill again, but in fact the President had not been keen on the visit.[83] Churchill had wished to set off for Washington almost as soon as he had won the election in October, but the President asked him to postpone his visit.[84] Both Truman and Acheson were afraid of the hostile reaction of the increasingly influential McCarthyites if they embarked on summit diplomacy with Moscow, and they also feared opposition in Congress to any economic or political deals entered into with their British visitors. During the early Cold War years the legislators on Capitol Hill had a tendency to suspect that any 'perfidious' British delegation would dominate the good-natured American politicians and extract commitments and understandings which would not only be costly but might also be politically unacceptable to Congress.[85]

Thus in advance of Churchill's visit a large number of position papers and memoranda was prepared.[86] The White House hoped to ensure that Churchill would 'return in a good mood' brought about by 'long, intimate and frank discussions' and 'the most courteous attention'. The United States needed Britain to continue playing its part in supporting America's Cold War strategy, not least in Korea. But Truman agreed with his advisers that 'no material concessions or changes in U.S. policy' should be promised.[87] It was therefore not Churchill's reputation, his age or his 'trouble-making capacity' that persuaded the Truman administration to treat Churchill kindly as is sometimes maintained.[88] Above all, it was Washington's desire to prevent a split in the western world's common front in Europe and the Far East that motivated American patience with the British visitors. Washington was also fully aware of the importance of the American strategic air bases in East Anglia as a launch pad for an atomic attack on the Soviet Union should this prove necessary; although the development of bases in Spain was being contemplated, the existence of crucial facilities in England was an important reason for humouring the British delegation.[89] Washington was aware that Churchill intended to exploit the importance of these bases to the US by driving a hard bargain for American economic support. He was bound to insist on prior consultation and the necessity of a joint decision if the bases were to be used to launch an atomic attack 'in an emergency'. Churchill believed that a 'firm commitment' in the matter had already been given during Attlee's visit in 1950.[90]

Naturally, the United States were also interested in generally improving Anglo-American relations. The relationship was perceived as having suffered under Herbert Morrison's stewardship of the Foreign Office and it was felt in Washington that it should be possible to restore the fairly smooth working relationship which had existed under Ernest Bevin. However, hardly anyone within the American government had any interest in reconstructing Anglo-American relations along the lines of the exceptional partnership between Roosevelt and Churchill, which, of course, had not been as close as Churchill liked to believe. The Americans feared that the Prime Minister wished to go back to the Anglo-American intimacy of the war years, once again making frequent use of the transatlantic telephone and proposing 'a Combined Chiefs of Staff in the economic and military fields'.[91]

Washington had no interest in going that far. While the American government was in favour of an 'ad hoc arrangement for early consultation' and believed in the exchange of 'the frankest views', Truman was strongly opposed to establishing a 'formal consultative machinery' between Britain and the USA. This would only impair relations with other friendly countries and might even restrict Washington's 'right to approach third countries' such as members of the British Commonwealth.[92] In the course of the six formal rounds of conversations, the President did not hesitate to repeatedly cut off 'the old man's powerful and emotional declarations of faith in Anglo-American co-operation' with a rude and wounding 'Thank you Mr Prime Minister', suggesting that their advisers should work that out. Truman thus avoided entering into any major new commitments or being pushed into the necessity of making more than the customary grand declarations.[93] Acheson concluded that from Washington's point of view the American strategy was 'brilliantly successful'.[94]

This was certainly the case as far as Churchill's pet subject, summit diplomacy, was concerned. Both Truman and Acheson continued to view the spectacle of a three- or four-power summit as wasteful and unproductive. 'Summit meetings of heads of government, except to ratify agreements already reached, were anathema to me,' wrote Acheson in his memoirs.[95] Churchill was confronted with this view during the initial informal talks on board the presidential yacht, the *Williamsburg*, on 5 January 1952. Apart from Truman, Acheson, Eden and the Prime Minister, eight advisers participated.

It became clear during their conversation that Acheson remained convinced of the necessity to build up the West's military strength, for example by means of the EDC and a West German contribution to the western defence. He believed that Moscow was intent on expanding its influence not by war, which was too risky, but by more subversive means. He did not expect a 'mass attack on Western Europe' but feared 'creeping actions' through the satellite states 'which would exhaust the Western powers'.[96] On the whole, the Secretary of State did not think that it would be possible to arrive at a settlement of the Cold War in the foreseeable future. At best it could be hoped that the West would be able 'to create sufficient forces to make any action by the Soviet Union in Europe too dangerous to be attempted'.[97]

As in the past, Eden largely agreed with Acheson's views on the East–West conflict. However, he emphasized his willingness to initiate informal talks with Moscow on more specific issues like Austria and, as outlined above, he had already begun to turn this strategy into practice with his attempts to arrange informal meetings with Soviet Foreign Minister Vyshinsky.[98] Churchill indicated his belief that 'the central factor in Soviet policy was fear'. He was convinced that Moscow 'feared our friendship more than our enmity'. The Prime Minister expressed the hope 'that the growing strength of the West would reverse this, so that they would fear our enmity more than our friendship and would be led thereby to seek our friendship'.[99] Thus, only very indirectly and in the most diplomatic way had Churchill indicated his interest in embarking on East–West negotiations.

Although nobody used the opportunity to begin talking about the Prime Minister's idea of attempting to organize a summit with Moscow, Churchill felt greatly encouraged by the frank and intimate atmosphere of the *Williamsburg* talks. In characteristic fashion, he deluded himself and entirely ignored the fact that he had not been able to make any progress in persuading the Truman administration of the value of his summit diplomacy. The Prime Minister later professed great enjoyment of the evening with the Americans: 'We talked as equals'.[100] Even Acheson spoke of an 'excellent atmosphere' and a 'most successful' meeting.[101] Churchill believed that the 'governance of the world' had been assembled 'not to dominate it ... but to save it'. The ever sober Acheson, however, 'had been more conscious of omnibrooding problems than of overshadowing salvation'.[102] The American had also noticed other signals. Although Acheson regarded Churchill as 'still formidable and quite magnificent', he came to believe that the Prime Minister was not quite as impressive as he had been when he had met him during the war and in 1946. The health and vigour of 'the old lion' appeared 'to be weakening'.[103]

Perhaps it came as no surprise to Acheson that Churchill did not defend his summit plans very vigorously when the topic eventually came up at the final round of formal discussions on 18 January, the day after his address to a joint session of Congress and after Eden's return to England.[104] Truman expressed the opinion that Stalin was not interested in genuine talks. The earlier failure of the Council of Foreign Ministers' meetings, the more recent unsuccessful Palais Marbre Rose conference, Vyshinsky's dire performance at the United Nations and his other insulting outbursts, including his referring to the American commanding general in Korea as a 'cannibal', seemed to allow no other conclusion. Moscow did not seem to be in a 'conciliatory mood'. Whilst Truman emphasized, as prescribed by his speaking notes, that he had no interest in a 'showdown' with Moscow, he warned about creating false expectations which would be impossible to fulfil even if a meeting was ever to take place. But he did not think that the Russians wanted a summit conference.[105]

Churchill agreed there was a danger that people in East and West would assume that war might be 'inevitable' if a summit meeting failed. He hoped that the power of the United States 'might induce the Russians to be reasonable', although he admitted that 'one could not be sure of this, and the

Russians might not be reasonable'.[106] Churchill then proceeded to outline a rather strange idea of how to put East–West relations back on track if a high-level meeting of the heads of governments had broken up in acrimony. He explained that after the breakdown of a summit meeting he would immediately introduce an 'intermediate stage' consisting of 'an intensification of the cold war' and an 'intense propaganda campaign' to inform the captive peoples in Eastern Europe of the true world situation. Such revelations would be greatly feared by the Soviet leaders. Then the summit conference 'might be resumed with greater hope of success'.[107]

It was no wonder that Truman and Acheson were not very impressed by these fanciful notions. Churchill's proposal appears to have contributed to undermining his authority and the general respect for him as a sensible world leader and elder statesman. Truman felt it necessary to inform him flatly that 'the time was not ripe' for summit diplomacy. Whilst the President proclaimed himself 'in favor of anything that would prevent war', he forcefully rejected the idea of travelling to Moscow. Instead, he expressed his willingness to meet at any time with Marshal Stalin in the USA, knowing perfectly well that this was a scenario Stalin was most unlikely to accept.[108] There was some fear in American circles that Churchill might propose to go to Moscow by himself, as it 'would help him politically in Britain'. The Prime Minister's tendency to speak 'for the Americans as well as [for] the British' meant that most politicians in Washington believed that such a journey would entail 'great dangers'.[109] However, Churchill did not propose this course of action during his American visit in early 1952.

Towards the end of the final plenary session, Truman 'concluded that while he still wished to reach agreement with the Russians, he was not going to give the world over to them'. Churchill professed to share his view and for the second time during the conversation emphasized his intention not to 'do anything to force the President's hand or make difficulties for him in dealing with the Russians'. He also doubted whether 'the Russians wanted such a conference' at this time.[110]

On the whole, and despite what he had regarded as a promising first evening on the *Williamsburg*, Churchill was disappointed by his visit to Washington and 'the most strenuous fortnight I can remember'.[111] He had achieved very little; even his personal relationship with President Truman had not become noticeably warmer.[112] But in spite of this setback Churchill was not prepared to exclude high-level talks for good. He left the door open for a conference with the Soviet Union when he informed Truman 'that in present circumstances he would not be in favour of proposing a meeting with the leaders of the Soviet Union. ... A different situation would, however, arise if at any time the Soviet leaders indicated that they were prepared to make a genuine effort to reach an understanding with the democracies.'[113] Despite the sobering experience of his visit to Truman, Churchill had by no means abandoned his summit diplomacy.

CHAPTER 9

Between Pessimism and New Hope
The Stalin Note and a New American President

Only two months after Churchill's return from Washington the topic of a summit conference was dramatically revived. On 10 March 1952 Stalin delivered a Note to the western allies in which he proposed the unification of Germany if the reunited nation agreed not to join an alliance directed against any of the victorious powers of the Second World War. The German borders agreed at Potsdam were to be confirmed and the Oder–Neisse line recognized as the permanent German-Polish border. Stalin expressed his readiness to accept the establishment of a small German army for self-defence and the limited production of military equipment. All allied occupation forces, however, would have to leave German territory within a year. An all-German government with representatives of the governments of West and East Germany should be installed which could then sign a German peace treaty. Free all-German elections would only be held once this had been accomplished. It was outlined that plans for a peace treaty and the setting up of an all-German government could be conveniently prepared at a meeting of the four powers. A detailed proposal for a German peace treaty was included with the Note.[1] Two weeks later, on 24 March, Stalin unexpectedly replied to the written questions of a group of American publishers, saying that he was in favour of a high-level meeting of the great powers and believed the time was ripe for German reunification.[2]

German Neutrality and the 'Battle of the Notes'

By means of his Note of March 1952 and subsequent comments Stalin did his best to tempt the Federal Republic away from the West. Effectively, he offered the release of the East Germans from Moscow's sphere of influence if the West

Germans left the western camp. Whether or not this proposal was seriously meant is still a matter of controversy in the scholarly literature. Historians like Rolf Steininger refer to the Stalin Note of 10 March 1952 as the first major 'missed opportunity' to bring about German reunification and, perhaps, overcome the Cold War.[3] Others, like Hermann Graml and Gerhard Wettig, regard this view as a 'myth' and a 'legend'; they claim that Stalin's primary aim was the disruption of the united western front on the German question, the destruction of the EDC, and the prevention of the Federal Republic's integration into the West.[4] The same divergence of view can be found in contemporary documents. While some American officials believed that the Stalin Note 'should be taken seriously' as it had 'a ring of considered policy rather than propaganda', other experts concluded 'that the note does not represent any change in Soviet policy and that the Russians are as unwilling as ever to relax their hold on East Germany'.[5] Neither then nor now was there any clear substantive evidence available to back either view. The relevant documents from the Soviet archives have still not been made available and perhaps they do not exist.[6]

Stalin's proposal greatly agitated West German Chancellor Adenauer. The western allies became concerned about the Note's potential impact on West German politics and western public opinion in general. In West Germany, the opposition Social Democrats (SPD) and a number of influential journalists, media outlets and representatives of other parties were not opposed to neutrality if this was the precondition for reunification. They came out clearly in favour of 'checking out' the sincerity of Stalin's offer at the conference table.[7] However, when Adenauer was informed of Stalin's offer he immediately made it clear that he rejected Stalin's last-minute attempt to destroy West Germany's close links with the West. The Chancellor believed that Stalin had only submitted his proposal in order to disrupt the imminent conclusion of the European Defence Community (EDC), planned for May 1952, and prevent the signing of the contractual agreements (or General Treaty), which was to take place one day before.[8] The treaty would turn West Germany into an almost sovereign country and an equal member of the western world. On the insistence of the French, the EDC treaty and the contractual agreements had been linked: both needed to be signed and ratified by the parliaments of the respective member countries (France, FRG, Italy, Benelux) to take effect; if only one of the two treaties was ratified both agreements were void.[9]

Despite some dissenting voices in western foreign ministries, the governments in Washington, London and Paris agreed with Adenauer that Stalin's Note was merely a 'spoiling operation' to prevent German rearmament and the Federal Republic's integration into the western world.[10] While the three western powers were privately in favour of retaining the Oder–Neisse line as Germany's eastern border, they informed the Kremlin that it had been agreed at Potsdam that Germany's final borders would be decided at a peace conference.[11] Adenauer had advocated a statement which left the border question officially open so as to conciliate right-wing groups in the Federal Republic, such as the influential expellee organizations. The western allies also told Stalin that his proposal for an independent German military force contrasted unfavourably with the integration of West German contingents into a defensive alliance like the EDC, which was intended to prevent the resurgence of German nationalistic militarism; an independent force would be 'a step backwards'. Adenauer did not like this phrase: not only did it refer to the possibility of renewed aggressive militarism on the part of West Germany, but it might also tie his hands and those of the western allies if the EDC failed.[12] Although he had told Churchill in December 1951 that he was not interested in creating a national German army, both Adenauer and the military experts in some western capitals were already cautiously considering alternative schemes in case the EDC foundered. As the EDC treaty faced a difficult parliamentary ratification process in almost all the member countries, particularly in France, an alternative solution, largely focusing on German membership of NATO, appeared to be vital to achieve Germany's rearmament and her integration into the West.[13]

The three western powers, like Adenauer, had no intention of allowing a united Germany to become a neutral state. They therefore did their best to convince public opinion that Stalin's offer was not meant seriously. A neutral Germany, they claimed, would in a matter of time mean a Germany dominated by the Soviet Union. To enter into 'a discussion of a peace treaty with Germany' and consider 'the question of the unification of Germany and the creation of an all-German government', as Stalin had suggested in his second Note of 9 April, seemed to be too risky.[14] Stalin's next Note, of 24 May, proposed four-power negotiations in an even more explicit way,[15] and the western powers feared that once the 'Big Four' discussed German reunification at the negotiating table the West German public might actually be prepared to accept unity in return for neutrality. Most Germans could be expected to be unaware of Soviet disingenuousness and the inherent dangers of embarking on such a course. At best, the Soviet solution would leave Germany swinging freely between East and West, at worst it would gradually lead to a united Germany dependent on Soviet goodwill; eventually, it was claimed, the country might even become incorporated into the Soviet sphere of influence. Moreover, it could be expected that the French government would be quick to use the opportunity to delay the signing of the controversial EDC treaty if preparations were set in motion for East–West negotiations that might make German rearmament unnecessary.[16]

Adenauer and the western powers were agreed that reunification had to be sacrificed, at least for the time being, to enable the Bonn Republic to join the western camp, though no one had the courage to admit this publicly. After all, this also meant that the 16 million captive East Germans were left to their fate. Only in private was the division of Germany viewed positively. For example, in late 1951 American officials admitted confidentially that while Washington 'publicly favored the unification of East and West Germany', not least in order 'to maintain the support of the German people',[17] it was clear that 'certain objectives can more readily be obtained while Germany is divided'. Within the confines of the Cabinet room, Foreign Secretary Eden came to the point in December 1952 and explained that the status quo of a divided Germany was greatly preferable to any alternative scenario. He explained that 'relations with Russia in respect of Germany were settling down on the basis of Russian consolidation in the east and Russian acceptance of our consolidation in the west.' While this situation 'could not be called satisfactory', it was not without 'certain advantages to all parties, not excluding the Germans themselves.'[18] At this time Churchill did not dissent from Eden's view.

However, for the sake of public opinion in Germany and elsewhere the western world could not reject Stalin's offer of March 1952 out of hand without being seen to make constructive counterproposals of how German unification should be achieved. After all, throughout the Cold War Adenauer and the western powers continually professed that they were genuinely interested in bringing about the reunification of a democratic Germany. Stalin's Note, therefore, led to a long-drawn out exchange of memoranda between the western capitals and Moscow. Adenauer and the western allies were agreed that the whole matter had to be delayed until the EDC treaty and the contractual agreements had been signed in May 1952.[19] Only two days after Stalin's first Note had been received, the British embassy in Washington was told by the Foreign Office that 'the Soviet initiative regarding a German peace treaty, makes it even more important to press on with the conclusion of the [EDC] negotiations . . . with all possible speed'.[20] Not much thought was wasted on the possibility of 'checking out' the sincerity of Stalin's proposal.

Eventually, the German contractual agreements and the EDC treaty were signed on 26 and 27 May 1952 in Bonn and Paris respectively.[21] Subsequently the State Department and the German Chancellery favoured terminating the exchange of Notes with the Kremlin. It was evident that with the Soviet Note submitted on 24 May, and in sharp contrast to Stalin's constructive and sober first two Notes of 10 March and 9 April, the exchange of messages was developing into a propaganda war. However, in view of the severe domestic problems an abrupt end to written communication with Moscow would have caused Adenauer, the exchange was continued.[22]

Throughout the exchange of Notes, the West stipulated five main requirements which were deemed non-negotiable: (1) the holding of free elections,
supervised by an international organization; (2) the establishment of an all-
German government on the basis of these elections; (3) the guarantee that an
all-German government must not be dominated by an outside power; (4) the
guarantee that an all-German government must have the right to join with
other nations in organizations and alliances for peaceful purposes; (5) the
guarantee that the all-German government must be able to participate as an
equal partner in the negotiations leading to an all-German peace treaty. It was
argued that meeting these requirements would demonstrate the sincerity of
Stalin's proposal of March 1952.[23]

The holding of free all-German elections prior to the establishment of an
all-German government and the signing of a German peace treaty was viewed
by the West as the first and main 'test' of Stalin's sincerity. Moscow's suggestion
that elections should be held at the end of the entire unification process was
unacceptable. Instead it was argued that the establishment of an all-German
government and the conclusion of a peace treaty could only occur in
conjunction with a freely elected all-German government. It was obvious that
Stalin was unlikely to accept this, as genuinely free elections would
undoubtedly have returned a strongly pro-western government without any
representatives from East Berlin. The three western powers (and Adenauer)
also insisted on asking a UN commission to investigate whether or not the
conditions for free elections existed in East and West Germany as well as in
East and West Berlin.[24] Moreover, the western allies wanted a freely elected all-
German government to be free to join any international bodies as it saw fit, if
these organizations were peaceful and recognized by the UN. It was assumed
that Stalin would also be unable to meet this second main 'test' of the sincerity
of his proposal. Both major western conditions would have resulted in a
Germany which, though nominally neutral, was in effect a close ally of the
western world. Although Stalin was not so easily defeated and proposed a four-
power commission to investigate electoral freedom in East Germany instead of
a UN commission,[25] it became clear in May and June 1952 that as far as the
majority of western public opinion was concerned, the western powers
possessed the better arguments. Eden was already convinced that the West 'had
won [the] battle of [the] notes'.[26]

While the insistence on free elections prior to the conclusion of an all-
German peace treaty and the free association of a reunited Germany with
international organizations were the western powers' most convincing
arguments, the West's constant refusal to meet the Soviets at a quadripartite
conference was clearly their most vulnerable point. After all, the British Prime

Minister had already advocated a high-level meeting with Moscow for a considerable period of time but when the opportunity suddenly presented itself, the western world made no efforts to exploit it. Thus, on occasion British and American officials as well as Anthony Eden considered the possibility of entering into four-power talks with the Soviet Union. Adenauer and Acheson continued to oppose strongly such a dangerous and risky strategy, and nothing came of it.[27]

In fact, it had been clear from the beginning that western politicians never really intended to embark on negotiations in order to arrive at a genuine compromise with the Soviet Union. On the few occasions when a meeting with the Soviet leaders was considered it became apparent that such a conference had nothing in common with Churchill's summit diplomacy. Like the strategy which was later pursued at the quadripartite Berlin foreign ministers' conference in early 1954, a high-level meeting with Moscow was only meant to expose Moscow's insincerity and demonstrate the West's apparent readiness to discuss any serious proposals.[28] Nevertheless, the West German Chancellor was not sure about this; he remained very worried about a possible four-power meeting. In particular, Bonn was greatly concerned that Churchill still played with the idea of convening a high-level conference for either trade-related reasons or in order to become more involved in the East–West conflict.[29] Yet, in 1952 these fears were largely unjustified. But it continued to be argued in the western capitals that even in the unlikely event that Stalin was prepared to accept an 'honestly non-Communist government' to prevent Germany's integration with the West, the West 'must tread very warily as we could arrive at the same stalemate as in Austria, with a government for the whole of the country but no progress toward a peace treaty or the end of the occupation or stability of any sort in Europe'.[30]

Thus even if Stalin had been prepared to reach a genuine compromise on the German question and accept the West's two main conditions, Washington, London, Paris and Bonn still adhered to their position that there were no clear advantages in giving up the Federal Republic's imminent integration with the West in favour of the reunification of Germany.[31] The status quo appeared to be a much more attractive option. Not even Adenauer was seriously interested in German reunification under the terms proposed by Stalin; what was required from the West's point of view was the irreversible integration of the Bonn Republic with the West. Moreover, there was a vague hope, given much prominence in public rhetoric, that the full integration of the Federal Republic with the western world might eventually lead to the unification of a westernized democratic all-German state.[32] While such an eventual development was regarded favourably by the US, it was viewed with very mixed feelings by the British and the French; much to their relief it seemed to be a very distant prospect. In view of their past experiences of German nationalism, Paris and London were privately quite satisfied with the continued division of Germany.[33]

The 'battle of the notes', a phrase coined by Anthony Eden, only petered out in September 1952 when, to the great relief of western politicians, Stalin did not reply to the last western message of 23 September, which once again outlined the western conception of how to bring about German unification.[34]

Surprisingly, Churchill did not become involved in the 1952 'battle of the notes'. Despite his pressure for talks with the USSR between 1946 and 1951, he did not regard the Stalin Note as an opportunity to realize his plans for summit diplomacy. Adenauer remained fearful about what Churchill might do and hoped that Acheson and John McCloy, the American High Commissioner in Germany, would attempt to influence the British government in the right way. Although Adenauer was only two years younger than Churchill, he regarded the Prime Minister as an 'old man' who dominated his Foreign Secretary.[35] However, for once, Churchill observed customary practice and left foreign policy to Eden and the Foreign Office.[36] In fact, British diplomats largely orchestrated the western responses to Stalin's Note of 10 March[37] without Churchill feeling the need to interfere. The Prime Minister merely advocated the acceptance of Moscow's proposal that representatives of the four powers should be sent to oversee the arrangements for free elections in East and West Germany instead of a UN delegation. This was in line with his views on the strengthening of mutual cooperation among the 'Big Four'. Churchill 'had this feeling that the Four Powers is a more manageable way of doing things than U.N.O.'. With reference to his summit diplomacy and bringing about East–West cooperation he thought that 'it fits in with our other ideas'.[38]

It is however difficult to see, as has been claimed, how this indicates 'that the Prime Minister was keen to see the continuation of exchanges with the Soviets and had little grasp of the danger that they might simply be seeking to destroy the Adenauer regime'.[39] In contrast to most other western politicians, including the diplomats in his own Foreign Office, Churchill often had doubts about the desirability of the continued partition of Germany. Despite his assurances to Adenauer in December 1951, he did not feel committed to supporting the continuation of the Chancellor's government under all circumstances. Churchill had come to believe that a dissatisfied German nation longing for unification would represent a major trouble spot and a potential source of nationalist agitation and instability in the middle of Europe.[40] Still, replacing a West German government led by Adenauer with a democratic all-German government would hardly have seemed to Churchill to entail the destruction of the German parliamentary regime.

Moreover, if Churchill had felt strongly that the Stalin Note presented an opportunity to initiate serious talks with the Soviets, he would surely have become actively involved, as he did after Stalin's death a year later. Instead, during the Cabinet meeting on 12 March 1952 Churchill made no objection to Eden's strategy of employing 'tests' to contain safely the proposals made in the Stalin Note. There are no indications that Churchill wished to prolong the 'battle of the notes' with the Soviet Union. Everyone present at the Cabinet meeting realized that it was most unlikely that Stalin would ever be prepared to accept any of the western conditions and 'tests'. It was much more likely that the dictator would either terminate the exchange of messages or allow them to develop into a propaganda battle.[41]

In the course of 1952, Churchill remained pessimistic about the prospect of resolving the East–West conflict by means of summit diplomacy. After his stroke in July he was also in relatively poor health, and many senior Conservative politicians encouraged him to take early retirement and hand over to Eden.[42] Churchill's health problems certainly contributed to the fact that he did not attempt to exploit the 'battle of the notes' to push for an early summit conference. Furthermore, at this stage he did not seriously believe in the possibility of fruitful negotiations with Moscow. The continuing war in Korea, the rather uncompromising attitude of Soviet Foreign Minister Vyshinsky, Truman's rejection of summit diplomacy, and the unpromising exchange of Notes with Stalin also greatly discouraged him. Not least, Churchill was deeply shocked and disappointed by the purges and show trials which took place in Czechoslovakia in 1951–52. He declared that under these conditions 'the chances of achieving anything with Stalin were almost nil, whereas the dangers of failure would be very great'.[43]

In the House of Commons, shortly before Stalin's death, he therefore was not prepared to give more than a non-committal response to questions as to whether he still considered negotiations with Stalin desirable.[44] Churchill appears to have come to the conclusion that negotiations with a Soviet delegation led by Stalin would be very difficult. Above all, such a scenario would clearly be impossible to sell to the American administration. It was most unlikely that during the remainder of Truman's second term in office, at the height of McCarthy's anti-Communist crusade and with the continuation of the war in Korea and a difficult election campaign ahead for presidential candidate Adlai Stevenson and the Democratic Party, the President could be persuaded to participate in negotiations with Moscow.

Churchill and President-elect Eisenhower

Despite his high hopes when he became Prime Minister in October 1951, Churchill soon found himself confronted with great obstacles to embarking on negotiations with Moscow and Washington. By late 1952 and early 1953 he had little hope left that he would succeed in creating an era of lasting détente by organizing a three- or four-power conference with the Soviet Union in the near future.

Nevertheless, during the American presidential election of 1952 the British Prime Minister left no stone unturned to convince the presidential candidates of the merits of his summit plans. Despite certain apprehensions about the Republican Party's likely foreign policy, he focused his attention on the Republican presidential candidate Dwight D. Eisenhower, the highly popular Second World War hero. Churchill declared in June 1952 'that if Eisenhower was elected President, he would have another shot at making peace by means of a meeting of the 'Big Three'. For that alone it would perhaps be worth remaining in office.'[45] Two months later he hinted that if Eisenhower were to become President, he hoped that a 'joint approach to Stalin' might be possible, 'proceeding perhaps to a congress in Vienna where the Potsdam Conference would be reopened and concluded'.[46] Thus, the disappointments of 1952 had not persuaded Churchill to renounce his pursuit of summit diplomacy. In the face of seemingly insurmountable difficulties he had merely postponed more intensive efforts.

Once Eisenhower had been elected in November 1952, Churchill cautiously took the initiative. He knew Eisenhower very well from the latter's days as Allied Commander in Chief during the war. He had also met him several times when Eisenhower was based in Paris as NATO's first Supreme Allied Commander.[47] Yet, much to the amusement of the five-star General, Churchill still regarded him as a high-ranking underling. In December 1951 Eisenhower wrote in his diary: 'I am back in Europe in a status that is not too greatly different, in his [Churchill's] mind, from that which I held with respect to him in World War II. To my mind, he simply will not think in terms of today but rather only those of the war years.'[48] Even after Eisenhower had been elected President Churchill believed that he would be able to influence the politically inexperienced General in favour of a high-level conference and the de-escalation of East–West tension.

While the Foreign Office viewed Eisenhower's election as President with little concern, the officials in London were greatly worried about the likelihood that John Foster Dulles would become Secretary of State. Dulles appeared to be too anti-Communist, with little sympathy for Britain's economic plight;

moreover, Eden had fallen out with him during the negotiations of the Japanese peace treaty in 1951.[49] Conservative MP Brendan Bracken, a member of Churchill's inner circle, wrote to their friend Lord Beaverbrook: 'Whitehall is already mourning the departure of Truman and Acheson. The preposterous Dulles has upset many people here, but that, of course, causes him no distress. Dollar diplomacy is now the order of the day ... Unless John Bull is financially independent he can play no worthy part in the world.'[50] Churchill was also suspicious of Dulles who seemed to be anti-British, lacked a sense of humour and had a 'great slab face'.[51] Eden even attempted to persuade Eisenhower to appoint New York Governor Thomas E. Dewey to head the State Department but to no avail; Eden had to telegraph London explaining that the 'Man we don't like is still making all the running he can. I am doing all that I discreetly can.'[52]

Eisenhower prevaricated for almost two weeks and considered John McCloy and Henry Cabot Lodge for the post as he feared that the Democrats in Congress would not be impressed by the divisive Dulles and might refuse to cooperate with Eisenhower's foreign policy. But on 20 November Dulles was offered the position of Secretary of State. He immediately accepted and undertook to support Eisenhower in working for a 'just and durable peace'.[53] However, in order to ensure that the State Department would not be too independent of the White House, Eisenhower appointed his old friend and confidant, General Walter Bedell Smith, former CIA director and ambassador to Moscow, as Under-Secretary of State and thus deputy to Dulles.[54] Eisenhower's long-standing friends Robert Murphy and Douglas MacArthur II were appointed Deputy Under-Secretary and Counsellor respectively. And much to Dulles's dislike, the new American ambassador to the UN, Henry Cabot Lodge, was given a seat in the Cabinet.[55] It appeared that Eisenhower wanted to ensure that Dulles was under the control of some of his most trusted confidants.

Moreover, the President-elect seemed to be unsure of how long Dulles would remain Secretary of State. At least Eisenhower indicated this when he responded to Eden's request not to entrust the State Department to Dulles. Eisenhower was 'almost apologetic' regarding the appointment of Dulles for 'at least a year'. He claimed with little conviction that Dulles's great experience as the representative of a 'bipartisan foreign policy' was the main reason for his decision to entrust him with the State Department.[56] Eisenhower's very mild reaction to Eden's almost unprecedented attempt to influence the selection of one of the most senior positions in the American government may well have encouraged Churchill to believe that he would be permitted to guide the new President towards a more flexible policy with regard to East–West relations. Churchill took immediate steps to contact the President-elect and could not be dissuaded from visiting the United States even before Eisenhower's inauguration.

In January 1953 Churchill set out on a private visit to the United States. In some respects he found his talks with the President-elect in Eisenhower's transition offices in a New York hotel on 5 and 7 January quite satisfactory.[57] John Colville, Churchill's Private Secretary, wrote in his diary: 'The Prime Minister told me, after Ike had left, that he had felt on top of him this time: Ike seemed to defer to his greater age and experience to a remarkable degree.'[58] Indeed, Eisenhower regarded Churchill as an 'extraordinary character' and a great statesman. He also viewed Britain as America's 'greatest natural friend' and found Churchill 'as charming and interesting as ever'.[59] However, the President-elect was not prepared to be led by London or to give international public opinion the impression of a two-power coalition between Britain and the United States.[60]

In fact, Eisenhower believed that Churchill was by now too old to be Prime Minister. He seemed to live too much in the past, 'trying to relive the days of World War II'. Eisenhower secretly wished that despite his 'personal affection' for Churchill and the admiration for his 'past accomplishments and leadership' he would 'turn over [the] leadership of the Conservative Party to younger men'.[61] As early as December 1951 the General had come to the conclusion that 'subconsciously my great friend is trying to re-live the days of his greatest glory'. Much to his regret he thought that 'the Prime Minister no longer absorbs new ideas; exhortation and appeals to the emotions and sentiment still have some effect on him – exposition does not.'[62] However, Eisenhower always treated Churchill with great politeness and respect, particularly at the beginning of his presidency. This in turn reinforced Churchill's belief that he would be able to persuade Eisenhower of the value of the political initiatives he wished to embark upon.[63] Throughout his peacetime government Churchill greatly valued the fairly regular correspondence he conducted with Eisenhower and 'looked forward with almost childish excitement to the arrival of the President's missives'.[64]

Nevertheless, Churchill was not entirely satisfied with his visit to the USA. He told Sir Roger Makins, the British ambassador to Washington, that on the whole 'he had been considerably disappointed by his talks in New York'. The American politicians he talked to had all been rather friendly but 'their views were a long way from ours'.[65] Churchill also appears to have overlooked the fact that Eisenhower, despite his relative political inexperience, was a very shrewd operator with 'exceptional analytical skills' and, according to his adviser General Andrew Goodpaster, possessed 'a quick mind and a very strong and vigorous personality'. During the war not only Churchill himself but General De Gaulle and other 'notoriously egocentric warleaders' had often 'yielded to the force of Eisenhower's logic and the charm of his personality'.[66] It would not be easy to persuade Eisenhower of anything he did not already believe.

During the conversations in New York on 7 January Churchill had been rather surprised when Eisenhower asked him if the Prime Minister would object if he, Eisenhower, were to meet Stalin alone for a conversation, in neutral Stockholm for example. The President-elect said he intended to make such a proposal in his inaugural speech, and would have no objections if Churchill also wished to meet Stalin.[67] Churchill replied: 'I would have objected strongly during the war when our contribution in forces was about equal. Now I don't mind.'[68] Yet, despite these words the Prime Minister appeared to fear Eisenhower's competition in the race to organize a summit conference with the dictator in the Kremlin. He advised the President not to rush matters too much and not to mention anything about his plan in his inaugural address: 'Don't be in a hurry. Get your reconnaissance in first.' It would be prudent if the new President would 'take a few months to get into a calmer atmosphere and learn the facts'.[69] Eisenhower should consider 'what the results might be if the vast hopes which such a meeting would raise were dashed and if nothing at all came of it.'[70] This was of course precisely the argument which Truman and other critics of Churchill's summit diplomacy had used to dampen his own enthusiasm for a high-level conference with the Soviets; it was an argument Churchill usually regarded as rather unconvincing when aimed at himself.

Although the Prime Minister was not keen on Eisenhower negotiating with Moscow without British participation, his reply may have been seriously meant. As outlined above, developments in 1952 had undermined his confidence in the prospects of summit diplomacy with the Soviet Union. Everything seemed to point to the fact that Stalin was not prepared to offer any concessions.[71] This was also the consensus view expressed in two important NATO Negotiating Papers on 'Trends in Soviet Policy' dated December 1952. It was agreed that there was 'no evidence that Soviet basic aims and strategy have changed'. It could be expected that Moscow's basic principle was still to create all sorts of 'mischief short of war' such as the disruption of NATO and the division of the western world including 'all forms of European integration'. While the Soviet leaders 'may yet renew proposals for a Four-Power Meeting in the hopes of paralysing the process of Western integration', the NATO ministers were agreed that Moscow had shown 'little sign of being able or willing to offer acceptable conditions for such a meeting'.[72] There was no indication that the Eisenhower administration, dominated as it was by rather conservative elderly people from the military and the business world, was likely to differ from the views expressed in the NATO papers.

The British Foreign Office too concluded that there was clear evidence that Moscow was not willing to contemplate a compromise on the German question. Even Churchill agreed: 'The present signs seem to be that the Soviet Government are busy with the task of turning Eastern Germany into a fully-fledged Satellite State, and show no indication of thinking that a settlement on Germany, on terms satisfactory to themselves, is likely to be attained in the near future.'[73] Thus, at the beginning of 1953 Churchill and the Foreign Office were still largely in agreement on Britain's policy towards the Soviet Union, a consensus that quickly broke down after Stalin's death in early March.[74] The consensus view in London was reinforced by the reports of the British ambassador to Moscow, Sir Alvary Gascoigne, who in late December 1952 had reported that the USSR seemed happy to merely observe the western difficulties in ratifying the EDC and the treaties giving sovereignty to West Germany. The ambassador believed that it was most unlikely 'that we should gain anything by attempting to start high level talks'.[75] Eden replied that this view of current Soviet foreign policy 'corresponds exactly with our own thoughts here.' Stalin's aim appeared to be to disseminate as much propaganda as possible 'to confuse and divide western opinion and embarrass the new American administration'. Eden continued: '[it is] conceivable, I suppose, that Stalin would actually like to meet Eisenhower, whether out of curiosity or because he still cherishes a hope of throwing Western policy back into the melting pot. But we are no more able than you to see any basis in Soviet policy for fruitful talks at the moment, and I entirely agree with you that we must not let ourselves be hustled into any premature meeting.'[76]

The State Department officials were surprised that during his talks with Eisenhower in early January 1953 Churchill appeared to have changed his mind about a meeting with Stalin. They wondered whether his vague reply was dictated by tactical considerations as he feared 'that he might be left out' or whether he was afraid that he would only be able to play a subordinate role in any negotiations. Soviet expert Charles Bohlen asked incredulously: 'Or had Mr. Churchill really changed his judgement on this?'[77] Still, following Churchill's advice, Eisenhower did not mention anything about a meeting with Stalin in his inaugural address on 20 January 1953.[78] A month later however, at a press conference on 25 February, Eisenhower could not restrain himself any longer. Replying to a question, he said: 'I would meet anybody anywhere, where I thought there was the slightest chance of doing any good, as long as it was in keeping with what the American people expect of their Chief Executive . . . because this business of defending freedom is a big job.'[79]

The new President intended to take his 'big job' seriously. He believed, however, that the American people were only prepared to accept a summit meeting at a 'suitable spot, let's say halfway between'. Moreover, Eisenhower was not willing to consider such a conference if it was unlikely that the meeting would result in concrete achievements.[80] After all, the pressures on Eisenhower were similar to those Truman had faced. The influence of McCarthyism and the strongly anti-Communist sentiments of American public opinion made it unwise for any President to attend a summit meeting with the Soviets before the war in Korea had come to an end. Eisenhower's brief visit to Korea shortly after winning the election and his frequent reiteration of his belief that the termination of the war there was the precondition for any improvement in East–West relations were highly popular.[81]

The President expressed no willingness to make the Korean War the topic of a meeting with Stalin; in fact, a meeting with Stalin would only be possible once the Korean War had been terminated. However, in a written interview with American journalist James Reston in late December 1952 Stalin had indicated that he believed a Soviet-American meeting would indeed make sense; he did not object to a meeting with Eisenhower to de-escalate the Cold War and, perhaps, overcome the Korean conflict.[82] Eisenhower's insistence that the end of the war in Korea was a precondition for an international summit conference aroused British suspicions. It appeared to London that Eisenhower was interested in the propaganda value of announcing his willingness to meet Stalin but his pre-condition appeared to ensure that he would never be called upon to travel to such a summit conference. Indeed, Sherman Adams, effectively Eisenhower's White House Chief of Staff and one of his most trusted advisers during his early presidency, declared in his memoirs that 'Eisenhower never felt that he would be able to negotiate successfully with Stalin.'[83]

From Churchill's point of view, it was rather disconcerting that neither Eisenhower nor Stalin appeared to find the participation of Britain necessary. Senior Foreign Office officials Frank Roberts and Paul Mason noted in February 1953 that they had observed a certain political naivety on Eisenhower's part as early as 1945.[84] Both heartily disliked the attempts by Charles Bohlen and the State Department to arrange a bilateral meeting with Stalin. They mistrusted Bohlen's motives, which seemed to be careerist rather than rooted in political developments in Moscow. 'We cannot help a slight suspicion', they wrote, 'that Bohlen may be canvassing these views to make his mark with the new Administration, in the knowledge that they will want to produce a Soviet policy with a new look.' Eden concurred; 'I have no confidence in Mr. Bohlen,' he wrote.[85]

Churchill was also disappointed with the new American administration. Eisenhower seemed to be as inflexible as the Truman administration during his visit twelve months earlier. Churchill's hopes that it might be possible to arrive at a *modus vivendi* with Moscow were not encouraged by his talks with the new President in New York. Moreover, the British including Churchill had a 'wary skepticism' with regard to Eisenhower's contemplated unilateral approach to Stalin.[86] Churchill reacted to Eisenhower's press conference on 25 February by declaring in the House of Commons on 2 March 1953 that he was prepared to meet both Stalin and Eisenhower at any time.[87] He had little hope that such an event was likely to occur soon.

For Churchill, the situation was transformed with the announcement of Stalin's death on 5 March: this convinced him that it might be possible to achieve a permanent 'settlement' with the Soviet Union after all. Lord Moran, Churchill's personal physician, noted: 'The P.M. feels that Stalin's death may lead to a relaxation in tension. It is an opportunity that will not recur.'[88] Stalin's unexpected demise transformed Churchill's pessimism in 1951–2 with regard to 'Big Three' summit diplomacy into renewed optimism. In view of his age and the increasing pressure on him to retire, Churchill felt that Stalin's death presented him with his final opportunity to engage in summit diplomacy and make a lasting impact on world affairs as a peacemaker. He would waste little time in exploiting the opportunity thus given to him.

Churchill realized that despite Eisenhower's upbeat pronouncements regarding his willingness to negotiate with Moscow it would not be easy to carry the Americans along. After all, during the Prime Minister's visit to the United States in early January 1953 the possibility of Stalin's death had been mentioned but, surprisingly, Stalin's eventual demise had not been considered as an opportunity to improve relations. According to the notes taken by a British officer during a dinner party for Churchill at the British embassy in Washington on 8 January, the American politicians present appeared to regard a change of leadership in the Kremlin with great scepticism.[89] On the whole the representatives of both the outgoing Truman and the incoming Eisenhower administrations believed that it might be easier to deal with a country that was dominated by Stalin than with a Soviet Union which was led by his much less familiar potential successors. Eisenhower's confidant Bedell Smith made a perceptive and partially correct prediction regarding the post-Stalin leadership:

> There was unanimous agreement that we were better off with Stalin alive than dead. The 'young hotheads' might prove a much worse set in their scrambles for power (Dean Acheson, next whom I was sitting, questioned in an aside who 'these young hotheads of 60' might be). Bedell [Smith] . . . said that the succession would probably take the form of a triumvirate – Malenkov, Molotoff [sic] and Beria, with the first possibly coming out on top but probably not for some years.[90]

CHAPTER 10

The Cold War After Stalin
Churchill, the United States, and the 'New' Men in the Kremlin

On 6 March 1953 Stalin's sudden death was announced. The international political lethargy and the stifling atmosphere of an all-pervasive Cold War gave way to a fresh dynamic. The new leadership in the Soviet Union seemed to be open to a world-wide relaxation of tension.[1] During the funeral oration for Stalin, Malenkov proclaimed that the Soviet Union believed in a policy 'of prolonged coexistence and peaceful competition of two different systems, capitalist and socialist'.[2] Soon the new leaders in Moscow became seriously interested in using their influence to obtain a truce in the Korean War. They were also ready to ease traffic restrictions between West Berlin and the Federal Republic of Germany, enter into discussions with the western allies about air safety in the Berlin air corridors, and waive Moscow's long-standing claims over Turkish territory. Such minor matters as the negotiation of a new fisheries agreement with Britain to replace the one the USSR had unilaterally terminated some months earlier were resolved in a surprisingly short time, and the instruction that the British and American embassies in Moscow would have to move from their prime locations near the Kremlin to smaller, uglier and less centrally situated buildings was cancelled.[3] The new collective leadership had embarked upon a general process of change before Stalin was even 'cold in his grave'.[4] The development of a general thaw in East–West relations no longer seemed impossible.[5]

The new leaders also began a modest process of internal liberalization and de-Stalinization in the Soviet Union. Measures such as a general amnesty for more than a million prisoners, including a great number of political prisoners, were rapidly implemented. The doctors accused of a plot to kill Stalin were released. Everything seemed to demonstrate that the new leadership was keen on placating the people so as to maintain its authority in the vast Soviet empire.[6]

Anxious to avoid the emergence of another sole dictator, Stalin's old comrades-in-arms decided to divide the reins of supreme power. Vyacheslav Molotov was once again appointed Foreign Minister; he had already served in this capacity between 1939 and 1949. Lavrenti Beria, the 'Soviet Himmler' as Stalin had described him to Roosevelt during the Yalta conference, was given responsibility for the amalgamated Interior and Security Ministries.[7] Georgi Malenkov headed the two most important state and Party organizations and was thus widely regarded as the *primus inter pares* in the new triumvirate.[8]

The Officials in London and Washington Respond

The foreign policy establishments in the United States, Britain and most western countries were suspicious about the sudden thaw. It was generally believed that Stalin's successors wanted to be more accommodating simply to gain time for the consolidation of their collective leadership. The British Foreign Office and the American State Department concluded independently that Malenkov and his colleagues felt very insecure, perhaps anticipating civil unrest and riots. At this juncture the Kremlin seemed to believe it was critically important to avoid trouble with their own population, the satellite countries and with the West. Although very little information was received in the western world, most experts assumed (correctly as it turned out) that a fierce power struggle was under way to succeed Stalin as the undisputed and sole leader of the Soviet empire.[9] Charles Bohlen thought that 'Bolshevism was facing its greatest crisis since the Hitler attack of 1941.'[10]

Most officials in London and Washington believed that a certain relaxation of international tension would ensue as a result of the complex situation confronting the new leaders, but that the Soviet Union would still be determined to advance world Communism and maintain a firm grip on the countries of Eastern Europe.[11] Thus, Stalin's death did little to change the thinking of the State Department, the Foreign Office or the West German and French foreign ministries. After 5 March 1953 the western powers were no more enthusiastic about entering into negotiations with the Soviet Union than at the time of the Stalin Note in 1952.[12]

Among western heads of government, only Churchill was seriously interested in embarking on summit diplomacy with the Malenkov government. As soon as Stalin's death was announced the American embassy in London warned the State Department that, according to British diplomats, the Prime Minister 'undoubtedly' would be 'itching' for a genuine high-level meeting with the new Soviet leaders.[13] Indeed, the period after Stalin's death would prove to be the high-point of Churchill's post-war pursuit of summit diplomacy. The changes in the Kremlin and the apparently more flexible foreign policy of Stalin's successors seemed to present a unique and rather unexpected opportunity to arrive at a 'settlement' with the Soviet Union, a policy Churchill had advocated since his 'iron curtain' speech in 1946.[14]

In the course of 1953 Churchill's efforts would lead to serious political clashes with Washington and Bonn, since both were strongly opposed to high-level talks with Malenkov at this juncture. Although a summit meeting was contemplated by the Americans from time to time, Eisenhower and most of his officials merely toyed with the idea of a propaganda conference which would end in failure but would persuade western public opinion that there had been no substantial changes in Moscow's policies. This would hasten the progress of the ratification of the European Defence Community (EDC), which was proceeding very slowly, and consolidate public opinion in favour of the Federal Republic's integration into the West. Similarly, the British Foreign Office viewed the Prime Minister's revived summit diplomacy with great scepticism. Churchill, however, remained firmly convinced that the death of Stalin had handed him a unique chance to organize a 'parley at the summit' to overcome the East–West conflict and the division of Europe. He believed that as the sole surviving member of the 'Big Three' of the Second World War he was the only statesman who was able to defuse the dangerous tensions of the Cold War for good. In the scholarly literature, the battle continues over the question whether or not an opportunity for winding down the Cold War was missed in the aftermath of Stalin's death.[15]

On 4 March, when the Kremlin published the first communiqué about Stalin's serious illness, Under-Secretary of State Bedell Smith told the National Security Council that Stalin was already 'dead as hell'.[16] Jacob Beam, the American chargé d'affaires in Moscow, was more circumspect.[17] He said that Stalin's stroke had greatly surprised the Soviet government, since throughout the previous winter he had appeared to be in good health and had received Argentine and Indian diplomats in February.[18] (In fact, Stalin had suffered a first stroke and a long illness soon after the war; he had a second stroke in 1947, and since at least 1949/50 suffered from hardening of the cerebral arteries, a condition that resulted in signs of senility and probably contributed to the increasing paranoia that marked the last years of his life.[19] Western observers were largely ignorant of Stalin's physical and mental decline and his death came as a surprise.) Beam tended to see 'confusion, uncertainty, and temporary restraint in [the] ruling group' in the Kremlin.[20]

The State Department largely agreed with this assessment, but there was almost as much confusion in Washington as in Moscow. America's foreign-policy establishment was not well prepared for the leadership change in Moscow. Since the end of the war, the State Department had expected that Stalin would gradually relinquish the 'active direction of affairs' and withdraw to an elder statesman role.[21] As a matter of routine, tentative plans for action in the event of Stalin's sudden departure had been considered in late 1952. However, the officials had not taken this task very seriously since no one expected Stalin's retirement or anticipated his imminent death.[22] During the transition from one President to another less urgent matters were frequently shelved. At a Cabinet meeting President Eisenhower complained in exasperation at the State Department's inexplicable lack of preparation for Stalin's demise.[23]

The American foreign policy establishment moved rapidly into action. On 4 March, an Intelligence Estimate on the 'Implications of Stalin's Collapse' was drawn up. It concluded that Stalin's heirs would undoubtedly face 'a tremendous readjustment problem', although the expected succession struggle would probably not be 'of a nature to disrupt the regime'.[24] The State Department did not anticipate any fundamental changes in the Soviet Union's domestic and foreign policies after Stalin's death. It was assumed that Stalin's heirs would not dare to change Moscow's foreign policy substantially as this would be likely to increase the instability of the new Soviet regime. The diplomats were convinced of Moscow's 'unremitting hostility' *vis-à-vis* the West and that there would be a 'continued "hard" Soviet policy on Korea, Germany, and all other outstanding issues between East and West.'[25]

Thus the Eisenhower administration assumed that Stalin's successors would not be interested in initiating more constructive relations with the western world. The dictator's death and the belief that the era of purges and persecutions had ended with him might even make international Communism more appealing to European intellectuals and the economically deprived developing world. The views of Secretary of State John Foster Dulles had been spelled out in his 1950 book, *War or Peace*. He believed that a blueprint for Moscow's strategies could be found in Stalin's volume *Problems of Leninism*, which called on Communists all over the world to adopt a policy of expediency, which might include tactical retreats and, on occasion, even cooperation with the West, to ensure the ultimate victory of world Communism and the eventual elimination of all capitalist states.[26] Dulles thought that it was unlikely that Stalin's successors would be capable of diverging from their mentor's mental framework.

Nor was the British Foreign Office impressed by the new developments in Soviet foreign policy in the immediate aftermath of Stalin's death. Indeed, at first Stalin's demise was deeply regretted among Britain's diplomats. Of all people, it was the fiercely anti-Communist Deputy Under-Secretary Frank Roberts who believed that 'the conservative, cautious hand of Stalin will be missing'.[27] Overlooking the fact that on more than one occasion in the past Stalin's initiatives had caused the development of dangerous crises, Sir Alvary Gascoigne, Britain's ambassador to Moscow, agreed, adding that there did not seem to be anyone left in Moscow with whom the western world could talk during a crisis like the Berlin blockade.[28] Shortly afterwards the ambassador said he very much doubted the correctness of the view, attributed to Dulles, that Stalin's death had improved the prospects for global peace.[29] Gascoigne expected the continuation of the Kremlin's policy 'on its present lines', although there might well be a new purge.[30]

Even Foreign Secretary Eden agreed with these sentiments. During a visit to Washington for talks on economic affairs in March 1953, he said he thought that Stalin's policies had not been overly adventurous to avoid endangering the continued existence of the Soviet empire. Eden arrived at the somewhat surprising conclusion that Stalin had always 'shown some sensitivity to outside affairs'.[31] The Foreign Secretary's view was shared by many in the British foreign service and military establishment.[32]

In general, the Foreign Office wished to adopt a 'wait-and-see' attitude[33] and kept reiterating that the West should not be tempted to embark on any rash policies which could be misunderstood by the new leadership in Moscow. Frank Roberts advised that 'our policies should be firm without being provocative'.[34] The Foreign Office agreed with the State Department that Stalin's death could easily provoke serious East–West tensions as it 'might shake both [the USSR's] governing apparatus and [the] country as a whole', and they advised that the situation could only be kept under control by exercising 'the greatest caution on [the] part of [the] West'.[35] London, like most western foreign ministries, expected that a collective leadership headed by either Molotov or Malenkov would take over power in the Kremlin.[36] British ambassador Gascoigne was convinced that the new leaders were likely 'to prove to be just as tough, ruthless and uncompromising as the former administration'. British policy had always assumed that Soviet policy could only change in a positive way under a Foreign Minister who was a 'man of calibre', and it was questionable whether Molotov was this man: he was 'steadfastly anti-western and as stubborn as a mule'.[37] There was clearly no desire among British diplomats to contemplate a high-level summit conference with the new Soviet leaders.

Churchill's and Eden's Reaction

Churchill took a different view. He was very keen to exploit the changes in the Kremlin for his summit diplomacy, but at first he proceeded in an unusually cautious way. Churchill waited until 11 March before writing to Eisenhower with respect to the new situation in the Soviet Union.[38] A day later the Foreign Office realized that Churchill was toying once again with his plan. In reply to a parliamentary question from Labour MP Arthur Lewis on 12 March, asking whether the Prime Minister was still thinking of organizing a high-level meeting with the American and Soviet leaders, Churchill, instead of answering that such a meeting was 'premature' as the Foreign Office had advised, said that he was re-considering his pessimistic attitude of the previous year and was currently unable to give an answer. He hoped the House of Commons would 'not assume that these issues are not regarded as of the highest importance at the present time'.[39] On 28 March, Churchill told Anthony Eden that he had made up his mind and would definitely like to meet the new Soviet leaders in Moscow, or perhaps elsewhere. As a first step, Eden should begin informal discussions with Molotov. Churchill had already drawn up the letter he intended to send to Molotov suggesting a meeting with Eden in Vienna; he believed that such talks 'might lead us all further away from madness and ruin'.[40]

Initially, Eden was intrigued by the idea.[41] 'A.E. is attracted ... Past troubles are forgotten in a new atmosphere of optimism,' his Private Secretary noticed.[42] However, Eden was soon persuaded otherwise by his Foreign Office advisers, who included the Permanent Under-Secretary William Strang, and the German expert Frank Roberts, as well as the Minister of State Selwyn Lloyd and his deputy, the young Anthony Nutting.[43] All of them were most concerned about Churchill's initiative. To them as to the vast majority of British officials it appeared that 'The Russians have not made any concession which is more than a trifle, but they look as if they were going to adopt a much cleverer policy for dividing and weakening the West than Stalin ever did. If so, we should be cautious and not rush in.'[44]

Eden became doubtful whether it made sense to convene an early meeting with Molotov. His officials said they were at a loss to understand 'what the agenda of such a meeting would be'. Most matters could be discussed only on a trilateral basis with the inclusion of the United States. The list of topics for bilateral talks was regarded as 'indeed rather thin' and any 'subject that it was safe to discuss would hardly be substantial enough to justify a high-level meeting.' Eventually Eden and his advisers agreed on a compromise. Ambassador Gascoigne would be asked to intensify his contact with Molotov 'on a narrow basis'. This appeared to be the best method 'to start the operation'. It was concluded that 'If it gets no further than this, no harm would have been done, and perhaps some good.' In a memorandum to Eden, Strang added: 'If we can broaden out in such a way as to lead to a meeting between you and Mr. Molotov, so much the better,'[45] but his lack of enthusiasm for this course of action was evident.

Churchill was strongly opposed to the Foreign Office's proposal to recall Gascoigne to London for consultations.[46] He pointed out to Eden, quite correctly as soon became clear, that Gascoigne 'knows nothing you do not know'. The Prime Minister regarded talks between Eden and Molotov as 'an important interim objective'.[47] Gascoigne's sceptical view of the developments in Moscow was no secret, and summoning him back to London would attract unnecessary attention without achieving anything. Churchill deviously attempted to exploit Eden's personal vanity by adding, 'Many people would think that you have not got a view of your own on the subject.' He went on: 'What is there, can you tell me, to ask for an audience about that you cannot telegraph direct to Molotov? I see no advantage in procedure for procedure's sake.' The Prime Minister emphasized: 'I do not want an interview between Gascoigne and Molotov, but between Molotov and you. At a later stage, if all went well and everything broadened, I and even Ike might come in too.'[48]

It was clear that Churchill still aimed at a summit meeting of the 'Big Three'. Drawing on Strang's lengthy memorandum, Eden pointed out that it was customary to consult the ambassador personally on complicated matters. Moreover, there were hardly any bilateral Anglo-Soviet topics he could discuss with Molotov; issues such as Korea, Austria, Germany and many other matters could only be sensibly considered if the USA participated in the talks. And then there was the German Chancellor: 'It is Adenauer who would be most anxious. A discussion of Germany's future without his being present must do him great harm.' Eden suggested that the Kremlin had merely changed its tactics without having offered any evidence for a truly new political departure, and, quoting Strang's memorandum almost word for word, continued: 'We have in the past been pretty sure that the Russians would not let us down by performing embarrassing conciliatory manoeuvres. It looks as though this is no longer true. Their peace propaganda will now have some more substance in it. Our own tactics will have to be to respond as freely as we can without surrendering vital positions like the North Atlantic Treaty: in this we may find the French to be very weak vessels.'[49]

Within a matter of days, the Foreign Office had succeeded in reversing Eden's initial enthusiasm for a meeting with Molotov.[50] Eden's inclination to rely entirely on the advice of his officials was often apparent – later in the year,

Conservative MP Douglas Dodds-Parker told an American diplomat that 'Eden has been too prone to depend upon the advice and subject himself to the influence of the permanent officials in the Foreign Office.'[51] However, leaving aside the persuasive skills of the officials, there were other reasons that made Eden hesitate to follow the policy advocated by Churchill. Chief among these was Eden's awareness that the new American administration did not believe the time was ripe for a summit meeting, and were it to change its view, Eisenhower would want to take the initiative; Washington was certainly not prepared to leave the first move to Britain. Eden therefore believed that a solitary initiative by Britain was unwise. In view of the economic and military aid which he and Rab Butler, the Chancellor of the Exchequer, had just negotiated in Washington, such an attempt might even be 'contra-productive'.[52] Strang's warning that a British meeting with Molotov or Malenkov 'would be jealously regarded in the United States' was certainly correct.[53]

On further reflection, Eden came to believe that Churchill intended to use summit diplomacy to delay his retirement and make Eden wait even longer to succeed him.[54] After more than a decade of being Churchill's heir-apparent Eden was running out of patience. Such considerations did not encourage Eden to support Churchill's vague summit plans. Instead, he eventually managed to persuade Churchill to agree to the return of ambassador Gascoigne to London.[55] The American embassy in London was informed that the ambassador had been called to London 'simply for general consultation'.[56]

The talks with the ambassador proceeded along the lines anticipated by everyone involved. Churchill's fears about Gascoigne's pessimistic and unimaginative advice were confirmed, as were the Foreign Office's hopes that Gascoigne would speak out against a high-level meeting at the present time. Not surprisingly, Gascoigne's de-briefing in London did not lead to any new insights.[57] The ambassador was very sceptical of anything that emanated from the Soviet Union; he regarded almost everything the Soviets did as an attempt to conceal a hidden agenda that sought to damage the interests of the western world.[58]

Gascoigne, who was due to retire soon, subscribed to the view that there was no real change in Soviet politics after Stalin's death, and even some Foreign Office experts regarded his analysis as deeply flawed. Harry Hohler, head of the Foreign Office's Northern Department, felt driven to comment that it was 'a mistake to be so hypnotised by the Soviet Union as to assume that every action which the Soviet Union takes must be to the disadvantage of the West'. Gascoigne even appeared to believe 'that the Kremlin's new methods may well prove to be substantially more dangerous than those adopted by Stalin in his comparatively straightforward Cold War'. Hohler's damning assessment of the ambassador's analysis concluded: 'this surely comes perilously near to saying what a pity the Russians have lowered the international temperature – it makes things so much more difficult for us'.[59]

What Gascoigne, Strang, Roberts and most other Foreign Office officials (and for that matter also the American and West German governments) feared was that Stalin's death had deprived the West of a formidable enemy image. This would make the unity of the western alliance and the continuation of the western world's expensive military build-up much more complicated to maintain. It also meant that it might become immensely difficult to justify the necessity of German rearmament and the establishment of the EDC and the need for the commitment of vast amounts of economic resources to the Cold War to western public opinion and the various parliamentary assemblies.

In the course of the first conversation with Gascoigne on 1 April the Foreign Office officials exploited the opportunity given to them by the ambassador's analysis of the situation in Moscow by bluntly telling Eden they did not believe in 'whoring after the Russians'. The allied powers, in particular the United States, would have been incredulous if 'Eden were gallivanting with Molotov' around the time of the forthcoming NATO meeting in late April.[60] Eden's Private Secretary Evelyn Shuckburgh did not think it was wise to embark on a race with the United States for the favour of Russia.[61] According to Shuckburgh, Eden had still been 'very keen' on talks with Molotov when the talks with Gascoigne began, but by the end of the discussions he had fully reversed his opinion:[62] 'A.E. was much impressed by all this and agreed with a lot of it.'[63] This was reflected in Eden's diary; on 2 April, he wrote: 'We all agreed that events were moving fast enough & that a meeting would endanger EDC, encourage [the] French to hang back & generally cause confusion at this time. If matters dragged this would be another question.'[64]

Eden believed he had also succeeded in convincing Churchill to adopt a wait-and-see attitude and allow matters to develop.[65] However, the following day he realized that the Prime Minister had either not understood his arguments or had no desire to understand them. Eden was surprised when Churchill rang up and took issue with his refusal to arrange a meeting with Molotov:

> I was taken aback by W[inston] ringing in the morning & saying somewhat challengingly 'So you have given up the idea of seeing Molotov. I don't like that at all.' He had entirely forgotten yesterday's conversation – went over it again with him carefully & he appeared to agree & and begin to recollect … When he did ring up [again] it was evident that he still did not, but he gave up idea of sending message himself [to Molotov or Malenkov].[66]

The Foreign Secretary found relations with Churchill increasingly exasperating. It was unclear whether Churchill's deafness and health problems or merely his obstinacy and stubbornness were responsible for many of the difficulties between the Prime Minister and his heir-designate. In a letter to his son the Foreign Secretary let off steam: 'All is well ... except that W[inston] gets daily older & is apt to ring up & waste a great deal of time. Between ourselves, the outside world has little idea how difficult all that becomes. Please make me retire before I am 80!'[67] After a further talk with Gascoigne on 6 April, Eden and his officials managed to reach an uneasy compromise with Churchill.[68] On 9 April Gascoigne returned to Moscow with the task of proposing to Molotov the clarification of a number of bilateral Anglo-Soviet matters. The British planned to use the negotiation of a new fisheries agreement as a test of Moscow's readiness to offer concessions in the Cold War. The ambassador was also to initiate talks about the freedom of movement of British diplomats in Moscow and raise the issue of the Soviet refusal to allow the Russian wives of British subjects to leave the USSR.[69]

To make Gascoigne's task easier, Churchill succeeded in persuading Eden to agree to a message to Molotov which Gascoigne was to deliver; Churchill insisted on having a hand in writing the telegram.[70] On the advice of Eden and the Foreign Office,[71] Churchill did not mention in his letter to Eisenhower on 5 April that Gascoigne's contact with Molotov was meant to lead ultimately to a meeting between Malenkov and Churchill himself.[72] On 11 April, Gascoigne was received by Molotov in a very friendly way; the Soviet Foreign Minister thanked the ambassador for Churchill's warm greetings and expressed the hope of an improvement of Anglo-Soviet relations, but nothing of import occurred.[73]

By the time Gascoigne met Molotov in the Kremlin Churchill had taken on the role of Acting Foreign Secretary. On 12 April 1953 Eden underwent an urgent gallbladder operation which, due to a surgeon's mistake, went badly wrong and necessitated two further operations. It would keep him out of office much longer than anticipated – he was only able to resume his post on 1 October.[74] The political work in the Foreign Office now rested on the shoulders of Selwyn Lloyd, the Minister of State, who soon complained that 'The P.M. is in theory in charge of the Foreign Office, but does not do any of the detailed work.'[75] Churchill focused entirely on the big issues, which meant that he concentrated almost exclusively on his summit diplomacy – after all, initially Eden was expected back at his desk within four or five weeks.[76] Churchill took over the Foreign Office with great enthusiasm, as it provided him with the unexpected opportunity of making progress with his summit diplomacy. The post of Foreign Secretary was also the only great office of state he had never held.

Still, Churchill had no desire to fall out with his sick Foreign Secretary. Somewhat disingenuously, he wrote to Eden: 'Happily we are fully agreed in outlook, and I will look after your foreign policy as well as your political interests',[77] a gentle reminder that Eden needed Churchill's support if he wanted to succeed him. The Prime Minister could well have concluded that Eden's illness would prevent him from continuing in active politics and that he would have to appoint a new Foreign Secretary, a course of action that would have wrecked Eden's prospects of becoming Prime Minister. A more ruthless operator than Churchill was on this occasion might well have used the opportunity to remove his heir-apparent, appoint a much less experienced man and thus decrease the mounting pressure on him to retire. Eden was undoubtedly worried about his political future, but he was also genuinely concerned about Britain's foreign policy and its relations with its western allies. He feared that Churchill would use his absence to meddle with Britain's policy towards the Soviet Union and cause a lot of mischief. Eden advised his Parliamentary Under-Secretary Anthony Nutting: 'Don't let the old man appease the Bear too much in my absence.'[78]

Eisenhower's Psychological Warfare and 'Roll-back' Strategy

Initially, however, it was not Churchill but the Eisenhower administration that took the initiative to formulate a speedy response to Stalin's death. Unlike Churchill, the American President and his advisers were not considering serious negotiations but a major psychological warfare offensive to exploit the inexperience and confusion of the new leaders in Moscow.[79] These differing views on how to respond to the situation arising from Stalin's death led to a cooling of Anglo-American relations, and placed considerable strains on the 'special relationship'.

Even before Stalin's death was confirmed, a strategy to seize the initiative had been discussed at a meeting of the American National Security Council (NSC) on the morning of 4 March 1953.[80] During the session the President made clear his 'desire to see whether and in what way the announcement of Stalin's illness could best be exploited for psychological purposes.' Eisenhower was thinking of making a speech to the Soviet peoples 'to penetrate the Iron Curtain', which he emphasized was 'a psychological and not a diplomatic move'.[81] Generating a general détente did not appear to be one of the President's priorities.[82] C.D. Jackson, a former *Time-Life* senior executive and journalist who was Eisenhower's newly appointed Special Assistant for Cold War Operations, thought a presidential statement addressed directly to the

Soviet people was an excellent idea. The present situation appeared to be 'the first really big propaganda opportunity offered to our side for a long time ... to stress our devotion to peace' and fight the Kremlin's 'hate America' campaign 'with real forcefulness'.[83] Most members of the NSC agreed but, somewhat surprisingly, Charles E. Wilson, the hard-line Secretary of Defense and former president of General Motors,[84] and John Foster Dulles, known for his aggressive liberation rhetoric during the 1952 election campaign,[85] warned that this kind of strategy might be dangerous. It would be a gamble from which the United States had more to lose than to gain.[86]

While opinion within the administration remained divided about how to react to Stalin's departure,[87] a consensus soon developed about what kind of policy the new leadership in the Kremlin could be expected to follow. Whereas the State Department's Intelligence Estimate of 4 March had concluded that no fundamental changes in Moscow's domestic and foreign policy would materialize in the near future, it was now assumed that the Kremlin might launch a peace campaign. Vice-President Richard Nixon pointed out that Congress was already putting pressure on the administration to reduce military expenditure; as a precaution, 'Congress should be warned that Stalin's successor might very well prove more difficult to deal with than Stalin himself.' Dulles wholeheartedly concurred.[88]

As requested by the National Security Council, Jackson drew up a policy document where, following the recommendation of the famous meeting of psychological warfare experts in Princeton in 1952, he suggested a presidential speech centred around 'A Message to the Soviet government and the Russian Peoples'.[89] Jackson thought that for maximum effect the President should deliver the speech the day after Stalin's funeral. A potential Soviet peace offensive which would almost certainly endanger the EDC and its ratification in the French parliament could thus be prevented. Jackson feared that the French and British Prime Ministers would use a more amenable Soviet policy as an excuse to press for negotiations with Moscow, which if successful would make West German rearmament and the whole EDC enterprise redundant.[90] MIT economist Walt Rostow, a member of the 'ad hoc group of government experts in "psychological warfare" '[91] led by Jackson and George Morgan, the director of the Psychological Strategy Board (PSB), drafted the presidential message on 6 March.[92] Rostow's drafts included the suggestion of a four-power conference at either head of state or foreign minister level. The conference was supposed to work out agreements on such complicated issues as the general control of armaments, special security arrangements for Europe in order to overcome the division of Germany by free elections, and the solution of the Austrian problem. Rostow emphasized, however, that any high-level meeting should be conditional on an end to the Korean War and perhaps the solution of other issues.[93]

Soon, critical voices from within the American government regretted the lack of political substance in the proposed initiative. Paul Nitze, who had succeeded George Kennan as director of the Policy Planning Staff (PPS) in January 1950, explained 'there was very little new in Jackson's plan and therefore that it amounted largely to a propaganda move'.[94] On 6 March Jackson, Emmet Hughes, another one of Eisenhower's speech-writers and also formerly a journalist for *Time-Life*, Charles Bohlen, Counsellor in the State Department and ambassador-designate to Moscow, and Nitze met to discuss the proposal.[95]

Hughes came to the point and outlined the main problem of the suggested policy offensive. He explained that the substance of the presidential statement very much depended on to whom the 'big speech' should be addressed. Would it be aimed at the Soviet satellite countries to encourage them to embark on an insurrection or would it be aimed 'over their bowed heads' at the Kremlin to embark on serious East-West negotiation? Hughes believed that the speech could not achieve both.[96]

Charles Bohlen also disagreed with the proposed course of action. In a memorandum dated 7 March 1953 Bohlen pointed out that a policy of active roll-back was unrealistic. The United States could help to stir up some anti-Soviet developments in China and the Eastern European satellite states but 'we cannot instigate them in the first instance.' Any dissenting group in the Soviet orbit would want 'assurances of material and not moral support. If we are not prepared to give such support it is better to say nothing.' Bohlen clearly advocated the latter course: 'a direct frontal political or psychological assault on the Soviet structure or leadership would only have the effect of consolidating their position and postponing the possibility of dissension in the top leadership'. Instead, the West should confront the Soviet Union with a genuinely new political and diplomatic situation which had not existed under Stalin. This would represent a genuine test of the new leaders' peaceful and cooperative intentions. Bohlen concluded that 'A suggestion of this nature might be the one for a meeting of the four foreign ministers for general discussion without an agenda and for a strictly limited period of time to exchange views.'[97]

Bohlen's proposal had nothing in common with the policy advocated by C.D. Jackson and Walt Rostow. They insisted on a fixed agenda and the pre-condition of a truce in Korea which would make the realization of an early four-power meeting nigh impossible. Bohlen's suggestion was remarkably close to Winston Churchill's unconventional ideas which, however, were not very popular in the White House. Consequently Bohlen's own similar proposal did not strengthen the ambassador-designate's influence in the White House. Although in general Eisenhower thought highly of him, Bohlen was distrusted by Dulles and hated by the McCarthyite wing of the Republican Party. After all he had been FDR's interpreter at Yalta and not least due to this fact was regarded as too liberal and too soft on Communism.[98]

On 11 March 1953, six days after Stalin's death had been announced, Churchill wrote to Eisenhower and reminded him that when they had met in New York in early January the President-elect had said he was interested in arranging a bilateral meeting with Stalin. Churchill asked Eisenhower if he was still interested in meeting the Soviet leaders unilaterally. He wondered whether 'now that the personalities are altered', the President had changed his mind, so that perhaps '*collective* action' might be possible instead. Churchill thought it was high time to 'turn over a leaf' in the Cold War.[99] According to British official Frank Roberts, Eisenhower was 'horrified' by Churchill's view.[100] In his reply of the same day, the President doubted 'the wisdom of a formal multilateral meeting' as this would enable Moscow once again to obstruct every serious effort on the part of the West, and to use the conference as a propaganda opportunity. Much to Churchill's distaste, Eisenhower indicated that he was contemplating making a speech very soon which would give the world 'some promise of hope, which will have the virtues of simplicity and correctness'. The President explained that within his administration a 'number of ideas have been advanced, but none of them has been completely acceptable'.[101]

Although hardly anyone among Britain's foreign policy experts agreed with Churchill's policy, the emerging US strategy of how to deal with the post-Stalin leadership in Moscow was viewed with great apprehension. On the day Stalin's death was announced, the British ambassador in Moscow summarized the Foreign Office's anxiety about an active American 'roll-back' policy. Gascoigne feared that 'elements of the US Government may try to replace our present policy of containment by a more forward and positive one in arguing that this is the moment to deal with Russia when the stability of her political situation has been impaired'.[102] His gloomy view of developments in Washington was widely shared in London. Already in late February 1953 Winthrop Aldrich, the new American ambassador to London, had reported that Churchill and the British Foreign Office were 'apprehensive over suggestions and rumors' that the Eisenhower government 'may regard "containment" as insufficient and may be embarking on stepped up psychological warfare and [a] more "positive and dynamic" policy towards [the] Soviets'.[103]

The British concerns were not unjustified but perhaps a little overblown. After all, many foreign policy experts within the Eisenhower administration, including John Foster Dulles, continued to oppose strongly an active policy of roll-back. They made their views known before the decisive NSC meeting scheduled for 11 March, the 'initial showdown' as Rostow called it,[104] where the paper of 6 March outlining the contents of a possible presidential message to the Soviet peoples would be discussed.[105] The day before several important memoranda were submitted to the NSC, all of them arguing strongly against a psychological warfare offensive.[106]

Among the senior State Department officials, one underlying rationale for opposing the President's planned initiative was the fact that the Eisenhower administration had not yet outlined a coherent foreign policy programme.[107] (Work on NSC 162/2, the administration's important framework of its 'New Look' Cold War strategy, was only begun on 30 July and the document was not finalized until the late summer; Eisenhower did not sign it into law until October 1953 and it continued to be developed thereafter.[108]) Beyond the preparation of a vague political warfare campaign, no one in the State Department seems to have known in the spring of 1953 what the substance of American policy was supposed to be. Did the President only intend to upset the new leaders in the Kremlin to make life more difficult for them, or had he actually embarked on the famous 'liberation' policy and the overthrow of the regime in the Soviet Union?[109]

During the NSC meeting on 11 March Dulles succinctly summarized all the arguments which had been put forward in papers by Nitze, Bohlen and Smith the day before. Dulles realized that Eisenhower was still keen on delivering a speech and so did not make any strenuous attempts to dissuade the President from giving the address but concentrated on attempting to alter its substance. Instead of Jackson's and Rostow's proposal for a foreign ministers' conference on European issues, an idea Dulles detested as it would almost inevitably include a discussion of disarmament and the unification of Germany, he referred to an idea proposed by Nitze, who thought the suggestion of a four-power conference to Moscow should be replaced by a call for the end of hostilities in Korea and Indochina.[110] Thus, Dulles proposed that the President's speech should not concentrate on European affairs but cover East–West tension in Asia. If a solution for the conflicts in Korea and Indochina materialized, 'the path would be open to further negotiations on other matters'. Dulles believed that such a strategy was more advantageous 'than to begin from the European end' with the attendant risk of undermining the Atlantic alliance.[111]

The Secretary of State was deeply worried that entering into close contact with the Soviet Union by convening a high-level conference, as advocated by Churchill and now even by some American experts, would endanger the stability of NATO. However, he was also strongly opposed to a policy of 'roll-back'. He warned the National Security Council that the US had a problem of its own:

> We too have a coalition to manage. In our attempt to destroy the unity of the Soviet orbit we must not jeopardize the unity of our own coalition. We must draw together and not fall apart at this moment in history, and it seem[s] especially doubtful ... as to whether this was the appropriate moment to carry the offensive direct to the Soviet Union. The Soviet Union [is] now involved in a family funeral and it might well be best to wait until the corpse was buried and the mourners gone off to their homes to read the will, before we begin our campaign to create discord in the family. If we move precipitately we might very well enhance Soviet family loyalty and disrupt the free world's.[112]

In the event of a four-power conference taking place after all, Dulles was against putting 'discussion of German unity on the agenda for such a Foreign Ministers meeting', which would ruin every prospect of the ratification of the EDC. The realization of the EDC was of vital importance to Dulles as the European army would cement the western alliance, leading to lasting Franco-German friendship and thus preventing future European wars.[113] The Secretary of State does not appear to have even considered the possibility of the heads of government summit that Churchill had in mind. Dulles assumed that the Kremlin would only 'dig up' all their old plans for high-level meetings and nothing positive would be achieved. He was 'pretty sure' that 'the proposal to discuss German unity with the Soviets in a foreign ministers' conference was tantamount to inviting the fall of the French, German and Italian Governments, and possibly even rendering Mr. Eden's position in the British government untenable'. Dulles therefore 'felt compelled to advise against this part' of the plan. It appeared obvious to him that 'if an attempt were made to create German unity by some other vehicle than the EDC, then certainly the EDC would be finished'.[114] This, incidentally, was also West German Chancellor Adenauer's greatest fear.[115]

In the course of the NSC meeting on 11 March, it also became clear that Eisenhower had changed his mind. He now agreed with Dulles that a four-power meeting was highly undesirable. The Soviet Union, the President believed, would stall indefinitely on the agenda for such a meeting. But 'something dramatic' was still needed, he said. 'A four-power conference would not do it, but the President might say that he would be ready and willing to meet with anyone anywhere from the Soviet Union provided the basis for the meeting was honest and practical.'[116] This, of course, was still not much of a new idea and was moreover a rather vague and imprecise proposal. The prospect of a bilateral US–USSR summit, however, was exactly what Churchill had gloomily anticipated ever since his meeting with Eisenhower in early January.[117] The NSC meeting concluded with an indecisive discussion of the timing and the place of the President's address. It was eventually agreed that C.D. Jackson and his advisers 'should immediately draft an address by the President in the light of the discussion at the meeting, for early delivery at a time and place to be determined'.[118]

Thus, the meeting concluded that Eisenhower should give a speech, albeit one which would not contain a proposal for a high-level East–West conference. The voices within the State Department advising against an early presidential statement had been ignored, though Nitze's insistence in his memorandum that a truce in Korea should be made a clear precondition for any improvement in relations with the Soviet Union had been accepted.[119] On the whole, the officials in the State Department received the impression that Eisenhower still planned to use his address to embark on a major campaign of political warfare.[120] Soon however, and entirely unexpectedly, the psychological warfare strategy was cancelled. Instead, Eisenhower's speech was determined by the unfolding Soviet peace campaign. In spite of his personal enthusiasm for a psychological warfare offensive, the President's 'Chance for Peace' address ultimately resembled much more closely the ideas of Dulles and the State Department than those of psychological warfare warriors around C.D. Jackson and Walt Rostow.

The Soviet Peace Campaign

The foreign policy experts in Washington and London were utterly surprised when the new Soviet leadership not only continued its cooperative gestures but initiated a vigorous and long drawn-out peace campaign.[121] Before a session of the Supreme Soviet on 15 March, Malenkov pointed out that 'there is no litigious or unresolved question which could not be settled by peaceful means on the basis of the mutual agreement of the countries concerned … including the United States of America.'[122] A few days later, the USSR suddenly expressed itself in favour of exchanging sick and disabled prisoners of war in Korea and gave several hints of being seriously interested in negotiating a truce; armistice talks resumed on 2 April.[123]

Soon, there were various other indications of the peace campaign. Traffic hold-ups around Berlin were lifted and the Kremlin even offered quadripartite negotiations on air safety in the Berlin air corridors.[124] The Soviet Union also waived its long-standing claim on military control of the Dardanelles and the

Bosphorus.[125] After months of firm refusal, Moscow agreed to the appointment of Dag Hammarskjöld as the new Secretary-General of the United Nations.[126] Even the long-standing 'hate America campaign' within the Soviet Union was allowed to peter out.[127] The Kremlin also approached a Norwegian representative at the United Nations indicating their interest in a meeting between Malenkov and Eisenhower which could be used to discuss disarmament and atomic energy control.[128]

In addition, a number of internal measures were introduced in the Soviet Union. A sudden relaxation of prison and labour camp regulations took place and a general amnesty was decreed for inmates serving prison terms of under five years and for some categories of political prisoners.[129] Moscow even acknowledged that the so-called 'doctors' plot' with its strong anti-Semitic tenor had been based on false accusations. In an extraordinarily frank statement, it was admitted that the confessions of the eight prominent physicians, whom Stalin during his last months had accused of having conspired to poison senior Soviet politicians including himself, had been achieved through 'impermissible methods of investigation'. The surviving doctors were released immediately.[130] To American diplomat Jacob Beam in Moscow all this seemed to be 'most concrete evidence' of the new regime's break with Stalinism.[131]

Most western foreign ministries did not share this conclusion. In London, the Permanent Under-Secretary William Strang commented that 'A few swallows do not make a summer'. Similarly, the British ambassador to Moscow still felt able to claim without much evidence that 'a really genuine change of heart which might bring about a basic change of policy [in Moscow] is out of the question'.[132] The American administration was also sceptical about Beam's analysis. Not only Eisenhower, C.D. Jackson and CIA chief Allen Dulles but also virtually all State Department officials did not believe in the possibility of a sudden end to the Cold War. It was assumed that Moscow's peace initiative was based entirely on the Soviet realization that certain compromises with the West had to be entered into in order to obtain a lull in the Cold War.[133] Adenauer agreed, warning the Americans not 'to succumb to the blandishments of a détente which for the time being was nothing but a pipedream'.[134]

Yet, in view of the popular appeal of the Soviet peace campaign American politicians became increasingly worried. Remembering the Stalin Note of March 1952, Charles Bohlen believed everything seemed to be 'building up towards a new offer on Germany'. It was even possible 'that with Stalin gone this offer might be a really big one involving Soviet withdrawal from Eastern Germany'.[135] As the western public was likely to greet such a proposal with enthusiasm, this would make the realization of the EDC and the integration of the Federal Republic of Germany with the West impossible. The influential journalist Walter Lippman commented that 'the Western diplomatic structure was fragile and highly vulnerable to a serious Soviet peace offensive'.[136] After all, the American position on the East–West conflict and German unification had not changed since 1951 when a policy paper concluded: 'Short of a complete change in Russian objectives which would remove existing tension with the West and would permit a general rather than a limited settlement of outstanding issues, there appears to be no basis for believing that the Western powers and the Soviet Union could agree to conditions permitting the unification of Germany'.[137]

As the Soviet peace campaign unfolded, hardly anyone in Washington believed that the Soviet Union was making genuine compromise proposals with the aim of de-escalating, let alone ending the Cold War. Bedell Smith told some visiting West German politicians that 'such a [Soviet] bid would not be sincere and would be nothing but an attempt to prevent or delay the establishment of a European Army'.[138]

Nevertheless, the peace campaign and its generally positive reception by western public opinion made Eisenhower's psychological warfare offensive inopportune. Jackson's draft presidential speech was revised several times, but no consensus between the White House and the State Department could be reached.[139] The result was the postponement of Eisenhower's address. After the original plan to deliver the speech on the day after Stalin's funeral on 9 March was shelved because of opposition to its substance from within the State Department, Jackson envisaged that the address would be delivered on 19 March before the UN General Assembly, or on television to the American people. The Soviet peace campaign, however, resulted in further haggling between Jackson and the State Department. By 17 March four new draft speeches had been drawn up by Jackson and Hughes, all of them geared towards delivery before the United Nations, but it was decided that the speech was not yet in a satisfactory state. Soon the idea of delivering it to the UN General Assembly was abandoned; Eisenhower believed that using the UN would only 'invite more sterile debate there'.[140]

The President felt increasingly uneasy, even threatened, by the almost universal popularity of the Soviet peace campaign. Giving a background talk to an Overseas Writers' luncheon, CIA director Allen Dulles admitted that no one 'predicted quite as sudden a Soviet Peace Offensive as has actually taken place'.[141] Eisenhower was greatly influenced by Malenkov's conciliatory speech to the Supreme Soviet on 15 March which included a proposal to commence negotiations for a German peace treaty. The President became more than ever 'disposed to move ahead' with his own address and thought that 'it was too bad that he had not made his speech before Malenkov'.[142] Any American propaganda move would now make much less impact on world opinion. After all, it was the Soviet Union and not the United States that had introduced a peace campaign; Washington would be seen as just reacting to the initiative by the Soviet Union. In view of the increasingly daring moves of the Soviet campaign, which even Rostow found 'quite impressive',[143] the President intervened decisively on 16 March. He had become rather disenchanted with his speech writers. Embarking on a psychological warfare campaign was now not enough and a change of tactics was urgently necessary. This time the American President had to offer something concrete.[144] According to Hughes, the President said to him in a highly emotional state:

> Look, I am tired ... of just plain indictments of the Soviet regime. I think it would be wrong ... for me to get up before the world now to make another of those indictments. Instead, just one thing matters: what have we got to offer the world? ... What are we trying to achieve? ... Let us talk straight: no double talk, no sophisticated political formulas, no slick propaganda devices. Let us spell it out, whatever we really offer ... withdrawal of troops here or there by both sides ... United Nations supervised free elections in another place ... and concretely all that we would hope to do for the economic well-being of other countries.[145]

It was clear that Eisenhower had become highly nervous of the implications of Malenkov's speech, which was not couched in the usual vague and general terms but contained some precise proposals of what could be done to relax East–West tension. The President began to move away from supporting Jackson's and Rostow's aggressive political warfare goals. After Malenkov's address, Eisenhower drew on his 'basic reservoir of common sense'[146] and decided that the speech-writing process had to be given new impetus and needed to move beyond considering merely a psychological warfare campaign. Accordingly, from now on Emmet Hughes became much more involved in the drafting of the speech, and C.D. Jackson's role became less important than it had been in the immediate aftermath of Stalin's death.[147] Hughes, strongly supported by Paul Nitze, approached the matter in a much more realistic and focused way. He intended to concentrate on the dangerous burden of the arms race and consequently on the importance of arms control.[148] Hughes was also careful to take into account the President's desire to emphasize issues such as raising the general standard of living in the world.[149]

Since Malenkov's speech, Eisenhower had moved much closer to the view of the State Department and also a little closer to Churchill's position, although the President was still not prepared to consider a genuine summit conference with the new men in the Kremlin. Neither Churchill's influence nor the persuasive powers of the State Department but rather the favourable impression of the Soviet peace campaign on world opinion was responsible for Eisenhower's changing mind. The President's first public response to the Kremlin's peace campaign came during a press conference on 19 March and indicated the evolution in his thinking: 'I can only say that that is just as welcome as it is sincere.'[150]

Dulles, however, was much less impressed by Malenkov's speech of 15 March than Eisenhower. He thought that the address had come about in a normal way 'and he had just added a few paragraphs aimed at us'.[151] Similarly, the British Foreign Office believed 'we should be wise to treat Malenkov's speech as being no different from previous Soviet declarations of peaceful intentions'.[152] Dulles was still convinced that the President's speech should not be too concrete, as the administration would have to cooperate with its European allies when attempting to convert the proposals into reality.[153] The Secretary of State was still firmly opposed to any direct or implied indication that there might be a need for an East–West conference as advocated by Churchill. This would almost certainly push the US into discussing the German question, which would inevitably lead to further postponement of the ratification of the EDC in France. At a meeting on the morning of 17 March Dulles explained in exasperation: 'What all this gets down to is the question of whether we are ready to start negotiating directly. The President hasn't seemed to feel this way, in his various exchanges with Churchill. But perhaps he has changed his mind.'[154] Yet regarding the British Prime Minister's summit ideas Eisenhower had not adopted a different attitude.[155]

In early April an almost final draft of the speech was submitted to Eisenhower. The President sent it to London and Paris, as he had decided that it was time the European allies be informed. French leader René Mayer wholeheartedly agreed with the speech and believed the address would serve a 'very useful purpose'.[156] It seemed sensible to put pressure on Moscow to obtain a peace treaty with Austria and the withdrawal of the Red Army from Austria, Hungary and Romania. Like many French parliamentarians, Mayer also hoped that the policy of the new Soviet leadership would make German reunification, which could well lead to a neutral Germany, superfluous. Only the simultaneous conclusion of a global disarmament treaty could make reunification acceptable. Mayer was opposed to a high-level meeting with Moscow as 'the Soviets would drag such a meeting out interminably'.[157]

On the advice of Dulles, Eisenhower also showed his draft speech to German Chancellor Adenauer, who was on his first state visit to Washington.[158] Adenauer thought the address 'excellent' but asked the President to incorporate a passage about the 300,000 German prisoners of war he believed were still held captive in the Soviet Union. This Eisenhower did, although in his speech he would not refer to German nationals in particular but to the POWs in general who were still imprisoned in the USSR.[159] Although in a subsequent conversation with British diplomat Christopher Steel, Adenauer referred to the American political approach as 'distinctly naif' [sic!], he told American politicians that he 'was pleased ... that their caution in dealing with the Russian peace drive matched his own attitude'.[160] Naturally, Adenauer was also very satisfied with the passage in Eisenhower's speech referring to the German question. This section of the speech repeated the traditional western requests for the creation of a 'free and united Germany with a government based upon free and secret elections', which Moscow was still most unlikely to accept.[161]

Churchill, however, was less happy with Eisenhower's speech when he received a copy from ambassador Aldrich on 9 April. Once again he was the odd one out. The Prime Minister criticized some of its content as sounding overly aggressive; he also suspected that Eisenhower was primarily interested in achieving a propaganda victory and impressing world opinion. In a letter to Eisenhower Churchill suggested the postponement of the delivery of the address until the purpose and full extent of the change of attitude in the Soviet leadership was clear. The Prime Minister employed the full force of his rhetorical skills to persuade Eisenhower to shelve his speech for the time being:

> The apparent change of Soviet mood is so new and so indefinite and its causes so obscure that there could not be much risk in letting things develop. We do not know what these men mean. We do not want to deter them from saying what they mean ... Great hope has arisen in the world that there is a change of heart in the vast, mighty masses of Russia and this can carry them far and fast and perhaps into revolution. It has been well said that the most dangerous moment for evil governments is when they begin to reform. Nothing impressed me so much as the doctor story ... We cannot see what you would lose by waiting till the full character and purpose of the Soviet change is more clearly defined and also is apparent to the whole free world.[162]

However, it was all to no avail; Eisenhower was not willing to postpone his speech. Instead, in Washington the suspicion grew – Emmet Hughes even speaks of a 'general concurrence' – that Churchill was less concerned with allowing the Soviet government more time than with the impact he himself wished to have on world opinion. It appeared that it was 'Churchill's deep, unspoken concern ... to guard and reserve for himself the initiative in any dramatic new approach to the Soviet leaders'. Dulles, however, exploited the opportunity given to him by Churchill's letter to voice once again his general doubt as to the 'need for any speech'.[163] In his prompt reply to Churchill, Eisenhower told the Prime Minister that he agreed that it was necessary to avoid appearing to threaten the new Soviet leadership and inducing them to 'retreat into their shell'. He promised to revise certain paragraphs of the address but explained to Churchill that 'he was obligated beyond any possibility of withdrawal to making a speech on this general subject'.[164]

Churchill was not impressed by Eisenhower's letter and sent a reply the same day. Although he grudgingly accepted that Eisenhower would give his speech on 16 April, the Prime Minister could not resist the temptation to point out once again the dangers inherent in such a course. 'It would be a pity,' he declared, 'if a sudden frost nipped spring in the bud', or 'if this could be alleged, even if there was no real spring.' He indicated that it might be a good idea to explain to Moscow 'separately' 'how glad we should be if we found there was a real change of heart'. Churchill also told the President that he himself would give a speech on 17 April which would focus on the statement that 'we are firm as rock against aggression but the door is always open to friendship'.[165] He also made some further suggestions of how to improve the President's speech which Eisenhower promised to incorporate 'one way or another'.[166] The importance with which Churchill viewed the matter explains the fact that he forwarded his correspondence with Eisenhower to the young Elizabeth II, much admired by Churchill, who had become Queen on the sudden death of her father in February 1952. In an accompanying letter he wrote: 'I hope your Majesty will feel that I have tried to save the spring-time buds – if any there be.'[167]

A Chance For Peace?

On 16 April 1953, Eisenhower, though suffering from severe food poisoning, delivered his speech to the American Society of Newspaper Editors in Washington. He called upon the Soviet Union to use the 'precious opportunity' provided by Stalin's death 'to awaken ... and to help turn the tide of history'. The President said that Moscow's first step had to be agreement to an end of the Korean War. Without mentioning an East–West conference, he declared that subsequently the discussion of the German and Austrian questions and a general disarmament treaty should be embarked upon. Eisenhower hoped the Kremlin would be prepared to submit to inspection by UN arms officials, and to permit the Eastern European countries to choose their own form of government. The financial savings achieved by a lessening of world tension could be used to increase the global standard of living with the aid of the UN. 'This would be a declared total war, not upon any human enemy but the brute forces of poverty and need.'[168]

The international reaction to Eisenhower's address was very positive. Even Andrei Gromyko, the outgoing Soviet ambassador in London, declared that the speech was 'not bad but too vague'.[169] The *New York Times* called the address 'magnificent and deeply moving' although, the paper commented, it had obviously been made to 'seize the peace initiative from the Soviets'. The *New Yorker* believed that Eisenhower had 'scored an immense triumph with both world and American opinion' which 'reestablished American leadership in the world'.[170] The American administration had indeed attempted to ensure that no one on earth would be able to ignore Eisenhower's address. The speech was broadcast live in the United States and in Britain. The text of the declaration was also given to all American embassies abroad, and diplomats were instructed to draw the attention of the politicians in their respective countries to particular points. The State Department sent out more than three million copies of the speech for distribution in Europe and Latin America. Film and tape recordings of the President delivering the speech were distributed all over the world. The *Voice of America* made sure that the address was repeatedly broadcast into all the Eastern European countries.[171]

Eisenhower's close adviser Sherman Adams called the speech 'the most effective ... of Eisenhower's public career, and certainly one of the highlights of his presidency'.[172] This is doubtful. The President had, after all, asked the new Soviet leadership to alter its entire foreign policy in exchange for American goodwill.[173] Nothing really changed because of it. No one within the Eisenhower administration thought of attempting to realize the global Marshall Plan, envisaged by C.D. Jackson as a result of the speech. The address was not followed up by any concrete action on the part of the United States.[174] Instead, in May the American administration threatened the use of atomic bombs to hasten the peace negotiations and so achieve a quick end to the war in Korea.[175]

All in all, a Soviet–American rapprochement proved as difficult as it had been before. Nor did this change when the Korean War eventually came to an end in the summer of 1953; on 27 July 1953 an armistice agreement was signed. As in the aftermath of the Second World War, the heavily fortified 38th parallel would continue to be the dividing line between North and South Korea. Yet, as the EDC treaty had still not been ratified and consequently the integration of the Federal Republic of Germany with the West had not yet been achieved, Dulles's and Eisenhower's opposition to a conference with the Soviet Union continued. It did not seem to matter that the end of the war in Korea had always been regarded as 'an essential prerequisite to any future improvement in the world situation'.[176] The risk that a four-power conference would wreck the EDC and prevent the irreversible integration of the Federal Republic of Germany into the West was still too great. Thus, Eisenhower's 'Chance for Peace' speech as well as his equally famous 'Atoms for Peace' speech in early December 1953 primarily constituted 'a direct challenge to the Soviet's near-monopoly of peace propaganda' in the aftermath of Stalin's death.[177] It certainly was not meant to be the beginning of an era of détente, negotiations and arms control.

In his own speech on 18 April 1953, only two days after Eisenhower's address and to a similar audience of newspaper editors, Secretary of State Dulles once again expressed doubts as to whether the Soviet peace moves were due to a basic change in policy or merely a tactical shift. Dulles still believed that the Kremlin was attempting 'to buy off a powerful enemy and gain a respite'. It certainly would be an 'illusion of peace', he said, if there was 'a settlement based on the status quo'. It was of the utmost importance, he added, that the United States made 'clear to the captive people that we do not accept their captivity as a permanent fact of history'.[178]

This was much closer to Dulles's election campaign speeches in 1952 and to C.D. Jackson's point of view than to the opinions Dulles had voiced in private to Eisenhower and his colleagues in the government during the previous weeks. He also made sure to mention in his own speech the 'Eisenhower tests' whose fulfilment was necessary for an era of mutual trust. One can only surmise that Dulles was mainly speaking to comfort the right wing of the Republican Party. Perhaps he also wanted to make sure that the Soviet Union did not misunderstand Eisenhower's superficially less belligerent although substantially very similar speech. As Lloyd Gardner expressed it: 'Dulles was playing "bad cop" to Ike's "good cop".'[179] The Secretary of State wanted to make sure that Moscow did not feel encouraged to propose a four-power conference, an idea which in view of the President's alleged 'peace offensive' the United States would have found difficult to turn down.[180] This must also have worried Eisenhower: it is highly unlikely that the President had not seen or had disagreed with Dulles's speech.

Churchill, however, was not happy with Dulles's speech. Above all, he was not content with allowing either Eisenhower's address or the Soviet peace campaign to dominate the international political agenda. He wished to guide the international discussion along lines favourable to his personal position and to the maintenance of Britain's great power status. The Prime Minister was certainly not diverted from conference diplomacy by the unenthusiastic reception his summit policy received from his Cabinet colleagues in late April.[181] Churchill would have been greatly encouraged, however, had he known that the Soviet Party Presidium (as the Politburo was called at the time) discussed his summit proposals as well as Eisenhower's 'Chance for Peace' speech on 24 April 1953. While the President's speech was largely viewed as 'propaganda and provocation' by Molotov and most members of the Presidium, Malenkov and Beria appear to have expressed interest in a summit conference as advocated by the Prime Minister. After all, participation in an international summit meeting would have helped them tremendously to boost their own authority in both international and domestic politics.[182]

On the whole, Stalin's death did not make much of a difference as far as both the State Department's and the Foreign Office's policies towards Moscow were concerned. A great lack of interest in a summit conference resulting from an equally profound lack of conviction that the post-Stalin Soviet Union had embarked on a genuinely new political course also dominated the Eisenhower White House. The only major western statesman who dissented from this position was the British Prime Minister. In view of the recalcitrant attitude of his own foreign policy experts and the even more adamant position of the new American administration not to fundamentally re-consider relations with Moscow, Churchill faced an uphill task with his attempt to open a new chapter in the East-West conflict after Stalin's death. Yet he was determined to begin with realizing his political vision for a new post-war order as soon as possible. Churchill was not averse to considering a 'solitary pilgrimage' to Moscow to persuade Malenkov and Molotov of his peaceful intentions and the necessity of conversation at the highest level. The British Prime Minister would use the opportunity of a major foreign affairs speech in the House of Commons in May 1953 to inform the world of his plans for achieving lasting global peace.

CHAPTER 11

Churchill's Vision
Proposals for Overcoming the Cold War

Four days after Eisenhower's 'Chance for Peace' speech on 16 April 1953, Churchill told the House of Commons of his hope that 'conversations on the highest level, even if informal and private, between some of the principal Powers concerned' would soon be possible.[1] On the same day Churchill asked Ambassador Gascoigne in Moscow to pass on the text of his parliamentary speech to Molotov.[2] The American embassy in London referred to Churchill's speech as the ' "warmest" statement Churchill has made since he assumed office on [the] question [of] negotiating with [the] Soviets'.[3] Indeed, in the second half of April it became ever clearer that Churchill was about to take the initiative to make progress with his cherished goal of a 'Big Three' summit conference to overcome the Cold War and ensure Britain's continued place in the sun. In particular Churchill's speech in Parliament on 11 May and his subsequent top secret memoranda addressed to the Foreign Office outlined the Prime Minister's vision of how to obtain the Soviet Union's agreement to a peaceful and enduring termination of the Cold War. Since Churchill's unconventional ideas threatened to undermine the entire western framework of how to conduct the Cold War they would prove highly controversial within the western world. The American administration was particularly upset by Churchill's approach.

A Solitary Pilgrimage to Moscow?

In the aftermath of Moscow's peace campaign and Eisenhower's 'Chance for Peace' address, Churchill decided it was time to embark on a more forceful initiative to realize his summit diplomacy. On 21 April 1953 he wrote to

Eisenhower asking him to consider the continuation of the Potsdam conference in neutral Stockholm; during their meeting in New York on 5 January Eisenhower had mentioned the Swedish capital as a possible meeting place with the Soviet leaders. But Churchill went further than merely once again suggesting a high-level conference; the Prime Minister was clearly losing patience. If a summit meeting did not prove to be acceptable to Eisenhower, he would meet Malenkov alone: 'If nothing can be arranged I shall have to consider seriously a personal contact.'[4]

Eisenhower was not impressed by Churchill's proposal. He was increasingly less keen on the correspondence with the British Prime Minister, and in early March had told Eden that he found Churchill's letters 'tiresome';[5] when he received Churchill's first letter he had thought immediately 'Here comes trouble'. By the end of the year ambassador Makins reported that 'the PM's messages irritated' Eisenhower and Dulles.[6] However, on 25 April the President replied in a reserved but friendly way to Churchill's letter, explaining that since their meeting in New York the situation had changed fundamentally. Eisenhower did not believe in 'premature action'; he favoured watching 'developments for a while longer before determining our further course'. The President realized of course that he could not actually forbid the Prime Minister to travel to Moscow. He therefore wrote that if Churchill, 'for some special and local reason' wished to enter into a personal contact with Moscow, he expected 'as much advance notice as you could possibly give us'. The President ended by saying that at some time in the future a high-level summit meeting might be sensible, but that he would have to insist on the participation of France.[7]

However, it was not that easy to dishearten Churchill. On 23 April Gascoigne had once again been received by Molotov in a warm and most encouraging way,[8] and Eisenhower's letter seemed to have left open the possibility that the President could be persuaded of the value of a summit meeting. The President had indicated that there was 'some feeling' for such a conference in the USA.[9] Thus, the Prime Minister did not give up his idea. On 2 May Churchill mentioned his plans to Deputy Under-Secretary Pierson Dixon. He said 'that he ought to offer himself ... to go to Moscow'. The official was greatly alarmed and advised against this policy but the Prime Minister declared that he would do his best to attempt to get 'back with the Soviet leaders on the old wartime basis'. He expressed the conviction that Moscow was afraid of the West and he, Churchill, might perhaps be able to 'allay their suspicions' by, for example, demonstrating understanding for the Soviet desire to obtain 'outlets to the sea'.[10]

Churchill was so convinced of the rightness of his assumption that on the evening of 3 May 1953 he decided to attempt to overcome the President's objections by means of a decisive initiative. He forwarded to Eisenhower the draft of a telegram which he intended to send to Molotov. In his capacity as Acting Foreign Secretary Churchill proposed that Molotov should invite him to Moscow at the end of May for three or four days of informal talks.

> I wonder whether you [Molotov] would like me to come to Moscow so that we could renew our own war-time relation[ship] and so that I could meet Monsieur Malenkov and others of your leading men. Naturally I do not imagine that we could settle any of the grave issues which overhang the immediate future of the world, but I have a feeling that it might be helpful if our intercourse proceeded with the help of friendly acquaintance and goodwill instead of impersonal diplomacy and propaganda. I do not see how this could make things worse.[11]

The following day Churchill met Selwyn Lloyd and William Strang, his most senior foreign policy advisers, and told them that if Eisenhower approved of his proposal he would ask the Cabinet to agree to his journey to Moscow. However, Churchill said he was in two minds: he was still doubtful whether to send the message to Molotov, 'though ... he probably would', and the whole matter was causing him 'great anxiety and had been a cause of deep heart-searching'. If he travelled to Moscow, his aim would be the renewal of contact between East and West, and before his journey he would make great efforts to explain this to Chancellor Adenauer. Strang tried to convince the Prime Minister of the risks of his enterprise: Churchill's own trip could easily be imitated by other western politicians, and if French politicians started visiting the USSR this could lead to an 'extremely dangerous' situation, 'given the hankering at the back of the French mind for a Franco-Russian agreement against Germany'. Churchill was not convinced: he said that France was not really important, and if Paris did not ratify the EDC, the Federal Republic would have to join NATO.[12]

Churchill's notion that a tête-à-tête with Malenkov and the other leaders in Moscow would lead to the re-establishment of good Anglo-Soviet relations was highly unrealistic. The Prime Minister entirely failed to understand the suspicion with which he was regarded in Moscow. Stalin's successors had been in important leadership positions during the war, and British policy in 1940–41, which the Kremlin regarded as a devious attempt by Churchill to provoke the Soviet Union to fight Hitler's Germany on behalf of the West, was still remembered with much resentment in Moscow. Nor had the Prime Minister's constant postponement of the Second Front and his many other confrontations with the Soviet government during the war been forgotten. The Yugoslav Communist Djilas summed up the Soviet view:

'One could tell in general that Churchill had left a deep impression on the Soviet leaders as a farsighted and dangerous "bourgeois statesman" – though they did not like him.'[13]

There was also Churchill's fierce and long-standing anti-Communism as displayed for example in his pronouncements and activities after the Russian revolution in 1917. Moreover, the Kremlin viewed his 1946 'iron curtain' speech as having started the Cold War; it was seen as a clarion call for 'the imperialist forces of the world to mobilize against the Soviet Union'.[14] Khrushchev, for example, believed that Churchill's choice of Fulton, Missouri, made his speech 'all the more threatening' as it was clear that in a third world war the USSR would have to face a western coalition led by the United States. Khrushchev thought the 'iron curtain' speech was largely responsible for Stalin's exaggeration of the strength of the West 'and their intention to unleash war on us'. He believed that for Stalin, and perhaps for many others in the Kremlin, 'Churchill's speech marked a return to prewar attitudes'.[15]

Moreover, Stalin's heirs appear to have interpreted Churchill's advocacy of a summit conference as an attempt to 'take advantage of the fact that the new Soviet Government wasn't yet fully formed and would therefore be more vulnerable to pressure'. Khrushchev suspected the Prime Minister of intending to 'wring some concessions out of Stalin's successors before we had our feet firmly on the ground'.[16] It also appears, as James Richter has pointed out, that Khrushchev, and perhaps others, did not have sufficient confidence in Malenkov's strength of character and his ability to defend Russian interests at a summit conference with devious western leaders. In his memoirs, Khrushchev refers to Malenkov as 'completely unpredictable' and 'unstable to the point of being dangerous because he was so susceptible to the pressure and influence of others'.[17] Furthermore, Molotov was unwilling to let Malenkov participate in a meeting of the 'Big Three' as he did not wish to allow him to reap the glory and the attention of the international media to the detriment of the Soviet Foreign Minister.[18]

The Kremlin was of course fully aware that Britain was politically and economically weakened and dependent on the United States. It was obvious that any 'Big Three' summit conference needed to be approved by Washington and that little progress towards overcoming the Cold War could be made in bilateral Anglo–Soviet talks. Moscow's suspicion of the Eisenhower administration and the fiercely anti-Communist Dulles made the new rulers conclude that reaching a genuine rapprochement with the USA would be impossible. While the collective leadership believed that Churchill was proposing summit negotiations because he had a secret agenda, Soviet intelligence circles thought that Eisenhower wished to prevent any unpredictable East–West negotiations.

Moscow's Small Committee of Information (KI), an intelligence organ headed by Deputy Foreign Minister Gromyko, concluded in the spring of 1953 that 'In reality the ruling circles of the USA would obviously do everything to postpone negotiations with the USSR for they fear that these negotiations could lead to a fiasco regarding ratification of the European Defence Community agreement and complicate the completion of aggressive US preparations for war against countries of the democratic camp.'[19]

The British Prime Minister seemed unaware of the mistrust with which he was viewed in Moscow, nor did he realize the Kremlin's other considerations. At least initially, Churchill believed that the new leadership would jump at the opportunity of a 'Big Three' summit or even a bilateral Anglo-Soviet conference. Churchill thought the chief obstacle to his plans was the American administration, not the Kremlin. He also assumed that once he had persuaded Eisenhower to go along with his policy, Chancellor Adenauer and the British Foreign Office would toe the American line, and the way would be open to his cherished summit diplomacy,

Churchill, however, failed to appreciate how far Eisenhower was from joining his initiative. The President was utterly dumbfounded by Churchill's draft telegram to Molotov. He replied immediately, though he downplayed his sentiments by merely expressing 'a bit of astonishment' about Churchill's proposed journey to Moscow. At the very least the Prime Minister should have chosen a neutral place for a meeting with Molotov: going to Moscow could easily be misinterpreted as 'weakness or over-eagerness'. Eisenhower also warned him not to underestimate the impact of such a 'solitary pilgrimage' on the policy of the western allies and the NATO alliance. On the whole, people would expect 'concrete and dramatic achievements' from the visit of the British Prime Minister to Moscow. Moreover, if Churchill intended to ignore the French government it could be expected that Paris would propose a four-power conference, 'and this, I am convinced, we are not ready for until there is some evidence, in deeds, of a changed Soviet attitude'.[20]

It is interesting that a first draft letter by Eisenhower, which was not sent, showed a much more understanding attitude towards Churchill's plans. In the draft, the President had declared that he could not travel to Moscow personally; although he would be 'more than glad to meet the man [Malenkov] unilaterally or multilaterally at any logical point', American public opinion might well misunderstand his visiting Moscow. Geneva, Stockholm 'or even Berlin' would be better meeting places. Eisenhower expressed the view that it might be possible to convince him of Moscow's serious interest in such talks, particularly if the Kremlin were to agree that 'each successive step' of the agreements achieved would 'carry its own guarantee of performance'.[21] In

effect, this meant that the President recognized the value of step-by-step agreements for building trust between East and West, whereas in his 'Chance for
Peace' speech he had insisted on the fulfilment of a whole series of conditions
before talks could commence.

The letter Eisenhower actually sent to Churchill concluded with the firm
statement that in the last resort Churchill himself had to decide whether he
could justify travelling to Moscow, but that the American government advised
strongly against it. The draft letter, however, had been much more accommodating: 'It is possible, of course, that your sources of information indicate that
much good might result from this kind of visit. In any event, you must do
whatever your own judgement and experience indicate to you as your best
possible contribution toward reaching the practical understandings so
essential to us today.'[22]

Perhaps it can be concluded that in early May 1953 Eisenhower was still not
entirely opposed to a summit meeting with Malenkov and Churchill. In
conversation with Churchill in early January and at his press conference in late
February, the President had indicated that he was interested in a meeting with
Stalin. His uncertainty in the course of developing the 'Chance for Peace'
speech as to whether or not he should suggest a four-power conference also
indicated his tentative interest. Thus the arguments put forward by the British
Prime Minister in favour of such a meeting appear to have had some effect. It
is not unreasonable to assume that in April the experts in the State
Department advised Eisenhower to firm up his letter to Churchill, since the
officials and the Secretary of State were still strongly opposed to a high-level
conference in view of the unpredictable consequences of an international
summit for the survival of the EDC and the entire Atlantic alliance.

Churchill of course was not aware of the first, more friendly draft of
Eisenhower's letter. The Prime Minister's reply, dated 7 May, was written
in a fairly reserved, even unfriendly tone. He repeated his reasons for his
wish to travel to Moscow,[23] emphasizing that he would like to meet the
Soviet Union's top leadership at a mutually agreed location as this appeared
to be 'the best chance of a good result'. He could not restrain his disappointment and outright anger about Eisenhower's 'weighty adverse advice'.
Churchill considered 'it difficult to believe that we shall gain anything by an
attitude of pure negation and your message to me certainly does not show
much hope.'[24]

In view of the strong opposition of the US and other western governments,
including West Germany's,[25] the Prime Minister did not dare to set out on his
'solitary pilgrimage' to see Malenkov. So far he had not even been able to gain
the support of his own Foreign Office.[26] Churchill told Eisenhower on 7 May

that he intended to consult his colleagues in the British government and would therefore delay sending the letter to Molotov until late June. To save face, he added that by then the coronation of the new Queen and the budget discussion in the American Congress, both of which complicated the pursuit of the Anglo-American international agenda, would have taken place. Perhaps in the autumn the President would 'feel able to propose some combined action'.[27]

Eisenhower was aware of Churchill's disenchantment. To keep on friendly terms, the President made a few pleasant remarks in his next letter to Churchill, dated 8 May, which mainly dealt with the situation in the Near East. Eisenhower agreed that 'consideration of protocol or of personal inconvenience' ought not to have the slightest impact on the possibility 'of advancing the cause of world peace'. Whenever Churchill felt he had a good idea he should immediately let him know.[28]

Yet, even these rather patronizing words seemed to indicate that to some extent the President was still in two minds about meeting the new Soviet leaders. Churchill arrived at the conclusion (informed by a good deal of wishful thinking) that there was still some hope that Eisenhower could eventually be persuaded to participate in a summit conference. Thus Eisenhower's consideration of Churchill's hurt feelings and his respect for the Prime Minister's age and past achievements may have contributed to Churchill's continued pursuit of his summit diplomacy in 1953.[29] This was certainly the opinion of Lord Salisbury, the Lord Privy Seal, whose views were much valued by the Prime Minister.[30] Salisbury warned the Prime Minister that the consequences of a unilateral Anglo-Soviet summit against the specific wishes of the American President would be disastrous; American public opinion and the American Congress would have no understanding of such a course.[31]

Churchill was still not convinced. Instead, he decided to use public opinion to change the President's mind. This was one of the primary motives for his dramatic speech in the House of Commons on 11 May 1953. Contrary to the view generally accepted in the literature, Churchill informed the American government about the contents of his forthcoming speech in a general way.[32] He even told Dulles that he intended 'to report certain conversations' with Eisenhower in the course of the speech. American objections, however, made him delete any such passages.[33] The President informed US Deputy Under-Secretary Bedell Smith that his correspondence with Churchill was either to remain 'completely confidential' or the Prime Minister had to be told that the exchange of letters would be terminated.[34] Although the gist of Eisenhower's statement was passed on to Churchill, the President's personal letters to Churchill never contained such rigorous statements. The British Prime Minister continued to hold the mistaken view that in the last resort he would be able to persuade his old comrade-in-arms of the value of a 'Big Three' summit conference.

Churchill, like many experts before and since, was misled by Eisenhower's smile and charming personality; he overlooked Eisenhower's underlying ruthlessness. However, a few contemporaries were aware of the President's resoluteness. Richard Nixon, who as Eisenhower's Vice-President had a rather uneasy relationship with him but knew him well, wrote that Eisenhower 'was a far more complex and devious man than most people realized'.[35] Lord Salisbury told Churchill after his meetings with Eisenhower in June 1953: 'I should add that I found the President, to my surprise, very strongly anti-Russian, far more so than Dulles.'[36] Konrad Adenauer was not misled either. On 20 April, on returning from his first state visit to the United States, he told British diplomat Frank Roberts at London airport that 'despite appearances, the President knew what he was doing and had his ship well under control. This applied particularly to external affairs.' Adenauer was convinced that 'American foreign policy was definitely that of President Eisenhower and Mr. Dulles's role was simply to execute it'.[37] Indeed, a year later Eisenhower would confirm this himself during a press conference when he stated that 'as far as I know Secretary Dulles has never made an important pronouncement without not only conferring and clearing with me, but sitting down and studying practically word by word what he is to say.'[38]

Churchill's Speech of 11 May 1953

Churchill's speech in the House of Commons, which the American ambassador described as 'dramatic and emotional',[39] offered a *tour d'horizon* of contemporary conflicts. However, by far the largest part of his address was dedicated to the possibility that Moscow's 'amicable gestures' were meant seriously. Moscow's accommodating behaviour since Stalin's death had 'taken the form of leaving off doing things, which we have not been doing to them', but he hoped that it did in fact represent a new Soviet policy. Churchill was in favour of initially concentrating on individual problems like how to bring about an end to the war in Korea and attempting to achieve a solution of the Austrian question. Agreements on these issues were bound to lead to further agreements. It would be a shame if the desire to terminate the Cold War once and for all 'were to impede any spontaneous and healthy evolution which may be taking place inside Russia'.[40]

Then the Prime Minister came to the main element of his speech. He became the first major western statesman to emphasize in public after Stalin's death that the West should not just focus on the threat posed by the Red Army. The western world also ought to take Russia's security interests and anxieties into consideration. He expressed understanding for the Soviet leaders' insistence on a friendly Poland: 'I do not believe that the immense problem of reconciling the security of Russia with the freedom and safety of Western Europe is insoluble ... Russia has a right to feel assured that as far as human arrangements can run the terrible events of the Hitler invasion will never be repeated, and that Poland will remain a friendly Power and a buffer, though not, I trust a puppet State.'[41]

Churchill outlined for the first time his conception of a security guarantee for the Soviet Union. He believed that the 'master thought' of the Locarno Treaty of 1925 ought to be revived and that Great Britain should be given the task of guaranteeing the maintenance of peace between the USSR and a reunited Germany. To Churchill it was clear that this meant that 'if Germany attacked France we should stand with the French, and if France attacked Germany we should stand with the Germans'.[42] The Prime Minister intended to transfer the 1925 security system for Western Europe to Central and Eastern Europe. Once again, he wished to make London responsible for maintaining the balance of power in Europe.[43]

In order to arrive at such a system Churchill continued to believe in the necessity of convening a summit meeting 'without long delay'. Such a conference 'should be confined to the smallest number of Powers and persons possible' and should also be characterized by 'a measure of informality and ... of privacy and seclusion'. Even if 'hard-faced agreements' might not result from the meeting, such a conference could not possibly do any damage. 'At the worst the participants in the meeting would have established more intimate contacts. At the best we might have a generation of peace.'[44]

In the scholarly literature the significance of Churchill's speech has often been misinterpreted. Its importance did not merely lie in the fact that he called for a 'summit' with Moscow. This he had often done before, most recently on 20 April.[45] The significance of the speech consisted of two elements: the emphasis on the link between German reunification and European security, and the passage in which Churchill underscored the fact that the Soviet Union had justified security interests which ought to be respected.[46] Churchill thereby criticized the willingness of the western world to accept the status quo and the division of Europe into East and West, and tolerate the enduring confrontation with the Soviet Union. A summit conference appeared to be necessary to overcome these unsatisfactory and dangerous situations. The Prime Minister was convinced that Moscow's justified security concerns could only be met if a reunited Germany was a genuinely neutral member of the international community and if the country was kept under firm control. A British guarantee to observe the peace between Germany and the USSR would provide this control and ensure that both Germany and the USSR would honour the agreement.

By May 1953, when Churchill gave his speech, the framework for a new European security system had already been contemplated elsewhere.[47] Ever since the 'battle of the notes' in 1952, the United States had been working on a German peace treaty that contained security clauses regarding the future status of Germany.[48] In the summer of 1952 the liberal West German politician and former diplomat Karl Pfleiderer had already referred to the Locarno Pact of 1925, proposing that East and West Germany should pull away from each other and disengage in the middle of Germany.[49] Very similar deliberations were taking place in Brussels. Early in 1953 Belgian Foreign Minister Paul van Zeeland made his tentative reflections available regarding a major disengagement plan in the middle of Europe, a plan officially submitted to the United States in September 1953. Van Zeeland believed that the establishment of a demilitarized zone, more or less equivalent in size to the territory of the German Democratic Republic (GDR) and complemented by militarily 'thinned out' territories to the east and west of this zone, would gradually lead to an end of the Cold War.[50]

It is doubtful whether Churchill was aware of all of these plans; there are no indications that he took them into consideration in the voluminous files in the British Public Record Office. Churchill was certainly not the originator of the various disengagement proposals. However, his very public pursuit of summit diplomacy after Stalin's death, including his speech on 11 May, encouraged West Germany, Belgium and the United States to speed up the existing tentative disengagement and European security plans in the summer and autumn of 1953.[51] More serious suggestions for demilitarized and neutral zones in the middle of Europe were embarked upon by van Zeeland in Belgium after Churchill's speech in the House of Commons, and top secret deliberations about a new European security structure were also conducted in the Chancellery in Bonn. The West German government knew it needed to prepare an alternative should the unpalatable plans worked out by van Zeeland and others come to fruition.[52]

The German scheme envisaged that only EDC troops would be stationed on West German territory after the successful reunification of Germany. Like van Zeeland, Adenauer expected that a large demilitarized zone would be established on the territory of the former GDR which would be guaranteed by the great powers. It would have meant that all allied troops would have had to leave Germany and the American and British troops would have to retreat at least to France and the Benelux countries.[53] This was the main reason why the British Foreign Office was not impressed by the tentative West German plans, once it heard about them; the ideas emanating from Bonn were regarded as 'very short-sighted'. After all, there was the danger that the American troops would leave Europe altogether, which for the British was a worst-case scenario. Obtaining an American guarantee for the security of Europe, including the continued stationing of American troops on the continent, had been the foremost aim of Britain's early Cold War strategy.[54] Not surprisingly Permanent Under-Secretary Strang commented: 'I think these Germans are getting rather above themselves.'[55]

Although Churchill did not know about the disengagement proposals considered in Bonn, he knew that Adenauer would hardly be impressed by his Locarno plans.[56] He therefore emphasized in his speech on 11 May that Adenauer 'may well be deemed the wisest German statesman since the days of Bismarck'. He also declared, thus contradicting the main gist of his speech, that Britain would of course fully honour its obligations towards the Federal Republic and not question the integration of the Bonn Republic with the western world.[57] Moreover, at the end of his address Churchill made a forceful appeal for the maintenance of the West's rearmament efforts 'up to the limit of our strength'; the western world should certainly not allow itself to become divided.[58]

This upbeat and forceful conclusion was Churchill's attempt to ensure a favourable response to his speech on the continent. In essence Churchill meant what he said about keeping an open mind regarding negotiations with Moscow while also maintaining the strength and unity of the West. He had demonstrated this, for example, when he intervened in the British-Soviet talks at High Commissioner level about safety regulations in the Berlin air corridors. These talks had been motivated by the shooting down of a British military aircraft on 12 March 1953, which had accidentally strayed from the Berlin air corridor into GDR air space, resulting in the death of the entire crew of seven. The talks began in Berlin on 31 March.[59] Due to Washington's reluctance even to contemplate negotiations with Moscow on an official level, talks between the British and the Soviets started before the Americans and the French joined in on 7 April.[60] During the second round of the Anglo-Soviet conversations the British hosts offered their Soviet guests drinks and a snack. Churchill immediately told the Foreign Office that he did not believe in 'too friendly an atmosphere in their talks',[61] demanding an explanation 'why British airmen were carousing at British expense with Russian airmen so soon after the murder of their comrades'.[62]

Churchill's surprising reaction was based on a misunderstanding regarding the size and nature of the event. However, the episode demonstrates that the

Prime Minister was not willing to appease the Soviet Union under all circum-stances. He was quite serious when he said that negotiations ought to take place but until decisive results had been achieved the West's policy of strength and rearmament should continue. On 18 June, in a rather sharp letter to Britain's delegates to the European parliament in Strasbourg, the Prime Minister also insisted on the fact that despite a 'new look' in Soviet foreign policy, it was still the West's intention to implement the plan for the EDC. 'We have not yet achieved a real détente between East and West, and my speech of May 11 merely foreshadowed the possibility'.[63]

Churchill's speech on 11 May horrified the western foreign ministries and met great resistance. For the first time Churchill had clarified the nature of his anticipated settlement with Moscow, indicating that he would accept 'even an improved modus vivendi' on the basis of the Cold War status quo, though he much preferred 'a friendly settlement' with Moscow.[64] During the Cold War, and even as late as 1989, it was generally assumed in the West that Moscow would only agree to European and German reunification on the basis of German neutrality.[65] Churchill had indirectly indicated in public for the first time that he favoured an agreement with the Soviet Union on the basis of a neutral and reunified Germany; at the very least he seemed not to be opposed to such a settlement.[66]

This idea was of course anathema to Bonn and Washington, but the Soviet leadership gave the speech its cautious approval. Not surprisingly, Moscow was impressed by the Prime Minister's proposal to combine the security of the Soviet Union with that of Western Europe. The Kremlin announced that it agreed with Churchill's reasoning and the view that, as he had said, it was a mistake to believe that nothing 'could be settled until all was settled'. However, as far as Germany was concerned, Moscow was sceptical. The Soviet leaders denied that Churchill's proposal was based on the Yalta and Potsdam agree-ments, and that on his terms it was unlikely that Germany could be reunited as a 'peace-loving and democratic state'; instead, 'military and fascist elements' would continue to survive in Germany.[67]

Neither the Soviet nor the American government agreed with Churchill's assumption that Britain would be in a position to guarantee peace between two great powers. This was a highly unrealistic idea, based on the international political situation of the 1920s and reflected Churchill's patriotic desire to give his country renewed importance as an international arbiter. The Prime Minister was clearly thinking in terms of the political constellations of yesteryear. The two superpowers (as they were soon to be called) did not believe that in the post-war period Britain was in a position to act as international arbiter, conciliator and guarantor. Khrushchev's declaration before the Central Committee of the CPSU in July 1953 – 'If a treaty [of neutrality] is not guaranteed by force, then it is worth nothing, and others will laugh at us and consider us naïve' – had an element of truth. Although he made the statement in connection with the fall of Beria, analysed below, its substance could also be applied to Britain and the country's post-war military weakness.[68]

However, it appears that to some extent Malenkov was impressed by Churchill's address. Shortly after the Prime Minister's speech, Malenkov wrote to Molotov proposing changes in Moscow's position on Austria to remove an obstacle for talks between the USSR and Britain. Molotov remained obstinate. He returned Malenkov's draft proposals for a new policy on Austria five times, asking for further revisions. In late May Molotov eventually made clear that in the current atmosphere of crisis in Eastern Europe, characterized by economic dissatisfaction and increasing unrest,[69] it would be unwise to change the Kremlin's position on Austria; this could be wrongly interpreted as a sign of Soviet weakness by the outside world. He also argued that Moscow had too little information about the western position on Austria and other Cold War issues and it would therefore be too risky to implement a new policy.[70] Churchill may well have been right in his gut feeling that an approach to Malenkov and a conference with a Soviet delegation headed by him rather than by the much more dogmatic Molotov might have been able to set matters in motion. Despite some positive noises, caution, restraint and mistrust dominated the Soviet response to Churchill's 11 May speech. It was also assumed in Moscow that Washington would do its best to undermine Churchill's initiative.[71]

This assessment soon proved to be correct. The reaction of American politicians was much less favourable than Moscow's. Senator William Knowland, the Republican majority leader, accused Churchill of pursuing a policy of 'appeasement'; he compared Churchill's speech with Chamberlain's journey to Munich to see Hitler.[72] The State Department and Eisenhower were more restrained. They merely referred to the President's 'Chance for Peace' speech and declared that a four-power conference could only take place if Moscow fulfilled the conditions the President had outlined.[73] American journalist Drew Pearson's assessment that Churchill's speech was 'likely to widen the chasm with Eisenhower, certainly with the United States' and lead to increasing 'dissension' between London and Washington would prove essentially accurate.[74]

It was not overlooked in Washington that in connection with the new European security order he proposed, Churchill had not once mentioned the United States. He had also entirely ignored the role of nuclear weapons; his thinking was based on the strategies of conventional warfare. Thus, he did not address the question whether Britain, as a guarantor of peace, would be able to drop or at least threaten to use nuclear bombs if the Red Army invaded a neutral Germany (militarized or not, the reunited country would be unlikely to be allowed to possess atomic bombs). Furthermore, what purpose would be achieved by destroying much of Central Europe (and all of Germany) with nuclear weapons in return for preventing the Soviet Union from occupying Germany? Could this even happen without the agreement and active support of the United States? Without the use of nuclear warfare, it was difficult to see how an economically and militarily weakened Britain could hope to intervene successfully in a conflict between Germany and the Soviet Union. The number of British troops and conventional weapons had been much reduced since 1945. Churchill clearly overestimated Britain's political and military strength while exaggerating the extent to which Washington would be prepared to leave a weakened Britain in charge of European security.

One of the driving forces behind Churchill's speech was his awareness that his country urgently needed a long and secure era of peace, which would enable the UK to replenish its economic resources. That his speech also served the aim of overcoming the Cold War in a way that would enable Britain to survive economically as a great power was immediately recognized by the West German press. The conservative *Frankfurter Allgemeine Zeitung*, one of Germany's largest and most distinguished broadsheets, commented, 'Nobody understands better than Churchill, the price which Britain had to pay for her victory.' The paper believed that Churchill's purpose was to 'secure a long period of peace and recovery'.[75]

The British Foreign Office immediately recognized the explosive material contained in the Prime Minister's speech. The FO officials had hardly been consulted, nor had Churchill requested the advice of his cabinet colleagues.[76] Although he had asked for some information from William Strang and Selwyn Lloyd and had shown them and Anthony Nutting the final draft of the speech on the morning of 11 May,[77] he had deliberately avoided involving the FO's Central Department. The officials in this department were responsible for Germany and Central Europe and it was known that they were firmly opposed to any four-power talks.[78] John Colville, Churchill's trusted Private Secretary, noted that the Prime Minister 'made this speech wholly contrary to Foreign Office advice since it was felt that a friendly approach to Russia would discourage the European powers working on the theme of Western union'.[79] Anthony Nutting referred to Churchill as 'an old man in a hurry' and informed Anthony Eden, who was recuperating in a clinic in Boston: 'There's no doubt that the Old Boy's speech in the foreign affairs debate has brought any momentum that remained behind the EDC virtually to a dead-stop and that it has given more comfort to our enemies than to our friends ... Inevitably it has encouraged all those elements in France who were seen casting about so desperately for an alternative to rearming Germany'.[80]

With the temporary exception of Selwyn Lloyd,[81] none of the politicians and Foreign Office officials shared Churchill's enthusiasm for summit diplomacy and his views on the German question. Among his few supporters were Field Marshal Montgomery and the Chiefs of Staff, above all Sir John Slessor, who had been in retirement since January 1953.[82] There was also support for Churchill's speech in the House of Commons, mostly from the Labour backbenches. The Labour and Conservative front benches as well as the Conservative Parliamentary Foreign Affairs Committee were much more muted in their response.[83]

The Foreign Office did not only object to the substance of Churchill's proposal. The officials also firmly rejected the idea that Churchill should negotiate with Eisenhower, Malenkov and perhaps the French Prime Minister alone and without the presence of his Foreign Office advisers. He had proposed in his speech that 'this conference should not be overhung by a ponderous or rigid agenda, or led into mazes and jungles of technical details, zealously contested by hordes of experts and officials drawn up in vast, cumbrous array.'[84] This was an insult to the professionalism of the Foreign Office, as it attacked their practice of anticipating risks and dangers and preparing themselves carefully for big international conferences. Furthermore, could one really entrust the ageing and backward-looking Prime Minister with negotiating on behalf of Britain without being 'taken for a ride' by the shrewd, experienced and in general much younger statesmen of the other participating countries?

Thus, despite Churchill's honourable intention of overcoming the East–West conflict it was concluded that in the last resort his policy might damage London's prestige and international standing as well as the coherence of the entire western alliance. Foreign Secretary Eden, who due to his illness was not able to influence developments, certainly shared this view. With hindsight he wrote in his diary in November 1954 (after the French parliament had failed to ratify the EDC in August 1954):

It must be long in history since any one speech did so much damage to its own side. In Italy, as de Gasperi openly stated to Winston, & I believe elsewhere, it lost de Gasperi the election ... In Germany, Adenauer was exasperated. Worst of all it probably cost us EDC in France. At any rate, the whole summer was lost in wrangling. The speech was made without any consultation with the Cabinet ... Nutting fought all he could against it. I, of course, never saw it at all, but W[inston] is not to blame for this for I was much too ill. He knew well though what I should have thought of it.[85]

Nevertheless, the great majority of the population in Britain, the United States and West Germany welcomed the Prime Minister's initiative.[86] The most positive response came from Paris. As early as 13 May, two days after Churchill's speech and clearly inspired by his address, the foreign policy committee of the French National Assembly passed a resolution calling for a high-level four-power conference to settle the East–West conflict.[87]

As early as April 1953, the French Prime Minister René Mayer and Foreign Minister Bidault had decided to put pressure on the United States to agree to a four-power conference on the German question. During the meeting of the North Atlantic Council in Paris in late April,[88] they had outlined their intention to call for a summit meeting. They had already formulated a letter to this effect, addressed to the American and British governments. However, American officials in Paris persuaded Mayer and Bidault not to send the letter and the French politicians, according to the Belgian NATO delegate Andre de Staerke, were therefore 'rather put out at the Prime Minister's speech, which they felt has stolen their thunder'.[89] Churchill's summit diplomacy as such was not resented but rather the fact that it was the British Prime Minister and not the French government who had proposed a new initiative and attracted so much international attention with his speech.

The politicians in Paris feared that Moscow, to prevent the Federal Republic's integration into the West, would soon issue an invitation to a four-power conference and express their readiness to accept German reunification including free elections and the sacrifice of the GDR, their East German puppet state. The West would find it difficult to refuse such an offer out of hand.[90] A British diplomat was told by his French colleague in mid-April that 'the Western Powers should keep a very open mind about any future Russian approaches, for instance on the question of German unity, and be careful to avoid any appearance of wishing to reject such approaches in advance or to discourage them by an over-rigid and over-cautious attitude.'[91]

During the NATO meeting in late April Bidault proposed a way of avoiding a development which would lead to German reunification on unacceptable terms. He suggested to his colleagues that disarmament would have to be at the top of the agenda of an international summit meeting to make German reunification more acceptable, if it could not be avoided altogether. By disarmament, Bidault meant the creation of an all-European security system,[92] to avoid a demilitarized vacuum in the middle of Europe. The Soviet Union would be keen to move into such a vacuum sooner or later 'with the result that the German menace would be added to the Russian menace'.[93] Moreover, if a genuine disarmament treaty could be concluded with the Soviet Union, the establishment of the controversial EDC and the rearmament of Germany would be superfluous.[94]

Thus, contrary to the views expressed in most of the literature, France was not opposed to convening a four-power meeting and had planned to submit such a plan to the United States before Churchill's speech on 11 May.[95] The French initiative was a reaction to the belief in Paris that it would be impossible to avoid a four-power conference. The proposal was meant to influence the discussion and to avoid German reunification or at least defuse its inherent dangers. However, both London and Washington rejected the French proposal for a summit meeting to conclude an international disarmament treaty. The British and the Americans did not believe that Moscow was about to initiate a dramatic development in the German question. Selwyn Lloyd summarized the Foreign Office view, with which Dulles fully agreed. He explained that London 'doubted whether the Russians would be willing to relinquish their position in Eastern Germany however large the reward for doing so might appear to be; that we saw no advantage in attempting to discuss disarmament before anything else; and that our own assessment of Soviet policy ... did not indicate that the Russians were likely at present to raise the question of German reunification'. 'It was tentatively thought' within the Foreign Office, 'that we could await progress on these questions before considering whether to make any move on Germany further to that of the three power Note of 23rd September, 1952 ...'[96]

A similar assessment had appeared in a memorandum by the Foreign Office's Central Department on 6 May 1953. The officials told Nutting that it made very little sense to discuss security questions and the German question together at a summit meeting. These were 'quite big enough subjects to be handled on their own'. The close connection between these topics, which would cause western politicians much concern until at least 1955, when West Germany's membership of NATO was achieved, was not recognized by the FO. There also was no readiness to be flexible on the German question as such. The director of the Central Department, Patrick Hancock, declared that the Soviet Union was still unsure 'what to do about the German problem and they may well hesitate before accepting the risk of abandoning their hold over the Eastern Zone of Germany'. He did not consider the possibility of exploiting Moscow's allegedly still uncertain frame of mind by favourable western actions and perhaps by attempting to enter into negotiations.[97] Such a course, it was reasoned, would undermine the integration of the Federal Republic into the

West and might possibly result in the creation of a reunited and neutral Germany instead. This was also the West German Chancellor's greatest fear.

Churchill, Adenauer, and a Unified and Neutral Germany

Adenauer was particularly upset about Churchill's speech on 11 May. His confidant Herbert Blankenhorn records that Churchill's Locarno proposal led to 'most critical' utterances in the Chancellery in Bonn.[98] In June 1953 Blankenhorn told his British friend Con O'Neill, a senior official in the Foreign Office, that the Chancellor had been 'scared stiff' and had not known 'whether he was now standing on his head or his heels' after Churchill's speech. Adenauer had been most concerned about the Prime Minister's 'unreliability'. The Chancellor had said he believed 'that the Prime Minister was obsessed with the idea that he was the only man in the world who could come to an arrangement with the Russians. Everything else in his mind was subordinate to this and would be sacrificed to it if necessary.'[99] In his memoirs, Adenauer himself only indicated that he was 'very surprised' about the speech.[100] Yet, even before the Chancellor departed for London on his second, long-arranged state visit to the UK in mid-May he was convinced that the British government would attempt to persuade him that contrary to American intentions the West had to change its attitude towards the Soviet Union.[101]

The Chancellor's anxiety that Churchill was ready to reconsider the integration of the Federal Republic into the West was confirmed during his visit to London between 14 and 16 May 1953.[102] Adenauer, regarded by British High Commissioner Ivonne Kirkpatrick as 'a very suspicious old gentleman',[103] made great efforts to convince the Prime Minister of the risk of such a step.[104] Similarly, the Foreign Office hoped the Chancellor could help persuade Churchill to abandon his summit diplomacy, or at least to pursue his policy with much greater caution. When Blankenhorn asked Deputy Under-Secretary Frank Roberts how the Chancellor should best approach the topic with Churchill, Roberts assured him that 'the Prime Minister would wish the Chancellor to explain his own difficulties and preoccupations very frankly and not to gloss over any anxieties he might feel'.[105]

The officials also intended to make sure as 'a matter of political importance' that everything discussed between Churchill and Adenauer would be known to the Foreign Office. Before the official dinner on the evening of 15 May, an informal private luncheon was planned for Adenauer, Churchill, Lady Churchill and an interpreter.[106] It was concluded with alarm that if this was Adenauer's personal interpreter 'the Foreign Office will have no means of ascertaining what passed at the luncheon'.[107] The officials' mistrust of their Prime Minister is abundantly clear. The Foreign Office feared that Churchill might use the opportunity to outline to Adenauer his real political intentions with respect to Germany, which might lead to a dramatic and possibly long-lasting deterioration of Anglo-German relations. In the end, the officials managed to insist on the participation of High Commissioner Kirkpatrick, who spoke fluent German.[108]

During three fairly frank conversations with the Prime Minister, Adenauer did not succeed in changing Churchill's political intentions as outlined in his 11 May speech.[109] Nor was the Prime Minister able to diminish Adenauer's apprehensions. Although he reassured Adenauer that London would not enter into any agreements to the detriment of or without the knowledge of the West Germans, he also declared 'that this should not be interpreted as excluding secret diplomacy'.[110] Thus, his statement to the Chancellor that he had 'specially inserted' in his 11 May speech the reassurance to Adenauer and the Germans that he would do nothing that would damage their interest was unable to allay Adenauer's fears.[111]

The Chancellor became particularly concerned when he recognized that the Prime Minister had noticeably aged since he had seen him last two years earlier. He observed that Churchill had difficulty concentrating and did not seem particularly well informed. Subsequently Blankenhorn told Con O'Neill that the Chancellor 'had the firm impression that the Prime Minister neither welcomed nor listened to advice. This perhaps would not have worried Dr. Adenauer so much (he has the same quality himself!) had he not the firm conviction that the Prime Minister really knew very little about the German problem or, for that matter, the problems of European unity.' Blankenhorn said Adenauer was fearful 'that the Prime Minister simply did not know enough about present day problems in Germany and the world to be able to form a wise and reliable judgement'. He added diplomatically: 'Without questioning the Prime Minister's motives, Dr. Adenauer simply could not trust him to conduct conversations with the Russians on German or other subjects.' Above all, the Chancellor 'had been amazed and somewhat angry to find at the official meeting that the Prime Minister paid no attention to what he was saying, did not seem to understand anything about the European problems involved and was obviously buried away in a world of his own far from the practical problems with which Dr. Adenauer and others had to deal.'[112]

Officially, Adenauer announced however that he had returned 'much reassured' from London.[113] Perhaps the Chancellor had indeed been relieved by Churchill's indication that when he referred to the Locarno Pact of 1925 in his

11 May speech he had not meant the precise clauses of the treaty but the 'spirit of Locarno'. This view of the meeting appeared in British reports of the discussions and later in Adenauer's memoirs. Churchill had also emphasized 'his concern that the Russian intention was only deceit',[114] and here Adenauer could not have agreed more. Still, on the whole neither Churchill nor the Foreign Office had managed to allay the Chancellor's fears.[115]

Back in Bonn, Adenauer attempted to play down the importance of Churchill's speech of 11 May. He pointed out the deterioration of the Prime Minister's health and the decline of Britain's great power role: 'Churchill is a very emotional man and, as you know, a man who is artistically very talented. He suffers from poor hearing. This condition results in the fact that sometimes he does not grasp everything during negotiations, in particular when – impatient as he is – he has put away his little machine.' He also emphasized Britain's resentment and jealousy of the United States, telling his party loyalists that 'there is a feeling of dissatisfaction which is widespread in Britain that America has taken over the leadership of the world and that Great Britain is only making global history by means of being taken in tow by America.'[116] In a confidential talk with journalists on 18 May the Chancellor elaborated his analysis by suggesting that Churchill, as a successful war politician, appeared to have the desire to play a decisive role by means of a policy which would lead to peace, and that in view of the leading position of the USA, Churchill had also wished to say something.

Subsequently, Adenauer warned that the Federal Republic should avoid getting involved in the current Anglo-American disagreements.[117] After all, it could be expected that eventually both countries would find yet another compromise and agree on a common line; Germany could only be damaged if it remained in an uneasy position between the Anglo-American allies.[118] On the whole, the Chancellor concluded after his visit to Britain that he had to be careful. Churchill would not cease doing everything in his power to bring about a détente between East and West along lines which Adenauer believed would be greatly disadvantageous to the Bonn Republic and would fail to find a solution to the German question.[119]

The Chancellor had every reason to be careful to avoid having his policy of the irreversible western integration of the Federal Republic sabotaged by Churchill. As the Foreign Office soon recognized to its dismay, Churchill was indeed aiming at the reunification of Germany on a neutral basis to arrive at a settlement with the Soviet Union.[120] On 16 May, on the very day of Adenauer's departure from London, Churchill told official Pierson Dixon 'that he had not closed his mind to the possibility of a unified and neutralised Germany'. Dixon elaborated in a memorandum: 'The PM made this remark in the context of a possible high-level discussion with the Russians, and his meaning, I think, was that it might be desirable to agree to such a solution for Germany as part of a settlement with the Russians.'[121]

Two days later Churchill expressed a similar view to William Strang and Selwyn Lloyd, but this time he added that the creation of a reunited and neutral Germany was only possible 'if the Germans wished, but only if they wished for this'.[122] This left open whether he was referring to the West German government or the German people in East and West. The Foreign Office became increasingly concerned about Churchill's summit diplomacy including his German policy and on 19 May Frank Roberts wrote a long memorandum entitled 'A unified, neutralised Germany' considering the imminent consequences of Churchill's ideas.[123]

Roberts expressed his conviction that Churchill's proposals would be 'a complete break' with the strategy pursued by the western allies since 1947. It would lead to a return to the Potsdam system of governing Germany and would therefore mean 'a reversal of alliances'; in fact it would represent a 'revolution' in Britain's external affairs. Roberts outlined the impossibility of uniting Germany at this stage. The aims of the western powers had not yet been achieved, and it was unlikely that they could be achieved for the time being as they included the integration of the Federal Republic with the West:

> [The western allies] have had as our common objective the closer associ-ation of the Federal Republic, and eventually of a reunited Germany, with the Western world ... our present not unsuccessful policies towards Germany and Western Europe cannot at present be reconciled with agreement with the Soviet Union on the German problem. As Dr. Adenauer himself said on May 15, German reunification *in freedom* will only come about if and when there is a possibility of a general settlement with the Soviet Union.[124]

Roberts painted a rather pessimistic picture of the likely consequences if Churchill's plans came to fruition. These might include the defeat of Adenauer in the forthcoming elections in West Germany and the victory of a weak socialist government which, sooner or later, might develop a tendency towards extreme nationalism. According to Roberts, it did not matter a lot whether a neutral Germany was demilitarized or had national armed forces. Without providing a shred of evidence, he claimed that in either case it could be expected that the country would look for accession to the Soviet Union. A demilitarized Germany would be fully 'at the mercy' of the Soviet Union and would represent as unreliable a factor in world politics as had Vichy France. If a reunited Germany had a national army the country would be tempted to use its economic strength in negotiations with East and West. And as Moscow was in possession of Germany's former eastern territories beyond the Oder–Neisse line the USSR would be able to offer much more to the Germans than the western powers. At best, the West could make concessions regarding the Saar territory, which was claimed by France. Therefore it could be expected that a neutral Germany would enter into an alliance with the Soviet Union. Roberts concluded that 'We should thus have created by our own action the most deadly danger to our security and to that of the world.'[125]

Moreover, Roberts believed that NATO's defence structure made it absolutely essential that the western allies had the territory of West Germany at their disposal. A neutral Germany would have to demand the withdrawal of all foreign troops, which might perhaps lead to the early withdrawal of all American troops from Europe. In such a case it was obvious that 'N.A.T.O. would no longer be an effective shield for Western Europe and the United Kingdom'. Europe would then be dependent on Soviet 'good will'. A West German defence contribution was necessary 'to complete the minimum defensive strength of N.A.T.O.'. Furthermore, German neutrality would have disastrous consequences for the creation of Franco-German friendship and the further development of European integration. In order to find counter arguments to Churchill's reasoning, Roberts showed a surprising pro-European attitude in his paper which so far had not been characteristic of the thinking within the British Foreign Office. In fact, he appeared to be convinced that a reunited Germany would withdraw from all European organizations like the Council of Europe, the ECSC and the EDC, and without Germany these organizations were unlikely to survive. Thus, sooner or later 'a return to German nationalism and a revival of the German quarrel with France and Western Europe' could be expected.[126]

In his memorandum, Roberts not only criticized strongly the policy of his own Prime Minister but also expressed himself in favour of the continuation of the Cold War status quo and its development towards the integration of the Federal Republic into the West. His colleague Pierson Dixon, who amended Roberts's memorandum with a few thoughts of his own, shared this view. Dixon explained on 19 May that a reversal of the West's German policy would 'bring the whole structure tumbling about our ears'. Moreover, this seemed to be entirely unnecessary as the Soviet Union 'would probably be satisfied with the "status quo" in Europe with a view to consolidating her position at home and exploiting opportunities in Asia'. In order to avoid a third world war it should be Britain's policy to strengthen the status quo but not to tamper with it. After all, the West was in possession of 'an effective Atlantic Alliance & united Europe & as much [as] 3/4ers of Germany, rearmed and anti-Russian'.[127]

Ten days later, on 29 May, Roberts alerted the Foreign Office that the West German press had begun 'to smell a rat' with regard to Churchill's plans for a neutral Germany.[128] On the same day, Parliamentary Under-Secretary Nutting impatiently asked his officials to obtain clarification regarding the Prime Minister's thinking.[129] Thus on 30 May Strang sent Roberts's memorandum, which he had edited and amended slightly, to the Prime Minister.[130] A day later Churchill replied and declared a little more cautiously than hitherto that he saw 'fully the awful consequences of a right-about turn'. However, he was still convinced that something had to be done as 'on present lines we are moving steadily towards war'. But it was obvious that 'our honour would prevent us letting Adenauer down. I promised him this and he quite understood.' While no longer referring to a possible neutralization of Germany, Churchill added: 'I have not yet come to any mental conclusions, but neither have I any final inhibitions.'[131] The Prime Minister pledged to study the memorandum once again.[132] Roberts suggested allowing him a little time to reconsider the situation: 'Our points have gone home and are to be studied further.'[133]

The Proposal for a Conference on Bermuda

By late May 1953 the officials in the Foreign Office had also become worried about the French initiative for a summit meeting. Spurred on by Churchill's 11 May speech, Prime Minister Mayer had sent a telegram to Eisenhower on 20 May asking him to agree to a summit conference of the western heads of government. Mayer intended to announce the conference on the following day just before a vote of confidence in his government was to take place in the National Assembly in Paris.[134] In the course of the western meeting Mayer wished to discuss the question whether or not a four-power meeting with the Soviet Union should be held. In contrast to Churchill's tendency to favour informal meetings, Mayer aspired to a conference with an 'agreed agenda and an agreed Western policy'. Adenauer was visiting Paris on 11 May and later told his party colleagues that the French government was astonished by Churchill's speech as the Prime Minister did not appear to regard France as one of the great powers.[135] Indeed, Mayer explained his sudden initiative as being necessary to ensure that his country would be represented at Churchill's summit conference, if the event were to take place.[136] Yet, above all, the French Prime Minister had been forced to resort to this desperate populist strategy by the increasingly difficult war in Indochina and severe domestic financial problems.[137]

Eisenhower received Mayer's telegram when he was on the golf course. He immediately returned to the White House and consulted the State Department as well as the British Prime Minister.[138] Despite the opposition from the State Department, which advised against a western conference due to the uncertain situation in the war in Korea,[139] this time Eisenhower agreed with Churchill. The President decided to accept Mayer's proposal, not least in order to help him in a difficult domestic situation. Eisenhower, Churchill and Mayer agreed to hold the conference on Bermuda, which was British territory but had an American military base; the meeting was to begin on 17 June. The President was careful enough to point out in his public announcement that the conference would be held 'to further develop common viewpoints'. In a letter to Churchill he said that the forthcoming Bermuda conference was 'not in any way ... tied to Four Power talks with the Soviet Union ... [or] considered as preliminary thereto'.[140] However, using the Bermuda conference to obtain agreement for a four-power meeting with Malenkov was exactly what Churchill intended to achieve. He replied to a question from Clement Attlee in the House of Commons concerning the aims of the conference that it was his 'main hope that we may take a definitive step forward to a meeting of far graver import.'[141]

Thus due to the French Prime Minister's proposal, Churchill's initiative to overcome the Cold War had already led to an important step in the 'right' direction less than two weeks after his speech on 11 May. The British Prime Minister clearly believed that the Bermuda conference would lead to a four-power conference with the new Soviet leaders which might well result in an era of détente in the near future and the termination of the Cold War in the medium to long term. Churchill was supremely confident that he would be able to persuade Eisenhower and the French leader to agree to a major inter-national big power conference to settle the world's post-war problems once and for all and allow Britain to continue playing a global role. However, Churchill's exuberance was misplaced. Events would develop in a very different way from that optimistically anticipated by the Prime Minister.

Moreover, both the Foreign Office and the German Chancellor continued to be greatly concerned about Churchill's plans. Similar apprehensions existed in Washington. Nevertheless, the British diplomats do not seem to have fully understood the western allies', and above all the Germans', deep concern about and general mistrust of the British government. On 1 June Selwyn Lloyd was told by the director of the Central Department that 'As regards Anglo-German problems, the present state of our relations with the Federal Republic is so happy that they are few in number.'[142] This was far from the truth. The number of problems may have been limited but their importance for Anglo-German relations was great. The German Chancellor's anxieties had hardly been allayed by his meeting with Churchill in May, and they were made worse by the forthcoming western foreign ministers' conference on Bermuda. Would Churchill succeed in persuading the other western governments to agree to a summit conference and perhaps even convince them of his Locarno ideas? The Chancellor was very concerned. The announcement of the Bermuda conference appeared to be the beginning of Churchill's cherished international summit diplomacy, which Adenauer feared and detested. After all, such a development might well have an impact on the outcome of the forthcoming general election in the Federal Republic in early September 1953.[143]

But Adenauer need not have worried. Almost immediately after Eisenhower and Churchill had agreed to accept French Prime Minister Mayer's proposal for convening a meeting of the three western heads of government on Bermuda, the scheme ran into difficulties. Mayer lost the vote of confidence in the National Assembly in Paris despite the announcement of the conference. For almost five weeks no French politician was able to form a new government. Although Churchill pressed the American President to convene a meeting without French participation (as 'the bloody Frogs can't make up their minds'), Eisenhower rejected this.[144] Eventually, on 19 June, the President agreed that the Bermuda conference should begin on 8 July – with or without a representative from France. Churchill had put great pressure on him and indicated that the 'recurring delays are very painful to me and [are] very bad for world affairs.'[145] Eisenhower may well have feared that Churchill might soon lose patience and embark on a 'solitary pilgrimage' to Moscow to talk to Malenkov alone.

Much to Eisenhower's relief, eventually on 27 June Joseph Laniel was sworn in as Prime Minister in Paris; French participation at the forthcoming Bermuda conference seemed assured.[146] However, Churchill's health deteriorated suddenly in late June 1953 leading to the further temporary postponement of the Bermuda conference. By then, the popular uprising in the GDR had taken place and as a result both Churchill and Eisenhower came to regard a western summit meeting with considerably less urgency than before (albeit for very different reasons). The events in East Germany had a major impact on the further course of the Cold War in the 1950s and beyond; they were also highly influential for the course of Churchill's personal diplomacy and in his ultimate failure to realize his grand objectives.

CHAPTER 12

Triumph and Tragedy
Britain, the USA, and the Uprising in East Germany

Churchill's speech in Parliament on 11 May 1953 had focused international attention on his vision for overcoming the Cold War. A few weeks later he was to lose the initiative again and was never to regain it during his remaining twenty-two months as Prime Minister. The uprising in the German Democratic Republic (GDR) which suddenly erupted on 16 and 17 June 1953 gave the opponents of Churchill's 'summitry' the opportunity to defeat his policies.

The events in East Germany, briefly described below, and similar though somewhat less dramatic developments in other Eastern European countries exposed not only the almost universal hostility of the East German people towards the GDR regime but also the insecurity of the Soviet Union's hold over its satellite states in Eastern Europe. The uprising in East Germany became another focus for Churchill's battle with the Eisenhower administration and the Foreign Office over the strategy the West should employ towards the new leaders in the Kremlin. None of the Western experts, including the increasingly isolated Prime Minister, shrank from using the events in the GDR to further their own political agenda. Despite the western leaders' public rhetoric, the fate of the East German people was less important to them than their tactical and strategic considerations of how the western world ought to react to the events behind the iron curtain.

The intentions of Stalin's successors regarding the future of the GDR were of vital importance for Churchill's summit diplomacy. To a large degree, Churchill's policy rested on the assumption that Stalin's heirs were ready to sacrifice the existence of the East German state and agree to a reunified and neutral Germany, on terms to be guaranteed by Great Britain. In return, the Soviets would obtain considerable material benefits from the West. While most western statesmen continued to believe that approaches from the new leaders in Moscow were mere political manoeuvres in the aftermath of Stalin's death, Churchill remained convinced, even after the uprising in the GDR, that informal high-level negotiations with Stalin's heirs might bring about an early end to the Cold War.

Causes and Motives of the Unrest in the GDR and the 'Beria Plan' for German Reunification

The uprising in East Berlin on 16 and 17 June 1953 was caused by the dire economic situation and rapidly deteriorating standard of living in the GDR. Within a matter of hours, the workers' protests developed into an expression of general popular dissatisfaction with the East German regime. The uprising soon spread to over 300 East German cities and even to the countryside; the protests involved more than half a million demonstrators.[1] The background lay in the fact that the Korean War and the intensifying Cold War had made Stalin insist on the increasingly rapid industrialization and rearmament of the Soviet Union, and similar efforts were demanded from the satellite countries. In addition, the Kremlin demanded the continued payment of punitively high reparations, which undermined the East German economy further. In July 1952, the Second Party Conference of the SED, the GDR's ruling Communist Party, decided on the enforced 'creation of socialism' in the GDR; this was soon approved by Stalin. In addition to a concentration on heavy industries, the collectivization of farms, the abandonment of almost all private enter-prises and the simultaneous neglect of the consumer industries, this also meant the final extinction of political liberties and the centralization of all political institutions: the GDR was to be modelled on Stalin's Soviet Union. These policies caused great hardship and provoked passionate resentment among the East German people.[2]

By the winter of 1952–53, GDR leader Walter Ulbricht's policies had produced a serious food crisis which soon led to a decline in industrial productivity and the standard of living.[3] Thousands of people left East Germany for the Federal Republic, a process which only worsened the economic situation in the first 'workers' and farmers' state on German soil', as the GDR was termed in official propaganda.[4] The SED asked Stalin for urgent economic assistance but received no positive response. When the East German elite went to Moscow to attend Stalin's funeral they were informed that no aid would be forthcoming; the Soviet Union had enough economic problems of its own. Further urgent GDR requests for Soviet aid in March, April and May 1953 were also largely turned down, though the delivery of some raw materials was promised on 18 April and the reparation payments were reduced. Earlier in the month, the Kremlin had hinted at the necessity of relaxing the GDR's Sovietization policy, but this was ignored by Ulbricht.[5]

Instead, the East German leadership now drew up their own plan to rescue the country from economic disaster. On 28 May 1953 the Party announced that there would have to be a 10 per cent increase of work norms in East German factories. This meant that in order to maintain existing wage levels workers were told to produce 10 per cent more goods; otherwise their wages would be cut accordingly. The people were further burdened when price increases and cuts in subsidies of certain goods and services were announced. These measures provoked an outcry. In several widely dispersed factories workers initiated protest strikes. The authorities arrested strike leaders but in most cases those detained had to be quickly released as public opinion was fiercely antagonistic to the regime's local and national apparatchiks. The crisis rapidly undermined the authority of the GDR leadership. Ulbricht was even faced with criticism of his performance from within the SED. In particular, Minister of State Security Wilhelm Zaisser and Rudolf Herrnstadt, Politburo candidate and chief editor of the SED party newspaper *Neues Deutschland*, strongly criticized Ulbricht's leadership style and his unrelenting attempts to create a Stalinist GDR.[6]

In early June, the Soviet Union instructed the SED to abolish the recently introduced economic measures and announce a 'New Course'.[7] Pressured by the stirrings of social and political unrest in Czechoslovakia as well as in Poland and Hungary,[8] Moscow had decided to resolve the spreading crisis by retreating at least temporarily from the creation of a purely socialist economy in East Germany. According to a fairly large though still incomplete collection of new documents which have recently become available, the Kremlin was well aware of the worrying developments in Eastern Europe.[9] To the astonishment of the East German population, on 11 June the price increases, the cuts in subsidies, the enforced establishment of agricultural collectives and the abolition of private firms were suddenly rescinded by means of a public announcement.[10] The SED leadership even admitted to having committed a few errors; however, it was clear that the instructions had come from Moscow.

Indeed, in April and May 1953 Soviet Foreign Minister Molotov had carefully analysed the situation in the GDR with the help of a select circle of advisers, who included Deputy Foreign Minister Andrei Gromyko and western European expert Vladimir Semenov, whose information added to the gloomy picture. Semenov drafted various papers on the crisis; in particular his memoranda of 2 May foreshadowed the solution eventually adopted.[11] Beria, who as Soviet interior and security minister was in charge of the Soviet intelligence services, may have been aware of the crisis situation in East Germany even earlier. He fully realized, as he stated in an intelligence report on 6 May, that it was not western propaganda, as claimed by some in Moscow and East Berlin, but the economic policy of the GDR which was responsible for the crisis.[12]

On 5 May, on 14 May and again on or about 20 May the matter was considered by the Presidium of the Council of Ministers in Moscow. Ulbricht was strongly criticized for his economic course as well as for the personality cult he had instigated in the GDR.[13] During the CPSU's Central Committee meeting in Moscow on 27 May the situation in East Germany was discussed in great detail and within a matter of days important decisions for the USSR's German policy were taken. The intense disputes and personality clashes which occurred in the course of the meeting and the question whether or not Beria openly advocated the creation of a neutral and reunited Germany based on a new treaty relationship with the Soviet Union *à la* Churchill are still shrouded in mystery; an analysis is attempted below.[14] The worsening situation in the GDR and other satellite countries increased the urgency for Moscow to deal with the developments in East Germany. Above all, the sudden escalation of the crises in Bulgaria and particularly in Czechoslovakia in early June forced Moscow to address the situation in the GDR to prevent a similar development in its model satellite state. In the aftermath of a currency reform, which greatly benefited the Czech state while undermining the savings and life insurance schemes of most citizens, widespread strikes and unrest had erupted in Pilsen and elsewhere in the CSSR. It took the combined strength and ruthlessness of the Czech police, border police and army units to contain the unrest on 1 and 2 June.[15]

On 2 June the GDR leaders Ulbricht and Otto Grotewohl (with Fred Oelssner to act as interpreter) were summoned to Moscow. In the meetings over the next three days (2–4 June), they were chided in no uncertain terms for their own timid reform proposals and instructed to implement Moscow's radical new policy for East Germany, as finalized in the Kremlin on 2 June.[16] The GDR leadership was to rescind the accelerated or 'enforced creation of socialism', at least for the time being; Ulbricht's strategy of turning his country into a socialist model state was to be abandoned.[17] Ulbricht had no choice but to follow Moscow's lead reluctantly, after cautiously attempting to defend his own political course. Ulbricht and Grotewohl were confronted with the displeasure of the entire collective leadership, but Beria was particularly rude to them.[18] On 28 May, Moscow had already announced that the Soviet Union's military rule over the GDR had been ended in favour of the establishment of a civilian authority on the model of the western powers' relations with West Germany. Semenov was appointed as the first Soviet High Commissioner in East Germany.[19] On 6 June, after his return to East Berlin, Semenov outlined Moscow's new policy to the East German Politburo.[20]

Three days later, on 9 June, after a number of hectic Politburo meetings, the GDR leaders decided how to transform the Kremlin's new strategy into a new East German policy: the result was the 'New Course' announced on 11 June. There had been much opposition within the GDR Politburo to the Soviet demands. In particular, the instruction to scrap the GDR's emphasis on heavy industry in favour of concentrating on the light and consumer industries was strongly opposed on the grounds that this would only increase the turmoil in the East German economy. Some politicians even demanded a Soviet Marshall Plan for the GDR to enable the country to produce both heavy and light industrial goods. But it was to no avail. Even the pleading of Ulbricht and his colleagues to delay the announcement of the 'New Course' by two weeks to prepare the East German population for the new policy was rejected by the Soviet High Commissioner.[21] Semenov pointed out to the shocked GDR leadership that 'in a fortnight you may not even have a state anymore'.[22]

While the Soviet Union had initially not intended to replace Ulbricht, his continued arrogance and dogmatic belief in the correctness of his policy of rapidly building up socialism in the GDR soon exasperated the Kremlin. Moscow began to support Ulbricht's intra-party opponents who, in the face of a worsening crisis, were increasingly outspoken in their criticism of Ulbricht's leadership style and his stubborn attempts to create a Stalinist GDR despite the regime's increasing unpopularity.[23]

In the literature, the interpretation of Moscow's 'New Course' and its implications for the USSR's German policy in the spring and summer of 1953 still causes controversy. Was the new policy merely a tactical manoeuvre to defuse the situation in the GDR without the intention of a long-term change of course, as most western politicians suspected? Or were Beria and/or his colleagues in the Kremlin genuinely interested in radically changing the Soviet Union's approach to the German question, as Churchill believed? After all, from Moscow's point of view, the GDR's economic instability, combined with the looming threat of the rearmament of West Germany and its integration into the EDC, may have made it imperative to find a genuine solution to overcome Moscow's difficulties with the West on the German question. The Kremlin may also have genuinely feared that West German rearmament might include the transfer of responsibility for atomic weapons to the Bonn government and to West German generals, some of whom had been Nazi officers.[24] Few scholars agree with Mark Kramer that Molotov was the driving force behind a new German policy and that there was a broad consensus on this strategy in Moscow but, as will be seen, his thesis deserves greater attention.[25] The long-standing alternative claim that Beria – perhaps initially supported by Malenkov and Semenov and the East German politicians Zaisser and Herrnstadt – was toying with the idea of sacrificing the GDR in favour of a reunited and democratic Germany is also still much debated.[26]

Beria's alleged plan for creating a reunited and neutral Germany, which he appears to have voiced in the course of the Central Committee meeting in the Kremlin on 27 May, was not dissimilar to the plans proposed by Churchill in London in April and May 1953. Despite the partial opening of Russian archives to western scholars, no clear evidence has so far emerged that Beria was influenced by Churchill and that he was working for a radical departure from Moscow's established German policy. However, it still cannot be ruled out. The files on Beria seem to have disappeared,[27] but recent oral testimony and memoirs by surviving aides of the Malenkov government point to the possibility that such a move was indeed contemplated by Beria, Malenkov and some of their advisers.[28]

According to the controversial and not always reliable memoirs of Pavel Sudoplatov, a Beria confidant and MVD general who was in charge of the Bureau of Special Tasks within the Ministry of State Security, his boss contacted him just before 1 May 1953. Beria was thinking of turning the GDR into an 'autonomous province' within a neutral and reunited new Germany which was to be ruled by a coalition government consisting of both Communist and non-Communist ministers. This solution was meant to act as 'a balancing factor between American and Soviet interests in Western Europe'. While the Soviet Union would have to make concessions to the western world, Beria hoped to obtain financial compensations from the West 'for demoting the Ulbricht government from its central role to a peripheral one'.[29] According to Sudoplatov and some additional information found by the Russian historian Lew Besymenski, it appears that Beria expected to extract a $10 billion aid programme from the West to prop up the ailing Soviet economy, rebuild the country and get rid of the $20 billion burden the GDR was expected to cost the USSR over the next ten years.[30]

Yet it seems that Beria was not merely motivated by improving the Soviet economy. He also had in mind the USSR's military preparedness to fend off either external or domestic threats. 'The money would be invested in badly needed modernization and extension of our highway and railway systems, which would allow us to move troops back and forth freely.'[31] Thus the argument put forward by some scholars that it was Molotov who kept the possibility of the outbreak of war with the West in mind, and that this was the main reason why he was opposed to Beria's plan, loses force. Molotov believed that a neutral Germany could never be truly peaceful; Moscow therefore needed to be in possession of German territory for strategic reasons.[32] Beria had not overlooked the military angle, but it is likely that he believed that a conventional war with the West was much less likely than a nuclear one, while the danger of domestic unrest that would have to be dealt with by military means was much greater than Molotov or anyone else in the Kremlin appreciated. As Vladislav Zubok has argued, Beria's unique knowledge about the imminent test of the first Soviet hydrogen bomb, which he had kept secret from his colleagues, may have made him discount the likelihood of a conventional conflict with the West.[33]

In addition, it has been pointed out that Beria may also have wished to enhance the role of the secret police, with whose help he eventually intended to obtain dictatorial powers, by making this body responsible for designing and executing a successful new German policy. By implication this would have led to a downgrading of the importance of the Party, which was largely dominated by Khrushchev, as the decisive body for introducing new ideological and strategic directions.[34] Ignoring the formidable opposition to his plans from Molotov and the inner circle of the ruling elite, Beria also appears to have expressed interest in designing new policies for Hungary, Yugoslavia and Austria. He intended to make Imry Nagy Prime Minister in Budapest after a reshuffle of the Hungarian government, conclude a treaty to solve the Austrian question, and embark on a rapprochement with Tito's Yugoslavia by accepting the view that there was more than one road to socialism.[35]

In early June 1953 the panicking Ulbricht regime in the GDR – and subsequently a number of historians – suspected that the imposition of the Soviet Union's new policy on the GDR was more than just a strategy for crisis management. The abrupt departure from Moscow's established thinking was regarded as proof of a radically new German policy developed by the collective leadership in the Kremlin since Stalin's death which might well result in the liquidation of the GDR. This interpretation is probably too simplistic. A coherent strategy of how to deal with the situation in the GDR did not evolve in the aftermath of Stalin's death. There were serious disputes about Moscow's German policy within the CPSU Presidium on 27 May 1953. Both Molotov and Beria had submitted quite different drafts on how to defuse the escalating crisis in East Germany. In the absence of the transcript of the meeting – which is still under lock and key in the Presidential archives in Russia – it is very difficult to ascertain what really happened.

It appears, however, that on 27 May Beria, tacitly supported by Malenkov, clashed seriously with Molotov, who much to his surprise found himself supported by Khrushchev.[36] While Molotov favoured the termination of the Soviet occupation authority in the GDR to boost Ulbricht's prestige and also advocated a temporary halt in the implementation of 'a forced policy of the construction of socialism in the GDR', Beria is said to have declared: 'We need only a peaceful Germany, it does not matter to us whether there will be socialism or not.' Beria therefore wished to abandon the attempt to construct socialism in the GDR altogether; he was losing patience with 'a permanently unstable socialist Germany whose survival relied on the support of the Soviet Union'.[37] Instead, Beria was in favour of allowing the introduction of capitalist elements into the East German economy and cancelling the establishment of the collective farms so detested by the East German population.[38] Despite their intense rivalry, Malenkov initially seems to have favoured Beria's plans. James Richter has argued convincingly that Malenkov was an opportunist who 'would have accepted easily a plan to reunify a neutral Germany, but would not insist upon it to the point of endangering his domestic position'. Indeed, in January 1955, during a meeting of the Central Committee of the CPSU, when Malenkov was being attacked by Khrushchev for having sided with Beria in 1953, Malenkov admitted (albeit under duress) that he had indeed supported the 'Beria plan' for Germany: 'Today I admit that I essentially took a wrong position on the German Question.'[39]

Despite this clear split in the collective leadership on 27 May 1953 between Beria/Malenkov and Molotov/Khrushchev, an uneasy compromise was achieved. A small committee consisting of Beria, Malenkov and Molotov (and perhaps Defence Minister Bulganin and also Khrushchev) was established after the 27 May meeting to deal with the differing positions and work out the details of a new policy. Eventually, after much further bickering and another attempt by Beria to get the Foreign Minister to agree to German reunification, Beria gave in. According to Molotov, Beria pronounced: 'To hell with you! Let's not have another meeting. I agree with your stand.'[40] It appears that it had been above all Molotov who persuaded Beria to fall in line, though it was Khrushchev who would claim credit for this in his memoirs.[41] In any case, the unanimity of the collective leadership was formally re-established. Thus, Molotov's draft paper (which was mostly based on Semenov's work) was largely adopted; it led to the document 'On Measures to Improve the Health of the Political Situation in the GDR', dated 2 June 1953, which outlined Moscow's envisaged policy for the GDR and led to the SED's 'New Course'.[42]

Thus, in late May and early June 1953 Beria and Malenkov professed to have come round to Molotov's and Khrushchev's position and agreed with their colleagues in the Presidium that it was of vital importance to the Soviet Union that the GDR should remain in existence. The creation of socialism in East Germany needed only to be slowed down until it became possible to accelerate the process again. Mark Kramer's contention about Molotov's strong position in the aftermath of Stalin's death does not seem unjustified; yet Molotov and Beria were not in agreement on Moscow's German policy.[43]

It appears, however, that Beria deceived Molotov and Khrushchev (and perhaps also Malenkov) and subsequently attempted to double-cross them. Instead of abandoning his plan after he had failed to get it accepted as official Soviet policy, Beria decided to use a different method for realizing his strategy. With the help of his extensive networks of secret agents in the eastern and western world, Beria attempted to conspire against his colleagues. He intended to embark on a policy that would provoke a western initiative to which the Kremlin would have to respond. In late April 1953 Beria had asked his close confidant Pavel Sudoplatov to make use of the German contacts of some of his secret agents 'to spread rumours that the Soviet Union was ready to make a deal on German unification'. Subsequently Beria intended to 'monitor the reactions in the Vatican, in American German policy circles, and from influential people around West Germany's chancellor Konrad Adenauer. By putting out these feelers, Beria hoped to begin negotiations with the Western powers.' He had emphasized to his confidant that the project was top secret and that Molotov's Foreign Ministry was not to know about it; it would only be allowed to get involved once talks with the West had commenced.[44] Thus, despite having professed to agree with Molotov's position in the aftermath of the Central Committee meeting on 27 May, Beria appears to have secretly embarked on a course to abolish the GDR.[45] He may well have hoped that eventually all four allied powers would cooperate in the process of German reunification.[46]

Surprisingly, in view of Churchill's long-standing and well-known advocacy of an international summit conference to overcome the Cold War and find a solution to the German question, Beria does not appear to have planned to approach London or to ask his agents to assess the reaction to his plans in British governmental circles.[47] The reasons are unknown. Perhaps Beria had a dim view of Britain's international importance and influence or – like the other Soviet leaders – he mistrusted Churchill too deeply and did not believe that the British Prime Minister might be a reliable partner in such an enterprise. In view of Molotov's rejection of a rapprochement with Britain on the Austrian question, as had been proposed by Beria in the aftermath of Churchill's 11 May speech, Beria had realized Molotov's and Khrushchev's deep mistrust of Churchill and may have believed that an approach to Britain would be counter-productive for eventually persuading his colleagues to support his plans for German reunification.[48] Still, it is puzzling that Beria should have had more confidence in Adenauer and Eisenhower and the Vatican than in Churchill. This, of course, begs the question whether Sudoplatov's memoirs can be trusted and whether Beria did indeed scheme for the creation of a reunited and neutral Germany, or whether this assumption is merely based on unsubstantiated hearsay, as a number of scholars maintain.[49] Yet, as outlined, Sudoplatov's, Molotov's and Khrushchev's memoirs and some other evidence point towards the fact that Beria had a plan to sacrifice the GDR and reunite Germany on a neutral basis. And, Beria seems to have continued with the pursuit of this policy even after the collective leadership had adopted an alternative strategy on 2 June 1953.

The enormous potential rewards for sacrificing the GDR and commencing a policy of rapprochement with the western world may have tempted Beria to embark on this course. A radically different German policy would have made economic help from the West much more likely. As indicated above, Beria effectively hoped to obtain the extension of German reparation payments to the Soviet Union for ten years while simultaneously freeing Moscow from having to deal with constant East German requests for economic and financial aid and subsidize the GDR 'with cheap raw materials and food' during these ten years.[50] If such an admittedly risky course had proven successful, it would have boosted Beria's standing within the Kremlin's ruling circle and would have made him almost unassailable. He was fully aware that despite his superficial friendship with Malenkov, his colleagues did not trust him and would not hesitate to get rid of him if the opportunity arose. As the ruthless long-standing head of the security services Beria knew too much and had too much power. Thus Beria was working for his own survival as well as bidding to become Stalin's sole successor. In the last resort he may also have hoped that a neutral, reunited and democratic Germany would eventually fall into the Soviet sphere of influence by default, as perhaps had also been Stalin's hope.

The Uprising

The 'New Course' announced on 11 June 1953 was warmly welcomed in the GDR. However, it was also seen as a sign of weakness in the new men in the Kremlin, and it also appeared to indicate the bankruptcy of the GDR regime. As Churchill often reminded his audiences, a dangerous situation tended to arise when a dictatorial state began to reform itself.[51] Rumours reached East Germany that Ulbricht was doomed and that there was an internal struggle for power among the leadership in the Kremlin, involving a battle between Beria and Molotov for the direction of the USSR's German policy.[52] There was a widespread perception in the GDR that the new leaders in Moscow were ready to give in to public pressure if enough pressure were applied.

The abolition of the new work norms as imposed on 28 May had not been included in the 'New Course'. These norms remained inflated, as the East

German leadership (and probably also the Soviet experts) were convinced that the GDR was economically so weak that it could not afford the consequences of returning to the pre-May production levels. The workforce had taken it for granted that a reduction in work norms was included in the SED's new policy. An article in the Party newspaper *Tägliche Rundschau* on 13 June announcing that 'the increase of the norms was utterly justified and would remain in force' was the spark that ignited the political powder keg.[53]

On 16 June 1953, construction workers from several building sites in East Berlin marched to the House of Ministers to protest against the maintenance of the higher norms. Instead of Secretary General Ulbricht and head of government Otto Grotewohl, a junior minister was sent to attempt negotiations but he was shouted down. When the government hastily announced that the increase in the work norms had been rescinded, it was no longer enough. The workers seized a loudspeaker car to announce a general strike for the next day. On 17 June almost 500,000 people demonstrated all over the GDR against the East German leadership. The protests had not been centrally organized by fascist or counter-revolutionary elements nor had they been inspired by the western world, as was soon claimed by East Berlin and Moscow.[54] In fact, the American High Commission in Bonn had explicitly forbidden the West Berlin radio station RIAS to use the word 'general strike' or any other inflammatory slogans.[55]

The initial phase of the strike was untarnished by any acts of violence. After lunch time, a further phase developed, characterized by looting, theft and the beating up of Party officials. In the early afternoon, when increasing demands for the resignation of the East German leadership and occasional cries of support for German reunification were heard, Soviet tanks were sent in and took only a few hours to crush the uprising. More than three decades later, Molotov explained when interviewed by Felix Chuev shortly before his death in 1986: 'We had passed a decision to use tanks. We had approved the use of drastic measures to put down the revolt, the most ruthless measures. Let the Germans rise up against us? Everything would have turned shaky, the imperialists would have taken action. There would have been a total collapse.'[56]

In the afternoon of 17 June it was even rumoured that Beria had flown to East Berlin to take charge of the Soviet counter measures, but this is unlikely.[57] When the Soviet soldiers arrived and martial law was declared, protesting crowds had begun to disperse; the East German police and Stasi (secret police) units had already been fairly successful in beating back the demonstrators. At least 25 demonstrators were killed and several executions and numerous arrests occurred in the following days and weeks. Some Soviet soldiers had refused to shoot at the unarmed protesters; they were later court-martialled and executed.[58]

The uprising in the GDR revealed the widespread hostility towards the East German regime and the fragility of the Soviet Union's hegemonic position in Eastern Europe. The western reaction to the events was characterized by dumbfounded surprise and by the determination to remain uninvolved at all costs. Of course, all three western allies and West German Chancellor Adenauer protested strongly to the Soviet High Commission and the Soviet City Commandant in East Berlin.[59] However, the West did not know what to do and western politicians were indeed rather helpless. No one wanted to provoke a direct confrontation between western and Soviet troops in Berlin. The United States even refused to supply an American military plane to the SPD mayor of West Berlin, Ernst Reuter, when he urgently requested transport from Vienna, where he had been attending a conference. The Americans feared that the popular mayor's presence in Berlin would only lead to a further destabilization of the situation; Reuter's forceful political rhetoric was well known.[60]

In London, Churchill rebuked the Commandant of the British Sector in Berlin, Major-General Coleman, for reporting that the USSR were using unrestrained force. Coleman had somewhat exaggerated the situation but Churchill was not so much interested in the substance of the Major-General's telegrams as in the possibility that Washington and the Foreign Office in London might get the wrong impression of the new leaders in Moscow. Churchill was concerned that the opponents of his summit diplomacy would use the uprising to make matters even more difficult for him.[61] This was indeed the case. To Eisenhower and Dulles, the uprising in the GDR seemed an opportunity to undermine Churchill's plans for good. How could one negotiate with a government which had just killed and wounded unarmed demonstrators? Dulles immediately realized that the uprising in the GDR presented an 'excellent propaganda opportunity'.[62]

The uprising was discussed by the National Security Council in Washington on 18 June. Most participants took satisfaction from the fact that the events in the GDR would create difficulties for the Soviet Union, and the Psychological Strategy Board was asked to work out proposals 'to exploit the unrest in the satellite states'. C.D. Jackson pointed out that it was now most unlikely that Moscow would be interested in participating in Churchill's summit conference: 'The East Berliners had pulled out the rug from under the Kremlin'. President Eisenhower also expressed relief that the British Prime Minister's cumbersome summit proposals could now easily be rejected, commenting that 'the uprisings certainly had provided us with the strongest possible argument to give Mr Churchill against a four-power meeting'.[63] The influential *Economist* in London also commented pointedly that the events in East Berlin were a 'reminder to [the] West that Churchill's musings on Locarno ignore the tragedy of the East'. The 'spirit of appeasement' that had taken root in Europe had to be reversed.[64]

Churchill soon realized what Washington and his own Foreign Office had in mind. He therefore attempted to play down the importance of the events in East Germany. In his capacity as Acting Foreign Secretary, he declared that the Soviet government's violent response to the uprising ought to be regarded as a reaction to a sudden emergency situation.[65] The West should not conclude that the various signs of the new Kremlin leadership's willingness to cooperate with the West had not been meant seriously. Churchill therefore disapproved of the activities of Major-General Coleman, and Acting British High Commissioner Jack Ward, who together with their American and French colleagues had sent a letter of protest to his Soviet counterpart Dibrova on 18 June. The three western High Commissioners also condemned 'the irresponsible recourse to military force', which had led to the death and injury of many people in East Germany. They protested against all the unrestrained activities of the Soviet soldiers under martial law and about the execution of the entirely innocent Willi Göttling from West Berlin who had been shot as a provocateur.[66] The British Prime Minister complained to Permanent Under-Secretary William Strang that he was rather surprised that the High Commissioners had sent their letter of protest to Dibrova without prior consultation with the Foreign Office. Moreover, they had simply overreacted. Churchill asked Strang rhetorically: 'Is it suggested that the Soviets should have allowed the Eastern zone to fall into anarchy and riot? I had the impression that they acted with considerable restraint in the face of mounting disorder.'[67]

Coleman and Jack Ward explained to Churchill that the High Commissioners had hoped to employ the letter of protest to stop the Soviet Union from conducting more executions. It had also been their intention to let the German population know that the western allies were on their side. 'To these ends its wording had necessarily to be strong.' The Americans and the French would certainly have received the wrong impression if the delivery of the letter had been delayed because Coleman first wished to consult London. However, Ward declared, he had succeeded in preventing the United States from formulating the letter of protest in a way 'which would have implied that the Allies approved of the riots'.[68]

The Prime Minister remained unconvinced. On 21 June he pointed to the alleged contradiction between Coleman's internal reports about the uprising and the text of the letter to Dibrova. In his memoranda, Coleman had declared that the Red Army 'acted with marked restraint and moderation and have clearly been under instruction to use minimum of force'.[69] This was confirmed by the opinion of the American High Commission. US diplomat Cecil C. Lyon wrote from Berlin on 30 June 'that the Soviet soldiers maintained remarkable reserve, that there was no wanton shooting into the crowds, and that they showed no animosity toward the demonstrators. This behavior of the Soviet soldiers contrasted sharply in an unfavorable light ... with that of the East German police'.[70] Churchill therefore wrote to Coleman angrily: 'If the Soviet Government, as the occupying Power, were faced as you have described with widespread movements of violent disorder they surely have the right to declare Martial Law in order to prevent anarchy ... We shall not find our way out of our many difficulties by making for purposes of local propaganda statements which are not in accordance with the facts.'[71]

Although the Foreign Office officials were opposed to Churchill's summitry, they agreed with the Prime Minister's legalistic reasoning. Deputy Under-Secretary Frank Roberts also believed that as one of the occupying powers the Soviet Union had the right to keep its zone under control. His opinion was shared by his colleague Christopher Warner, who telephoned the British High Commission in Germany and asked his counterpart there to let the Foreign Office 'know at once if the Russian troops were to open fire on the strikers. They have, of course, a right to do so as the occupying Power in order to preserve law and order.'[72]

A few days later, on 25 June, High Commissioner Sir Ivonne Kirkpatrick made a very similar, even more precise statement to the American High Commissioner James Conant, the former President of Harvard University and a wartime political adviser involved in atomic decision-making who had only recently arrived in Germany. Kirkpatrick regarded Conant as 'quite inexperienced in our jungle warfare'.[73] The British High Commissioner felt that as far as the control of the German population was concerned, the western powers and the Soviet Union faced similar situations. The Germans could not be allowed to instigate riots in the Soviet zone, which would carry the danger that something similar might occur in the western zones at some stage. Kirkpatrick was prepared to condemn the USSR for the infringement of basic human rights and bad administrative efforts in the GDR, but not for using its troops to quell the uprising. The High Commissioner overlooked entirely that the worsening economic situation and the lack of political freedom in the GDR had caused the uprising. He made it sound as if the population of the GDR had had no cause for protesting against their government.

Kirkpatrick, who was known within the Foreign Office for his strong anti-German sentiments, told Conant, who also was not in favour of German rearmament, that it seemed to him 'that whilst we should show sympathy with the Eastern Germans under their Communist yoke we must not close our eyes to the dangers inherent in the riots'.

The Germans were a hysterical people, rioting was contagious and if we deliberately inflamed passions for propaganda purposes we might one day find the Germans using violence to express disapproval of our own policy. In particular I called his attention to the consequences of attacking the Russians for using troops to restore order. Not only had they no alternative but we had expressly retained the right in the Bonn Treaty to declare a state of emergency, a right to which the Americans had attached special importance.

Kirkpatrick was certainly 'opposed to condemning' the Soviets 'for turning out their troops'.[74] Foreign Office official Frank Roberts approved of Kirkpatrick's sentiments and assured him that the Foreign Office 'fully agreed' with his statement.[75] The High Comissioner informed the Foreign Office that Conant 'professed to agree' with his views but Conant's memoirs show that this was not the case. 'Equating the legality of all occupation forces in Berlin', he wrote, 'may have been formally correct, but it in no way corresponded with the mood of the Berliners or the Americans in Berlin.' Conant mentions 'smoldering disagreements' among the western powers. 'The three governments were not of one mind as regards the uprising', he declared.[76]

However, in some American quarters the urge to exploit the momentary weakness of the Soviet Union in order 'to deal [the] Soviet [Union a] specious blow …' contributed to disagreements with the Foreign Office, which was much more cautious in this regard.[77] Eisenhower's trusted associates Walt Rostow and C.D. Jackson advised the President to revive his plans for a psychological warfare offensive. They believed 'that the chances of unifying Germany without [a] major war had vastly increased'. Rostow thought this might be the moment to encourage the population of the GDR to begin a 'full scale revolt'.[78] The chief of the CIA station in Berlin even asked his superiors in Washington to allow him to equip the demonstrators with guns. However, despite the uncertainty that beset the White House and most other western capitals when the news of the uprising first became known, Eisenhower kept his head; he was not convinced this was the moment to embark on a course of aggression. Although in principle the President and his National Security Council still favoured the employment of psychological warfare and other covert operations in Eastern Europe and East Germany (as was stated for example in the document NSC 160/1 of August 1953), Eisenhower realized the danger of helping to escalate the uprising. A full-scale revolution in the GDR might well result in a military clash between western and Soviet troops in Berlin.[79]

Although the Foreign Office agreed with Churchill that the Soviet Union had the right and possibly the obligation to bring the uprising to a quick end, the diplomats nevertheless believed that Coleman and Ward had acted correctly so far as the letter of protest to Dibrova was concerned. Since the principal Foreign Office officials strongly opposed the idea of convening a summit meeting with Moscow, they were much less sensitive about the possible consequences of the tone of the letter than Churchill. The diplomats believed that the note of protest to Dibrova had done no harm and Ward could not have withheld his signature. Otherwise, Adenauer's not entirely groundless suspicion 'that we [read Churchill] place the possibility of agreement with the Russians above all other issues' would have been confirmed.[80] However, in a minute to Minister of State Selwyn Lloyd Frank Roberts admitted that given the number of troops and tanks brought into East Berlin and the behaviour which could have been expected from the Red Army, the Kremlin had indeed acted with some restraint.[81]

Still, much to their delight Roberts and his colleagues in the Foreign Office believed that the crushing of the uprising on 17 June had effectively damaged Moscow's peace campaign irreparably. Churchill's summit plans now looked even more unrealistic than before. Roberts had written on 17 June: 'We are keeping a close eye on these interesting and encouraging, but also potentially dangerous developments. If the Russians have to fire, this will undo all the effect of their recent gestures.'[82] From Berlin, Major General Coleman concurred. The fact that the Soviets did intervene on a large scale 'will certainly prove a serious embarrassment for them in their new plan for Eastern Germany'.[83] Roberts summed up on 25 June: 'Recent developments have once again clearly and publicly nailed our flag to the mast of existing German and E.D.C. policies. They will, I hope, also have improved Dr. Adenauer's prospects of winning the elections.'[84]

This expectation was certainly correct. The Social Democrats may have criticized the Chancellor for being too passive during the uprising, but Adenauer believed that events in the GDR confirmed the wisdom of his *Westpolitik*.[85] He had been greatly worried about 'indications that Paris and London were prepared to make [a] deal with Moscow at [the] expense of Germany'. After the East German uprising he was optimistic that the 'latest events had convinced [the] French and [the] British that any "sell-out" of Germany would also spell doom for them'.[86] Only after full integration with the West had been achieved, the Chancellor declared in the Bundestag on 1 July 1953, would it be sensible to enter into negotiations with Moscow to achieve a solution to the German unification question.[87] Based on this reasoning Adenauer was able to exploit the uprising and gain the strong support of the western allies in his re-election campaign.

In the aftermath of the events in the GDR, the western allies did everything possible to help Adenauer's re-election in early September 1953. Less than a week after the uprising they agreed to elevate their High Commissioners in Bonn to the personal rank of ambassadors. The same would apply to the German diplomatic representatives in the respective western capitals. The decision conferring greater symbolic status and recognition on the Bonn government was announced at the end of June and took effect from 6 July. The British Foreign Office was well aware that 'the object of the exercise ... [was] to strengthen Dr. Adenauer's position, having regard to the coming elections'.[88] In particular Adenauer expected the Americans to 'help him get re-elected' though his personal relationship with American High Commissioner Conant proved to be increasingly cool.[89]

A few days after the uprising, the Chancellor had also asked the western heads of government to subscribe once again to his policy on German reunification and make this known to the general public.[90] Eisenhower, Churchill and Acting French Prime Minister Mayer immediately sent him supportive letters which were published at once. Minister of State Selwyn Lloyd reiterated the government's support for Adenauer's policies in the House of Commons on 24 June.[91] In the same statement Lloyd also commented that 'the Russians appear to have behaved so far with restraint'. Churchill had dictated this sentence to him and had insisted on leaving it in the speech.[92] Lloyd was thereby given the unpleasant task of defending Churchill's position against heavy attacks from fellow MPs.[93] The American embassy in London concluded quite correctly that the Prime Minister's 'real reason ... was that he felt this "non-provocative" statement would be appropriate at the present time' to rescue his summit diplomacy.[94]

A few weeks after the events in the GDR, Adenauer began reminding the United States of plans first voiced in May to offer the Soviet Union a joint and extensive 'food parcel scheme' for the benefit of the GDR population. The Chancellor wished to implement these plans at once. The scheme would not only help the suffering East German population but contribute to his popularity with the West German voters. As had been expected, Moscow turned down the proposal. But the East and West German populations were deeply impressed by the generous American offer, which had largely come about because of Adenauer's initiative. The British were told by Washington, however, that 'the State Department did not initiate the idea and that it seemed to have occurred to them and to Adenauer at about the same time'.[95]

Despite Moscow's rejection of the plan, within a few weeks and in close collaboration with Adenauer, Washington began to implement the 'food parcel scheme'. The United States began to organize free food collection centres for East Berliners on the border of the American zone in West Berlin.[96] The initiative certainly had 'humanitarian as well as propaganda aims',[97] yet the latter unquestionably dominated American and West German considerations. The forthcoming general election in the Federal Republic was never far from the minds of Adenauer and the Eisenhower administration. The 'food parcel scheme' was only terminated in early October, as both Bonn and Washington had deemed it advisable to continue until 'several weeks after [the] elections'.[98] In the immediate aftermath of his impressive election victory, Adenauer was naturally very grateful for all the help he had received from the Americans. His confidant Herbert Blankenhorn told British Deputy High Commissioner Jack Ward that 'Dr Adenauer considers that the existing distribution scheme has achieved a most favourable political result'.[99]

The Chancellor was much less impressed by the British government. Although London also supported Adenauer's election campaign, it did so in a much more reserved way. Some of Adenauer's wilder ideas on how to further his chances for re-election did not find British approval; the 'food parcel scheme', for example, was deemed inappropriate, since London believed that it provoked the Soviet Union unnecessarily and was therefore dangerous.[100] The Foreign Office was in favour of a return to normalcy in the GDR and allowing the Russians to 'save face'.[101] The British High Commission in Germany protested about the scheme for weeks, without being taken seriously by the Americans. Furthermore, the British as well as the French received little information about the progress of the scheme from the German and American authorities. At no stage were they consulted. This explains the rather cynical view of Patrick Hancock, the influential director of the Foreign Office's Central Department. He believed 'that the Americans are burning to take action in Germany. As long as they can do something, they do not seem greatly to care what.'[102]

Churchill shared this opinion. After all, the food parcel scheme was yet another obstacle to the realization of a friendly meeting with the new Soviet leadership. In early August he told Lord Salisbury that he regarded Eisenhower's move as 'an ill-timed act of charity and in line with what he told you about "harrying the Communists wherever possible" '.[103] On Churchill's advice, Kirkpatrick did his best to prevent the food parcel scheme coming into operation and at one point almost succeeded in doing so; in Conant's words, the British diplomat 'felt the risks were far too great' and that the entire plan represented a much too blatant political warfare operation.[104]

In the end, however, it was not so much the food parcel scheme or America's strong support for Adenauer's election campaign that proved decisive but the crushing of the East German uprising by Soviet tanks. This event ensured that voters in the Federal Republic lost all faith in any ideas about creating a neutral and united Germany and entering into a deal with the Kremlin – a concept which had found considerable support among SPD sympathizers. After the uprising, the vast majority of West Germans put their faith in Adenauer's and Dulles's *Westpolitik* and the build-up of 'positions of strength' to be followed by a policy of negotiation from strength. They hoped unification would come about in the long run. In the meantime they concentrated on exploiting the fruits of the economic miracle and largely ignored the fate of their brethren in the East.[105] The British High Commissioner in Bonn would even inform the Foreign Office at a later stage that the Germans in the Federal Republic were no longer keen on reunification; they were much more interested in the 'three B's – belly, BMW and building society accounts'.[106]

Within the Foreign Office, Selwyn Lloyd soon referred to the uprising as 'a great triumph'. It was of overriding importance that the Germans, 'whether Germany is united or not', regarded themselves as members of the western world and that the East Germans would not become 'loyal subjects of the Russian communists'. By then, Lloyd was also firmly opposed to Churchill's ideas of overcoming the division of Germany with the help of a summit conference and a deal on German neutrality. He believed that such a course was 'fraught with danger for all'. Lloyd was convinced that as long as the Cold War continued Germany should best remain divided as this was 'safer for the time being'. In public, however, he believed the western powers should continue to show support for a united Germany to appease those Germans who still believed in it.[107]

The Implications of the Uprising

Initially Beria appears to have refused to believe that the uprising in the GDR would have dire repercussions for the Soviet Union's relations with the western world. He is alleged to have told some of his advisers that after such an impressive demonstration of Soviet strength the West might well be more interested in any new Soviet proposals on the future of Germany than hitherto. According to Beria's confidant Sudoplatov, the Soviet agent Colonel Zoya Rybkina, the head of the German intelligence section in Moscow, was instructed to fly to Berlin on 24 June, where she was to meet the actress Olga Chekhova 'to start the intelligence probe on prospects of unification' as Beria had directed. The two women met on 26 June in Berlin to start the operation, but Beria's arrest on the same day put an end to these activities, which were immediately cancelled.[108]

Whether or not Beria's alleged new German policy was the main reason for his arrest on 26 June is not entirely clear.[109] However, assuming that the claims that Beria intended to sacrifice the GDR and use this to strengthen his own political position are essentially correct, it appears that it was above all his attempt to acquire an increasingly powerful position which aroused the suspicion of Khrushchev and other members of the collective leadership and led to his arrest. Beria was accused of being a British spy and of having aspired to rule the Soviet Union as a dictator. Shortly afterwards a special plenum of the Central Committee condemned Beria as an enemy of the Soviet people and the Communist Party and an agent of international imperialism.[110] Malenkov also stressed that Beria had had the audacity to take sole responsibility for going ahead with testing the hydrogen bomb and had not consulted his colleagues in the collective leadership. Yet, it seems in the last resort, it was not differences about substantive and ideological policy but Beria's striving for enhanced power that was decisive. He had, for example, attempted to remove his interior ministry and the intelligence services from the overall control of the Party; he also seemed to be scheming to discredit his colleagues. It appeared to the members of the Central Committee that Beria was preparing to become Stalin's sole successor. A successful new German policy and a rapprochement with the western world as envisaged in the 'Beria Plan' would have immensely strengthened his position in Moscow. Beria had also made the mistake of threatening Khrushchev's personal power base in the Ukraine and elsewhere.[111]

Why did Malenkov, Molotov and Khrushchev not implement Beria's plan for Germany? Proposing genuine talks about German reunification would have eased Moscow's relationship with the western world tremendously. After all, the East German uprising demonstrated how fragile Moscow's hold was on the GDR. As Hannes Adomeit has pointed out, there were several reasons for the Kremlin's decision not to sacrifice the GDR. Such a policy would in all likelihood have been interpreted as weakness by the population of the GDR and the other satellite states and might have led to a rapid unravelling of the entire Soviet position in Eastern Europe. It was also feared that it could well encourage the West to attempt to expand its influence in the region. As Molotov later commented, Khrushchev's patriotism would have regarded such a result as a major insult to the Soviet soldiers who had defeated Hitler. According to Molotov, Khrushchev was 'rotten through and through' yet he possessed 'a streak of Russian patriotism' which Beria lacked who was 'even more rotten'.[112] Molotov also emphasized his deep ideological belief that a 'bourgeois' Germany could not possibly be peaceful and neutral and would soon pose a military danger once again, thus the realization of Beria's plan would have been much too dangerous.[113] Finally, the Soviet Union needed the East German uranium sources for its nuclear weapons programme.

On the whole it seems that Moscow was convinced that despite the uprising in the GDR and its shaky position in Eastern Europe the Soviet Union could not be forced to abandon the GDR and its Eastern European empire; Moscow's power and territorial influence were too strong. Not only were there a considerable number of socialist countries with a population of almost 800 million people, the Kremlin also believed that western adventurism was safely contained by the Soviet Union's atomic arsenal.[114]

The uprising in the GDR and, above all, Beria's fall was a decisive turning-point in the Soviet Union's German policy. Instead of blaming Ulbricht's economic policies for the uprising and disposing of him, the Kremlin was afraid to show weakness. Sacrificing Ulbricht, as Beria and the senior Soviet personnel in East Berlin including High Commissioner Semenov had planned as late as 25 June,[115] might have been interpreted as a further sign of weakness by the East German people. Thus, instead of publicly accepting that Ulbricht's and by inference also Moscow's policy had been wrong and were responsible for the uprising, Ulbricht's position in the GDR was actually strengthened in the aftermath of the uprising.[116] Ulbricht was quick to exploit this. As early as 2 July he embarked on a strategy to undermine his internal opponents. At the end of the month, during the 15th Plenum of the East German Central Committee on 24–26 July 1953, Zaisser and Herrnstadt were condemned for having collaborated with Beria to establish a capitalist GDR. They were stripped of all positions and expelled from the Party. They benefited however from the changes introduced in Moscow after Stalin's death and were not imprisoned and executed, but they had to endure continued discrimination and harassment for the remainder of their lives.[117]

Beria's arrest resolved the internal struggle for power in the Kremlin, at least for the time being. Malenkov, Molotov and increasingly Khrushchev were able to consolidate their rule without having to fear that security minister Beria would attempt a coup with the help of the troops of his interior ministry and use his amassed secret documents to damage and probably exterminate his rivals. Instead, Beria himself was tried in secret and shot together with six of his alleged collaborators in December 1953.[118]

The uprising also had implications for Moscow's external politics. Before the uprising, the Kremlin had the impression that the United Kingdom and to a lesser extent the United States were seriously interested in negotiations on Germany, Austria and other outstanding questions. Churchill's speech on 11 May and earlier statements by him and by President Eisenhower clearly indicated this. The general conversations British ambassador Gascoigne had been instructed to conduct with Molotov soon after Stalin's death confirmed this further.[119] Yet, even before the uprising suspicion of Churchill's real intentions had prevailed among Stalin's successors. However, as discussed above, while Beria eventually intended to approach Washington and Bonn with his plan for a united and neutral Germany, he had no plans to make overtures to Churchill, although the British Prime Minister was the leading western advocate of a genuine rapprochement with Moscow.

After the uprising, it seemed – as the Foreign Office and the Eisenhower administration had anticipated and as Churchill had feared – that Moscow was in no mood to embark on summit diplomacy. Stalin's successors continued the peace campaign and kept on working for an armistice in Korea, but it now appeared to them to be too risky to enter into international summit negotiations with the West. With Beria's arrest – which only became known in the West on 10 July – Churchill's idea of talking to Malenkov about a neutral and reunited Germany was out of the question. A 'Big Three' summit, even if it did not focus on the German question, would raise hopes in the GDR and other satellite states that Moscow might be about to embark on a more liberal and tolerant policy; disappointing such a hope was bound to cause further unrest and protests all over Eastern Europe.[120]

Thus the uprising in East Germany was decisive in turning Stalin's successors away from the idea of a 'parley at the summit', however much Churchill attempted to push for it. Moreover, the uprising also provided the British Foreign Office and the Eisenhower administration with excellent arguments for rejecting Churchill's continued attempts to organize an informal 'Big Three' summit conference. The East German uprising and, paradoxically, Beria's arrest were severe blows for Churchill's strategy; these events undermined almost fatally the Prime Minister's policy of working for international détente and an easing of Cold War tension.

Churchill himself did not remain unaffected by Beria's arrest and the rather ambiguous role Malenkov had played in this connection. His conviction that Malenkov was 'a good man' with whom one could negotiate was shaken. Moreover, Churchill could not avoid pondering the question whether it might be possible that Malenkov could also be disposed of as quickly as the powerful Beria; in such a case all his efforts to achieve his elusive summit meeting with Malenkov would be worthless.[121] However, despite his increasing doubts, Churchill stuck to his summit policy; he did not give up his attempts to realize his vision. As will be outlined in the following chapter, Churchill genuinely believed that it was high time to give Stalin's successors a clear indication that the West was prepared to wind down the Cold War.

Moreover, Churchill also recognized with increasing urgency the necessity of creating a long period of peace to allow Britain to recover from the war. He wished to ensure that Britain would remain a great power through economic recovery and by playing a leading role as the chief guarantor of peace between the Soviet Union and Germany. Churchill's vision for the post-Cold War world was inherently logical but fairly unrealistic. It was quite obvious, and the Foreign Office realized this immediately, that even the partial achievement of Churchill's vision of peace was unlikely. The realities of the Cold War made this impossible. Mistrust between East and West was still much too great and could not easily be overcome. This would require a long-drawn out process. Neither the leading politicians in the West nor, ultimately, those in the East were prepared to give Churchill's vision the benefit of the doubt and attempt seriously to overcome the mutual aura of deep suspicion and distrust which characterized the Cold War in the 1950s. In May and June 1953 Churchill had been full of optimism regarding the possibility of pursuing his summit diplomacy after Stalin's death. After all, as a first step the Bermuda conference of western heads of government was to take place in early July 1953. Yet, developments since mid-June – above all the uprising in the GDR – seemed to have put him at an ever greater disadvantage. There was one further calamity he had to cope with which proved to be even more difficult to overcome: his deteriorating health.

CHAPTER 13

Churchill's Policy Undermined
Collusion and the Western Foreign Ministers' Talks in Washington

On the evening of 23 June 1953, after an official dinner in honour of the visiting Italian president, the 78-year-old Churchill suffered a stroke. Although he chaired a meeting of the Cabinet on the following day he was soon paralysed on one side and was hardly able to speak.[1] It was clear that Churchill would be unable to perform the duties of his office. However, he never appointed one of his colleagues Acting Prime Minister. Churchill insisted on remaining in his post. For the next few months his Private Secretary John Colville and a small number of other trusted officials were in effect governing the country.[2]

On 29 June it was merely announced that in the absence of both Churchill and the convalescent Eden, the Lord President, Lord Salisbury, would take over the Foreign Office as Acting Foreign Secretary.[3] The public as well as the British Parliament and most members of the Cabinet were left in the dark about the nature and the seriousness of Churchill's illness. A medical bulletin was published explaining that the Prime Minister was overworked and 'in need of a complete rest'. His medical consultants had advised him 'to abandon his journey to Bermuda and to lighten his duties for at least a month'.[4] Only almost two years later, in the course of a parliamentary speech on 2 March 1955, did Churchill himself reveal that he had suffered a stroke in June 1953.[5] Thus, throughout the summer of 1953 most of Churchill's colleagues and the country at large were confined to speculating about the real reasons for Churchill's need for a respite.[6] Stalin's successors in Moscow believed that the Prime Minister's 'rest' and the abandonment of the Bermuda conference were political in origin. Selwyn Lloyd, the Minister of State, and Conservative backbenchers Bob Boothby and Julian Amery were unable to convince Soviet diplomats in London of the genuineness of Churchill's need for a vacation.[7]

Apart from a very few trusted confidants, only President Eisenhower was put in the picture by Churchill about the real nature of his illness. Even before the publication of the medical bulletin, he had told him in a letter that due to his stroke he would be unable to attend the Bermuda meeting, the conference of western heads of government envisaged for early July.[8] The letter to Eisenhower dated 26 June was followed by a second one on 1 July. On 6 July, whilst lying in bed, Churchill dictated a long memorandum about his summit policy which was addressed to his cabinet colleagues.[9] This appears to be proof that Churchill's mental capacities had been hardly diminished by his illness. He suffered, however, ever more frequent lapses of concentration and his physical ability to move was seriously restricted during the first few weeks after his stroke. Naturally, the question arose whether Churchill should retire. If Eden, his 'heir apparent', had not also been ill a change of Prime Minister might well have taken place. However, as the Conservative party establishment was less than enthusiastic about Rab Butler, the most senior cabinet member after Eden, succeeding Churchill as PM, no decision was taken.[10]

Moreover, Churchill was soon recovering and did his best to undermine all discussions about appointing a new party leader. He even managed to use Eden's absence as a reason for persuading many doubters in the party that it would be unfair to his long-waiting Foreign Secretary if he resigned as Prime Minister now, thus robbing Eden of the chance to succeed him.[11] Churchill aimed at being fully back in office by the time of the Conservative party conference in October, where he would have to give the party leader's traditional address. If he was not able to achieve this he would retire, or so he told his closest advisers.[12]

In his letter to Eisenhower on 26 June, Churchill had proposed the postponement of the Bermuda conference. Instead, he favoured a visit to Washington by Acting Foreign Secretary Lord Salisbury for a bilateral talk with John Foster Dulles, his American counterpart. Salisbury would explain the British point of view to Dulles and perhaps Eisenhower himself 'and establish the intimate Anglo-American contact which is the keystone to our policy'.[13] Despite his illness, Churchill had by no means given up on his summit diplomacy. He hoped that Salisbury would be able to persuade the American administration to agree to an approach to Moscow. The Acting Foreign Secretary was on record as supporting such approaches: in February 1950 he had approved of Churchill's Edinburgh speech and in November that year he had spoken on similar lines in the House of Lords, calling on the Soviet Union to participate in a summit meeting.[14]

With his impressive aristocratic and political pedigree, the arch-conservative Salisbury enjoyed a good reputation in American political circles. At the end of June, US ambassador Aldrich described him as the 'best politician' in

England; though he appeared to be 'less flexible' than Churchill, Salisbury 'will not ... be so unpredictable, impulsive or so inclined to personal leadership'.[15] The ambassador also realized (correctly as it turned out) that despite Salisbury's pro-summit speech of November 1950 it could not be assumed that 'his opposition speeches necessarily reflect [the] views he would put forward as [a] representative of [the] government'.[16]

As Eisenhower had never been more than lukewarm about the Bermuda conference he was not sorry to see the meeting replaced with a much less time-consuming and burdensome event, but he still insisted on the participation of the French. On 29 June it was officially announced that trilateral talks between the western foreign ministers were to take place in Washington in mid-July.

Churchill Continues his Quest for Peace

In July 1953 Churchill still viewed the prospects for his policy in a fairly optimistic light. Though he was deeply depressed after his stroke he gradually began to recuperate and quickly regained confidence in his ability to shape world events. Despite the trust he put in Lord Salisbury the Prime Minister did not loosen his grip on the reins of power during his recovery. Moreover, on occasion as in July 1952, he spoke of Salisbury as 'tiresome' with 'frail health' and a 'defeatist frame of mind'.[17] Churchill had no intention of allowing the Foreign Office ideas on summit diplomacy to prevail unchallenged. Even from his sickbed Churchill was able to participate actively in the execution of British policy by way of written instructions and occasional discussions with his senior officials,[18] although after his stroke the Prime Minister became much more willing to enter into compromises with his advisers. He also appeared to be more understanding towards Washington's and Adenauer's determination to ratify the EDC first and only embark on East–West negotiations thereafter.

A week after his stroke, Churchill informed Eisenhower – quite untruthfully – that he had never envisaged a summit meeting before a final decision on the EDC had been reached.[19] He now even agreed that a high-level conference should not be convened before the West German elections had taken place. The convalescing Prime Minister had decided to placate his opponents: his sickness compelled him to curb his impatience. In the last resort, however, Churchill still aimed at convincing the Foreign Office and the United States of the importance of a speedy summit conference with the USSR. Despite his declarations to the contrary, he considered it of little importance whether or not the German elections or the ratification of the EDC, or for that matter any other important event, had taken place before a high-level 'parley at the summit' was convened.[20]

Eisenhower may have realized Churchill's change of tactic. The President hardly reacted to the Prime Minister's new considerations; he simply warned of the catastrophic effects on public opinion in the US and of Congress's willingness to provide funds for alternative European defence initiatives in the event of the EDC's failure. 'Possible alternatives to NATO's and E.D.C.'s success are too alarming to contemplate', he informed Churchill. The American people were always prepared to retreat into 'complete isolationism'.[21]

Churchill took this to heart; he began to work for a quick decision on the future of the EDC. A decision on the EDC had to be taken soon: one could not wait indefinitely for the French. In an important memorandum on 6 July to Salisbury and William Strang, the Foreign Office's most senior civil servant, dictated only two weeks after his stroke, Churchill again outlined the fundamental ideas behind his policy to prepare the British delegation for the forthcoming Washington talks. He declared that ratification of the EDC must be demanded from the French by the end of October;[22] otherwise, a revised NATO treaty should be implemented, possibly without French participation, whereby no member state could exert a veto over the integration of the Federal Republic of Germany into NATO.[23] Churchill was doubtful whether it would be possible to push the French towards a final EDC decision during the forthcoming talks in Washington, and whether the talks would lead to an announcement of a four-power conference. Instead, he was still ready to embark upon a 'solitary pilgrimage' once the West German elections were over.[24]

Regardless of the outcomes of the EDC ratification process and the elections in the Federal Republic, Churchill believed that 'We shall have to face very soon the problem of German unity. . . . There will always be "a German problem" and "a Prussian danger".' He sincerely believed that a unified, independent Germany would not become an ally of the Soviet Union. Using the kind of vocabulary that was customary during his younger days, Churchill thought that 'the German nation', due to its 'superior character', was well protected against the temptations of Communism. The fate of the oppressed eastern zone would act as a further deterrent. The hatred towards Bolshevism which had been instilled into the Germans by Hitler was still very strong. In sum, Churchill stressed that 'The eyes of Germany are turned against Soviet Russia in fear, hate and intellectual antagonism. For France there is only contempt and pity. What is Alsace-Lorraine compared with Silesia and the Western Neisse in Russian hands? *I am sure that Germany will not, in the next 20 years, join with Russia against the West or lose her moral association with the Free Powers of Europe and America.* That, at any rate, is the basis from which we ought to consider our terrible problem.'[25]

Churchill thought that even without the full integration of the Federal Republic into the West, the German people would not drift towards the eastern world. The question of integration into the West was therefore not as pressing as that of German unity. As the uprising in the GDR had shown, German dissatisfaction with their divided nation could be expected to remain at a dangerously high level; the inflammatory situation needed to be defused. This view was shared by others in Churchill's circle. Bob Boothby, for example, had 'reluctantly' concluded during a conversation with a Soviet diplomat in London 'that you could not keep them apart against their will'; the Soviet diplomat had replied: 'We have reached precisely the same conclusion.'[26] Contrary to the vast majority of western politicians, Churchill believed that German reunification, and not integration into the West, would bring about an era of international détente. The possibility of attempting to achieve both reunification and integration with the West as was realized in 1990 did not seem feasible to him.

In his memorandum of 6 July 1953 Churchill also returned to the danger of neglecting the security interests of the Soviet Union. Despite the numerous counter-arguments deployed by the Foreign Office, Churchill steadfastly upheld the views outlined in his 11 May speech. He emphatically declared: 'What must not be forgotten by us, and will I hope be remembered by the Soviets, is the safety of Russia against another Hitlerite invasion. It is along these lines of thought that ... our minds might adventurously travel.' He explained that at 'present I have only two practical points in Europe – the early ratification of E.D.C. followed by a Four-Power Conference. The whole policy being *simultaneously* announced.'[27] It was clear that Churchill had not changed the substance of his summit policy.

A few days after taking over as Acting Foreign Secretary, Lord Salisbury delivered a detailed memorandum to the Cabinet outlining the objectives he hoped to achieve during the discussions in Washington.[28] Salisbury's deliberations were based on a 'steering brief' completed by Frank Roberts in late June for the planned Bermuda conference.[29] Salisbury had also attempted to incorporate Churchill's thoughts on summit diplomacy and the German question and find a middle way between two opposite positions. But while Salisbury sought to placate Churchill, his memorandum leaned much more towards the ideas of the Foreign Office.[30]

The Lord President said that during his Washington meetings his aim would be 'to maintain the initiative' of Churchill's speech on 11 May and convince public opinion that the postponement of the Bermuda conference would not delay 'our joint efforts to reduce international tension'. Although he was not altogether sure that the Kremlin was seriously interested in negotiations it might well be advantageous, 'to test out what may prove to be a new situation in Russia. It is also my intention to try to persuade Mr. Dulles that high-level talks with the Russians, of the exploratory and informal character advocated by the Prime Minister, held in due time and after proper preparation, might do good and could do no harm, and that it would be a great mistake to take the responsibility upon ourselves of disappointing public expectations about such talks.' Salisbury believed that it might be possible 'to count on French support on both these issues.'[31]

The phrases 'due time' and 'proper preparation' indicated that Salisbury did not wholeheartedly support the Prime Minister's summit diplomacy. Moreover, he vigorously rejected Churchill's idea of a neutral reunified Germany. Although such a Germany would be 'the easiest way to reach agreement with the Soviet Union', Salisbury was of the firm opinion that such a course would be 'highly dangerous for the West'. It was still too early to strive for the imminent membership of Germany in NATO. 'We hold it, however, in reserve should the E.D.C. solution finally fail.' Salisbury thought it would be best if a summit meeting did not take place until after the general election in the Federal Republic and should not be held before the successful ratification of the EDC.[32] However, it became apparent from Salisbury's memorandum that the organization of a summit conference might well prove to be unavoidable and could not be delayed until the EDC ratification process had been completed.[33]

Churchill did not attend the Cabinet meeting of 6 July, but his lengthy memorandum was read and discussed along with Salisbury's paper. It was decided that the Lord President should pursue the strategy he had envisaged, and attempt to 'seek agreement to the conclusions set out in the Prime Minister's note'.[34] Churchill's idea of a 'Potsdam-type' conference had thus been more or less accepted by the Cabinet. John Young concludes that 'This showed that, when suitably hedged with limitations, Churchill's policy could win his Cabinet's support.'[35] However, this conclusion must be viewed with caution. The Cabinet knew full well that Eisenhower, Dulles and to some extent Salisbury would treat Churchill's ideas with politeness but were not ready to support the Prime Minister's plans. The Cabinet gave its apparent endorsement to Churchill's ideas in order to avoid a major argument and perhaps even a governmental crisis. It could be safely assumed that the Prime Minister's summit plans were most unlikely to be agreed. The events of summer 1954 would prove, however, that when there was the likelihood that Churchill's plans might come to fruition, the British Cabinet would risk the collapse of the government in order to block them.[36]

The British government was not particularly well informed about the opinion-forming process in Washington. The range of policy options discussed within the State Department, America's foreign policy elite and the White House confused the British. For example, the Foreign Office was horrified to learn that some members of the State Department's German Bureau had made the 'dangerous suggestion' that in the light of the GDR uprising the West's explicit conditions for German reunification as listed in the note of 23 September 1952 might have to be abandoned.[37] The British diplomats thought that there was no reason to change the solid western position of insisting on free elections as a precondition for an all-German government and a peace treaty. The Foreign Office remained convinced that after the GDR uprising the Kremlin was most unlikely to tempt the Germans with serious proposals for reunification.[38] However, much to the surprise of the British, this view was no longer shared in Washington.

Initially, British diplomats did not recognize that the Eisenhower administration had started to prepare a new strategy for the Washington discussions. Although ambassador Makins reported on 28 June that Dulles was convinced that 'a fresh look at the German problem is becoming urgent',[39] the ambassador did not appear to understand the radical change of course in American diplomacy which was taking place after the uprising in the GDR. While various indications about the American government's altered policy were not entirely overlooked in London, British officials still failed to interpret them correctly. They were therefore unaware of the new situation with which Salisbury would be confronted during the discussions in Washington. Thus at the beginning of July the British embassy in the US still told the Foreign Office that it was the aim of the American administration to 'eventually' seek negotiations with Moscow while initially attempting to expand the western position of strength. Soon, however, the surprised experts in London were told 'that the U.S. Government are not at all averse to negotiating with the Russians forthwith. But they want to begin with small things, and work their way up piecemeal towards the more fundamental issues. What they dislike is a meeting of Heads of Government at this early stage.'[40] Even this did not reflect the new American position entirely accurately.

In the aftermath of the uprising in the GDR, the general conviction had developed in the State Department that the Soviet Union would soon make an attractive offer for German reunification. In the event that a basis for agreement was not achieved in the West, the officials feared that the Soviet Union would be able to play the western powers off against each other.[41] Apprehensive voices pointed to the restrained attitude of the Soviet troops during the quelling of the uprising on 17 June, a fact that was accepted by most experts but continued to be disputed by American statesmen in public. The State Department believed that this restraint had already led some sections of the German public in East and West to see the distinct possibility of entering into serious discussions with Moscow, since the Kremlin appeared to them to have been more reasonable than could have been expected. Such a perception would also have a detrimental effect on Adenauer's prospects for re-election in September. In Washington it was believed that this dangerous view would only be strengthened 'if the West does nothing positive to bring about unification'.[42] The western world had to be seen to be actively working on a strategy to achieve German unification.

By early July 1953 the State Department had not yet reached a consensus on all aspects of the new strategy which the American diplomats hoped to agree at the Washington conference. But one issue had already been resolved: the Eisenhower administration had decided that at the conclusion of the discussions among the western foreign ministers, Moscow would be invited to a four-power conference on the German question. As early as 22 June – before Churchill's stroke and when the Bermuda conference was still expected to go ahead – a State Department memorandum had stressed that in view of the nationalist feeling which was running high in both Germanies after the uprising it was 'unrealistic to think that a Four-Power meeting with the USSR can be avoided in the relatively near future. On the assumption that Churchill will continue to press for a Four-Power meeting with the USSR, we should be prepared, in view of such important considerations as public pressures abroad and Allied unity, to retreat to a position of accepting a proposal for a Four-Power meeting with the USSR.'[43]

At this stage the State Department had still not committed itself as to whether a summit with the USSR should consist of a meeting of foreign ministers, heads of government, or a combination of both. The advantages and disadvantages of these possibilities were discussed over a prolonged period of time. Dulles and his colleagues were, however, in agreement that a meeting should be thoroughly prepared and that Adenauer needed to be closely consulted. They also concurred that under no circumstances should a conference with the Russians take place before the elections to the Bundestag in early September 1953. Furthermore, the British and the French would have to declare their readiness to do everything in their power to achieve the ratification of the EDC in at least some countries. It might well be most effective if Churchill were to decide to 'come out with a ringing declaration in support of the E.D.C. projects'. However, with regard to the ratification of the EDC in France, a new, more flexible stance appeared to be necessary. While the American officials believed that 'we should obtain from the French representatives solemn assurances that the French will continue to support EDC ratification', they agreed that ratification of the EDC in Paris ought not to become 'an absolute criterion prior to talks with the Soviets'.[44]

Thus, by late June/early July 1953 the White House felt ready to agree to a summit with Stalin's successors in the Kremlin in order to satisfy the Germans, improve Adenauer's election prospects and undermine any initiative Moscow might be planning. As the Eisenhower administration was prepared in principle to accept a high-level meeting, the State Department concluded that the United States might just as well 'seek to benefit by the advantages of naming the level, the date, the place, and the issues to be taken up'. It therefore recommended that 'we take [the] initiative with respect to the Four-Power talks and announce in the communiqué [of the Washington conference] ... that our three governments have despatched separate but identical notes to the Soviet Government proposing a meeting at Vienna ... on September 15'.[45]

However, the attitude of the German Chancellor posed a serious problem for implementing the new American strategy. Adenauer showed no readiness to change his mind. As late as 24 June the Chancellor had told the American High Commissioner James Conant, that 'he was no more desirous now than he had been before for Four-Power talks'.[46] On 30 June Dulles instructed Conant to consult the Chancellor once again. Two days later he reported that Adenauer still refused to listen to any suggestions of a four-power conference: the Chancellor was still strongly 'opposed to such discussions at any time unless there [was a] reasonable certainty that they will have positive results'. Conant explained that Adenauer 'would not consider it [an] acceptable result if [a] conference merely provided another demonstration of Soviet unwillingness to come to [a] genuine solution of [the] European or German problem. He was fearful that any four-power discussion, unless there was [a] reasonable assurance of success, would merely provide a propaganda platform for [the] Russians and lead to never-ending talks'.[47]

According to Conant, Adenauer remained convinced that instead of issuing a conference invitation to the Soviet Union at the end of the discussions in Washington, it would be preferable to send a protest note regarding the tyrannical behaviour of the GDR government, at the same time raising the question of the remaining German prisoners of war in the Soviet Union. The Chancellor also believed that it would be wise if the western powers were to repeat their readiness to negotiate on German reunification on the basis of the five conditions outlined in the note of 23 September 1952. At the same time it should be suggested that all-German elections must be internationally supervised. Adenauer had 'pointed out' that such a proposal 'would ensure [the] discussion of this matter by note exchange beyond [the] date of the September elections'.[48]

Conant himself advocated a three-power declaration on Germany at the end of the Washington discussions. A prolonged exchange of notes, as proposed by Adenauer to postpone a summit until at least after the Bundestag elections, would only lead to cynical comments in the Federal Republic.[49] On 26 June the High Commissioner had pointed to the fact that even the Chancellor was gradually beginning to acknowledge that in the aftermath of the East German uprising the vast majority of the West German public had begun to call for a four-power conference. Conant saw the contradiction between the Chancellor's private and public views: in public, Adenauer had begun to make some vague references which seemed to indicate a greater willingness on his part to compromise on the question of a summit conference, but in private he was as adamantly opposed as ever to a four-power conference.[50]

Although at first both the State Department and the Foreign Office had been certain that the GDR uprising would undermine Churchill's 'summitry' and end all talk of a summit conference with Moscow once and for all, exactly the opposite had occurred. In Britain, France and above all in the Federal Republic, the public desire for a summit had become stronger after 17 June. Moreover, it was assumed that since the Kremlin had been faced with such a drastic demonstration of the USSR's unpopularity in East Germany the new leaders in Moscow might be ready to compromise on the German question.[51] After all, Moscow had not pursued a more hard-line policy in the GDR after the rebellion; on the contrary, the Soviets appeared to be continuing their policy of accommodation, not only in the GDR but in other East European countries.[52] Conant concluded that if the Soviet Union continued its current 'peace campaign' there was the real possibility that due to 'the excited and competitive atmosphere' of the election campaign in the Federal Republic, West German public opinion might 'continue in the present direction' and insist on a compromise policy with the Soviet Union. This might well influence the electorate in favour of the Social Democrats.[53]

In his telegram to Dulles, the American High Commissioner recommended a strategy which, unbeknown to him, had already been adopted by the State Department. Soon Adenauer as well as the participants in the Washington conference would also subscribe to this new strategy. They all became convinced that it was the only realistic way of securing Adenauer's election victory. It seemed to be impossible for the Chancellor to continue ignoring the trend of German public opinion and the increasing strains within his coalition government. As Conant pointed out: 'The Chancellor may find it difficult to fight [an] effective electoral campaign, if he can be made [to] appear to be sacrificing unity to integration [into the West]. [The] Berlin and East Zone events have thus increased public pressure for talks on unity. . . . It does not follow that four-power talks at any level on German unity will be necessary or desirable before Federal Republic elections, but it may become important ... to indicate our views as to when such talks could begin.' Conant assumed correctly that 'for electoral reasons' Adenauer would soon 'be forced to abandon his delaying tactics'.[54] However, as Washington was not prepared to wait for Adenauer's electoral insights, the State Department decided to apply a little pressure themselves.

Despite hints from within the American government, the British, including Churchill, had still not detected any change of course in Washington. High Commissioner Kirkpatrick believed that the United States was simply planning a new psychological warfare initiative.[55] On 9 July the new strategy as formulated by the State Department around 22 June was once again outlined to Roger Makins. Deputy Under-Secretary Bedell Smith showed him a telegram from ambassador Bohlen in Moscow and added a few surprising comments of his own. In fact, Smith's statement was a ringing endorsement of the views which Churchill had expressed ever since Stalin's death in early March 1953. Smith told Makins that Bohlen's telegram

> confirmed what he himself had felt, and what he understood we also thought, that something more than window dressing was taking place in the Kremlin, and that here was a real opportunity for diplomacy if we played our cards well. He [Smith] added that it had long been clear to the Administration that they should meet Stalin's successors at the top level and before too long. The only question was at what stage. The nub of the problem was Germany. The firm United States position was that they would not meet the Russians at the top level until after the German elections, until the consolidation of Western Europe had proceeded a stage further 'for instance by getting E.D.C. through' and until the three Western Powers had reached a firm and concrete agreement on Germany.[56]

Makins did not grasp the implications of what he had been told; he was still unsure about what Smith was attempting to convey. Instead, the ambassador informed the Foreign Office that the 'U.S. administration seem disposed to wait and see'.[57] This was exactly what the Eisenhower government did not plan to do. In agreement with Adenauer, and, possibly after consultation with him, the US had decided to take the initiative during the Washington discussions and call for a four-power summit conference before the ratification of the EDC, as Churchill had long advocated. A summit meeting was to be announced before the Bundestag elections but would not take place until after the elections. Whether the summit was to be held at heads of government or foreign ministers' level was still uncertain; not surprisingly, Dulles clearly favoured the latter. The State Department had come to the conclusion that the

Soviet Union would soon propose negotiations on the German question and that the United States needed to counter Moscow's new tactics with a new strategy of its own.

Influenced by Churchill's speech in May and, above all, by the East German uprising, the State Department decided to change course. In order not to endanger the Chancellor's election victory, it was seen as imperative to convince Moscow to participate in a summit conference. In doing so it was hoped that once again the West would be able to grasp the initiative in the German question. Thus it might be possible to achieve a diplomatic victory over the new leadership in Moscow, which was undoubtedly weakened by the uprising in the GDR and probably unsure of how to deal with its consequences.[58]

It can, therefore, be assumed that the US was less surprised by Adenauer's proposals of 8 July 1953 than is usually claimed in the literature.[59] At long last the Chancellor proposed to the American government to invite the Soviet Union 'by autumn at the latest' to a summit conference on the basis of the five points contained in the Bundestag resolution of 10 June. During this meeting the EDC should be discussed as a starting point for the development of a European security system.[60] Only the method employed to convey this idea to the United States surprised the American government: Adenauer dramatically informed Dulles of his plans by means of a personal letter.[61] He instructed Herbert Blankenhorn to fly at once to Washington and deliver the letter, dated 8 July, personally.[62]

The Chancellor claimed that his initiative was prompted by information received from a reliable source that Moscow was on the brink of proposing a four-power conference. He professed to have drawn up his plan as a reaction to Moscow's anticipated proposal in the belief that the western world had to undermine the Kremlin's initiative by proposing such a conference itself.[63] Although High Commissioner Conant was totally disregarded by Adenauer during the entire episode, allegedly because he was not present in Bonn, Blankenhorn and Hallstein did pay a visit to Paris on 9 July to consult David Bruce, the American representative to the EDC temporary committee. Bruce then informed the State Department. Thus, at this stage, if not before, the State Department was aware of Blankenhorn's impending visit and the general content of Adenauer's letter. It can be assumed that the State Department would have been more than capable of asking Adenauer not to send Blankenhorn to Washington even at this late stage, if they had indeed wanted to do so. The American government was therefore hardly surprised when Blankenhorn arrived in Washington on 10 July.[64]

Washington had in fact contributed significantly to Adenauer's change of course and had done its best to persuade the Chancellor to go along with the new American strategy. In the absence of Adenauer's initiative, the American government would itself have proposed such a move during the Washington conference. In the scholarly literature it is usually assumed that it was the West German Chancellor who persuaded the US to call a summit conference without delay. Thus Adenauer has been given credit for having been responsible for the change of course during the Washington conference and for the restoration of the 'relative unity of the Western powers'.[65] Scholars have largely followed the account in Adenauer's memoirs and accepted his claim that his letter to Dulles had 'actively' influenced the course of the conference, resulting in the conference's invitation to the Soviet Union.[66]

However, this is a flawed account. As outlined above, even as late as 2 July, in conversation with Conant Adenauer was repeating his opposition to a summit conference with the USSR. Although less than a week after the East German uprising the State Department had already come to the conclusion that a summit could no longer be avoided and that the US would have to take the initiative itself in order to create favourable conditions for such a meeting and establish a unified western position, Adenauer had stubbornly rejected the new course for several weeks. Only by putting a great deal of political pressure on Adenauer and with the indirect help of German public opinion (due to the Chancellor's perceived vulnerability in the election campaign), the State Department had succeeded in convincing the Chancellor of the necessity of a change of course. The idea of Adenauer's dramatic letter to Dulles and Blankenhorn's unusual mission to Washington, however, had been conceived in the West German Chancellery. These initiatives made it appear as if it had been Adenauer himself who was astute enough to be able to persuade the American government to agree to a summit conference with Moscow to talk about German unification. Adenauer's election campaign strategy greatly benefited from this widespread perception.

The British, including the convalescent Churchill, were still unaware of this German-American collusion. They only expected a summit initiative from Bidault.[67] Even during the conference the British delegates remained in the dark. Salisbury reported to the Foreign Office towards the end of the Washington talks that it had 'not been easy' for Dulles 'to agree to the idea of a Four-Power meeting at all'.[68] He had still not realized that it had been the State Department's initiative in the first place. The Lord President was indeed so misled that he later remarked contentedly: 'There was … no sign at this meeting of any tendency towards a U.S.-German alignment.'[69] Nothing could have been more mistaken.

The Western Foreign Ministers' Conference in Washington

The conference of western foreign ministers in Washington took place between 10 and 14 July 1953. The talks would prove decisive for the fate of Churchill's summit diplomacy. Although in the course of the meeting the four foreign ministers decided to invite the Soviet Union to a high-level conference, it was not the kind of summit Churchill had in mind. The British Prime Minister envisaged a conference at heads of government level but the participants in the Washington meeting, including the Acting British Foreign Secretary, believed that it was too risky to endanger the western world's major Cold War objectives for the fanciful notion that agreement with Moscow on Germany and other East–West issues might be possible. Chancellor Adenauer, however, did not intend to rely merely on the support of Dulles and the other foreign ministers assembled in Washington to ensure that Churchill's plans for a 'Big Three' summit meeting would fail.

On 10 July, the first day of the Washington conference,[70] Herbert Blankenhorn arrived in the American capital. Under the rules of international diplomacy, Blankenhorn's uninvited appearance was a major *faux pas* which contradicted all rules of diplomatic courtesy. The three powers did not hesitate to make this clear in their talks with Adenauer's emissary.[71] The Chancellor had been aware of the unusual nature of Blankenhorn's mission but had swept aside all arguments against his intermediary's journey to Washington with the remark that the conference was decisive for 'Germany's fate'; it therefore appeared to him permissible to use tactics which did not fully correspond with the rules of international diplomacy.[72]

This was, of course, exaggerated. The fate of Germany was not so much on the line as Adenauer's election victory. The scholars who interpret Adenauer's exploitation of the Washington conference primarily in terms of his offensive against Churchill's policy largely follow the arguments which the Chancellor used in Germany to justify his change of course.[73] Adenauer and the State Department were well aware of the fact that Salisbury had no intention of using the Washington conference for a discussion of the neutralization of a united Germany. The bedridden Churchill was the only advocate of such a course and even he had shown a certain caution and hesitation. Bonn and Washington knew that the Foreign Office was firmly opposed to any such strategy.[74]

However, as will be seen, from a practical point of view Adenauer's interference in the Washington conference proved a great success.[75] Dulles could argue that even the German Chancellor welcomed the calling of a four-power conference; this helped to counter the strong resistance to a summit conference from Salisbury, which surprised the American and French foreign ministers. Of course, Salisbury's intervention ran counter to the plans of the British Prime Minister. Blankenhorn's presence in Washington enabled Adenauer to learn from a reliable source about the discussions taking place in the course of the meeting. The Chancellor clearly hoped that he would be able to influence the course of the discussions through his emissary if the need arose. However, this would not prove necessary.

At the beginning of the first day of the conference on 10 July 1953 Lord Salisbury immediately announced that London would not insist on the calling of a four-power meeting before the Bundestag elections. He recommended that the communiqué of the Washington conference should announce a meeting of the western heads of government in approximately three months' time to discuss thoroughly the post-election situation in Germany. Only at that point in time would it make sense 'to see if we should not make firmer plans ... for an announcement of a Four-Power meeting'.[76] Thus from the very beginning of the Washington meeting Salisbury was happy to restrict himself to merely suggesting a repetition of the Bermuda conference and hinting that Churchill would subsequently push for a summit with Moscow. Apart from this proposal Salisbury only expressed the vague hope 'that Four-Power talks would be held when practicable, and were accepted in principle'.[77]

Georges Bidault, the French foreign minister, was not as hostile to the idea of a summit conference as he had been two weeks earlier, when the uprising in the GDR had markedly influenced his attitude.[78] He was now primarily concerned with either securing the ratification of the EDC in the French parliament, or, if this proved to be impossible, with finding a way of dispensing with the EDC without making France accountable for the wholesale failure to breathe life into the EDC treaty. Bidault told Dulles that in view of the tremendous 'psychological attraction' that four-power talks had for French public opinion, the prospects for the ratification of the EDC remained very limited 'before the date is fixed for Four-Power talks'.[79] The West should propose to Moscow a conference of limited duration involving questions which were 'susceptible to settlement'. Discussions concerning a German peace treaty and a possible disarmament treaty could be taken up at a later stage.[80] The British minutes recorded that Bidault 'argued strongly that the French Parliament would not ratify the EDC until it was clear that there was no possible alternative German solution and that Germany would not shortly be reunited.'[81]

Salisbury concluded quite correctly that if it were to become clear that the prospects for German reunification were non-existent, as envisaged by the French foreign minister, then Bidault's proposed conference with the Soviet Union had to end in failure. In a telegram to the Foreign Office Salisbury pointed out that the Frenchman showed 'no enthusiasm for a Four Power meeting'. Instead Bidault focused on 'its difficulties and dangers [and] argued strongly that no progress was possible on the EDC until [the] French Parliament and public opinion had been convinced that no other solution was possible. He therefore favoured [an] early Four Power meeting with [a] clear time limit and on [a] specific agenda ... His suggestion clearly was that such a meeting would fail and that he could then secure French ratification of the EDC.'[82]

Salisbury was not impressed by Bidault's devious tactics, which would result in the further deterioration of relations with the Soviet Union, and he did not hesitate to make his view clear to the French minister. He tried to impress upon him the importance 'not to let it be known that in proposing a Four-Power meeting we were deliberately riding for a fall'.[83] In London, Churchill was horrified to learn of the French plans. He telegraphed Salisbury: 'Bidault's argument that we must have a Four Power Conference hoping for a breakdown in order to help the EDC through the French Parliament is lamentable. The Americans ought to do justice to what is happening in Russia and to the many favourable events which have occurred.'[84]

When Dulles took the floor during the first day of the conference, he declared to Salisbury's great relief that the western powers 'should not promote any open disturbances' in the Soviet satellite states. With regard to a summit conference, Dulles shared the view that a four-power conference could not possibly be held before the Bundestag election but that, 'it might be desirable to announce before the German elections that we would hold such a meeting'.[85] Salisbury's reaction showed that he was badly informed about the situation and did not understand the pressure of German public opinion. Moreover, he did not seem to be prepared to represent the policy of his Prime Minister. Instead, the Lord President raised the question of whether it would really be 'helpful to Adenauer' if a conference with Moscow were to be announced before the elections. In his view, German reunification should continue to be proposed on the basis of the September 1952 Note and not 'on some unspecified basis'.[86] Salisbury's declaration astounded Bidault. He declared that he was 'perplexed' by the assumption that if it were announced that the German question would be discussed with Moscow 'the Germans will be upset'. 'In this event, what could we say we would discuss?' Moreover, how was he to explain to the French parliament that no option other than the EDC existed, 'if it is not publicly announced, that we will discuss the German problem?'[87]

Until this point Dulles had skilfully delayed the announcement that Blankenhorn had delivered a letter from Adenauer. He now chose his opportunity to announce that even the Chancellor supported convening a four-power foreign ministers' conference in the autumn on the basis of the five points outlined in the Bundestag resolution of 10 June. Dulles also referred to Adenauer's desire that a new European security system should be devised. In this way the Secretary of State was able to undermine all of Salisbury's arguments against a conference with the USSR. Initially Bidault was also speechless. He had not expected to find himself in sudden agreement with Adenauer.[88] In London, Churchill reacted by demanding more information about Adenauer's ideas for a European security system from the Foreign Office. Shuckburgh explained to him somewhat disingenuously that Adenauer's idea was essentially a development of the Prime Minister's own 'Locarno' proposal and that it was not that new. Blankenhorn had already mentioned a similar scheme in June.[89]

The following day, 11 July, Salisbury fiercely contested Bidault's opinion that the West could afford to have successful discussions with Moscow before the ratification of the EDC.[90] He was convinced that 'it was important to obtain German military integration with the West before discussing the German problem with the Soviets, since otherwise the Soviets would have a chance to wreck the meeting and to gain their objectives'.[91] The Lord President also claimed that a summit held before the ratification of the EDC would 'be unpopular in the U.K. if held on this basis'.[92] This was nowhere near the truth and clearly contradicted the Prime Minister's policy. Churchill's summit diplomacy was still very favourably received by British public opinion, while the case for German rearmament, within or without the EDC, continued to be viewed with great suspicion by the majority of the British people.[93]

In contrast to Bedell Smith's recent and very different remarks to ambassador Makins, Dulles and Bidault did not dissent from Salisbury's assertion that the most recent developments in the Soviet Union 'represented no real change of policy'. The foreign ministers agreed that it was almost impossible to assess the internal situation in the Kremlin correctly. This was demonstrated by the arrest of Beria, which had only become known the previous day, 10 July, though it appeared already to have taken place on 26 June. Although on the basis of various sources of information the western powers, in particular the US, had been expecting Beria's downfall, his sudden arrest and incarceration nevertheless surprised them. However, the western foreign ministers' discussion regarding the reasons for Beria's fate was more or less based on pure speculation.[94]

Salisbury thought that despite the obvious power struggle in the Kremlin the USSR was still primarily seeking to block the rearmament and western integration of the Federal Republic. The very concept of a European army had been developed by the French in order to prevent Moscow from achieving its objectives. Salisbury went on to stress that the EDC offered the western powers 'the most effective possible control over German forces'. A few days before Salisbury had explained to the French ambassador that the Germans had to be attracted to the western side as the country 'might still become unified, and we should have no control over her at all'.[95] The Lord President was still convinced that the sudden development of a new 'German danger' could not be excluded, a view that by this time had been largely abandoned by the British Prime Minister, the Foreign Office and the American government. Salisbury's assessment of western relations with the Bonn Republic was clearly out of date. Nor did it reflect the opinion of the convalescent Foreign Secretary. Eden wrote to Rab Butler on 14 July: 'Adenauer is the man I want to help. . . . Therefore I should regard his appeal as decision.'[96]

Salisbury seems to have lacked the expertise on foreign policy that had been attributed to him by Churchill and American ambassador Aldrich. Although Salisbury enjoyed a great deal of respect among the diplomats in the Foreign Office, this can ultimately be attributed to the fact that the Lord President stood firm on the question of summit diplomacy and allowed the diplomats more room to manoeuvre than Eden or Churchill was prepared to give them.[97]

Throughout the second day of the conference, Salisbury's disputes with Dulles and Bidault continued. In the course of the discussions, Dulles and Bidault also became fully aware of the serious policy battles that were being fought within the British government. The French Foreign Minister could not conceal his astonishment. He declared that

> he was perplexed by the UK view that there should not be 4-power talks before the EDC was in effect. He repeated his statement that the idea of 4-power talks had been originated by Sir Winston Churchill. He had thought these talks held a high priority, but was now told that the German question should be settled first. The French thought that the best way to solve the German problem was to have 4-power talks first, and demonstrate the impossibility of this approach as a solution, after and as a result of which the French Government could get the EDC through Parliament.[98]

Dulles intervened; he had become concerned about the commitment of the French government to the entire European integration process and wanted to know whether Paris believed that a four-power conference would in some way invalidate the necessity for the EDC or whether the failure of a summit would highlight the importance of the EDC. Bidault replied that France was not attempting 'to find excuses for abandoning European integration'; he added that it was 'essential for our defence to have European integration'. Moreover, it was of vital importance to make further progress with the process of

European integration at any rate 'even if there were no defence problem involved'.[99] The Frenchman's statement meant in fact that in his view the EDC was not of prime importance for safeguarding the defence of Europe but for making sure that the definite and irreversible western integration of the Federal Republic would occur; the latter objective required the continued division of Germany.[100] Bidault's position was, therefore, diametrically opposed to Churchill's, but it coincided with the American standpoint to a considerable extent. Thus, following Bidault's statement Dulles concluded happily: 'The French viewpoint was clearly that if a 4-power meeting were held we would not go into it with the idea that the EDC was up in the air, and subject to change as a result of whatever the meeting might bring.'[101]

Lord Salisbury, however, still did not comprehend the situation. He answered 'that the U.K. continued to feel strongly that the EDC question should be settled before the holding of Four-Power talks'. But in view of the opinions that had been expressed he nevertheless reluctantly agreed to present Adenauer's proposal, as contained in the Chancellor's letter to Dulles, to his government.[102] In a letter to Eden he said that the Foreign Office diplomats had persuaded him to give way. 'Both Roger [Makins] and Frank Roberts are convinced that we could not hold back alone, especially as Winston started the whole idea. … though, in fact *his* [Churchill's] conception was a non-starter from the beginning. Apart from everything else, the President was finally opposed to it.'[103]

Despite its opposition to Churchill's summitry, the Foreign Office remained considerably more flexible than Salisbury: the British officials assessed the situation much more rationally than the Acting Foreign Secretary. They recognized immediately that London could not afford to take an opposing position to that of the other three western powers. After all, this was exactly what Churchill had achieved by disregarding the advice of the Foreign Office. For entirely different motives Salisbury was now in the process of emulating the Prime Minister's tactics. Whereas Eisenhower and Dulles might have allowed Churchill such extravagances, Salisbury could not rely upon American generosity. Eden also failed to be impressed by Salisbury's negotiating strategy and fiercely criticized the Lord President.

For no apparent reason the Acting Foreign Secretary had managed to marginalize himself; instead of attempting to influence the consensus reached between Washington and Paris and Bonn, Salisbury appeared merely to have adopted a strategy of opposition. Moreover, it seemed to Eden as though Salisbury did not properly understand Adenauer's precarious situation and the key role he played in the western integration of the Federal Republic. Eden told him:

I cannot see how you came to stand out against the views of the three other Powers, especially as Winston started the idea of a meeting, though admittedly, not this kind of meeting. The essential thing seems to me to give Adenauer all the help we can. The French, by their delay in ratifying EDC, are behaving as they did after the last war, and may be precipitating a German problem for us all.[104]

After Salisbury had reluctantly declared his readiness to consult with his government, Dulles summarized the point of view held in Bonn and Paris. Happily for Dulles, the German and French position largely complied with the strategy that had already been worked out by the State Department by 22 June. It was therefore not surprising that Dulles's verbal summary of 11 July consisted essentially of an outline of the West's policy as it was to be pursued thereafter.

The Secretary of State declared that 'in light of what Chancellor Adenauer had said on the subject of a 4-power meeting, he thought proposals for such a conference should be formulated'. Dulles explained that 'the Chancellor believed his position would be better if such a conference were announced. Because of this reason and the French position that it was not possible to ratify the EDC before such a meeting were held', Washington was 'disposed to go along with the French and German views on having the meeting, on the assumption that the question of European integration through the Schuman Plan, the EDC, and the EPC [European Political Community] would of course not be reopened'. Dulles went on to say that his country 'was disposed to announce promptly an invitation to the Soviet Union to hold a 4-power meeting at some date very soon after the German elections, such as September 15'. The Secretary concluded by saying that while he 'had not previously been enthusiastic about this subject' (he understandably remained quiet about Washington's role in bringing about Adenauer's change of mind), 'he felt that the circumstances were now such that we should go ahead' with inviting Moscow to a foreign ministers' conference.[105]

The decision over how to proceed in the question of Churchill's summit diplomacy had thus largely been taken.[106] This was confirmed when on 13 July the British Cabinet gave its approval to the holding of a four-power foreign ministers' conference before the ratification of the EDC. From his sickbed, Churchill expressed his hope that the heads of state 'might attend in the later stages and that the scope of the agenda would then be widened'. In view of the popularity of his initiatives with the British public, many members of Churchill's Cabinet felt it appropriate 'to give the impression in any public communiqué that, if progress were made, the talks would proceed to wider issues'. While Selwyn Lloyd was satisfied with the decisions taken during the talks, he was very critical of Dulles's conciliatory stance towards Adenauer. He proposed that London should give its agreement to a foreign ministers' conference with the USSR but this ought to be 'subject to the understanding that the Americans would not offer any further concessions to Dr. Adenauer before the elections'.[107]

During the remainder of the conference in Washington, the participants debated the passages concerning the EDC that were to be mentioned in the communiqué as well as the content of the text concerning an invitation to the Soviet Union to a four-power conference. Salisbury suddenly remembered the goals of his Prime Minister, to whom he was shortly due to present a report. In a telegram dated 13 July he had already declared to Churchill: 'I regret that I was not able to persuade my colleagues to drop their insistence upon this meeting being at Foreign Ministers' level. I pressed strongly.'[108]

That could hardly have been further from the truth. Salisbury showed no more interest in a meeting of the heads of state than Dulles and Bidault. In fact, in view of the domestic political difficulties that were bound to await him on his return, Salisbury informed Dulles and Bidault on the next day that 'While he had no doubt that any resulting meeting would in fact be a meeting of Foreign Ministers, he said he would prefer that the communiqué read "representatives of the French [sic!], United Kingdom, United States and the Soviet Union".'[109] However, Salisbury's request was rejected by Dulles. The US could only agree to a meeting at foreign ministers' level, although Dulles did not entirely rule out that a meeting of the heads of government might be possible, 'perhaps with or added to the Foreign Ministers' if the foreign ministers' conference should prove successful. This outcome was however most unlikely. As Bidault also preferred a meeting at foreign ministers' level Salisbury had to give in if he did not wish to provoke the failure of the Washington talks.[110]

In the note to the Soviet Union dated 14 July 1953, Moscow was invited to a meeting of the foreign ministers 'of limited duration' and 'at a place to be mutually agreed' for the end of September.[111] It was unlikely that Churchill would by then be in a position to represent Britain as Acting Foreign Secretary. For the moment his illness did not permit this and Eden's return to the Foreign Office was expected by the end of the summer. The western note to Moscow also pointed out that the West could not envisage the negotiation of a German peace treaty until after the formation of a freely elected all-German government.[112] Thus, it was made clear to the Soviet Union from the very beginning that they had to accept unequivocally the conditions in the September 1952 note and the Bundestag resolution of 10 June 1953; this amounted to the expectation that Moscow would have to surrender its position on the German question, or the conference would be doomed to failure. The conference invitation left no room for compromise.

As the Washington discussions had demonstrated, this was hardly surprising. In order to enable Adenauer to win the West German elections, the West was prepared to announce its readiness to become engaged in negotiations with Moscow after the West German elections, but only at foreign ministers' level. These negotiations, it had been decided, would have to result in failure to ensure the ratification of the EDC by the parliaments of the member countries, especially France, and thus the irreversible integration of the Federal Republic into the West. The final communiqué 'satisfied me a lot', Adenauer later wrote in his memoirs.[113]

Adenauer, Dulles and Bidault had every reason to be very pleased with the result of the Washington talks. It seemed that Churchill's summit diplomacy had finally been swept aside for good, and it had been possible to overcome Salisbury's almost dogmatic inflexibility. Bidault had managed to emphasize France's key position in deciding the fate of the EDC and had succeeded in making clear that his country still had a decisive role to play in international politics.[114] The Foreign Office also had no reason to complain; the officials noted happily that Churchill's summit diplomacy had not been supported by any of the ministers present in Washington. Eden's Private Secretary Evelyn Shuckburgh ventured the opinion that Salisbury would hardly have been able to achieve more. He noted with relief that the meeting 'has in fact brought us back to realities'.[115] The Washington conference demonstrated the growing significance of close German-American relations. The convalescing Eden wrote from Rhode Island that the talks in Washington had been 'one of the rare recent occasions when France and Germany and [the] U.S. agree'.[116] The participants in the meeting in the American capital, however, had become aware of the marginalization of Britain and the country's ever-diminishing influence in international politics. Although this had been excessively emphasized by Salisbury's inept negotiation strategy, there was no pretending that a really independent British position in world politics was any longer feasible.

Churchill's Increasing Frustration

Churchill, of course, was very disappointed by the outcome of the Washington discussions. Once more, he considered the idea of paying a visit to Malenkov. On 14 July he told his personal physician that he wanted to tell Eisenhower 'that I reserve the right to see Malenkov alone'.[117] The Prime Minister still believed that to move the situation forward it was imperative to speak to the Soviet

Prime Minister before a meeting of the foreign ministers took place. Despite Salisbury's warning Churchill wrote a letter to Eisenhower on 17 July and gave instructions that it should not to be made accessible to the Foreign Office.[118] Churchill asked Eisenhower to consider his idea that a four-power conference should begin 'with a preliminary survey by the heads of government of all our troubles in an informal spirit'. The western leaders could thus obtain an idea of the personality and thinking of Malenkov 'who has never seen anybody outside Russia'.[119] The President rejected Churchill's proposal. In his usual friendly but firm way Eisenhower replied on 20 July that he would only seek to meet on a 'very informal basis' with those whom he could trust.[120]

Churchill's growing frustration over the lack of success of his plan for summit diplomacy resulted in an increasingly critical attitude towards Eisenhower and Dulles. John Colville noted in his diary that the Prime Minister was 'very disappointed about Eisenhower whom he thinks both weak and stupid'.[121] Churchill was especially critical of the President's refusal to become personally involved in negotiating the political details of an East–West rapprochement at a high-level meeting. Like his officials, he had recognized that Eisenhower was 'determined not to attend any meeting with the Russians himself at least until some settlement is within sight, because he conceives it to be derogatory to his position as Head of State to get involved in bargaining and negotiations'.[122] Yet, Churchill attributed most of the blame to the Secretary of State. Only Dulles could be 'clever enough to be stupid on a rather large scale', he declared in exasperation.[123] As before, the Foreign Office was happy with Eisenhower's stance. It appeared that the officials could rely on the President's unyielding point of view; the President's position seemed to be 'quite firm'.[124]

Surprisingly enough, the Prime Minister did not initially reproach Lord Salisbury about the outcome of the Washington discussions. This can be attributed to the less-than-truthful minutes of the conference proceedings drawn up by the British delegation and to Salisbury's energetic final report which he presented to the Cabinet on 21 July.[125] As Anthony Nutting wrote in his memoirs, he had 'no doubt at all that it was largely due to Salisbury's personal reputation and his powers of persuasion that the U.S. Government were brought to accept even a Foreign Ministers' conference with the Soviets'.[126] Churchill even thought that Salisbury had 'done very well in the circumstances – no, in face of great difficulties, in face of Bidault and Dulles'.[127] When the conference was still in progress the Prime Minister had already telegraphed the Lord President that even the announcement of a meeting of the foreign ministers would be better than no result at all.[128] After all, this would indicate that the door to a 'Big Three' summit conference had not been closed altogether.[129]

Like Churchill, the British parliamentary opposition was very dissatisfied with the results of the Washington conference. During the foreign policy debate in the House of Commons on 21 and 22 July the Labour opposition vehemently attacked Lord Salisbury's negotiating tactics, claiming that Salisbury had sacrificed Churchill's far-sighted initiative of 11 May and had been unable to persuade the United States of the Prime Minister's policy. In particular, former Minister of State Kenneth Younger argued that the final communiqué of the Washington talks did not give any indication that dramatic changes had taken place in the world. The communiqué, he said, contained no words 'which could not have been written a year ago and long before the death of Stalin or any of the recent events'. Younger was convinced that 'in the limp hands of the acting Foreign Secretary, Lord Salisbury, the Prime Minister's policy has been sunk without trace'.[130]

The fairly tame speech, written by Frank Roberts, which Chancellor of the Exchequer Butler delivered was not able to deflect the attacks on Lord Salisbury's policies.[131] Colville commented that during Butler's speech many of the parliamentarians had asked themselves the question, 'Where is Winston's great peace initiative of May 11th? It is entombed in a guarded operation inspired by Frank Roberts (now a great power in the F.O.) who dislikes the P.M. and all his policies and who sat smiling contentedly beside me in the official box while Rab unfolded his dismal and pedestrian story.'[132] Even a large number of Conservative MPs was disappointed with the Lord President's negotiating tactics in Washington.[133] Salisbury's inept strategy was also condemned by the British press and British public opinion.[134]

The impression that the Washington meeting had buried Churchill's initiative once and for all appears to have been shared in Moscow. Soviet ambassador Malik explained in a conversation with a number of Conservative parliamentarians that

> he had regarded the Prime Minister's speech in May as meaning that Britain had recovered her independence from the U.S. He now felt, however, that [the UK] had fallen back under American control, and asked, more than once, how the Prime Minister could have been sincere in his May speech and yet agreed to the Washington communiqué.[135]

The foreign policy debate in the House of Lords on 29 July provided Salisbury with the opportunity to fend off the accusation 'that I have always been against Four-Power talks with Russia and that I did my best to prevent them'. In his speech, which Salisbury had largely written himself, he even claimed that 'If there was at any time any divergency of view between myself and the other Foreign Ministers at Washington, it was, I can assure your

Lordships, because of my continued advocacy of the Prime Minister's proposal of May 11'.[136] He explained that if the situation in the Soviet Union became clearer then the Prime Minister's summit policy might well be realized. During the Washington conference the only alternative option to the proposal contained in the communiqué had been no four-power conference at all.[137] In Paris, however, Bidault was not impressed by Salisbury's interpretation of the proceedings in Washington. He declared to an American diplomat 'that this was not a correct description of what happened …'.[138]

The historian reviewing the documentary evidence of the Washington conference cannot but agree with Bidault's assessment. Salisbury had in fact done his best to prevent the realization of the kind of summit meeting Churchill had in mind. However, even if he had fully supported Churchill's plans, it is very doubtful that Salisbury would have been able to overcome the opposition of Dulles, Bidault, and indeed Adenauer. It is most unlikely that Salisbury would have been able to change substantially the western strategy towards the planned foreign ministers' conference with the USSR adopted during the Washington meeting.

The uprising in East Germany in mid-June 1953 and, subsequently, Churchill's deteriorating health undermined the Prime Minister's attempt to overcome the Cold War. Soviet Foreign Minister Molotov continued to show little interest in Churchill's overtures. However, it was above all the American government which took the initiative to put an end to Churchill's vision. The Eisenhower administration realized that Churchill's calls for an international conference with the Soviet Union to negotiate an East–West détente was becoming ever more popular with the German people after the uprising in the GDR and something needed to be done. The organization of a four-power foreign ministers' conference without the presence of the unpredictable British Prime Minister looked like an acceptable compromise to appease western public opinion. As it had been determined during the Washington talks that such a meeting with the Soviets would have to result in failure, it also promised to be a fairly risk-free initiative.

CHAPTER 14

Churchill's Last Summit Conference
The Bermuda Meeting and the Continuation
of the Crusade

In the late summer of 1953 Churchill's health gradually recovered. He was even able to give a very well-received keynote speech at the Conservative party conference in Margate in October. After he had passed this self-imposed test of his ability to remain politically active, the Prime Minister abandoned any thoughts of tendering his resignation. Instead, Churchill once again began to intensify his crusade to bring about a summit conference with Malenkov. This led to increasingly tense relations with John Foster Dulles as well as with the officials in the Foreign Office and Churchill's Cabinet colleagues, among them Anthony Eden, who after his long illness also returned to active service. Churchill hoped that the western Bermuda conference would be decisive in convincing Eisenhower of the value of a summit meeting with Malenhov.

Cold War Stalemate

Despite the decision to invite the Soviet Union to a four-power foreign ministers' conference that was agreed at the Washington talks, the uneasy stalemate that characterized the Cold War in the aftermath of the East German uprising continued. The indecision that had gripped the Kremlin since Stalin's death persisted. It was generally assumed in the West that this was due to the deep shock induced by the events in East Germany; Moscow seemed to be cautious about embarking on any political strategies that might be controversial in the satellite countries. Despite the Soviet peace campaign and the official push for a global détente, the Kremlin had great reservations about the invitation to a foreign ministers' conference. Although in principle Moscow was prepared to take part in such a meeting, the Soviet politicians wished to delay the conference for the time being. In August 1953 the American government concluded that Moscow intended to wait until the situation in the GDR was under control.[1]

The Soviet government may well have hoped that the West German elections in early September would herald a change of government. The election of the SPD and the further postponement of a four-power conference might lead to the failure of the EDC and to more constructive East–West relations.[2] Above all, Moscow seems to have been aware of the fact that the western powers were 'clearly planning the failure of this conference in advance'.[3] The Kremlin realized that a dramatic collapse of the foreign ministers' conference, with Moscow being made responsible for such a failure, would jeopardize the credibility of the Kremlin's peace campaign and offer the West an opportunity to bring about the ratification of the EDC and the Federal Republic's integration with the western world.

In spite of the conclusion of a ceasefire agreement in Korea on 27 July 1953, originally hailed as the major test of Moscow's readiness for peace,[4] both the Foreign Office in London and the State Department in Washington remained convinced that Soviet policy had not changed. British diplomats also continued to believe that Churchill was still trying to implement his plan to create a neutral and demilitarized Germany. At the end of July, Evelyn Shuckburgh conveyed the Foreign Office's concerns to Anthony Eden, who spent two weeks in Britain before concluding his convalescence with a Mediterranean cruise. Shuckburgh informed him about the 'P.M.'s vagaries in foreign policy, his hankering after a neutral, unarmed Germany and agreement with the Soviets at high-level talks'.[5]

On 21 July Lord Salisbury had told the Cabinet that in the course of the Washington talks there had been rumours that the British government was still interested in the neutralization of Germany. He had done his best to deny that London harboured any such intentions as this was a 'highly dangerous' strategy, but he was unsure whether Dulles and Bidault had believed his protestations. Salisbury had no doubt that Britain's western partners regarded such a policy as 'suicidal on our part'.[6] David Carlton's assumption that Churchill's idea of German neutralization has been given a 'more significant' position in the literature 'than it deserves' does not appear to be justified.[7] More than seven weeks after his 11 May speech and over two months after Churchill had first mentioned the necessity of neutralizing Germany to his officials, the Foreign Office, as well as various other western foreign ministries, remained fearful that the Prime Minister was still thinking of reshaping the western world's entire Cold War framework. Nevertheless, during his short visit to London in late July Eden was advised not to raise Churchill's retirement during his talks with the Prime Minister. Norman Brook, the

Secretary to the Cabinet who enjoyed Churchill's full confidence, believed that Churchill felt that he was 'doing very well' and would therefore resent being 'asked when he is going to die'.[8] Indeed, at about the same time Churchill told his physician that he didn't 'like being kicked out till I've had a shot at settling this Russia business'.[9] Moscow, however, continued to stall.

The Soviet reply to the Washington invitation to a foreign ministers' conference was received on 4 August 1953. The Kremlin used the opportunity to reproach the western powers for their 'preliminary collusion' in Washington, which would have negative repercussions on the course of a four-power meeting.[10] The Soviet Union declared its fundamental readiness to consider the German question as well as the Austrian question during a conference but suggested that China should participate and other Cold War topics should also be discussed.[11] Moscow claimed that the Washington invitation had simply repeated the proposals contained in the western note of 23 September 1952. The envisaged meeting would, therefore, only lead to 'prolonged discussions'[12] which would serve to uphold the division of Germany, delay the conclusion of a German peace treaty, and improve the prospects for the remilitarization of West German society. Yet the Kremlin also ambiguously declared that it was important that the German problem should be discussed jointly by all four allies.[13]

In London the Soviet note of 4 August led to a major argument between Churchill and the Foreign Office. The officials in the Foreign Office had immediately analysed the note and drafted telegrams which were to be forwarded to the foreign ministries in Washington and Paris.[14] Churchill was appalled. He rejected the Foreign Office's very negative assessment of the Soviet note, describing the analysis as 'an ocean of verbiage'.[15] He was angry that the Foreign Office had forwarded their initial reactions to the State Department without consulting him personally. Churchill thought they had conveyed the impression that the British government had abandoned summit diplomacy in favour of an intensified course of confrontation. In particular, 'Mr Dulles may take advantage of this new attitude of Britain and confront us with proposals which would lead to the loss of the Four-Power talks'.[16] Still bitter about the outcome of the Washington conference, Churchill even demanded that the diplomats should inform the American and French governments that 'the Soviets had "naturally" responded to our invitation with a palpable manoeuvre because our invitation itself had simply been a manoeuvre'. He believed that the American and French governments had 'got us into this mess' due to their refusal to agree to 'top-level' talks. A foreign ministers' conference would only lead to another Palais Marbre Rose débâcle.[17] However, the Foreign Office, annoyed by Churchill's constant interference,[18] adhered to its view that the

Prime Minister's speech on 11 May was the cause of the West's current problems. Furthermore, the officials regarded Moscow's note as 'unhelpful'; it showed that 'Soviet foreign policy has not changed since Stalin's death'.[19]

Yet Churchill did not give in. He protested energetically about the officials' view of the Soviet note, proposed an alternative interpretation, and even drafted a reply. When Salisbury declined to accept Churchill's revisions, the Prime Minister demanded that the Lord President refrain from sending the telegrams to Washington and Paris until after the Cabinet meeting on 10 August.[20] Subsequently, Churchill proposed that the task of formulating a reply should be left to the Americans. As Washington and Paris were intent on conducting a 'fairly obvious manoeuvre', Britain ought not to assume a leading role in formulating the letter of reply to Moscow.[21]

Salisbury thought otherwise. He insisted upon the immediate dispatch of the Foreign Office telegrams to Washington and Paris. According to information received from ambassador Makins, it appeared that so far the State Department had overlooked 'all the extremely dangerous pitfalls set for us by the Russians'. In particular, it was not acceptable that Moscow should make the settlement of the Austrian question 'dependent on a German settlement'.[22] Although this view was largely shared in Paris,[23] Washington had indeed evaluated the Soviet note in a more optimistic way. The State Department had concluded that Moscow had after all agreed to the principle of a conference and merely criticized the proposed agenda.[24]

Salisbury was not impressed by this attitude; he even suggested that a reply to the Soviet note should be delayed until after the West German elections on 6 September. However, the American administration believed that 'the advantage lies in replying just before the German elections' and Salisbury had to accept this point of view.[25] Moreover, the Lord President had to comply with Churchill's instructions. He was not given permission to send further telegrams on the matter to Washington and Paris until after the next Cabinet meeting.[26] The Prime Minister, who was still confined to his sickbed after his stroke, summoned Salisbury and Permanent Under-Secretary Strang to Chequers, the British Prime Minister's country residence.[27] During the meeting on 8 August, 'in spite of contrary and long-winded drafts prepared by the Foreign Office', Churchill succeeded in gaining the upper hand. His Private Secretary concluded that 'The old man still gets his way: usually because it is simple and clear, whereas the "mystique" of the F.O. (as Selwyn Lloyd calls it) tends to be most pettifogging and over detailed.'[28]

This was only partly true. When really important decisions had to be taken, like whether a summit conference should be called at foreign ministers or heads of government level, the Foreign Office knew how to undermine Churchill's plans. But preventing the realization of the Prime Minister's policies demanded arduous detailed work and plenty of energy. Increasingly Salisbury was less able to perform this task. In addition to dealing with Churchill's summit diplomacy, the Lord President was fighting an exhausting battle with his officials over Britain's policy on China and the recognition of Mao's government. Salisbury soon became tired of the pressure attached to being Acting Foreign Secretary and began to consider his resignation. Referring to Churchill's summit diplomacy he told Shuckburgh that it was 'one thing to be a member of [the] Cabinet and to refrain from opposing such policies but quite another to be the responsible minister'.[29]

With the exception of the indecisive and 'very, very smooth' Chancellor of the Exchequer, who appeared to be keen to 'back a horse both ways',[30] no change of opinion in favour of Churchill's plans could be observed within the Cabinet and the Foreign Office. On the contrary, a gradual hardening of attitudes emerged, particularly since Churchill's diminishing powers of concentration could no longer be ignored. The Prime Minister's stubborn refusal to contemplate resignation embittered many government ministers. Eden was due to return soon and could have taken over as Prime Minister. Instead, Churchill frequently mentioned that he might stay in office until the summer of 1954 should his speech at the Conservative party conference in Margate in October prove to be a success.[31] This alarmed the Foreign Office and Eden's supporters. It was clear that Churchill's occasional talk about his imminent resignation, usually made during spells of depression, was not meant seriously.[32] Tension and conflict within the government grew, especially as the Prime Minister was contemplating a significant Cabinet reshuffle; he also chaired a Cabinet meeting on 18 August, the first since his stroke.[33]

At the same time, conducting business with Churchill became increasingly difficult as the Prime Minister insisted on being involved in all major foreign policy decisions. Shuckburgh wrote in his diary: 'All this week we are trying to conduct our foreign policy through the PM who is at Chartwell and always in the bath or asleep or too busy having dinner when we want urgent decisions. He had to be consulted about drafting points in the reply to the Soviets; about every individual "intelligence" operation (which he usually forbids for fear of upsetting the Russians); about telegrams to Persia and Egypt. We are constantly telephoning minutes and draft telegrams down to Chartwell'.[34] At the end of September Downing Street felt compelled to take the unusual step of publishing a declaration refuting the persisting rumours of serious diffi-culties between Churchill and his colleagues. The Prime Minister used the occasion to emphasize that it had not been Salisbury but the French and American foreign ministers who had objected to a summit meeting during the

Washington talks. Naturally the governments in Paris and Washington resented this not entirely truthful statement.[35]

In view of his domestic and external difficulties, Churchill was fortunate that his 'summitry' was given a new lease of life when Malenkov gave a speech emphasizing the necessity of an East–West détente.

Malenkov's address to the Supreme Soviet on 8 August 1953 attracted considerably more attention in the West than the Soviet note of 4 August.[36] While much of the speech concentrated on domestic issues and indicated that Moscow wished to improve the standard of living of its people by focusing more on the light industries and necessary agricultural reforms, Malenkov also took pains to emphasize the enhanced security situation of his country. He claimed that the international position of the Soviet Union was 'now stronger than ever', and the country was making great progress not only in the economic field but also in the military arena. He dramatically announced that the USSR had succeeded in breaking the American monopoly on the hydrogen bomb, though in fact the first Soviet explosion was not to take place until four days later.[37] In the foreign policy section of his speech, Malenkov called for peaceful cooperation on a global scale,[38] but he also indicated that the Soviet Union would continue to adhere to its policy of strength. In principle Moscow was prepared to take part in a summit conference, but Malenkov's fairly vague comments seemed to indicate that Moscow still intended to delay a four-power meeting for a while.[39] American diplomats in Bonn reported to Washington that in their view Malenkov's speech revealed that there was still a clash of opinion in the Kremlin; the collective leadership was unable to agree on a new policy and therefore 'it has clung to an old one'. Moreover, Malenkov's speech did not contain any 'hints of a new Soviet approach to the German problem'; instead it was 'full of warnings'. To the Americans it was obvious that the Kremlin was 'trying to hide its own nervousness'.[40]

While the foreign ministries in Washington, London and Paris, like the West German Chancellor's office in Bonn, were unimpressed by Malenkov's speech and maintained their sceptical positions, Churchill once again felt encouraged by Malenkov's words and confirmed in his views.[41] He was, however, aware that he would only be able to bring about a real summit at head of government level if his own health recovered quickly.[42] Eden's return to the Foreign Office was announced for the beginning of October. He would most certainly push for the Prime Minister's resignation and would command the support of a large number of Cabinet ministers on this issue.[43] Time was running out for Churchill. For the time being he accepted that it was useless to continue bombarding the American President with letters, but he was nevertheless disappointed when Eisenhower denied any knowledge of the idea that he was considering a visit to London, as the American ambassador had indicated.[44] Two months passed before Churchill resumed his correspondence with Eisenhower. Churchill briefly contemplated travelling to the US himself in mid-September to talk to the President in person, but then changed his mind.[45]

Instead, Churchill decided to concentrate his efforts (unsuccessfully) on obtaining permission from his Cabinet to meet with Malenkov alone in Zurich.[46] After all, his health was improving. On 18 and 25 August Churchill had managed to chair his first two Cabinet meetings since his stroke in late June, and considering that each session lasted almost three hours, the Prime Minister was pleased that he was able to cope with the ordeal. Soon he felt physically strong enough to receive the American ambassador for talks, to appear in public at the Doncaster races in September on his forty-fifth wedding anniversary, and to take a holiday at Lord Beaverbrook's villa in Monte Carlo. He also began to follow international political developments in a more regular way.[47]

Malenkov's announcement that the Soviet Union had the capacity to produce an H-bomb and the news, published in the *Manchester Guardian* on 20 August, that the US had already tested such a bomb in November 1952, had severely shocked the Prime Minister. Like most politicians, he had not known about the American test explosion on Eniwetok Atoll. While most western statesmen suspected that Washington was capable of producing an H-bomb, it had generally been assumed that so far the United States had refrained from testing the weapon.[48] Ever since Churchill had learnt about the American and Soviet H-bomb explosions, he had been pursued by the horrific vision of a world war waged with such destructive weapons. A *tête-à-tête* with Moscow now appeared to be all the more urgent to him. In a world faced with nuclear extinction, resigning his position as British Prime Minister no longer seemed to be an option. Instead, Churchill hoped that the 'ghastly invention' of the hydrogen bomb 'might perhaps present humanity with a real chance of lasting peace, since war would now be impossible'. Therefore, he reasoned, the Kremlin might well be interested in reaching a speedy agreement with the West along the lines outlined in his speech in the Commons on 11 May and elsewhere. 'Defence by suicide', a phrase coined by military historian Liddell Hart, would hardly make sense to the new leaders in the Kremlin.[49]

Meanwhile, yet another full-scale battle of notes with the Soviet Union had begun. Moscow's reply to the western invitation to a foreign ministers' conference on 4 August heralded a six-month East–West exchange consisting of eleven notes in total. On 15 August the Kremlin sent a second note which dealt exclusively with the 'abnormal situation' in Germany. It was obvious that the Soviet Union was addressing the West German electorate.[50] On 2 September, four days before the Bundestag election, the western powers replied to the Soviet note. In general they were concerned to shorten the exchange of notes with Moscow without however slamming the door on a foreign ministers' conference.[51] The West therefore proposed holding a conference on the German and Austrian questions in the Swiss town of Lugano on 15 October.[52] The Soviet answer, dated 28 September, entirely ignored this proposal and instead suggested the calling of two conferences: a five-power conference (including China), which was to be principally concerned with the topics of détente and disarmament, and a four-power meeting to deal with the German question.[53]

As it could be safely predicted that the US would not react favourably to the Soviet proposals, it appeared that the note was merely meant to delay the convening of a foreign ministers' conference.[54] Even Churchill had to concede that the 'latest Soviet answer showed little desire for talks at any level (but he admitted he hadn't read it)'.[55] Adenauer's surprisingly impressive election victory on 6 September gave Moscow no reason to adopt a different policy on the German question or with respect to a high-level conference. American diplomats concluded that the new leaders in Moscow 'appear to be confused'.[56] The Chancellor's party did, after all, gain 45.2 per cent of the vote and won more than half of all Bundestag mandates (the Social Democrats gained only 28.8 per cent). Along with the small Liberal party (9.5 per cent) and the patriotic expellee party BHE (5.9 per cent) this enabled Adenauer to form a new government which commanded a two thirds majority in parliament. Nothing appeared to stand in the way of the completion of the Federal Republic's parliamentary ratification of the EDC. Given such an impressive parliamentary majority, it was unlikely that the West German constitutional court and the Federal President would continue their opposition to the EDC treaty.[57]

Yet West German public opinion still demanded a four-power conference. The western powers acknowledged therefore that it was 'too early to try to break off the exchange of notes'. Still, after Adenauer's election victory the State Department began to wonder whether it was really necessary to convene a four-power foreign ministers' conference with the Soviet Union. Dulles asked his advisers: 'Do we really want a meeting?'[58] The Secretary of State had realized that Adenauer was 'still basically afraid of [a] Four Power conference'.[59] However, London and Paris insisted upon attempting to convene the envisaged four-power meeting. The pressure applied by Churchill's enthusiasm for summit diplomacy and in turn by British and French public opinion would have made it very difficult to explain the cancellation of the conference agreed upon at the Washington talks in July. Although deeply deplored in governmental circles in the United States, in Britain and to some extent in France, Churchill's speech on 11 May had 'hit the jackpot' with regard to western public opinion.[60]

Moreover, in France the assumption prevailed that the ratification of the EDC could only be pushed through the French parliament after a failed conference with Moscow had demonstrated that a deal with the Soviets was impossible and that the EDC was the only way to control the Germans. Thus, in order to achieve the convening of a conference with the Soviet Union in the near future it was concluded that the western notes to the Kremlin should 'be as forthcoming as possible'.[61] Still, behind the scenes the Foreign Office attempted to support Adenauer's opposition to four-power talks with Moscow but the officials did not dare to do this in too obvious a fashion. While the British diplomats were still strongly opposed to a foreign ministers' conference with the Soviet Union, they had no wish to be held responsible for preventing such an event.[62]

In spite of all the scepticism about a foreign ministers' meeting that became evident after the West German elections, the western powers decided to adhere to the plan agreed at the Washington talks, namely that a four-power foreign ministers' conference with Moscow should be convened without further delay.[63] However, the key to unlocking the situation was in Moscow's hands. The Soviet Union still needed to agree to such a meeting; and Moscow had still not made up its mind whether or not to attend. William Hayter, the new British ambassador to Moscow, believed that the Soviet leaders knew that 'they can have a Four-Power meeting to discuss Germany whenever they wish. But since the events of June 17, and perhaps before, they have clearly decided that the present division of Germany suits them better than any alternative, and as long as this is so there is nothing for them to gain by a meeting on Germany.'[64]

During the following weeks, both the State Department and the Foreign Office endeavoured to overcome Moscow's hesitations. It was becoming increasingly urgent to bring about a situation that would persuade the French National Assembly to ratify the EDC, and thus solve the German question on western terms and obtain a stable and peaceful *modus vivendi* in Europe.

Eden's Return and Churchill's Continued Search for a Summit

After nearly six months' absence Anthony Eden returned to the Foreign Office in reasonably good health on 5 October. He had successfully resisted any move to a domestic ministry, which Churchill had offered him repeatedly as a means of maintaining greater freedom of manoeuvre for his summit policy.[65] Eden's officials realized with relief 'that A.E. has been following the Prime Minister's Malenkov policy closely and strongly disapproves'.[66] Eden's opposition to Churchill's 'summitry' was not only political but also increasingly personal.

His Private Secretary Evelyn Shuckburgh realized that Eden was 'scared of the popularity of the PM's project and cannot see any effective role for himself in the House of Commons until it has been "decently buried" '. Shuckburgh was, however, aware of Churchill's resilience: 'I fear the burial service may revive the corpse'.[67]

Shortly after his return, Eden, Salisbury and Butler met Churchill over dinner. In his diary Eden described the occasion as 'a depressing evening'. The discussion had centred on foreign affairs but Churchill had kept complaining about his colleagues' lack of enthusiasm for his 'summitry'. He even went so far as to criticize Salisbury for his lack of loyalty.[68] Churchill dismissed Shuckburgh's proposal to ask Dulles to come to London to discuss East–West relations. As the idea had initially come from the American ambassador, it was clear that the State Department greatly favoured such a course of action.[69] To Churchill it appeared much more constructive if he himself were to meet with Eisenhower in the Azores. Within a few days, and to the great annoyance of the Foreign Office, Churchill had even succeeded in convincing Eden to agree that a letter containing this proposal should be sent to Eisenhower.[70] Shuckburgh, Colville and Moran report in their diaries that Eden was still unable to impress his will on a Prime Minister weakened by a serious stroke. In all important questions, including the issue of Churchill's retirement, Eden did not manage to insist on his preferred policies. 'I haven't got a log heavy enough to hold this elephant,' he told his Private Secretary. Despite his better judgement, Eden did not even dare to take up Shuckburgh's suggestion and include in his forthcoming speech for the Conservative party conference a passage critical of Churchill's summit diplomacy.[71]

In his letter to Eisenhower dated 7 October Churchill proposed a bilateral meeting in the Azores. As an alternative he suggested a meeting in Washington for 15 and 16 October 'to clear up a great many things'. If the President were to request the participation of the French, he would agree. However, Eisenhower succeeded once again in avoiding a meeting with the British Prime Minister. He explained to Churchill that he had already scheduled a number of important appointments which could not be moved, and hinted that it would be a good idea if Eden were to come to Washington to speak to Dulles.[72] Churchill drafted 'a terrible second message to Ike' but before sending it he thought better of it; this may have been due to Colville's calming influence on the Prime Minister.[73] Instead, he merely conveyed his regret to the President that the proposed meeting in the Azores was not feasible and said that Eden planned to invite Dulles and Bidault for talks in London.[74] With the failure of his initiative to organize a personal meeting with Eisenhower, Churchill had retracted his objections to the Foreign Office plan.

On 10 October 1953 Churchill gave the Prime Minister's speech at the Conservative party conference in Margate. He had anticipated the occasion with considerable nervousness. This was, after all, his first political appearance since his stroke. Fortified by Lord Moran's tablets, which contained a good dose of amphetamines, Churchill managed very well indeed.[75] Colville described the fifty-minute speech as 'a complete success' – 'one could see but little difference, as far as his oratory went, since before his illness'.[76] The American embassy described the Prime Minister's speech as a 'considerable personal triumph', characterizing the party conference as a 'well controlled decorous assembly, devoted largely to platitudes and self-congratulation'.[77]

In the course of his address Churchill emphasized that his speech was meant to be a continuation of his speech to the House of Commons on 11 May. At the centre of his hopes remained his desire to convene a 'Big Three' summit conference. In this context Churchill deviously suggested that Eden and Salisbury also believed 'that we should persevere in seeking such a meeting between the heads of governments', a far from truthful account of their thinking. Churchill reiterated his long-standing conviction that 'the leading men of the various nations ought to be able to meet together without trying to cut attitudes before excitable publics or using regiments of experts to marshal all the difficulties and objections, and let us try to see whether there is not something better for us all than tearing and blasting each other to pieces, which we can certainly do'.[78]

He admitted that he had not yet been able 'to persuade our trusted allies to adopt' his policy 'in the form I suggested' but he insisted that it was entirely inaccurate to say that his summit diplomacy was 'dead'. With regard to reviving the Locarno treaty, Churchill remarked that in his speech in May he had of course referred to the idea 'of everybody going against the aggressor, whoever he may be, and helping the victims, large and small'. Although the Second World War had taken place in spite of the Locarno treaty, it was important to remember that in contrast to the present situation Washington had not been a party to the treaty. The Prime Minister could still not explain how he envisaged the Americans would participate in a new European security system but at least unlike in his speech in May he recognized that the United States had to be given a prominent role in any new political and military framework. Churchill once again indicated that his summit policy was concerned with maintaining Britain's role as a global power, and even claimed that London's influence on Bonn and Moscow was gaining importance. It was Britain's 'duty' to 'use what I believe is our growing influence, both with Germany and with Russia, to relieve them of any anxiety they may feel about each other'.[79]

After Churchill's triumphant performance at the party conference it was clear that he would not be prepared to retire as Prime Minister in the

immediate future.[80] Churchill had hinted at this in his speech and he subsequently told his Private Secretary that he definitely had no intention of
leaving office before May 1954, when the Queen was due to return from an
extended visit to Australia and other Commonwealth countries.[81] After the
party conference, Eden became convinced that Churchill would only resign
after a summit meeting had taken place, and he therefore concluded that a
summit should be held earlier rather than later to give a new party leader
time to prepare for the next general election, which was due to be held in 1956
at the latest. Eden thus resigned himself to the fact that paradoxically he had
to support Churchill's summit diplomacy in order to reveal its inadequacy:
only the failure of a 'Big Three' or 'Big Four' conference would bury
Churchill's dreams and compel him to resign. Thus, after Churchill's party
conference speech in October 1953, British summit diplomacy became a
political football in the rivalry between the two competing prima donnas in
British politics.[82]

In his address in Margate, Churchill had also said a few words regarding
Germany's return to a place 'among the great powers of the world'. Much to the
displeasure of France, the US and Adenauer, he had suggested that should the
EDC fail, 'some new arrangement', perhaps by way of tying Germany in with
NATO, would be necessary in order to 'join the strength of Germany to the
Western allies'.[83] The Chancellor's confidant Blankenhorn subsequently
informed the Foreign Office that Adenauer 'considered it a mistake to have
suggested that there was an alternative to the EDC'.[84] Yet, Churchill had not
been the first leading British politician to openly suggest NATO as an alternative to the EDC: at the end of September a similar suggestion had been made
by Anthony Nutting, the Under-Secretary of State, in the course of a one-day
visit to the Federal Republic,[85] and in the light of the stagnation of the issue in
France, alternatives to the EDC were also discussed in Washington.[86] The
important document NSC-160/1 from the middle of August and to some
extent NSC 162/2, the Eisenhower administration's 'New Look' document of
September 1953, referred to it.[87] However, it was decided in Washington that
one last attempt to bring about the EDC ought to be made.

The US was prepared to allow the French government a breathing space
until 1 January 1954 to ratify the EDC.[88] This delay was tolerable since the
American administration thought that 'the risk of general war seemed at the
moment less than at any time in recent years'.[89] Dulles came to the conclusion
– a real change of heart for him – that 'the urgency to rearm Germany was
perhaps not so great as we had thought'. Dulles and Defense Secretary Charles
Wilson agreed 'that alternatives to [the] EDC should, indeed, have been
studied earlier, and ... that the study of alternatives by the Planning Board
should be started at once'.[90] However, during the NSC meeting on 1 October it

became apparent that Eisenhower still had great reservations as to the feasibility of any alternative to French membership of the EDC.[91] This was also the opinion of ambassador Conant in Bonn.[92]

Shortly afterwards, during the 166th NSC meeting on 13 October, it was decided in Washington that 1 April 1954 would be the deadline 'on which the German military build-up will effectively begin ... assuming prior EDC ratification'.[93] Dulles and Eisenhower were aware that this was little more than wishful thinking. Although Dulles sometimes considered alternatives to the EDC, this was largely out of despair and he was not convinced of the effectiveness of options such as the development of a German national army and West German membership of NATO; he believed such schemes would be 'most unsatisfactory alternative[s] to European unity'. Yet Dulles was convinced that the western world was 'at the crossroads'. Somewhat enigmatically (and partially foreshadowing his 'agonizing reappraisal' statement of December 1953), he expressed the view that in the event that the EDC was not ratified, the consequences might have to be 'more radical than merely to bring Germany into NATO. Of course, Churchill and many of our military people would doubtless favour that course.'[94]

On 15 October 1953, the American and French foreign ministers arrived in London for three-day talks to discuss their reply to the Soviet note of 28 September and other East–West issues.[95] On the evening of the first day, Dulles and US ambassador Aldrich dined with Churchill, Eden and Salisbury. Not surprisingly, the subject which dominated the conversation was a possible summit conference with Moscow. Churchill rehearsed all his usual arguments in favour of a summit and Dulles again explained Eisenhower's reasons for rejecting one. He added, however, that if Churchill was prepared to delay his plans for a summit conference until after the ratification of the EDC, he would ask the President to rethink his position.[96] Churchill appears to have interpreted this as Eisenhower's promise to participate in a meeting with Moscow following EDC ratification.[97] This further encouraged him in his belief that Eisenhower was not opposed in principle to a summit with Malenkov but was unduly influenced by his devious Secretary of State. After all, to the alarm of the Foreign Office and the British ambassador to Washington, Eisenhower had recently told Lord Cherwell, Churchill's scientific adviser, that the Prime Minister could of course meet with the Soviet leaders if he wished to do so.[98]

As the evening progressed, it became clear however that the British Prime Minister was no longer ready to delay pursuing an East–West summit conference until after the creation of the EDC. He had suggested shortly after his stroke that he would, but this had only been a tactical device to soften the opposition of Eisenhower and the Foreign Office. In fact, the Prime Minister's negative attitude towards the EDC had hardly changed. Dulles reported to Eisenhower that 'Winston made [his] usual uncomplimentary references [to the] EDC with grudging acquiescence in [the] importance [of an] early decision one way or another.' When Churchill mentioned that he might well embark on a solitary journey to Moscow to meet up with Malenkov, Dulles had had enough. He energetically opposed Churchill's idea and a fierce and heated discussion developed.[99] Dulles was heartened that Eden and Salisbury did not share Churchill's view: Eden told him that 'he doubted [the] wisdom [of a] "summit" although he would, of course, loyally support his chief'. In principle, Eden, like Dulles, was convinced that a summit meeting should only be allowed to take place after the successful ratification of the EDC; in that event, a high-level conference would be 'much less dangerous'.[100]

In view of the recent political developments the conversation moved to the crisis in Trieste and the exchange of notes with the Soviet Union,[101] but ambassador Aldrich feared that in spite of a certain conciliatory tone which Churchill adopted and his declaration that for the time being he would not seek to pursue plans for an immediate summit, the Prime Minister continued to think of a 'lonely pilgrimage' to Moscow.[102] This was, indeed, the case. Churchill was encouraged by a declaration at the end of October from new Soviet UN ambassador Vyshinsky that Moscow was in favour of convening a meeting of the heads of governments of the great powers. According to the *Daily Telegraph*, this was the first time the Kremlin 'had accepted an invitation of this kind'. Moreover, in a recent conversation with former Labour Cabinet minister Harold Wilson, Molotov had referred to Churchill's summit proposal as 'very interesting'.[103]

Speaking in the House of Commons on 3 November and shortly afterwards at the Mansion House, Churchill did not disclose any deviation from the restraint he had conveyed during the London talks.[104] Lord Moran attributed this mainly to Anthony Eden's influence.[105] But Churchill was very happy with his performances: he had made clear that he did not believe that the Soviets were intent on external expansion and he had expressed his conviction that a deal with Moscow might still be possible even though it might take a little longer than anticipated. Therefore the speech on 3 November also demonstrated Churchill's ability to remain in control of the House of Commons, regarded by some as the precondition for his continuing as Prime Minister.[106]

Churchill had deliberately played down his interest in summit diplomacy. The *New York Times* claimed to have detected a fundamental change in Churchill's summit policy, but that was not the case and American diplomats fully realized this. In reply to Bedell Smith's query with regard to the developments in Churchill's thinking, the American embassy in London confirmed that Churchill appeared to persist in the pursuit of his summit ideas. Churchill was 'well aware his health gives him relatively little time and is therefore prone to push proposals at [a] pace which under normal circumstances would be against his better judgement'. The American diplomats had the 'definite impression' that 'practically all members of [the British] government are now convinced of [the] unwisdom of continuing to press for four-power top level talks and we believe that [the] Cabinet would be solidly opposed to any solitary pilgrimage by Churchill to Moscow'.[107] Nevertheless, it was 'probable' that 'Churchill still desires to bring about [a] four-power top level conference and regards [a] meeting with President Eisenhower as [a] step on [the] road to Moscow'.[108]

Indeed, with the gradual recovery of his health, Churchill once again contemplated reviving the idea of a conference of western heads of government in Bermuda. As in June, when the Bermuda meeting had been first considered, Churchill was optimistic that this might present him with the opportunity to persuade Eisenhower of the value of his summit diplomacy and thus allow him to implement finally his policy of overcoming the Cold War and strengthening Britain's great power position.

On 18 October 1953 the western reply to the Soviet note of 28 September was sent to Moscow.[109] As agreed during the foreign ministers' talks in London, Moscow's proposal for a five-power meeting to consider questions of disarmament and the reduction of East–West tension was not rejected outright, but the West suggested that as a preliminary, a separate four-power conference to resolve the German and Austrian questions should begin in Lugano on 9 November.[110] The western proposal was not meant seriously. Dulles told Eisenhower he did not expect France to ratify the EDC before January 1954, and that the West 'ought not seriously to seek discussions with the Soviets until decisions have been taken on EDC'.[111] Moscow replied just two weeks later, on 3 November, in rather negative and ambiguous terms. Whilst the Soviet Union neither rejected nor agreed to the proposed Lugano meeting, Moscow still insisted on the participation of China, suggested the development of a new European security order in very general terms and still fiercely opposed the rearmament of West Germany.[112] The exchange of notes appeared to be approaching a dead end.

This was also Churchill's impression. 'So why not let us try Bermuda again?' he asked Eisenhower in a letter dated 5 November. 'We could then take stock of the whole position and I think quite a lot of people will be pleased that we are doing so.'[113] However, Eden and the majority of the British Cabinet rejected Churchill's initiative. Ambassador Aldrich also advised the Eisenhower administration to avoid such a meeting, particularly since the Soviet Union's somewhat negative response might open the door to a speedy ratification of the EDC.[114] Surprisingly, however, Eisenhower changed his mind about a meeting with the Prime Minister: he told Churchill that 'there may be considerable value in a good talk between us and the French in order to survey the situation in which we now find ourselves'.[115] While it was not entirely clear why Eisenhower suddenly agreed to a conference with Churchill, subsequent events showed that the President wished to use the meeting to terminate the British Prime Minister's summit policy once and for all and bring about the strategy designed by the State Department on 22 June and agreed with the allies at the Washington conference in July.[116]

Eisenhower proceeded cautiously. In order to avoid any misunderstandings, he told Churchill that the 'false impression' should be avoided 'that our purpose in meeting is to issue another invitation to the Soviets. There is nothing to be gained by showing too much concern over their intransigence.' The President believed 'that instead of relating our meeting to any Soviet word or act, past or future, we should merely announce that we are meeting to discuss matters of common interest'.[117] Eisenhower also intended to use the Bermuda conference to impress upon the French the urgency of the ratification of the EDC.[118]

Despite the presidential words of restraint, Churchill was 'delighted'. He no longer minded that the French Prime Minister would also attend the meeting.[119] He also did his best to ensure that Anglo-American preparations for the conference proceeded smoothly. Relations with French Prime Minister Laniel proved awkward, however. Laniel was annoyed that Churchill had arranged the meeting with Eisenhower and that the Foreign Office had even informed the German Chancellor without having consulted Paris. And Churchill was not pleased when his personal invitation to Laniel to participate in the conference was answered via impersonal official channels.[120] Thus, even before the Bermuda conference had begun, tension had developed between Churchill and the French.

The American government certainly wished to conduct the negotiations in Bermuda 'on the most general terms'. The State Department had been unable to find out 'Churchill's probable line on [the] USSR' as he did not seem to have asked his officials for the preparation of detailed position papers.[121] The American experts therefore hoped that the Prime Minister 'will not press specific suggestions for any chiefs of state meeting'. Still, ambassador Aldrich warned the State Department not to forget that Churchill was 'imaginative, unpredictable, firm in [the] belief in his own genius, and apparently determined to attempt one last crowning act on [the] world stage'.[122]

The Eisenhower administration also realized that its plan to persuade Laniel and Foreign Minister Bidault to start the ratification process of the EDC would not please the French delegation. The French government had been putting pressure on both Washington and London for some time to enter into a commitment to base troops on the European continent for the next 20 years, hoping this guarantee would prevent the military domination of the continent by the Federal Republic.[123] Since Washington was determined not to enter into any commitments to station American troops in Europe on a permanent basis, serious clashes of opinion could be expected. The Foreign Office in London wondered whether Paris would regard it as sufficient for beginning the EDC ratification process if it were promised that American and British troops would be based on the European continent 'at least for [the] next few years'.[124] In fact, for some time it already had been 'a part of the British plan' regarding an alternative to the EDC that London would commit itself to the permanent stationing of 'certain force levels on the continent'.[125]

However, it was unlikely that the French government would be swayed. Moreover, Bidault's view that the political status quo in Europe ought to be accepted for the time being ran counter to Churchill's vision of an early end to the Cold War and promised to lead to controversial discussions in Bermuda. The French foreign minister 'felt that we should ... take [the] approach that we were now settling down for the long term, during which Europe would be divided as at present for many years, and that we must find means of adapting ourselves to this long range situation and of maintaining the necessary defence as economically as possible'. At least in public, the German Chancellor, who had not been invited to attend the Bermuda conference, could hardly be expected to support the continued partition of Europe and Germany.[126]

On 10 November, the British public was informed by the Prime Minister that the Bermuda conference, initially scheduled for early July, was now to take place between 4 and 7 December 1953. On the same day Churchill wrote to Molotov expressing the hope that the Bermuda meeting would contribute to world peace.[127] Almost immediately the international media began to focus on the differences of opinion among the western leaders regarding a summit conference with the USSR. Then, suddenly on 13 November Molotov held an unprecedented press conference in Moscow to enlighten the world about the content of the Kremlin's latest note of November.[128] The Soviet foreign minister declared that the Kremlin was not refusing to participate in a four-power foreign ministers' conference. While there existed differences of opinion between the West and the Soviet Union with respect to the aims of such a conference, the necessity of convening a meeting was not contentious. Molotov still regarded the western proposal for a conference in Lugano as inferior to the

Soviet suggestion to convene a five-power conference including Mao's China; only a five-power meeting would be able to overcome East–West tension.[129]

The western allies reacted five days later.[130] While the invitation to a conference issued to Moscow on 18 October remained open, it seemed as though Moscow was currently not interested in negotiations. The West therefore avoided proposing yet another date for a conference.[131] Once again, it appeared as if a battle of notes with the Kremlin was petering out without any concrete results. Like his predecessor Alvary Gascoigne, and almost the entire Foreign Office in London, William Hayter, the new British ambassador in Moscow, was also unable to detect any 'real change' in the Soviet Union's policy since Stalin's death.[132]

However, this time the Soviet Union took a tougher line. In a note dated 26 November, the Kremlin strongly attacked the 'remilitarization' of the Federal Republic and the planning for a 'European Army'. Moscow once again continued to insist on the participation of China in any conference dealing with global East–West tension. However, in the last section of the note the Soviet Union declared its willingness to attend a separate conference of foreign ministers on Germany, and suggested that the foreign ministers' conference regarding the German question should be convened in Berlin in the near future.[133]

The western foreign ministries were very surprised at the Kremlin's change of mind. The American ambassador to Moscow, Charles Bohlen, believed that the Soviet Union might have been moved by the negative reaction of its supporters in the western world to its note of 3 November. Bohlen did not believe the new leaders in the Kremlin were interested in a return to an intensively conducted Cold War. They also felt more secure as the situation in the GDR had been stabilized in the meantime.[134] In general, Bohlen thought that the Soviet note represented an 'important shift' in Moscow's 'tactical handling of [the] German question'. He did not believe, however, that it indicated a fundamental change of Soviet policy. There still appeared to be differences of opinion in the Kremlin on how to deal with the German question, and he advised that the Soviet Union's suggestion should be taken up. After all, Moscow had compromised and this was a 'distinct victory for Western diplomacy'.[135] The State Department largely agreed with Bohlen's assessment and Dulles even announced this during a press conference on 1 December.[136] The Secretary of State was not 'particularly concerned' about whether the conference took place in Berlin or elsewhere, but Adenauer's view had to be taken into consideration.[137]

True to form, Adenauer was not enamoured of the proposal for a four-power conference; in fact he strongly opposed it. He told American ambassador

Conant that though he could not oppose Berlin as the venue of the conference, 'personally he had considerable doubts'.[138] Conant informed Washington that '[the] Chancellor felt strongly that it would be dangerous in [the] extreme for [the] Bermuda meeting to agree to [a] meeting of [the] four foreign ministers in [the] too near future'. Adenauer 'felt that for [the] three Allies to meet with [the] Russians before there was another three power meeting with a French Government, which had been put in power after [the] French presidential elections [in late December], would be foolish and might well be disastrous.' The government in Paris agreed with Adenauer; they too rejected Berlin as the venue for the conference. Conant reported that the Chancellor proposed to delay any reply to the Soviet Union in order to 'gain time.'[139]

The British Foreign Office, however, had little understanding for Adenauer's strategy of delay. Eden advised Dulles to accept the Soviet proposal. Berlin was a perfectly acceptable venue for the conference, and mid-January would be suitable for the beginning of the meeting. He thought the exact reply to the Soviet Union could be worked out in the course of the Bermuda conference; at least this would give the western heads of government something to do during their superfluous meeting in the West Indies. He also hoped it would help to shift the focus of the conference from Churchill's summit diplomacy to a more specific task.[140] The British Foreign Secretary had made up his mind to exploit Moscow's more lenient attitude to put an end to Churchill's summit diplomacy.

The highly strung Eden was rapidly losing patience with the Prime Minister, who became more and more difficult to deal with. For instance, on 19 November Churchill had refused to give Eden permission to present a memorandum to the Cabinet which spelled out his view that Moscow had only made 'certain gestures' since Stalin's death but not any genuine political sacrifices.[141] Eden also feared that the introductory visit which ambassador Sir William Hayter had been asked to pay Malenkov on 28 November might well lead to difficulties with Churchill.[142] As early as 7 November the Foreign Office had been expecting that Hayter would receive an opportunity to meet Malenkov, but Churchill had been deliberately kept in the dark about it.[143] The Foreign Secretary and his officials tried to do everything in their power to prevent interference by the Prime Minister. Eden had explicitly instructed his advisers that all diplomatic telegrams from Moscow which mentioned the possibility of a talk between Malenkov and Hayter 'should remain departmental'; they were not to be passed on to 10 Downing Street.[144] Churchill's various attempts to communicate directly with Molotov were 'quite enough in present circumstances'.[145]

Dulles agreed with Eden on the proposed four-power foreign ministers' conference in Berlin. Just before the beginning of the Bermuda conference,

Dulles persuaded Adenauer to drop his opposition to a western foreign ministers' conference with Moscow. In a conversation with West German State Secretary Walter Hallstein on 1 December, Dulles explained that it was 'highly improbable' that 'anything of substance' would be achieved in the course of the Berlin conference. If the process of ratifying the EDC was prolonged until May or June 1954, however, the American Congress was bound to adopt a very rigid attitude towards granting further American financial aid to Western Europe.[146] It was therefore best 'to get the four power meeting over and get it over with fast'. Adenauer should not harbour the illusion that the US was prepared 'to work with Germany to the exclusion of France'.[147] The Secretary of State came to the point by asking Hallstein whether 'in fact the Chancellor's purpose in his suggestions was to evade or escape any four power meeting at all'; Hallstein 'acknowledged that this was a fact'.[148]

In order to persuade Adenauer to agree to the Berlin conference, Dulles disclosed to Hallstein the western strategy for a conference with Moscow. A letter from ambassador Conant to Dulles reveals that the Secretary of State informed Adenauer's confidant about the plan for the four-power conference decided on during the western talks in Washington in July. Hallstein was told that the Berlin foreign ministers' meeting was necessary so that it could fail; the failure of the conference would ensure the subsequent ratification of the EDC in France. Hallstein passed this on to Adenauer and on 4 December Conant was able to tell Dulles that Adenauer had adopted an entirely different point of view: the Chancellor has 'now completely changed as a result of your arguments transmitted through Professor Hallstein. He is in favour of a four power conference as soon as possible, [and] only hopes it will be brief and ... will persuade the French that they must proceed with [the] ratification of the EDC.'[149]

Thus, by early December it had become clear that a four-power foreign ministers' meeting would take place soon. Although this did not coincide with Churchill's idea of a 'real' summit, it appeared to be a start. Perhaps agreement on a heads of government summit conference might be possible after this meeting in Berlin, so Churchill thought.[150] Eden, however, had quite different plans. He thought the expected failure of the Berlin conference with Moscow would serve to bury Churchill's summit diplomacy for good and make Churchill retire as Prime Minister. On 3 November, in view of Churchill's imaginative attempts to hang on to power, Eden had been so frustrated as to consider resigning as Foreign Secretary, and towards the end of the month he sent a letter of resignation to Churchill, which he was then persuaded to withdraw. However, his Private Secretary soon concluded that Eden had become more optimistic again; cheered by the possibility that the Bermuda conference might be used to obtain Churchill's retirement, Eden became

'keenness itself'.[151] Nevertheless, Eden secretly feared that Eisenhower would
not be strong enough to withstand Churchill's charm and powers of
persuasion, and might be talked into agreeing to Churchill's cherished summit
conference with Malenkov.[152] However, this was improbable. It was most
unlikely that the strategy decided upon at the Washington talks in July would
be overturned. Only Churchill believed that he would be able to persuade the
American President to give his agreement to a speedy East–West summit
conference at heads of government level.[153]

Churchill's Last Summit: The Bermuda Conference

The conference held by the heads of government and foreign ministers of the
United States, Great Britain and France in Bermuda between 4 and 8
December 1953 was not a great success.[154] Although almost all current topics in
international politics were covered, hardly any agreement could be reached.
The personal relationship of the three heads of government also left much to
be desired. Moreover, the three delegations were internally divided: French
Prime Minister Laniel and his Foreign Minister Bidault hardly talked to each
other,[155] and on the second day of the conference Laniel declared that he was
ill and needed to stay in bed; he was hardly seen again during the course of the
meetings. This contributed significantly to the difficulties of holding the
conference proceedings in an orderly fashion.

In addition, Anthony Eden was close to despair at Churchill's infatuation
with a summit, his personal idiosyncrasies and his constant changes of
mood. When the British delegation arrived on Bermuda on 2 December,
Eden wrote his wife: 'I am hating the whole thing even more than I had
expected ... The whole thing is a complete circus.' Two days later, on the first
day of the conference, he wrote: 'Here we appear to be living in a night-mare
... so far it is chaotic & my fear is that we shall end up committed to new
perils without any advantage of peace anywhere.'[156]

Moreover, Churchill ignored the French delegation as much as possible
and behaved in rather insulting ways. On the very first day, when he and
Laniel were awaiting the arrival of Eisenhower at the airport, Churchill
apparently preferred to preoccupy himself with a goat, the attending honour
guards' mascot, rather than engage in polite conversation with the French
Prime Minister.[157] During private discussions in the course of the conference,
Churchill reverted to describing the French as 'bloody frogs'. On the plane to
Bermuda, and then on the verandah of the Mid Ocean Club where the
conference was held, he read C.S. Forester's novel *Death to the French* but
promised to conceal it before meeting the French delegation.[158] Churchill

also insisted on discussing certain topics like Egypt and the atomic bomb without the participation of the French delegation.[159]

Soon, all participants became aware of Churchill's increasing frailty. The Prime Minister had not prepared any of his speeches, nor was he capable of focusing on Eisenhower's and Bidault's contributions; his increasing deafness prevented this. At one point he even mistook his own official Frank Roberts for an American participant.[160] Furthermore, as on previous occasions, none of the assembled politicians and officials was prepared to agree with the principles of his summit ideas. The French delegation ensured that there were plenty of leaks of the conference proceedings so that the press remained fully informed of the differences of opinion between Churchill and Eisenhower and Churchill and Bidault.[161] However, this did not appear to annoy the Prime Minister, who was convinced that his summit proposal remained very popular with the British public and press. 'Everything I have said will do good in England,' he declared confidently.[162] Before this conference, the Prime Minister had made clear that he hoped to use British public opinion to remain in office and pursue his summit diplomacy; in late November, he told Eden that he did not regret his speech of 11 May. 'It is a cheap way of being popular'.[163]

On the evening of the first day of the conference, a joint meeting took place between the three heads of government and their foreign ministers.[164] In his lengthy opening speech, Bidault's central message was that the Soviet Union's change of attitude since Stalin's death was not due to any 'fundamental policy changes' but was simply a shift in tactics. Churchill strongly disagreed. He claimed that western resistance to Soviet expansionism after the war, along with the Soviet Union's economic problems, had led to a modification of policy, and that he was in favour of entering into closer contact with Malenkov. This would do the West no harm although the Kremlin feared any infiltration of the Iron Curtain by Western goods and ideas. Churchill made it clear, however, that the West's defence commitments should be maintained, and reiterated the double-track policy he had advocated in the late 1940s and early 1950s: 'We should have a two-fold policy of strength and readiness to look for any hope of an improved state of mind, even if it were necessary to run a slight mental risk.' Churchill also repeatedly emphasized the value of 'infiltrating' the Soviet Union by means of trade and commercial links and other East–West points of contact.[165] To some extent he was proposing the policy which was to be at the centre of Richard Nixon's and Henry Kissinger's détente policy and Willy Brandt's *Ostpolitik* of the 1970s. While Eden and most of his advisers, in particular Frank Roberts and Evelyn Shuckburgh, regarded Churchill's statement as a 'disaster', John Colville and Denis Allen, the new director of the Foreign Office's Central Department, viewed it as 'statesmanlike'.[166]

The contrast between Churchill's speech and Bidault's anti-Soviet attitude could not have been greater. Even so, the Prime Minister could not attempt to push the assembled politicians into holding a summit conference with Malenkov.[167] Eisenhower's reaction to his comments had simply been too fierce. The President had commended Bidault's speech for the 'positive quality of its approach' but he reacted very differently to Churchill's deliberations. Shuckburgh wrote in his diary: 'He came down like a ton of bricks, very rude I thought and vulgar.'[168] In the minutes of the meeting, it was reported more soberly that Eisenhower 'did not want to approach this problem on the basis that there had been any change in the Soviet policy of destroying the Capitalist free world by all means, by force, by deceit or by lies. This was their long-term purpose. From their writings it was clear there had been no change since Lenin. If he had misinterpreted the Prime Minister, he would be happy if Sir Winston would correct him. President Eisenhower then adjourned the conference.'[169]

With this heated exchange of views the discussions of a summit meeting with Malenkov were already over. Eisenhower had made it perfectly clear that his and Churchill's stance in 1945, when Churchill had been the anti-Soviet hard-liner and Eisenhower had assumed a more conciliatory stance, had been reversed.[170] Thus Churchill's hopes of being able to convince Eisenhower of the merits of a summit by means of his personal powers of persuasion were dashed on the very first day of the Bermuda conference. Yet, as before, the Prime Minister by and large blamed Dulles for the President's negative attitude: he still deluded himself by thinking that Dulles and not Eisenhower dictated American foreign policy. He believed that 'everything is left to Dulles. It appears that the President is no more than a ventriloquist's doll ... This fellow [Dulles] preaches like a Methodist Minister, and his bloody text is always the same: That nothing but evil can come out of meeting with Malenkov.' Churchill believed that 'Dulles is a terrible handicap ... Ten years ago I could have dealt with him. Even as it is I have not been defeated by this bastard. I have been humiliated by my own decay.'[171]

Instead of considering a summit with Malenkov, discussions during the rest of the Bermuda conference focused on the details of the reply to Moscow. With the change of topic, Churchill lost interest in the conference.[172] The members of the trilateral working group responsible for drawing up the note to the Kremlin agreed that the Soviet proposal of 26 November should be accepted in principle; merely the place and timing of the conference remained disputed.[173] Subsequently this was discussed by the three foreign ministers. In general, Dulles and Eden believed that an early conference date would be desirable and that Berlin should be accepted as a conference venue. 'Time was running out,' Dulles fretted. He explained that his country was 'ready to accept a four-power meeting on the assumption that it will be over quickly and not converted into a Soviet propaganda weapon to upset Western European progress. The US was under no illusion about the Soviet concept of the meeting ... Sabotage was the obvious intent of the Soviets.'[174]

The discussions showed that with the exception of Churchill none of those present had even the remote expectation that the Berlin conference would succeed or that agreement over German reunification might be reached. What would happen if the conference with the Soviets was successful was not even discussed in Bermuda. For Dulles the problem merely consisted of 'how do you get it [the conference] over with, with as little damage as possible[?]'.[175] After consultation with the bedridden Laniel and with Eisenhower and Churchill, the three foreign ministers agreed to propose to the Soviet Union that a four-power foreign ministers' meeting should begin in Berlin in the headquarters of the Allied High Commission on 4 January. Adenauer had already accepted this proposal.[176]

When Eden initially expressed concern that this early date would leave very little time for preparing the meeting, the US once again used the tactics employed at the Washington talks: the President invoked Adenauer's authority. Eisenhower declared that the Chancellor 'had sent word on the previous day that he had completely changed his mind and felt that the earlier the conference were held the better'. In view of Adenauer's apparent change of mind, the British Foreign Secretary's objections paled into insignificance as far as Eisenhower was concerned. The western powers agreed to propose 4 January as the opening date for the conference in Berlin.[177] The politicians also stipulated that the conference ought to be concluded after about three weeks, but it did not seem appropriate to inform the Soviet Union of this.[178] After consultation with Adenauer and West Berlin's Governing Mayor Schreiber, identical western notes were conveyed to the USSR. There had been another dispute with Churchill regarding the wording of the note to Moscow, but Churchill had been overruled.[179]

With the drafting of the note to Moscow, the Bermuda conference had been successful in securing at least one concrete result. Otherwise there existed only severe differences. Serious clashes on the EDC question emerged on the first day of the conference, when the French delegation was faced with fierce reproaches.[180] Naturally, Bidault resented this; he defended the French government against accusations of not having done enough to ensure the ratification of the EDC, and blamed Britain's non-participation in the EDC for the difficulties in securing ratification by the French parliament. Bidault attempted to persuade the British and US governments to offer further concessions, expressing the hope that the British would 'be willing to associate themselves much more closely with the EDC'. He also expected firm assurances from the US 'that it did not intend to pull out of Europe, thus leaving France and Germany virtually alone on the continent'.[181]

An American pull-out also worried Churchill. He was as afraid as anyone that the Americans would leave Europe if the EDC could not be implemented and no alternative could be found. In such circumstances, it could soon be expected that 'the Russian armies would be in occupation of Western Europe' and eventually 'a third World War would become inevitable'.[182] Churchill's concern demonstrates one of the reasons why he was so deeply convinced that his policy of détente with the Soviet Union was of overwhelming importance.[183]

The Americans showed some understanding for the anxieties of the Europeans. The members of the Eisenhower government, in particular the National Security Council officers, were therefore instructed not to give speeches that indicated, even remotely, the possibility of a 're-deployment of American troops in Europe'. Words to such effect would 'throw France and the others in panic, and then the President and/or the Secretary of State have got to issue a strong denial which makes the situation more rigid than ever, at the precise time when we want to keep it fluid and leave it to American diplomacy to work out the answer'.[184]

On 5 December, the second day of the conference, Eisenhower and Dulles had a private conversation with Laniel and endeavoured to convince him of the urgency of ratifying the EDC. Although the bedridden French Prime Minister claimed to be an enthusiastic proponent of the European army, he believed that a precondition of agreement on this was a solution of the Saar question: the coal-rich territory on the border with France that had been annexed by France in all but name after the end of the war and was fiercely contested between Bonn and Paris.[185] Bidault subsequently declared that France might be willing to accept the Europeanization of the Saar area but would never accept its return to Germany. He declared that it was not easy to become involved in a supranational institution with a state whose borders were defined neither to the East (Oder–Neisse line) nor to the west (the Saar). 'There was no pleasure in integration.'[186]

Churchill was still fretting about his defeat on the summit question and had little understanding for the prolonged time this part of the discussion consumed; he regarded it as unimportant and marginal. The Prime Minister replied scornfully to Bidault's statement that he 'did not feel we should be mixed up with a few fields in the Saar valley. We should maintain a sense of proportion.'[187] The French persisted. Laniel explained that France would be immensely relieved if Great Britain were to declare its intent to place even only one of its divisions under the command of the EDC,[188] and Bidault pointed out that in the event of the integration of the Federal Republic into NATO there were no guarantees to prevent the rapid rearmament of Germany. The Germans might well use their new army to re-conquer Königsberg. West German integration into NATO did not provide a solution: 'There was no guarantee against German rearmament in NATO which was on the basis of the general consent of those taking part. Any alternative solution would be extremely difficult to apply if indeed desirable. The very basis of NATO was non-discrimination. There were no limitations on strength, on the financial or economic strength of any country, regardless of the imbalance which might result there from.'[189]

Churchill increasingly lost patience. He declared that his country was not in a position to commit itself over the stationing of its troops on the continent. As in the past, he expressed his disquiet at the alleged necessity for establishing a supranational European defence organization. A coalition army, structured with national forces and with a joint supreme commander similar to NATO, was all that was needed. Instead, three years had been 'completely wasted'. A 'good strong German army' could have been set up three years ago. If this were to be achieved by way of the EDC in the next eight to ten weeks, then this would be an acceptable solution for the western world and France.[190] The Prime Minister did not hesitate to openly threaten the French delegation: if the EDC failed, he would be compelled to ask Washington to allow German rearmament within NATO by altering the structure of NATO so that the French would no longer have a veto over the admission of new members. Churchill also envisaged NATO-imposed controls on the new German army. Thus, the Prime Minister had indicated an eventual alternative to the EDC, suggesting a solution that was eventually enforced in the autumn of 1954.[191] If this were not accomplished and if the US was to pull out of Europe, Britain would do the same: 'the British would stay only as long as the United States.'[192] Not surprisingly, British diplomats continued to persist in urging the State Department to follow the example of the Foreign Office and begin exploring serious alternatives to the EDC.[193]

Eisenhower disagreed with Churchill's view that the West had lost three years. After all, the Germans should not be integrated into the West simply with an army but also 'with heart, will and economic ties as well'. The primary task was to integrate the West Germans 'in a federation from which they could not break loose'; 'they must never be in a position where they could blackmail the other powers'.[194] The President explained that Churchill had overlooked the fact that the Germans under Adenauer's leadership were no longer inter- ested in possessing a national army. Eisenhower was firmly convinced 'that to resort to a national army was a second choice so far behind [the] EDC that there could be no comparison'.[195] Although the President agreed with

Churchill regarding the serious consequences that would arise if the EDC failed to be ratified in Paris, he endeavoured to ensure that the remaining discussions in Bermuda would be conducted in a quieter, more conciliatory fashion.[196] After the end of the conference, however, he expressed the opinion that the Bermuda conference had not helped to secure progress with the EDC; he thought the Bermuda meeting 'was probably the least decisive of any that has taken place'.[197]

The subsequent meetings during the conference were almost entirely devoted to atomic matters and to the Far East and Middle East. A considerable period of time was also taken up with the discussion of NATO's 'New Look' and 'Long Haul' policy.[198] Eisenhower's 'Candor' or 'Atoms for Peace' speech, which he was to deliver to the General Assembly of the United Nations on 8 December, was also debated.[199] This speech, a call for the peaceful and cooperative use of atomic energy, was another attempt to outdo the Soviet Union's peace campaign once and for all.[200] It is not surprising that Churchill expressed the same opinion as he had voiced before Eisenhower's 'Chance for Peace' speech in April, 'that he had some reservations as to the wisdom of delivering it'; this time Eden fully agreed with his Prime Minister.[201] Churchill feared that Eisenhower's address would deflect the attention of the international media from the Bermuda conference and the forthcoming foreign ministers' meeting with Moscow. To be on the safe side, after Eisenhower's speech on 8 December Churchill sent a telegram to Molotov in which he stressed that Eisenhower's address did not represent a political manoeuvre; instead it was 'a real endeavour to find new ways of dealing with this terrible threat to the world'.[202]

It was only on the concluding day of the western Bermuda conference that discussions began on a security guarantee that could be proposed to Moscow in the course of the forthcoming Berlin foreign ministers' conference. Although the previous day Churchill had suggested in passing that it would make sense if the participants discussed his 'Locarno security idea', he had received no positive response.[203] On the last day of the conference, Churchill once again raised the security policy expressed in his 11 May speech. 'We should do something to reassure' the Soviets, he announced. While he did not intend to accept the status quo that prevailed in the East European satellite states, this situation should not be overcome by the use of force but rather 'by allowing time, patience and perhaps good fortune to work'. The Prime Minister hoped that certain conciliatory phrases, which he termed 'Locarnoism', would find their way into the final communiqué of the Bermuda conference. Churchill reminded his colleagues that:

Since the communiqué of the Conference was to strike so many notes of strength, we could surely afford to strike one which would give at any rate some sense of wishing the Soviet Union no harm or even of being ready to help them against unjustified assault and would indicate that the world instrument would, as was intended, play its part on their side on occasions when they were in the right.[204]

Bidault, however, cared little for extending over-hasty security guarantees. Such assurances, he declared, should only be given at the end of the four-power conference but not before it had begun. Moreover, the Soviet Union feared Germany above all, and so 'the guarantees and assurances that the Russians wanted should come from Germany'. Without it being mentioned, it was evident that France was also interested in such assurances. Dulles rejected Bidault's proposal. Unlike the years after the First World War, the Germans ought not to be regarded as the power expected to embark first on aggression. It was, after all, the aim of the western Allies to prevent the emergence of a second Hitler, not to help build him up. Eden succeeded in finding a compromise, suggesting the Germans be asked if they would be willing to announce unilaterally a declaration guaranteeing security. Churchill, was not happy with this solution. Such a statement was bound to merely paraphrase the declarations that had already been made many times before; nothing new would be said. However, Eden's compromise was agreed upon and the session was brought to a close to allow sufficient time for the editing of the final communiqué; the delegations had already been working on this since the beginning of the conference but without having been able to reach agreement.[205]

When the final communiqué was discussed by the foreign ministers and heads of government fierce conflicts of opinion re-emerged. Bidault insisted on finding a solution to the Saar problem before progress with the EDC was possible: 'He asked that consideration be given to the consequences of the return of the Saar to the Reich [sic!].' Bidault demanded that the communiqué should include a reference to the fact that the EDC could only be established if a way was found to overcome the difficulties 'with which France has long been faced'. This was a blatant attempt to ensure that any blame would be attributed to France's allies, especially London, if the French parliament failed to ratify the EDC. Dulles joined the British delegation in rejecting Bidault's demand. When Eden proposed that it might perhaps be better to openly admit to existing differences of opinion, Eisenhower categorically turned this down. Every word that would adversely affect support for the EDC would make it more difficult for the American annual assistance programme to get through Congress.[206]

In his diary, Shuckburgh describes 'outbursts by Eisenhower and Winston, former left the conference table in a rage, came back … sat another four hours'. Exhausted, the President informed Dulles: 'Never again will I come to one of these, unless it is all prepared and agreed beforehand.' To the annoyance of the French, Eisenhower left the conference before the communiqué had been finally agreed. Churchill announced: 'The EDC is dead. We want a German army.'[207] Right at the beginning of the arguments, the Prime Minister had told Eden of his disappointment that there was not one sentence in the final communiqué which attempted to establish better relations with Moscow. Instead, it appeared as though the West was intent on maintaining and even stabilizing the partition of Europe. Churchill told his Foreign Secretary that he could not find anything 'in this communiqué which shows the slightest desire for the success of the conference or for an assessment in relations with Russia.'

> We are to gang up against them without any reference to the 'Locarno' idea. The statement about Europe ends with the challenge about a united Germany in EDC or NATO, for which Russia is to give up the Eastern Zone. Many people would think that we are deliberately riding for a fall. Perhaps we are … We cannot accept as justified or permanent the present division of Europe.[208]

Discussions about the communiqué continued until one o'clock in the morning. At last a compromise was found. The politicians agreed that the 'intimate and durable co-operation' of Great Britain and the US with the EDC should be stressed in the statement. It was also decided to point out that the French Foreign Minister had 'explained the problems facing his government in regard to the European Defence Community'.[209] Eden commented: 'We have had a hell of a time.' Churchill was now finally convinced that the EDC had failed. He announced that it was 'obvious' that 'there was no agreement between us, and that the French would not accept EDC'.[210]

Although it had been possible to more or less paper over the differences that existed within the western camp, a solution was still a long way off. Apart from failure to reach agreement over the EDC, it had not been possible to reach agreement on a declaration of a security policy guarantee for the USSR nor on a summit with Malenkov. Not surprisingly, both the British and American delegates showed signs of exasperation with the cumbersome and tiring behaviour of Bidault and Laniel.[211] There had also been differences over the western world's policy in the Far and Middle East and disputes regarding the use of the atomic bomb. Churchill proved entirely incapable of renewing the 'special relationship' on atomic matters.[212] Above all, when drafting the communiqué the participants had not even considered mentioning

Churchill's summit diplomacy and his ideas on a new European security policy. Even the Prime Minister himself had not seriously attempted to ensure that such a passage was contained in the final report. He simply no longer had the physical stamina to continue battling with his colleagues. Following his fierce encounter with Eisenhower at the beginning of the conference, it appeared very much as though Churchill had parted from his dreams of summit diplomacy for the time being.

Despite Eden's disappointment with the chaotic proceedings of the meeting and his difficulties with Churchill, the Foreign Secretary appeared to be the only one who was genuinely happy with the outcome of the conference. Eisenhower seemed to have robbed Churchill of his political illusions for good. On his return to London, Eden explained to the American ambassador that 'he thought the Bermuda meeting although, as anticipated, not productive of startling results, had been a very useful means of improving co-operation and ironing out certain difficulties. He said he was particularly impressed by the admirably effective manner with which the President had chairmanned the meeting.'[213]

Eden assumed that Churchill was greatly frustrated with the outcome of the Bermuda conference and would thus finally see the impossibility of achieving his aim to organize a three- or four-power summit meeting. The Foreign Secretary hoped that his failure to obtain agreement for a 'Big Three' 'parley at the summit' with Malenkov would induce the Prime Minister to retire in the very near future. However, Eden was mistaken. Churchill had not yet given up on his vision to overcome the Cold War, create an international détente and ensure Britain's continued position as a European great power by means of his personal summit diplomacy.

CHAPTER 15

Preparing a Final Attempt
Churchill's Perseverance and Perceived Agreement with Eisenhower

In the aftermath of the Bermuda conference Churchill had no choice but to postpone any new summit initiative for a while. Bermuda had made clear that Eisenhower was still strongly opposed to Churchill's vision of how to overcome the Cold War. Moreover, the meeting of the North Atlantic Council in Paris in mid-December 1953 not only reiterated the belief of the western countries that the Soviet Union's political objectives had not changed since Stalin's death[1] but it also led to Dulles's 'agonizing reappraisal' statement, in which the Secretary of State publicly threatened the French government with a reorientation of American policy if the EDC continued to be opposed by the French parliament.[2] Churchill and many others assumed that due to American pressure the EDC might well be ratified soon after the Berlin foreign ministers' conference. Following a Soviet proposal the four powers had agreed to commence the Berlin meeting in late January 1954. However, in view of the tacit deal entered into by the western foreign ministers at the Washington talks in July 1953, Churchill was not very hopeful that the conference would lead to any constructive results.

The Impact of the Berlin Conference and the H-Bomb on Churchill's Plans

The four-power conference of foreign ministers on Germany and Austria took place in Berlin between 25 January and 18 February 1954. It was the first such meeting for almost four years. While public expectations ran high, it was most unlikely that the conference would be a success. Agreement with the Soviet Union would only have been possible if Moscow had assented to the reunification of Germany on conditions similar to those it was to accept in entirely different political and economic circumstances in October 1990. In 1954, when the Soviet Union had just succeeded in testing its first H-bomb and was hoping to make further dramatic technological and economic progress, this was an unlikely scenario.[3] If, contrary to Churchill's expectations, agreement over the German question were to be reached during the Berlin conference, he was prepared to fly to Berlin and sign a final document together with Eisenhower and Malenkov.[4]

However, the so-called 'Eden-Plan' for German reunification contained all the well-known western preconditions that were unacceptable to the Soviet Union and consequently no progress was made.[5] The Soviet Foreign Minister's proposals were in turn unacceptable to the West. Molotov essentially suggested a return to the Potsdam system of four-power control of Germany, advocating that free elections should only take place after the formation of an all-German government from representatives of the West German Bundestag and the East German Volkskammer. Prior to this, however, all occupation troops had to be withdrawn, and if Germany were to be united it was to be neutral. He envisaged that both NATO and the EDC should be replaced by a new European security system that excluded the United States.[6]

Neither in the plenary sessions nor in the bilateral talks before and after the official rounds of negotiations did Molotov reveal any serious indications that Moscow was prepared to become more flexible on the German question, though on a personal level he was somewhat less reserved than he had been during similar encounters in the past. Molotov had detested Eden's predecessor Ernest Bevin but he liked Churchill's Foreign Secretary. Although he regarded Eden as 'delicate' and 'quite helpless', he believed 'I could deal with him'.[7] However, when towards the end of the conference Eden attempted to reach an agreement with Molotov on limiting the number of police troops in eastern and western Germany, hoping that at least a tentative agreement could be reached to ask the four High Commissioners to examine the issue further, even such a very limited accord did not materialize.[8]

Nevertheless, when the Berlin conference drew to a close on 18 February credit was due to Anthony Eden and the French Foreign Minister Bidault for having managed to prevent the real breakdown of the conference and the worsening of East–West relations, given a difficult American ally and an unrelenting Molotov. Indeed, the British Foreign Secretary achieved the very difficult task of finding a compromise with 'the bear without parting us from the eagle'.[9] While the western powers focused above all on exposing Molotov's insincerity with regard to the German and Austrian questions,[10] Eden managed to obtain an agreement on holding a five-power conference (including China) on Korea and Indochina in the near future.

Initially, Dulles and the American delegation had been less than enthusiastic about such a meeting and continued to refuse to give equal status to Mao's China. While Eden wished to return home with some kind of diplomatic achievement, Dulles feared that American public opinion would never forgive him if he accepted Mao's China, which the US adamantly refused to recognize diplomatically, as one of the 'Big Five'; this might well become his 'Yalta'.[11] In the end it was agreed that a 'Big Four' conference on the Far East was to take place in Geneva in the summer of 1954, with China and the Vietminh being allowed to participate as the locally affected parties to the conflict.[12] This result also placated Churchill to some extent. He expected that Eden would be so occupied with the foreign ministers' conference during the summer that he would hardly have the time to press too hard for Churchill's resignation as Prime Minister. Moreover, while the Berlin conference had proved disappointing, at least contact with the Soviet Union had not collapsed altogether and a foreign ministers' meeting on the Far East might well keep the idea of summit diplomacy with Moscow alive.[13]

In the western world most leading politicians were much happier than Churchill with the results of the Berlin conference; after all, the West had achieved the outcome it had had in mind since the summer of 1953. On 15 February 1954, three days before the end of the Berlin conference, the State Department had recorded with satisfaction that it was 'safe to state that, once all the returns are in on the Berlin Meeting, we will have clear and impressive up-to-the minute evidence of Soviet intransigence, hypocrisy and dishonesty. The true intentions of the Kremlin and the entire Soviet conspiracy will have been laid bare as they rarely have been exposed before'.[14] The Soviet peace campaign was bound to look very hollow now. The German Chancellor was also most relieved at the absence of any results regarding the German and Austrian questions at the Berlin meeting; Dulles was able to tell the American National Security Council that Adenauer 'was extremely pleased with the outcome of the conference'.[15]

After the Berlin meeting Churchill no longer spoke of his plan to discuss the German question with Malenkov. In early 1953 he had been firmly convinced that his Locarno proposal and the creation of a neutral, reunified Germany could solve the East–West conflict for good, as he had indicated in his speech on 11 May.[16] Subsequently, however, he had become much more pessimistic; the Foreign Office's work of persuasion and perhaps also Adenauer's and Eisenhower's influence had paid dividends. During the Berlin conference, the Prime Minister had written to Eden that he found it 'hard to believe that any settlement can be reached about Germany. We must stand by the principle of a German contingent either to EDC or an amended NATO. This alone gives the West the chance of obtaining the necessary strength by creating a European or internationalized German Army but not a national one'.[17]

Churchill also professed his loyalty to the West German Chancellor: 'I think we are bound in good faith to Adenauer to bring this about and we should in no circumstances agree to Germany being reduced to a neutralised, defenceless hiatus which would be the preliminary to another Czechoslovakia process.' While in 1953 he had been firmly convinced that the Soviets would agree to a neutral and reunited Germany, by early 1954 he found it 'hard to believe that the Soviets will relinquish their grip on Eastern Germany'.[18] The Prime Minister even thought that it had been a blunder to attempt to discuss Germany and Austria with the Soviets in Berlin, which had only put 'them on the spot'; the West ought to be 'nicer to the Russians'. Eden's Private Secretary Evelyn Shuckburgh commented wryly: 'What should we have talked to them about, one wonders, just peace and loving kindness, presumably, without hordes of experts or [a] specific agenda.'[19]

On 25 January 1954, shortly after the end of the conference, Churchill gave a speech in the House of Commons during which he reflected on the meeting in Berlin. Despite Foreign Office official Frank Roberts's best efforts to get 'the worst features removed' from the Prime Minister's 'terrible' speech, as it was viewed in the Foreign Office,[20] Churchill nonetheless emphasized that he intended to continue with his top-level and agenda-free summit diplomacy, based on the 'Locarno spirit', as outlined in his speech in May 1953. Churchill expressed the belief that the Berlin conference had led to an improvement in 'personal relations and comprehension of each other's point of view'. Indeed, he declared that the conference had been 'very remarkable'. Although 'very little' had been agreed and in this respect the meeting had been unsatisfactory, 'no offence' had been given to either side and 'new contacts have been established'. Above all, the Berlin conference was able to restore 'the reputation of such meetings after some very unfortunate examples' and further meetings, like the forthcoming conference in Geneva on Indochina, had thus become possible.[21] Regarding 'the liberation of Austria' he believed that the door had not been closed at Berlin and he did 'not feel inclined to take "No" for an answer in this matter'.[22]

In the course of his speech Churchill also admitted that after having considered schemes for the creation of 'a united, neutralised, disarmed Germany', he had abandoned this idea as it now seemed to him 'full of the gravest dangers'. Germany should not be allowed to become 'a kind of no-man's land in Europe' with 'a sort of leper status'. This would pose the danger of the country falling under Soviet influence or turning into a militaristic power again. Instead, the democratic and pro-western Chancellor Adenauer, 'a strong champion of the European idea', deserved the western world's fullest support. Indeed, Churchill had once again come to the conclusion that Adenauer was 'one of the greatest men Germany has produced since Bismarck'. The Prime Minister also emphasized that an international détente with Moscow could be achieved while 'building up the defensive strength of the free world against Communist pressure' and making sure that the Federal Republic would remain a member of the western world. Indeed, he believed that only by 'this two-fold policy of peace through strength ... we shall get a chance of getting anything of it at all.'[23] A day later he told his doctor that he liked 'to be on speaking terms with everyone. I like to have the Germans on my side, but I don't want to quarrel with the Russians. I want to keep in with both sides.'[24]

By early 1954 Churchill had clearly changed from an advocate of a reunited and neutralized Germany into an equally strong defender of the continued division of the country; in effect, he had become a supporter of Adenauer's and Dulles's German policy and thus of the western integration of the Federal Republic. In characteristic fashion, Churchill now greatly exaggerated his enthusiasm for the status quo in the German question. He even intended to say in his parliamentary address on 25 February that Germany was Britain's 'sword on the Continent', but the Foreign Office managed to convince him to delete this passage from his speech in the Commons.[25]

However, Churchill could not be persuaded to drop any reference to the kind of summit conference he desired. As in May 1953, he reiterated that he had in mind 'a meeting like we used to have in the war of the heads of States and Governments, with the Foreign Secretaries, and I still think that this procedure should not be ruled out'. He emphasized that 'Patience and perseverance must never be grudged when the peace of the world is at stake. Even if we had to go through a decade of cold-war bickerings punctuated by vain parleys, that would be preferable to the catalogue of unspeakable and also unimaginable horrors which is the alternative.' 'Every channel' should be used and he therefore trusted that 'we shall always hold the resource of a meeting of the heads of States and Governments in reserve.' He was convinced that 'any meeting' with the Soviets 'was better than no meeting at all'.[26]

Thus, in early 1954 it became evident that the Prime Minister was still intent on continuing with his summit diplomacy. He therefore searched for further suitable topics for a summit conference other than the German question. The mere convening of a summit meeting rather than the actual topics to be discussed became ever more important to him. Churchill clearly wished to receive credit as the originator of an internationally significant event to bring about global peace. He desired to go down in history as the politician who had not only won the Second World War but also succeeded in overcoming the

Cold War. His Private Secretary believed that Churchill's 'genuine yearning to be considered a peace-maker was an extremely powerful motivation of his policies'. Churchill was therefore deeply disappointed when he learnt that he had not won the 1953 Nobel Peace Prize but the prize for literature; however, he still appreciated the prize money though he did not bother to collect it in person.[27]

Nor can it be overlooked that from the spring of 1954 the summit theme also became Churchill's instrument with which he hoped to postpone his retirement a little longer. An official at the American embassy in London had gained the impression that Churchill still had 'a very strong feeling that when he steps down it must be after one last dramatic gesture on the world stage'. He told the State Department that although it could be assumed 'that Churchill will not remain as Prime Minister in another Government', it had to be concluded that it was 'virtually impossible to predict when and how such an extraordinary individualist of such unique talents will retire'.[28] Indeed, in early April 1954 the Prime Minister informed Lord Moran outright: 'I shall not relinquish office until I meet Malenkov.' As an afterthought he added: 'I would pop over to America first to make it all right with them.'[29]

The Prime Minister also knew that nothing could be done until after the Indochina conference, which was to begin in Geneva on 26 April. He was keen to see whether the Far East, unlike Germany, proved to be an area where the West and Moscow could arrive at some compromise which, perhaps, would set the ball rolling for a more general détente. In the last resort Churchill was deeply convinced that a meeting with Malenkov would be necessary whatever the actual outcome of the Geneva conference. 'If the conference fails, I shall pick up the bits. If it triumphs, I shall go to meet Malenkov to exploit the victory.'[30]

Following the Berlin conference the US and Britain intensified their attempts to push Paris into ratifying the EDC. According to Eden, this was now 'the most urgent question' of the day.[31] In London and Washington, it was assumed that the French National Assembly would begin the EDC debate in early April. Moreover, Eden had returned from Berlin with the conviction that the Soviet Union would not regard the establishment of the EDC as a serious threat that would need to be answered militarily. He even believed 'that M. Molotov had recognized that the EDC was itself an insurance against future German aggression'.[32] This was, however, an exaggerated interpretation of a remark made by Soviet ambassador Malik to Under-Secretary of State Nutting during a conversation at the end of January. Malik had said that the maintenance of the partition of Germany was perhaps unavoidable and that the western integration of the Federal Republic would have to be accepted.[33]

Although Washington remained fairly optimistic, if exasperated, in the spring of 1954, the government in London had come to the view that it was increasingly improbable that the EDC would ever be ratified in Paris. The British Cabinet began concentrating on the question of finding an alternative solution to German rearmament so that a different scheme could be rapidly implemented; this alone would prevent the eventual failure of the EDC leading to a prolonged crisis in the West.[34] Since Eden 'regarded it as doubtful whether the EDC would go through', he therefore believed it was time to consider 'whether the United States and we could not assume the role of controlling Germany ourselves by some strengthening of the NATO obligations and machinery'. Eden stressed that his considerations needed to remain confidential, 'as we must give no hint to the French that there was an acceptable alternative to [the] EDC'.[35] In a conversation with ambassador Makins, Dulles severely criticized Eden's proposal to look for an alternative to the EDC, but in the course of the summer the Secretary of State agreed to allow his officials to ponder alternatives to the EDC scheme. This was a fundamental change of course; hitherto Dulles and other senior American politicians had refused even to think about the possibility of failure of the EDC plan.[36]

Churchill also believed that it was high time to consider seriously alternatives to the EDC, and this was one reason why he remained relatively passive in the aftermath of the Berlin conference. He intended to await developments with regard to the EDC and the forthcoming Geneva conference on Korea and Indochina. Thus instead of immediately reverting to his summit policy, he attempted to stimulate more intensive East–West commercial contacts, not least to improve his country's balance of trade. On 25 February he had pointed out to the House of Commons that an improvement of trade relations with the Soviet Union would ease tension and increase the eastern and western world's material well-being: 'Friendly infiltration can do nothing but good.'[37] The Prime Minister proposed to a more than reluctant Eisenhower that the West should remove a considerable number of goods from the CoCom list and thus make them acceptable for East–West trade.[38] Yet, as John Young has perceptively remarked, in the first few months of 1954 the question of East–West trade also enabled Churchill 'to keep alive hopes of détente until a new issue emerged which reinvigorated his hopes of a Summit'.[39]

Once again Churchill also considered his retirement. He was now thinking of either May/June 1954, shortly after the Queen had returned from a Commonwealth visit, or just before the parliamentary summer recess in July.[40] Eden, his designated successor, along with the American embassy in London, firmly expected the Prime Minister's imminent resignation as there was increasing reluctance in the Cabinet and the Conservative Party to tolerate the rapidly deteriorating Churchill as head of government much longer.[41] The Prime Minister was hardly able to concentrate any more and preferred to read novels to Cabinet papers. He was also increasingly deaf and showed definite signs of physical and mental decline. His interest was limited to some very few foreign policy topics, each concerning the continuation of Britain's role as a world power.

Apart from his summit diplomacy, his primary political objective, Churchill was also still greatly concerned about the maintenance of Britain's position in Egypt.[42] The Prime Minister firmly rejected the policy supported by Eden and the Foreign Office of a step-by-step evacuation of the British military base on the Suez Canal and the conclusion of a treaty with the Egyptian nationalists under General Nagib and Colonel Nasser, who had recently come to power with clandestine American help. Despite the Suez Canal being of reduced strategic importance to Britain since the independence of India, the Prime Minister believed that the continued British presence in Egypt was still vital for the maintenance of Britain's role as a global power.[43] It became clear to the Foreign Office that Churchill even hoped to provoke the Egyptians into a violent campaign to expel the British troops on the Suez Canal. In such an eventuality he hoped London would have an excuse to re-assert Britain's presence on the Canal by using counter-force and thus maintain its presence in Egypt.[44]

This plan clearly contradicted his own summit diplomacy. Here he strove for a meeting with Malenkov and Eisenhower to end the Cold War and bring about a long period of peace. The link between Churchill's apparently contradictory intentions was that both served the purpose of maintaining Britain's position as a global power – the constant factor in Churchill's political thinking since he had first entered politics at the beginning of the century.[45] It was thus perhaps not surprising that on 16 June 1954 the Defence Policy Committee (DPC), which was chaired by the Prime Minister, took the decision to produce a British hydrogen bomb,[46] thus asserting Britain's role as a world power. However, the danger to world peace resulting from the almost inevitable proliferation of nuclear weapons worried Churchill a great deal.

Since early 1954 he had become increasingly concerned about the risk of an atomic catastrophe if a major military conflict were ever to break out again. During the Bermuda conference in December 1953 he had clearly failed to re-create the Anglo-American collaboration on atomic matters which he felt he had established with the Quebec Agreement in August 1943, when he and Roosevelt had agreed on 'full and effective' cooperation in this area and 'mutual consent' if an atomic bomb were ever to be deployed.[47] Despite the discussion of his 'Atoms for Peace speech', Eisenhower had not expressed any great interest in East–West nuclear armaments at the Bermuda conference. It

was therefore a particularly unwelcome surprise to Churchill when on 16
February 1954 a speech by Sterling Cole, the Chairman of the Joint Congressional Committee on Atomic Energy, alerted the western public to the huge
explosive power of the various hydrogen bombs tested by the United States.

Codenamed 'Mike', the first hydrogen bomb had been tested on Eniwetok
Atoll, one of the South Pacific Marshall Islands as early as November 1952.
With the equivalent of 10.4 million tons of TNT, the device was a thousand
times larger than the bombs which had devastated Hiroshima and Nagasaki.
Churchill and the British government had not known about these tests; and to
make matters worse, five more test explosions had taken place in the Pacific
Ocean over the subsequent months. The most powerful explosion was
codenamed 'Bravo' and took place on Bikini Atoll on 1 March 1954. This was
not merely a test device as the previous ones but the first 'genuine, deliverable'
H-bomb. 'Bravo' led to the destruction of several of the Marshall Islands and,
as the winds changed without warning, the massive explosion equivalent to 15
million tons of TNT (three times as much as expected) resulted in an
unexpected radioactive cloud and the contamination with nuclear fall-out of
several hundred Pacific islanders. The radioactive fall-out even reached a
Japanese fishing boat some eighty miles away from the centre of the explosion
(ground zero).[48]

Both Western European and Asian opinion was much antagonized by these
events. Cole's speech in mid-February and the revelation soon afterwards of
the enormous force of the test explosion on 1 March 1954 caused Churchill
much renewed anxiety about the threatening nuclear catastrophe should the
two superpowers ever wage war against each other.[49] He became even more
deeply concerned about Washington's apparently uninhibited policy of
nuclear testing in the atmosphere when during a joint press conference a few
weeks later Eisenhower and Lewis Strauss, the chairman of the U.S. Atomic
Energy Commission, revealed some of the details; the latter also explained that
an H-bomb could easily wipe out the entire city of New York.[50] Subsequently,
Churchill succeeded in putting pressure on the BBC not to show documen-
taries or broadcast in-depth discussions about nuclear matters and the likely
effects of an atomic attack on Britain.[51]

On occasion the Prime Minister secretly feared that the US planned a
preventive attack on the USSR while Washington still commanded atomic
supremacy. After all, in early February 1954 Eisenhower had declared in a letter
to Churchill that it was necessary for the West to sharpen the swords 'for the
struggle that cannot possibly be escaped'. Even the Foreign Office expressed
concern, and insisted that in his reply Churchill ask the President whether he
was referring to a military conflict or to the 'spiritual struggle' with the Soviet

Union's atheistic materialism. The President was quick to confirm that he had merely referred to the ideological battle with the Kremlin,[52] but the British continued to be concerned. By late March Churchill remarked that he was 'more worried by the hydrogen bomb than by all the rest of my troubles put together'.[53] This theme, which could be conveniently linked with the necessity of organizing an East–West summit meeting, began to dominate his remaining period in office and became the centrepiece of his forthcoming speech in Parliament. A debate had been initiated by the Labour Party's call for an international summit meeting to discuss the need for global disarmament, and Churchill intended to use the opportunity to emphasize both the dangers of the hydrogen bomb and the benefits of a 'Big Three' meeting.

On 5 April 1954 he therefore delivered a lengthy speech in Parliament on the dangers of the hydrogen bomb and the necessity of a mutual disarmament effort, but the Prime Minister's speech was a disaster since it revealed to the world Churchill's physical and mental deterioration. In reply to a short, common-sense address by Clement Attlee, Churchill accused Attlee of having given up the British right of veto over the deployment of nuclear bombs by the US during his time as Prime Minister.[54] This was entirely incorrect and the House of Commons erupted in turmoil. Eden and the Foreign Office had warned Churchill against using the speech to start a party political quarrel. However, influenced by his old friend and science adviser Lord Cherwell, the Prime Minister could not be dissuaded.[55]

What had initially been an uncontroversial debate, according to *The Times*, 'degenerated into a sterile, angry and pitiful party wrangle'.[56] Shuckburgh wrote in his diary: 'So the Old Man made his speech the way he wanted it, and brought the House down on top of himself. I have never seen such a row. Attlee red in the face, quivering with rage … the backbenchers shouting and booing, the Tories glum and silent; all the tough guys putting on shocked expressions and yelling "disgriceful [sic!], shockin [sic!], another red letter, resign"; and the Old Man looking utterly dumbfounded, plunging further and further where he had not intended to go.'[57] Even the members of his own party were unable to defend their leader. When Churchill eventually stumbled towards the end of his speech, the initial turmoil had given way to embarrassed silence. 'All expression had gone from his voice, which quavered into the high-pitched voice of a very old man; he had somehow to get through a set piece before he sat down, and he gabbled through it as if his only purpose was now to get to the end.'[58]

In the press, and especially within the Conservative Party itself, the calls for Churchill's resignation now became increasingly louder. Eden and the majority of the Cabinet were firmly convinced 'that W. S. C. can in no circumstances be allowed to attend a top-level conference'.[59] During the next few days, ad hoc meetings took place between leading members of the Cabinet to discuss how the Prime Minister could be persuaded to retire gracefully. The day after Churchill's disastrous speech Eden and Lord Woolton agreed that the Prime Minister ought to tender his resignation on 7 June and that shortly thereafter Parliament should be dissolved and new elections held.[60] Churchill, however, firmly rejected all talk about his imminent retirement. If anything, the débâcle of his speech on 5 April 1954 had made him even more adamant that he would not retire under these circumstances. He intended to undo his dismal performance and prove that he was still capable of fulfilling the duties of Prime Minister; he 'hoped to do better next time'.[61] On 13 April Churchill took the initiative himself by convening a Cabinet meeting to consider the date of the next general election. In the course of the meeting, he blandly declared that he assumed that the various private discussions among Cabinet members had nothing to do with him personally. He certainly intended to remain in office for the time being.[62]

It was little wonder that Anthony Eden, still Churchill's heir apparent, became increasingly frustrated and began to resort to desperate measures. Once again he pondered whether or not a summit conference at heads of government level should be convened to achieve Churchill's resignation as fast as possible, asking his advisers whether he should encourage the Prime Minister to propose a summit conference immediately 'so as to get it over and done with'. But even if Malenkov were to declare his readiness to participate, which was by no means certain, Eisenhower would still be unlikely to accept the invitation. Eden's officials therefore pointed to the risk that a situation might develop in which London would find itself in a coalition of interests with Moscow, which could well result in an Anglo-Soviet summit conference being held in face of American opposition. Eden's desperate idea was abandoned.[63]

Churchill did not wait long before reviving his summit plans. Only a few days after his dismal performance in Parliament, he was once again contemplating the possibility of a conference with Malenkov. He had been encouraged by a discussion between his son-in-law Christopher Soames, and Georgi Rodionov, the chargé d'affaires of the Soviet embassy in London, from which Soames and his wife gathered that the Soviet Prime Minister would welcome a summit meeting with Churchill.[64]

In a speech on 12 March, Malenkov had rejected the continuation of the East–West conflict; he had expressed his belief that a war fought with modern weapons of mass destruction would spell the end of all civilization. He called for the easing of East–West tension and negotiations to overcome 'the so-called Cold War', which he believed would almost inevitably lead to a new world war. Nothing like this had ever been heard from Moscow before; historian David Holloway believes that Malenkov had been deeply impressed by the massive American H-bomb explosion on 1 March and the speech was testimony to this.[65] However, the CPSU's Central Committee, in particular Molotov and Khrushchev, subsequently decided that Malenkov's statement had gone too far and he had to revert to a more traditional declaration in late April. In early 1955, after Malenkov had been relieved of his post as Chairman of the Council of Ministers (and thus of his post as Prime Minister as it was seen in the West), Khrushchev declared that the speech had been 'theoretically mistaken and politically harmful'.[66]

Although Eisenhower, referring to Churchill's summit diplomacy during a press conference in early March 1954, had said that he had disagreed with the Prime Minister on this topic before and failed 'to see at this moment what good could come out of it', Churchill decided to ignore this clear indication that his policy was still not welcome in Washington.[67] Instead he stuck to his intention of convening a meeting of the heads of government of the 'Big Three' as soon as possible. In contrast to his proposals presented in the immediate aftermath of Stalin's death, Churchill now declared that only one major topic should be debated at such a summit: the enormous dangers connected with atomic warfare and the possibility of cooperation in the field of atomic energy.[68]

Without disputing Churchill's genuine concern over the hydrogen bomb, this much more concrete proposal for the calling of a summit conference was inspired at least in part by tactical considerations. The Prime Minister was skilfully connecting his policies with Eisenhower's 'Atoms for Peace' speech before the United Nations the previous December: how could the President possibly reject a proposal for a great power conference that was based on his very own suggestion of five months ago? Churchill appeared to believe that the dangers of the hydrogen bomb could bring East and West to the negotiating table.

The Indochina War and Eisenhower's Interest in Meeting Churchill

In mid-April 1954 the American Secretary of State paid a brief visit to London. He primarily intended to discuss the war in Indochina with Eden but he also passed on an interesting message from the President. He told the British that Eisenhower had briefly considered whether he should initiate a meeting with

Churchill and Eden in Newfoundland, but had decided against it, due to the 'crisis atmosphere' it would have caused.[69] Although Churchill may well still have been 'sore over the rebuff Eisenhower gave him at Bermuda',[70] this was the opening Churchill had been waiting for.

On 16 April he instructed the British embassy in Washington to find out Eisenhower's schedule over the coming months,[71] and already on 22 April he wrote to the President saying that he would like to arrange a detailed discussion with him. As he had learnt that Eisenhower would be in Washington between 20 and 24 May and did not seem to have any important engagements, this might perhaps be an ideal opportunity to embark on Anglo-American talks. However, Churchill had proposed an awkward time: the Geneva conference was to open on 26 April and might well last much longer than mid-May, a fact of which the Prime Minister seems to have been unaware. Churchill did not elaborate on the topics he planned to discuss with Eisenhower in Washington,[72] but it was clear that the Prime Minister's main objective was still to persuade Eisenhower of the necessity of a meeting with Malenkov.[73] Much to the surprise of the officials in London and Washington, the President replied by expressing his interest in a meeting. However, what he had in mind was not a discussion of Churchill's tiresome summit policy. Instead he wanted to discuss a very different and in his view much more pressing issue: the increasingly dangerous developments in the Far East.[74]

The military position of the French in Indochina, where they had been fighting the Communist nationalists with American financial aid since 1946, had become increasingly hazardous since January 1954. As Dulles had made explicit in a speech on 29 March, Washington was in favour of the 'united action' of a large coalition army of various western and Far Eastern states to help the French out of their predicament. It was to be expected that Congress would refuse to give its approval to any unilateral intervention by Washington, and the American military was less than enthusiastic about getting involved in Vietnam.[75]

Dulles believed that during his discussions with Eden in London in mid-April he had persuaded the British to participate in a joint Anglo-American enterprise, and thus in direct military intervention in Indochina, and to agree to the build-up of a South-East Asian defensive organization.[76] 'The dual approach of seeking united action and working to obtain congressional approval' was Eisenhower's method of managing the Dien Bien Phu crisis. Since early March 1954 the 13,000 forces strong French military base at Dien Bien Phu in north-west Vietnam was besieged by almost 50,000 Viet Minh forces who encircled the base, which could only be supplied by air, ever more tightly.[77] However, it soon became clear that London had no plans to participate in military action in Vietnam. The British government feared that the war would spread and that Washington might even be considering the employment of atomic bombs.[78] The British refusal led to a considerable increase of tension between London and Washington and especially between Eden and Dulles. The Secretary of State felt betrayed by Eden, who in his view had promised British military participation in the war in Indochina during his visit to London in mid-April.[79] Yet according to Eden the British 'were at no time willing to support such action'.[80]

Due to the escalating crisis in the Far East, Eisenhower took a more open-minded view with regard to conducting discussions with Churchill. The President's readiness to meet the Prime Minister had nothing to do with summit diplomacy and everything to do with the situation in Indochina. Eisenhower thus suddenly became unusually flexible. 'I agree with you,' he wrote to Churchill on 23 April, 'that it is high time that we make certain of our common understanding of current and impending events.'[81] Eisenhower's change of mind was so surprising to the British that initially even Churchill was quite unsure as to whether Eisenhower was genuinely willing to embark on bilateral talks.[82]

In fact, the President was much less interested in talking to Churchill than in negotiating with Eden, the future Prime Minister, but Eisenhower was certain that Churchill would not allow the Foreign Secretary to go to Washington without him, whatever the American administration would say. It was also essential to avoid the possibility that Churchill might appear in Washington without Eden. Eisenhower expressed to British ambassador Makins his hope that Eden would definitely accompany the Prime Minister. Makins reported to Eden, who was undoubtedly flattered, that the President thought it would be 'much more satisfactory from every point of view', if he were with the Prime Minister throughout the conversation.[83]

It is not the case, as has been suggested, that the President 'showed some reticence' over a visit to Washington by the Prime Minister but that Churchill eventually succeeded in persuading him to take part in a bilateral meeting.[84] The exchange of letters between the President and the Prime Minister contradicts this view. As the military situation in Indochina became more critical, and the opposing positions of London and Washington and the increasing antagonism between Dulles and Eden more obvious, Eisenhower came to believe that only a personal meeting could overcome Anglo-American difficulties regarding Indochina.

On 4 April Eisenhower had dramatically informed Churchill that he feared 'that the French cannot alone see this thing through … If they do not see it through, and Indochina passes into the hands of the Communists, the ultimate effect on our and your global strategic position with the consequent shift in the power ratio throughout Asia and the Pacific could be disastrous'. The President believed that such a development 'would be a great threat to the whole free community, and that in our view this possibility should now be met by united action and not passively accepted'. Aware that Churchill viewed the policies of his glorious past as a model for the solution of contemporary problems, Eisenhower reminded him of the mistakes which had led to the Second World War: 'We failed to halt Hirohito, Mussolini and Hitler by not acting in unity and time.' Similar errors should not be made now.[85]

On 26 April, Eisenhower pressed the point, reminding Churchill that due to the 'drastic critical changes in the world situation'[86] and the 'seemingly wide differences' between London and Washington a meeting in the American capital would be desirable.[87] On 3 May Dulles stormed out of the Geneva meeting, and returned to Washington full of indignation that no compromise over Korea had been possible during the first phase of the conference. Throughout his stay in Geneva he had refused to meet the Chinese delegation; Eden explained in the House of Commons that the differences over Korea were 'very deep and were not to be reconciled'.[88]

Subsequently Washington sent Under-Secretary of State Bedell Smith to represent the USA in Geneva but Smith was also soon recalled to the US, leaving the third-ranking member of the American delegation in charge until Smith returned to the conference for the final few days. Dulles was also annoyed with Eden, who after consulting the Cabinet and the Chiefs of Staff in London had once again rejected military intervention in Indochina in spite of the perilous situation of the French at Dien Bien Phu. Moreover, during the conference proceedings Eden seemed to be getting on better with Molotov and Chinese Foreign Minister Chou En-lai than with his western allies.[89]

On 7 May, shortly before Indochina was to be discussed during the second phase of the Geneva conference, the French surrendered at Dien Bien Phu and the last major French fortress in Indochina fell into the hands of the Vietminh. The impossible had become reality: France had lost the war to the Chinese-supported Communist nationalists. Due to his refusal to send British troops to Indochina, Churchill was viewed in Paris as a '1954 version of Chamberlain at Munich'.[90]

A week later, on 12 May, Eisenhower wrote to Churchill proposing a meeting 'some time' in June; by then, more clarity would exist over the further course of the Geneva conference 'where I think a greater show of unity is essential'. The final analysis of the American hydrogen bomb tests would be completed and could also be discussed.[91] The date envisaged was 18 June, but due to the continuing and ever more difficult proceedings of the Geneva conference, at the beginning of June Eden suggested that the meeting with Eisenhower should be postponed by a week.[92] Churchill proposed to the Cabinet that he travel alone to the US, as Eden's presence in Washington was not really required. However, the British Cabinet was not impressed: nor were the Americans; Eden's participation was seen as vital in view of the complex situation in Geneva and the strained Anglo-American relationship. Above all, Eden would make sure that Churchill would not spring any surprise proposals on the Americans; the Prime Minister had to be kept under control.[93]

Although Churchill had certainly not lost hope of achieving a 'Big Three' summit meeting with Malenkov, the proceedings in Geneva had made him not only deeply concerned about global peace but also very worried about transatlantic relations. The Prime Minister felt he had no choice but to delay his retirement once again. In mid-June 1954, Churchill informed his Foreign Secretary, who was still in Geneva, that he could not possibly stand down in July as envisaged. The global political situation was too dangerous; his presence at the helm of British politics was required. He declared dramatically: 'I have a gift to make to the country, a duty to perform. It would be cowardly to run away from such a situation.'[94] He told Harold Macmillan, the Minister for Housing, that he could hardly negotiate successfully with Eisenhower 'with the sense of only having a few weeks more of power'. The Prime Minister also told his doctor that he intended to postpone his retirement until September,[95] and proposed 25 June to Eisenhower as the new date for the Washington meeting, as had been suggested by Eden.[96]

Once again the President showed considerable flexibility; after all he was greatly interested in making sure that the meeting would take place. Eisenhower was anxious to maintain good relations with Britain as events unfolded. In France, the Laniel government had fallen and the new Prime Minister, Pierre Mendès-France, who also acted as foreign minister, intended to arrive at a peace treaty on Indochina within four weeks or resign. Washington feared that to obtain Moscow's support for a compromise solution on Indochina, the new French Prime Minister might be willing to trade a successful outcome of the Geneva conference for the failure of the EDC.[97] Even at this late stage massive American military intervention in Indochina had not been ruled out entirely in the State Department and British support was still seen as crucial. Eisenhower therefore replied to Churchill: 'It is easy for me to make the change of one week'.[98]

During the exchange of letters with Eisenhower before his journey to Washington, Churchill did not mention his intention to use his visit to convince Eisenhower of the merits of a meeting with Malenkov. However, the American administration knew that Churchill would raise this topic for discussion.[99] And indeed, Lord Moran secretly wrote in his diary that the

Prime Minister still believed that if he 'can only talk with Malenkov he is sure things will happen'. Churchill's doctor believed: 'This idea has completely taken possession of him. It has indeed become an article of faith and is never out of his head for long.'[100] Although Churchill said the nuclear issue was the topic he wished to discuss in Washington, it is doubtful whether he did indeed succeed 'in obscuring his main purpose in Washington from the FO, Eden, and Eisenhower'.[101] In view of his past and indeed very recent utterances regarding the importance of an informal 'Big Three' summit, there could hardly be any doubt about what Churchill intended to achieve with his visit.

Moreover, in the days before the departure of the British delegation Churchill made little secret of his continued belief that all political problems in the world could be solved with the help of an international summit conference, as had been the case during the Second World War. It appeared to him that the Indochina question could also best be solved by a summit, instead of relying on the tiresome endeavours of foreign ministers and diplomats in Geneva. Churchill told his doctor to look up his speech on 11 May, where he would see how he 'gave warning that nothing can come of these talks at a lower level. They go on, day after day, endlessly. The Foreign Office keeps on splitting hairs. There is no one to say: "Bloody well go and do it". When I read what had happened at Geneva I felt a great sense of defiance. It was just like the war.'[102]

Neither the American nor the British officials expected that Churchill would attempt, as in 1953, to endanger the western integration of the Federal Republic of Germany in order to make progress with his summit diplomacy, nor did it seem necessary to draw up position papers dealing with Churchill's Locarno ideas. Despite this development in Churchill's thinking, which was regarded with much relief in Washington, the assessment dominated that 'Eden is O.K. and that if he were on his own we would have much less difficulty'.[103]

Nor was the Foreign Secretary misled about Churchill's real intentions but he was not too worried about curbing the Prime Minister this time. The prevailing mood was that 'No one, save Winston, seems to think that much will come out of this visit to Washington.'[104] Eden had come to the conclusion that the meeting in Washington might be useful after all. He hoped that Anglo-American differences over the Far East could be put aside and agreement on an Indochina solution might be possible.[105] After all, on 16/17 June 1954 a significant breakthrough had been reached at Geneva when the Chinese delegation had declared its readiness to agree to a ceasefire and to the partition of Indochina into a Communist and a western half. Soon afterwards it was agreed that the Geneva conference would go into recess.

On 20 June Eden returned to London via Paris, where he had lunch with Mendès-France. Soon afterwards he delivered a speech in the House of

Commons where he spoke favourably of Molotov and Chou En-lai and expressed cautious optimism that the 'long and difficult negotiations' in Geneva would lead to a mutually 'acceptable result'. While he said that he had 'worked closely together' with Bedell Smith, Eden did not mention Dulles's efforts in Geneva.[106] This did no go unnoticed in Washington. Moreover, in the course of his speech Eden even harked back to Churchill's speech of May 1953 by advocating a 'Locarno' for reaching a settlement in the Far East. Like Churchill on a European settlement, Eden believed that a solution to the Indochina problem ought to be supported by an 'international guarantee' by the great powers.[107]

The House of Commons was greatly impressed by Eden's speech. The Leader of the Opposition even used the opportunity to express his hope that the negotiations in Geneva would lead to a meeting with Malenkov and result in a genuine 'Big Three' summit conference, which Attlee proposed should take place in London. After all, why should the Prime Minister always have to go abroad; Churchill was fully entitled to be host of a 'Big Three' meeting.[108] The Prime Minister liked Attlee's pressure for a summit meeting; as Kenneth Harris has pointed out, this enabled Churchill to continue to claim that 'the country wanted one'.[109] None of this won approval in the United States. Dulles and the State Department regarded the Foreign Secretary's 'Locarno' proposal with great misgivings and Eden soon dropped the idea again.[110] In view of the strained 'special relationship,' it was timely that only a few days after Eden's speech and accompanied by their senior advisers, the Foreign Secretary and his Prime Minister set out on their visit to Washington.

Churchill's Final Visit to Washington as Prime Minister

From 25 to 29 June 1954 the British delegation was in the American capital.[111] Churchill's doctor believed that the journey to Washington had given the Prime Minister 'a new lease of life',[112] but the American participants noticed a distinct deterioration in Churchill's strength since the Bermuda conference. The President told his press official that 'The Prime Minister has moments when he does not seem to be entirely aware of everything that is going on. It is merely old age, but it is becoming increasingly more noticeable.'[113] Although Churchill was treated with the utmost courtesy and respect, Dulles and Eisenhower nonetheless directed most of their statements towards Eden. Eisenhower found it 'awfully difficult' to converse with Churchill. As the Prime Minister refused to use his hearing aid, the President needed to shout to make himself understood.[114] Yet the talks succeeded in improving Anglo-American relations; Eden and Dulles also managed to get on better with each other.[115] With regard to Indochina, Dulles gave his agreement to a solution on the basis of the country's partition; he no longer pressed for American and British military intervention.[116]

The EDC and the German rearmament question were also intensively discussed in Washington. Both the American and the British governments were becoming more and more impatient with French hesitation to ratify the EDC. Eisenhower described the French, who had not been invited to Washington, as 'a hopeless, helpless mass of protoplasm'.[117] Dulles declared that if the French parliament had not ratified the EDC by the summer break, consideration should be given to dissolving the connection between the Bonn and the EDC treaties. Perhaps the Bonn treaty should come into force immediately. Eden agreed in principle. The Federal Republic ought to have received its sovereignty by October 1954. Some recent comments by Mendès-France had confirmed most British diplomats in their opinion that it was highly unlikely that the EDC would ever be ratified in Paris.[118]

Churchill did not regret this. He still preferred a NATO solution to bring about German rearmament. He believed that 'We must not let ourselves imagine that if the EDC does fail, it is impossible to build up European security under NATO'.[119] Although Eisenhower did not share this view, he urged investigation of 'what must be done and what was feasible in the event the French failed to ratify this summer'. The politicians agreed to set up a joint Anglo-American working group in London to discuss alternatives to the EDC and deal with the question of how the link between the Bonn treaty and the EDC could be suspended. However, with regard to public opinion the conference participants believed that 'it would be extremely unwise to indicate that we were jointly considering alternatives to the EDC'.[120]

The actual German question itself, that is German reunification or even the neutrality of the country, was not discussed in Washington. This did not appear to be necessary in the aftermath of the Berlin conference. Nor did the continued exchange of notes with Moscow in recent months sway the conference participants. Instead, once again it was agreed that the irreversible integration of the Federal Republic with the West had to be brought about in the very near future.[121] This view was shared by Churchill. He no longer referred to undoing the partition of Germany and sacrificing the Federal Republic's integration with the West for a meeting with Malenkov.[122] All of his 1953 ideas on changing the western world's German policy appeared to be forgotten. In the months before his journey to Washington, Churchill had buried his Locarno proposals for good.

Perhaps this was the reason why the Prime Minister was a little more successful in his attempt to convince Eisenhower of the merits of a summit conference. Indeed, along with the President's pity for the rapidly deteriorating leader, the Prime Minister's change of attitude regarding the integration of the Federal Republic appears to have been the crucial factor in Eisenhower's more conciliatory position on the summit question. However, despite claims to the contrary in the literature, Churchill did not succeed in persuading the President to support his summit plans.[123] Eisenhower had simply begun to waver a little and had expressed his thoughts more hesitantly; he never indicated his agreement to Churchill's 'summitry'.

The President's more accommodating position was already evident on the first day of the talks in Washington. When Churchill suggested that 'summit diplomacy' be added to the list of topics proposed by the Americans, the President had no objections. Eisenhower even volunteered his own ideas on summit diplomacy without being prompted by Churchill. He reiterated that it would be impossible for him as both head of government and head of state to take part in an international conference over a relatively long period of time. Perhaps Dulles or Vice-President Nixon could participate in such a meeting. If matters developed successfully the President could attend during the final three or four days of such a conference.[124]

Churchill realized, of course, that in spite of the President's increased flexibility his ideas were still rather vague and that preparations for the kind of meeting Eisenhower had in mind would take up a good deal of time. He therefore proposed that it might be appropriate if he alone should initially undertake 'a first reconnaissance in force' to find out 'if anything promising developed'. Churchill explained that he was interested 'in finding out what sort of a man' Malenkov was who 'had never been outside his own country'. The Prime Minister 'believed there was a deep underlying demand on the part of the Russian people to enjoy a better life, particularly after suffering oppression for more than fifty years'.[125] However, Eisenhower was not impressed by Churchill's idea of a solitary pilgrimage to meet Malenkov. He evaded the issue by suggesting that Churchill should put his ideas down in writing, so that they could be considered in greater detail. John Colville's note in his diary that it was a 'first and vast surprise' for Churchill and himself when Eisenhower 'at once agreed to talks with the Russians'. This was a clear misinterpretation of the President's response.[126]

Churchill too was convinced of the correctness of this version of the events of the first day of his visit. According to Lord Moran, the Prime Minister was full of enthusiasm, believing that he had 'achieved some understanding with Ike about meeting the Russians'. Moran could 'think of nothing else' that would explain Churchill's elated mood.[127] Indeed, later that evening the Prime Minister expressed his great satisfaction with the proceedings; he believed that Eisenhower had more or less agreed to a summit conference with Malenkov.

He told his doctor that the day had been 'an incredible success. It is astounding how well things have gone ... This may lead to results which will be received by the world with a gasp of relief and amazement.'[128] The Prime Minister revealed his hope of travelling to Moscow in July. Although Eden would be asked to accompany him, Churchill assured his doctor: 'It is my show entirely. I have been working for this for a long time.'[129] Churchill also attempted to convince himself that it would be advantageous to meet Malenkov in the USSR rather than in a neutral country. He was still convinced, as he had explained to Eden earlier in the year, that 'one can get better treatment out of the Russians when you are on their ground than when they are on yours'.[130]

The following day, 26 June, Eisenhower returned to the subject. He was against holding a summit meeting in any country controlled by the Soviet Union but had no objections to Stockholm or London. Nonetheless the President attempted to persuade the Prime Minister to extend diplomatic feelers first and also to include France. Churchill was not convinced. He still intended to limit a summit conference to the 'Big Three': the Soviet Union, the US and Britain. 'Two is company, three is hard company, four is a deadlock', he declared. Churchill proposed to contact Malenkov directly. Eisenhower warned about giving the Soviet leader the opportunity of rejecting a western summit proposal and thereby allowing him 'to hit the free world in the face'. When he suggested that Churchill should use his age as the reason for entering into direct contact with Malenkov, the Prime Minister indignantly refused.[131]

In spite of Churchill's assurance, 'I swear to you that I will not compromise you in the slightest', Eisenhower was still not prepared to commit himself. Instead, he proposed that the Prime Minister discuss the matter with Dulles. In totally uncharacteristic fashion, the President declared that 'he was unsure as to exactly what was [the] right thing to do'. Eisenhower still feared that a summit with Moscow would lead to the emergence of great expectations. He reminded those present of his proposal to take part on the first day of the conference and perhaps be present during the final days, leaving Dulles and Vice-President Nixon to conduct the actual negotiations.[132] Anthony Seldon's conclusion that 'Churchill managed to charm Eisenhower into going at least some way with his plans' is understandable, but somewhat misleading.[133] The American President had not agreed to Churchill's idea of travelling alone on a reconnaissance mission. Nor had the convening of a 'Big Three' or 'Big Four' summit conference been agreed, though Churchill had decided to assume that such an understanding had been arrived at. Over dinner that night Churchill justified his long-standing preference for top-level negotiations by coining the memorable phrase: 'To jaw-jaw is always better than to war-war'.[134]

The following day, 27 June, Churchill had a lengthy discussion with Dulles. He explained to him that he would seek to convene a bilateral meeting with Malenkov in Stockholm in preparation for a three-power conference 'to see whether there were "consenting minds" '.[135] Dulles was less obliging and less courteous than the President. He told the Prime Minister that it would be 'extremely dangerous' to arrange such a meeting without being certain of success. The failure of an East–West meeting could even give the impression that the only other alternative was war. Dulles asked Churchill what concrete results he hoped to achieve and received the reply that Churchill was thinking of obtaining an Austrian peace treaty. Although the Prime Minister had spoken vaguely about this aim a number of times before, he had not acquainted himself with the complexities of Allied policy on the issue.[136] Churchill seemed to believe that professing to tackle the Austrian problem with the Soviets was less controversial than his 1953 suggestions on how to overcome the German question. Surprisingly, Churchill did not tell Dulles that he intended to talk to Malenkov about the dangers of the hydrogen bomb.

In any case, the Secretary of State was unimpressed by Churchill's reply. He declared that during the Berlin conference everything had been attempted to find a solution to the Austrian question. He was sceptical 'about the possibility of getting it by this method'. Dulles urged Churchill to weigh the matter 'very carefully … before any positive decision was made'. Later the Secretary of State conveyed his conclusion to his officials that Churchill 'was still obsessed with the idea of going to Moscow for a meeting … Of course, we are unalterably opposed to such a trip but it may be if we do not go, Churchill will go anyway.'[137]

In spite of Dulles's negative stance and in the absence of any firm agreement with Eisenhower, at the end of his final visit to Washington as Prime Minister, Churchill still believed that the President would not object to his proposed fact-finding mission to Moscow.[138] The Prime Minister persuaded himself (as well as his Private Secretary John Colville), that he had succeeded in gaining Eisenhower's approval for a visit to Malenkov.[139] Although the President's ambiguous statements had contributed to Churchill's belief, it was mainly a matter of wishful thinking. Moreover, Eisenhower's tendency to leave it to Dulles to present some unpleasant truths to Churchill may have given the Prime Minister the impression that though the tiresome Secretary of State continued to oppose his summit plans, the President himself objected much less to his policy and had eventually been persuaded by his weighty arguments to consent to an approach to Malenkov.[140] On the whole Churchill believed that he had 'never had a more agreeable or fruitful visit' and 'never had the feeling of general good will more strongly borne in upon him.'[141]

Above all, Churchill was aware that if he still wished to organize an international summit conference, the final opportunity had arrived. It was now or never. In view of his increasing health problems and the growing pressure on him from Eden and his Cabinet colleagues to retire, Churchill knew that he could not prolong his time as Prime Minister much longer. At this juncture it was Eisenhower's restraint and his lack of open resistance to his plans which convinced Churchill that he now had to take a calculated risk and approach Moscow if he wanted to succeed in his ultimate aim of overcoming the Cold War, maintaining Britain's great power role and making a final and enduring contribution to preserving world peace, thus ensuring his place in world history not only as a war leader but also as an international peacemaker.[142]

CHAPTER 16

At the End of the Day
Outrage in London, Consternation in Washington, and Disinterest in Moscow

Churchill regarded his visit to Washington as Prime Minister in late June 1954 as a personal triumph. He was convinced that he had succeeded in finally obtaining President Eisenhower's agreement to his summit diplomacy. Despite John Foster Dulles's negative comments, Churchill was certain that Eisenhower himself seemed to have been agreeable to his visiting Moscow and holding a bilateral Anglo-Soviet summit conference. Thus, despite the immense resentment and opposition he could expect to arouse in many circles in London and Washington, Churchill lost no time in approaching Moscow with a proposal for a bilateral 'parley at the summit'. He was firmly convinced that the time for the implementation of his summit diplomacy had finally arrived.

Contacting Moscow

On 30 June 1954, after a one-day stay in Canada, the British delegation returned to Britain. The Prime Minister had chosen to return home by sea from New York to Southampton as this would give him a few days' rest. Eden hoped to use the opportunity of the voyage to raise the succession issue with him. However, Churchill had different plans. Instead of unwinding, he began preparing his summit offensive on board the *Queen Elizabeth*. Ignoring Eden's serious doubts, the Prime Minister contemplated sending a telegram to Moscow to arrange his visit.[1] Surprisingly, he intended to send the message to Foreign Minister Molotov and not to Malenkov. So far no convincing explanation has been found for Churchill's reasoning.[2] After all, Churchill's counterpart in the Kremlin was not the Soviet Foreign Minister but rather the

Soviet head of government; moreover, Malenkov not Molotov was the person he had desired to meet since Stalin's death in March 1953.

Believing that Eisenhower had in principle agreed with his plan, Churchill was thinking of travelling to Moscow in early August. He told John Colville: 'Ike has crossed a gulf of thought. He has taken a very important step. He has made up his mind that Communism is not something which we must at all costs wipe out, but rather something we have got to learn to live with, and alongside.' To Churchill, 'peaceful coexistence' seemed to be the new code word of international affairs. The term had been used by Anthony Eden in his parliamentary speech on 23 June 1954 and soon became accepted western terminology.[3]

On 2 July Churchill dictated a long telegram addressed to Molotov. Even after the message had been revised and shortened, the Foreign Secretary still disapproved of the whole project. Eden feared that it would only lead to false expectations in the public mind. Moreover, he anticipated serious differences with the American government. The Foreign Secretary was not convinced that Eisenhower had agreed to Churchill's plans and he was well aware of John Foster Dulles's strong opposition to the Prime Minister's summit diplomacy. Coming on top of Anglo-American difficulties with regard to finding a solution to the war in Indochina, Eden feared negative consequences for the united western front against Moscow. The Foreign Secretary was also strongly opposed to Churchill's intention to send his telegram to Moscow without consulting the Cabinet. He thought the message to Molotov should be debated by the entire Cabinet; there did not seem to be any necessity to rush things. This would also allow him to hand the telegram in person to the Soviet Foreign Minister in Geneva, where the Indochina conference was to continue in a few days' time.[4]

The Prime Minister described Eden's objections as 'nonsense' and declared that his telegram represented merely an 'unofficial enquiry'. If Molotov agreed that he should visit Moscow, he would consult the Cabinet on whether or not to accept the invitation.[5] This meant of course that the members of the Cabinet would hardly be able to block Churchill's trip without antagonizing Moscow and embarrassing the Prime Minister. By encouraging Molotov to ask him to come to Moscow, the Prime Minister in fact committed the British government to accepting an invitation. Churchill brushed aside such counter-arguments. He declared that he planned to make the matter a vote of confidence: if the Cabinet were to reject his initiative, this would be the right time to stand down. Again, this was a rather dubious argument. Churchill was aware that the Conservative Party could not afford to bring about the retirement of the country's most distinguished international statesman in such circumstances. Such a scenario would lead to a serious crisis in Westminster and bestow on the new Eden government the reputation of not only being unappreciative of Churchill's past achievements, but also hostile to achieving a détente in the Cold War.[6]

Eventually, after a series of unpleasant arguments, Churchill and Eden agreed on an uneasy compromise. Churchill assured Eden on board the *Queen Elizabeth* that he would make the telegram available to the Cabinet if he could add that the Foreign Secretary agreed with the message to Molotov in principle. Although this did not reflect the view on the matter held by his heir apparent, 'Eden weakly gave in.' Yet Eden had only relented in order to ensure that the Prime Minister would retire immediately after his trip to Moscow. Churchill had solemnly promised his Foreign Secretary that he would resign from office on 21 September, following his visit to Malenkov.[7] However, as on previous occasions, the Prime Minister did not appear to mean what he had said. Only hours later he told his doctor: 'I do not think I shall retire … I don't think Anthony expects me to.' A couple of days later he wondered again whether or not to resign in mid-September after all,[8] but then he wavered and thought he would retire on 18 September though he 'would have liked to go on' as he had 'everything at my finger-tips. They are fools', he said; 'I can do it all so much better than anyone else.'[9]

On Saturday 3 July, the telegram with the proposed message to Molotov was sent to the Chancellor of Exchequer, Rab Butler, the most senior minister left in Britain.[10] Moran believed that Eden 'once more bowed to Winston's tenacity and strength of will'.[11] Colville, who had the unenviable task of mediating between the two politicians during the voyage home, shared this view. 'I am afraid the P.M. has been ruthless and unscrupulous in all this, because he must know at the moment, for both internal and international reasons, Eden cannot resign – though he told me, while all this was going on and I was acting as intermediary, that he had thought of it.'[12]

In London, the Foreign Office was appalled when Churchill's entirely unexpected message to Molotov arrived. The officials were determined that Churchill should not be allowed to travel to Moscow alone and without the agreement of the American government. In particular, it was unacceptable that the Prime Minister did not seem to be prepared to make the telegram to Molotov accessible to the Cabinet and the Foreign Office; instead he had sent it to Butler as a 'private and personal' communication. Following Churchill's telegram to Butler with the message to Molotov, the Foreign Office had just about succeeded in obtaining the Chancellor of the Exchequer's pledge to ask Churchill to delay sending his message to Moscow until after the Cabinet had been consulted when a second message from the Prime Minister arrived.

Churchill cunningly cabled Butler: 'Presume my message to the Bear has gone out. It in no way commits the Cabinet to making an official proposal. Time is important.'[13]

The Chancellor no longer dared to raise any further objections as he appeared to believe that 'this was A. E.'s way of holding the Prime Minister to his promise to retire, and did not feel he could interfere with that'.[14] Butler may also have felt that it might be disadvantageous to his own career to oppose the Prime Minister. He had secret hopes himself of being chosen as Churchill's successor, and had been encouraged by Churchill's frequent expressions of doubt as to whether Eden was really capable of succeeding him as Prime Minister.[15] Butler swiftly replied to Churchill's second telegram and made only very few suggestions on how to improve the communication. The Chancellor of the Exchequer 'appeared generally satisfied with the main idea'. He did, however, point out that Churchill's message sounded as though the Prime Minister planned to travel to Moscow. It would be better if the venue of the meeting was only vaguely mentioned so that a neutral country could be chosen.[16]

On board the *Queen Elizabeth* Churchill's mood improved after receipt of Butler's fairly tame reply. Once the Prime Minister had agreed to the alterations,[17] Butler relayed the telegram to Molotov on 4 July. Churchill's doctor was informed that Churchill no longer planned to travel to Moscow. He intended to meet Malenkov in Vienna to persuade him to sign an Austrian peace treaty. 'If that came off people would whoop with joy. I might pay a courtesy visit to Moscow after Vienna – perhaps staying forty-eight hours.'[18] In the telegram to Molotov, however, Churchill had only mentioned that he was thinking 'of a friendly meeting' without any firm agenda; he merely had the objective of finding 'a reasonable way of living side by side in growing confidence, easement and prosperity'. The meeting, wherever it might be, would only last a few days and would be 'simple' and 'informal'.[19] Shortly afterwards, ambassador Hayter in Moscow reported that when he handed over Churchill's note to Molotov, the Soviet Foreign Minister's only comment had been that 'he realized its importance and that there would be no delay in replying'.[20]

The Foreign Office in London continued to disapprove strongly of the telegram to Molotov. Frank Roberts, Anthony Nutting and Selwyn Lloyd were outraged and considered resigning. Ambassador Hayter was equally 'dismayed'. He regarded Churchill's message as superfluous. It could not be ruled out that Moscow might regard Britain as 'a negligible force' and that bilateral talks would therefore not be considered of great value; the Kremlin might well insist on the participation of the United States before committing itself to any talks. Thus, Churchill's suggestion might fall on deaf ears in Moscow which would be highly embarrassing.[21] Roberts and also Harold

Macmillan, the Minister of Housing and Local Government, cabled Eden on the *Queen Elizabeth* and informed him of the view of the Foreign Office and the potentially dire consequences of Churchill's activities for Britain's standing in international affairs.[22]

Not surprisingly, when the British delegation eventually arrived back in London on 6 July 1954, the Foreign Secretary was strongly reproached by his officials. It had been his task to keep Churchill under control in Washington and on the return voyage; they had not expected Eden to support the Prime Minister's unrealistic plans. The Foreign Office believed that Churchill was allowing himself to be deceived by the Soviet Union's peace campaign and the Kremlin's talk of 'peaceful coexistence'. The officials remained convinced that no major change had taken place in the Soviet Union since Stalin's death – the Kremlin was only interested in weakening the West's vigilance in order to neutralize Western Europe and embark on Moscow's ultimate objective of world revolution.[23] Evelyn Shuckburgh, until recently Eden's Private Secretary, was full of contempt for Eden's behaviour. 'It looks as though there was a compact,' he wrote in his diary, ' "You let me go to Malenkov and after that I will resign". What is to prevent everyone else – Adenauer, Tito – running after the Russians in Winston's wake?' Moreover, Eden had always sworn to him 'that the *one* thing he would not allow was a visit to Moscow without the Americans'.[24]

From the Foreign Office point of view, matters were made even worse by Molotov's answer. On 5 July the Soviet Foreign Minister sent a 'very friendly and encouraging reply' to the Prime Minister's enquiry and endorsed Churchill's travel plans.[25] The Foreign Minister declared that Churchill's proposal was being favourably considered and explained that he was looking forward to welcoming Churchill and Eden in Moscow. It might well be advantageous to convene a high-level summit conference to bring about an international détente. However, Molotov hinted at the fact that he attached importance to the presence of the United States.[26]

The British Cabinet only learnt of Churchill's initiative and Molotov's reply on the morning of 7 July, the day after the return of the British delegation from Washington.[27] Almost every minister was stunned and deeply dismayed. Conservative Party Chairman Lord Woolton and Harry Crookshank, the Leader of the House, threatened to resign.[28] The Minister for Commonwealth Affairs, Lord Swinton, and the Lord Chancellor, Lord Simonds, intended to ask the Queen to intervene to save the government from itself.[29] Lord Salisbury, whose relationship with Churchill had rapidly deteriorated since the autumn of 1953, declared that he was outraged and would resign if the project was pursued in the face of Eisenhower's objections. However, some of the Foreign

Office experts had realized that 'whatever Ike says, we are surely hooked; we cannot get out of it'.[30] For example the diplomat Harold Caccia recognized that after having antagonized the United States, there was the danger that London would also alienate Moscow. In the event of the Kremlin's acceptance of Churchill's proposal, the British government could no longer turn down a summit meeting. Churchill was bound by his word and Eden would, therefore, have to accompany him to Moscow. 'They are in a thorough mess.'[31] After all, it appeared as if the Soviet government might be highly interested in a meeting with Churchill held in Moscow. Moreover, when Frank Roberts mentioned in a conversation with Soviet ambassador Malik that the place and time of the meeting were still uncertain, the ambassador declared: 'time, yes, but the place is Moscow'.[32]

In view of the embarrassing disputes and the heightened tension among ministers, the Cabinet meeting was soon adjourned to await Washington's response to Churchill's initiative.[33] Immediately after the Cabinet meeting Churchill informed Eisenhower by letter of his communication with Molotov. He enclosed only an edited version of his note to the Soviet Foreign Minister so as not to anger the President, since he had taken the liberty of mentioning the likelihood of a three-power conference after a bilateral Anglo-Soviet meeting.[34] To all intents and purposes it seemed that the Prime Minister firmly expected that Eisenhower would support his initiative and that this would suffice in persuading the Cabinet to agree to his travel plans. Most Foreign Office officials also placed their hopes in Eisenhower: 'So there is hope still that Ike will bring us to our senses'.[35]

And indeed the American President was flabbergasted when he read Churchill's letter of 7 July and learned of the Prime Minister's message to Molotov.[36] Eisenhower replied instantly. According to Shuckburgh the President's response was 'about as scathing and negative as it could be without actually being rude'.[37] Eisenhower stressed that he had never agreed to such an initiative on the part of the Prime Minister during their meetings in Washington. He still considered that Churchill's initiative was inadvisable; the President was quite annoyed about the Prime Minister's activities and he told him so. 'You did not let any grass grow under your feet. When you left here, I had thought, obviously erroneously, that you were in an undecided mood about this matter, and that when you had cleared your own mind I would receive some notice if you were to put your program into action.' The American media would undoubtedly suspect that Churchill's initiative had been discussed during his Washington visit and would assume that he had received the approval of the American government. Thus Eisenhower felt that he would 'probably' have to say 'something to the effect that while you were here the possibility of a Big Three Meeting was discussed'. Yet, the President believed that he had to state that he was unable to 'see how it could serve a useful purpose at this time' and that he had told Churchill that if he 'did undertake such a mission, your plan would carry our hopes for the best but would not engage our responsibility'.[38]

Cabinet Crisis in London

Churchill was very disappointed by Eisenhower's letter. In a special Cabinet meeting on 8 July 1954, during which the President's reply was read out, the Prime Minister announced that he had prepared another message to Eisenhower. He hoped that 'a more favourable response might be elicited from the President'. Churchill proposed to the Cabinet not to take a final decision before Eisenhower had replied to his second letter. The Prime Minister also felt that he had to make it clear that he did not intend to accept an invitation to travel to Moscow. Instead, he would try to meet the Soviet head of government on neutral ground.[39]

During the Cabinet meeting of 8 July Churchill was on the defensive. He was strongly criticized for not having delayed sending the telegram until the Cabinet had been consulted. Salisbury once again threatened to resign and asked Churchill 'Was the message so urgent?' Churchill had to admit that 'he might have taken an exaggerated view of the urgency of the matter'. He attempted to talk his way out of the embarrassing situation by insisting that his letter had simply been an informal message to Molotov, the kind of message he had frequently sent to foreign governments during the war. This had in no way infringed upon the Cabinet's freedom of decision. Moreover, he claimed that Eden had given his approval to the message on board the *Queen Elizabeth*.[40]

Whereas Churchill attempted to divert some of the criticism to Eden, the Foreign Secretary tried to pass the blame to Butler, claiming that the Chancellor should have attempted to consult some of his colleagues. However, Butler managed to argue convincingly that he had received the impression that Churchill was not interested in consulting the Cabinet as most of its members were dispersed over the whole country that weekend.[41] This, of course, was essentially correct and most Cabinet members knew it. And indeed a few days later Churchill confirmed this general impression when he told his Private Secretary in confidence that he had intentionally refrained from consulting the Cabinet before sending the telegram to Molotov. 'He admitted to me if he had waited to consult the Cabinet after the *Queen Elizabeth* had returned, they would almost certainly have raised objections and caused delays.'[42]

During the Cabinet meeting on 8 July Eden suggested that it would be 'much more natural' if, after the Geneva conference, Molotov and he were to go on a short trip to Berne and take up bilateral Anglo-Soviet discussions together with Churchill and Malenkov.[43] Churchill incorporated Eden's proposal in his letter to Eisenhower of the same day. The Prime Minister also informed the President of his hope that he would be able to obtain a promise from Moscow to complete an Austrian peace treaty 'to liberate Austria and Vienna from Russian military domination'. If he succeeded, it might perhaps be meaningful to convene a summit conference of the three or four great powers in London. To appease Eisenhower, Churchill no longer even excluded the participation of France. He also mentioned that the joint use of atomic energy for peaceful purposes, the topic of Eisenhower's speech to the UN in December 1953, should be discussed during the meeting in Berne.[44]

Once again Eisenhower replied immediately. However, this time he wrote a fairly mellow letter and he even politely reassured the Prime Minister of his complete faith in him. The President appeared to have resigned himself to the fact that Churchill's plans could no longer be prevented.[45] However, he still did not agree with the Prime Minister's intention, and a few days later pointed out to him that he was unsure what the response of American public opinion would be. He hoped that most Americans would generally accept Churchill's 'sincerity and lofty motivations', even though they would hardly take them seriously. In fact, the President was quite insulting when he told Churchill that the majority of the American public would probably consider his plan as a 'noble experiment' in the way they had also viewed the less than successful experiment with Prohibition during the interwar years.[46]

On 9 July another Cabinet meeting took place in London to deal with Churchill's initiative. Macmillan described the meeting in his diary as 'the most dramatic Cabinet which I have attended'.[47] The Prime Minister read out another draft letter to Eisenhower which he had just completed. He repeated his intention to obtain a sign of goodwill from Moscow, such as the signing of an Austrian treaty, before a 'Big Three' or 'perhaps' a 'Big Four' summit meeting was to be convened, and promised to keep the President informed of any initiative.[48] Salisbury was not impressed and once again threatened to resign. Churchill again proposed waiting for Eisenhower's response and not taking any final decisions on the matter for the time being. The Cabinet agreed to this. It also appeared wise to await the outcome of the Geneva Indochina conference. If the US were to distance itself from the outcome of the conference, a bilateral Anglo-Soviet meeting would give the impression of a deep rift between London and Washington. On the other hand, a meeting with Malenkov might well have a reassuring effect on public opinion if no agreement had been reached in Geneva. Under most difficult circumstances, Churchill succeeded in rescuing his initiative for the time being.[49]

Harold Macmillan, like many other senior members of the government, had come to the conclusion that Churchill was 'now quite incapable – mentally as well as physically – of remaining Prime Minister'. He believed that Churchill's judgement was 'distorted': 'He thinks about one thing all the time – the Russian visit and his chance of saving the world – till it has become an obsession.'[50] The combined resistance of the Cabinet, Eisenhower, the Foreign Office and Eden compelled Churchill to act with considerable caution. Nonetheless, it was clear that the crisis in London had not been resolved. Lord Salisbury was still threatening resignation. Churchill declared that 'he didn't give a damn' but he and others convinced Salisbury to delay such a drastic step since Churchill was unlikely to remain in office much longer while a resignation would damage Eden's ability to take over smoothly.[51] The Foreign Office had already reluctantly begun drafting position papers in preparation for a bilateral meeting with Malenkov. However, there was still a consensus among the officials that such an event entailed great dangers as a 'failure to achieve any concrete results does not simply leave matters where they stand but in a much worse and more dangerous position'.[52]

On 12 July Churchill explained the results of his visit to Washington to the House of Commons. He was however careful not to be tempted into giving anything away about his approach to Molotov or the crisis atmosphere in his government.[53] On the same day Eden returned to Geneva for the continuation of the Indochina conference. By way of sceptical comments from Geneva, which were mostly based on confidential talks with Molotov, Eden attempted to undermine Churchill's plans and lend greater credibility to the opposition of the Foreign Office, though the Prime Minister failed to be impressed by Eden's arguments.[54]

Immediately on arriving in Geneva, the Foreign Secretary mentioned the Prime Minister's telegram to Molotov. The Soviet Foreign Minister did not show much interest in the matter. When Eden explained that London would not accept a conference venue in the Soviet Union but would prefer a neutral country, Molotov declared 'that he must tell me frankly that his Government had not as yet considered questions of time and place'. In any case, before all else, the outcome of the Geneva conference would have to be awaited.[55] Eden once again recommended to the Prime Minister to drop the entire project as the Soviet government did not seem to be interested: 'You will have seen from my telegram No.943 that the Russians may not themselves be keen for such a meeting at the present time, since they may well calculate that the prospects of compromises and wedge-driving are not present. On our side, there is also the risk that if such a meeting took place and failed, the state of our relations would be left even worse than before. I would therefore myself be against pressing them if they show any hesitation.'[56]

Churchill, however, did not heed Eden's advice. A day after, on 13 July, in yet another Cabinet meeting, Churchill declared that Molotov, during his talks with Eden in Geneva, had in no way ruled out a bilateral summit in London or Berne. Churchill also told the Cabinet about a more positive letter from Eisenhower; the President seemed to be happy with the Prime Minister's course of action as decided during the Cabinet meeting on 9 July. Churchill still did not dare to push for a decision in the matter and the meeting was adjourned again.[57]

Meanwhile Churchill had banished all thoughts of retirement.[58] This fact, along with the danger that the Cabinet threatened to break apart as Salisbury was still talking about resigning, compelled Macmillan to approach Lady Churchill on 16 July and ask her to influence her husband in the matter. Together with John Colville she did indeed succeed in making Churchill realize that Salisbury's resignation would have serious consequences for the survival of the government and for the public image of the Conservative Party.[59]

Nevertheless, Churchill continued to be preoccupied with how to persuade his Cabinet colleagues to agree to another message to Molotov. He even wrote to Eden in Geneva, cheekily asking for his assistance. However, Eden had learned his lesson from the episode on board the *Queen Elizabeth*. He bluntly told Churchill that he could not support him:

> As I have repeatedly told you I do not myself believe that anything of any value will be gained from such a meeting. I am more than ever convinced of it since my recent conversation with Molotov. You, however, continue to believe that it can serve some useful purpose and that with your authority some result can be achieved and wish to make the attempt. If that is still your determination … I consider that you should have the chance to do this, as long as the meeting is not on Russian soil. But I cannot pretend tomorrow to the Cabinet that I like it.[60]

Hardly ever had Eden been so frank with Churchill. He also managed to persuade Bedell Smith to visit Churchill in London on his way back from Geneva. While Churchill tried to impress on his American visitor the importance of accomplishing an Austrian treaty and engaging in a 'final try for peaceful co-existence' by means of negotiations with Malenkov, Smith was mindful of majority leader Knowland's warning against the 'Trojan horse of coexistence'.[61] Smith explained to the Prime Minister that Malenkov 'was not actually filling Stalin's shoes'. Smith thought that Molotov's influence was currently much greater than Malenkov's but the Soviets 'were trying to get along without a supreme "boss"'. When Smith asked Churchill what he would do if the Soviets were only prepared to meet in Moscow, the Prime Minister said that 'he did not know' and 'this would have to be thought over'.[62] Churchill still seemed to be quite prepared to go to Moscow.

On the whole, Eisenhower's confidant came to the conclusion that Churchill was as stubborn as ever but was now both physically and mentally on his last legs. Smith was most disconcerted that Churchill did not understand that he had come from Geneva and not from Washington. Despite several attempts at explaining this to him, Churchill mentioned five times his astonishment that Smith had made the long journey from America for such a brief visit.[63]

The crucial Cabinet meeting regarding the future of the government and Churchill's summit plans took place on the last weekend in July, immediately after the Geneva conference had been successfully concluded on 21 July, with the agreement to partition Vietnam into a western and Communist half and to hold all-Vietnamese elections in 1956. It had thus been demonstrated that it was not impossible to reach a deal with Molotov.[64] Credit for achieving a constructive outcome of the Geneva conference on Indochina was largely due to Anthony Eden, who had thus scored an impressive diplomatic victory. Before the Cabinet meeting on 23 July Churchill told his doctor: 'Today's Cabinet will be decisive. They must support me or I shall go.'[65]

Churchill had not been persuaded to drop his plans by Eden's report of his discussion with Molotov on the last day of the Geneva conference. During the conversation between the two foreign ministers it had become clear, at least according to Eden's subsequent report, that Moscow had still no more than polite interest in Churchill's proposal.[66] Not surprisingly, during the Cabinet meeting on Friday, 23 July, 'a flaming row' developed.[67] Eden opposed Churchill's journey to Moscow; Salisbury, supported by Harry Crookshank, once again threatened to resign; an outraged Prime Minister also talked about resigning. The fate of the government appeared to be hanging on a thread.[68]

Moreover, Churchill proceeded to inform the Cabinet of the telegram that he wanted to send to Molotov as a reply to the latter's message of 5 July. Eden had actually helped him to draft the message. The Prime Minister intended to propose a bilateral meeting in Berne, Stockholm or Vienna. He did not forget to attempt to appease his colleagues by adding 'that other ministers, besides the Prime Minister and the Foreign Secretary, might attend'. However, the Cabinet indignantly rejected Churchill's proposal to send the telegram to Molotov marked 'personal and private'. Once again the constitutional aspects of Churchill's telegram to Molotov dated 3 July were discussed. The Prime Minister strongly rejected the charge of 'any constitutional impropriety'.

Eventually Macmillan proposed, with the support of several other ministers, that the Cabinet should no longer concern itself with the past but should concentrate on the future.[69]

However, Lord Salisbury explained that it was not only the constitutional aspects that worried him but also the international consequences of Churchill's plans. In his view world peace was less threatened by the Soviet Union than by the danger of the US succumbing to the temptation of using its atomic supremacy to exercise a preventive attack on Moscow. For this reason the main task of the British government ought to be the preservation of 'the unity and coherence of the Atlantic Alliance'. Only then would London be able to influence American decision-making. Churchill's plan should therefore be rejected. After all, he explained: 'Could we expect the Americans to respect the unity of that Alliance if, without their agreement, we embarked on bilateral discussions with the Russians? Was there not a great risk that they would thereby be encouraged to pursue independent policies and to take less account of our views on international affairs?'[70]

Eden tried to play for time. While he was opposed to Churchill's plan, he claimed somewhat ambiguously that he was prepared to accompany him if he insisted on journeying to Moscow. The Foreign Secretary recommended that the decision should again be postponed. As Salisbury had already pointed out, the Soviet reaction to the outcome of the Geneva conference had only been published that morning and appeared to indicate that Moscow was intensifying its anti-American propaganda. If this was the case, Eden believed, London could not take part in a bilateral meeting. The Foreign Secretary wanted time to study the Soviet comments in greater detail. Eden also pointed out that Moscow might well publish the exchange of notes with Churchill, and he had therefore most reluctantly decided to support convening a meeting with Moscow. The British government would 'be put in an embarrassing position if it were disclosed that, having made this offer, we had then withdrawn it'.[71]

The Foreign Secretary recommended that a second telegram be sent to Molotov. Perhaps it would be advantageous if London proposed that further members of the collective leadership should participate in the conference. Eden expressed the hope that it could not be ruled out that Moscow might reject a meeting if Britain were to insist on a venue outside the Soviet Union. Any additional telegram to Molotov would automatically become the responsibility of the entire Cabinet. The public, as well as the Kremlin, would in any case hold the whole Cabinet responsible, irrespective of the type of correspondence.

Eden's proposal was met with general approval. The Cabinet agreed to ask the Prime Minister to convey a further message to Molotov 'as this project had now been carried so far'. It was decided, however, that before such a message was sent, members of the government should be given the opportunity to use the weekend to reflect on the issue. Thus, the Cabinet meeting was once again adjourned.[72]

Paradoxically, it was the Soviet Union that unwittingly helped the British government to escape from the dilemma created by Churchill. On Saturday, 24 July, Moscow sent a note to the three western powers and China proposing a conference of all European states and the United States and China (as observers) at foreign ministers' level to talk about questions concerning European security including German reunification. This was a suggestion Molotov had already submitted in the course of the Berlin conference but the Soviets had not pursued the issue afterwards.[73]

The West concluded that the Kremlin's surprising proposal had the aim of preventing, or at least considerably delaying, the realization of the EDC and thus the integration of the Federal Republic into the West. Moreover, Moscow had merely repeated the unacceptable ideas on European security and the German question which the West had already rejected at Berlin. Further, the preparation and holding of the proposed multilateral conference would take many months. It could be expected that it would prove difficult to achieve a consensus in negotiating with so many different nations; and even if this could be reached, all participating states would still have to ratify the negotiated treaties. Thus, years of uncertainty would lie ahead if the Soviet proposal were accepted. There was no hope of ratifying the EDC while multilateral negotiations over a fundamental reform of the European power system were in progress. The West, therefore, assumed that the Soviet proposal aimed at further delaying the implementation of the EDC; this was clearly unacceptable.[74]

Even Churchill had to admit that the initiative appeared to represent the beginning of a new Soviet propaganda campaign. It was clear to both Churchill and the Cabinet that in view of the Soviet offensive the British Prime Minister could no longer participate in a bilateral meeting with the Soviet head of government. Churchill commented: 'Foreign Secretaries of the world unite; you have nothing to lose but your jobs.'[75] Clearly, he assumed that Molotov had done his best to torpedo a summit conference which would give increased prestige to Malenkov. Churchill, of course, also knew that Eden was not unhappy either about the need to shelve the envisaged summit meeting for the time being.

Together Churchill and Eden formulated a new telegram to Molotov. The Prime Minister intended to tell the Soviet foreign minister that he had no choice but to postpone the proposed meeting with Malenkov until the question of Moscow's suggested multilateral conference had been clarified. Churchill also wished to inform Molotov that he had been about to propose a bilateral meeting for the end of August or the beginning of September. However, Moscow's proposal for a conference on European security questions, 'which I presume the heads of government would not be expected to attend', did not match his expectations for an informal meeting with Malenkov which could have led to a 'Big Three' summit conference.[76]

During a calm and peaceful meeting on Monday, 26 July, the Cabinet agreed to this plan of action.[77] The day after, Churchill made a vague statement in the House of Commons to the effect that the government needed a little time to consider the Soviet note.[78] Although in his telegram of 31 July Molotov attempted to persuade Churchill that the bilateral Anglo-Soviet meeting did not need to await the proposed European security conference, the Prime Minister felt he could not relent.[79] The British Cabinet crisis had been resolved in an unexpected way. Evelyn Shuckburgh commented that the Churchill government being saved from its 'own embarrassment by a clumsy action on the part of the Soviets' was 'quite like old Stalin times. I do not understand why Malenkov and Molotov have let us off so lightly.'[80]

So far scholars have not been able to answer this question. It is still unclear why Molotov did not delay sending the note concerning a security conference to the western powers. After all, he must have expected that Churchill would shortly propose a date for a bilateral meeting. Eden had personally told him this in Geneva on 21 July.[81] Through his diplomatic and intelligence channels, Molotov must also have been aware of the fierce arguments in the western camp over Churchill's 'summitry'.

It is likely that the Kremlin's deep distrust of Churchill had made the Soviet Union doubt the seriousness of the British Prime Minister's summit diplomacy. A comment by Soviet diplomat Rodionov appears to hint at this. In the course of a talk with Frank Roberts in mid-August 1954, Rodionov made the surprising admission that Moscow was partly responsible for Churchill's 'summitry' not becoming reality. '[Rodionov] indicated that the Russian leaders were by no means sure what the Prime Minister really wanted to do at such a meeting and, with their naturally suspicious outlook, were reluctant to commit themselves to something the outcome of which they could not quite foresee.' On the whole, Roberts reported, Rodionov appeared to be surprised by his own country's action. Western diplomats concluded that originally the Kremlin had favoured a meeting with Churchill but then the issue had been reconsidered in Moscow – perhaps due to Malenkov's waning influence.[82] Thus the continuing leadership battle in Moscow for Stalin's mantle contributed to Molotov's unwillingness to allow Malenkov to enjoy the media attention which a meeting with Churchill would undoubtedly bring.[83] Both Moscow's continuing deep mistrust of Churchill as well as Molotov's efforts to prevent any event which would enable Malenkov to play a prominent role on the international stage and thus gain a more advantageous position in the leadership battle in the Kremlin were responsible for Moscow not being prepared to meet Churchill half-way.

London and Washington, however, were vastly relieved at the failure of Churchill's summit plans. Even the Prime Minister did not appear to be too unhappy. He had not expected so much opposition to his travel plans and had certainly not anticipated that his government might break apart over the issue. There are also indications that in the light of the formidable American opposition to his plans and with his deteriorating health Churchill was even somewhat relieved that his initiative had come to nothing; all sorts of difficulties with Washington could be avoided, while no one could blame him for not having tried hard enough. In early July Churchill had confided to his doctor that if his approach to Moscow were to fail, 'then with a clear conscience and an easy mind I can go to my Maker'.[84] A few weeks later John Colville wrote in his diary that Churchill, 'feeling that he has at least made the effort and is justified as far as his frequent policy statements over the last two years are concerned, is content – at least on the surface. Lord Salisbury is smiling again.'[85]

Thus, by the end of July 1954 Churchill's final major attempt to bring about a bilateral meeting with Malenkov and a subsequent 'Big Three' summit conference had ended in failure. Churchill tried to ignore this fact for a further few months; he continued speaking of the importance of a 'parley at the summit', and on 3 August, in yet another memorandum to the Cabinet, he even referred to the urgent necessity for a meeting with Malenkov. However, the likelihood of ever achieving his post-war dream was now quite remote.[86]

CHAPTER 17

A Prolonged Farewell
Churchill's Last Months as Prime Minister

Following the effective defeat of his summit diplomacy in July and August 1954, the question of the Prime Minister's resignation came to the fore. Even President Eisenhower gently pointed out to Churchill that it was time to go. In a letter of late July 1954, Eisenhower reminded Churchill that during their talks in Washington he had mentioned his intention 'to shift the responsibility of the Premiership to other shoulders'. As he assumed that Churchill would want to make one final statesmanlike gesture of lasting value, which after all had been one of the underlying factors of his summit policy, the President proposed to him 'a thoughtful speech on the right of self-government'.[1] The Prime Minister, Eisenhower wrote, would 'electrify the world' if he announced that the independence of the colonies ought to be achieved within twenty-five years. If the colonial peoples were provided with material and educational assistance, the American President seemed to believe, they would 'cling more tightly to the mother country and be a more valuable part thereof' and such a development would be immensely helpful to the West in the Cold War.[2]

However, the proposed topic was not to Churchill's liking; after all, he still believed firmly in the value of the British Empire. He therefore replied to Eisenhower that he was 'a bit sceptical about universal suffrage for the Hottentots even if refined by proportional representation'. Churchill declared that he liked to give priority to 'The Unity of the English-speaking peoples'. Eisenhower concluded: 'My steel struck no spark from his flint.'[3]

Churchill was hurt by Eisenhower's hint that it was time to think about retirement. The longer he thought about life without office and politics, the worse he felt. The Prime Minister therefore attempted to find all kinds of excuses as to why he should not retire in September 1954, as he had envisaged only a short while before. When he said he would like to stay in office in order to be able to receive the national and international congratulations on his 80th birthday on 30 November, his colleagues found it hard to argue. He also indicated that he might even contest another general election or form a coalition government with Labour or the Liberals.[4] His Private Secretary John Colville summarized the ageing leader's feelings: 'As the days went by he became less reconciled to giving up office and adumbrated all sorts of reasons why he should not.'[5] No wonder that Churchill detested the portrait painted by Graham Sutherland which the House of Commons presented to him on his birthday. He believed that the painting depicted him as a drunkard unfit for high office; his wife later destroyed the picture.[6]

During Churchill's remaining nine months as Prime Minister he attempted several times to revive his summit diplomacy; yet, all his efforts came to nothing. Four major factors prevented a renewed summit offensive by the Prime Minister: the visit by a Labour Party delegation to Moscow; the failure of the EDC; Malenkov's fall from power; and not least his own deteriorating health and pressure by his colleagues to consider retirement.

The End of a Dream

Late on the evening of 10 August 1954 a delegation of the British Labour Party led by Clement Attlee arrived in Moscow. Although the delegation's desti-nation was Beijing, where they were to explore Mao's policy towards South-East Asia, they had decided to slot in a two-day stay in the Soviet capital. Attlee and his delegation, as well as ambassador Hayter, were invited to dinner with Malenkov and other leading Soviet politicians on 10 and 11 August. Numerous topics in international politics were discussed. However, Churchill's summit diplomacy was not mentioned at all.[7]

Churchill was deeply frustrated about Attlee's trip. What the incumbent head of government had failed to achieve during his last two years in office, former Prime Minister Attlee had managed to effect without any great problems. 'There would have been an outburst of joy if I'd seen Malenkov,' Churchill declared to his doctor. 'Now Attlee has done it'.[8] He now tried again to find ways to enter into talks with Moscow. After all, Attlee was merely Leader of the Opposition; it would be of much greater importance if the head of government of one of the leading western nations was to meet his Soviet counterpart. Moreover, the Labour delegation's visit to Moscow had not resulted in any new insights about Soviet policy. Thus, on 18 August Churchill submitted yet another memorandum to the Cabinet, the second within two

weeks, regarding a meeting with Malenkov. He was convinced that such an
event would be much appreciated by the British public.[9] The West had
formally rejected the Soviet proposal for a multilateral European security
conference on 10 September and Churchill felt free to revive his attempts to
enter into a constructive dialogue with Malenkov.[10]

However, Churchill had to postpone his summit diplomacy once again. This
time it was the failure of the EDC that prevented another big summit
initiative. When Mendès-France visited Chartwell on 23 July, he failed to elicit
any support from the Prime Minister for a wholesale reconsideration of the
entire EDC treaty; any delay in ratifying the EDC would also mean a
postponement of Churchill's efforts to bring about a meeting with Malenkov.[11]

On 30 August 1954 the EDC was effectively rejected by the French National
Assembly, throwing the western alliance into turmoil. The rearmament and
the sovereignty of the Federal Republic and the entire European integration
process needed to be reconsidered. West German Chancellor Adenauer called
it a 'black day' for Europe, and Eisenhower and Dulles were equally depressed.[12]
In this crisis situation a revival of Churchill's 'summitry' was unthinkable since
a bilateral Anglo-Soviet summit would have created even more instability in
the western alliance. It would certainly prevent the success of the precarious
negotiations to find an alternative solution which Eden, Dulles, Adenauer and
other western politicians were to conduct with Mendès-France.[13]

Although C.D. Jackson, Eisenhower's former speech writer, continued to be
concerned about Churchill's 'summitry' and his apparent inclination to
appease the Russians,[14] it was Eden's attempts to find an alternative to the EDC
which dominated the following months. During two rapidly convened conferences in London and Paris in September and October 1954, and by way of an
earlier whirlwind journey through the European capitals, Eden was able to
convince his partners to agree to West German membership of NATO on a
non-discriminatory basis. This was the solution to the German rearmament
question which had always been preferred by Britain.[15] French agreement was
won after the negotiation of Bonn's prior admission to the Western European
Union (WEU). This was the renamed Brussels Treaty Organization (BTO) of
1948, a military alliance of Britain, France and the Benelux countries which
since the founding of NATO in 1949 had been largely only symbolic in
character. As a result of West German membership of the WEU, France and the
other member states were to secure a veto over the rearmament and arms
procurement activities of the Federal Republic.[16]

During the London conference Eden also announced that Britain would not
withdraw its Rhine Army and tactical airforce based in West Germany without
the agreement of its WEU partners.[17] Although this had often been hinted at

since late 1953, so far it had nonetheless been regarded as irreconcilable with British sovereignty and indeed it had not been easy to overcome Churchill's opposition to this clause.[18] The WEU solution to controlling German rearmament and Britain's commitment to permanently deploy troops on the European continent were decisive in France's decision to withdraw its opposition to West Germany's membership of NATO.

Largely due to Eden's efforts to find an alternative solution to the EDC and convince his European partners to accept the scheme, the Federal Republic's integration with the West was achieved without agitating the French too much. The unity of the western alliance had been preserved. Moreover, much to London's relief, the NATO/WEU solution meant that all supranational elements were dropped.[19] While this displeased Dulles and Adenauer, Bonn and Washington nonetheless declared their support for the British solution. They had no other choice in the autumn of 1954. After all, over five years had passed since the Federal Republic had come into existence, and in view of Moscow's constant attempts to undermine West Germany's attachment to the western world, it was high time that the integration of the Federal Republic with the West was completed.

Two Soviet notes on 23 October and 13 November suggesting that a European security conference should be urgently convened confirmed western suspicions that the Soviet initiatives were merely meant to disrupt French consideration of the WEU/NATO solution to German rearmament. The West emphasized in its reply of late November that a four-power conference could only be convened after the Paris treaties had been accepted by all countries concerned.[20] Although the so-called Paris Treaties were signed on 23 October 1954, they still had to be ratified by the countries involved. Western politicians nervously had to await the end of the year before France gave its final agreement.[21] In a first unsuccessful ballot on 24 December, the National Assembly refused to give its approval to the creation of the WEU. A vote on the whole of the Paris agreements, however, had been wisely delayed until after Christmas. A stern British warning issued after the first ballot had the desired effect: London declared that British troops would only remain on the continent in the event that all participating nations accepted the Paris Treaties.[22]

Eventually, on 30 December 1954 the treaties were accepted by the French parliament with a small majority; Mendès-France had linked the issue with a vote of confidence in his government. Subsequently, in late March, the French Senate passed the treaties and on 5 May 1955 the deposition of the two last ratification documents by France and Britain meant that the Paris Treaties came into effect. West Germany was admitted to the WEU and NATO and was declared a sovereign state.[23] The western integration of the Federal Republic had finally been achieved and the coherence and strength of the western alliance had been maintained and indeed improved.

During the months of hectic diplomatic activity to find an alternative to the EDC, Churchill continued to pursue his plan to organize an international summit meeting with Malenkov and Eisenhower; at times he thought he might be able to exploit the EDC crisis to unite the West and bring about a 'Big Four' summit meeting.[24] To facilitate this (and further postpone his retirement), he hoped to persuade the President to come on a state visit to London, but Eisenhower was adamant that he was unable to visit London for the time being.[25]

Churchill's address to the annual Conservative party conference in Blackpool in October 1954 was generally regarded as a poor performance but although there was some subdued criticism of his address, Churchill believed his speech had been 'a huge success' and was greatly encouraged by it. Adenauer, for example, had expressed his gratitude to Churchill for the kind remarks about the German people and his policy in the speech.[26] His audience had, of course, expected some hints as to when he would retire but Churchill did not say a word about it. On 18 October 1954 he even carried out a Cabinet reshuffle, which included Macmillan's promotion to Secretary of Defence. The Prime Minister thus sent out a further signal that he was fully in control of his government and intended to stay in power for the time being.[27]

However, a speech Churchill gave at a girls' school in his Woodford constituency on 23 November 1954 undermined the impression that he was capable of continuing as Prime Minister. In the course of the speech, Churchill claimed that at the end of the Second World War he had asked Field Marshal Montgomery to make preparations for gathering the arms of the surrendering German soldiers 'so that they could easily be issued again to the German soldiers whom we should have to work with if the Soviet advance continued'.[28] The speech aroused a public controversy. An odd combination of *The Times*, the *Daily Herald* and the *Daily Worker* strongly attacked Churchill. The *Daily Mirror*, together with former Labour Defence Minister Emanuel Shinwell, depicted Churchill as a politician who, despite his recent peace overtures to Moscow, was not really interested in détente with the Soviet Union; the paper's description of him in 1951 as a 'warmonger' appeared to have been proved correct.[29] Yet, in all likelihood, at Woodford Churchill only wanted to reiterate his commonsense policy, and emphasize his wise foresight of basing the development of a good relationship with the Kremlin on a policy of strength, as he had always advocated. He had intended to clarify in his speech that his policy was by no means one of appeasement but was based on two equally important pillars: strength and negotiations.

However, Churchill's instruction to Montgomery had never been mentioned before and there was no mention of the event in the final volume of his memoirs of the Second World War.[30] Neither the Prime Minister nor his civil servants were able to find any documentary evidence in the old wartime files, which were frantically investigated to rebut the impression that Churchill's mental capacities were no longer up to standard. Indeed, it was discovered that three years previously, Churchill's historical adviser Lieutenant General Sir Henry Pownall, who had assisted in the preparation of his memoirs, had attempted to locate the telegram but was unable to find any trace of it 'and concluded the P.M. must have decided at the last moment not to send it'.[31] Churchill eventually had to admit in Parliament that he had been mistaken and had in fact never given such an order, though he claimed that what he had said in Woodford reflected his thoughts at the time.[32]

Initially the Prime Minister was not too worried about his gaffe; he was too busy receiving the congratulations and gifts for his 80th birthday which were pouring into Downing Street.[33] However, after having read the scathing attack on his statement in Woodford in the Soviet official newspaper *Pravda* on 28 November, Churchill became greatly concerned about the effect of his mistake on his summit diplomacy. His remarks were unlikely to boost Malenkov's interest in meeting him and would strengthen the anti-détente forces in the Kremlin hierarchy. Churchill told his doctor: 'If my slip has done harm with the Russians I may pull out sooner than I intended.'[34] In his statement in Parliament on 1 December he emphasized that both in 1945 and since Stalin's death he had been greatly interested in an understanding with Russia which could be brought about by a personal meeting. The establishment of 'closer contact with Russia' was 'the only explanation' of his remaining in office as British Prime Minister.[35] In fact Churchill was much less upbeat and later, in retirement, he was convinced that his Woodford speech had undermined the respect in which he (mistakenly) believed he was generally held in Moscow; his 'usefulness with the Russians was diminished', he reasoned.[36]

In the late 1990s, however, there came to light a 29-page report dated 22 May 1945 ('Operation Unthinkable') which considered a major though not a 'total' war against the Soviet Union beginning on 1 July 1945. It was to be launched by means of an Anglo-American attack consisting of some 500,000 British and American troops (47 divisions) based between Dresden and the Baltic. The rearming of up to ten German divisions (some 100,000 soldiers) and the deployment of ten Polish divisions was also considered. It was expected that in retaliation Stalin would invade Turkey, Greece and Norway, and embark on major sabotage activities in the Iranian and Iraqi oil fields and in France, Belgium and the Netherlands. The battle plan, which Churchill described at the time as 'a purely hypothetical contingency', was eventually rejected by Churchill and the Chiefs of Staff in 1945 and replaced with a more defensive plan to guard against any Soviet invasion of Western Europe.[37]

This scheme submitted to Churchill only two weeks after the end of the Second World War in Europe shows that he was not entirely mistaken in his Woodford speech. In 1954 Churchill seems to have mixed up his consideration of various hypothetical scenarios at the end of the Second World War, and indeed at the end of the First World War, with his actual activities at the time. His statement in his parliamentary speech on 1 December 1954 that the gist of the Woodford speech was 'not contrary to my thoughts' in 1945 was essentially correct.[38] Still, the fact that Churchill had proved to be rather unsure about the historical facts and scenarios of such importance at the end of the war and that he could not recall them nine years later did not reflect well on his mental agility. As he frankly admitted in Parliament, when he was preparing his Woodford speech he had forgotten to ask the Foreign Office to check the facts mentioned in his address, as was customary. It was clear that by the time of his 80th birthday celebrations in late November 1954 Churchill's health and mental vigour had greatly deteriorated and were continuing to do so.

Yet, Churchill was unwilling to recognize this. Instead, on 7 December he informed Eisenhower that he still expected to succeed in organizing a summit meeting: 'It is in the hope of helping forward such a meeting that I am remaining in harness longer than I wished or planned.'[39] But even Churchill realized that it would be irresponsible to endanger the final ratification of the Paris Treaties by both the National Assembly in Paris and the French Senate by organizing a conference with the Soviet Union at this time. Thus, in reply to a parliamentary question he explained that before a summit could take place the treaties would have to be fully ratified by the French parliamentary assemblies.[40] In late November and again in mid-January 1955, when Mendès-France talked of a détente initiative and proposed a summit conference with Moscow, albeit initially at foreign ministers' level, Churchill firmly rejected these moves. Not only did he believe that Paris was attempting to prevent the rearmament and western integration of Germany at the very last moment, he was also not prepared to tolerate any diplomatic competition concerning his 'summitry'.[41]

As soon as the Paris Treaties had been accepted, Churchill intended to embark once again on his 'summitry'. Yet, at the beginning of 1955 the Prime Minister felt greatly discouraged by comments from Malenkov. In a press interview on 1 January, the Soviet head of government felt unable to confirm that 'he would welcome diplomatic talks leading to a four-Power conference'. Instead, he said that the efforts to bring about German rearmament with the help of the Paris Treaties 'were not compatible' with convening a high-level conference.[42] These negative remarks were rather surprising. Only recently, on 8 November, Malenkov had had a long and constructive talk with the British and American ambassadors at a reception in the Kremlin during which he had emphasized the importance of 'peaceful coexistence' between the Soviet Union and the western world.[43] Still, in mid-January 1955 the Soviets sent another note to the western capitals declaring that the ratification of the Paris Treaties would make four-power talks on German unification unnecessary and would have dire consequences for East–West relations in general.[44]

What was decisive in undermining Churchill's 'summitry' for good was the 'bombshell' of the announcement of Malenkov's resignation as the head of the Soviet Council of Ministers (and thus effectively as Prime Minister) on 8 February 1955.[45] Churchill had been warned by Colville the day before that Moscow appeared to have decided to increase heavy industrial production at the expense of consumer products, which seemed to be a reversal of policy; Churchill had initially 'thought that the abandonment of this policy after Stalin's death was one of the most hopeful signs'.[46] Churchill was entirely unprepared for Malenkov's fall. The new official head of government was Marshal Nikolai Bulganin, the former Defence Minister, but there were clear signs that the most powerful man in the Kremlin was Nikita Khrushchev.[47]

The British embassy in Moscow reported that there was an 'outward smoothness' about Malenkov's removal from office, although in the West it led to much speculation about the power struggle in the Kremlin.[48] Malenkov was not arrested, as would have been the case under Stalin, but was simply relegated to the unimportant post of Deputy Chairman of the Council of Ministers (Deputy Prime Minister) and Energy Minister.[49] A year later he visited Britain in this capacity and Foreign Office official Evelyn Shuckburgh was able to 'shake the hand of Malenkov' at the Soviet embassy.[50] On the day of the announcement of Malenkov's demotion, Molotov made a vicious personal attack on Churchill and said that a nuclear war, which would destroy capitalism, could not be ruled out. Churchill was much upset by Molotov's statement, which slammed the door on a 'Big Three' conference.[51]

In spite of the Kremlin power struggle, of which the West had been aware, hardly any western expert had expected Malenkov's rapid fall from power. The reasons for Malenkov's resignation and whether domestic, economic or foreign policy factors had proved decisive in his downfall still remain unclear. There are indications, however, that his failed attempt to expand the consumer goods industry at the expense of heavy industry, together with the unresolved problems in the Soviet agricultural sector, may have led to his forced resignation. Malenkov's foreign policy may also have played a role: many in the Soviet leadership regarded his external policies as too lenient. The Foreign

Office, however, was not convinced of this; it recognized that for some sections of public opinion it was 'attractive' to argue that 'western intransigence over Germany and Austria contributed to the good man's eclipse'. Most Foreign Office officials would have agreed with the *Economist*'s effort to 'debunk the halo which is growing round Malenkov's head'.[52] In the unfolding leadership battle in the Kremlin, not only Malenkov but soon also his rival Molotov lost out to Khrushchev, who was to dominate Soviet politics until 1964 when he in turn was forced to retire.[53]

Once Malenkov had fallen from power it was a moot point whether or not the West could have bolstered his prestige in the power battle within the Kremlin by supporting Churchill's summit diplomacy and organizing a 'Big Three' conference.[54] While Malenkov himself may well have been more interested than either Molotov or Khrushchev in a 'parley at the summit' in 1953 and 1954, there is no evidence that a top-level meeting without any striking achievements would have strengthened his position. Even Churchill did not expect any major results during the initial rounds of talks. With hindsight, Charles Bohlen believed that after Stalin's death he should not have advised Eisenhower to reject 'Churchill's call for a "meeting at the summit" … with Malenkov',[55] but so far it has not been possible to unearth any proof that Malenkov would have been an easier person to deal with than Khrushchev turned out to be. Once Khrushchev had consolidated his position in the Kremlin, he did not, as was generally expected in the western world, 'adopt a more belligerent foreign policy'. Instead, he became ready to negotiate about Austria, sign an Austrian State Treaty, and embark on a summit meeting with the three western powers in Geneva.[56]

Retirement Approaches

Three days after Malenkov's fall Shuckburgh was informed by Anthony Nutting that the Prime Minister was planning to stand down in the very near future.[57] A few days later, Churchill told his doctor that he would lay down office at the beginning of April, shortly before Parliament's Easter break.[58] Since the beginning of January the Prime Minister had seriously begun to contemplate an appropriate date for his retirement so as to give his successor the chance to settle in before having to hold an election. It was clear that Churchill had neither the strength nor the support of his colleagues to fight another general election. Some of his closest confidants even expected that in view of his frustrating experiences with summit diplomacy he might announce his retirement as early as 2 February.[59]

Although Churchill continued to believe that he was still needed to bring about top-level negotiations towards global disarmament efforts and the prevention of a nuclear catastrophe, Malenkov's resignation was decisive in his decision on whether or not to remain Prime Minister. Soon after Malenkov's downfall, and despite frequent second thoughts, Churchill decided to retire from office in early April 1955. Observers at the time did not overlook the connection. Charles Moran thought that until Malenkov's fall from power the Prime Minister 'believed that he, and he alone, could help to make the Russians see reason. He would make them see that their self-interest would be served by an understanding with the West. When Malenkov went, the bottom fell out of Winston's plans.'[60]

In early 1955 Churchill still wavered, not least because he was fearful about a nuclear holocaust. Considerations of the NATO Council, enshrined in Plan MC-48 of mid-December 1954 to enable the American Supreme Allied Commander of NATO to use tactical nuclear weapons if Moscow commenced an invasion of Western Europe, frightened him. Churchill believed that only the nuclear powers, and thus the American and British governments, should be able to decide on whether to order the use of nuclear weapons. He also resented the USA's belief that NATO should threaten 'first use' of atomic weapons; the Prime Minister was convinced that such fearful weapons should only be used in retaliation to a major Soviet attack. While Churchill was in favour of a British bomb and the build-up of a massive western nuclear capacity, he still believed that the West ought to talk to the Soviet leaders from a position of strength before the nuclear arms race escalated further.[61]

While carefully avoiding revealing NATO secrets, Churchill spoke along these lines in Parliament on 1 March 1955, when he introduced the government's new Defence White Paper and used the opportunity to present a thorough review of the dangers to world peace.[62] By all accounts Churchill's speech was sincere and impressive. Due to Malenkov's fall, his pending retirement and the remoteness of summit diplomacy with Moscow, Churchill felt he could be very outspoken. Indeed, as in his final major foreign affairs speech two weeks later, to some extent Churchill seemed to be at pains to re-emphasize his knowledge of Communist duplicity and the Soviet threat, and downplay his intensive but unsuccessful attempts to negotiate with Moscow in the post-war era.

The Prime Minister spoke of the 'continued aggression and advance of Communism in Asia and in Europe', declaring that 'Facts are stubborn things.' Churchill expressed the belief (as he had already done in a March 1949 speech at the Massachusetts Institute of Technology) that 'but for American nuclear superiority' the European continent 'would already have been reduced to satellite status and the Iron Curtain would have reached the Atlantic and the Channel'.[63] He spoke of the dangers of 'fall-out', the approach of 'saturation' and the possibility of 'mutual annihilation'. In three or four years' time, after the current 'period of transition', both the US and the Soviets would each be capable 'of inflicting crippling or quasi-mortal injury on the other' with the weapons they had developed even if the other power possessed a greater number of nuclear devices.[64] Although a 'worldwide international agreement on disarmament' would be the best way of putting a stop to this development, one could not rely on this being achieved and the build-up of a western nuclear 'deterrent' and the improvement of western conventional forces were consequently the best ways forward. 'Unless the N.A.T.O. Powers had effective forces there on the ground and could make a front, there would be nothing to prevent piecemeal advance and encroachment by the Communists in this time of so-called peace. By successive infiltration, the Communists could progressively undermine the security of Europe. Unless we were prepared to unleash a full-scale nuclear war as soon as some local incident occurs in some distant country, we must have conventional forces in readiness to deal with such situations as they arise.'[65]

In the course of this speech he repeatedly emphasized his two main goals throughout his long political life: the maintenance of Britain's global influence and the continuation of the 'special relationship' with the United States. However, he also pointed out that despite having always advocated the closest possible Anglo-American cooperation, he believed that Britain had to go ahead with the development of its own hydrogen bomb. Only such a course of action would 'strengthen our influence within the free world'.[66] He continued: 'Personally, I cannot feel that we should have much influence over ... [American] policy or actions, wise or unwise, while we are largely dependent, as we are today, upon their protection.' He therefore recommended that 'We, too, must possess substantial deterrent power of our own. We must never allow ... the growing sense of unity and brotherhood between the United Kingdom and the United States and throughout the English-speaking world to be injured or retarded. Its maintenance, its stimulation and its fortifying is one of the first duties of every person who wishes to see peace in the world and wishes to see the survival of this country.'[67]

When in the course of the ensuing debate the Labour MP Nye Bevan accused Churchill and his government of having cancelled the planned Bermuda conference in June 1953 due to American pressure, Churchill intervened decisively, declaring that this was 'absolutely wrong'. Britain was not at the mercy of Washington and had not been dictated to by the United States. He went on to say that while it was 'quite true' that he would have liked to see a top-level conference shortly after Malenkov came to power, he had been 'struck down by a very sudden illness which paralysed me completely, physically'. For the first time it was thus revealed to a stunned House of Commons that Churchill had suffered a severe stroke in late June 1953: 'That is why I had to put it all off.'[68]

Although, in early February 1955, Churchill decided to retire in April, there were several occasions when he was tempted to reverse his decision. A minor financial crisis in February appeared to present an excuse for postponing his departure yet again, but Churchill could not assert himself against his Cabinet colleagues.[69] His deteriorating health and the numerous failures of his summit diplomacy in the previous months had weakened his will. Colville quotes him as saying: 'I have lost interest; I am tired of it all.'[70] There were nevertheless times when Churchill fought back. According to Shuckburgh there were 'a number of last-minute efforts by the Old Man to escape the inevitable. He misread a lot of telegrams from William Hayter about meetings with the Russians, thinking they related to "top-level" meetings'.[71]

Churchill's very last hope of achieving a summit conference and being able to remain in office a little longer arose because of a message from Roger Makins, the British ambassador to Washington, on 10 March 1955.[72] According to the ambassador, Dulles had mentioned that Eisenhower was considering whether he should pay a state visit to Paris on 8 May, the anniversary of the Allied victory over Hitler, so that he could make sure that the French would indeed accept the Paris Treaties and not consider any last minute excuses not to do so. Although Lord Woolton assumed that Eisenhower would call a summit conference with the USSR during his visit to Paris, Dulles had only mentioned that the President planned to 'lay plans for a meeting with the Soviets'.[73] Eisenhower merely wanted to discuss with the western allies in Paris a possible foreign ministers' or summit conference of the four powers; he never considered inviting the Soviet leadership to the French capital.[74]

Eden and the Foreign Office nonetheless urgently warned of the dangers of a presidential visit to Paris, which would antagonize the German government and appear to be an attempt to blackmail France. Eisenhower's visit might therefore have dire consequences for the final acceptance of the Paris Treaties by the French. Above all, it was feared in London that if Eisenhower visited Paris it would not be possible to dissuade Churchill from also travelling to the French capital. After all, the Prime Minister had already told Woolton that he was 'tremendously keen about the whole idea'.[75] Less than three weeks before his possible departure Churchill mentioned that he might delay his retirement once again. These considerations led to a fierce argument between Eden and Churchill during the Cabinet meeting on 14 March 1955.[76]

In desperation, the Foreign Secretary and a few of his Cabinet colleagues decided to involve the American ambassador in London so that it could be explained to Eisenhower and Dulles why the President should in no way pursue his plans any further.[77] However, on 15 March, before the reply to the ambassador's letter to Dulles had arrived, Churchill had been persuaded to stick to his decision to retire in early April.[78] The Cabinet had managed to explain to him that Eisenhower as head of state could not take part in any serious negotiations at a four-power conference and for the present was not thinking of paying a visit to London. According to Lord Woolton, the Prime Minister thought that Eisenhower 'was quite wrong to take this view, but if he was taking it then he – the P.M. – could with a clear conscience leave the matter to others, and in those circumstances he had no desire to take any further part'. Woolton also noticed that Churchill 'seemed to me to be vastly relieved; the truth is there is no fight in him, but a very natural desire to remain on the stage … It's very pathetic, but how difficult it is to know when to go.'[79]

Indeed, Churchill wondered increasingly whether he still had the strength to conduct negotiations in person. When towards the end of March new Soviet Prime Minister Bulganin hinted at the possibility of four-power talks, Churchill was intrigued while Eden became deeply annoyed. On the advice of John Colville, the Foreign Secretary remained amicable however and managed to persuade Churchill to stick to his promise to retire in early April 1955.[80]

On 14 March 1955, after the stormy Cabinet meeting in the morning of the same day, Churchill delivered what was to be his last foreign policy speech in the House of Commons (his imminent retirement had not yet been announced). The Prime Minister reported in great detail on his various attempts since Stalin's death to organize a two-, three- or four-power conference. In particular, he stressed his last initiative in the summer of 1954 and his attempts to convene a two-power Anglo-Soviet conference by contacting Molotov on his return from Washington. This meeting was meant to be 'simple' and 'informal' 'with no agenda and no objective but living side by side in growing confidence, easement and prosperity'. After all, during the war Churchill had seen a lot of Molotov and 'sometimes' he was even 'very cordial and human'.[81]

The Prime Minister felt it necessary to emphasize that during his visit to Washington no agreement on a top-level meeting had been reached, but 'There was, on the other hand, certainly no slamming of the door, no slamming down of the idea, of the plan.' Due to the Soviet proposal for a major international European security conference, this plan 'superseded for the time being the small informal meeting' Churchill had had in mind which might have been the 'prelude to a four-Power meeting at the top level'.[82]

Compared with the more radical proposals in his address of May 1953 and his subsequent attempts to persuade his allies to meet with Malenkov, Churchill's farewell speech was much more cautious. Eisenhower, Dulles, Adenauer and the British Foreign Office would not have found much fault with it. For example, while throughout 1953 and 1954 Churchill had looked down on the French claim to be one of the great powers and had done his best to convene a high-level meeting of the 'Big Three' without them, he now sounded very different. He even declared that a four-power top-level meeting had always been his ultimate goal; anything else would only give offence to the French.[83]

Churchill also stressed, as in his parliamentary speech on 25 February 1954, that he did not think that the partition of Germany ought to be overcome on the basis of the creation of a neutral country. Instead, he said that it was of the utmost importance to range 'the mighty German race and nation with the free world'. He continued: 'Earnestly as I desire to get a peaceful arrangement for co-existence brought about with Russia, I should regard it as an act of insanity to drive the German people into the hands of the Kremlin.' While he believed that the value of adding twelve West German divisions to NATO was more 'a symbol rather than a physical factor', it would contribute to his aim of achieving 'peace through strength'. Churchill declared that 'weakness makes no appeal to Moscow' and 'without [western] unity there can be no strength'.[84] He emphasized that from the moment 'the Russian-Communist menace became apparent' he had promoted 'an alliance of the free world against it'.[85]

Although ever since Stalin's death Churchill had been firmly convinced that a summit conference with Malenkov might have been able to overcome the Cold War if only Washington and the Foreign Office had declared their consent, he now told the House of Commons that this was not necessarily the case. The 'New Look' which he had wanted to explore in 1953 had just been replaced by another 'New Look'. While some 'may no doubt contend that this change might have been averted if a meeting had taken place', Churchill now doubted 'very much whether this assertion has any foundation at all'. He explained that the Soviet Union's 'new "New Look"' had 'not raised any extravagant hopes of improvement. But anyhow it is easy to assume, as is done in some influential quarters, that all would have been well if only Mr Malenkov had had due encouragement from us and of course from the United States. This is all pure guesswork'.[86]

Furthermore, in stark contrast to his endeavours throughout 1953 and 1954, Churchill emphasized not only that the mere convening of a summit conference was important. He now also argued that the time and circumstances of such a high-level meeting were of great importance. 'It would be wrong and foolish', he declared, 'in timing our procedure, to run the risk of dividing the allies of the Free World.'[87] Churchill thereby attempted to respond to the Labour Party's repeated criticism of his unsuccessful summit diplomacy. Perhaps he also attempted to rationalize why he could retire in peace without having achieved his cherished 'Big Three' summit meeting to end the Cold War.

The outgoing Prime Minister made use of the arguments that the Foreign Office diplomats had constantly employed during the past two years in opposing his summit diplomacy. Churchill's capitulation could not have been more obvious but his deteriorating health, the opposition to his policy in Washington and London as well as Moscow's apparent disinterest left him no other choice. He declared: 'I must here, however, say very seriously to the House that it is a mistake to suppose that to bring about such a meeting of any of these classes is an end in itself. It is only a means to an end. It is by no means certain that the end will be agreeable. To have a conference at an ill-chosen moment, or in unfavourable circumstances, would only raise false hopes and probably finish by leaving things worse than before.'[88]

Before concluding, Churchill also hinted at his real political aims and spelled out his legacy for his successor. He explained that he considered with great satisfaction 'the increase of our friendship and understanding with our ally the United States'. He also made clear that his 'summitry' had been a serious policy and had not merely been an attempt to postpone his retirement or a way of finding a suitable theme for his last years in power. Indeed, ever since Churchill had first become a Cabinet Minister in 1908 his belief in personal diplomacy and informal high-level negotiations had been a defining characteristic of his foreign policy. In his final major speech as Prime Minister Churchill did not hesitate to highlight this:

> I have tried very hard to set in motion this process of a conference at the top level and to bring about actual results. Although I do not pretend to measure what the recent changes in the Soviet oligarchy imply, I do not feel that they should in any way discourage us from further endeavours.[89]

> I still believe that, vast and fearsome as the human scene has become, personal contacts of the right people in the right place, at the right time may yet have a potent and valuable part to play in the cause of peace which is in our hearts.[90]

On 5 April 1955 Churchill stood down as Prime Minister.[91]

'Summitry' After Churchill

Within a month of Churchill's retirement and only two weeks before the general election in the UK, the western powers sent a note to the Soviet Union with an invitation to a summit meeting in Geneva.[92] Some subtle pressure exerted on the American government by the new Prime Minister Anthony Eden contributed decisively to this development.[93] In fact, in late March, when Churchill was still in office, Eden had already raised the idea of a four-power conference with his colleagues.[94] On 5 May, the day before the dissolution of Parliament, Eden wrote to Eisenhower expressing his belief that the time had come when '"top level" talks between Heads of Government, could play a useful part in the reduction of world tension'. Although he informed the President that his summit proposal 'may be rather a surprise to you', Eden hoped Eisenhower would 'give it earnest consideration' and would agree to 'issue the invitation promptly' as 'much' in Britain depended on it.[95]

Eden and Harold Macmillan, the new Foreign Secretary, expected that the British electorate would appreciate the announcement of a summit conference and the new Prime Minister's attempt to continue Churchill's policy of rapprochement with the Soviet Union, and that the Eden government would be rewarded with an increased electoral majority on 26 May.[96] This calculation proved largely correct. The British voters appreciated Eden's long service as Foreign Minister during the war and his diplomatic achievements since 1951. In particular, Eden was still able to bask in the success of his 1954 'annus mirabilis', when he received most of the credit for negotiating a solution to both the Indochina war and the German rearmament/EDC question. Eden was probably never more highly regarded by British public opinion than in the spring and summer of 1955; indeed his 'third spell' as Foreign Secretary had 'marked the high point of Eden's political career'.[97]

Eden was also fortunate. The Soviet Union's sudden agreement to the Austrian State Treaty during negotiations with a delegation to Moscow led by Chancellor Julius Raab in April 1955, after years of disagreement with the West over the future of the country, indicated Moscow's willingness to initiate a more constructive European policy. On 15 May, just 11 days before the British general election, the four allied powers and Austria signed the Austrian State Treaty, which terminated the country's occupation status and established a fully sovereign Austria in its 1938 borders.[98] During the election campaign, Eden could highlight his persistent attempts to persuade Moscow to agree to the long-overdue settlement of the Austrian question. Thus he contributed to an important relaxation of international tension.[99]

The Austrian State Treaty resulted in the removal of all occupation forces from Austria within five months; the first time that the Soviet Union had withdrawn its troops (in return for reparation payments) from a European country it had occupied during the Second World War. The Austrian peace treaty also banned any future *Anschluss* between Austria and Germany, a proviso warmly approved by the peoples of both the USSR and Britain. Most importantly, the conclusion of the State Treaty encouraged the Austrian parliament on 26 October to pass a constitutional law establishing the country's perpetual neutrality on the Swiss model. This ensured that Austria's political sympathies would remain heavily tilted towards the western world; the country's neutrality consisted largely of military rather than genuine political neutrality.[100] As the American embassy in Vienna had recognized early on, Austria desired to be neutral on the side of the West and, on the whole, it managed to achieve this objective.[101] Thus, the Austrian State Treaty could certainly be interpreted as a diplomatic victory for the West and thus also for Anthony Eden, one of the western world's most experienced statesmen, who was about to embark on another major détente initiative at the Geneva summit conference.

On 26 May 1955 Eden won the British general election with an overall majority of 59 seats, 42 seats more than Churchill had gained in October 1951. Indeed, the election provided a Conservative government with an increased parliamentary majority for the first time in 90 years.[102] Not only Eden's dramatic summit initiative but rising living standards and Labour's proposals for another nationalization programme may have convinced a sizeable number of the electorate to switch their votes to the Conservatives or abstain. Eden also benefited from the ideological clashes within the Labour Party; the party was split between the Bevanite left wing and a more mainstream group represented by Attlee and Hugh Gaitskell, who would become Labour leader in the autumn of 1955.[103]

With scant modesty, Churchill believed, however, that the Conservative Party's overwhelming victory had little to do with Eden but was largely due to the fact that the electors had been impressed by the performance of his peacetime government and his personal leadership during the previous three and a half years. Churchill therefore concluded that he 'could not have gone in a more fitting manner'. He even admitted that he was glad that he had left office. 'I could have gone on, but it would have been an effort.'[104] However, this was uttered on one of his good days. At other times, Churchill was unable to achieve the degree of coolness and remoteness towards political affairs which he attempted to maintain in retirement. While he professed not to be really interested in the election campaign, it was 'hurtful' that Eden and the

Conservative Party believed that they did not need him as an electoral asset and could do well, and perhaps even better, without making use of his immense experience and popularity.[105] Churchill also deeply resented the strenuous efforts made by his successor to organize a 'Big Three' summit meeting as soon as he had been removed as Prime Minister. Churchill remembered very well Eden's and Macmillan's persistent scepticism and outright opposition to his 'summitry' in 1953 and 1954. When he learnt of Eden's summit plans soon after his successor had moved into Downing Street, Churchill cynically commented from retirement: 'How much more attractive a top-level meeting seems when one has reached the top!'[106]

Although Churchill attempted to assume an air of detachment towards Eden's summit enthusiasm, the more he thought about the Geneva conference, the more wounded he felt about the sudden readiness to invite the Soviet leaders to an international summit conference only weeks after he had left office. Emmet Hughes, an American visitor to Churchill's home at Chartwell ten days before the opening of the Geneva summit conference, reported:

> the old man could not suppress great emotion as he contemplated the imminent conference. He had so ardently hoped for the meeting to occur during his last months as Prime Minister, to mark a climactic initiative for peace. And now his pale blue eyes welled with tears, as he looked back upon the unhappy timing of his resignation barely three months earlier. 'I did not want to leave,' he explained, 'but I think the people realized that I did it for the general good, do you not believe?'[107]

Prompted by Hughes's report on his visit, Eisenhower felt sorry for Churchill and, swayed by his former aide's advice, wrote Churchill a comforting letter referring to the former Prime Minister's important contribution to East–West relations. The President emphasized the importance of Churchill's policy for having laid the groundwork for an East–West summit conference and, quite disingenuously, expressed regret that for reasons of Soviet antagonism to NATO it had not been possible to arrange the conference at an earlier time. He wrote of his 'feeling of sadness' that Churchill was out of office and would thus not attend the meeting.[108] Macmillan wrote to Churchill in a similar vein: 'It is sad to think that you will not be at the "top level" meetings yourself, but you have the satisfaction of having been the pioneer.'[109] In his memoirs, Eisenhower reflected further on 'What a disappointment it must have been to Winston Churchill not to have been able to represent Her Majesty's government in this critical period'.[110] However, neither the President, nor Eden or Macmillan, considered inviting Churchill to Geneva as an honorary guest. Despite their pious words in July 1955 they were all glad that the unpredictable Churchill was in retirement. However, both Eden and Macmillan were polite enough to keep Churchill informed of the proceedings in Geneva by occasionally making diplomatic telegrams available to him.[111]

To some extent Eden's views regarding the envisaged summit meeting with Khrushchev and Bulganin were not unlike those which Churchill had expounded throughout his peacetime government. For example, in a letter to Eisenhower in late May, Eden expressed the opinion that he wanted to meet the Russians 'to test the temperature'; he explained that 'in my experience it is the informal contacts which are often the more useful with the Russians'. Although the Russians were still 'deeply suspicious and slow-moving animals', Eden believed, like Churchill before him, that the Russians appeared to be 'more ready for serious discussion now than they have been since the war'.[112] Despite the fact that these thoughts greatly resembled Churchill's thinking on 'summit diplomacy' with Stalin's successors, on the whole Eden and new Foreign Secretary Macmillan had in mind a summit somewhat different to the one to which Churchill had aspired.

The Eden government attempted to design an event which would be most unlikely to end in failure. Instead of the informal agenda-free and wide-ranging meeting with the presence of only very few advisers that Churchill had desired, it was deemed safer to ask the four heads of government to focus on the investigation of certain limited topics such as disarmament and, once again, the German question. The three western powers were also agreed on working out a unified position prior to the summit meeting through meetings of the western foreign ministers and various working groups in Paris. Dulles even suggested bilateral Anglo-American 'private talks' without the French. Otherwise, he feared, leaks would occur and the Russians would become familiar with the western strategy for Geneva.[113] Furthermore, while the Geneva summit conference was to be restricted to an initial exploration of some of the major problems in East–West relations, the foreign ministers were to continue the talks in Geneva by considering the same problems in much greater detail a few months later. For the heads of government this had the advantage that they would be able to avoid getting bogged down and divided over controversial East–West topics. It was envisaged that in particular European security issues should be dealt with by the foreign ministers in the autumn. Macmillan foresaw 'a continuing process of conferences and discussions with the Russians' and hoped that in the course of a number of constructive meetings the foreign ministers might eventually be able to arrive at mutually acceptable agreements in certain Cold War areas.[114]

This character of the conference appealed to President Eisenhower, who was still opposed to becoming involved in the bickering over political positions which was bound to occur if detailed negotiations were to take place at a high-level conference. Although initially the President was still fairly unenthusiastic about Eden's suggestion and raised questions regarding the agenda and the necessity of preparatory meetings, he also realized that in view of the electoral advantages Eden hoped for it was important not to delay issuing a conference invitation to the Soviet Union.[115] Still, the British ambassador in Washington thought that the President had 'grave misgivings' about Eden's idea; his colleague in Paris reported politely that Dulles was 'not himself very happy about this project' either.[116] However, there were at least two crucial aspects which made it much easier for Eisenhower and his British and French colleagues to convene a summit conference. Not only had the Austrian question been solved but the full and watertight integration of the Federal Republic of Germany with the western world had been achieved by early May 1955 when West Germany joined NATO and the WEU and became an (almost) sovereign country in its own right. Moscow's persistent attempts during the previous five years to prevent West German rearmament, undermine the cohesion of NATO and destabilize the American leadership of NATO and the western world had thus been defeated.

From the western point of view, convening a summit with the Soviet leaders had thus become much less dangerous politically. Furthermore, once the Soviets had agreed to sign the Austrian State Treaty a continued western refusal to participate in a summit meeting would have found very little sympathy with western public opinion. This was underlined by the fact that also in May, after almost nine years of stalling, Moscow 'made a considerable move', if not a 'spectacular move', and submitted a wide-ranging arms control plan to the UN disarmament subcommittee in London. The Kremlin was clearly signalling its seriousness about making progress with the improvement of East–West relations when it proposed a reduction of conventional weapons and the inspection of nuclear arms facilities.[117] Shortly afterwards, Khrushchev and Bulganin embarked on a dramatic rapprochement with Tito's Yugoslavia by visiting Belgrade between 26 May and 2 June,[118] and on 7 June 1955 the West German Chancellor received an invitation to visit Moscow to establish diplomatic and trade relations with the Soviet Union. The Soviet Union hoped that 'personal contact' with Adenauer and a number of his representatives could be established in the 'interests of peace and European security'.[119] In the West, the note from Moscow was regarded as 'a diplomatic sensation of the first order'.[120] The general 'vigour and freshness and apparent conciliatory attitude of the new Soviet regime' convinced western statesmen that Moscow might be genuinely interested in a constructive summit meeting.[121]

Indeed, by the spring of 1955 Moscow had realized that the further pursuit of the theme of German unification was no longer a viable political strategy. Instead, Moscow seemed increasingly inclined to accept the peaceful status quo of a partitioned Germany and a divided Europe. Khrushchev decided to embark on the 'two state theory' and thus a policy focused on maintaining the permanent division of Germany and Europe. Already in late March 1954 the Kremlin had declared the GDR a sovereign state and on 20 September 1955 a formal Soviet–East German treaty of sovereignty was signed which gave the GDR responsibility for its own foreign policy. The establishment of the Warsaw Pact on 14 May 1955, which extended membership to the East German government in East Berlin in early 1956, also pointed in this direction. After the West German accession to NATO, Moscow had begun to accept the power political realities in Europe, effectively giving up hope of ever achieving German unification on Soviet terms; therefore, the USSR was no longer prepared to sacrifice the existence of its East German ally.[122] By 1955 Europe had definitely been divided into East and West. Moreover, Khrushchev also recognized the very real danger of a nuclear holocaust if Cold War tension continued unabated; a certain rapprochement with the West was required.[123]

Thus by the spring of 1955 President Eisenhower and many of his advisers (though not John Foster Dulles) were inclined to view a formal East–West summit meeting with an agreed agenda much less negatively. While Dulles still focused on the risk of raising too many hopes, Eisenhower believed that the danger of meeting with the Soviets was not 'quite so great as it was once'. The American people and the media had begun to realize that the conference was 'merely a beginning and not an end'. According to the President, a 'greater maturity' had developed which made people understand the significance but also the limitations of such a high-level conference.[124] Moreover, after the successful conclusion of the Austrian State Treaty and the end of the wars in Korea and Indochina, Eisenhower also considered that most of the conditions for meeting the Soviet leaders that he had spelled out in his 'Chance for Peace' speech on 16 April 1953 had actually been met. He told a press conference that he was prepared to 'pick up and go from any place to Timbuktu to the North Pole to do something about this question of peace'.[125] He nevertheless declined Eden's invitation to visit London before travelling to Geneva.[126]

It was also clear that Churchill's departure was viewed with relief in Washington and contributed to Eisenhower's readiness to consider participating in a summit meeting with Moscow. Eisenhower was confident that the sober, reliable and much more predictable Eden would not turn a summit conference into a destablizing and tumultuous affair by proposing dramatic and ill-thought out plans for how to overcome the Cold War. This, and the fact that the American administration was quite prepared to help Eden in his attempt to be elected Prime Minister in his own right, contributed to

Eisenhower's decision to announce that he was ready to participate in the four-power summit conference in Geneva.[127]

Forgotten were his earlier declarations that any American President would find it very difficult to leave his country for a prolonged period of time to participate in international negotiations. Eisenhower even managed to persuade the West German Chancellor of the necessity of the Geneva summit.[128] The President also decided to ignore the warning issued by the still sceptical John Foster Dulles to be careful not to flash his famous big smile when being photographed with Khrushchev and to avoid meeting the Soviets in private. Dulles feared that the American people might otherwise receive a wrong impression; one that disguised the high degree of mutual suspicion that still characterized East–West relations.[129] Perhaps the confidence Eisenhower initially placed in Eden's position as Prime Minister also explains his anger and ruthless response to Eden's Suez adventure in late 1956, when the US was entirely ignored by the British, French and Israeli collaborators.[130]

Between 18 and 23 July 1955 Eisenhower, Eden, the new French Prime Minister Faure and Bulganin and Khrushchev took part in the first summit conference at heads of government level since the Potsdam conference in 1945.[131] Despite Eisenhower's dramatic 'open skies' suggestion on the fourth day of the meeting – a proposal for an agreement on mutual aerial inspection and the exchange of military intelligence between East and West – the Geneva conference was not a serious attempt to terminate the Cold War, as had been the aim of Churchill's summit diplomacy. Not surprisingly, in the summer of 1955 it did not prove possible to solve any of the many outstanding Cold War problems and no sensational results were recorded.[132] The major result of the Geneva conference consisted of the insight that the status quo, and thereby the division of the world into East and West, ought to be mutually accepted. Macmillan strongly believed that the new Soviet moderation, which became evident at Geneva, resulted from the American hydrogen bomb; thus the improvement in East–West relations was 'really due to fear, not to love' and Macmillan called it 'the first dividend of the nuclear weapons'.[133]

Although at first sight it would be fair to label the Geneva conference 'an exercise in procrastination', something more substantial was achieved. As American journalist Richard Rovere wrote shortly after the summit, 'A decision to accept a status quo can be every bit as important and, in certain circumstances, as helpful as a decision to rearrange things.' Thus, the 'negative agreements and diplomacy' of the Geneva summit, together with the effort of all the participants to be pleasant and get to know each other by means of constructive negotiations and conversations, contributed to the development of the much praised but evanescent 'spirit of Geneva'.[134] To some extent Eisenhower, who dominated the Geneva conference and stole the limelight from Eden, Faure and Khrushchev, was right when he told the American people shortly before the event that the conference was meant 'to change the spirit that has characterized the intergovernmental relationships of the world during the past ten years'.[135]

However, at least with hindsight Khrushchev saw this differently. In an ill-tempered passage in his memoirs he attacked both the Geneva summit and Churchill's premature 'summitry' after Stalin's death, when Moscow had not been 'really ready' for such an initiative, by claiming that although Churchill 'was already retired, his unrealistic ideas dominated the [Geneva] meeting. Certainly his influence on the proceedings was greater than Eisenhower's.'[136] Despite Khrushchev's belated and fairly exaggerated outburst, which was tape-recorded in the mid- to late 1960s after he had lost power, the Geneva summit conference demonstrated that it was possible to contain the escalation of the Cold War in Europe. In the course of the summit conference both sides agreed to disagree; a policy which was soon referred to as 'peaceful coexistence'.

While the development of the Geneva rapprochement was a real achievement and represented in fact the first genuine thaw in East–West relations since 1945, the Geneva 'spirit' gradually evaporated in the course of the next few years. During the subsequent meeting of foreign ministers in October/November 1955 it was already difficult to discern any constructive spirit of engagement. Both Macmillan and Molotov once again submitted interesting but also highly contentious proposals about East–West dis-engagement and the establishment of demilitarized zones in the middle of Europe. In fact, Macmillan attempted to make progress with Eden's contro-versial disengagement proposal (the so-called Eden Plan) for the creation of a neutral zone in the middle of Germany to de-escalate East–West tension along the German–German border which the Prime Minister had proposed in the course of the Geneva summit conference.[137] These ideas were immediately rejected as unrealistic by the West German government (which was only unofficially represented in Geneva) although, as in 1953, Adenauer and his advisers had also reluctantly begun to draw up their own disengagement proposals. There was little support for disengagement in Washington.[138]

Still, the 'spirit of Geneva' resulted in a certain relaxation of the Cold War until the crises of 1956 in Suez and Hungary and Khrushchev's ultimatum of November 1958, which led to the Berlin crisis and eventually to the building of the Berlin Wall in August 1961. During the long Berlin crisis, Prime Minister Harold Macmillan, who had succeeded Eden in January 1957, exasperated Eisenhower with his penchant for attempting to arrange an international summit conference with Khrushchev to save world peace. Unlike his mentor

Churchill, Macmillan did not hesitate to travel to Moscow in February 1959, despite strong American objections, to investigate the situation for himself. Yet, while Macmillan's summit diplomacy helped him win the British general election in early October 1959, he only achieved a very moderate alleviation of East–West tension.[139] More decisive progress in improving East–West relations only occurred in late 1962. The very real possibility of mutually assured destruction if one or the other side resorted to war, as seemed a serious possibility during the Cuban Missile Crisis of October 1962, effectively resulted in an enforced stabilization of the Cold War and thus also contributed to the ever deeper division of the world along the river Elbe in the middle of Germany.

Shortly before the Geneva summit in July 1955, Gladwyn Jebb, London's ambassador to France and one of Britain's most senior and experienced diplomats, had written in a 'think piece' that pressure by western public opinion would 'not permit us to be completely uncompromising' at Geneva. The western world 'should not, however, be alarmed if "tension" rises again after some temporary abatement' due to the Geneva summit. 'To be quite candid', Jebb continued, 'some "tension" – in the sense of common fear, if not war at any rate or revolutionary change – is necessary to keep the Western World together: if it were removed altogether there is little doubt that we should be in for a period of what the Russians always refer to as "capitalist contradictions".'[140] Thus, according to this cynical view, the West should actually welcome a certain degree of Cold War tension to ensure the further development of the Atlantic alliance and the capitalist character of the countries of the western world. However, by the early 1960s the threat to the survival of the world, whether capitalist or Communist, made it highly dangerous to further pursue this kind of orthodox Cold War attitude which Churchill had been unable to defeat during his peacetime government. Instead, in the 1960s serious attempts at rapprochement were undertaken.

In the wake of the nuclear diplomacy of the Cuban Missile Crisis which brought the world to the brink of nuclear disaster,[141] one of the first attempts to embark on a constructive working relationship to prevent the likelihood of a nuclear holocaust was the August 1963 international Test Ban Treaty which made nuclear test explosions in the atmosphere illegal.[142] The installation of a 'hot' telephone line between Washington and Moscow as well as for example American President Johnson's May 1964 call for the 'building of bridges' between the two blocs and his proposal of October 1966 for the 'peaceful engagement' of East and West were other consequences of the Cuban Missile Crisis. NATO's Harmel report of December 1967 also explicitly spoke of the necessity and western aim to 'further a détente in East–West relations'.[143] It was recognized that East–West détente and not further Cold War tension was the only option to ensure the world's long-term survival.

It was only in the late 1960s and early 1970s that the so-called era of super-power détente and West German *Ostpolitik* managed to break through the highly dangerous tension which still dominated international politics and, by means of constructive negotiations at various governmental levels, succeeded in establishing new Cold War paradigms. In the aftermath of Richard Nixon's and Henry Kissinger's policies of détente with Moscow and Beijing and West German Chancellor Willy Brandt's rapprochement with Moscow and the Soviet Union's Eastern European satellite states, a somewhat more relaxed, though still uneasy and dangerous East–West relationship commenced.[144] The Cuban Missile Crisis, the Vietnam War including the danger of massive Chinese intervention, the proliferating conflicts by proxy in the developing world and, not least, the ever escalating nuclear arms race made politicians recall Churchill's dictum that 'To jaw-jaw is always better than to war-war'.[145]

Churchill's Final Political Activities

By this stage, however, Churchill was long past being able to participate in international affairs. Even in the summer of 1955 Churchill would hardly have been able to attend the Geneva conference if he had still been Prime Minister. On 2 June he had suffered his third severe stroke and by August his condition had worsened; he could hardly speak and deteriorated rapidly. His personal physician did not expect Churchill to live for much longer. Even when Churchill very slowly recuperated, he was advised to avoid appearing in the House of Commons and elsewhere so as not to reveal his physical and indeed mental decline.[146]

Eventually, however, Churchill did recover to the extent of being able to travel to Aachen in May 1956 to receive the Charlemagne Prize for his contribution to European Integration. This was the first time that he had travelled to Germany since the Potsdam conference eleven years before. When he gave his short speech in Aachen accepting the prize it happened to be the anniversary of his becoming Prime Minister in the war against Germany in 1940. Churchill did not visit Berlin during his stay in West Germany, but he travelled to Bonn to see Adenauer and visited the British troops based in the FRG.[147]

Although Churchill never managed to meet Malenkov during the latter's 23 months at the helm of Soviet politics, Churchill did meet new Soviet leader Khrushchev when a high-ranking Soviet delegation visited the UK in April 1956, shortly after Khrushchev's dramatic speech which began the process of de-Stalinization in the USSR. Eden had issued an invitation for Khrushchev's visit during the Geneva summit in the previous year.[148] Over dinner at Downing Street, Churchill was seated next to Khrushchev and they had an amicable conversation but it does not seem to have included any important political topics past or current. Churchill believed that the Russians had been 'delighted to see him'; he thought however that Khrushchev, who was clearly the most senior Soviet politician present, was a minor figure compared to Stalin.[149] In his memoirs Khrushchev, however, speaks very unflatteringly of his encounter with Churchill; he refers to him as 'very old and fat and doddering' and remarked that they only exchanged 'occasional phrases, not really saying much of anything to each other'.[150]

During the first few years of his retirement Churchill made a number of speeches of modest importance and a few contributions in the House of Commons. He travelled often to the south of France to paint and relax, cruised frequently in the Mediterranean, and otherwise stayed at his London house at Hyde Park Gate and at his country home in Chartwell. Some of the precious time during which he was able to concentrate on intellectual matters was devoted to making some revisions to the last volume of *A History of the English Speaking Peoples*, which was published in 1958. After having contemplated travelling to the USA in 1957 and 1958, Churchill was eventually well enough to embark on his last journey to America in May 1959. He stayed with Eisenhower in the White House and at the President's farm in Gettysburg, and also managed to visit the ailing General Marshall and John Foster Dulles, who was in hospital and died only two weeks later.[151] In the same year Churchill also made several speeches during the election campaign of 1959; he was returned unopposed as MP for Woodford.

It became, however, increasingly obvious that Churchill was no longer able to participate in the political dialogue and make any noteworthy contributions.[152] Although Churchill's strength was ebbing, this did not stop him from receiving Chancellor Adenauer in London in November 1959. In late 1960 he met President De Gaulle in Nice; in 1958 he had received the Cross of the Liberation, France's highest honour. However, not so much relations with continental Europe as the relationship with the United States was uppermost in Churchill's mind.[153] In fact, he regarded it as his last important mission in life to support new Prime Minister Macmillan and help him mend fences with the United States after the Suez Crisis and re-establish the 'special relationship' of the war years. His advice to the Queen to appoint Harold Macmillan rather than Rab Butler as Eden's successor in January 1957 was perhaps one of Churchill's last important political contributions.[154]

Soon, the political issues of the day were gradually passing him by. After 1960 Churchill's physical and mental health continued to deteriorate; before long he was unable to read, his memory vanished and he became increasingly inarticulate. In 1963 his son Randolph received the honorary citizenship of the United States from President Kennedy on his father's behalf. In 1964 Churchill formally retired from the House of Commons. He celebrated his ninetieth birthday on 30 November 1964 at his London house in Hyde Park Gate and his last public appearance was in December at the Savoy Hotel at a dinner of 'The Other Club', a dining club of distinguished members which he had founded together with Lord Birkenhead and Lloyd George in 1911. On 10 January 1965 Churchill suffered a fatal stroke; he passed away two weeks later. Allegedly his last words were 'I am so bored with it all.'[155]

Churchill's Legacy

When Churchill died on 24 January 1965, almost ten years after he had left office as Prime Minister, the era of détente he had worked so hard to bring about was still in the future. Due to his long and debilitating illness, the former Prime Minister had been unable to participate in political affairs during his last years. In retirement Churchill neither had the strength, the will nor the interest to continue making a political contribution to Britain's well-being. During his last difficult years he had hardly been aware of the world around him. Churchill's coffin was transported by coach and boat from Westminster Hall to St Paul's Cathedral and from there to Tower Pier and to Waterloo Station. From Waterloo Station the former Prime Minister embarked on his final journey by train to his last resting place in Bladon churchyard near Blenheim Palace, where he was born over 90 years before. Along the route the people of his country gave him a tremendous final farewell. 'Britain was treated to a spectacular funeral in the style of the war heroes of the previous century, most notably those of Nelson and Wellington. He was hailed as "The Great Englishman".'[1]

This was overwhelmingly due to Churchill's lasting achievement as Britain's wartime Prime Minister. While there were many people who also remembered him for having warned of the looming danger from the Soviet Union at the beginning of the Cold War with his 1946 'iron curtain' speech, there were very few who appreciated him for his persistently pursued 'summitry' and personal diplomacy. Indeed, Churchill's lifelong attempts to maintain Britain's political and economic well-being and its great power status by means of his remarkable dedication to personal diplomacy and summit negotiations are seldom recalled by either professional historians or the general public interested in international affairs.

Although Churchill was not always successful with his 'parleys at the summit', his personal diplomacy must be viewed as an essential part of his political legacy. With his efforts to end the Anglo-German naval race by attempting to negotiate with the Kaiser and Admiral Tirpitz between 1908 and 1914 he had endeavoured to contribute to the preservation of the stability of the European 'concert of nations' to avoid the First World War. During the Second World War he deployed this strategy to negotiate with Roosevelt and Stalin and maintain Britain's seat at the table of the 'Big Three', particularly in 1940–42 and after the Tehran conference when Britain's declining importance in the strenuous battles to defeat Hitler could no longer be overlooked. During the Second World War, conference diplomacy with Roosevelt and Stalin was Churchill's preferred and not altogether unsuccessful strategy for maintaining his country's global role and minimizing the decline in influence of Britain on allied military policy and on allied planning for the post-war world.

During the Cold War, both in opposition and after he became Prime Minister again in late 1951, Churchill desperately tried to use his summit diplomacy to bring about a détente with the Soviet Union. He called for the resumption of East–West talks to arrive at an early end of the Cold War and fervently believed in the possibility of reaching a 'settlement' with Moscow this way. Even his 'iron curtain' speech in 1946 contained many conciliatory elements. Churchill pursued a dualistic policy during the Cold War years. He strove for informal negotiations with Moscow at heads of government level whilst at the same time stressing that the military build-up of the West and the 'policy of strength' should not be neglected. In the early phase of the Cold War, as Leader of the Opposition between 1945 and 1951 and also in 1951–52 as Prime Minister, he sometimes doubted whether the political realities and Stalin's policies and personality would actually allow for a resolution of the East–West conflict through negotiations. But he realized that the Cold War had to be overcome if the world was to become a safer place, free from the threat of nuclear annihilation, and if his country was to recover from the sacrifices of the Second World War. Churchill was therefore greatly encouraged when Stalin suddenly died in early March 1953 and was succeeded by a collective leadership led by Georgi Malenkov, who seemed to be more flexible and much more interested in a constructive relationship with the West.

Unlike the vast majority of his contemporaries, Churchill realized that only a rapid de-escalation and indeed termination of the Cold War would enable Britain to survive as one of the world's great powers. Only if his country were able to re-focus its energies away from concentrating on fighting the Cold War and the development of ever more expensive weapons of mass destruction towards economic development and technological improvement of its economy would Britain be able to survive as one of the 'Big Three'. At an early stage Churchill recognized that his country needed a relaxation of the tense global situation in order to be able to reduce its excessive military expenditure and by implication make more resources available for the development of its manufacturing and export industries. Moreover, it appeared to him that only an East–West détente would ensure that funds would become available for the further development of the British atomic bomb, the construction of its own hydrogen bomb and the production of British rockets capable of launching these weapons without American assistance. Even if a relaxation of the Cold War could be achieved, he still believed that Britain needed to possess nuclear weapons to maintain its position as one of the 'Big Three'. At the time reliance on nuclear arms was regarded as much less expensive than conventional weapons; it would also ensure Britain's continued sovereignty and the country's ability to remain at the forefront of technological progress. Churchill felt all of this to be necessary for maintaining the great power role of the British Isles and, despite his constant emphasis on the significance of the 'special relationship' with the United States for regaining military and financial independence from Washington. Thus, the final objective of Churchill's life-long policies was to increase the international influence of his country or, at least, preserve it and avoid its further diminution.

With the Locarno idea, presented in his important speech on 11 May 1953, he proposed that Great Britain be made a guarantor power of a settlement between Germany and the USSR. Although this was not very realistic, it convincingly demonstrated whose interests the Prime Minister really sought to defend. Churchill's security policy ideas, and in particular the notion of a reunified, neutral Germany, which he seriously toyed with in 1953, were primarily directed towards ending the Cold War and maintaining Britain's role as a global power. The interests of Germany and the Soviet Union were of only secondary importance to Churchill. In 1953 the Prime Minister's view was that the reunification of the two German states was necessary to conciliate German nationalism and thereby remove a dangerous potential crisis situation from the centre of Europe. The uprising in the GDR in June 1953 appeared to prove him right in this respect.

During his entire peacetime premiership, and in particular in 1954–55, Churchill was greatly troubled by the development of the hydrogen bomb. He feared that the aggressive anti-Communist comments made by the American government, above all by Secretary of State John Foster Dulles whom he thoroughly disliked, were perhaps not just empty rhetoric. The Prime Minister asked himself if Washington might possibly seek to strike pre-emptively at the Soviet Union in an attempt to end the Cold War the American way. Churchill was convinced that the destructive power of the H-bomb, the proliferation of nuclear weapons, Soviet atomic aggression or the expected nuclear response from Moscow, if there ever was an atomic first-strike by the West, would mean the end of all civilization and, above all, the end of the old continent. Churchill therefore believed that East–West summit talks would make peace much more secure, enable East and West to overcome the Cold War and thus preserve global stability and, ultimately, ensure the world's physical survival.

Churchill hoped to solve all the main problems of his time: resolving the Cold War; avoiding a nuclear disaster; removing a dangerous crisis area in Europe; fulfilling German, French and Soviet ambitions while preventing renewed German nationalism including another European civil war, and, above all, maintaining Britain's great power role. Churchill was convinced that because of his own great prestige he would be able to successfully arrange a 'summit' and persuade the Soviet Union to resolve the Cold War through personal discussions with Malenkov. On the basis of his extensive experience and unique charisma and as the only survivor of the wartime 'Big Three' club, Churchill believed that he was the only politician capable of this. This largely explains his 'summit' enthusiasm after the Second World War.

However, the United States and the Soviet Union did not share Churchill's convictions. Both countries distrusted the other too much even though both were interested in an acceptable *modus vivendi*. The British Prime Minister and his country were no longer influential enough to bring about substantial changes in international affairs. Moreover, Churchill was deeply mistrusted in Moscow. While Churchill never realized the extent of the suspicion, even loathing, he still aroused in the Kremlin, the belief the Prime Minister was merely attempting to deceive Moscow and obtain western advantages in the Cold War helped to undermine Malenkov's and Beria's modest interest in Churchill's summit diplomatic proposals after Stalin's death.

Above all, despite a certain albeit limited degree of Soviet interest in Churchill's proposals in 1953, the initiative had to come from the United States if the Kremlin was to be induced to embark on a more constructive relationship with the West. But politicians in Washington were much too concerned with psychological warfare considerations to be able to exploit the opportunity of Stalin's sudden death in a more flexible and forward looking way.[2] There was absolutely no interest in Churchill's proposals among the senior members of the Eisenhower administration. It was also well known that the Prime Minister did not enjoy the support of his own Cabinet and the Foreign Office for his unconventional ideas for changing the western world's entire strategy of how to conduct the Cold War. This greatly undermined Churchill's summit diplomacy in Washington.

Churchill also had his own career and its historical significance in sight. As well as being a great statesman of the war, he also sought to go down in history as a politician of peace. He was greatly disappointed when he was awarded the 1953 Nobel Literature Prize rather than the one for peace. Moreover, in 1954 and 1955 he did not hesitate to exploit his summit diplomacy to further postpone his retirement. It was after his successful speech at the Conservative party conference in Margate in October 1953, once both the Prime Minister and his Foreign Secretary and heir apparent Anthony Eden had recovered from their long and serious illnesses, that Eden realized that, contrary to all his many promises, Churchill still had no plans to retire. From the end of 1953 summit diplomacy thereby increasingly became the political football of the personal rivalries and animosities between Churchill and Eden.

However, Churchill's memoranda, letters and other documentary and oral evidence dealing with the 'summit' theme throughout the period 1945–55 and particularly in 1953 and 1954 are so deeply felt that it is impossible to conclude that Churchill merely used the topic to postpone his resignation. There is no evidence either that Churchill was merely driven by a strong and vicious anti-Communism in his years as peacetime Prime Minister and earlier, as David Carlton argues rather unconvincingly.[3] Instead, it is evident that the Prime Minister was entirely convinced of his 'missionary task' and his personal 'manifest destiny' to overcome the Cold War and maintain Britain's great power role. It would however have been surprising if Churchill had not also realized that he could conveniently use his genuinely pursued political objectives to achieve other goals like the postponement of his dreaded retirement which Eden and others were demanding ever more impatiently. In the summer of 1954 his personal diplomacy came to a head when, ignoring President Eisenhower's wishes, he embarked on his final major attempt to organize a bilateral 'parley at the summit' and travel to Moscow to meet Malenkov.

Yet, for the reasons outlined in this book, Churchill's political vision fell on deaf ears among the political elites in the United States and the Soviet Union. Even in his own country, the Foreign Office and most of his Cabinet colleagues could not be persuaded to go along with his views. While the British people as well as the peoples in many other countries instinctively felt that there might be an element of insight and political vision in Churchill's thinking, his political contemporaries largely dismissed his ideas. Arguably, his two immediate successors as Prime Minister, Anthony Eden and Harold Macmillan, who after all had closely collaborated with him since early in the Second World War, were greatly influenced by Churchill's summit diplomacy and also quite keen on this kind of policy. Despite their strong opposition to Churchill's 'summitry' in 1953–55, both Eden and Macmillan were no less ardent admirers of personal diplomacy and summit meetings than Churchill once they had reached the top of the 'greasy pole' themselves. After all, already in 1951/2 Eden had actively attempted to embark on his own personal 'summitry' with the then Soviet Foreign Minister Vyshinsky. Immediately after Churchill's retirement the new Prime Minister Eden pressed for the Geneva four-power conference in mid 1955, the first 'real' summit since Potsdam. When Macmillan was Prime Minister he travelled to Moscow in 1959 to negotiate personally with Khrushchev and subsequently continued pestering both Eisenhower and his successor John F. Kennedy about convening a 'Big Four' summit meeting to resolve the dangerous Berlin crisis. Like Churchill, his successors fully recognized the political as well as personal (and electoral) advantages of 'parleys at the summit'.

Yet, after the abortive four-power summit in Paris in May 1960 when Macmillan desperately but unsuccessfully attempted to mediate between Eisenhower and Khrushchev to save the conference from collapsing, summit diplomacy became largely a bilateral matter for the two superpowers. In particular after the building of the Berlin Wall in August 1961 and the Cuban Missile Crisis of October 1962, Britain and France hardly ever participated in international summit events. As Churchill had already gloomily anticipated during the Second World War and after, these events only seemed to require the presence of the American President and the Soviet Secretary General. The Europeans, including the British, were fortunate if they were informed about the progress of the talks rather than just about the results. The exceptions were the negotiations which concerned the German question. Both in the high-level talks which led to the 1971/2 quadripartite Berlin Agreement and the two-plus-four negotiations which resulted in German unification in 1990 Britain and France were active though junior participants.[4]

To some extent it might be tempting to see Churchill as the forerunner of the détente of the 1970s and the first practitioner of personalized informal East–West negotiations which by means of the Reagan/Bush–Gorbachev summits in the mid to late 1980s helped to terminate the Cold War. However, this would exaggerate the importance of Churchill's political vision and his summit diplomacy. Although, as mentioned in the introduction to this book, Reagan's Secretary of State George Shultz was aware of Churchill's détente policy and summit vision of the 1940s and 1950s, Churchill's policy was hardly the role model for Reagan's and Gorbachev's summit encounters in the 1980s.

However, his summit diplomacy did leave a legacy. Churchill managed to reverse the deep suspicions and unpopularity of international 'summitry' which had been much maligned in the aftermath of the controversial conferences in Yalta and Potsdam towards the end of the Second World War and in the course of the various contentious four-power foreign ministers' meetings during the early post-war period. To a large extent, as recognized by Khrushchev in his memoirs, the Geneva conference in 1955 took place due to Churchill's long-standing relentless pressure for a summit conference with the Soviet Union.[5] The general perception that the Geneva summit conference had led to a positive result – the evanescent 'spirit of Geneva' – and that personal diplomacy was indeed valuable proved important. It influenced subsequent attempts to overcome the lack of communication between East and West by means of multilateral conference diplomacy and bilateral summit meetings. In the long term this led to West and East gradually resuming closer contact with one another, a development which culminated in the important 1975 Helsinki conference, and the imminent threat of nuclear war began to recede. To some extent Churchill's summit policy did have a positive, albeit indirect, impact on the development of East–West détente.

With regard to the maintenance of Britain's great power status, Churchill's legacy was perhaps less successful. Both Eden and Macmillan, and arguably their successors Alec Douglas-Home and Harold Wilson, were still acting within a 'Churchillian' great power framework for Britain. While they were also aware, as Churchill had recognized, that Britain needed to recuperate economically and improve its economic and industrial performance to enable the country to continue its global role, this insight was only acted upon half-heartedly. The pursuit of a consistent and realistic economic and industrial policy was not a strong point of any British government between the 1950s and 1970s. In fact, despite all the rhetoric to the contrary, it was a rather neglected area.[6] Moreover, none of these governments, including Churchill's peacetime administration, was ready to accept the new post-war realities and adopt a more genuinely pursued European policy for Britain.

After the governments of the early to mid-1950s, led in turn by Attlee, Churchill and Eden, had refused to join the Schuman Plan and participate in the EEC, Prime Minister Harold Macmillan's decision to apply for EEC membership in the early 1960s was merely a rather belated and less than enthusiastically pursued change of policy. Harold Wilson's attempt to make Britain a member of the European Community in 1967 was also rather unconvincing. Not only President De Gaulle but also the majority of Britain's western allies and the British people themselves were not yet convinced that Britain had decided to narrow its international concentration from a global and Commonwealth focus to a European outlook. This would have to await the government of Edward Health in the early 1970s.[7]

Throughout the remainder of the twentieth century and the early years of the twenty-first doubts were expressed frequently within and without the UK as to whether the country was fully committed to regarding itself as a European country. Britain still appeared to be much more interested in the 'special relationship' with the United States including participation in events at the summit of international affairs and in the remnants of its former global Empire than in the pursuit of a genuine European role. Still, even at the beginning of the twenty-first century, when considering Britain's hesitation to commit itself fully to Europe by adopting the Euro, the common European currency, and Prime Minister Tony Blair's global shuttle diplomacy in the efforts to fight international terrorism and strut the world as Washington's closest global ally, Dean Acheson's statement of the early 1960s that Britain had lost an Empire but not yet found a new role does not seem to be entirely without relevance.[8] Yet even as a very old man in retirement, Churchill deeply resented Acheson's statement; he repudiated its implication that Britain must be regarded as playing only a 'tame and minor role in the world'.[9]

Still, Churchill's pursuit of a global role for Britain by means of his summit diplomacy throughout his political life, not least in the years after 1945, must bear some responsibility for prolonging Britain's failure to accept political realities. It made it even more difficult for the country to grapple with the legacies of Empire, like the impact of de-colonization on Britain's internal and external policies, and to accept the growing Europeanization of British politics than would otherwise have been the case. Although Churchill had embarked on designing a limited and perhaps contradictory post-war European strategy for his country during the Second World War and in the immediate post-war years, he never developed a fuller and more coherent vision for Britain's European future.[10] He too was caught in the legacies of his country's 'glorious past', as he and most of his fellow citizens saw it, and despite attempting to show a visionary way forward to overcome the Cold War, Churchill's thinking could not escape the global framework within which his country had traditionally conducted its foreign policy.

Thus, while Churchill may have succeeded in postponing Britain's decline as a great power as seen and perceived by the British people, at the same time he made it more difficult for his country to accept the new post-war realities and leave behind the 'Churchillian' framework of international affairs within which the country had been able to act for so long. Churchill attempted to develop a visionary policy for stabilizing and even increasing Britain's influence in the world while at the same time being unable to break out of the traditional great power frame of reference within which his country was accustomed to act, and that he himself had decisively helped to shape, but which by the 1950s increasingly constrained Britain's ability to accept and adapt to its changing role in world affairs.

However, a historical assessment of Churchill's summit diplomacy has to be set in the context of his time: the first half of the twentieth century. Within this frame of reference it might be asking too much of any politician to foresee global developments in the second half of the twentieth century. Within the political and historical framework in which Churchill had to act, he must be given credit for having clearly recognized throughout his long political career, and as early as the first decade of the twentieth century, that both world peace and the continuation of Britain's great power role were endangered. Britain's global influence and importance could only be maintained by acknowledging two interlinked factors: the necessity of the preservation of world peace including global disarmament efforts and a greater focus on the management of his country's diminishing resources to maintain its international competitiveness. Churchill's stubbornly pursued personal summit diplomacy attempted to achieve this; after 1945 he wished to free Britain from the Cold War and thus many of its military burdens to enable his country to focus more on its manifold other challenges.

With his attempts to negotiate with Tirpitz and de-escalate the Anglo-German naval race, with his efforts to make Britain's voice heard during the meetings and conferences of the Second World War, and not least by way of his post-war summit diplomacy to overcome the Cold War and avoid a nuclear holocaust, he attempted to do his best to further guarantee his country's strength and significant role in international affairs. It was his important and persistently pursued personal summit diplomacy between 1908 and 1955 that was Churchill's main instrument for attempting to maintain Britain's continued place in the sun.

Abbreviations

BD Foreign Affairs	*British Documents on Foreign Affairs: Reports and Papers from the Foreign Office Confidential Print.* Part I, Series F, Vol. 21: *Germany, 1909–1914* (ed. by David Stevenson; general editors: K. Bourne and D.C. Watt). Frederick Md.: University Publications of America, 1990.
BD Origins	*British Documents of the Origins of the War, 1898–1914* (ed. by G.P. Gooch and H. W. V. Temperley)
BL	Bodleian Library, Oxford University, Oxford
BTO	Brussels Treaty Organization
BUA	Birmingham University Archive, UK
CFM	Council of Foreign Ministers
CIA	Central Intelligence Agency (USA)
Cmd.	Command Papers published by the British Government
COCOM	Co-ordinating Committee (for East–West trade issues)
COS	Chiefs of Staff (GB)
CWIHB	*Cold War International History Bulletin*
CWIHP	Cold War International History Project (Woodrow Wilson Centre, Washington, D.C.)
DBPO	*Documents on British Policy Overseas*
EAC	European Advisory Commission
EDC	European Defence Community
EL	Eisenhower Presidential Library, Abilene, Kans.
FRG	Federal Republic of Germany (West Germany and post-1990 Germany)
FRUS	Foreign Relations of the United States
FO	Foreign Office
GDR	German Democratic Republic (GDR)
GP	*Die Grosse Politik der europäischen Kabinette, 1871–1914; Sammlung der diplomatischen Akten des Auswärtigen Amtes* (ed. by J. Lepsius, A. Mendelssohn Bartholdy and F. Thimme). Berlin: Deutsche Verlagsgeschaft für Politik und Geschichte, 1922–7
HC	House of Commons

H.C. *Parl. Deb.*	House of Commons, London: *Parliamentary Debates* (Hansard). Fourth Series and Fifth Series
HL	House of Lords Records Office, London
H.L. *Parl. Deb.*	House of Lords, London: *Parliamentary Debates* (Hansard)
HMSO	Her Majesty's Stationery Office
JCOS	Joint Chiefs of Army Staff (USA)
LOC	Library of Congress, Washington D.C., Manuscript Division
MI5/6	Secret Intelligence Services (GB)
NA	National Archives, Washington, D.C.
NATO	North Atlantic Treaty Organization
NSC	National Security Council
PRO	Public Record Office, London/Kew
PPS	Policy Planning Staff (USA)
PSB	Policy Strategy Board (USA)
PUA	Princeton University Archive (Seeley G. Mudd Library), Princeton, N.J.
RIIA	Royal Institute of International Affairs (Chatham House, London)
SACEUR	Supreme Allied Commander, Europe
TLS	*Times Literary Supplement*
UN	United Nations

Notes

INTRODUCTION

1. A.J.P. Taylor, 'The Statesman,' in A.J.P. Taylor et al., *Churchill: Four Faces and the Man* (London, 1969), 32.
2. W.F. Kimball (ed.), *Churchill and Roosevelt: The Complete Correspondence, Vol. 1* (London, 1984), 3–20 (introduction); see in general also W.S. Churchill, *Thoughts and Adventures* (London, 1932), 51–61 (chapter 'Personal Contacts').
3. P. Boyle (ed.), *The Churchill-Eisenhower Correspondence, 1953–1955* (Chapel Hill, N.C., 1990).
4. R.R. James, *Gallipoli* (London, 1984), 4–12, 25–6, 35ff.; T. Morgan, *Churchill: Young Man in a Hurry 1874–1915* (New York, 1982), 490ff.; R.R. James, *Churchill: A Study in Failure, 1900–1939* (London, 1970), 81ff.; G. Penn, *Fisher, Churchill and the Dardanelles* (Barnsley, 1999); M. Gilbert, *Winston S. Churchill Vol. 3: 1914–16* (London, 1971), 188ff.; M. Howard, 'Churchill and the First World War,' in R. Blake and W.R. Louis (eds), *Churchill* (Oxford, 1993), 129–45; also the rather uncritical account J.D. Wallin, *By Ships Alone: Churchill and the Dardanelles* (Durham, N.C., 1981). See also W.S. Churchill, *The World Crisis, Vol. 2: 1915* (London, 1923), 46–9, 92ff., 190–344, 432–99, 500–17; and D.G. Boadle, *Winston Churchill and the German Question in British Foreign Policy, 1918–1922* (The Hague, 1973), xv.
5. P. Clarke, 'Churchill's Economic Ideas, 1900–1930', in Blake and Louis (eds), *Churchill*, 79–95; M. Gilbert, *Winston S. Churchill, Vol. 5: Prophet of Truth, 1922–1939* (London, 1976), 92ff.; James, *Study in Failure*, 202, 204, 206–11; P. Addison, *Churchill on the Home Front, 1900–1955* (London, 1993), 244–50. See also J.M. Keynes, *The Economic Consequences of Mr. Churchill* (London, 1925); and R. Skidelsky, *Keynes* (Oxford, 1996), 26; R. Skidelsky, *John Maynard Keynes, Vol. 2: The Economist as Saviour, 1920–1932* (London, 1992), 197–207.
6. For Churchill's reaction to the failure of the Gallipoli expedition which resulted in the death of 120,000 British soldiers and numerous troops from other nations, see Churchill, *The World Crisis, Vol. 4: 1916–1918, Part 2* (London, 1927), 293–4; James, *Study in Failure*, 85–90. For his initial depression and ultimately his unshakeable confidence in his strategy as contained in private letters written by Churchill, see *Sunday Times* (No. 9,014), 1/6/1997, p. 5.
7. In Nov./Dec. 1895 Churchill was an observer in the Cuban civil war; from Aug. to Sept. 1897 he served with the Malakand Field Force in India; a year later, from August to October 1898, he was fighting in the Sudan; and the following year from October 1899 until early 1900 he covered the Boer War as war correspondent for the London *Morning Post*. See Churchill's own books on his adventures: *The Malakand Field Force: An Episode of Frontier War* (London, 1898); *The River War: A Historical Account of the Reconquest of the Soudan* (London, 1902); *The Boer War: London to Ladysmith via Pretoria/Ian Hamilton's March* (London, 1989); and above all *My Early Life: A Roving Commission* (London, 1930), 88ff., 115ff., 136ff., 176ff., 243ff. See also F. Woods (ed.), *Young Winston's Wars: The Original Despatches of Winston S. Churchill, War Correspondent, 1897–1900* (London, 1972); also H. Pelling, *Winston Churchill* (London, 1977), 44–65; W. Manchester, *The*

Last Lion: Winston S. Churchill, Visions of Glory, 1874–1932 (London, 1983), 219ff.; Morgan, *Churchill*, 74–127; B. Roberts, *Churchills in Africa* (London, 1970), 119ff., esp. 235ff.

8. Quoted in J. Charmley, *Churchill: The End of Glory. A Political Biography* (London, 1993), 76.

9. See C.P. Snow, *Variety of Men* (Harmondsworth, 1969), 137; also Taylor, 'The Statesman,' 16–17; R.R. James, 'The Politician', in A.J.P. Taylor et al., *Churchill*, 63–4, 83–4; also R.R. James, 'Churchill the Parliamentarian, Orator, and Statesman,' in Blake and Louis (eds), *Churchill*, 503–17.

10. As Fritz Stern wrote of Chaim Weizmann: 'Devotion to cause merged with personal ambition; cause and self served each other. Surely that is a common characteristic of great leaders ...'. See F. Stern, *Einstein's German World* (Harmondsworth, 1999), 228. For recent assessments of Churchill's career and politics, see *Transactions of the Royal Historical Society*, 6th series, Vol. XI (Cambridge, 2001), 179 ff.

11. This phrase was contained in the letter of acceptance his son Randolph Churchill read on his father's behalf when Churchill received honorary American citizenship from President Kennedy in 1963. See A.M. Schlesinger Jr, 'History's Impressario', Keynote address to the International Churchill Society, Boston, 28 October 1995 [webpage: www.winstonchurchill.org/p94rschles. htm]. See also A.M. Schlesinger Jr, *A Life in the Twentieth Century: Innocent Beginnings, 1917–1950* (Boston, 2000), 385–6.

12. Henry Kissinger, amongst others, has acknowledged this. See his *Diplomacy*, paperback edn (New York, 1994), 512, 513–14.

13. Quoted in F. Duchene, *Jean Monnet: The First Statesman of Interdependence* (New York, 1994), 81.

14. Quoted in H. Young, *This Blessed Plot: Britain and Europe from Churchill to Blair* (London, 1998), 24. At the time the respected Tizard was chief scientific adviser at the Ministry of Defence.

15. See Boyle (ed.), *Correspondence*, 48: letter Churchill to Eisenhower, 4/5/1953.

16. While, in the words of A.J.P. Taylor, Churchill 'had no doubt of his own consistency', Taylor believed that his 'consistency was less obvious to others'. Taylor, 'The Statesman', 32.

17. For a good and brief account of these events, see G. Best, *Churchill: A Study in Greatness* (London, 2001), 39–41; and for a much more lengthy treatment, see R. Jenkins, *Churchill: A Biography* (London, 2001), ch. 10. Jenkins concludes with regard to Tonypandy that 'On any objective analysis it is difficult to fault Churchill ... for any sign of aggression or vindictiveness towards labour' (p. 199). One of the best accounts of Churchill's domestic policies is still Addison's *Churchill on the Home Front*.

18. For Gallipoli, see nn. 4 and 6, above; and for the return to the gold standard, see n. 5, above. All these episodes are dealt with in detail in the many good biographical overviews of Churchill's life and entire political career which have appeared recently. See for example N. Rose, *Churchill: An Unruly Life* (London, 1994); F. Bédarida, *Churchill* (Paris, 1999); Best, *Churchill: A Study in Greatness*; P. Brendon, *Churchill: A Brief Life*, 2nd edn (London, 2001; 1st edn, 1984); and Jenkins's massive volume *Churchill: A Biography*. See also the still valuable books by H. Pelling, *Winston Churchill* (London, 1974) and K. Robbins, *Churchill* (Harlow, 1992); and the popular account by R. Blake, *Churchill* (1998). Of particular value are the the thematic accounts by Blake and Louis (eds), *Churchill* and Ian S. Wood, *Churchill* (Basingstoke, 2000); there also is of course Martin Gilbert's massive multi-volume Churchill biography and companion volumes which appeared (initially in cooperation with Randolph Churchill) from the mid-1960s to the late 1980s. For a good biographical overview, see B.B. Barrett (ed.), *Churchill: A Concise Bibliography* (Westport, Conn., 2000).

19. For a persuasively argued early criticism of Churchill's Far East policies, see S. Roskill, *Churchill and the Admirals* (London, 1977). Churchill's 'history' quote is cited in Schlesinger (see n. 20, below).

20. See A.M. Schlesinger Jr, 'History's Impressario', Keynote address to the International Churchill Society, Boston, 28 Oct. 1995 [webpage: www.winstonchurchill.org/p94rschles.htm]. However, despite its sometimes overly critical point of view, the book by Clive Ponting is an at times stimulating account. See C. Ponting, *Churchill* (London, 1994); J. Charmley, *Churchill: The End of Glory* (London, 1993), esp. p. 649; see above all his *Churchill's Grand Alliance: A Provocative Reassessment of the 'Special Relationship' between England and the U.S. from 1940 to 1957* (New York, 1995).

21. A. Clarke, 'A Reputation Ripe for Revision', *The Times*, 2 January 1993.

22. M. Cowling, *The Impact of Hitler* (London, 1975); and his revealing article 'Why We Should not have gone to War with Hitler', *Sunday Telegraph*, 20 Aug. 1989; D. Irving, *Churchill's War. Vol. 1: The Struggle for Power* (Bullsbrook, Australia, 1987); now also available, *Vol. 2: Triumph in Adversity* (2001). For the recent trial about Irving's manipulation of historical facts in connection with the Holocaust, see R.J. Evans, *Lying About Hitler: History, Holocaust, and the David Irving*

Trial (New York, 2001); D.D. Guttenplan, *The Holocaust on Trial* (New York, 2001); E. Menasse, *Der Holocaust vor Gericht: der Prozess um David Irving* (Berlin 2000). See also the earlier books dealing with the historical distortions of Irving and others: E. Jaeckel, *David Irving's Hitler: A Faulty History Dissected* (Port Angeles, Wash., 1993); and D.E. Lipstadt, *Denying the Holocaust: The Growing Assault on Truth and Memory* (New York, 1993).

23. See Charmley, *Churchill's Grand Alliance*, in particular, chs 1, 2 and 29. One of the last sentences of Charmley's book summarizes his position neatly: 'Churchill's "misguided sentimental investment" paid few dividends for Britain, but it made the road to world power for America smoother' (p. 361). For one of the best accounts of recent Churchill revisionism, see P. Addison, 'Churchill and the Price of Victory' in: N. Tiratsoo (ed.), *From Blitz to Blair: A New History of Britain since 1939* (London, 1998), 53–6, esp. 58–60. For a strong defence of Charmley's writing by a close friend, see A. Roberts, 'Churchill and the revisionists', *History Today* (March, 1997).

24. Quoted in Addison, 'Churchill and the Price of Victory', 63. For the inclination of Lord Halifax and others to commence peace negotiations with Nazi Germany, see Chapter 2, n. 1, below.

25. See Schlesinger, 'History's Impressario'.

26. Addison, 'Churchill and the Price of Victory', 76. For recent fairly level-headed books on Churchill, see n. 18 above. Moreover, whether the establishment of the welfare state including a model health service and the gradual breaking-up of Britain's entrenched class barriers were disadvantageous to the country in the post-1945 world, as some of the right-wing Churchill revisionists argue, must very much be doubted. For a very critical though not entirely negative assessment of Churchill's war-time performance, which appeared when this book went to press, see C. Hitchens, 'The Medals of his Defeats', *Atlantic Monthly* (April 2002), 118–37. (I am grateful to Prof. Günter Bischof for bringing this to my attention).

27. His domestic policy in the 1950s has been much less controversial. It is generally agreed that with some exceptions he largely continued the development of the welfare state established by the Labour governments and was careful to maintain industrial peace. The main controversy refers to the question whether Churchill's lack of decisive leadership contributed to Britain's economic placidity and whether or not Britain 'missed the bus' with regard to joining the Schuman Plan and the EEC. For a more detailed discussion of the latter, see Chapter 7, below. For Churchill's domestic policies, see the literature in n. 18 above; also A. Seldon, *Churchill's Indian Summer: The Conservative Government, 1951–55*, (London, 1981) and R. Jenkins, 'Churchill: The Government of 1951–55', in Blake and Louis (eds), *Churchill*, 491–502.

28. Kissinger, *Diplomacy*, quote: 513.

29. See J. Foschepoth, 'Churchill, Adenauer und die Neutralisierung Deutschlands', *Deutschland-Archiv* 17 (1984), 1300.

30. Quotes: A. Glees, 'Churchill's Last Gambit: What the Secret Documents Reveal […]', *Encounter* 64 (April 1985), 32; R. Callahan, *Churchill: Retreat from Empire* (Wilmington, Del., 1984), 263; J.W. Young, *Winston Churchill's Last Campaign: Britain and the Cold War, 1951–55* (Oxford, 1996); see also J.W. Young, 'Churchill, the Russians and the Western Alliance: The Three-Power Conference at Bermuda, December 1953', *English Historical Review* 101 (1986), 912. See also the interesting account by S. Lambakis, *Winston Churchill: Architect of Peace. A Study in Statesmanship and the Cold War* (Westport, Conn., 1993).

31. Quotes: Seldon, *Churchill's Indian Summer*, 421; J.W. Young, 'Cold War and Détente with Moscow', in J.W. Young (ed.), *The Foreign Policy of Churchill's Peacetime Government, 1951–55* (Leicester, 1988), 75. See also Brendon, *Churchill: A Brief Life*, 219.

32. See D. Carlton, 'Grossbritannien und die Gipfeldiplomatie', in B. Thoß and H.E. Volkmann (eds), *Zwischen Kaltem Krieg und Entspannung* (Boppard, 1988), 53; also D. Carlton, *Churchill and the Soviet Union* (Manchester, 2000), esp. chs 5–7; see also Best, *Churchill: A Study in Greatness*, 300.

33. Quote: Young, *Churchill's Last Campaign*, 341.

34. See n. 32. But see also the contemporary accounts by E. Shuckburgh, *Descent to Suez: Diaries, 1951–56* (London, 1986), 91, 134–5, 141; Lord Moran, *Churchill: The Struggle for Survival, 1940–65* (London, 1966), 403–7; and in general for leadership and old age, see J.M. Post and R.S. Robin, *When Illness Strikes the Leader: The Dilemma of the Captive King* (New Haven, Conn., 1993), 20–4.

35. For a good analysis of these factors, see I. Clark, *Globalization and Fragmentation: International Relations in the Twentieth Century* (Oxford, 1997).

36. Mentioned during a conversation with President Eisenhower on 26 June 1954. See FRUS 1952–54, Vol. 6, 1108–9: memorandum of conversation. See also Chapter 15, below, 338.

37. A summarizing analysis of Churchill's legacy is contained in the Conclusion of this book (see 383ff.).

38. Quoted in H.W. Brands, 'Who Won the Cold War? 1984–1991', reprinted in K. Larres and A. Lane (eds), *The Cold War. Essential Readings in History* (Oxford, 2001), 191. In his famous speech in the House of Commons on 11 May 1953 Churchill had said that it was a mistake to believe 'that nothing could be settled until all was settled'. For the speech, see H.C. *Parl.Deb.*, 5th series, Vol. 515, 11/5/1953, 883–98; for a detailed analysis of this important speech, see Chapter 11, below, 222–32.

CHAPTER 1: CHURCHILL'S PERSONAL DIPLOMACY BEFORE THE FIRST WORLD WAR

1. For a good account of the complex relationship between Churchill and Lloyd George, see J. Grigg, 'Churchill and Lloyd George', in: R. Blake and W. R. Louis (eds), *Churchill* (Oxford, 1993), 97–111. See also C.A. Amlund, 'Lloyd George and Winston Churchill: Contrasts and Similarities', *Contemporary Review* 259 (1991), 263–6.
2. Quoted in P.M. Kennedy, *The Rise and Fall of British Naval Mastery* (London, 1976), 215.
3. For a good overview, see PRO: ADM 116/940B; see also D. Stevenson, *Armaments and the Coming of War; Europe, 1904–1914* (Oxford, 1996), 165ff.; V.R. Berghahn, *Der Tirpitz Plan: Genesis und Verfall einer innenpolitischen Krisenstrategie unter Wilhelm II* (Düsseldorf, 1971); J. Steinberg, *Yesterday's Deterrent: Tirpitz and the Birth of the German Battle Fleet* (London, 1965); P.M. Kennedy, *The Rise of the Anglo-German Antagonism, 1860–1914* (London, 1980), 223ff., 441ff.; M. Epkenhans, *Die wilhelminische Flottenrüstung 1908–1914: Weltmachtstreben, industrieller Fortschritt, soziale Integration* (Munich, 1991); I.N. Lambi, *The Navy and German Power Politics, 1862–1914* (Boston, 1984). Still very useful are L. Woodward, *Great Britain and the German Navy* (Oxford, 1935) and A.J. Marder, *From the Dreadnought to Scapa Flow: The Royal Navy in the Fisher Era, 1904–1919, Vol.1* (Oxford, 1961). The Kaiser's personal role, though very important, should not be exaggerated; 'the German military-industrial complex proved to be very powerful'. See for example J. Retallack, *Germany in the Age of Kaiser Wilhelm II* (Basingstoke, 1996), quote: 79; see also convincingly J.C.G. Röhl, *The Kaiser and his Court: Wilhelm II and the Government of Germany* (Cambridge, 1987); J. van der Kiste, *Kaiser Wilhelm II: Germany's Last Emperor* (Stroud, 1999); and for a good overview: C. Clark, *Kaiser Wilhelm II: Profiles in Power* (Harlow, 2000), 71 ff.
4. See the excellent FO summary covering the years until late 1909: 'Précis of Correspondence Showing the Attitude of the German Government Towards the Question of the Limitation of Naval Armaments', 12/1/1910, in D. Stevenson (ed.), *British Documents on Foreign Affairs: Reports and Papers from the Foreign Office Confidential Print, Part I, Series F, Vol. 21: Germany, 1909–1914 [hereafter: BD Foreign Affairs]* (Washington, D.C., 1990), 29–43; also ibid., 312–17: Report by Captain Watson, 13/10/1913; also Kennedy, *Antagonism*, 447ff.; Z.S. Steiner, *Britain and the Origins of the First World War* (Basingstoke, 1977), 53–4, 70ff.; D.G. Herrmann, *The Arming of Europe and the Making of the First World War* (Princeton, N.J., 1996), 113ff., 147ff.; J. Steinberg, 'The German Background to Anglo-German Relations, 1905–1914,' in F.H. Hinsley (ed.), *British Foreign Policy under Sir Edward Grey* (Cambridge, 1977), 193ff.; D.W. Sweet, 'Great Britain and Germany, 1905–1911,' in Hinsley (ed.), ibid., 216ff.; K. Hildebrand, *Das vergangene Reich: Deutsche Außenpolitik von Bismarck bis Hitler, 1871–1945* (Stuttgart, 1995), 263–8; for a discussion of the literature and an overview of these crises, see J. Lowe, *The Great Powers, Imperialism and the German Problem, 1865–1925* (London, 1994), 166ff.; also V. Ullrich, *Die nervöse Großmacht 1871–1918. Aufstieg und Untergang des deutschen Kaiserreichs* (Frankfurt/M., 1999), 193ff.
5. For the British considerations regarding the possible motives for Germany's rearmament programme, see for example J. Steinberg, 'Diplomatie als Wille und Vorstellung: Die Berliner Mission Lord Haldanes im Februar 1912,' in H. Schottelius and W. Deist (eds), *Marine und Marinepolitik im kaiserlichen Deutschland, 1871–1914*, 2nd edn (Düsseldorf, 1981), 268–9.
6. Admiral Fisher, the First Sea Lord, was convinced that 'The Navy is the first, second, third, fourth, fifth … ad infinitum Line of Defence! … It's not invasion we have to fear if the Navy is beaten, IT'S STARVATION!' Quoted in P.M. Kennedy, 'Strategic Aspects of the Anglo-German Naval Race,' in P.M. Kennedy, *Strategy and Diplomacy, 1870–1945: Eight Studies* (London, 1983), 155; see also A.L. Friedberg, *The Weary Titan: Britain and the Experience of Relative Decline, 1895–1905* (Princeton, N.J., 1988); and K. Neilson, ' "Greatly Exaggerated": The Myth of the Decline of Britain before 1914,' in *International History Review* 13 (1991), 695–725.

7. On Grey's foreign policy, see above all Z.S. Steiner, *The Foreign Office and Foreign Policy, 1898–1914* (Cambridge, 1969), 83ff.; Hinsley (ed.), *British Foreign Policy*; K. Robbins, *Sir Edward Grey: A Biography* (London, 1971); E. Grey, *Twenty-Five Years, 1892–1916* (London, 1925).

8. Kennedy, 'Strategic Aspects,' 135–6. He concludes that what Tirpitz and the German government wanted to obtain was 'recognition and respect in peacetime, and a good chance of victory in wartime' (p. 136). See also Marder, *Dreadnought*, 105ff.; Kennedy, *The Realities behind Diplomacy: Background Influences on British External Policy, 1865–1980* (London, 1981), 130–1; Hildebrand, *Das vergangene Reich*, 253. For a contrary view see K.M. Wilson, *The Policy of the Entente: Essays on the Determinants of British Foreign Policy, 1904–1914* (Cambridge, 1985), 100–20. On the Schlieffen Plan, see Hildebrand, *Das vergangene Reich*, 172–3, 230–1, 274; Herrmann, *Arming of Europe*, 44–51, 121–2, 158–60; A. Bucholz, *Moltke, Schlieffen, and Prussian War Planning* (Oxford, 1991); and G. Ritter's classic *Der Schlieffenplan. Kritik eines Mythos* (Munich, 1956). For a discussion of *Weltpolitik* see also Lowe, *Great Powers*, 140–53; I. Geiss, *Der lange Weg in die Katastrophe: Die Vorgeschichte des Ersten Weltkrieges 1815–1914* (Munich, 1990); Ullrich, *Die nervöse Großmacht*, 194–9. For the development of *Weltpolitik*, see P. Winzen, *Bülows Weltmachtkonzept. Untersuchungen zur Frühphase seiner Außenpolitik* (Boppard, 1977); and K. Canis, *Von Bismarck zur Weltpolitik. Deutsche Außenpolitik 1890–1902* (Berlin, 1997). For an interesting review of some of the newer literature, see N. Ferguson, 'Germany and the Origins of the First World War: New Perspectives,' *Historical Journal* 35 (1992), 725–52.

9. For the 'continental commitment strategy', see Kennedy, *Rise and Fall*, 205–37; Kennedy, *Realities*, 110–39; M.L. Dockrill, *The Formulation of a Continental Foreign Policy by Great Britain, 1908–1912* (New York, 1986).

10. For a comparision of both country's naval strength, see PRO: CAB 37/97/27, 'Great Britain and Germany in April 1909'.

11. See V.R. Berghahn, *Germany and the Approach of War* (London, 1973), 54ff.; and F. Fischer, *Germany's War Aims in the First World War* (London, 1967); F. Fischer, *War of Illusions* (London, 1973); see also the literature cited in Ullrich, *Die nervöse Großmacht*, 216ff., 238ff..

12. See Steiner, *First World War*, 99, 48ff.; Lowe, *Great Powers*, 155–7; Wilson, *Policy of the Entente*, 100–20. Wilson argues for example that in view of Britain's relative decline, weakness and the vulnerability of the Empire, the invention of the German naval threat 'fulfilled important psychological needs. The more unflattering the portrayal of Germany, the more flattering that of Great Britain. The greater the menace of Germany, the better able were some people to persuade themselves that they had a role to play' (p. 118).

13. This change of policy was, however, only admitted publicly in 1912. The Two-Power Standard was defined by Lord Selborne in 1902 as referring 'to the two strongest naval powers at any given moment'; thus London intended to maintain the policy that the Royal Navy should always be as strong as the next two navies combined. In 1908 Prime Minister Asquith explained somewhat optimistically that it also meant a 10 per cent superiority of the combined power of the next two navies so that a fourth navy would not be able to hold the balance. See Kennedy, 'Strategic Aspects,' 139 (quote: ibid.); Stevenson, *Armaments*, 170; Sweet, 'Great Britain and Germany,' 223–4; also H.C. *Parl. Deb.*, 4th series, Vol. 5, 26/5/1909, 1290–6.

14. See R.K. Massie, *Dreadnought: Britain, Germany, and the Coming of the Great War* (London, 1992), 468ff. The Dreadnoughts, the first one was laid down in late 1905, had a much greater fire-power and a higher speed than the existing battleships. Thus, with the introduction of the Dreadnought, the Anglo-German rivalry assumed the nature of both a quantitative and a qualitative race (see Berghahn, *Approach of War*, 49). However, Dreadnoughts cost almost twice as much as the pre-Dreadnought battleships and required almost 50 per cent more personnel. Moreover, it became clear that instead of widening the gap as had been expected in London, the development of the Dreadnoughts enabled Germany to close the gap in the naval superiority between Germany and Britain much more quickly than would otherwise have been the case.

15. Kennedy, *Rise and Fall*, 211ff.; Kennedy, *Antagonism*, 441ff.; Steiner, *First World War*, 22ff.; on the shift in Britain's strategy from a 'balance of power' to a policy of ever closer relations with and greater support for its increasingly important entente partners, see C. Gade, *Gleichgewichtspolitik oder Bündnispflege? Maximen britischer Außenpolitik, 1909–1914* (Göttingen, 1997), 49ff., 209–19; also Wilson, *Policy of the Entente*, esp. 37ff. Since 1906 (and in particular towards late 1908 and in September 1911 and July/August 1912) unofficial conversations between British and French military experts had taken place which only became known to the Cabinet in late 1911; they culminated in the Grey–Cambon exchange of late 1912. See Robbins, *Grey*, 238–9, 244–7; Gade,

Gleichgewichtspolitik, 153ff.; D. Lloyd George, *War Memoirs, Vol. 1* (London, 1933), 49–51; and S.R. Williamson, *The Politics of Grand Strategy: Britain and France Prepare for War, 1904–1914* (Cambridge, MA, 1969).

16. PRO: ADM 116/940B, final report Dumas, Berlin, to Sir F. Lascelles, London, 30/7/1908; Lascelles regarded the report as serious enough to pass it on to Grey a day later (No. 335).

17. For an analysis of Churchill's attitude towards the German Reich, see D.G. Boadle, *Winston Churchill and the German Question in British Foreign Policy, 1918–22* (The Hague, 1973), 10ff.; G.A. Craig, 'Churchill and Germany,' in Blake and Louis (eds), *Churchill*, 21–40.

18. See W. Manchester, *The Last Lion: William S. Churchill. Visions of Glory, 1874–1932* (London, 1983), 168–70; Massie, *Dreadnought*, 818; see also W.S. Churchill's 'The Ex-Kaiser', in his *Great Contemporaries* (London, 1937; 1990 edn), 12–25, esp. 20.

19. See, for example, T. Morgan's *Churchill: Young Man in a Hurry 1874–1915* (New York, 1982); in great detail also R. Jenkins, *Churchill* (London, 2001), 65 ff.

20. See note 18 above.

21. Quote: G.A. Craig, 'Churchill and Germany,' 25; Manchester, *Last Lion*, 424–6; M. Gilbert, *Churchill: A Life* (London, 1993), 125, 128, 144–5; Boadle, *German Question*, 9–10. However, on another trip to Germany in September 1907 he was deeply impressed by the country's labour exchanges and social insurance schemes. See Addison, *Home Front*, 72; also R.S. Churchill, *Winston S. Churchill, Vol. 2: Young Statesman, 1901–1914* (London, 1967), 194–7, 221, 224–5, 312.

22. There was some justification in the outburst of Grey's Private Secretary in late August 1911 that it was 'depressing to find that after six years' experience of Germany the inclination here is still to believe that she can be placated by small concessions'. Quoted in Steiner, *First World War*, 42; see also Massie, *Dreadnought*, 819.

23. See Addison, *Home Front*, 68–9; H. Weinroth, 'Left-Wing Opposition to Naval Armaments in Britain before 1914,' *Journal of Contemporary History* 6 (1971), 96ff.; also H. Weinroth, 'The British Radicals and the Balance of Power, 1902–1914,' *Historical Journal* 13 (1970), 653–82.

24. See Ullrich, *Die nervöse Großmacht*, 202–3.

25. See Sweet, 'Great Britain and Germany,' 218; see also *British Documents on the Origins of the War, 1898–1914, Vol.6: Anglo-German Tension, Armaments and Negotiations, 1907–12* [hereafter: *BD Origins*] (London, 1930), ch. 42. The Kaiser's November 1907 visit to Windsor (which was reciprocated by Edward VII's visit to Berlin in early 1909) had not been able to improve relations substantially.

26. See B.B. Gilbert, *David Lloyd George: A Political Life. The Architect of Change, 1863–1912* (London, 1987), 345–6. The construction of four German ships annually had come about by shortening the replacement period for each ship from 25 to 20 years. Once this had been implemented the building rate would go down to two new ships annually from 1912 and three ships from 1918 onwards unless a new naval bill was introduced as Tirpitz envisaged despite the opposition of the German Chancellor.

27. See Gilbert, *Lloyd George*, 345–7; Steiner, *First World War*, 52; W.S. Churchill, *The World Crisis, Vol. 1: 1911–14* (London, 1923), 34; for the wider background see Sweet, 'Great Britain and Germany,' 222–4; Stevenson, *Armaments*, 167–9; Robbins, *Grey*, 190; Lloyd George, *War Memoirs, Vol. 1*, 7ff.; also M. Pugh, *Lloyd George* (London, 1988), 69–73; for the 1908–9 attempts, see *BD Origins, Vol. 6*, chs 43–5. For the Lloyd George–Churchill relationship, see also Morgan, *Churchill*, 245ff.

28. One can differentiate among the 'economists' who wished to reduce Britain's military expenditure, the 'navalists' with their strong conviction that the strengthening of the country's navy was imperative, and the 'Potsdam Party' who favoured an accommodation with Germany for political reasons. The members of the so-called 'Potsdam Party' were partially identical with the 'economists' (e.g. Lloyd George and Churchill). See for example, Steiner, *Foreign Office*, 86ff.

29. Two weeks later he had another interview with Metternich but this time Grey was not present. See M.G. Fry, *Lloyd George and Foreign Policy: The Education of a Statesman, 1890–1916* (Montreal, 1977), 94–8.

30. This, however, did not restrain the German press from expressing the view in July 1910 (with reference to a speech in the Commons) that 'praise from an English mouth is very suspicious'. *BD Foreign Affairs*, Vol. 21, 114: Goschen to Grey, 18/7/1910.

31. On Lloyd George's and Churchill's activities in 1908, see Gilbert, *Lloyd George*, 346–52; Fry, *Lloyd George*, 94–103; also R.S. Churchill, *Young Statesman*, 270, 511–17. For Lloyd George's pro-German sympathies, see also K.O. Morgan, 'Lloyd George and Germany,' *Historical Journal* 39/3 (1996), 756–58.

32. See V. Bonham Carter, *Winston Churchill As I Knew Him* (London, 1965), 168–74 ('untrustworthy' quote: p.169). Other quotes: R.S. Churchill, *Young Statesman*, 512, 513. See also Morgan, *Churchill*, 252–3.

33. See PRO: CAB 37/94/108, August 1908.
34. See F. Broeze, 'Shipping Policy and Social-Darwinism: Albert Ballin and the *Weltpolitik* of the Hamburg–America Line, 1886–1914', *The Mariner's Mirror* 79/4 (1993), 419–36. Broeze concludes that 'Ballin's behaviour was characterized by the same social-darwinist concepts of struggle and the decisive use of raw power in a world of national and racial inequality as those which existed in the political arena'. He believes that Ballin's 'unrestricted shipping Weltpolitik' was a 'disturber of the peace' (pp. 431–2). See also P.F. Stubmann, *Ballin. Leben und Werk eines deutschen Reeders*, 2nd rev. edn (Berlin, 1927).
35. Quote: Berghahn, *Approach of War*, 78; see also Steiner, *Foreign Office*, 99; L. Cecil, *Wilhelm II, Vol. 2: Emperor and Exile, 1900–1941* (Chapel Hill, N.C., 1996), 123–45. For a good summary of the *Daily Telegraph* affair and the Bosnian crisis, see Ullrich, *Die nervöse Großmacht*, 219–20, 210–11. On Ballin and Cassel, see Massie, *Dreadnought*, 792ff. (for the 1908 and 1909 negotiations, see p. 801); E. Straub, *Albert Ballin. Der Reeder des Kaisers* (Berlin, 2001); S. Wiborg, *Albert Ballin* (Hamburg, 2000); L. Cecil, *Albert Ballin: Business and Politics in Imperial Germany, 1988–1918* (Princeton, N.J., 1967), 193ff.; also B. Huldermann, *Albert Ballin* (Berlin, 1922), 208ff.; K. Pinette, *Albert Ballin und die deutsche Politik: Ein Beitrag zur Geschichte von Staat und Wirtschaft 1900–1918* (Hamburg, 1938), 68; also Broeze, 'Shipping Policy', 433, n. 7. For the attempts at an Anglo-German rapprochement between 1908–11, see good summaries in Steiner, *First World War*, 52ff., Stevenson, *Armaments*, 171–2; Cecil, *Wilhelm II, Vol. 2*, 152–68. Very little literature exists on Cassel; but see B.A. Nidder, *Sir Ernest Cassel, International Financier: A Biography* (A.B., honors thesis, Harvard University, 1935).
36. Quoted in Addison, *Home Front*, 69.
37. Quotes: Steinberg, 'Diplomatie,' 273; Churchill, *World Crisis, Vol. 1*, 36–7. Moreover, in April 1909 the German Acting Foreign Minister Kiderlen-Wächter indicated that Berlin was interested in an arrangement with London. See *BD Origins, Vol. 6*, 265–66: Goschen to Grey, 16/6/1909.
38. See Steiner, *Foreign Office*, 98; Wilson, *Policy of the Entente*, 35–6; also Morgan, *Churchill*, 263–70. Asquith regarded Lloyd George's and Churchill's veiled threats of resignation as 'bluff' though he became rather exasperated with them. See Bonham Carter, *As I Knew Him*, 170; M. Bonham Carter and M. Pottle (eds), *Lantern Slides: The Diaries and Letters of Violet Bonham Carter, 1904–14* (London, 1997), 169–70.
39. Churchill, *World Crisis, Vol. 1*, 36–8 (quote: 37); for details see H.C., *Parl. Deb.*, 4th series, Vol. 8, 26/7/1909, 855–71; Robbins, *Grey*, 196–204; Lowe, *Great Powers*, 156–7; also Gilbert, *Lloyd George*, 364–8; Fry, *Lloyd George*, 105ff.; and also very detailed Marder, *Dreadnought, Vol. 1*, 151ff.; *BD Foreign Affairs, Vol. 21*, 83–97: Annual Report, 1909, Goschen to Grey, dated 24/6/1910.
40. For a literature review and a good assessment of Bethmann's 'moderate imperialism' and 'reforming conservatism' and an evaluation of the 'significance of individual personality' and 'the power of structural constraints', see K.H. Jarausch, 'Revising German History: Bethmann Hollweg Revisited', *Central European History* 21/3 (1988), 224–43. On the whole Jarausch concludes that 'Bethmann incorporated both the best and worst traits of his contemporaries. Decency and dependability, surprising courage and independence of mind struggled with indecisiveness and pessimism, exasperating conventionality, and subservience to the military' (p. 240). See also G. MacDonogh, *The Last Kaiser: William the Impetuous* (London, 2000), ch. 13 (on Bethmann-Hollweg).
41. See *BD Origins, Vol. 6*, 283: Goschen to Grey on his conversation with Bethmann Hollweg, 21/8/1909. For an overview of Bethmann Hollweg's political strategy see Hildebrand, *Das vergangene Reich*, 249ff.; K.H. Jarausch, *The Enigmatic Chancellor: Bethmann-Hollweg and the Hubris of Imperial Germany* (New Haven, Conn., 1973); also Huldermann, *Ballin*, 216ff., 248; Cecil, *Wilhelm II, Vol. 2*, 146ff., 169. See also Gade, *Gleichgewichtspolitik*, 49ff., who ignores the admittedly modest role of Churchill, Lloyd George and Cassel and Ballin in these talks.
42. See *BD Foreign Affairs, Vol. 21*, 25–6: Goschen to Grey, 3/1/1910; 95: Annual Report, 1909, dated 24/6/1910.
43. Quotes: *BD Origins, Vol. 6*, 285: Grey to Goschen, 23/8/1909; Gilbert, *Churchill: A Life*, 143; see also Sweet, 'Great Britain and Germany,' 227ff.; Robbins, *Grey*, 205–7; Steiner, *Foreign Office*, 90.
44. See for example *BD Origins, Vol. 6*, 284: Goschen to Grey, 21/8/1913; 285–7: Memorandum by C. Hardinge, 25/8/1909; Mallet to Grey, 26/8/1909; Goschen to C. Hardinge, 28/8/1909; *BD Foreign Affairs, Vol. 21*, 83–97: Annual Report, 1909, dated 24/6/1910; also Jarausch, *Enigmatic Chancellor*, 114–16. On *Weltpolitik*, see also note 8, above.
45. Quotes: Jarausch, *Enigmatic Chancellor*, 113, 114; see also *BD Origins, Vol. 6*, 288–9: Notes and minutes by Grey, 31/8–1/9/1909.

46. See Steiner, *First World War*, 54–5; Robbins, *Grey*, 206–7; Steinberg, 'Diplomatie,' 273; Sweet, 'Great Britain and Germany,' 229–33; Stevenson, *Armaments*, 172–3; Hildebrand, *Das vergangene Reich*, 255–8; Jarausch, *Enigmatic Chancellor*, 116ff.; also *BD Origins, Vol. 6*, 434ff., 575–6: Grey to Goschen, 16/12/1910. For an excellent account of the domestic background of Bethmann's policies, see Berghahn, *Approach of War*, 85ff.; and for a succinct British characterization of Tirpitz, see *BD Foreign Affairs, Vol. 21*, 117–18: Report by Captain Heath, 6/8/1910; for the March 1910 Reichstag debate regarding the second reading of Tirpitz's naval estimates, see also ibid., 68–73.
47. Quotes: Churchill, *World Crisis, Vol. 1*, 39–40, see also 50–2; also Addison, *Home Front*, 83; also D. Stafford, *Churchill and Secret Service* (London, 1997), 28. As early as August 1908 Chancellor Bülow had already recognized that Germany 'could not simultaneously have the best army in the world ..., pursue the most generous and most expensive social policy among all peoples and build up and renew a huge navy'. Quoted in Ullrich, *Die nervöse Großmacht*, 220 (my translation).
48. PRO: ADM 116/940B, Goschen, Berlin, to Grey, London, No. 215, 6/8/1910 with the enclosed final report by Captain Heath, the British naval attaché. Heath also wrote that Tirpitz seemed to be almost looking for an excuse to feel insulted by the British: it 'might almost be said' of Tirpitz that he was 'seeking for an excuse to consider himself insulted, or his word doubted by English ministers'.
49. Grey told the Cabinet in late July 1910, that it was inexpedient to enter 'into any engagements with Germany which would be of such a character as to lead to misunderstanding and perhaps loss of friendship with France'. Quoted in Robbins, *Grey*, 222.
50. See *BD Origins, Vol. 6*, 496ff.; also Cecil, *Wilhelm II, Vol. 2*, 159–60.
51. *BD Origins, Vol. 6*, 590–1: Nicolson to Hardinge, 2/3/1911; see also 577ff.; and Steinberg, 'Diplomatie,' 271; see also Sweet, 'Great Britain and Germany,' 234–5.
52. The committee seems to have been abolished again on 21 July 1911. The FO officials believed that it was an attempt to keep an eye on Grey and ensure the realization of Anglo-German talks. See Steiner, *Foreign Office*, 90.
53. See *BD Origins, Vol. 6*, 598ff.; 631–7: Memoranda Grey, 24/5. and 1/6/1911; 781–90. Extract from Grey's speech to the Committee of Imperial Defence, 26/5/1911; also Robbins, *Grey*, 233–4; and *Die Grosse Politik, Vol. 31: Das Scheitern der Haldane-Mission und ihre Rückwirkung auf die Tripelentente 1911–1912* [hereafter: *GP*] (Berlin, 1926), 1ff.
54. See *BD Origins, Vol. 6*, 612ff.; also *BD Foreign Affairs, Vol. 21*, 140–1: Watson to Goschen, 17.2.1911; 145–52: Goschen to Grey, 31/3/1911; Steiner, *First World War*, 54–7; Sweet, 'Great Britain and Germany,' 234–5; Stevenson, *Armaments*, 173–5; Hildebrand, *Das vergangene Reich*, 253, 255, 265; Steiner, *Foreign Office*, 90–91. See also p. 25, below.
55. Berghahn, *Approach of War*, 94.
56. See E. Oncken, *Panthersprung nach Agadir: Die deutsche Politik während der zweiten Marokkokrise 1911* (Düsseldorf, 1973); G. Barraclough, *From Agadir to Armageddon: Anatomy of a Crisis* (New York, 1982); Gade, *Gleichgewichtspolitik*, 94–8; Hildebrand, *Das vergangene Reich*, 260ff.; Th. Meyer, '*Endlich eine Tat, eine befreiende Tat ...*'. *Alfred von Kiderlen-Wächters 'Panthersprung nach Agadir' [...]* (Husum, 1996). See also the accounts in Robbins, *Grey*, 239ff.; Jarausch, *Enigmatic Chancellor*, 120–6; Cecil, *Wilhelm II, Vol. 2*, 160–6. It is generally accepted that it was not so much Bethmann-Hollweg but the uncontrollable strong-willed Foreign Minister Kiderlen-Wächter (who suddenly died in late 1912) whose influence was decisive for German policy throughout the crisis. See also *BD Origins, Vol. 7: The Agadir Crisis* (London, 1932), 322ff.; *GP, Vol. 29: Die Zweite Marokkokrise 1911* (Berlin, 1925), 139ff.; *BD Foreign Affairs, Vol. 21*, 107–8: Goschen to Grey, 30/6/1910.
57. Letter to his wife, 5/7/1911. Quoted in R.S. Churchill, *Young Statesman*, 522. See also Steiner, *Foreign Office*, 141–2; see also Morgan, *Churchill*, 328–35; and in general H. Weinroth, 'The British Radicals and the Agadir Crisis', in *European Studies Review* 3 (1973), 39–61. On this crisis, see also *BD Foreign Affairs, Vol. 21*, 270–86: Annual Report, 1911, Goschen to Grey, dated 21/2/1913.
58. See Churchill, *World Crisis, Vol. 1*, 50–2 (quote: 51); see also R.S. Churchill, *Young Statesman*, 525–6; Gilbert, *Churchill: A Life*, 162–3. For Churchill's early interest and involvement with Britain's young secret service, see the excellent account in Stafford, *Churchill and Secret Service*, 28ff., 40ff.
59. W.S. Churchill, *Great Contemporaries* (London, 1937, 1990 edition), 10.
60. *BD Origins, Vol. 7*, 387–417 (quote: 391); Churchill, *Great Contemporaries*, 46–50; *BD Foreign Affairs, Vol. 21*, 184–6: Grey to Granville, 13/10/1911, Corbett to Grey, 24/10/1911; 192: Goschen to Grey, 3/11/1911; Lloyd George, *War Memoirs, Vol. 1*, 43–5; Grey, *Twenty-Five Years*, 224–31; *GP, Vol.*

29, 206ff.; Marder, *Dreadnought, Vol. 1*, 239ff.; and T. Boyle, 'New Light on Lloyd George's Mansion House Speech', in *Historical Journal* 23 (1980), 431–3; K. Wilson, 'The Agadir Crisis, the Mansion House Speech, and the Double-Edgedness of Agreements,' *Historical Journal* 15/3 (1972), 513–32.

61. Letter to his wife, 6/8/1911. Quoted in R.S. Churchill, *Young Statesman*, 529.

62. Craig, 'Churchill and Germany,' 26; Robbins, *Grey*, 241–4; Churchill, *World Crisis, Vol. 1*, 37–9; R.S. Churchill, *Young Statesman*, 523ff.

63. Churchill's letter to the Liberal backbencher William Royle is quoted in R.S. Churchill (ed.), *Young Statesman, Companion, Vol. 3: 1911–1914* (London, 1969), 1360–1; see also Stevenson, *Armaments*, 195.

64. See Ullrich, *Die nervöse Großmacht*, 228; also W.J. Mommsen, 'Der Topos vom unvermeidlichen Krieg. Außenpolitik und öffentliche Meinung im deutschen Reich im letzten Jahrzehnt vor 1914', in J. Dülffer and K. Holl (eds), *Bereit zum Krieg. Kriegsmentalität im wilhelminischen Deutschland 1890–1914* (Göttingen, 1986), 194–224.

65. There was much less unanimity about *how* to defend France. Temporarily, Lloyd George and Churchill were even 'enthusiastically working for a war' with Germany in defence of France (Steiner, *Foreign Office*, 125–6, quote: 126); see also Churchill's undated memorandum, published in R.S. Churchill, *Young Statesman*, 523. See also Kennedy, *Realities*, 132; Kennedy, *Rise and Fall*, 235–6; Stevenson, *Armaments*, 180ff.; Robbins, *Grey*, 250. For a hostile discussion of Churchill's selfish motives regarding the adoption of an anti-German standpoint, see J. Charmley, *Churchill: The End of Glory. A Political Biography* (London, 1992) 75–7, 84.

66. These were the words of the Austro-Hungarian foreign minister Alois von Aehrenthal, quoted in Lowe, *Great Powers*, 153.

67. See PRO: FO 93/36/74; and above all, M. Fröhlich, *Von Konfrontation zur Koexistenz: die deutsch-englischen Kolonialbeziehungen in Afrika zwischen 1884 und 1914* (Bochum, 1990); F. H. Bode, *Der Kampf um die Bagdadbahn, 1903–1914: ein Beitrag zur Geschichte der deutsch-englischen Beziehungen* (Aalen, 1982).

68. See *BD Foreign Affairs, Vol. 21*, 202–4: Grey to Goschen, 20/11/1911.

69. See Berghahn, *Approach of War*, 118, see also 111–20; and Stevenson, *Armaments*, 205–06; Robbins, *Grey*, 223; Steiner, *First World War*, 105–9; R.T.B. Langhorne, 'Great Britain and Germany, 1911–1914,' in Hinsley (ed.), *British Foreign Policy*, 308–14; Hildebrand, *Das vergangene Reich*, 277ff.; and *BD Origins, Vol. 10, Part 2: The Last Years of Peace* (London, 1938), chs 91–5; also *BD Foreign Affairs, Vol. 21*, 200–1: Watson to Goschen, 6/12/1911.

70. The 'risk theory' meant that Germany intended to obtain a fleet powerful enough 'not only to defend her coasts but also able to threaten the *overall* maritime superiority of the most powerful navy existing'. Thus if Britain were to attack such a strong German fleet, it 'might lose so many warships that the Royal Navy would be inferior to its other rivals, particularly the Franco-Russian naval forces'. As the British were expected to realize this, the German fleet would therefore be immune from a British attack. However, Tirpitz was aware that until such a fleet had been developed there was a 'danger zone' and he therefore attempted quite unsuccessfully to play down the size and speed of Germany's naval construction programme. Kennedy, 'Strategic Aspects,' 133–8 (quotes: 133); also Lowe, *Great Powers*, 155.

71. Churchill, *World Crisis, Vol. 1*, 111ff., 151ff. (quote: 113); *BD Origins, Vol. 10, 2*, 612ff. See Kennedy, *Rise and Fall*, 226–7; Massie, *Dreadnought*, 825–7; also R.S. Churchill, *Young Statesman*, 588–6; *BD Origins, Vol. 10, 2*, 580ff.; Woodward, *Great Britain and the German Navy*, 380ff. Within the British government and in various departments like the Foreign Office and the Admiralty, which opposed the almost total withdrawal of British warships from the Mediterranean, the whole problem was extensively discussed, in particular between May and July and again in November/December 1912 (see *BD Origins, Vol. 10, 2*, 580ff.). The Grey–Cambon exchange of letters took place in October/November 1912 and renewed naval conversations with the French had been entered into in July/August 1912 (see n. 15 above). By spring 1913 plans for Anglo-French naval cooperation in case of a war with Germany had been worked out. Although it was made clear that this did not mean that common action would be automatically embarked upon in case of war, it was agreed 'if there was a menace of war, the two Governments should consult together'. On the whole Grey believed that he had ensured that Britain's flexibility and independence of action were preserved. Robbin, *Grey*, 262–3 (quote: 262); Hildebrand, *Das vergangene Reich*, 268, 271; Steiner, *First World War*, 99–104.

72. For example J. Steinberg, 'Diplomatie,' 272, claims that by early 1912 Britain was not really neutral anymore as the entente with France approximated a military alliance. See also Charmley, *End of Glory*, 82; R.S. Churchill, *Young Statesman*, 596–9; on the great naval debate of 1912, also Robbins, *Grey*, 260ff.

73. Quoted in Kennedy, *Rise and Fall*, 223–4; see also Gade, *Gleichgewichtspolitik*, 158ff. On another occasion, in February 1911, he had already written that 'the sea is all one, and naval supremacy must be settled at the central point'. Quoted in R.S. Churchill, *Young Statesman*, 520. Lord Selborne and the Admiralty had already come to the same conclusion in 1901/02. See Kennedy, 'Strategic Aspects,' 140–1.

74. Churchill, *World Crisis, Vol. 1*, 70ff.; Craig, 'Churchill and Germany,' 26; D. Sommer, *Haldane of Cloan: His Life and Times, 1856–1928* (London, 1960), 245–9; Robbins, *Grey*, 255. For Churchill's time at the Admiralty, see in general S. Roskill, *Churchill and the Admirals* (London, 1977); Morgan, *Churchill*, 340ff.; R. Ollard, 'Churchill and the Navy,' in Blake and Louis (eds), *Churchill*, 375–95; R. Hough, *Former Naval Person: Churchill and the Wars at Sea* (London, 1985), 42–52; also Churchill, *World Crisis, Vols 1 and 2*.

75. Churchill, *World Crisis, Vol. 1*, 71ff.; Charmley, *End of Glory*, 74.

76. Most of the memorandum is published in R.S. Churchill, *Young Statesman*, 577–80 (quotes: 577, 579); see also the account in H.H. Asquith, *The Genesis of the War* (London, 1923), 77ff.

77. These were the words of FO official Eyre Crowe, quoted in Steiner, *Foreign Office*, 143.

78. The announcement in late November 1911 that there had been ongoing secret Anglo-French military talks only increased the criticism of Grey's allegedly too confrontational foreign policy. See Steiner, ibid., 126–7; Gade, *Gleichgewichtspolitik*, 102–15; also J.A. Murray, 'Foreign Policy Debated: Sir Edward Grey and His Critics, 1911–1912', in W.C. Askew and L.P. Wallace (eds), *Power, Public Opinion and Diplomacy* (Durham, N.C., 1959), 140–1.

79. Churchill, *World Crisis, Vol. 1*, 94. See also R. Prior, *Churchill's World Crisis as History* (London, 1983).

80. Letter Churchill to Sir Ernest Cassel, 7/1/1912. Quoted in R.S. Churchill (ed.), *Young Statesman, Companion, Vol. 3*, 1491–2 (also in R.S. Churchill, *Young Statesman*, 560). See also Churchill's letter to Cassel, dated 14/4/1912, in R.S. Churchill (ed.), ibid., 1537–8). See also Taylor, 'The Statesman,' 15–16. At this stage Churchill was considered 'as by no means anti-German' in Germany. See Huldermann, *Ballin*, 247.

81. According to Lloyd George's *War Memoirs, Vol. 1*, 46–51, this strategy only reciprocated the habit of Grey and the Foreign Office to leave most members of the Cabinet in the dark regarding important foreign policy matters.

82. It is still somewhat uncertain whether the initiative came from Ballin or Cassel though all indications and most of the secondary literature as well as the editors of *Die Grosse Politik*, the monumental collection of documents published and very carefully selected by the German Foreign Office in the 1920s (they thus have to be used with great caution), point to Ballin. In late January 1912 and particularly after the failure of the Haldane mission both governments tried to emphasize that the initial approach to enter into negotiations had originated with the other side. However, it appears to have been Ballin's own private initiative which was not inspired by Wilhelm; the Kaiser probably did not even know about it. Amateur diplomacy which initially excluded both countries' ambassadors contributed to the resulting confusion and mutual misunderstanding. See *GP, Vol. 31*, footnote on p. 97; Cecil, *Ballin*, 182; Huldermann, *Ballin*, 248; Steinberg, 'Diplomatie,' 275–6; Langhorne, 'Great Britain and Germany,' 289–90; Stevenson, *Armaments*, 206; also Robbins, *Grey*, 256. For the contemporary German perspective, see Wilhelm II, *Ereignisse und Gestalten 1978–1918* (Leipzig, 1922), 122–34. H. Begbie, *The Vindication of Great Britain* (London, 1916) believes that the initiative had come from the German government (see pp. 133, 135). However, Begbie was largely writing on behalf of Haldane, who after 1914 found himself strongly attacked for his alleged pro-German sympathies, and Begbie had been extensively briefed by Haldane. See S.E. Koss, *Lord Haldane: Scapegoat for Liberalism* (New York, 1969), 88–94, esp. 93.

83. B. Huldermann, *Ballin* (English edn, London, 1922, reprinted 1984 and 2000), 165 (p. 256 in the German edition); see also Massie, *Dreadnought*, 802.

84. Letter Churchill to Sir Ernest Cassel, 7/1/1912, quoted in R.S. Churchill (ed.), *Young Statesman, Companion, Vol. 3*, 1491–2; see also Massie, ibid.; Steinberg, 'Diplomatie,' 274; Manchester, *Last Lion*, 449.

85. Cassel's letter to Ballin was dated 9 January 1912. See Huldermann, *Ballin*, 165. In the German edition (p. 246) it is said more precisely that such an opportunity had to develop in a natural way ('müßte dann auf natürliche Weise entstehen').

86. Steinberg, 'Diplomatie,' 274.

87. Langhorne, 'Great Britain and Germany,' 290, 305; Haldane mentions in his *An Autobiography* (London, 1929), 239, that Churchill told only 'certain of his colleagues'.

88. Grey, *Twenty-Five Years*, 250.
89. Massie, *Dreadnought*, 802–4; Steinberg, 'Diplomatie,' 274–5. According to Bethmann Hollweg's memoirs (as correctly summarized by Churchill) the memorandum consisted of three major points which London put to Berlin: 1. German acceptance of British naval superiority and no further increase and possibly a reduction of the German navy programme; 2. Britain would be favourably disposed towards supporting Germany's colonial ambitions; 3. an agreement that the two countries would not embark on or take part in any aggression against each other. See Churchill, *World Crisis*, Vol. 1, 95; Th. von Bethmann Hollweg, *Reflections on the World War* (London, 1920), 46–9; also F. Maurice, *Haldane, 1856–1915: The Life of Viscount Haldane of Cloan* (London, 1937), 291; Jarausch, *Enigmatic Chancellor*, 127; Massie, ibid., 803. However, a British pledge of absolute neutrality – the main German aim – was missing. Whether Asquith knew of the developments at this stage is uncertain. Grey regularly consulted with Asquith but foreign policy was controlled by the Foreign Secretary and 'Asquith was not one to override expert knowledge'. G.H. Cassar, *Asquith as War Leader* (London, 1994), 4; Steiner, *Foreign Office*, 86; Sommer, *Haldane*, 257.
90. See Cecil, *Wilhelm II*, Vol. 2, 169–70; R.S. Churchill (ed.), *Young Statesman, Companion*, Vol. 3, 1503: Churchill's letter to Grey, dated 31/1/1912; see also *GP, Vol. 31*, 97ff.
91. Hildebrand, *Das vergangene Reich*, 272; Cecil, ibid., 170.
92. *GP, Vol. 31*, Bethmann Hollweg to Metternich, 30/1/1912; Churchill, *World Crisis*, Vol. 1, 95.
93. Churchill, ibid. For the complex domestic battle in Germany between Tirpitz and Bethmann (and the Treasury) regarding the necessity and timing of yet another (the fifth) naval law and the increasing competition between the army and the navy, see Berghahn, *Approach of War*, 98ff.; see also R. Scheck, *Alfred von Tirpitz and German Right-Wing Politics, 1914–1930* (Atlantic Highlands, N.J., 1998).
94. Churchill, ibid.
95. See Stevenson, *Armaments*, 208; Massie, *Dreadnought*, 804; Letter Churchill to Grey, 31/1/1912, quoted in R.S. Churchill, *Young Statesman*, 561–2.
96. Langhorne, 'Great Britain and Germany,' 290; Steinberg, 'Diplomatie,' 275.
97. Quotes in Robbins, *Grey*, 257; see also Maurice, *Haldane*, 292–3.
98. Sommer, *Haldane*, 258; Maurice, ibid., 293; *BD Origins*, Vol. 6, 667–70: 2/2–7/2/1912; 674–5: 10/2/1913; 690–2: 13/2/1913; 726ff.
99. Quotes: *BD Origins*, Vol. 6, 687: Bertie, British Ambassador in Paris, to Nicolson, 11/2/1912; also Grey, *Twenty-Five Years*, 251–2; Koss, *Lord Haldane*, 79–80; Langhorne, 'Great Britain and Germany,' 290; Robbins, *Grey*, 257.
100. Quoted in Langhorne, 'Great Britain and Germany,' 290.
101. Churchill, *World Crisis*, Vol. 1, 98; Wilhelm II, *Ereignisse und Gestalten*, 126–7.
102. Massie, *Dreadnought*, 803. The German government seems to have expected that either Grey or Churchill would go to Berlin. See Koss, *Lord Haldane*, 79; Huldermann, *Ballin*, 252–3.
103. See Churchill, *World Crisis*, Vol. 1, 100–2; also *BD Foreign Affairs*, Vol. 21, 220–2, 226–9: German newspaper reports. For the text of the speech, see R.S. Churchill, *Young Statesman*, 563–4; also Bonham Carter, *As I Knew Him*, 246–7. Surprisingly, Churchill's claim seems to have been accepted in the literature without further questioning. See for example Stevenson, *Armaments*, 207; R. Langhorne, 'The Naval Question in Anglo-German Relations, 1912–1914,' *Historical Journal* 14 (1971), 360; Charmley, *End of Glory*, 75; Massie, ibid., 820–1; N. Rose, *Churchill: An Unruly Life* (London, 1994), 101; C. Ponting, *Churchill* (London, 1994), 127.
104. Ponting, ibid., 126.
105. Letter Lichnowsky to Bethmann Hollweg, 30/4/1913. Quoted in Prince Lichnowsky, *Heading for the Abyss: Reminiscences* (London, 1928), 336, see also p. 64; *GP, Vol. 39: Das Nahen des Weltkrieges 1912–1914* (Berlin, 1926), 38–9.
106. See Bethmann-Hollweg's memorandum dated 4/2/1912, in *GP, Vol. 31*, 103–4 (also in Huldermann, Ballin, [German edn], 252; A.v. Tirpitz, *Politische Dokumente, Vol. 2: Der Aufbau der deutschen Weltmacht*, Stuttgart, 1924, 280–1); also *BD Foreign Affairs*, Vol. 21, 214–15: summary of Bethmann's Reichstag speech, 15/2/1912.
107. Letter Cassel to Ballin, 3/2/1912, quoted in Churchill, *World Crisis*, Vol. 1, 98. see also R.S. Churchill (ed.), *Young Statesman, Companion*, Vol. 3, 1515.
108. Churchill, *World Crisis*, Vol. 1, 97.
109. Quoted in Langhorne, 'Germany and Great Britain,' 291 (also in Steiner, *First World War*, 95). See also letter Churchill to Grey, 31/1/1912, quoted in R.S. Churchill (ed.), *Young Statesman, Companion*, Vol. 3, 1504–05.

110. See *BD Foreign Affairs, Vol. 21*, 218: Enclosure with Memorandum from Granville, 29/2/1912; 210–14: Memorandum by F. Oppenheimer on the Reichstag elections, dated 9/2/1912. The SPD gained 34.8 per cent of the vote and thus their best result so far and, having gained 110 mandates, became the strongest party in the Reichstag. Yet, the Conservative bloc parties together still had 165 mandates. See Ullrich, *Die nervöse Großmacht*, 243–4.

111. See *BD Foreign Affairs, Vol. 21*, 237: Corbett to Grey, 10/4/1912.

112. See ibid.; Massie, *Dreadnought*, 848–9; Epkenhans, *Flottenrüstung*, 361–2; J.H. Maurer, 'Churchill's Naval Holiday: Arms Control and the Anglo-German Naval Race, 1912–1914,' *Journal of Strategic Studies* 15 (1992), 119; Stevenson, *Armaments*, 339–40; Hildebrand, *Das vergangene Reich*, 254, 270–2.

113. See the correspondence between Ballin and Cassel in early February as partially quoted in Huldermann, *Ballin*, 249–60 (German edn), and also *GP, Vol. 31*, 105ff.

114. *BD Foreign Affairs, Vol. 21*, 236: Corbett to Grey, 10/4/1912.

115. For details, including Haldane's diary entries, see Lord Haldane's account in *Before the War* (London, 1920), 56ff.; Haldane, *Autobiography*, 238–46; *BD Origins, Vol. 6*, 672ff.; *GP, Vol. 31*, 109ff.; *BD Foreign Affairs, Vol. 21*, 330–45: Annual Report, 1912, Goschen to Grey, dated 19/12/1913; Begbie, *Vindication*, 137ff.; Huldermann, *Ballin*, 248ff.; Maurice, *Haldane*, 293ff., 302ff.; Koss, *Lord Haldane*, 71–81 (see also footnote on p.78); Sommer, *Haldane*, 260ff.; Robbins, *Grey*, 257–60; Marder, *Dreadnought*, 272–87; Jarausch, *Enigmatic Chancellor*, 127ff.; Cecil, *Wilhelm II, Vol. 2*, 170–2; also Gade, *Gleichgewichtspolitik*, 146–52; also for a general account J.G. Hall and D.F. Martin, *Haldane: Statesman, Lawyer, Philosopher* (Chichester, 1996), 200–2.

116. See the previous note.

117. Ibid.; also Massie, *Dreadnought*, 810–12.

118. *BD Origins, Vol. 6*, 710–11: Memorandum by Haldane, 12/3/1912; Maurice, *Haldane*, 298–9; Robbins, *Grey*, 259; Sommer, *Haldane*, 266.

119. Regarding the latter, see the detailed discussions in the literature in n. 115, above. It appears that on the British ambassador's insistence Ballin and Cassel were asked to 'drop out' of the negotiations. See *BD Origins, Vol. 6*, 674–5: Goschen to Nicolson, 10/2/1912; *GP, Vol. 31*, 108: Memorandum Bethmann Hollweg, 8/2/1912; see also the illuminating and detailed account in *BD Foreign Affairs, Vol. 21*, 330–45: Annual Report, 1912; also Langhorne, 'The Naval Question,' 304–5; Steinberg, 'Diplomatie,' 276–82. See also Massie, *Dreadnought*, 805–17; Kennedy, *Antagonism*, 451–2; Stevenson, *Armaments*, 205ff.; Hildebrand, *Das vergangene Reich*, 273ff.; also Bethmann Hollweg, *Reflections*, 49–61.

120. Langhorne, 'The Naval Question,' 359; also Maurice, *Haldane*, 297–8. A provisional version had already been brought back to London by Cassel in early January 1912.

121. Churchill, *World Crisis, Vol. 1*, 102–3; Massie, *Dreadnought*, 813, 821; Herrmann, *Arming of Europe*, 161ff.; Hildebrand, *Das vergangene Reich*, 273ff.; R.S. Churchill, *Young Statesman*, 565–6.

122. Jarausch, *Enigmatic Chancellor*, 108. On the power struggle between Tirpitz and Bethmann, see for example *BD Foreign Affairs, Vol. 21*, 229–31: Goschen to Grey, 21/3/1912.

123. Steiner, *First World War*, 96; Hildebrand, *Das vergangene Reich*, 250ff., 269ff.

124. Massie, *Dreadnought*, 814–5; Stevenson, *Armaments*, 208–9; Hildebrand, ibid., 274–5; Robbins, *Grey*, 258; Jarausch, *Enigmatic Chancellor*, 129–30. On the army law, see *GP, Vol. 39*, 143ff.; on the efforts to strengthen the German army, see for example Berghahn, *Approach of War*, 129ff.

125. See Huldermann, *Ballin*, 264–5.

126. Cecil, *Ballin*, 193–95. Cecil writes that Ballin 'was simply blinded by a noble but, under the circumstances, a foolish hope' (p. 195). However, Ballin himself believed that any rapprochement with England was made impossible by Tirpitz and his 'strong and unscrupulous personality' (p. 198).

127. Langhorne, 'Great Britain and Germany,' 300–1; Cecil, *Ballin*, 195–6.

128. Quoted in Steiner, *First World War*, 96; Robbins, *Grey*, 259–60; see also Asquith, *Genesis*, 54ff., 97–102; Langhorne, ibid., 298–9; Grey, *Twenty-Five Years*, 253; *BD Origins, Vol. 6*, 718–19: Grey to Goschen, 16/4/1912; *GP, Vol. 31*, 181–3: Metternich to Auswärtiges Amt, 17/3/1912; 185–7: Bethmann Hollweg to Wilhelm II, 17/3/1912.

129. Quoted in Koss, *Lord Haldane*, 86. See also the Kaiser's letter to Ballin, dated 19 March (quoted in Huldermann, *Ballin*, 266). It makes clear that Berlin regarded the negotiations as broken off; this is also apparent from a letter by Bethmann Hollweg to Ballin (quoted in ibid.). In his letter the Emperor mentioned that in addition to the unsatisfactory formula submitted by Grey, Churchill's 'impertinent' speech in the House of Commons in early March (see below) represented a provocation of Germany and, above all, it did not contain any apology for his Glasgow speech. See also

BD Origins, Vol. 6, 719–20: Grey to Goschen, 19/3/1912; also 722ff.; *GP, Vol. 31*, 188–9: Bethmann Hollweg to Metternich, 18/3/1912; 191–2, Metternich to Auswärtige Amt, 18/3/1912.

130. Grey later wrote in his memoirs that 'the Germans were not really willing to give up the naval competition, and that they wanted a political formula that would in effect compromise our freedom of action. We could not fetter ourselves by a promise to be neutral in a European war. ... We were bound to keep our hands free and the country uncompromised as to its liberty of judgement, decision and action'. Grey, *Twenty-Five Years*, 253; see also Steiner, *First World War*, 97; Sweet, 'Great Britain and Germany', 226.

131. See Langhorne, 'Great Britain and Germany', 299; Massie, *Dreadnought*, 816–17.

132. For the entire speech see H.C. *Parl. Deb.*, 5th series, Vol. 35, 18/3/1912, 1549–74. See also *GP, Vol. 31*, 194–7; Massie, *Dreadnought*, 821–2; R.S. Churchill, *Young Statesman*, 565ff., 598–600.

133. Epkenhans, *Flottenrüstung*, 347–8; also A.J.P. Taylor, *Struggle for Mastery in Europe* (Oxford, 1971), 501–2; Lichnowsky, *Heading for the Abyss*, 332ff.; see also Bonham Carter, *As I Knew Him*, 248–50.

134. Quoted in Lord Blake, 'Churchill and the Conservative Party,' in R. Crosby Kemper III (ed.), *Winston Churchill: Resolution, Defiance, Magnanimity, Good Will* (Columbia, Mo., 1996), 143. Blake believes that 'Almost from the beginning of his parliamentary career Churchill was far closer to the right wing of the Liberal Party than to the orthodox Conservatives' (p. 144). Blake is convinced that the Conservative Party's shabby treatment of his father was an important factor in Churchill's lifelong suspicion and mistrust of the Conservatives.

135. See Maurer, 'Naval Holiday,' 112, 123–4; Koss, *Lord Haldane*, 74. Maurer, 123, concludes: 'Domestic political imperatives played a large part in moving Churchill to make the holiday proposal'. For the FO's views, see Steiner, *Foreign Office*, 147.

136. Churchill, *World Crisis, Vol. 1*, 107–10 (quote: 109). See also H.C. *Parl. Deb.* 5th series, Vol. 35, 18/3/1912, 1549–74.

137. See Maurer, 'Naval Holiday,' 104–5. In this respect there was a certain similarity with his 'iron curtain' speech 33 years later in 1946 which was also characterized by a 'carrot and stick' approach. See Chapter 6 below, 124–7.

138. Churchill, *World Crisis, Vol. 1*, 109.

139. See for example *BD Foreign Affairs, Vol. 21*, 199 (27/11/1911).

140. Ibid. See also *GP, Vol. 31*, 107–8; for the feared social repercussions, see Berghahn, *Approach of War*, 129. Churchill's proposal was much better received by the German press. See *BD Foreign Affairs, Vol. 21*, 249–50: Grey to Goschen on his conversation with the new German ambassador Baron Marschall, 8/8/1912, also 351–2: Annual Report, 1912.

141. See Langhorne, 'The Naval Question,' 361; Stevenson, *Armaments*, 290ff.; Massie, *Dreadnought*, 817; Hildebrand, *Das vergangene Reich*, 276ff.; Haldane, *Autobiography*, 246; on Anglo-German relations since August 1912, see *BD Origins, Vol. 10*, 2, 655ff.

142. *GP, Vol. 39*, 119–25: Lichnowsky to Bethmann Hollweg, 3/12/1912; Memorandum Wilhelm II, no date; PRO: FO 244/806, 1913; also Robbins, *Grey*, 268; H.P. Ullmann, *Das deutsche Kaiserreich, 1871–1918* (Darmstadt, 1997), 217–9; A. Hillgruber *Deutschlands Rolle in der Vorgeschichte der beiden Weltkriege*, 3rd edn (Göttingen 1986), 32–4; R.J. Crampton, *The Hollow Détente: Anglo-German Relations in the Balkans, 1911–14* (London, 1980). For a good overview, see Ullrich, *Die nervöse Großmacht*, 231–8; also G. Schöllgen, *Imperialismus und Gleichgewicht. Deutschland, England und die orientalische Frage 1871–1914* (Munich, 1984), 374ff.

143. Quoted in Langhorne, 'Great Britain and Germany', 306. See *BD Origins, Vol. 10*, 2, 675ff.; Massie, *Dreadnought*, 829, see also 848–9. On Tirpitz's speech, see *BD Foreign Affairs, Vol. 21*, 259–61, 293–302.

144. H.C. *Parl. Deb.*, 5th series, Vol. 50, 26/3/1913, 1750–94; R.S. Churchill, *Young Statesman*, 600ff.; also *GP, Vol. 39*, 23ff.

145. *BD Origins, Vol. 10*, 2, 690–3; Goschen to Grey, 28/3 and 29/3/1913; *GP, Vol. 39*, 23ff.; for the German reaction, see *BD Foreign Affairs, Vol. 21*, 303–4: Goschen to Grey, 29/3/1913; 306–8: Oppenheimer to Goschen, 21/7/1913.

146. Ibid., 705–6: Goschen to Grey, 3/7/1913; also Massie, *Dreadnought*, 830–1: Maurer, 'Naval Holiday,' 106, 119–20. For Bethmann's speech, see *BD Foreign Affairs, Vol. 21*, 304–6, 12/4/1913.

147. Ibid., 253: Granville to Grey, 19/9/1912.

148. *BD Origins, Vol. 10*, 2, 706: Minute Churchill to Grey, 8/7/1913.

149. *BD Origins, Vol. 10*, 2, 722: Grey to Goschen, 28/10/1913; also Stevenson, *Armaments*, 336–7; Maurer, 'Naval Holiday,' 112–13.

150. *BD Origins, Vol. 10*, 2, 718–19; Goschen to Grey, 22/10/1913; 720: Goschen to A. Nicolson, 24/10/1913; 721: Churchill to Grey, 24/10/1913; also *BD Foreign Affairs, Vol. 21*, 318–20: Goschen to

Grey, 22/10/1913 and Corbett to Grey, 24/10/1913; Maurer, 'Naval Holiday', 107, Massie, *Dreadnought*, 831 (quote: ibid.); Woodward, *Great Britain and the German Navy*, 423; *GP, Vol. 39*, 52ff.; also C. Mauch, 'Pazifismus und politische Kultur', in R. Fiebig-von Hase and J. Heideking (eds), *Zwei Wege in die Moderne: Aspekte der deutsch-amerikanischen Beziehungen, 1900–1918* (Trier, 1998), 278–84.

151. In both Britain and Germany there was particular concern about the rising might of the Russian navy. See Stevenson, *Armaments*, 337.

152. Quote: Stevenson, ibid. For the potential disadvantages to Britain's strategic position if the 'naval holiday' proposal had been accepted, see Maurer, 'Naval Holiday', 116–18.

153. *BD Origins, Vol. 10, 2*, 734–7: Grey to Goschen, 5/2/1914; Goschen to Grey, 6/2/1914; Goschen to Nicolson, 6/2/1914; Goschen to Grey, 10/2/1914; *GP, Vol. 39*, 74–6: Aide-mémoire Goschen, 6/2/1914. See also Steiner, *First World War*, 98. Later in the month Tirpitz officially rejected the 'holiday proposal' in a speech to the Budget Committee of the Reichstag. While proclaiming that Berlin had never received any official proposal, he also listed a number of technical reasons why the suggestion was unacceptable. See Maurer, ibid., 107–8; *GP, Vol. 39*, 74–80: 6/2–10/2/1914.

154. Massie, *Dreadnought*, 833–6; Churchill, *World Crisis, Vol. 1*, 177–8: see Lloyd George's *Daily Chronicle* article on 1 January and his speech in mid-January 1914 denouncing the 'organized insanity' of the armaments race which caused a great stir in Germany. *BD Origins, Vol. 10, 2*, 729–30: Corbett to Grey, 13/1/1914; *BD Foreign Affairs, Vol. 21*, Corbett to Grey, 13/1/1914; Pugh, *Lloyd George*, 73; also Weinroth, 'Left-Wing Opposition', 96ff.

155. In December 1913 it had been revealed to the Cabinet that the naval estimates had to be increased by £3 million which would take them to the exorbitant sum of almost £51 million. Against much heated opposition within the Cabinet, in the end it was decided to spend almost £53 million though the year after they were to be substantially reduced. See Massie, *Dreadnought*, 833–7 (see also the calculation on p. 832 that the Liberal government had spent £229 million on the navy in the six years between 1907 and 1913). See also R.S. Churchill, *Young Statesman*, 655ff.; Marder, *Dreadnought*, 311ff.; Charmley, *End of Glory*, 90–3. For Churchill's speech, see H.C. *Parl. Deb.*, 5th series, Vol. 59, 17/3/1914 1896–1938; Stevenson, *Armaments*, 338; Robbins, *Grey*, 279–80; Massie, *Dreadnought*, 836–37; *GP, Vol, 39*, 82–99: 18/3 and 30/3/1914.

156. Cecil, *Wilhelm II, Vol 2*, 179.

157. Churchill, *World Crisis, Vol. 1*, 179–80. Ballin's plan was probably more than just a 'diplomatische Arabeske' as claimed by Epkenhans, *Flottenrüstung*, 363. See also *GP, Vol. 39*, 99–100: 25/4 and 27/4/1914, and 7/5/1914; *BD Origins, Vol. 10, 2*, 744–9: 18–26/5/1914.

158. Letter Churchill to Grey, 8 May 1914, quoted in R.S. Churchill (ed.), *Young Statesman, Companion, Vol. 3*, 1977.

159. Quote: Cecil, *Ballin*, 199; see Lichnowsky, *Heading for the Abyss*, 346–7; *GP, Vol. 39*, 101–3: 10/5/1914; also Massie, *Dreadnought*, 850. The German Foreign Ministry was however less enthusiastic and vetoed the idea immediately. Huldermann, *Ballin*, 275–6; Pinette, *Ballin*, 73.

160. Quoted in Epkenhans, *Flottenrüstung*, 364, and confirmed by Churchill's letter to Grey on 20 May 1914 (see the following note). This contradicts the older accounts based on the German view in Cecil, *Ballin*, 199; Huldermann, *Ballin*, 192; and also in *GP, Vol. 39*, 100–13: 27/4–10/5/1914, where it is claimed that Wilhelm II vetoed an invitation to Churchill as he wished to receive a prior enquiry about the visit from the British government. The German Foreign Office regarded the invitation as a mere propaganda coup and Tirpitz allegedly proclaimed that he felt 'ashamed deep into his German soul' about the Kaiser's action (Epkenhans, ibid., 364).

161. See Churchill's letter to Asquith and Grey, 20/5/1914, quoted in R.S. Churchill (ed.), *Young Statesman, Companion, Vol. 3*, 1978–1980; also in *BD Origins, Vol. 10, 2*, 746–8. See also Churchill, *World Crisis, Vol. 1*, 180; Gilbert, *Churchill, Vol. 3*, 1–2; Taylor, 'The Statesman', 16–17; Manchester, *Last Lion*, 449. This was similar to Lord Haldane's belief that Anglo-German antagonism was based on 'mutual misapprehension'. Koss, *Lord Haldane*, 66.

162. Churchill's letter to Asquith and Grey, 20/5/1914 (see previous note); also Churchill, *World Crisis, Vol. 1*, 180–1. According to Churchill, ibid., 180, and contrary to the statement in Hough, *Former Naval Person*, 51, the Foreign Office was opposed to Churchill's journey to Berlin. The FO merely 'wished a British squadron to visit German ports simultaneously with other naval visits'. The visit of a high-ranking politician was of an entirely different quality, in particular if it was the unpredictable Churchill who had already antagonized the FO with his holiday proposal.

163. For details, see Chapters 10, 11 and 15, below.

164. See for example D. Carlton, 'Großbritannien und die Gipfeldiplomatie 1953–55', in B. Thoß and H.E. Volkmann (eds), *Zwischen Kaltem Krieg und Entspannung. Sicherheits- und Deutschland-*

politik der Bundesrepublik im Mächtesystem der Jahre 1953–1956 (Boppard, 1988), 53–4; and E. Shuckburgh, *Descent to Suez: Diaries, 1951–1956* (London, 1986), 91, 134–5, 141.

165. This is the sub-title of the hardback edition of T. Morgan's book *Churchill* (New York, 1982).

166. Churchill's letter to Asquith and Grey, 20/5/1914, in R.S. Churchill (ed.), *Young Statesman, Companion, Vol. 3*, 1979–80; see also Churchill, *World Crisis, Vol. 1*, 181. Churchill was able to ignore all of this with regard to the USSR in the 1950s. The power political realities were much clearer and were more openly admitted.

167. *BD Origins, Vol. 10, 2*, 748–9: Memorandum Grey, 25/5/1914 (quotes: 748).

168. Churchill, *World Crisis, Vol. 1*, 181.

169. Grey's letter to Asquith and Churchill, 25/5/1914, in R.S. Churchill (ed.), *Young Statesman, Companion, Vol. 3*, 1980; see also *BD Origins, Vol. 10, 2*, 748–9: Memorandum Grey, 25/5/1914, 748.

170. Remarks by House in two letters to Walter Hines Page, the American ambassador in London, Dec. 1913 and 4 Jan. 1914. Quoted in Asquith, *Genesis*, 157, 158, see also 154–63.

171. For the whole episode, see above all J.G. Williams, *Colonel House and Sir Edward Grey: a Study in Anglo-American Diplomacy* (Lanham, MD, 1984), ch. 3, esp. 39–47; C. Seymour, *The Intimate Papers of Colonel House, Vol. 1: Behind the Political Curtain, 1912–1915* (London, 1926), 232–75; see also the brief outline in Maurer, 'Naval Holiday', 109–10; and *GP, Vol. 39*, 107–6.

172. See for Grey's statement: H.C. *Parl. Deb.*, 5th series, Vol. 63, 11/6/1914, 457–8; Ullrich, *Die nervöse Großmacht*, 238.

173. See the literature dealing with House's European diplomacy mentioned in n. 171 above. Churchill's idea of a naval holiday was subsequently taken up by American Secretary of State Charles Evans Hughes in November 1921 during the Washington Disarmament Conference. See for example K.J. McDonald, 'The Washington Conference and the Naval Balance of Power, 1921–2,' in J.B. Hattendorf and R.S. Jordan (eds), *Maritime Strategy and the Balance of Power* (Basingstoke, 1989), 189–213.

174. See the British reports on the Kiel week in *BD Foreign Affairs, Vol. 21*, 414–15: Rumbold to Grey, 2/7/1914; 416–18: Henderson to Rumbold, 3/7/1914 (quote: 416). The Kiel week proved to be a success and the naval teams of the British and German ships attending the event got on very well (see p. 418).

175. *BD Origins, Vol. 10, 2*, 748–9: Memorandum to Grey, 25/5/1914 (quote: 749).

176. Quoted in Rose, *Churchill*, 160. For Churchill's Irish policy, see above all M.C. Bromage, *Churchill and Ireland* (Notre Dame, Ind., 1964); also I.S. Wood, *Churchill* (Basingstoke, 2000), 140–56.

177. See A.M. Schlesinger Jr, 'History's Impressario', Keynote address to the International Churchill Society, Boston, 28 Oct. 1995 [webpage: www.winstonchurchill.org/p94rschles.htm].

178. E. Hanfstaengl, *Hitler: The Missing Years* (London, 1957), 184. Hanfstaengl is however mistaken about the time of the year; it was late August 1932 not April 1932 as he writes in his memoirs.

179. For a brief account of Hanfstaengl's earlier life and acquaintance with Hitler, see P. Metcalfe, *1933*, paperback edn (London, 1990), 47–77. For good overviews of Hitler's tactics and his rise in German politics in the early 1930s, see J. Fest, *Hitler: Eine Biographie*, paperback edn (Frankfurt/M., 1987), 437ff.; I. Kershaw, *Hitler: 1896–1936. Hubris* (London, 1998), ch. 9, esp. 370ff.

180. For an account of the 1932 episode which is entirely based on Churchill's memoirs (e.g. the author repeats Churchill's belief of having stayed in the Regina hotel in Munich though in fact it was the hotel Continental), see Ch. Graf von Krockow, *Churchill: Eine Biographie des 20. Jahrhunderts*, 2nd edn (Hamburg, 1999), 137–8; G.Best, *Churchill: A Study in Greatness* (London, 2001), 155, also largely follows Churchill's reasoning; so does R. Jenkins, *Churchill* (London, 2001), 468–9. For Churchill's own account, see *The Second World War, Vol. 1: The Gathering Storm* (London, 1948), 75–6, quote: 76.

181. Hanfstaengl, *Hitler: The Missing Years*, 184–5.

182. Ibid., 186; Churchill, *The Second World War*, Vol.1, 75.

183. Hanfstaengl, ibid., 186–7. See also the interesting but somewhat inaccurate account, which ignores some of Hanfstaengl's statements in his memoirs, in M. Gilbert, *Winston S. Churchill, Vol. 5: 1922–1939* (London, 1976), 447–8. In 1933 Hanfstaengl became the NSDAP's foreign press spokesperson but after having fallen out with the Nazi regime in 1937 he managed to escape to Zurich and then to Britain, where he was interned as an enemy alien. He was shipped to Canada and eventually made it to the US, where he intermittently advised the Roosevelt administration on German affairs, before being returned to Britain as an internee and, after the war, to Germany; he was released in 1946. He died in 1975. See Hanfstaengl, ibid., 287ff.; Gilbert, ibid., 447, n. 2.

184. Quote: Churchill, *Second World War*, Vol. 1, 224. Lord Halifax visited Hitler in November 1937. Lloyd George received the controversial impression that Hitler was pursuing a defensive policy.

For a succinct summary of Lloyd George's perception of and attitude to Hitler's policies, see J. Grigg, 'Churchill and Lloyd George', in Blake and Louis (eds), *Churchill*, 107–8. Eden, the Lord Privy Seal, had first met Hitler on 20 February 1934; he saw him again in April 1934 and March 1935. See A. Eden, *Facing the Dictators. Memoirs* (London, 1962), 61, also 133.

185.　Churchill, *Second World War, Vol. 1*, 224; see also Jenkins, *Churchill*, 469.

186.　Churchill, ibid., 75. He continued writing: 'I admire men who stand up for their country in defeat, even though I am on the other side. He had a perfect right to be a patriotic German if he chose.'

187.　Churchill's essay, 'Hitler and his Choice, 1935', was reprinted in his *Great Contemporaries* (London, 1937, 1990 edn), 223–31 (quote: 230). See also Ponting, *Churchill*, 393ff.

188.　See G. Stewart, *Burying Caesar: Churchill, Chamberlain, and the Battle for the Tory Party* (London, 1999).

CHAPTER 2: THE POLITICS OF WAR

1.　See for example the documentation in PRO: PREM 4/100/8 (June 1940–Oct. 1944). See for a good brief summary 'Rethinking Negotiation with Hitler', *New York Times* (Arts & Ideas Section), 25/1/00; and also R.A.C. Parker, *Churchill and Appeasement* (Basingstoke, 2000); J. Lukacs, *Five Days in London, May 1940* (New Haven, Conn., 1999); E. Barker, *Churchill and Eden at War* (London, 1978), 140–7; P. Calvocoressi, *Fall Out: World War II and the Shaping of Postwar Europe* (London, 1997), 37–43; J. Costello, *Ten Days to Destiny: the Secret Story of the Hess Peace Initiative and British Efforts to Strike a Deal with Hitler* (New York, 1991), and G. L. Weinberg, *A World At Arms: A Global History of World War II* (Cambridge, 1994), 142–3 (and the lit. discussed on pp. 971–2, n 77). For a brief discussion of John Charmley's controversial argumentation (as argued before him already by Maurice Cowling and Alan Clark) in *Churchill: The End of Glory. A Political Biography* (London, 1993) that Churchill should have entered into a compromise peace with Hitler in 1940/41 to prevent Britain's decline, the disintegration of the Empire, and America's dominance in the post-war period, see the introduction to this book, xvii–xix. For a good account of why such considerations of the 'big five' within the British Cabinet (Churchill, Chamberlain, Halifax, Attlee, Greenwood) were discussed but not seriously pursued, see B. Martin, 'Churchill and Hitler, 1940; Peace or War?', in R.A.C. Parker (ed.), *Winston Churchill: Studies in Statesmanship* (London, 1995), esp. 88–95; also B. Martin, *Friedensinitiativen und Machtpolitik im Zweiten Weltkrieg, 1939–1942* (Düsseldorf, 1975); for the considerations of a compromise peace with Hitler, see also P. Addison, Churchill and the Price of Victory: 1939–1945', in N. Tiratsoo (ed.), *From Blitz to Blair: A New History of Britain since 1939*, paperback edn (London, 1998), 58–64; and D. Reynolds, 'Churchill the appeaser? Between Hitler, Roosevelt and Stalin in World War Two', in M. Dockrill and B. McKercher (eds), *Diplomacy and World Power: Studies in British Foreign Policy, 1890–1950* (Cambridge, 1996), 198–205.

2.　PRO: PREM 4/100/8, esp. for example Minute Churchill to Eden on telegram No. 281 from Berne, 28/6/1940; Minute Eden entitled 'Peace Overtures' to Churchill, P.M.41/108, and Churchill's reply to Eden, PM's Personal Minute, M.888/1, 10/9/1941 (quote from M.888/1). For a summary of the principal peace feelers between Sept. 1939–March 1941 and April 1941–June 1942, see ibid., C4216/610/G and C7180/416/G. See also D. Reynolds, 'Churchill's Writing of History: Appeasement, Autobiography and *The Gathering Storm*', in *Transactions of the Royal Historical Society*, 6th series, Vol. XI (Cambridge, 2001), 221–47.

3.　See J.L. Gaddis, 'Dividing the World', reprinted in K. Larres and A. Lane (eds), *The Cold War: The Essential Readings* (Oxford, 2001), 41.

4.　However, before accepting he had consulted Prime Minister Neville Chamberlain. See W.F. Kimball (ed.), *Churchill & Roosevelt: The Complete Correspondence, Vol. 1: Alliance Emerging* (London, 1984), 6–7, 23–5; also J.P. Lash, *Roosevelt and Churchill, 1939–41: the Partnership that Saved the West* (London, 1976), 21ff; D. Reynolds, *The Creation of the Anglo-American Alliance, 1937–41: a Study in Competitive Cooperation* (Chapel Hill, N.C., 1981), 86–8; see also B.R. Farnham, *Roosevelt and the Munich Crisis: A Study of Political Decision-making* (Princeton, N.J., 1997). For their brief earlier meeting in 1918 in London and Churchill's efforts to keep in touch once Roosevelt had become governor of New York, see Kimball, 'Wheel within a Wheel: Churchill, Roosevelt, and the Special Relationship,' in R. Blake and W. R. Louis (eds), *Churchill* (Oxford, 1993), 297.

5.　See Kimball (ed.), ibid.; see also the brilliant study by F. Harbutt, *The Iron Curtain: Churchill,*

America, and the Origins of the Cold War (New York, 1986), 22; also Barker, *Churchill and Eden*, 22–23, 26.

6. W.S. Churchill, *The Second World War*, Vol. 1: *The Gathering Storm* (London, 1948), 254–5; for an excellent interpretation, see L.C. Gardner, *Spheres of Influence: The Partition of Europe, from Munich to Yalta* (London, 1993), 3–7, 8ff; also Reynolds, 'Churchill the appeaser?', 19–23, 31–3.

7. See Reynolds, *Creation*, 95ff.; Lash, *Roosevelt and Churchill*, 93ff., 154ff. For good overviews regarding the Churchill-FDR relationship, see also for example Barker, *Churchill and Eden*, 125–138; and Kimball, 'Wheel within a Wheel,' 291–307; W.F. Kimball, *Forged in War: Churchill, Roosevelt and the Second World War* (London, 1998); J. Charmley, *Churchill's Grand Alliance: A Provocative Reassessment of the 'Special Relationship' between England and the U.S. from 1940 to 1957* (New York, 1995); and, with the emphasis on the intelligence dimension, D. Stafford, *Roosevelt & Churchill: Men of Secrets* (London, 1999). For an absurd anti-American diatribe, see J. Charmley, 'Churchill's Roosevelt', in A. Lane and H. Temperley (eds), *The Rise and Fall of the Grand Alliance, 1941–45* (Basingstoke, 1995), 90–107. Much useful information also in Weinberg, *A World at Arms*.

8. See R. Hough, *Former Naval Person: Churchill and the Wars at Sea* (London, 1985), 157–62; P. Goodhart, *Fifty Ships that Saved the World. The Foundation of the Anglo-American Alliance* (Garden City, N.Y., 1965), 177 ff., and 3ff. for the earlier history.

9. See W.S. Cole, *Roosevelt and the Isolationists, 1932–45* (Lincoln, Neb., 1983); also W. Heinrichs, *Threshold of War: Franklin D. Roosevelt and American Entry into World War II* (Oxford, 1988).

10. For a good interpretive account, see R. Overy, *The Battle* (Harmondsworth, 2000); and for a detailed and exhaustive treatment, S. Bungay, *The Most Dangerous Enemy: A History of the Battle of Britain* (London, 2000).

11. See the still useful essay by D. Waley, 'Lend-Lease,' in W. McNeill, *America, Britain, and Russia: their Cooperation and Conflict, 1941–46* (London, 1953), 772–89; and W.F. Kimball, 'The Most Unsordid Act': *Lend-Lease, 1939–41* (Baltimore, 1969); also Reynolds, *Creation*, 145–68: A.P. Dobson, *US Wartime Aid to Britain, 1940–46* (London, 1986); W.F. Kimball, *The Juggler: Franklin Roosevelt as Wartime Statesman* (Princeton, N.J., 1991), 127–57.

12. See above all R.E. Sherwood, *Roosevelt and Hopkins: An Intimate History* (New York, 1948), 176–77, 275ff.; W.A. Harriman and E. Abel, *Special Envoy to Churchill and Stalin* (New York, 1975), 56ff.; D. Stafford, *Churchill and Secret Service* (London, 1997), 197–99; for good accounts of the visits of Roosevelt's envoys, see also M. Gilbert, *Winston S. Churchill, Vol. 6: Finest Hour, 1939–41* (London, 1983), 981–1000, 1033 ff.; for Welles's visit and his long conversation with Eden, see in particular PRO: PREM 4/25/2, 13/3/1940. See also F.J. Harbutt, 'Churchill, Hopkins and the Other Americans: An Alternative Perspective on Anglo-American Relations, 1941–45', *International History Review* Vol. 8 (1986), 236–62.

13. For this meeting, see L.C. Gardner, *Spheres of Influence*, 91ff. (quote: 99); also D. Brinkley and D.R. Facey-Crowther (eds), *The Atlantic Charter* (Basingstoke, 1994); T.A. Wilson, *The First Summit: Roosevelt and Churchill at Placentia Bay 1941* (London, 1969, rev. edn 1991), 8ff., esp. 166–7, 173ff.; also K.V. Morton, *Atlantic Meeting [...]* (London, 1946); R. Dallek, *Franklin D. Roosevelt and American Foreign Policy, 1932–1945* (New York, 1979), 281–86; W.F. Kimball, 'Anglo-American War Aims, 1941–43, The First Review: Eden's Mission to Washington,' in A. Lane and H. Temperley (eds), *The Rise and Fall of the Grand Alliance, 1941–45* (Basingstoke, 1995), esp. 1–3.

14. See in greater detail Chapters 3 and 4 of this book. Point three of the Atlantic Charter's eight 'common principles' (and effectively four major goals) expressed 'the right of all peoples to choose the form of government under which they will live' and it endorsed the desire 'to see sovereign rights and self-government restored to those who have been forcibly denied them'. Point four dealt with the right of all states to have equal access to trade and raw materials. Quoted in Gardner, *Spheres of Influence*, 99. See W.R. Louis, 'American Anti-Colonialism and the Dissolution of the British Empire,' in W.R. Louis and Hedley Bull (eds), *The 'Special Relationship': Anglo-American Relations since 1945* (Oxford, 1986), 61–83; W.R. Louis, *Imperialism at Bay: The United States and the Decolonization of the British Empire, 1941–45* (New York, 1978), esp. 3–26, 48–67, 121–33, 548–3; Kimball, *The Juggler*, 127–52; R.B. Woods, *A Changing of the Guard: Anglo-American Relations, 1941–46* (Chapel Hill, N.C., 1990), 43–62.

15. See PRO: PREM 4/27/9, letter Halifax, Washington, to Churchill, 9/12/1941, reporting on his conversation with Roosevelt. Churchill's talks with FDR were continued in January by their respective military experts who began to discuss joint strategy; this laid the basis for the Anglo-American Combined Chiefs of Staff which was soon established. See W.S. Churchill, *The Second World War, Vol. 3: The Grand Alliance* (London, 1950), 608–9; J. Baylis, *Anglo-American Defence Relations, 1939–1980: The Special Relationship* (New York, 1981), 5–7.

16. See also the literature in n. 7 above; and K. Sainsbury, *Churchill and Roosevelt at War: The War They Fought and the Peace They Hoped to Make* (London, 1994); D. Reynolds et al. (eds), *Allies at War: the Soviet, American, and British Experience, 1939–45* (New York, 1994); M.S. Stoler, *Allies and Adversaries: The Joint Chiefs of Staff, the Grand Alliance, and US Strategy in World War Two* (Chapel Hill, N.C., 2001).

17. Quoted in Churchill, *Second World War, Vol. 3*, 539. For the controversy about whether or not Churchill passed on all information regarding the Japanese attack on Pearl Harbor, see Kimball, 'Wheel within a Wheel,' 298; also Kimball, *Forged in War*, 120–23; see also the controversial and misleading book by J. Rusbridger and E. Nave, *Betrayal at Pearl Harbor: How Churchill Lured Roosevelt into World War II* (New York, 1991).

18. PRO: PREM 4/27/9, letter Halifax, Washington, to Churchill, 11/10/1941, reporting his conversation with Roosevelt on 10/10/1941.

19. Ibid., letter Halifax, Washington, to Churchill, 9/12/1941, reporting his conversation with Roosevelt. Yet, the Americans resented the fact that Churchill referred in a speech to America's entry into the war as something he had 'dreamt of, aimed at and worked for'. It sounded like a Macchiavellian Churchillian policy of getting 'American boys' into the war: 'first our arms, then our money, then our boys'. Ibid., letter Halifax to Eden, 24/2/1942. For the new developments in the international history of the Second World War, see 'The Future of World War II Studies: A Roundtable', *Diplomatic History* 25/3 (2001), 347 ff.

20. Churchill fully believed Lord Halifax's assessment: 'I have no doubt that the more you can maintain your private communications with him and tell him everything that you can, the better. He continually gets … rather partial and limited impressions from many of their people, and if you could manage to give him from time to time the picture as you yourself see it, it would be an inevitable correction to other stuff that is pouring in on him all the time'. PRO: ibid., letter Halifax, Washington, to Churchill, 11/10/1941, reporting his conversation with Roosevelt on 10/10/1941. See also Churchill, *Second World War, Vol. 3*, 207–9, 377, 380, 384, 608–9, 594–6. The closeness of the Churchill–Roosevelt relationship should however not be exaggerated. Despite relatively few initial differences of opinion about immediate war aims (long-term post-war aims were a very different matter; see Chapters 3 and 4, below) and the sharing of the atomic secret and both country's code-breaking capabilities, the image of intimacy and total candour in their relations with each other as portrayed by Churchill and many subsequent historians is misleading. For a good critical overview, see already Sherwood, *Roosevelt and Hopkins*; and Kimball, 'Wheel within a Wheel,' 291ff.; also D. Reynolds, 'Roosevelt, Churchill, and the Wartime Anglo-American Alliance, 1941–45: towards a New Synthesis', in Louis and Bull (eds), *Special Relationship*, 17–41; P. Boyle, 'The Special Relationship: An Alliance of Convenience?', *Journal of American Studies* 22 (1988), 457–65. For the sharing of intelligence information see, B. Smith, 'Sharing ULTRA in World War II', *International Journal of Intelligence and Counterintelligence* 2 (1988), 59–72; and his *Sharing Secrets with Stalin: How the Allies Traded Intelligence, 1941–45* (Lawrence, Kan., 1996).

21. See Kimball, 'Wheel within a Wheel,' 298; Kimball, *The Juggler*, 173–83.

22. For a succinct summary, see Harbutt, *Iron Curtain*, 47–8. For the Second Front issue, see also the literature in nn. 72 and 79, below.

23. See Kimball, 'Wheels within a Wheel,' 296. Usually, however, Churchill had to travel to Washington or they met in third countries; FDR never came to London during the war.

24. See Kimball (ed.), *Churchill & Roosevelt*, Vol. I, 4, 11–13, 15; Barker, *Churchill and Eden*, 130.

25. See for example PRO: PREM 4/100/8, minute Eden to Churchill, P.M./43/198, 2/7/1943. See also Weinberg, *World at Arms*, 289, 462, 609–11; I. Fleischhauer, *Die Chance des Sonderfriedens: Deutsch-sowjetische Geheimgespräche 1941–1945* (Berlin, 1986); also for example McNeill, *America, Britain, and Russia*, 168–70, 275–6, 324–5. For Churchill's suspicion of Stalin, see concisely Harbutt, *Iron Curtain*, 23 ff., 67–8.

26. See in detail Chapters 3 and 4, below.

27. See K. Sainsbury, *The Turning Point: the Cairo, Moscow and Teheran Conferences* (London, 1985), 9–10, 293ff.; Weinberg, *World at Arms*, 591ff., 625 ff.; also Sainsbury, *Churchill and Roosevelt at War*, esp. ch. 9. See below for further details.

28. The deeper roots and the gradual development of the so-called Anglo-American 'special relationship' cannot be considered here. See the literature in n. 4, above; and also H.C. Allen, *Great Britain and the United States. A History of Anglo-American Relations, 1783–1952* (Watford, 1954); D.C. Watt, *Succeeding John Bull: America in Britain's Place, 1900–1975 [...]* (Cambridge, 1984); Louis and Bull (eds), *The Special Relationship*; Reynolds, *Creation*; D. Dimbleby and D.

Reynolds (eds), *An Ocean Apart; the Relationship between Britain and America in the 20th Century* (London, 1988); C.J. Bartlett, 'The Special Relationship': *A Political History of Anglo-American Relations since 1945* (London, 1992); A.P. Dobson, *Anglo-American Relations in the Twentieth Century* (London, 1995). See also Barker, *Churchill and Eden*, 199–217. For relations on the 'home front', see D. Reynolds, *Rich Relations: the American Occupation of Britain, 1942–45* (London, 1995); I. Parmar, *Special Interests: The State and the Anglo-American Alliance, 1939–1945* (London, 1998). See also the populist books by K. Halle (ed.), *Winston Churchill on America and Britain. A Selection of his Thoughts on Anglo-American Relations* (New York, 1970), esp. 48ff.; and R.H. Pilpel, *Churchill in America, 1895–1961: An Affectionate Portrait* (New York, 1976).

29.   See Kimball (ed.), *Churchill & Roosevelt*, Vol. I, 9–10, 12–13. However, he met Stalin only twice without Roosevelt: in 1942 and 1944, both times in Moscow. Eden very much resented Churchill's tendency to monopolize contacts with both Roosevelt and Stalin. See D. Dutton, *Anthony Eden: A Life and a Reputation* (London, 1997), 183. See also S.M. Miner, *Between Churchill and Stalin: the Soviet Union, Great Britain and the Origins of the Grand Alliance* (Chapel Hill, N.C., 1988); also R. Edmonds, 'Churchill and Stalin,' in Blake and Louis (eds), *Churchill*, 309–26. For revealing selections of documents, see G. Ross (ed.), *The Foreign Office and the Kremlin: British Documents on Anglo-Soviet Relations, 1941–45* (Cambridge, 1984).

30.   For some of the best overviews on Stalin's life and political views, see E. Radzinsky, *Stalin* (New York, 1996), 495ff.; D.A Volkogonov, *Stalin: Triumph and Tragedy* (London, 1991), 483–93; R. H. McNeal, *Stalin: Man and Ruler* (Basingstoke, 1988); I. Deutscher, *Stalin: A Political Biography*, rev. edn (Harmondsworth, 1990), 451ff.

31.   M. Djilas, *Conversations with Stalin* (London, 1963), 61. See also Stalin's reference to Roosevelt and Churchill as his 'comrades-in-arms' during the Tehran conference. He quickly added 'if it is possible for me to consider Mr Churchill my friend'. FRUS, *The Conferences at Cairo and Tehran, 1943*, 837: Memorandum Bohlen, December 1943.

32.   In August 1943 Churchill and Roosevelt agreed not to share the results of this research with anyone; Churchill explained that he regarded the atomic bomb as a weapon which could be used to contain Moscow after the end of the war. See Kimball, *The Juggler*, 87. For an excellent account of the Soviet nuclear programme, see D. Holloway, *Stalin and the Bomb: The Soviet Union and Atomic Energy, 1939–56* (New Haven and London, 1994).

33.   Even as late as March 1949 Churchill still expressed deep regret about the failure of the Versailles peace conference to strangle Bolshevism. See his speech at the Massachusetts Institute of Technology on 13/3/1949 as reported in the *New York Times*, 1/4/1949. For the clipping, see LOC: Harriman Papers, Box 266, Folder: General Correspondence, Churchill, Winston (1949–50).

34.   For Churchill's attitude towards revolutionary Russia and the Allied intervention, see above all the detailed account in R.R. James, *Churchill: A Study in Failure, 1900–1939* (London, 1970), 132–60; also R.C. Horning, *Winston Churchill and British Policy Towards Russia, 1918–19* (unpubl. diss., Washington, DC., 1958), esp. 1–18, 377–89; Harbutt, *Iron Curtain*, xi–35; and despite its title, see also D.G. Boadle, *Winston Churchill and the German Question in British Foreign Policy, 1918–22* (The Hague, 1973), 31ff., 56ff. For a good general account of the war, see O. Figes, *A People's Tragedy: The Russian Civil War* (London, 1996); see also the following note.

35.   For the allied intervention, see above all R. Ullmann, *Anglo-Soviet Relations, 1917–1921*, 3 vols (Princeton, N.J., 1961–8); I. Somin, *Stillborn Crusade: The Tragic Failure of Western Intervention in the Russian Civil War, 1918–20* (New Brunswick, N.J., 1996); also M. Kettle, *Russia and the Allies, 1917–20*, 3 vols (New York, 1981–92), esp. *Vol. 3: Churchill and the Archangel Fiasco* (New York, 1992); F. Northedge and A. Wells, *Britain and Soviet Communism: The Impact of a Revolution* (London, 1982), 25–32; C. Keeble, *Britain and the Soviet Union, 1917–89* (Basingstoke, 1990), 12–79.

36.   For Churchill's 'royalism' see Barker, *Churchill and Eden*, 299–306; W.S. Churchill, *Great Contemporaries* (London, 1937; 1990 edn), 24–5; P. Ziegler, 'Churchill and the Monarchy', in Blake and Louis (eds), *Churchill*, 187–98. Charmley, *End of Glory*, 152, quotes Lloyd George's comment: 'his [Churchill's] blood revolted at the wholesale slaughter of Grand Dukes'. See also D. Cannadine, 'Churchill and the British Monarchy', in *Transactions of the Royal Historical Society*, 6th series, Vol. XI (Cambridge, 2001), 249–72; also M. Gilbert, *Winston S. Churchill, Vol. 4: World in Torment, 1917–22* (London, 1975), 219 ff. For Churchill's own interpretation, see *The World Crisis, Vol. 5: The Aftermath* (London, 1929), 59–60, 70–103. On 'Churchill's unalterable faith in the firmly conceived scheme of human relationships' and his belief 'in a specific world order', see also I. Berlin, *Mr. Churchill in 1940* (London, 196), 17–18 (quotes: ibid.). On the assassination of the Czar and his family, see M.D. Steinberg and V.M. Khrustalev, *The Fall of the Romanovs: Political Dreams*

and Personal Struggles in a Time of Revolution (New Haven, 1995); J.C. Perry and C. Pleshakov, *The Flight of the Romanovs: A Family Saga* (New York, 1999).

37. Quoted in N. Rose, *Churchill: An Unruly Life* (London, 1994), 146. Churchill's most vicious comments about the nature of Bolshevism can be found in Vol. 5 of his *World Crisis*, e.g. p. 263.

38. Quoted in C. Ponting, *Churchill* (London, 1994), 229.

39. See Gilbert, *World in Torment*, 226; Boadle, *German Question*, 82, 88–90; Harbutt, *Iron Curtain*, xi, 24, 26.

40. James, *Study in Failure*, 140–1, also 154–6; Boadle, ibid., 57–9.

41. Quoted in Rose, *Churchill*, 143; Edmonds, 'Churchill and Stalin,' 311; Harbutt, *Iron Curtain*, 26. For Churchill's respect for Germany and its military in particular, see also his contribution on Hindenburg and Ludendorff in his book *Great Contemporaries* (this is pointed out in A. Montague Browne, *Long Sunset: Memoirs of Winston Churchill's Last Private Secretary*, London, 1995, 159).

42. Quoted in Rose, ibid., 143.

43. For Churchill's activities at the Ministry of Munitions, 1917–19, see E.E. Beriger, *Churchill, Munitions and Mechanical Warfare: The Politics of Supply and Strategy* (New York, 1997).

44. See Rose, *Churchill*, 143; and for example Boadle, *German Question*, 66–69; Harbutt, *Iron Curtain*, 23–4.

45. Quoted in Rose, ibid., 144.

46. Quoted in Charmley, *End of Glory*, 153; Ponting, *Churchill*, 232, 237.

47. Quoted in Edmonds, 'Churchill and Stalin,' 301; Harbutt, *Iron Curtain*, 25.

48. Quoted in Charmley, *End of Glory*, 154.

49. The quoted words were written by FO official Eyre Crowe. Quoted in Ponting, *Churchill*, 235.

50. See James, *Study in Failure*, 141–2; Boadle, *German Question*, 79–81. On Wilson's policy see D.S. Foglesong, *America's Secret War Against Bolshevism: US Intervention in the Russian Civil War, 1917–1920* (Chapel Hill, N.C., 1995), 188ff.; also V.M. Fic, *The Collapse of American Policy in Russia and Siberia, 1918: Wilson's Decision not to Intervene* (Boulder, Co., 1995); and P. Boyle, *American-Soviet Relations: From the Russian Revolution to the Fall of Communism* (London, 1993), 6–16; also G.F. Kennan, *Russia and the West under Lenin and Stalin* (New York, 1961), 124–6.

51. See James, ibid.; Foglesong, ibid 229; FRUS, *1919, Paris Peace Conference*, Vol. 11, 67–8; also for example Ponting, *Churchill*, 233–4; Rose, *Churchill*, 145; D. Lloyd George, *War Memoirs, Vol. 3* (London, 1934), 1605–7; also *Vol. 6* (London, 1936), 3157ff.

52. See Harbutt, *Iron Curtain*, 24; Horning, *British Policy*, 381–6; James, *Study in Failure*, 157–8; W. Pelling, *Winston Churchill* (London, 1977), 253–9; Gilbert, *World in Torment*, 234ff.

53. See for example Ponting, *Churchill*, 231, 235ff.; James, ibid., 155–7; M. Pugh, *Lloyd George* (London, 1988), 137–8.

54. Formal diplomatic relations with the Soviet Union were entered into in early 1924. Diplomatic relations were interrupted by Stanley Baldwin's Conservative government in late May 1927 and resumed again in early October 1929.

55. Quoted in Harbutt, *Iron Curtain*, 25; also in Edmonds, 'Churchill and Stalin,' 311.

56. See F. Stern, *Einstein's German World* (Harmondsworth, 1999), 240; see also N. Rose, 'Churchill and Zionism', in Blake and Louis (eds), *Churchill*, 147–66.

57. Quoted in Rose, *Churchill*, 146. See also Harbutt, *Iron Curtain*, 25.

58. Quoted in Harbutt, ibid., 27.

59. See above all Harbutt, ibid., 23ff.; Churchill, *World Crisis, Vol. 5*, 59–60, 70ff. For his early enthusiasm about America as influenced by his youthful admiration for the American politician and family friend Bourke Cockran, see J.H. Andrews, 'Winston Churchill's Tammany Hall Mentor', *New York History* (April 1990), 133–71.

60. Quoted in Harbutt, ibid., xii, see also 16–18.

61. See Harbutt, ibid., 30–31; Lord Blake, 'Churchill and the Conservative Party,' in R. Crosby Kemper III (ed.), *Winston Churchill: Resolution, Defiance, Magnanimity, Good Will* (Columbia, Mo., 1996), 152; for Churchill and Mussolini, see A. Spinosa, *Churchill: Il nemico degli italiani* (Milan, 2001).

62. See Harbutt, ibid., xii, 16–17, 31–2. For an overview of Churchill's statements on the Soviet Union between 1918 and 1940, see the collection of quotes and cartoons by Victor (ed.), *Mon Alié Staline de Winston Churchill* (Paris, 1942); also C.R. Coote (ed.), *Sir Winston Churchill: A Self-Portrait* [...] (London, 1954), 72–83.

63. Quoted in Edmonds, 'Churchill and Stalin,' 312; see also W.S. Churchill, *The Second World War, Vol. 1 The Gathering Storm* (London, 1949), 289–308; D.C. Watt, *How War Came*, paperback edn. (London, 1990), 370–72; R. Overy with A. Wheatcroft, *The Road to War*, rev. and updated edn

(London, 1999); C. Thorne, *The Approach of War, 1938–39* (London, 1967), 140–47; G. Niedhart, *Großbritannien und die Sowjetunion, 1934–39 [...]* (Munich, 1972), 390–425.

64. Churchill to Cripps, the British ambassador in Moscow, 28/10/1941. Quoted in W.S. Churchill, *The Second World War, Vol. 4: The Hinge of Fate* (London, 1951), 443.

65. Churchill, *Second World War, Vol. 3*, 331. For Churchill's similar explanation for his change of view to Soviet ambassador Ivan Maisky in 1938, see Edmonds, 'Churchill and Stalin,' 311. See also for an interesting analysis, D. Carlton, 'Churchill and the "two Evil Empires" ', in *Transactions of the Royal Historical Society*, 6th series, Vol. XI (Cambridge, 2001), 331–51.

66. See Harbutt, *Iron Curtain*, 33; also for a good concise overview of Anglo-Soviet relations during the war, V. Rothwell, *Britain and the Cold War, 1941–47* (London, 1982), 74ff., 151ff.; and the good detailed account by M. Kitchen, *British Policy towards the Soviet Union during the Second World War* (Basingstoke, 1986); see also G. Warner, 'From ally to enemy: Britain's relations with the Soviet Union, 1941–48', in Dockrill and McKercher (eds), *Diplomacy and World Power*, 221–43.

67. See above all G. Gorodetsky, *Grand Delusion: Stalin and the German Invasion of Russia* (New Haven, Conn., 1999), ch.8; see also the excellent review by R. Overy in the *TLS*, 11 August 2000. See also Gardner, *Spheres of Influence*, 86–7; Stafford, *Secret Service*, 221–3; O. Ordietsky, 'Churchill's Warning to Stalin: A Reappraisal', *Historical Journal* 29/4 (1986), 979–90; also A. Resis (ed.), *Molotov Remembers: Inside Kremlin Politics. Conversations with Felix Chuev* (Chicago, 1993), 28. There has still not been any evidence found for the controversial theory that Hitler's invasion was a preventive war as Stalin was mobilizing for an immediate attack on Germany. See Gorodetsky, ibid., and B. Pietrow-Ennker (ed.), *Präventivkrieg? Der deutsche Angriff auf die Sowjetunion* (Frankfurt/M., 2000).

68. See Gorodetsky, ibid., ch. 12, esp. 267–74; I. Kershaw, *Hitler, 1936–1945: Nemesis* (London, 2000), 369 ff.; P. Padfield, *Hess: Flight from the Führer*, new edn (London, 2001); also R.F. Schmidt, *Rudolf Hess, 'Botengang eines Toren?' Der Flug nach Grossbritannien vom 10. Mai 1941* (Düsseldorf, 1997); and for the confusion in London caused by Hess's flight, R.F. Schmidt, 'Der Hess-Flug und das Kabinett Churchill. Hitlers Stellvertreter im Kalkül der britischen Kriegsdiplomatie Mai-Juni 1941', *Vierteljahrshefte für Zeitgeschichte* 42/1 (1994), 1–38. See also Martin, *Friedensinitiativen und Machtpolitik*, 425–47; U. Schlie, *Kein Friede mit Deutschland: Die geheimen Gespräche im Zweiten Weltkrieg, 1939–1941* (Munich, 1994), 290–324; also Costello, *Ten Days to Destiny*.

69. See the previous note.

70. On the day after the German invasion, Churchill broadcast: 'No one has ever been a more consistent opponent to Communism than I have for the last twenty-five years. I will unsay no word that I have spoken about it. But all this fades away before the spectacle which is now unfolding. We shall give whatever help we can to Russia and the Russian people ... The Russian danger is therefore our danger, and the danger of the United States, just as the cause of any Russian fighting for his hearth and home is the cause of free men and free peoples in every quarter of the globe ...' Quoted in Edmonds, 'Churchill and Stalin,' 313.

71. For the negotiations, see the documents in O.A. Rzheshevsky (ed.), *War and Diplomacy: The Making of the Grand Alliance, Documents from Stalin's Archives* (Amsterdam, 1996), Part I, pp. 1–62; for a summary of the history of British-Soviet relations, see also Ross (ed.), *The Foreign Office and the Kremlin*, 3–9, 10ff.

72. See for example J. Haslam, 'Soviet War Aims', in Lane and Temperley (eds), *The Grand Alliance*, 36–7; also J. Erickson, 'Stalin, Soviet Strategy and the Grand Alliance', in ibid., 136–41; R. Edmonds, *The Big Three: Churchill, Roosevelt and Stalin in Peace and War* (London, 1991), 282ff.

73. PRO: PREM 3/366/8, W.P. (43)430, 5/10/1943: Record of a meeting between Churchill and Dominion Representatives in Washington held at the British embassy, Washington, on 10 September 1943.

74. Quoted in Harbutt, *Iron Curtain*, 46. Churchill's letter was dated 28/10/1941.

75. Ministry of Foreign Affairs of the USSR (ed.), *Correspondence between the Chairman of the Council of Ministers of the USSR and the Presidents of the USA and the Prime Ministers of Great Britain during the Great Patriotic War of 1941–45* (Moscow, 1957), 33–4 (Doc. No. 20), and for Churchill's reply, 34–5 (Doc. No. 21).

76. He told Polish Prime Minister in exile, General Sikorski, that his government 'had such evidence of the deep suspicion which had implanted itself in the Soviet Government's mind that there was no alternative but for him to go'. Quoted in Rothwell, *Britain and the Cold War*, 85.

77. PRO: PREM 4/30/8, Record of Interview between the Foreign Secretary and M. Stalin, 16 December 1941. See also the following note.

78. Eden had also attempted to obtain Molotov's agreement to the idea that both London and Moscow would not conclude any bilateral treaties with the Eastern European countries as this would only lead to a competition for allies. On Eden's talks in Moscow and Molotov's negotiations in London, see the Soviet documents in Rzheshevsky (ed.), *War and Diplomacy*, Parts I, II and IV; A. Eden (Lord Avon), *The Reckoning* (London, 1965), 275 ff, esp. 289–303, 327–30; also Dutton, *Anthony Eden*, 185–96; V. Mastny, *Russia's Road to the Cold War: Diplomacy, Warfare and the Politics of Communism, 1941–45* (New York, 1979), 41–5; also R. Overy, *Russia's War* (London, 1998). It was Eden and not so much Churchill who argued particularly strongly in favour of aid to the Soviet Union. See S. Lawlor, 'Britain and the Russian Entry into the War,' in R. Langhorne (ed.), *Diplomacy and Intelligence during the Second World War* (Cambridge, 1985), 168–83. For the thinking of the FO, see also G. Ross, 'Foreign Office Attitudes to the Soviet Union, 1941–45,' *Journal of Contemporary History* 16 (1981), 522–4.

79. For Churchill's meetings with Stalin and the reports and telegrams he sent to Roosevelt and British Deputy Prime Minister Clement Attlee, see Kimball (ed.), *Churchill & Roosevelt*, Vol. 1, 560–2; also Kitchen, *British Policy*, 124ff., esp. 132ff. Operation OVERLORD, the Normandy invasion, only took place in February 1944. In the meantime Churchill endeavoured to convince Washington that it was necessary to invade the Balkans and strengthen the Mediterranean militarily, a policy which above all served to strengthen Britain's great power role in this region and the Near East. See W. Loth, *Die Teilung der Welt, 1941–1955* (Munich, 1980), 51ff., 71–5, esp. 72. See also T. Ben-Moshe, 'Winston Churchill and the "Second Front": A Reappraisal,' in *Journal of Modern History* 62 (1990), 503–37; also M.A. Stoler, *The Politics of the Second Front: American Military Planning and Diplomacy in Coalition Warfare, 1941–43* (Westport, Conn., 1977); Kimball (ed.), ibid., 6, 13; R. Douglas, *From War to Cold War*, (New York, 1981), 9–11.

80. Quoted in Churchill, *Second World War, Vol. 4*, 443.

81. Quoted in Kimball (ed.), *Churchill & Roosevelt*, Vol. 1, 571–2: Churchill to Roosevelt, 18/8/1942. See also Churchill, ibid., 428–50; Harbutt, *Iron Curtain*, 47; Barker, *Churchill and Eden*, 224.

82. See Barker, ibid., esp. 15–28, 125–47; Kimball (ed.), ibid., Vol. 3, 180: Churchill to Roosevelt, 11/6/1944.

83. Thus, Churchill was not averse to slightly dramatizing his role from time to time. 'He lived for crisis. He profited from crisis. And when crisis did not exist, he strove to invent it'. Quoted in A.J.P. Taylor, 'The Statesman,' in A.J.P. Taylor et al., *Churchill: Four Faces and the Man* (London, 1969), 50. In a similar vein, see Barker, ibid., 27: also Earl of Birkenhead, *Churchill, 1874–1922* (London, 1989), 152. On the 1950s, see Chapters 8–17 in this book.

84. Edmonds, 'Churchill and Stalin,' 316. On Churchill's romantic vision in foreign affairs, see also I. Berlin, *Churchill in 1940* (London, 1964), 18.

85. Not without reason did Stalin receive the pet name 'Uncle Joe' in Britain and America. Hardly anyone would have dreamed of inventing a similar nickname for Soviet Foreign Minister Molotov. Allegedly Stalin was not too pleased about this nickname. See W.F. Kimball (ed.), *Churchill & Roosevelt: the Complete Correspondence, Vol. 3: Alliance Declining* (London, 1984), 573; W.S. Churchill, *The Second World War, Vol. 6: Triumph and Tragedy* (London, 1954), 345.

86. See for example Churchill, *Second World War, Vol. 4*, 441; PRO: PREM 4/100/7, PM's Personal Minute M.474/2 to Eden, 21/10/1942; C.P. Snow, *Variety of Men* (Harmondsworth, 1969) 213–14; Harbutt, *Iron Curtain*, 47. During the war people like for example Ernest Bevin and George Kennan shared this view at times. See Barker, *Churchill and Eden*, 221–2, 224. For Churchill's view of Beria during and after the war, see Chapter 10, n. 7 (p. 462 below).

87. Western illusions and Stalin's charisma were so powerful that even after the end of the Second World War American Presidents Truman and Eisenhower were on occasion and despite clear evidence to the contrary influenced by this myth. See for example the memorandum of the 136th NSC meeting, in FRUS 1952–4, Vol. 8, 1118, 11/3/1953.

88. For Roosevelt's policy towards Stalin, see for example Harbutt, *Iron Curtain*, 38–45; Sainsbury, *Turning Point*, 7–10; J.L. Gaddis, *The United States and the Origins of the Cold War, 1941–1947* (New York, 1972), 4ff., 32ff.; also Loth, *Teilung der Welt*, 27ff.; J.L. Gaddis, *Russia, the Soviet Union and the United States. An Interpretive History* (New York, 1978), 147ff.; Edmonds, *The Big Three*, 363ff.; Kimball, *The Juggler*, 159ff.; also A. Perlmutter, *FDR & Stalin: A Not So Grand Alliance, 1943–45* (Columbia, Mo., 1993).

89. After the German invasion of the Soviet Union American public opinion became noticeably more sympathetic to Russia. See R.B. Levering, *American Opinion and the Russian Alliance, 1939–1945* (Chapel Hill, N.C., 1976), 43–62. Regarding 'lend-lease' aid for Moscow see Sherwood, *Roosevelt and Hopkins*, 318–22, 323ff.; G.C. Herring, *Aid to Russia, 1941–46: Strategy, Diplomacy, and the*

Origins of the Cold War (New York, 1973), 8ff.; L. Martel, *Lend-lease: Loans and the Coming of the Cold War. A Study of the Implementation of Foreign Policy* (Boulder, Co., 1979), 25–56. For FDR's 'grand design' and long-term collaboration with Moscow, see D. Yergin, *Shattered Peace: the Origins of the Cold War and the National Security State* (Boston, 1977), 55–8; Loth, *Teilung der Welt*, 40–1.

90. Quoted in Kimball (ed.), *Churchill & Roosevelt*, Vol. 1, 421: Roosevelt to Churchill, 18/2/1942.

91. For Davies' convictions, see E.K. MacLean, *Joseph E. Davies: Envoy to the Soviets* (Westport, Conn., 1992) and D.J. Dunn, *Caught between Roosevelt and Stalin: America's Ambassadors to Moscow* (Lexington, 1998), 61–94.

92. See Kimball (ed.) *Churchill & Roosevelt*, Vol. 1, 12–4; and the correspondence between the two leaders in ibid., Vol. 2, 233–4, 245–6, 259–61, 278–79, 283–4. See also Sherwood, *Roosevelt and Hopkins*, 733–4; Loth, *Teilung der Welt*, 71–4; Sainsbury, *Turning Point*, 8–11. Apart from the decreasing importance which Britain was to have in the post-war world and which could already be recognized by 1943, Washington was also concerned about Churchill's old-fashioned Victorian views which seemed to pose a problem for the progressive restructuring of the post-war world. See Kimball, 'Wheel within a Wheel,' 299, also 304–5. See in much greater detail Chapters 3 and 4, below.

93. See Dutton, *Anthony Eden*, 154.

94. See FRUS, *Conferences at Cairo and Tehran, 1943*, 482–6, 529–33, 594–6; also for example Sainsbury, *The Turning Point*, 218ff.; McNeill, *America, Britain and Russia*, 355–7, 364–5, but see 368 ff. for their greater understanding during the second Cairo conference in December 1943, just before the Tehran conference.

95. See Harbutt, *Iron Curtain*, 45, 49; Dallek, *Franklin D. Roosevelt*, 403–5.

96. See previous note.

97. See Harbutt, *Iron Curtain*, 49. For a good analysis of why the Allies were eventually able to defeat Germany, see R. Overy, *Why the Allies Won*, paperback edn (London, 1996), esp. 63 ff.; and for Russia's role, see in particular the same author's book *Russia's War* (Harmondsworth, 1997), esp. 154 ff. One of the most authoritative recent accounts of the battle of Stalingrad is A. Beevor, *Stalingrad* (London, 1998).

98. PRO: PREM 3/366/8, W.P.(43)430, 5/10/1943: Record of a meeting between Churchill and Dominion Representatives in Washington held at the British embassy, Washington, on 10th September 1943.

99. See for example Harbutt, *Iron Curtain*, 50; Dallek, *Franklin D. Roosevelt*, 410–11.

100. For a good and succinct overview, see Harbutt, ibid., 53ff. See also the somewhat simplified account by K. Eubank, *The Summit Conferences, 1919–1960* (Norman, Okla., 1966), esp. 55–7, 58ff. For excellent overviews of the conference and the developments leading up to it, see Mastny, *Russia's Road*, 111–44; Sainsbury, *Turning Point*, 12ff esp. 217–80, Weinberg, *World at Arms*, 619–31; also R. Jenkins, *Churchill* (London, 2001), ch. 37, esp. 719–78. See also 86–7, below.

101. For a detailed analysis of this aspect, see Ch. 4 below.

102. See FRUS, *Conferences at Cairo and Tehran, 1943*, esp. 487 ff., 529–552, 565ff., 576ff.; see also the literature in n. 92 above, and in particular for a convincing interpretation Harbutt, *Iron Curtain*, 53–60.

103. This is for example Fraser Harbutt's position. He also argues convincingly (ibid., p.59) that while Roosevelt informed Stalin that he intended to demolish the British Empire after the war, Churchill attempted to ingratiate himself with Stalin and 'scramble back to the summit' at the expense of Poland and Turkey for which Britain had assumed treaty responsibilities.

104. PRO: PREM 3/366/8, W.P.(43)430, 5/10/1943: Record of a meeting between Churchill and Dominion Representatives in Washington held at the British embassy, Washington, on 10 September 1943.

105. See for example Stalin's extraordinary political and personal attacks on Churchill during a tripartite dinner meeting on 29/11/1943: FRUS, *Conferences at Cairo and Tehran, 1943*, 553–5.

106. See A. Hillgruber, *Der Zweite Weltkrieg: Kriegsziele und Strategie der großen Mächte*, 2nd edn (Stuttgart, 1983). 124–8, 157; also Sainsbury, *Turning Point*, 293ff.; Barker, *Churchill and Eden*, 28. Warren Kimball convincingly differentiates among four stages in the Churchill–Roosevelt relationship: 1. up to June 1940: the 'get acquainted stage'; 2. up to Pearl Harbor: Churchill was wooing Roosevelt to become an ally; 3. from 1942 to mid/late 1943: equal partners' stage; 4. after Tehran at the latest: junior-senior partner relationship existed. See Kimball, 'Wheel within a Wheel,' 305.

107. Churchill said this to Violet Bonham-Carter and made a similar statement to the Czechoslovakian President Beneš in February 1945. Quoted in Colville's essay in J. Wheeler-Bennett (ed.), *Action this Day: Working with Churchill* (London, 1984), 96, n. 1; see also Edmonds, *The Big Three*,

318. During the first Quebec conference (14/8–28/8/1943) the United States had first insisted on its view in an important military-strategic decision against British doubts. Since the victory at Stalingrad in Feb. 1943 the Soviet Union's influence made itself also increasingly felt. See for example Hillgruber, *Der Zweite Weltkrieg*, 125–6; for the Tehran conference, see note 100 above, and also K. Eubank, *Summit at Teheran* (New York, 1985); Mastny, *Russia's Road to the Cold War*, 73ff., 111ff.; Rothwell, *Britain and the Cold War*, 100–14; Sainsbury, *Turning Point*, 12ff.; also P.D. Mayle, *Eureka Summit: Agreement in Principle and the Big Three at Tehran, 1943* (Newark, Del., 1987). The following two chapters of this book are devoted to an analysis of Churchill's ideas for the post-war world and the defeat of his conceptions by Stalin's and Roosevelt's opposition.

108. Quoted in A.J.P. Taylor, *The War Lords* (Harmondsworth, 1978), 93–4.

109. Harbutt, *Iron Curtain*, 62.

110. Quoted in Rose, *Churchill*, 189, see also 216ff.

111. Churchill made this remark on 10 November 1942 in the course of a speech during the Lord Mayor's Luncheon in London. Quoted in Louis, *Imperialism at Bay*, 200.

112. Quoted in Taylor, 'The Statesman,' 22, 18. See also Hillgruber, *Der Zweite Weltkrieg*, 156–7; and Churchill's remarks in the chapter 'On Britain and the Empire,' in Coote (ed.), *Sir Winston Churchill. A Self-Portrait*, 212–35, on India, ibid., 240–6. For Churchill's views on the British Empire, see also R.A. Callahan, *Churchill: Retreat from Empire* (Wilmington, Del., 1984), 249; and above all K. Emmert, *Winston S. Churchill on Empire* (Durham, N.C., 1989); R. Hyam, 'Churchill and the British Empire,' in Blake and Louis (eds), *Churchill*, 167–85; and S. Gopal, 'Churchill and India,' in ibid., 457–71.

113. W.S. Churchill, *The World Crisis, Vol. 1: 1911–4* (London, 1923), 181.

114. PRO: PREM 4/100/7, PM's Personal Minute M.474/2 to Eden, 21/10/1942; also in Churchill, *Second World War, Vol. 4*, 504.

115. Quote: T.H. Anderson, *The United States, Great Britain and the Cold War, 1944–47* (Columbia, Mo., 1981), 10. On 23 Nov. 1954 Churchill gave a speech at his Woodford constituency during which he claimed that at the end of the Second World War he asked Field Marshall Montgomery to make preparations for rearming German soldiers to use them against a further western advance of the Red Army. The speech aroused much controversy and a few days later Churchill admitted that he had been mistaken and had never given such an order. For details, see Chapter 17, below, 360–2.

116. Quoted in J. Colville, *The Fringes of Power: 10 Downing Street Diaries, 1939–55* (London, 1985), 312–13: diary entry, 13 Dec. 1940; see also Montague Browne, *Long Sunset*, 159; Gilbert, *Finest Hour*, 943.

117. Quote: Anderson, *The United States, Great Britain*, 10–11. See also J. Wheeler-Bennett and A. Nicholls, *The Semblance of Peace: The Political Settlement After the Second World War* (London, 1972), 290.

118. For the COS, see L. Woodward, *British Foreign Policy in the Second World War, Vol. 5* (London, 1976), 189–90; Ross, 'Foreign Office Attitudes,' 528–33; also Erickson, 'Stalin, Soviet Strategy and the Grand Alliance', 139.

119. Lord Moran, *Churchill: The Struggle for Survival, 1940–65* (London, 1966), 173 (21/8/1944).

120. See Barker, *Churchill and Eden*, 221–32, 286–95. These conflicting views were also held by Foreign Secretary Eden who, in this regard, tended to be even more optimistic than his superior.

121. Quoted in Douglas, *From War to Cold War*, 11–12 (quote: 12). See also Barker, ibid., 223.

122. For Stalin's territorial conquests towards the end of the war, see for example in great detail Weinberg, *World at Arms*, 587 ff.; Overy, *Russia's War*, 237 ff.

123. See Edmonds, *The Big Three*, 384–86. However, later Churchill himself did not shrink from ordering the bombardment of German cities, as in the case of Dresden as late as February 1945, which caused the unnecessary death of many thousands of innocent civilians. Also his thinking about the use of poison gas (above all mustard gas) in the bombardment of German cities is well known. See G.W. Gellermann, *Der Krieg der nicht stattfand* [...] (with the facsimile of a memo by Churchill on the issue, dated 6/7/1944) (Koblenz, 1986), 249–51.

124. For a good comprehensive overview see Kimball (ed.), *Churchill & Roosevelt*, Vol. 3, 348–51. Quotes: p. 353; for the percentage deal with which the two politicans agreed on dividing up the Balkans between them, see W.S. Churchill, *Second World War, Vol. 6*, 197–212; Edmonds, 'Churchill and Stalin,' 320–21; Kimball, *The Juggler*, 159–83; A. Resis, 'The Churchill-Stalin Percentages Agreement,' *American Historical Review* 82/2 (1978), 368–87.

125. PRO: FO 371/43 336/N 7650/G, 27/11/1944.

126. Quoted in Churchill, *Second World War*, Vol. 6, 351. On 5 March 1945 Churchill wrote to Eden with respect to the strong criticism of the Foreign Office regarding Soviet activities in Romania: 'We

really have no justification for intervening in this extraordinary vigorous manner for our late Roumanian enemies …' Quoted in D. Carlton, *Anthony Eden: A Biography* (London, 1986), 254. See also Kimball (ed.), *Churchill & Roosevelt*, Vol. 3 545–6. Eden appears to have been much more sceptical about Stalin at Yalta than Churchill. See R.R. James, *Anthony Eden* (London, 1987), 288–92. For the Yalta conference, see the still valuable work by D.S. Clemens, *Yalta* (New York, 1970); also R.D. Buhite, *Decisions at Yalta: An Appraisal of Summit Diplomacy* (Wilmington, Del, 1986).

127. Quote: R.M. Hathaway, *Ambiguous Partnership: Britain and America, 1944–47* (New York, 1981), 39. See also Moran, *Struggle for Survival*, 272ff.

128. Barker, *Churchill and Eden*, 294; Kimball, 'Wheel within a Wheel,' 302–5; see also R.H. Ferrell, *The Dying President: Franklin D. Roosevelt, 1944–45* (Columbia, Mo., 1998).

129. Quoted in Churchill, *Second World War, Vol. 6*, 433–4.

130. Kimball (ed.), *Churchill & Roosevelt*, Vol. 3, 17: Churchill to Roosevelt, 4/3/1944. There was a strong nationalistic streak in Churchill's imperialism; he was fully aware that without the Empire Britain would never have become a global power.

CHAPTER 3: CHURCHILL AND 'THE UNITED STATES OF EUROPE' DURING THE SECOND WORLD WAR

1. Quoted in E. Roosevelt, *As He Saw It* (New York, 1946), 115–16.

2. In the following the terms 'federal Europe', 'federalists', 'federalism', etc. are employed in the way they were usually applied by Churchill and his contemporaries. They took these terms to refer to a Europe organized on a more or less supranational basis with decisions largely made by majority rule. It implied a considerable decrease in the importance and relevance of the individual nation state. It also represented almost the exact opposite to traditional intergovernmental cooperation among fully sovereign and independent states. The relationship between supranationalism and intergovernmentalism is analysed in A. Milward (with G. Brennan and F. Romero), *The European Rescue of the Nation State* (London, 1992). See also B. Rosamond, *Theories of European Integration* (Basingstoke, 2000).

3. See A. Shlaim, *Britain and the Origins of European Unity, 1940–1951* (Reading, 1978), 14–18, 20 ff.; and the very convincing article by R. Boyce, 'Britain's first "No" to Europe: Britain and the Briand Plan, 1929–30', *European Studies Review* 10 (1980), 17–45; for a good overview and analysis, see also P.M.R. Stirk, *A History of European Integration since 1914* (London, 1996), 34–8. Briand first outlined his vision to the Assembly of the League of Nations in Geneva in early September 1929. At the request of German Foreign Minister Stresemann he explained his reasoning in greater detail in a lengthy though still rather vague memorandum submitted to the League's European members on 1 May 1930. See Boyce, ibid., 32–4. See also B. Oudin, *Aristide Briand: la paix. Une Idée neuve en Europe* (Paris, 1987); F. Siebert, *Aristide Briand, 1862–1932. Ein Staatsmann zwischen Frankreich und Europa* (Zurich, 1973). For brief but good overviews, see W. Loth, *Der Weg nach Europa*, 3rd edn (Göttingen, 1996), 12–13; W. Lipgens, *Die Anfänge der europäischen Einigungspolitik 1945–1950, Vol. 1, Teil: 1945–47* (Stuttgart, 1977), 40–1.

4. See for example R.W.G. Mackay's argumentation in his *Federal Europe* (London, 1940), 107ff.; for a good analysis, see A.J. Crozier, 'Federalism and Anti-Federalism in the United Kingdom', in F. Knipping (ed.), *Federal Conceptions in EU Member States: Traditions and Perspectives* (Baden-Baden, 1994), 164. In Britain, the reception of Briand's memorandum of May 1930 was much cooler than the reception of his September 1929 speech (this was also the case in Germany). The predominance of political over economic aspects (a reversal of his original intention) was not welcomed by the Foreign Office whose long delay in responding was interpreted as a negative assessment and effectively killed any support for Briand's memorandum in the other European capitals. In London it was feared that his proposal had become too federalist and was still too anti-American in tenor. It was also assumed that the implementation of Briand's ideas would damage imperial free trade and Britain's links with its Empire and Commonwealth. The Foreign Office certainly felt that London could not support any ideas leading to a European political union. See Boyce, ibid.

5. Quoted in C. Ponting, *Churchill* (London, 1994), 737; see also Churchill's similar post-war remarks in a speech at a meeting of the European Movement in London, 28/11/1949, in R.S. Churchill (ed.), *In the Balance: Speeches 1949 and 1950* (London, 1951), 152.

6. See A. Bosco, 'The British Federalist Tradition and the Origins of the Churchill Proposal of Union with France in 1940', in Knipping (ed.), *Federal Conceptions in EU Member States*, 178–9; also A. Bosco (ed.), *The Federal Idea, Vol. 1: The History of Federalism from the Enlightenment to 1945* (London, 1991), 3 ff. See also in particular J. Pinder and R. Mayne, *Federal Union: the Pioneers. A History of Federal Union* (Basingstoke, 1990). For a good account of the thinking on Europe after the First World War, see C.H. Pegg, *Evolution of the European Idea, 1914–1932* (Chapel Hill, N.C., 1983); and for brief introductions, see P. Rich, 'Visionary Ideas of European Unity after World War I'; and P. Wilson, 'The New Europe Debate in Wartime Britain', both in P. Murray and P. Rich (eds), *Visions of European Unity* (Boulder, Col., 1996), 21–37, 39–62. For the round table movement, see A. Bosco and A. May (eds), *The Round Table, the Empire/Commonwealth and British Foreign Policy* (London, 1997). For a good overview, see J. Pinder, 'British Federalists 1940–1947: From Movement to Stasis', in M. Dumoulin (ed.), *Wartime Plans for Postwar Europe, 1940–1947* (Brussels, 1995), 247–74.

7. Streit never doubted that a federal Europe ought to be established under the firm leadership of the United States with Britain in a supporting role. In 1941 he published his second book entitled *Union Now with Britain* which also became very popular. The exhaustive Clarence Streit papers and the Atlantic Union Committee papers in the Manuscript Division of the Library of Congress in Washington, DC, offer interesting insights into Streit's tireless campaigns (until his death in 1986 at the age of 90), his limited political influence and the reception of his ideas in Britain. See also R.A. Wilford, 'The Federal Union Campaign', *European Studies Review* 10 (1980), 101–14.

8. Churchill first met the Count in February 1938; see Shlaim, *Britain and the Origins of European Unity*, 22, also 20ff.; M. Gilbert, *Winston S. Churchill, Vol. 8: Never Despair, 1945–65*, paperback edn (London, 1990), 243. The date early 1939 as assumed by Onslow is incorrect. See S. Onslow, *Backbench Debate within the Conservative Party and its Influence on British Foreign Policy, 1948–57* (Basingstoke, 1997), 16. See also R.N. Coudenhove-Kalergi's books *Pan-Europe* (New York, 1926), *Europa Erwacht* (Zurich, 1934), *Crusade for Pan-Europe: Autobiography of a Man and a Movement* (New York, 1943); and his memoirs *An Idea Conquers the World* (London, 1953). For a good overview, see R. White, 'The Europeanism of Coudenhove-Kalergi', in P.M.R. Stirk (ed.), *European Unity in Context: The Interwar Period* (London, 1989), 23–40; see also Stirk, *History of European Integration*, 26–8.

9. For Davies and the New Commonwealth Society, see Bosco, 'The British Federalist Tradition', 184–5.

10. Lipgens, *Anfänge der europäischen Einigungspolitik, Vol. 1, Teil: 1945–47*, 62–3. Vice President was Duff Cooper.

11. See C. Ponting, 'Churchill and Europe: a revision', in R. Bideleux and R. Taylor (eds), *European Integration and Disintegration: East and West* (London, 1996), 36–45 (quote: 37).

12. Quote: M. Gilbert (ed.), *The Churchill War Papers, Vol. 2: Never Surrender, May 1940–December 1940* (New York, 1995), 643: John Colville diary, 10/8/1940; also J. Colville, *The Fringes of Power: 10 Downing Street Diaries, 1939–55* (London, 1985), 215: diary entry, 10/8/1940; also M. Gilbert, *Winston S. Churchill, Vol. 6: Finest Hour, 1939–41* (London, 1983), 986.

13. For details, see 61ff. below; also Chapter 4.

14. See Crozier, 'Federalism and Anti-Federalism', 165–6; J. Monnet, *Mémoires* (Paris, 1976), 147–51; F. Duchene, *Jean Monnet: The First Statesman of Interdependence* (New York, 1994), 76–81. Later Monnet also became an important member of Charles De Gaulle's government in exile.

15. Quote: A. Spinelli, 'The Growth of the European Movement since the Second World War', reprinted in M. Hodges (ed.), *European Integration: Selected Readings* (Harmondsworth, 1972), 46; see also Crozier, ibid.; also J. Pinder (ed.), *Altiero Spinelli and the British Federalists: Writings by Beveridge, Robbins and Spinelli* (London, 1998). For a brief account of Spinelli's lasting influence, see P. Murray, 'Spinelli and European Union', in Murray and Rich (eds), *Visions of European Unity*, 109–30. Even Anthony Eden spoke on occasion of 'some kind of federation' including 'a defence scheme, a European customs union and common currency' as 'the only possible solution'. Quoted in Stirk, *History of European Integration*, 71.

16. First quote: Spinelli, ibid. Second quote: H.J. Heiser, *British Policy with Regard to the Unification Efforts on the European Continent* (Leyden, 1959), 21. For the proposal, see also W.S. Churchill, *The Second World War, Vol 2: Their Finest Hour* (London, 1949), 183–4.

17. For the Franco-British union proposal, see above all A. Shlaim, 'Prelude to Downfall: The British Offer of Union to France, June 1940', *Journal of Contemporary History* 9/3 (1974), 27–63; A. Bosco, 'Federal Union, Chatham House, the Foreign Office and Anglo-French Union in spring 1940', in Bosco (ed.), *The Federal Idea, Vol. 1*, 291–325; M. Beloff, 'The Anglo-French Union Project of June 1940', in M. Beloff, *The Intellectual in Politics* (London, 1970), 172–99; Bosco, 'The British Feder-

alist Tradition', 173–8; for good overviews, see also Stirk, *History of European Integration since 1914*, 62; Loth, *Weg nach Europa*, 14. On the fall of France, see for example A. Horne, *To Lose a Battle: France, 1940*, rev. edn (London, 1999); A. Shennan, *The Fall of France, 1940* (Harlow, 2000).

18.   Quote: M. Beloff, 'Churchill and Europe', in R. Blake and W.R. Louis (eds), *Churchill* (Oxford, 1993), 445; see also E. Barker, *Britain in a divided Europe, 1945–70* (London, 1971), 18–19. A. Shlaim also agrees with this view, see his *Britain and the Origins of European Unity*, 29–31; so does Bosco, 'The British Federalist Tradition', 177. For a contrary view, see for example Pinder, 'British Federalists 1940–1947', 252–5.

19.   Churchill's proposal therefore cannot be given credit as the 'event which gave birth to the post-war development of European integration' which led to the establishment of the Council of Europe in 1949. For this view see Heiser, *British Policy*, 21. W. Lipgen's assumption that Churchill's proposal was meant to be the 'Keimzelle weiterer europäischer Integration' is similarly misguided. See Lipgens, *Anfänge der europäischen Einigungspolitik, Vol. 1, Teil: 1945–1952*, 63.

20.   For example, Lipgens, ibid., 64, believes that it is difficult to understand why Churchill missed the opportunity to do so in the summer of 1941. He partially blames Eden and his inability to feel sympathy for the idea of a united Europe.

21.   See for example D. Weigall, 'British Ideas of European Unity and Regional Confederation in the Context of Anglo-Soviet Relations, 1941–5', in M.L. Smith and P.M.R. Stirk (eds), *Making the New Europe: European Unity and the Second World War* (London, 1990), 156.

22.   For an excellent account of the manifold motivating forces among Resistance leaders, see Lipgens, *Anfänge der europäischen Einigungspolitik, Vol. 1. Teil: 1945–47*, 43–57. The author emphasizes quite correctly that only in 1944–5 was the necessity for a federally organized Europe explained with the requirement to preserve Europe as a strong power between the overwhelming strength of the USA and the USSR (see ibid., 54–5). See D. Brandes, 'Confederation Plans in Eastern Europe during World War II' and W. Loth, 'Die Résistance und die Pläne fur Europäischen Einigung', both in Mamoulin (ed.), *Wartime Plans*, 83ff. and 47ff.

23.   See the previous note.

24.   See D .W. Urwin, *The Community of Europe: A History of European Integration since 1945*, 2nd edn (London, 1995), 10, 8. Altiero Spinelli's 1941 *Ventotene Manifesto*, which led to the 1943 creation of the European Federalist Movement, was perhaps the most important early development. For an overview of the evolution of plans by the various Resistance groups for uniting Europe and the development of the incorporation of supranational principles in these plans, see Lipgens, ibid., 43–61; also Loth, *Weg nach Europa*, 16ff. For interesting discussions of Nazi Germany's 'New Order' as 'a form of European unity' in a geopolitical and ideological sense, see M.L. Smith, 'Introduction: European Unity and the Second World War', in Smith and Stirk (eds), *Making the New Europe*, 3–12; and P.M.R. Stirk, 'Authoritarian and Nationalist Socialist Conceptions of Nation, State and Europe', in Stirk (ed.), *European Unity in Context*, 125–8.

25.   Quoted in Stirk, *History of European Integration*, 64. For a good account of the attitude of the FO towards a Polish-Czech and a Yugoslav-Greek confederation, see Deputy Under-Secretary of State Orme Sargent's memorandum of June 1942, publ. in L. Woodward, *British Foreign Policy in the Second World War*, Vol. 5 (London, 1976), 18–21. The FO hoped initially that these confederations could be extended to other countries (even partially by force) and turned into a Central European confederation, a Balkan Union and a South-Eastern European confederation. For Foreign Secretary Eden's much more sceptical view, see ibid., 42–3. For a good account of these plans, see P.S. Wandycz, *Czechoslovak-Polish Confederation and the Great Powers, 1940–43* (Indiana, 1956, reprinted ed. Westport, Conn., 1979); also S.M. Terry, *Poland's Place in Europe: General Sikorski and the Origin of the Oder-Neisse Line, 1939–43* (Princeton, N.J., 1983).

26.   See for example W.H. McNeill, *America, Britain and Russia: Their Co-operation and Conflict, 1941–1946* (London, 1953), 323; Lipgens, *Anfänge der europäischen Einigungspolitik, Vol. 1. Teil: 1945–47*, 66; Loth, *Weg nach Europa*, 16–17. See for greater details for the plans on East European confederations, W. Lipgens, 'East European Plans for the Future of Europe: the Example of Poland'; and F. Gross and M. Kamil Dziewanowski, 'Plans by Exiles from East European Countries', in W. Lipgens (ed.), *Documents on the History of European Integration* (Berlin, 1984), Vol. 1, pp. 609–58; and Vol. 2, pp. 353–413.

27.   Moreover, as Wilfried Loth has pointed out, it soon became clear that some kind of federalist solution to the German question and the participation of the 'Big Three' needed to be achieved before progress with this plan could be made. See Loth, *Weg nach Europa*, 18–20.

28.   See J.E. Meade, *Negotiations for Benelux: An Annotated Chronicle, 1943–56* (Princeton, N.J., 1957).

29.   See K. Sainsbury, *The Turning Point: Roosevelt, Stalin, Churchill, and Chiang-Kai-Shek. The*

Moscow, Cairo and Teheran Conferences (Oxford, 1986), 83–4; also D. Dutton, *Anthony Eden: A Life and Reputation* (London, 1997), 203.

30. The committee was chaired by Deputy Prime Minister Clement Attlee; in the summer of 1943 it developed into the 'Ministerial Committee on Armistice Terms'; see PRO: PREM 4/30/3, War Cabinet Conclusions 107 (43), 29/7/1943. For the initial discussions regarding the Committee, including its membership, see PRO: PREM 4/100/4 (August–December, 1940: Committee on War Aims).

31. First quote: PRO, PREM 4/100/8, 9/9/1941; second quote: PREM 4/30/10, Churchill to Eden, M. 1191/4, 6/12/1944.

32. See W.S. Churchill, *The Second World War, Vol. 3: The Grand Alliance* (London, 1950), 331; quote: 637. See also Charmley, *Churchill's Grand Alliance: A Provocative Reassessment of the 'Special Relationship' between England and the U.S. from 1940 to 1957* (New York, 1995), 66.

33. For the Western European bloc idea, see Chapter 4, below, 90ff. For British planning on Germany, see in great detail the useful book by L. Kettenacker, *Krieg zur Friedenssicherung: die Deutschlandplanung der britischen Regierung während des Zweiten Weltkrieges* (Göttingen, 1989); also A. Tyrell, *Großbritannien und die Deutschlandplanung der Alliierten 1941–5* (Frankfurt, 1987). The following account does not focus on the role of Germany in allied post-war planning; the emphasis lies on plans for a united or a more integrated Europe.

34. See C. Hull, *Memoirs*, Vol. 2 (London, 1948), 1626, 1631–3.

35. See Woodward, *British Foreign Policy*, Vol. 5, 1–3; and L. Woodward's earlier one-volume history confusingly also entitled *British Foreign Policy in the Second World War* (London, 1962), 429–33. See also G. Jebb, *The Memoirs of Lord Gladwyn* (London, 1972), 111.

36. Quoted in G. Ross (ed.), *The Foreign Office and the Kremlin: British Documents on Anglo-Soviet Relations, 1941–45* (Cambridge, 1984), 81; see also Stirk, *History of European Integration*, 69.

37. For the latter, see the extensive documentation in PRO: PREM 3/449/1 and 2. The Atlantic Charter was also the first public formulation of tentative Anglo-American war aims. See Woodward, *British Foreign Policy*, Vol. 5, 1–3; and Woodward, *British Foreign Policy* (1962), 429–33. For the Atlantic Charter and the relevant literature, see Chapter 2, 36 and nn 13 and 14 (p. 410).

38. This remark was made on 25 January 1941 during Harry Hopkins' visit. Quoted in Gilbert, *Finest Hour*, 995.

39. PRO: FO 954/7, PM's Personal Minute M. 461/2, Churchill to Eden from Chequers, 18/10/1942 (also in PREM 4/100/7). See also J. Baylis, 'British wartime thinking about a post-war European security group', *Review of International Studies* 9/2 (1983), 278. Only when it became clear in the course of the battle of Stalingrad in late 1942/early 1943 that the Nazis were unlikely to win the war did the Foreign Office make rapid progress with the development of a plan, which was, however, rather ambiguous, for the future of Europe. The resulting *Four-Power Plan* is analysed below.

40. Jebb, *Memoirs*, 118.

41. See for example D. Dutton, *Anthony Eden: A Life and a Reputation* (London, 1997), 282.

42. 'Sporadic bursts of imaginative energy did not represent a coherent policy', is the critical assessment of one author. See E.J. Hughes, 'Winston Churchill and the Formation of the United Nations Organization', *Journal of Contemporary History* 9/4 (1974), 193.

43. For details, see Lipgens, *Anfänge der europäischen Einigungspolitik, Vol. 1. Teil: 1945–47*, 62–7.

44. See for example Stirk, *History of European Integration*, 58–9, 63. Keynes submitted the paper in December.

45. See J.R. Colville, 'The Personality of Sir Winston Churchill', in R. Crosby Kemper III (ed.), *Winston Churchill: Resolution, Defiance, Magnanimity, Good Will* (Columbia, Mo., 1996), 122–3; also PRO: CAB 65/6, W.M. 67 (40), 13/3/1940.

46. See Gilbert (ed.), *Churchill War Papers, Vol. 2*, 643: John Colville diary, 10/8/1940; also Colville, *Fringes of Power*, 215–16: diary entry, 10/8/1940.

47. PRO: CAB 65/8, W.M. 233 (40), 23/8/1940; also publ. in Gilbert (ed.), ibid., 708; see also already CAB 65/6, W.M. 67 (40), 13/3/1940.

48. Colville, *Fringes of Power*, 312–14 (quotes: 314, 313): diary entry, 13/12/1940. Colville was Churchill's trusted Private Secretary. See also M. Charlton, *The Price of Victory* (London, 1983), 18–25. This valuable book is a collection of interviews with politicians and civil servants active between 1940 and 1963.

49. Colville, ibid.; see also Colville, 'The Personality of Sir Winston Churchill', 122–3.

50. Quoted in Colville, *Fringes of Power*, 312–14; see also Gilbert, *Finest Hour*, 943–4.

51. Colville, ibid. The wording in Gilbert, ibid., 943–4, is slightly different. Churchill's view that 'Britain would be part of Europe but she would also be part of the English-speaking world' was

not dissimilar to his speech to the Congress of Europe on 7 May 1948, as published in R.S. Churchill (ed.), *Europe Unite: Speeches 1947 and 1948* (London, 1950), 314–15.

52. Quoted from the Churchill papers in Gilbert, *Finest Hour*, 943–4. Churchill may also have been influenced by John Maynard Keynes's memorandum of December 1940 in which Keynes pointed out the impossibility of constructing a prosperous post-war Europe without German reconstruction and participation in post-war prosperity. See Stirk, *History of European Integration*, 63.

53. See Chapter 6, below, 137–9.

54. Ponting, 'Churchill and Europe', 38.

55. Quoted in J. Wheeler-Bennett (ed.), *Action this Day* (London, 1968), 97–8; see also Shlaim, *Britain and the Origins of European Unity*, 28; Colville, *Fringes of Power*, 331–5; Gilbert, *Finest Hour*, 983–9.

56. The importance Churchill attached to the Anglo-American pillar became particularly clear when the *Atlantic Charter* was signed in August 1941. Churchill believed that with the help of a new world organization as successor to the League of Nations the USA could be prevented from withdrawing into isolationism after the war. See Hughes, 'Formation of the UNO', 179–81.

57. McNeill, *America, Britain and Russia*, 316.

58. See Weigall, 'British Ideas of European Unity', 161. Weigall points out that the terminology used 'was exactly reminiscent of Stalin's response to the Briand Plan in 1930'. See also Dutton, *Anthony Eden*, 203; Stirk, *History of European Integration*, 69.

59. See for example the discussion of the Soviet borders and the future of Germany at the Tehran conference: FRUS, *Conferences at Cairo and Tehran, 1943*, 599–604: Tripartite Political Meeting of the Heads of Government, 1 Dec. 1943 (Bohlen minutes). For a good discussion of British-Soviet relations between 1939–41, see G. Gorodetsky, *Grand Delusion: Stalin and the German Invasion of Russia* (New Haven, Conn., 2000).

60. Molotov explained this to Eden during the October 1944 Foreign Ministers' conference in Moscow. See W.F. Kimball, *Forged in War: Churchill, Roosevelt and the Second World War* (London, 1997), 229; Lipgens, *Anfänge der europäischen Einigungspolitik, Vol. 1. Teil: 1945–47*, 70.

61. See PRO: PREM 4/30/8, Record of Interview Between the Foreign Secretary and M. Stalin, December 16, 1941; also A. Eden, *The Reckoning* (London, 1965), 289–92; O.A. Rzheshevsky (ed.), *War and Diplomacy: The Making of the Grand Alliance. Documents from Stalin's Archives* (Amsterdam, 1996), 11–27: documents 4, 5–6; Lipgens, ibid., 68–9; Woodward, *British Foreign Policy* (1962), 191–2; Ross (ed.), *Foreign Office and the Kremlin*, 82.

62. FRUS, *Conferences at Cairo and Tehran, 1943*, 845–6 (quote: 846): Memorandum Bohlen, 15/12/1943.

63. When Stalin discussed the amount of time it would take Germany to recover during the war he spoke of 20–30 years and sometimes of 15–20 years; after 1945 he frequently mentioned only 12–15 years. See J. Haslam, 'Soviet War-Aims', in A. Lane and H. Temperley (eds), *The Rise and Fall of the Grand Alliance 1941–45* (Basingstoke, 1995), 36; FRUS, ibid., 847, 15/12/1943.

64. See Lipgens, *Anfänge der europäischen Einigungspolitik, Vol. 1. Teil: 1945–47*, 69–70; also Stirk, *History of European Integration*, 62–3, 69–70; Weigall, 'British Ideas of European Unity', 158–9, 161; also in much greater detail Wandycz, *Czechoslovak-Polish Confederation*. By the summer of 1942 the lack of Soviet support had persuaded Beneš to abandon the idea of a Czech-Polish confederation. Instead, in December 1943 he entered into an alliance with the Soviet Union (see Wandycz, ibid., 75–83).

65. See PRO: PREM 4/30/8, Record of Interview Between the Foreign Secretary and M. Stalin, December 16, 1941.

66. See Sainsbury, *Turning Point*, 84ff.; Dutton, *Anthony Eden*, 203; Stirk, *History of European Integration*, 69.

67. See Wandycz, *Czechoslovak-Polish Confederation*, 75 ff.

68. See for example, Loth, *Weg nach Europa*, 23–4; also Lipgens, *Anfänge der europäischen Einigungspolitik, Vol. 1 Teil: 1945–47*, 69–70.

69. See Stirk, *History of European Integration*, 70–1; also Woodward, *British Foreign Policy*, Vol. 5, 9.

70. PRO: PREM 3/59, W.P.(42)480, 'Post-war Atlantic bases' (Eden memorandum to the Cabinet), 22/10/1942.

71. For details, see Chapter 2, above. The detailed planning for post-war defence cannot be explored here. For an excellent analysis, see J. Lewis, *Changing Direction: British Military Planning for Post-war Strategic Defence, 1942–47* (London, 1988), esp. chs 1–2; also Baylis, 'British wartime thinking'.

72. See for example PRO: PREM 4/100/8, Minute Eden to Churchill, P.M./43/198, 2/7/1943; and for Molotov's strong denial of any interest in German overtures: Clark Kerr, Moscow, to FO, No. 293, 22/4/1943. See also G.L. Weinberg, *A World at Arms: A Global History of World War II* (Cambridge, 1994), 609; Lipgens, *Anfänge der europäischen Einigungspolitik, Vol. 1. Teil: 1945–47*, 70.

73. See D. Reynolds, 'Churchill the appeaser? Between Hitler, Roosevelt and Stalin in World War Two', in M. Dockrill and B. McKercher (eds), *Diplomacy and World Power: Studies in British Foreign Policy, 1890–1950* (Cambridge, 1996), 207, 212; V. Mastny, *Russia's Road to the Cold War* (New York, 1979), 73–85; Lipgens, ibid., 70; McNeill, *America, Britain and Russia*, 324–5.

74. For the Second Front issue in allied relations, see also Chapter 2, above, 47–8.

75. See for example McNeill, *America, Britain and Russia*, 323–4; also Lipgens, *Anfänge der europäischen Einigungspolitik, Vol. 1, Teil: 1945–47*, 70. For Stalin's and Molotov's continuing opposition to Churchill's confederation plans as expressed to the British ambassador in the spring of 1943, see PRO: PREM 4/30/1 (March 1943).

76. For a good and convincing account, see A. Gietz, *Die Neue Alte Welt. Roosevelt, Churchill und die europäische Nachkriegsordnung* (Munich, 1986); from a revisionist point of view, see G. Kolko, *The Politics of War: The World and United States Foreign Policy, 1943–45* (New York, 1968). For a good overview of the American thinking, see J.L. Gaddis, 'Dividing the World', reprinted in K. Larres and A. Lane (eds), *The Cold War: The Essential Readings* (Oxford, 2001), 45–6 (and for Stalin's concept, 46–9).

77. See W.F. Kimball, *The Juggler: Franklin Roosevelt as Wartime Statesman* (Princeton, 1991), 85. See also J.L. Gaddis, *The United States and the Origins of the Cold War, 1941–1947* (New York, 1972), 103–5. On Roosevelt's trustee idea, see also W.F. Kimball, 'Anglo-American War Aims, 1941–3, "The First Review": Eden's Mission to Washington', in Lane and Temperley (eds), *Grand Alliance*, 8.

78. See Kimball, ibid., 85.

79. Quoted in ibid., 85. Molotov agreed with the importance of uniting the armed forces of 'several dominant powers' but asked whether France would be excluded from this forum. Roosevelt confirmed this. See Edmonds, *The Big Three: Churchill, Roosevelt and Stalin in Peace and War* (London, 1991), 343–4.

80. See for example Lipgens, *Anfänge der europäischen Einigungspolitik, Vol. 1. Teil: 1945–47*, 72.

81. Quoted in Kimball, *The Juggler*, 85–6; see also Woodward, *British Foreign Policy*, Vol. 5, 33–6.

82. For the ideas of Sumner Welles and the Advisory Committee regarding the future of Europe, which were strongly influenced by Welles's European journey in the spring of 1940 and included three regional organizations but not yet a world organization, see Lipgens, *Anfänge der europäischen Einigungspolitik, Vol. 1. Teil: 1945–47*, 64–5, 65 n. 103. For Welles's visit to London, see PRO: PREM 4/25/2, 13/3/1940.

83. See the account in Hull, *Memoirs*, Vol. 2, 1642–3.

84. See Edmonds, *The Big Three*, 342.

85. Quotes: Kimball, *Forged in War*, 229; Kimball, 'Anglo-American War Aims', 11.

86. Edmonds, *The Big Three*, 342.

87. See Eden, *The Reckoning*, 371 ff.; Dutton, *Anthony Eden*, 161; Woodward, *British Foreign Policy*, Vol. 5, 32 (account of conversation between Eden and Roosevelt, Washington, March 1943); also Jebb, *Memoirs*, 127–8.

88. Hull, *Memoirs*, Vol. 2, 1638; see also Kimball, *Forged in War*, 229–30. The following outline of Hull's views is largely based on the views expressed in his quite open and revealing memoirs.

89. Hull, ibid., 1638.

90. Ibid., 1644, see also 1646.

91. Ibid., 1645.

92. Ibid., 1644–5.

93. Ibid., 1644, 1646.

94. Ibid., 1640 ff.; also already McNeill, *America, Britain and Russia*, 322.

95. Kimball, *Forged in War*, 229.

96. For the Four-Power Declaration, see PRO: PREM 4/30/5, Campbell, Washington, to Eden, No. 3690, August 1943; and see the memorandum to the War Cabinet, ibid., W.P.(43)389, 4/9/1943.

97. PRO: PREM 4/30/5, Churchill to Eden, PM's Personal Minute, T.1807/3, 1/11/1943. Churchill expressed himself 'very pleased with the combined Four-Power Declaration'. Similar general satisfaction is indicated in various other minutes contained in this file.

98. Hull, *Memoirs*, Vol. 2, 1648; also 1646–7.

99. See McNeill, *America, Britain and Russia*, 315.

100. See Stirk, *History of European Integration*, 71–3. In some American memoranda, therefore, warnings against the British imposition of a 'super-government for Europe' were voiced.

101. See PRO: PREM 4/100/4, W.A.(40)14, 13/12/1940, 'Draft Statement on War Aims', circulated by Eden to the War Cabinet's Committee on War Aims. Churchill had underlined the quoted words in pencil and put a question mark in the left hand margin. First quote in Dutton, *Anthony Eden*, 281.

102. Quote: Dutton, ibid.; see also Stirk, *History of European Integration*, 61. See also 56–7, above.
103. It is therefore largely correct to state that Eden shared 'Churchill's views on most of the key issues, particularly the need to create some sort of political barrier to Soviet expansion into Central Europe'. See Kimball, *Forged in War*, 228.
104. See for example PRO: PREM 4/30/3, PM's Personal Telegram to Eden, T.441/3, 30/3/1943. Churchill wrote: 'A proposal to rank France lower than China even in matters affecting Europe, and to subjugate all Europe after disarmament to the four Powers, would certainly cause lively discussion. . . . You were right to protest about France.'
105. Eden expressed this belief on 30 May 1944. Quoted in Dutton, *Anthony Eden*, 169. For Eden's insistence towards Roosevelt, during his visit to Washington in March 1943, that France ought not to be delegated to secondary status, see for example Woodward, *British Foreign Policy*, Vol. 5, 35–6; almost the entire FO shared this view (see ibid., pp. 36–7). For the role of France in both Eden's and Churchill's thinking, see F. Kersaudy, *Churchill and de Gaulle* (New York, 1982).
106. See for example Eden, *The Reckoning*, 424; and Halifax's report from Washington in PRO: PREM 4/27/9, letter Halifax to Churchill, 13/3/1941.
107. See PRO: CAB 66/63, W.P.(43)31, 16/1/1943.
108. Quoted in Dutton, *Anthony Eden*, 282; for a good analysis of Eden's attitude towards the USA and the USSR, see ibid., chs 6 and 7.
109. Quoted in ibid., 144. Churchill made this remark in September 1943
110. For the resulting memorandum by Richard Law, the Parliamentary Undersecretary of State for Foreign Affairs, to the Cabinet, see PRO: FO 371/31 515/U1187/27/70 (W.P.(42)492), 21/10/1942. He emphasized the broad agreement on the political and economic structure of the post-war world which existed within the US government and also referred to Washington's suspicion of British imperialism; however, there also existed 'a genuine anxiety to work with us'. See also Jebb, *Memoirs*, 108–9.
111. See Woodward, *British Foreign Policy*, Vol. 5, 1 ff. As early as 17 December 1941, the House of Lords had urged the government to 'prepare without delay the proposals they intend to make for World Settlement after the War'. See PRO: PREM 4/100/8.
112. Jebb, *Memoirs*, quote: 117; see also Woodward, *British Foreign Policy*, Vol. 5, 3–5.
113. Woodward, ibid., 3–4.
114. See Dutton, *Anthony Eden*, 156.
115. See for example Woodward, *British Foreign Policy*, Vol. 5, 32.
116. See Jebb, *Memoirs*, 109–10.
117. Although the Four-Power Plan was subsequently revised, the January 1943 *United Nations Plan* was very similar to the original *Four-Power Plan*; indeed, as is outlined below, even the final *United Nations Plan for Organising Peace* of July 1943 was still very similar to the initial plan. The *Four-Power Plan* of Oct. 1942 – both the long version of 38 pages, and a summary of 11 pages – is in PRO: PREM 4/100/7; the Plan is also in FO 371/31 515/U742/742/70, see also U216/71/71 (Reconstruction Dept.); the similar *United Nations Plan* of Jan. 1943 is publ. in Woodward, *British Foreign Policy*, Vol. 5, 14–18.
118. Jebb, *Memoirs*, 115. For a good analysis of the Foreign Office view, see Lewis, *Changing Direction*, 30 ff., esp. 35–39, 45 ff., 65–72.
119. Woodward, *British Foreign Policy*, Vol. 5, 11; see also ibid, 15: *The United Nations Plan*, submitted by Eden to the Cabinet on 16/1/1943; see also Jebb, ibid., 137–8.
120. For a detailed analysis, see Woodward, ibid., 3ff.; also Jebb, ibid., 112–18; also Lewis (see n. 118).
121. Jebb, ibid., 114. For the importance the FO attached to enabling France to assume her traditional role as a great power, see also Woodward, ibid., 7.
122. See Jebb, ibid., 112–13.
123. Ibid., 116–17 (quotes: 117); see also Woodward, *British Foreign Policy*, Vol. 5, 8.
124. PRO: PREM 4/100/7 and FO 371/31515/U742/742/70, 'The Four-Power Plan', October 1942. See also Jebb, *Memoirs*, 112–13.
125. Jebb, ibid., 118. Indeed Churchill's later agreement with Stalin in October 1944, the notorious percentage agreement, was at least partially aimed at maintaining some degree of British influence in Central and South Eastern Europe. However, it only confirmed long-held American suspicions about British imperialism. Churchill had attempted to include the Americans in the deal but not surprisingly Washington declined and then refused even to officially acknowledge the Soviet-British understanding. See Gaddis, *The United States and the Origins of the Cold War*, 15–17; W. Loth *Die Teilung der Welt, 1941–1955* (Munich, 1980), 87; for a case study regarding the exaggerated importance which has been given to the 1944 agreement, see M. Percival, 'Churchill

and Romania: The Myth of the October 1944 "Betrayal" ', *Contemporary British History* 12/3 (1998), 41–61. See also Chapter 2, n. 124, above.

126. Woodward, *British Foreign Policy*, Vol. 5, 17: Point 23 of *The United Nations Plan*, submitted by Eden to the Cabinet on 16/1/1943; see also in a very similar vein PRO: PREM 4/100/7 and FO 371/31515/U742/742/70, 'The Four-Power Plan', October 1942.

127. Woodward, ibid., 17: Point 22 of *The United Nations Plan*, 16/1/1943; also PRO: ibid.

128. Ibid.

129. Woodward, ibid., 7; also PRO: PREM 4/100/7 and FO 371/31515/U742/742/70, 'The Four-Power Plan', Oct. 1942.

130. PRO: PREM 4/100/7, W.P. (42) 516, 'The "Four-Power Plan"', 8/11/1942.

131. Woodward, *British Foreign Policy, Vol. 5*, 9, 10.

132. Jebb, *Memoirs*, 119. Henry R. Luce (1898–1967), the founder and proprietor of popular magazines such as *Time, Fortune* and *Life* and author of an influential article on the new global role of the USA entitled 'The American Century' (*Life*, 17 February 1941) was well known for his strong Republican and anti-Communist views which he wished to see reflected in the magazines he owned. He 'celebrated internationalism in a rather nationalistic vein'; this could also be said of Amery. Quoted characterization of Luce: G. Lundestad, '"Empire by Invitation" in the American Century', *Diplomatic History* 23/2 (1999), 189. For the Cabinet meeting, see PRO: CAB 65/28, W.M. (42), 161, 27/11/1942; also Beloff, 'Churchill and Europe', 446–7.

133. PRO: PREM 4/100/7, W.P.(42)532, 19/11/1942. Cripps was also Lord Privy Seal and for a few months in 1942 Churchill's rival for premiership. See also Jebb, ibid.; Woodward, *British Foreign Policy*, Vol. 5, 11–12. Cripps also foresaw a 'Council of Asia' under the leadership of China; a proposal which Churchill did not approve of.

134. PRO: PREM 4/100/7, W.P.(42)524, Nov. 1942 (Amery's memorandum).

135. See the discussion in PRO: CAB 65/28, W.M. (42), 161, 27/11/1942; also Jebb, *Memoirs*, 118–19.

136. Woodward, *British Foreign Policy*, Vol. 5, 13.

137. The plan is publ. in ibid., 14–18.

138. Quote: Jebb, *Memoirs*, 128. *The United Nations Plan for Organising Peace and Welfare* of 7 July 1943 can be found in PRO: PREM 4/30/3, W.P.(43)300, 7/7/1943. The Plan is publ. in Woodward, ibid., 51–62. For a detailed paper by Leo Amery giving his assessment of the new plan, see PRO: PREM 4/30/3, W.P.(43)321, 19/7/1943, 'Post-War Settlement and the United Nations Plan'. See also Eden's memorandum 'Post-War Settlement', W.P.(43)292, 1/7/1943 and Churchill's paper W.P.(43)233 earlier in the month; see also Amery's memorandum W.P.(43)244, 'The Relation of the British Commonwealth to the Post-war International Political Organisation', 15/6/1943.

139. Woodward, ibid., 52–3: The *United Nations Plan for Organising Peace and Welfare*, 7/7/1943, Point 5, also 12.

140. Eden mentioned this in a parliamentary speech on 2 December 1942; but see also his telegram to Washington, No. 7724, 8/12/1942, in: PRO: FO 371/31 515.

141. This was already emphasized in the January version of the plan. Quote: Woodward, *British Foreign Policy*, Vol. 5, 17: Point 24 of the United Nations Plan, 16/1/1943. For the initial negative American reaction to this idea, see ibid., 36–8.

142. The EAC met frequently between Jan. 1944 and July 1945 until it was dissolved during the Potsdam conference. See Kettenacker, *Krieg zur Friedenssicherung;* Tyrell, *Großbritannien;* and H.G. Kowalski, 'Die EAC als Instrument alliierter Deutschlandplanung, 1943–45', *Vierteljahrshefte für Zeitgeschichte* 19 (1971) 261ff.; also Shlaim, *Britain and the Origins of European Unity*, 42–3; Hughes, 'Formation of the UNO', 181–2; Woodward, ibid., 48–9; Stirk, *History of European Integration*, 72–4; also Jebb, *Memoirs*, 118–24, 127–8.

143. See already Eden's memorandum to the War Cabinet dealing with these issues. PRO: CAB 66/34/W.P.(43)96, 8/3/1943; also Woodward, ibid., 25; also Baylis, 'British wartime thinking', 267; Jebb, *Memoirs*, 113–18.

144. Woodward, ibid., 8, also 38.

145. PRO: FO 371/31 515, Halifax, Washington, to FO, No. 5891, 5/12/1942, reporting on his conversation with Welles.

CHAPTER 4: THE EMERGENCE OF THE POST-WAR WORLD

1. F. Harbutt, *The Iron Curtain: Churchill, America, and the Origins of the Cold War* (New York, 1986), 65.

2. PRO: PREM 4/100/7, PM's Personal Minute M.474/2 to Eden, 21/10/1942; also quoted in W.S. Churchill, *The Second World War, Vol. 4: The Hinge of Fate* (London, 1951), 504. See also W. Lipgens, *Die Anfänge der europäischen Einigungspolitik, 1945–1950, Vol. 1, Teil: 1945–1947* (Stuttgart, 1977), 64; also D. Weigall, 'British Ideas of European Unity and Regional Confederation in the Context of Anglo-Soviet Relations, 1941–45', in M.L. Smith and P.M.R. Stirk (eds), *Making the New Europe: European Unity and the Second World War* (London, 1990), 160.

3. For details of his vision as outlined in 1940, see Chapter 3, above, 61ff.

4. PRO: PREM 4/100/7, PM's Personal Minute M.474/2 to Eden, 21/10/1942; also in Churchill, *Second World War*, Vol. 4, 504.

5. See PRO: PREM 4/30/2, the 'most secret' original is dated 31/1/1943. The text of his 'Morning Thoughts, Note on Post War Security by the Prime Minister', dated 1/2/1943, is publ. in M. Howard, *Grand Strategy*, Vol. 4: August 1942–September 1943 (London, 1972), Appendix 5, 637–9. The passage on Europe and the necessity to set up confederations is also publ. in Churchill's, *Second World War*, Vol. 4, 636–7. See also the interpretation in C. Hull, *Memoirs*, Vol. 2 (London, 1948) 1640–1; and the illuminating discussion in M. Charlton, *The Price of Victory* (London, 1983), 11ff.

6. PRO: ibid.; also Churchill, *Second World War*, Vol. 4, 636–7; and FRUS, *The Conferences at Washington and Quebec, 1943*, 702–6.

7. A. Shlaim, *Britain and the Origins of European Unity, 1940–1951* (Reading, 1978), 44–5, 28–9 (quotes: 45, 29).

8. PRO: PREM 4/27/9, letter Halifax, Washington, to Churchill, 5/2/1943.

9. See Charlton, *Price of Victory*, 14 ff. (quotes: 14–17).

10. G. Jebb, *The Memoirs of Lord Gladwyn* (London, 1972), 130–1, also 121–3; see also V. Rothwell, *Britain and the Cold War, 1941–47* (London, 1982), 31ff.

11. See Charlton, *Price of Victory*, 17–18.

12. For Stalin's and Molotov's reaction, see the reports from Sir A. Clark Kerr, the British ambassador in Moscow, and other material in PRO: PREM 4/30/1 (March 1943).

13. FDR received the information from Churchill on 2 February. See W.F. Kimball (ed.), *Churchill & Roosevelt: The Complete Correspondence, Vol. 2: Alliance Forged* (London, 1984), 129–32: Churchill to Roosevelt, 2/2/1943, C-259–A/1. See also D. Weigall and P.M.R. Stirk (eds), *The Origins and Development of the European Community* (Leicester, 1992), 33; also P.M.R. Stirk, *A History of European Integration since 1914* (London, 1996), 72.

14. The Foreign Office had been strongly opposed to Churchill displaying his support of the Congress by making a broadcast. Kalergi was believed to be 'more favourably inclined to Germany than any of us are likely to be' and the FO thus advised against any officials attending the conference in New York. Moreover, Kalergi was regarded as a man with a 'somewhat erratic' career 'owing to his addiction for forming Unions out of some ill-assorted partners'. See PRO: PREM 4/33/4, letter Harold Butler, Washington to Nevill Butler, FO, 1/2/1943 and Minister of Information to T.L. Rowan, Downing Street, 24/3/1942.

15. The text of the broadcast entitled 'A Four Year's Plan' is publ. in C. Eade (ed.), *The War Speeches of Winston Churchill, Vol. 2: Onwards to Victory* (London, 1944), 33–45.

16. See Weigall, 'British Ideas of European Unity', 161.

17. This phrase was coined by Herbert Feis. Quoted in W.F. Kimball, 'Anglo-American War Aims, 1941–43, "The First Review": Eden's Mission to Washington', in A. Lane and H. Temperley (eds), *The Rise and Fall of the Grand Alliance, 1941–45* (Basingstoke, 1995), 6.

18. See PRO: PREM 4/30/3, Eden to Churchill, PM's Personal Telegram T.397/3 (=Halifax to FO, No. 1470), 28/3/1943: report on Eden's talks with FDR, Hull, Welles, Hopkins and Ambassador Winant (also in FO 954/22); see also D. Dutton, *Anthony Eden: A Life and Reputation* (London, 1997), 282; L. Woodward, *British Foreign Policy in the Second World War*, Vol. 5 (London, 1976), 33–6; also R.E. Sherwood, *The White House Papers of Harry L. Hopkins* (London, 1949), 715–16. This argument was also similar to the one used by Hull when attempting to persuade Roosevelt of his global approach. See Chapter 3, above, 68–70.

19. See the previous note.

20. See FRUS 1943, Vol. 3, 35–6, 38–9: memorandum Hopkins, 22/3/1943; PRO: FO 954/22, PWP/43/13, Churchill to Eden, 29/3/1943; PREM 4/1004, Eden to Churchill, 29/3/1943; see also J. Charmley, *Churchill's Grand Alliance: A Provocative Assessment of the 'Special Relationship' between England and the U.S. from 1940 to 1957* (New York, 1995), 65–6, 107.

21. See Kimball, 'Anglo-American War Aims', 7. Kimball speaks of the American 'image of a powerful, London-led combine'. See also W.F. Kimball, *Forged in War: Churchill, Roosevelt and the Second World War* (London, 1997), 233–4.

22. See Woodward, *British Foreign Policy*, Vol. 5, 39.
23. PRO: PREM 4/30/3, W.P.(43)233, 'The Structure of the Post-war Settlement', 10/6/1943 – 'to be kept under lock and key' it was emphasized. The memorandum is published in Kimball (ed.), *Churchill & Roosevelt*, Vol. 2, 222–7: memorandum C-297/1, 28/5/1943.
24. Kimball (ed.), ibid., 223.
25. Ibid., 222–23.
26. Ibid., 224. See also Hull, *Memoirs*, Vol. 2, 1641–2.
27. Quote: Kimball (ed.), *Churchill & Roosevelt*, Vol. 2, 224; also quoted in Woodward, *British Foreign Policy*, Vol. 5, 40.
28. PRO: PREM 4/30/3, letter Churchill to Halifax, 26/5/1943 commenting on Halifax's draft memorandum of the luncheon meeting and reflecting on the American view of what he had said.
29. See Churchill, *Second World War*, Vol. 4, 717–22; Kimball (ed.), *Churchill & Roosevelt*, Vol. 2, 225–6 (memorandum C-297/1), 28/5/1943; also Woodward, *British Foreign Policy*, Vol. 5, 40; Shlaim, *Britain and the Origins of European Unity*, 48; A. Eden, *The Reckoning* (London, 1965), 443.
30. The speech of 6 Sept. 1943 is publ. in Eade, *War Speeches*, Vol. 2, 181–6. See also the reference to his speech, which he claimed was even welcomed by members of the Republican Party, in PRO: PREM 3/366/8, W.P.(43)430, 5/10/1943: Record of a meeting between Churchill and Dominion Representatives in Washington held at the British embassy, Washington, on 10 September 1943.
31. PRO: PREM 4/27/9, letter Halifax, Washington, to Churchill, 28/5/1943. Stafford Cripps also viewed Churchill's outline of his thinking to the Americans as 'most encouraging'. PREM 4/30/3, handwritten letter from Cripps to Churchill, 12/6/1943.
32. Stirk, *History of European Integration*, 72.
33. Woodward, *British Foreign Policy*, Vol. 5, 42–4, also 48–9, 62; also Jebb, *Memoirs*, 128. Yet, Churchill was not convinced. He proposed that a small committee of the War Cabinet should study the views put forward by himself and the Foreign Office regarding the post-war settlement. Although this committee held four meetings in the course of August 1943, in view of the decisions of the 'Big Three' in the same month and his subsequent 'defeat' at the Tehran conference, Churchill lost all interest in defending his European vision; the committee was not convened again. As is outlined below, Churchill had no choice but to go along with Roosevelt's and Stalin's preferences.
34. See Lipgens, *Anfänge der europäischen Integration, Vol. 1, Teil: 1945–47*, 73–4; H.A. Notter, *Postwar Foreign Policy Preparation, 1939–1945* (Washington, D.C., 1949), 146–8, 167 ff.; McNeill, *America, Britain, and Russia: Their Co-operation and Conflict, 1941–1946* (London, 1953), 322–3; Loth, *Der Weg nach Europa*, 3rd edn (Göttingen, 1996), 23; also W. Lipgens, *Europa-Föderationspläne der Widerstandsbewegungen, 1940–45. Eine Dokumentation* (Munich, 1968), 417 ff.
35. Ibid.
36. Ibid., esp. Lipgens, *Anfänge der europäischen Integration, Vol. 1, Teil: 1945–47*, 75.
37. See for example PRO: PREM 4/30/5, Eden, at Quebec, to Sargent, FO (WELFARE 313), 23/8/1943, reporting on the meeting between Churchill and Roosevelt on 23/8/1943. For Quebec, see also the massive material in PREM 4/73/1.
38. See PRO: PREM 4/30/5, Cambell, Washington, to FO No. 3692 and Eden at Quebec No. 3, August 1943; also Woodward, *British Foreign Policy*, Vol. 5, 70–3.
39. Jebb, *Memoirs*, 130; for Jebb's conversation with the two officials, see also PRO: PREM 4/30/5, Campbell, Washington, to Eden, No. 3690, August 1943; and Cambell, to FO No. 3692 and Eden at Quebec No. 3, Aug. 1943. For Jebb's conversation with Canadian officials before arriving in the US, see FO 371/31 515/U1430/27/70, 11/11/1944.
40. For details see K. Sainsbury, *The Turning Point: Roosevelt, Stalin, Churchill, and Chiang-Kai-Shek. The Moscow, Cairo and Teheran Conferences* (Oxford, 1986), 83–4, 88–92; C. Ponting, 'Churchill and Europe: A Revision', in R. Bideleux and R. Taylor (eds), *European Integration and Disintegration: East and West* (London, 1996), 39; Dutton, *Anthony Eden*, 206–7; also Woodward, *British Foreign Policy*, Vol. 5, 73–8.
41. For the 'Four-Power Declaration', see the British memorandum to the War Cabinet, PRO: FO 371/31 515, W.P.(43)389, 4/9/1943. For Hull's speech, see also Chapter 3, above, 70.
42. See Lipgens, *Die Anfänge europäischer Integration, Vol. 1, Teil: 1945–47*, 75.
43. FRUS, *The Conferences at Cairo and Tehran, 1943*, 596–604, esp. 602: minutes Bohlen of the Tripartite Political Meeting, 1/12/1943; see also Loth, *Weg nach Europa*, 22; R. Edmonds, *The Big Three: Churchill, Roosevelt and Stalin in Peace and War* (London, 1991), 357; also Woodward, *British Foreign Policy*, Vol. 5, 78–79.
44. FRUS, ibid., 259: minutes of Roosevelt's meeting with the Joint Chiefs of Staff, 19/11/1943; also 594–6: minutes Bohlen of the Roosevelt-Stalin meeting, 1/12/1943; and above all, pp. 529–33,

esp. 530–2, Bohlen minutes of Roosevelt-Stalin meeting on 29/11/1943. See also Edmonds, ibid., 353–4.

45. FRUS, ibid., 847: attachment to memorandum by Bohlen on 'Attitude of the Soviet Government on European Political Questions as Expressed by Marshall Stalin during the Tehran Conference', 15/12/1943.

46. See Loth, *Weg nach Europa*, 22–3; for a good account of the Tehran discussions, see Sainsbury, *The Turning Point*, 240ff. For greater details, see Chapter 2, above, 48–9.

47. Kimball, 'Anglo-American War Aims', 16.

48. This phrase is from M.L. Smith, 'Introduction: European Unity and the Second World War', in M.L. Smith and P.M.R. Stirk (eds), *Making the New Europe: European Unity and the Second World War* (London, 1990), 16, see also 15–16.

49. Soviet and American motives were, of course, very different. See McNeill, *America, Britain, and Russia*, 323; Loth, *Weg nach Europa*, 23–4; Weigall, 'British Ideas of European Unity', 161; and for a good general overview, see Sainsbury, *The Turning Point*, 53ff.

50. For details, see Chapter 2 above, 48–9.

51. The further discussions and deliberations within the FO cannot be explored here. For a very detailed narrative of the Foreign Office thinking, including the FO's extensive five memoranda on the shape of the envisaged world organization which Eden submitted to Churchill in early May 1944, see Woodward, *British Foreign Policy*, Vol. 5, 89ff., esp. 110–11, 115ff.; also with regard to British military planning, see J. Lewis, *Changing Direction: British Military Planning for Post-war Strategic Defence, 1942–47* (London, 1988), 98ff.

52. See M. Beloff, 'Churchill and Europe', in R. Blake and W.R. Louis (eds), *Churchill* (Oxford, 1993), 445–7.

53. Ibid., 448; for a concise summary of the thinking of eastern and southern European politicians, see Shlaim, *Britain and the Origins of European Unity*, 33–40; Loth, *Weg nach Europa*, 16–22.

54. PRO: PREM 4/30/7, P.M.M.(44)5, 'The Post-War World Settlement. Note by the Prime Minister of the United Kingdom', 8/5/1944. For the meeting with the Dominion Prime Ministers, see also the bound volume of minutes and memoranda in PREM 4/42/5 (May 1944).

55. Ibid., 'The Post-War World Settlement'.

56. PRO: PREM 4/30/7, minutes of the meeting of Prime Ministers at Downing Street, 11/5/1944, and especially the confidential annex P.M.M.(44) 12th meeting 'The Post-War World Settlement', 11/5/1944. Of particular interest regarding the rejection of Churchill's scheme are the extensive statements by the Canadian Prime Minister MacKenzie King and the New Zealand Prime Minister P. Fraser. See also Woodward, *British Foreign Policy*, Vol. 5, 117–19; Eden, *The Reckoning*, 442–3; E.J. Hughes, 'Winston Churchill and the Formation of the United Nations Organization', *Journal of Contemporary History* 9/4 (1974), 188–9; Shlaim, *Britain and the Origins of European Unity*, 50–1; and W.R. Louis, *Imperialism at Bay. The United States and the Decolonization of the British Empire, 1941–45* (New York, 1978), 337–50.

57. PRO: PREM 4/30/7, letter P. Fraser, New Zealand Prime Minister, to Eden, 18/5/1944.

58. Ibid., minute Eden to Churchill, P.M./44/355, 19/5/1944.

59. Ibid., Churchill to Eden, PM's Personal Minute, M.614/4, 25/5/1944.

60. PRO: PREM 4/30/8, Churchill to Stalin, PM's Personal Telegram, T.2183/4, 25/11/1944.

61. Loth, *Weg nach Europa*, 24; W. Loth, *Die Teilung der Welt, 1941–1955* (Munich, 1980), 81–2.

62. It is therefore an unfair exaggeration to claim that after Churchill's regional plans had been defeated by late 1943 'the prime minister made no attempt to adapt to the realities of the American and Russian position'. See Hughes, 'Formation of the UNO', 194.

63. For details, see Chapter 2, above, 47ff.

64. Quote: R. Hathaway, *Ambiguous Partnership: Britain and America, 1944–47* (New York, 1981), 154. See also A. Hillgruber, *Der Zweite Weltkrieg. Kriegsziele und Strategie der großen Mächte* (Stuttgart, 1983), 124–8, 157; Sainsbury, *The Turning Point*, 28.

65. See Chapter 2 above, 49ff.

66. The further development of the new United Nations organization as agreed at Dumbarton Oaks and later can not be analysed here. Rich material can be found in PRO: PREM 4/30/6 (Dumbarton Oaks, 1944) and above all in PREM 4/30/7 (April–October 1944: Schemes for World Organization); also FO 371/40 720, Dumbarton Oaks conference. See also R.C. Hildebrand, *Dumbarton Oaks: the Origins of the United Nations and the Search for Postwar Security* (Chapel Hill, N.C., 1990); also G.M. Schild, *Bretton Woods and Dumbarton Oaks: American Economic and Political Postwar Planning in the Summer of 1944* (Basingstoke, 1995).

67. D. Healey, *When Shrimps Learn to Whistle: Signposts for the Nineties* (London, 1990), 68.

68. Quote: Woodward, *British Foreign Policy*, Vol. 5, 193. See for a good overview of Churchill's assessment of the weakness of continental Europe, PRO: PREM 4/30/8, Churchill to Eden, PM's Personal Minute, M.1144/4, 25/11/1944.

69. PRO: PREM 4/30/8, Churchill to Stalin, PM's Personal Telegram, T.2183/4, 25/11/1944.

70. Ibid., Churchill to Stalin, PM's Personal Telegram, T.2234/4, 1/12/1944. For the Soviet attitude to the Western bloc, see FO 371/40 723/U 8430/G/180/70, Clark Kerr, Moscow, to FO, No. 3549, 29/11/1944. For British thinking on post-war relations with the Soviet Union at this stage, see FO 371/43 336/N 4957/G, W.P.(44)436, memorandum Eden 'Soviet Policy in Europe', 9/8/1944; and ibid., N 6177/G, minutes of meeting between Eden, Orme Sargent and the COS, 4/10/1944.

71. For Cooper's thinking, see in particular J. Charmley, *Duff Cooper* (London, 1986); and J. Charmley, 'Duff Cooper and Western European Union, 1944–47', *Review of International Studies* 11 (1985), 53–64.

72. By late 1943 Jean Monnet, de Gaulle's economic adviser, was already prepared to accept a loss of French sovereignty in return for the establishment of close European economic cooperation. De Gaulle himself added the important security dimension to Monnet's thoughts. He believed that future security requirements in Europe, in particular in order to control Germany militarily, would not only make economic but also military co-operation between France and the Benelux countries and perhaps Britain necessary. See J.W. Young, *France, the Cold War and the Western Alliance, 1944–49: French Foreign Policy and Post-war Europe* (Leicester, 1990), 11; also in general J. Lacouture, *De Gaulle: The Rebel, 1890–1944* (New York, 1990), ch. 35. By early 1944 the Dutch had arrived at a similar conclusion. For the thinking in London, see PRO: FO 371/39 020/C 681/681/22, memorandum, Harrison, Central Dept., 13/1/1944.

73. PRO: PREM 4/30/8, W.P.(44)409, memorandum Eden 'Policy in Western Europe' which included a copy of a despatch by Duff Cooper on a Western Bloc, 25/7/1944. For the later thinking with regard to Britain assuming the leadership of Western Europe, see the various brief comments by officials in PRO: FO 371/40 720/U 7943/180/70, October 1944; also ibid., U 7810/180/70, October 1944; see also Charmley, *Duff Cooper*, 184–8; Weigall, 'British Ideas of European Unity', 164–5.

74. For the final agreed draft of this paper entitled 'Western Europe', see PRO: ibid., Annex A, minute Eden to Churchill, P.M./44/732, 29/11/1944. For the following, see in greater detail, S. Greenwood, *The Alternative Alliance: Anglo-French Relations Before the Coming of NATO, 1944–1948* (London, 1996); K. Larres, 'A Search for Order: Britain and the Origins of a Western European Union, 1944–55', in B. Brivati and H. Jones (eds), *From Reconstruction to Integration: Britain and Europe since 1945* (Leicester, 1993), 71–7; L. Woodward, *British Foreign Policy in the Second World War*, Vol. 3, (London, 1971), 95–103; Vol. 5, 181–97.

75. PRO: CAB 80/44, COS(44)113, dated 3/6/1944 (for the final and quite similar draft, see note 74 above); see also already PREM 4/30/7, Foreign Office Aide-Memoire, 1/7/1943, point 9; and ibid., 'Future World Organisation: Suggested redraft of certain paragraphs of Memoranda A and B' (of P.M.M.(44)4, 31/5/1944). See also J. Baylis, 'Britain, the Brussels Pact and the Continental Commitment', *International Affairs* 60 (1984), 616–17; Woodward, ibid., Vol. 5, 183–9.

76. PRO: CAB 80/44, COS(44)113, dated 3/6/1944 (for the final and quite similar draft, see n. 74, above).

77. On the 'defence in depth' issue, see also the later consideration in PRO: PREM 4/30/8, minute Eden to Churchill, P.M./44/732, 29/11/1944; also Woodward, *British Foreign Policy*, Vol. 5, 186–9.

78. See for example PRO: PREM 4/30/8, minute Eden to Churchill, P.M./44/732, 29/11/1944 (reply to Churchill's minute M.1144/4, 25/11/1944).

79. The COS report 'Security in Western Europe and the North Atlantic' (P.H.P.(44)17(0) (Final); C.O.S.(44)248th Meeting, minute 14, confidential annex, 26/7/1944) is publ. in Lewis, *Changing Directions*, 349–53 (Annex 8: 'C.O.S. Attitudes to the Soviet Union in 1944'); quote: 350. See also Woodward, *British Foreign Policy*, Vol. 5, 189–90.

80. The 1942 Anglo-Soviet friendship treaty, for example, had done little to assuage Stalin's mistrust of Churchill. For Churchill's and Stalin's distrust (as well as admiration) of each other, see Chapter 2 above, 38ff., 42ff; also Chapter 9, below, 181.

81. Regarding the hesitation with which the US embassy was told about the conversations with Spaak and the entire Western European bloc idea, see for example PRO: FO 371/40 723/U 8415/180/70, Minute Roberts, 7/11/1944, and various comments by other officials.

82. See PRO: PREM 4/30/8, Churchill to Eden, PM's Personal Minute, M.1144/4, 25/11/1944; and for example for Churchill's attitude in the 1950s, Charlton, *Price of Victory*, 124ff.

83. See Charmley, 'Duff Cooper and Western European Union, 1944–47', 53–64, esp. 55–7; Woodward, *British Foreign Policy*, Vol. 5, 190–1.

84. Ibid.

85. PRO: PREM 4/30/8, Churchill to Eden, PM's Personal Minute, M.1144/4, 25/11/1944.

86. See Woodward, *British Foreign Policy*, Vol. 5, 197.

87. See in detail, Lewis, *Changing Direction*, ch. 4, esp. 110ff.; also Lewis, ch. 3, for an analysis of the work of 'The Post-Hostilities Planning Sub-Committee'.

88. PRO: CAB 81, PHP(44)27 (9/11/1944). See Baylis, 'Britain, the Brussels Pact and the Continental Commitment', 617; B. Zeeman, 'Britain and the Cold War: An Alternative Approach. The Treaty of Dunkirk Example', *European History Quarterly* 16 (1986), 350–1.

89. Moreover, progress towards a Western Union was also prevented by Churchill's and the Foreign Office's hostile attitude towards the self-righteous De Gaulle. See S. Greenwood, 'Return to Dunkirk: The Origins of the Anglo-French Treaty of March 1947', *Journal of Strategic Studies* 4 (1984), 320–1; Young, *France, the Cold War and the Western Alliance*, 14ff.

90. PRO: PREM 4/30/8, Churchill to Eden, PM's Personal Minute, M.1144/4, 25/11/1944; see also CAB 21/1614, PM's Personal Telegram T.2183/4, November 1944; also Lewis, *Changing Direction*, 337.

91. Eden explained: 'I think we should have to reconcile ourselves to making a rather larger land contribution than the famous two divisions which was all we had to offer last time [in 1939]'. Quoted in E. Barker, *Britain in a Divided Europe, 1945–70* (London, 1971), 20–1.

92. See S. Greenwood, 'Ernest Bevin, France and Western Union: August 1945–February 1946', *European History Quarterly* 14 (1984), 319–38; also Greenwood, *The Alternative Alliance*. See also K. Larres, 'North Atlantic Treaty Organization', in A. DeConde et al. (eds), *Encyclopedia of American Foreign Relations: Studies of the Principal Movements and Ideas*, 2nd rev. edn (New York, 2002), Vol. 2, 573–93. For a good overview of the 'third force' policy, see for example S. Croft, *The End of Superpower: British Foreign Office Conceptions of a Changing World, 1945–51* (Aldershot 1994), 70–108. For Bevin's policy, see also Chapter 5, below, 108ff. and n. 59 (p. 435).

93. Quoted in Beloff, 'Churchill and Europe', 447. After all, it appeared as if the USA were still busy pursuing the realization of its illusory 'one world' concept. See for example Gietz, *Die neue Alte Welt*, 92–4, 97–9; E. Roosevelt, *As He Saw It* (New York, 1946), 35–6, 115–16, 155–6.

94. See Beloff, 'Churchill and Europe', 448, 447.

95. See the literature on the 'percentage deal', in Chapter 2, n. 124 (p. 417), and Chapter 3, n. 125 (p. 424), above.

96. See Lipgens, *Die Anfänge der europäischen Integration, Vol. 1, Teil: 1945–47*, 77.

97. For the development of his thinking on this issue, see Chapter 7 below.

98. See W.S. Churchill, *The World Crisis, Vol. 1: 1911–1914* (London, 1923), 14.

99. See Churchill's speech at the Royal Albert Hall, London, 14/5/1947, when he attended a 'United Europe Meeting', in R.S. Churchill (ed.), *Europe Unite: Speeches 1947 and 1948* (London, 1950), 83–5 (quote: p. 83).

100. See Churchill's speech to the Council of the European Movement, Brussels, 26/2/1949, in R.S. Churchill (ed.), *In the Balance: Speeches 1949 and 1950* (London, 1951), 29.

101. For good overviews on the Truman administration's policy towards the USSR during the transition from war to Cold War, see M. Trachtenberg, *A Constructed Peace: The Making of the European Settlement, 1945–1963* (Princeton, N.J., 1999), 4ff.; M.J. Hogan, *A Cross of Iron: Harry S. Truman and the Origins of the National Security State, 1945–54* (Cambridge, 1998); R.L. Messer, *The End of an Alliance: James F. Byrnes, Roosevelt, Truman, and the Origins of the Cold War* (Chapel Hill, N.C., 1982), 66ff.; N.A. Graebner, 'Yalta, Potsdam, and Beyond: The British and American Perspectives,' in Lane and Temperley (eds), *Grand Alliance*, 230ff.; A.L. Hamby, *Man of the People: A Life of Harry S. Truman* (New York, 1995), 293ff.; M.J. Lacey (ed.), *The Truman Presidency* (New York, 1991, 1st publ. 1989), esp. chs 7–10; M.P. Leffler, *A Preponderance of Power: National Security, the Truman Administration, and the Cold War* (Stanford, Ca., 1992), 30ff.; R. Edmonds, *Setting the Mould: The United States and Britain, 1945–1950* (Oxford, 1986), 77ff.; also R.J. Maddox, *From War to Cold War: the Education of Harry S. Truman* (Boulder, Col., 1988).

102. Quotes: Hathaway, *Ambiguous Partnership*, 137; Edmonds, *Setting the Mould*, 21.

103. See FRUS, *The Conference of Berlin (Potsdam), 1945*, Vol. 1, p. 9: Churchill to Truman, 12/5/1945; also Woodward, *British Foreign Policy*, Vol. 3, 577–8, see also 490–595; W.S. Churchill, *The Second World War, Vol. 6: Triumph and Tragedy* (London, 1954), 498–9; also 523, for the second telegram to Truman containing the phrase, dated 4 June 1945. Nazi propaganda minister Goebbels had used the expression 'iron curtain' in a newspaper article on 25 February 1945, Ethel Snowden had used it in the 1920 book *Through Bolshevic Russia*, and the novelist H.G. Wells had employed it as early as 1904 when referring to the barrier between a scientist and the world in his novel *The Food of the Gods*. See W. Mieder, ' "Make Hell While the Sun Shines": Proverbial Rhetoric in Winston Churchill's *The Second World War*', *De Proverbio: An Electronic Journal of International Proverb Studies*, 1/2 (1995), 12–13 [http:/info.utas.edu.au/docs/flonta/DP,1,2,95/CHURCHILL.html]; also M.

Gilbert, 'The Origins of the "Iron Curtain" Speech', in R. Crosby Kemper III (ed.), *Winston Churchill: Resolution, Defiance, Magnanimity, Good Will* (Columbia, Mo., 1996), 35–60; and for a good analysis, Harbutt, *Iron Curtain*, esp. 81ff., 183ff.

104. Woodward, ibid., Vol. 3, 578.

105. See H.B. Ryan, *The Vision of Anglo-America: the US-UK Alliance and the Emerging Cold War, 1943–46* (Cambridge, 1987), 113–16; Edmonds, *Setting the Mould*, 51–2; Hathaway, *Ambiguous Partnership*, 163–4; Woodward, ibid., 579–84.

106. Quoted in Hamby, *Man of the People*, 321.

107. Truman hoped that the first atomic test-explosion would have taken place prior to the conference. See Edmonds, 'Churchill and Stalin', 324; Edmonds, *Setting the Mould*, 51–2.

108. In August 1946 it was passed into legislation as the Atomic Energy Act. See H.S. Truman, *Memoirs, Vol. 2: 1946–52. Years of Trial and Hope* (New York, 1996 edn), 11ff.; M. Gowing, *Independence and Deterrence: Britain and Atomic Energy, 1945–1952, Vol. 1: Policy Making* (London, 1974), 1ff. For Anglo-American relations and the Soviet threat in the period of transition from war to Cold War, see for example R.B. Woods, *A Changing of the Guard: Anglo-American Relations, 1941–46* (Chapel Hill, N.C., 1990); Ryan, *The Vision of Anglo-America*; R. Ovendale, *The English-Speaking Alliance: Britain, the United States, the Dominions and the Cold War, 1945–51* (London, 1985); Hathaway, *Ambiguous Partnership*, 132ff.; T.H. Anderson, *The United States, Great Britain and the Cold War, 1944–47* (Columbia, Mo., 1981), 66–102. For primary sources, see *Documents of British Policy Overseas*, Series I, Vol. 3: *Britain and America: Negotiation of the United States Loan, 3 Aug.–7 Dec., 1945* (London, 1986); and Series I, Vol. 4: *Britain and America: Atomic Energy, Bases and Food, 12 Dec. 1945–31 July 1946* (London, 1987); also P.A. Karber and J.A. Combs, 'The United States, NATO, and the Soviet Threat to Western Europe: Military Estimates and Policy Options, 1945–1963', *Diplomatic History* 22/3 (1998), esp. 399–419; also R. Spencer, 'Alliance Perceptions of the Soviet Threat, 1950–1988', in C.C. Schweitzer (ed.), *The Changing Western Analysis of the Soviet Threat* (New York, 1990), 9–48.

109. See Chapter 7, below.

CHAPTER 5: EARLY COLD WAR YEARS

1. Labour gained 393 seats, the Conservatives merely 213 including 15 seats for the National Liberals. The independent Liberal Party won 12 seats. See D. Butler and G. Butler, *British Political Facts, 1900–1985* (Basingstoke, 1986), 226. For the reasons for the Conservative defeat, see R.B. McCallum and A. Readman, *The British General Election of 1945* (London, 1947), 247–71; M. Bentley, '1931–1945', in A. Seldon (ed.), *How Tory Governments Fall: The Tory Party in Power since 1783* (London, 1996), 309–12; J. Ramsden, *The Age of Churchill and Eden, 1940–1957* (London, 1995), 5–6, 86–92; also J. Ramsden, *An Appetite for Power: A History of the Conservative Party since 1830* (London, 1998), 303–15 (Ramsden writes that Churchill's 'stewardship of his own party [since Chamberlain's death in late 1940] had been an unqualified disaster', pp. 310–11); M.D. Kandiah, 'The Conservative Party and the 1945 General Election', *Contemporary Record* 9/1 (1995), 22ff., esp. 36–43; also M. Franklin and M. Ladner, 'The Undoing of Winston Churchill: Mobilization and Conversion in the 1945 Realignment of British Voters', *British Journal of Political Science* 25 (1995), 429–52.

2. See J. Ramsden, 'From Churchill to Heath', in Lord Butler (ed.), *The Conservatives: A History from their Origins to 1965* (London, 1977), 414; M. Gilbert, *Churchill's Political Philosophy* (Oxford, 1981), 109; Lord Moran, *Winston Churchill: The Struggle for Survival, 1940–1965* (London, 1966), 286–90.

3. R. Blake, *The Conservative Party from Peel to Churchill*, expanded edn (London, 1997), 258, believes that 'Churchill was more interested in the world scene. . . . He had never been very good on "bread and butter" politics.'

4. Quote: P. Addison, *Churchill on the Home Front, 1900–1955*, paperback edn (London, 1993), 390; for Churchill's inactivity as Leader of the Opposition see also ibid., esp. 388–401; and J. Ramsden, 'Winston Churchill and the Leadership of the Conservative Party, 1940–51', in *Contemporary Record* 9/1 (1995), 99–119.

5. See T.F. Lindsay and M. Harrington, *The Conservative Party 1918–1979*, 2nd edn (London, 1979), 147–8; Blake, *Conservative Party*, 257–8. See also the stimulating essay by P. Addison, 'Churchill and the Price of Victory: 1939–1945', in N. Tiratsoo (ed.), *From Blitz to Blair: A New History of Britain since 1939*, paperback edn (London, 1998), 65–76. For a brief overview of Labour's domestic political

programme, see in the same collection of essays the article by J. Tomlinson, 'Reconstructing Britain: Labour in Power, 1945–1951', 77–101; also K. Jefferys, *The Attlee Governments, 1945–51* (London, 1992).

6. Ramsden, *Age of Churchill and Eden*, 7; see also his 'Leadership of the Conservative Party', 109, 112.

7. J. Ramsden, 'From Churchill to Heath' (1977), 414–15; also his 'Leadership of the Conservative Party', 109. Paul Addison arrives at a similar positive conclusion. See his 'Churchill in British Politics, 1940–1955', in J.M.W. Bean (ed.), *The Political Culture of Modern Britain* (London, 1987), 243–61; also his *Churchill on the Homefront*, 387ff. But see the interesting memorandum highlighting Churchill's passivity, dated March 1950, by R.A. Butler. He calls it somewhat cynically 'a description of policy-making with WSC'. It is published in J. Ramsden, *The Making of Conservative Party Politics: The Conservative Research Department since 1929* (London, 1980), 146–7. For Churchill's general activities during this time, see for example C. Ponting, *Churchill* (London, 1995), 726–31; R. Jenkins, *Churchill* (London, 2001), 803ff.

8. Towards the end of the war, while Eden was in Potsdam, his favourite son had been killed in action, Eden's mother had also died and he was recovering from an ulcer operation in the 'disastrous summer of 1945'. Subsequently, Eden considered applying for the post of Secretary General of the newly founded United Nations. See B. Pimlott (ed.), *The Political Diary of Hugh Dalton* (London, 1986), 367; H. Dalton, *High Tide and After: Memoirs, 1945–1960* (London, 1962), 104; R.R. James, *Anthony Eden*, paperback edn, (London, 1986), 312–13; V.H. Rothwell, *Anthony Eden: A Political Biography, 1931–57* (Manchester, 1992), 95; D. Dutton, *Anthony Eden: A Life and Reputation* (London, 1997), 232–3; see also the review essay by D. Reynolds, 'Eden the Diplomatist, 1931–56: Suezide of a Statesman?', *History* 74 (1989), esp. 64–71.

9. See Lindsay and Harrington, *Conservative Party*, 148. On the influence of the 1922 Committee, see P. Goodhart with U. Branston, *The 1922: The Story of the Conservative Backbenchers' Parliamentary Committee* (London, 1973), 140–57; Addison, *Churchill on the Homefront*, 388–9.

10. See M. Gilbert, *Winston S. Churchill, Vol. 8: Never Despair, 1945–1965*, paperback edn (London, 1990), 132ff., 151ff., 180ff., 450ff. For the many other shorter and longer trips taken by Churchill in the years 1945–51, a glance at Gilbert's index is informative; also D. Carlton, *Anthony Eden: A Biography*, paperback edn (London, 1989), 259.

11. The almost 'social-democratic' character of the *Industrial Charter* did not indicate any Conservative opposition to Keynesian politics, the NHS or to public ownership of the nationalized industries. See for example Butler (ed.), *The Conservatives*, 417, 421–6; Ramsden, *Conservative Party Policy*, 108–14; Blake, *Conservative Party*, 258–9; Ramsden, *Age of Churchill and Eden*, 138ff., esp. 148ff.; Ramsden, *Appetite for Power*, 321–4; J. Charmley, *A History of Conservative Politics, 1900–1996* (Basingstoke, 1996), 136–7.

12. See D.S. McLellan and D.C. Acheson (eds), *Among Friends: Personal Letters of Dean Acheson* (New York, 1980), 61: letter Acheson to Mary A. Bundy, 30/7/1945. In the same letter Acheson also said that he thought that 'A leftist government in England will find it harder to work with Moscow than a rightist one. A paradox perhaps, but true.'

13. Lord Woolton, *Memoirs* (London, 1959), 331ff.; by 1950 membership had risen from 1.2 million in 1947 to 2.5 million (and to 2.8 million in 1952, and even 3 million incl. Scotland), see A. Clark, *The Tories: Conservatives and the Nation State, 1922–1997*, paperback edn (London, 1999), 328. The best overview regarding the streamlining of the Conservative party structure is Ramsden, *Age of Churchill and Eden*, 103ff.; see also Ramsden, *Appetite for Power*, 335ff.; A. Gamble, *The Conservative Nation* (London, 1974), 40ff.; Blake, *Conservative Party*, 259–62; Lindsay and Harrington, *Conservative Party*, 149ff. For an older but still very useful analysis of the internal developments in the Conservative Party and in British domestic politics, see J.D. Hoffmann, *The Conservative Party in Opposition, 1945–51* (London, 1964), esp. 81ff. See also Z. Layton-Henry, 'The Young Conservatives, 1945–73', *Journal of Contemporary History* 8/2 (1973), 143–56. For a good overview regarding the structural hierarchy of the Conservative Party during this time, see R.N. Kelly, *Conservative Party Conferences; The Hidden System* (Manchester, 1988), 28–35; from a wider perspective, see also the various articles in A. Seldon and S. Ball (eds), *Conservative Century: The Conservative Party since 1900* (Oxford, 1994).

14. See Rothwell, *Eden*, 96–102; Lord Butler, *The Art of the Possible: Memoirs* (London, 1971), 133–53; good overviews also in I. Gilmour and M. Garnett, *Whatever Happened to the Tories: The Conservative Party since 1945* (London, 1997), 30–40; and B. Evans and A. Taylor, *From Salisbury to Major: Continuity and Change in Conservative Politics* (Manchester, 1996), 76–100; in general also S. Ball, *The Conservative Party and British Politics, 1902–1951* (London, 1995), 103–16; Charmley, *History of Conservative Politics*, 123–39.

15. R.R. James, 'The Politician,' in A.J.P. Taylor et al., *Churchill: Four Faces and the Man* (London,

1969), 65. See also John Colville's diary entry (9/11/1940) with regard to the speech Churchill made when assuming the leadership of the Conservative Party; he seems to have felt it necessary to justify his membership of the Conservative Party. J. Colville, *The Fringes of Power: 10 Downing Street Diaries, 1939–55* (London, 1985), 259.

16. Quoted in James, ibid., 58–9. See also Lord Blake, 'Churchill and the Conservative Party', in R. Crosby Kemper III (ed.), *Winston Churchill: Resolution, Defiance, Magnanimity, Good Will* (Columbia, Mo., 1996), 141–56.

17. See A. Seldon, 'The Churchill Administration, 1951–5, in P. Hennessy and A. Seldon (eds), *Ruling Performance: British Governments from Attlee to Thatcher* (London, 1987), 69–73; A. Seldon, *Churchill's Indian Summer: The Conservative Government, 1951–55* (London, 1981), 36–8; R.A. Callahan, *Churchill: Retreat from Empire* (Wilmington, Del., 1984), 252–4. See also S. Ball, 'Churchill and the Conservative Party', in *Transactions of the Royal Historical Society*, 6th series, Vol. XI (Cambridge, 2001), 307–30.

18. P. Addison, 'Churchill and the Price of Victory: 1939–1945', 70. Not surprisingly, the 1946 Conservative Party Conference as well as the 1922 Committee rejected the proposed change of the party's name as advocated by Churchill and others. For the decision to keep the party's name, see Butler (ed.), *The Conservatives*, 416–17; Blake, *Conservative Party*, 261–2; Ramsden, 'Leadership of the Conservative Party,' 114–16; Addison, *Churchill on the Home Front*, 392–3; Goodhart, *The 1922*, 148–9; Clark, *The Tories*, 324; Ramsden, *Appetite for Power*, 317–18; H. Macmillan, *Tides of Fortune, 1945–55* (London, 1969), 292–3.

19. Quote: I. Zweiniger-Bargielowska, 'Rationing, Austerity and the Conservative Recovery after 1945,' *Historical Journal* 37/1 (1994), 176.

20. These were RAB Butler's words. See his memoirs *Art of the Possible*, 126.

21. For the Attlee consensus, see P. Addison, *The Road to 1945: British Politics and the Second World War* (London, 1994, 1st edn 1975), esp. 13–21, 270–92; K. Jefferys, *The Churchill Coalition and Wartime Politics, 1940–45* (Manchester, 1991); also his 'British Politics and Social Policy during the Second World War', *Historical Journal* 30/1 (1987), 123–44; see also R. Lowe, 'The Second World War, Consensus and the Foundation of the Welfare State,' *Twentieth Century British History* 1/2 (1990), 152–82; and D. Dutton, *British Politics since 1945: The Rise, Fall, and Rebirth of Consensus*, 2nd edn (Oxford, 1997); D. Kavanagh, 'Debate: The Postwar Consensus', *Twentieth Century British History* 3/2 (1992), 175–90. Sometimes 'Attlee's consensus' is also referred to as 'Churchill's consensus', see the review article 'Churchill and Consensus' by R.A.C. Parker, *Historical Journal* 39/2 (1996), 563–72.

22. For rather sceptical views, see for example B. Pimlott, 'The Myth of Consensus,' in L.M. Smith (ed.), *The Making of Britain: Echoes of Greatness* (London, 1988), 129–41; J.D. Marlow, *Questioning the Postwar Consensus Thesis: Towards an Alternative Account* (Aldershot, 1996); also H. Jones and M. Kandiah (eds), *The Myth of Consensus: New Views on British History, 1945–64* (Basingstoke, 1996); also the remarks by P. Addison in his review of Ramsden, *The Age of Churchill and Eden*, in 'The British Conservative Party from Churchill to Heath: Doctrine or Men?', *Contemporary European History* 8/2 (1999), 294–5; J. Turner, 'The British Conservative Party in the Twentieth Century: from Beginning to End?', *Contemporary European History* 8/2 (1999), 284–5; I. Zweiniger-Bargielowska, *Austerity in Britain: Rationing, Controls, and Consumption, 1939–1955* (Oxford, 2000).

23. Quote: D. Kavanagh and P. Morris, *Consensus Politics from Attlee to Thatcher* (Oxford, 1989), 111 (see esp. 1–22, 110ff.). Thus, on the whole, the consensus was characterized by a 'style of government' in the sense of 'institutionalized consultation' as well as by a 'range of policies' (pp. 3–4). The authors believe that the consensus referred to issues such as the mixed economy, full employment, conciliation of trade unions, welfare, and foreign policy. Although recognizing the many disagreements among the major political parties, on the whole Kavanagh and Morris define the post-war settlement as 'a set of parameters which bounded the set of policy options regarded by senior politicians and civil servants as administratively practicable, economically affordable and politically acceptable' (p. 13). Addison speaks of 'a Whitehall consensus' within a 'deeply divided society'. See *The Road to 1945*, 281–2; also J.D. Smith, *The Attlee and Churchill Administrations and Industrial Unrest, 1945–55: a Study in Consensus* (London, 1990).

24. See J. Ramsden, 'A Party for Owners or a Party for Earners? How far did the British Conservative Party really change after 1945?,' in *Transactions of the Royal Historical Society*, 5th series, Vol. 37 (1987), 49–63 (quote: 63).

25. Oliver Poole to R.A. Butler, 28/2/1949. Quoted in J. Turner, 'A Land Fit for Tories to Live in: The Political Ecology of the British Conservative Party, 1944–1994,' *Contemporary European History* 4/2 (1995), 193.

26. Quote: Zweiniger-Bargielowska, 'Rationing, Austerity', 176. The author argues that the party actively used popular dissatisfaction with the 'age of austerity' to 'regain much of the [electoral] support lost in 1945' (p. 194). For the 'age of austerity' in general, see the book with the same title by M. Sissions and P. French, eds (London, 1963). See also Charmley, *History of Conservative Politics*, 128–30; and the very detailed book by Zweiniger-Bargielowska, *Austerity in Britain*.

27. See Ramsden, 'Leadership of the Conservative Party', 117; Ramsden, *Appetite for Power*, 316. See also Butler (ed.), *The Conservatives*, 407, 412, 414–16; and in general also the rather superficial account, which regards Churchill as an 'effective' opposition leader, by F.A. Mayer, *The Opposition Years: Winston S. Churchill and the Conservative Party, 1945–51* (New York, 1992).

28. See letter Harriman to Truman, 13/3/1950, in LOC: Harriman Papers, Box 266, Folder: General Correspondence, Acheson, Dean.

29. See S. Onslow, *Backbench Debate within the Conservative Party and Its Influence on British Foreign Policy, 1948–57* (Basingstoke, 1997), 24–32, 48–53. For Churchill's post-1945 policy towards Europe, see in particular Chapter 7, below.

30. See Carlton, *Anthony Eden*, 259, 266–7; James, *Anthony Eden*, 314, 315–16; Gilbert, *Never Despair*, 227–8; N. Nicolson (ed.), *The Diaries and Letters of Harold Nicolson, 1945–60* (London, 1960), 36, 63–5. For a good overview of the strain on Eden due to being Prime Minister in waiting for almost five years under Chamberlain and then fifteen years under Churchill as well as for the complex relationship between Eden and Churchill, see Dutton, *Anthony Eden*, 217–46. Moreover, at times there was great competitive tension among Eden, Butler, Macmillan and the occasional other contender for Churchill's succession.

31. See Carlton, ibid., 266; Ponting, *Churchill*, 746; Dutton, *Anthony Eden*, 234–5; H. Pelling, *Churchill's Peacetime Ministry, 1951–55* (Basingstoke, 1997), 4; Onslow, *Backbench Debate*, 27–8.

32. Quote: Onslow, ibid., 27.

33. Quote: P. Addison in his review of J. Ramsden's, *The Age of Churchill and Eden*, *Contemporary European History* 8/2 (1999), 291. For Churchill's popularity during the opposition years, see for example G.H. Gallup (ed.), *The Gallup International Public Opinion Poll: Great Britain, 1937–1975, Vol. 1: 1937–1964* (London, 1976), 204, 206, 227, also 296. For other internal party political reasons why Churchill was able to remain in power (e.g. the gratitude felt towards Britain's wartime leader and the general expectation that he would not intend to fight another election but would retire soon), see Ramsden, 'Leadership of the Conservative Party', 106–9; also Butler, *Art of the Possible*, 132–3.

34. This led to his frequent cerebrovascular problems. Until his retirement in April 1955 Churchill would have two more serious strokes: in July 1952 and June 1953. For his disease, see a letter by R. Lovell, 'Lord Moran's prescriptions for Churchill', *British Medical Journal*, Vol. 310 (1995), 1537–8; also R. Lovell, *Churchill's Doctor: A Biography of Lord Moran* (London, 1992). For his first slight stroke, see M. Soames, *Clementine Churchill* (London, 1979), 407, 428–9; for the second, see Ch. 13 below, 263–4.

35. Memorandum by Averell Harriman about a luncheon with Churchill on 17/11/1949. LOC: Harriman Papers, Box 266, Folder: General Correspondence, Churchill, Winston (1949–50).

36. See Dutton, *Anthony Eden*, 230–6. Blake, *Conservative Party*, 253, concludes with respect to the 1945 general election that Churchill 'was still a highly popular figure. If the British premiership had been an elective office like the American presidency and the voter could have split his ticket, Churchill, like Eisenhower in 1956, might have been elected, but he would have faced a legislature dominated by the other party. The Conservatives fared badly in 1945, but who can say how much worse they might have done without Churchill?'

37. See Ramsden, 'Leadership of the Conservative Party', 106–9; Ramsden, *Age of Churchill and Eden*, 101–3, 177–84; Ramsden, *Appetite for Power*, 328–9; Dutton, *Anthony Eden*, 231–46; Addison, *Churchill on the Home Front*, 386.

38. Quoted in Carlton, *Anthony Eden*, 267. See also Blake, 'Churchill and the Conservative Party', 155.

39. For Labour's economic difficulties, see for example K.O. Morgan, *Labour in Power, 1945–51*, paperback edn (Oxford, 1984), 330ff. (quote: 331); also A.J. Robertson, *The Bleak Midwinter 1947* (Manchester, 1987); J. Tomlinson, *Democratic Socialism and Economic Policy: the Attlee Years, 1945–1951* (Cambridge, 1997).

40. See Ramsden, *Age of Churchill and Eden*, 7.

41. D. Willetts, *Modern Conservatism* (London, 1992), 33.

42. Goodhart, *The 1922*, 143–8; see in particular the strong criticism of Churchill by the *Economist*, quoted here on pp. 144–6; see also Macmillan, *Tides of Fortune*, 286–7.

43. For details, see Chapter 7, below.

44. On the widespread belief within the Labour Party that 'Left understands Left' and the importance of the pursuit of a 'socialist foreign policy', see for example P. Jones, *America and the British Labour Party: The Special Relationship at Work* (London, 1997), 20–1.

45. Allegedly Churchill made this attack under the influence of Friedrich von Hayek's book *The Road to Serfdom*; see Willetts, *Modern Conservatism*, 33. See also Kandiah, '1945 General Election,' 37; Ramsden, 'Leadership of the Conservative Party,' 110; 'bulldog' quote in A. Nutting, 'Sir Anthony Eden,' in H. van Thal (ed.), *The Prime Ministers, Vol. 2* (London, 1975), 330. The election campaign was however dominated by domestic affairs rather than by foreign policy issues.

46. Again Churchill successfully attempted to be his own historian. See his *The Second World War: Vol. 6: Triumph and Tragedy* (London, 1954), 287ff.

47. J. Ramsden, '*That will depend on who writes the history': Winston Churchill as his own Historian*. Inaugural Lecture (London, 1997), 2; see also Ramsden, 'How Winston Churchill Became "The Greatest Living Englishman"', *Contemporary British History* 12/3 (1998), 1–40; also Ramsden, *Appetite for Power*, 316, 327. For a detailed analysis of the 'iron curtain' speech within the context of Churchill's summit diplomacy, see Chapter 6, below, 124ff.

48. See F. Harbutt, *The Iron Curtain: Churchill, America, and the Origins of the Cold War* (Oxford, 1986), 205ff.

49. See Ramsden, '*That will depend [...]*', 21–3.

50. Quoted in Turner, 'Land fit for Tories,' 194.

51. Quoted in ibid., 194; see also in general for Macmillan's Cold War views, A. Horne, *Harold Macmillan, Vol. 1: 1984–1956* (London, 1988), 306–7.

52. B. Schwarz, 'The Tide of History. The Reconstruction of Conservatism, 1945–51', in N. Tiratsoo (ed.), *The Attlee Years* (London, 1991), 158. Ramsden also believes that by 1951 Churchill's 'anti-Communism was in tune with a national mood'. See his 'Leadership of the Conservative Party', 110.

53. See M. Blackwell, *Clinging to Grandeur: British Attitudes and Foreign Policy in the Aftermath of the Second World War* (Westport, Conn., 1993), 163. For the Foreign Office views, see in detail G. Ross, 'Foreign Office Attitudes to the Soviet Union, 1941–45', *Journal of Contemporary British History* 16 (1981), 521–40; A. Adamthwaite, 'Britain and the World, 1945–49: the View from the Foreign Office', *International Affairs* 61 (1985), 223–35.

54. Morgan, *Labour in Power*, 278.

55. Attlee wrote this in his 1937 book *The Labour Party in Perspective*. Here quoted in Jones, *America and the British Labour Party*, 18. Schwarz (see n. 52, above) also sees a foreign policy consensus later on in his article but fails to resolve the puzzle in how far the Cold War would have helped Conservative election prospects if both parties were equally adamant in their condemnation of Stalin. For the foreign policy consensus, see for example Kavanagh and Morris, *Consensus Politics*, 90ff.

56. For Churchill's inconsistency in his policies and personal relations with Stalin, see Chapter 2, above. This is not the place to discuss the very different 'orthodox' and 'revisionist' scholarly views of Bevin's foreign policy. A good overview of the literature can be obtained from P. Weiler, 'Britain and the First Cold War: Revisionist Beginnings', *Twentieth Century British History* 9/1 (1998), 127–38. For a very critical look at Labour's foreign policy, see also P. Weiler, *Ernest Bevin* (Manchester, 1993); for what has become the most influential standard account, see A. Bullock, *Ernest Bevin: Foreign Secretary, 1945–1951* (London, 1983). See also K. Harris, *Attlee*, rev. edn (London, 1995); T. Burridge, *Clement Attlee: A Political Biography* (London, 1985); R. Ovendale, *The English-Speaking Alliance: Britain, the United States, the Dominions and the Cold War, 1945–51* (London, 1985); V. Rothwell, *Britain and the Cold War, 1941–1947* (London, 1982); J. Saville, *The Politics of Continuity: British Foreign Policy and the Labour Government, 1945–46* (London, 1993).

57. 'Debate on the Address', H.C. Parl. Deb., 5th series, Vol. 413, 20/8/1945, 291.

58. Quoted in H. Pelling, *The Labour Governments, 1945–51* (London, 1984), 121; see also A. Clark Kerr's record of Bevin's frank and 'hard-line' conversation with Molotov in London, 23/9/1945, publ. in DBPO, Series I, Vol. 2, 316–23 (Doc. 108).

59. Quotes from Pelling, ibid., 121, 131; see also Ovendale, *English-Speaking Alliance*, 29ff.; Rothwell, *Britain and the Cold War*, 222ff. The lack of American support at this stage also explains why in late 1945 Bevin pursued the development of a British-led coalition of European states as a 'third force' between the superpowers; it led to the 1947 Franco-British Dunkirk Treaty and the 1948 Brussels Treaty. However, Bevin's 'third force' concept was abandoned in early 1949 with the prospect of the realization of NATO and firm American commitment to the defence of the European continent. On Bevin's 'third force' concept, see G. Warner, 'Ernest Bevin and British Foreign Policy, 1945–51', in G.A. Craig and F.L. Loewenheim (eds), *The Diplomats, 1939–1979* (Princeton, N.J., 1994), 110–14;

S. Greenwood, *The Alternative Alliance: Anglo-French Relations before the Coming of NATO, 1944–48* (London, 1996); also S. Greenwood, 'The Third Force Policy of Ernest Bevin', in M. Dumoulin (ed.), *Wartime Plans for Postwar Europe, 1940–1947* (Brussels, 1995) 419–36; and K. Larres, 'A Search for Order: Britain and the Origins of a Western European Union, 1944–1955', in B. Brivati and H. Jones (eds), *From Reconstruction to Integration: Britain and Europe since 1945* (Leicester, 1993), 71–87; W. Loth, *Der Weg nach Europa*, 3rd edn (Göttingen, 1996), 28ff.

60. The American policy towards both the Soviet Union and Britain during the transition from war to Cold War has been covered in numerous excellent books and articles. See for example, A.A. Offner, *Another Such Victory: President Truman and the Cold War, 1945–1953* (Stanford, CA., 2002); M. Trachtenberg, *A Constructed Peace: The Making of the European Settlement, 1945–1963* (Princeton, N.J., 1999), 12ff.; M. Leffler, *A Preponderance of Power: National Security, the Truman Administration, and the Cold War* (Stanford, Cal., 1992), 27ff.; R.L. Messer, *The End of an Alliance: James F. Byrnes, Roosevelt, Truman, and the Origins of the Cold War* (Chapel Hill, N.C., 1982). Other good accounts are Harbutt, *Iron Curtain*, 99ff.; J.L. Gaddis, *The United States and the Origins of the Cold War, 1941–1947* (New York, 1972), 230–83; B.R. Kuniholm, *The Origins of the Cold War in the Near East: Great Power Conflict and Diplomacy in Iran, Turkey, and Greece* (Princeton, N.J., 1980), 303ff.; B. Rubin, *The Great Powers in the Middle East, 1941–47: the Road to the Cold War* (London, 1980); J.L. Gaddis, *Strategies of Containment: A Critical Appraisal of Postwar American National Security Policies* (New York, 1982), 17ff.; D. Yergin, *Shattered Peace: the Origins of the Cold War and the National Security State* (Boston, 1977), 163ff.

61. Kennan's 'long telegram' is published in George F. Kennan, *Memoirs, 1925–50* (London, 1968), 547–59. See also J.L. Gaddis, *Strategies of Containment*, 19ff., 25ff.; A. Stephanson, *Kennan and the Art of Foreign Policy* (Cambridge, Ma., 1989), 45–53; W. Hixson, *George F. Kennan: Cold War Iconoclast* (New York, 1989), 21–45.

62. See Leffler, *Preponderance of Power*, 100ff. Despite their denials, Truman and Byrnes were well acquainted with the text of Churchill's speech prior to its delivery. Attlee, Bevin and Dalton were also familiar with the broad outlines of what Churchill was going to say, in spite of their subsequent statements to the contrary. They had even facilitated that Churchill was given confidential material for the preparation of his speech (see, for example, Pimlott (ed.) *Political Diary of Hugh Dalton*, 366, diary entry: 25/2/1946). While Attlee and Bevin did not disagree with Churchill's statements, they felt the need to distance themselves from the speech in view of the anger of the Labour Party's left wing. Lord Halifax also knew the speech beforehand. See Yergin, *Shattered Peace*, 175; F.J. Harbutt, 'American Challenge, Soviet Response. The Beginning of the Cold War, February–May 1946,' *Political Science Quarterly* 96 (1981–2) 626; Bullock, *Bevin*, 224–6; T.H. Anderson, *The United States, Great Britain, and the Cold War, 1944–47* (Columbia, Mo., 1981), 113; R.M. Hathaway, *Ambiguous Partnership: Britain and America, 1944–47* (New York, 1981), 238–42; Morgan, *Labour in Power*, 245–6, 273–4; A. Roberts, *'The Holy Fox': A Biography of Lord Halifax* (London, 1991), 295. For Stalin's public reaction, see Harbutt, *Iron Curtain*, 209–16; also H. Feis, *From Trust to Terror: The Onset of the Cold War, 1945–50* (London, 1970), 78–9.

63. Halifax to FO, 10/3/1946. Quoted in P. Boyle, 'The British Foreign Office View of Soviet-American Relations, 1945–46,' *Diplomatic History* 3 (1979), 314. For the importance of Churchill's speech see Gaddis, *United States and the Origins of the Cold War*, 289, 315; Harbutt, 'American Challenge,' 633; Yergin, *Shattered Peace*, 171–4; H.B. Ryan, 'A New Look at Churchill's "Iron Curtain" Speech', *Historical Journal* 22, (1979), 895–920; Harbutt, *Iron Curtain*, 183ff., esp. 197–208; Leffler, *Preponderance of Power*, 107–10.

64. H.S. Truman, *Memoirs, Vol.1: Year of Decisions, 1945* (New York, 1955), 492–3; also M.M. Poen (ed.), *Strictly Personal and Confidential: The Letters Harry Truman Never Mailed* (Boston, 1982), 38–41. It is unclear whether Truman really addressed Byrnes with these words. For J. Byrnes's view of policy with the USSR, see his revealing memoirs *Speaking Frankly* (London, 1947), 91ff.; also Messer, *End of an Alliance*; P.D. Ward, *The Threat of Peace: James F. Byrnes and the Council of Foreign Ministers, 1945–1946* (Kent, Oh., 1979); K.A. Clements (ed.), *James F. Byrnes and the Origins of the Cold War* (Durham, N.C., 1982); D. Robertson, *Sly and Able: a Political Biography of James F. Byrnes* (New York, 1994).

65. FRUS, 1946, Vol. 1, 1165–6: JCOS to Byrnes, 29/3/1946.

66. These were the words of Congressman Emmanuel Celler. Quoted in R.N. Gardner, *Sterling-Dollar Diplomacy in Current Perspective [...]* (New York, 1980, 1st publ. 1956), 237. See also for example Jones, *America and the British Labour Party*, 34–50; C. Anstey, 'The Projection of British Socialism. Foreign Office Publicity and American Opinion, 1945–50', *Journal of Contemporary History* 19 (1984), 417ff.

67. For Bevin's foreign policy, see above all Bullock, *Bevin*; and very critically Weiler, *Ernest Bevin*; also Morgan, *Labour in Power*; M.A. Fitzsimmons, *The Foreign Policy of the British Labour Government, 1945–1951* (Notre Dame, Ind., 1953). For Bevin's early Cold War policy with regard to Germany and Western Europe, see for example A. Deighton, 'Towards a "Western" Strategy: The Making of British Policy Towards Germany, 1945–46', in A. Deighton (ed.), *Britain and the First Cold War* (Basingstoke, 1990), 53ff.

68. Minute from Attlee to Churchill, 23/7/1945 (written during the Potsdam conference), in DBPO, Series I, Vol. 1 (London, 1984), 573–4 (document No.237). See also the document cited in the following note.

69. See for example PRO: FO 800/475, ME/46/22, letter Attlee to Bevin, 1/12/1946.

70. Ibid.

71. Memorandum Attlee, 'Future of the Italian Colonies', 1/9/1945, publ. in DBPO, Series I, Vol 2, 42–3 (doc.18); also publ. in Harris, *Attlee*, 396–7. Initially Attlee had high hopes for the new United Nations organization and its ability to mediate international conflicts but during 1946 he became rather disappointed by the ineffectiveness of the UN and its Security Council. See R. Smith and J. Zametica, 'The Cold Warrior: Attlee Reconsidered, 1945–47', *International Affairs* 61 (1985), 241, 243, 250; also Ovendale, *English-Speaking Alliance*, 40–1.

72. Minute Attlee to Eden, 18/7/1945 (written during the Potsdam conference), in DBPO, Series I, Vol. 1, 363–4 (document No.179). See also PRO: FO 800/475, ME/46/22, letter Attlee to Bevin, 1/12/1946. For interesting analyses of Attlee's thinking, see above all Smith and Zametica, ibid., 237–52; R. Smith, 'Ernest Bevin, British Officials and British Soviet Policy, 1945–47', in Deighton (ed.), *Britain and the First Cold War*, 32–52; Saville, *Politics of Continuity*, 112–48; R.J. Aldrich and J. Zametica, 'The Rise and Decline of a Strategic Concept: the Middle East', in R.J. Aldrich (ed.), *British Intelligence, Strategy and the Cold War, 1945–51* (London, 1992), 236–74; R. Pearce, *Attlee* (London, 1997), 162–64; Burridge, *Clement Attlee*, 188–9; Weiler, *Ernest Bevin*, 161–2; Ovendale, *English-Speaking Alliance*, 40ff; J. Kent, *British Imperial Strategy and the Origins of the Cold War, 1944–49* (Leicester, 1993), ch. 3; W.R. Louis, *The British Empire in the Middle East, 1945–51* (Oxford, 1984), 27ff.

73. See C.J. Bartlett, *British Foreign Policy in the Twentieth Century* (Basingstoke, 1989), 74. For a shrewd analysis of Britain's strategic needs and political dilemmas from the Foreign Office's point of view, see the memorandum by Gladwyn Jebb, 29/7/1945 (written during the Potsdam conference), in DBPO, Series I, Vol. 1, 990–4 (doc. No. 459). For the development of a British atomic bomb, see still the classic work by M. Gowing, *Independence and Deterrence: Britain and Atomic Energy, 1945–52*, Vol. 1: *Policy Making* (London, 1974), chapter 6, esp. 179–85; see also B. Cathcart, *Test of Greatness: Britian's Struggle for the Atomic Bomb* (London, 1994); and P. Hennessy, *The Secret State: Whitehall and the Cold War* (London, 2002).

74. PRO: CAB 131/2, DO (46) 27, memorandum Attlee, 2/3/1946. See also Louis, *British Empire*, 107. For a good overview of Britain's traditional role in the Middle East, see G. Balfour-Paul, 'Britain's Informal Empire in the Middle East', in J.M. Brown and W.R. Louis (eds), *The Oxford History of the British Empire*, Vol. 4: *The Twentieth Century* (Oxford, 1999), 490–514.

75. See J. Tomlinson, 'The Attlee Government and the Balance of Payments, 1945–51,' *Twentieth Century British History* 2/1 (1999), 47–66.

76. PRO: CAB 131/1 DO (46) 5th Conclusions, 15/2/1946; CAB 131/2 DO (46)27, memorandum Attlee, 2/3/1946; see also for a good analysis, Kent, *British Imperial Strategy*, 97–8; also E. Barker, *The British between the Superpowers, 1945–50* (Basingstoke, 1983), 49; Louis, *British Empire*, 107–8.

77. See Onslow, *Backbench Debate*, 28. For Churchill's post-1945 European policy initiatives, see Chapter 7, below.

78. Joint memorandum by Attlee and A.V. Alexander, the Minister of Defence, 22/2/1946. Quoted in Barker, *Superpowers*, 49. See also R. Edmonds, *Setting the Mould: The United States and Britain, 1945–50* (Oxford, 1986), 120–1.

79. PRO: FO 800/475, ME/46/22, letter Attlee to Bevin, 1/12/1946.

80. Pimlott (ed.), *Political Diary of Hugh Dalton*, 368–69: diary entry, 22/3/1946. See also Dalton, *High Tide and After*, in which he quotes a very similar statement but dates it 9/3/1946 (p. 105) and refers to a conversation with Attlee on 16 or 17 February 1946 during which Attlee was 'fresh-minded on Defence' and expressed almost identical sentiments (p. 101). In contrast, see the document JIC(46) I (O) of 1 March 1946, a long analysis of 'Russia's Strategic Interests and Assumptions' by the Joint Intelligence Committee. See Hennessy, *The Secret State*, 12–22.

81. Memorandum Bevin, 25/8/1949, Quoted in Bullock, *Bevin*, 113. Dalton commented that Bevin was 'rather fascinated by the Middle East'. Quoted in Pimlott (ed.), ibid., 369: diary entry, 22/3/1946.

For good accounts of the defence dimension, see M.J. Cohen, *Fighting World War Three from the Middle East: Allied Contingency Plans, 1945–1954* (London, 1997); D.R. Devereux, *The Formulation of British Defence Policy Towards the Middle East, 1948–1956* (Basingstoke, 1990).

82. PRO: FO 371/52 312, minute by the British diplomat J. Thyne Henderson, 30/3/1946. Quoted in full in Louis, *British Empire*, 19. For good accounts, see M.J. Cohen and M. Kolinksy (eds), *Demise of the British Empire in the Middle East: Britain's Responses to Nationalist Movements, 1943–55* (London, 1998).

83. First quote: PRO: FO 800/476/, ME/47/4, letter Bevin to Attlee, 9/1/1947; second quote: Louis, ibid., 20, see also 4, 8, 16–21. See also P.W. Kingston, *Britain and the Politics of Modernization in the Middle East, 1945–1956* (Cambridge, 1996).

84. PRO: FO 800/476/, ME/47/4, letter Bevin to Attlee, 9/1/1947. Bevin also argued: 'This was once a rich region and could be made so again with good government and modern methods. If we help it to build itself up, it can become economically prosperous and a valuable market for us.'

85. In a memorandum dated 13/3/1947 Bevin explained: 'we are the last bastion of social democracy. It may be said that this now represents our way of life as against the red tooth and claw of American capitalism and the Communist dictatorship of Soviet Russia. Any weakening of our position in the Mediterranean area will, in my view, lead to the end of social democracy there and submit us to a pressure which would make our position untenable.' See PRO: CAB 131/2, DO (46)40; see also Louis, *British Empire*, 88; L.D. Epstein, *Britain – Uneasy Ally* (Chicago, 1954), 114–15.

86. These were the words of Labour MP Michael Foot in the House of Commons. Quoted in Epstein, ibid., 115.

87. See Louis, *British Empire*, 18–19.

88. For Bevin's grand illusions, see the excellent account in E. Monroe, *Britain's Moment in the Middle East, 1914–71*, 2nd rev. edn (London, 1981), 155–6, 160–1; also Bullock, *Bevin*, 50–1; Adamthwaite, 'Britain and the World', 226–31; for the lack of British experts willing to go to the Middle East, see Louis, ibid., 18.

89. See for example Bullock, ibid., 34–5, 113–15, 350; Kent, *British Imperial Strategy*, ch. 3; see also the Preface, with detailed information on the relevant documents, in DBPO, Series I, Vol. 2; and the illuminating documents published in G. Ross (ed.), *The Foreign Office and the Kremlin: British Documents on Anglo-Soviet Relations, 1941–45 (Cambridge, 1984)*, 199–281 (documents 35–46, April–December 1945). There were two CFM meetings in 1946 (in Paris, 25 April to 12 July with a break from mid May to mid June; and in New York, 4 November to 11 December); the Paris Peace conference took place from 29 July to 15 October, 1946.

90. PRO: FO 800/475, ME/46/24, memorandum Dixon to Bevin, 9/12/1946. The traditionalist and anti-Communist view of the Foreign Office and the British military is well summarized in Attlee's minute and memorandum (entitled 'Near Eastern Policy') to Bevin, dated 5/1/1947. See PRO: FO 800/476, ME/47/1, Prime Minister's Personal Minute, No. M. 15/47.

91. Bevin during a meeting of the Cabinet Defence Committee, 5/4/1946; quoted in Bullock, *Bevin*, 29. See also the document cited in the previous note.

92. PRO: CAB 131/2, DO (46)47, 'Strategic Position of the British Commonwealth', memorandum by the Chiefs of Staff, 2/4/1946. See also Louis, *British Empire*, 28. For the importance of Africa in Bevin's thinking, see above all Kent, *British Imperial Strategy*, chs 3 and 5; and also for example: Louis, *British Empire*, 16, 108–9; J. Gallagher, 'The Decline, Revival and Fall of the British Empire', in A. Seal (ed.), *The Decline, Revival and Fall of the British Empire* (Cambridge, 1982), 145–50.

93. See for example Bevin's memorandum for the British Overseas Reconstruction Committee, 'The Future of the Italian Colonies and the Italian Mediterranean Islands', 25/8/1945, publ. in DBPO, Series I, Vol. 2, 26–35 (doc. No. 12), also Bevin's memorandum, 10/9/1945, in ibid., 81–3 (doc. No. 33); also Bevin's explanations of British policy in the Record of the 4th meeting of the CFM, London, 14/9/1945, publ. in ibid., 158–66 (doc. No. 53).

94. Louis, *British Empire*, 6, see also 107–8, 274–5, 277. The phrase 'deficit areas' was contained in Attlee's memorandum dated 2/3/1946 (PRO: CAB 131/2, DO (46) 27).

95. For details, see Kent, *British Imperial Strategy*, 100–1; also Louis, ibid., 21–35, 108ff.; Edmonds, *Setting the Mould*, 117–21. Initially, the British COS held very different views; they hoped to organize a confederation under British leadership consisting of Syria, the Lebanon and Saudi Arabia to strengthen the British position with regard to any Soviet designs on the Middle East. See Louis, ibid., 22–5, 108ff.; Bullock, *Bevin*, 243.

96. See for example Attlee's thoughts as reported by Hugh Dalton, in Pimlott (ed.), *Political Diary of Hugh Dalton*, 368–9: diary entry, 22/3/1946. Attlee expressed the belief that in case of a withdrawal from the Middle East 'We should ... constitute a line of defence across Africa from Lagos to Kenya

and concentrate a larger part of our forces in the latter'. See also Dalton, *High Tide and After*, 101, 105, where he cites very similar statements.

97. First quote: PRO: CAB 131/2, DO (46)47, 'Strategic Position of the British Commonwealth', memorandum by the Chiefs of Staff, 2/4/1946 (see also the discussion in Louis, *British Empire*, 27–32, 265ff., esp. 271–80). Second quote: PRO: FO 800/475, ME/46/24, memorandum Dixon to Bevin, 9/12/1946.

98. See Louis, ibid., 15; Kent, *Britain's Imperial Strategy*, 98–100; also R. Frazier, *Anglo-American Relations with Greece: The Coming of the Cold War, 1942–47* (Basingstoke, 1991), 141–5.

99. PRO: FO 371/57 173, minute by Oliver Harvey, 11/3/1946; see also the minute in ibid. by G. Jebb, 8/3/1946, who feared the negative impact on America's perception of the UK; also CAB 131/2, DO (46)40, 13/3/1947, memorandum Bevin, 13/3/1947; also FO 800/475, ME/46/24, memorandum Dixon, 9/12/1946.

100. PRO: FO 371/57 173, minute by Orme Sargent, 12/3/1946; also quoted at length in Kent, *British Imperial Strategy*, 99.

101. For a good account of the difficulties induced by the hard winter 1947, see Robertson, *Bleak Midwinter 1947*.

102. See PRO: FO 800/475, ME/46/22, letter Attlee to Bevin, 1/12/1946.

103. Ibid., ME/46/25, minute J.N. Henderson, 28/12/1946.

104. PRO: CAB 131/1 DO (46)22nd Conclusions, 19/7/1946; CAB 131/2 DO (46)27, 2/3/1946; DO (46)47, 2/4/1946; DO (46)80, 18/6/1946.

105. PRO: FO 800/476, ME/47/1, memorandum Attlee to Bevin, 5/1/1947; also Ovendale, *English-Speaking Alliance*, 46–53. Attlee cancelled British military exercises in the area, see F. Beckett, *Clem Attlee* (London, 1997), 227–8.

106. PRO: FO 800/475, ME/46/22, letter Attlee to Bevin, 1/12/1946; and FO 800/476, ME/47/1, Prime Minister's Personal Minute to Bevin, No. M.15/47, with enclosed memorandum 'Near Eastern Policy', dated 5/1/1947.

107. PRO: FO 800/475, ME/46/22, letter Attlee to Bevin, 1/12/1946. The Foreign Office agreed that Russia might have an 'exaggerated sense of security'; yet it was 'almost undistinguishable from an imperialist instinct' which would result in Moscow attempting 'to fill a vacuum, if it was there to fill'. Ibid., ME/46/24, memorandum Dixon, 9/12/1946.

108. See for example his reply to Attlee's memorandum, dated 5/1/1947, PRO: FO 800/476, ME/47/4, 9/1/1947.

109. For 1945–51, see Chapters 6 and 7, below; and for 1953–4, see Chapters 10–15, below.

110. Quoted in Smith and Zametica, 'The Cold Warrior', 250.

111. The Prime Minister explained that 'Unless we are persuaded that the U.S.S.R. is irrevocably committed to a policy of world domination and that there is no possibility of her alteration, I think that before being committed to this strategy we should seek to come to an agreement with the U.S.S.R. after consideration with Stalin of all our points of conflict'. PRO: FO 800/476, ME/47/1, memorandum Attlee to Bevin, 5/1/1947. See also Bullock, *Bevin*, 348–51. See also Attlee's speech in the House of Commons on 18 November 1946: H.C. *Parl. Deb.*, 5th series, Vol. 430, 577–90.

112. PRO: ibid.

113. PRO: FO 800/475, ME/46/24, Dixon's long memorandum to Bevin, 9/12/1946. See also FO 800/476, ME/47/2, note by Dixon on the meeting between Bevin, Dixon, Hayter, Warner, 8/1/1947, and Bevin's long letter to Attlee, dated 9/1/1947, which was based on this meeting and Dixon's memorandum, FO 800/476/, ME/47/4. This kind of argument was also very popular in Washington.

114. See the previous note.

115. Ibid.

116. PRO: FO 800/476, ME/47/4, letter Bevin to Attlee, 9/1/1947; ME/47/2, note by Dixon on a meeting between Bevin, Dixon, Hayter, Warner, 8/1/1947

117. Ibid.

118. PRO: FO 800/476, ME/47/5, minute Dixon, 10/1/1947.

119. See Smith and Zametica, 'The Cold Warrior', 251; Ovendale, *English-Speaking Alliance*, 51–3.; also for example Barker, *Superpowers*, 49; P.S. Gupta, 'Imperialism and the Labour Government of 1945–51', in J. Winter (ed.), *The Working Class in Modern British History* (Cambridge, 1983), 286. Moreover, Attlee needed Bevin's support within the Cabinet and with respect to the trades union movement.

120. Weiler, *Ernest Bevin*, 161.

121. See Louis, *British Empire*, 250–3; P.L. Hahn, *The United States, Great Britain, and Egypt, 1945–1956* (Chapel Hill, N.C., 1991), 34–5; and in great detail H. Rahman, *A British Defence Problem in the Middle East: The Failure of the 1946 Anglo-Egyptian Negotiations* (Reading, 1994).

122. See for example Louis, ibid., 345ff.

123. Quoted in Dalton, *High Tide and After*, 101 (based on a diary entry, 18/2/1946). Louis, ibid., 88, says that as early as February/March 1946 London heard about tentative indications of future American aid for the region. See also R. Ovendale, *Britain, the United States, and the Transfer of Power in the Middle East, 1945–1952* (Leicester, 1996).

124. PRO: FO 800/475, ME/46/22, letter Attlee to Bevin, 1/12/1946.

125. Ibid.

126. Quotes in Louis, *British Empire*, 91–2.

127. PRO: FO 371/67 040/R5397, letter Dalton to Bevin, 18/4/1947.

128. See Louis, *British Empire*, 88–102; for a good account of the Greek crisis and the development of American interest in supporting and then replacing Britain's position there, see Frazier, *Anglo-American Relations with Greece*, 108–19; also G.M. Alexander, *The Prelude to the Truman Doctrine: British policy in Greece, 1944–47* (Oxford, 1982). There is no evidence for the myth that Attlee and Bevin skilfully pulled the Americans into the region and into the support of the British Empire by 'suddenly' and 'unexpectedly' announcing the British withdrawal from Greece.

129. FRUS, 1946, Vol. 1, 1165–6: JCOS to Byrnes, 29/3/1946.

130. Ibid., 1170: memorandum by Matthews, Dept. of State, 1/4/1946.

131. See P. Boyle, 'The British Foreign Office View of Soviet-American Relations, 1945–46', 307–20; Adamthwaite, 'Britain and the World,' 223–35.

132. PRO: FO 800/476, ME/47/8, Foreign Office note on 'The British and Economic Bases of British Policy in the Middle East', 24/1/1947.

133. See for example the interesting articles by R. Frazier, 'Did Britain start the Cold War? Bevin and the Truman Doctrine', *Historical Journal* 27 (1984), 715ff.; and J.L. Gaddis, 'Was the Truman Doctrine a Real Turning Point?', *Foreign Affairs* 52 (1973–4), 386 ff.; for a more recent account see Leffler, *Preponderance of Power*, 121–7, 142–7; also E.D. Smith, *Victory of a Sort: the British in Greece, 1941–46* (London, 1988); H. Jones, '*A New Kind of War': America's Global Strategy and the Truman Doctrine in Greece* (New York, 1989); and R. Clogg, *Concise History of Greece* (London, 1992). For a succinct discussion of the literature, see also H. Jones and R.B. Woods, 'Origins of the Cold War in Europe and the Near East: Recent Historiography and the National Security Imperative', in M. J. Hogan (ed.), *America in the World: The Historiography of American Foreign Relations since 1941* (New York, 1995), esp. 247ff.; also T. D. Sfikas, 'War and Peace in the Strategy of the Communist Party of Greece, 1945–1949', *Journal of Cold War Studies* 3/3 (2001), 5–30; also T.D. Sfikas, *The British Labour Government and the Greek Civil War, 1945–49: The Imperialism of Non-Intervention* (Keele, 1994).

134. After all, as was formulated a few years later, it was in America's 'interest to take such measures as we can to strengthen the British position generally and in specific areas' so that London could continue assuming 'a large share of the overall responsibility' for fighting the Cold War. Moreover: 'We want them to carry the load wherever they can and especially in those areas where we can not carry it.' FRUS 1951, Vol.4, 981, 986: PPS paper 'The Nature of the US-UK Relationship', 20/11/1951. See also Louis, *British Empire*, 100–2.

135. Churchill College Cambridge, Churchill Papers 2/158: letter Churchill to Truman, 12/5/1947.

136. PRO: FO 800/475, ME/46/22, letter Attlee to Bevin, 1/12/1946.

137. Dalton, *High Tide and After*, 101.

138. Warner, 'Ernest Bevin and British Foreign Policy', 107. Warner believes that 'It was not until the London meeting of the Council of Foreign Ministers in November-December 1947 that he finally gave up on the Russians' (p. 108). See also B. Jones, *The Russia Complex: The British Labour Party and the Soviet Union* (Manchester, 1977), 103ff., 121ff.

139. See H.C. *Parl. Deb.*, 5th series, Vol. 525, 30/3/1954, 1842–44.

140. See for example G. Gallup (ed.), *The Gallup International Public Opinion Poll, Great Britain, 1937–1975, Vol. 1: 1937–1964* (Westport, Conn., 1975), 232, 234, 243, 259, 288, 300, 302, 312, 328–9, 331, 333, 344, 347–8, 355, 365 (1950–5).

CHAPTER 6: WAITING IN THE WINGS

1. For an excellent assessment of Britain's weakened but still formidable role in the world as the third global power, see the famous Foreign Office memorandum, written by Sir Orme Sargent, 'Stocktaking after VE-Day', PRO: FO 371/50912, 11/7/1945; a shorter version (incl. Annexes) is publ. in DBPO, Series I, Vol. 1, 181–92 (doc. No. 102). Churchill always talked about 'the Empire'; he never warmed to the expression 'Commonwealth'. See PRO: CAB 128/28, CM(55)28th, 5/4/1955.

2. Churchill, 'The Sinews of Peace', 5/3/1946, Westminster College, Fulton, Missouri, in: R.R. James (ed.), *Winston S. Churchill: His Complete Speeches, 1987–1963, Vol. 7: 1940–49* (London, 1974), 7292 (my emphasis). For a similar statement, see Churchill's speech 'The Darkening International Scene', 15/3/1946, Waldorf Astoria Hotel, New York, in ibid., 7299–301. The best scholarly analysis of Churchill's 'iron curtain' speech and Anglo-American relations in the early Cold War is still F.J. Harbutt, *The Iron Curtain: Churchill, America, and the Origins of the Cold War* (Oxford, 1986); see also J.W. Muller (ed.), *Churchill's 'Iron Curtain' Speech Fifty Years Later* (Columbia, Mo., 1999).

3. Churchill, 'Sinews of Peace', ibid., 7293.

4. For Churchill's earlier references to this phrase and its origins, see Chapter 4, above, 97–8.

5. Churchill, 'Sinews of Peace', 7292. For the very negative response to his speech by former Vice-President and Secretary of Commerce Henry Wallace and the American media and his general characterization as a 'warmonger', see K.W. Thompson, *Winston Churchill's World View: Statesmanship and Power* (Baton Rouge, La., 1983), 21–2, 23–4, 81–4; also H. Wallace, 'Churchill's Crusade', in *New Republic* 116 (13/1/1947), 22–3; A.L. Hamby, 'Henry A. Wallace, the Liberals and Soviet-American Relations', in *Review of Politics* 30 (1968), 157–8; R.J. Walton, *Henry Wallace, Henry Truman, and the Cold War* (New York, 1976).

6. See Thompson, ibid., 21–4, 81–4; J.L. Gaddis, *The United States and the Origins of the Cold War, 1941–1947* (New York, 1972), 313; Harbutt, *Iron Curtain*, 196ff.; M. Gilbert, *Winston S. Churchill, Vol. 8: Never Despair, 1945–65*, paperback edn (London, 1990), 203ff. For UN-Secretary General Trygve Lie's view, see his *In the Cause of Peace* (New York, 1954), 37–8.

7. Churchill, 'Speech on Foreign Affairs', H.C. *Parl. Deb.*, 5th series, Vol. 427, 5/6/1946, 2030.

8. Churchill, 'Speech on Defence', H.C. *Parl. Deb.*, 5th series, Vol.472, 16/3/1950, 1288–9; 'Speech on Foreign Affairs.' H.C. *Parl. Deb.*, 5th series, Vol. 473, 28/3/1950, 191–2. For the debate about German rearmament, see the still useful book by A.C. Azzola, *Die Diskussion um die Aufrüstung der BRD im Unterhaus und in der Presse Großbritanniens November 1949–Juli 1952* (Meisenheim, 1971), 13ff.

9. Churchill was convinced that the difficult global political situation was a temporary phenomenon though he did not speculate about its duration. See Churchill, 'Speech on Foreign Affairs', H.C. *Parl. Deb.*, 5th series, Vol. 446, 23/1/1948, 560–1.

10. See for example Churchill's, 'The Al Smith Memorial Lecture', recorded in London and broadcast after dinner in New York on 14/10/1947. Published in James (ed.), *Complete Speeches*, Vol. 7, 7539.

11. Neither the historians of the Cold War and British foreign policy nor most of Churchill's biographers pay much attention to Churchill's détente proposals between 1946 and 1951. The writings on Churchill's détente policy in 1953/4 also neglect this important episode. The exception is J.W. Young, *Winston Churchill's Last Campaign: Britain and the Cold War, 1951–55* (Oxford, 1996). In a recent article Young also argues that Churchill's détente policy 'was quite consistent with his anti-Communism'; see his 'Churchill and East-West Détente', in *Transactions of the Royal Historical Society*, 6th series, Vol. XI (Cambridge, 2001), 373–92 (quote: 373).

12. W.S. Churchill, 'Speech on Foreign Affairs', in H.C. *Parl. Deb.*, 5th series, Vol. 446, 23/1/1948, 548–61, esp. 560–1.

13. For the Council of Foreign Ministers' conferences, see M. Kessel, *Westeuropa und die deutsche Teilung. Englische und französische Deutschlandpolitik auf den Außenministerkonferenzen von 1945 bis 1947* (Munich, 1989); A. Deighton, *The Impossible Peace: Britain, the Division of Germany and the Origins of the Cold War* (Oxford, 1990).

14. Ernest Bevin, 'Speech on Foreign Affairs', H.C. *Parl. Deb.*, 5th series, Vol 446, 22/1/1948, 388.

15. Churchill, 'Speech on Foreign Affairs', ibid., 23/1/1948, 552; see also H.C. *Parl. Deb.*, Vol. 428, 23/10/1946, 1687–9.

16. H.C. *Parl. Deb.*, 5th series, Vol. 446, 23/1/1948, 552–3.

17. Ibid., 560, 561. See also the surprising similarity between Churchill's statements and Acheson's speech on 8/2/1950. The latter one is partially quoted in C. Bell, *Negotiation from Strength: A Study in the Politics of Power* (London, 1962), 14, and more extensively in RIIA, *Documents on International Affairs, 1949–50* (London, 1952), 50–4, esp. 53.

18. Churchill, 'Debate on the Address,' H.C. *Parl. Deb.*, 5th series, Vol. 413, 16/8/1945, 80.

19. See Lord Moran, *Churchill: The Struggle for Survival, 1940–65* (London, 1966), 294, 300.

20. See G.A. Donaldson, *Truman Defeats Dewey* (Lexington, 1998); H.I. Gullan, *The Upset that Wasn't: Harold S. Truman and the Crucial Election of 1948* (Chicago, 1998); Z. Karabell, *The Last Campaign: How Harry Truman won the 1948 Election* (New York, 2000).

21. See J. Chace, *Acheson: The Secretary of State Who Created the American World* (New York, 1998), 270–1; M. Leffler, 'Negotiating from Strength: Acheson, the Russians, and American Power', in D. Brinkley (ed.), *Dean Acheson and the Making of U.S. Foreign Policy* (Basingstoke, 1993), 176–210; Bell, *Negotiation*, 13, also 14–16; D. Acheson, *Present at the Creation: My Years in the State Department* (New York, 1969), chs 38 and 41. For Acheson's development into a Cold Warrior, see R.L. Beisner, 'Dean Acheson Joins the Cold Warriors', *Diplomatic History* 20/3 (1996), 321–55. Thompson, *Churchill's World View*, 17–24, 81–5, indicates that Churchill invented this concept of how to face the Soviet Union in the post-war world. This is of course incorrect. For Acheson's foreign policy, see also in this book, below 132ff. See also J.T. McNay, *Acheson and Empire: The British Accent in American Foreign Policy* (Columbia, Mo., 2001).

22. See Bell, *Negotiation*, 16, 22–7, 188–214; also Chace, ibid.; Leffler, ibid.

23. Churchill, 'Speech on Foreign Affairs,' H.C. *Parl. Deb.*, 5th series, Vol. 446, 23/1/1948, 560.

24. Ibid., H.C. *Parl. Deb.*, 5th series, Vol 473, 28/3/1950, 191; Vol 481, 30/11/1950, 1332. See also Churchill's speech in Plymouth, 15/7/1950, on the Korean War and the international situation, in *Keesing's Contemporary Archive. Vol. 8: 1950–52*, 10837.

25. Churchill, 'Speech on Foreign Affairs,' H.C. *Parl. Deb.*, 5th series, Vol. 473, 28/3/1950, 191; 'Speech on Defence,' Vol. 478, 12/9/1950, 985–87; Vol. 478, 27/7/1950, 702–14, esp. 709–13. See also the memorandum dated 17/11/1949 on the luncheon meeting between Churchill and Averell Harriman, at the time American co-ordinator of the European Recovery Plan, in London, in LOC: Harriman Papers, Box 266, Folder: General Correspondence, Churchill, Winston (1949–50). On 11/8/1950, during a speech in Strasbourg, Churchill emphasized again: 'We are still under the shield of the atomic bomb. … In my judgement we have a breathing space. … If in the next two years or so we can create a trustworthy system of defence against Communist invasion, we shall at least have removed the most obvious temptation to those who seek to impose their will by force upon the free democracies. This system of defence in the West will alone give the best chance of a final settlement by negotiation with the Soviets on the basis of strength and not of our weakness, but there is not a day to be lost or a scrap of available strength to be denied'. Quoted in *Keesing's*, ibid., 11086.

26. Churchill, 'Speech on Foreign Affairs,' H.C. *Parl. Deb.*, 5th series, Vol. 487, 10/5/1951, 2161.

27. For American and Soviet nuclear competition, see above all D. Holloway, *Stalin and the Bomb: The Soviet Union and Atomic Energy, 1936–1956* (New Haven, 1994), 300–2.

28. See Bell, *Negotiation*, 188–214. For the development of the myth of a 'missile gap' in the late 1950s, see for example C.J. Pach and E. Richardson, *The Presidency of Dwight D. Eisenhower*, rev. edn (Lawrence, Ks., 1991), 174, 213–16, 233–4; and above all P.J. Roman., *Eisenhower and the Missile Gap* (Ithaca, N.Y., 1995).

29. LOC: Harriman Paper, Box 233, Folder: Churchill, Winston, 1946–8, letter dated 28/4/1948.

30. Churchill, 'Perils Abroad and At Home,' 9/10/1948, Speech given at the Annual Conservative Conference, Llandudno, Wales, in James (ed.), *Complete Speeches*, Vol. 7, 7708.

31. However, see his utterance to his personal physician Lord Moran in May 1954; he seems to indicate that he may have meant it. Moran, *Struggle for Survival*, 545: diary entry, 4/5/1954; see also D. Carlton, *Churchill and the Soviet Union* (Manchester, 2000), 162–3.

32. See A. Bullock, *Ernest Bevin: Foreign Secretary, 1945–1951* (London, 1983), 558–9; A.B. Ulam, *The Rivals, America and Russia since World War II* (New York, 1971), 145–7; J.S. Walker, '"No More Cold War": American Foreign Policy and the 1948 Soviet Peace Offensive', in *Diplomatic History* 5 (1981), 75–91; FRUS 1948, Vol. 4, 834–59; RIIA, *Documents on International Affairs, 1947–48* (London, 1952), 153–5. See for Henry Wallace's involvement and his correspondence with Stalin: RIIA, ibid., 160–4; also RIIA, *Survey of International Affairs, 1947–48* (London, 1950), 54–9; *Annual Register 1948* (London, 1949), 213; *Keesing's*, Vol. 6: 1946–48, 9261–2.

33. See Ulam, ibid., 148–50, esp. 149; H. Feis, *From Trust to Terror: The Onset of the Cold War, 1945–50* (London, 1970), 333ff.; A. and J. Tusa, *The Berlin Blockade* (London, 1988), 149ff.; A. Shlaim, *The United States and the Berlin Blockade, 1948–49: A Study in Crisis Decision-Making* (Berkeley, Ca., 1983), 195ff.; Bullock, ibid., 547ff.; R.G. Miller, *To Save A City: the Berlin Airlift, 1948–49* (College Station, Tx., 2000); also V. Koop, *Kein Kampf um Berlin? Deutsche Politik zur Zeit der Berlin-Blockade 1948/49* (Bonn, 1998).

34. For these talks, see W.B. Smith, *Moscow Mission, 1946–49* (Melbourne, 1950), 228–44, esp. 233ff.; Bullock, ibid., 590–2; Feis, ibid., 343ff., esp. 347–51; Tusa, ibid., 199–218; Shlaim, ibid., 312–26.

35. See H.S. Truman, *Memoirs, Vol 2: Years of Trial and Hope* (Garden City, N.Y., 1956), 213–19 (quotes: 214–15).

36. For good accounts, see A.L. Hamby, *Man of the People: A Life of Harry S. Truman* (New York, 1995), 460–1; D. McCullough, *Truman* (New York, 1992), 685–8; C. Clifford with R. Holbrooke, *Counsel to the President* (New York, 1991), 232–4.

37. Churchill, 'Perils Abroad and At Home,' 9/10/1948, in James (ed.), *Complete Speeches*, Vol. 7, 7709. See also 'Speech on Defence,' H.C. *Parl. Deb.*, 5th series, Vol. 478, 27/7/1950, 711.

38. Churchill, speech on 31/3/1949. Quoted in *Keesing's, Vol. 7: 1948–50*, 9918. See also the report of the *New York Times* on 1/4/1949; clipping in LOC: Harriman Papers, Box 266, Folder: General Correspondence, Churchill, Winston (1949–50).

39. Churchill, 'Speech on Foreign Affairs,' H.C. *Parl. Deb.*, 5th series, Vol. 459, 10/12/1948, 721.

40. Churchill said this during a speech in which he expressed himself in favour of the closer integration of the Western European nations. However, this view was characteristic of Churchill's attitude towards both western and eastern states. H.C. *Parl. Deb.*, 5th series, Vol. 473, 28/3/1950, 196.

41. Ibid., H.C. *Parl. Deb.*, 5th series, Vol. 404, 27/10/1944, 493.

42. See *The Times* (London), 2/2/1950, 4–5; 4/2/1950, 4; 5/2/1950, 3.

43. See *Europa-Archiv*, Vol. 4/1 (Jan.-June, 1949), 2116; Feis, *Trust to Terror*, 355–6; Bullock, *Bevin*, 666–7; RIIA, *Survey of International Affairs, 1949–50* (London, 1953), 62–3; Acheson, *Present at the Creation*, 267–9; *The Times* (London), 3/2/1950, 4.

44. For the discussion on 7/2/1949 in the House of Commons over the question of a possible meeting between Truman and Stalin, see for example H.C. *Parl. Deb.*, 5th series, Vol. 461, 28 f., 132–63.

45. See FRUS, 1949, Vol. 3: *Council of Foreign Ministers, Germany and Austria*, 694–855; C.P. Mayhew (Under-Secretary of State for Foreign Affairs), 'Oral Answers: Berlin Situation,' H.C. *Parl. Deb.*, 5th series, Vol. 464, 4/5/1949, 999–1000; Bullock, *Bevin*, 666–7; Acheson, *Present at the Creation*, 267–74; D.S. McLellan, *Dean Acheson: The State Department Years* (New York, 1976), 155–6.

46. See ibid.; also Bevin, 'Statement on Berlin Blockade,' H.C. *Parl. Deb.*, 5th series, Vol. 464, 5/5/1949, 1220–1; Tusa, *Berlin Blockade*, 329 ff., 357 ff.

47. See Acheson, *Present at the Creation*, 269–74, 291–301; Truman, *Years of Trial and Hope*, 138; Tusa, ibid., 170–2, 329 ff.

48. The conference took place from 23 May to 20 June 1949. See Acheson, ibid., 291–301; see also the anonymous article entitled 'Der "Modus vivendi" in Europa. Die Ost-West Beziehungen und die Pariser Außenministerkonferenz von 1949,' *Europa-Archiv* 4/2 (July–December, 1949), 2389; Tusa, *Berlin Blockade*, 65–72.

49. See *Europa-Archiv*, ibid., 2383–4; Ann and John Tusa view the Paris Foreign Ministers' conference as a 'negative success': 'the Soviet Union had not abrogated the New York agreement [between Malik and Jessup] nor had the West renounced its dedication to liberal and democratic institutions in the western sectors and zones' (see ibid., 372). See also A. Riklin, *Das Berlinproblem, Historisch-Politische und völkerrechtliche Darstellung des Viermächtestatus* (Cologne, 1964), 138–41; and the very critical account by American diplomat R. Murphy, *Diplomat among Warriors* (London, 1964), 391–4. See also McLellan, *Dean Acheson*, 157–63, who mistakenly refers to the meeting as the Palais Marbre Rose conference (p. 162).

50. See Lord Dunglass (Douglas-Home), 'Speech on Foreign Affairs,' H.C. *Parl. Deb.*, 5th series, Vol. 473, 28/3/1950, 303; Bell, *Negotiation*, 15; Acheson, *Present at the Creation*, 371–80.

51. Acheson's statement during his press conference is published in *Vital Speeches of the Day* (15/2/1950), 261–3; also in RIIA, *Documents, 1949–50*, 51–3 (quote: 53). See also Acheson, ibid., 274–5; McGeorge Bundy (ed.), *The Pattern of Responsibility. Edited from the Record of the Secretary of State Dean Acheson* (Cambridge, Ma., 1952), 26–31; Chace, *Acheson*, 270–1.

52. This speech was only published on 9 March but its major points were already known. The speech is partly quoted in Bell, *Negotiation*, 13. For Acheson's view regarding negotiations with Moscow, see the good account in Bell, 12 ff.; see also the commentary and the extensive quotes from Acheson's speeches in Bundy, ibid., 19–43, esp. 24–35; and Acheson, *Present at the Creation*, 274–5; also P. Nitze, *From Hiroshima to Glasnost: At the Centre of Decision. A Memoir* (London, 1989), 117–20.

53. See the previous note.

54. For example, in a speech in the White House on 16/2/1950 in front of company directors, Acheson explained: 'It is only when they come to the conclusion that they cannot so exploit them that they

will make agreements, and they will let it be known when they have reached that decision'. Quoted in Bell, *Negotiation*, 12; see also Chace, *Acheson*, 270–71.

55. NA: PPS, 64D563, Box 17, Folder: Great Britain, 1948–50: D.O.(50)45, dated 7/6/1950, Report by the Chiefs of Staff entitled, 'Defence Policy and Global Strategy', dated 7/6/1950. For a good analysis, see A.M. Johnston, 'Mr Slessor goes to Washington: The Influence of the British Global Strategy Paper and the Eisenhower New Look', *Diplomatic History* 22/3 (1998), 361–98.

56. NA: PPS, 64D563, Box 17, Folder: Great Britain, 1948–50: memorandum of a meeting between Sir John Slessor with American officials from the State Dept. and the PPS in Washington DC, 1/11/1950.

57. See H.G. Nicholas, *The British General Election of 1950* (London, 1951), 102.

58. See ibid., 101–2, 107, 304; also Young, *Churchill's Last Campaign*, 28–33.

59. Most of Churchill's speech in Edinburgh is published in RIIA, *Documents, 1949–50*, 55–6 (quote: 56) and also partially in R.R. James (ed.), *Winston S. Churchill: His Complete Speeches, 1987–1963, Vol. 8: 1950–63* (London, 1974), 7936–44. For an analysis, see Nicholas, ibid., 102–3.

60. In general the literature concurs with this view. The accusation of the Labour government that Churchill only dwelt on the topic because of electoral reasons cannot be dismissed entirely, though he also had some more profound reasons. See Nicholas, ibid., 103–5.

61. See ibid., 103–5, 109–12 (quote: 103). See also Churchill, 'Speech on Foreign Affairs,' H.C. *Parl. Deb.*, 5th series, Vol. 473, 28/3/1950, 199; Kenneth Younger, 'Speech on Foreign Affairs,' ibid., 209. See also Bell, *Negotiation*, 17–19. The US government also often referred its critics to the UN-negotiations between East and West. However, Thompson, *Churchill's World View*, 318, quite rightly believes that 'No one familiar with the difficulties of negotiating ... inside the United Nations would construe this as anything but a refusal to have a positive policy on negotiations.'

62. See Nicholas, *British General Election*, 103–4.

63. See *Keesing's, Vol. 7: 1948–50*, 10550–1.

64. Quoted in Conservative Party Archive, Bodleian Library Oxford, CRD 2/34/6: 'General Brief for Foreign Affairs Debate' by Ursula Branston, FAC 50 (7), 27/11/1950. See also Churchill, 'Speech on Foreign Affairs,' H.C. *Parl. Deb.*, 5th series, Vol. 473, 200. See also Lie, *In the Cause of Peace*, 261.

65. The Conservatives obtained 298 seats, Labour 315, the Liberals gained 9 seats and there were 3 other seats.

66. For Bevin's last months in office (he died on 14 April 1951) and for the many sick Labour ministers, see Bullock, *Bevin*, 803–35; K.O. Morgan, *Labour in Power, 1945–51* (Oxford, 1984), 460ff. On Morrison, see B. Donoughue and G.W. Jones, *Herbert Morrison: Portrait of a Politician* (London, 1973).

67. See Morgan, *Labour in Power*, 441–56.

68. For a good American analysis describing the Attlee Cabinet as 'tired and rather disillusioned', see FRUS 1951, Vol. 4, 972–5 (quote: 974): memorandum Perkins, 26/9/1951; also Morgan, ibid., 462–85.

69. FRUS 1952–4, Vol. 6, 855: meeting Churchill-Truman, 18/1/1952.

70. See Churchill, 'Speech on Foreign Affairs,' H.C. *Parl. Deb.*, 5th series, Vol. 473, 28/3/1950, 199–201 (quote: 199). See also *Keesing's, Vol. 7: 1948–50*, 10694–5.

71. Quote: Churchill, ibid., 201. See also the 'Speeches on Foreign Affairs,' by Julian Amery, ibid., 218–23, esp. 221–3; and Raymond Blackburn, ibid., 223–30, esp. 228–30; also *Keesing's*, ibid.

72. Anthony Eden, 'Speech on Foreign Affairs,' H.C. *Parl. Deb.*, 5th series, Vol. 473, 28/3/1950, quotes: 317–18.

73. Quoted in Bell, *Negotiation*, 24.

74. Letter Harriman to Truman, 13/3/1950, in LOC: Harriman Papers, Box 266, Folder: General Correspondence, Acheson, Dean.

75. Ibid.

76. See Churchill, 'Speech on Foreign Affairs,' H.C. *Parl. Deb.*, 5th series, Vol. 473, 28/3/1950, 199–201; also *Keesing's, Vol. 7: 1948–50*, 10694–5.

77. Acheson, *Present at the Creation*, 480, 484. For the developments in the Korean War and the relevant literature, see chapter 8, n. 77, below (pp. 454–5).

78. Kenneth Younger, 'Speech on Foreign Affairs,' H.C. *Parl. Deb.*, 5th series, Vol. 473, 28/3/1950, 209.

79. But contrary to the general view, West German Chancellor Adenauer did not expect a Soviet invasion of West Berlin. See N. Wiggershaus, 'Aspekte westdeutscher Bedrohungsperzeptionen 1946–1959,' in J. Rohwer (ed.), *Feindbilder und Militärstrategien seit 1945* (Bremen, 1992), 54–5; also N. Wiggershaus, 'Bedrohungsvorstellungen Bundeskanzler Adenauers nach Ausbruch des Korea-Krieges,' *Militärgeschichtliche Mitteilungen* 25 (1979), 79–122.

80. Quoted in *Keesing's, Vol. 8: 1950–52*, 10837.
81. Churchill, 'Speech on Defence', H.C. *Parl. Deb.*, 5th series, Vol. 478, 27/7/1950, 711.
82. Churchill, 'Speech on the International Situation,' H.C. *Parl. Deb.*, 5th series, Vol. 482, 14/12/1950, 1367.
83. The conference focused on the German question but it proved impossible even to agree on an agenda; therefore it was postponed indefinitely. The developments leading up to the unusual Palais Marbre Rose event are complex: during a conference in Prague in October 1950 the eastern bloc countries strongly opposed West German rearmament which was being considered in the West. They demanded a four-power foreign ministers' conference to negotiate a German peace treaty and the withdrawal of all occupation forces; in fact the neutralization of a united Germany was seen as the solution to the German question. In the West the proponents and opponents of German rearmament were divided in their views regarding a four-power foreign ministers' conference; eventually a compromise was reached. It was decided that a pre-conference should take place prior to a proper foreign ministers' conference. This pre-conference could resolve some of the items which would otherwise clutter the agenda of a full foreign ministers' conference and not least it could be used to assess whether or not a four-power conference was likely to succeed. The Palais Marbre Rose conference took place from 5 March-21 June 1950. See Nitze, *From Hiroshima to Glasnost*, 71–7; H.P. Schwarz, *Die Ära Adenauer. Gründerjahre der Republik 1949–1957*, new edn (Wiesbaden, 1994), 140–1; S.W. Mawby, 'Détente Deferred: The Attlee Government, German Rearmament and Anglo-Soviet Rapproachement, 1950–51', *Contemporary British History* 12/2 (1998), 13–18.
84. For a discussion of the myth surrounding the Yalta conference and its impact on British and American post-war foreign policy, see D.C. Watt, 'Britain and the Historiography of the Yalta Conference and the Cold War', *Diplomatic History* 13 (1989), 76ff.
85. Churchill's 'Three Circles' speech was officially entitled 'Perils Abroad and At Home', and held at the Annual Conservative Party Conference, Llandudno, Wales, 9/10/1948. See James (ed.), *Complete Speeches*, Vol. 7, 7712. He made a very similar statement during the Conservative Party Conference in London a year later. See *Keesing's, Vol. 7: 1948–50*, 10288.
86. Churchill, 'Speech in Loughton.' Quoted in *The Times* (London), 8/10/1951, 2. See also Thompson, *Churchill's World View*, 216.
87. For a very forceful defence of the Empire, see Churchill, 'Debate on the Address,' H.C. *Parl. Deb.*, 5th series, Vol. 457, 28/10/1948, 242–53. See also Emerys Roberts, 'Speech on Foreign Affairs,' ibid., Vol. 473, 28/3/1950, 295–7. Prime Minister Attlee largely agreed with Churchill. He explained in his Guildhall speech in London on 9/11/1948: '… great as is our interest in the affairs of Europe, we have, of course, far closer ties with the peoples of the British Commonwealth and Empire.' However, while Churchill always concentrated on the Empire, Attlee appeared to emphasize the comparatively recent British Commonwealth of Nations. Quoted in *Keesing's, Vol. 7: 1948–50*, 9616.
88. Quoted in *Keesing's*, ibid., 10550. For the high regard in which Churchill held Britain's international reputation, see the end of his 'Speech on Foreign Affairs,' on 17/11/1949, H.C. *Parl. Deb.*, 5th series, Vol. 469, 2232–3.
89. Churchill, 'Perils Abroad and At Home,' 9/10/1948, in James (ed.), *Complete Speeches*, Vol. 7, 7712. Churchill expressed very similar sentiments during the Annual Party Conference in 1950.
90. Quoted in *Keesing's, Vol. 7: 1948–50*, 10129.
91. Churchill, 'Speech on Foreign Affairs,' H.C. *Parl. Deb.*, 5th series, Vol. 459, 10/12/1948, 707.
92. For details, see Chapter 11, below, 222ff.
93. Quoted in James (ed.), *Complete Speeches*, Vol. 8, 8257, 8/10/1951. See also Churchill's, 'Oral Answers, Foreign Ministers' Deputies' Conference (Termination),' H.C. *Parl. Deb.*, 5th series, Vol. 489, 25/6/1951, 1002–5; also 'Written Answers, Foreign Ministers' Conference, Paris,' ibid., 6.
94. See R.R. James, *Anthony Eden*, paperback edn (London, 1986), 338–9; Morgan, *Labour in Power*, 484; D. Butler, *The British General Election of 1951* (London, 1952), 118–28; also D. Butler, *British General Elections since 1945* (Oxford, 1989), 11–13. For the Iran crisis, see Donoughue and Jones, *Herbert Morrison*, 491ff.; J. Martschukat, *Antiimperialismus, Öl und die 'Special Relationship'. Die Nationalisierung der Anglo-Iranian Oil Company im Iran 1951–54* (Münster, 1995).
95. See Churchill's speech in the Home Park football ground in Plymouth, 23/10/1951, in James (ed.), *Complete Speeches*, Vol. 8, 8282.

CHAPTER 7: EVER CLOSER UNION?

1. See Churchill's speech at the Albert Hall, London, 14/5/1947, when he attended a 'United Europe Meeting', in R.S. Churchill (ed.), *Europe Unite: Speeches 1947 and 1948* (London, 1950), 83–5; quote: 83.
2. See for example Churchill's speech to the Congress of Europe in The Hague, 7/5/1948, in R.S. Churchill (ed.), ibid., 310–17.
3. Churchill's speech to the Council of the European Movement, Brussels, 26/2/1949, in R.S. Churchill (ed.), *In the Balance: Speeches 1949 and 1950* (London, 1951), 29.
4. See Chapter 3, 67ff., above.
5. All quotes from the Fulton speech from R.S. Churchill (ed.), *The Sinews of Peace: Postwar Speeches* (London, 1948), 98–104.
6. See also Churchill's brief speech at the reception of the Lord Mayor and civic authorities of New York at the Waldorf Astoria, New York, on 15/3/1946, in ibid., 115–20. The tenor of the speech was similar to what he said in the 'iron curtain' speech.
7. For details of the 'Three Circles' speech, see Chapter 6, 138, above. See also the convincing arguments in S. Onslow, *Backbench Debate within the Conservative Party and Its Influence on British Foreign Policy, 1948–1957* (Basingstoke, 1997), 22–3, also 15.
8. For the Foreign Office's attitude to Coudenhove-Kalergi, see Chapter 4, n. 14, above (p. 426).
9. See Onslow, *Backbench Debate*, 16–19 (quote: 18). Other Conservative pro-Europeans who supported and influenced Churchill's European themes were Boothby, Macmillan, Maxwell Fyfe, Eccles, Thorneycroft and a few others – Anthony Eden, however, was not among them; he was much more sceptical and in fact resented Churchill's overly enthusiastic pronouncements. See ibid., 19ff. (on Eden: 25–7).
10. Churchill's Zurich speech; quoted in R.S. Churchill (ed.), *Sinews of Peace*, 198–202; quotes: 199–200, 202; see also the interesting account in H. Young, *This Blessed Plot: Britain and Europe from Churchill to Blair* (London, 1998), 16–18; also W. Mauter, 'Churchill and the Unification of Europe', *The Historian* 161, No. 7 (Fall, 1998), 67–84.
11. Churchill's Zurich speech; quoted in R.S. Churchill (ed.), ibid., quote: 201.
12. Churchill, 'Speech on Foreign Affairs', in H.C. *Parl. Deb.*, 5th series, Vol. 427, 5/6/1946, 2030.
13. Churchill's Zurich speech, quoted in R.S. Churchill (ed.), *Sinews of Peace*, quote: 201.
14. Churchill, 'Speech on Foreign Affairs', in H.C. *Parl. Deb.*, 5th series, Vol. 427, 5/6/1946, 2029; also Churchill, 'Speech on Foreign Affairs', in ibid., Vol. 459, 10/12/1948, 711. See also G.A. Craig, 'Churchill and Germany', in R. Blake and W.R. Louis (eds), *Churchill* (Oxford, 1993), 37–40; and for a more general perspective, see the articles in C. Wurm (ed.), *Western Europe and Germany: The Beginnings of European Integration* (Oxford, 1995).
15. For example Averell Harriman – the influential American businessman and politician who had been a confidant of Roosevelt's and was now one of President Truman's close advisers – also held this view. See for example, *Akten zur Auswärtigen Politik der Bundesrepublik Deutschland, 1951*, 164–5: Krekeler, Consul General in Washington, to Adenauer, on his conversation with Harriman, 3/3/1951.
16. Churchill, 'Speech on Foreign Affairs', in H.C. *Parl. Deb.*, 5th series, Vol. 427, 5/6/1946, 2028, 2031. Churchill's realism contrasts with the opinion of the British military who still believed in mid-1950 that 'It is very unlikely that the present division of Germany can be permanent'. See NA: PPS, 64D563, Box 17, Folder: Great Britain, 1948–50: D O (50)45, Report by the Chiefs of Staff entitled 'Defence Policy and Global Strategy', dated 7/6/1950, p. 7.
17. Churchill's Zurich speech, quoted in R.S. Churchill (ed.), *Sinews of Peace*, 201–2. For Churchill's European ideas during the Second World War, see Chapters 3 and 4 above.
18. Quotes: ibid., 202.
19. See H. Young, *This Blessed Plot*, 17.
20. For details, see Chapter 4, 64–90 above.
21. For details of his 1930 article on the theme, see the beginning of Chapter 3, above, 54ff. See also Churchill's speech at a meeting of the European Movement in London, 28/11/1949, in R.S. Churchill (ed.), *In the Balance*, 152.
22. Quoted in M. Gilbert, *Winston S. Churchill, Vol. 8: Never Despair, 1945–1965* (London, 1990) paperback edn, 267.
23. See Onslow, *Backbench Debate*, 13.
24. For the strong support (and financial resources) the European Movement received from the CIA, see F. S. Saunders, *Who Paid the Piper? The CIA and the Cultural Cold War* (London, 1999), 99, 329; see also S. Dorril, *MI6: Fifty Years of Special Operations* (London, 2000), 455ff., esp. 458–61, 467ff.

25. See Onslow, *Backbench Debate*, 15–16.
26. See for example his speech at the Albert Hall, London, 14/5/1947, when he attended a 'United Europe Meeting', in R.S. Churchill (ed.), *Europe Unite*, 84; see also his 'United Europe Exhibition' speech, Dorland Hall, London, 17/11/1948, in ibid., 466; and above all his speech on the Schuman Plan to the House of Commons, 27/6/1950, in R.S. Churchill (ed.), *In the Balance*, 287–303. See also Onslow, ibid., 23.
27. H. Young, *This Blessed Plot*, 6.
28. Quotes: G. Warner, 'The Labour Governments and the Unity of Western Europe, 1945–51', in R. Ovendale (ed.), *The Foreign Policy of the British Labour Governments, 1945–51* (Leicester, 1984), 67–8. For a similar view see M. Camps, *Britain and the European Community, 1955–63* (London, 1964), 11–12. For Britain and European unity since 1945, see also the contributions in K. Larres (ed. with E. Meehan), *Uneasy Allies: British-German Relations and European Integration since 1945* (Oxford, 2000), and the 'Introduction', pp. 4, 11.
29. See for example the brief overviews in D.W. Urwin, *The Community of Europe: A History of European Integration since 1945*, 2nd edn (London, 1995), 1 ff.; D. Dinan, *Ever Closer Union? An Introduction to the European Community*, 2nd edn (Basingstoke, 1999), 9ff.
30. See Onslow, *Backbench Debate*, 38. However, this figure may well be a little high.
31. According to Onslow, ibid., 244, n. 39, 28 sitting MPs, 7 Conservative candidates and Leo Amery participated, thus 36 Conservative delegates in total. H. Young, *Blessed Plot*, 19, speaks of 140 British participants in total. Onslow states that, in total, 730 delegates attended the Congress while Young refers to *c.* 800.
32. For a most interesting contemporary impression of Churchill's European policy in 1948–9 by one of his closest and most long-standing female friends, see V. Bonham Carter, *Daring to Hope: Diaries and Letters 1946–1969*, ed. by M. Pottle (London, 2000), 40–74; for the Congress at the Hague, see 48–51.
33. Ibid., 53, n. 1 (quoting the impression of Peter Fleming).
34. Ibid., 50 (Churchill said this on 8 May 1948).
35. See R.S. Churchill (ed.), *Europe Unite*, 310–17 (quote: 317); for the Congress, see also H. Young, *This Blessed Plot*, 19–22, 41; Onslow, *Backbench Debate*, 38–42.
36. See for example Stirk, P.M.A. *A History of European Integration since 1914*, (London, 1996) 103–4.
37. See J.T. Grantham, 'British Labour and The Hague "Congress of Europe": National Sovereignty Defended', *Historical Journal* 24 (1981), 443–52; also G. Warner, 'Die britische Labour-Regierung und die Einheit Westeuropas', *Vierteljahrshefte für Zeitgeschichte* 28 (1980), 316ff.; also Dorrill, *MI6*, 462–3.
38. Onslow, *Backbench Debate*, 42.
39. See R.S. Churchill (ed.), *Europe Unite*, 347–52 (quote: 352). See also Churchill, 'Speech on Foreign Affairs', H.C. *Parl. Deb.*, 5th series, Vol. 481, 30/11/1950, 1333; and 'Speech on Defence', Vol. 484, 15/2/1951, 631–5.
40. For a still useful book, see G. Wettig, *Entmilitarisierung und Wiederbewaffnung in Deutschland 1943–1955* (Munich, 1967); and D.C. Large, *Germans to the Front: West German Rearmament in the Adenauer Era* (Chapel Hill, N.C., 1996); R. McGeehan, *The German Rearmament Question: American Diplomacy and European Defence after World War II* (Urbana, Ill., 1971).
41. NA: PPS, 64D563, Box 17, Folder: Great Britain, 1948–50: D.O. (50)45, Report by the Chiefs of Staff entitled 'Defence Policy and Global Strategy', dated 7/6/1950, p. 7.
42. On the difficulties with the EDC and its eventual failure in August 1954 and the consequences for Churchill's summit diplomacy, see Chapters 15 and 16, below.
43. NA: PPS, 64D563, Box 17, Folder: Great Britain, 1948–50: memorandum of a meeting between Sir John Slessor, Chief of the Air Staff, and officials from the State Dept. and the PPS in Washington, DC, 1/11/1950. Slessor emphasized that the French feared above all 'the re-emergence of a German General Staff'. He recommended that ultimately German forces would have to be treated on a basis of equality with other NATO forces and explained that he did not feel 'that the Germans will ever turn against the West again or join the U.S.S.R because it must be perfectly clear to them that if there is a third world war, German industry … would be completely destroyed.'
44. On the EDC and the British attitude, see above all still E. Fursdon, *The European Defence Community* (London, 1980); and now K. Ruane, *The Rise and Fall of the European Defence Community; Anglo-American Relations and the Crisis of European Defence, 1950–55* (Basingstoke, 2000); also S. Dockrill, *Britain's Policy for West German Rearmament, 1950–55* (Cambridge, 1991); H.-E. Volkmann and W. Schwengler (eds), *Die Europäische Verteidigungsgemeinschaft. Stand und Probleme der Forschung* (Boppard, 1985), esp. the article by P. Jones, 'Labour-Regierung, deutsche

Wiederbewaffnung und die EVG 1950–51', 51–80; L. Köllner et al. (eds) *Die EVG-Phase* (Boppard, 1990); and S. Mawby, *Containing Germany: Britain and the Arming of the Federal Republic* (Basingstoke, 1999), chapters 1–3.

45. Quoted in L. Galambos (ed.), *The Papers of Dwight D. Eisenhower: NATO and the Campaign of 1952*, Vol. XII (Wilmington, Del., 1989), 394: letter Eisenhower to Ralph A. Bard, 29/6/1951.

46. For the development of the ECSC, see for example D. Spierenburg and R. Poidevin, *The History of the High Authority of the ECSC* (London, 1994); M. Kipping, *Zwischen Kartellen und Konkurrenz. Der Schuman-Plan und die Ursprünge der europäischen Einigung, 1944–1952* (Berlin, 1996).

47. See R.S. Churchill (ed.), *In the Balance*, 287–303 (quotes: 302–3). For the Labour government's decision not to participate in the Schuman Plan, which is often seen as the beginning of Britain 'missing the bus' in the European integration process, see for example R. Bullen, 'The British Government and the Schuman Plan, May 1950–March 1951', in K. Schwabe (ed.), *The Beginning of the Schuman Plan 1950/51* (Baden-Baden, 1988), 199–210; E. Dell, *The Schuman Plan and the British Abdication of Leadership in Europe* (London, 1995); for a very good account, see also H. Young, *This Blessed Plot*, 44–68; also Onslow, *Backbench Debate*, 57–69.

48. Quoted in H.S. Truman, *Memoirs*, Vol. 2: *Years of Trial and Hope* (Garden City, N.Y., 1956), 259; see also L. Galambos (ed.), *Papers of Dwight D. Eisenhower*, Vol. XII (Baltimore, 1989), 781–2.

49. FRUS 1952–4, Vol. 6, 739: Memorandum by Acheson on the dinner meeting between Churchill and Truman and their respective delegations, aboard the presidential yacht *Williamsburg*, 5/1/1952.

50. Draft telegram Harriman to Acheson, 2/3/1949, LOC: Harriman Papers, Box 266, Folder: General Correspondence, Churchill, Winston (1949–50).

51. See Chapter 10, 199ff., below.

52. Draft telegram Harriman to Acheson, 2/3/1949, LOC: Harriman Papers, Box 266, Folder: General Correspondence, Churchill, Winston (1949–50).

53. See Churchill, 'Perils Abroad and At Home', 9/10/1948, in James (ed.), *Complete Speeches, Vol. 7*, 7712. See also A. Deighton, 'Britain and the Three Interlocking Circles', in A. Varsori (ed.), *Europe, 1945–1990s: The End of an Era* (London, 1995), 155–69.

54. Macmillan developed this analogy in conversation with Labour politician Richard Crossman in 1943 at Allied Forces Headquarters in Algiers. See J. Dumbrell, *A Special Relationship: Anglo-American Relations in the Cold War and After* (Basingstoke, 2001), 13–14.

55. Quote: Camps, *Britain and the European Community*, 4. For the view of the Labour governments, see for example K.O. Morgan, *Labour in Power, 1945–51* (Oxford, 1984), 66ff., 271ff., 389–98, 417–21; Warner, 'The Labour Governments', 61ff.; S. Croft, 'British Policy towards Western Europe, 1945–51', in P.M.R. Stirk and D. Willis (eds), *Shaping Postwar Europe: European Unity and Disunity, 1945–57* (London, 1991), 77ff.

56. For Adenauer's opinion with regard to Churchill's view of European integration, see his *Erinnerungen 1945–1953* (Stuttgart, 1965), 507.

57. All quotes: D. Healey, *When Shrimps Learn to Whistle: Signposts for the Nineties* (London, 1990), 76; see also H. Young, *This Blessed Plot*, 30.

58. See Chapter 4, 90ff., above.

59. See Bevin, 'Speech on Foreign Affairs', H.C. *Parl. Deb.*, 5th series, Vol. 446, 387–409. For good overviews of all these issues, see Stirk, *History of European Integration*, ch. 4; J.W. Young, *Britain, France and the Unity of Europe, 1945–51* (Leicester, 1984); also J.W. Young, *Britain and European Unity, 1945–1992* (Basingstoke, 1993).

60. See for an overview of the literature K. Larres, 'A Search for Order: Britain and the Origins of a Western European Union, 1944–55', in B. Brivati and H. Jones (eds), *From Reconstruction to Integration: Britain and Europe since 1945* (Leicester, 1993), 71–2, 85–6; also Warner, 'The Labour Governments', 61–82; J. Schneer, 'Hopes deferred or shattered: the British Labour Left and the Third Force Movement, 1945–59', *Journal of Modern History* 56/2 (1984), 197–226.

61. Ibid. See also M. Hogan, *The Marshall Plan: America, Britain, and the Reconstruction of Western Europe, 1947–52* (Cambridge, 1987), 46–8. For the development of NATO and the relevant literature, see K. Larres, 'North Atlantic Treaty Organization', in A. DeConde et al. (eds), *Encyclopedia of America Foreign Relations: The Principal Movements and Ideas*, 2nd edn (New York, 2002), Vol. 2, 573–93; G. Schmidt (ed.), *A History of NATO* (Basingstoke, 2001).

62. See A. Deighton, 'British-West German Relations, 1945–1972', in Larres (ed.), *Uneasy Allies*, 30–1. As John Young has persuasively shown, this also applied to the 'pro-Europeans' within the Conservative Party like Macmillan, Maxwell Fyfe, Eccles, etc. who were somewhat more prepared than Churchill and Eden to associate Britain with the European continent. However they did not

think in terms of integration with a federal supranational Europe either. See J.W. Young, 'Churchill's "No" to Europe: The "Rejection" of European Union by Churchill's Post-war Government, 1951–52', *Historical Journal* 28 (1985), 923–37.

63. See Hogan, *Marshall Plan*, 47–8; Warner 'The Labour Governments', 61ff.; Croft, 'British Policy towards Western Europe', 77ff.; Camps, *Britain and the European Community*, 3.

64. See Warner, ibid., 65ff. For Acheson's view, see for example FRUS 1949, Vol. 4, 472: telegram to US embassy in Paris, 19/10/1949.

65. See K. Schwabe, ' "Ein Akt konstruktiver Staatskunst" – die USA und die Anfänge des Schuman-Plans', in Schwabe (ed.), The *Beginning of the Schuman Plan*, 214–15. For American-German relations at this time, see H.J. Schröder, 'USA und westdeutscher Wiederaufstieg (1945–52)', in K. Larres and T. Oppelland (eds), *Deutschland und die USA im 20. Jahrhundert: Geschichte der politischen Beziehungen* (Darmstadt, 1997), 95–118.

66. F. Romero, 'U.S. Attitudes towards Integration and Interdependence: The 1950s,' in F.H. Heller and J.R. Gillingham (eds), *The United States and the Integration of Europe: Legacies of the Postwar Era* (London, 1996), 103–21; J. Killick, *The United States and European Reconstruction, 1945–1960* (Edinburgh, 1997), 65ff., 171ff.; also G. Lundestad, *'Empire' by Integration: The United States and European Integration, 1945–1997* (Oxford, 1997).

67. It seems to be more appropriate to speak of 'enlightened self-interest'. See Killick, ibid., 185.

68. See n. 66, above.

69. For still a most useful book on containment, see J.L. Gaddis, *Strategies of Containment: A Critical Appraisal of Postwar American National Security Policy* (Oxford, 1982).

70. See for example FRUS, 1955–7, Vol. 4, 349, 21/11/1955.

71. See n. 66, above; and Lundestad, *'Empire' by Integration*, 18, 71; A. Grosser, *The Western Alliance: European-American Relations since 1945* (London, 1980); P. Winand, *Eisenhower, Kennedy and the United States of Europe* (London, 1993). President Eisenhower came to hope that the unity of Western Europe would not only 'solve the peace of the world' but, perhaps, even result in the roll-back of the Soviet Union. He expected that Western Europe's democratic and prosperous way of life would 'ultimately attract to it all the Soviet satellites'. FRUS, 1955–7, Vol. 4, 349, 21/11/1955.

72. See J. Gillingham, *Coal, Steel, and the Rebirth of Europe, 1945–55: The Germans and the French from Ruhr Conflict to Economic Community* (Cambridge, 1991), 120–33; Camps, *Britain and the European Community*, 6–8; H. Young, *This Blessed Plot*, 38–9.

73. For a good account of the various theories of European integration, see B. Rosamund, *Theories of European Integration* (Basingstoke, 2000).

74. See Churchill's 'United Europe Exhibition' speech, Dorland Hall, London, 17/11/1948, in R.S. Churchill (ed.), *Europe Unite*, 466 (quote: ibid.). See also Warner, 'The Labour Governments', 68–70.

75. See Churchill's speech before the Consultative Assembly of the council of Europe, Strasbourg, 17/8/1949, in R.S. Churchill (ed.), ibid., 81–2 (quotes: 80); see also his speech to the same forum on 11/8/1950, in ibid., 347ff.

76. See A.J. Zurcher, *The Struggle to Unite Europe, 1940–1958*, reprint of the 1958 edn (Westport, Conn., 1975), 40–56; also A.H. Robertson, *The Council of Europe* (London, 1956).

77. See for example, *Akten zur Auswärtigen Politik, 1951*, 194: memorandum Blankenhorn on his conversation with McCloy and Reber, 28/11/1951.

78. See Young, 'Churchill's "No" to Europe', 923–37; H. Young, *This Blessed Plot*, 2–5; Onslow, *Backbench Debate*, 24.

79. Quoted in Galambos (ed.), *Papers of Dwight D. Eisenhower*, Vol. XII, 790 (letter Eisenhower to Churchill, 14/12/1951), 842 (letter Eisenhower to Truman, 4/2/1952).

80. *Akten zur Auswärtigen Politik, 1951*, 605–6: memorandum of conversation between Blankenhorn and Monnet, 8/11/1951.

81. See for example Eisenhower's disappointment about the Churchill government's attitude to the European army idea as cautiously expressed in a letter to Anthony Eden, dated 8/12/1951, and to American Secretary of Defense Bob Lovett, dated 13/12/1951, in Galambos (ed.), *Papers of Dwight D. Eisenhower*, Vol. XII, 767, 779–85.

82. See Young, 'Churchill's "No" to Europe', 923–7; Warner, 'The Labour Governments', 67–8; A. Nutting, *Europe Will Not Wait: a Warning and a Way Out* (London, 1960); A. Montague Browne, *Long Sunset: Memoirs of Winston Churchill's Last Private Secretary* (London, 1995), 270–6. See also the various articles in G. Schmidt (ed.), *Grossbritannien und Europa – Grossbritannien in Europa* (Bochum, 1989).

83. See Young, ibid., 927, 932–6; Nutting, ibid., 42–6; Spierenburg and Poidevin, *History of the High Authority of the ECSC*, 202–4; A. Eden, *Full Circle: Memoirs* (London, 1960), 47–8; D. Dutton,

Anthony Eden: A Life and Reputation (London, 1997), 298–300; V.H. Rothwell, *Anthony Eden: A Political Biography, 1931–1957* (Manchester, 1992), 108–12.

84. See the previous note; also Young, 'German Rearmament and the European Defence Community', in J.W. Young (ed.), *The Foreign Policy of Churchill's Peacetime Government, 1951–55* (Leicester, 1988), 81–107.

85. PRO: CAB 129/48, C(51)32nd Conclusions, 29/11/1951; see also Montague Browne, *Long Sunset*, 271–2.

86. See n. 44, above, and the articles by D.C. Watt, 'Großbritannien und Europa 1951–1959. Die Jahre Konservativer Regierung,' in *Vierteljahrshefte für Zeitgeschichte* 28 (1980), 389–409; and 'Die Konservative Regierung und die EVG,' in Volkmann and Schwengler (eds), *Die Europäische Verteidigungsgemeinschaft*, 81–99; also K. Adenauer, *Erinnerungen 1945–53*, 169ff.; H.-J. Rupieper, *Der besetzte Verbündete. Die amerikanische Deutschlandpolitik 1949–55* (Opladen, 1991).

87. For details on the EDC and Churchill's 'summitry' in 1954, see Chapters 15 and 16 below.

88. See the very critical book by Nutting, *Europe Will Not Wait*; also R. Boothby, *My Yesterday, Your Tomorrow* (London, 1962), 73ff.; H. Macmillan, *Tides of Fortune, 1945–55* (London, 1969), 461ff.; E. Shuckburgh, *Descent to Suez: Diaries, 1951–56* (London, 1986), 24–45; the articles in Schmidt (ed.), *Grossbritannien und Europa*; and above all the two articles by D.C. Watt, referred to in n. 86, above; Young, 'Churchill's "No" to Europe', 923–37; M. Beloff, 'Churchill and Europe,' in Blake and Louis (eds), *Churchill*, 443–55.

89. See A. Cairncross, *Years of Recovery: British Economic Policy, 1945–51* (London, 1985), esp. ch 10. See also the extensive literature on 'British decline', for example A. Orde, *The Eclipse of Great Britain: the United States and British Imperial Decline, 1895–1956* (London, 1996), 160–92; P. Clarke and C. Trebilcock (eds), *Understanding Decline: Perceptions and Realities of British Economic Performance* (Cambridge, 1997); A. Gamble, *Britain in Decline: Economic Policy, Political Strategy, and the British State*, 4th edn (Basingstoke, 1994); D. Coates and J. Hillard (eds), *The Economic Decline of Modern Britain: The Debate between Left and Right* (London, 1986); for a good summary of the older literature, see W. Krieger, 'Die britische Krise in historischer Perspektive,' in *Historische Zeitschrift* 247 (1988), 585–602. See also the interviews and discussions with contemporary politicians and civil servants in M. Charlton (ed.), *The Price of Victory* (London, 1983), esp. 89ff.

90. See for example Charlton, ibid., 89ff.; and K. Larres (ed.), 'Witness Seminar: British Attitudes to German Rearmament and Reunification in the 1950s', *Contemporary Record* 5 (1991), 302ff.

91. Quoted in H.J. Heiser, *British Policy with Regard to the Unification Efforts on the European Continent* (Leyden, 1959), 84.

92. Speech in Plymouth, Home Park Football Ground, 23/10/1951, in James (ed.), *Complete Speeches*, Vol. 8, 8282.

Chapter 8: Against All Odds

1. On 25 October 1951 the Conservative Party won 321 seats, the Liberals 6 and Labour 295 seats. Although the Labour Party obtained 231,000 more votes than the Conservatives, due to the 'first-past-the-post' electoral system, Churchill gained a very narrow majority of seats. See D. Butler and G. Butler (eds), *British Political Facts, 1900–1985* (Basingstoke, 1986), 226.

2. Already in mid-December 1951 French diplomats concluded that 'Churchill had aged very considerably in recent weeks'. A few weeks later Walter Gifford, the US ambassador in London, came to the same conclusion: 'Churchill is definitely aging and is no longer able to retain his full clarity and energy for extended periods. Also he is increasingly living in the past …'. FRUS 1951, Vol. 4, 994: Bruce, Paris, to Acheson, 19/12/1951; FRUS 1952–4, Vol 6, 721: Gifford, London, to State Dept., 29/12/1951. See also M. Soames, *Clementine Churchill* (London, 1979), 431.

3. R. Jenkins, 'Churchill: The Government of 1951–1955', in R. Blake and W.R. Louis (eds), *Churchill* (Oxford, 1993), 497; also R. Jenkins, *Churchill* (London, 2001), 843ff. For good overviews of the domestic and foreign policy of this administration, see also A. Seldon, *Churchill's Indian Summer: The Conservative Government, 1951–55* (London, 1981); and H. Pelling, *Churchill's Peacetime Administration* (Basingstoke, 1997).

4. See for example E. Shuckburgh, *Descent to Suez: Diaries, 1951–56* (London, 1986), 24ff. For Churchill's unsuccessful attempt to make his government more effective than its predecessor by introducing a grand 'overlord system' based on his war experiences, see P. Hennessey and D.

Welsh, 'Lords of all they surveyed? Churchill's ministerial "overlords", 1951–53', *Parliamentary Affairs* 51/1 (1998), 62–70. For Churchill's understanding of the office of the Prime Minister, see P. Hennessy, 'Churchill and the Premiership', in *Transactions of the Royal Historical Society*, 6th series, Vol. XI (Cambridge, 2001), 295–306.

5. FRUS 1952–4, Vol 6, 861: R.A. Lovett, US Secretary of Defense, to D. Eisenhower, Supreme Allied Commander, Europe, 24/1/1954.

6. Churchill, 'Debate on the Address', H.C. *Parl. Deb.*, 5th series, Vol. 493, 6/11/1951, 68–9.

7. See chapter 7 above.

8. Churchill, 'Debate on the Address', H.C. *Parl. Deb.*, 5th series, Vol. 493, 6/11/1951, 79–80 (quote: 80).

9. Churchill, ibid., 644, also 6.

10. On Adenauer, see above all the critical biography by H. Köhler, *Adenauer: Eine politische Biographie* (Frankfurt, 1994); also H.P. Schwarz, *Adenauer. Der Aufstieg, 1876–1952*, 2nd edn (Stuttgart, 1986); H.P. Schwarz, *Adenauer. Der Staatsmann, 1952–1967* (Stuttgart, 1991); and C. Williams, *Adenauer: The Father of the New Germany* (London, 2000) which, however, contains a fair number of factual mistakes. For a brief overview, see also K. Larres, 'Konrad Adenauer (1876–1967)', in T. Oppelland (ed.), *Deutsche Politiker, 1949–1969*, Vol. 1 (Darmstadt, 1999), 13–24; see also the still valuable essays in J. Foschepoth (ed.), *Adenauer und die Deutsche Frage* (Göttingen, 1988).

11. NA: PPS, 64D563, Box 16, Folder: Germany, 1950–52: memorandum Philip C. Jessup to Paul Nitze 'Notes on Trip To Frankfurt, May 26 and 27, 1951', dated 1/6/1951.

12. For Adenauer's general fear that the western allies would arrive at some understanding with Russia at the expense of Germany (his so-called 'Potsdam complex'), see K. Adenauer, *Erinnerungen 1953–1955* (Stuttgart, 1966), 63–6; D. Acheson, *Present at the Creation: My Years in the State Department* (New York, 1969), 584–5; J. Chace, *Acheson: The Secretary of State Who Created the American World* (New York, 1998), 333; Schwarz, *Adenauer: Der Aufstieg*, 827–50; Köhler, *Adenauer*, 641ff. For Adenauer's general view of Britain, see Schwarz, ibid., 894–97, esp. 896, 828–9, 848, 857; H.P. Schwarz, 'Churchill and Adenauer', in R.A.C. Parker (ed.), *Winston Churchill: Studies in Statesmanship* (London, 1995), 172–82; also K. Schwabe, 'Adenauer und England', in L. Kettenacker et al. (eds), *Studien zur Geschichte Englands und der deutsch-britischen Beziehungen* (Munich, 1981), 353–74; D. Gossel, *Briten, Deutsche und Europa. Die Deutsche Frage in der britischen Außenpolitik 1945–1962* (Stuttgart, 1999); and the somewhat uncritical book by B. Leupold, 'Weder anglophil noch anglophob'. *Großbritannien im politischen Denken Konrad Adenauers* (Frankfurt/M., 1997).

13. For the visit which Adenauer regarded as highly important, see above all K. Adenauer, *Erinnerungen 1945–1953* (Stuttgart, 1965), 500–12; Leupold, ibid., 213ff.; Schwarz, *Adenauer. Der Aufstieg*, 894–97.

14. PRO: PREM 11/1852, C 1052/4, memorandum of the meeting between Churchill and Adenauer in London, 4/12/1951. Churchill had crossed out the words 'even to avoid a war' in red ink in the draft minutes of the meeting. For Adenauer's account along very similar lines, see his *Erinnerungen 1945–1953*, 508–9. See also the West German memorandum of the talk between Churchill and Adenauer on 4 December: *Akten zur Auswärtigen Politik*, 1951, 646–97.

15. PRO: ibid. See also Adenauer, ibid., 510; R. Morsey and H.P. Schwarz (eds), *Adenauer: Teegespräche 1950–54* (Berlin, 1985), 172; H. Blankenhorn, *Verständnis und Verständigung. Blätter eines politischen Tagebuchs 1949 bis 1979* (Frankfurt/M., 1980), 130. For Adenauer's 'Potsdam complex', see also n. 12, above.

16. Churchill had written to Stalin on 4 November: 'You sent me a message when I left office in 1945. Now that I am again the head of His Majesty's Government I wish to acknowledge that message with the word "Greetings"'. See FRUS 1951, Vol. 4, 695: letter Churchill to Truman, 9/11/1951 (and editorial comments); also PRO: FO 371/94 841/134, 4/11/1951; see also NA: PPS, 64D563, Box 17, Folder: Great Britain, 1951: minute James E. Webb, 'Meeting with the President', 5/11/1951 (the words but not the gist of Churchill's message to Stalin are quoted slightly differently here).

17. See for example Eden, 'Speech on Foreign Affairs', H.C. *Parl. Deb.*, 5th series, Vol.473, 28/3/1950, 317–18. John Young appears to exaggerate the continuity of Eden's approval of summit diplomacy in his otherwise convincing book. See his *Winston Churchill's Last Campaign: Britain and the Cold War, 1951–1955* (Oxford, 1996), e.g. 50.

18. Eden, 'Speech on Foreign Affairs', H.C. *Parl. Deb.*, 5th series, Vol. 484, 12/2/1951, 44–5.

19. For the conference, see P. Nitze, *From Hiroshima to Glasnost: At the Centre of Decision. A Memoir* (London, 1989), 71–7; for further literature, see Chapter 6, n. 83, above (p. 445).

20. Eden, 'Speech on Foreign Affairs', H.C. *Parl. Deb.*, 5th series, Vol. 484, 12/2/1951, 44–5.

21. PRO: CAB 21/1792, memorandum Makins, undated, 'Paris Talks: Brief on Relations with the USSR', written in preparation for Churchill's and Eden's visit to Paris in early December 1951. See also A. Eden, *Full Circle: Memoirs* (London, 1960), 11. For a good summary of Eden's political approach, see Young, *Last Campaign*, 50–1. He emphasizes that Eden did not view the world through ideological lenses, believed in the 'efficacy of secret, personal diplomacy', had an 'idealistic streak', was 'steeped in the logic of the balance of power' and preferred foreign ministers' meetings and 'incremental advances' to Churchill's grand diplomacy.

22. Eden, *Full Circle*, 9. Eden's aim was similar to Churchill's; he told the journalist Iverach McDonald of *The Times* that his 'one long-term aim in returning to the Foreign Office is to help in reducing tension between the two camps'. Quoted in V. Rothwell, *Anthony Eden: A Political Biography, 1931–1957* (Manchester, 1992), 113.

23. The meetings lasted from early November 1951 to 5 February 1952; an overview of the conclusions can be found in *Europa-Archiv*, VII/I, 5/3/1952, 4738–9.

24. PRO: FO 800/832, telegram No. 198, Eden to Bateman, Warsaw, 30/10/1951.

25. Ibid.

26. PRO: FO 800/694, letter Eden to S. Lloyd, 24/1/1952.

27. Ibid., telegram No. 574, Eden, Paris, to Foreign Office, 21/11/1951. For the internal discussions in the Foreign Office and the FO's Russia Committee, a think-tank concerned with the Soviet world which was chaired by P. Dixon and had originally been set up by Ernest Bevin, see Young, *Last Campaign*, 51, 53. In general most officials were in favour of attempting to re-open lines of communication with Moscow.

28. E. Shuckburgh, *Descent to Suez: Diaries, 1951–56* (London, 1986), 26. See also D.R. Thorpe, *Selwyn Lloyd* (London, 1989), who quotes Lloyd with the words: 'He [Vyshinsky] could be offensive in debate, but was always courteous in private' (p. 158). For Vyshinsky's 'diatribe of an hour and three-quarters', see also Acheson, *Present at the Creation*, 580.

29. *Akten zur Auswärtigen Politik, 1951*, 599: letter Blankenhorn to Adenauer, 7/11/1951.

30. PRO: FO 800/832, telegram No.574, Eden, Paris, to FO, 21/11/1951.

31. PRO: FO 800/832, telegram No. 961, FO to Eden in New York, 17/11/1951.

32. Ibid. The FO reminded Eden to ensure that Adenauer would be informed through the British High Commissioner in Bonn. He ought to be told that there was 'no question of doing a deal [with Moscow] behind Germany's back.'

33. PRO: FO 800/694, draft telegram reporting on Eden's conversation with the Soviet ambassador at the FO on 28/12/1951. See also the various minutes by Eden and his advisers in FO 371/100 825/1023/5, January 1952; also Shuckburgh, *Descent to Suez*, 50.

34. For Churchill's and Eden's talks with Truman, see 161ff., below. The British delegation returned to England on 28/1/1952. Although R.R. James, *Anthony Eden*, paperback edn (London, 1986), 358, claims that the Foreign Secretary did not participate in the visit, this is not correct; however, Eden returned a week earlier than Churchill. See for example, Eden, *Full Circle*, 18–20; Shuckburgh, *Descent to Suez*, 30–4; M. Gilbert, *Winston S. Churchill*, Vol. 8: *Never Despair, 1945–1965*, paperback edn (London, 1990), 672ff.

35. PRO: FO 800/694, letter Eden to S. Lloyd, 24/1/1952.

36. Ibid.

37. See Rothwell, *Anthony Eden*, 113. On the whole this also seems to be the view of Young, *Last Campaign*, 51–3, though he is somewhat more circumspect in his judgement.

38. See Rothwell, ibid., 112–14 (quote: 114).

39. See for example D. Carlton, *Anthony Eden: A Biography*, paperback edn (London, 1981), 331–2. In the literature Eden's initiative in 1951/2 is seldom mentioned. A notable exception is Young's *Last Campaign*, 51–3, also 113. For example Seldon, *Churchill's Indian Summer*, only refers to it in a footnote (p. 618, n. 20). Moreover, Seldon regards Eden's two attempts to arrange talks with Vyshinsky in November 1951 and January 1952 as two entirely separate episodes. He does not realize that they have to be seen as one interconnected policy. Rothwell also appears to assume this, see his *Anthony Eden*, 112–13.

40. Churchill, 'Debate on the Address,' H.C. *Parl. Deb.*, 5th series, Vol. 493, 6/11/1951, 80. Moreover, when Eden was ill in the summer of 1952, Churchill missed his advice a great deal and was relieved when he returned in August. See M. Soames (ed.), *Speaking for Themselves: The Personal Letters of Winston and Clementine Churchill*, paperback edn (London, 1998) 569: letter Churchill to his wife, 4/8/1952.

41. PRO: FO 800/696, letter Eden to Lloyd, 14/7/1953.

42. Lloyd, 'Speech on Foreign Affairs', H.C. *Parl. Deb.*, 5th series, Vol. 495, 5/2/1952, 926. See also Thorpe, *Selwyn Lloyd*, 161.

43. See for example, *Akten zur Auswärtigen Politik der Bundesrepublik Deutschland, 1952*, 32–3: memorandum Krekeler, West German Consul General in Washington, to Auswärtige Amt, on his conversation with Henry Byroade, the head of the German Section in the State Dept, who was present at some of the Churchill talks, 10/1/1952. For NATO Supreme Commander Eisenhower's attempt to enlist Truman's help to persuade Churchill to make 'a ringing statement' in British support of the EDC, see L. Galambos (ed.), *The Papers of Dwight David Eisenhower: NATO and the Campaign of 1952*, Vol. XII (Baltimore, Md., 1989), 841–2: letter Eisenhower to Truman, 4/1/1952.

44. For good overviews of Churchill's and Eden's visit, see above all Acheson, *Present at the Creation*, 595–606; also Eden, *Full Circle*, 35–7; Chace, *Acheson*, 334–7; PRO: CAB 21/3057, 3058; FRUS 1951, Vol. 4, 972–99; FRUS 1952–4, Vol. 6, 693ff.; Gilbert, *Never Despair*, 672–95; Young, *Last Campaign*, 67–87. Regarding the controversy over the Atlantic Command, see the memorandum on the final round of the discussions: FRUS 1952–4, Vol. 6, 846–57, 18/1/1952. For the initial British and American ideas regarding the agenda for the talks, see LOC: Harriman Papers, Box 332, Folder (i): Meeting Truman–Churchill, January 1952: TCT Memo-5 (message Churchill to Truman), dated 26/12/1951; letter Truman to Churchill, 27/12/1951; and TCT Memo-8 (message Eden), dated 2/1/1951; TCT Memo-9a ('Tentative Order of Subjects'), dated 5/1/1952.

45. For the speech, see R.R. James (ed.), *Winston S. Churchill: His Complete Speeches, 1987–1963, Vol. 8: 1950–63* (London, 1974), 8323–9.

46. See Young, *Last Campaign*, 87.

47. J. Colville, *The Fringes of Power: 10 Downing Street Diaries, 1939–1955* (New York, 1985), 637; LOC: Harriman Papers, Box 332, Folder (i), Meeting Truman-Churchill: Gifford, US ambassador to the UK, to Acheson, No.2903, 29/12/1951; FRUS 1952–4, Vol. 6, 709–12: State Dept, Paper, 21/12/1951; ibid., 720–1: Gifford to Dept. of State, 29/12/1951; also LOC: ibid., Negotiating Paper TCT D-2/1b, dated 28/12/1951, entitled 'Nature of the U.S.–U.K. Relationship'. See also A.P. Dobson, 'Informally Special? The Churchill-Truman Talks of January 1952 and the State of Anglo-American Relations', *Review of International Studies* 23/1 (1997), 27–47.

48. FRUS 1951, Vol. 4, 994: Bruce, ambassador to France, to Acheson, 19/12/1951; FRUS 1952–4, Vol. 6, 712: State Dept. Paper, 21/12/1951; LOC: Harriman Papers, Box 332, Folder (i), Gifford to Acheson, No.2903, 29/12/1951.

49. FRUS, ibid., 978: State Dept. paper, undated, *c.* late October 1951.

50. Ibid., Webb, Acting Secretary of State, to US embassy, London, 25/10/1951. These issues were above all Korea, Germany and disarmament problems.

51. LOC: Harriman Papers, Box 332, Folder (i), Meeting Truman-Churchill: Negotiating Paper TCT D-1/3a, dated 26/12/1951, entitled 'Big Four Meeting or Other High-Level Negotiations with the USSR'.

52. FRUS 1951, Vol. 4, 983: PPS paper 'The Nature of the US-UK Relationship', 20/11/1951; ibid., 987: Record of a joint staff meeting between Dept of State and the Joint Chiefs of Staff, Pentagon, 21/11/1951.

53. Ibid., Vol. 4, 991: memorandum Bohlen, 5/12/1951; see also the similar statement by Paul Nitze, 21/11/1951, ibid., 987; and Ambassador Gifford's views in FRUS 1952–4, Vol. 6, 724–5, 29/12/1951.

54. Ibid., Vol. 4, 987: Dept of State-Joint Chiefs of Staff Meeting, 21/11/1951.

55. LOC: Harriman Papers, Box 332, Folder (i), Meeting Truman-Churchill: Gifford, London, to Acheson, No. 2898, 28/12/1951; also No. 2903, 29/12/1951.

56. Ibid., Negotiating Paper TCT D-1/6, dated 6/1/1951, entitled 'Future Policy Toward the USSR' (drafted by the Policy Planning Staff and approved by State Dept. official Matthews).

57. For a good analysis of the differing views in the literature, see H. Jones and R.B. Woods, 'Origins of the Cold War in Europe and the Near East: Recent Historiography and the National Security Imperative', in M.J. Hogan, *America in the World: The Historiography of American Foreign Relations since 1941* (New York, 1995), 251–4. For Kennan's strategy, see J.L. Gaddis, *Strategies of Containment: A Critical Appraisal of Postwar American National Security Policy* (Oxford, 1982), chapters 2–4; also R. L. Russell, *George F. Kennan's Strategic Thought: The Making of an American Political Realist* (Westport, Conn., 1999).

58. FRUS 1951, Vol. 4, 983: PPS paper 'The Nature of the US–UK Relationship', 20/11/1951; ibid., 987: Record of a joint staff meeting between Dept of State and the Joint Chiefs of Staff, Pentagon, 21/11/1951.

59. LOC: Harriman Papers, Box 332, Folder (i), Meeting Truman-Churchill: TCT D-1/5a, dated 6/1/1952, entitled 'Political Warfare against USSR' (this is a shorter version of a previous paper approved by officials from both the State Dept. and the Pentagon, declassified in April 1998). The paper summa-

rizes the British position succinctly as follows: 'The British, in short, appear to believe that the immediate dangers of provokation overbalance the long-range deterrent results of political warfare carried on within Moscow's own orbit'. See also already Carlton, *Anthony Eden*, 331.

60.   Ibid. For the Truman administration and psychological warfare, see W.L. Hixson, *Parting the Curtain: Propaganda, Culture, and the Cold War, 1945–1961* (Basingstoke, 1998), 10–21.

61.   PRO: CAB 21/1792, memorandum Makins to Churchill entitled 'Paris Talks: Brief on Relations with the USSR, Annex II: Policy Towards Soviet Russia', undated, *c.* December 1951.

62.   NA: PPS, 64D563, Box 17, Folder: Great Britain, 1948–50: D.O.(50)45, dated 7/6/1950, Report by the Chiefs of Staff, 'Defence Policy and Global Strategy'. For further details, see also Chapter 6, 132, above.

63.   Ibid., Folder: Great Britain, 1952–3: British paper 'Future Policy Towards Soviet Russia', received from the British embassy, 7/1/1952, Top Secret (declassified in February 2000).

64.   For further details of Churchill's insights, see Chapter 11, below.

65.   NA: PPS, 64D563, Box 17, Folder: Great Britain, 1948–50: minute Thurston to Ferguson, 23/1/1952; also ibid., State-Joint Strategic Survey Committee meeting, 22/5/1952; memorandum 'Topics for Discussion with Policy Planning Group', undated; see also the memorandum 'U.S.-U.K. Political Military Talks', dated 5/2/1952. For NSC-68; see S.N. Drew (ed.), *NSC-68: Forging the Strategy of Containment* (Washington, DC, 1994); E. May (ed.), *American Cold War Strategy: Interpreting NSC 68* (Boston, 1993).

66.   NA: ibid., memorandum 'Topics for Discussion with Policy Planning Group', undated.

67.   Ibid., memorandum 'Comments on the British Paper entitled Future Policy Towards Soviet Russia', 25/3/1952.

68.   Ibid., memorandum, dated 25/4/1952, by the Policy Planning Staff on the British paper 'Future Policy Towards Soviet Russia'. This memorandum was itself rather extreme in its disparaging comments about the British concerns.

69.   Ibid.

70.   There is no clear evidence available for the perhaps not unreasonable assumption in view of the FO's opposition to Churchill's summit diplomacy that Britain's foreign policy experts attempted to undermine Churchill's talks in Washington by submitting a paper which would displease the American government.

71.   FRUS 1951, Vol. 4, 987: Record of a joint staff meeting between Dept. of State and the Joint Chiefs of Staff, Pentagon, 21/11/1951.

72.   J. Charmley, *Churchill's Grand Alliance: A Provocative Reassessment of the 'Special Relationship' between England and the US from 1940 to 1957* (New York, 1995), 254. There were, however, the occasional earlier pronouncements on the usefulness of 'spheres of influences' and the balance-of-power concept. See for example General Marshall's memorandum to the Under-Secretary, 'Subject: Cabinet Meeting', 7/11/1947; also the memoranda by J. Davies, 'Destruction of the Complex Balance of Power' and 'Peculiarities of the Current Struggle for Power', both dated 5/12/1949; and D. Fosdick, 'Nature of the Present Balance of Power', 6/12/1949; NA: PPS, 64D563, Box 10, Folder: General.

73.   FRUS 1951, Vol. 4, 987: memorandum Bohlen, 5/12/1951.

74.   Ibid.

75.   See for example Acheson, *Present at the Creation*, 633–4; and for a good account, see Young, *Last Campaign*, 55–6. For Truman's political paralysis due to McCarthy's crusade, see the classic account, R. Rovere, *Senator Joe McCarthy* (London, 1959), 15–19; also G.F. Kennan, *Memoirs, 1950–1963* (New York, 1972), ch. 9, esp. 226–8. See also A. Theoharis, *Seeds of Repression: Harry S. Truman and the Origins of McCarthyism* (Chicago, 1971); and in general E. Schrecker, *Many are the Crimes: McCarthyism in America* (Boston, 1998). See also the long review essay of relevant books on American anti-Communism by M. E. Parish, 'Soviet Espionage and the Cold War', *Diplomatic History* 25/1 (2001), 105–20.

76.   FRUS 1951, Vol. 4, 980–9: PPS Paper, 20/11/1951, Joint Meeting Dept. of State-Joint Chiefs of Staff, 21/11/1951; ibid., 991–3: memorandum Bohlen, 5/12/1951; FRUS 1952–4, Vol. 6, 720–9: Gifford, ambassador to the UK, 28 and 29/12/1951. On the Foreign Office and the State Department's somewhat differing Cold War strategies, see Young, *Last Campaign*, 68–72.

77.   See for example FRUS, 1951, Vol. 4, 975: memorandum Raynor, Director of the Office of British Commonwealth and Northern European Affairs, 18/10/1951. For good overviews of the development of the Korean War, see R. Whelan, *Drawing the Line: the Korean War, 1950–53* (London, 1990); R. Foot, *A Substitute for Victory: the Politics of Peacemaking at the Korean Armistice Talks* (Ithaca, N.Y., 1990); S.N. Goncharev, *Uncertain Partners: Stalin, Mao, and the Korean War* (Stanford, Calif., 1993); W.W. Stueck, *The Korean War: An International History* (Princeton, N.J.,

1995); P.G. Pierpaoli, *Truman and Korea: the Political Culture of the early Cold War* (Columbia, Miss., 1999); R.C. Thornton, *Odd Man Out: Truman, Stalin, Mao and the Origins of the Korean War* (Washington, DC, 2000); and for a recent brief history see S.H. Lee, *The Korean War* (Harlow, Essex, 2001). For a critical overview of the extensive literature, see P.M. Edwards (ed.), *The Korean War: An Annotated Bibliography* (Westport, Conn., 1998).

78. FRUS 1952–4, Vol. 6, 696–8 (quote: 698): memorandum McMahon to Truman, 5/12/1951; see also 699, n. 4; 702–3: memorandum of conversation between Webb and Truman, 10/12/1951. Truman told Churchill in a letter dated 13 December that he felt 'that conversations covering problems of such magnitude run along more smoothly if conducted according to a general plan of procedure. I am also having a list of subjects prepared' (ibid., 706); see also Churchill's letter to Truman, dated 10/12/1951 (ibid., 704–5).

79. LOC: Harriman Papers, Box 332, Folder (i), Meeting Truman-Churchill: TCT Memo-8, dated 2/1/1951 (message from Eden). However when reading the account of the final round of discussions on 18 January one gains the impression that Truman regretted not having dedicated more time to a personal chat with Churchill. See FRUS 1952–4, Vol. 6, 854, 18/1/1952. LOC: ibid., Gifford, London, to Acheson, No. 2898, 28/12/1951.

80. LOC: ibid., Gifford, London, to Acheson, No. 2898, 28/12/1951. See also n. 2, above. It was however rather condescending (though it did contain an element of truth) when in the same telegram Gifford praised Anthony Eden, at the time one of the world's most experienced foreign ministers, for 'developing real independent stature' and for the fact that despite Churchill's frequent opposition Eden was 'more and more inclined to stand up for his views'.

81. NA: PPS, 64D563, Box 17, Folder: Great Britain, 1947–53: memorandum 'U.S. Objectives in the Talks between President Truman and Prime Minister Churchill', dated 15/12/1951. The author of the paper viewed Britain's prospects to recover its economic fortunes in such a negative light that he believed that eventually the merger of Britain's sovereignty with the US and Canada would be necessary. He was, however, certainly right when he also concluded that the UK people were undergoing a 'still far from complete' change of view from 'an outward-looking, imperial, great power attitude toward an inward-looking, insular, secondary power attitude'. In an earlier paper official R.W. Tufts strongly believed that 'an offer by the United States of union with Western Europe might make the difference' regarding the general resolve and ability of Western Europe to resist Soviet Communism. See ibid., Box 10, Folder: General (memorandum Tufts to Nitze on the current world situation, 19/7/1950).

82. The Americans were for example most critical of Britain's 1952 'Defence Policy and Global Strategy' paper. The British seemed to downgrade the danger of Soviet Communism and the outbreak of war due to the country's dire economic situation. In fact, the UK had developed its own kind of 'new look' policy by attempting to rely much more than hitherto on the American atomic deterrence. Washington concluded that 'The British "judgment [sic] as to what the real requirements" of the Cold War were appeared to be clouded by "unrealistic rationalizations" for economic reasons'. The US also believed that 'the danger of a hot war in the near future was rather greater than did the United Kingdom'. See NA: PPS, 64D563, Box 17, Folder: Great Britain, 1952–3, Report by the UK Chiefs of Staff, dated 9/7/1952; memorandum on US-UK Politico-Military meeting regarding the COS's report, Washington, dated 9/7/1952; memorandum entitled 'Points to be Covered in Discussion with British', dated 31/7/1952. For a good analysis of the 1952 Global Strategy paper, see A.M. Johnston, 'Mr Slessor Goes to Washington: The Influence of the British Global Strategy Paper on the Eisenhower New Look', *Diplomatic History* 22/3 (1998), 361–98; and J. Baylis and A. Macmillan, 'The British Global Strategy Paper of 1952', *Journal of Strategic Studies* 16/2 (1993), 200–6.

83. H. Truman, *Memoirs, Vol. 2: Years of Trial and Hope, 1946–1952* (New York, 1955), 259.

84. FRUS 1952–4, Vol. 6, 693–5, 699–700 (early November 1951); PRO: FO 371/90 937/1,2,3 (early November 1951)

85. For Truman's dealing with Congress in 1947–8, see S.M. Hartmann, *Truman and the 80th Congress* (Columbia, Miss., 1971); for Congress and Churchill's visit, see Acheson, *Present at the Creation*, 592, 594, 596, 599, 601; see also Dulles's apprehension in January 1953 that Congress would gain the wrong impression if Churchill himself headed negotiations about Britain's financial problems, NA: PPS, 64D563, Box 17, Folder: Great Britain, 1952–3: 'Report by Mr. Dulles on Churchill Talks', 8/1/1953.

86. See the editorial note in FRUS 1952–4, Vol. 6, 729–30; and ibid., 693ff.

87. Acheson, *Present at the Creation*, 594; FRUS ibid., 860: R.A. Lovett, US Secretary of Defense, to D.D. Eisenhower, Supreme Allied Commander, Europe, 24/1/1954.

88. See Young, *Last Campaign*, 87.

89. For the importance the Americans attached to Britain playing its part in the Far East and elsewhere, see for example FRUS 1951, Vol. 4, 981: PPS paper 'The Nature of the US-UK Relationship', 20/11/1951. For a discussion considering the development of bases in Spain, see NA: PPS, 64D563, Box 17, Folder: Great Britain, 1952–3: State-Joint Strategic Survey Committee Meeting, 22/5/1952. For the role of Spain in the Cold War, see J. Edwards, *Anglo-American Relations and the Franco Question, 1945–1955* (Oxford, 1999), esp. chs 14 and 15.

90. See LOC: Harriman Papers, Box 332, Folder (i), Meeting Truman-Churchill: Gifford, London, to Acheson, No.2898, 28/12/1951; also FRUS 1951, Vol. 4, 988: Dept of State-Joint Chiefs of Staff Meeting, 21/11/1951; FRUS 1952–4 Vol. 6, 695: memorandum McMahon, Chairman of the Joint Committee on Atomic Energy, 5/12/1951; quote: Joint Communiqué by Truman and Churchill, 9/1/1952, ibid., 837. On Britain's economic position, see also the memorandum of the first formal meeting on 7 January 1952: FRUS 1952–4, Vol. 6, 746–5; also the memorandum of the Luncheon meeting on 8 January, ibid., 786–92; the memorandum of the internal meeting of the Dept. of the Treasury, 9/1/1952, ibid., 813–21; and for the eventual decision to grant economic aid of $300 million, see memorandum Bonbright, 3/3/1952, ibid., 865–7.

91. See FRUS 1951, Vol. 4, 986: Record of a joint meeting between the Dept. of State and the Joint Chiefs of Staff, Pentagon, 21/11/1951; FRUS 1952–4, Vol. 6, 703: memorandum of conversation between Webb, Under-Secretary of State, and Truman, 10/12/1951; also FRUS 1951, Vol. 4, 993: Bruce, ambassador to France, to Acheson, 19/12/1951. On the Churchill-Roosevelt relationship, see in detail Chapters 2–4, above.

92. LOC: Harriman Papers, Box 332, Folder (i), Meeting Truman-Churchill: Negotiating Paper TCT D-2/1b, dated 28/12/1951, entitled 'Nature of the U.S.–U.K. Relationship'. See also NA: PPS, 64D563, Box 17, Folder: Great Britain, 1947–53: memorandum Acheson to Lovett, 18/1/1951; memorandum of telephone conversation between Lovett and Acheson, 18/1/1951; memoranda: Lovett to Acheson, 24/1/1951; Jessup to Acheson, 2/2/1951; Acheson to Lovett, 7/2/1951; Lovett to Acheson, 9/2/1951.

93. Shuckburgh, *Descent to Suez*, 32: diary entry, 5/1/1952. Shuckburgh concluded: 'It was impossible not to be conscious that we are playing second fiddle.' See also FRUS, 1951, Vol. 4, 986: Policy Planning Staff Paper, 20/11/1951.

94. Acheson, *Present at the Creation*, 594.

95. Ibid., 580. Later Acheson concluded: 'No wonder foreign ministers dislike meetings at the summit, where their chiefs are likely to take the bit in their teeth and have a gay canter across country!' (ibid., 599).

96. FRUS 1952–4, Vol. 6, 736–7: memorandum Acheson on the talks on the *Williamsburg* on 5/1/1952 (his memorandum is dated 8/1/1952).

97. Ibid. 737.

98. See Acheson, *Present at the Creation*, 597–9; PRO: FO 371/124 998/12, 5/1/1952; on the Austrian question, see also FRUS 1952–4, Vol. 6, 839–41: memorandum of a talk between Eden and Acheson, 10/1/1952.

99. FRUS, ibid. 736. See also ibid., 740: memorandum regarding the evening on board the *Williamsburg* by Gen. Omar Bradley, the Chairman of the Joint Chiefs of Staff, undated.

100. Lord Moran, *Churchill: The Struggle for Survival, 1940–1965* (London, 1966), 355: diary entry, 5/1/1952. During his visit to Ottawa, just over a week later and before returning and completing his talks in Washington, Churchill still expressed 'unreserved expressions [of] satisfaction' with respect to his negotiations in Washington. See LOC: Harriman Papers, Box 332, Folder (ii): Meeting Truman-Churchill, Jan. 1952: telegram No. 114, Woodward, Ottawa, to Acheson, 14/1/1952.

101. FRUS 1952–54, Vol.6, 731: memorandum Acheson regarding the talks on board the *Williamsburg* on 5/1/1952 (his memorandum is dated 8/1/1952).

102. Acheson, *Present at the Creation*, 597.

103. Ibid., 595. Other American observers came to similar, and occasionally even to more devastating conclusions about the state of Churchill's health and attention span; see also Shuckburgh, *Descent to Suez*, 32–3; Moran, *Struggle for Survival*, 351–71.

104. For Churchill's assessments of his talks in Washington as conveyed to the Canadian authorities, see LOC: Harriman Papers, Box 332, Folder (ii): Meeting Truman-Churchill, Jan. 1952: telegram No. 114, Woodward, Ottawa, to Acheson, 14/1/1952. For the final round of talks, see above all PRO: CAB 21/3058, and CAB 21/3057, folder 9/102, accounts of the 5th plenary session; FRUS 1952–4, Vol. 6, 846–57: Final Truman-Churchill meeting, 18/1/1952; see also the accounts in Gilbert, *Never Despair*, 691–2; M. Gilbert, *Churchill: A Life* (London, 1991), 903; and more detailed Young, *Last Campaign*, 84–7. See also the articles published in the *Daily Telegraph* and the *Morning Post*, in PRO: CAB 21/3057, folder 9/102.

105. PRO: CAB 21/3058, 5th plenary meeting, 18/1/1952; FRUS 1952–4, Vol. 6, 848–9.
106. Ibid.
107. PRO: ibid.; also Gilbert, *Never Despair*, 691–2.
108. PRO: CAB 21/3057, Folder 9/102, dated 8/2/1952; also FRUS 1951, Vol. 4, 987: Joint staff meeting between the Dept. of State and the Joint Chiefs of Staff, 21/11/1951. See also Shuckburgh, *Descent to Suez*, 32: diary entry, 5/1/1952. Truman would repeat this offer frequently.
109. FRUS 1951, ibid.
110. FRUS 1952–4, Vol. 6, 852, 849: Final Truman-Churchill meeting, 18/1/1952.
111. Letter Churchill to his wife, 20/1/1952, in: Soames (ed.), *Speaking for Themselves*, 563.
112. This is also Clive Ponting's conclusion; see his *Churchill* (London, 1995), 766. Yet, *Newsweek* wrote: 'Not since the war had relations between Britain and the United States been put on such a friendly cooperative basis.' This put a rather exaggerated gloss on the Anglo-American meetings. See R.H. Pilpel, *Churchill in America, 1895–1961: An Affectionate Portrait* (New York, 1976), 250–1 (quote: 251); less optimistic was Moran, *Struggle for Survival*, 371: diary entry, 26/1/1952.
113. PRO: CAB 21/3057, Folder 9/102, dated 8/2/1952.

CHAPTER 9: BETWEEN PESSIMISM AND NEW HOPE

1. The so-called Stalin Note including the proposed text for a German peace treaty is published in RIIA, *Documents on International Affairs, 1952* (London, 1955), 85–9. The Note and the ensuing 'battle of the notes' is also well documented in FRUS 1952–4, Vol. 7, Part 1, 169–327: Exchanges of Notes with the Soviet Union [...], March 10–Sept. 23, 1952; see also RIIA, *Documents, 1952*, 85–105, 175–7, 186–97. See also the still valuable collections of documents by E. Jäckel (ed.), *Die deutsche Frage 1952–56. Notenwechsel und Konferenzdokumente der Vier Mächte* (Frankfurt/Berlin, 1957); I. von Münch (ed.), *Dokumente des geteilten Deutschland*, Vol. 1 (Stuttgart, 1968). See also the British Command Papers Cmd.8501 (10/25 March), Cmd.8551 (9/13 May), Cmd.8610 (10/24 July, 23 August, 23 September 1952). For the internal British reaction to the notes, see PRO: PREM 11/168, FO telegram No. 1126 to Embassy Washington, 13/3/1952; also No.1182, 15/3/1952; No. 1206, 18/3/1952; also FO 371/97 877–92; and PREM 11/168; FO 800/793; FO 800/777, Eden to Prime Minister, PM/52/26, 18/3/1952 (regarding the attitude of the Foreign Affairs Committee). For the American reaction, see FRUS ibid., 172ff.; for an analysis of the French government's reaction, see N. Meyer-Landrut, *Frankreich und die deutsche Einheit. Die Haltung der französischen Regierung und Öffentlichkeit zu den Stalin-Noten 1952* (Munich, 1988); for Adenauer's and the West German reaction, see K. Adenauer, *Erinnerungen, 1953–55* (Stuttgart, 1966), 66–131; also H. Köhler, *Adenauer: Eine politische Biographie* (Frankfurt, 1994), 681–97.
2. See RIIA, *Survey of International Affairs, 1952* (London, 1953), 178, n.2; RIIA, *Documents, 1952*, 240.
3. See R. Steininger, *The German Question: The Stalin Note of 1952 and the Problem of Reunification* (New York, 1990). See also the contemporary criticism in an interesting memorandum written by Labour left-winger Richard Crossman, 'Notes on the Russian "Peace Offensive" ', 20/3/1952, PRO: CAB 127/211. For the most recent comprehensive analyses by many of the experts in the field, see J. Zarusky (ed.) *Die Stalin-Note vom 10. Mätz 1952. Neue Quellen und Analysen* (Munich, 2002).
4. H. Graml, 'Die Legende von der verpaßten Gelegenheit. Zur sowjetischen Notenkampagne des Jahres 1952', *Vierteljahrshefte für Zeitgeschichte* 29 (1981) 307–41; G. Wettig, 'Stalin and German Reunification: Archival Evidence on Soviet Foreign Policy in Spring 1952', *Historical Journal* 37/2 (1994), 411–19; G. Wettig, *Bereitschaft zu Einheit in Freiheit? Die sowjetische Deutschland-Politik 1945–1955* (Munich, 1999), 215–34; M. Kittel, 'Zur Genesis einer Legende. Die Diskussion um die Stalin-Noten in der Bundesrepublik 1952–1958', *Vierteljahrshefte für Zeitgeschichte* 41 (1993), 355–90. For reliable overviews see also, H. Booms, 'Einleitung', in Booms (ed.), *Die Kabinettsprotokolle der Bundesregierung*, Vol. 5: 1952 (Boppard, 1988), li–lvi; P. März, *Die Bundesrepublik zwischen Westintegration und Stalin-Noten* [...] (Frankfurt/M., 1982); H. Adomeit, *Imperial Overstretch: Germany in Soviet Policy from Stalin to Gorbachev* (Baden-Baden, 1998), 87–92. See also the continuation of the debate about Moscow's German policy between 1945–52 in *Deutschland-Archiv* 33/2 (2000), 391–8 (W. Daschitschew) and 399–416 (G. Wettig).
5. First quote: NA: PPS 64D563, Box 16, Folder: Germany, 1950–3: memorandum R.M. Scammon and R.W. Tufts to P. Nitze, 'Outline of factors bearing on the Western reply to the Soviet note on

Germany', 14/3/1952. Second quote: ibid., memorandum J.H. Ferguson to P. Nitze, 'Possible Russian Reactions to Alternative Western Replies to Russian Note on Germany', 18/3/1952.

6. For regular updates on the declassification of newly available archival material, see above all the information in the *Bulletins* of the *Cold War International History Project* at the Woodrow Wilson Center in Washington, D.C. (website: cwihp.si.edu) and the *Parallel History Project on NATO and the Warsaw Pact* (PHP) (website: www.isn.ethz.ch/php); see also the Cold War website of the PRO: http://learningcurve. pro.gov.uk/coldwar/.

7. See for example, the views of the influential West German Liberal MP Karl Georg Pfleiderer, *Politik für Deutschland, Reden und Aufsätze 1948–1956* (Stuttgart, 1961), 83ff.; and for a good analysis, see K.H. Schlarp, 'Alternativen zur deutschen Außenpolitik 1952–5. Karl-Georg Pfleiderer und die deutsche Frage', in W. Benz and H. Graml (eds), *Aspekte deutscher Außenpolitik im 20. Jahrhundert* (Stuttgart, 1976), 211–48. For the position of the SPD, see for example G.D. Drummond, *The German Social Democrats in Opposition, 1949–1960. The Case against Rearmament* (Norman, Okl. 1982); D.C. Large, *Germans to the Front: West German Rearmament in the Adenauer Era* (Chapel Hill, N.C., 1996). The most prominent journalist arguing in favour of 'checking out' the Stalin Note was Paul Sethe of the *Frankfurther Allgemeine Zeitung*. See his book *Öffnung nach Osten. Weltpolitische Realitäten zwischen Bonn, Paris und Moskau* (Frankfurt/M., 1966), 44–6.

8. See Adenauer, *Erinnerungen, 1953–55*, 69–73.

9. For the western negotiations leading to the contractual agreements, see FRUS 1952–4, Vol. 7, 1–168; the documents give a good though not a complete overview of the discussions.

10. This was Dean Acheson's phrase, see his *Present at the Creation: My Years in the State Department* (New York, 1969), 630. See also *Akten zur Auswärtigen Politik, 1952*, 244: memorandum Blank to Adenauer, 29/3/1952. Adenauer's defence expert Theodor Blank believed that it was only because of the intervention of French Foreign Minister Schuman and NATO Supreme Commander Eisenhower that the American and British governments reconsidered their position and did not reply in a friendly way to Stalin and propose a four-power conference, to be convened in May, as they had initially intended.

11. See for example FRUS 1952–4, Vol. 7, 186–8; Bonsal, Paris, to Dept. of State, 20/3/1952; ibid., 189–90: Acheson to US High Commission in Bonn, 22/3/1952; Acheson, ibid., 631.

12. FRUS, ibid., 189–90: Acheson to US High Commission in Bonn, 22/3/1952 (quote: 190); also ibid., 192–3: Acheson to US embassy in London, 25/3/1952; ibid., 194–9: memorandum Pollack, 2/4/1052; see also Acheson, *Present at the Creation*, 631.

13. For Adenauer's declaration to Churchill, see his *Erinnerungen 1945–53*, 506. For American considerations on the EDC, see the interesting memoranda reflecting the thinking of George Kennan, NA: PPS 64D563, Box 16, Folder: Germany, 1950–3: US embassy London to Paul Nitze, Parts I and II, 26/9/1952. It becomes clear that for many American officials (and probably for Adenauer too) the EDC was an instrument to appease the French; the EDC was not regarded as an alternative to German membership of NATO. In fact, the EDC was seen as a stepping stone to Germany's eventual NATO membership.

14. See FRUS, 1952–4, Vol. 7, 199–202, 9/4/1952 (quote: p. 201).

15. Ibid., 247–52, 24/5/1952; Adenauer, *Erinnerungen, 1953–55*, 98–105.

16. For the western considerations, see FRUS, ibid., 202–42 (10/4–12/5/1952); also 252–88 (25/5–8/7/1952). See also Adenauer, *Erinnerungen 1953–55*, 76–98, 98ff.; also the interesting discussions taking place within the US Policy Planning Staff. NA: PPS 64D563, Box 16, Folder: Germany, 1950–3: e.g. memorandum Tufts to Nitze, 12/3/1952; memorandum Ferguson to Nitze, 18/3/1952; memorandum Ferguson to Acheson, 27/3/1952.

17. NA: PPS 64D563, Box 16, Folder: Germany, 1950–53: memorandum H. Koch 'Preconditions for German Unification', 26/10/1951.

18. Eden referred to the West Germans; he does not seem to have been too concerned about the fate of the East Germans in the GDR. PRO: CAB 128/25, C.C. (52) 102nd Conclusions, 4/12/1952. The Commonwealth Prime Ministers of Canada, New Zealand, Ceylon, Australia, Pakistan, Rhodesia and the Finance Ministers of South Africa and India attended the Cabinet meeting as guests.

19. See for example Adenauer, *Erinnerungen 1953–55*, 75; A. Eden, *Full Circle: Memoirs* (London, 1960), 45–6; Blankenhorn, *Verständnis und Verständigung: Blätter eines politischen Tagebuchs 1949 bis 1979* (Frankfurt/M., 1980), 132–8.

20. PRO: PREM 11/171, telegram FO to Washington, No 1107, 12/3/1952.

21. Both treaties including all appendices are published in RIIA, Documents, 1952, 105–70. For an excellent summary of the complicated negotiations which led to the signing of the treaties, see

H. Booms, 'Einleitung', in Booms (ed.), *Kabinettsprotokolle der Bundesregierung*, Vol. 5: 1952, xxx–xlvi.

22. See FRUS, 1952–4, Vol. 7, 255: Bruce, Acting Secretary of State, to US embassy in France, 26/5/1952; also Eden, *Full Circle*, 46; Adenauer, *Erinnerungen 1953–55*, 66ff., 104ff.; also H.P. Schwarz, *Die Ära Adenauer. Gründerjahre der Republik 1949–1957*, new edn (Wiesbaden, 1994), 156ff.

23. For the four western notes of 25 March, 13 May, 10 July and finally 23 Sept., see FRUS 1952–4, Vol. 7, 189–90, 242–7, 288–91, 324–6 (the western conditions for German unification are particularly well summarized in the final note as, at the time, it was of course unknown that the Kremlin would not reply to this note). See also NA: PPS 64D563, Box 16, Folder: Germany, 1950–3: memorandum Tufts to Nitze, 12/3/1952; memorandum Ferguson to Nitze, 18/3/1952; memorandum Ferguson to Acheson, 27/3/1952.

24. See for example NA: PPS 64D563, Box 16, Folder: Germany, 1950–2: minute L.H. Pollack, 'Notes on April 11 Meeting in Mr Nitze's Office to Discuss Problems of Free Elections in Germany', 11/4/1952; also B.H. Morris, 'Memorandum for the Files: United States Policy on Four-Power Talks and Investigation of Conditions for Free Elections in Germany'.

25. FRUS 1952–4, Vol. 7, 200: Soviet note of 9 April 1952.

26. Ibid., 256: Eden, as quoted in Acheson, Paris, to Dept. of State, 28/5/1952. For the western strategy, see also the good analysis in T.A. Schwartz, *America's Germany: John J. McCloy and the Federal Republic of Germany* (Cambridge, Mass., 1991), 263–9.

27. In his memoirs Acheson claims that Adenauer came out in favour of a four-power meeting in response to the Stalin Note of 10 March 1952 (see *Present at the Creation*, 630). This is clearly wrong; Acheson may have mixed up Adenauer's position with the one he assumed a year later in response to Churchill's proposal. See Chapter 13, 274ff., below.

28. For evidence, see the various minutes and memoranda in PRO: PREM 11/168; FO 371/100 830/1,3; FO 371/100 841, 8, 9; FO 371/97 877/11–15 (all January–March 1952). For the Berlin conference, see Chapter 15, below, 318ff.

29. *Akten zur Auswärtigen Politik, 1952*, 493–4, n. 2: memorandum Krapf, Consul in Paris, to Auswärtiges Amt, c. 25/6/1952. It was also thought that Churchill was under pressure from the Labour opposition.

30. Acheson, *Present at the Creation*, 631.

31. See NA: PPS 64D563, Box 16, Folder: Germany, 1950–3: memorandum H. Koch, 'Preconditions for German Unification', 26/10/1951.

32. For Churchill's vague hope in this respect, see for example, Adenauer, *Erinnerungen 1945–1953* (Stuttgart, 1965), 508. It could of course be argued, and some scholars do so, that Adenauer and the western powers ultimately achieved their objective in 1989/90 with a delay of a few decades. While at first sight this seems to be correct, it entirely ignores the dynamic driven by détente, West German *Ostpolitik* and the Helsinki process in the 1970s which decisively contributed to this outcome. It also ignores the developments in 1989/90 which were driven much more by the internal situation in the USSR and its satellite states than by the activities of the western world. Thus, without the developments begun in the 1970s and the internal events in the East in 1989/90 it is very doubtful that the West's strategy of the 1950s alone would have been sufficient to achieve the general acceptance of the reunification of Germany on a westernized democratic basis and fully integrated into both the EU and NATO.

33. See for example Selwyn Lloyd's famous statement that 'everyone – Dr. Adenauer, the Russians, the Americans, the French and ourselves – feel in our hearts that a divided Germany is safer for the time being. But none of us dare say so openly because of the effect upon German public opinion. Therefore we all publicly support a united Germany, each on his own terms' (PRO: FO 371/103 665/C 1071/56, memorandum Lloyd to Churchill, PM/MS/53/254, 22/6/53). This also explains, of course, British Prime Minister Thatcher's and French President Mitterrand's initial hesitancy in supporting German unification in 1989/90. See L. Kettenacker, 'Britain and German Unification, 1989/90', in K. Larres (ed. with E. Meehan), *Uneasy Allies: British-German Relations and European Integration since 1945* (Oxford, 2000), 99–123; also K. Larres, 'Ein Englisches Dilemma. Wie Margaret Thatcher die Wiedervereinigung verhindern wolte […], *Die Zeit*, No. 40 (28 September 2000), 7–6.

34. For the note, see FRUS 1952–4, Vol. 7, 324–6, 23/9/1952.

35. *Akten zur Auswärtigen Politik, 1952*, 482: memorandum of conversation between Adenauer and McCloy, 17/6/1952.

36. See A. Hillgruber, *Alliierte Pläne für eine 'Neutralisierung' Deutschlands 1945–55* (Opladen, 1987), 21. There are no documents in the British Public Record Office which indicate that Churchill had any great interest in 'the battle of the notes'.

37. See Schwartz, *America's Germany*, 265.

38. PRO: PREM 11/168, minute Churchill to Eden, M.235/52, 13/4/1952 (see also FO 800/793).

39. See J.W. Young, *Winston Churchill's Last Campaign: Britain and the Cold War, 1951–1955* (Oxford, 1996) 97–98.

40. In particular, he would demonstrate this in the months after Stalin's death. See Chapters 12–14.

41. PRO: CAB 128/24, CC(52)29, 12/3/1952.

42. For a good overview of Churchill's health problems in 1952, see Young, *Last Campaign*, 88–90; Lord Moran, *Churchill: The Struggle for Survival, 1940–1965* (London, 1966), 351–95.

43. PRO: FO 371/106 537, 1044/2/53 G, reported in letter Steel, British embassy Washington, to Mason, FO, 16/1/1953. See also J. Colville, *The Fringes of Power: 10 Downing Street Diaries, 1939–1955* (New York, 1985), 660: diary entry, 5/1/1953.

44. See Churchill, 'Oral Answers: International Situation,' in H.C. *Parl. Deb.*, Vol. 511, 9/2/1953, 28–32; ibid., 12/2/1953, 597–8.

45. Colville, *Fringes of Power*, 650: diary entry, 13–15.6.1952.

46. Ibid., 654: diary entry, 22–5/8/1952. See also J. Colville's essay in J. Wheeler-Bennett (ed.), *Action this Day. Working with Churchill* (London, 1984), 129.

47. See for example S. E. Ambrose, 'Churchill and Eisenhower in the Second World War', in R. Blake and W.R. Louis (eds), *Churchill* (Oxford, 1993), 397–405. For the time when Eisenhower was NATO's Supreme Commander, see L. Galambos (ed.), *The Papers of Dwight David Eisenhower: Nato and the Campaign of 1952* (Baltimore, Md., 1989), Vol. XII, 399–400, 414–15, 621–2, 665–6, 790–803, 809–10. Churchill, however, had not always dealt particularly tactfully with Eisenhower after 1945 (see e.g. Galambos (ed.), ibid., 174–5, 191.

48. Galambos (ed.), ibid., 810. This is also confirmed by Churchill's Private Secretary, see A. Montague Browne, *Long Sunset: Memoirs of Winston Churchill's Last Private Secretary* (London, 1995), 154–5.

49. The British government would have preferred to see Democratic candidate Adlai Stevenson win the presidential election. See BUA: Avon Papers, AP/20/16/23, letter Makins to Eden, 9/1/1953. See also Colville, *Fringes of Power*, 654: diary entry, 9/11/1952; also P. Boyle, 'Introduction,' in P. Boyle (ed.), *The Churchill-Eisenhower Correspondence, 1953–1955* (Chapel Hill, N.C., 1990), 3. Interview with Sir Anthony Nutting, former Deputy Under-Secretary and Minister of State in the FO, on 23/1/1991 in London.

50. HL: Beaverbrook Papers, BBK, C/57, Bracken B, 1948–53, letter Bracken to Beaverbrook, dated 12/2/1953.

51. As reported by Anthony Montague Browne, one of Churchill private secretaries who eventually accompanied him into private life as his trusted aid after his retirement in 1955. See Montague Browne, *Long Sunset*, 146. For Dulles's earlier career, see the excellent book by R. W. Pruessen, *John Foster Dulles. The Road to Power* (New York, 1982); also K. Larres, 'Die Welt des John Foster Dulles (1939–1953)', *Historische Mitteilungen* 9/2 (1996), 256–82.

52. PRO: PREM 11/323, Eden from New York to Churchill, telegram No. 780 (PM's Personal Telegram T.212/52), 12/11/1952; see also Boyle (ed.), *Correspondence*, 11; Colville, *Fringes of Power*, 661–2: diary entry, 6/11/1953.

53. See R. H. Immerman, *John Foster Dulles: Piety, Pragmatism, and Power in U.S. Foreign Policy* (Wilmington, Del., 1999), 44–5. The accounts in the literature are often contradictory on this matter. See T. Hoopes, *The Devil and John Foster Dulles* (Boston, 1973), 135–6; R. Drummond and G. Coblentz, *Duel at the Brink: John Foster Dulles' Command of American Power* (London, 1960), 31; S.E. Ambrose, *Eisenhower, Vol. 2: The President, 1952–1969* (London, 1984), 20–2; and R.A. Divine, *Eisenhower and the Cold War* (Oxford, 1981), 20–1.

54. For Eisenhower's relationship with Smith, see W. Snyder, 'Walter Bedell Smith. Eisenhower's Chief of Staff', *Military Affairs* 48 (1984), 6–14. For Eisenhower's motives, see also P. Grose, *Gentleman Spy: The Life of Allen Dulles* (Boston, 1994), 334–5.

55. See Drummond and Coblentz, *Duel at the Brink*, 31–2; Hoopes, *The Devil*, 145–6.

56. However, according to Immerman, *Dulles*, 45, it was exactly the fact that Dulles could not be regarded as representing a bipartisan foreign policy and his 'oversimplification' in his public rhetoric which had made Eisenhower hesitate to appoint him Secretary of State. PRO: PREM 11/323, Eden from Washington to PM, No. 852 (PM's Personal Telegram No. T.221/52), 20/11/1952; PREM 11/323/AU 1018/68 G, dated 4/12/1952, memorandum C. Steel on Eden's conversation with Eisenhower on 20/11/1952 (the phrases quoted were used in this memorandum). See also E. Shuckburgh, *Descent to Suez: Diaries, 1951–56* (London, 1986), 55, also 50, 52.

57. Churchill and Eisenhower saw each other at the home of Bernard Baruch, where the Prime Minister stayed during his visit to New York, in the late afternoon and then for dinner on 5 January (the day

Churchill arrived in New York); they telephoned on 6 January and saw each other again on 7 January. Churchill spoke twice with Dulles on 6 and 7 January before flying to Washington on 8 January to say farewell to Truman; he left for a holiday on Jamaica the day after. See Galambos (ed.), *Papers of Dwight D. Eisenhower*, Vol. XIII (see note 47 above), notes on pp. 1483–4, 1451. See also M. Gilbert, *Winston S. Churchill, Vol. 8: Never Despair, 1945–1965*, paperback edn (London, 1990) 789–94; Young, *Last Campaign*, 113–20. During his talks with Dulles Churchill did not mention his summit diplomacy; instead Britain's enforced non-participation in the ANZUS treaty, the EDC, Iran and the UK's economic situation were discussed. Churchill even suggested to stay an extra week in Jamaica and then return to Washington for talks on the convertibility of sterling and similar issues but Dulles convinced him that it would be more appropriate if such talks were to take place with Eden and Chancellor of the Exchequer Butler in February/March 1953. See NA: PPS, 64D563, Box 17, Folder: Great Britain, 1952–53: 'Report by Mr. Dulles on Churchill Talks', 8/1/1953.

58. Colville, *Fringes of Power*, 661: diary entry, 7/1/1953. For the Churchill-Eisenhower talks, see PRO: CAB 21/3057; PREM 11/422, 373; FO 371/106 537; FO 800/836; FRUS 1952–4, Vol. 6, 881–7; EL: John Foster Dulles Papers, Subject Series, Folder: Classified Material, 'Churchill may propose', 5/1/1953; Colville, ibid., 657ff.; D.D. Eisenhower, *The White House Years, Vol. 1: Mandate for Change, 1953–1956* (London, 1963), 97.

59. Quotes: L. Galambos (ed.), *The Papers of Dwight D. Eisenhower, Vol. VII: Eisenhower. The Chief of Staff* (Baltimore, Md., 1978), 686; R. Ferrell (ed.), *The Eisenhower Diaries* (New York, 1981), 222: diary entry, 6/1/1953; see also R. Griffith (ed.), *Ike's Letters to a Friend, 1941–58* (Lawrence, Ks., 1985), 140; Galambos (ed.), ibid., Vol. XIII, 1481: diary entry, 6/1/1953.

60. FRUS 1952–4, Vol. 6, 882: Memorandum of a conversation between Dulles and Churchill, 8/1/1953; Galambos (ed.), ibid., Vol. XIII, 1481–2: diary entry, 6/1/1953; Eisenhower even spoke of Churchill's 'almost childlike faith that all of the answers are to be found merely in British-American partnership' (p. 1482). See also NA: PPS, 64D563, Box 17, Folder: Great Britain, 1952–3: 'Report by Mr. Dulles on Churchill Talks', 8/1/1953. See also D.C. Watt, 'Churchill und der Kalte Krieg', *Schweizer Monatshefte* 61, No. 11 (1981), 18.

61. See Ferrell (ed.), *Eisenhower Diaries*, 222–4: diary entry, 6/1/1953; Galambos (ed.), ibid., 1482–3. Eisenhower believed that Churchill thought he and the American President were still 'sitting on some rather Olympian platform with respect to the rest of the world, and directing world affairs from that point of vantage' although even during the Second World War this had been at best partially true. While Churchill was not proposing to 'resort to power politics' the new President was convinced that Churchill tended to 'take the rather old-fashioned, paternalistic, approach' to international affairs. See Galambos (ed.), ibid.

62. Galambos (ed.), ibid., Vol. XII, 810: diary entry, 21/12/1951. At the time Eisenhower also noticed that Churchill was getting rather deaf; in early July 1951 Churchill had even admitted this to Eisenhower himself. See ibid., 822 (28/12/1951), 415 (early July 1951).

63. Churchill's correspondence with Eisenhower in the first six months of 1953 conveys this impression. See Boyle (ed.), *Correspondence*, 16ff. This correspondence can also be found in PRO: PREM 11/422 and partially in FRUS 1952–4, Vol. 6, 975ff., and Vol. 8, 1166ff.

64. Quote: Montague Browne, *Long Sunset*, 155. It is difficult, however, to agree with Montague Browne's recollection that Eisenhower's letters to Churchill 'were bland, and generally negative' with 'the mark of several drafters'. Ibid.

65. BUA: Avon Papers, AP/20/16/23, letter Makins to Eden, 9/1/1953. For a similar account, see Lord Beaverbrook's letter to Bracken, 15/1/1953, HL: Beaverbrook Papers, BBK, C/57, Bracken B., 1948–53. For a similar assessment, see Young, *Last Campaign*, 118–20.

66. Quotes: C.J. Pach and E. Richardson, *The Presidency of Dwight D. Eisenhower*, rev. edn (Lawrence, Ks., 1991), 40, 7.

67. PRO: PREM 11/422, Churchill from New York to Eden and Butler, No. 34, 8/1/1953; FO 371/106 537/NS 1071/29/6, minutes by Colville of the conversation between Eisenhower and Churchill, 7/1/1953; Moran, *Struggle for Survival*, 462: diary entry, 26/8/1953; see also J. Foschepoth, 'Churchill, Adenauer und die Neutralisierung Deutschlands', *Deutschland-Archiv* 17 (1984), 1287; Gilbert, *Never Despair*, 790–1.

68. Shuckburgh, *Descent to Suez*, 74: diary entry, 16/1/1953.

69. PRO: PREM 11/422, Churchill from New York to Eden and Butler in London, No. 34, 8/1/1953. See also FO 371/106 537/NS 1044/2/53G, letter Steel, British embassy in Washington, to Mason, FO, 16/1/1953.

70. PRO: FO 371/106 537/NS 1071/29/6, minutes by Colville of the conversation between Eisenhower and Churchill, 7/1/1953. See also PREM 11/422, ibid.

71. For documentation regarding Stalin's interview at this time, see n. 82, below.

72. LOC: Harriman Papers, Box 339, Folder: 'Trends in Soviet Policy': Documents NATOP D-5c (NATO Ministerial Meeting, Paris), dated 14/12/1952; C-M(52)116 (report by a Working Group establ. on 8/10/1952 by the North Atlantic Council), dated 1/12/1952.

73. Ibid., NS 1071/30/6, letter Mason, FO, to C. Steel, British embassy Washington, 3/2/1953. See also FO 371/106 524/NS 1021/19/G, Joint Services Staff College, 'Basic Factors in Soviet Policy. The Communist State in Theory and Practice', Part 2, ii and iii, c. 27/2 and 30/3/1953.

74. However, the FO's Russia Committee, the think-tank of senior FO officials dealing with Soviet affairs, did not agree with Churchill's view that the danger of war emanating from Moscow had decreased. See PRO: FO 371/106 524/NS 1021/11, minute Roberts to Mason, 19/1/1953. See Chapter 10, below, for the time after Stalin's death.

75. Ibid., NS 1021/8, letter Gascoigne, Moscow, to Eden, FO, 23/12/1952.

76. Ibid., letter Eden to Gascoigne, 12/1/1953.

77. Ibid., 1044/2/53 G, letter Steel, Washington, to Mason, FO, 16/1/1953.

78. The inaugural address is publ. in *Public Papers of the Presidents of the USA: Dwight D. Eisenhower, 1953* (Washington, DC, 1954), 1–8.

79. FRUS 1952–4, Vol. 8, 1079 (editorial note); Eisenhower, ibid., 69–70; also PRO: PREM 11/422.

80. Quote: FRUS, ibid.; see also Foschepoth, 'Churchill, Adenauer', 1287.

81. See for example Pach and Richardson, *Presidency of Dwight D. Eisenhower*, 26, 45–6; Immerman, *Dulles*, 68; also E.C. Keefer, 'President Dwight D. Eisenhower and the End of the Korean War', *Diplomatic History* 10/3 (1986), 267–89; B. Pierson, *Ike: The Life and Times of Dwight D. Eisenhower* (London, 1987), 226–7, 236–7. For the military developments in Korea, see Chapter 8, 167, above.

82. For the interview see, RIIA, *Survey, 1952*, 179, n. 2; RIAA, *Documents, 1952*, 244. See also PRO: FO 371/106 524/NS 1021/3, Dixon to Eden, 29/12/1952; NS 1071/5, William D. Allen to the FO's Northern Dept., 2/1/1953; NA: 761.11/1/853, Lyon, Berlin, to Dulles, No. 1016, 8/1/1953; 611.61/1–2653, reports of two Costa Rican papers, *La Prensa* and *La Republica*, on a possible meeting between Stalin and Eisenhower, 27/1/1953; see also Young, *Last Campaign*, 115–16.

83. S. Adams, *First-Hand Report: The Inside Story of the Eisenhower-Administration* (London, 1961), 96. For a brief assessment of Adams' important position, see Pach and Richardson, *Presidency of Dwight D. Eisenhower*, 39, 43. See also the interesting review article by John Lukacs, 'The Fifties: Another View. Revising the Eisenhower Era', *Harper's Magazine* (Jan. 2002), 64–70.

84. PRO: FO 371/106 537/NS 1071/30/6, letter Mason, FO, to C. Steel, Washington, 3/2/1953.

85. Ibid.

86. Quote in NA: 611.61/3/353, Holmes, US embassy in London, to State Dept., No.4896, 3/3/1953.

87. Churchill, 'Oral Answers. World Peace (Mr Eisenhower's Statement)', in H.C. *Parl. Deb.*, 5th series, Vol. 512, 2/3/1953, 18–19.

88. Moran, *Struggle for Survival*, 403: diary entry, 7/3/1953. On Moran, see R.R.H. Lovell, *Churchill's Doctor: A Biography of Lord Moran* (Carlton, Victoria, 1993). For an interesting reaction to Stalin's death, see also the diary entry on 6/3/1953 by the former Permanent Under-Secretary, the FO's most senior civil servant, Sir A. Cadogan: Churchill College, Cambridge, Cadogan Papers, 1/24, Diary 1953.

89. Those present included President Truman who, however, left early after having entertained Churchill by playing the piano.

90. Liddell-Hart Archive London: Elliot Papers, 5/1/55a, report on the dinner party which Ambassador Makins gave for Churchill, 8/1/1953. However, Bedell Smith had already made a very similar prophecy in his 1949 book *My Three Years in Moscow* (New York, 1949). He wrote that he thought that Stalin's succession would be divided among Molotov, Malenkov and Beria; he was convinced that 'no struggle is likely to occur that is in any way commensurate with the battle of giants which took place after Lenin's death' (p. 95).

CHAPTER 10: THE COLD WAR AFTER STALIN

1. See for example PRO: FO 371/106 504, 505 (October 1952–July 1953), 106 515–19 (March–December 1953); FRUS 1952–4, Vol. 8, 1125–9: Special Estimate 39 (12/3/1953); also M.S. Fish, 'After Stalin's Death. The Anglo-American debate over a new Cold War', *Diplomatic History* 10 (1986),

333ff.; W.W. Rostow, *Europe After Stalin. Eisenhower's Three Decisions of March 11, 1953* (Austin, Tex., 1982).

2. Quoted in G.D. Embree, *The Soviet Union between the 19th and 20th Party Congress, 1952–1956* (The Hague, 1959), 37. For Beam's report on Stalin's funeral, see FRUS 1952–4, Vol. 8, 1105–6; also R.J. Donovan, *Eisenhower: The Inside Story* (New York, 1956), 72. Stalin's funeral only three days after his death seemed to have been organized with 'almost indecent haste' as the British diplomat Paul Grey wrote; the people of Moscow had been able to pay their respects to Lenin for over a week PRO: FO 371/106 504/NS 1013/19, Grey, counsellor at the British embassy in Moscow, to FO, No. 54 (first quarterly report 1953), 8/4/1953.

3. PRO: PREM 11/384 (July 1952–April 1953); PRO: FO 371/106 533/NS 1051/2 (7/3/1953), NS 1051/17 (27/3/1953), NS 1013/17 (27/3–2/4/1953); FRUS 1952–4, Vol. 8, 1138. For the reaction of the Soviet peoples to Stalin's death, the atmosphere in Moscow and elsewhere as well as for the immediate reaction of the new leaders (e.g. the call-up of troops in case of a popular uprising, the various announcements to exercise a calming influence on the population, etc.), see above all the contemporary account by H.E Salisbury, *Moscow Journal* (Chicago, 1962), 340ff.; also Embree, *The Soviet Union between the 19th and 20th Party Congress*, 28ff.; G. Bortoli, *The Death of Stalin* (London, 1975), esp. 145ff.; A. Awtorchanow, *Das Rätsel um Stalins Tod* (Frankfurt/M., 1984); and for an overview, also W. Leonhard, *The Kremlin since Stalin* (London, 1962), 63ff.

4. This was the way the British diplomat Paul Grey expressed it in a despatch to London. PRO: FO 371/106 504/NS 1013/19, telegram No. 54 (first quarterly report, 1953), 8/4/1953. An excellent overview of the various internal and external measures by the new government is given in the document 'Chronology of Principal Events in Soviet Affairs, January–June, 1953,' dated 16/7/1953 (draft paper), in PRO: FO 371/106 510/NS 1015/39; also EL: Jackson Papers, Record 1953–4, 'Soviet Lures and Pressures Since Stalin's Death, March 5 to 25, 1953', annex, 26/3/1953; and a document with the same title for the period from March 26 to April 13, annex, 15/4/1953. See also Salisbury, *Moscow Journal*, 364–6, 369–71; and NA: 761.00/5–2153, telegram No. 480, 21/5/1953.

5. See for example PRO: FO 371/106 504, 505 (October 1952–July 1953), 106 515–19 (March–December 1953); FRUS, 1952–4, Vol. 8, 1125–9: Special Estimate 39 (12/3/1953); also Fish, 'After Stalin's Death', 333ff.

6. See A. Knight, *Beria: Stalin's First Lieutenant* (Princeton, N.J., 1993) 184–5. On the Doctor's Plot, see also n. 130, below. It was Beria who was behind the new leaders' attempt to curry favour with the Soviet peoples. Already in 1938, when Beria became deputy leader of the NKVD and thus occupied his first important post in Moscow, this had been his method to become popular and unassailable by any of his rivals. See for example A. Antonow-Owsejenko's and N. Khrushchev's separate accounts in V.F. Nekrassow (ed.), *Berija. Henker in Stalins Diensten. Ende einer Karriere* (Augsburg, 1997), 91–2, 298–9; N. Khrushchev, *Khrushchev Remembers* (Boston, 1970), 96–104, 324ff.

7. For Stalin's 'Himmler' expression, see A. Gromyko's account in V.F. Nekrassow (ed.), *Berija. Henker in Stalins Diensten*, 274. For Churchill's dislike and suspicion of Beria during the Yalta conference, see the contemporary accounts mentioned in Knight, *Beria*, 131. Churchill's distrust of Beria explains why throughout 1953–4 Churchill wished to believe that it was Malenkov who was in charge. Churchill had met Malenkov in the course of the Second World War but he did not know him well. Churchill found most unpalatable the prospect that he might have to negotiate with the torturer Beria (until his arrest was announced in late June) or the dour and difficult Molotov whom Churchill and Eden knew comparatively well from Second World War days. The best impression of Molotov's views and activities can be gained from A. Resis (ed.), *Molotov Remembers: Inside Kremlin Politics. Conversations with Felix Chuev* (Chicago, 1993); and V. Zubok and C. Pleshakov, *Inside the Kremlin's Cold War: From Stalin to Khrushchev* (Cambridge, Mass., 1996), 78–109.

8. Malenkov's importance was often exaggerated in the West as he was initially both chairman of the Presidium of the Council of Ministers and of the CPSU's Secretariat and thus leader of both state and Party. British diplomat Grey thought for example that Malenkov 'had a middle class upbringing which he conceals by wearing rather untidy party clothes'. However, Malenkov had to relinquish the latter position on 14 March 1953. This only became known on 21 March but it caused great confusion in the West. Moreover Khrushchev was initially underestimated and his rise to power overlooked. Even in 1955–6, after Malenkov's downfall, many western politicians believed in his comeback. See for example British ambassador W. Hayter's memoirs *The Kremlin and the Embassy* (London, 1962), 123–5. For a good characterization of both Malenkov and Beria, see also Zubok and Pleshakov, ibid., 138–73; also J.G. Richter, *Khrushchev's Double Bind: Interna-*

tional Pressures and Domestic Coalition Politics (Baltimore, Md., 1994), 36–52. See also PRO: FO 371/106 504/NS 1013/19, Grey to FO, No. 54, 8/4/1954; also FO 371/106 542/NS 1075/1, Gascoigne to FO, No. 510, 11/7/1953. For a detailed discussion of the post-Stalin leadership arrangements, see M. Kramer, 'The Early Post-Stalin Succession Struggle and Upheavals in East-Central Europe', *Journal of Cold War Studies* 1/1 (1999), 7–9. Kramer emphasizes the much overlooked importance of Molotov as the driving force behind Soviet policy in 1953 and 1954; U. Bar-Noi also comes to this conclusion, see 'The Soviet Union and Churchill's Appeals for High-Level Talks, 1953–4: New Evidence from the Russian Archives', *Diplomacy & Statecraft* 9/3 (1998), 110–33; see also Knight, ibid., 180–3. On Khrushchev, see S.N. Khrushchev, *Nikita Khrushchev and the Creation of a Superpower* (Philadelphia, Pa., 2000); W. Taubman, S. Khrushchev and A. Gleason (eds), *Nikita Krushchev* (New Haven, 2000), esp. chs 2 and 3.

9. For details and a discussion of the extensive literature and the available documentary evidence from the former USSR and its satellite countries, see the important article (in three parts) by Kramer, 'The Early Post-Stalin Succession Struggle and Upheavals in East-Central Europe', *Journal of Cold War Studies*, 1/1 (1999), 3–55; 1/2 (1999), 3–38; 1/3 (1999), 3–66. See also V. Zubok, ' "Unverfroren und grob in der Deutschlandfrage ..." Berija, der Nachfolgestreit nach Stalins Tod und die Moskauer DDR-Debatte im April–Mai 1953', in C. Kleßmann and B. Stöver (eds), *1953 – Krisenjahr des Kalten Krieges in Europa* (Cologne, 1999), 29–48.

10. See FRUS 1952–4, Vol. 8, 433–4; C. Bohlen, *Witness to History, 1929–1969* (London, 1973), 336.

11. PRO: PREM 11/540: FO paper NS 1022/4 (9/4/1953) 'Soviet policies after Stalin's death'; FRUS 1952–4, Vol. 8, 1100–43.

12. See PRO: FO 371/125 037/ZP 9/19, 25/4/1953; for the Stalin Note and the 'battle of the notes', see Chapter 9, above.

13. NA: 741.00/3–653: telegram No. 4964 US embassy London to State Dept., 6/3/1953; see also 741.00/2–2653, telegram No. 4808 US embassy London to State Dept., 26/2/1953.

14. For details, see Chapter 6, above.

15. For details and good overviews of the scholarly debates, see the articles in the recent books by Kleßmann and Stöver (eds), *1953 – Krisenjahr*; A.B. Hegedüs and M. Wilke, *Satelliten nach Stalins Tod* (Berlin, 2000); K. Larres and K. Osgood (eds), *The Cold War After Stalin: A New International History* (forthcoming, 2003). See also G. Wettig, *Bereitschaft zu Einheit in Freiheit? Die sowjetische Deutschland-Politik 1945–1955* (Munich, 1999), 235ff.; also G. Wettig, 'Die beginnende Umorientierung der sowjetischen Deutschland-Politik im Frühjahr und Sommer 1953', *Deutschland-Archiv* 28/5 (1995), 495–507; and G. Wettig, 'Zum Stand der Forschung über Berijas Deutschland-Politik im Frühjahr 1953', *Deutschland-Archiv* 4/26 (1993), 674–82. See also the article by M. Reiman and the reply by G. Wettig and another reply by Reiman in *Deutschland-Archiv* 32/3 (1999), 456–60 and 32/4 (1999), 644–9. For a discussion from a political science point of view, see D.W. Larson, *Anatomy of Mistrust: US-Soviet Relations during the Cold War* (Ithaca, N.Y., 1997), 39ff.

16. FRUS 1952–4, Vol. 8, 1093: 135th NSC meeting, 4/3/1953. As will be seen, Sherman Adams's statement that Stalin's death 'caused no great excitement in the White House' was clearly incorrect. See S. Adams, *First-Hand Report: The Inside Story of the Eisenhower Administration* (London, 1961), 95. The events surrounding Stalin's death are still shrouded in mystery. For example, the question whether or not there was a deliberate decision by Beria and others to delay the arrival of medical help for the dictator, who had lain paralysed and mostly unconscious at his dacha since his stroke late at night on 1 March or early in the morning of 2 March, is still unsolved. The same applies to the subsequent power struggle between, above all, Khrushchev and Beria and the plot against Beria in June; many details are still unclear. For a good overview, see Knight, *Beria*, 176–200; D. Volkogonov, *Stalin: Triumph and Tragedy* (London, 1991), 570–6; and E. Radzinsky, *Stalin* (London, 1996), 566–80; R.H. McNeal, *Stalin: Man and Ruler* (London, 1988), 300–9; and for a very illuminating analysis, see V. Mastny, *The Cold War and Soviet Insecurity: The Stalin Years* (New York, 1996), 166–70. See also the forthcoming article by V. Mastny in Larres and Osgood (eds), *The Cold War After Stalin*. See also N. Khrushchev's still useful version of the events: *Khrushchev Remembers*, 315ff.; also *Khrushchev Remembers: The Glasnost Tapes* (Boston, 1990), 38ff. See also the respective articles by N. Barsukov and E. Zubkova in W. Taubman et al. (eds), *Nikita Khrushchev*, 44–66, 67–84.

17. At the time of Stalin's death there was not even an American ambassador in Moscow, which meant that Jacob Beam, the Chargé d'Affaires, was in charge of the Moscow embassy. Ambassador George Kennan had been declared *persona non grata* in September 1952 by the Soviet government; the nomination of Charles Bohlen as his successor was still pending before the Senate. In his memoirs Bohlen drew a very positive picture of Beam. He wrote: 'He [Beam] had not been in

Moscow very long [since December, 1952], but he was an astute observer and had kept Washington fully informed of the period when Stalin was ill and of events following the dictator's death. I had been impressed by Beam's telegrams ... and hoped to retain him as counsellor ...' (*Witness to History*, 338, also 309–36). See also Beam's memoirs, *Multiple Exposure: An American Ambassador's Unique Perspectives on East-West Issues* (New York, 1978), 28ff.; FRUS 1952–4, Vol. 8, 1082–3, 1130–1; G.F. Kennan, *Memoirs, 1950–1963* (Boston, 1972), 145–67, 168ff.

18. For Argentinian ambassador Bravo's talk with Stalin, see PRO: FO 371/106 524/NS 1021/15, conversation Eden-Bidault in London, 13/2/1953 (also FO 800/821; PREM 11/436); for the Indian diplomats Menon and Kitchlews separate conversations with the dictator, see FO 371/106 602/NS 1903/8, Gascoigne to FO, No. 85, 18/2/1953; NS 1903/11, Gascoigne to Hohler, 26/2/1953; NS 1903/13, Gascoigne to Mason, 27/2/1953. See also NA: 761.11/2/2753, 27/2/1953; FRUS 1952–4, Vol. 8, 1078–9; and R. Payne, *The Rise and Fall of Joseph Stalin* (London, 1966), 669–73; M. Rush, *Political Succession in the USSR* (New York, 1968), 42–3.

19. See R. Richardson, *The Long Shadow: Inside Stalin's Family*, paperback edn (London, 1994), 210–11; Knight, *Beria*, 144, 153–4, 172. Stalin celebrated his 70th birthday in December 1949. M. Djilas seems to have detected clear signs of Stalin's senility already during his third conversation with the dictator in early 1948. See his *Conversations with Stalin* (London, 1963), 147–8, 152–61.

20. FRUS, 1952–4, Vol. 8, 1084: Beam to State Dept., 4/3/1953.

21. Ibid., 1087: Dept. of State, Intelligence Estimate, 'Implications of Stalin's Collapse', 4/3/1953; also 1080–1: memorandum E. Lewis Revey, Office of Policy and Plans, 25/2/1953.

22. Acting on a request made by the Political Strategy Board (PSB) in a paper entitled 'Psychological Preparation for Stalin's Passing from Power' in November 1952, the State Department had forwarded stand-by instructions for use in the period immediately following the dictator's death to the PSB on 21 January 1953, the day after Eisenhower's inauguration. This paper (PSB D-24) is partially published in FRUS, ibid., 1059–60. See also EL: Ann Whitman File, Administration Series, Box 29, Folder: Psychological Warfare, memorandum C.D. Jackson to National Security Adviser General Robert Cutler, 4/3/1953; FRUS, ibid., memorandum E. Lewis Revey, 25/2/1953. On the work of the PSB in the early 1950s, see S. Lucas, 'Campaigns of Truth: The Psychological Strategy Board and American Ideology, 1951–3', *International History Review* 18 (1996), 279–302. For the view of Eisenhower's National Security Adviser, see R. Cutler, *No Time To Rest* (Boston, 1965), 320ff.

23. He said: 'Ever since 1946, I know that all the so-called experts have been yapping about what would happen when Stalin dies and what we as a nation should do about it. Well, he's dead. And you can turn the files of our government inside out – in vain – looking for any plans laid. We have no plan. We are not even sure what difference his death makes'. Quoted in E. Hughes, *The Ordeal of Power: A Political Memoir of the Eisenhower Years* (London, 1963), 101. The Cabinet meeting took place on 6 March. See also FRUS, 1952–4, Vol. 8, 1098; S.E. Ambrose, *Eisenhower, Vol. II: The President, 1952–1969* (London, 1984), 67–8. As a former military man Eisenhower placed great importance on proper planning procedures, see A.K. Nelson, 'The "Top of Policy Hill": President Eisenhower and the National Security Council,' *Diplomatic History* 7 (1983), 324; also J.G. Bock, *The White House Staff and the National Security Assistant: Friendship and Friction at the Water's Edge* (New York, 1987), 31–42.

24. FRUS 1952–4, Vol. 8, 1086, 1088: Dept. of State, Intelligence Estimate, 4/3/1953. For the nature of American Intelligence Estimates, see S.E. Ambrose with R.H. Immerman, *Ike's Spies: Eisenhower and the Espionage Establishment* (Garden City, N.Y., 1981), 252–64. For a contemporary criticism of the usefulness of intelligence estimates, see the minute by R.W. Tufts, 6/6/1951, NA: PPS, Box 10, Folder: General.

25. FRUS 1952–4, ibid., 1089–90. It was assumed that in the near future 'the policy decisions by Stalin will tend to be frozen for a more or less prolonged period with no one Soviet leader strong enough, or daring enough, to attempt changes' (ibid., 1090).

26. For details, see my article 'Die Welt des John Foster Dulles (1939–1953)', *Historische Mitteilungen* 9/2 (1996), 256–82. After Stalin's death Dulles referred to these beliefs for example in his remarks to the Advertising Council in the White House on 24/3/1953. Similar convictions and the belief that Moscow had laid a trap to provoke the break-up of the western alliance can be found in Dulles's subsequent remarks to the Senate's Foreign Relations Committee in late April. See L. Gardner, 'Poisoned Apples: American Responses to the Russian "Peace Offensive" ', in K. Larres and K. Osgood (eds), *The Cold War After Stalin* (forthcoming, 2003).

27. C.L. Sulzberger, *A Long Row of Candles: Memoirs and Diaries, 1934–1954* (New York, 1969), 847: diary entry, 4/3/1953 (talk with F. Roberts); see also F. Roberts, *Dealing with Dictators: The*

Destruction and Revival of Europe, 1930–70 (London, 1991), 165. For the British reaction, see also J.W. Young, *Winston Churchill's Last Campaign: Britain and the Cold War, 1951–55* (Oxford, 1996), 135–8.

28. PRO: FO 371/106 515/NS 10110/2, Gascoigne to FO, No. 122, 6/3/1953.

29. PRO: FO 371/106 509/NS 1015/20, Gascoigne to Eden, 11/3/1953.

30. PRO: FO 371/106 515/NS 10110/2, Gascoigne to FO, No. 122, 6/3/1953; for a similar view, see also NS/10110/33.

31. PRO: FO 371/125 031/ZP 3/15/G, conversation Eden and Chancellor of the Exchequer Rab Butler with representatives of the British Commonwealth in the British embassy in Washington, DC, 7/3/1953. On these talks, see A. Dobson, *The Politics of the Anglo-American Economic Special Relationship, 1940–1987* (Brighton, 1988), 148ff.

32. Defence Minister Alexander and General Strong explained to American journalist Cy Sulzberger on 3 March 'that as long as Stalin was around there was very little risk of war'; the dictator was aware of America's atomic superiority. Sulzberger, *Long Row of Candles*, 843–4: diary entry, 3/3/1953 (quote: 844). West German Chancellor Adenauer had a very similar opinion. See G. Buchstab (ed.), *Adenauer, 'Es mußte alles neu gemacht werden'* [...] (Stuttgart, 1986), 428–9.

33. This was also recommended by the British ambassador to Moscow. See PRO: FO 371/106 509/NA 1015/20, Gascoigne to Eden, 11/3/1953.

34. PRO: FO 371/106 509/NS 1015/18, Roberts to Mason about his talk with C. Sulzberger of the *New York Times* on 5/3/1953. For Roberts's views, see also his memoirs *Dealing with Dictators*, 165–8; and his views as expressed in K. Larres (ed.), 'Witness Seminar: British Attitudes to German Rearmament and Reunification in the 1950s', *Contemporary Record* 5 (1991), 314ff.

35. See Sulzberger, *Long Row of Candles*, 846–7: diary, 4/3/1953 (talk with Frank Roberts).

36. See for example the fairly correct prophecies of the West German foreign policy experts, NA: 761.00/3–653, Conant, US High Commissioner in Germany, to Dulles, No. 4137, 6/3/1953, on his talk with the German official Bräutigam; also Bedell Smith's prediction of early January 1953, KCL: Liddell–Hart Archive: Elliot Papers, 5/1/55a. CIA chief A. Dulles's correct prediction that initially Malenkov would be more important than Molotov impressed Eisenhower. See P. Grose, *Gentleman Spy: The Life of Allen Dulles* (Boston, 1994), 350.

37. PRO: FO 371/106 509/NS 1015/14, Gascoigne to FO, No. 130, 9/3/1953. This view was shared by Khrushchev. See *Khrushchev Remembers: The Glasnost Tapes*, 75–6. For Churchill's 11 March letter to Eisenhower and the President's reply as well as for their subsequent correspondence, see below, 202ff.

38. P. Boyle (ed.), *The Churchill-Eisenhower Correspondence, 1953–1955* (Chapel Hill, N.C., 1990), 31: Churchill to Eisenhower, 11/3/1953. See also below, 202ff.

39. PRO: FO 371/106 537/NS 1071/22, 12/3/1953. See also 'Oral Answers, Three-Power Talks', H.C. *Parl. Deb.*, 5th series, Vol. 512, 12/3/1953, 1502.

40. PRO: PREM 11/422, Churchill to Eden, 28/3/1953.

41. For Eden's earlier interest in high-level diplomacy, see Chapter 8, 158–61, above.

42. E. Shuckburgh, *Descent to Suez: Diaries, 1951–56* (London, 1986), 83–5: diary entry, 24–30/3, 1/4/ and 2/4/1953 (quote: 83). See also A. Seldon, *Churchill's Indian Summer: The Conservative Government, 1951–55* (London, 1981), 397. Allegedly Churchill told Eden when they discussed who among the collective leadership would reply to the letter: 'If it is Mol, you go. But if it is Mal, it's me'. See Shuckburgh, ibid., 83; also Seldon, ibid., 398; M. Gilbert, *Winston S. Churchill, Vol. 8: Never Despair 1945–1965*, paperback edn (London, 1990), 812, n. 1.

43. Nutting was Joint Parliamentary Under-Secretary of State for Foreign Affairs; he became Minister of State in October 1954 and resigned over the Suez Affair in November 1956. For Frank Robert's strong opposition to the idea that civil servants would be able or willing to influence and manipulate the politicians they work for, see his comments in Larres (ed.), 'Witness Seminar', 314–16 (see also n. 50, below). The officials who advised Eden in the matter were above all Strang and Roberts as well as Deputy Under-Secretaries Mason and Dixon, his Private Secretary Shuckburgh and Harry Hohler, the Director of the Northern Dept. See PRO: FO 371/106 537/NS 1071/41/G, memorandum Strang to Eden, 28/3/1953; also Shuckburgh, ibid., 83, diary entry: 1/4/1953.

44. Shuckburgh, ibid.; also PRO: ibid.

45. PRO: ibid. Strang also said: 'To plunge straight into a meeting with Mr. Molotov would cause questionings in Germany, would greatly increase French hesitation to ratify the E.D.C. Treaty and would be jealously regarded in the United States'.

46. See also R. Steininger, 'Ein vereintes, unabhängiges Deutschland? Winston Churchill, der Kalte Krieg und die deutsche Frage im Jahre 1953', *Militärgeschichtliche Mitteilungen* 34 (1984), 1105–6.

47. PRO: FO 371/106 537/NS 1071/G, Churchill to Eden, 28/3/1953.
48. Ibid.
49. Ibid., Eden to Churchill, 28/3/1953.
50. Even with hindsight Frank Roberts always rejected that anyone except Churchill was interested in a high-level meeting after Stalin's death. In November 1990 he said: 'Well, I think the idea of British officials, manipulating Adenauer, manipulating Ernest Bevin, is so fantastic that I don't think it's worth wasting any time on. You advanced a view, they either accepted it or they didn't. But the problem with Churchill at the time is that he suddenly had this idea that before he died he had to do something to recreate the old relationships. The problem was that we were faced with a new situation. . . . I did actually have to oppose Churchill's policy, knowing that Anthony Eden who was ill was opposed to it, knowing that by and large the Cabinet was opposed to it … knowing above all that the Chancellor of Germany was opposed and that the President of the United States was opposed to it and that the French were opposed to it. These are the facts of the matter, it's very nice to say why didn't we let Churchill have his way, but it didn't rest with us, I mean that was the prevailing situation.' Quoted in Larres (ed.), 'Witness Seminar', 317.
51. NA: 741.13/7–1753, memorandum of the conversation between Dodds-Parker and Joseph Palmer, Second Secretary at the American embassy in London, 16/7/1953. See also Dodds-Parker's memoirs, *Political Eunuch* (Ascot, 1986), 61ff.
52. See Shuckburgh, *Descent to Suez*, 83–84: diary entry, 1/4/1953. Quote: FRUS 1952–4, Vol. 8, 1111–13: memorandum Smith to Morgan, 10/3/1953.
53. PRO: FO 371/106 537/NS 1071/41/G, memorandum Strang to Eden, 28/3/1953.
54. For the lengthy arguments in 1953–5 between Eden and Churchill regarding the latter's retirement and Eden's succession, see above all Seldon, *Churchill's Indian Summer*, 38ff.; D. Carlton, 'Großbritannien und die Gipfeldiplomatie 1953–55', in B. Thoß and H.E. Volkmann (eds), *Zwischem Kalten Krieg und Entspannung. Sicherheits- und Deutschlandpolitik der Bundesrepublik im Mächtesystem der Jahre 1953–1956* (Boppard, 1988), 51ff.; R.R. James, *Anthony Eden*, paperback edn (London, 1986), 355ff.; V. Rothwell, *Anthony Eden: A Political Biography, 1931–57* (Manchester, 1992), 163–203; D. Dutton, *Anthony Eden: A Life and Reputation* (London, 1997), 217–46; M. Gilbert, *Never Despair*; H. Pelling, *Churchill's Peacetime Ministry, 1951–55* (Basingstoke, 1997), esp. Ch. 7. See also the published diaries and memoirs by Shuckburgh (*Descent to Suez*), J. Colville (The *Fringes of Power: 10 Downing Street Diaries, 1939–1955*, London, 1985) and Lord Moran (*Churchill: The Struggle for Survival, 1940–1965*, London, 1966). There are also numerous details in Anthony Eden's diaries for the years 1953–5 (BUA: AP 20/1/29, 30 and 31) and in his other private papers (AP 20/16/112, 123ff., 140–59, AP 20/17/79, 138, 191–3, 195ff., 200); see also the interesting remarks in Lord Woolton's diary (Bodleian Library, Oxford, 1942–1960, 115ff.) and Rab Butler's papers (Trinity College Cambridge: G 26/55, 56–8, 59ff., G 27/18–19, 98, 103–6, 108–13, G 46/8); see also the Colville Papers (Churchill College, Cambridge, 3/5) and the Beaverbrook Papers (HL: BBk C/58 Breckan, C/250 Moran). For a brief but interesting account of the Churchill–Eden relationship after 1951, see A. Montague Browne, *Long Sunset: Memoirs of Winston Churchill's Last Private Secretary* (London, 1995), 122–4, 132.
55. On 29 March Eden asked Gascoigne to return to London. Already on the day before he had asked him for his views on a meeting with Molotov. See BUA: Avon Papers, AP 20/16/10, Strang to Gascoigne No. 141, 28/3/1953; and No. 142, 29/3/1953. See also the account in Young, *Last Campaign*, 142ff.
56. On Eden's advice Churchill did not tell American ambassador Aldrich anything about his envisaged summit diplomacy. See NA: 761.00/4–153, Aldrich, London, to State Dept., No. 84, 1/4/1953; also PRO: PREM 11/422, minute on the conversation between Churchill and Aldrich, M. 61/53, 30/3/1953.
57. See also Sir William Hayter's view of Gascoigne, his predecessor as British ambassador in Moscow, in Larres (ed.), 'Witness Seminar', 311; also BUA: Avon Papers, AP 20/1/29: diary 1953 (2/4 and 3/4/1953); see also Shuckburgh, *Descent to Suez*, 83–5. For Hayter's view of Soviet politics after Stalin's death (he arrived in Moscow in October 1953), see his book *The Kremlin and the Embassy*, 62ff., 114ff.
58. PRO: FO 371/106 524/NS 1021/29, 26/3/1953; 106 526/NS 1021/67/G, 68, 69, June 1953.
59. PRO: FO 371/106 526/NS 1021/69, 26/6/1953. Hohler confirmed this opinion in an interview in Washington, D.C. on 7 September 1990. The Northern Dept. was responsible for following developments in much of Eastern Europe including the Soviet Union.
60. Shuckburgh, *Descent to Suez*, 83–4: diary entry, 1/4/1953 (quote: 84). A list of the various other topics discussed with Gascoigne can be found in BUA: Avon Papers, AP 20/16/10B, 1/4/1953.

61. Shuckburgh wrote in his diary: 'I tried to illustrate the truth that this hankering after a meeting with Molotov is equivalent to a willingness, for the sake of popularity, to abandon policies hitherto pursued: running after the Russians in case our allies do it first. And fancy not telling the NATO powers'. Shuckburgh, ibid., 84.

62. Seldon, *Indian Summer*, 398, claims that 'although all the Foreign Office team were opposed to the idea, they did not press their objections, solely because they felt that Eden was so keen'. This is incorrect. On the contrary the officials uttered so many forceful objections that they were able to persuade Eden to change his mind.

63. Shuckburgh, *Descent to Suez*, 83, 84: diary entry, 1/4/1953.

64. BUA: Avon Papers, AP 20/1/29: diary entry Eden, 2/4/1953; see also James, *Anthony Eden*, 361.

65. BUA: ibid.

66. Ibid., diary entry Eden, 3/4/1953.

67. The letter is dated 10/4/1953. Quoted in James, *Anthony Eden*, 362. On 1 April Churchill said in the House of Commons with respect to a question by the Labour MP Lewis about his summit diplomacy that there was no 'distinction between my personal point of view and that of Her Majesty's Government'. However, this was plainly incorrect at this stage. See Churchill, 'Oral Answers, Three Power Talks', H.C. *Parl. Deb.*, 5th series, Vol. 513, 1210.

68. This was at least Gascoigne's third talk with Eden and not the first and final one as claimed by Seldon. See his *Indian Summer*, 618, n. 24. Gascoigne was in London from 1–9 April. See *The Times*, 10/4/1953.

69. See Boyle (ed.), *Correspondence*, 36–7: Churchill to Eisenhower, 5/4/1953.

70. This is reported in Gilbert, *Never Despair*, 812. Fish's claim that Churchill instructed Eden already on 2 April to send a telegram to Molotov is clearly wrong (see his 'After Stalin's Death', 337). See also Steininger, 'Ein vereintes, unabhängiges Deutschland?', 111–12; PRO: PREM 11/422, FO to embassy Moscow, No. 171, 8/4/1953. A first draft of the telegram to Molotov is dated 3 April but the eventual final version was only sent to Eisenhower on 8 April. These versions are very similar to Churchill's initial draft of 28 March.

71. For the exchange of views between Churchill and Eden on 3 and 4 April 1953, see PRO: ibid.

72. See Boyle (ed.), *Correspondence*, 36–7: Churchill to Eisenhower, 5/4/1953; also Shuckburgh, *Descent to Suez*, 83–4: diary entry, 1/4/1953. For an attempt to construct 'phases' in Churchill's summit diplomacy, see J. Foschepoth, 'Churchill, Adenauer und die Neutralisierung Deutschlands', *Deutschland-Archiv* 17 (1984), 1288. Churchill merely informed the President: 'For our part we are sending our Ambassador back to Moscow with instructions to try to settle with Molotov a number of minor points which concern Britain and Russia alone and have caused trouble in the last few years. None of these is of major importance …' (quoted in Boyle, ibid., 36).

73. PRO: PREM 11/422, Gascoigne, Moscow, to FO No. 233, 234–7, 11/4/1953.

74. The highly strung Eden had suffered from stomach and gall bladder problems for some time. On 4 April he was informed that he had to undergo an urgent operation. It took place on 12 April in London but was not successful. A second operation on 29 April became necessary. The surgeons blundered and Eden only narrowly survived. After a prolonged convalescence the exhausted and very weak Foreign Secretary underwent a third operation in a specialist clinic in Boston, New Jersey. This time his treatment proved to be more successful. After a long period of recovery which included a cruise in the Mediterranean, he was only fit enough to return to the Foreign Office on 1 October. See BUA: Avon Papers, AP 20/1/29, dairy entries Eden 2/4 and 4/4/1953; AP 20/1/29A, diary Eden: 'Convalescence Cruise', August – September 1953; diary entry, 1/10/1953. See also Shuckburgh, *Descent to Suez*, 85. For details of Eden's illness, see above all James, *Anthony Eden*, 361–6; D. Carlton *Anthony Eden: A Biography*, paperback edn (London, 1981), 327–28; Gilbert, *Never Despair*, 814–15, 817, 820; A. Eden, *Full Circle: Memoirs*, paperback edn (London, 1960), 51–2.

75. Quoted in D.R. Thorpe, *Selwyn Lloyd* (London, 1989), 170.

76. BUA: Avon Papers, AP 19/1/76, letter Churchill to Eden, 6/4/1953.

77. Ibid.

78. Quoted in Carlton, *Anthony Eden*, 333; and confirmed in an interview with Sir A. Nutting in London, 23/1/1991. See also Thorpe, *Selwyn Lloyd*, 171.

79. For a stimulating article which essentially arrives at a very similar conclusion, see K. Osgood, 'Form before Substance: Eisenhower's Commitment to Psychological Warfare and Negotiations with the Enemy', *Diplomatic History* 24/3 (2000), 405–33. This article also analyzes the very different revisionist and post-revisionst assessments of Eisenhower's psychological warfare strategies. See also J.J. Yurechko, 'The Day Stalin Died: American Plans for Exploiting the Soviet Succession Crisis of 1953', *Journal of Strategic Studies* 13/1 (1990), 44–73. For a good account, see

also W.L. Hixson, *Parting the Curtain: Propaganda, Culture, and the Cold War, 1945–1961* (New York, 1997), pp. 21–7, 57ff.; also S. Lucas, *Freedom's War: The US Crusade against the Soviet Union, 1945–56* (Manchester, 1999), 163ff. For a much more positive vision of Eisenhower's policies, see R.R. Bowie and R.H. Immerman, *Waging Peace: How Eisenhower Shaped an Enduring Cold War Strategy* (New York, 1998), e.g. 109–22. For a general account of American political warfare, see P. Grose, *Operation Rollback: America's Secret War behind the Iron Curtain* (Boston, 2000).

80. For Eisenhower's use of formal meetings of the NSC and informal talks with his advisers to arrive at sensible decisions, see Nelson, 'The "Top of Policy Hill" ', 310ff.; and A.K. Nelson, 'The Importance of Foreign Policy Process: Eisenhower and the National Security Council', in S.E. Ambrose and G. Bischof (eds), *Eisenhower: A Centenary Assessment* (Baton Rouge, Louis., 1995), 111–25.

81. Before the NSC Council met, Eisenhower had already consulted C.D. Jackson, his newly appointed Special Assistant for Cold War Operations, and CIA chief Allen Dulles, about a special announcement on Stalin's death which he wished to make. Harold Stassen, the Director of Mutual Security, and Eisenhower's press secretary Jim Hagerty attended the meeting as well. See H. Stassen and M. Houts, *Eisenhower: Turning the World toward Peace* (St. Paul, 1990), 154. The memorandum of the discussion of the 135th NSC meeting on 4/3/1953 is published in FRUS 1952–4, Vol. 8, 1091–5, quotes: 1091.

82. The psychological warfare activities of the Eisenhower era had effectively commenced in the summer of 1952, with the convening of two seminars in Princeton. The CIA, the State Dept., the PSB, the National Committee for a Free Europe, and the Center for International Studies (CENIS) were represented. The participants agreed that Truman's policy of containment had to be substituted by 'a more dynamic and positive policy'. Jackson, and representatives from Radio Free Europe, believed that eventually the 'ultimate liberation of the enslaved nations' should be achieved (quotes in B.W. Cook, *The Declassified Eisenhower: A Divided Legacy* (Garden City, N.Y., 1981, 177–8). On 24 January 1953, immediately after Eisenhower's inauguration, the so-called William H. Jackson committee was established and given the task to reform the structure of the NSC. The recommendation of the committee was responsible for the eventual foundation of the Operation Coordinating Board (OCB) in the summer of 1954 as a replacement for Truman's PSB which had been established in 1951. The OCB thus became responsible for psychological warfare actions. See Cook, ibid., 175–9; Osgood, 'Form before Substance', 410–22; also Lucas, *Freedom's War* and Hixson, *Parting the Curtain*, 23–7, 63ff.; see also the persuasive book by G. Mitrovich, *Undermining the Kremlin: America's Strategy to Subvert the Soviet Bloc, 1947–56* (Ithaca, N.Y., 2000), 129ff.

83. FRUS 1952–4, Vol. 8, 1092. According to Stassen and Houts, *Eisenhower*, 156, Jackson also speculated that 'if the President were to remain silent we would not only miss the opportunity he had outlined, but the very silence of the Chief Executive would be subject to misinterpretation by those who sought to misinterpret him'. Jackson had already aided Eisenhower in psychological warfare policies during the 1942 African campaign and the 1944 Normandy invasion. For Jackson's policies, see also V. Ingimundarson, ' "Der Chef des Kalten Krieges". C.D. Jackson, psychologische Kriegführung und die deutsche Frage 1953/54', *Vierteljahrshefte für Zeitgeschichte* 46/2 (1998), 221–51.

84. Wilson became known for his refusal to divest himself of his GM shares until Eisenhower forced him to do so and for his explanation during his confirmation hearings that 'What was good for the country was good for General Motors and vice versa'. See D.D. Eisenhower, *The White House Years, Vol. 1: Mandate for Change, 1953–1956* (London, 1963), 110.

85. FRUS 1952–54, Vol. 8, 1092. For an interesting account of the NSC meeting by a participant, see Stassen and Houts, *Eisenhower*, 154–62.

86. FRUS, ibid. See also H.W. Brands, *Cold Warriors: Eisenhower's Generation and American Foreign Policy* (New York, 1988), 19, 123. M. Beglinger however is mistaken when he regards Wilson as a member of the group around C.D. Jackson. See his *'Containment' im Wandel. Die amerikanische Aussen- und Sicherheitspolitik im Übergang von Truman zu Eisenhower* (Stuttgart, 1981), 83. Sherman Adams also confuses the situation. He claims: '… Eisenhower agreed with Dulles and Jackson that the psychological time had arrived … to deliver a major speech …' (*First-Hand Report*, 96). On Defense Secretary Wilson's rather unimpressive role within the Eisenhower administration, see E.B. Geelhoed, *Charles E. Wilson and the Controversy at the Pentagon, 1953 to 1957* (Detroit, 1979). See also R.H. Immerman, *John Foster Dulles: Piety, Pragmatism, and Power in U.S. Foreign Policy* (Wilmington, Del., 1999), 47ff.

87. An early division in the administration was revealed: the political warfare enthusiasts in the White House led by Eisenhower and C.D. Jackson, versus the more cautious Dulles and Wilson and the

Departments of State and Defense. The NSC document reveals that also Secretary of the Treasury George Humphrey agreed with Eisenhower. According to Stassen and Houts, *Eisenhower*, 161–2, this NSC meeting 'became the President's first official break with Dulles'.

88. FRUS 1952–4, Vol. 8, 1093. See also the speaking notes, dated 16/4/1953, for Bedell Smith's use in his talks with Congressional leaders, in NA: PPS, Box 8, Folder: Congressional, 1950–53. Smith was advised to say: 'It would be very foolish of us, however, to regard anything that has happened so far as proof that Stalin's death has brought about a real change in the nature of the Soviet regime or that its hostility to the non-communist world is any less than is has been in the past'. The 'free world' still needs to pursue a policy 'of continued strength and clear-headed recognition of the dangers'. Thus, a 'sharp, sudden reduction in our own military strength or in the aid we are furnishing our friends and allies would be to invite disasters'. The US had to 'bear the cost of achieving' a 'bold and firm foreign policy'.

89. On the Princeton meeting, see n. 82 above. The National Security Council also instructed the CIA to provide a new evaluation of the impact of Stalin's death. The NSC asked not only Jackson but also the State Dept. to recommend appropriate courses of action by 9 March. Ibid., 1094. See also Rostow, *Europe after Stalin*, 103–4: 'Extracts from the Author's Notes on the Origin of the President's Speech of April 16, 1953', 102–10; this document is also published in FRUS, ibid., 1173–83. The following quotes are taken from Rostow's book.

90. Regarding the close connection between the EDC, German rearmament and the various proposals to convene a summit conference with Moscow, see S. Dockrill, *Britain's Policy for West German Rearmament, 1950–55* (Cambridge, 1991), 124ff.; J.G. Hershberg, 'German Rearmament and American Diplomacy, 1953–1955,' *Diplomatic History* 16 (1992), 511ff.; B.R. Duchin, 'The "Agonizing Reappraisal": Eisenhower, Dulles and the EDC', *Diplomatic History* 16/2 (1992), 201–21; D.C. Large, *Germans to the Front: West German Rearmament in the Adenauer Era* (Chapel Hill, N.C., 1996), 111ff.; and S. Mawby, *Containing Germany: Britain and the Arming of the Federal Republic* (Basingstoke, 1999), 104ff. Rostow asserts that Jackson appears to have believed 'not that a negotiation was likely to succeed, but, rather, that it might unite the Free World around a position which would make EDC a necessary and logical step, not negatively to oppose the USSR but positively to move towards a European settlement …' (*Europe after Stalin*, 110). This was a rather fanciful assumption.

91. Hughes, *Ordeal of Power*, 101.

92. Rostow, *Europe after Stalin*, 87. The proposed message ended with the words 'We must remake eight years of bad history'. Lloyd Gardner has pointed out that this phrase was highly unpopular within the State Dept. as the 'We' implicated both the USSR and the US for the Cold War and did not merely make Soviet deceit and aggression responsible for the East-West conflict. See his 'Poisoned Apples' in Larres and Osgood (eds), *The Cold War After Stalin* (forthcoming, 2003).

93. The paper also made clear that until alternative measures of collective security had been agreed upon, the United States would continue to develop its military strength. Moreover, there would be no second Yalta as every nation about which action was to be taken should participate in the negotiations. For a discussion of the myth surrounding the Yalta conference and its impact on British and American post-war foreign policy, see D.C. Watt, 'Britain and the Historiography of the Yalta Conference and the Cold War,' *Diplomatic History* 13 (1989), 76ff.

94. Nitze in a memorandum to Dulles, dated 19/3/1953. Published in Rostow, *Europe after Stalin*, 140–1. Nitze had a very tense relationship with Dulles who asked him in May 1953 to transfer to the Defense Department to work under Charles Wilson. In June, however, Nitze was also dismissed from this post; he was still regarded as having been too close to the Truman administration. By ridding itself of Nitze, the Eisenhower administration attempted to appease the Republican Party's McCarthyite wing. See W. Isaacson and E. Thomas, *The Wise Men. Six Friends and the World They Made: Acheson, Bohlen, Harriman, Kennan, Lovett, McCloy* (New York, 1986), 570; S. Talbott, *The Master of the Game: Paul Nitze and the Nuclear Peace* (New York, 1988), 60–2; P. Nitze with A.M. Smith and S.L. Rearden, *From Hiroshima to Glasnost: At the Center of Decision – A Memoir* (New York, 1989), 146–8. When he showed the draft to George Morgan, Jackson commented that the 'opening gun in the political warfare campaign would be a Presidential statement of some sort'. Quoted in Rostow, *Europe after Stalin*, 105.

95. Rostow, ibid., 3–5.

96. Hughes, *Ordeal of Power*, 102. In his memoirs Hughes claims that he was the one who was mainly responsible for drafting Eisenhower's speech and he praises the valuable help he received from Paul Nitze. At this stage this is, however, not borne out by the documents nor by the account given by

Rostow. Hughes only became involved more intensively after the Soviet peace campaign had taken off (see below for details). See Hughes, ibid., 108, 119–20; FRUS 1952–4, Vol. 8, 1107–8: memorandum Nitze, 10/3/1953; Rostow, ibid., 104–5. By 1 April Charles Bohlen still believed that the administration had not yet clarified 'what it expects to accomplish by this speech, i.e. whether it is to be in the field of propaganda only or whether it is to be a serious political move designed for some constructive result'. PUA: John F. Foster Dulles Papers, Drafts of Presidential Correspondence, Box 1, PPS, memorandum Bohlen to O'Connors, 1/4/1953.

97. FRUS, ibid., 1101–2: memorandum Bohlen, 7/4/1953. See also T.M. Ruddy, *The Cautious Diplomat. Charles E. Bohlen and the Soviet Union, 1929–1969* (Kent, Ohio/London, 1986), 127–8. Young, *Last Campaign*, 147, claims that it was Bedell Smith who made the proposal for a four-power conference. This is not borne out by the American documents; in fact, as outlined below, Smith was strongly opposed to a four-power meeting. Moreover, Bohlen was quite serious about his proposal; he did not make the suggestion in the expectation that the Soviets would reject it and thus enable the US to score a propaganda victory. In fact, in his memoirs Bohlen later claimed that the failure in conducting negotiations with Malenkov proved to be a missed opportunity as his successor Khrushchev was a much less rational and cultivated person to deal with. See Bohlen, *Witness to History*, 370.

98. While Eisenhower also had misgivings about Bohlen's participation in the Yalta conference, he was much more impressed by Bohlen's qualities than Dulles. The latter offered him the post in Moscow in order to sideline him and to ensure that he would not play any role in decision-making in Washington. See Ruddy, ibid., 109–24; for a brief but succinct portrait, see D. Mayers, *The Ambassadors and America's Soviet Policy* (New York, 1995), 192–200. Very illuminating with respect to Eisenhower's and Dulles's opportunism towards McCarthy is the article by T.G. Corti and T.M. Ruddy, 'The Bohlen and Thayer Affairs: A Case Study in the Eisenhower Administration's Response to Senator Joseph McCarthy,' *Mid-America: An Historical Review* 72 (1990), 119ff. On the tense relationship between Dulles and Bohlen, see Ruddy, *The Cautious Diplomat*, 109ff.; Isaacson and Thomas, *The Wise Men*, 566–9.

99. Boyle (ed.), *Correspondence*, 31: Churchill to Eisenhower, 11/3/1953.

100. Roberts, *Dealing with Dictators*, 165.

101. Boyle (ed.), *Correspondence*, 31–2: Eisenhower to Churchill, 11/3/1953.

102. PRO: FO 371/106 515/NS 1010/2, telegram No. 122, 6/3/1953.

103. FRUS 1952–4, Vol. 6, 891: Aldrich to State Dept., 26/2/1953. For the British view of psychological and political warfare initiatives in general, see Chapter 8, 163 ff., above.

104. Rostow, *Europe after Stalin*, 6.

105. According to Rostow, ibid., 5, the originally planned formal discussion of the matter with Eisenhower on 9 March was postponed to 11 March as Dulles was not in Washington; he only returned in the late afternoon of 10 March.

106. Nitze, Bohlen and Bedell Smith submitted very critical papers. See FRUS, 1952–4, Vol. 8, 1107–12. Basically, the whole State Dept., including Dulles and Robert Bowie – who became Nitze's successor as Director of the PPS in May 1953 – agreed that quiet, secret negotiations were much more sensible than a public media spectacle. See T.F. Soapes, 'A Cold Warrior Seeks Peace: Eisenhower's Strategy for Nuclear Disarmament,' *Diplomatic History* 4 (1980), 61. Bohlen considered the forces of nationalism within the Soviet Empire as the chief element working against the continuation of its control over the satellite countries. He emphasized, however, that 'the process of increased nationalism may be a very long-term process'. See FRUS, 1952–4, Vol. 8, 1108–11: memorandum Bohlen, 10/3/1953, quotes: 1109–11. See also Bowie and Immerman, *Waging Peace*, 113–18.

107. This criticism was well expressed in a memorandum which Robert W. Tufts, a member of the PPS, wrote about a discussion he had with C.D. Jackson, while they were working on the 'crash plan' for the psychological exploitation of Stalin's death. See FRUS, ibid., 1113, n. 4: memorandum Tufts, 10/3/53. On Tufts, see D. Callahan, *Dangerous Capabilities: Paul Nitze and the Cold War* (New York, 1990), 148–9.

108. See FRUS 1952–4, Vol. 2, 399–434. For recent analyses of the document and its development, see Bowie and Immerman, *Waging Peace*, 139–46, and for the preceding 'Solarium Exercise' which began in early May, see 123–38; see also S. Dockrill, *Eisenhower's New Look National Security Policy, 1953–61* (Basingstoke, 1996), 19ff.; M. Bosse, *Shaping and Signalling Presidential Policy: The National Security Decision Making of Eisenhower and Kennedy* (College Station, Tex., 1998); M. Hogan, *A Cross of Iron: Harry S. Truman and the Origins of the National Security State, 1945–1954* (Cambridge, 1998), 366ff.; also A. Wenger, *Living with Peril: Eisenhower, Kennedy, and Nuclear*

Weapons (Lanham, Md., 1997). See also for a good assessment A.M. Johnston, 'Mr Slessor goes to Washington: The Influence of the British Global Strategy Paper and the Eisenhower New Look', *Diplomatic History* 22/3 (1998), 361–98.

109. See Bohlen's memorandum of 7/3/1953, in FRUS 1952–4, Vol. 8, 1101–2; and Hughes, *Ordeal of Power*, 102.

110. See FRUS, ibid., memorandum Nitze, 10/3/1953.

111. FRUS, ibid., 1120 (memorandum Dulles, 11/3/1953). See also PRO: FO 371/103 660/C 1016/32, 19/5/1953.

112. FRUS, ibid.

113. F.W. Marks III, 'The Real Hawk at Dienbienphu: Dulles or Eisenhower?', *Pacific Historical Review* 59 (1990), 299ff., rightly emphasizes the 'overriding importance' of the EDC for Dulles's diplomacy (quote: 299). See also n. 90, above. See also F.W Marks III, *Power and Peace: The Diplomacy of John Foster Dulles* (Westport, Conn., 1993); D. Felken, *Dulles und Deutschland. Die amerikanische Deutschlandpolitik 1953–1959* (Bonn, 1993), 136ff., 222ff.

114. FRUS, 1952–4, Vol. 8, 1121, 11/3/1953.

115. NA: 761.00/3–653, Conant, US High Commissioner, Bonn, to Dulles, No. 4137, 6/3/1953.

116. FRUS, 1952–4, Vol. 8, 1122, 11/3/1953.

117. The President did not exactly distinguish himself as an expert on Soviet affairs during the NSC meeting. For some reason he came to the extraordinary conclusion 'that Stalin had never actually been undisputed ruler of the Soviet Union'. The minutes of the NSC meeting state: 'Contrary to the views of many of our intelligence agencies, the President persisted in believing that the Government of the Soviet Union had always been something of a committee government. . . . [and] had Stalin at the end of the war, been able to do what he wanted with his colleagues in the Kremlin, Russia would have sought more peaceful and normal relations with the rest of the world … [but] Stalin had had to come to terms with other members of the Kremlin ruling circle.' Ibid., 1118. This quote can certainly be taken as a prime example of Eisenhower's tendency to think aloud at NSC meetings. See E.C. Keefer, 'President Dwight D. Eisenhower and the End of the Korean War', *Diplomatic History* 10/3 (1986), 277. Eisenhower had already expressed a very similar attitude on 4 March at the NSC meeting on 4 March. See Stassen and Houts, *Eisenhower*, 161.

118. FRUS, 1952–4, Vol. 8, 1124–5, 11/3/1953.

119. Allegedly this is what Jackson told Rostow immediately after he emerged from the NSC meeting. See Rostow, *Europe after Stalin*, 6–7. The condition of a prior Korean truce for a summit conference is not mentioned in the minutes of the NSC meeting. Rostow had referred to it in his memorandum of 6 March without, however, drawing particular attention to it. See also Jackson's supporting statement, dated 11/3/1953, published in Rostow, ibid., 87–90; quotes: 87–9.

120. See for example Jackson's 'supporting memorandum', dated 8/3/1953, published in *Declassified Documents*, 1978, No. 115 D. Moreover, a few months later, in view of the uprising in the GDR on 17 June 1953, Jackson and Rostow once again advised Eisenhower to embark upon a psychological warfare offensive. They believed, 'that the chances of unifying Germany without major war had vastly increased'. Rostow even tended to believe that the US should encourage the GDR population to begin a 'full scale revolt'. Quoted in Brands, *Cold Warriors*, 124.

121. For good details on the Soviet peace initiatives, see for example Zubok and Pleshakov, *Inside the Kremlin's Cold War*, 138ff., esp. 155ff.; Mastny, *The Cold War and Soviet Insecurity*, 171–98; also Richter, *Khrushchev's Double Bind*, 30ff.; and still valuable A. Ulam, *Expansion and Coexistence. Soviet Foreign Policy, 1917–1973* (New York, 1974), 496ff.

122. The text of Malenkov's address on 15 March is published in RIIA, *Documents on International Affairs, 1953* (London, 1956), 11–13, quote: 12–13. See also FRUS 1952–4, Vol 8, 1131, n. 2: Editorial Note; and ibid., 1105–6, n. 3: Beam to State Department, 9/3/1953. The reaction of the British FO can be found in PRO: FO 371/106 524/NS 1021/21, 17/3/1953.

123. PRO: FO 371/106 533/NS 1051/17: Gascoigne, Moscow, to Hohler, FO, 27/3/1953; FRUS, ibid., 1138: memorandum Carlton Savage to Nitze, 1/4/1953. For Soviet-Chinese agreement on the need to enter a truce in Korea, see above all K. Weatherby, 'New Russian Documents of the Korean War. Introduction and Translation', *Cold War International History Bulletin* 6–7 (1995–6), 80–4; see also Zubok and Pleshakov, *Inside the Kremlin's Cold War*, 155.

124. Moscow hoped that the negotiations would be helpful in preventing further accidents like the shooting down of a British bomber which had strayed from the Berlin air corridor into GDR air space on March 12 (see also Chapter 11, 225, below). The Kremlin apologized for the incident. PRO: CAB 128/26, Part II, C.C. (53)20th Conclusions, minute 7, 17/3/1953; 21st Conclusions,

minute 1, 20/3/1953; 22nd Conclusions, minute 7; 24/3/1953; PRO: FO 371/106 090; and FRUS, ibid., 1130: memorandum of telephone conversation between Dulles and Eisenhower, 16/3/1953. See also PRO: PREM 11/896; Shuckburgh, *Descent to Suez*, 82–3: diary entry, 24–30/3/1953.

125. Boyle (ed.), *Correspondence*, 66–7: Churchill to Eisenhower, 4/6/1953; see also Gilbert, *Never Despair*, 834–5.

126. See Shuckburgh, *Descent to Suez*, 82–3: diary entry, 24–30/3/1953; RIIA, *Survey of International Affairs, 1953* (London, 1956), 17–18.

127. FRUS 1952–4, Vol. 8, 1137: Beam to State Dept., 20/3/1953. On 18 March Beam informed the State Dept. that Stalin's long-standing anti-America campaign had only increased the fear of the Soviet population that a war between the superpowers could break out. He concluded that 'one [of the] most popular measures [the new] regime could adopt would probably be [the] cessation [of the] anti-US campaign' (quote: ibid., 1132).

128. Ibid., 1138: memorandum Savage to Nitze, 1/4/1953; PUA: John Foster Dulles Papers, Telephone Conversation Series, Box 1, telephone conversation between Dulles and UN Ambassador Lodge, 31/3/1953; EL: Jackson Papers, Record 1953–54, 'Soviet Lures and Pressures since Stalin's Death, March 5 to 25, 1953', 26/3/1953.

129. This also applied to pending court cases with sentences expected to be less than five years imprisonment. For the view of the British FO on the amnesty, see PRO: FO 371/106 583. See also RIIA, *Survey, 1953,* 10; A.B. Ulam, *The Rivals: America and Russia Since World War II* (New York, 1971), 198.

130. FRUS 1952–4, Vol. 8, 1140–3: Beam to State Dept., 4/4/1953, quote: 1140. For the Doctors' Plot, see Knight, *Beria*, 169–75 (she believes that it may well have been Khrushchev who 'was somehow behind the case of the Doctors' Plot', p. 173); see also the memoir of one of the doctors: Y. Rapoport, *The Doctors' Plot: Stalin's Last Crime* (London, 1991), 177ff.; and in general for Stalin's and Soviet anti-Semitism, see L. Rapoport, *Stalin's War against the Jews: The Doctors' Plot and the Soviet Solution* (New York, 1990); B. Pinkus, *The Soviet Government and the Jews, 1948–1967: A Documented Study* (Cambridge, 1984). For a good discussion whether or not the Doctor's Plot was the beginning of a new purge directed against Stalin's closest advisers, see Mastny, *The Cold War and Soviet Insecurity,* 158–70.

131. FRUS, ibid., 1141: Beam to State Dept., 4/4/1953.

132. PRO: FO 371/106 533/NS 1051/17, 27/3/1953).

133. Beam, *Multiple Exposure,* 31. See also D.C. Goar, 'A Chance for Peace – the Eisenhower Administration and the Soviet Peace Offensive of 1953', *Mid-America: An Historical Review* 76/3 (1994), 241–78.

134. K. Adenauer, *Memoirs, 1945–53* (translated by B. Ruhm von Oppen; London, 1966), 438; see also 434–7.

135. PRO: FO 371/106 532/NS 10345/9, minute Roberts to his superior Permanent Under-Secretary William Strang about his conversation with Bohlen, 9/4/1953. Roberts, however, seems to have doubted that the Soviets were prepared to embark upon a new policy towards Germany on the basis of reunification. See H. Blankenhorn, *Verständnis und Verständigung. Blätter eines politischen Tagebuchs 1949 bis 1979* (Frankfurt/M., 1979), 144–5. On 11 April 1953, Ambassador Bohlen commenced his duties at the American embassy in Moscow. See Isaacson and Thomas, *Wise Men,* 575. For the Stalin note and the battle of the notes, see Chapter 9, above.

136. PRO: FO 371/103 659/C 1016/9, article by Lippman entitled 'Today and Tomorrow. Dr. Adenauer in Washington', publ. in the *New York Herald Tribune*, 7/4/1953.

137. NA: PPS, Box 16, Folder: Germany, 1950–3, memorandum by H. Koch, a State Dept. official, entitled 'Preconditions for German Unification', 26/10/1951.

138. FRUS, 1952–4, Vol. 7, 410–11: memorandum of conversation between Smith and the prominent West German MPs Gerhard Schröder, Franz-Josef Strauss, Karl Pfleiderer and Hans von Merkatz in Washington on 30/3/1953. Smith subsequently explained to Roger Makins, the British Ambassador in Washington, that convening a summit conference 'might well be enough to kill the E.D.C.'. PRO: FO 800/778, Makins to FO, telegram No 726, 6/4/1953.

139. The PSB furthermore set up the so-called 'Working Group (Stalin)' (WGS) which was made responsible for following up Eisenhower's speech by coordinating the action 'on the psychological exploitation of the situation' and to 'discourage some rather extreme suggestions …'. FRUS 1952–4, Vol. 8, 1135–6: PSB Implementation of NSC Action 734 d (3), 19/3/1953 (quote: 1136). The influence of this working group, however, seems to have been negligible. See NA: lot 64D563, PPS Records, 1947–53, Box 29, Folder: Europe, 1952–3, minute by Edmund A. Guillion, 18/5/1953, and the accompanying document 'Follow-up on President's Speech of April 16, 1953'.

140. Memorandum of a telephone conversation between Hughes and Dulles on 16/3/1953. Published in Rostow, *Europe after Stalin,* 57. A proposal that the speech should be delivered to the Pan-American Union on 12 April was also given up. Ibid., 52–4.

141. PUA: Allen Dulles Papers, Selected Correspondence, Box 56, memorandum Walter Waggoner to the journalists Krock and Whitney about Allen Dulles's talk, 3/4/1953. See also Eisenhower, *Mandate for Change*, 148–9. For some of the rather ineffective proposals of how to react to Stalin's death put forward by Allen Dulles, see Grose, *Gentleman Spy*, 349–54.

142. FRUS 1952–4, Vol. 8, 1130: memorandum of a telephone conversation between Dulles and Eisenhower, 16/3/1953.

143. Rostow, *Europe after Stalin*, 144.

144. Nitze, *From Hiroshima to Glasnost*, 143.

145. Hughes, *Ordeal of Power*, 103–4. In all probability Eisenhower said this on 16 March 1953. See ibid., 107; Rostow, *Europe after Stalin*, 56.

146. In a different context this expression is used by Keefer, 'President Dwight D. Eisenhower', 288.

147. Hughes, *Ordeal of Power*, 105ff., esp. 107–8.

148. Rostow, *Europe after Stalin*, 58; Hughes, ibid., 108–10, 119–20. Admittedly, Walt Rostow and C.D. Jackson had already made a very similar proposal. When recommending a four-power meeting during the first few days following the announcement of Stalin's illness, they had suggested that the United States should express its willingness 'to enlarge its contribution to the development of underdeveloped areas' if the four-power meeting succeeded in reducing the burden of armaments. They hoped that this proposal would 'develop an attractiveness equivalent to the Marshall Plan'. See Rostow, ibid., 87.

149. Eisenhower's ideas consisted of somewhat unrealistic proposals which the journalist Sam Lubell had suggested to him in a letter. See FRUS 1952–4, Vol. 8, 1122. See also Stassen and Houts, *Eisenhower*, 168; Bowie and Immerman, *Waging Peace*, 113–15. Already in the course of the NSC meeting on 11 March the President had said that 'what we should do now is propose that the standard of living throughout the world be raised at once, not at some indefinite time in the future. Such an appeal as this might really work. . . . the economic incentive would have terrific attraction in Russia' and this, he believed, 'might even result in a settlement in Korea.' Apart from saying that the 'emphasis in the current psychological plan, and notably in his speech, must be on the simple theme of a higher living standard for all the world ...', Eisenhower, unfortunately, did not elaborate on how this could be achieved. None of his aides thought it advisable to ask too many detailed questions. See ibid., 1122–4.

150. *Public Papers of the Presidents of the USA: Dwight D. Eisenhower, 1953* (Washington, DC, 1954) 104.

151. Memorandum of a telephone conversation between Hughes and Dulles, 16/3/1953. Published in Rostow, *Europe after Stalin*, 56–7.

152. PRO: FO 371/106 524/NS 1021/21, minute Hohler, 17/3/1953. Harry Hohler still expressed the same opinion during an interview in Washington, DC, on 27/9/1990. See also NS 1021/23, Gascoigne to FO, telegram No. 40, 20/3/1953.

153. Memorandum of a telephone conversation between Hughes and Dulles, 16/3/1953. Published in Rostow, *Europe after Stalin*, 56–7.

154. Quoted in Hughes, *Ordeal of Power*, 106.

155. Still, some officials in the State Department believed that preparations for the eventuality of four-power talks ought to be made. For example, on 1 April Carlton Savage, a member of the Policy Planning Staff, informed his director that he felt that 'these Soviet moves might lead to general negotiations between the U.S. and the Soviet Union'. It appeared to be high time 'to determine the position that [the] U.S. should take in such negotiations.' FRUS 1952–4, Vol. 8, 1138: memorandum Savage to Nitze, 1/4/1953. For possible four-power talks and the problems this would create for the EDC and America's German policy, see the illuminating memoranda by State Dept. official L. Fuller to P. Nitze, NA: PPS 64D563, Germany 1950–3, Box 16: 'EDC and a German Settlement', 17/3/1953; 'German Thinking Concerning German Unity', 17/4/1953; 'Possible Four-Power Talks on Germany', 17/4/1953.

156. FRUS 1952–4, Vol 6, 1342–4: Dillon, Paris, to State Dept., 9/4/1953 (quote: 1343). Mayer was shown a summarized version of the speech by the American ambassador to Paris. The speech was not shown to French Foreign Minister Bidault as the US believed that he would leak the draft to the press. Roger Makins, the British ambassador in Washington, believed that consequently 'Bidault of course will be hopping mad'. PRO: FO 800/839, telegram Makins to FO, No. 791, 14/4/1953. See also PRO: PREM 11/429. For the reaction of the French government to Eisenhower's draft speech, see FRUS 1952–4, Vol. 6, 1342–4; PRO: FO 800/698, memorandum Duff, Paris, 28/4/1953. See also J.L. Gerson, *John Foster Dulles* (New York, 1967), 129–30; Fish, 'After Stalin's Death', 335.

157. FRUS, ibid., 1343. See also Gerson, ibid., 129–30; Fish, ibid., 335. For Bidault's very similar view, see PRO: FO 800/698, memorandum Duff, Paris, to FO on a conversation with Lloyd and the

Canadian External Affairs Minister Lester Pearson, 28/4/1953; also FRUS, ibid., 1346: Dillon, Paris, to State Dept., 16/4/1953.

158. See Rostow, *Europe after Stalin*, 132: memorandum Dulles to Eisenhower, 6/4/1953. Adenauer's first state visit to the USA took place from 6–9 April 1953. After Churchill's visit in January, Eden's and Butler's economic talks and the visit of the French Prime Minister in March, Adenauer was the latest one of the 'cardinals of Europe [who] want to make the pilgrimage to pay their respects to the new Pope' as an American diplomat expressed it. FRUS 1952–54, Vol. 6, 1327: Dunn, Paris, to State Dept., 13/1/1953. For Adenauer's visit, see K. Adenauer, *Erinnerungen 1945–1953*, (Stuttgart, 1965), 564–89; H. Köhler, *Adenauer. Eine politische Biographie* (Frankfurt/M., 1994), 767–71.

159. See FRUS 1952–4, Vol. 7, 447. The rather exaggerated figure of 300,000 was mentioned by Adenauer during his first conversation with Eisenhower and Dulles on 7/4/1953. See ibid., 434; also Rostow, *Europe after Stalin*, 51; FRUS 1952–4, Vol. 8, 1151.

160. PRO: FO 371/103 951/CW 10345/9, Makins to FO, No. 762, 10/4/1953.

161. Quoted from Eisenhower's 'Chance for Peace' speech. See FRUS 1952–4, Vol. 8, 1152, 16/4/1953.

162. Boyle (ed.), *Correspondence*, 41–2: Churchill to Eisenhower, 11/4/1953; see also PRO: FO 800/821, 10/4/1953.

163. Hughes, *Ordeal of Power*, 111.

164. Boyle (ed.), *Correspondence*, 42–3: Eisenhower to Churchill, 11/4/1953; also PRO: FO 800/839, Makins, Washington, to FO, telegram No. 791, 14/4/1953.

165. Boyle (ed.), ibid., 43–4: Churchill to Eisenhower, 12/4/1953. See also PRO: PREM 11/429.

166. PRO: FO 800/839, Makins, Washington, to FO, No. 791, 14/4/1953. Among other issues Churchill also mentioned his high regard for Adenauer: 'I am entirely with you on not letting Adenauer down. He seems to be the best German we have found for a long time'. Boyle (ed.), ibid.; see also Boyle, 45: Eisenhower to Churchill, 13/4/1953; and PRO: PREM 11/429; FO 800/839; Foschepoth, 'Churchill, Adenauer', 1288.

167. PRO: PREM 11/429, 14/4/1953. Elizabeth II was twenty-six when she became Queen; her official coronation took place with much pomp in mid-1953.

168. FRUS 1952–4, Vol. 8, 1151–4, quotes: 1051, 1053, 16/4/1953.

169. PRO: FO 800/698, Selwyn Lloyd's memorandum about his conversation with French ambassador Massigli in London who informed Lloyd of his recent talk with Gromyko, 20/4/1953. On the Soviet reaction, see also Stassen and Houts, *Eisenhower*, 173.

170. See T. Hoopes, *The Devil and John Foster Dulles* (Boston, 1973); 173; Donovan, *Eisenhower*, 74; Hughes, *Ordeal of Power*, 113–14.

171. Donovan, ibid., 110; Cook, *Declassified Eisenhower*, 180–1.

172. Adams, *First-Hand Report*, 97.

173. See also R.F. Burk, *Dwight D. Eisenhower: Hero and Politician* (Boston, 1986), 136.

174. In view of Eisenhower's general lack of effort to pursue vigorously the realization of his ideas, J.L. Gaddis even speaks of Eisenhower's 'persistent failure to follow through on his usually quite sound initial instincts, a curious unwillingness to grasp the reins of power at all levels' (*Strategies of Containment: A Critical Appraisal of Postwar American National Security Policy*, New York, 1982, 163). See also T.E. Forland, ' "Selling Firearms to the Indians": Eisenhower's Export Control Policy, 1953–4,' *Diplomatic History* 15 (1991), 243–4.

175. See Keefer, 'President Dwight D. Eisenhower', 276–80.

176. FRUS 1952–4, Vol. 8, 1156: Bohlen to State Dept. about his conversation with Soviet politician Voroshilov, 20/4/1953.

177. Quoted in Osgood, 'Form before Substance', 431. See also M.J. Medhurst, 'Atoms for Peace and Nuclear Hegemony: The Rhetorical Structure of a Cold War Campaign', *Armed Forces & Society* 23/4 (1997), 571ff.

178. Dulles's speech, entitled 'The Eisenhower Foreign Policy, a world-wide peace offensive', is published in Rostow, *Europe after Stalin*, 122–31 (quotes: 127, 130).

179. See Gardner, 'Poisoned Apples', in Larres and Osgood (eds), *The Cold War After Stalin*, (forthcoming, 2003). This was already the strategy employed by Eisenhower and Dulles during the 1952 election campaign. See K. Larres, 'Die Welt des John Foster Dulles (1939–1953)', *Historische Mitteilungen 9/2* (1996), 265–7; see also regarding Dulles's rhetoric, G.A. Olson, 'Eisenhower and the Indochina Problem', in M.J. Medhurst (ed.), *Eisenhower's War of Words: Rhetoric and Leadership* (East Lansing, 1994), 110–11.

180. See for example Nitze's memorandum to Dulles, 19/3/1953. Published in Rostow, *Europe after Stalin*, 140–1. See also PUA: John Foster Dulles Papers, Drafts of Presidential Correspondence,

Box 1, President's Speech, April 1953 (i), memorandum Nitze to Dulles, 2/4/1953. Immerman, *John Foster Dulles*, also believes that 'Dulles correctly conceived of the two speeches as complementary, as the proverbial two sides of the same coin ...' (p. 55).

181. See PRO: CAB 128/26, CC(53)29th conclusions, 28/4/1953.
182. See Zubok and Pleshakov, *Inside the Kremlin's Cold War*, 157.

CHAPTER 11: CHURCHILL'S VISION

1. Churchill, 'World Peace (President Eisenhower's Declaration)', H.C. *Parl. Deb.*, 5th series, Vol. 514, 20/4/1953, 649–50. See also PREM 11/429, memorandum of a conversation among the American, British and French foreign ministers in Paris, 25/4/1953.

2. He also instructed Gascoigne to tell Molotov: 'I asked Gromyko to give you my good wishes, which no doubt he has done'. PRO: PREM 11/422, FO to Gascoigne, No. 228, 20/4/1053; FO 371/106 505/NS 1013/22AG, Gascoigne to FO, No. 18, 29/4/1953 ('Weekly Summary' of the week 23–29/4/1953). Churchill had seen Gromyko for a farewell visit on 17 April; Gromyko returned to Moscow and was replaced as Soviet ambassador to London by Yakov Malik. However, Churchill did not tell Gromyko what he really thought of Eisenhower's speech and he did not propose a new initiative himself to Moscow. Instead, he merely expressed his sympathies for Soviet demands to prevent any renewed German militarism. See U. Bar-Noi, 'The Soviet Union and Churchill's Appeals for High-Level Talks, 1953–4: New Evidence from the Russian Archives', *Diplomacy & Statecraft* 9/3 (1998), 113.

3. NA: 741.00/4–2053, Aldrich, London, to State Dept., No. 5686, 20/4/1953.

4. P. Boyle (ed.), *The Churchill-Eisenhower Correspondence, 1953–1955* (Chapel Hill, N.C., 1990), 46: Churchill to Eisenhower, 21/4/1953. Churchill, however, was not interested in French participation. See also Churchill's similar statement during the Cabinet meeting on 28/4/1953. PRO: CAB 128/26, Part 1, C.C. (53)29th Conclusions, minute 1. See also M. Gilbert, *Winston S. Churchill, Vol. 8; Never Despair, 1945–65*, paperback edn (London, 1990), 819–20.

5. BUA: Avon Paper, AP 20/1/29, Eden's diary entry, 4/3/1953.

6. See BUA: Avon Papers, AP 20/1/29, Eden's diary entry, 4/3/1953; and AP/20/16/9, letter Makins to Eden, 23/12/1953. On 8 May, however, Eisenhower wrote quite untruthfully to Churchill: 'I like having your letters'. See Boyle (ed.), *Correspondence*, 52.

7. Boyle (ed.), ibid., 47: Eisenhower to Churchill, 25/4/1953.

8. Although the conversation did not lead to any concrete results, Churchill felt encouraged nevertheless. Molotov had asked the ambassador to give his very best wishes to the Prime Minister. PRO: PREM 11/422, Gascoigne to FO, No. 209, 23/4/1953.

9. See Boyle (ed.), *Correspondence*, 47: Eisenhower to Churchill, 25/4/1953.

10. PRO: FO 800/821, minute Dixon to Strang on his conversation with Churchill, 2/5/1953.

11. Boyle (ed.), *Correspondence*, 48: Churchill to Eisenhower, 4/5/1953.

12. PRO: FO 800/821, SU/53/33, memorandum Strang on his conversation with Churchill, 4/5/1953. Strang wrote by hand on the memorandum that so far he had only shown Pierson Dixon Churchill's telegrams to Eisenhower and Molotov. Therefore, only Lloyd, Strang and Dixon were informed thus far.

13. M. Djilas, *Conversations with Stalin* (London, 1963), 115. For the Anglo-Soviet confrontations during the war, see Chapters 2–4 above.

14. Quote: N. Khrushchev, *Khrushchev Remembers* (Boston, 1970), 361. For details on the western involvement in the Russian civil war and for the 'iron curtain' speech, see Chapters 2, 38–42, and 6, 124ff above. Khrushchev, for example, believed that Churchill was responsible for initiating the Cold War. See N. Khrushchev, *Khrushchev Remembers: The Glasnost Tapes* (Boston, 1990), 68; N. Khrushchev, *Khrushchev Remembers: The Last Testament* (Boston, 1974), 353. Molotov held the same view, see A. Resis (ed.), *Molotov Remembers: Inside Kremlin Politics: Conversations with Felix Chuev* (Chicago, 1993), 60; so did Beria's confidant Pavel Sudoplatov. See P. and A. Sudoplatov (with J.L. and L.P. Schecter), *Special Tasks: The Memoirs of an Unwanted Witness – A Soviet Spymaster* (Boston, 1994), 221.

15. Quotes: N. Khrushchev, *Khrushchev Remembers: The Last Testament*, 355.

16. Quotes: *Khrushchev Remembers*, 393; *Khrushchev Remembers: The Last Testament*, 362.

17. N. Khrushchev, *Khrushchev Remembers*, 393. See also J. Richter, 'Reexamining Soviet Policy

towards Germany during the Beria Interregnum', *CWIHP*, Working Paper No. 3 (Washington, DC, 1992), 24–5.

18. See for convincing arguments and evidence Bar-Noi, 'The Soviet Union and Churchill's Appeals', 115ff., 129–30. Molotov had a much more powerful position within the Soviet hierarchy in the aftermath of Stalin's death than is often realized in the literature. See Chapter 10, above, n. 8.

19. Quoted in V.M. Zubok, 'Soviet Intelligence and the Cold War: The "Small" Committee of Information, 1952–53', *CWIHP*, Working Paper No. 4 (Washington, DC, 1992), 14.

20. Boyle (ed.), *Correspondence*, 49–50: Eisenhower to Churchill, 5/5/1953.

21. EL: Ann Whitman File, International Series, Box 16, Folder: President-Churchill, Vol. 1 (4), draft of a letter from Eisenhower to Churchill, 4–5/5/1953.

22. Ibid.

23. Churchill's vanity had probably also been encouraged by Polish ambassador Michalovski's statement as reported to the PM by Roberts and Lloyd. The ambassador had said 'that it was a pity that there was no longer a President Roosevelt about to seize this great opportunity for lessening world tension'. PRO: PREM 11/540, PM/MS/53/108, minute Lloyd to Churchill, 4/5/1953.

24. Boyle (ed.), *Correspondence*, 50–1: Churchill to Eisenhower, 7/5/1953.

25. See PRO: FO 371/106 225/NS 1021/52, minute Nutting on his conversation with Robert Schuman in Paris, 22/4/1953; FO 371/106 538/NS 1071/69, minute Roberts to Strang and Nutting on his talk with the Swedish ambassador M. Hägglöff, 1/5/1953.

26. Frank Roberts, for example, was still talking of the 'unduly enthusiastic reception' of the Soviet 'new look' by the Prime Minister. PRO: FO 371/125 037/ZP 9/19, minute Roberts to Strang and Nutting, 25/4/1953.

27. Boyle (ed.), *Correspondence*, 53: Churchill to Eisenhower, 7/5/1953.

28. Ibid., 53–4: Eisenhower to Churchill, 8/5/1953.

29. This view is shared by D. Carlton, 'Großbritannien und die Gipfeldiplomatie 1953–55', in B. Thoß and H.E. Volkmann (eds), *Zwischen Kaltem Krieg und Entspannung. Sicherheits und Deutschlandpolitik der Bundesrepublik im Mächtesystem der Jahre 1953–1956* (Boppard, 1988), 54. Carlton also believes that Eisenhower's reactions were characterized by a tendency to tone down his annoyance and be overly polite to Churchill.

30. PRO: PREM 11/428, letter Salisbury to Churchill, 11/6/1953. Salisbury was a nephew of Queen Victoria's long-serving Prime Minister and Foreign Secretary of the same name.

31. Salisbury wrote: 'It wouldn't matter that the President himself might have shown an understanding attitude about our going forward alone. American public opinion would never understand it'. PRO: ibid.

32. However, Churchill did not send a draft version of his speech to Washington. For the misunderstanding in the literature, see for example Carlton, 'Großbritannien und die Gipfeldiplomatie', 54; J.W. Young, 'Cold War and Détente with Moscow', in J.W. Young (ed.), *The Foreign Policy of Churchill's Peacetime Government, 1951–1955* (Leicester, 1988), 61; J.W. Young, *Winston Churchill's Last Campaign: Britain and the Cold War, 1951–55* (Oxford, 1996), 159.

33. PRO: FO 800/821, minute Dixon to Strang on his talk with Churchill on 2/5/1953.

34. FRUS 1952–4, Vol. 6, 983–84: memorandum of a telephone conversation between Smith and Eisenhower, 11/5/1953.

35. Nixon made this statement in his 1962 book *Six Crises*. Quoted in F.I. Greenstein, *The Hidden-Hand Presidency: Eisenhower as Leader* (New York, 1982), 9.

36. PRO: PREM 11/419, T. 221/53, 16/6/1953. See in a similar vein: CAB 128/26, Part II, C.C. (53)44th Conclusions, minute 4, 21/7/1953.

37. PRO: PREM 11/446: minute Roberts, 20/4/1953.

38. *Public Papers of the Presidents of the USA: Dwight D. Eisenhower, 1954* (Washington, DC, 1960), 387 (7/4/1954).

39. NA: 741.00/5–1153, Aldrich, London, to State Dept., No. 6028, 11/5/1953. See also ibid., Aldrich to State Dept., No. 6041, 12/5/1953.

40. Churchill, 'Foreign Affairs speech', H.C. *Parl. Deb.*, 5th series, Vol. 515, 11/5/1953, 883–98 (quote: 895).

41. Ibid., 896. For a contemporary view, see I.F. Stone, *The Haunted Fifties* (New York, 1963), 55–8 (reprint of a newspaper article of 30 May 1953). For an interesting analysis of Churchill's policy after Stalin's death, see also S. Lambakis, *Winston Churchill: Architect of Peace. A Study in Statesmanship and the Cold War* (Westport, Conn., 1993).

42. H.C. *Parl. Deb.*, ibid.

43. Young, *Last Campaign*, 159, points out that Churchill had already written in a positive way about the Locarno Treaty in the first volume of his war memoirs and emphasized that Britain had been

the 'arbiter and umpire' between Germany and France. It does not seem to have concerned Churchill too much in 1953 that Britain had been unable to fulfil this role in 1939/40.

44. Churchill, 'Foreign Affairs speech', H.C. *Parl. Deb.*, 5th series, Vol. 515, 11/5/1953, 897.

45. See for example Churchill, 'World Peace (President Eisenhower's Declaration)', H.C. *Parl.Deb.*, 5th series, Vol. 514, 20/4/1953, 649–50. This was also recognized in Moscow. See RIIA, *Documents on International Affairs, 1953* (London, 1956), 66–7. For a similar argumentation, see A. Hillgruber, *Alliierte Pläne für eine 'Neutralisierung' Deutschlands 1945–55* (Opladen, 1987), 21, and partially also J. Foschepoth, 'Churchill, Adenauer und die Neutralisierung Deutschlands', *Deutschland-Archiv* 17 (1984), 1289–91. Thus, claiming that the call for a summit meeting was the 'bombshell in the speech' (Young, *Last Campaign*, 160) is an exaggeration. It ignores the much greater importance of the other crucial aspects of Churchill's speech which are outlined in the following. See also the interesting discussion in S. Mawby, *Containing Germany: Britain and the Arming of the Federal Republic* (Basingstoke, 1999), 106–12.

46. To some extent the latter aspect has also been pointed out by the following authors: H. Haftendorn, 'Adenauer und die europäische Sicherheit', in D. Blumenwitz et al. (eds), *Konrad Adenauer und seine Zeit. Politik und Persöhnlichkeit des ersten Bundeskanzlers*, Vol. 2 (Stuttgart, 1976), 99; H.J. Rupieper, 'Wiedervereinigung und europäische Sicherheit. Deutsch-amerikanische Überlegungen für eine entmilitarisierte Zone in Europa 1953', *Militärgeschichtliche Mitteilungen* 39 (1986), 91, 93, 100. Yet, Foschepoth, ibid., 1291, believes that the question of a security guarantee was not the most crucial element of the speech as already the British-Soviet and the French-Soviet treaties of friendship of 1942 and 1944 had promised the USSR protection from Germany. However, this statement overestimates the importance Moscow attached to the treaties concluded with western powers during the war in an entirely different political climate. A considerable number of authors ignore the security aspect entirely. See for example M.S. Fish, 'After Stalin's Death. The Anglo-American Debate over a new Cold War', *Diplomatic History* 10 (1986), 338; Young, 'Cold War', 60–1; and in particular S. Dockrill, *Britain's Policy for West German Rearmament, 1950–55* (Cambridge, 1991), 125–26.

47. For an overview of the non-governmental plans drawn up by individuals for the time after 1948/9, see G. Scheuer, 'Materielle Voraussetzungen für eine Wiedervereinigung Deutschlands in der Sicht nichtamtlicher Vorschläge', *Europa-Archiv* 6 (1960), 177–92. For an interesting but rather incomplete compilation, see E. Hinterhoff, *Disengagement* (London, 1959), 139ff.

48. See D. Felken, *Dulles und Deutschland. Die amerikanische Deutschlandpolitik 1953–1959* (Bonn, 1993), 198ff.; H.J. Rupieper, 'Deutsche Frage und europäische Sicherheit. Politisch-strategische Überlegungen 1953/55', in Thoß and Volkmann (eds), *Zwischen Kaltem Krieg und Entspannung*, 180–1 (quote: 181); Rupieper, 'Wiedervereinigung und europäische Sicherheit', 92; H.J. Rupieper, *Der besetzte Verbündete. Die amerikanische Deutschlandpolitik 1949–55* (Opladen, 1991), 300ff.

49. See K. Pfleiderer, *Politik für Deutschland. Reden und Aufsätze 1948–1956* (Stuttgart, 1961), esp. 83ff., 100ff. See also K.H. Schlarp, 'Alternativen zur deutschen Außenpolitik 1952–5. Karl Georg Pfleiderer und die "Deutsche Frage" ', in W. Benz and H. Graml (eds), *Aspekte deutscher Außenpolitik im 20. Jahrhundert* (Stuttgart, 1976), 213–14, 217–18, 222–5, 233–7; also A. Baring, *Im Anfang war Adenauer. Die Entstehung der Kanzlerdemokratie*, 3rd edn, paperback (Munich, 1984), 300–1; Hinterhoff, *Disengagement*, 157, 161; and for very critical views, see W.G. Grewe, *Deutsche Außenpolitik in der Nachkriegszeit* (Stuttgart, 1960), 174–81; K. Erdmenger, *Das folgenschwere Mißverständnis. Bonn und die sowjetische Deutschlandpolitik 1949–55* (Freiburg, 1967), 132ff. For German Foreign Minister Stresemann's original Locarno treaty, see P. Krüger, *Die Außenpolitik der Republik von Weimar* (Darmstadt, 1985), 269–334. For the differing interpretations of the Locarno treaty, see RIIA, *Documents, 1953*, 68; RIIA, *Survey of International Affairs, 1953* (London, 1956), 22; PRO: FO 371/106 527/NS 1021/110, memorandum of the FO Research Dept., 29/10/1953.

50. See Rupieper, 'Wiedervereinigung und europäische Sicherheit', 93–4; Haftendorn, 'Adenauer und die europäische Sicherheit', 101; also Hinterhoff, ibid., 164–5. See also V. Dujardin and M. Dumoulin, *Paul van Zeeland* (Brussels, 1997).

51. In the literature the connection between Churchill's speech and the various disengagement proposals of 1953 (which were partially revived between 1955 and 1958) has still not been considered. It is for example ignored in P. Siebenmorgen's book dealing with Adenauer's policy of détente (whatever this may have been): *Gezeitenwechsel. Aufbruch zur Entspannungspolitik* (Bonn, 1990), e.g. 71–2, 79–80.

52. At least Herbert Blankenhorn referred to this during his visit to Washington and London in early and mid-June. At this time Blankenhorn was the official who was the West German Chancellor's

most trusted confidant in matters of foreign policy. Initially London and Washington were only informed verbally about the work taking place in Bonn in great secrecy and no concrete written plans were submitted. Rupieper refers to talks between German official W.W. Schütz and the American official L.W. Fuller in Washington on 9 April. See Rupieper, 'Wiedervereinigung und europäische Sicherheit', 95–6. Schütz worked for Jakob Kaiser whose Ministry for All-German Questions had already begun in April – independently from the Chancellery with whom it co-existed in intense competition – to consider disengagement proposals (see point 6 of the 'Schütz-plan', in ibid., 96). However, the exact development of the West German plan is still unclear. Rupieper even believes that Adenauer was not familiar with the plan; in view of the Chancellor's suspicion and firm grip on anything important that went on within his government this is most unlikely. See ibid., 94–7; Haftendorn, 'Adenauer und europäische Sicherheit' 98–9; also K. Adenauer, *Erinnerungen 1953–55* (Stuttgart, 1966), 225–6; H. Blankenhorn, *Verständnis und Verständigung. Blätter eines politischen Tagebuchs 1949 bis 1979* (Frankfurt/M., 1979), 158–62. Blankenhorn mentioned the German considerations not only during his visit to Washington in early July 1953 as assumed in the literature but had already made references to the plan a month earlier during his visits to Washington (2–5 June) and London (on 15 June). See PRO: FO 371/103 704/C 1073/10, minute Colville to Shuckburgh, 27/7/1953, commenting on telegram No. 1461, dated 11/7/1953, from the British embassy in Washington. See also Rupieper, ibid., 95; Blankenhorn, ibid., 158–59; H.P. Schwarz, *Adenauer. Der Staatsmann 1952–1967* (Suttgart, 1991), 86–7. See also FO 371/103 665/C 1071/60/G, memorandum Roberts to Strang, 17/6/1953, on his conversation with British official Con O'Neill who in turn had spoken to Blankenhorn during the latter's visit to London on 15 June. See also FO 371/103 704/C 1073/10, 17/6/1953. See also Felken, *Dulles und Deutschland*, 198ff.

53. It remained unclear to which kind of Germany Adenauer referred, i.e. a Germany with or without the territories beyond the Oder–Neisse line. It was thus unspecified behind which line the Soviet troops would have to withdraw. See PRO: FO 371/103 665/C 1071/60/G, memorandum Roberts to Strang, 17/6/1953 on his conversation with Con O'Neill.

54. See Chapter 4 above, 93ff.

55. PRO: FO 371/103 665/C 1071/60/G, minute Strang, 18/6/1953, commenting on Roberts's memorandum regarding his conversation with Con O'Neill. The more or less final version of the West German plan was only received by the American High Commissioner, and subsequently by the British, on 16 September 1953.

56. See PRO: FO 800/794, GE/53/11 (also C 1074/14), p. 18.

57. Churchill declared: 'Strong as is our desire to see a friendly settlement with Soviet Russia, or even an improved modus vivendi, we are resolved not in any way to fail in the obligations to which we have committed ourselves about Western Germany. Dr. Adenauer is visiting us here in a few days, and we shall certainly assure him that Western Germany will in no way be sacrificed or – I pick these words with special care – cease to be master of its own fortunes within the agreements we and other N.A.T.O. countries have made with them.' Churchill, 'Foreign Affairs speech', H.C. *Parl. Deb.*, 5th series, Vol. 515, 11/5/1953, 889–90.

58. Ibid., 898.

59. See PRO: FO 371/106 510/NS 1016/39; CAB 128/26, Part II, C.C. (53)22nd Conclusions, minute 7, 24/3/1953. It appears that the plane may well have been on an espionage mission.

60. For the relative success of the talks, see PRO: FO 371/104 052–060; PREM 11/896. For the bilateral Anglo-Soviet talks, see PRO 371/104 049–051.

61. PRO: FO 800/794, minute Colville, 25/4/1953.

62. Ibid., memorandum Roberts to Strang on telegram No.410 by Kirkpatrick, British High Commissioner in Germany, 20/4/1953. See also in a similar vein: FO 800/821, minute Churchill to Lloyd and Strang, M 97/53, 21/4/1953.

63. PRO: FO 800/701, letter Churchill to the parliamentarians Boothby, Amery, Hope, Beamish et al., 18/6/1953. See also PREM 11/427, minute Nutting to Churchill and others, 17–18/6/1953 and Churchill's reply, 19/6/1953. Whether or not the uprising in the GDR led to Churchill's letter is unclear.

64. Churchill, 'Foreign Affairs speech', H.C. *Parl. Deb.*, 5th series, Vol. 515, 11/5/1953, 890.

65. For example, an article containing this assumption by a former general of the West German armed forces was published in April 1989. See G. Kießling, 'Zum Begriff der Neutralität in der deutschlandpolitischen Diskussion', *Deutschland-Archiv* 22 (1989), 384–90.

66. For a similar conclusion based on a different argumentation, see Foschepoth, 'Churchill, Adenauer', 1291 (the author basically follows Adenauer's line of thinking in his *Erinnerungen*,

1953–55, 211). Foschepoth explains that a new Locarno treaty would have necessitated a German peace treaty including firm agreement on Germany's eastern borders. Thus, according to Foschepoth (and Adenauer), a Locarno treaty would have led to a 'definitive decision in the question of the country's western integration'. 'The thought of a neutralisation of Germany was therefore only a logical consequence arising out of Churchill's policy of détente'. A. Hillgruber is not convinced however. He writes that Churchill had said nothing about a neutralization of Germany in his speech (see his *Alliierte Pläne*, 22). However, Hillgruber misunderstands the implications of the statements contained in Churchill's address.

67. RIIA, *Survey, 1953*, 23. The detailed Soviet reaction to Churchill's speech was published in the Communist party newspaper *Pravda* on 24 May. It is also publ. in RIIA, *Documents, 1953*, 66–71; further information also in PRO: PREM 11/421; FO 371/106 505/NS 1013/22AG; NS 1013/25–7; FO 371/103 664/C 1071/8. The Canadian government also supported Churchill's plans. See PRO: FO 371/103 705/C 1074/10, minute Roberts to Strang on his conversation with Mr Crean from the Canadian High Commission in London, 18/5/1953. See also G. Wettig, *Bereitschaft zu Einheit in Freiheit? Die sowjetische Deutschland-Politik 1945–1955* (Munich, 1999), 241; G. Wettig, 'Berijas deutsche Pläne im Licht neuer Quellen', in C. Kleßmann and B. Stöver (eds), *1953 – Krisenjahr des Kalten Krieges in Europa* (Cologne, 1999), 54.

68. Quoted in V. Zubok, 'The Case of Divided Germany', in W. Taubman, S. Khrushchev and A. Gleason (eds), *Nikita Khrushchev* (New Haven, Conn., 2000), 280. For the 'Beria affair' and the latter's proposal for the creation of a reunited neutral Germany in May/June 1953, see Chapter 12, 241ff., below.

69. For details, see Chapter 12, below.

70. See V. Zubok, ' "Unverfroren und grob in der Deutschlandfrage …" Berija, der Nachfolgestreit nach Stalins Tod und die Moskauer DDR-Debatte im April–Mai 1953', in Kleßmann and Stöver (eds), *Krisenjahr des Kalten Krieges*, 34; also V. Zubok, 'Soviet Intelligence and the Cold War: The "Small" Committee of Information, 1952–53', *Diplomatic History* 19/3 (1995), 462.

71. See Bar-Noi, 'The Soviet Union and Churchill's Appeals', 114–15.

72. However, the American reaction to Churchill's speech was also influenced by Attlee's speech in the same foreign affairs debate on 11 May. The British Leader of the Opposition had criticized the alleged poor working of the American constitution and American domestic politics. This led to a strong anti-British attack by Senator McCarthy, who demanded an apology, and also intensified the negative response by Senator Knowland to Churchill's speech. See *Annual Register of World Events, 1953* (London, 1954), 164; RIIA, *Survey, 1953*, 21, n. 5. See also Adenauer, *Erinnerungen 1953–55*, 206; Fish, 'After Stalin's Death', 338.

73. See RIIA, ibid. 23–4; RIIA, *Documents, 1953*, 65–6; Eisenhower, *Public Papers, 1953*, 285; H.S. Parmet, *Eisenhower and the American Crusade* (New York, 1972), 282–3. For the American reaction, see also Blankenhorn, *Verständnis und Verständigung*, 149.

74. D. Pearson, *Diaries, 1949–59*, ed. by T. Abell (New York, 1974), 269.

75. Quoted according to a summary of the article compiled for Churchill by the Foreign Office, PRO: FO 371/103 704/C 1073/4, FAZ, 14/5/1953. See also C 1073/3, FAZ, 12/5/1953; see also D.C. Watt, 'Churchill und der Kalte Krieg', *Schweizer Monatshefte*, 61/11, Sonderbeilage (1981), 18.

76. See H. Macmillan, *Tides of Fortune, 1945–55* (London 1969), 511.

77. For example at an early stage Churchill had asked Strang for a draft on considerations of 'The Locarno Principle'. See PRO: FO 800/699, Strang to Churchill, PM/WS/53/81, 27/4/1953; also PREM 11/373, letter Strang to Churchill, 20/4/1953. See also Strang's letter to David Pitblado, one of Churchill's private secretaries, dated 20/4/1953, Con/53/38, FO 800/759. Lloyd's biographer writes that in the weeks before the 11 May speech Lloyd and Churchill collaborated closely. See D.R. Thorpe, *Selwyn Lloyd* (London, 1989), 171. For the question whether or not Churchill had consulted the FO and whether or not the diplomats had agreed with his speech, see A. Seldon, *Churchill's Indian Summer: The Conservative Government, 1951–55* (London, 1981), 400–1; Young, *Last Campaign*, 159–60; A. Nutting, *Europe Will Not Wait: A Warning and a Way Out* (London, 1960), 50; also G. Buchstab (ed.), *Adenauer, 'Es mußte alles neu gemacht werden'* […], (Stuttgart, 1986), 519; R. Morsey and H.P. Schwarz (eds), *Adenauer. Briefe, 1951–53* (Berlin, 1987), 373.

78. See PRO: FO 371/103 664/C 1071/9, minute Hancock, director of the Central Dept., 6/5/1953.

79. Colville referred to the EDC. See J. Colville, *The Fringes of Power: 10 Downing Street Diaries, 1939–1955* (London, 1985), 667. The British ambassador-designate to Moscow, Sir William Hayter, declared: 'Churchill's speech was a disaster'. See C.L. Sulzberger, *A Long Row of Candles: Memoirs and Diaries, 1934–1954* (New York, 1969), 873: diary entry, 15/5/1953.

80. BUA: Avon Papers, AP 20/16/127, letter Nutting to Eden, 26/6/1953.

81. Colville and Lloyd's biographer report that the Minister of State viewed the speech in a positive light and therefore 'a certain cooling' of his relationship with Eden could be noticed. Indeed, on 12 May Lloyd gave a fairly optimistic speech in which he welcomed a summit conference (see also Young, *Last Campaign*, 164). However, documents from the end of April and mid-June 1953 do not confirm this view. In June Lloyd and Nutting collaborated to dissuade Churchill from pursuing his plans. Perhaps in early May Lloyd was briefly affected by Churchill's enthusiasm and had begun to support the Prime Minister's summit diplomacy only to revert to a more sceptical attitude after consulting his colleagues in the Foreign Office. See Colville, *Fringes of Power*, 667; Thorpe, *Selwyn Lloyd*, 171; Watt, 'Churchill und der Kalte Krieg', 19; Seldon, *Indian Summer*, 400–1; Young, 'Cold War', 61; Lloyd, 'Foreign Affairs speech', H.C. *Parl. Deb.*, 5th series, Vol. 515, 12/5/1953, 1071–2. See also NA: 741.00/5–1253, Aldrich to State Dept., No. 6052, 12/5/1953; BUA: Avon Papers, AP 20/16/127, letter Nutting to Eden, 25/6/1953. See also the memorandum from Lloyd to Churchill indicating the correctness of the above, 22/6/1953, FO 371/103 665/C 1071/56; also FO 371/106 537/NS 1071/57, minute Hohler, 25/4/1953; PREM 11/429, memorandum of conversation between the American, British and French foreign ministers in Paris, 25/4/1953; FO 371/125 032/ZP 3/29, FO telegram to the High Commissioners in the 'old' Commonwealth countries, 30/4/1953.

82. See KCL: Liddell–Hart-Archive, Ismay Papers III/12/5 and 6/1: Montgomery's memoranda to Churchill, 26/6 and 2/7/1953; ibid., III/12/7a, Ismay's reply, dated 6/7/1953. Even as late as April 1959 Montgomery criticized Eisenhower in a television interview for his lack of enthusiasm about attending a summit meeting and suggested that soldiers should stay out of politics. See Gilbert, *Never Despair*, 1294, n. 4; also A. Montague Browne, *Long Sunset: Memoirs of Winston Churchill's Last Private Secretary* (London, 1995), 263. See also Hillgruber, *Alliierte Pläne*, 23; Dockrill, *Britain's Policy*, 125–26. Regarding Slessor, see also Hinterhoff, *Disengagement*, 145, 174–5. Later Slessor would view Churchill's summit diplomacy in a very critical light. See his *What Price Coexistence? Policy for the Western Alliance* (London, 1962), 37–40.

83. For a good overview, see Young, *Last Campaign*, 161–3.

84. Churchill, 'Foreign Affairs speech', H.C. *Parl. Deb.*, 5th series, Vol. 515, 11/5/1953, 897.

85. BUA: Avon Papers, AP 20/1/30, diary entry Eden, 27/11/1954. See also R.R. James, *Anthony Eden*, paperback edn (London, 1986), 365.

86. For the reaction of the West German press, see PRO: FO 371/103 704/C 1073/3–4; and FO 371/103 664/C 1071/8. See also E. Noelle and E.P. Neumann (eds), *Antworten. Politik im Kraftfeld der öffentlichen Meinung* (Allensbach, 1954), 119–64; and Noelle and Neumann (eds), *The Germans: Public Opinion Polls, 1947–1966* (London, 1967), 214ff. For public opinion in Britain, see G.H. Gallup (ed.), *The Gallup International Opinion Poll. Great Britain, 1937–1975, Vol. 1: 1937–64* (London, 1976), 253ff., 295ff.; and for public opinion in the USA, see H.G. Erskine, 'The Cold War. Report from the Polls', *Political Science Quarterly* 25 (1961), 302–3; Erskine, 'The Polls. Defense, Peace, and Space', in ibid., 487–89; R.G. Niemi et al. (eds), *Trends in Public Opinion. A Compendium of Survey Data* (New York, 1989), 52–70.

87. See RIIA, *Survey, 1953*, 21.

88. The meeting took place from 23 to 25 April 1953. See for the NATO meeting and the tripartite ministerial talks, FRUS 1952–4, Vol. 5, 368–97; HMSO, Cmd. Paper No. 8838; HMSO, Miscellaneous No. 5 'Report of the North Atlantic Ministerial Meeting held in Paris 23–25 April 1953'. For London's points of view as formulated during the meetings, see PRO: PREM 11/369.

89. PRO: FO 371/106 538/NS 1071/82, Hayter, Paris, to Roberts, FO, about a conversation with de Staercke and the British diplomat Derek Hoyer Millar, 14/5/1953.

90. Bidault's interpretation of Moscow's intention rested largely on the Kremlin's reaction to Eisenhower's 'Chance for Peace' speech as published in *Pravda*. This *Pravda* article is partially publ. in RIIA, *Documents, 1953*, 51–7. See also Churchill, 'Oral Answers', H.C. *Parl. Deb.*, 5th series, Vol. 514, 29/4/1953, 2142; R. Steininger, 'Ein vereintes, unabhängiges Deutschland? Winston Churchill, der Kalte Krieg und die deutsche Frage im Jahre 1953', *Militärgeschichtliche Mitteilungen* 34 (1984), 115–16. George Kennan wrote an interesting analysis of Moscow's reaction. Like Bidault, Kennan concluded that Stalin's successors were 'definitely interested in pursuing with us the effort to solve some of the present international difficulties'. EL: Jackson Papers, Records, 1953–4, Box 4, Folder: Kennan, memorandum Kennan, 25/4/1953. For Bidault's attempts to persuade his American and British colleagues of the French position, see PRO: FO 371/106 538/NA 1071/61, memorandum of a trilateral meeting, Paris, 25/4/1953; FO 371/106 094/N 1191/12, Harvey, Paris, to FO, No. 150, 25/4/1953.

91. PRO: FO 371/103 951/CW 10345/9, minute Allen, 13/4/1953, on his conversation with French diplomat Lebel.

92. PRO: PREM 11/429, memorandum of a trilateral conversation, Paris, 25/4/1953; PRO: FO 371/106 537/NS 1071/57, minute Holer, 25/4/1953. FO 371/125 032/ZP 3/25, memorandum of a trilateral ministerial meeting, Paris, c. 22/4/1953; Steininger, 'Ein vereintes, unabhängiges Deutschland?', 116, emphasizes that Bidault aimed at a summit meeting to discuss the German question as a priority. This is incorrect. Above all, Bidault wished to talk about rearmament; he did not intend to convene a summit meeting along traditional lines (e.g. by once again talking about Germany). To him the conclusion of a rearmament treaty prior to discussing Germany was necessary to find an acceptable solution to the German question. See PRO: PREM 11/429.

93. PRO: PREM 11/429, memorandum of a conversation among the French, British and American foreign ministers during the NATO meeting, 25/4/1953. For French Cold War strategy, see W.I. Hitchcock, *France Restored: Cold War Diplomacy and the Quest for Leadership in Europe, 1944–1954* (Chapel Hill, N.C., 1998).

94. Blankenhorn told McCloy on 15/3/1953 that Bidault only gave 'lip service' to the EDC but that he was not interested in the realization of the European army concept. See FRUS 1952–4, Vol. 8, 406. See also Dockrill, *Britain's Policy*, 114; F. Giles declares that Bidault 'was always liable to personal mood and petty jealousy'. See his book *The Locust Years. The Story of the Fourth French Republic, 1946–58* (London, 1991), 183. For Bidault's views see also the very informative letter by the British ambassador in Paris, O. Harvey, to Roberts, dated 29/6/1953: FO 371/103 666/C 1071/62. Hancock commented on the letter on 1/7/1953: 'The fact is that M. Bidault and a lot of other Frenchmen want neither the EDC nor a reunited Germany. They want, in fact, to maintain the present situation, just as King Canute did' (ibid.).

95. This interpretation still differs from the view of most scholars to date who have largely ignored both Bidault's proposal for a disarmament conference and the letter he intended to send to propose a summit conference. So far most authors claim that the French government viewed Churchill's speech negatively as it strengthened the opponents of the EDC in the National Assembly and because Churchill did not show any interest in French participation in his summit conference. Although the latter claim, but not the former, is correct, by itself it does not explain the French position sufficiently. Thus, it is difficult to agree with the interpretations by Young, *Last Campaign*, 166–7; Steininger, 'Ein vereintes, unabhängiges Deutschland?', 118; Carlton, 'Großbritannien und die Gipfeldiplomatie', 55–6; Gilbert, *Never Despair*, 833; Young, 'Cold War', 61; J.W. Young, 'Churchill, the Russians and the Western Alliance: The Three-Power Conference at Bermuda, December 1953', *English Historical Review* 101 (1986), 891–3. Young does mention Bidault's disarmament proposal but does not include it in his discussion. See also Rupieper, *Der besetzte Verbündete*, 315–16; also R. Massigli, *Une comédie des erreurs 1943–1966. Souvenirs et réflections sur une étape de la reconstruction européenne* (Paris, 1978), 374ff.; V. Auriol, *Journal du septennat, 1947–1954* (Paris, 1978), 163ff. My analysis is confirmed by Selwyn Lloyd's minute on his conversation with French ambassador Massigli on 19 May in London. Subsequently Lloyd wrote to Churchill: 'Contrary to what has appeared in the press, he [Massigli] did not make any adverse criticism of your suggestion for a meeting of the Great Powers'. PRO: FO 800/700, PM/MS/53/155, 19/5/1953. See also quite correct Köhler, *Adenauer*, 811.

96. PRO: FO 371/125 032/ZP 3/29, telegram to the British High Commissioners in Canada, Australia, New Zealand and South Africa with information about the ministerial talks during the NATO meeting in Paris, dated 30/4/1953. The Central Dept. sent a similar analysis to Nutting on 6 May in preparation for his parliamentary speech on 12 May. See Chapter 12, below for an analysis of the new Soviet leaders' policy towards German unification.

97. PRO: FO 371/103 664/C 1071/9, memorandum Hancock, 6/5/1953.

98. Blankenhorn, *Verständnis und Verständigung*, 148; see also FRUS 1952–4, Vol. 7, 456–7: Draper, US NATO representative to State Dept., 13/5/1953. See also EL: Ann Whitman File, International Series, Box 13, Folder: Germany 1953 (5), memorandum Smith to Eisenhower, undated, c. mid-May 1953.

99. PRO: FO 371/103 665/C 1071/60G, memorandum Roberts to Strang, 17/6/1953 on a conversation between Blankenhorn and Con O'Neill in London on 15/6/1953. See also Blankenhorn, ibid., 155.

100. Adenauer, *Erinnerungen 1953–55*, 205.

101. Morsey and Schwarz (eds), *Adenauer. Briefe 1951–53*, 363: letter Adenauer to Karl Arnold, 9/5/1953.

102. See Adenauer, *Erinnerungen 1953–55*, 295–8; Blankenhorn, *Verständnis und Verständigung*, 150–1; H. Booms (ed.), *Die Kabinettsprotokolle der Bundesregierung, Vol. 6: 1953* (Boppard, 1988), 301; Foschepoth, 'Churchill, Adenauer', 1290–1; Schwarz, *Adenauer, Der Staatsmann*, 72–4; also B. Leupold, '*Weder anglophil noch anglophob'. Großbritannien im politischen Denken Konrad Adenauers* (Frankfurt/M., 1997), 248–50; for a more general account of Adenauer's policy towards

Britain, see also A. Pütz, 'Aber ein Europa ohne Grossbritannien kann ich mir nicht vorstellen!' Die Englandpolitik der Ära Adenauer, 1949–63 (Bochum, 1996); also S. Lee, Victory in Europe: Britain and Germany since 1945 (London, 2001), chs 3 and 4.

103. PRO: FO 371/103 927/CW 10113/48, letter Kirkpatrick to Roberts, 5/5/1953.

104. However, in talks with journalists and later in his memoirs Adenauer remained rather discreet about his aim. See PRO: FO 371/103 704/C 1073/6; Adenauer, Erinnerungen 1953–55, 205–17.

105. PRO: FO 371/103 705/C 1074/5, memorandum of a conversation between Roberts and Blankenhorn, 15/5/1953.

106. PRO: FO 371/104 131/CW 1633/11, minute Roberts to Central Dept., 17/4/1953; CW 1633/9, letter Colville to British diplomat Priestman, 14/4/1953. See also Blankenhorn, Verständnis und Verständigung, 151; R. Morsey and H.P. Schwarz (eds), Adenauer. Teegespräche 1950–54, 2nd edn (Berlin, 1985), 464–5.

107. PRO: ibid.; minute Roberts to either Anthony Montague-Brown or David Pitblado (who together with Colville were Churchill's private secretaries) on his talk with Colville, 20/4/1953. It is noteworthy that the FO did not believe it necessary to invite the American or French ambassador to the official dinner for Adenauer. They had been invited in December 1951 when Adenauer first visited London to avoid the impression 'that we were cooking something up with Dr Adenauer'. But this did not seem to be necessary anymore as the Chancellor's ' "independent status" has progressed considerably since then'. Ibid., minute Roberts, 18/4/1953.

108. See for the memorandum of the conversation between Churchill and Adenauer on 15/5/1953: PRO, FO 800/794/GE/53/11; also FO 371/103 705/C 1074/14; C 174/16. For Adenauer's press conference on 16/6/1953, see C 1074/5.

109. Ibid., memorandum, 15/5/1953.

110. Ibid.

111. PRO: FO 800/794, GE/53/11 (also C 1074/14), p. 18.

112. PRO: FO 371/103 665/C 1071/60 G, memorandum Roberts to Strang, 17/6/1953, on a conversation between Blankenhorn with O'Neill in London on 15/6/195. See also for a similar account, Blankenhorn, Verständnis und Verständigung, 150–1.

113. PRO: FO 371/103 664/C 1071/10, Roberts to Strang, 27/5/1953, on his conversation with Humphrey Trevelyan, the financial and economic adviser at the British High Commission in Wahnerheide near Bonn on 26/5/1953.

114. PRO: FO 800/794, GE/53/11, memorandum of the conversation between Churchill and Adenauer, 15/5/1953 (quote: p.20); see also FO 371/103 705/15, minute Roberts to Strang, 16/5/1953; 103 894/CW 1013/19, Kirkpatrick to FO, No. 376, 19/5/1953. Strang made similar statements to the Turkish ambassador on 10/6/1953. See PRO: FO 371/103 704/C 1073/7. See also Adenauer, Erinnerungen 1953–55, 207, 210–11 (quote: 211); Buchstab (ed.), Adenauer, 'Es mußte alles neu gemacht werden', 519; Morsey and Schwarz (eds), Adenauer. Teegespräche, 464–6; also H.P. Schwarz, Die Ära Adenauer. Gründerjahre der Republik, 1949–1957 (Wiesbaden, 1981), 206.

115. PRO: FO 371/103 705/C 1074/15, minute Roberts to Strang, 16/5/1953; see also D. Gossel, Briten, Deutsche und Europa: die deutsche Frage in der britischen Außenpolitik, 1945–1962 (Stuttgart, 1999), 65–83.

116. Buchstab (ed.), Adenauer. 'Es mußte alles neu gemacht werden', 518–19.

117. See Morsey and Schwarz (eds), Adenauer: Teegespräche, 467.

118. See Buchstab (ed.), Adenauer, 'Es mußte alles neu gemacht werden', 519–20. See also A. Baring, Sehr geehrter Herr Bundeskanzler! Heinrich von Brentano im Briefwechsel mit Konrad Adenauer 1949–1964 (Hamburg, 1974), 128; Morsey and Schwarz (eds), Adenauer: Briefe 1951–53, 368.

119. Adenauer, Erinnerungen 1953–55, 205, 208–9. For Adenauer's concern about Churchill's plans, see also FRUS 1952–4, Vol. 7, 458–9: Bruce, Paris, to Conant, Bonn, 29/5/1953; FO 371/103 664/C 1071/34, minute Roberts on his conversation with the Dutch ambassador Stikker, 10/6/1953.

120. Roberts diplomatically ignores this in his memoirs. He writes: 'Churchill maintained that his ideas need not have interfered with our Western plans for the future of Germany, but I think he was alone in that view'. See F. Roberts, Dealing with Dictators: The Destruction and Revival of Europe, 1930–70 (London, 1991), 166.

121. PRO: FO 371/103 660/C 1016/32, minute Dixon to Strang and Roberts, 19/5/1953, on his conversation with Churchill on 16/5/1953.

122. Ibid., minute Strang to Dixon, 19/5/1953, on his conversation with Churchill on 18/5/1953.

123. Ibid., memorandum Roberts to Strang: 'A unified, neutralised Germany', 19/5/1953. The edited memorandum which Strang sent to Churchill (but not the first version written by Roberts on which the following remarks are based) is publ. in Steininger, 'Ein vereintes, unabhängiges Deutschland?', 126–8; see also Foschepoth, 'Churchill, Adenauer', 1292–3.

124. PRO: ibid. See also my introduction in K. Larres (ed.), 'Witness Seminar: British Attitudes to German Rearmament and Reunification in the 1950s', *Contemporary Record* 5 (1991), 291ff.

125. PRO: FO 371/103 666/C 1016/32, memorandum Roberts to Strang, 'A unified, neutralised Germany', 19/5/1953. Similar fears regarding a new German Rapallo policy were also expressed by Pierson Dixon. See FO 371/103 660/C 1016/34, minute Dixon to Strang and Roberts, 1/6/1953. For the issue in general, see K. Larres, 'Germany and the West: the "Rapallo Factor" in German Foreign Policy from the 1950s to the 1990s', in K. Larres and P. Panayi (eds), *The Federal Republic of Germany since 1949: Politics, Society and Economy before and after Unification* (London, 1996), 278–326.

126. PRO: ibid. See also the interviews in M. Charlton, *The Price of Victory* (London, 1983), 124ff; and in Larres (ed.), 'Witness Seminar', 302ff.

127. Ibid., C 1016/32, minute Dixon, 19/5/1953, on Roberts's memorandum 'A unified, neutralised Germany', dated 19/5/1953.

128. Ibid., C 1016/33, Roberts to Strang, 29/5/1953, on an editorial in *Die Welt* of 27/5/1953.

129. PRO: FO 371/106 538/NS 1071/110/G, memorandum Nutting to Lloyd and Strang, 29/5/1953.

130. PRO: PREM 11/449 (also in FO 800/794), memorandum Strang, 'A unified, neutralised Germany', including an accompanying letter by Strang to Churchill, PM/WS/185, both dated 30/5/1953.

131. Ibid., Churchill to Strang, M. 178/53, 31/5/1953.

132. At the same time Churchill pointed to the analogy between a united Germany and the fate of Czechoslovakia which nobody understood despite the attempts at interpretation by Pierson Dixon. See PRO: FO 371/103 660/C 1016/34, minute Dixon to Strang and Roberts, 1/6/1953.

133. Ibid., minute Roberts, 3/6/1953.

134. PRO: PREM 11/1074; Steininger, 'Ein vereintes, unabhängiges Deutschland?', 118; Young, 'Churchill, the Russians and the Western Alliance', 889, 893–4; Young, *Last Campaign*, 167–8.

135. See Buchstab (ed.), *Adenauer. 'Es mußte alles neu gemacht werden'*, 519.

136. The French were fighting the war with ten well-equipped divisions which were therefore not available for use in the context of the EDC. Paris increasingly feared that West Germany would not only be stronger economically (the West German economic miracle could already be observed) but also militarily in Western Europe. See PRO: FO 800/700, letter ambassador Massigli to Lloyd, 15/5/1953; Giles, *The Locust Years*, 194–7.

137. PRO: ibid., minute Lloyd to Churchill, PM/MS/53/115, 19/5/1953, on his conversation with Massigli on 15/5/1953; also PREM 11/449: minute Lloyd to Churchill, 14/6/1953 with a memorandum on a conversation between Roberts and French diplomat Crouy-Chanel, 12/6/1953. See also Massigli, *Une comédie des erreurs 1943–1966*, 377–9; Auriol, *Journal du septennat, 1947–1954*, 146, 163, 193, 742; Young, 'Churchill, the Russians and the Western Alliance', 893.

138. See PRO: CAB 128/26, Part 1, C.C. (53)33rd Conclusions, minute 2, 21/5/1953; Boyle (ed.), *Correspondence*, 56: Eisenhower to Churchill, 21/5/1953; EL: Ann Whitman File, Dulles-Herter Series, Box 1, Folder: Dulles, May 1953, memorandum Eisenhower to Bedell Smith, 20/5/1953.

139. Only a few hours before, the NSC had agreed with a proposal from the Joint Chiefs of Staff to employ the new tactical atomic weapons north of the Yalu river and thus against China if armistice negotiations should fail again.

140. Boyle (ed.), *Correspondence*, 56–7: Eisenhower to Churchill, 21/5/1953; Churchill to Eisenhower, 21/5/1953; PRO: PREM 11/520, Makins to FO No. 1084, 21/5/1953; Churchill to Makins, No. 2171, T160/53, 22/5/1953.

141. Churchill, 'Oral Answers', H.C. *Parl. Deb.*, 5th series, Vol. 515, 21/5/1953, 2263 (see also Churchill's announcement of the conference, ibid., 2262). Churchill repeated this in the House of Commons on 9/6/1953. See ibid., Vol. 516, 29.

142. PRO: FO 371/103 956/CW 1051/11, minute Hancock to Lloyd, 1/6/1953.

143. See Schwarz, *Adenauer. Der Staatsmann*, 74.

144. For Churchill's 'frog' quote, see Lord Moran, *Churchill: The Struggle for Survival, 1940–1965* (London, 1966), 406: diary entry, 16/6/1953.

145. Boyle (ed.), *Correspondence*, 75: Churchill to Eisenhower, 19/6/1953; see also 72–5 (correspondence, 13/6–19/6). On the Bermuda plan and the discussions within the FO, see also Young, *Last Campaign*, 169–76.

146. See NA: 741.13/5–2853, Aldrich to State Department, No. 6295, 28/5/1953; PRO: PREM 11/520; Boyle (ed.), ibid., 61–80. For the governmental crisis in France, see PRO: PREM 11/434; Giles, *Locust Years*, 183; also FRUS 1952–4, Vol. 6, 1358–9.

CHAPTER 12: *TRIUMPH AND TRAGEDY*

1. For the question whether the unrest was mainly driven by the workers in East Berlin and elsewhere or whether it was something approximating a general revolutionary uprising, see T. Diedrich, 'Zwischen Arbeiterbewegung und gescheiterter Revolution in der DDR. Retrospektive zum Stand der zeitgeschichtlichen Aufarbeitung des 17. Juni 1953', *Jahrbuch für Historische Kommunismusforschung* (1994), 288–305. For a good evaluation of the nature of the uprising with emphasis on the long-term development of the unrest and its continuation for weeks after 17 June, see A Mitter, 'Die Ereignisse im Juni und Juli 1953 in der DDR. Aus den Akten des Ministeriums für Staatssicherheit', *Aus Politik und Zeitgeschichte*, B5 (1991), 31–41. See also the valuable introduction by C. Kleßmann and B. Stöver, 'Einleitung: Das Krisenjahr 1953 und der 17. Juni in der DDR in der historischen Forschung', in C. Kleßmann and B. Stöver (eds), *1953 – Krisenjahr des Kalten Krieges in Europa* (Cologne, 1999), 9–28, esp. 21–2.

2. See W.S. Semjonow's (or in English: Semenov) criticism of Ulbricht in his memoirs, *Von Stalin bis Gorbatschow. Ein halbes Jahrhundert in diplomatischer Mission 1939–1991* (Berlin, 1995), 274. A large amount of literature has been produced on the uprising in East Germany. Among the most important works are the following: the still very useful books by A. Baring, *Der 17. Juni 1953* (Cologne, 1957; 3rd edn 1983) [English edn: *Uprising in East Germany: June 17, 1953*, London, 1972] and M. Jänicke, *Der dritte Weg. Die anti-stalinistische Opposition gegen Stalin seit 1953* (Cologne, 1964); the various articles in I. Spittmann and K.W. Fricke (eds), *17 Juni 1953. Arbeiteraufstand in der DDR*, 2nd edn (Cologne, 1988); A. Mitter and S. Wolle, *Untergang auf Raten. Unbekannte Kapitel der DDR-Geschichte* (Munich, 1993); T. Diedrich, *Der 17. Juni 1953 in der DDR. Bewaffnete Gewalt gegen das Volk* (Berlin, 1991); M. Hagen, *DDR-Juni'53. Die erste Volkserhebung im Stalinismus* (Stuttgart, 1992); G. Baier, *Wir wollen freie Menschen sein. Der 17. Juni 1953: Bauleute gingen voran* (Frankfurt/M., 1993); and the accounts in H. Weber, *Geschichte der DDR* (Munich, 1985); H. Weber, *Die DDR, 1945–1990*, 3rd revd edn (Munich, 2000); D. Staritz, *Geschichte der DDR 1949–90*, revd edn (Darmstadt, 1997), 100ff.; also U. Mählert, *Kleine Geschichte der DDR* (Munich, 1998), 62–79; and the first part of the book by A.B. Hegedüs and M. Wilke (eds), *Satelliten nach Stalins Tod* (Berlin, 2000).

3. See for example C. Buchheim, 'Wirtschaftliche Hintergründe des Arbeiteraufstandes vom 17. Juni 1953 in der DDR', *Vierteljahrshefte für Zeitgeschichte* 38 (1990), 415ff.

4. During the second half of 1952 each month approximately between 15,000 and 23,000 people left the GDR. In 1952–3 just under half a million people moved from East to West Germany; in the first half of 1953 alone a total of 226,000 people emigrated. Predominately members of the younger generation including many members of the SED and its youth organizations left East Germany for good. See K.W. Fricke, 'Der Arbeiteraufstand: Vorgeschichte, Verlauf, Folgen', in Spittmann and Fricke (eds), *Der 17. Juni*, 7–8; see also the table in M. Kramer, 'The Early Post-Stalin Succession Struggle and Upheavals in East-Central Europe: Internal-External Linkages in Soviet Policy Making', Part 1, *Journal of Cold War Studies* 1/1 (1999), 13. The older book by Jänicke, *Der dritte Weg* quotes the following numbers: January 1952: only 7,227 people fled East Germany; however, since December 1952 a steady increase in refugees could be observed; the maximum was reached in March 1953 when 58,605 registered refugees left the GDR (p. 25). See also Hagen, *DDR*, 27–8; and the statistics quoted in Bundesministerium für innerdeutsche Beziehungen (ed.), *Der Volksaufstand vom 17. Juni 1953* (Bonn, 1953), 9; and Baring, *Der 17. Juni*, 18–21. See also V. Ingimundarson, 'Cold War Misperceptions: The Communist and Western Responses to the East German Refugee Crisis in 1953', *Journal of Contemporary History* 29 (1994), 463–81.

5. See C.F. Ostermann, ' "This is Not a Politburo but a Madhouse": The Post-Stalin Succession Struggle […]', *CWIHP*, Bulletin 10 (March 1998), 62–3; and the Soviet document 'On Further Measures on the German Question', c. 28/4/1953, ibid., 72–4.

6. See N. Stulz-Herrnstadt (ed.), *Rudolf Herrnstadt. Das Herrnstadt-Dokument. Das Politbüro der SED und die Geschichte des 17. Juni 1953* (Reinbek bei Hamburg, 1990); also K. Schirdewan, *Ein Jahrhundert Leben. Erinnerungen und Visionen. Autobiographie* (Berlin, 1998); other relevant and interesting earlier memoirs of East German politicians who later fled to the FRG are H. Brandt, *Ein Traum der nicht entführbar ist. Mein Weg zwischen Ost und West* (Berlin, 1977); and F. Schenk, *Im Vorzimmer der Diktatur. Zwölf Jahre Pankow* (Colgone, 1962). For a brief summary, see D. Childs and R. Popplewell, *The Stasi: The East German Intelligence and Security Service*, paperback edn (Basingstoke, 1999), 54–9.

7. For an analysis of the 'New Course' and other Russian financial and economic measures before and after the uprising, see the paper prepared in the FO Research Department, PRO: FO 371/103 850/CS 1018/1 (13/10/1953).

8.   See the articles by J.M. Rainer (on Hungary), J. Pernes (on the CSSR) and A. Malkiewics/K.
     Ruchniewicz (on Poland) in Kleßmann and Stöver (eds), *Krisenjahr des Kalten Krieges*, 71ff., 93ff.,
     181ff.; also the various contributions in K. Larres and K. Osgood (eds), *The Cold War After Stalin:
     A New International History* (forthcoming, 2003). See also the articles in Hegedüs and Wilke
     (eds), *Satelliten nach Stalins Tod*; and in J. Foitzik (ed.), *Entstalinisierungskrise in Ostmitteleuropa
     1953–1956. Vom 17. Juni bis zum ungarischen Volksaufstand* [...] (Paderborn, 2001).
9.   See C.F. Ostermann (ed.), 'The Post-Stalin Succession Struggle and the 17 June Uprising in East
     Germany: The Hidden History' (unpublished documentary reader, Washington, DC., 1996) (now
     mostly published as *Uprising in East Germany 1953: The Cold War, the German Question and the First
     Major Upheaval behind the Iron Curtain*, Budapest, 2001). For an illuminating introduction, see
     Ostermann, 'This is Not a Politburo', 61–72. For other good overviews of the complicated episode in
     the literature, see H. Adomeit, *Imperial Overstretch: Germany in Soviet Policy from Stalin to
     Gorbachev* (Baden-Baden, 1998), 92–100; G. Wettig, *Bereitschaft zu Einheit in Freiheit? Die
     sowjetische Deutschland-Politik 1945–1955* (Munich, 1999), 235ff.; W. Loth, *Stalins ungeliebtes Kind.
     Warum Moskau die DDR nicht wollte* (Berlin, 1994), 193ff. (see also Loth's reply to his critics in his
     article 'Stalin, die deutsche Frage und die DDR. Eine Antwort an meine Kritiker', *Deutschland-
     Archiv* 28/3, 1995, 290–98). Of great interest are also the contributions by G. Wettig and V. Zubok in
     Kleßmann and Stöver (eds), *Krisenjahr des Kalten Krieges*; and the article by E. Scherstjanoi, 'Die
     sowjetische Deutschlandpolitik nach Stalins Tod 1953. Neue Dokumente aus dem Archiv des
     Moskauer Außenministeriums', *Vierteljahrshefte für Zeitgeschichte* 46 (1998), 497–549. Scherstjanoi
     provides one of the best overviews of the scholarly debates so far (see 498ff.).
10. This also included a review of the already established agricultural collectives. Beria appears to
     have insisted on this. See Stulz-Herrnstadt (ed.), *Das Herrnstadt-Dokument*, 69–70. The SED
     Politburo had taken the decision on 9 June. The communiqué as announced on 11 June is publ.
     in R. Steininger, *Deutsche Geschichte seit 1945. Darstellungen und Dokumente in vier Bänden*, Vol.
     2: 1948–55 (Frankfurt/M., 1996), 267–9.
11. See A. Resis (ed.), *Molotov Remembers: Inside Kremlin Politics: Conversations with Felix Chuev*
     (Chicago, 1993), 333–4. Semenov had been recalled to Moscow from his work in the Soviet Control
     Commission in East Berlin on 22 April. For details and a good analysis of the thinking in the Soviet
     Foreign Ministry, see Scherstjanoi, 'Sowjetische Deutschlandpolitik nach Stalins Tod', 505–13; V.
     Zubok, ' "Unverfroren und grob in der Deutschlandfrage ..." Berija, der Nachfolgestreit nach
     Stalins Tod und die Moskauer DDR-Debatte im April–Mai 1953', in Kleßmann and Stöver (eds),
     Krisenjahr des Kalten Krieges, 35–7. Ostermann, 'This is Not a Politburo', 63, and Zubok, ibid., report
     that initial memoranda were written by Foreign Ministry experts on 18 and 21 April for use in the
     Presidium meeting on 22 April. Molotov remained sceptical about the proposed solutions which
     included the suggestion to establish a provisional all-German government while maintaining two
     separate German states; the papers lacked, however, any concrete ideas on how to address the
     economic crisis in the GDR. Semenov's role is still unclear. He attempted to remain on good terms
     with both Molotov and Beria – and succeeded in doing so. Moreover, after Molotov had fallen out
     of favour in 1955 he even became deputy foreign minister. From 1978 to 1985 Semenov was Soviet
     ambassador to Bonn and was highly influential in this position.
12. See Wettig, *Bereitschaft zu Einheit*, 242–3; also D. Murphy, S.A. Kondrashev and G. Bailey, *Battle-
     ground Berlin: CIA vs. KGB in the Cold War* (New Haven, Conn., 1997), 156–8. According to Wettig
     a memorandum on the situation in the GDR written by Heinz Lippmann, the East German
     advisor to the Soviet Control Commission (who later fled to West Germany), and submitted to
     Moscow as well as a visit to Moscow by GDR politician Ernst Wollweber who reported on the
     opposition to Ulbricht within the SED may have impressed further the urgency of the situation
     on Beria. See ibid., and G. Wettig, 'Berijas deutsche Pläne im Licht neuer Quellen', in Kleßmann
     and Stöver (eds), *Krisenjahr des Kalten Krieges*, 55; P. and A. Sudoplatov (with J.L. and L.P.
     Schecter), *Special Tasks: The Memoirs of an Unwanted Witness – A Soviet Spymaster* (Boston, 1994),
     364–5; also L. Besymenski, 'Sowjetischer Nachrichtendienst und Wiedervereinigung Deutsch-
     lands: Der Berija-Plan von 1953', in W. Krieger and J. Weber (eds), *Spionage für den Frieden?
     Nachrichtendienste in Deutschland während des Kalten Krieges* (Munich, 1997), 157.
13. See Wettig, ibid., 243; Scherstjanoi, 'Die sowjetische Deutschlandpolitik nach Stalins Tod 1953',
     515–17. The Presidium of the Council of Ministers was chaired by Malenkov and, for a little while,
     this body was superior to the Politburo of the CPSU which at the time was also called Presidium.
14. See, below, 244–9.
15. The unrest was followed by widespread arrests and subsequent prosecution and other forms of
     repression. Yet, in August and September 1953 a new political and financial course was soon also

embarked upon in the CSSR. See J. Pernes, 'Die politische und wirtschaftliche Krise in der Tschechoslowakei 1953 und Versuche ihrer Überwindung', in Kleßmann und Stöver (eds), *Krisenjahr des Kalten Krieges*, 98–111. For the crisis in the CSSR and in Bulgaria, see also Kramer, 'The Early Post-Stalin Succession Struggle', Part I, 15–22. For the US view of these crises, see L. Borhi, 'Rollback, Liberation, Containment, or Inaction? U.S. Policy and Eastern Europe in the 1950s', *Journal of Cold War Studies* 1/3 (1999), 67–110. There were strikes in Bulgarian factories and prisons as well as in Soviet camps and prisons, see A. Graziosi, 'The Great Strikes of 1953 in Soviet Labor Camps in the Accounts of their Participants: A Review', *Cahiers du Monde Russe et Soviétique* 33/4 (1992), 419–46.

16. The new policy was made available to the Soviet Council of Ministers on 2 June and thus must have been completed between 27 May and 1 June. See J. Richter, 'Reexamining Soviet Policy towards Germany during the Beria Interregnum', CWIHP, Working Paper No. 3 (Washington, DC, 1992), 10.

17. See the brief note on the meeting by O. Grotewohl, publ. in Ostermann, 'This is not a Politburo', 81; also Loth, *Stalins ungeliebtes Kind*, 203–4. The Soviet instructions to the SED have become available: 'Ein Dokument von grosser historischer Bedeutung vom Mai 1953', *Beiträge zur Geschichte der Arbeiterbewegung* 32/5 (1990), 648–54.

18. See Stulz-Herrnstadt (ed.), *Das Herrnstadt-Dokument*, 58–61.

19. See A. Knight, *Beria: Stalin's First Lieutenant* (Princeton, N.J., 1993), 192; Marshall Chuikov, the commander of the Soviet forces and chairman of the Soviet military control commission in the GDR, was recalled to Moscow.

20. See Semjonow, *Von Stalin bis Gorbatschow*, 291–4; Stulz-Herrnstadt (ed.), *Das Herrnstadt-Dokument*, 62–78.

21. For the disputes in the East German Politburo, see Ostermann, 'This is not a Politburo', 66–7; Stulz-Herrnstadt (ed.), ibid., 62ff.; and the document 'Dokumente zur Auseinandersetzung in der SED 1953', *Beiträge zur Geschichte der Arbeiterbewegung* 32/5 (1990), 655–72.

22. Quoted in Stulz-Herrnstadt, ibid., 74 (my translation): 'In 14 Tagen werden Sie vielleicht schon keinen Staat mehr haben'. See also E. Scherstjanoi, ' "In 14 Tagen werden Sie vielleicht schon keinen Staat mehr haben". Vladimir Semenov und der 17. Juni 1953', *Deutschland-Archiv* 31/6 (1998), 907–37.

23. See ibid.; Ostermann, 'This is not a Politburo', 66–7. It now appears clear that Zaiser and Herrnstadt, Ulbricht's most critical internal opponents, never intended to give up the GDR as a socialist state or to merge the GDR with the FRG as later alleged by Ulbricht. They merely wished to tone down Ulbricht's arrogant leadership style and, probably, delay the overly rapid policy of turning the GDR into a fully-fledged socialist state. For details, see G. Wettig, 'Berijas deutsche Pläne im Licht neuer Quellen', 64–9; H. Müller-Enberg, *Der Fall Rudolf Herrnstadt. Tauwetterpolitik vor dem 17. Juni* (Berlin, 1993).

24. For Moscow's rearmament fears, see Richter, 'Reexamining Soviet Policy' (CWIHP), 8–9. See also V. Zubok and C. Pleshakov, *Inside the Kremlin's Cold War: From Stalin to Khrushchev* (Cambridge, MA, 1996), 159–60.

25. See Kramer, 'The Early Post-Stalin Succession Struggle', Part I, 10–11, 22ff.

26. While for example Loth (*Stalins ungeliebtes Kind*) and Scherstjanoi ('Sowjetische Deutschlandpolitik nach Stalins Tod') argue strongly in favour of the existence of a 'Beria Plan' for giving up the GDR, above all G. Wettig equally strongly maintains that this was not the case (see his books and articles cited above). Other stimulating literature dealing with the issue includes Knight, *Beria*, 190ff.; W. Otto, 'Sowjetische Deutschlandpolitik 1952/53: Forschungs- und Wahrheitsprobleme', *Deutschland-Archiv*, 26/8 (1993), 948–54; J. Foitzik, '"Hart und Konsequent ist der neue politische Kurs zu realisieren". Ein Dokument zur Politik der Sowjetunion gegenüber der DDR nach Berijas Verhaftung im Juni 1953', *Deutschland-Archiv* 1/33 (2000), 32–49; and the articles by G. Wettig, 'Zum Stand der Forschung über Berijas Deutschland-Politik im Frühjahr 1953', *Deutschland-Archiv* 6/26 (1993), 674–82; 'Neue Erkenntnisse über Berijas Deutschland-Politik', *Deutschland-Archiv* 26/12 (1993), 1412–13. Still useful older writings include B. Bonwetsch, 'Deutschlandpolitische Alternativen der Sowjetunion, 1949–1955', *Deutsche Studien* 24 (1986), 20–40; B. Meissner, 'Die Sowjetunion und die deutsche Frage 1949–1955', in D. Geyer (ed.), *Osteuropahandbuch, Sowjetunion: Außenpolitik II, 1955–1973* (Cologne, 1976), 473–501; R. Löwenthal, 'Vorwort', in: Baring, *Der 17. Juni* (revd edn, Cologne, 1965), 1–6.

27. It appears that just before the collapse of the Soviet Union in December 1991 the Central Committee of the CPSU asked for Beria's files which were deposited in the archives of the Soviet High Court and in the KGB archives. It never returned them. See L. Besymenski, '1953-Berija will die DDR beseitigen', *Die Zeit* 42/1993 (15 October 1993), 81.

28. See above all Sudoplatov, *Special Tasks*, 363–7; Besymenski, ibid., 81–3; Resis (ed.), *Molotov Remembers*, 333ff.; and the transcripts of the meetings of the Central Committee of the CPSU after Beria's arrest: D.M. Stickle (ed.), *The Beria Affair: The Secret Transcripts of the Meetings Signalling the End of Stalinism* (New York, 1992); Stulz-Herrnstadt (ed.), *Das Herrnstadt-Dokument*, 14–23, 64ff, 162ff., 207, 222–4; also V.M. Zubok, 'Soviet Intelligence and the Cold War: The "Small" Committee of Information, 1952–53', *CWIHP*, Working Paper No. 4 (Washington, DC, 1992), 15–17.

29. Sudoplatov, *Special Tasks*, 363–4 (quotes: 364); see also Zubok and Pleshakov, *Inside the Kremlin's Cold War*, 159–62. Sudoplatov was arrested himself shortly after Beria's arrest in mid-1953. He was imprisoned and endured torture and solitary confinement until his release in 1968.

30. See Sudoplatov, ibid.; Besymenski, 'Sowjetischer Nachrichtendienst', 157–8.

31. Sudoplatov, ibid., 365; Besymenski, ibid. The claim that Beria and Malenkov held the view 'that Soviet nuclear weapons were sufficient to deter the West' is therefore unconvincing. See Richter, 'Reexamining Soviet Policy' (CWIHP), 15.

32. See Richter, ibid., 17; also Resis (ed.), *Molotov Remembers*, 336.

33. See Zubok, 'Unverfroren und grob', 46–7.

34. Richter, 'Reexamining Soviet Policy' (CWIHP), 15. However, this may be a little far-fetched.

35. See Zubok and Pleshakov, *Inside the Kremlin's Cold War* 157–8. Sudoplatov, *Special Tasks*, 367. Wettig, 'Berijas deutsche Pläne', 61. On Yugoslavia, see Zubok, 'Soviet Intelligence and the Cold War', 464; Richter, 'Reexamining Soviet Policy' (CWIHP), 16–17. For Beria's and Malenkov's conversations with the Hungarian leadership in Moscow on 13 June, see the transcript of the talks in Ostermann, 'This is not a Politburo', 81–6; also Kramer, 'The Early Post-Stalin Succession Struggle', Part I, 35–7; for Beria's letter to Malenkov from prison on 1 July 1953 where he mentions his proposal about Nagy, see Ostermann, ibid., 99.

36. Resis (ed.), *Molotov Rembers*, 334–6. Khrushchev had a very low opinion of Malenkov; he called him an 'errand boy' without any 'independent thought or initiative' who thought it 'profitable to play up to Beria'. N. Khrushchev, *Khrushchev Remembers* (Boston, 1970), 323. V. Mastny's interpretation, for example, is more optimistic. He believes that the dispute over the policy towards the GDR has been exaggerated. See his *The Cold War and Soviet Insecurity: The Stalin Years* (New York, 1996), 178–85.

37. Quote: Sudoplatov, *Special Tasks*, 364; see also Resis (ed.), ibid. Khrushchev claimed this as early as July 1963 and it is also reported in A. Gromyko's *Memories* (London, 1989), 315. In a letter to Malenkov from prison on 1 July 1953 Beria admits his 'inadmissable rudeness and insolence' towards Khruschev and Bulganin when discussing the German question and he admits his guilt. The letter is publ. in Ostermann, 'This is not a Politburo', 99. Molotov later said: 'We believed that the building of socialism in the GDR must unfold gradually in order not to alienate the population. Otherwise revolts might flare up, and then we would have to forcibly repress the very Germany we had only just started to rebuild. The work had not really begun yet, and we had to be patient and proceed slowly so as not to have to use force. Yet Beria said: "Don't follow this policy! The policy of building socialism should not be pursued in the GDR" ' (Resis, ed., ibid., 336). See also J. Richter, 'Reexamining Soviet Policy towards Germany in 1953', *Europe-Asia Studies* 45/4 (1993), 676–7; also Richter, 'Reexamining Soviet Policy' (CWIHP), 13ff.; V. Zubok, 'Soviet Intelligence and the Cold War: The "Small" Committee of Information, 1952–53', *Diplomatic History* 19/3 (1995), 463.

38. See the account in Zubok and Pleshakov, *Inside the Kremlin's Cold War*, 160–1 (quote: 161); see also in detail Zubok, 'Unverfroren und grob', 39–42; and above all Scherstjanoi, 'Sowjetische Deutschlandpolitik nach Stalins Tod', 517–25. Beria is also said to have declared: 'What does it amount to, this GDR? It's not even a real state. It is only kept in being by Soviet troops' (ibid., 161).

39. See Richter, 'Reexamining Soviet Policy' (CWIHP), 19–20 (quote: 19). Malenkov quoted in Ostermann, 'This is not a Politburo', 64.

40. Resis (ed.), *Molotov Remembers*, 335.

41. See Khrushchev, *Khrushchev Rembers*, 325–6. According to Semenov's (Semjonow's) memoirs it appears that Molotov was more influential in this context. See his *Von Stalin bis Gorbatschow*, 290. See for Kramer's interpretation that 'Molotov and Beria worked closely together to compile the final draft', in his article 'The Early Post-Stalin Succession Struggle', Part I, 28–9 (quote: 28).

42. So far this document is only available in its draft versions and in a publ. German and English translation of these versions. See 'Ein Dokument von großer historischer Bedeutung vom Mai 1953', *Beiträge zur Geschichte der Arbeiterbewegung* 32/5 (1990), 648–54; Ostermann, 'This is not a Politburo', 79–81.

43. There is no clear evidence available for Kramer's claim that 'the Molotov-Beria document strongly reaffirmed Moscow's broad commitment to the "unification of Germany on a

peaceloving and democratic basis" '. See Kramer, 'The Early Post-Stalin Succession Struggle', Part I, 30. For the 27 May discussion and its aftermath, see Resis (ed.), *Molotov Remembers*, 334–6; also the careful analyses of the available evidence in Adomeit, *Imperial Overstretch*, 96–7; Zubok and Pleshkov, *Inside the Kremlin's Cold War*, 161–2; Richer, 'Reexamining Soviet Policy' (CWIHP), 13–26, esp. 20–2; and Wettig, *Bereitschaft zu Einheit*, 244ff. Adomeit rightly says that accusations against Beria for being a 'bourgeois provocateur' and for having collaborated with western intelligence services against the GDR were made only after Beria's arrest during the Central Committee meeting in July 1953 when Malenkov, Molotov and Khrushchev were interested in exaggerating Beria's crimes. See also Resis, (ed.) 340.

44. Sudoplatov, *Special Tasks*, 364. Besymenski mentions that Beria believed he had plenty of time for these activities which were planned for June and July. See his 'Sowjetischer Nachrichtendienst', 158.

45. For supporting evidence see the accounts by Sudoplatov, ibid., 363–4; Besymenski, '1953-Berija will die DDR beseitigen', 81–3.

46. See Besymenski, ibid., 81–2; Wettig, 'Neue Erkenntnisse', 1412.

47. This has also been emphasized by Wettig, *Bereitschaft zu Einheit*, 249. The author explains that although Beria could not expect to obtain financial aid from London, receiving political support from Britain would have been 'very important'. Wettig also emphasizes that it is rather strange that Ernst Wollweber who is alleged to have been one of Beria's German contacts (together with Zaisser and Herrnstadt) was subsequently put in charge of the East German security services. See also Wettig, 'Berijas deutsche Pläne im Licht neuer Quellen', 59, 62.

48. For Moscow's suspicion of Churchill before and after Stalin's death, see Chapter 11, above, 217–19.

49. See in particular Gerhard Wettig's writings mentioned above.

50. Sudoplatov, *Special Tasks*, 365. See Besymenski, '1953-Berija will die DDR beseitigen', 82. Wettig is sceptical about this explanation; he argues that due to the reparations Moscow still received from the GDR at this point in time, there were no substantial costs to the Soviet Union to maintain its empire. See Wettig, 'Berijas deutsche Pläne', 61.

51. See for example, P. Boyle (ed.), *The Churchill-Eisenhower Correspondence, 1953–1955* (Chapel Hill, N.C., 1990), 41: 'It has been well said that the most dangerous moment for evil governments is when they begin to reform' (letter Churchill to Eisenhower, 11/4/1953). Churchill appropriated a well-known statement by Tocqueville which is for example quoted in Kramer, 'The Early Post-Stalin Succession Struggle', Part 1, 44.

52. See for example Sudoplatov, *Special Tasks*, 365–6; Foitzik, 'Hart und Konsequent', 36; for further evidence, see also I.S. Kowalczuk et al. (eds), *Der Tag X – 17. Juni 1953. Die 'Innere Staatsgründung' der DDR als Ergebnis der Krise 1952/54* (Berlin, 1996).

53. Quoted in Karl-Wilhelm Fricke, 'Der Arbeiteraufstand. Vorgeschichte, Verlauf, Folgen', in Spittmann and Fricke (eds), *17. Juni 1953*, 11 (my translation). See also: PRO: FO 371/103 839/CS 1016/35–59, 81; 103 841/CS 1016/118 (June 1953).

54. See Ostermann, 'This is not a Politburo', 67; and the documents of the reactions of Soviet representatives in East Berlin on 16 June and 17–19 June, ibid., 86–97.

55. See B.S. Chamberlin and J. Wetzel, 'Der 17. Juni und der RIAS', in: Spittmann and Fricke (eds), *17. Juni 1953*, 212–15; also M. Wackel, 'Wir sprechen zur Zone. Die politischen Sendungen des RIAS in der Vorgeschichte der Juni-Erhebung 1953', *Deutschland-Archiv* 26/9 (1993), 1035–48; M. Rexin, 'Der 16. und 17. Juni 1953 in West Berlin', *Deutschland-Archiv* 26/8 (1993), 985–94.

56. Resis (ed.), *Molotov Remembers*, 346. Allegedly, Beria telephoned the Soviet High Commission in East Berlin asking why Semenov appeared to be economical with using live ammunition. See Semjonow, *Von Stalin bis Gorbatschow*, 295. Molotov's quoted statement, albeit made many years later, does not indicate that the Soviet representatives in the GDR as well as the ruling elite in the Kremlin concluded immediately that the uprising had been organized by the West as Ostermann believes to have detected. See his 'This is not a Politburo', 67. Indeed in view of the Kremlin's careful analyses of the deteriorating situation in the GDR prior to the uprising, it must be assumed that the collective leadership was well aware of the real causes of the unrest. This is confirmed by former GDR 'spymaster' Markus Wolf. See his memoirs *Spionagechef im Kalten Krieg. Erinnerungen* (Munich, 1997), 79. For the Soviet and East German reaction to the uprising, see also Kramer, 'The Early Post-Stalin Succession Struggle', Part 1, 40–55.

57. See Semjonow, *Von Stalin bis Gorbatschow*, 294; see also the brief discussion of the Soviet functionaries who were sent to East Berlin in Foitzik, 'Hart und Konsequent', 37–8.

58. See Baring, *Der 17. Juni*, 56–7; see also: PRO: PREM 11/673 (June 1953); PRO: FO 371/103 840/CS 1016/85/G (16, 17, 18/6/1953); Mitter, 'Die Ereignisse im Juni und Juli 1953 in der DDR', 31–41;

Diedrich, *Der 17. Juni 1953 in der DDR*. Eighteen Soviet soldiers were court-martialled and executed for having refused to shoot at the demonstrators. See Hagen, *DDR*, 119–20.

59. See William Strang's minute to the Prime Minister M.215/53 (19/6/1953), PRO: FO 371/103 841/CS 1016/107, also 103 842–3, PRO: PREM 11/673 (June 1953).

60. See Baring, *Der 17. Juni*, 62.

61. PRO: PREM 11/673; PRO: FO 800/794 (June 1953).

62. NA: 762B.00/6–1753, State Department to HICOG Berlin (No. 5536) and Bonn (No. 564), 17/6/1953. See also D.G. Coleman, 'Eisenhower and the Berlin Problem, 1953–1954', *Journal of Cold War Studies* 2/1 (2000), 3–34, esp. 11–19.

63. All quotes: FRUS 1952–4, Vol. 7, 1587–8: meeting of the NSC, 18/6/1953. See also Coleman, 15–18.

64. NA: 762B.00/6–2253, Aldrich, London, to Dulles, No. 6712, 22/6/1953.

65. After 12 April 1953 Churchill was also in charge of the Foreign Office as Anthony Eden had to undergo several serious operations which would keep him out of office until his return to the FO on 1 October 1953.

66. PRO: PREM 11/673, Ward, Wahnerheide, to FO, No. 555, 18/6/1953. The brief letter is published in RIIA, *Documents on International Affairs, 1953* (London, 1956), 159. Göttling was in fact not as young as he is usually portrayed in the literature. He was thirty-five years old. See NA: 762B.00/6–1853, Lyon, Berlin, to Dulles, No. 1694, 18/6/1953.

67. PRO: ibid., minute Churchill to Strang, 19/6/1953. See also A. Nutting, *Europe Will Not Wait: A Warning and a Way out* (London, 1960), 53; M. Gehler, 'Der 17. Juni aus der Sicht des Foreign Office', *Aus Politik und Zeitgeschichte*, B25/93 (18/6/1993), 27–9.

68. PRO: ibid., Ward, Wahnerheide, to FO, No.560, 20/6/1953; Coleman, Berlin, to FO, No. 133, 20/6/1953 (also in FO 800/794). The western protest was repudiated by Dibrova on 20 June. See ibid., Berlin to FO, No. 139, 21/6/1953. Dibrova's answer is published in: RIIA, *Documents, 1953*, 159–60. On 24 June the western commandants denied Dibrova's accusation that the West had instigated the uprising. See ibid., 160–1.

69. PRO: PREM 11/673, letter Churchill to Coleman, 21/6/1953 (= FO to Berlin, No. 168, 22/6/1953).

70. NA: 761.5/6–3053, Lyon, Berlin, to High Commission in Bonn. Some Soviet soldiers did indeed react in a markedly restrained way and were subsequently court-martialled (see n. 58, above).

71. PRO: ibid., letter Churchill to Coleman, 21/6/1953 (= FO to Berlin, No. 168, 22/6/1953). See also Churchill's letter to Ward on 21 June (= FO to Wahnerheide, No. 483, 22/6/1953). Churchill referred to Coleman's telegram, No. 126, dated 18 June, in: ibid.

72. PRO: ibid., minute Warner, 17/6/1953 (also in FO 371/103 840/CS 1016/71). When answering the question of a journalist whether or not his government agreed to the deployment of Soviet tanks against the East German people, GDR Deputy Prime Minister Otto Nuschke said in a very similar vein: 'Selbstverständlich, weil sie ein Interesse daran hat, daß Ruhe und Ordnung zurückkehrt. Wenn das nicht mit polizeilichen Mitteln möglich ist, dann muß eben selbstverständlich die Besatzungsmacht, jede Besatzungsmacht, ihre Machtmittel einsetzen.' Quoted in K.W. Fricke, *Opposition und Widerstand in der DDR. Ein politischer Report* (Cologne, 1984), 94.

73. PRO: See FO 371/103 985/CW 10715/5, 25/6/1953. Because of the events in the GDR Kirkpatrick had just been recalled from his annual holiday; he had only been appointed High Commissioner less than five months earlier. In general, Conant was sceptical about West Germany's political maturity and he thus doubted the wisdom of German rearmament. On Conant's career, see J. Hershberg's very readable *James B. Conant: Harvard to Hiroshima and the Making of the Nuclear Age* (Stanford, Calif., 1995). On Conant's defence of his atomic decision-making, see B.J. Bernstein, 'Seizing the Contested Terrain of Early Nuclear History: Stimson, Conant, and their allies explain the decision to use the Atomic Bomb', *Diplomatic History* 17/1 (1993), 35–72.

74. PRO: ibid.

75. PRO: FO 371/103 985/CW 10715/5, minute Roberts to Strang, 26/6/1953.

76. J.B. Conant, *My Several Lives: Memoirs of a Social Inventor* (New York, 1970), 601. See also J.G. Hershberg, ' "Explosion in the Offing": German Rearmament and American Diplomacy, 1953–1955', *Diplomatic History* 16 (1992), 523–6; Fish, 'After Stalin's Death', 340; Hershberg, *Conant*, 912–13, n. 56.

77. NA: 762B.00/6–2653, Conant, Bonn, to Dulles, No. 5486, 26/6/1953.

78. Quotes in H.W. Brands, *Cold Warriors: Eisenhower's Generation and American Foreign Policy* (New York, 1988), 124. For the USA and the East German uprising, see C.F. Ostermann, ' "Keeping the Pot Simmering": The United States and the East German Uprising', *German Studies Review* 19/1 (1996), 61–89; C.F. Ostermann, ' "Die beste Chance für eine Rollback?" Amerikanische Politik und der 17. Juni 1953', in Kleßmann and Stöver (eds), *Krisenjahr des Kalten Krieges*, esp. 119–26; V.

Ingimundarson, 'The Eisenhower Administration, the Adenauer Government, and the Political Uses of the East German Uprising of 1953', *Diplomatic History* 20/3 (1996), 381–409.

79. See Hershberg, *Conant*, 659–60, also 661–3. Hershberg reports that Conant admitted later that 'We were all caught unawares, without any plans, for which all of us got sufficient blame ... There really wasn't much to do' and that despite the uprising the High Commissioner himself took his time to return to Germany from Washington where he had been testifying on budgetary issues (quote: 660). For American (and British) covert operations in Eastern Europe, see B. Heuser, 'Subversive Operationen im Dienste der "Roll-Back"-Politik 1948–1953', *Vierteljahrshefte für Zeitgeschichte* 37 (1989), 279–97.

80. PRO: FO 371/103 840/CS 1016/71, minute Roberts to Lloyd, 20/6/1953.

81. Moreover, as early as May 1952, when after the signing of the EDC treaty the West had expected a rather unpleasant reaction by the Soviet Union, the western High Commissioners had been given the authority to act without prior consultation with their governments in emergency situations. See ibid.

82. PRO: PREM 11/673, minute Roberts to Strang, 17/6/1953 (also in FO 371/103 840/CS 1016/71).

83. Ibid., Berlin to FO, No. 128, 19/6/1953.

84. PRO: FO 371/103 960/CW 1055/1 G, minute Roberts to Strang, 25/6/1953.

85. See for example NA: 762A.00/6–2453, Conant, Bonn, to Dulles, No. 5445, 24/6/1953.

86. NA: 762B.00/6–1953, Conant, Bonn, to Dulles, No. 5400, 19/6/1953.

87. Deutscher Bundestag, *Verhandlungen der I. Wahlperiode, Stenographische Berichte*, Vol. 17, 278th session, 1/7/1953, 13872. See also PRO: FO 371/103 665/C 1071/45, Ward, Wahnerheide, to FO, No. 472, 20/6/1953.

88. PRO: FO 371/104 178/CW 1893/19, minute Hancock to Roberts, 23/6/1953. See also ibid., CW 1893/14, 22, 23; PREM 11/382, minute Lloyd to Churchill, PM/MS/53/248, 20/6/1953; PREM 11/449, minute Churchill to Lloyd, M 218/53, 23/6/1953; ibid., minute Lloyd to Churchill, 26/6/1953; H.C. *Parl. Deb.*, Vol. 517, 13/7/1953, 1703.

89. Quote: Hershberg, *Conant*, 663. On Adenauer's tense relationship with Conant, see ibid., 656, 658, 668–9. Adenauer and Conant were very different personalities. But apart from a lack of personal trust between the two men, Bonn had also recognized that Dulles's confidence in Conant was not as high as Acheson's in McCloy, Conant's predecessor. Moreover, Conant's lack of courage in standing up for his staff in Germany against McCarthy's anti-communist attacks met little understanding in Bonn.

90. Adenauer's letter to Eisenhower, dated 21 June, is published in RIIA, *Documents, 1953*, 161. His letter to Churchill is in PRO: PREM 11/449, 22/6/1953.

91. For Eisenhower's reply see RIIA, *Documents, 1953*, 161–2; for Churchill's letter see PRO: FO 371/103 665/C 1071/57, FO to Wahnerheide, No. 497, 24/6/1953 (see also CAB 126/28, Part I, C.C.(53)36th conclusions, minute 3, 24/6/1953). For Lloyd's statement see H.C. *Parl. Deb.*, 5th series, Vol. 516, 24/6/1953, 1906–7; see also NA: 762B.00/6–2153, minute Kellermann to Riddle-berger, 23/6/1953.

92. NA: 762B.00/6–2653, Courtney, London, to State Department, No. 6193, 25/6/1953.

93. See H.C. *Parl. Deb.*, 5th series, Vol. 516, 24/6/1953, 1906–8.

94. NA: 762B.00/6–2653, Courtney, London, to State Department, No. 6193, 25/6/1953.

95. See PRO: FO 371/103 870/CS 1301/14, Makins, Washington, to FO, No.1440, 9/7/1953. For the American-Soviet exchange of notes regarding the 'food parcel scheme' between 10–23 July, see RIIA, *Documents, 1953*, 164–7. In a personal letter Ambassador Conant to Eisenhower, dated 19/10/1953, Conant claims however that 'the brilliant idea had been developed in Washington'. The enterprise seems to have succeeded largely because of the wholehearted support of Ernst Reuter, the SPD's governing mayor of West Berlin. EL: Ann Whitman File, Administration Series, Box 10, Folder: Conant (2); also W. Brandt and R. Löwenthal, *Ernst Reuter* (Munich, 1957), 674–87.

96. For further details on the food scheme, see Ingimundarson, 'The Political Uses of the East German Uprising of 1953', 381–409; and Ostermann, ' "Die beste Chance für ein Rollback?" ', 126–39; Ostermann, 'Keeping the Pot Simmering', esp. 73ff.; also Hagen, *DDR* 94–104; D. Prowe, *Weltstadt in Krisen: Berlin, 1949–1958* (Berlin, 1973), 114–25.

97. Quoted in German in H.P. Schwarz, *Die Ära Adenauer. Gründerjahre der Republik 1949–1957* (Wiesbaden, 1981), 190 (my translation).

98. NA: 862B.49/8–2053, Dulles to US HICOG, Bonn and Berlin, Nos 787 and 167, 5/9/1953.

99. PRO: FO 371/103 873/CS 1301/83, Ward to FO, No. 905, 28/9/1953.

100. For the British government's criticism, see above all PRO: FO 371/103 870–3. For the background of the scheme, see the memorandum 'Food Crisis in Eastern Germany', dated December, 1952, in PRO:

FO 975/67. For the American views, see the telegrams and memoranda in NA: 862B.49/ff. According to Ostermann the 'food scheme' was indeed a huge success among the East Berlin population and unnerved the GDR leadership to a considerable extent; on the whole it 'heightened tensions in the already explosive situation' ('Keeping the Pot Simmering', 73). Thus, British concerns about the 'food parcel scheme' leading to an increase in Cold War tension appear to have been fully justified.

101. PRO: FO 3781/103 843/CS 1016/161, minute Roberts to Strang, 6/7/1953.

102. PRO: FO 371/103 870/CS 1301/14, minute Hancock, 10/7/1953. See also for example ibid., CS 1301/18, minute Warner, 24/7/1953; ibid., CS 1301/24, Kirkpatrick, Wahnerheide, to FO, No.212, 24/7/1953; ibid., CS 1301/30, memorandum Roberts to Nutting, 28/7/1953. For the non-inclusion of the British, see also EL: Ann Whitman File, Administration Series, Box. No. 10, Folder Conant (2), letter Conant to Eisenhower, 19/10/1953.

103. PRO: FO 371/103 871/CS 1301/35, minute Churchill to Salisbury, M 256/53, 6/8/1953 (also in PREM 11/673).

104. Quoted in Ostermann, 'Keeping the Pot Simmering', 75.

105. PRO: FO 371/118 151/WG 1013/5, 27/1/1955. See also Schwarz, Ära Adenauer, 220–1; E. Noelle and E.P. Neumann (eds), Jahrbuch der öffentlichen Meinung, 1947–55, 2nd edn (Allensbach, 1956), 313–20; see also M. Krämer, Der Volksaufstand vom 17. Juni 1953 und sein politisches Echo in der Bundesrepublik Deutschland (Bochum, 1996).

106. PRO: FO 371/118 151/WG 1013/5, Hoyer Millar, Bonn, to FO, No.52 (Weekly Report), 27/1/1955. See also Schwarz, ibid., 220–1. See also the results of contemporary opinion polls on 'reunification' in West Germany in Noelle and Neumann (eds), ibid., 313–20.

107. PRO: PREM 11/673, memorandum Lloyd to Churchill, PM/MS/53/254, 22/6/1953 (also in PREM 11/449 and FO 371/103 665/C 1071/56).

108. Sudoplatov, Special Tasks, 366; also Loth, Stalins ungeliebtes Kind, 207; Besymenski, 'Sowjetischer Nachrichtendienst', 159.

109. See above all Kramer's careful analysis of the plot to remove Beria, 'The Early Post-Stalin Succession Struggle', Part 2, Journal of Cold War Studies 1/2 (1999), 2ff.

110. For the five sessions of the plenum of the Central Committee of the CPSU in early July 1953, see D.M. Stickle (ed.), The Beria Affair: The Secret Transcripts of the Meetings Signalling the End of Stalinism (New York, 1992), 1 ff., esp. 41 ff.

111. The overwhelming importance of power politics (rather than ideology and the German question per se) in the Kremlin after Stalin is for example also emphasized by Zubok, 'Unverfroren und grob', 46–8 and by Adomeit, Imperial Overstretch, 96; see also V. Baras, 'Beria's Fall and Ulbricht's Survival', Soviet Studies 27/3 (1975), 381–95; Loth, Stalins ungeliebtes Kind, 209–10. For details of Beria's arrest – which was mainly plotted by Khrushchev who eventually suceeded in persuading Malenkov to turn against Beria – and his subsequent trial and execution, see Kramer, 'The Early Post-Stalin Succession Struggle', Part 2, 9ff., esp. 21–38; Knight, Beria, 194–200, 201ff.; also Resis (ed.), Molotov Remembers, 343–6; Khrushchev Remembers, 321ff., esp. 333ff.; T. Wittlin, Comissar: The Life and Death of Lavrenty Pavlovich Beria (New York, 1972), 393–401.

112. Resis (ed.), Molotov Remembers, 336.

113. Ibid., 336–7.

114. This was of course similar to the West's belief that the existence of nuclear weapons was limiting Moscow's willingness to take risks. See the excellent discussion in Adomeit, Imperial Overstretch, 97–9.

115. Zubok and Pleshakov, Inside the Kremlin's Cold War, 162–6; Richter, 'Reexamining Soviet Policy' (CWIHP), 13.

116. See Wettig, Bereitschaft zu Einheit, 259ff.; Ostermann, 'This is not a Politburo', 68–9; and the interesting interpretation based on a newly released Soviet document by Foitzik, 'Hart und Kosequent', 32–49. See also Kramer's detailed analysis: 'The Early Post-Stalin Succession Struggle', Part 3, Journal of Cold War Studies 1/3 (1999), 4–33. Similarly, after the uprising the Stasi was given greater importance in the long run although the East German intelligence organization had failed to predict the uprising. The number of full-time employees increased from 4,000 in 1952 to 10,000 in 1955 and the 'Inoffiziellen Mitarbeiter' (the part-time informers) had doubled to 30,000 by 1954. After all, Ulbricht realized the necessity of preventing another uprising similar to the one which had almost led to his loss of power. See Childs and Popplewell, The Stasi, 59; Wolf, Spionagechef, 80ff.; Mählert, Kleine Geschichte der DDR, 79.

117. See Richer, 'Reexamining Soviet Policy' (CWIHP), 14; Stulz-Herrnstadt (ed.), Das Herrnstadt-Dokument, 34ff.

118. For an account of Beria's execution by one of the soldiers involved, see M. Franchetti, 'Kremlin Guard Reveals How He Shot Hated Beria', *Sunday Times*, 4 January 1998, p. 19. Curiously enough Semenov and Malenkov remained unscathed (the latter, however, only until 1955). On Beria's fate, see also PRO: FO 371/106 517 (March-July 1953), FO 371/111 678 (Dec. 1953–June 1954); FRUS 1952–4, Vol. 8, 1206–7; Meissner, 'Die Sowjetunion und die deutsche Frage', 484–85; R. Conquest, *Power and Politics in the USSR: The Study of Soviet Dynastics* (London, 1961), 195–227, 440–7.

119. For Churchill's 11 May speech, see Chapter 11 above, 222ff. For Gascoigne's conversations with Molotov, see PRO: PREM 11/422 (23/4/1953) and PRO: FO 371/106 533–4 (April 1953). See also Chapter 10, above, 196–8.

120. See for example E. Scherstjanoi's article 'Die sowjetische Deutschlandpolitik nach Stalins Tod', 497ff. The author strongly believes in Beria's plan to embark on negotiations about German unification before the uprising occurred. Moscow decided to crush the uprising in order to be able to negotiate from a position of strength and to make an attractive offer to the West for which a high price was to be extracted from the West (see esp. 528–30).

121. PRO: PREM 11/419, minute Churchill to Salisbury, PM/M. 257/53, 6/8/1953. See also Lord Moran, *Churchill: The Struggle for Survival, 1940–1965* (London, 1966), 448: diary entry, 5/8/1953; FO 371/106 257/NS 1021/108/G, memorandum Gascoigne regarding his conversation with Churchill in London, 19/8/1953. Gascoigne asked the FO not to mention to Downing Street that he had written a memorandum on his farewell meeting (due to his retirement) with the Prime Minister. For Beria's arrest, see also the FO's assessment of 25/8/1953: FO 371/106 512/NS 1016/12.

CHAPTER 13: CHURCHILL'S POLICY UNDERMINED

1. See J. Colville, *The Fringes of Power: 10 Downing Street Diaries, 1939–1955* (London, 1985), 668–70; Lord Moran, *Churchill: Struggle for Survival, 1945–1965* (London, 1966), 408–74; M. Gilbert, *Winston S. Churchill, Vol. 8: Never Despair, 1945–65*, paperback edn (London, 1990), 846–92; M. Soames, *Clementine Churchill* (London, 1979), 434–6; Trinity College, Cambridge: Butler Papers, G 24/47–54, memorandum on Churchill's stroke, *c.* end June 1953; also J. M. Post and R. S. Robins, *When Illness Strikes the Leader: The Dilemma of the Captive King* (New Haven and London, 1993), 20–4.

2. In effect John Colville, Conservative MP Christopher Soames (who was Churchill's son in law) and Cabinet Secretary Norman Brook governed Britain. See for example Churchill College, Cambridge: Fife–Clark Papers, 2/2/8 (three newspaper articles dated January 1970 which dealt with the issue); P. Hennesey, *Whitehall* (London, 1980), 140; Colville, ibid., 668–70, also J.W. Young, *Winston Churchill's Last Campaign: Britain and the Cold War, 1951–55* (Oxford, 1996), 179–82.

3. As Salisbury was a member of the House of Lords, the Chancellor of the Exchequer was the most senior politician in the absence of Churchill and Eden. Butler therefore had to speak for the government on foreign policy issues in the House of Commons. See Butler, 'Oral Answers', H.C. *Parl. Deb.*, 5th series, Vol. 517, 29/6/1953, 27–32, and 1/71953, 403–6.

4. The medical bulletin, dated 27 June 1953, is publ. in P. Boyle (ed.), *The Churchill–Eisenhower Correspondence, 1953–1955* (Chapel Hill, N.C., 1990), 81–2.

5. See H.C. *Parl. Deb.*, 5th series, Vol. 537, 2/3/1955, 2116. See also Chapter 17, 366–7, below.

6. For example French Foreign Minister Bidault reported quite correctly to his government that Churchill had had a stroke, was paralysed on one side and could not walk. This was soon also reported in American newspapers but subsequently denied by London. See PRO: PREM 11/517, undated, *c.* end July/early August 1953; ibid., Fife–Clark, press spokesman for the British government, to Lord Swinton, 29/6/1953, regarding the reports in French newspapers. See also Moran, *Struggle for Survival*, 441: diary entry, 23/7/1953.

7. PRO: FO 371/106 526/NS 1021/77G, Boothby to Lloyd, 6/7/1953; also FO 371/106 534/NS 1051/59, letter Julian Amery to Lloyd, 21/7/1953, on his conversation with Soviet ambassador Malik and Chargé d'Affaires Georgi Rodionov. For a good account of Soviet suspicion, see U. Bar-Noi, 'The Soviet Union and Churchill's Appeals for High-Level Talks, 1953–4: New Evidence from the Russian Archives', *Diplomacy & Statecraft* 9/3 (1998), 119.

8. Boyle (ed.), *Correspondence*, 81: Churchill to Eisenhower, 26/6/1953.

9. For details regarding this memorandum, see, below, 266–7. See also Young, *Last Campaign*, 184–5, who emphasizes Montgomery's support for Churchill's thinking.

10. See Colville, *Fringes of Power*, 671: diary entry, 19/7/1953; Trinity College, Cambridge: Butler

Papers, G26/55–8, 59ff.; Churchill College, Cambridge: Woolton Papers, 3, diary 1942–60, 115ff.; HL: Beaverbrook Papers, BBk, C/250/ letters from Moran to Beaverbrook, 30/6 and 2/7/1953 and Beaverbrook's reply dated 31/7/1953; BUA: Avon Papers, AP 20/16/123/25 (various letters to Eden from the end of June 1953), 128–9: letters from Colville to Eden, dated 1/7 and 4/7/1953, 140–59: various letters to Eden, July–September 1953.

11. See E. Shuckburgh, *Descent to Suez: Diaries, 1951–56* (London, 1986), 88–103: diary entry after 20/7/1953. For the discussions of American diplomats regarding Churchill's potential successors, see NA: 741.13/7/753, Aldrich, London, to Dulles, No. 102, 7/7/1953.

12. See Colville, *Fringes of Power*, 673: diary entries, 31/7–4/8/1953; also Moran, *Struggle for Survival*, 476–7: diary entries, 6/10 and 10/10/1953. 'Never before … has so much depended on a single bloody speech', Churchill told his doctor (p. 477).

13. Boyle (ed.), *Correspondence*, 81: Churchill to Eisenhower, 26/6/1953.

14. This had not been forgotten in the USA either. See NA: 741.13/6–2953, Smith to US embassy in London, A–16, 2/7/1953. See also Salisbury, 'Foreign Affairs speech', H.L., *Parl. Deb.*, 5th series, Vol. 169, 15/11/1953, 275–86.

15. NA: 741.13/6–2953, Aldrich, London, to State Dept., No. 6866, 29/6/1953.

16. Ibid., Aldrich to Dulles, No. 103, 7/7/1953.

17. M. Soames (ed.), *Speaking for Themselves: The Personal Letters of Winston and Clementine Churchill* (London, 1998), 568: letter Churchill to his wife, 21/7/1952.

18. For example on 7 July he once again explained his views to Salisbury in detail. See Moran, *Struggle for Survival*, 425: diary entry, 7/7/1953.

19. Churchill realized that the British and American experts assumed that a summit conference with the Soviet Union after ratification of the EDC could hardly endanger the Western integration of the Federal Republic anymore and for that reason would be relatively safe. Churchill was aware that his political opponents would especially seek to block a summit before the completion of the EDC. See also J.W. Young, 'Churchill, the Russians and the Western Alliance: The Three-Power Conference at Bermuda, December 1953', *English Historical Review* 101 (1986), 896: 'Churchill was willing now to meet some of the criticisms of his "open approach" to Russia.'

20. Boyle (ed.), *Correspondence*, 83: Churchill to Eisenhower, 1/7/1953. Churchill also said in his letter that 'ten years of easement plus productive science might make a different world'. He thus hinted at this hope that after a prolonged détente and efforts at economic improvements Britain would again be in a position to perform its traditional and independent role in world politics.

21. Ibid., 85: Eisenhower to Churchill, 6/7/1953. Dulles made similar remarks in a conversation with Salisbury in Washington on 10 July. PRO: PREM 11/373/WU 1197/489G.

22. The memorandum was made available to all Cabinet members. PRO: CAB 129/61, C(53)194, memorandum Churchill to Salisbury and Strang, 6/7/1953 (also in PREM 11/323, 420, 449); FO 371/125 052/ZP 23/101. See also Moran, *Struggle for Survival*, 425: diary entry, 6/7/1953.

23. This strategy was soon characterized as the policy of the 'empty chair'. See for example S. Dockrill, *Britain's Policy for West German Rearmament, 1950–55* (Cambridge, 1991), 131, 140, 149.

24. See PRO: CAB 129/61, C(53)194, 6/7/1953. Moreover, it was clear, although Churchill did not mention it, that his health would not allow him to embark on such a journey before this point in time.

25. Ibid. (emphasis in the original).

26. PRO: FO 371/106 526, memorandum of the third conversation between Boothby and Chivotovski, 6/7/1953. On Boothby, see R.R. James, *Bob Boothby: A Portrait* (London, 1991).

27. PRO: CAB 129/61, C(53)194, memorandum Churchill, 6/7/1953 (emphasis in the original). For Churchill's views, see also Moran, *Struggle for Survival*, 428–9: diary entry, 10/7/1953.

28. PRO: CAB 129/61, C(53)187, 3/7/1953; also in PREM 11/323, 420, 425.

29. This memorandum was entitled 'The Problem of Germany'. See PRO: FO 371/103 666/C 1071/c. late June 1953. See also FO 371/125 052/ZP 23/82, minute Roberts to Mason, 15/6/1953, which makes clear that Roberts was the author of the memorandum.

30. PRO: FO 371/125 052/ZP 23/103/6, minute Dixon, 2/7/1953. See also A. Seldon, *Churchill's Indian Summer: The Conservative Government, 1951–55* (London, 1981), 402: 'in Lord Salisbury they [the FO] had an acting Foreign Secretary very much on their side'. A. Nutting, *Europe Will Not Wait: A Warning and a Way out* (London, 1960), 53, also declares that it was well-known that Salisbury was 'a protagonist of the "tough" line with Russia'.

31. PRO: CAB 129/61, C(53)187, memorandum Salisbury, 3/7/1953.

32. Ibid. Dixon also regarded this as the 'ideal programme'. PRO: FO 371/125 052/ZP 23/103/G, minute Dixon, 2/7/1953.

33. PRO: CAB 129/61, C(53)187, memorandum Salisbury, 3/7/1953.

34. PRO: CAB 128/26, Part 2, C.C. (53)39th Conclusions, minute 3, 6/7/1953 (also in PREM 11/373, 419, 1074).

35. Young, 'Churchill, the Russians', 897; see also J.W. Young, 'Cold War and Détente with Moscow', in J.W. Young (ed.), *The Foreign Policy of Churchill's Peacetime Government, 1951–1955* (Leicester, 1988), 62; and Young, *Last Campaign*, 185–5; also D. Carlton, 'Großbritannien und die Gipfeldiplomatie 1953–55', in B. Thoß and H.E. Volkmann (eds), *Zwischen Kaltem Krieg und Entspannung. Sicherheits- und Deutschlandpolitik der Bundesrepublik im Mächtesystem der Jahre 1953–1956* (Boppard, 1988), 56. Carlton's claim that Churchill himself suggested a foreign ministers' conference to ensure the survival of his summit diplomacy, however, is not correct.

36. See Chapter 16, below, 345ff.

37. The FO believed that it might be necessary to make concessions for example with respect to a UN commission to observe the elections in Germany but 'surely there is no need to volunteer it'. PRO: FO 371/103 665/C 1071/22, letter Hancock to Porter, 10/6/1953. A compromise on the question of the UN commission had already been suggested by Churchill in 1952. For the September 1952 note and the western conditions for German unification, see Chapter 9, above, 174ff., esp. 178–80.

38. PRO: FO 371/103 665/C 1071/49, minute Palliser, 26/6/1953.

39. PRO: FO 371/125 042/ZP 23/58/6, Makins to FO, No. 1376, 28/6/1953.

40. PRO: FO 371/106 532/NS 103 45/16G, letter Watson, British embassy Washington, to Hohler, FO, 8/7/1953. See also NS 103 45/12, letter Makins to Strang, 4/6/1953.

41. This view was shared by Bohlen. See NA: 761.00/7–1453, memorandum entitled 'Ambassador Bohlen's views on the situation in Russia', 14/7/1953.

42. NA: 761.5/6–3053, Cecil Lyon, Berlin, to High Commissioner Conant in Bonn, 30/6/1953. See also FRUS 1952–4, Vol. 8, 90: report by Lyon on the Vienna conference of US ambassadors in Eastern Europe, 21/9/1953.

43. EL: C.D. Jackson Records, 1953–4, Box No. 2, Folder: 'Bermuda Conference (5)', revised memorandum Thurston which incorporated Dulles's views entitled 'Bermuda Conference. Four-Power Meeting with the USSR', BCD–10e, 22/6/1953.

44. Ibid. See also FRUS 1952–4, Vol. 5, 1 1593: Conant, Bonn, to Dulles, 6/7/1953.

45. EL: C.D. Jackson Records, 1953–4, Box No. 2, Folder: 'Bermuda Conference (5)', memorandum Thurston 'Bermuda Conference. Four–Power Meeting with the USSR', BC D–10e, 22/6/1953.

46. Adenauer had added: 'In particular, he was dead set against talks between the Western High Commissioners and Mr Semenov'. PRO: FO 371/103 665/C 1071/58, minute Hancock, 25/6/1953.

47. FRUS 1952–4, Vol. 5, 1587: Conant to Dulles, 2/7/1953.

48. Ibid., 1588. Adenauer also explained to Conant that he felt 'that an all-German Government will not be free to have a national army and make an alliance with Russia'. When Conant pointed out that paragraph 5 of the Bundestag resolution of 10 June addressed the freedom of alliance for the Federal Republic, the Chancellor declared that the 'Bundestag resolution was not to be read too literally'.

49. See ibid., 1591–3: Conant to Dulles, 6/7/1953. See also ibid., 1603–4: memorandum MacArthur II, Counsellor in the State Dept., entitled 'Major Objectives in US–UK–French Talks', 9/7/1953.

50. NA: 762A.00/6–2653, Conant, Bonn, to Dulles, No. 5482, 26/6/1953. See also Felken, *Dulles*, 184.

51. See in NA: ibid. the summary of the comments of various West German newspapers. The SPD demanded an immediate meeting of the four High Commissioners. This met with the strong resistance of Adenauer who did not wish to see a revival of the old control commission of the four High Commissioners. See 762B.00/6–1953, Conant, Bonn, to State Dept, No. 5400, 19/6/1953; PRO: FO 371/103 839/CS 1016/57, Ward, Wahnerheide, to FO, No. 553, 18/6/1953. For the view of British parliamentarians, see for example the debates on 21 July 1953 in H.C. *Parl. Deb.*, 5th series, Vol. 518, 211ff.

52. Only early in 1954 was the 'New Course' gradually replaced. For Moscow's policy in the GDR after the uprising, see for example H. Weber, *Geschichte der DDR, 1945–87* (Munich, 1986), 245 ff.; M. Jänicke, *Der dritte Weg. Die anti-stalinistische Opposition gegen Stalin seit 1953* (Cologne, 1964), 39 ff.; D. Staritz, *Geschichte der DDR 1949–90*, revd edn (Darmstadt, 1997), 136 ff.; see also J. Foitzik (ed.), *Entstalinisierungskrise in Ostmitteleuropa 1953–56. Vom 17. Juni bis zum ungarischen Volksaufstand* [...] (Paderborn, 2001). NA: ibid., High Commission Bonn to State Dept., 'Larger Implications of June 17', 6/7/1953. For British analyses, see PRO: PREM 11/540, PREM 11/673, 'Note on East Germany', undated, *c.* August 1953, without author, FO 371/103 849, FO 371/103 850/CS 1018/1, memorandum of the Research Department 'Communist Political Ends and Means in the Soviet Zone of Germany', 13/10/1953.

53. NA: 762A.00/6–2653, Conant, Bonn, to Dulles, No. 5485, 26/6/1953.

54. Ibid. He also explained that 'if Adenauer 'should attempt to recommend [the] postponement of four-power talks into [the] indefinite future on [the] ground that [the] time is not ... ripe, he will find himself increasingly out of step with his coalition.' See also NA: PPS 64 D 563, Box 20029, Folder: 'Germany, 1953', memorandum Beam to Bowie 'Tactics in Presenting a Western Plan for a United Germany', 30/6/1953.

55. PRO: FO 371/103 666/C 1071/78, letter Kirkpatrick, Wahnerheide, to Roberts, FO, 7/7/1953.

56. PRO: FO 371/106 526/NS 1021/75, Makins, Washington, to FO, No. 1441, 9/7/1953.

57. Ibid.

58. NA: 762B.00/6-2653, Lyon, Berlin, to Conant (and passed on to Dulles, No. 5486, by Conant, 26/6/1953).

59. See the literature mentioned in the following note.

60. The letter is publ. in K. Adenauer, *Erinnerungen 1953-55* (Stuttgart, 1966), 225-6, quote: 225. Dockrill, *Britain's Policy*, 127, misunderstands the situation however. For the alleged surprise expressed by Dulles, see for example J. Foschepoth, 'Churchill, Adenauer und die Neutralisierung Deutschlands', *Deutschland-Archiv* 17 (1984), 1296-9; R. Steininger, 'Ein vereintes, unabhängiges Deutschland? Winston Churchill, der Kalte Krieg und die deutsche Frage im Jahre 1953', *Militärgeschichtliche Mitteilungen* 34 (1984), 121-2; H.P. Schwarz, *Die Ära Adenauer. Gründerjahre der Republik 1949-1957* (Wiesbaden, 1981), 211; H.P. Schwarz, *Adenauer. Der Staatsmann 1952-1967* (Stuttgart, 1991), 85-6. The five points of 10 June 1953 were almost identical with the conditions for German reunification as expressed in the western note to Moscow of 23 September 1952. See for this note Chapter 9, above, 178-80.

61. According to Adenauer's confidant Blankenhorn the plans were based on the ideas of State Secretary Walter Hallstein. See H. Blankenhorn, *Verständnis und Verständigung. Blätter eines politischen Tagebuchs 1949 bis 1979* (Frankfurt/M., 1979), 159.

62. See Adenauer, *Erinnerungen 1953-55*, 224-6. For an interesting analysis, see PRO: PREM 11/419, British embassy Washington to FO, No. 1461, 11/7/1953.

63. NA: 396.1-WA/7-1753, personal letter Conant to Dulles, 17/7/1953; PRO: ibid., Salisbury to FO, No. 1465, 11/7/1953, on a conversation with Roberts and Blankenhorn.

64. FRUS 1952-4, Vol. 7, 484-5: excerpt from Bruce's diary, 9/7/1953. See also Blankenhorn, *Verständnis und Verständigung*, 160; NA: 396.1-WA/7-953, Bruce to Dulles, No. Coled 11, 9/7/1953; 7/1053, Conant, Bonn, to Dulles, No. 168, 10/7/1953. M.S. Fish, 'After Stalin's Death. The Anglo-American Debate Over a New Cold War', *Diplomatic History* 10 (1986), 345, assumes that Dulles only received Adenauer's message on 10 July, shortly before the first meeting of the foreign ministers in Washington; this is however most unlikely.

65. See Foschepoth, 'Churchill, Adenauer', 1296-9 (quote: 1296); Steininger, 'Ein vereintes, unabhängiges Deutschland?', 121-2; Schwarz, *Adenauer. Der Staatsmann*, 85-9; H. Rupieper, *Der besetzte Verbündete. Die amerikanische Deutschlandpolitik 1949-55* (Opladen, 1991), 325; also J. Hershberg, *James B. Conant: Harvard to Hiroshima and the Making of the Nuclear Age* (Stanford, Calif., 1995), 665. Fish expresses a somewhat different view and appears to believe that the new tactic was developed simultaneously in Washington and Bonn. But he claims the two governments had not colluded with each other on the question (see ibid., 185).

66. Adenauer, *Erinnerungen 1953-5*, 226.

67. PRO: FO 800/778, WU 1197/480, memorandum of the conversation between Salisbury and Massigli, 8/7/1953.

68. PRO: PREM 11/419, Salisbury to FO, No. 1471, 11/7/1953.

69. PRO: CAB 128/26, Part 2, C.C.(53) 44th Conclusions, minute 4, 21/7/1953 (also in FO 800/761; PREM 11/419).

70. For other accounts of the Washington conference based on primary sources, see for example Foschepoth, 'Churchill, Adenauer', 1294-9; Fish, 'After Stalin's Death', 342-6; Steininger, 'Ein vereintes, unabhängiges Deutschland?', 121-2; Dockrill, *Britain's Policy*, 127-9; Young, *Last Campaign*, 187-94. While Foschepoth and Steininger exaggerate the importance of Adenauer's interference in the conference with the help of Blankenhorn, Young appears to neglect Adenauer's activities too much; see his 'Churchill, the Russians', 897, and also to a lesser extent his *Last Campaign*, ibid.

71. See Blankenhorn, *Verständnis und Verständigung*, 160-1; PRO: FO 371/103 667/C 1071/85, Makins, Washington, to FO, No. 1465, 11/7/1953 (also in PREM 11/419), minute of the conversation between Roberts and Blankenhorn. Even Adenauer mentions in his memoirs that he had given Blankenhorn a very difficult task and that his emissary was not received with enthusiasm by the western allies as he had the instruction to stay in Washington for the duration of the

conference (see *Erinnerungen 1953–5*, 226). Adenauer also claims that he sent Blankenhorn to the USA as Krekeler, the German diplomatic representative in Washington, was not yet accredited as the German ambassador. However, this was incorrect. In order to support Adenauer's election campaign the allied powers had just agreed to elevate Germany's diplomatic representatives to the rank of ambassadors (with effect from 6 July). Conant even feared that Krekeler's authority might become undermined by Blankenhorn's journey. See NA: 396.1–WA/7–1053, Conant, Bonn, to Dulles, No. 168, 10/7/1953.

72. Blankenhorn, *Verständnis und Verständigung*, 159.

73. See Foschepoth, 'Churchill, Adenauer', 1296–9; Steininger, 'Ein vereintes, unabhängiges Deutschland?', 121–2.

74. Electioneering tactics were Adenauer's reasons for his agreement to a conference with Moscow. This is confirmed by a memorandum dated 10 July and authored by James Riddleberger, the director of the Bureau of German Affairs within the State Dept., regarding a conversation with Blankenhorn: 'Mr Blankenhorn then emphasized that the Chancellor's present feeling is that his whole position is in danger because of the prevalence of the idea that he is somewhat against German unification. Therefore, the Chancellor must demonstrate his support of German unification and he would very much like to publish eventually the letter which he addressed to the Secretary'. FRUS 1952–4, Vol. 5, 1606–7, 10/7/1953. See also in a similar vain NA: 396.1-WA/7/1053, Conant, Bonn, to Dulles and Riddleberger, No. 169, 10/7/1953.

75. This was also Conant's opinion as expressed in a letter to Dulles on 17/7/1953. See NA: ibid., 7–1053.

76. The memorandum concerning the first trilateral session of the Washington conference on 10/7/1953 is publ. in FRUS 1952–4, Vol. 5, 1608–21 (quote: 1613). See also NA: ibid., 7-1153; FO 371/106 542/NS 1075/1, Salisbury, Washington, to FO, No. 1460, 10/7/1953. A bound book of the British minutes and the telegrams and reports of the British delegation on the meetings in Washington is in PRO: PREM 11/425 (see also PREM 11/419) and in FO 371/125 033/ZP 3/34/G. The following interpretation is largely based on the American reports. The British minutes appear to exaggerate the importance of Salisbury's contributions. Moreover, differences of opinion between Salisbury and his colleagues tend to be played down and reported in a somewhat ambiguous way.

77. FRUS 1952–4, Vol. 5, 1613, 10/7/1953. Fish, 'After Stalin's Death', 344–6, takes Salisbury's memorandum of 3 July too literally and assumes mistakenly that Salisbury did indeed attempt to secure a summit conference along the lines of Churchill's wishes. Young's conclusion in 'Churchill, the Russians', 897, is equally mistaken: 'Once in Washington … Salisbury pressed Churchill's views but was opposed strongly by Bidault'. As will be explained below, Bidault was indeed opposed to Salisbury's point of view but this was due to Salisbury's rather dogmatic views and not because Salisbury attempted to realize Churchill's ideas. Salisbury made no great efforts to push Churchill's summit policy.

78. For the attitude of the French foreign ministry, see NA: 762.0221/7–753, Achilles, US chargé d'affaires in Paris, to Dulles, No. 96, 7/7/1953.

79. FRUS 1952–4, Vol. 5, 1614–15, 10/7/1953.

80. Bidault added that the proposal he made in April to talk about disarmament questions with the USSR first was no longer feasible because of shifting western public opinion and the events of the last few months. See FURS, ibid., 1614–15, 1617, 10/7/1953.

81. PRO: PREM 11/425, Salisbury, Washington, to FO, No. 1460, 10/7/1953 (also in PREM 11/419). See also FRUS, ibid., 1614–15, 10/7/1953.

82. PRO: ibid. Fish, 'After Stalin's Death', 344, believes that Bidault had to be persuaded by Dulles to agree to four-power talks on Germany. However, this was not the case.

83. PRO: ibid., minute of the conversation between Salisbury and Bidault in the British embassy in Washington, 12/7/1953; also CAB 21/3073, 21–2.

84. PRO: PREM 11/425 (also in PREM 11/419), FO to Washington, No. 2772, T.218/53, 11/7/1953. See also ibid. No. 2779, T.219/53, 12/7/1953; and Moran, *Struggle for Survival*, 431: diary entry, 12/7/1953.

85. FRUS 1952–4, Vol. 5, 1617, 10/7/1953.

86. Ibid., 1617–18, 10/7/1953. For British ambassador Gascoigne's very similar view, see PRO: FO 371/106 542/NS 1075/1, Gascoigne, Moscow, to FO, No. 510, 11/7/1953. Gascoigne explained that an invitation 'might … assist Moscow over the stile … I would let the Kremlin stew in its own juice for a while longer.' See also FO 371/106 505/NS 1013/34, Gascoigne to FO, No. 141, 'Quarterly Report, April–June 1953', 9/7/1953.

87. FRUS, 1952–4, Vol. 5, 1618–19, 10/7/1953.

88. FRUS ibid.

89. See PRO: PREM 11/373, letter Colville to Shuckburgh, 27/7/1953; reply Shuckburgh to Colville, 31/7/1953.
90. The memorandum dealing with the second trilateral meeting on 11/7/1953 is publ. in ibid., 1621–31; see also NA: 396.1-WA/7-1153; PRO: FO 371/103 667/C 1071/86.
91. FRUS 1952–4, Vol. 5, 1625–6, 11/7/1953.
92. Ibid., 1626, 11/7/1953.
93. See for example the interesting parliamentary speech by former Prime Minister and Leader of the Opposition Clement Attlee, H.C. *Parl. Deb.*, 5th series, Vol. 518, 21/7/1953, esp. 229–31.
94. See for the reports and the speculations about Beria's arrest the documents in NA: 761.00, esp./7/653, Bohlen, Moscow, to Dulles, No. 28, 6/7/1953; /7-1053, Lyon, Berlin, to Dulles, No. 153, 10/7/1953; memorandum Armstrong 'Significance of Beria's Downfall', 10/7/1953; /7-1153, Conant to Dulles, No. 193, 11/7/1953; /7-1453, memorandum Bohlen 'Ambassador Bohlen's views on the situation in Russia', 14/7/1953; PRO: FO 371/106 505/NS 1013/32–5, 'Quarterly reports' from Moscow, April–June 1953. The USSR announced on 24 December 1953 that Beria had been sentenced to death together with some collaborators and that the sentence had been carried out on the same day. See A. Knight, *Beria: Stalin's First Lieutenant* (Princeton, N.J., 1993), 194 ff., 217 ff.; also Young, *Last Campaign*, 194–5. For details of the Beria affair, see Ch. 12 above, 258ff.
95. PRO: FO 800/794, memorandum of the conversation Salisbury–Massigli, 30/6/1953 (also in FO 371/125 051/ZP23/74). With regard to Adenauer's suggestion to make the resolution of the Bundestag of 10 June 1953 the basis of negotiations with the USSR Salisbury also held a view different from Bidault's. Not without displaying a lack of common sense, Salisbury believed 'that the UK would prefer to discuss Germany with the Soviets on the basis of the Allied declaration of September 1952, but pointed out the differences in substance between the two documents were few'. FRUS 1952–4, Vol. 5, 1625, 11/7/1953.
96. Trinity College, Cambridge: Butler Papers, G 26/65–7, letter Eden to Butler, 14/7/1953. However, on occasion Dulles also displayed some pessimism in the matter.
97. See for example Shuckburgh's diary entry on 21/7/1953: 'We are all enjoying having the Foreign Secretary in the House of Lords, where there is less politics and a calmer and more objective attitude'. Shuckburgh, *Descent to Suez*, 90.
98. FRUS 1952–4, Vol. 5, 1626–7, 11/7/1953.
99. Ibid.
100. See also Salisbury's 'Foreign Affairs speech' in the House of Lords: H.L. *Parl. Deb.*, 5th series, Vol. 183, 29/7/1953, 1031–2.
101. FRUS 1952–4, Vol. 5, 1627, 11/7/1953.
102. Ibid., 1628, 11/7/1953.
103. BUA: Avon Papers, AP 20/16/137, letter Salisbury to Eden, 12/7/1953 (emphasis in the original).
104. Ibid., letter Eden to Salisbury, 14/7/1953.
105. FRUS 1952–4, Vol. 5, 1628, 11/7/1953.
106. The memoranda dealing with the remaining meetings of the conference are publ. in ibid., 1631–96.
107. PRO: CAB 128/26, Part 2, C.C.(53)42nd Conclusions, minute 1, 13/7/1953 (also in PREM 11/419). See also ibid., 44th Conclusions, minute 4, 21/7/1953; PREM 11/419, FO to Salisbury, No. 2790, 13/7/1953; FRUS 1952–3, Vol. 5, 1663, 13/7/1953.
108. PRO: PREM 11/419, Salisbury to FO, No. 1490, 13/7/1953.
109. FRUS 1952–4, Vol. 5, 1673, 14/7/1953.
110. Ibid., 1674. See also PRO: PREM 11/419, Salisbury to FO, No. 1490, 13/7/1953; CAB 128/26, Part 2, C.C.(53)42nd Conclusions, minute 1, 13/7/1953. See also ibid., 44th Conclusions, minute 4, 21/7/1953.
111. Adenauer regarded the date of 15 September which the USA envisaged as the opening date of the conference as too soon. After the general election in West Germany it would take a considerable while to form a new government. See FRUS 1952–4, Vol. 5, 1691–2.
112. The invitation to Moscow to attend a foreign ministers' conference dated 15 July 1953 is publ. in ibid., 1701–2. The Washington conference's communiqué is publ. in ibid., 1703–6. Regarding Adenauer's influence, see Salisbury's speech on 14 July which was based on Kirkpatrick's conversation with the Chancellor in Bonn. See ibid., 1691–2.
113. Adenauer, *Erinnerungen 1953–55*, 228. Kirkpatrick reported that Adenauer was 'delighted' with the results of the conference as the SPD could not 'criticize anymore that Adenauer pays only lip service to the idea of reunification through Four power talks'. PRO: FO 371/103 895/CW 1013/27, Kirkpatrick to FO, No. 554, 21/7/1953.

114. Some authors believe that the conference was above all a success for Bidault. See for example Foschepoth, 'Churchill, Adenauer', 1296; Carlton, 'Großbritannien und die Gipfeldiplomatie', 57.
115. Shuckburgh, *Descent to Suez*, 89: diary entry, 21/7/1953.
116. Trinity College, Cambridge: Butler Papers, G26/65/67, letter Eden to Butler, 14/7/1953.
117. Moran, *Struggle for Survival*, 433-4: diary entry, 14/7/1953.
118. PRO: PREM 11/419, Churchill to British embassy Washington, No. 2876, T.222/53, 17/7/1953.
119. Boyle (ed.), *Correspondence*, 86-7: Churchill to Eisenhower, 17/7/1953.
120. Ibid., 87: Eisenhower to Churchill, 20/7/1953. See also Moran, *Struggle for Survival*, 439-40: diary entry, 21/7/1953.
121. Colville, *Fringes of Power*, 672: diary entry, 24/7/1953.
122. Shuckburgh, *Descent to Suez*, 89: diary entry, 21/7/1953. The officials believed that Eisenhower was 'therefore embarrassed by our Old Man's constant return to this theme'.
123. Moran, *Struggle for Survival*, 440: diary entry, 22/7/1953.
124. Shuckburgh, *Descent to Suez*, 89: diary entry, 21/7/1953.
125. For the British conference reports, see PRO: PREM 11/419; also CAB 128/26, Part 2, C.C. (53)44th Conclusions, minute 4, 21/7/1953.
126. Nutting, *Europe Will not Wait*, 54.
127. Moran, *Struggle for Survival*, 436: diary entry, 16/7/1953. For a similar statement by Salisbury, see his 'Foreign Affairs speech', in H.L. *Parl. Deb.*, 5th series, Vol. 183, 29/7/1953, 1029.
128. PRO: PREM 11/425, FO to British embassy, Washington, No. 2779, T.219/53, 12/7/1953. See also Moran, ibid., 431-4: diary entries, 12, 13 and 14/7/1953.
129. PRO: CAB 128/26, Part 2, C.C. (53) 44th Conclusions, minute 4, 21/7/1953; see also D. Carlton *Anthony Eden: A Biography*, paperback edn (London, 1981), 333.
130. K. Younger, 'Foreign Affairs speech', H.C. *Parl. Deb.*, 5th series, Vol. 518, 22/7/1953, quotes: 387-7, 392.
131. See Shuckburgh, *Descent to Suez*, 90: diary entry, 22/7/1953.
132. Colville, *Fringes of Power*, 671-2: diary entry, 21/7/1953.
133. See Kenneth Younger's statement in his 'Foreign Affairs speech' in the House of Commons: H.C. *Parl. Deb.*, 5th series, Vol. 518, 22/7/1953, 386-7; also Colville, ibid., 671.
134. For a summary of the reaction of the British press, see PRO: FO 371/125 052/ZP 23/114, 15/7/1953.
135. PRO: FO 371/106 534/NS 1051/59, letter Julian Amery to Lloyd, 21/7/1953, on his, Boothby's and Soames's conversation with Soviet ambassador Malik and Chargé d'Affaires Georgi Rodionov.
136. Salisbury, 'Foreign Affairs speech', H.L. *Parl. Deb.*, 5th series, Vol. 183, 29/7/1953, 1024-5. For Salisbury's speech, see also the German Chancellor's view: Adenauer, *Erinnerungen 1953-55*, 232-6.
137. Salisbury, ibid., 1028.
138. FRUS 1952-4, Vol. 6, 1364: Dillon, Paris, to State Dept., 31/7/1953.

CHAPTER 14: CHURCHILL'S LAST SUMMIT CONFERENCE

1. See FRUS 1952-4, Vol. 7, 607-14: various analyses of the Soviet note by Beam (5/8), Smith (6/8) and C.D. Jackson (8/8/1953). For the State Dept's assessment of Moscow's policy towards Germany, see ibid. 510-21: NSC 160/1 'United States position with Respect to Germany'; also NA: 611.62A/8-753, memorandum Bonbright on NSC 160, 7/8/1953; PPS 64D563, Box 20029 'Germany, 1953', and memorandum Fuller, 'Establishment of an All-German Government', 13/8/1953.
2. See the previous note.
3. From a document of the Soviet foreign ministry's espionage section 'Committee of Information' (KI); quoted in V.M. Zubok, 'Soviet Intelligence and the Cold War: The "Small" Committee of Information, 1952-53', *CWIHP*, Working Paper No. 4 (Washington, DC, 1992), 25 (see also Chapter 13, 276ff., above).
4. See for example Eisenhower's 'Chance for Peace speech' in April 1953. See Chapter 10, 199ff., 211ff. above.
5. E. Shuckburgh, *Descent to Suez: Diaries, 1951-56* (London, 1986), 92: diary entry, 27/7/1953.
6. PRO: CAB 128/26, Part 2, C.C.(54)44th Conclusions, minute 4, 21/7/1953.
7. See D. Carlton, 'Großbritannien und die Gipfeldiplomatie 1953-55', in B. Thoß and H.E. Volkmann (eds), *Zwischen Kaltem Krieg und Entspannung. Sicherheits- und Deutschlandpolitik der Bundesrepublik im Mächtesystem der Jahre 1953-1956* (Boppard, 1988), 56.
8. PRO: FO 800/760, FO to the British UN delegation in New York, Salisbury to Eden, No. 615,

24/7/1953. See also Shuckburgh, *Descent to Suez*, 92ff.: diary entries since 26/7; also J. Colville, *The Fringes of Power: 10 Downing Street Diaries, 1939–1955* (London, 1985), 672ff.; A. Seldon, *Churchill's Indian Summer: The Conservative Government, 1951–55* (London, 1981), 402ff.; R.R. James, *Anthony Eden*, paperback edn (London, 1986), 369–70.

9. Lord Moran, *Churchill: Struggle for Survival, 1945–1965* (London, 1965), 444, 25/7/1953.

10. Immediately after the Washington conference the Soviet Union's official daily *Pravda* had already argued in a very similar vein. See RIIA, *Survey of International Affairs, 1953* (London, 1956), 28–9.

11. PRO: PREM 11/419, Gascoigne, Moscow, to FO, No. 563, 4/8/1953. See also Bidault's analysis as conveyed in Adenauer's memoirs *Erinnerungen 1953–55* (Stuttgart, 1966), 236–8, also 244–5; also FRUS 1952–4, Vol. 7, 608–9: memorandum Beam, 5/8/1953.

12. The Soviet reply of 4 August is publ. in RIIA, *Documents on International Affairs, 1953* (London, 1956), 81–4; quote: 83; it is also publ. in FRUS, ibid., 604–7.

13. See RIIA, ibid.

14. PRO: PREM 11/419, memorandum Salisbury to the British embassies in Washington and Paris, c. 5/8/1953. See also ibid., Gascoigne Moscow, to FO, No. 566, 5/8/1953.

15. Ibid., minute Churchill to Salisbury, PM/M. 257/53, 6/8/1953. See also Shuckburgh, *Descent to Suez*, 96: diary entry, 6/8/1953.

16. Ibid., minute Churchill to Salisbury and Butler, PM/M, 263/53, 10/8/1953.

17. PRO: FO 371/106 257/NS 1021/108/G, memorandum Gascoigne regarding his conversation with Churchill in London, 19/8/1953; Shuckburgh, *Descent to Suez*, 96: diary entry, 6/8/1953. For the Palais Marbre Rose pre-conference, see Chapter 6, above, n. 83 (p. 445); Chapter 8, above, n.19 (p. 451).

18. See Shuckburgh, ibid., 97: diary entry, 7/8/1953.

19. RRO: CAB 128/26, Part 2, C.C.(53)48th Conclusions, minute 2, 10/8/1953: statement by Lord Salisbury; See also Shuckburgh, ibid., 96: diary entry, 6/8/1953; and for Frank Roberts's similar view, see ibid., 95: diary entry, 4/8/1953.

20. PRO: PREM 11/419, minute Churchill to Salisbury, PM/M. 257/53, 6/8/1953.

21. Ibid., PM/M. 258/53, 7/8/1953.

22. Ibid., minute Salisbury to Churchill, PM/S/53/278, 7/8/1953. See also ambassador Makins' telegrams from Washington in which he tried to explain the State Dept.'s 'bland acceptance' of the Soviet proposals regarding the discussion of the German question. Ibid., Washington to FO, Nos 1744 and 1758, 12/8/1953. See also FRUS 1952–4, Vol. 7, 608: analysis by Beam, 5/8/1953.

23. See for Bidault's changed view as explained to Adenauer during their meeting in Baden-Baden on 7 and 8 Aug. 1953, Adenauer, *Erinnerungen 1953–55*, 236–8; also FRUS ibid., 610: Smith to American embassy in Seoul, 6/8/1953.

24. FRUS, ibid., 607–14: analyses of the Soviet note by Beam (5/8), Smith (6/8) and C.D. Jackson (8/8/1953).

25. PRO: PREM 11/419, Makins, Washington, to FO, No. 1744, 12/8/1953.

26. Ibid., minute Churchill to Salisbury, PM/M. 258/53, 7/8/1953; minute Salisbury to Churchill, PM/S/53/278, 7/8/1953.

27. Ibid., memorandum of the Chequers meeting on 8/8/1953; present were Churchill, Salisbury, Butler, Colville and a few other officials. See also Shuckburgh, *Descent to Suez*, 97: diary entry, 7/8/1953; Moran, *Struggle for Survival*, 449: diary entry, 8/8/1953; Colville, *Fringes of Power*, 674: diary entry 6–9/8/1953; M. Gilbert, *Winston S. Churchill, Vol. 8: Never Despair, 1945–65*, paperback edn (London, 1990), 872; see also J.W. Young, *Winston Churchill's Last Campaign: Britain and the Cold War, 1951–55* (Oxford, 1996), 199, who perhaps underestimates the nature of the meeting; it essentially consisted of a prime ministerial reprimand for Salisbury and the FO.

28. Colville, ibid.; see also PRO: PREM 11/419, minute Churchill to Salisbury and Butler, PM/M. 263/53, 10/8/1953; also FO to Washington, No. 3156, 10/8/1953.

29. Shuckburgh, *Descent to Suez*, 100: diary entry, 26–7/8/1953. In mid-September Salisbury offered his resignation to Churchill but the Prime Minister refused to accept it. See ibid., 102: diary entry, 1/10/1953; also BUA: Avon Papers, 1 AP 20/1/29A: Diary 1953: Convalescent Cruise, 22/9/1953.

30. Indeed, Butler seemed to be intent on exploiting Eden's absence to promote himself as Churchill's potential heir. Quote: Moran, *Struggle for Survival*, 449: diary entry, 8/8/1953; also 483: diary entry, 11/10/1953; Colville, *Fringes of Power*, 671: diary entry, 19/7/1953; Shuckburgh, ibid., 97: diary entry, 7/8/1953. For an assessment of Churchill's fairly cool view of Butler, see A. Montague Browne, *Long Sunset: Memoirs of Winston Churchill's Last Private Secretary* (London, 1995), 125.

31. See Moran, ibid., 448: diary entry, 5/8/1953; also 476–7: diary entries, 6/10 and 10/10/1953; Shuckburgh, ibid., 94–5: diary entry, 4/8/1953; also 97–9: diary entry, 11/8/1953. See also Gilbert, *Never Despair*, 871.

32. See for example, Colville, *Fringes of Power*, 675: diary entries, 14–15/8/1953, 17/8/1953.

33. See Shuckburgh, *Descent to Suez*, 100: diary entry, 26–7/8/1953; M. Soames, *Clementine Churchill* (London, 1979), 436.

34. Ibid., 99–100: diary entry, 26–7/8/1953. Indeed, Churchill 'took charge' of the clandestine Anglo-American operation to remove Iranian Prime Minister Mussadeq ('Operation Boot'). See W.R. Louis, 'How Mussadeq was ousted: the untold story behind the CIA–M16 coup', *Times Literary Supplement* No. 5126 (29 June 2001), 13–15.

35. See Seldon, *Indian Summer*, 402 (the declaration was publ. on 28/9/1953); also Young, *Last Campaign*, 191–2. Due to Churchill's statement, the difficulties of the French government in attempting to push the EDC through the National Assembly may well have increased further.

36. See RIIA, *Survey, 1953*, 29; see also the letter regarding yet another meeting between Boothby and the Soviet diplomat Chivotovsky in London: PRO: FO 371/106 527/NS 1021/94/G, letter Boothby to Lloyd, 7/8/1953.

37. For a discussion whether or not it was a 'real' hydrogen bomb or merely a 'boosted fission' (atomic) bomb, see D. Holloway, *Stalin and the Bomb: The Soviet Union and Atomic Energy, 1939–54* (New Haven, 1994), 306–10. In a speech during a banquet in the Kremlin on 23/8/1953 Malenkov mentioned again the fact that Moscow had broken the American monopoly on the hydrogen bomb. See PRO: FO 371/103 947; also FO 371/106 527/NS 1021/103, letter Grey, Moscow, to Mason, FO, 27/8/1953.

38. Malenkov's long speech before the Supreme Soviet on 8/8/1953 is partially publ. in RIIA, *Documents, 1953*, 22–33. The entire speech can be found in PRO: FO 371/106 511/NS 1015/51.

39. See for example FRUS 1952–4, Vol. 8, 1212: Bohlen, Moscow, to State Dept., 10/8/1953; also RIIA, ibid., 30.

40. NA: 761.11/8–2553, C.R. Harvey, Office of Political Affairs, US High Commission Bonn, to State Dept., 25/8/1953. See also the detailed analysis of Malenkov's speech of 8/8/1953 which was enclosed with the telegram.

41. For the reaction of the western foreign ministries, see for example, PRO: FO 371/106 526/NS 1021/88, Makins, Washington, to FO No. 675, 11/8/1953; NS 1021/92, Makins to FO No. 685, regarding a speech by Dulles on 12/8, 14/8/1953; NS 1021/85, Gascoigne, Moscow, to FO No. 577, 9/8/1953; FO 371/106 511/NS 1015/47, memorandum Hohler to Salisbury, 10/8/1953; NS 1015/49, memorandum Gascoigne on the meeting of the Supreme Soviet, 11/8/1953; FO 371/106 527/NS 1021/102, letter, Grey, Moscow, to Salisbury, 28/8/1953; FRUS 1952–4, Vol. 8, 1210–12: Bohlen to State Dept., 10/8/1953. For Churchill's reaction, see for example, Colville, *Fringes of Power*, 675: diary entry, 11–12/8/1953.

42. See Moran, *Struggle for Survival*, 448: diary entry, 5/8/1953.

43. See Colville, *Fringes of Power*, 679: diary entry, October 1953 (no more precise date given).

44. See PRO: FO 800/840, various minutes, 7/8/1953; also Colville, ibid., 673: diary entry, 31/7–4/8/1953; Shuckburgh, *Descent to Suez*, 97: diary entry, 10/8/1953; P. Boyle (ed.), *The Churchill-Eisenhower Correspondence, 1953–1955* (Chapel Hill, N.C., 1990), 88–9: Churchill to Eisenhower, 3/8/1953, Eisenhower to Churchill, 8/8/1953; see also Young, *Last Campaign*, 210–11.

45. On 8 August Eisenhower had replied to Churchill's letter dated 3 August. Only on 7 October did Churchill write again to the President. See Boyle (ed.), ibid., 88–9; Moran, *Struggle for Survival*, 452: diary entry, 16/8/1953.

46. See Shuckburgh, *Descent to Suez*, 95: diary entry, 4/8/1953; also 96: diary entry, 6/8/1953; and Moran, ibid. See also Churchill's explanations in his conversation with Gascoigne in London on 19/8/1953: PRO: FO 371/106 257/NS 1021/108/G.

47. See Moran, ibid., 455–6. 459–62. 470: diary entries, 18/8, 25/8, 11/9/1953; H. Macmillan, *Tides of Fortune, 1945–55* (London 1969), 522–3; Colville, *Fringes of Power*, 676; FRUS 1952–4, Vol. 6, 1002–3: memorandum of conversation Churchill–Aldrich, 10/9/1953; Young, *Last Campaign*, 201–2; also M. Soames (ed.), *Speaking for Themselves: The Personal Letters of Winston and Clementine Churchill* (London, 1998), 571; Soames, *Clementine Churchill*, 437–8.

48. See Gilbert, *Never Despair*, 772, 875; Colville, ibid., 675–6: diary entry, 14–15/8/1953; Moran, ibid., 451: diary entry, 16/8/1953. For further details, see Chapter 15, 325–7 below.

49. See Colville, ibid., diary entries, 14–15/8, 17/8/1953; quote: 676. See also Gilbert, ibid., 772, 873–4; and Churchill's parliamentary speech in early November 1953 as quoted and commented on by Moran, ibid., 492–4: diary entry, 3/11/1953. See also PRO: ibid., for the conversation between Churchill and Gascoigne. For Liddell Hart's phrase, see Liddell–Hart-Archive, London: Liddell–Hart-Papers, 11/1954/5b, 30/6/1954.

50. See PRO: PREM 11/419, Gascoigne, Moscow, to FO No. 567, 16/8/1953; also No. 598, 17/8/1953; for Salisbury's comments, see CAB 128/26, Part 2, C.C.(53)49th Conclusions, minute 8, 18/8/1953. For

the reaction of the West German press, see PREM 11/419, Ward, Wahnerheide, to FO No. 761, 18/8/1953. See also Bedell Smith's analysis in FRUS 1952-4, Vol. 7, 624-7, 17/8/1953; see also NA: 761.11/8-2553, memorandum, US High Commission, Bonn, dated 28/8/1953. For this exchange of notes, see also Young, *Last Campaign*, 198-201.

51. See FRUS, ibid., 626: Smith to US High Commission, Bonn, 17/8/1953.
52. The western reply is publ. in RIIA, *Documents, 1953*, 89-91; and in FRUS, ibid., 630-2. For American thinking in the matter, see FRUS, ibid., 632-3, 634-5.
53. The Soviet note is partially publ. in RIIA, ibid., 91-5; and in full in FRUS, ibid., 639-45. For the Soviet note and the western Lugano proposal, see also PRO: PREM 11/449, Grey, Moscow, to FO, No. 705 and 707, 28/9 and 29/9/1953.
54. See PRO: PREM 11/419. The West continued with its preparations for a conference in Lugano though hardly anyone expected that this meeting would take place. See ibid., GEN 443/2, 30/9/1953; also C.C.(53)57th Conclusions, minute 2, 13/10/1953.
55. BUA: Avon Papers, AP 20/1/29A, diary Eden: Convalescent Cruise, 1/10/1953.
56. FRUS 1952-4, Vol. 8, 90: statement by Lyon during the conference of American ambassadors to Eastern Europe, 22/9/1953; see also p. 99: Bohlen's statement on 23/9/1953 in the course of the same meeting.
57. See H.P. Schwarz, *Die Ära Adenauer. Gründerjahre der Republik 1949–1957* (Wiesbaden, 1981), 194-6; for the international reaction to the West German election and the speculations shortly before election day, see PRO: FO 371/103 947, 'Soviet Press Reactions to events in FRG, April–Sept. 1953'; ibid., CW 10338/3, Grey, Moscow, to FO No. 659, 7/9153, 'Probably Soviet Reaction to the results of the elections in FRG'; PREM 11/440/CW 10113/111, Kirkpatrick, Bonn, to Salisbury, 15/8/1953; CW 1013/183, Ward, Bonn, to Salisbury, 5/10/1953; also FRUS 1952-4, Vol. 7, 531-8. The western allies, however, anticipated that relations with the self-confident Adenauer would become even more difficult now. See FO 371/103 706/C 1075/1–23 (May–October 1953); FRUS, ibid., 531ff., 628-30; Vol. 8, 88-9; EL: Ann Whitman File, Administrative Series, Folder: Conant (2), letter to Eisenhower, 8/9/1953; PUA: John F. Dulles Papers, Selected Correspondence, Box 72, letter McCloy to Dulles, 23/9/1953.
58. FRUS 1952-4, Vol. 7, 645-8: memorandum of a conversation between Dulles and his advisers, 30/9/1953.
59. Ibid., 655: telegram Dulles to the US embassy in London, 13/10/1953.
60. Quoted in Young, *Last Campaign*, 200.
61. Ibid., 648: Dulles to the US embassy in London, 3/10/1953. Regarding the considerations whether or not to cancel the conference, see also ibid., 628-9, 632-3: letters Conant to State Dept. on his conversations with Adenauer, 31/8/1953 and 10/9/1953; 634-8, 645-8: talks between Dulles and his advisers on 26/9 and 30/9/1953.
62. For the opposition of the FO, see FRUS 1952-4, Vol. 7, 653-4: Conant to State Dept., 12/10/1953; and for Adenauer's opposition to a four-power meeting, see ibid., 654-6: Dulles to US embassy in London, 13/10/1953.
63. See for example the opinion of Berthoud, the British ambassador to Copenhagen, PRO: FO 371/106 527/NS 1021/112, letter Berthoud to Mason, FO, 4/11/1953.
64. Ibid., NS 1021/118, Hayter to FO No. 250, 24/11/1953. Hayter had resided in Moscow since October 1953.
65. See Shuckburgh, *Descent to Suez*, 98, 101: diary entries, 11/8 and 8/9/1953; Colville *Fringes of Power*, 675: diary entry, 11–12/8/1953; James, *Anthony Eden*, 369.
66. Shuckburgh, ibid., 61: diary entry, 30/9/1953. See also D. Carlton, *Anthony Eden: A Biography*, paperback edn (London, 1981), 333. Adenauer was pleased about Eden's continuation of Salisbury's hostile policy with regard to a summit with Moscow. See PRO: FO 371/103 956/CW 1051/15, letter Hoyer Millar to Roberts, 6/10/1953. Hoyer Millar was the new High Commissioner to West Germany. On 1 October he had replaced his predecessor Kirkpatrick who succeeded William Strang as Permanent Under-Secretary and thus the FO's most senior official in London on 1 November 1953. Strang retired. For the comments of the West German press on Kirkpatrick's promotion which had already been announced in May, see ibid., CW 1051/8, 12/5/1953.
67. Shuckburgh, ibid., 105: diary entry, 5/10/1953.
68. BUA: Avon Papers, AP 20/1/29A, diary Convalescent Cruise, 1/10/1953. Indeed, Churchill's last Private Secretary believes that Churchill had a fairly 'cool' view of Salisbury. See Montague Browne, *Long Sunset*, 126.
69. PRO: PREM 11/892, Eden to Makins, Washington, undated; NA: 741.13/9–1453, Aldrich to Dulles, No. 1095, 14/9/1953; Shuckburgh, *Descent to Suez*, 105: diary entry, 5/10/1953.
70. Shuckburgh, ibid., 106: diary entry, 7/10/1953.

71. Ibid., 107: diary entry, 9/10/1953; see also ibid., 106: diary entry, 7/10/1953; BUA: Avon Papers, AP 20/2: diary entry, 2/10/1953; Colville, *Fringes of Power*, 679–80: diary entry, Oct. 1953; Moran, *Struggle for Survival*, 475ff.: diary entries for October 1953; PRO: PREM 11/892, Eden to Makins, Washington, undated

72. Boyle (ed.), *Correspondence*, 89–90: Churchill to Eisenhower, 7/10/1953; Eisenhower to Churchill, 8/10/1953; further details are contained in PRO: PREM 11/892, Churchill to Eisenhower, PM/T.259/53, FO to Washington, No. 3892, 7/10/1953; Eisenhower to Churchill, 8/10/1953.

73. See Shuckburgh, *Descent to Suez*, 107: diary entry, 9/10/1953; BUA: Avon Papers, AP 20/1/29A, diary Eden, Convalescent Cruise, 1/10/1953. Shuckburgh's and Eden's diary entries show a surprising similarity; even certain phrases can be found in both diaries; it can be assumed that Shuckburgh was given access to Eden's writing. See also Colville, *Fringes of Power*, 679: diary entry, October 1953; James, *Anthony Eden*, 371.

74. See Boyle (ed.), *Correspondence*, 90–1: Churchill to Eisenhower, 9/10/1953; PRO: PREM 11/892, Eden to British embassy in Washington, No. 3967, 9/10/1953. See also ibid., minute Eden to Churchill, undated, c.9/10/1953. For the background to the talks, see FRUS 1952–4, Vol. 7, 687 (editorial note); and 687–8: Dulles to US embassy in Paris, 12/10/1953. See also PRO: CAB 128/26, Part 2, C.C.(53)57th Conclusions, minute 1, 13/10/1953.

75. According to Richard Lovell, Moran prescribed Drinamyl and Edrisal tablets which he fine-tuned with the help of d-amphetamines and other substances like aspirin and phenacetin. At the time this appears to have been a very imaginative treatment for cerebrovascular disease which, however, became the standard treatment years later. Lovell concludes therefore that Moran 'may unwittingly have prolonged' Churchill's life. See R. Lovell, 'Lord Moran's prescriptions for Churchill', *British Medical Journal*, Vol. 310 (1995), 1537–8.

76. Colville, *Fringes of Power*, 679: diary entry, October 1953. See also the detailed report in Moran, *Struggle for Survival*, 475–81: diary entries, 6, 9, and 10/10/1953; also Soames, *Clementine Churchill*, 438–9.

77. NA: 741.13/10–1153, Aldrich to Dulles, No. 1547, 11/10/1953; ibid., 741.00/10–1253, Penfield, US embassy, London, to Dulles, No. 1567, 12/10/1953.

78. Churchill's speech in Margate on 10/10/1953 is publ. in R.R. James (ed.), *Winston S. Churchill: His Complete Speeches, 1987–1963, Vol. 8: 1950–63* (London, 1974), quotes: 8495–6. The speech is also partially publ. in RIIA, *Documents, 1953*, 95–7.

79. Quoted in James (ed.), ibid., 8496.

80. Eden's speech in Margate was also very successful. See the very detailed memorandum on the party conference by the American diplomat Margaret J. Tibetts, NA: 741.00/10–1953, Tibetts to State Dept., No. 1475, 19/10/1953.

81. See James (ed.), *Complete Speeches*, Vol. 8, 8496–7; Colville, *Fringes of Power*, 679: diary entry, October 1953; Moran, *Struggle for Survival*, 479–80: diary entry, 10/10/1953. See also James, *Anthony Eden*, 372; Gilbert, *Never Despair*, 895. The Queen intended to embark on her visit in November 1953.

82. See also Carlton, 'Großbritannien und die Gipfeldiplomatie', 55. According to Carlton, personal disputes and rivalry had always been more important than disagreements over Churchill's summit diplomacy. However, it appears that only after the autumn of 1953 did the personal factor become more important than issues of political substance. This is also the view of James, *Anthony Eden*, 372–4. After the autumn of 1953 James believes that the Churchill–Eden relationship resembled the one between Gladstone and Roseberry in 1892–94.

83. Quoted in James (ed.), *Complete Speeches*, Vol. 8, 8495. For the great displeasure which Churchill's speech caused in France, see A. Werth, *France, 1940–1955* (London, 1956), 645–6. Werth believes that the speech was a 'landmark' as for the first time it had been stated in public by a senior western statesman that it was unlikely that the EDC would be ratified; 'until then it was somehow assumed that, sooner or later, she would' (p. 646).

84. PRO: FO 371/103 956/CW 1051/29, minute of the conversation between Blankenhorn and British diplomat Chaput de Saintonge, 2/11/1953.

85. Ibid., CW 1051/12, Hoyer Millar, Wahnerheide, to FO, No. 761, 29/9/1953. See also CAB 128/26, Part 2, C.C.(53)52nd Conclusions, minute 7, 16/9/1953: discussion of a memorandum by Salisbury [C.(53)256, to be found in CAB 129/63] on 'possible alternative forms of a security guarantee between the Soviet Union and the Western Powers'. But see also Eden's proposals for a certain intensification of Britain's association with the EDC, in CAB 128/26, Part 2, C.C.(53)72nd Conclusions, minute 4, 26/11/1953; and Eden's memorandum in the matter in CAB 129/64, C.(53)332, November 1953. For further details, see Young, *Last Campaign*, 202ff.

86. See for example in detail H. Rupieper, *Der besetzte Verbündete. Die amerikanische Deutschland-politik 1949–55* (Opladen, 1991), 348ff.; also H.H. Jansen, *Großbritannien, das Scheitern der EVG und der NATO-Beitritt der Bundesrepublik Deutschland* (Bochum, 1992), 40ff.; S. Mawby, *Containing Germany: Britain and the Arming of the Federal Republic* (Basingstoke, 1999), ch. 4; and very detailed, T.U. Schöttli, *USA und EVG. Truman, Eisenhower und die Europa-Armee* (Bern, 1994), 319ff.

87. NSC 160/1, dated 17/8/1953, is publ. in FRUS 1952–54, Vol. 7, 510–20; see above all, 515–16, 518–19. For a good analysis of NSC 162/2, the New Look document, see S. Dockrill, *Eisenhower's New Look National Security Policy, 1953–61* (Basingstoke, 1996), 19ff.; and S.F. Wells, 'The Origins of Massive Retaliation', *Political Science Quarterly* 96/1 (1982), 31–52; H.W. Brands, 'The Age of Vulnerability: Eisenhower and the National Insecurity State', *American Historical Review* 94/4 (1989), 963–89.

88. FRUS, ibid., 515–16, n. 2.

89. Ibid., 501–8: memorandum of the 159th NSC meeting, 13/8/1953; quote: 504. This view was shared by most NATO members including Britain. See PRO: PREM 11/369, C.C.(53)50th Conclusions, minute 2, 25/8/1953: discussion of a memorandum by Lord Salisbury, 'A Revised Policy Directive for the North Atlantic Treaty Organisation' (memorandum to be found in CAB 129/62, C.(53)234, 17/8/1953).

90. FRUS, ibid., 506: memorandum of the 159th NSC meeting, 13/8/1953.

91. Ibid., 542: memorandum of the 164th NSC meeting, 1/10/1953.

92. Ibid., 553–4: letter Conant, Bonn, to Dulles, Washington, 13/11/1953. On 20 November Dulles had informed him by letter that 'Certainly, the United States is not now considering alternatives'. EL: John Foster Dulles Papers, Subject Series, Box 8, Folder: Germany, 1953–4 (2).

93. See FRUS 1952–4, Vol. 7, 543: 166th NSC meeting, 13/10/1953 (editorial note). However, the work on alternative plans proceeded although they were given less attention. Lower level officials in the State Dept., the Pentagon and the PPS continued considering alternative solutions to the EDC. See for example NA: 762A.00/11–1953, memorandum of a draft telegram by Lewis, Office of German Affairs, to Merchant, 20/11/1953; PPS 64D563, Box 722, 'Europe, 1952–53', memorandum Owen, 'Alternatives to EDC', 24/111953; also Box 20035, 'Europe, 1952–53', memorandum Fuller to Bowie, 'Alternatives to EDC', 1/12/1953; also Box 721, memorandum Beam to Bowie, 'Defense Department Paper on Alternatives to EDC', 9/12/1953.

94. See FRUS, ibid., 553: letter Dulles to Conant, Bonn, 9/11/1953; also EL: John Foster Dulles Papers, Subject Series, Box 8, Folder: Germany, 1953–4 (2), letter Dulles to Conant, 20/11/1953. For Dulles's December 1953 statement, see Dockrill, *Eisenhower's New Look National Security Policy*, 85–8.

95. Ibid., 688: Dulles to US embassy in Paris, 12/10/1953. For the meeting, see also Young, *Last Campaign*, 210–14.

96. Ibid., 691: Dulles to Eisenhower, 16/10/1953; for the conversations in London, see also PRO: PREM 11/892; and FO 371/125 123/ZP 3/1/G, Nos 1–22.

97. See Colville's views which appear to have been based on statements by Churchill as conveyed in Shuckburgh, *Descent to Suez*, 108: diary entry, 18/10/1953.

98. See BUA: Avon Papers, AP 20/16/15, 18/10/1953. Lord Cherwell, the former F.A. Lindemann, was to retire at the end of the month. For an account of Cherwell's relationship with Churchill during the Second World War, see T. Wilson, *Churchill and the Prof* (London, 1997); for an interesting brief portrait, see also Montague Browne, *Long Sunset*, 126–8.

99. FRUS 1952–4, Vol. 7, 691: Dulles to Eisenhower, 16/10/1953. Quote: 718: memorandum of the 167th NSC meeting, 22/10/1953 (Dulles's report on the London meeting). For the session on 16/10/1953, see also Shuckburgh, *Descent to Suez*, 108: diary entry, 18/10/1953.

100. FRUS, ibid., 692: Dulles to Eisenhower, 16/10/1953; 719: memorandum of the 167th NSC meeting, 22/10/1953. Salisbury even told the American ambassador that he liked Dulles's attitude. For the London meeting, see also Carlton, *Anthony Eden*, 334.

101. See Shuckburgh, *Descent to Suez*, 107–9: diary entry, 18/10/1953; FRUS, ibid., 692ff.; see also the bound volume of the minutes of the London talks, PRO: FO 371/125 123/ZP 3/1/G, No. 1–22.

102. See FRUS, ibid., 716–17: memorandum US ambassador Aldrich on his luncheon with Churchill, 19/10/1953.

103. PRO: PREM 11/420, *Daily Telegraph* article, dated 28/10/1953, and minute Colville, 10/11/1953.

104. See Churchill, 'Foreign Affairs speech', H.C. *Parl. Deb.*, 5th series, Vol. 520, 3/11/1953, 28–31. His Mansion House speech is publ. in James (ed.), *Complete Speeches*, Vol. 8, 8506–8.

105. Moran, *Struggle for Survival*, 492–4: diary entry, 3/11/1953.

106. See Young, *Last Campaign*, 214, n.17.

107. NA: 741.00/11–1153, Aldrich to Dulles, No. 2474, 5/11/1953.

108. Ibid.
109. For the western discussions, see FRUS 1952–4, Vol. 7, 651–2.
110. The western note is publ. in RIIA, *Documents, 1953*, 98–100.
111. EL: John F. Dulles Papers, Drafts of Presidential Correspondence, Box 1, 'Memorandum for the President, Atomic Speech', 23/10/1953.
112. The Soviet note of 3 November is partially publ. in RIIA, *Documents, 1953*, 100–6; the note can be found in full, including an interesting analysis by ambassador Hayter, in PRO: PREM 11/419, Hayter to FO, No. 802, 3/11/1953.
113. Boyle (ed.), *Correspondence*, 93: Churchill to Eisenhower, 5/11/1953. See also PRO: PREM 11/418, C.C. (53)64th Conclusions, Minute 2, 9/11/1953.
114. EL: Ann Whitman File, International Series, Box 17, Folder: President-Churchill, Vol. 3 (4), Aldrich to Dulles, No. 1979, 6/11/1953.
115. NA: 611.41/11–1953, memorandum 'United States Objectives at Bermuda', 10/11/1953 (without author). See also EL: John F. Dulles Papers, Subject Series, Box 8, Folder: Germany, 1953–4 (2), letter Dulles to Conant, 20/11/1953.
116. John Young's explanation that Eisenhower found it difficult to reject the conference as Bermuda had only been 'postponed' in June is not entirely convincing (*Last Campaign*, 216). The President tended to be quite imaginative when he wished to avoid meetings with Churchill or other politicians.
117. Boyle (ed.), *Correspondence*, 94: Eisenhower to Churchill, 6/11/1953.
118. NA: 611.41/11–1953, memorandum 'United States Objectives at Bermuda', 10/11/1953 (without author). See also EL: John Foster Dulles Papers, Subject Series, Box 8, Folder: Germany, 1953–4 (2), letter Dulles to Conant, 20/11/1953.
119. Boyle (ed.), *Correspondence*, 95: Churchill to Eisenhower, 7/11/1953.
120. PRO: PREM 11/418, Harvey, Paris, to FO, No. 453, 10/11/1953. See also J.W. Young, 'Churchill, the Russians and the Western Alliance: The Three-Power Conference at Bermuda, December 1953', *English Historical Review* 101 (1986), 899. After Churchill's speech in Margate, which had been criticized in Paris for the suggestion that an alternative to the EDC ought to be devised (see above, 299), this episode was already the second disagreement between Downing Street and Paris within a month. For further details, see Young, *Last Campaign*, 217.
121. A very few position papers of which the American embassy had been unaware can be found in PRO: ibid. See also FRUS 1952–4, Vol. 5, 1714–15: 170th NSC meeting, 13/11/1953, quote: 1715; ibid., 1716–17: memorandum Raynor, director of the Office of British Commonwealth and Northern European Affairs, to MacArthur II, 16/11/1953.
122. FRUS, ibid., 1721: Aldrich, London, to State Dept., 27/11/1953.
123. For the American unwillingness at this stage to enter into any binding and long-term commitments to base troops on the European continent, see FRUS, ibid., 1729–36.
124. These kind of considerations would eventually lead to the development of an alternative to the EDC when the French National Assembly failed to approve the EDC in late August 1954. However, the idea of making use of the Brussels treaty of 1948 was not mentioned at this stage. See FRUS, ibid., 1723–5: Aldrich, London, to Dulles, 27/11/1953. Young, 'Churchill, the Russians', 900, goes too far with the assumption that the Foreign Office rejected all of Churchill's ideas for considering alternatives to the EDC. In fact, in the autumn the FO had begun to seriously embark on considering alternatives to the EDC while also still attempting to bring the EDC itself into being.
125. F. Roberts, *Dealing with Dictators: The Destruction and Revival of Europe, 1930–70* (London, 1991), 172; see also PRO: CAB 128/26, Part 2, C.C.(53)72nd Conclusions, minute 4, 26/11/1953; CAB 129/64, C(53)332.
126. FRUS 1952–4, Vol. 7, 1719: Achilles, Paris, to State Dept., 17/11/1953.
127. The Prime Minister had only informed the British Cabinet of the forthcoming conference on the previous day. See Churchill, 'Oral Answers', H.C. *Parl. Deb.*, 5th series, Vol. 520, 10/11/1953, 773–4; also PRO: CAB 128/26, Part 2, C.C. (53)64th Conclusions, minute, 2, 9/11/1953; 65th Conclusions, minute 2, 10/11/1953; also FO 800/822, telegram to Molotov, 10/10/1953; also Boyle (ed.), *Correspondence*, 97: Churchill to Eisenhower, 12/11/1953; Churchill only told Eisenhower after a delay of two days about his message to Molotov.
128. See FRUS 1952–4, Vol. 7, 678: Bohlen, Moscow, to State Dept., 27/11/1953.
129. See RIIA, *Survey, 1953*, 35.
130. See FRUS 1952–4, Vol. 7, 722 (editorial note). A bound volume with the minutes and memoranda, mostly authored by Frank Roberts, of the 'Tripartite Official Talks on Germany and Austria' which convened in Paris between 21 October and 2 November to prepare the western reply, can be found in PRO: PREM 11/449 (also in PREM 11/419). See also the interesting memorandum by

Eden, which was based on the work of the Tripartite Group, entitled 'Germany, Austria and Security Arrangements', PREM 11/449, C.(53)316, 13/11/1953.

131. The western reply is publ. in RIIA, *Documents, 1953*, 106–7.

132. PRO: FO 371/106 527/NS 1021/118, Hayter to FO, No. 250, 24/11/1953.

133. However, Moscow made clear that at such a conference the Soviet representative would insist on a subsequent more general five-power conference. The Soviet note of 26 November is publ. in FRUS 1952–4, Vol. 7, 673–7; quote: 675. The note is also partially publ. in RIIA, *Documents, 1953*, 107–9.

134. FRUS, ibid., 1662–3: Lyon, Berlin, to US High Commission in Bonn, 21/10/1953.

135. Ibid., 677–9: Bohlen, Moscow, to State Dept., 27/11/1953; quote: 677, 679. See also ibid., Vol. 8, 1218–20: Bohlen to State Dept., 5/12/1953.

136. See RIIA, *Survey, 1953*, 36.

137. FRUS 1952–4, Vol. 7, 680: Dulles to US embassy, London, 28/11/1953.

138. Ibid., 683: Conant, Bonn, to State Dept., 30/11/1953.

139. Ibid., 682–3; for the French position, see ibid., 680, n. 4.

140. Ibid., 680, n. 2: Dulles to the US embassy, London, 28/11/1953. See also C.L. Sulzberger, *A Long Row of Candles: Memoirs and Diaries, 1934–1954* (New York, 1969), 930: diary entry, 3/12/1953; also Seldon, *Indian Summer*, 403–4. NATO Secretary General Lord Ismay, who had been asked to join the participants in Bermuda towards the end of the conference, was also sceptical. 'I am not looking forward much to Bermuda: as I haven't an idea what I am expected to do.' Liddell–Hart-Archive, London: Ismay Papers, IV/Gru/B, letter Ismay to General Gruenther, 2/12/1953.

141. PRO: PREM 11/418, Eden to Churchill and Churchill to Eden, 19/11/1953; see also FO 371/105 180/20; and Young, 'Churchill, the Russians', 900.

142. See Hayter's report, dated 3/12/1953, on his meeting with Malenkov on 28 November which was of little importance though it caused quite a stir at the time. After all, this was the first time that Malenkov had welcomed a new western ambassador. PRO: FO 371/106 535/NS 1051/88, 89. See also W. Hayter, *The Kremlin and the Embassy* (London, 1966), 34–5; *A Double Life* (London, 1974), 99–101; and for Hayter's general impression of Soviet foreign policy, see his *The Diplomacy of the Great Powers* (London, 1960), 20ff.

143. PRO: ibid., NS 1051/85, minute Shuckburgh of a conversation with Eden, 16/11/1953.

144. Ibid., 13/11/1953.

145. Ibid., NS 1051/78, minute Roberts, 8/11/1953.

146. For the expected difficulties with Congress if the EDC was not ratified by mid-January, see FRUS 1952–4, Vol. 6, 1392–3: Merchant, State Dept., to Dillon, Paris, 28/10/1953.

147. NA: PPS 64D563, Box 17, 'Germany', 1/12/1953. See also EL: John F. Dulles Papers, Subject Series, Box 8, Folder: 'Germany, 1953–54 (2)', letter Dulles to Conant, 20/11/1953; Ann Whitman File, ACW Diary, Box 1, Diary November–December 1953 (2), 'Conference on Bermuda', 2/12/1953.

148. NA: PPS 64D563, Box 17, 'Germany', 1/12/1953.

149. FRUS 1952–4, Vol. 7, letter Conant to Dulles, 5/12/1953.

150. Moreover, as David Carlton believes, this meant Eden would be fully occupied and would thus not be in a position to insist on Churchill's retirement. See his *Churchill and the Soviet Union* (Manchester, 2000) 184.

151. Shuckburgh, *Descent to Suez*, 111: diary entry, 1/12/1953.

152. BUA: Avon Papers, 20/45/33, letter Eden to his wife, 4/12/1953.

153. See Moran, *Struggle for Survival*, 504: diary entry, 3/12/1953.

154. Good impressions regarding the proceedings and results of the Bermuda conference can be obtained from the following diaries: Colville, *Fringes of Power*, 681–90; Moran, ibid., 503–12; Shuckburgh, *Descent to Suez*, 112–17; see also Young, 'Churchill, the Russians', 902–12; and Young, *Last Campaign*, 222ff. For the American and British minutes of the proceedings of the conference, see FRUS 1952–4, Vol. 5, 1737–1837; PRO: FO 371/125 138/ZP 23/2/G, bound volume with the minutes of the trilateral and bilateral meetings and conversations (documents 1–13).

155. For the 'sharp split between the views of Laniel and Bidault', see FRUS 1952–4, Vol. 5, 1728, 4/12/1953.

156. BUA: Avon Papers, 20/45/31, 33, letters Eden to his wife, 2/12 and 4/12/1953. See also Shuckburgh, *Descent to Suez*, 112: diary entry, 3/12/1953.

157. See Werth, *France, 1940–1955*, 650ff.

158. However, he was photographed with the book in his hand; it is a novel about the Napoleonic Wars. See Moran, *Struggle for Survival*, 508, 504: diary entries, 7/12 and 3/12/1953; Montague Browne, *Long Sunset*, 156.

159. EL: Ann Whitman File, Administration Series, Box 16, Folder: 'Governor's Conference', memorandum Eisenhower, 'Bermuda Conference', 10/12/1953, p. 9.

160. On this case of mistaken identity, see Roberts, *Dealing with Dictators*, 167; James, *Anthony Eden*, 375; also reported in Young, *Last Campaign*, 227.

161. In all likelihood the French received information about the confidential Anglo-American talks from some of the American diplomats. In particular, Eden held C.D. Jackson responsible for the leaks; however Eden's suspicion of Jackson must be regarded with caution as he was ill-disposed towards him; Jackson had been his first wife's lover. See BUA: Avon Papers, AP 20/45/33, letter Eden to his (second) wife, c. 4/12/1953; interview with Sir Anthony Nutting, London, 23/1/1991.

162. Moran, *Struggle for Survival*, 505: diary entry, 4/12/1953.

163. Shuckburgh, *Descent to Suez*, 111: diary entry, 30/11/1953.

164. See FRUS 1952–4, Vol. 5, 1754–61, 4/12/1953; see also Colville, *Fringes of Power*, 683: diary entry, 4/12/1953.

165. FRUS, ibid., 1759.

166. See Colville, *Fringes of Power*, 683: diary entry, 4/12/1953.

167. This is also Young's conclusion, see his 'Churchill, the Russians', 903; *Last Campaign*, 225–6. However, M.S. Fish concludes: 'Churchill spent a large portion of the talks pressing Eisenhower to agree to a heads-of-government meeting with the Soviets'. This is clearly wrong ('After Stalin's Death. The Anglo-American Debate Over a New Cold War', *Diplomatic History* 10, 1986, 352).

168. Shuckburgh, *Descent to Suez*, 113: diary entry, 3/12/1953.

169. FRUS 1952–4, Vol. 5, 1761, 4/12/1953. The British minutes quote Eisenhower's statement as follows: 'He [Eisenhower] would be ready to consider whether this was a new dress or the old dress with a new patch on it; but he hoped that no one was under any illusion that the woman wearing it had changed her profession … he did not believe that there had been any significant change in the basic policy and design of the Soviet Union to destroy the capitalist system and the free world by force, lies and corruption'. PRO: FO 371/125 138/ZP 23/2/G, Document No. 2, 4/12/1953.

170. For this point, see Carlton, *Churchill and the Soviet Union*, 184. For an illuminating account of the first day of the conference, see Moran, *Struggle for Survival*, 505–6: diary entry, 5/12/1953.

171. Moran, ibid., 508; diary entry, 7/12/1953.

172. Ibid.

173. See FRUS 1952–4, Vol. 5, 1761–2: Meeting of the Tripartite Working Group, 5/12/1953.

174. Ibid., 1763–65, 5/12/1953: Second Tripartite Foreign Ministers Meeting; quotes: 1764. See also PRO: FO 371/125 138/ZP 23/2/G, Document No. 3, 5/12/1953; also Shuckburgh, *Descent to Suez*, 113: diary entry, 5/12/1953.

175. EL: Ann Whitman File, ACW Diary, November–December 1953 (2), Vol. 3, 'Conference in the President's Office to discuss Bermuda and other problems', 2/12/1953. See also FRUS, ibid., 1763–5.

176. FRUS 1952–4, Vol. 5, 1766–7, 5/12/1953.

177. Ibid., 1775–78: Second Plenary Tripartite Meeting, 5/12/1953; quote: 1777. Ibid., 1788: Third Tripartite Foreign Ministers' Meeting, 6/12/1953. See also PRO: FO 371/125 138/ZP 23/2/G, Document No. 4, 5/12/1953.

178. FRUS, ibid., 1763–7, 5/12/1953.

179. For the dispute with Churchill, see PRO: FO 371/125 138/ZP 23/2/G, Document No. 5, 6/12/1953; also Colville, *Fringes of Power*, 686; diary entry, 6/12/1953; BUA: Avon Papers, AP 20/1/29, diary Eden 1953, entry 5/12/1953. The western note is publ. in FRUS, ibid., 1837.

180. FRUS, ibid., 1740: memorandum Dulles of a conversation between Eisenhower and Churchill, 4/12/1953. See also Colville, ibid., 687: diary entry, 6/12/1953; Shuckburgh, *Descent to Suez*, 114: diary entry, 5/12/1953.

181. FRUS, ibid., 1742: memorandum of the conversation between MacArthur II, Counsellor in the State Dept., and Laniel, 4/12/1953. For the disagreements over the EDC question, see also Eisenhower's memorandum, dated 10/12/1953, in EL: Ann Whitman File, Administration Series, Box 16, Folder: 'Governor's Conference', 7/12/1953, pp. 3–8.

182. PRO: PREM 11/618, minute Churchill to Eden, 6/12/1953, also publ. in Carlton, *Churchill and the Soviet Union*, 185–6.

183. David Carlton, however, argues that Churchill's summit diplomacy and détente enthusiasm was insincere as he was concerned that the US would leave Europe and that subsequently Soviet forces would overrun the European continent; thus Carlton assumes that Churchill did not really believe in the good intentions of the new Soviet leadership (see his *Churchill and the Soviet Union*, 184–6. While on occasion Churchill did have these fears (though sometimes he also simply liked to agree with some of Eisenhower's sentiments), on the whole his consistently pursued summit diplomacy over a prolonged period of time points to his deep insincerity in the matter.

184. EL: ibid., Box 21, Folder: 'Jackson 1953 (1)', memorandum C.D. Jackson to Cutler, 9/12/1953.

185. FRUS 1952–4, Vol. 5, 1770–3: memorandum Vernon Walters of a conversation between Eisenhower and Laniel, 5/12/1953.

186. Ibid., 1798. For the complex Saar question, see above all B. Thoß, 'Die Lösung der Saarfrage

1954/55', *Vierteljahrshefte für Zeitgeschichte* 38 (1990), 225ff.; R. Hudemann and R. Poidevin (eds), *Die Saar 1945–1955: ein Problem der europäischen Geschichte* (Munich, 1992); M. Kerkhoff, *Großbritannien, die Vereinigten Staaten und die Saarfrage, 1945 bis 1954* (Stuttgart, 1996).

187. FRUS, ibid., 1802–4: Third Plenary Tripartite Meeting, 6/12/1953; see also PRO: FO 371/125 138/ZP 23/2/G, Document No. 7, UK delegation, Bermuda, to FO, No. 150, 6/12/1953.

188. FRUS, ibid., 1770–3, 5/12/1953.

189. Ibid., 1784–5: Second Plenary Tripartite Conference, 5/12/1953. See also PRO: FO 371/125 138/ZP 23/2/G, Document No. 4, 5/12/1953; and Document No. 7, 6/12/1953.

190. However, Churchill greatly exaggerated in his statement. In fact, Churchill as well as NATO Secretary General Ismay and the American Supreme Commander Gruenther had come to the conclusion that German rearmament was not as urgent as had been believed initially; the military might of the USSR had been vastly over-estimated. See Liddell–Hart-Archive, London: Ismay Papers, III/22/6a, minute Ismay of his conversation with Eisenhower, 8/12/1953; PRO: PREM 11/771, letter Ismay to Churchill, 29/1/1954; Moran, *Struggle for Survival*, 510: diary entry, 9/12/1953.

191. Churchill explained: 'If it were impossible to put EDC into operation in the next few weeks, eight or ten; … then he would be bound to say that he would propose to make a new version of NATO achieving the same hope as EDC, with controls over the German army by the NATO organization so as to make it quite clear that this army could not be used against France or to precipitate war to regain the Eastern territories.' FRUS 1952–4, Vol. 5, 1781: Second Plenary Tripartite Meeting, 5/12/1953. See also PRO: FO 371/125 138/ZP 23/2/G, Document No. 7, 6/12/1953; also BUA: Avon Papers, AP 20/1/29, diary Eden, 1953, 5/12/1953. For the solution found in late 1954, see Chapter 17, 358ff., below.

192. FRUS, ibid., 1802–4: Third Plenary Tripartite Meeting, 6/12/1953. See also PRO: ibid.

193. See NA: 740.5/1–12–54, memorandum of the conversation regarding the EDC between British ambassador Makins and Robert Murphy, Deputy Under-Secretary, Dept. of State, 12/1/1954.

194. FRUS, 1952–4, Vol. 5, 1783, 5/12/1953.

195. Ibid.. See also PRO: FO 371/125 138/ZP 23/2/G, Document No. 7, 6/12/1953.

196. FRUS, ibid., 1804–6: Third Plenary Tripartite Meeting, 6/12/1953; also Shuckburgh, *Descent to Suez*, 115: diary entry, 6/12/1953.

197. EL: Ann Whitman File, Administration Series, Box 16, Folder: 'Governor's Conference', Eisenhower memorandum, 'Bermuda Conference', 10/12/1953.

198. See FRUS 1952–4, Vol. 5, 1787–95: Third Tripartite Foreign Ministers' Meeting, 6/12/1953; Fourth Tripartite Foreign Ministers' Meeting, 6/12/1953; Third Plenary Tripartite Meeting, 6/12/1953 (quote: 1795). See also PRO: FO 371/125 138/ZP 23/2/G, Document No. 5, 6/12/1953; Document No. 6, 6/12/1953.

199. See FRUS, ibid., 1751, 4/12/1953; EL: John F. Dulles Papers, Drafts of Presidential Correspondence, Box 1. The speech is publ. in RIIA, *Documents, 1953*, 116–21.

200. This is also Piers Brendon's view (*Ike: The Life and Times of Dwight D. Eisenhower*, London, 1987, 258–9), even though he regards Eisenhower's speech on 16 April as a serious American peace initiative. Ken Osgood, however, views 'Atoms for Peace' as 'above all a political warfare initiative, predicated on exposing as fraudulent the post-Stalin peace campaign and elevating the U.S. position as the foremost champion of peace and disarmament' (see his 'Form before Substance: Eisenhower's Commitment to Psychological Warfare and Negotiations with the Enemy', *Diplomatic History* 24/3 (2000), 425–33, quote: p. 431). Young, 'Churchill, the Russians', 905, writes that Eisenhower's speech consisted of 'a rather different approach to co-operation with Russia' as his concern had been raised with the Soviet H-bomb explosion. See more differentiating, his *Last Campaign*, 230–4. For the speech, see also R.G. Hewlett and J.M. Holl, *Atoms for Peace and War, 1953–61: Eisenhower and the Atomic Energy Commission* (Berkeley, Calif., 1989), 198ff.; and C. Pruden, *Conditional Partners: Eisenhower, the United Nations, and the Search for a Permanent Peace* (Baton Rouge, La., 1998); also C. Campbell, *Destroying the Village: Eisenhower and the Thermonuclear War* (New York, 1998); M.J. Medhurst, 'Atoms for Peace and Nuclear Hegemony: The Rhetorical Structure of a Cold War Campaign', *Armed Forces & Society* 23/4 (1997), 571–93.

201. See FRUS 1952–4, Vol. 5, 1769: memorandum by Admiral Strauss of a conversation between Eisenhower and Churchill, 5/12/1953. See also Colville, *Fringes of Power*, 684–5: diary entries, 5/12/ and 6/12/1953; also Churchill's letters to Eisenhower on 6/12 and 7/12/1953, in Boyle (ed.), *Correspondence*, 110–11.

202. PRO: FO 800/822, draft of a telegram to Moscow; minute Eden to Churchill, PM/53/341, 12/12/1953.

203. FRUS 1952–4, Vol. 5, 1806: Third Plenary Tripartite Meeting, 6/12/1953.

204. PRO: FO 371/125 138/ZP 23/2/G, Document No. 11, Minutes of the 6th Plenary Meeting, 7/12/1953.
205. FRUS 1952–4, Vol. 5, 1830–3: Fifth Plenary Tripartite Meeting, 7/12/1953; see also the considerably shorter British minutes: ibid.
206. See PRO: FO 371/125 138/ZP 23/2/G, Document No. 12: minutes of the 7th Plenary Meeting, 7/12/1953.
207. Shuckburgh, *Descent to Suez*, 116: diary entry, 7/12/1953.
208. PRO: PREM 11/418, minute Churchill to Eden, M.330/53, 7/12/1953 (also in FO 800/760).
209. Shuckburgh, *Descent to Suez*, 116: diary entry, 7/12/1953. See also PRO: FO 371/125 138/ZP 23/2/G, Document No. 12: minutes of the 7th Plenary Meeting, 7/12/1953. The final communiqué of the Bermuda conference is publ. in FRUS 1952–4, Vol. 5, 1838–9.
210. Moran, *Struggle for Survival*, 508–9: diary entry, 7/12/1953.
211. For a good assessment of the French performance at Bermuda, see Young, *Last Campaign*, 228–9.
212. See FRUS 1952–4, Vol. 5, 1769: memorandum Strauss of the conversation between Eisenhower and Churchill, 5/12/1953; see also 1739: memorandum Dulles of the conversation between Eisenhower and Churchill, 4/12/1953; Colville, *Fringes of Power*, 484–5, 687–8: diary entries, 5/12, 6/12, 7/12/1953; Shuckburgh, *Descent to Suez*, 114–15: diary entries, 5/12 and 6/12/1953; EL: Ann Whitman File, Administration Series, Box 16, Folder: 'Governor's Conference', memorandum Eisenhower, 'Bermuda Conference', 10/12/1953, pp. 11, 13–14; BUA: Avon Papers, AP 20/1/29, diary Eden, 1953, 7/12/1953.
213. NA: 741.00/12–1253, Aldrich, London, to State Dept., No. 2578, 12/12/1953.

CHAPTER 15: PREPARING A FINAL ATTEMPT

1. For the paper of the NATO conference dealing with the Soviet Union, see FRUS 1952–4, Vol. 5, 458–8; PRO: CAB 134/766, AOC (53)33, 14/12/1954.
2. Dulles used the expression in his speech before the North Atlantic Council as well as in his subsequent press conference. See FRUS 1952–4, Vol. 5, 461–9. See also PRO: PREM 11/369, Steel, Paris, to FO, No. 910, 14/12/1953; Hoyer Millar, Bonn, to FO, No. 1129, 15/12/1953; WU 1072/168, 'Statement by the Secretary of State at the Ministerial Meeting of the North Atlantic Council, 15/12/1953'; Annex of C.O.S.(53)144th meeting, 22/12/1953; 'Report by the Chief of the Imperial General Staff on the NATO Meetings in Paris, 7–16 December, 1953'; WU 1072/180 G, 'Record of the Restricted Meeting of Ministers of the North Atlantic Council on December 16, 1953'. See also FO 800/698, minute of the conversations between Dulles and Eden in Paris, 15/12/1953; P. Boyle (ed.), *The Churchill–Eisenhower Correspondence, 1953–1955* (Chapel Hill, N.C., 1990), 115: Churchill to Eisenhower, 19/12/1953; B.R. Duchin, 'The "Agonizing" Reappraisal: Eisenhower, Dulles and the EDC', *Diplomatic History* 16 (1992), 201–1.
3. See PRO: CAB 128/27, Part 1, C.C.(54)3rd Conclusions, minute 3, 18/1/1954; also Eden's memorandum, 'The Problem of Security in Europe' and 'Prospects for the Berlin Meeting' in CAB 129/65, C.(54)1st Conclusions, minute 1, 7/1/1954; C.C.(54)2nd Conclusions, minute 1, 12/1/1954; C.C.(54)5th Conclusions, minute 3, 26/1/1954; C.C.(54)9th Conclusions, minute 4, 17/2/1954; and Eden's final report in C.C.(54)10th Conclusions, minute 1, 22/2/1954.
4. See E. Shuckburgh, *Descent to Suez: Diaries, 1951–56* (London, 1986), 131: diary entry, 3/2/1954.
5. The Eden Plan was based on the western conditions for German reunification as listed in the note to Moscow in September 1952 (see Chapter 9, above, 178–80). The plan had been drawn up by the trilateral working group in Paris. As Eden introduced the plan since it was his turn to speak in Berlin, much to the delight of the FO the plan was associated with Eden's name. See H.P. Schwarz, *Die Ära Adenauer. Gründerjahre der Republik 1949–1957* (Wiesbaden, 1981), 214; R.R. James, *Anthony Eden*, paperback edn (London, 1986), 375; D. Carlton, *Anthony Eden: A Biography*, paperback edn (London, 1981), 338. For the Eden plan, see A. Eden, *Full Circle: Memoirs* (London, 1960), 67–70; K. Adenauer, *Erinnerungen, 1953–55* (Stuttgart, 1966), 247–8; FRUS 1952–4, Vol. 7, 871–7, 1177–80; HMSO, *Documents Relating to the Meeting of Foreign Ministers in Berlin* (1954), Annex A, 120–2 (Cmd. 9080); and RIIA, *Documents on International Affairs, 1954* (London, 1957), 72–5.
6. For Molotov's proposals submitted on 4 and 10 February 1954, see FRUS, ibid., 1182–93; RIIA, ibid., 75–6, 77; also Adenauer, ibid., 249–50.
7. See A. Resis (ed.), *Molotov Remembers: Inside Kremlin Politics: Conversations with Felix Chuev* (Chicago, 1993), 50.

8. For the proceedings of the Berlin conference, see above all PRO: FO 371/109 269–302; PREM 11/664, 665; FRUS, ibid., 601ff., 804–1207; Eden, *Full Circle*, 53–76; Adenauer, *Erinnerungen 1953–55*, 245–59. For detailed analyses of the negotiations as well as the conversations before and after the plenary sessions, see N. Katzer, *Eine Übung im Kalten Krieg. Die Berliner Viermächtekonferenz von 1954* (Cologne, 1994); H. J. Küsters, *Der Integrationsfriede. Viermächte-Verhandlungen über die Friedensregelung mit Deutschland 1945–1990* (Munich, 2000), 657–9; H.J. Rupieper, 'Die Berliner Außenministerkonferenz von 1954. Ein Höhepunkt der Ost-West-Propaganda oder die letzte Möglichkeit zur Schaffung der deutschen Einheit?', *Vierteljahrshefte für Zeitgeschichte* 34 (1986), 427–53; R. Steininger, 'Deutsche Frage und Berliner Konferenz 1954', in W. Venohr (ed.), *Ein Deutschland wird es sein* (Erlangen, 1990), 39–88; N. Katzer, 'Die Berliner Viermächtekonferenz von 1954 und die Deutsche Frage', in D. Blumenwitz et al. (eds), *Die Deutschlandfrage vom 17. Juni 1953 bis zu den Genfer Viermächtekonferenzen von 1955* (Berlin, 1990), 49–74. For the discussions on Austria, see G. Stourzh, *Um Einheit und Freiheit. Staatsvertrag, Neutralität und das Ende der Ost-West Besetzung Österreichs 1945–1955*, 4th edn (Vienna, 1998), 301–19. For Eden's private conversations with Molotov, see PRO: FO 800/761; see also the British parliamentary debate: H.C. *Parl. Deb.*, 5th series, Vol. 524, 24/2/1954, 401–519; also Shuckburgh, *Descent to Suez*, 132–3: diary entries, 11/2, 17/2/, 18/2/1954.

9. Quoted in J.W. Young, *Winston Churchill's Last Campaign: Britain and the Cold War, 1951–55* (Oxford, 1996), 244. However, in the US politicians were much less enthusiastic than in Britain. For a good discussion, see A. Combs, 'The Path Not Taken: The British Alternative to U.S. Policy in Vietnam, 1954–56', *Diplomatic History* 19/1 (1995), 33–57. For Bidault's role, see W.I. Hitchcock, *France Restored: Cold War Diplomacy and the Quest for Leadership in Europe, 1944–1954* (Chapel Hill, N.C., 1998), 186–7. For a good biography of the French Foreign Minister, see J.C. Demory, *Georges Bidault. 1899–1983: Biographie* (Paris, 1995).

10. See for example PRO: FO 800/761, Johnston, British High Commission, to Hancock, FO, 20/2/1954. For the final four-power communiqué of the conference and the western three-power statement of 19 February, see RIIA, *Documents, 1954*, 78–9, 79–80.

11. See Shuckburgh, *Descent to Suez*, 132–3: diary entries, 11/2 and 17/2/1954; L.A. Kusnitz, *Public Opinion and Foreign Policy: America's China Policy, 1949–79* (London, 1984). The literature on Washington's China policy is proliferating, see for example W.I. Cohen, *America's Response to China: A History of Sino-American Relations*, 3rd edn (New York, 1990); G.H. Chang, *Friends and Enemies: The United States, China, and the Soviet Union, 1948–1972* (Stanford, Calif., 1990); also X. Li and H. Li (eds), *China and the United States: A New Cold War History* (Lanham, Md., 1997).

12. See FRUS 1952–4, Vol. 7, 1005–7, 1031–4; and above all K. Ruane, 'Anthony Eden, British Diplomacy and the Origins of the Geneva Conference of 1954', *Historical Journal* 37/1 (1994), 153–72. Unlike Britain, the US had not recognized Mao's China diplomatically; until late 1971, and thus until shortly before President Nixon's visit to Beijing in early 1972, Washington recognized Taiwan as the official representative of the Chinese nation.

13. Churchill expressed this opinion in his parliamentary speech on 25/2/1954. See below, 321–2.

14. NA: 396.1-BE/2-1554, memorandum, Robert C. Hickock, State Dept., to Montgomery, Office of European Affairs, 15/2/1954. For interesting analyses of the Berlin conference, see the literature in n. 8 above, and also Young, *Last Campaign*, 238–47; however, Young largely overlooks the fact that the western powers (but not Churchill) intended to bring about the failure of the Berlin conference and that therefore no great efforts were made to arrive at any genuine compromises on the German and other questions. See for details of the 'devious' western strategy, Chapter 13, above, 276ff.

15. FRUS 1952–4, Vol. 7, 1229: memorandum of the 186th NSC meeting, 26/2/1954. For Adenauer's reaction, see also ibid., 1208–15: conversation with Dulles, 20/2/1954; see also PRO: FO 371/109 292/C 1071/701, minute Nutting to Eden of his conversation with Blankenhorn, 8/2/1954; H.P. Schwarz, *Adenauer. Der Staatsmann 1952–1967* (Stuttgart, 1991), 131. On 18 February, before his return to Washington, Dulles had an extensive conversation with Adenauer at Cologne airport. See Adenauer, *Erinnerungen, 1953–55*, 259–64.

16. For details of this speech, see Chapter 11, above, 222ff.

17. PRO: FO 800/761, Con/54/6, Churchill, London, to Eden in Geneva, 27/1/1954.

18. Ibid.

19. Shuckburgh, *Descent to Power*, 134: diary entry, 22/2/1954; see also PRO: CAB 128/27, C.C.(59),9th Conclusions, 17/2/1954, 10th Conclusions, 22/2/1954.

20. Shuckburgh, ibid., 134–5: diary entries, 22/2/ and 23/2/1954; see also Lord Moran, *Churchill: The Struggle for Survival, 1945–1965* (London, 1966), 528: diary entry, 23/2/1954.

21. H.C. *Parl. Deb.*, 5th series, Vol. 524, 25/2/1954, 584, 585.

22. Ibid., 586.
23. Ibid., 589–91. He also said: 'Peace is our aim and strength is the only way of getting it' (ibid., 591). See also Eden's very similar view regarding Germany as expressed later in the debate on the same day, ibid., 689–92. In mid-March 1955 Churchill again referred to Adenauer as a 'valiant patriot and idealist'. See H.C. *Parl. Deb.*, 5th series, Vol. 538, 14/3/1955, 964.
24. Moran, *Struggle for Survival*, 528: diary entry, 26/2/1954; see also ibid., 590–1.
25. Shuckburgh, *Descent to Suez*, 135: diary entry, 22/2/1954.
26. H.C. *Parl. Deb.*, 5th series, Vol. 524, 25/2/1954, 590, 587, 584.
27. See A. Montague Browne, *Long Sunset: Memoirs of Winston Churchill's Last Private Secretary* (London, 1995), 133; M. Soames (ed.), *Speaking for Themselves: The Personal Letters of Winston and Clementine Churchill* (London, 1998), 575: letter Churchill to his wife, 16/10/1953. David Carlton's conclusion that Churchill was merely egotistically interested in continuing in power and did not care about anything else apart from his strong anti-Communism is a vast exaggeration (see his *Churchill and the Soviet Union*, Manchester, 2000, ch. 7).
28. NA: 741.13/1-2854, J.K. Penfield to State Dept., No. 2589, 28/1/1954.
29. Moran, *Struggle for Survival*, 540: diary entry, 8/4/1954; see also Boyle (ed.), *Correspondence*, 124, 126: Churchill to Eisenhower, 9/3/1954; Eisenhower to Churchill, 19/3/1954.
30. Moran, ibid., 541: diary entry, 8/4/1954; see also Shuckburgh, *Descent to Suez*, 162: diary entry, 9/4/1954; also p. 149: diary entry, 17/3/1954. See also Churchill's statement in the course of his speech, in H.C. *Parl. Deb.*, 5th series, Vol. 526, 5/4/1954, 58.
31. PRO: CAB 128/27, Part 1, C.C.(54)10th Conclusions, minute 1, 22/2/1954. See in detail, S. Dockrill, *Britain's Policy for West German Rearmament, 1950–55* (Cambridge, 1991), 134–8; K. Maier, 'Die Auseinandersetzungen um die EVG als europäisches Unterbündnis der NATO 1950–54. Die EVG als supranationales Instrument für die kontrollierte Bewaffnung der Bundesrepublik', in L. Herbst et al. (eds), *Vom Marshall-Plan zur EWG. Die Eingliederung der Bundesrepublik Deutschland in die westliche Welt* (Munich, 1990), 455ff.; S. Mawby, *Containing Germany: Britain and the Arming of the Federal Republic* (Basingstoke, 1999), 136ff.; K. Ruane, *The Rise and Fall of the European Defence Community: Anglo-American Relations and the Crisis of European Defence, 1950–55* (Basingstoke, 2000), 70ff.
32. PRO: ibid.
33. PRO: CAB 129/65, C.(54)36, 30/1/1954, memorandum of the conversation between Nutting and Malik on 26/1/1954; also C.(54)44, 11/2/1954, memorandum of the conversation between Roberts and Malik, 30/1/1954.
34. See already PRO: FO 800/778, memorandum of the conversation between Eden and Massigli on 25/11 and 22/12/1953; also minute Eden to Lord Alexander, Minister of Defence, FS/53/20, 12/12/1953; FO 800/840, FO to embassy Washington, No. 5366, Churchill to Eisenhower, 22/12/1953 (this letter is not included in the correspondence between Churchill and Eisenhower edited by P. Boyle).
35. PRO: FO 800/698, minute of the conversation between Eden and Dulles on 15/12/1953 in Paris.
36. PRO: PREM 11/667, Makins, Washington to FO, No. 1258, 24/6/1954. See also the discussions and decisions regarding the EDC during Churchill's visit to Washington in June 1954 (see, below, 336).
37. H.C. *Parl. Deb.*, 5th series, Vol. 524, 25/2/1954, 587–8 (quote: 588).
38. See PRO: CAB 128/27, Part 1, C.C.(54)9th Conclusions, minute 4, 17/2/1954; C.C.(54)10th Conclusions, minute 1, 22/2/1954. See also Churchill's parliamentary speech on 25/2/1954, in H.C. *Parl. Deb.*, 5th series, Vol. 524, esp. 587–91; also Boyle (ed.), *Correspondence*, 127–30: Eisenhower to Churchill, 19/3/1954; Churchill to Eisenhower, 24/3/1954. In March 1954 Harold Stassen, the Director of the American Mutual Security Agency, visited London and a compromise on the Co Com list could be reached. See in great detail with further literature: Young, *Last Campaign*, 247–55; J.W. Young, 'Winston Churchill's Peacetime Administration and the Relaxation of East–West Trade Controls, 1953–54', *Diplomacy & Statecraft* 7/1 (1996), 125–40; and I. Jackson, ' "The Limits of International Leadership": The Eisenhower Administration, East–West Trade and the Cold War, 1953–54', *Diplomacy & Statecraft* 11/3 (2000), 113–38; also I. Jackson, *The Economic Cold War: America, Britain, and East–West Trade, 1948–1968* (Basingstoke, 2001); T.W. Zeiler, 'Managing Protectionism: American Trade Policy in the Early Cold War', *Diplomatic History* 22/3 (1998), 337–60.
39. Young, *Last Campaign*, 254–5.
40. Churchill told his Chancellor of the Exchequer in mid-March. See Lord Butler, *The Art of the Possible: Memoirs* (London, 1971), 173; also A. Seldon, *Churchill's Indian Summer: The Conservative Government, 1951–55* (London, 1981), 45; H. Macmillan, *Tides of Fortune, 1945–55* (London, 1969), 531.

41. See Shuckburgh, *Descent to Suez*, 145ff.; NA: 741.13/1-2754, B.M. Hulley, First Secretary at the American embassy in London, to State Dept., No. 2565, 27/1/1954; ibid., 1–2854, J.K. Penfield, Counsellor at the US embassy, to State Dept., No.2589, 28/1/1954; see also Seldon, ibid., 45–6.

42. See Shuckburgh, ibid., 149: diary entry, 17/3/1954; Montague Browne, *Long Sunset*, ch. 17. It is largely correct to say that in order to preserve his resources Churchill essentially tended 'to concentrate on one major issue to the exclusion of other matters'. See Montague Browne, ibid., 137.

43. See K. Kyle, *Suez* (London, 1991), 39–51; Wm. R. Louis, 'Churchill and Egypt, 1946–1956', in R. Blake and W.R. Louis (eds), *Churchill* (Oxford, 1993), 473–90; P.L. Hahn, *The United States, Great Britain, and Egypt, 1945–1956* (Chapel Hill, N.C., 1991), chs 7 and 8.

44. See the conversations, discussions and considerations as reported in Shuckburgh's diary entries: *Descent to Suez*, 140ff.; also p.136: diary entry, 25/2/1954; and Seldon, *Indian Summer*, 411–13.

45. For details, see Chapter 1, above.

46. The full Cabinet was only informed about this decision on 7 July and then also proceeded to give its agreement to the development of a British H-bomb in the Cabinet meeting on 26 July 1954. See the excellent new analysis based on recently declassified documents by Peter Hennessy in his *The Secret State: Whitehall and the Cold War* (London, 2002), 52–8; see also 30. See also M. Gilbert, *Winston S. Churchill, Vol. 8: Never Despair, 1945–65*, paperback edn (London, 1990), 993, 995, 1019–20; PRO: CAB 128/27, C.C.(54)47th, 48th and 53rd Conclusions. For the development of British atomic policy after the war, see M. Gowing, *Independence and Deterrence: Britain and Atomic Energy, 1945–52*, Vol. 1 (London, 1974), 495 ff.; J. Baylis, *Ambiguity and Deterrence: British Nuclear Strategy, 1945–1964* (Oxford, 1995); I. Clark and N. Wheeler, *The British Origins of Nuclear Strategy, 1945–1955* (Oxford, 1989); and the important account by L. Arnold, *Britain and the H-Bomb* (Basingstoke, 2001).

47. The understanding also included an agreement that atomic information would not be passed on to third parties unless both Washington and London agreed on this and that the US would share its atomic research results with the British. See for example W.F. Kimball, *Forged in War: Churchill, Roosevelt and the Second World War* (London, 1998), 220–1.

48. Subsequently one of the twenty-three fishermen died. See J. Newhouse, *War and Peace in the Nuclear Age* (New York, 1989), 81; J.P.D. Dunbabin, *The Cold War: The Great Powers and their Allies* (Harlow, 1994), 165; D. Holloway, *Stalin and the Bomb: The Soviet Union and Atomic Energy, 1939–54* (New Haven and London, 1994), 303; R. Crockatt, *The Fifty Years War: The United States and the Soviet Union in World Politics, 1941–1991* (London, 1995), 155. For detail, see R.A Divine, *Blowing in the Wind. The Nuclear Test Ban Debate, 1954–1960* (New York, 1978).

49. See Moran, *Struggle for Survival*, 544–5: diary entry, 4/5/1954; Boyle (ed.), *Correspondence*, 122–4, 131–3: Churchill to Eisenhower, 9/3/1954; Churchill to Eisenhower, 29/3/1954 and 1/4/1954; see also Macmillan, *Tides of Fortune*, 153–7: diary entries, 26/3–31/3/1954. Shuckburgh commented: 'The newspapers today say that the H-bomb explosion on 1 March was three times more powerful than the scientists themselves expected. In other words, it was out of control' (ibid., 153, 26/3/1954). See also very informative: Gilbert, *Never Despair*, 952, 959–60. See also Churchill's parliamentary speeches during which he mentioned the topic in detail: H.C. *Parl. Deb.*, 5th series, Vol. 525, 30/3/1954, 1840–49; Vol. 526, 5/4/1954, 45–7; also Vol. 530, 12/7/1954, 34–6 and Vol. 537, 1/3/1955, 1895. For Eisenhower's reaction during a press conference on 17 March, see *Public Papers of the Presidents of the USA: Dwight D. Eisenhower, 1954* (Washington, DC, 1960), 320–1. According to John Newhouse, the bomb 'dug a crater in the Pacific a mile long and 175 feet deep. An island called Eleugelab disappeared' (*War and Peace in the Nuclear Age*, 80).

50. The press conference took place on 31 March. See Divine, *Blowing in the Wind*, 6–9, 13; J.L. Gaddis, *We Now Know: Rethinking Cold War History* (New York, 1997), 225–6, also 226–43; also R.A. Divine, *Eisenhower and the Cold War* (New York, 1981), 114–15; see also Eisenhower's very cautious statements *Public Papers, 1954*, 346–7 (24/3/1954), 374–6 (5/4/1954), 381–2 (7/4/1954). For Churchill's distress, see his letter to Eisenhower on 9 March, in Boyle (ed.), *Correspondence*, 123–4.

51. See 'Churchill axed BBC broadcast of A-bomb program', *Japan Policy & Politics* (Kyodo News International) (23 August 1999).

52. See Boyle (ed.), ibid., 121, 124: Eisenhower to Churchill, 9/2/1954; Churchill to Eisenhower, 9/3/1954; also PRO: PREM 11/1074, Eden to Churchill, PM/54/40, 2/3/1954. For the episode, see also Carlton, *Churchill and the Soviet Union*, 163–4.

53. Moran, *Struggle for Survival*, 530: diary entry, 26/3/1954. Anthony Montague Browne, Churchill's last Private Secretary, also reports that Churchill was deeply impressed by Nevil Shute's novel *On the Beach* which described the effects of global nuclear contamination resulting in the elimination of all life (see his *Long Sunset*, 157). See also J. Rosenberg, 'Before the Bomb and After: Winston

Churchill and the Use of Force', in J.L. Gaddis et al. (eds), *Cold War Statesmen Confront the Bomb: Nuclear Diplomacy Since 1945* (Oxford, 1999), 188–91.

54. This was the Quebec Agreement of 1943. When Churchill quoted clauses from the agreement in his speech (and later circulated the agreement), he was the first politician to reveal details of the agreement in public. See also Eisenhower's response during a press conference regarding the exchange of atomic information with Britain, Eisenhower, *Public Papers, 1954*, 385 (7/4/1954).

55. See Moran, ibid., 537: diary entry, 5/4/1954; NA: 741.13/4–754, Aldrich, US embassy, London, to State Dept., No. 4405, 7/4/1954; Shuckburgh, *Descent to Suez*, 158: diary entry, 5/4/1954.

56. Moran, *Struggle for Survival*, 538: diary entry, 6/4/1953; also 534–7: diary entry, 5/4/1954. See also Bodleian Library, Oxford: Woolton Papers, 3, Diary, 1942–60, 6/4/1954, 122–4; Young, *Last Campaign*, 256–7; Seldon, *Indian Summer*, 46.

57. Shuckburgh, ibid.; also Moran, ibid., 534–7: diary entry, 5/4/1954. See also Churchill's parliamentary speech in H.C. *Parl. Deb.*, 5th series, Vol. 526, 5/4/1954, 54–7. Kenneth Harris speaks of 'Churchill's least fine hour' and 'his worst ever' performance as Prime Minister (see his *Attlee*, revd edn, London, 1995, 517).

58. Moran, ibid., 536: diary entry, 5/4/1954. See also Montague Browne, *Long Sunset*, 179–81.

59. Shuckburgh, *Descent to Suez*, 160: diary entry, 6/4/1954. The following statement summarizes the situation neatly: 'Almost certainly Churchill was no longer capable, by any objective criteria, of running the government effectively. At times he seemed perfectly normal, but at others he was obviously very feeble and his mind tended to wander, usually to irrelevant wartime analogies. Growing deafness and an unwillingness to use a hearing aid only exacerbated the problem. At international conferences he was little short of an embarrassment ...'. Quoted from D. Dutton, *Anthony Eden: A Life and Reputation* (London, 1997), 243.

60. See Bodleian Library, Oxford: Woolton Papers, 3, Diary, 1942–60, 6/4/1954, 124–5; see also Seldon, *Indian Summer*, 46.

61. NA: 741.13/4-1954, Aldrich, US embassy, London, to State Dept., No. 4405, 7/4/1954.

62. See ibid., /5-2854, Aldrich to State Dept., No. 5398, 28/5/1954 on his conversation with Walter Monckton, the Minister of Labour; also Shuckburgh, *Descent to Suez*, 160: diary entry, 6/4/1954; Bodleian Library, Oxford: Woolton Papers, 3, Diary, 1942–60, 6/4/1954, 126–9.

63. Shuckburgh, ibid.

64. See Shuckburgh, ibid., 149: diary entry, 17/3/1954; Moran, *Struggle for Survival*, 540: diary entry, 8/4/1954; J.W. Young, 'Cold War and Détente with Moscow', in J.W. Young (ed.), *The Foreign Policy of Churchill's Peacetime Government, 1951–1955* (Leicester, 1988), 66. Already in December Churchill and some of his advisers had met with Rodionov and Soviet ambassador Malik at Chequers but he did not receive any particular Soviet encouragement regarding his summit diplomacy. Moreover, Julian Amery and Bob Boothby had conducted several meetings with Soviet embassy officials throughout 1953 but again the Soviet attitude to Churchill's policy was ambiguous and difficult to interpret in any clear way. For these meetings, see above Chapter 13, n. 7 (p. 493), n. 26 (p. 494), n. 135 (p. 499); Chapter 14, n. 36 (p. 501). See also Shuckburgh, ibid., 124: diary entry, 22/12/1953; see also Young, *Last Campaign*, 237, n. 113 and 114. For the close relationship between Churchill and Christopher Soames, see M. Soames, *Clementine Churchill* (London, 1979), 415.

65. Holloway, *Stalin and the Bomb*, 337; see also Gaddis, *We Now Know*, 228–9.

66. Quotes: V. Zubok and C. Pleshakov, *Inside the Kremlin's Cold War: From Stalin to Khrushchev* (Cambridge, MA, 1996), 166, 168; for the debate regarding Malenkov's speech, see Holloway, ibid., 336–40; see also J.G. Richter, *Khrushchev's Double Bind: International Pressures and Domestic Coalition Politics* (Baltimore, Md., 1994), 48–52. In a speech on 27 April 1954 Malenkov was compelled to announce that an atomic war would merely lead to the disappearance of capitalism and the forces of imperialism and not to the elimination of all civilization. The point was, as for example Molotov fully realized, if socialism could not win a world war, then peace would appear more important than continuing the fight against capitalism and imperialism and this seemed to be 'tantamount to abandoning the communist cause' (Holloway, ibid., 339). In the literature this episode and the months March/April 1954 tend to be seen as the beginning of the end of Malenkov's political influence (for example, in February 1955, after Malenkov's downfall, Molotov like Khrushchev before him severely criticized Malenkov's speech on 12 March 1954). In any case, from the spring of 1954 Malenkov became increasingly marginalized within the Kremlin hierarchy; the reasons appear to lie partially in his unsuccessful economic, agricultural and foreign policies but perhaps primarily in the still continuing power battle in the Kremlin. See for example Zubok and Pleshakov, ibid., 168–9; also already R. Conquest, *Power and Policy in the USSR: A Study of Soviet Dynasties* (London, 1961), 260–2, 333–4.

67. For Eisenhower's press conference, see PRO: FO 371/125 139/ZP 24/1 A, Makins, Washington, to FO, No. 422, 10/3/1954; also Eisenhower, *Public Papers, 1954*, 303, 10/3/1954.

68. See H.C. *Parl. Deb.*, 5th series, Vol. 526, 5/4/1954, 48–9, 57–60.

69. FRUS 1952–4, Vol. 6, 1024–5: memorandum of conversation among Dulles, Churchill, Eden and ambassador Aldrich on 12/4/1954 (quote: 1015). Between 11–13 April Dulles was in London.

70. D. Pearson, *Diaries, 1949–59*, ed. by T. Abell (New York, 1974), 316: diary entry, 28/5/1954 (reporting a remark by Joseph Davies, America's Second World War ambassador to the Soviet Union). It is however unlikely that Churchill's resentment resulted in the Prime Minister's 'cool' reaction to American 'overtures on Indochina' as Davies thought (ibid.).

71. PRO: PREM 11/1074, 16/4/1954.

72. Boyle (ed.), *Correspondence*, 139: Churchill to Eisenhower, 22/4/1954; J. Colville, *The Fringes of Power: 10 Downing Street Diaries, 1939–1955* (London, 1985), 691: diary entry, 24/6/1954. Harold Macmillan's (and also historian John Charmley's) assumption that Churchill decided only in early June 1954 to travel to Washington again is incorrect. See H. Macmillan, *Tides of Fortune, 1945–55* (London 1969), 530; J. Charmley, *Churchill's Grand Alliance: A Provocative Reassessment of the 'Special Relationship' between England and the U.S. from 1940 to 1957* (New York, 1995), 287.

73. See Lord Moran, *Churchill: Struggle for Survival, 1945–1965* (London, 1966), 559: diary entry, 24/6/1954; also Colville, ibid.

74. See Boyle (ed.), *Correspondence*, 136–8, 140: Eisenhower to Churchill, 4/4/1954 and on 26/4/1954.

75. See R. Buzzanco, 'Prologue to Tragedy: U.S. Military Opposition to Intervention in Vietnam, 1950–54', *Diplomatic History* 17/2 (1993), 201–22; also from a different angle: J.R. Arnold, *The First Domino: Eisenhower, the Military, and America's Intervention in Vietnam* (New York, 1991); on Dulles's 29 March speech before the Overseas Press Club, see also G.A. Olson, 'Eisenhower and the Indochina Problem', in M.J. Medhurst (ed.), *Eisenhower's War of Words: Rhetoric and Leadership* (East Lansing, 1994), 108–11.

76. See FRUS 1952–4, Vol. 13, 1302ff.; Vol. 6, 1025ff.

77. Quote: Olson, 'Eisenhower and the Indochina Problem', 106, see also, 102–8. Olson pays particular attention to the sensitivities of Congress which Eisenhower had to take on board as the Korean War had been fought under executive order; Truman never asked Congress to pass a war resolution.

78. See also Eden's parliamentary speech on 13/4/1954, in H.C. *Parl. Deb.*, 5th series, Vol. 526, 969–75. For the British fears and the Churchill government's belief in the interconnection between Indochina and the EDC and the West's NATO policy, see K. Ruane, 'Refusing to Pay the Price: British Foreign Policy and the Pursuit of Victory in Vietnam, 1952–54', *English Historical Review* 90, No. 435 (1995), 70–92.

79. For this episode, see Eden, *Full Circle*, 95–9; A. Short, *The Origins of the Vietnam War* (London, 1989), 138–44; J. Cable, *The Geneva Conference of 1954 on Indochina*, 2nd edn (Basingstoke, 2000), 53ff.; P. Devillers and J. Lacouture, *End of a War: Indochina 1954* (London, 1969), 71ff.; I.M. Wall, *The United States and the Making of Postwar France, 1945–54* (Cambridge, 1991), 233ff., esp. 256ff.; Carlton, *Anthony Eden*, 340–50; James, *Anthony Eden*, 376–80; R.H. Immerman, 'Between the Unattainable and the Unacceptable: Eisenhower and Dienbienphu', in R.A. Melanson and D. Mayers (eds), *Reevaluating Eisenhower: American Foreign Policy in the 1950s* (Urbana, Ill., 1987), 120ff.

80. Eden, 'Foreign Affairs speech', H.C. Parl. Deb., Vol. 529, 435, also 429, 23/6/1954.

81. Boyle (ed.), *Correspondence*, 139: Eisenhower to Churchill, 23/4/1954.

82. Shuckburgh, *Descent to Suez*, 173: diary entry, 24/4/1954.

83. PRO: PREM 800/841, Makins, Washington, to FO, No. 1040, 27/5/1954, to Eden ('Private and Personal'). See also in a very similar vein, ibid., letter Makins to Eden, 29/5/1954.

84. This is claimed by Young, 'Cold War', 66; see also his *Last Campaign*, 260. Similarly, Eisenhower's press official speaks of the President's annoyance that Churchill was pushing for a visit. FRUS 1952–54, Vol. 6, 1064–5: Hagerty, diary entry, 14/6/1954; see also Eisenhower's press conference on 28/5/1954, in Eisenhower, *Public Papers, 1954*, 88–9. However, these assumptions are mistaken; this time the President was keen on talking to the British.

85. Boyle (ed.), *Correspondence*, 136–8: Eisenhower to Churchill, 4/4/1954. For major works on Eisenhower's Vietnam policy, see M. Billings-Yun, *Decision against War: Eisenhower and Dien Bien Phu, 1954* (New York, 1988); L.C. Gardner, *Approaching Vietnam: From World War II through Dienbienphu* (New York, 1988); D.L. Anderson, *Trapped by Success: the Eisenhower Administration and Vietnam, 1953–1961* (New York, 1991); and for a good brief analysis, see Olson, 'Eisenhower and Indochina', 99ff., esp. 108–18.

86. On 23 April 1954 (some two weeks before the fall of Dien Bien Phu as it turned out) Dulles may have offered to place two atomic bombs at France's disposal for use in the Indochina war. However, this is controversial; it may well never have happened. See the discussions in L.S. Kaplan, D. Artaud and M.R. Rubin (eds), *Dien Bien Phu and the Crisis of Franco-American Relations, 1954–55* (Wilmington, Del., 1990); Short, *Origins of the Vietnam War*, 140; and F. Giles, *The Locust Years. The Story of the Fourth French Republic, 1946–58* (London, 1991), 204; see also Olson, 'Eisenhower and the Indochina War', 112, and the literature mentioned there; see also the literature in n. 85, above.

87. Boyle (ed.), *Correspondence*, 140: Eisenhower to Churchill, 26/4/1954.

88. H.C. *Parl. Deb.*, Vol. 529, 23/6/1954, 430.

89. See ibid., 439–40. See also Short, *Origins of the Vietnam War*, 147–8; also FRUS 1952–4, Vol. 6, 1035: Smith, Geneva, to State Dept., 30/5/1954; Eden, *Full Circle*, 108ff. For the proceedings of the Geneva conference on Indochina, see above all Cable, *Geneva Conference*, 66 ff.; Devillers and Lacouture, *End of a War*, 121ff.; Carlton, *Anthony Eden*, 354–6; Shuckburgh, *Descent to Suez*, 168–204; and the interesting comment in Charmley, *Churchill's Grand Alliance*. Charmley reports that Shuckburgh's diary entries were manipulated in order to expunge some of Eden's frank comments to Molotov regarding American behaviour and intentions when his diary was prepared for publication by Charmley (see p. 284).

90. FRUS 1952–4, Vol. 6, 1062: Dillon, Paris, to State Dept., 10/5/1954. Yet, in his parliamentary speech on 23 June, Eden emphasized diplomatically that 'we have at no time been reproached by our French allies for our decision'. See H.C. *Parl. Deb.*, 5th series, Vol. 529, 435. See also J.P. Rioux, *The Fourth Republic, 1944–1958* (Cambridge, 1987), 216–18; G.C. Herring, ' "A Good Stout Effort": John Foster Dulles and the Indochina Crisis, 1954–55', in R.H. Immerman (ed.), *John Foster Dulles and the Diplomacy of the Cold War* (Princeton, N.J., 1990), 213–33; see also the articles in L.S. Kaplan et al. (eds), *Dien Bien Phu*. For the battle, see H. Türk, *Dien Bien Phu. Die Schlacht, die einen Kolonialkrieg beendete*, 3rd edn (Berlin, 1994). For good overviews on the whole episode, see R.D. Schulzinger, *A Time for War: The United States and Vietnam, 1941–1975* (New York, 1997), 70ff.; and G. Herring, *America's Longest War: The United States and Vietnam, 1950–1975*, 2nd edn (New York, 1986), 43ff.

91. Boyle (ed.), *Correspondence*, 140: Eisenhower to Churchill, 12/5/1954.

92. Ibid., 144: Churchill to Eisenhower, 10/6/1954.

93. See PRO: CAB 128/27, Part 1, C.C.(54)39th Conclusions, minute 3, 5/6/1954; also Macmillan, *Tides of Fortune*, 530–1; Seldon, *Indian Summer*, 404.

94. Moran, *Struggle for Survival*, 555: diary entry, 10/6/1954.

95. Ibid., 556: diary entry, 15/6/1954; Macmillan, *Tides of Fortune*, 531; also Shuckburgh, *Descent to Suez*, 220: diary entry, 14/6/1954.

96. See Boyle (ed.), *Correspondence*, 144: Churchill to Eisenhower, 10/6/1954.

97. For Mendès-France's policy, see Wall, *The US and the Making of Postwar France*, 256ff., 263ff.; Giles, *The Locust Years*, 194ff.; and for two good recent assessments, see Hitchcock, *France Restored*, 190–202; and Ruane, *Rise and Fall of the EDC*, 89–93. For a still useful biography, see J. Lacouture, *Pierre Mendès-France* (Paris, 1981); also J.L. Rizzo, *Mendès-France, ou, La Rénovation en Politique* (Paris, 1993); P. Guillen, 'The Role of the Soviet Union as a Factor in the French Debates on the European Defence Community', *Journal of European Integration History* 2/1 (1996), 71–83.

98. Boyle (ed.), *Correspondence*, 145: Eisenhower to Churchill, 11/6/1954.

99. See FRUS 1952–4, Vol. 6, 1066: Aldrich, London, to State Dept., 18/6/1954. See also Churchill's references in his speech on the occasion of the 'Grand Habitation of the Primrose League', London, 30/4/1954, in R.R. James (ed.), *Winston S. Churchill: His Complete Speeches, 1987–1963, Vol 8: 1950–63* (London, 1974), 8563–5, esp. 8565; and in his speech 'Anglo-American Friendship', English Speaking Union Dinner for General Gruenther, London, 8/6/1954, in ibid., 8573–4.

100. Moran, *Struggle for Survival*, 562: diary entry, 26/6/1954.

101. This is claimed by Young, *Last Campaign*, 265.

102. Moran, *Struggle for Survival*, 556: diary entry, 15/6/1954.

103. However, this assessment referred to the Indochina situation. FRUS, 1952–4, Vol. 6, 1074: memorandum Raynor, director of the Office of British Commonwealth and Northern European Affairs, to Merchant, Office for European Affairs, 24/6/1954.

104. Moran, *Struggle for Survival*, 560: diary entry, 25/6/1954; also Seldon, *Indian Summer*, 404–5; Shuckburgh, *Descent to Suez*, 220–1. On 1 June 1954 Evelyn Shuckburgh became new Under-Secretary in the Foreign Office with responsibility for the Near East. His successor as Eden's private secretary was Anthony Rumbold. Although Shuckburgh's diary remains an important

source for the policy of Churchill's peace time government, after the summer of 1954 it proved to be less important than before as Shuckburgh was not consulted as closely by Eden as previously.

105. See Eden, *Full Circle*, 128–31; Macmillan, *Tides of Fortune*, 532. See also Makins letter to Eden which contained a similar view: PRO, FO 800/842, 21/6/1954. Moreover, Eisenhower's insistence that Eden should accompany Churchill will have flattered the vain Foreign Secretary. Carlton's assumption that Eden 'insisted' on accompanying 'his chief' is mistaken; it was above all Eisenhower and the Cabinet who insisted on this; there was no need for Eden to insist on it. See Carlton, *Churchill and the Soviet Union*, 190. See also Short, *Origins of the Vietnam War*, 160–3: Cable, *Geneva Conference*, 72ff.; also Eden's parliamentary speech on 23/6/1954, in H.C. *Parl. Deb.*, 5th series, Vol. 529, 428–41.

106. He also praised French Foreign Minister Bidault and the Commonwealth leaders. See H. C. *Parl. Deb.*, 5th series, Vol. 529, 428, 431–2, 439–41 (quote: 441).

107. Ibid., 433. He said: 'In other words, we could have a reciprocal arrangement in which both sides take part, such as Locarno'.

108. Ibid., 444–5.

109. Harris, *Attlee*, revd edn, 520.

110. See Churchill's remark in Parliament stating that they expected to be faced with 'a storm of hostile opinion' in the US, H.C. *Parl. Deb.*, 5th series, Vol. 530, 12/7/1954, 35; Young, *Last Campaign*, 264; V. Rothwell, *Anthony Eden: A Political Biography, 1931–57* (Manchester, 1992), 148.

111. A list of the British participants is in Colville, *Fringes of Power*, 691.

112. Moran, *Struggle for Survival*, 560: diary entry, 25/6/1954; similar Colville, ibid., 692ff.

113. R. Ferrell (ed.), *The Diary of James C. Hagerty* (Bloomington, Ind., 1983), 80: diary entry, 29/6/1954.

114. Ibid., 77: diary entry, 26/6/1954. See also S.E. Ambrose, *Eisenhower, Vol. II: The President, 1952–1969* (London, 1984), 197–8. Ambrose reports that since Bermuda Churchill had suffered two more strokes. However, this is incorrect; Ambrose merely repeats a statement made in Hagerty's diary (see Ferrell, ed., ibid., 77).

115. See FRUS 1952–4, Vol. 6, 1077ff.; for a good summary, see J.W. Young, 'Churchill's Bid for Peace with Moscow, 1954', *Historical Journal* 28 (1985), 433; also Moran, *Struggle for Survival*, 559–60: diary entry, 24/6/1954.

116. See FRUS, ibid., 1086–94, 1118–22: memoranda of conversation between Dulles and Eden, 26/6/1954 and 29/6/1954; ibid., 1094–6: British position paper 'A South-East Asia Settlement', 25/6/1954; ibid., 1127–8: 'Agreed Minute on Southeast Asia', 27/6/1954.

117. Colville, *Fringes of Power*, 693: diary entry, 27/6/1954.

118. NA: 762.0221/6-1854, Aldrich, London, to State Dept., No. 5824, on his conversation with Anthony Nutting, 18/6/1954. See also the minutes of the first meeting of the Anglo-American working group on 7/7/1954. The topic of discussion was entitled 'Restrictions on German Rearmament which might be feasible in the event of German admission to NATO'. The delegates gradually arrived at the NATO/WEU solution which was then realized in September/October 1954. NA: 762A.5/7-754, 7/7/1954. See also 762A.00/7-654, memorandum of a conversation between Dulles and Merchant on 2/7/1954 're Plans for Germany', dated 6/7/1954.

119. FRUS 1952–4, Vol. 6, 1103: notes by Hagerty for Eisenhower during a luncheon which the American Congress gave for Churchill, 26/6/1954.

120. Ibid., 1080–1: memorandum of a conversation between Eisenhower and Churchill, 25/6/1954; see also 1126–7: 'Agreed Minute on Germany and EDC'. See also RIIA, *Survey of International Affairs, 1954* (London, 1957), 141. For the work and proposals of the Anglo-American working group, which was chaired by Frank Roberts and Cecil Lyon and met in London between 5 and 12 July, see FRUS, ibid., Vol. 5, 997ff. This was also Adenauer's view. Contrary to the recurring claim in the literature that the Chancellor blindly put his trust in the EDC until its ultimate failure, in fact he had already instructed his advisers to look into alternative solutions. Adenauer believed that if the EDC failed the West 'should have an alternative plan of action to put into operation immediately'. NA: 762A.00/6-2354, memorandum Merchant, to Dulles, on his conversation with West German ambassador Krekeler in Washington on 23/6/1954. See also Schwarz, *Adenauer. Der Staatsmann*, 121–40. For a very illuminating discussion of Adenauer's plans and thinking on the EDC, see H. Köhler, *Adenauer. Eine politische Biographie* (Frankfurt/M., 1994), 821–38.

121. In the aftermath of the Berlin conference another exchange of notes with the Soviet Union unfolded which continued throughout 1954. For this exchange, see PRO: FO 371/109 203–302; FRUS, 1952–4, Vol. 5, 487ff., 684ff, and summarizing: FRUS, ibid., Vol. 7, 1232–3 (editorial note); RIIA, *Survey, 1954*, 156–61; RIIA, *Documents, 1954*, 88ff. For a good overview, see Schwarz, *Ära Adenauer*, 169ff.

122. Clive Ponting's assumption that Churchill was 'still attracted by the idea of a unified and neutralised Germany' during his visit to Washington is mistaken (see his *Churchill*, London, 1994, 792).

123. See for example the statements in Carlton, *Churchill and the Soviet Union*, 190; White, *Britain, Détente, and Changing East–West Relations* (London, 1992), 53–4; Colville, *Fringes of Power*, 692: diary entry, 25/6/1954.
124. FRUS 1952–4, Vol. 6, 1079–80: memorandum of conversation, 25/6/1954.
125. Ibid., 1080.
126. Colville, *Fringes of Power*, 692: diary entry, 25/6/1954. For a somewhat different interpretation, see Young, *Last Campaign*, 268–9.
127. Moran, *Struggle for Survival*, 562: diary entry, 26/6/1954.
128. Moran, ibid., 561: diary entry, 25/6/1954.
129. Ibid.
130. PRO: FO 800/823, note Churchill to Eden, M.9/54, 14/1/1954.
131. FRUS 1952–4, Vol. 6, 1098: memorandum of a conversation between Eisenhower and Churchill, 26/6/1954.
132. Ibid. Colville's account of this conversation is not correct; he misunderstood the situation. Colville wrote in his diary: 'The Russian visit project has now been expanded (by the President, so the P.M. says) to a meeting in London, together with the French and West Germans, at the opening of which Ike himself would be present.' *Fringes of Power*, 693: diary entry, 26/6/1954. Perhaps Colville's account reflected to some extent what Churchill himself mistakenly believed to have been the result of his talk with Eisenhower.
133. Seldon, *Indian Summer*, 405.
134. FRUS 1952–4, Vol. 6, 1108–9: memorandum of conversation between Eisenhower and Churchill, 26/6/1954; see also Young, *Last Campaign*, 269.
135. FRUS 1952–4, Vol. 6, 1111: memorandum of a conversation between Dulles and Churchill, 27/6/1954.
136. See for example PRO: FO 371/109 292/C 1071/704, minute Roberts to Eden, 22/2/1954; minute Roberts to Eden and Kirkpatrick, 23/2/1954; Churchill, 'Foreign Affairs speech', H.C. *Parl Deb.*, 5th series, Vol. 524, 25/2/1954, 586–7. In November 1953 Churchill had even mentioned to Eden that he did not think it made sense to talk to Moscow about Germany *and* Austria in a concrete way. This would only ensure that a conference would be doomed to failure. See PRO: FO 800/822, minute Churchill to Eden, M.3 19/53, *c.* early November, as mentioned in minute Eden to Churchill, PM/53/328, 9/11/1953. See also B. Thoβ, 'Modellfall Österreich? Der österreichische Staatsvertrag und die deutsche Frage 1954/55', in B. Thoβ and H.E. Volkmann (eds), *Zwischen Kaltem Krieg und Entspannung. Sicherheits- und Deutschlandpolitik der Bundesrepublik im Mächtesystem der Jahre 1953–1956* (Boppard, 1988), 93–136. The standard work on the policies of the West and the Soviet Union with respect to the Austrian state treaty is the 4th edition of Stourzh, *Um Einheit und Freiheit*, 320ff. (for the developments since the Berlin conference). For a very good overview of the Austrian question since Stalin's death, see G. Bischof, *Austria in the First Cold War, 1945–1955: The Leverage of the Weak* (Basingstoke, 1999), 130ff.
137. FRUS 1952–4, Vol. 6, 1111–12: memorandum of a conversation between Dulles and Churchill, 27/6/1954 (see also p. 1111, n. 1).
138. Churchill visited Washington for the last time in retirement. In early May 1959 he spent three days with President Eisenhower in the White House and was able to pay farewell visits to Dulles and General Marshall who were both seriously ill (Dulles died two weeks later and Marshall in October 1959). For details, see Gilbert, *Never Despair*, 1291–6; Montague Browne, *Long Sunset*, 260–3.
139. See Colville, *Fringes of Power*, 693: diary entry, 27/6/1954.
140. On the whole, this is also John Young's impression. See his *Last Campaign*, 270.
141. He explained this during his parliamentary speech on 12 July 1954 when he reported on the results of his visit. See H.C. *Parl. Deb.*, 5th series, Vol. 524, 35.
142. See for example Churchill's considerations as reflected in Moran, *Struggle for Survival*, 562–3: diary entry, 26/6/1954.

CHAPTER 16: AT THE END OF THE DAY

1. For interesting accounts of Churchill's activities after his visit to Washington, see H. Macmillan, *Tides of Fortune, 1945–55* (London, 1969), 534–41; R.R. James, *Anthony Eden*, paperback edn, (London, 1986), 380–1; D. Carlton, *Anthony Eden: A Biography*, paperback edn, (London, 1981), 351–5; M. Gilbert, *Winston S. Churchill, Vol. 8: Never Despair, 1945–65*, paperback edn (London, 1990), 996ff., 1018ff.; J.W. Young, *Winston Churchill's Last Campaign: Britain and the Cold War*,

1951–55 (Oxford, 1996), 270ff.; J.W. Young, 'Churchill's Bid for Peace with Moscow, 1954', *Historical Journal* 28 (1985), 343–4; A. Seldon, *Churchill's Indian Summer: The Conservative Government, 1951–55* (London, 1981), 406–7.

2. See for example Frank Roberts's statement in K. Larres (ed.), 'Witness Seminar: British Attitudes to German Rearmament and Reunification in the 1950s', *Contemporary Record* 5 (1991), 314–16.

3. Lord Moran, *Churchill: The Struggle for Survival, 1945–1965* (London, 1966), 572: diary entry, 2/7/1954, p. 575: diary entry, 4/7/1954, p. 574: diary entry, 3/7/1954. For Churchill's praise of Eden's use of the phrase, see H.C. *Parl. Deb.*, 5th series, Vol. 530, 12/7/1954, 46.

4. J. Colville, *The Fringes of Power: 10 Downing Street Diaries, 1939–1955* (London, 1985), 697–8: diary entry, 2/7/1954; Moran, ibid., 573–4: diary entry, 3/7 and 4/7/1954.

5. Colville, ibid.

6. Ibid., 698.

7. Ibid., 697.

8. Moran, *Struggle for Survival*, 572: diary entry, 2/7/1954.

9. Ibid., 574: diary entry, 4/7/1954.

10. PRO: FO 371/125 139/ZP 24/5/G, Eden to FO, No. 11, 2/7/1954. Quote: Colville, *Fringes of Power*, 698: diary entry, 2/7/1954.

11. Moran, *Struggle for Survival*, 575: diary entry, 4/7/1954.

12. Colville, *Fringes of Power*, 698: diary entry, 2/7/1954. Macmillan later expressed the belief that Eden 'ought to have resigned on the boat'. Quoted in A. Horne, *Macmillan, 1894–1956*, Vol. 1 (London, 1988), 348.

13. PRO: FO 125 139/ZP 24/5/G, Churchill to Butler, 3/7/1954.

14. E. Shuckburgh, *Descent to Suez: Diaries, 1951–56* (London, 1986), 221–2: diary entries, 5/7/1954 and 6/7/1954 (quote: p. 222).

15. Later, however, Churchill would recommend Macmillan rather than Butler to succeed Eden as Prime Minister in early 1957. For Butler's ambitions in 1954, see the obsequious telegram from Butler to Churchill on 3 July which points in this direction. See PRO: FO 371/125 139/ZP 24/5/G, Butler to Churchill, No. 29, 3/7/1954. In his memoirs Butler does not mention the episode at all. Young assumes that Butler had not recognized the significance of the affair. However, in view of the arguments around Churchill's 'summitry' during the previous months this seems to be unlikely. See Young, 'Churchill's Bid', 436. The evening before his retirement Churchill famously said 'with vehemence' to his Private Secretary: 'I don't think Anthony can do it' (see Colville, *Fringes of Power*, 708). Yet, as David Dutton has written, 'it is probably correct to assume that Churchill would have felt the same "nagging doubts" about "any nominated successor" and never seriously considered any other heir than Eden'. See Dutton, *Anthony Eden: A Life and Reputation* (London, 1997), 237–8 (quote: 237). See also P. Hennessy, *The Prime Minister: The Office and its Holders since 1945* (London, 2000), 209, who takes Churchill's doubts much more seriously and also quotes Lord Swinton's doubts.

16. Colville, *Fringes of Power*, 699: diary entry, 3/7/1954; PRO: FO 125 139/ZP 24/5/G, Butler to Churchill, No. 29, 3/7/1954. See also Moran, *Struggle for Survival*, 575: diary entry, 4/7/1954.

17. PRO: ibid., Churchill to FO for Butler, No. 27, 3/7/1954.

18. Moran, *Struggle for Survival*, 574: diary entry, 4/7/1954.

19. For the telegram to Molotov, see PRO: FO 371/125 139/ZP 24/5/G, FO to Moscow, No. 873, 4/7/1954. See also P. Boyle (ed.), *The Churchill-Eisenhower Correspondence, 1953–1955* (Chapel Hill, N.C., 1990), 152: Churchill to Eisenhower, 7/7/1954. Churchill elaborated in detail on the episode in his last major parliamentary speech on 14/3/1955, see H.C. *Parl. Deb.*, 5th series, Vol. 538, 958ff; see also Ch. 17 below, 368–70. As a reaction to Churchill's speech in Parliament on 14/3/1955, Moscow published the correspondence between Churchill and Molotov which had taken place in July and August 1954. The British government then also published the correspondence (see Cmd. No. 9418).

20. PRO: ibid., Hayter, Moscow, to FO for Churchill and Eden, No. 656, 4/7/1954.

21. PRO: ibid., ZP 24/8/G, letter Hayter, Moscow, to Kirkpatrick, FO, 9/7/1954; see also Hayter's comment to the American journalist C.L. Sulzberger in the latter's *A Long Row of Candles: Memoirs and Diaries, 1934–1954* (New York, 1969), 873.

22. See Shuckburgh, *Descent to Suez*, 221–2: diary entry, 6/7/1954; see also F. Roberts, *Dealing with Dictators: The Destruction and Revival of Europe, 1930–70* (London, 1991), 166.

23. PRO: FO 371/125 139/ZP 24/12/G, letter Roberts to the diplomat Harald Caccia in Geneva, 13/7/1954, with an enclosed memorandum entitled 'Probable Soviet line in any general talks'; see also ibid., ZP 24/14/G, FO to British delegation in Geneva, No. 1503, Roberts to Caccia, 19/7/1954. See also the FO thinking about the term 'peaceful coexistence', FO 371/111 706/NS 1073/1, 6, 9, 11, 12, 14, 23 (late July/early August 1954).

24. Shuckburgh, *Descent to Suez*, 221–2: diary entries, 5/7 and 6/7/1954.

25. These were the words Churchill used in his parliamentary speech on 14/3/1955 during which he referred to the episode in detail. See H.C. *Parl. Deb.*, 5th series, Vol. 538, 961 (for this speech see Chapter 17, below, 368–70). For Churchill's view of Molotov's reply, see also his letter to Eisenhower dated 8/7/1954, in Boyle (ed.), *Correspondence*, 155.

26. Boyle (ed.), ibid., 152–53: Churchill to Eisenhower, 7/7/1954.

27. See PRO: CAB 128/27, Part 2, C.C. (54)47th Conclusions, minute 4, 7/7/1954. The actual discussion of Churchill's initiative was included separately in a 'confidential annex'. This was also the case in the subsequent Cabinet meetings which dealt with the matter.

28. Ibid.; also Shuckburgh, *Descent to Suez*, 222: diary entry, 7/7/1954; also Seldon, *Indian Summer*, 406.

29. See Colville, *Fringes of Power*, 437: diary entry, 7/7/1954.

30. Shuckburgh, *Descent to Suez*, 222: diary entry, 7/7/1954. On Salisbury, see also Young, *Last Campaign*, 273–4. Whether the Cabinet disputes were mainly a clash between Churchill and Salisbury, as Young indicates (see pp. 277–8), is doubtful. It was rather Churchill vs the entire Cabinet with a few politicians like Salisbury and Crookshank a little more outspoken than others.

31. Quoted in Shuckburgh, ibid., 223: diary entry, 12/7/1954.

32. Ibid.

33. PRO: CAB 128/27, Part 2, C.C. (54)47th Conclusions, 7/7/1954.

34. See Shuckburgh, *Descent to Suez*, 222: diary entry, 7/7/1954; Boyle (ed.), *Correspondence*, 152: Churchill to Eisenhower, 7/7/1954.

35. Shuckburgh, ibid.

36. See Macmillan, *Tides of Fortune*, 535. Macmillan reports that Eisenhower was 'naturally surprised' and 'somewhat hurt'.

37. Shuckburgh, *Descent to Suez*, 223: diary entry, 13/7/1954.

38. Boyle (ed.), *Correspondence*, 153–4: Eisenhower to Churchill, 7/7/1954.

39. PRO: CAB 128/27, Part 2, C.C.(54)48th Conclusions, minute 3, 8/7/1954, Confidential Annex.

40. Ibid.

41. Ibid. See also A. Howard, *R.A.B.: The Life of R.A. Butler* (London, 1987), 207–8.

42. Colville, *Fringes of Power*, 702: diary entry, 16/7/1954.

43. PRO: CAB 128/27, Part 2, C.C.(54)48th Conclusions, minute 3, 8/7/1954, Confidential Annex.

44. Boyle (ed.), *Correspondence*, 158–60: Churchill to Eisenhower, 9/7/1954; pp. 154–5: Churchill to Eisenhower, 8/7/1954. See also Shuckburgh, *Descent to Suez*, 223: diary entry, 12/7/1954.

45. See Boyle (ed.), ibid., 156: Eisenhower to Churchill, 8/7/1954. This is also Young's conclusion; see his *Last Campaign*, 279. Young, 'Churchill's Bid', 439, refers to Eisenhower's letter as 'more positive' than the preceding one. However, it is doubtful whether this letter undermined Salisbury's resistance to Churchill's plans (see also similarly his *Last Campaign*, 277).

46. Boyle (ed.), ibid., 161: Eisenhower to Churchill, 12/7/1954.

47. Quoted in Horne, *Macmillan, Vol. 1*, 348.

48. Boyle (ed.), *Correspondence*, 157–9: Churchill to Eisenhower, 9/7/1954.

49. See also Macmillan, *Tides of Fortune*, 536.

50. Quoted in Horne, *Macmillan, Vol. 1*, 348.

51. Colville, *Fringes of Power*, 702: diary entry, 16/7/1954. For this episode and for a letter from Macmillan to Eden dated 15 July 1954 (not June as is sometimes claimed) about the necessity to prevent Salisbury's resignation, see also Horne, ibid., 348. On occasion Churchill expressed genuine concern regarding the consequences of Lord Salisbury's resignation on the stability of the government. See for example PRO: FO 371/125 139/ZP 24/11/G, FO to British delegation in Geneva, No. 1486, personal message Churchill to Eden.

52. PRO: ibid., letter Roberts to Caccia in Geneva, 13/7/1954, with enclosed memorandum 'Probable Soviet line in any general talks'. See also ibid., letter Caccia to Roberts, without date, c. 14/7 or 15/7/1954; ibid., ZP 24/14/G, FO to British delegation in Geneva, No. 1503, Roberts to Caccia, 19/7/1954.

53. For Churchill's speech, see H.C. *Parl. Deb.*, 5th series, Vol. 530, 12/7/1954, 34–49; for his reply whether he had considered a 'Big Three' meeting or meeting Malenkov by himself, see 47–8. He said vaguely that the issue was 'always' in his mind and that it was more a question 'of timing than of anything else'.

54. See Shuckburgh, *Descent to Suez*, 223, 225–6: diary entries, 12/7/1954 and 19/7/1954; also A. Eden, *Full Circle: Memoirs* (London, 1960), 138. Young, *Last Campaign*, 280–1, believes that both Eden and the FO managed to 'sow doubts in Churchill's mind' about a meeting with the Soviets. This seems unlikely.

55. PRO: FO 800/823, Eden, Geneva, to FO, No. 898, 12/7/1954. See also the discussion of Eden's telegram during the Cabinet meeting on 13/7/1954: CAB 128/27, Part 2, C.C.(54)50th Conclusions, minute 2, Confidential Annex, 13/7/1954.

56. Ibid., No. 957, 17/7/1954. For telegram No. 943, see ibid., Eden to FO for Churchill, 16/7/1954.
57. PRO: CAB 128/27, Part 2, C.C.(54)50th Conclusions, minute 2, Confidential Annex, 13/7/1954. See also Young, *Last Campaign*, 278.
58. See Shuckburgh's conversation with Jane Portal, Churchill's secretary, as reported in Shuckburgh, *Descent to Suez*, 224: diary entry, 14/7/1954; see also Moran, *Struggle for Survival*, 581: diary entry, 20/7/1954.
59. See Colville, *Fringes of Power*, 702: diary entry, 16/7/1954; M. Soames, *Clementine Churchill* (London, 1979), 449.
60. PRO: FO 800/823, letter Eden, Geneva, to Churchill, PM/54/111, 22/7/1954.
61. Quoted in E. Hughes, *The Ordeal of Power: A Political Memoir of the Eisenhower Years* (London, 1963), 164.
62. See FRUS 1952–4, Vol. 6, Part I, 1049–50: memorandum Smith, dated 26/7/1954, on his conversation with Churchill on 22 July.
63. Ibid.; see also Young, *Last Campaign*, 282–83.
64. This was pointed out, for example, by left-wing Labour MP Arthur Lewis, see H.C. *Parl. Deb.*, 5th series, Vol. 531, 27/7/1954, 232. The line of partition was to run further north than the West had first feared. The United States largely agreed with the outcome of the conference without however signing the agreement; they issued a separate statement. Washington insisted on the creation of the equivalent to NATO in Asia to contain Communism: the South-East-Asia Treaty Organization (SEATO) was established later in 1954. The free elections in Vietnam never took place. For the details of the outcome of the Indochina conference, see for example PRO: CAB 129/69, C.(54)227, 8/7/1954; Eden, *Full Circle*, 138–42; J. Cable, *The Geneva Conference of 1954 on Indochina*, 2nd edn (Basingstoke, 2000), 115ff.; also G.A. Olson, 'Eisenhower and the Indochina Problem, in M.J. Medhurst (ed.), *Eisenhower's War of Words: Rhetoric and Leadership* (East Lansing, 1994), 115–17.
65. Moran, *Struggle for Survival*, 581: diary entry, 23/7/1954.
66. PRO: FO 371/125 139/ZP 24/16/G, Eden to Churchill, PM/54/110, 22/7/1954, with the enclosed memorandum of the conversation between Eden and Molotov on 21/7/1954.
67. See Shuckburgh, *Descent to Suez*, 227: diary entry, 23/7/1954. Harry Crookshank called it a 'terrible' Cabinet, see Seldon, *Indian Summer*, 406.
68. See Colville, *Fringes of Power*, 702: diary entry, August 1954. See also Young, 'Churchill's Bid', 441–2.
69. PRO: CAB 127/28, Part 2, C.C.(54)52nd Conclusions, minute 3, Confidential Annex, 23/7/1954.
70. Ibid.
71. Ibid.
72. Ibid.
73. For the Soviet Note dated 24 July, see also RIIA, *Survey of International Affairs, 1954* (London, 1957), 157–8; the note is partially publ. in RIIA, *Documents on International Affairs, 1954* (London, 1957), 46–51.
74. PRO: FO 371/125 139/ZP 24/17/G, minute Churchill to Eden, M/138/54, 4/8/1954; also FO 371/111 706/NS 1073/13, minute Richardson, FO, 31/8/1954. See also PREM 11/668.
75. Colville, *Fringes of Power*, 702: diary entry, August 1954.
76. PRO: FO 800/762, FO to British embassy in Moscow, No. 987, Churchill to Molotov, 26/7/1954. See also FO 371/125 139, minute Eden to Churchill, PM/54/115, 30/7/1954; ibid., minute Churchill to Eden, 1/8/1954 and M/138/54, 4/8/1954. See also Macmillan, *Tides of Fortune*, 537–8.
77. See PRO: CAB 128/27, Part 2, C.C.(54)53rd Conclusions, minute 2, Confidential Annex, 26/7/1954.
78. Churchill, 'Oral Answers: International Situation', H.C. *Parl. Deb.*, 5th series, Vol. 531, 27/7/1954, 232–3.
79. PRO: FO 371/125 139/ZP 24/18/G, Molotov to Churchill, 31/7/1954; ibid., Churchill to Molotov, 31/7/1954 (also: FO 800/762, FO to embassy Moscow, No. 1024, Molotov to Churchill, 5/8/1954; ibid., FO to embassy Moscow, No. 1026, Churchill to Molotov, 5/8/1954.). See also ibid., minute Churchill to Kirkpatrick, 31/7/1954; ibid., Molotov to Churchill, 11/8/1954 (= FO to embassy Moscow, No. 1070, 14/8/1954). See also Seldon, *Indian Summer*, 620–1, n. 96; and Churchill, 'Disarmament speech', H.C. *Parl. Deb.*, 5th series, Vol. 538, 14/3/1955, 962–3; Macmillan, *Tides of Fortune*, 537–8; see also U. Bar-Noi, 'The Soviet Union and Churchill's Appeals for High-Level Talks, 1953–4: New Evidence from the Russian Archives', *Diplomacy & Statecraft* 9/3 (1998), 126–8.
80. Shuckburgh, *Descent to Suez*, 235: diary entry, 28/7/1954. See also ambassador Hayter's fairly wild speculations, PRO: FO, 800/823, letter Hayter to Kirkpatrick, 6/8/1954. Hayter, like the majority of the Cabinet and the FO, had expected that Moscow would welcome Churchill's initiative with great enthusiasm.
81. See PRO: FO 371/125 139/ZP 24/16/G, memorandum of a conversation between Eden and Molotov on 21/7/1954 in Geneva, PM/54/110, 22/7/1954. Eden had told Molotov that he would 'be seeing the

Prime Minister on [his] return and no doubt an official message would be coming in the next few days from Her Majesty's Government'.

82. PRO: FO 800/823, Kirkpatrick to Churchill, PM/IK/54/131, 16/8/1954, with an enclosed memorandum regarding the conversation between Roberts and Rodionov on 14/8/1954. Churchill made the memorandum available during the Cabinet meeting on 18/8/1954, see CAB 129/70, C.(54)271. Young, *Last Campaign*, 285, mentions a previous meeting between Rodionov and members of the US embassy on 26 July.

83. This was John Foster Dulles's shrewd conclusion in mid-July 1954. See for example Young, *Last Campaign*, 280.

84. Moran, *Struggle for Survival*, 575: diary entry, 4/7/1954.

85. Colville, *Fringes of Power*, 703: diary entry, August, 1954.

86. PRO: CAB 129/70, C.(54)263, 3/8/1954; Moran, *Struggle for Survival*, 588–89: diary entry: 6/8/1954; also Boyle (ed.), *Correspondence*, 167: Churchill to Eisenhower, 8/8/1954.

CHAPTER 17: A PROLONGED FAREWELL

1. P. Boyle (ed.), *The Churchill-Eisenhower Correspondence, 1953–1955* (Chapel Hill, N.C., 1990), 162–5: Eisenhower to Churchill, 22/7/1954. Quotes: 162, 163.

2. Quoted in G.A. Olson, 'Eisenhower and the Indochina Problem', in M.J. Medhurst (ed.), *Eisenhower's War of Words: Rhetoric and Leadership* (East Lansing, 1994), 98.

3. Boyle (ed.), *Correspondence*, 167: Churchill to Eisenhower, 8/8/1954; last quote: Olson, ibid.

4. See J.W. Young, *Winston Churchill's Last Campaign: Britain and the Cold War, 1951–55* (Oxford, 1996), 286, who argues that Churchill's threat of a coalition government had to be taken quite seriously.

5. J. Colville, *The Fringes of Power: 10 Downing Street Diaries, 1939–1955* (London, 1985), 703: diary entry, August 1954.

6. See P. Brendon, *Churchill: A Brief Life*, 2nd edn (London, 2001), 219–20.

7. For the preparation of the Labour delegation's journey, see the telegram from the Moscow embassy, PRO: FO 371/111 765, NS 1635/10, 13, 14, 16. A convenient summary is contained in Hohler's minute to Ward, dated 5/8/1954, in ibid., NS 1635/18. For the talks of the Labour politicians with Malenkov and other Soviet leaders, see NS 1635/19, Hayter, Moscow, to FO, No. 785, 11/8/1954; see also NS 1635/21, Hayter to FO No. 790, 12/8/1954; NS 1635/28/G, memorandum by the diplomat Brimelow, dated 11/8/1954; ibid., Hayter to FO, No. 818, 12/8/1954. See also PREM 11/697; and see the narrative in W. Hayter, *The Kremlin and the Embassy* (London, 1966), 37–9. In most of Attlee's biographies, the China trip is not mentioned. Harris, *Attlee*, revd edn, (London, 1995), 520–1, does mention the trip to China but has nothing to say about Attlee's meeting with Malenkov. Subsequently, the Labour delegation visited Japan (without Attlee) while Attlee went to Australia.

8. Lord Moran, *Churchill: Struggle for Survival, 1945–1965* (London, 1966), 590: diary entry, 12/8/1954. See also PRO: CAB 129/70, C(54)271, 18/8/1954, memorandum Churchill entitled 'Anglo-Russian Relations'.

9. PRO: ibid.

10. The Soviet note of 24 July with the suggestion to convene a thirty-two-nation European security conference had been followed by another Soviet note on 4 August. This note proposed a pre-conference of the foreign ministers of the four powers in August or September to pave the way for the general European security conference. The western powers believed that the note was directly linked to the EDC debate in the French parliament in August 1954. In the western reply of 10 September, the West was only prepared to agree to the Kremlin's proposed four power conference if Moscow first signed an Austrian peace treaty and allowed free elections in the whole of Germany. The rejection of this proposal was expected. See RIIA, *Survey of International Affairs, 1954* (London, 1957), 157–8; PREM 11/668. The exchange of notes is publ. in RIIA, *Documents on International Affairs, 1954* (London, 1957), 39ff.

11. PRO: PREM 11/672, 23/7/1954; and ibid., WU 1197/783 G, 23/8/1954 (memorandum of conversation between Churchill and Mendès-France); see also ibid., FO to Paris, No. 1938, Churchill to Mendès-France, T.283/54, 17/8/1954; Jebb, Paris, to FO, 17/8, and to Churchill, 18/8/1954; Churchill to Eden, T. 284/54, 18/8/1954; also W.I. Hitchcock, *France Restored: Cold War Diplomacy and the Quest for Leadership in Europe, 1944–1954* (Chapel Hill, N.C., 1998), 195.

12. See K. Adenauer, *Erinnerungen 1953–55* (Stuttgart, 1966), 289ff.; D.D. Eisenhower, *The White House Years, Vol. 1: Mandate for Change, 1953–1956* (London, 1963), 402–8; D. Felken, *Dulles und*

Deutschland. Die amerikanische Deutschlandpolitik 1953–1959 (Bonn, 1993), 245–6; R.H. Immerman, *John Foster Dulles: Piety, Pragmatism, and Power in U.S. Foreign Policy* (Wilmington, Del., 1999), 103–6.

13. See Boyle (ed.), *Correspondence*, 180: Churchill to Eisenhower, 7/12/1954.

14. See EL: C.D. Jackson papers, box 70, Henry & Clare Luce, 1954 (1): letter Jackson to Clare Luce, 29.9.1954; letter Jackson to Henry Luce, 20.9.1954 (I am grateful to Kenneth Osgood for pointing these documents out to me).

15. For the London nine-power conference (28/9–3/10/1954), which was the crucial meeting for drawing up an alternative to the EDC, see above all PRO: FO 371/125 146 (September–October 1954); FO 371/109 773–6 (October 1954). For the attempts to overcome the crisis, see A. Eden, *Full Circle: Memoirs* (London, 1960), 146ff.; Adenauer, *Erinnerungen 1953–55*, 305ff.; Felken, *Dulles und Deutschland*, 246–77; S. Mawby, *Containing Germany: Britain and the Arming of the Federal Republic* (Basingstoke, 1999), 160–82; K. Ruane, *The Rise and Fall of the European Defence Community: Anglo-American Relations and the Crisis of European Defence, 1950–55* (Basingstoke, 2000), 152–72.

16. Adenauer had also 'voluntarily' agreed that the FRG would never aspire to obtain ABC weapons. See the dramatic narrative in Adenauer, ibid., 347–8; see also H.P. Schwarz, *Adenauer. Der Staatsmann 1952–1967* (Stuttgart, 1991), 154–7; H. Köhler, *Adenauer. Eine politische Biographie* (Frankfurt/M., 1994), 820ff. For Churchill's view of a Western European bloc, see Chapter 4, above, 90ff.

17. See Eden, *Full Circle*, 167–9. See also S. Dockrill, *Britain's Policy for West German Rearmament, 1950–55* (Cambridge, 1991), 148; H. Rupieper, *Der besetzte Verbündete. Die amerikanische Deutschlandpolitik 1949–55* (Opladen, 1991), 389–96.

18. Churchill only gave in during a meeting on 28 September, see PRO: PREM 11/843, 28/9/1954. However, Eden had left a way out for Britain as would become clear in the next few years. Although Britain could not withdraw its troops from the continent without the agreement of its partners, there was nothing preventing it from reducing its troop strength; this did not require consultation with or the agreement of the other WEU members. See also Harold Macmillan's memorandum to Butler of 10/8/1955 (PRO: FO 800/668) in which he considered such a possibility a few months after he became Foreign Minister in early April 1955.

19. For the rapid solution to the EDC crisis in September/October 1954 and the debate whether credit was largely due to Eden, Mendès-France or even Dulles, see the recent works by Hitchcock, *France Restored*, 195–202; Ruane, *Rise and Fall of the EDC*, 111ff.; Mawby, *Containing Germany*, 157ff.; for a good overview of Eden's efforts, see A. Deighton, 'Britain and the Creation of the Western European Union, 1954', in M. Dumoulin (ed.), *The European Defence Community: Lessons for the Future?* (Brussels, 2000), 283–308.

20. The notes are publ. in RIAA, *Documents, 1954*, 58–64 (Soviet note, 13/11), 61–4 (western reply, 29/11), 96–101 (Soviet note, 23/10/1954); see also the various documents dealing with the issue in PRO: FO 371/109 295–9 (October–November 1954); see also Young, *Last Campaign*, 292–3.

21. The Paris Treaties are publ. in RIIA, *Documents, 1954*, 102–7. For the concern about further delays, due to both Mendès-France's resignation and Malenkov's resignation in early 1955, see PRO: FO 371/118 258/WG 1074/10, 12, 34, 37, 69 (February–March 1955). For the British assessment of Mendès-France's government and policy, see also PREM 11/900 (July 1954–February 1955).

22. For this important issue and for Anglo-American plans to go ahead without French agreement, see FRUS 1952–4, Vol. 5, 1519–29; PRO: PREM 11/891, FO 800/843 (December 1954).

23. For the considerable literature on the failure of the EDC and the rapid development of the alternative WEU/NATO solution, see the literature in n. 19, above, and: H.H. Jansen, *Großbritannien, das Scheitern der EVG und der NATO-Beitritt der Bundesrepublik Deutschland* (Bochum, 1992), 143ff.; R. Steininger, 'Das Scheitern der EVG und der Beitritt der Bundesrepublik zur NATO', *Aus Politik und Zeitgeschichte*, B 17 (27/4/1985), 4ff.; T. Vogelsang, 'Großbritanniens Politik zwischen Mendès-France und Adenauer im August/September 1954', in D. Blumenwitz et al. (eds), *Konrad Adenauer und seine Zeit. Politik und Persönlichkeit des ersten Bundeskanzlers*, Vol. 2 (Stuttgart, 1976), 37–52; P. Noack, *Das Scheitern der europäischen Verteidigungsgemeinschaft. Entscheidungsprozesse vor und nach dem 30. August 1954* (Düsseldorf, 1977); R. Aron and D. Lerner (eds), *France Defeats EDC* (New York, 1957); S. Dockrill, 'Britain and the Settlement of the West German Rearmament Question in 1954', in M. Dockrill and J.W. Young (eds), *British Foreign Policy, 1945–1956* (Basingstoke, 1989), 149–72; J.W. Young, 'German Rearmament and the European Defence Community', in J.W. Young (ed.), *The Foreign Policy of Churchill's Peacetime Government, 1951–1955* (Leicester, 1988), 96–107; B. Thoß, 'Sicherheits- und deutschlandpolitische Komponenten der europäischen Integration zwischen EVG und EWG, 1954–57', in L. Herbst et al. (eds), *Vom Marshall-Plan zur EWG. Die Eingliederung der Bundesrepublik Deutschland in die westliche Welt* (Munich, 1990), 475–500.

24. See PRO: PREM 11/618, 29/8/1954; also Young, *Last Campaign*, 289.
25. Eisenhower's letter was friendly but firm. See Boyle (ed.), *Correspondence*, 180: Churchill to Eisenhower, 7/12/1954, and p. 182: Eisenhower to Churchill, 14/12/1954.
26. PRO: PREM 11/676, letter Adenauer to Churchill, 15/10/1954.
27. For a very detailed consideration, see M. Gilbert, *Winston S. Churchill, Vol. 8: Never Despair, 1945–65*, paperback edn (London, 1990), 1063–6. See also, Moran, *Struggle for Survival*, 599, 603–4: diary entries, 1/10 and 10/10/1954 (quote: 604); also C. Ponting, *Churchill* (London, 1994), 797. For the increasing attempts by various members of his government to persuade Churchill to consider retirement, see A. Seldon, *Churchill's Indian Summer: The Conservative Government, 1951–55* (London, 1981), 48–54.
28. The fairly short Woodford speech is published in R.R. James (ed.), *Winston S. Churchill: His Complete Speeches, 1987–1963, Vol. 8: 1950–65* (London, 1974), 8604–5.
29. See PRO: PREM 11/915 (November 1954–March 1955); Moran, *Struggle for Survival*, 611: diary entry, 28/11/1954; for Shinwell's speech, see H.C. *Parl. Deb.*, 5th series, Vol. 535, 1/12/1954, 159–69. For the 'warmonger' accusation during the 1951 election campaign, see Chapter 6, above, 139.
30. See Churchill's parliamentary speech in reply to Shinwell, H.C. *Parl. Deb.*, ibid., 170; also Moran, ibid., 609–12; Young, *Last Campaign*, 294. Young emphasizes that Churchill's speech was well prepared, he did not merely make a few ad hoc statements (ibid., n. 16).
31. Moran, ibid., 613. For the entire episode, see also A.L. Smith, *Churchill's German Army: Wartime Strategy and Cold War Policies* (Beverly Hills, Calif., 1977), 11–24; Gilbert, *Never Despair*, 1078–81; and PRO: 371/109 302/1095 (December 1954). David Carlton uses the episode unconvincingly as evidence that Churchill had always remained strongly anti-Communist, which once again was revealed in the Woodford speech, and had only embarked on his 'summitry' to postpone his retirement (see his *Churchill and the Soviet Union*, Manchester, 2000, 193–4).
32. See Churchill's speech, H.C. *Parl. Deb.*, 5th series, Vol. 535, 1/12/1954, 171.
33. See for example Soames, *Clementine Churchill* (London, 1979), 445–7.
34. Moran, *Struggle for Survival*, 612: diary entry, 29/11/1954. In the House of Commons he claimed however that he was 'not unduly disheartened' by the Russian reaction to his Woodford speech. See H.C. *Parl. Deb.*, 5th series, Vol. 535, 1/12/1954, 175.
35. H.C. *Parl. Deb.*, ibid., 175.
36. Moran, *Struggle for Survival*, 612, 655: diary entries, 29/11/1954 and 11/5/1955.
37. For 'Operation Unthinkable', see *Daily Telegraph*, 1 October 1998, 1, 8–9; also the press release by *The Associated Press*, 1 October 1998, 2:47 a.m. For a discussion of various tentative remarks by General Sir Alan Brooke, C.I.G.S., to 'the unthinkable war' in his memoirs and elsewhere, see J. Lewis, *Changing Direction: British Military Planning for Post-war Strategic Defence, 1942–7* (London, 1988), 242–3. Lewis was unable to trace any documentation of 'Operation Unthinkable' in the PRO documents.
38. Quote: H.C. *Parl. Deb.*, 5th series, Vol. 535, 1/12/1954, 174. See PRO: PREM 11/915 (November 1954–March 1955; See also H.C., Parl. Deb., 5th series, Vol. 535, 1–14.12.1954: 160–80, 602, 1109–16, 1575, 1579–81; also Smith, *Churchill's German Army*, 11–24. For Churchill's thoughts in November 1918 and again in April 1919 about using captured German troops to fight in the Russian civil war against Lenin's and Trotzky's Bolshevik forces, see Chapter 2, above, p. 39.
39. Boyle (ed.), *Correspondence*, 180: Churchill to Eisenhower, 7/12/1954.
40. See H.C. *Parl. Deb.*, 5th series, Vol. 535, 16/12/1954, 178 (in reply to a question by Labour MP Lewis). See also ibid., 185: Churchill to Eisenhower, 12/1/1955; see also his final major speech as Prime Minister, 'World Disarmament', on 14/3/1955, in H.C. *Parl. Deb.*, 5th series, Vol. 538, 957–8, and Attlee's call for not making high-level talks dependent on the intricacies of French policies, ibid., 953–6.
41. Mendès-France sent a letter to this effect to Churchill on 12 January 1955. See Churchill, 'World Disarmament', ibid., 966; also J.W. Young, 'Churchill's Bid for Peace with Moscow, 1954', *Historical Journal* 28 (1985), 444. For the entire episode, see in great detail, Gilbert, *Never Despair*, 1089–90 (incl. Churchill's angry letter to Mendès-France on 10 January 1955); also A. Nutting, *Europe will not wait: A Warning and a Way out* (London, 1960), 80. For a good detailed analysis, see also Young, *Last Campaign*, 295–6, 298–300.
42. Churchill, 'World Disarmament', H.C. *Parl. Deb.*, 5th series, Vol. 538, 14/3/1955, 965–66; also Seldon, *Indian Summer*, 407.
43. See C. Bohlen, *Witness to History, 1929–1969* (London, 1973), 369–70; W. Hayter, *A Double Life* (London, 1974), 114; also Young, *Last Campaign*, 293.
44. The Soviet note of 15 January 1955 is publ. in RIIA. *Documents on International Affairs, 1955* (London, 1958), 240–3.

45. American politicians referred to the event as a 'bombshell'. See EL: Ann Whitman File, Administration Series, Box 22, Memorandum 'Operation Kremlin Kracks', p. 3, 16/2/1955.

46. PRO: PREM 11/1015/NS1103/1, minute Colville, 7/2/1955.

47. See for example PRO: FO 371/116 631/NS 1015/14, Minute Ward to Hohler, FO, 9/2/1955. For British and American and some other assessments of the change, see also FO 371/116 632/NS 1015/29, 30, 34, 37 (March–May 1955); FO 371/116 633/NS 1015/40, 44, 46, 48, 49, 51 (June–August 1955); FO 371/116 634/NS 1015/52, 53, 57, 61, 69 (July–December 1955); FO 371/116 637/NS 1017/1, 2, 4, 5, 8, 9, 10, 11, 14, 22, 27, 28, 29, 31 (February 1955); FO 371/116 637/NS 1017/29, 31 (February 1955); FO 116 638/NS 1017/35, 38, 44–9 56 (February 1955).

48. PRO: FO 371/116 106, Minute G.G. Brown, Moscow, to FO, 24/2/1955; FO 371/116 631/NS 1015/1. Watson, Washington, to FO, 6/1/1955; NS 1015/5, Washington to FO, No. 60, 29/1/1955; NS 1015/6, Makins, Washington, to FO, No. 366, 8/2/1955; No. 396, 11/2/1955 (with the CIA's assessment of Malenkov's resignation).

49. The announcement of Malenkov's new post to the Supreme Soviet was received in 'complete silence'. See PRO: FO 371/116 631/NS 1015/9, Hayter, Moscow, to Eden, No. 26 'S', 11/2/1955; also NS 1015/7, Hayter to FO, No. 124, 9/2/1955.

50. E. Shuckburgh, *Descent to Suez: Diaries, 1951–56* (London, 1986), 350: diary entry, 29/3/1956. Malenkov also held talks with Hugh Gaitskell, the new leader of the Labour opposition, at the Soviet embassy on 29 and 30 March 1956. See PRO: FO 800/720.

51. For extracts from Molotov's speech, see RIIA, *Documents, 1955*, 217–18, 262–3; see also PRO: FO 371/116 650–51 (February 1955).

52. PRO: FO 371/116 651/NS 1021/21, minute Harrison to Ward, 21/2/1955.

53. For the analysis of Malenkov's downfall and Khrushchev's rise by the FO and the State Department, see PRO: PREM 11/1015; FRUS 1955–7, 22–7, 30, 69, 158–9; also W. Leonard, *The Kremlin since Stalin* (Oxford, 1962), 90–4; L. Shapiro, *The Communist Party of the Soviet Union* (London, 1970), 561–2; V. Zubok and C. Pleshakov, *Inside the Kremlin's Cold War: From Stalin to Khrushchev* (Cambridge, Mass., 1996), 168ff.; J.G. Richter, *Khrushchev's Double Bind: International Pressures and Domestic Coalition Politics* (Baltimore, 1994), 49–52, 53ff.; see also W. Taubman, S. Khrushchev and A. Gleason (eds), *Nikita Khrushchev* (New Haven, 2000).

54. Yet, to some extent the issue was debated within the British government and the FO. Churchill still believed that 'Malenkov would have played' and that 'the opportunity was lost'. See Moran, *Struggle for Survival*, 634: diary entry, 1/3/1955; also Young, *Last Campaign*, 303–4. However, this contradicted his statements in his last major parliamentary speech on 14 March. See below, 368–70.

55. Bohlen, *Witness to History*, 371.

56. See ibid., 372, 373ff. (quote: 372).

57. See Shuckburgh, *Descent to Suez*, 249: diary entry, 11/2/1955.

58. See Moran, *Struggle for Survival*, 632: diary entry, 16/2/1955; also Shuckburgh, ibid., 250: diary entry, 17/2/1955.

59. See Moran, ibid., 631, 632: diary entries, 2/2 and 16/2/1955; Shuckburgh, ibid., 243–4: diary entry, 17/12/1954; also Colville, *Fringes of Power*, 705–7: diary entry, 29/3/1955; Soames, *Clementine Churchill*, 451; Seldon, *Indian Summer*, 51. See also R. Cockett (ed.), *My Dear Max: The Letters of Brendan Bracken to Lord Beaverbrook, 1925–58* (London, 1990), 177: Bracken to Beaverbrook, 21/2/1955.

60. Moran, ibid., 634: diary entry, 1/3/1955.

61. This brief outline follows the account in Young, *Last Campaign*, 306–7.

62. For the 'Defence speech', see H.C. *Parl. Deb.*, 5th series, Vol. 537, 1/3/1955, 1893ff. For an analysis of the Defence White Paper, Cmd. 9391, of February 1955, see Young, ibid., 309; and Gilbert, *Never Despair*, 1098–101. See also Moran, *Struggle for Survival*, 634: diary entry, 1/3/1955; Colville, *Fringes of Power*, 706: diary entry, 29/3/1955. For the Labour opposition's role in the debate, see Harris, *Attlee*, revd edn, 527–9.

63. H.C. *Parl. Deb.*, ibid., 1896. For his MIT speech on 31/3/1949, see Chapter 6, 130, above. For Moscow's fairly critical reaction as publ. in *Pravda*, see PRO: FO 371/116 742/NS 1242/7 and 10, dated 4/3 and 18/3/1955.

64. H.C. *Parl. Deb.*, ibid., 1898–902. He also spoke of a situation 'where safety will be the sturdy child of terror, and survival the twin brother of annihilation' (ibid., 1899). See also J. Rosenberg, 'Before the Bomb and After: Winston Churchill and the Use of Force', in J.L. Gaddis et al. (eds), *Cold War Statesmen Confront the Bomb: Nucelar Diplomacy Since 1945* (Oxford, 1999), 188, 191–2.

65. H.C. *Parl. Deb.*, ibid., 1903.

66. Quote: ibid., 1897; for the continued importance of conventional weapons as otherwise any minor conflict would lead to a nuclear war, see ibid., 1895–6, 1903–4.

67. Ibid., 1905.
68. See ibid., Vol. 537, 2/3/1955, 2115–16.
69. See H. Macmillan, *Tides of Fortune, 1945–55* (London, 1969), 554–5; Seldon, *Indian Summer*, 52.
70. Colville, *Fringes of Power*, 705: diary entry, 29/3/1955.
71. Shuckburgh, *Descent to Suez*, 254: diary entry, 1/4/1955.
72. See Gilbert, *Never Despair*, 1102–11; also Young, *Last Campaign*, 311–12; and the not very reliable account in Seldon, *Indian Summer*, 52–3. See above all, PRO: FO 800/763 and PREM 11/893.
73. PRO: FO 800/763, Makins, Washington, to FO, No. 539, 10/3/1955 (also in Bodleian Library, Oxford: Woolton Papers, 3, Diary 1942–60, p. 151). Seldon, ibid., follows Woolton's remarks too uncritically.
74. See the American clarification, in PRO: ibid., Makins to FO, No. 583, which enclosed a message from Dulles to Eden, 16/3/1955. See also Woolton Papers, ibid., p. 146, 14/3/1955; also PRO: FO 800/844, Makins to FO, No. 568, 15/3/1955, and Rumbold, FO, to Makins, 15/3/1955; and Seldon, ibid.
75. Woolton Papers, ibid., 147, 14/3/1955.
76. PRO: CAB 128/28, C.C.(55),23rd Conclusions, 14/3/1955; also Colville, *Fringes of Power*, 705–6: diary entry, 29/3/1955. See in detail, Gilbert, *Never Despair*, 1105–8; also R.R. James, *Anthony Eden*, paperback edn (London, 1986), 401–2.
77. See PRO: FO 800/844, Rumbold, FO, to Makins for Dulles, 15/3/1955; also Seldon, *Indian Summer*, 52–3.
78. See PRO: ibid., Makins to FO, with message from Dulles, No. 583, 16/3/1955. See also Churchill's informative letter, dated 15/3/1955, on the Cabinet meeting on 14 March and the letter by R. Makins, publ. in M. Soames (ed.), *Speaking for Themselves: the personal letters of Winston and Clementine Churchill* (London, 1998), 589–90.
79. Bodleian Library, Oxford: Woolton Papers, 3, Diary 1942–60, p. 150, 15/3/1955. See also PRO: CAB 128/28, C.C.(55)24th Conclusions, 15/3/1955.
80. Colville, *Fringes of Power*, 707–8: diary entry, 29/3/1955.
81. See 'World Disarmament speech', H.C. *Parl. Deb.*, 5th series, Vol. 538, 14/3/1955, 959–63 (quotes: 960, 961).
82. Ibid.
83. Ibid., 957–58.
84. H.C. *Parl. Deb.*, 5th series, Vol. 538, 14/3/1955, 964. For his as well as General Gruenther's and Ismay's conviction that German rearmament ought to occur more for political rather than for military reasons, see K. Larres, 'Unification or Integration with the West? Britain and the Federal Republic of Germany in the early 1950s', in R.J. Aldrich and M.F. Hopkins (eds), *Intelligence, Defence and Diplomacy: British Policy in the Post-war World* (London, 1994), 42–75. For his speech on 25 February, see Chapter 15, 321–2 above.
85. H.C. *Parl. Deb.*, ibid., 963.
86. Ibid., 965–6.
87. Ibid., 967–8
88. Ibid., 967.
89. Ibid., 967.
90. Ibid., 970
91. For details of the hand-over and the internal farewell wishes, see Gilbert, *Never Despair*, ch. 58. As there was a national newspaper strike, Churchill's resignation was a rather subdued affair as far as public opinion was concerned 'with the result that it obtained neither the news coverage nor the valedictory acclaim which it would otherwise have attracted' (ibid., 1125). However, it also 'spared [Churchill] the full pressure of press comment and speculation which would have been inevitable in these last few weeks'. See Soames, *Clementine Churchill*, 451.
92. The western note, dated 10 May 1955, and the Soviet reply of 25 May are publ. in RIIA, *Documents, 1955*, 2–4. See also RIIA, *Survey, 1955–1956* (London, 1960), 150–55; for an interesting account, see Eden, *Full Circle*, 288–90, 278–83. Eden's original proposal to meet in Berlin was strongly opposed by Adenauer as the conference would then look like a continuation of the failed 1954 Berlin meeting. See PRO: FO 800/673, Hoyer Millar, Bonn, to FO, No. 297, 14/5/1955.
93. See Macmillan, *Tides of Fortune*, 585; PRO: PREM 11/893 (April/May 1955); R. Lamb, *The Failure of the Eden Government* (London, 1987), 10. Eisenhower was not keen on the return of a Labour government in Britain
94. Eden, *Full Circle*, 289.
95. PRO: FO 800/666, letter Eden to Eisenhower, 5/5/1955. Although, as George Peden believes, Eden may have been 'the last prime minister to believe that Britain was an independent world power',

Eden well remembered the American opposition to Churchill's 'summitry' and fully realized that he had to persuade Eisenhower to give his agreement to the envisaged conference. See G. Peden, 'Robert Anthony Eden, First Earl of Avon', in R.R. Eccleshall and G. Walker (eds), *Biographical Dictionary of British Prime Ministers* (London, 1998), 315.

96. See for example PRO: FO 371/118 204 and 205 (April 1955); FRUS 1955–57, Vol. 5, 137: Memorandum of conversation between British and American diplomats, State Dept., Washington, 1/4/1955.

97. A. Nutting, 'Anthony Eden', in H. Van Thal (ed.), *The Prime Ministers, Vol. 2* (London, 1975), 336; also V. Rothwell, *Anthony Eden: A Political Biography, 1931–57* (Manchester, 1992), 164–5.

98. For the best and most comprehensive account of the negotiation of the Austrian state treaty and Moscow's sudden readiness to compromise, see G. Stourzh, *Um Einheit und Freiheit. Staatsvertrag, Neutralität und das Ende der Ost-West Besetzung Österreichs 1945–1955*, 4th edn (Vienna, 1998), 335ff. See also Macmillan's interesting memorandum on the negotiations and Austrian neutrality in PRO: CAB 129/75, C.P. (55)12, 26/4/1955.

99. See for example D. Carlton, *Anthony Eden: A Biography*, paperback edn (London, 1981), 373.

100. It was agreed that for the purpose of securing neutrality 'in all future times Austria will not join any military alliances and will not permit the establishment of any foreign military bases on its territory'. See RIIA, *Documents, 1955*, 239. Apart from Stourzh, *Um Einheit und Freiheit*, 4th edn, 335ff., see also G. Bischof, 'Österreichische Neutralität, die deutsche Frage und europäische Sicherheit 1953–1955', in R. Steininger et al. (eds.), *Die doppelte Eindämmung: Europäische Sicherheit und deutsche Frage in den Fünfzigern* (Munich, 1993), 133–76; R. Steininger, '1955: The Austrian State Treaty and the German Question', *Diplomacy & Statecraft*, 3/3 (1992), 494–522; G. Bischof, *Austria in the First Cold War, 1945–1955: The Leverage of the Weak* (Basingstoke, 1999), 142ff.; G. Bischof, 'Eisenhower, the Summit and the Austrian Treaty, 1953–55', in S.E. Ambrose and G. Bischof (eds), *Eisenhower: A Centenary Assessment* (Baton Rouge, La., 1995), 136–61.

101. In fact, as early as May 1950 the US embassy in Vienna had mentioned this in a report. See W. Blasi, 'Die Libanonkrise 1958 und die US-Überflüge', in E.A. Schmidl (ed.), *Österreich im Frühen Kalten Krieg, 1945–1958* (Cologne, 2000), 239. The article provides a good case study of Austrian difficulties to maintain political neutrality in face of American pressure to grant overflight permission for U.S. warplanes.

102. Eden gained 3.3 per cent more votes than the Labour Party although both parties lost votes; in 1951 Churchill had actually secured fewer votes than the Labour Party but due to the British electoral system had obtained more parliamentary seats than Labour. For the most detailed account of the election, see D. Butler, *The British General Election of 1955* (London, 1955). For Eden's succession as Conservative party leader and the 1955 election campaign, see also T.F. Lindsay and M. Harrington, *The Conservative Party 1918–1979*, 2nd edn (London, 1979), 184–6; A. Clark, *The Tories: Conservatives and the Nation State, 1922–97*, paperback edn (London, 1999), 350–3; Macmillan, *Tides of Fortune*, 582–5; James, *Anthony Eden*, 404–9; Carlton, *Anthony Eden*, 370–4.

103. See for example B. Pimlott, *Harold Wilson* (London, 1992), 191–3.

104. Moran, *Struggle for Survival*, 657: diary entry, 29/5/1955; Lamb, *Failure of the Eden Government*, 11.

105. Soames, *Clementine Churchill*, 453; see also Moran, ibid., 653–5: diary entries, 4/5 and 11/5/1955; 656–7: diary entry, 19/5/1955.

106. Quoted in Macmillan, *Tides of Fortune*, 587; see also Moran, ibid., 655: diary entry 11/5/1955.

107. E. Hughes, *The Ordeal of Power: A Political Memoir of the Eisenhower Years* (London, 1963), 167–8.

108. Quote: Boyle (ed.), *Correspondence*, 213: extract from letter Eisenhower to Churchill, 18/7/1955. See also Hughes, ibid., and Moran, *Struggle for Survival*, 679: diary entry, 18/7/1955.

109. PRO: FO 800/679, letter Macmillan to Churchill, 15/6/1955.

110. Eisenhower, *Mandate for Change*, 530.

111. See for example PRO: FO 800/666, UK delegation, Geneva, Macmillan to FO, No. 22, 18/5/1955, with message from Eden to Churchill; ibid., Macmillan to FO, No. 75, 22/7/1955, with message to Churchill.

112. PRO: FO 800/666, FO to Washington, No. 2555, PM's Personal Telegram, T(E)35/55, with letter from Eden to Eisenhower, 29/5/1955.

113. PRO: FO 800/689, Record of Conversation between Macmillan and Dulles at the British embassy in Paris, 12/5/1955. For an important conversation between Macmillan and Dulles illuminating the different views of the UK and the US regarding the western positions on German unification and European security at Geneva, see PRO: FO 800/670, Jebb, Paris, to FO, No. 256, from Macmillan to Eden, 15/7/1955; also No. 259, 15/7/1955.

114. Quote: PRO: FO 800/666, Macmillan to Eden, PM/55/99, 6/8/1955; see also ibid., Macmillan to Eden, PM/55/33, 12/4/1955; ibid., letter Eden to Eisenhower (FO to Washington, No. 2139), 5/5/1955;

ibid., reply Eisenhower to Eden (Washington to FO, 1071), 6/5/1955; ibid., Record of Meeting at the US embassy in Vienna between Dulles, Macmillan, Pinay and Molotov, 14/5/1955. For the British aims at Geneva, see also a draft paper for the US in FO 800/673, Macmillan to Eden, PM/55/79, 30/6/1955. See also Eden, *Full Circle*, 289–90; Macmillan, *Tides of Fortune*, 585–92; see also Young, *Last Campaign*, 317.

115. Otherwise, he wrote, it would 'defeat the purposes you [Eden] may be seeking'. PRO: FO 800/666, Makins, Washington, to FO, No. 1071, with Eisenhower's letter to Eden, 6/5/1955.

116. Ibid., Makins to FO, No. 1073, 6/5/1955; and Jebb, Paris, to FO, No. 190, 8/5/1955; also No. 187, 7/5/1955.

117. See PRO: FO 800/684, FO to Paris, No. 847, 11/5/1955 (first quote); FO 800/666, letter Nutting to Macmillan, 13/5/1955 (second quote). See also for example, R.A. Divine, *Eisenhower and the Cold War* (New York, 1981), 117

118. For Yugoslav conclusions regarding the Soviet rapprochement as passed on to British diplomats, see PRO: FO 371/116 652/NS 1021/42, minute W.H. Young, 10/6/1955; see also S. Clissold (ed.), *Yugoslavia and the Soviet Union, 1939–1973: a Documentary Survey* (London, 1975); P. Maurer, *La Reconciliation Sovieto-Yougoslave, 1954–1958: Illusions et Desillusions de Tito* (Fribourg, CH, 1991).

119. The note is published in RIIA (ed.), *Documents, 1955*, 245–8, quotes: 248, 245. See also FRUS 1955–7, Vol. 5, 544: Bohlen, Moscow, to State Dept., 6/8/1955. Regarding Adenauer's invitation and subsequent journey to Moscow, see above all Josef Foschepoth, 'Adenauers Moskaureise 1955' in *Aus Politik und Zeitgeschichte*, Vol. 22 (31/5/1986), 30–46; Felken, *Dulles und Deutschland*, 320–6; Köhler, *Adenauer*, 872–89; Schwarz, *Adenauer. Der Staatsmann*, 189–222. See also the memoirs from members of Adenauer's delegation, above all: W. G. Grewe, *Rückblenden, 1976–1951* (Berlin, 1979), 229–51; H. Blankenhorn, *Verständnis und Verständigung. Blätter eines politischen Tagebuchs 1949 bis 1979* (Frankfurt/M., 1979), 224–35; C. Schmidt, *Erinnerungen* (Bern, 1979), 564–85; and, of course, Adenauer himself, *Erinnerungen 1953–55*, 487–556. See also N. Khrushchev, *Khrushchev Remembers: The Last Testament* (Boston, 1974), 357–62.

120. *Christian Science Monitor*, 8/6/1955, quoted in RIIA (ed.), *Survey, 1955–56*, 138.

121. RIIA, ibid., 69. For the British considerations in connection with Adenauer's visit, see the extensive documentation in PRO: FO 371/118 178–83 (June–October 1955)

122. See K. Larres, 'Britain and the GDR, 1949–1989', in K. Larres (ed. with E. Meehan), *Uneasy Allies: British-German Relations and European Integration since 1945* (Oxford, 2000), 70–1.

123. For the latter, see V. M. Zubok, 'Soviet Policy Aims at the Geneva Conference, 1955', in G. Bischof and S. Dockrill (eds), *Cold War Respite: The Geneva Summit of 1955* (Baton Rouge, La., 2000), 60–67; V. M. Zubok, 'The Case of Divided Germany, 1953–64', in W. Taubman et al. (eds), *Nikita Khrushchev*, 283–6. For a good general account, see also H. Adomeit, *Imperial Overstretch: Germany in Soviet Policy from Stalin to Gorbachev* (Baden-Baden, 1998), 100ff.

124. *Public Papers of the Presidents of the United States, Dwight D. Eisenhower, 1955*, (Washington, DC, 1960), 503–4 (quotes: 504): remarks by Eisenhower and Dulles during the latter's television report on his European visit, 17/5/1955; see also Eisenhower's news conference of 18/5/1955, ibid., 507–9, 515–16.

125. Quoted in Divine, *Eisenhower and the Cold War*, 117. For an interesting assessment regarding when the Soviets could be regarded as having fulfilled the President's conditions, see PRO: PREM 11/670, minute Kirkpatrick to Churchill, PM/IK/54/150, 23/8/1954. For Eisenhower's 'Chance for Peace speech', see Chapter 10, 211ff., above.

126. PRO: 800/689, Eden to Eisenhower (FO to Washington, Nos 2555 and 2627), 29/5 and 3/6/1955.

127. See for example Macmillan, *Tides of Fortune*, 585–7; Lamb, *Failure of the Eden Government*, 10.

128. For Adenauer's view of the 1955 conferences, see his *Erinnerungen 1953–55* (Stuttgart, 1966), 437ff.; *Erinnerungen 1955–59* (Stuttgart, 1967), 31–62.

129. See Felken, *Dulles und Deutschland*, 293ff.; Immerman, *John Foster Dulles*, 136–43; C.J. Pach and E. Richardson, *The Presidency of Dwight D. Eisenhower*, revd edn (Lawrence, Kans., 1991), 109; also P. Brendon, *Ike: His Life and Times* (London, 1986), 305–10.

130. See for example K. Kyle, *Suez* (London, 1991); W.R. Louis and R. Owen, *Suez 1956: The Crisis and its Consequences* (Oxford, 1989); C.C. Kingseed, *Eisenhower and the Suez Crisis of 1956* (Baton Rouge, La., 1995); D. B. Kunz, *The Economic Diplomacy of the Suez Crisis* (Chapel Hill, N.C., 1991); L. Richardson, *When Allies Differ: Anglo-American Relations during the Suez and Falklands Crises* (Basingstoke, 1996).

131. For the proceedings of the Geneva summit conference, see FRUS 1955–7, Vol. 5, 119ff. (preparatory talks), 361ff. (four-power meetings and talks); PRO: CAB 133/141 (bound volume with the Geneva proceedings); see also CAB 129/76, C.P. (55) 99, 27/7/1955; C.P.(55) 100, 12/8/1955, minutes and memoranda on the Geneva summit; some interesting documentation is also in FO 800/673. For

extensive documentation on the preparations (including the western meetings of foreign ministers and the various western working parties) and the conferences themselves, see FO 371/118 195–254 (January–December 1955), esp. FO 371/116 150. For Eden's impressions, see his *Full Circle*, 295–311; and for Eisenhower's views, see his *Mandate for Change*, 503–31. See also RIIA, *Survey, 1955–1956*, 155ff. The official statements during the summit are publ. in RIIA, *Documents, 1955*, 5ff.; and during the subsequent foreign ministers conference, ibid, 5off. For the most recent and convincingly argued analyses of the 1955 Geneva conferences, see the various contributions in Bischof and Dockrill (eds), *Cold War Respite*. See also R.W. Pruessen, 'Beyond the Cold War-Again: 1955 and the 1990s', *Political Science Quarterly* 108/1 (1993), 59–84; H. J. Küsters, *Der Integrationsfriede. Viermächte-Verhandlungen über die Friedensregelung mit Deutschland 1945–1990* (Munich, 2000), 698ff.; D. Gossel, *Briten, Deutsche und Europa: die deutsche Frage in der britischen Außenpolitik, 1945–1962* (Stuttgart, 1999), 106–16.

132. See J. Prados, 'Open Skies and Closed Minds: American Disarmament Policy at the Geneva Summit', in Bischof and Dockrill (eds), ibid., 215–33; for a rather positive interpretation, see W. W. Rostow, *Open Skies: Eisenhower's Proposal of July 21, 1955* (Austin, Tx., 1982); for a brief overview, see also Pach and Richardson, *Presidency of Dwight D. Eisenhower*, 110–12. For an interesting interpretation, see also M.J. Hogan, 'Eisenhower and Open Skies: A Case Study in "Psychological Warfare" ', in M.J. Medhurst (ed.), *Eisenhower's War of Words: Rhetoric and Leadership* (East Lansing, Mich., 1994), 137–55.

133. PRO: FO 800/668, 'memorandum Macmillan on Disarmament (to clear his mind)', 8/8/1955; see also his memorandum to Butler in ibid., 10/8/1955.

134. Quotes: R.H. Rovere, *The Eisenhower Years* (New York, 1956), 283, 291, 293. For the very high satisfaction of American and Western European public opinion with the Geneva conference, see the polls in EL: Ann Whitman File, Administration Series, Box 30, Report by Nelson A. Rockefeller, 30/11/1955 (Rockefeller had succeeded C.D. Jackson as Eisenhower's psychological warfare adviser).

135. Quoted in Divine, *Eisenhower and the Cold War*, 119.

136. Khrushchev, *Khrushchev Remembers: The Last Testament*, 362.

137. See S. Dockrill, 'The Eden Plan and European Security'; and J.W. Young, 'The Geneva Conference of Foreign Ministers, October–November 1955: The Acid Test of Détente', both in Bischof and Dockrill (eds), *Cold War Respite*, 161–89, 271–91. See also Eden, *Full Circle*, 292–4, 298–9, 302–5; and for details and discussions of the Eden Plan, see PRO: FO 800/670, Nutting, FO, to Macmillan, Geneva, 2/11/1955, with letter from Eden to Adenauer, also FO 800/673, Macmillan to Eden, PM/55/83, 4/7/1955; FO 800/673, Jebb, Paris, to FO, Nos 260 and 261, with letter Macmillan to Eden, 15/7/1955; also FO 953/1527/PG 14517/6 (incl. Annexes). While the implementation of the Eden Plan was never seriously contemplated, the Plan did lead to the development of various similar disengagement plans in 1956–8 (like the Rapacki Plan and George F. Kennan's 1957 considerations). See Felken, *Dulles und Deutschland*, 453–61. For still useful overviews, see also E. Hinterhoff, *Disengagement* (London, 1959); M. Howard, *Disengagement* (Harmondswoth, 1958).

138. See EL: Ann Whitman File, Administration Series, Box 29, Memorandum by the Joint Chiefs of Staff for the President, 17/6/1955; and memorandum Eisenhower to Admiral Radford, with Adenauer's plan for Europe, 13/6/1955; see also the documents in PRO: FO 371/118 191 (January–December 1955). See also E. Conze, 'No Way Back to Potsdam: The Adenauer Government and the Geneva Summit', in Bischof and Dockrill (eds), *Cold War Respite*, 190–214. For Adenauer's fears that Moscow would attempt to exploit the solution of the creation of a neutral Austria as a model for resolving the German question and that he would be faced with proposals to this effect during his September 1955 visit to Moscow, see his *Erinnerungen 1953–55*, 437ff., esp. 441–6, 468–80, 487ff. For Macmillan's impressions of the Geneva foreign ministers' conference, see his *Tides of Fortune*, 643–50; and A. Horne, *Macmillan, 1894–1956*, Vol. 1 (London, 1988), 361–2.

139. See J.P.S. Gearson, *Harold Macmillan and the Berlin Wall Crisis: The Limits of Interests and Force 1958–62* (Basingstoke, 1998), 75–8; H. Macmillan, *Riding the Storm, 1956–1959* (London 1971), 592–634; and for the international history of the entire Berlin crisis, see R. Steininger, *Der Mauerbau. Die Westmächte und Adenauer in der Berlinkrise 1958–1963* (Munich, 2001).

140. PRO: FO 800/673, letter Jebb, Paris, to Kirkpatrick, FO, 11/7/1955, with enclosed ten-page paper 'The Cold War and the Future'. For a later, much more sober paper by an unknown official, see FO 371/116 114, 'Brief for the Secretary of State's Tour, Autumn 1955: The Present State of the Cold War', undated.

141. See for example J. Weldes, *Constructing National Interests: The United States and the Cuban Missile Crisis* (Minneapolis, Minn., 1999); L.V. Scott, *Macmillan, Kennedy and the Cuban Missile Crisis: Political, Military, and Intelligence Aspects* (Basingstoke, 1999); A. Fursenko and T. Naftali, *'One Hell of a Gamble': Khrushchev, Castro, Kennedy, and the Cuban Missile Crisis, 1958–64* (London,

1997); M.J. White, *The Cuban Missile Crisis* (Basingstoke, 1996); J.A. Nathan (ed.), *The Cuban Missile Crisis Revisited* (New York, 1993); M.R. Beschloss, *The Crisis Years: Kennedy and Khrushchev, 1960–3* (London, 1991). For the second Berlin Crisis, see the literature in n. 139, above, and H.M. Catadul, *Kennedy and the Berlin Wall Crisis: A Case Study in US Decision Making* (Berlin, 1980); and on the double crisis Berlin–Cuba, see J.C. Ausland, *Kennedy, Khrushchev, and the Berlin-Cuba Crisis, 1961–4* (Oslo, 1996); also Richter, *Khrushchev's Double Bind*, 101ff., 129ff.; and L. Freedman, *Kennedy's Wars: Berlin, Cuba, Laos, and Vietnam* (Oxford, 2000).

142. See for good accounts O. Kendrick, *Kennedy, Macmillan, and the Nuclear-test Ban Debate, 1961–3* (Basingstoke, 1998); R.J. Terchek, *The Making of the Test Ban Treaty* (The Hague, 1970).

143. See for example R. L. Garthoff, *Détente and Confrontation: American-Soviet Relations from Nixon to Reagan*, revd edn (Washington, 1994), 123–4, 127–8.

144. See ibid., and also for example, H. Kissinger, *Diplomacy* (London 1994), ch. 28; A. de Tinguy, *US-Soviet Relations during the Détente* (New York, 1999); K.L. Nelson, *The Making of Détente: Soviet-American Relations in the Shadow of Vietnam* (Baltimore, Md., 1995); R.S. Litwak, *Détente and the Nixon Doctrine: American Foreign Policy and the Pursuit of Stability, 1969–76* (Cambridge, 1984); R.W. Stevenson, *The Rise and Fall of Détente: Relaxations of Tension in US-Soviet Relations. 1953–84* (Basingstoke, 1985); R. Davy, *European Détente: A Reappraisal* (London, 1992); J. van Oudenaren, *Détente in Europe: The Soviet Union and the West since 1953* (Durham, N.C., 1991); S.R. Ashton, *In Search of Détente: The Politics of East–West Relations since 1945* (Basingstoke, 1989). On *Ostpolitik* in particular, see W. Brandt, *My Life in Politics* (New York, 1992), ch. 3; W. E. Griffith, *The Ostpolitik of the Federal Republic of Germany* (Cambridge, Mass., 1978); R. Tilford (ed.), *The Ostpolitik and Political Change in Germany* (Farnborough, Hants., 1975); A. Stent, *From Embargo to Ostpolitik: the Political Economy of West German-Soviet Relations, 1955–80* (Cambridge, 1981); M. Uschner, *Die Ostpolitik der SPD: Sieg und Niederlage einer Strategie* (Berlin, 1991); P. Bender, *Die 'Neue Ostpolitik' und ihre Folgen: Vom Mauerbau bis zur Vereinigung*, 4th edn (Munich, 1996).

145. See FRUS 1952–4, Vol. 6, 1108–9: memorandum of a conversation between Eisenhower and Churchill, 26/6/1954.

146. Moran, *Struggle for Survival*, 660–1, 665, 681ff.: diary entries, 2/6/1955, 6/6/1955; 2/8/1955ff.; also for full details about Churchill's remaining years, see Gilbert, *Never Despair*, 1144ff.

147. Churchill had already accepted the prize in early 1954. For Churchill's visit to Aachen and the preparation of the visit which was originally planned for May or June 1955, see PRO: FO 371/118 189/WG 10151/1; also FO 371/118 190 (January–December, 1955); Moran, ibid., 696–8: diary entries, 6/5 and 14/5/1955; Gilbert, ibid., 1197. Later in the year, Churchill went again to Germany, this time on a private racing excursion to see his horses perform. See Gilbert, ibid., 1200–1.

148. For details, see PRO: FO 800/684, Macmillan, Geneva, to FO, No. 50, 20/7/1955 (also passed on to Churchill from Eden); FO to Moscow, No. 1370, 28/7/1955. For Adenauer's view of the international repercussions of the Soviet visit to London, see his *Erinnerungen 1955–59*, 128–32; and for the dramatic 20th Party Congress in Moscow, pp. 109–13.

149. See Moran, *Struggle for Survival*, 694–5: diary entry, 22/4/1956.

150. N. Khrushchev, *Khrushchev Remembers* (Boston, 1970), 410–11.

151. For his final visit to the U.S., see Gilbert, *Never Despair*, 1293–6; A. Montague Browne, *Long Sunset: Memoirs of Winston Churchill's Last Private Secretary* (London, 1995), 260–3.

152. For detailed information about the last ten years of Churchill's life, see Gilbert, ibid., 1131ff.; Montague Browne, ibid., 187ff.; Soames, *Clementine Churchill*, 454ff.

153. Gilbert, ibid., 1306, 1316.

154. See Gilbert, ibid., 1225; for Churchill's views on and reactions to the Suez Crisis, see ibid., 1201ff. For Macmillan's policy, see the interesting articles in R. Aldous and S. Lee (eds), *Harold Macmillan and Britain's World Role* (Basingstoke, 1996); and R. Aldous and S. Lee (eds), *Harold Macmillan: Aspects of a Political Life* (Basingstoke, 1999), esp. chs 3, 6, 13, 15; J. Turner, *Macmillan* (London, 1994), chs 6–9; A. Horne, *Harold Macmillan, Vol. 2: 1957–1986* (London, 1989), 29ff.

155. See N. Rose, *Churchill: An Unruly Life* (London, 1994), 341.

CONCLUSION: CHURCHILL'S LEGACY

1. Quote: P. Stansky and P. Wainright, 'Winston Leonard Spencer Churchill', in R.R. Eccleshall and G. Walker (eds), *Biographical Dictionary of British Prime Ministers* (London, 1998), 304. For details of the world-wide mourning and Churchill's funeral, see M. Gilbert, *Winston S. Churchill, Vol. 8:*

Never Despair, 1945–1965, paperback edn (London, 1990), 1360–4. Eisenhower, the former American President, also attended the funeral and read one of the lessons. Finally he had come to London though in 1953–5 he had constantly refused Churchill's requests to do so.

2. Even in the summer of 1955 Eisenhower's psychological warfare advisers Nelson Rockefeller and Walt Rostow were still talking of the possibility of the Free World's 'victory in the Cold War' and the continued development of overwhelming American and western military strength so that the Cold War could be won without the enemy daring to resort to war. See EL: Ann Whitman File, Administration Series, Box 30, Rockefeller's memoranda to the President, 13/6/1955; ibid., letter Rostow to Rockefeller, 17/6/1955. See also ibid., Ann Whitman File, Miscellaneous Series, 'Report of the Quantico Vulnerabilities Panel', 10/6/1955.

3. See for example David Carlton's 'Conclusion' in his *Churchill and the Soviet Union* (Manchester, 2000), 200–19; also his ch 7.

4. For the Berlin negotiations in the early 1970s, see D.M. Keithly, *Breakthrough in the Ostpolitik: The 1971 Quadripartite Agreement* (Boulder, Colo., 1986); P. Bender, *Die 'Neue Ostpolitik' und ihre Folgen: Vom Mauerbau bis zur Vereinigung*, 4th edn (Munich, 1996), 185–93; and also A. Wilkens, *Der unstete Nachbar. Frankreich, die deutsche Ostpolitik und die Berliner Vier-Mächte-Verhandlungen, 1969–1974* (Munich, 1990). For the two-plus-four negotiations in 1990, see H.J. Küsters, *Der Integrationsfriede. Viermächte-Verhandlungen über die Friedensregelung mit Deutschland 1945–1990* (Munich, 2000), 827ff.; and C.S. Maier, *Dissolution: The Crisis of Communism and the End of East Germany* (Princeton, N.J., 1997), 244–84; also P. Zelikow and C. Rice, *Germany Unified and Europe Transformed: A Study in Statecraft* (Cambridge, Mass. 1995), 149ff.

5. See N. Khrushchev, *Khrushchev Remembers: The Last Testament* (Boston, 1974), 362.

6. For an excellent overview, from a left-of-centre point of view, see N. Tiratsoo (ed.), *From Blitz to Blair: A New History of Britain since 1939* (London, 1997); R. Hattersley, *Fifty Years On: A Prejudiced History of Britain since the War* (London, 1997). For a more conservative outlook focusing on the Attlee government, see C. Barnett, *The Lost Victory: British Dreams, British Realities, 1945–50* (London, 1995); also Barnett's interesting *The Verdict of Peace: Britain between her Yesterday and the Future* (London, 2001); for a re-interpretation from a political science angle, see D. Marsh et al. (eds), *Postwar British Politics in Perspective* (Oxford, 1999). For a very critical account of British foreign policy, see M. Curtis, *The Ambiguities of Power: British Foreign Policy since 1945* (London, 1995).

7. See for example H. Young, *This Blessed Plot: Britain and Europe from Churchill to Blair* (London, 1998), 99ff.; D. Reynolds, *Britannia Overruled: British Policy and World Power in the 20th Century* (London, 1991), chs 7–10; W. Kaiser, *Using Europe. Abusing the Europeans: Britain and European Integration, 1945–63* (Basingstoke, 1996); J. Ellison, *Threatening Europe: Britain and the Creation of the European Community, 1955–58* (Basingstoke, 2000); J. Tratt, *The Macmillan Government and Europe: A Study in the Process of Policy Development* (New York, 1996); J. Campbell, *Edward Heath: A Biography* (London, 1993), 334ff.; S. Ball and A. Seldon (eds), *The Heath Government: A Reappraisal* (London, 1996). For further literature see my introduction in K. Larres (ed. with E. Meehan), *Uneasy Allies: British-German Relations and European Integration* (Oxford, 2000), esp. 4, n. 9.

8. See D. Brinkley, 'Dean Acheson and the "special relationship": The West Point speech of December 1962', *Historical Journal* 33 (1990), 599–608 (the relevant paragraph of the speech is quoted on p. 601). See also D. Sanders, *Losing an Empire, Finding a Role* (Basingstoke, 1990), esp. ch. 5.

9. As already mentioned in the introduction to this book, this phrase was contained in the letter of acceptance that Randolph Churchill read on his father's behalf when Churchill received honorary American citizenship from President Kennedy in 1963. See A.M. Schlesinger Jr, 'History's Impressario', Keynote address to the International Churchill Society, Boston, 28 October 1995 [webpage: www.winstonchurchill.org/p94rschles.htm]. For greater details of this occasion, see A.M. Schlesinger Jr, *A Life in the Twentieth Century: Innocent Beginnings, 1917–1950* (Boston, 2000), 385–6.

10. Here I agree with John Charmley's argument that 'by encouraging the belief that the road to power lay through Washington, Churchill's myth encouraged British statesmen, including himself during his peacetime premiership, to neglect Europe in favour of the special relationship'. See Charmley, 'Churchill and the American Alliance', in *Transactions of the Royal Historical Society*, 6th series, Vol. XI (Cambridge, 2001), 370–1.

Bibliography

Primary Sources

National Archives

Public Record Office, London/Kew

ADM 116   Records of the Admiralty, Naval Forces, Royal Marines ...

Records of the Cabinet Office

CAB 21   Registered Files, 1916–65.
CAB 37   Photographic Copies of Cabinet Papers
CAB 65   War Cabinet and Cabinet: Minutes: WM and CM Series
CAB 66   War Cabinet and Cabinet: Memoranda: WP and CP Series
CAB 80   War Cabinet and Cabinet: Chiefs of Staff Committee. Memoranda
CAB 81   War Cabinet and Cabinet: Committees and Sub-committees of the Chiefs of Staff Committee
CAB 127   Cabinet Office: Private Collections of Ministers' and Officials' Papers
CAB 128   Minutes: CM and CC Series
CAB 129   Memoranda: CP and C Series
CAB 131   Defence Committee: Minutes and Papers (DO, D and DC Series)
CAB 133   Commonwealth and International Conferences and Ministerial Visits to and from the UK
CAB 134   Miscellaneous Committees: Minutes and Papers (General Series)

Foreign Office Files

FO 93   Protocols of Treaties
FO 244   Embassy and Consulates: Germany (formerly Prussia). General Correspondence
FO 371   Foreign Office: General Correspondence
FO 800   Foreign Office: Private Papers Collections
FO 954   Private Papers of Sir Anthony Eden, Earl of Avon
FO 975   Information Research Department: Information Reports

Prime Minister's Office

PREM 3   Operational Correspondence and Papers
PREM 4   Confidential Correspondence and Papers
PREM 11 Correspondence and Papers, 1951–64.

National Archives, Washington, D.C.

Central Files. Record Group 59
Decimal Files and Lot Files (State Dept. Files) including PPS Records

Private Papers

Dean Acheson Papers: Truman Presidential Library, Independence, Missouri.
Avon Papers (papers of Anthony Eden): BUA
Lord Beaverbrook Papers: HL
Charles Bohlen Papers: LOC
R.A. Butler Papers: Trinity College, Cambridge University, Cambridge
Alexander Cadagon Papers: Churchill College, Cambridge University, Cambridge
John Colville Papers: Churchill College, Cambridge University, Cambridge
Winston S. Churchill Papers: Churchill College, Cambridge University, Cambridge
Conservative Party Archives: BL
Allen Dulles Papers: PUA
John F. Dulles Papers: PUA
John F. Dulles Papers: EL – Subject Series; Telephone Conversations; Draft of Presidential Correspondence
Anthony Eden Papers: PRO
Dwight D. Eisenhower Papers: EL
    Ann Whitman Files: Administrative Series; International Series; Dulles-Herter Series; Ann C. Whitman Diary
    White House Office: Confidential File and National Security Office and Affairs
General Walter Elliot Papers: King's College London: Liddell–Hart-Archive Centre
Fife–Clark (William Clark) Papers: Churchill College, Cambridge University, Cambridge
Averell W. Harriman Papers: LOC
Lord Ismay Papers: King's College, London: Liddell–Hart-Archive Centre
C.D. Jackson Papers: EL
Liddell–Hart Papers: King's College, London: Liddell–Hart-Archive Centre
Selwyn Lloyd Papers: PRO
Lord Swinton Papers: Churchill College, Cambridge University, Cambridge
Harry S. Truman Papers: Truman Presidential Library, Independence, Missouri
Lord Woolton Papers: BL

Published Collections of Documents

Akten zur Auswärtigen Politik der Bundesrepublik Deutschland; main editor: Hans-Peter Schwarz on behalf of the Auswärtige Amt of the Federal Republic of Germany. Munich: R. Oldenbourg.
    Vol. 1950: ed. by Rainer A. Blasius with Daniel Kosthorst and Michael F. Feldkamp (1997);
    Vol. 1951: ed. by Rainer A. Blasius with Matthias Jaroch (1999).
Akten zur Auswärtigen Politik der Bundesrepublik Deutschland. Adenauer und die Hohen Kommissare:
    Vol. 1: *1951* and Vol. 2: *1952* (both vols ed. by Hans-Peter Schwarz and Reiner Pommerin with F.L. Kroll and M. Nebelin). Munich: R. Oldenbourg, 1989–90.
Booms, Hans (ed.). *Die Kabinettsprotokolle der Bundesregierung.* Vol. 5: *1952* (ed. by Kai von Jena); Vol. 6: *1953* (ed. by Ulrich Enders and Konrad Reiser). Boppard: Boldt, 1989.
British Documents on the Origins of the War, 1898–1914 (ed. by G.P. Gooch and H.W.V. Temperley). London: H.M.S.O.
    Vol. 6: *Anglo-German Tension, Armaments and Negotiations, 1907–12* (1930).
    Vol. 7: *The Agadir Crisis* (1932). Vol. 10, Part 2: *The Last Years of Peace* (1938).
British Documents on Foreign Affairs: Reports and Papers from the Foreign Office Confidential Print. Part I, Series F, Vol. 21: *Germany, 1909–1914* (ed. by David Stevenson; general editors: K. Bourne and D.C. Watt). Frederick, MD.: University Publications of America, 1990.
Buchstab, Günter (ed.). *Adenauer, 'Es musste alles neu gemacht werden'. Die Protokolle des CDU-Bundesvorstandes 1950–1953.* Stuttgart: Klett-Cotta, 1986.
Chandler, Alfred D. and Galambos, Louis (eds) *The Papers of Dwight D. Eisenhower.* Vol. 7–9: *The Chief of Staff.* Baltimore, Md.: Johns Hopkins University Press, 1978.
Charlton, Michael. *The Price of Victory.* London: British Broadcasting Corporation, 1983.
Churchill, Randolph S. (ed.) *Winston S. Churchill. The Official Biography: Companion Volumes.* London:

Heinemann. Vol. 1, Part I: *1874–1896;* Part II: *1896–1900* (1967). Vol. 2: Part I: *1901–1907;* Part II: *1907–1911;* Part III: *1911–1914* (1969).

Deutscher Bundestag, *Verhandlungen der I. Wahlperiode, Stenographische Berichte,* Vol. 17, 278th session, 1/7/1953, 13872 (Bonn, 1953).

Documents on British Policy Overseas. London: H.M.S.O. Series I, Vol. 1: *The Conference at Potsdam, July–August 1945* (ed. by R. Butler and R.E. Pelly with H.J. Yasamee. 1984). Vol. 2: *Conferences and Conversations 1945. London, Washington and Moscow* (ed. by R. Bullen and M.E. Pelly with H.J. Yasamee and G. Bennett. 1985). Vol. 3: *Britain and America: Negotiations of the United States Loan, 3 August–7 December, 1945* (ed. by R. Bullen and M.E. Pelly with H.J. Yasamee and G. Bennett. 1986). Vol. 4: *Britain and America: Atomic Energy, Bases and Food, 12 December 1945–31 July 1946* (ed. by R. Bullen and M.E. Pelly with H.J. Yasamee and G. Bennett. 1987).

'Dokumente zur Auseinandersetzung in der SED 1953', *Beiträge zur Geschichte der Arbeiterbewegung* 32/5 (1990), 655–72.

'Ein Dokument von grosser historischer Bedeutung vom Mai 1953', *Beiträge zur Geschichte der Arbeiterbewegung* 32/5 (1990), 648–54.

Drew, S. Nelson (ed.). *NSC-68: Forging the Strategy of Containment* (with analyses by Paul H. Nitze) Washington, DC: National Defense University Press, 1994 [mostly a selection of documents].

Foreign Relations of the United States. Diplomatic Papers (Dept. of State: Office of the Historian; Washington, D.C.: Government Printing Office): *The Paris Peace Conference, 1919, Vol. 11 (1945); The Conferences at Cairo and Tehran, 1943 (1961); 1943,* Vol. 2: *Europe (1964); The Conferences at Washington and Quebec, 1943* (1970); *1943:* Vol. 3: *The British Commonwealth, Eastern Europe and the Far East* (1964); *The Conference of Berlin (The Potsdam Conference), 1945* (1960); *1946,* Vol. 1: *General, The United Nations* (1972); *1948,* Vol. 4: *Eastern Europe, The Soviet Union* (1974); *1949,* Vol. 3: *Council of Foreign Ministers, Germany and Austria* (1975); *1951,* Vol. 4: (in two parts): *Europe. Political and Economic Developments* (1985); *1952–1954, Vol. 2* (in two parts*): National Security Affairs* (1984); *1952–1954,* Vol. 5 (in two parts): *Western European Security* (1983); *1952–1954,* Vol. 6 (in two parts): *Western Europe and Canada* (1986); *1952–1954,* Vol. 7 (in two parts): *Germany and Austria* (1986); *1952–1954,* Vol. 8: *Eastern Europe, Soviet Union, Eastern Mediterranean* (1988); *1952–1954,* Vol. 13 (in two parts): *Indochina* (1982); *1955–1957,* Vol. 4: *Western European Security and Integration* (1986); *1955–1957,* Vol. 5: *Austrian State Treaty; Summit and Foreign Ministers Meetings, 1955* (1988).

Galambos, Louis (ed.). *The Papers of Dwight D. Eisenhower.* Vols 12–13: *NATO and the Campaign of 1952.* Baltimore, MD: Johns Hopkins University Press, 1989.

Gilbert, Martin (ed.). *Winston S. Churchill. The Official Biography: Companion Volumes.* London: Heinemann. Vol. 3, Part I: *Documents, July 1914–April 1915;* Part II: *Documents, May 1915–December 1916* (1972). Vol. 4, Part I: *Documents January 1917–June 1919;* Part II: *Documents, July 1919–March 1921;* Part III: *April 1921–November 1922* (1977). Vol. 5, Part I: *Documents, The Exchequer Years, 1922–1929* (1979); Part II: *Documents, The Wilderness Years, 1929–1935* (1981); Part III: *Documents, The Coming of War, 1936–1939* (1982).

Gilbert, Martin (ed.). *The Churchill War Papers.* London: Heinemann. Vol. 1: *At the Admiralty: September 1939–May 1940* (1993); Vol. 2: *Never Surrender: May 1940–December 1940* (1994); *The Ever-Widening War, 1941* (2000).

Die Grosse Politik der europäischen Kabinette, 1871–1914: Sammlung der diplomatischen Akten des Auswärtigen Amtes (ed. by J. Lepsius, A. Mendelssohn Bartholdy and F. Thimme). Berlin: Deutsche Verlagsgesellschaft für Politik und Geschichte, 1922–27. Vol. 29: *Die Zweite Marokkokrise 1911* (1925); Vol. 31: *Das Scheitern der Haldane-Mission und ihre Rückwirkung auf die Tripelentente 1911–1912* (1926); Vol. 39: *Das Nahen des Weltkrieges 1912–1914* (1926).

Her Majesty's Government: *Command Papers,* Fourth Series. H.M.S.O.: Cmd.8501, 8551, 8610 (all 1952), 8838 (1953), 9080 (1954).

House of Commons, London: *Parliamentary Debates* (Hansard). Fourth Series and Fifth Series.

House of Lords, London: *Parliamentary Debates* (Hansard). Fifth Series.

Jäckel, Eberhard (ed.). *Die Deutsche Frage 1952–1956: Notenwechsel und Konferenzdokumente der Vier Mächte.* Frankfurt/M.: A. Metzner, 1957.

Keesing's Contemporary Archive. (London: Keesing's Ltd.), Vol. 6: *1946–48;* Vol. 7: *1948–50;* Vol. 8: *1950–52;* Vol. 9: *1953–54.*

Lipgens, Walter (ed.). *Europa-Föderationspläne der Widerstandsbewegungen 1940–1945: Eine Dokumentation.* Munich: R. Oldenbourg, 1968.

Lipgens, Walter (ed.). *Documents on the History of European Integration.* Vol. 2. Berlin: De Gruyter, 1985.

Münch, Ingo von (ed.). *Dokumente des Geteilten Deutschland: Quellentexte zur Rechtslage des Deutschen Reiches, der Bundesrepublik Deutschland und der Deutschen Demokratischen Republik.* Vol. 1. Stuttgart: Kröner, 1968.

Ostermann, Christian F. (ed.), *The Post-Stalin Succession Struggle and the 17 June Uprising in East Germany: The Hidden History* [unpubl., documentary reader] Washington, DC., 1996.

Ostermann, Christian F. (ed.). '"This is Not a Politburo but a Madhouse": The Post-Stalin Succession Struggle ...' [selection of Soviet, German and Hungarian documents], *Cold War International History Bulletin* (CWIHB) 10 (March 1998), 72–110.

Ostermann, Christian F. (ed.). *Uprising in East Germany 1953: The Cold War, the German Question, and the First Major Upheaval behind the Iron Curtain.* National Security Archive Cold War Readers. Budapest/New York: Central European University Press, 2001.

Ross, Graham. *The Foreign Office and the Kremlin: British Documents on Anglo-Soviet Relations 1941–45.* Cambridge/New York: Cambridge University Press, 1984.

Royal Institute of International Affairs, London (Chatham House). *Documents on International Affairs: 1947–48* (ed. by Margaret Carlyle, 1952); *1949–50* (ed. by Margaret Carlyle, 1951); *1951* (ed. by Denise Folliot, 1954); *1952* (ed. by Denise Folliot, 1955); *1953* (ed. by Denise Folliot, 1956); *1954* (ed. by Denise Folliot, 1957); *1955* (ed. by Noble Frankland with Patricia Woodcock, 1958).

Rzheshevsky, Oleg A. *War and Diplomacy: The Making of the Grand Alliance. Documents from Stalin's Archives. Edited with a Commentary.* Amsterdam: Harwood Academic Publishers, 1995.

Scherstjanoi, Elke. 'Die sowjetische Deutschlandpolitik nach Stalins Tod 1953. Neue Dokumente aus dem Archiv des Moskauer Außenministeriums', *Vierteljahrshefte für Zeitgeschichte* 46 (1998), 497–549.

Sherwood, Robert E. *The White House Papers of Harry L. Hopkins: An Intimate History.* London: Eyre & Spottiswoode, 1949.

Stickle, D.M. (ed.), *The Beria Affair: The Secret Transcripts of the Meetings Signalling the End of Stalinism.* New York: Nova Science Publishers, 1992.

Interviews

Sir Douglas Dodds-Parker
Sir William Hayter
Mr Harry Hohler
Sir Anthony Nutting
Sir Roger Makins (Lord Sherfield)
Mr Ian Mikado
Sir Anthony Montague Browne
Sir Frank Roberts
Sir David Pitblado

Correspondence and Speeches

Baring, Arnulf (ed.). *Sehr verehrter Herr Bundeskanzler! Heinrich von Brentano im Briefwechsel mit Konrad Adenauer 1949–1964.* Hamburg: Hoffmann und Campe, 1974.

Boyle, Peter G. (ed.). *The Churchill-Eisenhower Correspondence, 1953–1955.* Chapel Hill: University of North Carolina Press, 1990.

Bundy, McGeorge (ed.). *The Pattern of Responsibility: Edited from the Record of the Secretary of State Dean Acheson.* Boston: Houghton Mifflin, 1952.

Churchill, Randolph, S. (ed.). *Winston S. Churchill. The Sinews of Peace: Post-War Speeches.* London: Cassell, 1948.

Churchill, Randolph S. (ed.). *Winston S. Churchill. Europe Unite: Speeches, 1947 and 1948.* London: Cassell, 1950.

Churchill, Randolph S. (ed.). *Winston S. Churchill. In the Balance: Speeches, 1949 and 1950.* London: Cassell, 1951.

Cockett, Richard (ed.). *My Dear Max: The Letters of Brendan Bracken to Lord Beaverbrook, 1925–1958.* London: Historians' Press, 1990.

Eade, Charles (ed.). *The War Speeches of Winston S. Churchill: Vol. 2: Onwards to Victory, 1943.* London: Cassell, 1944.

Halle, Kay. *Winston Churchill on America and Britain: A Selection of his Thoughts on Anglo-American Relations.* New York, 1970.

Griffith, Robert (ed.). *Ike's Letters to a Friend, 1941–1958.* Lawrence, Kan.: University Press of Kansas, 1984.

James, Robert Rhodes (ed.). *Winston S. Churchill: His Complete Speeches, 1897–1963.* 8 vols. London/New York: Chelsea House in association with Bowker, 1974. Vol. 7: 1940–1949; Vol. 8: 1950–1963

Kimball Warren, F. (ed.) *Churchill and Roosevelt: The Complete Correspondence. Vol. 1: Alliance Emerging, 1933–1942; Vol. 2: Alliance Forged, November 1942–February 1944; Vol. 3: Alliance Declining, February 1944–April 1945.* London: Collins, 1984.

McLellan, David S. and David C. Acheson (eds). *Among Friends: Personal Letters of Dean Acheson.* New York: Dodd Mead, 1980.

Ministry of Foreign Affairs of the USSR (ed.). *Correspondence between the Chairman of the Council of Ministers of the USSR and the Presidents of the USA and the Prime Ministers of Great Britain during the Great Patriotic War of 1941–1945.* Moscow: Progress, 1957.

Morsey, Rudolf and Hans-Peter Schwarz (eds), in association with Hans Peter Mensing, *Konrad Adenauer. Briefe 1951–1953.* Berlin: Siedler, 1987.

Pfleiderer, Karl Georg. *Politik für Deutschland: Reden und Aufsätze 1948–1956.* Stuttgart: Deutsche Verlags-Anstalt, 1961.

Pinder, John. *Altiero Spinelli and the British Federalists: Writings by Beveridge, Robbins and Spinelli, 1937–1943.* London: Federal Trust for Education & Research, 1998.

Poen, Monte M. (ed.). *Strictly Personal and Confidential: The Letters Harry Truman Never Mailed.* Boston: Little, Brown, 1982.

Public Papers of the Presidents of the USA: Dwight D. Eisenhower, 1953/1954/1955: Containing the Public Messages, Speeches, and Statements of the President. Washington, DC: Government Printing Office, 1959–60.

Schwarz, Hans-Peter and Rudolf Morsey (eds), in association with Hanns Jürgen Küsters. *Adenauer. Teegespräche 1950–1954.* 2nd edn, Berlin: Siedler, 1985.

Soames, Mary (ed.). *Speaking for Themselves: The Personal Letters of Winston and Clementine Churchill.* London/New York: Doubleday, 1998; paperback edn, 1999.

Victor (ed.). *Mon Alié Staline de Winston Churchill* [statements on Russia made by W.L.S. Churchill between 1919 and 1940. With reproduction of political cartoons from British and American newspapers]. Paris, 1942.

Vital Speeches of the Day: 1950 (New York: The City News Pub. Co., 1950).

Memoirs, Autobiographies, and Diaries

Acheson, Dean. *Present at the Creation: My Years in the State Department.* New York; London: W.W. Norton, 1969.

Adams, Sherman. *First-Hand Report: The Inside Story of the Eisenhower Administration.* New York: Harper, 1961

Adenauer, Konrad. *Erinnerungen 1945–1953.* Stuttgart: Deutsche Verlags-Anstalt, 1965 (English edn, trans. by Beate Ruhm von Oppen, *Memoirs, 1945–1953,* London: Weidenfeld and Nicolson, 1966).

Adenauer, Konrad. *Erinnerungen 1953–1955.* Stuttgart: Deutsche Verlags-Anstalt, 1966.

Adenauer, Konrad. *Erinnerungen 1955–1959.* Stuttgart: Deutsche Verlags-Anstalt, 1967.

Asquith, Herbert H. *The Genesis of the War.* London: Cassell, 1923.

Auriol, Vincent. *Journal du Septennat 1947–1954.* Vol. VII: 1953–54. Paris: Armand Colin, 1971.

Beam, Jacob D. *Multiple Exposure: An American Ambassador's Unique Perspective on East–West Issues.* New York: Norton, 1978.

Bethmann Hollweg, Theodor von. *Reflections on the World War* (trans. from the German by G. Young). London: Thornton Butterworth, 1920.

Blankenhorn, Herbert. *Verständnis und Verständigung: Blätter eines Politischen Tagebuchs 1949 bis 1979.* Frankfurt/M.: Propyläen, 1980.

Bohlen, Charles E. *Witness to History, 1929–1969.* London: Norton, 1973.

Bonham Carter, Violet. *Winston Churchill As I Knew Him.* London: Eyre & Spottiswoode, 1965.

Bonham Carter, Mark and Mark Pottle. *Lantern Slides: The Diaries and Letters of Violet Bonham Carter, 1904–1914.* London: Weidenfeld and Nicolson, 1996.

Boothby, Robert John Graham. *My Yesterday, Your Tomorrow.* London: Hutchinson, 1962.

Brandt, Heinz. *Ein Traum der nicht entführbar ist. Mein Weg zwischen Ost und West.* 2nd edn, Berlin: Berlin Verlag, 1977.

Brandt, Willy. *My Life in Politics.* New York/London: Hamish Hamilton, 1992.

Butler (Lord), Richard Austen. *The Art of the Possible: The Memoirs of Lord Butler, K.G., C.H.* London: Hamish Hamilton, 1971.

Byrnes, James Francis. *Speaking Frankly.* London: Heinemann, 1947.

Churchill, Winston. *The Boer War: London to Ladysmith Via Pretoria; Ian Hamilton's March.* London: Leo Cooper, 1989.

Churchill, Winston. *The Story of the Malakand Field Force: An Episode of Frontier War*. Longman's Colonial Library. London: Longmans Green, 1898.

Churchill, Winston. *The River War: an Historical Account of the Reconquest of the Soudan*. London, New York and Bombay: Longmans Green, 1899.

Churchill, Winston S. *The World Crisis*. 6 vols (London: Thornton Butterworth, 1923–31. Vol. 1: *1911–1914* (1923); Vol. 2: *1915* (1923); Vol. 3: *1916–1918, Part I* (1927); Vol. 4: *1916–1918, Part II* (1927); Vol. 5: *The Aftermath* (1929); Vol. 6: *The Eastern Front* (1931).

Churchill, Winston. *My Early Life: A Roving Commission*. London: Butterworth, 1930.

Churchill, Winston. *Thoughts and Adventures*. London: Thornton Butterworth, 1932.

Churchill, Winston S. 'The Ex-Kaiser', in Churchill, Winston S., *Great Contemporaries* (London: Leo Cooper, 1990), 12–25 (first publ., London: Thornton Butterworth, 1937).

Churchill, Winston S. *The Second World War*, 6 vols. Vol. 1: *The Gathering Storm*; Vol. 2: *Their Finest Hour*; Vol. 3: *The Grand Alliance*; Vol. 4: *The Hinge of Fate*; Vol. 5: *Closing the Ring*; Vol. 6: *Triumph and Tragedy*. London: Cassell, 1948–54.

Clifford, Clark, M. (with Richard C. Holbrooke). *Counsel to the President: A Memoir*. New York: Random House, 1991.

Colville, John. 'The Personality of Sir Winston Churchill', in Kemper III, R. Crosby (ed.), *Winston Churchill: Resolution, Defiance, Magnanimity, Good Will*. Columbia, Mo.: University of Missouri Press, 1996, 108–25.

Colville, John. *The Fringes of Power: 10 Downing Street Diaries, 1939–1955*. London: Hodder & Stoughton, 1985.

Conant, James B. *My Several Lives: Memoirs of a Social Inventor*. New York: Harper & Row, 1970.

Coudenhove-Kalergi, Richard Nicolaus. *Crusade for Pan-Europe: Autobiography of a Man and a Movement*. New York: Putnam, 1943.

Coudenhove-Kalergi, Richard Nicolaus. *An Idea Conquers the World* (with a Preface by Sir Winston Churchill). London: Hutchinson, 1953.

Cutler, Robert. *No Time for Rest*. Boston: Little, Brown, 1966.

Dalton, Hugh. *High Tide and After: Memoirs, 1945–1960*. London: F. Muller, 1962.

Djilas, Milovan. *Conversations with Stalin* (translated by M.B. Petrovich). London: Penguin, 1963.

Dodds-Parker, Douglas. *Political Eunuch*. Ascot, Berks.: Springwood Books, 1986.

Eden, Anthony (Lord Avon). *Full Circle. The Eden Memoirs*. London: Cassell, 1960.

Eden, Anthony (Lord Avon). *Facing the Dictators. The Eden Memoirs*. London: Cassell, 1962.

Eden, Anthony (Lord Avon). *The Reckoning. The Eden Memoirs*. London: Cassell, 1965.

Eisenhower, Dwight D. *The White House Years*. Vol. 1: *Mandate for Change, 1953–1956*. London: Heinemann, 1963.

Ferrell, Robert H. (ed.). *The Eisenhower Diaries*. New York: W.W. Norton, 1981.

Ferrell, Robert H. (ed.). *The Diary of James C. Hagerty: Eisenhower in Mid-Course 1954–1955*. Bloomington: Indiana University Press, 1983.

Grewe Wilhelm, G. *Rückblenden, 1976–1951*. Frankfurt/M.: Propyläen, 1979.

Grey, Edward. *Twenty-Five Years, 1892–1916*. New York: Frederick A. Stokes, 1925.

Gromyko, Andrei Andreevich. *Memories* (trans. from the Russian by H. Shukman). London: Hutchinson, 1989.

Haldane, (Lord) Richard B. *Before the War*. London/New York: Cassell, 1920.

Haldane, (Lord) Richard B. *An Autobiography*. London: Hodder & Stoughton, 1929.

Hanfstaengl, Ernst. *Hitler: The Missing Years*. London: Eyre & Spottiswoode, 1957 (repr. New York: Arcade Pub./Little, Brown, 1994).

Harriman, W. Averell, and Elie Abel. *Special Envoy to Churchill and Stalin, 1941–1946*. New York: Random House, 1975.

Hayter, William. *The Kremlin and the Embassy*. London: Hodder & Stoughton, 1966.

Hayter, William. *A Double Life*. London: Hamilton, 1974.

Hughes Emmet, John. *The Ordeal of Power: A Political Memoir of the Eisenhower Years*. London: Macmillan, 1963.

Hull, Cordell. *The Memoirs of Cordell Hull: Vol. 2*. London: Hodder & Stoughton, 1948.

Jebb, Gladwyn Hubert. *The Memoirs of Lord Gladwyn*. London: Weidenfeld and Nicolson, 1972.

Kennan George, F. *Memoirs, 1925–1950*. London: Hutchinson, 1968.

Kennan George, F. *Memoirs, 1950–1963*. Boston: Little, Brown, 1972.

Khrushchev, Nikita Sergeevich. *Khrushchev Remembers* (trans. and ed. by Edward Crankshaw and Strobe Talbott). Boston: Little, Brown, 1970.

Khrushchev, Nikita Sergeevich. *Khrushchev Remembers: the Last Testament* (trans. and ed. by Strobe Talbott). Boston: Little, Brown, 1974.

Khrushchev, Nikita Sergeevich. *Khrushchev Remembers: The Glasnost Tapes* (trans. and ed. by Jerrold L. Schecter and Vyacheslav V. Luchkov). Boston: Little, Brown, 1990.

Larres, Klaus (ed.), 'Witness Seminar: British Attitudes to German Rearmament and Reunification in the 1950s'. *Contemporary Record* 5/2 (1991), 291–320.

Lichnowsky, (Prince) Karl Max. *Heading for the Abyss: Reminiscences* (translated from the German by F. Sefton Delmer). London: Constable, 1928.

Lie, Trygve. *In the Cause of Peace: Seven Years with the United Nations.* New York: Macmillan, 1954.

Lloyd George, David. *War Memoirs.* London: I. Nicholson & Watson. Vol. 1. (1933), Vol. 3 (1934), Vol. 6 (1936).

Macmillan, Harold. *Tides of Fortune: 1945–1955.* Memoirs, Vol. 3. London: Macmillan, 1969.

Macmillan, Harold. *Riding the Storm, 1956–1959.* Memoirs, Vol. 4. London: Macmillan, 1971.

Massigli, René L.D. *Une Comédie des Erreurs, 1943–1956: Souvenirs et Réflexions sur une étape de la Construction Européenne.* Paris: Plon, 1978.

Monnet, Jean. *Mémoires.* Paris: Fayard, 1976.

Montague Browne, Anthony. *Long Sunset: Memoirs of Winston Churchill's Last Private Secretary.* London: Cassell, 1995.

Moran, (Lord) Charles McMoran Wilson. *Winston Churchill: The Struggle for Survival 1940–1965: Taken from the Diaries of Lord Moran.* London: Constable, 1966.

Murphy, Robert, D. *Diplomat Among Warriors.* Garden City, N.Y.: Doubleday, 1964.

Nicolson, Nigel (ed.). *The Diaries and Letters of Harold Nicolson, 1945–1962.* London: Collins, 1968.

Nitze, Paul H. (with Ann M. Smith and Steven L. Rearden). *From Hiroshima to Glasnost: At the Centre of Decision. A Memoir.* London: Weidenfeld and Nicolson, 1989.

Nutting, Anthony. 'Sir Anthony Eden', in Herbert van Thal (ed.), *The Prime Ministers*, Vol. 2 (London: Allen and Unwin, 1975), 327–43.

Nutting, Anthony. *Europe Will Not Wait: A Warning and a Way Out.* London: Hollis & Carter, 1960.

Pearson, Drew. *Diaries, 1949–1959* (ed. by Tyler Abell). London: Cape, 1974.

Pimlott, Ben (ed.). *The Political Diary of Hugh Dalton 1918–40, 1945–60.* London: Cape, 1986.

Pottle, Mark (ed.). *Daring to Hope: The Diaries and Letters of Violet Bonham Carter, 1946–1969.* London: Weidenfeld and Nicolson, 2000.

Rapoport, Yakov A. L. *The Doctors' Plot: Stalin's Last Crime* (translated from the Russian). London: Fourth Estate, 1991.

Resis, Albert (ed.) *Molotov Remembers: Inside Kremlin Politics. Conversations with Felix Chuev.* Chicago: I.R. Dee, 1993.

Roberts, Frank. *Dealing with Dictators: The Destruction and Revival of Europe 1930–70.* London: Weidenfeld and Nicolson, 1991.

Roosevelt, Elliott. *As He Saw It.* New York: Duell Sloan & Pearce, 1946.

Salisbury, Harrison Evans. *Moscow Journal: The End of Stalin.* Chicago, Ill.: University of Chicago Press, 1961.

Schenk, Fritz. *Im Vorzimmer der Diktatur. Zwölf Jahre Pankow.* Revised edn. Würzburg: Naumann, 1989.

Schirdewan, Karl. *Ein Jahrhundert Leben. Erinnerungen und Visionen. Autobiographie.* Berlin: Edition Ost, 1998.

Schlesinger, Arthur M. Jr. *A Life in the Twentieth Century: Innocent Beginnings, 1917–1950.* Boston: Houghton Mifflin, 2000.

Schmid, Carlo. *Erinnerungen.* Bern: Scherz, 1979.

Semenov, Vladimir S. (German: Semjonow, V.S.). *Von Stalin bis Gorbatschow. Ein halbes Jahrhundert in diplomatischer Mission 1939–1991* (trans. from the Russian by H. and H. Ettinger). Berlin: Nicolai, 1995.

Shuckburgh, Evelyn. *Descent to Suez: Diaries 1951–56* (selected by John Charmley) London: Weidenfeld and Nicolson, 1986.

Smith, Walter Bedell. *Moscow Mission, 1946–1949.* Melbourne/London: Heinemann, 1950 (U.S. edn, publ. as *My Three Years in Moscow.* Philadelphia: Lippincott, 1949).

Stassen, Harold Edward and Marshall Houts. *Eisenhower: Turning the World toward Peace.* St. Paul: Merrill/Magnus, 1990.

Stulz-Herrnstadt, Nadja (ed.), *Rudolf Herrnstadt. Das Herrnstadt-Dokument. Das Politbüro der SED und die Geschichte des 17. Juni 1953.* Reinbek bei Hamburg: Rowohlt, 1990.

Sudoplatov, Pavel and Anatoli (with Jerrold L. and Leona P. Schecter). *Special Tasks: The Memoirs of an Unwanted Witness. A Soviet Spymaster.* Boston: Little, Brown and Company, 1994.

Sulzberger, Cyrus L. *A Long Row of Candles: Memoires and Diaries, 1934–1954.* New York: The Macmillan Company, 1969.

Tirpitz, Alfred von. *Politische Dokumente, Vol. 2: Der Aufbau der deutschen Weltmacht.* Stuttgart: Cotta, 1924.

Truman Harry, S. *Memoirs, Vol. 1: Year of Decisions: 1945*. Garden City, N.Y.: Doubleday, 1955.
Truman Harry, S. *Memoirs, Vol. 2: Years of Trial and Hope: 1946–1953*. London: Hodder & Stoughton, 1956 (new edn, New York, 1996).
Wheeler-Bennett, John Wheeler (ed.). *Action This Day: Working with Churchill*. Memoirs by Lord Normanbrook, John Colville and others. London: Macmillan, 1968.
Wilhelm II. *Ereignisse und Gestalten aus den Jahren 1878–1918*. Leipzig/Berlin: K.F. Koehler, 1922.
Wolf, Markus. *Spionagechef im Kalten Krieg. Erinnerungen*. Munich: List Verlag, 1997.
Woolton, Marquis Frederick James. *The Memoirs of the Rt Hon the Earl of Woolton*. London: Cassell, 1959.

Public Opinion Polls and Election Details

Butler, David (ed.). *British General Elections since 1945*. Oxford: Basil Blackwell, 1989.
Butler, David (ed.). *The British General Election of 1951*. London: Macmillan, 1952.
Butler, David (ed.). *The British General Election of 1955*. London: Macmillan, 1955.
Butler, David and Gareth Butler (eds). *British Political Facts, 1900–1985*. London: Macmillan, 1986.
Erskine, H.G. 'The Cold War. Report from the Polls'. *Political Science Quarterly* 25/2 (1961), 300–15.
Erskine, H.G. 'The Polls. Defense, Peace, and Space'. *Political Science Quarterly* 25/3 (1961), 478–89.
Gallup, George H. (ed.). *The Gallup International Public Opinion Poll: Great Britain, 1937–1975*. Vol. 1: 1937–64. New York: Random House, 1976.
McCallum, Ronald Buchanan and Violet Alison Readman. *The British General Election of 1945*. London/New York: Oxford University Press, 1947.
Nicholas, H.G. and David Butler (eds). *The British General Election of 1950*. London: Macmillan, 1951.
Niemi, Richard G., Tom W. Smith and John Mueller (eds). *Trends in Public Opinion: A Compendium of Survey Data*. New York/London: Greenwood Press, 1989.
Noelle, Elisabeth and Erich Peter Neumann (eds). *Antworten: Politik im Kraftfeld der öffentlichen Meinung*. Allensbach: Verlag für Demoskopie, 1954.
Noelle, Elisabeth and Erich Peter Neumann (eds). *Jahrbuch der öffentlichen Meinung, 1947–55*. 2nd edn Allensbach: Verlag für Demoskopie, 1956.
Noelle-Neumann, Elisabeth and Neumann Erich Peter (eds). *The Germans: Public Opinion Polls 1947–1966*. Allensbach: Verlag für Demoskopie, 1967.

Secondary Works

Adamthwaite, Anthony. 'Britain and the World, 1945–49: the View from the Foreign Office', *International Affairs* 61/2 (1985), 223–35.
Addison, Paul. 'Churchill in British Politics, 1940–1955', in Bean, J.M.W. (ed.), *The Political Culture of Modern Britain: Studies in Memory of Stephen Koss*. London: Hamish Hamilton, 1987, 243–61.
Addison, Paul. *Churchill on the Home Front, 1900–1955*. London: Cape, 1992 (paperback edn, Pimlico, 1993).
Addison, Paul. *The Road to 1945: British Politics and the Second World War*. London: Pimlico, 1994 (1st edn, London: Jonathan Cape, 1975).
Addison, Paul. 'Churchill and the Price of Victory', in Tiratsoo, Nick (ed.), *From Blitz to Blair: A New History of Britain since 1939*, London: Phoenix, 1998, 53–76.
Addison, Paul. 'The British Conservative Party from Churchill to Heath: Doctrine or Men?' (review of John Ramsden's *The Age of Churchill and Eden*), *Contemporary European History*, 8/2 (1999), 289–98.
Addison, Paul. 'The Three Careers of Winston Churchill', in *Transactions of the Royal Historical Society*, 6th series, Vol. XI, Cambridge: Cambridge University Press, 2001, 183–99.
Adomeit, Hannes. *Imperial Overstretch: Germany in Soviet Policy from Stalin to Gorbachev. An Analysis Based on New Archival Evidence, Memoirs, and Interviews*. Baden-Baden: Nomos, 1998.
Aldous, Richard and Sabine Lee (eds). *Harold Macmillan and Britain's World Role*. Basingstoke: Macmillan, 1996.
Aldous, Richard and Sabine Lee (eds). *Harold Macmillan: Aspects of a Political Life*. Basingstoke: Macmillan, 1999.
Aldrich, Richard J. and John Zametica. 'The Rise and Decline of a Strategic Concept: the Middle East', in Aldrich, Richard J. (ed.), *British Intelligence, Strategy and the Cold War, 1945–51*. London: Routledge, 1992, 236–74.
Alexander, G.M. *The Prelude to the Truman Doctrine: British Policy in Greece 1944–1947*. Oxford: Clarendon Press, 1982.

Allen, H.C. *Great Britain and the United States: A History of Anglo-American Relations, 1783–1952.* London: Odhams Press, 1954.

Ambrose, Stephen E. (with Richard H. Immerman). *Ike's Spies: Eisenhower and the Intelligence Community.* Garden City, N.Y.: Doubleday, 1981.

Ambrose Stephen, E. *Eisenhower.* Vol. 2: *The President, 1952–1969.* London: George Allen & Unwin, 1984.

Ambrose, Stephen E. 'Churchill and Eisenhower in the Second World War', in Blake, Robert and William Roger Louis (eds). *Churchill.* Oxford/New York: Oxford University Press, 1993, 397–405.

Amlund, Curtis Arthur. 'Lloyd George and Winston Churchill: Contrasts and Similarities', *Contemporary Review* 259/1510 (1991), 263–6.

Anderson, David L. *Trapped by Success: The Eisenhower Administration and Vietnam, 1953–1961.* New York: Columbia University Press, 1991.

Anderson Terry, H. *The United States, Great Britain, and the Cold War 1944–1947.* Columbia, Mo./London: University of Missouri Press, 1981.

Andrews, J.H. 'Winston Churchill's Tammany Hall Mentor', *New York History* (April, 1990), 133–71.

Annual Register. A View of the History, Politics and Literature for the Year. 1948, 1953. London: Dodsley, 1949, 1954.

Anstey, Caroline. 'The Projection of British Socialism. Foreign Office Publicity and American Opinion, 1945–50'. *Journal of Contemporary History* 19 (1984), 417–51.

Arnold, James R. *The First Domino: Eisenhower, the Military, and America's Intervention in Vietnam.* New York: W. Morrow, 1991.

Arnold, Lorna (with Katherine Pyne). *Britain and the H-Bomb.* Basingstoke: Palgrave, 2001.

Aron, Raymond and Daniel Lerner. *France Defeats E.D.C.* New York: Praeger, 1957.

Ashton, Stephen R. *In Search of Détente: The Politics of East-West Relations since 1945.* Basingstoke: Macmillan, 1989.

Ausland, John C. *Kennedy, Khrushchev, and the Berlin-Cuba Crisis, 1961–1964.* Oslo: Scandinavian University Press, 1996.

Avtorchanov, Abdurachman. *Das Rätsel um Stalins Tod.* Frankfurt/M., Ullstein, 1984.

Azzola, Axel Christian. *Die Diskussion um die Aufrüstung der BRD im Unterhaus und in der Presse Grossbritanniens, November 1949–Juli 1952.* Meisenheim am Glan: A. Hain, 1971.

Baier, Gerhard. *Wir wollen freie Menschen sein. Der 17. Juni 1953: Bauleute gingen voran.* Frankfurt/M.: Büchergilde Gutenberg, 1993.

Balfour-Paul, Glen. 'Britain's Informal Empire in the Middle East', in Brown, Judith M. and William Roger Louis (eds), *The Oxford History of the British Empire*, Vol. 4: *The Twentieth Century.* Oxford: Clarendon Press, 1999, 490–514.

Ball, Stuart. *The Conservative Party and British Politics, 1902–1951.* London/New York: Longman, 1995.

Ball, Stuart. 'Churchill and the Conservative Party', in *Transactions of the Royal Historical Society*, 6th series, Vol. XI. Cambridge: Cambridge University Press, 2001, 307–30.

Ball, Stuart and Anthony Seldon (eds). *The Heath Government, 1970–1974: A Reappraisal.* London: Longman, 1996.

Baras, Victor. 'Beria's Fall and Ulbricht's Survival', *Soviet Studies* 27/3 (1975), 381–95.

Baras, Victor. 'Stalin's German Policy after Stalin', *Slavic Review* 37 (1978), 259–67.

Baring, Arnulf. *Der 17. Juni 1953.* Cologne: Kiepenheuer & Witsch, 1957, 3rd edn 1983 [English edn: *Uprising in East Germany: June 17, 1953*, London/Ithaca, N.Y.: Cornell University Press, 1972].

Baring, Arnulf. *Im Anfang war Adenauer. Die Entstehung der Kanzlerdemokratie*, 3rd paperback edn Munich: Deutscher Taschenbuch Verlag, 1984 (1st edn, 1969; original title: *Außenpolitik in Adenauers Kanzlerdemokratie. Bonns Beitrag zur Europäischen Verteidigungsgemeinschaft*).

Barker, Elisabeth. *Britain in a Divided Europe, 1945–1970.* London: Weidenfeld and Nicolson, 1971.

Barker, Elisabeth. *Churchill and Eden at War.* London: Macmillan, 1978.

Barker, Elisabeth. *The British between the Superpowers, 1945–50.* London: Macmillan, 1983.

Barnett, Correlli. *The Lost Victory: British Dreams, British Realities, 1945–1950.* London: Macmillan, 1995.

Barnett, Correlli. *The Verdict of Peace: Britain between Her Yesterday and the Future.* London: Macmillan, 2001.

Bar-Noi, Uri. 'The Soviet Union and Churchill's Appeals for High-Level Talks, 1953–54: New Evidence from the Russian Archives', *Diplomacy & Statecraft* 9/3 (1998), 110–33.

Barraclough, Geoffrey. *From Agadir to Armageddon: Anatomy of a Crisis.* New York: Holmes and Meier, 1982.

Barret, Buckley Barry. *Churchill: A Concise Bibliography.* Westport, Conn.: Greenwood Press, 2000.

Bartlett, Christopher J. *British Foreign Policy in the Twentieth Century.* Basingstoke: Macmillan, 1989.

Bartlett, Christopher J. *'The Special Relationship': A Political History of Anglo-American Relations since 1945.* London: Longman, 1992.

Baylis, John. *Anglo-American Defence Relations 1939–1980: The Special Relationship.* London: Macmillan, 1981.

Baylis, John. 'British wartime thinking about a post-war European security group', *Review of International Studies* 9/4 (1983), 265–81.

Baylis, John. 'Britain, the Brussels Pact and the Continental Commitment', *International Affairs* 60 (1984), 615–29.

Baylis, John. *Ambiguity and Deterrence: British Nuclear Strategy, 1945–1964.* Oxford/New York: Clarendon Press, 1995.

Baylis, John and Alan Macmillan. 'The British Global Strategy Paper of 1952'. *Journal of Strategic Studies* 16/2 (1993), 200–26.

Beckett, Francis. *Clem Attlee.* London: Richard Cohen Books, 1997.

Bédarida, François. *Churchill.* Paris: Fayard, 1999.

Beevor, Antony. *Stalingrad.* New York: Viking, 1998; paperback edn, Penguin, 1999.

Begbie, Harold. *The Vindication of Great Britain: A Study in Diplomacy and Strategy with Reference to the Illusions of Her Critics and the Problems of the Future.* London: Methuen, 1916.

Beglinger, Martin. *'Containment' im Wandel. Die Amerikanische Aussen- und Sicherheitspolitik im Übergang von Truman zu Eisenhower.* Stuttgart: Steiner Verlag, 1988.

Beiriger, Eugene Edward. *Churchill, Munitions, and Mechanical Warfare: The Politics of Supply and Strategy.* New York: Peter Lang, 1997.

Beisner, Robert L. 'Dean Acheson Joins the Cold Warriors', *Diplomatic History* 20/3 (1996), 321–55.

Bell, Coral. *Negotiation from Strength: A Study in the Politics of Power.* London: Chatto & Windus, 1962.

Beloff, Max. 'The Anglo-French Union Project of June 1940', in Beloff, Max. *The Intellectual in Politics and other Essays.* London: Weidenfeld and Nicolson, 1970, 172–99.

Beloff, Max. 'Churchill and Europe', in Blake, Robert and William Roger Louis (eds). *Churchill.* Oxford/New York: Oxford University Press, 1993, 443–55.

Bender, Peter. *Die 'Neue Ostpolitik' und ihre Folgen. Vom Mauerbau bis zur Vereinigung.* Revised 4th edn, Munich: Deutscher Taschenbuch Verlag, 1996.

Ben-Moshe, Tuvia. 'Winston Churchill and the "Second Front": A Reappraisal', *Journal of Modern History* 62 (1990), 503–37.

Bentley, Michael, '1931–1945', in Seldon, Anthony (ed.). *How Tory Governments Fall: The Tory Party in Power since 1783.* London: Fontana Press, 1996, 285–312.

Berghahn Volker, R. *Der Tirpitz-Plan: Genesis und Verfall einer innenpolitischen Krisenstrategie unter Wilhelm II.* Düsseldorf: Droste Verlag, 1971.

Berghahn, Volker R. *Germany and the Approach of War.* London: Macmillan, 1973; 2nd edn, 1993.

Berlin, Isaiah. *Mr. Churchill in 1940.* London: John Murray, 1964.

Bernstein, Barton J. 'Seizing the Contested Terrain of Early Nuclear History: Stimson, Conant, and their Allies explain the Decision to Use the Atomic Bomb', *Diplomatic History* 17/1 (1993), 35–72.

Beschloss, Michael R. *The Crisis Years: Kennedy and Khrushchev, 1960–1963.* London: Faber and Faber, 1991.

Best, Geoffrey. *Churchill: A Study in Greatness.* London: Hambledon, 2001.

Besymenski, Lev. '1953–Berija will die DDR beseitigen', *Die Zeit* 42/1993 (15 October 1993), 81–3.

Besymenski, Lev. 'Sowjetischer Nachrichtendienst und Wiedervereinigung Deutschlands: Der Berija-Plan von 1953', in Krieger, Wolfgang and Jürgen Weber (eds), *Spionage für den Frieden? Nachrichtendienste in Deutschland während des Kalten Krieges.* Munich: Olzog, 1997.

Billings-Yun, Melanie. *Decision against War: Eisenhower and Dien Bien Phu, 1954.* New York: Columbia University Press, 1988.

Birkenhead (Earl of), Frederick Winston Furneaux Smith (ed. by John Colville). *Churchill, 1874–1922.* London: Harrap, 1989.

Bischof, Günter. 'Österreichische Neutralität, die deutsche Frage und europäische Sicherheit 1953–1955', in Steininger, Rolf et al. (eds). *Die doppelte Eindämmung: Europäische Sicherheit und Deutsche Frage in den Fünfzigern.* Munich: v. Hase & Koehler, 1993, 133–76.

Bischof, Günter. 'Eisenhower, the Summit, and the Austrian Treaty, 1953–55', in Ambrose, Stephen E. and Günter Bischof (eds). *Eisenhower: A Centenary Assessment.* Baton Rouge, Louis., 1995, 136–61.

Bischof, Günter. *Austria in the First Cold War, 1945–55: The Leverage of the Weak.* Basingstoke: Macmillan, 1999.

Blackwell, Michael. *Clinging to Grandeur: British Attitudes and Foreign Policy in the Aftermath of the Second World War.* Westport, Conn.; London: Greenwood Press, 1993.

Blake, Robert and William Roger Louis (eds). *Churchill*. Oxford/New York: Oxford University Press, 1993.

Blake, Robert. 'Churchill and the Conservative Party', in Kemper, R. Crosby. *Winston Churchill: Resolution, Defiance, Magnanimity, Good Will*. Columbia: University of Missouri Press, 1996, 141–56.

Blake, Robert. *The Conservative Party from Peel to Major*. Expanded edn London: Heinemann, 1997.

Blake, Robert. *Winston Churchill*. Pocket Biographies. Stroud: Sutton, 1998.

Blasi, Walter. 'Die Libanonkrise 1958 und die US-Überflüge', in Schmidl, Erwin A. (ed.). *Österreich im Frühen Kalten Krieg 1945–1958*. Cologne: Böhlau, 2000, 239–59.

Boadle, Donald Graeme. *Winston Churchill and the German Question in British Foreign Policy, 1918–1922*. The Hague: Martinus Nijhoff, 1973.

Bock, Joseph G. *The White House Staff and the National Security Assistant: Friendship and Friction at the Water's Edge*. New York/London: Greenwood Press, 1987.

Bode, Friedrich Heinz. *Der Kampf um die Bagdadbahn, 1903–1914: Ein Beitrag zur Geschichte der Deutsch-Englischen Beziehungen*. Aalen: Scientia-Verlag, 1982. (first publ. as Breslauer Historische Forschungen, Heft 15. Breslau: Priebatschs Buchhandlung, 1941).

Bonwetsch, Bernd. 'Deutschlandpolitische Alternativen der Sowjetunion, 1949–1955', *Deutsche Studien* 24 (1986), 20–40.

Borhi, Laszlo. 'Rollback, Liberation, Containment, or Inaction? U.S. Policy and Eastern Europe in the 1950s', *Journal of Cold War Studies* 1/3 (1999), 67–110.

Bortoli, Georges. *The Death of Stalin* (trans. from the French by R. Rosenthal). London: Phaidon Press, 1975.

Bosco, Andrea (ed.). *The Federal Idea*. Vol. 1: *The History of Federalism from the Enlightenment to 1945*. London: Lothian Foundation Press, 1991.

Bosco, Andrea. 'Federal Union, Chatham House, the Foreign Office and Anglo-French Union in spring 1940', in Bosco, Andrea (ed.). *The Federal Idea*. Vol. 1: *The History of Federalism from the Enlightenment to 1945*. London: Lothian Foundation Press, 1991, 291–325.

Bosco, Andrea, 'The British Federalist Tradition and the Origins of the Churchill Proposal of Union with France in 1940', in Knipping, Franz (ed.), *Federal Conceptions in EU Member States: Traditions and Perspectives*. Baden-Baden: Nomos, 1994, 173–88.

Bosco, Andrea and Alex May (eds). *The Round Table: The Empire/Commonwealth and British Foreign Policy*. London: Lothian Foundation Press, 1997.

Bose, Meena. *Shaping and Signaling Presidential Policy: The National Security Decision Making of Eisenhower and Kennedy*. College Station: Texas A & M University Press, 1998.

Bowie, Robert and Richard H. Immerman. *Waging Peace: How Eisenhower Shaped an Enduring Cold War Strategy*. New York: Oxford University Press, 1998.

Boyce, Robert. 'Britain's First "No" to Europe', *European Studies Review* 10 (1980), 17–45.

Boyle, Peter. 'The British Foreign Office View of Soviet-American Relations, 1945–46', *Diplomatic History* 3/3 (1979), 307–20.

Boyle, Peter. 'The Special Relationship: An Alliance of Convenience?', *Journal of American Studies* 22 (1988), 457–65.

Boyle, Peter. *American-Soviet Relations: From the Russian Revolution to the Fall of Communism*. London: Routledge, 1993.

Boyle, Timothy. 'New Light on Lloyd George's Mansion House Speech', *Historical Journal* 23 (1980), 431–3.

Brandes, Detlef. 'Confederation Plans in Eastern Europe During World War II', in Dumoulin, Michel (ed.), *Wartime Plans for Postwar Europe, 1940–1947*. Brussels: Nomos-Verlag, 1995, 83–94.

Brands, Henry W. *Cold Warriors: Eisenhower's Generation and American Foreign Policy*. New York: Columbia University Press, 1988.

Brands, Henry W. 'The Age of Vulnerability: Eisenhower and the National Insecurity State', *American Historical Review* 94/4 (1989), 963–89.

Brands, Henry W. 'Who Won the Cold War? 1984–1991', reprinted in Larres, Klaus and Ann Lane (eds), *The Cold War. Essential Readings*. Oxford: Basil Blackwell, 2001, 185–230.

Brandt, Willy and Richard Löwenthal. *Ernst Reuter. Ein Leben für die Freiheit. Eine Politische Biographie*. Munich: Kindler, 1957.

Brendon, Piers. *Ike: The Life and Times of Dwight D. Eisenhower*. London: Secker & Warburg, 1987.

Brendon, Piers. *Winston Churchill: A Brief Life*. 2nd edn, London: Pimlico, 2001 (1st edn, London: Secker & Warburg, 1984).

Brinkley, Douglas. 'Dean Acheson and the "special relationship": The West Point speech of December 1962', *Historical Journal* 33 (1990), 599–608.

Brinkley, Douglas and David R. Facey-Crowther. *The Atlantic Charter*. Basingstoke: Macmillan, 1994.

Broeze, F. 'Shipping Policy and Social-Darwinism: Albert Ballin and the *Weltpolitik* of the Hamburg-America Line, 1886–1914', *The Mariner's Mirror* 79/4 (1993), 419–36.

Bromage, Mary Cogan. *Churchill and Ireland*. Notre Dame, Ind.: University of Notre Dame Press, 1964.

Buchheim, Christoph. 'Wirtschaftliche Hintergründe des Arbeiteraufstandes vom 17. Juni 1953 in der DDR', *Vierteljahrshefte für Zeitgeschichte* 38 (1990), 415–33.

Bucholz, Arden. *Moltke, Schlieffen, and Prussian War Planning*. Oxford: Berg, 1991.

Buhite, Russell D. *Decisions at Yalta: An Appraisal of Summit Diplomacy*. Wilmington, Del.: Scholarly Resources, 1986.

Bullen, Roger. 'The British Government and the Schuman Plan, May 1950–March 1951', in Schwabe, Klaus (ed.). *The Beginnings of the Schuman-Plan: Contributions to the Symposium in Aachen, May 28–30, 1986*. Baden-Baden: Nomos, 1988, 199–210.

Bullock, Alan. *Ernest Bevin: Foreign Secretary 1945–1951*. London: Heinemann, 1983.

Bundesministerium für innerdeutsche Beziehungen (ed.). *Der Volksaufstand vom 17. Juni 1953*. Bonn: Bundesministerium für innerdeutsche Beziehungen, 1953.

Bungay, Stephen. *The Most Dangerous Enemy: A History of the Battle of Britain*. London: Aurum Press, 2000.

Burk, Robert Fredrick. *Dwight D. Eisenhower: Hero and Politician*. Boston, Mass.: Twayne Publishers, 1986.

Burridge, Trevor. *Clement Attlee: A Political Biography*. London: Cape, 1985.

Buzzanco, Robert. 'Prologue to Tragedy: U.S. Military Opposition to Intervention in Vietnam, 1950–54', *Diplomatic History* 17/2 (1993), 201–22.

Cable, James. *The Geneva Conference of 1954 on Indochina*. 2nd edn, Basingstoke: Macmillan, 2000 (first publ., 1986).

Cairncross, Alec. *Years of Recovery: British Economic Policy, 1945–51*. London/New York: Methuen, 1985.

Callahan, David. *Dangerous Capabilities: Paul Nitze and the Cold War*. New York: Harper & Row, 1990.

Callahan, Raymond. *Churchill: Retreat from Empire*. Wilmington, Del.: Scholarly Resources, 1984.

Calvocoressi, Peter. *Fall Out: World War II and the Shaping of Postwar Europe*. London: Longman, 1997.

Campbell, John. *Edward Heath: A Biography*. London: Jonathan Cape, 1993.

Camps, Miriam. *Britain and the European Community, 1955–1963*. London: Oxford University Press, 1964.

Canis, Konrad. *Von Bismarck zur Weltpolitik. Deutsche Außenpolitik 1890–1902*. Berlin: Akademie Verlag, 1997.

Cannadine, David. 'Churchill and the British Monarchy', in *Transactions of the Royal Historical Society*, 6th series, Vol. XI. Cambridge: Cambridge University Press, 2001, 249–72.

Carlton, David. *Anthony Eden: A Biography*. Paperback edn, London: Allen Lane, 1981.

Carlton, David. 'Grossbritannien und die Gipfeldiplomatie', in Thoß, Bruno and Hans-Erich Volkmann (eds), *Zwischen Kaltem Krieg und Entspannung. Sicherheits- und Deutschlandpolitik der Bundesrepublik im Mächtesystem der Jahre 1953–1956*. Boppard: Boldt, 1988, 51–69.

Carlton, David. *Churchill and the Soviet Union*. Manchester: Manchester University Press, 2000.

Carlton, David. 'Churchill and the Two Evil Empires', in *Transactions of the Royal Historical Society*, 6th series, Vol. XI. Cambridge: Cambridge University Press, 2001, 331–51.

Cassar, George H. *Asquith as War Leader*. London/Rio Grande, Ohio: Hambledon Press, 1994.

Cathcart, Brian. *Test of Greatness: Britain's Struggle for the Atom Bomb*. London: John Murray, 1994.

Catudal, Honoré M. *Kennedy and the Berlin Wall Crisis: A Case Study in US Decision Making*. Berlin: Berlin Verlag, 1980.

Cecil, Lamar. *Albert Ballin: Business and Politics in Imperial Germany, 1988–1918*. Princeton, N.J.: Princeton University Press, 1967.

Cecil, Lamar. *Wilhelm II, Vol. 2: Emperor and Exile, 1900–1941*. Chapel Hill, N.C.: University of North Carolina Press, 1996.

Chace, James. *Acheson: The Secretary of State Who Created the American World*. New York/Cambridge, Mass.: Simon & Schuster and Harvard University Press, 1999.

Chamberlin, Brewster and Jürgen Wetzel. 'Der 17. Juni und der RIAS', in Spittmann, Ilse and Karl Wilhelm Fricke (eds), *17. Juni 1953. Arbeiteraufstand in der DDR*. 2nd edn, Cologne: Edition Deutschland Archiv, 1988, 212–15.

Chang Gordon, H. *Friends and Enemies: The United States, China, and the Soviet Union, 1948–1972*. Stanford, Calif.: Stanford University Press, 1990.

Charmley, John. 'Duff Cooper and Western European Union, 1944–47', *Review of International Studies* 11 (1985), 53–64.

Charmley, John. *Duff Cooper: The Authorized Biography*. London: Weidenfeld and Nicolson, 1986.

Charmley, John. 'Churchill's Roosevelt', in Lane, Anne and Howard Temperley (eds). *The Rise and Fall of the Grand Alliance, 1941–45*. Basingstoke: Macmillan, 1995, 90–107.

Charmley, John. *Churchill, the End of Glory: A Political Biography*. London: Hodder & Stoughton, 1993.

Charmley, John. *Churchill's Grand Alliance: A Provocative Reassessment of the 'Special Relationship' between England and the US from 1940 to 1957*. New York/London: Harcourt Brace & Company, 1995.

Charmley, John. *A History of Conservative Politics in Britain, 1900–1996: The Quest for Power*. Basingstoke: Macmillan, 1996.

Charmley, John. 'Churchill and the American Alliance', in *Transactions of the Royal Historical Society*, 6th series, Vol. XI. Cambridge: Cambridge University Press, 2001, 353–71.

Childs, David and Popplewell Richard. *The Stasi: The East German Intelligence and Security Service*. Paperback, 2nd edn, Basingstoke: Macmillan, 1999.

'Churchill axed BBC broadcast of A-bomb program', *Japan Policy & Politics* (Kyodo News International), 23 August 1999.

Churchill, Randolph S. *Winston S. Churchill. The Official Biography*. London: Heinemann. Vol. 1: *Youth, 1874–1900* (1966); Vol. 2: *Young Statesman, 1901–1914* (1967).

Clark, Alan. 'A Reputation Ripe for Revision'. *The Times* (London), 2 January 1993.

Clark, Alan. *The Tories: Conservatives and the Nation State 1922–1997*. Paperback edn, London: Phoenix, 1999 (first publ., London: Weidenfeld and Nicolson, 1997).

Clark, Christopher M. *Kaiser Wilhelm II*. Profiles in Power. Harlow, Essex/New York: Longman, 2000.

Clark, Ian. *Globalization and Fragmentation: International Relations in the Twentieth Century*. Oxford: Oxford University Press, 1997.

Clark, Ian and Nicholas J. Wheeler. *The British Origins of Nuclear Strategy, 1945–1955*. Oxford/New York: Oxford University Press, 1989.

Clarke, Peter F. 'Churchill's Economic Ideas, 1900–1930', in Blake, Robert and William Roger Louis (eds). *Churchill*. Oxford/New York: Oxford University Press, 1993, 79–95.

Clarke, Peter F. and Clive Trebilcock (eds). *Understanding Decline: Perceptions and Realities of British Economic Performance. Essays presented to Barry Supple*. Cambridge: Cambridge University Press, 1997.

Clemens, Diane Shaver. *Yalta*. New York: Oxford University Press, 1972.

Clements, Kendrick A. *James F. Byrnes and the Origins of the Cold War*. Durham, N.C: Carolina Academic Press, 1982.

Clissold, Stephen. *Yugoslavia and the Soviet Union, 1939–1973 : A Documentary Survey*. London/New York: Published for the Royal Institute of International Affairs by Oxford University Press, 1975.

Clogg, Richard. *A Concise History of Greece*. Cambridge: Cambridge University Press, 1992.

Coates, David and John Hillard. *The Economic Decline of Modern Britain: The Debate between Left and Right*. London: Wheatsheaf Books, 1986.

Cohen, Michael J. *Fighting World War Three from the Middle East: Allied Contingency Plans, 1945–1954*. London: Frank Cass, 1997.

Cohen, Michael J. and Martin Kolinsky (eds). *Demise of the British Empire in the Middle East: Britain's Responses to Nationalist Movements, 1943–55*. London: Frank Cass, 1998.

Cohen, Warren I. *America's Response to China: An Interpretative History of Sino-American Relations*. 3rd edn, New York: Wiley, 1990.

Cole, Wayne S. *Roosevelt & the Isolationists, 1932–45*. Lincoln, Nebr./London: University of Nebraska Press, 1983.

Coleman, David G. 'Eisenhower and the Berlin Problem, 1953–1954', *Journal of Cold War Studies* 2/1 (2000), 3–34.

Conquest, Robert. *Power and Policy in the USSR: The Study of Soviet Dynastics*. London/New York: Macmillan, 1961.

Conze, Eckard. 'No Way Back to Potsdam: The Adenauer Government and the Geneva Summit', in Bischof, Günter and Saki Dockrill (eds), *Cold War Respite: The Geneva Summit of 1955*. Baton Rouge, LA.: Louisiana State University Press, 2000, 190–214.

Cook, Blanche Wiesen. *The Declassified Eisenhower: A Divided Legacy*. Garden City, N.Y.: Doubleday, 1981.

Coote, Colin R. (ed.). *Sir Winston Churchill: A Self-Portrait*. London: Eyre & Spottiswoode, 1954.

Corti, T.G. and T. Michael Ruddy. 'The Bohlen and Thayer Affairs: A Case Study in the Eisenhower Administration's Response to Senator Joseph McCarthy'. *Mid-America: An Historical Review* 72 (1990), 119–33.

Costello, John. *Ten Days to Destiny: The Secret Story of the Hess Peace Initiative and British Efforts to Strike a Deal with Hitler*. New York: W. Morrow, 1991.

Coudenhove-Kalergi, Richard Nicolaus. *Pan-Europe*. New York: Knopf, 1926.

Coudenhove-Kalergi, Richard Nicolaus. *Europa Erwacht*. Zürich: Paneuropa, 1934.

Cowling, Maurice. *The Impact of Hitler: British Politics and British Policy, 1933–40*. London: Cambridge University Press, 1975.

Cowling, Maurice. 'Why we should not have gone to war with Hitler'. *Sunday Telegraph* (London), 20 August 1989.

Craig, Campbell. *Destroying the Village: Eisenhower and Thermonuclear War*. New York: Columbia University Press, 1998.

Craig, Gordon A. 'Churchill and Germany', in Blake, Robert and William Roger Louis (eds). *Churchill*. Oxford/New York: Oxford University Press, 1993, 21–40.

Crampton, Richard J. *The Hollow Detente: Anglo-German Relations in the Balkans, 1911–1914*. London: G. Prior, 1980.

Crockatt, Richard. *The Fifty Years War: The United States and the Soviet Union in World Politics, 1941–1991*. London/New York: Routledge, 1995.

Croft, Stuart. 'British Policy Towards Western Europe, 1945–51', in Stirk, Peter M.R. and David Willis (eds), *Shaping Postwar Europe: European Unity and Disunity, 1945–1957*. London: Pinter, 1991, 77–89.

Croft, Stuart. *The End of Superpower: British Foreign Office Conceptions of a Changing World, 1945–51*. Aldershot/Brookfield, Vt.: Dartmouth, 1994.

Crozier, Andrew J. 'Federalism and Anti-Federalism in the United Kingdom', in Knipping, Franz (ed.), *Federal Conceptions in EU Member States: Traditions and Perspectives*. Baden-Baden: Nomos, 1994, 160–72.

Curtis, Mark. *The Ambiguities of Power: British Foreign Policy since 1945*. London: Zed Books, 1995.

Dallek, Robert. *Franklin D. Roosevelt and American Foreign Policy 1932–1945*. Oxford: Oxford University Press, 1981.

Davis Smith, Justin. *The Attlee and Churchill Administrations and Industrial Unrest, 1945–55: A Study in Consensus*. London: Pinter, 1990.

Davy, Richard. *European Détente: A Reappraisal*. London: Sage, 1992.

Deighton, Anne. *The Impossible Peace: Britain, the Division of Germany and the Origins of the Cold War*. Oxford: Clarendon Press, 1990.

Deighton, Anne. 'Towards a "Western" Strategy: The Making of British Policy Towards Germany, 1945–46', in Deighton, Anne (ed.), *Britain and the First Cold War*. Basingstoke: Macmillan, 1990, 53–70.

Deighton, Anne. 'Britain and the Three Interlocking Circles', in Varsori, Antonio. *Europe, 1945–1990s: The End of an Era?* London: Macmillan, 1995, 155–69.

Deighton, Anne. 'Britain and the Creation of the Western European Union, 1954', in Dumoulin, Michel (ed.). *The European Defence Community, Lessons for the Future?* Brussels/New York: Peter Lang, 2000, 283–308.

Deighton, Anne. 'British-West German Relations, 1945–1972', in Larres, Klaus (ed. with E. Meehan), *Uneasy Allies: British-German Relations and European Integration since 1945*. Oxford: Oxford University Press, 2000, 27–44.

Dell, Edmund. *The Schuman Plan and the British Abdication of Leadership in Europe*. Oxford: Oxford University Press, 1995.

Demory, Jean-Claude. *Georges Bidault: 1899–1983: Biographie*. Paris: Julliard, 1995.

'Der "Modus Vivendi" in Europa. Die Ost-West Beziehungen und die Pariser Aussenministerkonferenz von 1949', *Europa-Archiv* 4/2 (July–December, 1949), 2389.

Deutscher, Isaac. *Stalin: A Political Biography*. Political Leaders of the Twentieth Century. London: Penguin, 1990 (first publ., 1949).

Devereux David, R. *The Formulation of British Defence Policy Towards the Middle East, 1948–56*. Basingstoke: Macmillan, 1990.

Devillers, Philippe and Jean Lacouture. *End of a War: Indochina, 1954* (transl. from the French by A. Lieven and A. Roberts). London: Pall Mall Press, 1969.

Diedrich, Torsten. *Der 17. Juni 1953 in der DDR: Bewaffnete Gewalt gegen das Volk*. Berlin: Dietz, 1991.

Diedrich, Torsten. 'Zwischen Arbeiterbewegung und gescheiterter Revolution in der DDR. Retrospektive zum Stand der zeitgeschichtlichen Aufarbeitung des 17. Juni 1953', *Jahrbuch für Historische Kommunismusforschung* (1994), 288–305.

Dimbleby, David and David Reynolds. *An Ocean Apart: The Relationship between Britain and America in the Twentieth Century*. London: Hodder & Stoughton and BBC Books, 1988.

Dinan, Desmond. *Ever Closer Union? An Introduction to European Integration*. 2nd edn, London: Macmillan Press, 1999 (1st edn, 1994).

Divine, Robert A. *Blowing on the Wind: The Nuclear Test Ban Debate, 1954–1960*. New York: Oxford University Press, 1978.

Divine, Robert A. *Eisenhower and the Cold War*. Oxford: Oxford University Press, 1981.

Dobson, Alan P. *U.S. Wartime Aid to Britain 1940–1946*. London/Dover, N.H: Croom Helm, 1986.

Dobson, Alan P. *The Politics of the Anglo-American Economic Special Relationship, 1940–1987*. Brighton, Sussex: Wheatsheaf Books, 1988.

Dobson, Alan P. *Anglo-American Relations in the Twentieth Century: Of Friendship, Conflict and the Rise and Decline of Superpowers*. London/New York: Routledge, 1995.

Dobson, Alan P. 'Informally Special? The Churchill-Truman Talks of January 1952 and the State of Anglo-American Relations', *Review of International Studies* 23/1 (1997), 27–47.

Dockrill, Michael L. *The Formulation of a Continental Foreign Policy by Great Britain, 1908–1912*. New York: Garland, 1986.

Dockrill, Saki. 'Britain and the Settlement of the West German Rearmament Question in 1954', in Dockrill, Michael L. and John W. Young John (eds). *British Foreign Policy, 1945–56*. Basingstoke: Macmillan, 1989, 149–72.

Dockrill, Saki. *Britain's Policy for West German Rearmament, 1950–55*. Cambridge: Cambridge University Press, 1991.

Dockrill, Saki. *Eisenhower's New-Look National Security Policy, 1953–61*. Basingstoke: Macmillan, 1996.

Dockrill, Saki. 'The Eden Plan and European Security', in Bischof, Günter and Saki Dockrill (eds), *Cold War Respite: The Geneva Summit of 1955*. Baton Rouge, La.: Louisiana State University Press, 2000, 161–89.

Donaldson, Gary A. *Truman Defeats Dewey*. Lexington: University Press of Kentucky, 1998.

Donovan Robert, J. *Eisenhower: The Inside Story*. New York: Harper, 1956.

Dorril, Stephen. *MI6: Fifty Years of Special Operations*. London: Fourth Estate, 2000.

Douglas, Roy. *From War to Cold War, 1942–48*. New York: St. Martin's Press, 1981.

Drummond, Gordon D. *The German Social Democrats in Opposition, 1949–1960: The Case against Rearmament*. Norman, Okla.: University of Oklahoma Press, 1982.

Drummond, Roscoe and Gaston Coblentz. *Duel at the Brink: John Foster Dulles' Command of American Power*. London: Weidenfeld and Nicolson, 1961.

Duchêne, François. *Jean Monnet: The First Statesman of Interdependence*. New York: W.W. Norton, 1994.

Duchin, Brian R. '"The Agonizing Reappraisal": Eisenhower, Dulles and the EDC', *Diplomatic History* 16/2 (1992), 201–21.

Dujardin, Vincent and Michel Dumoulin. *Paul Van Zeeland, 1893–1973*. Brussels: Racine, 1997.

Dumbrell, John. *A Special Relationship: Anglo-American Relations in the Cold War and After*. Basingstoke: Macmillan, 2001.

Dunbabin, J.P.D. *The Cold War: The Great Powers and Their Allies. International Relations since 1945*, Vol. 1. Harlow, Essex/New York: Longman, 1994.

Dunn, Dennis, J. *Caught between Roosevelt & Stalin: America's Ambassadors to Moscow*. Lexington, Ky.: University Press of Kentucky, 1998.

Dutton, David. *British Politics since 1945: The Rise, Fall and Rebirth of Consensus*. 2nd edn, Oxford: Basil Blackwell, 1997 (1st edn, 1991).

Dutton, David. *Anthony Eden: A Life and Reputation*. London/New York: Arnold, 1997.

Edmonds, Robin. *Setting the Mould: The United States and Britain 1945–1950*. Oxford: Clarendon Press, 1986.

Edmonds, Robin. *The Big Three: Churchill, Roosevelt, and Stalin in Peace & War*. London: Hamish Hamilton, 1991.

Edmonds, Robin. 'Churchill and Stalin', in Blake, Robert and William Roger Louis (eds). *Churchill*. Oxford/New York: Oxford University Press, 1993, 309–26.

Edwards, Jill. *Anglo-American Relations and the Franco Question, 1945–1955*. Oxford: Clarendon Press, 1999.

Edwards, Paul M. *The Korean War: An Annotated Bibliography*. Westport, Conn.: Greenwood Press, 1998.

Ellison, James. *Threatening Europe: Britain and the Creation of the European Community, 1955–1958*. Basingstoke: Macmillan, 2000.

Embree, George Daniel. *The Soviet Union between the 19th and 20th Party Congresses, 1952–1956*. The Hague: Martinus Nijhoff, 1959.

Emmert, Kirk. *Winston S. Churchill on Empire*. Studies in Statesmanship. Durham, N.C.: Carolina Academic Press and Claremont Institute for the Study of Statesmanship and Political Philosophy, 1989.

Epkenhans, Michael. *Die wilhelminische Flottenrüstung 1908–1914: Weltmachtstreben, industrieller Fortschritt, soziale Integration*. Munich: R. Oldenbourg, 1991.

Epstein, Leon D. *Britain: Uneasy Ally*. Chicago: Chicago University Press, 1954.

Erdmenger, Klaus. *Das folgenschwere Mißverständnis. Bonn und die sowjetische Deutschlandpolitik 1949–1955*. Freiburg: Rombach,1967.

Erickson, John. 'Stalin, Soviet Strategy and the Grand Alliance', in Lane, Anne and Howard Temperley (eds). *The Rise and Fall of the Grand Alliance, 1941–45*. Basingstoke: Macmillan, 1995, 136–73.

Eubank, Keith. *The Summit Conferences, 1919–1960*. Norman, Okla.: University of Oklahoma Press, 1966.

Evans, Brendan and Andrew Taylor. *From Salisbury to Major: Continuity and Change in Conservative Politics*. Manchester/New York: Manchester University Press, 1996.

Evans, Richard J. *Lying About Hitler: History, Holocaust, and the David Irving Trial*. New York: Basic Books, 2001.

Farnham, Barbara R. *Roosevelt and the Munich Crisis: A Study of Political Decision-Making*. Princeton, N.J.: Princeton University Press, 1997.

Feis, Herbert. *From Trust to Terror: The Onset of the Cold War, 1945–1950*. London: Anthony Blond, 1970.

Felken, Detlef. *Dulles und Deutschland. Die Amerikanische Deutschlandpolitik 1953–1959*. Bonn: Bouvier, 1993.

Ferguson, Neil. 'Germany and the Origins of the First World War: New Perspectives,' *Historical Journal* 35 (1992), 725–52.

Ferrell, Robert H. *The Dying President: Franklin D. Roosevelt, 1944–1945*. Columbia, Mo./London: University of Missouri Press, 1998.

Fest, Joachim. *Hitler: Eine Biographie*. Paperback edn, Frankfurt/M.: Propyläen, 1987.

Fic, Victor M. *The Collapse of American Policy in Russia and Siberia, 1918: Wilson's Decision Not to Intervene (March–October, 1918)*. Boulder, Colo./New York: East European Monographs/Columbia University Press, 1995.

Figes, Orlando. *A People's Tragedy: A History of the Russian Revolution*. New York: Cape, 1996.

Fischer, Fritz. *Germany's Aims in the First World War* (trans. from the German). London: Chatto & Windus, 1967.

Fischer, Fritz. *War of Illusions: German Policies from 1911 to 1914* (trans. from the German by M. Jackson). London: Chatto & Windus, 1975.

Fish, M. Steven. 'After Stalin's Death: The Anglo-American Debate over a new Cold War', *Diplomatic History* 10 (1986), 333–55.

Fitzsimons, Matthew A. *The Foreign Policy of the British Labour Government, 1945–1951*. Notre Dame, Ind.: University of Notre Dame Press, 1953.

Fleischhauer, Ingeborg. *Die Chance des Sonderfriedens. Deutsch-sowjetische Geheimgespräche 1941–1945*. Berlin: Siedler, 1986.

Foglesong David, S. *America's Secret War against Bolshevism: U.S. Intervention in the Russian Civil War, 1917–1920*. Chapel Hill/London: University of North Carolina Press, 1995.

Foitzik, Jan. '"Hart und Konsequent ist der neue politische Kurs zu realisieren". Ein Dokument zur Politik der Sowjetunion gegenüber der DDR nach Berijas Verhaftung im Juni 1953', *Deutschland-Archiv* 1/33 (2000), 32–49.

Foitzik, Jan (ed.). *Entstalinisierungskrise in Ostmitteleuropa 1953–1956. Vom 17. Juni bis zum ungarischen Volksaufstand. Politische, militärische, soziale und nationale Dimensionen*. Paderborn: Schöningh, 2001.

Foot, Rosemary. *A Substitute for Victory: The Politics of Peacemaking at the Korean Armistice Talks*. Ithaca, N.Y.: Cornell University Press, 1990.

Forland, Tor Egil. ' "Selling Firearms to the Indians": Eisenhower's Export Control Policy, 1953–54', *Diplomatic History* 15 (1991), 221–44.

Foschepoth, Josef. 'Churchill, Adenauer und die Neutralisierung Deutschlands', *Deutschland-Archiv* 17 (1984), 1286–301.

Foschepoth, Josef. 'Adenauers Moskaureise 1955', *Aus Politik und Zeitgeschichte* B22 (31 May 1986), 30–46.

Foschepoth, Josef (ed.). *Adenauer und die Deutsche Frage*. Göttingen: Vandenhoeck & Ruprecht, 1988.

Franchetti, Mark. 'Kremlin Guard Reveals How He Shot Hated Beria', *Sunday Times* (4 January 1998), p.19.

Franklin, Mark and Matthew Ladner. 'The Undoing of Winston Churchill: Mobilization and Conversion in the 1945 Realignment of British Voters', *British Journal of Political Science* 25/4 (1995), 429–52.

Frazier, Robert. 'Did Britain Start the Cold War? Bevin and the Truman Doctrine', *Historical Journal* 27 (1984), 715–27.

Frazier, Robert. *Anglo-American Relations with Greece: The Coming of the Cold War, 1942–47.* Basingstoke: Macmillan, 1991.

Freedman, Lawrence. *Kennedy's Wars: Berlin, Cuba, Laos, and Vietnam.* Oxford: Oxford University Press, 2000.

Fricke, Karl Wilhelm. *Opposition und Widerstand in der DDR. Ein politischer Report.* Cologne: Verlag Wissenschaft und Politik, 1984.

Fricke, Karl Wilhelm. 'Der Arbeiteraufstand: Vorgeschichte, Verlauf, Folgen', in Spittmann, Ilse and Karl Wilhelm Fricke (eds), *17. Juni 1953. Arbeiteraufstand in der DDR,* 2nd edn. Cologne: Edition Deutschland Archiv, 1988, 5–22.

Friedberg, Aaron L. *The Weary Titan: Britain and the Experience of Relative Decline, 1895–1905.* Princeton, N.J.: Princeton University Press, 1988.

Fröhlich, Michael. *Von Konfrontation zur Koexistenz: die deutsch-englischen Kolonialbeziehungen in Afrika zwischen 1884 und 1914.* Bochum: N. Brockmeyer, 1990.

Fry, Michael G. *Lloyd George and Foreign Policy: The Education of a Statesman, 1890–1916.* Montreal: McGill-Queen's University Press, 1977.

Fursdon, Edward. *The European Defence Community: A History.* London: Macmillan, 1980.

Fursenko, Aleksandr and Timothy Naftali. *'One Hell of a Gamble': Khrushchev, Castro, Kennedy and the Cuban Missile Crisis 1958–1964.* London: John Murray, 1997.

'The Future of World War II Studies: A Roundtable', *Diplomatic History* 25/3 (2001), 347–499.

Gaddis, John Lewis. *The United States and the Origins of the Cold War, 1941–1947.* New York: Columbia University Press, 1972.

Gaddis, John Lewis. 'Was the Truman Doctrine a Real Turning Point?' *Foreign Affairs* 52/2 (1973–4), 386–402.

Gaddis, John Lewis. *Russia, the Soviet Union and the United States: An Interpretive History.* New York/Chichester: Wiley, 1978.

Gaddis, John Lewis. *Strategies of Containment: A Critical Appraisal of Postwar American National Security Policy.* New York: Oxford University Press, 1982.

Gaddis, John Lewis. *We Now Know: Rethinking Cold War History.* New York/Oxford: Oxford University Press, 1997.

Gaddis, John Lewis. 'Dividing the World' (from *We Now Know: Rethinking Cold War History,* Oxford University Press, 1997), reprinted in Larres, Klaus and Ann Lane (eds). *The Cold War.* Essential Readings. Oxford: Basil Blackwell, 2001, 41–64.

Gade, Christian. *Gleichgewichtspolitik oder Bündnispflege? Maximen britischer Außenpolitik, 1909–1914.* Göttingen: Vandenhoeck & Ruprecht, 1997.

Gallagher, John. 'The Decline, Revival and Fall of the British Empire', in Seal, Anil (ed.), *The Decline, Revival and Fall of the British Empire: The Ford Lectures and other Essays by John Gallagher.* Cambridge: Cambridge University Press, 1982, 73–153.

Gamble, Andrew. *The Conservative Nation.* London/Boston: Routledge & Kegan Paul, 1974.

Gamble, Andrew. *Britain in Decline: Economic Policy, Political Strategy and the British State.* 4th edn, Basingstoke: Macmillan, 1994.

Gardner, Lloyd C. *Approaching Vietnam: From World War II through Dienbienphu, 1941–1954.* New York: W.W. Norton, 1988.

Gardner, Lloyd C. *Spheres of Influences: the Great Powers Partition Europe, from Munich to Yalta.* London: John Murray, 1993.

Gardner, Lloyd. 'Poisoned Apples: American Responses to the Russian "Peace Offensive"', in Larres, Klaus and Kenneth Osgood (eds). *The Cold War After Stalin: A New International History.* Lanham, Md./Oxford: Rowman & Littlefield, 2003 [forthcoming].

Gardner, Richard N. *Sterling-Dollar Diplomacy: Anglo-American Collaboration in the Reconstruction of Multilateral Trade.* Oxford: Clarendon Press, 1956.

Garthoff, Raymond L. *Détente and Confrontation: American-Soviet Relations from Nixon to Reagan.* Revd edn, Washington, D.C: Brookings Institution, 1994.

Gearson, John P.S. *Harold Macmillan and the Berlin Wall Crisis: The Limits of Interest and Force, 1958–1962.* Basingstoke: Macmillan, 1998.

Geelhoed, E. Bruce. *Charles E. Wilson and Controversy at the Pentagon, 1953 to 1957.* Detroit, Mich.: Wayne State University Press, 1979.

Gehler, Michael. 'Der 17. Juni aus der Sicht des Foreign Office', *Aus Politik und Zeitgeschichte,* B25 (18 June 1993), 22–31.

Geiss, Imanuel. *Der lange Weg in die Katastrophe: Die Vorgeschichte des Ersten Weltkrieges 1815–1914.* Munich: Piper, 1990; 2nd edn, 1991.

Gellermann, Günther W. *Der Krieg der nicht stattfand: Möglichkeiten, Überlegungen und Entscheidungen der deutschen Obersten Führung zur Verwendung chemischer Kampfstoffe im Zweiten Weltkrieg.* Koblenz: Bernard & Graefe, 1986.

Gerson Louis, L. *John Foster Dulles.* New York: Cooper Square Publishers, 1967.

Gietz, Axel. *Die Neue Alte Welt: Roosevelt, Churchill und die Europäische Nachkriegsordnung.* Munich: W. Fink, 1986.

Gilbert, Bentley B. *David Lloyd George: A Political Life. The Architect of Change, 1863–1912.* London: Batsford, 1987.

Gilbert, Martin. *Winston S. Churchill. The Official Biography.* London: Heinemann. Vol. 3: 1914–16 (1971); Vol. 4 *World in Torment, 1917–1922* (1975); Vol. 5: *Prophet of Truth, 1922–1939* (1976); Vol. 6: *Finest Hour, 1939–1941* (1983); Vol. 7: *Road to Victory, 1941–1945* (1986); Vol. 8: *Never Despair, 1945–1965* (1988; paperback edn, London: Minerva, 1990).

Gilbert, Martin. *Churchill's Political Philosophy.* Thank-Offering to Britain Fund Lectures 24, 25 and 27 November 1980. Oxford: Published for the British Academy by Oxford University Press, 1981.

Gilbert, Martin. *Churchill: A Life.* London: Heinemann, 1991 (paperback edn, London: Mandarin, 1993).

Gilbert, Martin. 'The Origins of the "Iron Curtain" Speech', in Kemper, R. Crosby. *Winston Churchill: Resolution, Defiance, Magnanimity, Good Will.* Columbia: University of Missouri Press, 1996, 35–60.

Giles, Frank. *The Locust Years: The Story of the Fourth French Republic, 1946–1958.* London: Secker & Warburg, 1991.

Gillingham, John. *Coal, Steel, and the Rebirth of Europe, 1945–1955: The Germans and French from Ruhr Conflict to Economic Community.* Cambridge: Cambridge University Press, 1991.

Gilmour, Ian and Mark Garnett. *Whatever Happened to the Tories: The Conservative Party since 1945.* London: Fourth Estate, 1997.

Glees, Anthony. 'Churchill's Last Gambit: What the Secret Documents Reveal [...]', *Encounter* 64 (April, 1985), 27–35.

Goar, D.C. 'A Chance for Peace – the Eisenhower Administration and the Soviet Peace Offensive of 1953', *Mid-America: An Historical Review* 76/3 (1994), 241–78.

Goncharov, S. N., John Wilson Lewis and Litai Xue. *Uncertain Partners: Stalin, Mao, and the Korean War.* Stanford, Calif.: Stanford University Press, 1993.

Goodhart, Philip. *Fifty Ships that Saved the World: The Foundation of the Anglo-American Alliance.* London: Heinemann, 1965.

Goodhart, Philip and Ursula Branston. *The 1922: The Story of the Conservative Backbenchers' Parliamentary Committee.* London: Macmillan, 1973.

Gopal, Sarvepalli. 'Churchill and India' in Blake, Robert and William Roger Louis (eds). *Churchill.* Oxford/New York: Oxford University Press, 1993, 457–71.

Gorodetsky, Gabriel. 'Churchill's Warning to Stalin: A Reappraisal', *Historical Journal* 29/4 (1986), 979–90.

Gorodetsky, Gabriel. *Grand Delusion: Stalin and the German Invasion of Russia.* New Haven/London: Yale University Press, 1999.

Gossel, Daniel A. *Briten, Deutsche und Europa: Die Deutsche Frage in der britischen Aussenpolitik 1945–1962.* Stuttgart: Steiner Verlag, 1999.

Gowing, Margaret (with Lorna Arnold). *Independence and Deterrence: Britain and Atomic Energy, 1945–1952.* Vol. 1: *Policy Making.* London: Macmillan [for the United Kingdom Atomic Energy Authority], 1974.

Graebner, Norman A, 'Yalta, Potsdam, and Beyond: The British and American Perspectives' in Lane, Anne and Howard Temperley (eds). *The Rise and Fall of the Grand Alliance, 1941–45.* Basingstoke: Macmillan, 1995, 226–54.

Graml, Hermann. 'Die Legende von der verpaßten Gelegenheit. Zur sowjetischen Notenkampagne des Jahres 1952'. *Vierteljahrshefte für Zeitgeschichte* 29 (1981), 307–41.

Grantham, John T. 'British Labour and the Hague "Congress of Europe": National Sovereignty Defended', *Historical Journal* 24 (1981), 443–52.

Graziosi, Andrea. 'The Great Strikes of 1953 in Soviet Labor Camps in the Accounts of their Participants: A Review', *Cahiers du Monde Russe et Soviétique* 33/4 (1992), 419–46.

Greenstein, Fred I. *The Hidden-Hand Presidency: Eisenhower as Leader.* New York: Basic Books, 1982.

Greenwood, Sean. 'Return to Dunkirk: the Origins of the Anglo-French Treaty of March 1947', *Journal of Strategic Studies* 6/4 (1983), 49–65.

Greenwood, Sean. 'Ernest Bevin, France and Western Union: August 1945–February 1946', *European History Quarterly* 14 (1984), 319–38.

Greenwood, Sean. 'The Third Force Policy of Ernest Bevin', in Dumoulin, Michel (ed.), *Wartime Plans* for *Postwar Europe, 1940–1947*. Brussels: Nomos-Verlag, 1995, 419–36.

Greenwood, Sean. *The Alternative Alliance: Anglo-French Relations before the Coming of NATO, 1944–48*. London: Minerva Press, 1996.

Grewe, Wilhelm Georg. *Deutsche Aussenpolitik der Nachkriegszeit*. Stuttgart: Deutsche Verlags-Anstalt, 1960.

Griffith, William E. *The Ostpolitik of the Federal Republic of Germany*. Cambridge, Mass.: MIT Press, 1978.

Grigg, John. 'Churchill and Lloyd George', in Blake, Robert and William Roger Louis (eds). *Churchill*. Oxford/New York: Oxford University Press, 1993, 97–111.

Grose, Peter. *Gentleman Spy: The Life of Allen Dulles*. Boston: Houghton Mifflin, 1994.

Grose, Peter. *Operation Rollback: America's Secret War Behind the Iron Curtain*. Boston: Houghton Mifflin, 2000.

Gross, F. and M. Kamil Dziewanowski. 'Plans by Exiles from East European Countries', in Lipgens, Walter (ed.), *Documents on the History of European Integration* (Berlin, 1984), Vol. 1, 609–58; Vol. 2, 353–413.

Grosser, Alfred. *The Western Alliance: European-American Relations since 1945*. London: Macmillan, 1980.

Guillen, Pierre. 'The Role of the Soviet Union as a Factor in the French Debates on the European Defence Community', *Journal of European Integration History* 2/1 (1996), 71–83.

Gullan, Harold I. *The Upset That Wasn't: Harry S. Truman and the Crucial Election of 1948*. Chicago: Ivan R. Dee, 1998.

Gupta, Partha Sarathi. 'Imperialism and the Labour Government of 1945–51', in Winter, J.M. (ed.), *The Working Class in Modern British History: Essays in Honour of Henry Pelling*. Cambridge: Cambridge University Press, 1983, 99–124.

Guttenplan, D.D. *The Holocaust on Trial*. London: Granta, 2001.

Haftendorn, Helga. 'Adenauer und die europäische Sicherheit', in Blumenwitz, Dieter et al. (eds). *Konrad Adenauer und seine Zeit: Politik und Persönlichkeit des Ersten Bundeskanzlers*. Vol. 2: *Beiträge der Wissenschaft*. Stuttgart: Deutsche Verlags-Anstalt, 1976, 92–110.

Hagen, Manfred. *DDR-Juni'53. Die erste Volkserhebung im Stalinismus*. Stuttgart: Steiner Verlag, 1992.

Hahn Peter, L. *The United States, Great Britain, and Egypt, 1945–1956: Strategy and Diplomacy in the Early Cold War*. Chapel Hill, N.C.: University of North Carolina Press, 1991.

Hall, Jean Graham and Douglas F. Martin. *Haldane: Statesman, Lawyer, Philosopher*. Chichester: B. Rose Law Publishers, 1996.

Hamby, Alonzo L. 'Henry A. Wallace, the Liberals and Soviet-American Relations', *Review of Politics* 30 (1968), 153–69.

Hamby, Alonzo L. *Man of the People: A Life of Harry S. Truman*. New York/Oxford: Oxford University Press, 1995.

Harbutt, Fraser J. 'American Challenge, Soviet Response. The Beginning of the Cold War, February–May 1946', *Political Science Quarterly* 96/4 (1981–2), 623–39.

Harbutt, Fraser J. 'Churchill, Hopkins and the Other Americans: An Alternative Perspective on Anglo-American Relations, 1941–45', *International History Review* 8 (1986), 236–62.

Harbutt, Fraser J. *The Iron Curtain: Churchill, America, and the Origins of the Cold War*. Oxford/New York: Oxford University Press, 1986.

Harris, Kenneth. *Attlee*. Revised edn, London: Weidenfeld and Nicolson, 1995 (1st edn, 1982).

Haslam, Jonathan. 'Soviet War-Aims', in Lane, Anne and Howard Temperley (eds). *The Rise and Fall of the Grand Alliance, 1941–45*. Basingstoke: Macmillan, 1995, 22–42.

Hathaway, Robert M. *Ambiguous Partnership: Britain and America, 1944–1947*. New York/Guildford: Columbia University Press, 1981.

Hattersley, Roy. *Fifty Years On: A Prejudiced History of Britain since the War*. London: Abacus, 1998.

Hayter, William. *The Diplomacy of the Great Powers*. London: Hamish Hamilton, 1960.

Healey, Denis. *When Shrimps Learn to Whistle: Signposts for the Nineties*. London: Michael Joseph, 1990.

Hegedüs, Andras B. and Manfred Wilke (eds). *Satelliten nach Stalins Tod: Der 'Neue Kurs', 17. Juni 1953 in der DDR, Ungarische Revolution 1956*. Berlin: Akademie Verlag, 2000.

Heinrichs, Waldo H. *Threshold of War: Franklin D. Roosevelt and American Entry into World War II*. New York/Oxford: Oxford: Oxford University Press, 1988.

Heiser, Hans Joachim. *British Policy with Regard to the Unification Efforts on the European Continent*. Leyden: A. W. Sythoff, 1959.

Hennessy, Peter. *Whitehall*. London: Secker & Warburg, 1989.

Hennessy, Peter. *The Prime Minister: The Office and Its Holders since 1945*. London: Allen Lane, 2000.

Hennessy, Peter. 'Churchill and the Premiership', in *Transactions of the Royal Historical Society*, 6th series, Vol. XI. Cambridge: Cambridge University Press, 2001, 295–306.

Hennessy, Peter. *The Secret State. Whitehall and the Cold War*. London: Allen Lane and Penguin, 2002.

Hennessy, Peter and David Welsh. 'Lords of all they surveyed? Churchill's ministerial "overlords", 1951–53', *Parliamentary Affairs* 51/1 (1998), 62–70.

Herring George, C. *Aid to Russia, 1941–1946: Strategy, Diplomacy, the Origins of the Cold War*. New York/London: Columbia University Press, 1973.

Herring, George C. *America's Longest War: The United States and Vietnam, 1950–1975*. 3rd edn, New York/London: McGraw-Hill, 1986.

Herring, George C. '"A Good Stout Effort": John Foster Dulles and the Indochina Crisis, 1954–55', in Immerman, Richard H. (ed.). *John Foster Dulles and the Diplomacy of the Cold War*. Princeton, N.J.: Princeton University Press, 1990, 213–33.

Herrmann, David G. *The Arming of Europe and the Making of the First World War*. Princeton, N.J.: Princeton University Press, 1996.

Hershberg, James G. ' "Explosion in the Offing": German Rearmament and American Diplomacy, 1953–1955', *Diplomatic History* 16 (1992), 511–49.

Hershberg, James G. *James B. Conant: Harvard to Hiroshima and the Making of the Nuclear Age*. Stanford, Calif.: Stanford University Press, 1995.

Heuser, Beatrice. 'Subversive Operationen im Dienste der "Roll-Back"-Politik 1948–1953', *Vierteljahrshefte für Zeitgeschichte* 37 (1989), 279–97.

Hewlett, Richard G. and Jack M. Holl. *Atoms for Peace and War, 1953–1961: Eisenhower and the Atomic Energy Commission*. Berkeley, Calif.: University of California Press, 1989.

Hildebrand, Klaus. *Das vergangene Reich: Deutsche Außenpolitik von Bismarck bis Hitler, 1871–1945*. Stuttgart: Deutsche Verlags-Anstalt, 1995.

Hilderbrand, Robert C. *Dumbarton Oaks: The Origins of the United Nations and the Search for Postwar Security*. Chapel Hill, N.C.: University of North Carolina Press, 1990.

Hillgruber, Andreas. *Der Zweite Weltkrieg 1939–1945: Kriegsziele und Strategie der Grossen Mächte*. Stuttgart: Kohlhammer, 1982; 2nd edn., 1983, 4th edn., 1985.

Hillgruber, Andreas. *Deutschlands Rolle in der Vorgeschichte der beiden Weltkriege*, 3rd edn, Göttingen: Vandenhoeck & Ruprecht, 1986.

Hillgruber, Andreas. *Alliierte Pläne für eine 'Neutralisierung' Deutschlands 1945–1955*. Opladen: Westdeutscher Verlag, 1987.

Hinterhoff, Eugene. *Disengagement*. London: Stevens and Sons, 1959.

Hitchcock William, I. *France Restored: Cold War Diplomacy and the Quest for Leadership in Europe, 1944–1954*. Chapel Hill, N.C.: University of North Carolina Press, 1998.

Hitchens, Christopher. 'The Medals of His Defeats', *The Atlantic Monthly* (April, 2002), 118–37.

Hixson, Walter L. *George F. Kennan: Cold War Iconoclast*. New York: Columbia University Press, 1989.

Hixson, Walter L. *Parting the Curtain: Propaganda, Culture, and the Cold War, 1945–1961*. Basingstoke: Macmillan, 1997.

Hoffman, John David. *The Conservative Party in Opposition, 1945–51*. London: MacGibbon & Kee, 1964.

Hogan, Michael J. *The Marshall Plan: America, Britain, and the Reconstruction of Western Europe, 1947–52*. Cambridge: Cambridge University Press, 1987.

Hogan, Michael J. 'Eisenhower and Open Skies: A Case Study in "Psychological Warfare"', in Medhurst, Martin J. (ed.), *Eisenhower's War of Words: Rhetoric and Leadership*. East Lansing: Michigan State University Press, 1994, 137–55.

Hogan, Michael J. *A Cross of Iron: Harry S. Truman and the Origins of the National Security State, 1945–54*. Cambridge: Cambridge University Press, 1998.

Holloway, David. *Stalin and the Bomb: the Soviet Union and Atomic Energy, 1939–1956*. New Haven/London: Yale University Press, 1994.

Hoopes, Townsend. *The Devil and John Foster Dulles: The Diplomacy of the Eisenhower Era*. Boston: Little, Brown, 1973.

Horne, Alistair. *To Lose a Battle: France 1940*. Revised edn, London: Papermac, 1990 (first publ., 1969).

Horne, Alistair. *Macmillan 1894–1956, Vol. 1 of the Official Biography*. London: Macmillan, 1988.

Horne, Alistair. *Macmillan 1957–1986, Vol. 2 of the Official Biography*. London: Macmillan, 1989.

Horning, Ross Charles. 'Winston Churchill and British Policy towards Russia, 1918–19.' Unpubl. dissertation, George Washington University, Washington, DC, 1958.

Hough, Richard Alexander. *Former Naval Person: Churchill and the Wars at Sea*. London: Weidenfeld and Nicolson, 1985.

Howard, Anthony. *Rab: The Life of R.A. Butler*. London: Cape, 1987.

Howard, Michael. *Disengagement*. Harmondsworth: Penguin, 1958.

Howard, Michael. *Grand Strategy. Vol. 4: August 1942–September 1943*. History of the Second World War. London: H.M.S.O., 1972.

Howard, Michael. 'Churchill and the First World War', in Blake, Robert and William Roger Louis (eds). *Churchill*. Oxford/New York: Oxford University Press, 1993, 129–45.

Hudemann, Rainer and Raymond Poidevin (with Annette Maas). *Die Saar 1945–1955: Ein Problem der Europäischen Geschichte*. Munich: R. Oldenbourg, 1992 (2nd edn, 1995).

Hughes, E.J. 'Winston Churchill and the Formation of the United Nations Organization', *Journal of Contemporary History* 9/4 (1974), 177–94.

Huldermann, Bernhard. *Albert Ballin*. Oldenburg i.O./Berlin: G. Stallin, 1922 (English edition of the same title trans. by W.J. Eggers, London/New York: Cassell, 1922; repr. Westport, Conn.: Greenwood Press, 1984, 2000).

Hyam, Ronald. 'Churchill and the British Empire', in Blake, Robert and William Roger Louis (eds). *Churchill*. Oxford/New York: Oxford University Press, 1993, 167–85.

Immerman, Richard H. 'Between the Unattainable and the Unacceptable: Eisenhower and Dienbienphu', in Melanson, Richard A. and David Mayers (eds). *Reevaluating Eisenhower: American Foreign Policy in the 1950s*. Urbana, Ill.: University of Illinois Press, 1987, 120–54.

Immerman, Richard H. (ed.). *John Foster Dulles and the Diplomacy of the Cold War*. Princeton, N.J.: Princeton University Press, 1990.

Immerman, Richard H. *John Foster Dulles: Piety, Pragmatism, and Power in U.S. Foreign Policy*. Wilmington, Del.: Scholarly Resources, 1999.

Ingimundarson, Valur. 'Cold War Misperceptions: The Communist and Western Responses to the East German Refugee Crisis in 1953', *Journal of Contemporary History* 29 (1994), 463–81.

Ingimundarson, Valur. 'The Eisenhower Administration, the Adenauer Government, and the Political Uses of the East German Uprising of 1953', *Diplomatic History* 20/3 (1996), 381–409.

Ingimundarson, Valur. '"Der Chef des Kalten Krieges". C.D. Jackson, psychologische Kriegführung und die deutsche Frage 1953/54', *Vierteljahrshefte für Zeitgeschichte* 46/2 (1998), 221–51.

Irving, David. *Churchill's War. Vol. 1: The Struggle for Power*. Bullsbrook, W.A.: Veritas, 1987.

Irving, David. *Churchill's War. Vol. 2: Triumph in Adversity*. London: Focal Point, 2001.

Isaacson, Walter and Evan Thomas. *The Wise Men: Six Friends and the World they Made: Acheson, Bohlen, Harriman, Kennan, Lovett, Mccloy*. New York: Simon & Schuster, 1986.

Jackson, Ian. '"The Limits of International Leadership": The Eisenhower Administration, East-West Trade and the Cold War, 1953–54', *Diplomacy & Statecraft* 11/3 (2000), 113–38.

Jackson, Ian. *The Economic Cold War: America, Britain and East-West Trade, 1948–63*. Basingstoke: Palgrave, 2001.

Jaeckel, Eberhard. *David Irving's Hitler: A Faulty History Dissected*. Port Angeles, Wash., 1993.

James, Robert Rhodes. 'The Politician', in A.J.P. Taylor et al., *Churchill: Four Faces and the Man*. London: Allen Lane, 1969, 53–115.

James, Robert Rhodes. *Churchill: A Study in Failure, 1900–1939*. London: Weidenfeld and Nicolson, 1984 (1st edn 1970).

James, Robert Rhodes. *Gallipoli*. London: Pan Books, 1984 (1st edn 1965).

James, Robert Rhodes. *Anthony Eden*. Paperback edn, London: Papermac, 1986.

James, Robert Rhodes. *Bob Boothby: A Portrait*. London: Hodder & Stoughton, 1991.

James, Robert Rhodes. 'Churchill the Parliamentarian, Orator, Statesman', in Blake, Robert and William Roger Louis (eds). *Churchill*. Oxford/New York: Oxford University Press, 1993, 503–17.

Jänicke, Martin. *Der dritte Weg. Die anti-stalinistische Opposition gegen Stalin seit 1953*. Cologne: Neuer Deutscher Verlag, 1964.

Jansen, Hans-Heinrich. *Grossbritannien, das Scheitern der EVG und der Nato-Beitritt der Bundesrepublik Deutschland*. Bochum: Brockmeyer, 1992.

Jarausch, Konrad H. *The Enigmatic Chancellor: Bethmann Hollweg and the Hubris of Imperial Germany*. New Haven/London: Yale University Press, 1973.

Jarausch, Konrad H. 'Revising German History: Bethmann Hollweg Revisited', *Central European History* 21/3 (1988), 224–43.

Jefferys, Kevin. 'British Politics and Social Policy during the Second World War', *Historical Journal* 30/1 (1987), 123–44.

Jefferys, Kevin. *The Churchill Coalition and Wartime Politics, 1940–1945*. Manchester: Manchester University Press, 1991.

Jefferys, Kevin. *The Attlee Governments, 1945–1951*. London/New York: Longman, 1992.

Jenkins, Roy. 'Churchill: the Government of 1951–55', in Blake, Robert and William Roger Louis (eds). *Churchill*. Oxford/New York: Oxford University Press, 1993, 491–502.

Jenkins, Roy. *Churchill*. London: Macmillan, 2001.

Johnston, Andrew M. 'Mr Slessor Goes to Washington: The Influence of the British Global Strategy Paper and the Eisenhower New Look', *Diplomatic History* 22/3 (1998), 361–98.

Jones, Bill. *The Russia Complex: The British Labour Party and the Soviet Union*. Manchester: Manchester University Press, 1977.

Jones, G. W. and Bernard Donoughue. *Herbert Morrison: Portrait of a Politician.* London: Weidenfeld and Nicolson, 1973.

Jones, Harriet and Michael D. Kandiah (eds). *The Myth of Consensus: New Views on British History, 1945–64.* Basingstoke: Macmillan, 1996.

Jones, Howard. '*A New Kind of War*': *America's Global Strategy and the Truman Doctrine in Greece.* New York: Oxford University Press, 1989.

Jones, Howard and Randall B. Woods. 'Origins of the Cold War in Europe and the Near East: Recent Historiography and the National Security Imperative', in Hogan, Michael J. (ed.). *America in the World: The Historiography of American Foreign Relations since 1941.* New York: Cambridge University Press, 1995, 234–69.

Jones, Peter. 'Labour-Regierung, deutsche Wiederbewaffnung und die EVG 1950–51', in Volkmann, Hans-Erich and Walter Schwengler (eds). *Die Europäische Verteidigungsgemeinschaft: Stand und Probleme der Forschung.* Boppard am Rhein: Boldt, 1985, 51–80.

Jones, Peter M. *America and the British Labour Party: The Special Relationship at Work.* London: I.B. Tauris, 1996.

Kaiser, Wolfram. *Using Europe, Abusing the Europeans: Britain and European Integration, 1945–63.* Basingstoke: Macmillan, 1996.

Kandiah, Michael D. 'The Conservative Party and the 1945 General Election', *Contemporary Record* 9/1 (1995), 22–47.

Kaplan, Lawrence S., Denise Artaud and Mark R. Rubin (eds). *Dien Bien Phu and the Crisis of Franco-American Relations, 1954–1955.* Wilmington, Del.: Scholarly Resources, 1990.

Karabell, Zachary. *The Last Campaign: How Harry Truman Won the 1948 Election.* New York: Knopf, 2000.

Karber, Phillip A. and Jerald A. Combs. 'The United States, NATO, and the Soviet Threat to Western Europe: Military Estimates and Policy Options, 1945–1963', *Diplomatic History* 22/3 (1998), 399–419.

Katzer, Nikolaus. 'Die Berliner Viermächtekonferenz von 1954 und die Deutsche Frage', in Blumenwitz, Dieter (ed.). *Die Deutschlandfrage vom 17. Juni 1953. Bis zu den Genfer Viermächtekonferenzen von 1955.* Berlin: Duncker & Humblot, 1990, 49–74.

Katzer, Nikolaus. *Eine Übung im Kalten Krieg: Die Berliner Aussenministerkonferenz von 1954.* Cologne: Verlag Wissenschaft und Politik, 1994.

Kavanagh, Denis. 'Debate: The Postwar Consensus', *Twentieth Century British History* 3/2 (1992), 175–90.

Kavanagh, Dennis and Peter Morris. *Consensus Politics from Attlee to Thatcher.* Oxford/New York: Basil Blackwell, 1989.

Keeble, Curtis. *Britain and the Soviet Union, 1917–89.* Basingstoke: Macmillan, 1990.

Keefer, Edward C. 'President Dwight D. Eisenhower and the End of the Korean War', *Diplomatic History* 10/3 (1986), 267–89.

Keithly, David M. *Breakthrough in the Ostpolitik: The 1971 Quadripartite Agreement.* Boulder, Col.: Westview Press, 1986.

Kelly, Richard N. *Conservative Party Conferences: The Hidden System.* Manchester/New York: Manchester University Press, 1989.

Kendrick, Oliver. *Kennedy, Macmillan and the Nuclear Test-Ban Debate, 1961–3.* Basingstoke: Macmillan, 1998.

Kennan, George Frost. *Russia and the West under Lenin and Stalin.* New York: Mentor Books, 1961.

Kennedy, Paul M. *The Rise of the Anglo-German Antagonism 1860–1914.* London: Allen & Unwin, 1980.

Kennedy, Paul M. *The Realities behind Diplomacy: Background Influences on British External Policy, 1865–1980.* Paperback edn, London: Fontana, 1981.

Kennedy, Paul M. 'Strategic Aspects of the Anglo-German Naval Race', in Kennedy, Paul M. *Strategy and Diplomacy, 1870–1945: Eight Studies.* London/Boston: Allen & Unwin, 1983, 129–60.

Kent, John. *British Imperial Strategy and the Origins of the Cold War 1944–49.* Leicester: Leicester University Press, 1993.

Kerkhoff, Martin. *Grossbritannien, die Vereinigten Staaten und die Saarfrage, 1945 bis 1954.* Stuttgart: Steiner Verlag, 1996.

Kersaudy, François. *Churchill and De Gaulle.* New York: Atheneum, 1982.

Kershaw, Ian. *Hitler: 1896–1936. Hubris.* London: Allen Lane, 1998.

Kershaw, Ian. *Hitler: 1936–1945: Nemesis.* London: Allen Lane, 2000.

Kessel, Martina. *Westeuropa und die deutsche Teilung: Englische und französische Deutschlandpolitik auf den Aussenministerkonferenzen von 1945 bis 1947.* Munich: R. Oldenbourg, 1989.

Kettenacker, Lothar. *Krieg zur Friedenssicherung: Die Deutschlandplanung der britischen Regierung während des Zweiten Weltkrieges.* Göttingen: Vandenhoeck & Ruprecht, 1989.

Kettenacker, Lothar. 'Britain and German Unification, 1989/90', in K. Larres (ed. with E. Meehan). *Uneasy Allies: British-German Relations and European Integration since 1945*. Oxford: Oxford University Press, 2000, 99–123.

Kettle, Michael. *Russia and the Allies, 1917–1920*. 3 vols. Vol. 1: *The Allies and the Russian Collapse, March 1917*; Vol. 2: *The Road to Intervention, March–November 1918*; Vol. 3: *Churchill and the Archangel Fiasco, November 1918–July 1919*. London/New York: Routledge, 1981, 1988, 1992.

Keynes, John Maynard. *The Economic Consequences of Mr. Churchill*. London: L. and V. Woolf, 1925.

Khrushchev, Sergei. *Nikita Khrushchev: Creation of a Superpower*. University Park, Pa.: Pennsylvania State University Press, 2000.

Kidder, Randolph A. *Sir Ernest Cassel, International Financier: A Biography*. Cambridge, Mass.: Harvard University, 1935 (A.B. Honors Thesis).

Kießling, Günter. 'Zum Begriff der Neutralität in der deutschlandpolitischen Diskussion', *Deutschland-Archiv* 22 (1989), 384–90.

Killick, John. *The United States and European Reconstruction, 1945–1960*. Edinburgh: Keele University Press, 1997.

Kimball Warren, F. *The Most Unsordid Act: Lend-Lease, 1939–1941*. Baltimore/Ann Arbor: Johns Hopkins University Press, 1969.

Kimball, Warren F. *The Juggler: Franklin Roosevelt as Wartime Statesman*. Princeton, N.J.: Princeton University Press, 1991.

Kimball, Warren F. 'Wheel within a Wheel: Churchill, Roosevelt, and the Special Relationship', in Blake, Robert and William Roger Louis (eds). *Churchill*. Oxford/New York: Oxford University Press, 1993, 291–307.

Kimball, Warren F. 'Anglo-American War Aims, 1941–43. The First Review: Eden's Mission to Washington', in Lane, Anne and Howard Temperley (eds). *The Rise and Fall of the Grand Alliance, 1941–45*. Basingstoke: Macmillan, 1995, 1–21.

Kimball Warren, F. *Forged in War: Churchill, Roosevelt and the Second World War*. Paperback edn, London: HarperCollins, 1998.

Kingseed, Cole C. *Eisenhower and the Suez Crisis of 1956*. Baton Rouge, La.: Louisiana State University Press, 1995.

Kingston, Paul W. T. *Britain and the Politics of Modernization in the Middle East, 1945–1958*. Cambridge: Cambridge University Press, 1996.

Kipping, Matthias. *Zwischen Kartellen und Konkurrenz: Der Schuman-Plan und die Ursprünge der Europäischen Einigung 1944–1952*. Berlin: Duncker & Humblot, 1996.

Kissinger, Henry. *Diplomacy*. New York/London: Simon & Schuster, 1994.

Kiste, John van der. *Kaiser Wilhelm II: Germany's Last Emperor*. Stroud: Sutton, 1999.

Kitchen, Martin. *British Policy Towards the Soviet Union During the Second World War*. Basingstoke: Macmillan, 1986.

Kittel, Manfred. 'Zur Genesis einer Legende. Die Diskussion um die Stalin-Noten in der Bundesrepublik 1952–1958', *Vierteljahrshefte für Zeitgeschichte* 41 (1993), 355–90.

Kittel, Manfred. *Die Legende von der 'Zweiten Schuld': Vergangenheitsbewältigung in der Ära Adenauer*. Berlin: Ullstein, 1993.

Kleßmann, Christoph and Bernd Stöver. 'Einleitung: Das Krisenjahr 1953 und der 17. Juni in der DDR in der historischen Forschung', in Kleßmann, Christoph and Bernd Stöver (eds), *1953 – Krisenjahr des Kalten Krieges in Europa*. Cologne: Böhlau, 1999, 9–28.

Knight, Amy W. *Beria: Stalin's First Lieutenant*. Princeton, N.J.: Princeton University Press, 1993.

Köhler, Henning. *Adenauer. Eine politische Biographie*. Frankfurt/M.: Propyläen, 1994.

Kolko, Gabriel. *The Politics of War: Allied Diplomacy and the World Crisis of 1943–1945*. New York: Random House, 1968.

Köllner, Lutz et al. (ed.). *Die EVG-Phase. Anfänge Westdeutscher Sicherheitspolitik, 1945–1956*, Vol. 2. Munich: Oldenbourg, 1990.

Koop, Volker. *Kein Kampf um Berlin? Deutsche Politik zur Zeit der Berlin-Blockade 1948/1949*. Bonn: Bouvier, 1998.

Koss, Stephen E. *Lord Haldane: Scapegoat for Liberalism*. New York: Columbia University Press, 1969.

Kowalczuk, Ilko-Sascha, Armin Mitter and Stefan Wolle. *Der Tag X – 17. Juni 1953. Die 'Innere Staatsgründung' der DDR als Ergebnis der Krise 1952/54*. Berlin: Ch. Links, 1995.

Kowalski, Hans-Günter. 'Die EAC als Instrument alliierter Deutschlandplanung 1943–45', *Vierteljahrshefte für Zeitgeschichte* 19 (1971), 261ff.

Krämer, Martin. *Der Volksaufstand vom 17. Juni 1953 und sein politisches Echo in der Bundesrepublik Deutschland*. Bochum: Brockmeyer, 1996.

Kramer, Mark. 'The Early Post-Stalin Succession Struggle and Upheavals in East-Central Europe: Internal-External Linkages in Soviet Policy Making (Part 1)', *Journal of Cold War Studies* 1/1 (1999), 3–55.

Kramer, Mark. 'The Early Post-Stalin Succession Struggle and Upheavals in East-Central Europe: Internal-External Linkages in Soviet Policy Making (Part 2)', *Journal of Cold War Studies* 1/2 (1999), 3–38.

Kramer, Mark. 'The Early Post-Stalin Succession Struggle and Upheavals in East-Central Europe: Internal-External Linkages in Soviet Policy Making (Part 3)', *Journal of Cold War Studies* 1/3 (1999), 3–66.

Krieger, Wolfgang. 'Die britische Krise in historischer Perspektive', *Historische Zeitschrift* 247 (1988), 585–602.

Krockow, Christian Graf von. *Churchill: Eine Biographie des 20. Jahrhunderts.* 2nd edn, Hamburg: Hoffman und Campe, 1999.

Krüger, Peter. *Die Außenpolitik der Republik von Weimar.* Paperback edn, Darmstadt: Wissenschaftliche Buchgesellschaft, 1985.

Kuniholm, Bruce R. *The Origins of the Cold War in the Near East: Great Power Conflict and Diplomacy in Iran, Turkey, and Greece.* Princeton, N.J.: Princeton University Press, 1980.

Kunz, Diane B. *The Economic Diplomacy of the Suez Crisis.* Chapel Hill, N.C.: University of North Carolina Press, 1991.

Kusnitz, Leonard A. *Public Opinion and Foreign Policy: America's China Policy, 1949–1979.* Londn/Westport, Conn.: Greenwood Press, 1984.

Küsters, Hanns Jürgen. *Der Integrationsfriede: Viermächte-Verhandlungen über die Friedensregelung mit Deutschland 1945–1990.* Munich: R. Oldenbourg, 2000.

Kyle, Keith. *Suez.* London: Weidenfeld and Nicolson, 1990.

Lacey, Michael J. *The Truman Presidency.* Washington, D.C./Cambridge/New York: Woodrow Wilson International Center for Scholars & Cambridge University Press, 1989.

Lacouture, Jean. *Pierre Mendès France.* Paris: Seuil, 1981.

Lacouture, Jean. *De Gaulle: The Rebel 1890–1944* (trans. from the French by P. O'Brian). New York/London: W.W. Norton, 1990.

Lamb, Richard. *The Failure of the Eden Government.* London: Sidgwick & Jackson, 1987.

Lambakis, Steven James. *Winston Churchill, Architect of Peace: A Study of Statesmanship and the Cold War.* Westport, Conn.: Greenwood Press, 1993.

Lambi, Ivo N. *The Navy and German Power Politics, 1862–1914.* Boston/London: Allen & Unwin, 1984.

Lane, Anne and Howard Temperley (eds). *The Rise and Fall of the Grand Alliance, 1941–45.* Basingstoke: Macmillan, 1995.

Langhorne, Richard T.B. 'The Naval Question in Anglo-German Relations, 1912–1914,' *Historical Journal* 14/2 (1971), 359–70.

Langhorne, Richard T.B. 'Great Britain and Germany, 1911–1914,' in Hinsley, F.H. (ed.). *British Foreign Policy under Sir Edward Grey.* Cambridge: Cambridge University Press, 1977, 308–14.

Large, David Clay. *Germans to the Front: West German Rearmament in the Adenauer Era.* Chapel Hill, N.C.: University of North Carolina Press, 1996.

Larres, Klaus. 'A Search for Order: Britain and the Origins of a Western European Union, 1944–55', in Brivati, Brian and Harriet Jones (eds), *From Reconstruction to Integration: Britain and Europe since 1945.* Leicester: Leicester University Press, 1993, 71–87.

Larres, Klaus. 'Unification or Integration with the West? Britain and the Federal Republic of Germany in the early 1950s', in Aldrich, Richard J. and Michael F. Hopkins (eds). *Intelligence, Defence and Diplomacy: British Policy in the Post-war World.* London: Frank Cass, 1994, 42–75.

Larres, Klaus. 'Preserving Law and Order: Britain, the United States and the East German Uprising of 1953', *Twentieth Century British History* 5/3 (1994), 320–50

Larres, Klaus. *Politik der Illusionen. Churchill, Eisenhower und die deutsche Frage.* Göttingen: Vandenhoeck & Ruprecht, 1995 (Veröffentlichungen des Deutsschen Historischen Instituts, London, 35).

Larres, Klaus. 'Eisenhower and the First Forty Days after Stalin's Death: The Incompatibility of Détente and Political Warfare', *Diplomacy & Statecraft* 6/2 (1995), 431–69.

Larres, Klaus. 'Die Welt des John Foster Dulles (1939–1953)', *Historische Mitteilungen* 9/2 (1996), 256–82.

Larres, Klaus. 'Integrating Europe or Ending the Cold War? Churchill's post-war foreign policy,' *Journal of European Integration History* 2/1 (1996), 15–49.

Larres, Klaus. 'Germany and the West: The "Rapallo Factor" in German Foreign Policy from the 1950s to the 1990s', in Larres, Klaus and Panikos Panayi (eds). *The Federal Republic of Germany since 1949: Politics, Society and Economy before and after Unification.* London: Longman, 1996, 278–326.

Larres, Klaus. 'Konrad Adenauer (1876–1967)', in Oppelland, Torsten (ed.). *Deutsche Politiker 1949–1969.* Darmstadt: Wissenschaftliche Buchgesellschaft, 1999, Vol. 1., 13–24.

Larres, Klaus. 'Ein englisches Dilemma. Wie Margaret Thatcher die Wiedervereinigung verhindern wollte [...]', *Die Zeit*, No.4 (28 September 2000), 76 (Zeitläufte).

Larres, Klaus. 'Britain and the GDR, 1949–1989', in Larres, Klaus (ed. with E. Meehan), *Uneasy Allies: British-German Relations and European Integration since 1945*. Oxford: Oxford University Press, 2000, 63–98.

Larres, Klaus (ed. with Elizabeth Meehan), *Uneasy Allies: British-German Relations and European Integration since 1945*. Oxford: Oxford University Press, 2000.

Larres, Klaus. 'North Atlantic Treaty Organization', in De Conde, Alexander, Richard Dean Burns and Frederik Logevall (eds). *Encyclopedia of American Foreign Relations: Studies of the Principal Movements and Ideas*, Vol. 2, 2nd revd edn, New York: Scribner, 2002, 573–93.

Larres, Klaus and Kenneth Osgood (eds). *The Cold War After Stalin: A New International History*. Landham, MD/Oxford: Rowman & Littlefield, 2003 [forthcoming].

Larson, Deborah Welch. *Anatomy of Mistrust: U.S.-Soviet Relations During the Cold War*. Ithaca, N.Y.: Cornell University Press, 1997.

Lash, Joseph P. *Roosevelt and Churchill, 1939–1941: The Partnership that Saved the West*. London: Deutsch, 1976.

Lawlor, Sheila. 'Britain and the Russian Entry into the War', in Langhorne, Richard (ed.). *Diplomacy and Intelligence During the Second World War: Essays in Honour of F.H. Hinsley*. Cambridge: Cambridge University Press, 1985, 168–83.

Layton-Henry, Zig. 'The Young Conservatives, 1945–73', *Journal of Contemporary History* 8/2 (1973), 143–56.

Lee, Sabine. *Victory in Europe: Britain and Germany since 1945*. Harlow: Longman, 2001.

Lee, Steven Hugh. *The Korean War*. Harlow, Essex/New York: Longman, 2001.

Leffler, Melvyn P. *A Preponderance of Power: National Security, the Truman Administration, and the Cold War*. Stanford, Calif.: Stanford University Press, 1992.

Leffler, Melvyn P. 'Negotiating from Strength: Acheson, the Russians, and American Power', in Brinkley, Douglas (ed.), *Dean Acheson and the Making of U.S. Foreign Policy*. Basingstoke: Macmillan, 1993, 176–210.

Leonhard, Wolfgang. *Kreml ohne Stalin*. Cologne: Verlag für Politik und Wirtschaft, 1959, 2nd edn, 1960; English ed. (trans. by E. Wiskeman and M. Jackson), *The Kremlin since Stalin*. New York: Praeger, 1962 (republ. Westport, Conn.: Greenwood Press, 1975).

Leupold, Bernd. '*Weder Anglophil Noch Anglophob*': Grossbritannien im politischen Denken Konrad Adenauers. Ein Beitrag zur Geschichte der Deutsch-Britischen Beziehungen. Frankfurt/M.: Peter Lang, 1997.

Levering, Ralph B. *American Opinion and the Russian Alliance, 1939–1945*. Chapel Hill, N.C.: University of North Carolina Press, 1976.

Lewis, Julian. *Changing Direction: British Military Planning for Post-War Strategic Defence, 1942–1947*. London: Sherwood Press, 1988.

Li, Xiaobing and Hongshan Li (eds). *China and the United States: A New Cold War History*. Lanham, MD/Oxford: University Press of America, 1997.

Lindsay, Thomas F. and Michael Harrington. *The Conservative Party, 1918–1979*. 2nd edn, London/New York: Macmillan, 1979.

Lipgens, Walter (with two contributions by Wilfried Loth). *Die Anfänge der Europäischen Einigungspolitik 1945–1950. Pt 1: 1945–1947*. Stuttgart: Ernst Klett, 1977.

Lipgens, Walter. 'East European Plans for the Future of Europe: the Example of Poland', in Lipgens, Walter (ed.), *Documents on the History of European Integration*. Vol. 1. Berlin: De Gruyter, 1984, 609–58.

Lipstadt, Deborah E. *Denying the Holocaust: The Growing Assault on Truth and Memory*. New York: Free Prees, 1993.

Litwak, Robert S. *Détente and the Nixon Doctrine: American Foreign Policy and the Pursuit of Stability, 1969–1976*. Cambridge: Cambridge University Press, 1984.

Loth, Wilfried. *Die Teilung der Welt: Geschichte des Kalten Krieges 1941–1955*. Munich: Deutscher Taschenbuch-Verlag, 1980 (English edn, London: Routledge, 1988).

Loth, Wilfried. 'Die Résistance und die Pläne zur Europäischen Einigung', in Dumoulin, Michel (ed.), *Wartime Plans for Postwar Europe, 1940–1947*. Brussels: Nomos-Verlag, 1995, 47–57.

Loth, Wilfried. 'Stalin, die deutsche Frage und die DDR. Eine Antwort an meine Kritiker', *Deutschland-Archiv* 28/3 (1995), 290–8.

Loth, Wilfried. *Der Weg nach Europa: Geschichte der Europäischen Integration 1939–1957*. 3rd edn, Göttingen: Vandenhoeck & Ruprecht, 1996 (1st edn, 1990).

Loth, Wilfried. *Stalins ungeliebtes Kind. Warum Moskau die DDR nicht wollte*. Berlin: Rowohlt, 1994 (English transl.: Macmillan, 1998).

Louis, William Roger. *Imperialism at Bay, 1941–1945: The United States and the Decolonization of the British Empire.* New York: Oxford University Press, 1978.

Louis, William Roger. *The British Empire in the Middle East 1945–1951: Arab Nationalism, the United States, and Postwar Imperialism.* Oxford: Clarendon Press, 1984.

Louis, William Roger. 'American Anti-Colonialism and the Dissolution of the British Empire', in Louis, William Roger and Hedley Bull (eds). *The 'Special Relationship': Anglo-American Relations since 1945.* Oxford/New York: Clarendon Press, 1989, 61–83.

Louis, William Roger. 'Churchill and Egypt', in Blake, Robert and William Roger Louis (eds). *Churchill.* Oxford/New York: Oxford University Press, 1993, 473–90.

Louis, William Roger. 'How Mussadeq was ousted: the untold story behind the CIA-MI6 coup', *TLS,* No. 5126 (29 June 2001), 13–15.

Louis, William Roger and Hedley Bull (eds). *The 'Special Relationship': Anglo-American Relations since 1945.* Oxford/New York: Clarendon Press, 1989.

Louis, William Roger and Roger Owen (eds). *Suez: The Crisis and its Consequences.* Oxford: Clarendon Press, 1989.

Lovell, Richard. *Churchill's Doctor: A Biography of Lord Moran.* London: Royal Society of Medicine Services, 1992.

Lovell, Richard. 'Lord Moran's Prescriptions for Churchill', *British Medical Journal* 310 (1995), 1537–8.

Lowe, John. *The Great Powers, Imperialism, and the German Problem, 1865–1925.* London/New York: Routledge, 1994.

Lowe, Rodney. 'The Second World War, Consensus and the Foundation of the Welfare State', *Twentieth Century British History* 1/2 (1990), 152–82.

Löwenthal, Richard. 'Vorwort', in Baring, Arnulf. *Der 17. Juni.* Revd edn, Cologne: Kiepenheuer & Witsch, 1965, 1–6.

Lucas, Scott. 'Campaign of Truth: The Psychological Strategy Board and American Ideology, 1951–1953', *International History Review* 18 (1996), 279–302.

Lucas, Scott. *Freedom's War: The US Crusade Against the Soviet Union, 1945–56.* Manchester: Manchester University Press, 1999.

Lukacs, John. *Five Days in London, May 1940.* New Haven/London: Yale University Press, 1999.

Lukacs, John. 'The Fifties: Another View. Revising the Eisenhower Era', *Harper's Magazine* (January, 2002), 64–70.

Lundestad, Geir. *'Empire' by Integration: The United States and European Integration, 1945–1997.* Oxford: Oxford University Press, 1997.

Lundestad, Geir. ' "Empire by Invitation" in the American Century', *Diplomatic History* 23/2 (1999), 189–217.

McCullough, David G. *Truman.* New York: Simon & Schuster, 1993.

McDonald, James Kenneth. 'The Washington Conference and the Naval Balance of Power, 1921–22,' in Hattendorf, John B. and Robert S. Jordan (eds). *Maritime Strategy and the Balance of Power: Britain and America in the Twentieth Century.* Basingstoke: Macmillan, 1989, 189–213.

MacDonogh, Giles. *The Last Kaiser: William the Impetuous.* London: Weidenfeld and Nicolson, 2000.

McGeehan, Robert. *The German Rearmament Question: American Diplomacy and European Defense after World War II.* Urbana, Ill: University of Illinois Press, 1971.

Mackay, Ronald William Gordon. *Federal Europe: Being the Case for European Federation, Together with a Draft Constitution of a United States of Europe.* London: Michael Joseph, 1940.

MacLean, Elizabeth K. *Joseph E.Davies: Envoy to the Soviets.* Westport, Conn./London: Praeger, 1992.

McLellan, David S. *Dean Acheson: The State Department Years.* New York: Dodd Mead & Co., 1976.

McNay, John T. *Acheson and Empire: The British Accent in American Foreign Policy.* Columbia, Mo.: University of Missouri Press, 2001.

McNeal, Robert H. *Stalin: Man and Ruler.* Houndmills, Basingstoke: Macmillan, 1988.

McNeill William Hardy. *America, Britain and Russia: Their Cooperation and Conflict, 1941–1946* (Royal Institute of International Affairs. Survey of International Affairs, 1939–1946, Vol. 3). London: Oxford University Press, 1953 (repr., 1970).

Maddox, Robert James. *From War to Cold War: The Education of Harry S. Truman.* Boulder, Colo./London: Westview Press, 1988.

Mählert, Ulrich. *Kleine Geschichte der DDR.* Munich: Beck, 1998.

Maier, Charles S. *Dissolution: The Crisis of Communism and the End of East Germany.* Princeton, N.J.: Princeton University Press, 1997.

Maier, Klaus. 'Die Auseinandersetzungen um die EVG als europäisches Unterbündnis der NATO 1950–54. Die EVG als supranationales Instrument für die kontrollierte Wiederbewaffnung der

Bundesrepublik', in Herbst, Ludolf, Werner Bührer and Hanno Sowade (eds). *Vom Marshallplan zur EWG: Die Eingliederung der Bundesrepublik Deutschland in die Westliche Welt*. Munich: R. Oldenbourg, 1990, 447–74.

Malkiewicz, Andrzej and Krzysztof Ruchniewicz. 'Das polnische Echo auf den Juni-Aufstand in der DDR im Jahre 1953', in Kleßmann, Christoph and Bernd Stöver (eds), *1953 – Krisenjahr des Kalten Krieges in Europa*. Cologne: Böhlau, 1999, 181–97.

Manchester, William Raymond. *The Last Lion. Winston Spencer Churchill: Visions of Glory, 1874–1932.* Boston: Little, Brown, 1983.

Marder, Arthur J. *From the Dreadnought to Scapa Flow: The Royal Navy in the Fisher Era, 1904–1919. Vol. 1: The Road to War, 1904–1914.* Oxford: Oxford University Press, 1961 (revd edn, 1978).

Marks III, Frederick W. 'The Real Hawk at Dienbienphu: Dulles or Eisenhower?', *Pacific Historical Review* 59/3 (1990), 297–322.

Marks III, Frederick W. *Power and Peace: The Diplomacy of John Foster Dulles.* Westport, Conn.: Praeger, 1993.

Marlow, James D. *Questioning the Postwar Consensus Thesis: Towards an Alternative Account.* Aldershot/Brookfield, Vt.: Dartmouth, 1996.

Marsh, David. *Post-War British Politics in Perspective.* Oxford: Basil Blackwell, 1999.

Martel, Leon. *Lend-Lease, Loans, and the Coming of the Cold War: A Study of the Implementation of Foreign Policy.* Boulder, Colo.: Westview Press, 1979.

Martin, Bernd. *Friedensinitiativen und Machtpolitik im Zweiten Weltkrieg, 1939–1942.* Düsseldorf: Droste, 1974.

Martin, Bernd. 'Churchill and Hitler, 1940: Peace or War?' in Parker, Robert A.C. (ed.). *Winston Churchill: Studies in Statesmanship.* London: Brassey's, 1995, 83–96.

Martschukat, Jürgen. *Antiimperialismus, Öl und die 'Special Relationship'. Die Nationalisierung der Anglo-Iranian Oil Company im Iran 1951–54.* Münster: Lit, 1995.

März, Peter. *Die Bundesrepublik zwischen Westintegration und Stalin-Noten: Zur Deutschlandpolitischen Diskussion 1952 in der Bundesrepublik vor dem Hintergrund der Westlichen und der Sowjetischen Deutschlandpolitik.* Frankfurt/M.: Peter Lang, 1982.

Massie, Robert K. *Dreadnought: Britain, Germany, and the Coming of the Great War.* London: Cape, 1992.

Mastny, Vojtech. *Russia's Road to the Cold War: Diplomacy, Warfare, and the Politics of Communism, 1941–1945.* New York: Columbia University Press, 1979.

Mastny, Vojtech. *The Cold War and Soviet Insecurity: The Stalin Years.* New York: Oxford University Press, 1996.

Mauch, Christof. 'Pazifismus und politische Kultur', in Fiebig-von Hase, Ragnhild and Jürgen Heideking (eds), *Zwei Wege in die Moderne: Aspekte der deutsch-amerikanischen Beziehungen, 1900–1918.* Trier: Wissenschaftlicher Verlag, 1998, 261–92.

Maurer, John H. 'Churchill's Naval Holiday: Arms Control and the Anglo-German Naval Race, 1912–1914,' *Journal of Strategic Studies* 15 (1992), 104ff.

Maurer, Pierre. *La Réconciliation Soviéto-Yougoslave, 1954–1958: Illusions et Désillusions de Tito.* Fribourg, CH: DelVal, 1991.

Maurice, Frederick. *Haldane, 1856–1915: the Life of Viscount Haldane of Cloan, K.T., O.M.* London: Faber and Faber, 1937 (repr.: Westport, Conn.: Greenwood Press, 1970).

Mauter, Wendell R. 'Churchill and the Unification of Europe', *Historian* (Fall, 1998) [http://www.winstonchurchill.org/ITJ102.htm].

Mawby, Spencer W. 'Détente Deferred: The Attlee Government, German Rearmament and Anglo-Soviet Rapprochement, 1950–51', *Contemporary British History* 12/2 (1998), 1–21.

Mawby, Spencer W. *Containing Germany: Britain and the Arming of the Federal Republic.* Basingstoke: Macmillan, 1999.

May, Ernest R. *American Cold War Strategy: Interpreting NSC 68.* Boston: Bedford Books of St. Martin's Press, 1993.

Mayer, Frank A. *The Opposition Years: Winston S. Churchill and the Conservative Party, 1945–1951.* New York: Peter Lang, 1992.

Mayers, David Allan. *The Ambassadors and America's Soviet Policy.* New York: Oxford University Press, 1995.

Mayle, Paul D. *Eureka Summit: Agreement in Principle and the Big Three at Tehran, 1943.* Newark, Del./London: University of Delaware Press, 1987.

Mayne, Richard and John Pinder. *Federal Union: The Pioneers: A History of Federal Union.* Basingstoke: Macmillan, 1990.

Meade, J. E. *Negotiations for Benelux : An Annotated Chronicle, 1943–1956.* Princeton, N.J.: International Finance Section: Department of Economics and Sociology Princeton University, 1957.

Medhurst, Martin J. 'Atoms for Peace and Nuclear Hegemony: The Rhetorical Structure of the Cold War Campaign', *Armed Forces & Society* 23/4 (1997), 571–93.

Meissner, Boris. 'Die Sowjetunion und die deutsche Frage 1949–1955', in Geyer, Dietrich (ed.), *Osteuropahandbuch, Sowjetunion: Außenpolitik II, 1955–1973*. Cologne, 1976, 473–501.

Menasse, Eva. *Der Holocaust vor Gericht: der Prozess um David Irving*. Berlin: Siedler, 2000.

Messer Robert, L. *The End of an Alliance: James F. Byrnes, Roosevelt, Truman, and the Origins of the Cold War*. Chapel Hill, N.C.: University of North Carolina Press, 1982.

Metcalfe, Philip. *1933*. Paperback edn, London: Black Swan, 1990.

Meyer, Thomas. *Endlich eine Tat, eine befreiende Tat: Alfred Von Kiderlen-Wächters "Panthersprung nach Agadir" unter dem Druck der Öffentlichen Meinung*. Husum: Matthiesen, 1996.

Meyer-Landrut, Nikolaus. *Frankreich und die Deutsche Einheit: Die Haltung der Französischen Regierung und Öffentlichkeit zu den Stalin-Noten 1952*. Munich: R. Oldenbourg, 1988.

Mieder, Wolfgang. ' "Make Hell While the Sun Shines": Proverbial Rhetoric in Winston Churchill's *The Second World War*', *De Proverbio: An Electronic Journal of International Proverb Studies* 1/2 (1995) [http://info.utas.edu.au/docs/flonta/DP,1,295/CHURCHILL.html].

Miller, Roger G. *To Save a City: The Berlin Airlift, 1948–1949*. College Station, TX: Texas A&M University Press, 2000.

Milward Alan, S. (with the assistance of George Brennan and Federico Romero). *The European Rescue of the Nation-State*. London/New York: Routledge, 1992 (new edn 2000).

Miner, Steven Merritt. *Between Churchill and Stalin: The Soviet Union, Great Britain, and the Origins of the Grand Alliance*. Chapel Hill, N.C.: University of North Carolina Press, 1988.

Mitrovich, Gregory. *Undermining the Kremlin: America's Strategy to Subvert the Soviet Bloc, 1947–1956*. Ithaca, N.Y.: Cornell University Press, 2000.

Mitter, Armin. 'Die Ereignisse im Juni und Juli 1953 in der DDR. Aus den Akten des Ministeriums für Staatssicherheit', *Aus Politik und Zeitgeschichte*, B5 (1991), 31–41.

Mommsen, Wolfgang J. 'Der Topos vom unvermeidlichen Krieg. Außenpolitik und öffentliche Meinung im deutschen Reich im letzten Jahrzehnt vor 1914', in Dülffer, Jost and Karl Holl (eds), *Bereit zum Krieg. Kriegsmentalität im wilhelminischen Deutschland 1890–1914*. Göttingen: Vandenhoeck & Ruprecht, 1986, 194–224.

Monroe, Elizabeth. *Britain's Moment in the Middle East 1914–1956*. New and revd 2nd edn. London: Chatto & Windus, 1981 (1st ed., 1964).

Morgan, Kenneth O. *Labour in Power 1945–1951*. Oxford: Clarendon Press, 1984.

Morgan, Kenneth O. 'Lloyd George and Germany', *Historical Journal* 39/3 (1996), 755–66.

Morgan, Ted. *Churchill: Young Man in a Hurry, 1874–1915*. New York: Simon & Schuster, 1982.

Morton, H. V. *Atlantic Meeting: An Account of Mr Churchill's Voyage in H.M.S. Prince of Wales, in August 1941, and the Conference with President Roosevelt, Which Resulted in the Atlantic Charter*. London: Methuen, 1943.

Muller, James W. (ed.). *Churchill's 'Iron Curtain' Speech Fifty Years Later*. Columbia, Mo.: University of Missouri Press, 1999.

Müller-Enberg, Helmut. *Der Fall Rudolf Herrnstadt. Tauwetterpolitik vor dem 17. Juni*. Berlin: Links-Druck Verlag, 1993.

Murray, J.A. 'Foreign Policy Debated: Sir Edward Grey and His Critics, 1911–1912', in Askew, William C. and Lillian Parker Wallace (eds), *Power, Public Opinion and Diplomacy. Essays in Honor of Eber Malcolm Carroll*. Durham, N.C.: Duke University Press, 1959, 140–71.

Murray, P. 'Spinelli and European Union', in Murray, Philomena and Paul Rich (eds), *Visions of European Unity*. Boulder, Col.: Westview Press, 1996, 109–30.

Murphy, David E., Sergei A. Kondrashev and George Bailey. *Battleground Berlin: CIA vs. KGB in the Cold War*. New Haven/London: Yale University Press, 1997.

Nathan, James A. (ed.). *The Cuban Missile Crisis Revisited*. New York: St. Martin's Press, 1992.

Neilson, K. '"Greatly Exaggerated": The Myth of the Decline of Britain before 1914', *International History Review* 13 (1991), 695–725.

Nekrassow, Vladimir F. (ed.). *Berija. Henker in Stalins Diensten. Ende einer Karriere* (trans. from the Russian by B. and L. Lehnhardt). Augsburg: Bechtermünz Verlag, 1997 (first publ., Moscow, 1991).

Nelson, Anna K. 'The "Top of Policy Hill": President Eisenhower and the National Security Council', *Diplomatic History* 7 (1983), 307–26.

Nelson, Anna K. 'The Importance of Foreign Policy Process: Eisenhower and the National Security Council', in Ambrose, Stephen E. and Günter Bischof (eds). *Eisenhower: A Centenary Assessment*. Baton Rouge, Louis., 1995, 111–25.

Nelson, Keith L. *The Making of Détente: Soviet-American Relations in the Shadow of Vietnam*. Baltimore, Md./London: Johns Hopkins University Press, 1995.

Newhouse, John. *War and Peace in the Nuclear Age.* New York: Knopf, 1989.

Niedhart, Gottfried. *Grossbritannien und die Sowjetunion 1934–1939. Studien zur britischen Politik der Friedenssicherung zwischen den beiden Weltkriegen.* Munich: W. Fink, 1972.

Noack, Paul. *Das Scheitern der Europäischen Verteidigungsgesellschaft. Entscheidungsprozesse vor und nach dem 30. August 1954.* Düsseldorf: Droste, 1977.

Northedge, F. S. and Audrey Wells. *Britain and Soviet Communism: The Impact of a Revolution.* London/Basingstoke: Macmillan, 1982.

Notter Harley, A. *Postwar Foreign Policy Preparation, 1939–1945.* Washington, D.C.: U.S. Government Printing Office, 1949 (repr.: Westport, Conn.: Greenwood Press, 1975).

Offner, Arnold A. *Another Such Victory: President Truman and the Cold War, 1945–1953.* Stanford, Calif.: Stanford University Press, 2002.

Ollard, Richard. 'Churchill and the Navy,' in Blake, Robert and William Roger Louis (eds). *Churchill.* Oxford/New York: Oxford University Press, 1993, 375–95.

Olson, Gregory A. 'Eisenhower and the Indochina Problem', in Medhurst, Martin J. (ed.), *Eisenhower's War of Words: Rhetoric and Leadership.* East Lansing: Michigan State University Press, 1994, 97–135.

Oncken, Emil. *Panthersprung nach Agadir: Die deutsche Politik während der zweiten Marokkokrise 1911.* Düsseldorf: Droste, 1973 (2nd edn, 1981).

Onslow, Sue. *Backbench Debate within the Conservative Party and Its Influence on British Foreign Policy, 1948–57.* Basingstoke/New York: Macmillan/St. Martin's Press, 1997.

Orde, Anne. *The Eclipse of Great Britain: The United States and British Imperial Decline, 1895–1956.* London: Macmillan, 1996.

Osgood, Kenneth. 'Form before Substance: Eisenhower's Commitment to Psychological Warfare and Negotiations with the Enemy', *Diplomatic History* 24/3 (2000), 405–33.

Ostermann Christian, F., *The United States, the East German Uprising of 1953, and the Limits of Rollback.* Working Paper. Cold War International History Project, No. 11. Washington, D.C.: CWIHP and Woodrow Wilson International Center for Scholars, 1994.

Ostermann, Christian F. '"Keeping the Pot Simmering": The United States and the East German Uprising', *German Studies Review* 19/1 (1996), 61–89.

Ostermann, Christian F. '"This is Not a Politburo but a Madhouse": The Post-Stalin Succession Struggle […]' [Introduction], *Cold War International History Bulletin* (CWIHB) 10 (March 1998), 61–72.

Ostermann, Christian F. '"Die beste Chance für ein Rollback?" Amerikanische Politik und der 17. Juni 1953', in Kleßmann, Christoph and Bernd Stöver (eds), *1953 – Krisenjahr des Kalten Krieges in Europa.* Cologne: Böhlau, 1999, 115–39.

Otto, Wilfriede. 'Sowjetische Deutschlandpolitik 1952/53: Forschungs- und Wahrheitsprobleme', *Deutschland-Archiv*, 26/8 (1993), 948–54.

Oudenaren, John van. *Détente in Europe: The Soviet Union and the West since 1953.* Durham, N.C./London: Duke University Press, 1991.

Oudin, Bernard. *Aristide Briand: La Paix, Une Idée Neuve en Europe.* Paris: Editions Robert Laffont, 1987.

Ovendale, Ritchie. *The English-Speaking Alliance: Britain, the United States, the Dominions and the Cold War 1945–1951.* London/Boston: G. Allen & Unwin, 1985.

Ovendale, Ritchie. *Britain, the United States and the Transfer of Power in the Middle East, 1945–1962.* London: Leicester University Press, 1996.

Overy, Richard J. *Why the Allies Won.* Paperback edn, London: Pimlico, 1996.

Overy, Richard J. *Russia's War.* London: Allen Lane, 1998.

Overy, Richard J. (with Andrew Wheatcroft). *The Road to War.* Revd and updated edn, London/New York: Penguin, 1999.

Overy, Richard J. *The Battle.* Harmondsworth: Penguin, 2000.

Overy, Richard. Review of Gabriel Gorodetsky. *Grand Delusion: Stalin and the German Invasion of Russia* (1999), *TLS*, 11 August 2000.

Pach, Chester J. and Elmo Richardson. *The Presidency of Dwight D. Eisenhower.* Lawrence, Kan.: University Press of Kansas, 1991.

Padfield, Peter. *Hess: Flight for the Führer.* London: Weidenfeld and Nicolson, 1991 (new edn, London: Cassell, 2001).

Parish, Michael E. 'Soviet Espionage and the Cold War', *Diplomatic History* 25/1 (2001), 105–20.

Parker, Robert A. C. (ed. in association with Correlli Barnett and Churchill College, Cambridge). *Winston Churchill: Studies in Statesmanship.* London: Brassey's, 1995.

Parker, Robert A.C. 'Churchill and Consensus' (review article), *Historical Journal* 39/2 (1996), 563–72.

Parker, Robert A.C. *Churchill and Appeasement.* Basingstoke: Macmillan, 2000.

Parmar, Inderjeet. *Special Interests, the State and the Anglo-American Alliance, 1939–1945.* London/Portland, Oreg.: Frank Cass, 1995.

Parmet, Herbert S. *Eisenhower and the American Crusades.* New York: Collier-Macmillan, 1972.

Payne, Robert. *The Rise and Fall of Stalin.* London: W.H. Allen, 1966.

Pearce, Robert. D. *Attlee.* Profiles in Power. London: Longman, 1997.

Peden, George. 'Robert Anthony Eden, First Earl of Avon', in Eccleshall, Robert R. and Graham Walker (eds). *Biographical Dictionary of British Prime Ministers.* London: Routledge, 1998, 315–20.

Pegg Carl, H. *Evolution of the European Idea, 1914–1932.* Chapel Hill, N.C./London: University of North Carolina Press, 1983.

Pelling, Henry. *The Labour Governments, 1945–51.* London: Macmillan Press, 1984.

Pelling, Henry. *Winston Churchill.* New York: Dutton, 1974 (2nd edn, Basingstoke, Hampshire: Macmillan, 1989).

Pelling, Henry. *Churchill's Peacetime Ministry, 1951–1955.* Basingstoke: Macmillan, 1997.

Percival, Mark. 'Churchill and Romania: The Myth of the October, 1944 "Betrayal"', *Contemporary British History* 12/3 (1998), 41–61.

Perlmutter, Amos. *FDR & Stalin: A Not So Grand Alliance, 1943–1945.* Columbia, Mo./London: University of Missouri Press, 1993.

Pernes, Jiří. 'Die politische und wirtschaftliche Krise in der Tschechoslowakei 1953 und Versuche ihrer Überwindung', in Kleßmann, Christoph and Bernd Stöver (eds), *1953 – Krisenjahr des Kalten Krieges in Europa.* Cologne: Böhlau, 1999, 98–111.

Perry, John Curtis and Konstantin Pleshakov. *The Flight of the Romanovs: A Family Saga.* New York: Basic Books, 1999.

Pierpaoli, Paul G. *Truman and Korea: The Political Culture of the Early Cold War.* Columbia, Mo.: University of Missouri Press, 1999.

Pietrow-Ennker, Bianka (ed.) *Präventivkrieg? Der deutsche Angriff auf die Sowjetunion.* 2nd edn, Frankfurt/M.: Fischer Taschenbuch Verlag, 2000.

Pilpel Robert, H. *Churchill in America, 1895–1961: An Affectionate Portrait.* London: New English Library, 1977.

Pimlott, Ben. 'The Myth of Consensus', in Smith, Lesley M. (ed.), *The Making of Britain: Echoes of Greatness.* London: Macmillan, 1988, 129–41.

Pimlott, Ben. *Harold Wilson.* London: HarperCollins, 1992.

Pinder, John. 'British Federalist 1940–1947: From Movement to Stasis', in Dumoulin, Michel (ed.), *Wartime Plans for Postwar Europe, 1940–1947.* Brussels: Nomos-Verlag, 1995, 247–74.

Pinette, Kaspar. *Albert Ballin und die deutsche Politik: Ein Beitrag zur Geschichte von Staat und Wirtschaft 1900–1918.* Hamburg: Hansischer Gildenverlag, 1938.

Pinkus, Benjamin. *The Soviet Government and the Jews, 1948–1967: A Documented Study.* Cambridge: Cambridge University Press, 1984.

Ponting, Clive. *Churchill.* London: Sinclair-Stevenson, 1994.

Ponting, Clive. 'Churchill and Europe: a Revision', in Bideleux, Robert and Richard Taylor (eds). *European Integration and Disintegration: East and West.* London: Routledge, 1996, 36–45.

Post, Jerold M. and Robins, Robert S. *When Illness Strikes the Leader: The Dilemma of the Captive King.* New Haven/London: Yale University Press, 1993.

Prados, John. 'Open Skies and Closed Minds: American Disarmament Policy at the Geneva Summit', in Bischof, Günter and Saki Dockrill (eds), *Cold War Respite: The Geneva Summit of 1955.* Baton Rouge, La.: Louisiana State University Press, 2000, 215–33.

Prior, Robin. *Churchill's 'World Crisis' as History.* London: Croom Helm, 1983.

Prowe, Diethelm. *Weltstadt in Krisen. Berlin 1949–1958.* Berlin/New York: Walter de Gruyter, 1973.

Pruden, Caroline. *Conditional Partners: Eisenhower, the United Nations and the Search for a Permanent Peace.* Baton Rouge: Louisiana State University Press, 1998.

Pruessen, Ronald W. *John Foster Dulles: The Road to Power.* New York: Free Press, 1982.

Pruessen, Ronald W. 'Beyond the Cold War – Again: 1955 and the 1990s', *Political Science Quarterly* 108/1 (1993), 59–84.

Pugh, Martin. *Lloyd George.* Profiles in Power. London: Longman, 1988.

Pütz, Alexandra. *'Aber ein Europa ohne Grossbritannien kann ich mir nicht vorstellen!' Die Englandpolitik der Ära Adenauer 1949–1963.* Bochum: Brockmeyer, 1996.

Radzinsky, Edvard. *Stalin: The First in-Depth Biography Based on Explosive New Documents from Russia's Secret Archives.* London: Hodder & Stoughton, 1996.

Rahman, H. *A British Defence Problem in the Middle East: The Failure of the 1946 Anglo-Egyptian Negotiations.* Reading: Ithaca Press, 1994.

Rainer, Janos M. 'Der neue Kurs in Ungarn 1953', in Kleßmann, Christoph and Bernd Stöver (eds), *1953 – Krisenjahr des Kalten Krieges in Europa*. Cologne: Böhlau, 1999, 71–92.

Ramsden, John. 'From Churchill to Heath', in Butler (Lord), Richard Austen (ed.). *The Conservatives: A History from their Origins to 1965*. London/Boston: George Allen & Unwin, 1977, 405–52.

Ramsden, John. *The Making of Conservative Party Policy: The Conservative Research Department since 1929*. London/New York: Longman, 1980, 405–52.

Ramsden, John. 'A Party for Owners or a Party for Earners? How far did the British Conservative Party really change after 1945?' *Transactions of the Royal Historical Society*, 5th series, Vol. XXXVII (1987), 49–63.

Ramsden, John. *The Age of Churchill and Eden, 1940–1957*. A History of the Conservative Party, Vol. 5. London: Longman, 1995.

Ramsden, John. 'Winston Churchill and the Leadership of the Conservative Party, 1940–51', *Contemporary Record* 9/1 (1995), 99–119.

Ramsden, John. '"That Will Depend on Who Writes the History": Winston Churchill as His Own Historian: An Inaugural Lecture Delivered by Professor John Ramsden on 22 October 1996'. London: Department of History Queen Mary and Westfield College, 1997.

Ramsden, John. 'How Winston Churchill Became the "Greatest Living Englishman"', *Contemporary British History* 12/3 (1998), 1–40.

Ramsden, John. *An Appetite for Power: A History of the Conservative Party since 1830*. London: Harper Collins, 1998.

Rapoport, Louis. *Stalin's War against the Jews: The Doctors' Plot and the Soviet Solution*. New York: Free Press, 1990.

Resis, Albert. 'The Churchill-Stalin Percentages Agreement', *American Historical Review* 82/2 (1978), 368–87.

Retallack, James. *Germany in the Age of Kaiser Wilhelm II*. Basingstoke: Macmillan, 1996.

'Rethinking Negotiations with Hitler', *New York Times* (Arts & Ideas Section), 25 January 2000.

Rexin, Manfred. 'Der 16. und 17. Juni 1953 in West Berlin', *Deutschland-Archiv* 26/8 (1993), 985–94.

Reynolds, David. *The Creation of the Anglo-American Alliance, 1937–1941: a Study in Competitive Cooperation*. Chapel Hill, N.C.: University of North Carolina Press, 1981.

Reynolds, David. 'Eden the Diplomatist, 1931–56: Suezide of a Statesman?' *History* 74 (1989), 64–84.

Reynolds, David. 'Roosevelt, Churchill, and the Wartime Anglo-American Alliance, 1941–45: Towards a New Synthesis', in Louis, William Roger and Hedley Bull (eds), *The 'Special Relationship': Anglo-American Relations since 1945*. Oxford/New York: Clarendon Press, 1989, 17–41.

Reynolds, David. *Britannia Overruled: Power and Policy in the Twentieth-Century World*. London: Longman, 1991 (new edn, 2000).

Reynolds, David, Warren F. Kimball and A.O. Chubarian (eds). *Allies at War: The Soviet, American, and British Experience, 1939–1945*. New York: St. Martin's Press, 1994.

Reynolds, David. *Rich Relations: The American Occupation of Britain, 1942–1945*. London: Harper Collins, 1995.

Reynolds, David. 'Churchill the Appeaser? Between, Hitler, Roosevelt and Stalin in World War Two', in Dockrill, Michael L. and Brian J.C. McKercher (eds), *Diplomacy and World Power: Studies in British Foreign Policy, 1890–1950*. Cambridge/New York: Cambridge University Press, 1996, ch. 10.

Reynolds, David. 'Churchill's Writing of History: Appeasement, Autobiography and "The Gathering Storm"', *Transactions of the Royal Historical Society*, 6th series, Vol. XI. Cambridge: Cambridge University Press, 2001, 221–47.

Rich, Paul. 'Visionary Ideas of European Unity after World War I', in Murray, Philomena and Paul Rich (eds), *Visions of European Unity*. Boulder, Col.: Westview Press, 1996, 21–37.

Richardson, Louise. *When Allies Differ: Anglo-American Relations During the Suez and Falklands Crises*. Basingstoke: Macmillan, 1996.

Richardson, Rosamond. *The Long Shadow: Inside Stalin's Family*. Paberback edn, London: Abacus, 1994 (first publ., 1993).

Richter, James G. 'Reexamining Soviet Policy towards Germany during the Beria Interregnum'. Working Paper, No. 3. Washington: Cold War International History Project (CWIHP), 1992.

Richter, James. 'Re-examining Soviet Policy towards Germany in 1953', *Europe-Asia Studies* 45/4 (1993), 671–91.

Richter, James G. *Khrushchev's Double Bind: International Pressures and Domestic Coalition Politics*. Baltimore, Md.: Johns Hopkins University Press, 1994.

Riklin, Alois. *Das Berlinproblem: Historisch-Politische und völkerrechtliche Darstellung des Viermächtestatus*. Cologne: Verlag Wissenschaft und Politik, 1964.

Rioux, Jean-Pierre. *The Fourth Republic, 1944–1958*. Cambridge: Cambridge University Press, 1987.

Ritter, Gerhard. *Der Schlieffenplan. Kritik eines Mythos*. Munich: R. Oldenbourg, 1956 (English transl.: *The Schlieffen Plan: Critique of a Myth*. Westport, Conn.: Greenwood Press, 1979).

Rizzo, Jean-Louis. *Mendès-France, ou, La Rénovation en Politique*. Paris: Presses de la Fondation nationale des sciences politiques, 1993.

Robbins, Keith. *Sir Edward Grey: A Biography of Lord Grey of Fallodon*. London: Cassell, 1971.

Robbins, Keith. *Churchill*. Harlow/New York: Longman, 1992.

Roberts, Andrew. *'The Holy Fox': A Biography of Lord Halifax*. London: Weidenfeld and Nicolson, 1991.

Roberts, Andrew. 'Churchill and the Revisionists', *History Today* (March, 1997).

Roberts, Brian. *Churchills in Africa*. London: Hamilton, 1970.

Robertson, A. H. *The Council of Europe : Its Structure, Functions and Achievements*. New York: Praeger, 1961 (first publ. London: Stevens, 1956).

Robertson, Alex J. *The Bleak Midwinter: 1947*. Manchester: Manchester University Press, 1987.

Robertson, David. *Sly and Able: A Political Biography of James F. Byrnes*. New York: W.W. Norton, 1994.

Röhl, John C.G. *The Kaiser and his Court: Wilhelm II and the Government of Germany* (transl. from the German by T.F. Cole). Cambridge: Cambridge University Press, 1987.

Roman, Peter J. *Eisenhower and the Missile Gap*. Ithaca, N.Y.: Cornell University Press, 1995.

Romero, Federico. 'U.S. Attitudes towards Integration and Interdependence: The 1950s', in Heller, Francis H. and John R. Gillingham (eds), *The United States and the Integration of Europe: Legacies of the Postwar Era*. London: Macmillan, 1996, 103–21.

Rosamond, Ben. *Theories of European Integration*. Basingstoke/New York: MacMillan/St. Martin's Press, 2000.

Rose, Norman. 'Churchill and Zionism', in Blake, Robert and William Roger Louis (eds), *Churchill*. Oxford/New York: Oxford University Press, 1993, 147–66.

Rose, Norman. *Churchill: An Unruly Life*. London/New York: Simon & Schuster, 1994.

Rosenberg, Jonathan. 'Before the Bomb and After: Winston Churchill and the Use of Force', in Gaddis, John Lewis, Philip H. Gorden, Ernest R. May and Jonathan Rosenberg (eds), *Cold War Statesmen Confront the Bomb : Nuclear Diplomacy since 1945*. New York: Oxford University Press, 1999, 171–93.

Roskill, Stephen W. *Churchill and the Admirals*. London: Collins, 1977.

Ross, Graham. 'Foreign Office Attitudes to the Soviet Union, 1941–45', *Journal of Contemporary History* 16 (1981), 521–40.

Rostow, Walt W. *Open Skies: Eisenhower's Proposal of July 21, 1955*. Austin, Tex.: University of Texas Press, 1982.

Rostow, Walter W. *Europe after Stalin: Eisenhower's Three Decisions of March 11, 1953*. Austin, Tex.: University of Texas Press, 1982.

Rothwell, Victor H. *Britain and the Cold War 1941–1947*. London: Cape, 1982.

Rothwell, Victor. *Anthony Eden: A Political Biography 1931–1957*. Manchester: Manchester University Press, 1992.

Rovere, Richard H. *The Eisenhower Years: Affairs of State*. New York: Farrar Straus & Cudahy, 1956.

Rovere, Richard H. *Senator Joe McCarthy*. London: Methuen, 1959.

Royal Institute of International Affairs, London (Chatham House): *Survey of International Affairs* (London: Oxford University Press): *1947–48* (by Peter Calvocoressi, with Sheila Harden, 1952); *1949–50* (by Peter Calvocoressi, with Sheila Harden, 1953); *1951* (by Peter Calvocoressi, with Konstanze Isepp, 1954); *1952* (by Peter Calvocoressi, with Konstanze Isepp, 1955); *1953* (by Peter Calvocoressi, with Coral Bell, 1956); *1954* (by Corall Bell, 1957); *1955–1956* (by Geoffrey Barraclough, 1960).

Ruane, Kevin. 'Anthony Eden, British Diplomacy and the Origins of the Geneva Conference of 1954', *Historical Journal* 37/1 (1994), 153–72.

Ruane, Kevin. 'Refusing to Pay the Price: British Foreign Policy and the Pursuit of Victory in Vietnam, 1952–54', *English Historical Review* 90/435 (1995), 70–92.

Ruane, Kevin. *The Rise and Fall of the European Defence Community: Anglo-American Relations and the Crisis of European Defence, 1950–55*. Basingstoke: Macmillan, 2000.

Rubin, Barry. *The Great Powers in the Middle East 1941–1947: The Road to the Cold War*. London: Frank Cass, 1980.

Ruddy, T. Michael. *The Cautious Diplomat: Charles E. Bohlen and the Soviet Union, 1929–1969*. Kent, Ohio/London: Kent State University Press, 1986.

Rupieper, Hermann-Josef. 'Die Berliner Außenministerkonferenz von 1954. Ein Höhepunkt der Ost-West-Propaganda oder die letzte Möglichkeit zur Schaffung der deutschen Einheit?' *Vierteljahrshefte für Zeitgeschichte* 34 (1986), 427–53.

Rupieper, Hermann-Josef. 'Wiedervereinigung und europäische Sicherheit. Deutsch-amerikanische Überlegungen für eine entmilitarisierte Zone in Europa 1953', *Militärgeschichtliche Mitteilungen* 39 (1986), 91–130.

Rupieper, Hermann-Josef. 'Deutsche Frage und europäische Sicherheit. Politisch-strategische Überlegungen 1953/55', in Thoß, Bruno and Volkmann, Hans-Erich (eds), *Zwischen Kaltem Krieg und Entspannung. Sicherheits- und Deutschlandpolitik der Bundesrepublik im Mächtesystem der Jahre 1953–1956.* Boppard: Boldt, 1988, 179–209.

Rupieper, Hermann-Josef. *Der besetzte Verbündete: die amerikanische Deutschlandpolitik 1949–1955.* Opladen: Westdeutscher Verlag, 1991.

Rusbridger, James, and Eric Nave. *Betrayal at Pearl Harbor: How Churchill Lured Roosevelt into World War II.* New York: Michael O'Mara, 1991.

Rush, Myron. *Political Succession in the U.S.S.R.* New York: Columbia University Press, 1965 (paperback edn, 1968).

Russell, Richard L. *George F. Kennan's Strategic Thought: The Making of an American Political Realist.* Westport, Conn.: Praeger, 1999.

Ryan, Henry Butterfield. 'A New Look at Churchill's "Iron Curtain" Speech', *Historical Journal* 22 (1979), 895–920.

Ryan, Henry Butterfield. *The Vision of Anglo-America: The US-UK Alliance and the Emerging Cold War, 1943–1946.* Cambridge: Cambridge University Press, 1987.

Sainsbury, Keith. *The Turning Point: Roosevelt, Stalin, Churchill, and Chiang-Kai-Shek, 1943. The Moscow, Cairo and Teheran Conferences.* London/Oxford: Oxford University Press, 1985.

Sainsbury, Keith. *Churchill and Roosevelt at War: The War They Fought and the Peace They Hoped to Make.* Basingstoke: Macmillan, 1994.

Sanders, David. *Losing an Empire, Finding a Role: An Introduction to British Foreign Policy since 1945.* Basingstoke: Macmillan, 1990.

Saunders, Frances S. *Who Paid the Piper? The CIA and the Cultural Cold War.* London: Granta Books, 1999.

Saville, John. *The Politics of Continuity: British Foreign Policy and the Labour Government, 1945–46.* London/New York: Verso, 1993.

Schapiro, Leonard Bertram. *The Communist Party of the Soviet Union.* Revd 2nd edn, London: Methuen, 1970.

Scheck, Raffael. *Alfred von Tirpitz and German Right-Wing Politics, 1914–1930.* Atlantic Highlands, N.J.: Humanities Press, 1998.

Scherstjanoi, Elke. '"In 14 Tagen werden Sie vielleicht schon keinen Staat mehr haben". Vladimir Semenov und der 17. Juni 1953', *Deutschland-Archiv* 31/6 (1998), 907–37.

Scherstjanoi, Elke. 'Die sowjetische Deutschlandpolitik nach Stalins Tod 1953. Neue Dokumente aus dem Archiv des Moskauer Außenministeriums', *Vierteljahrshefte für Zeitgeschichte* 46 (1998), 497–549.

Scheuer, Gernot. 'Materielle Voraussetzungen für eine Wiedervereinigung Deutschlands in der Sicht nichtamtlicher Vorschläge', *Europa-Archiv* 6 (1960), 177–92.

Schild, Georg. *Bretton Woods and Dumbarton Oaks: American Economic and Political Post-War Planning in the Summer of 1944.* Basingstoke: Macmillan, 1995.

Schlarp, Karl-Heinz. 'Alternativen zur deutschen Außenpolitik 1952–55. Karl-Georg Pfleiderer und die deutsche Frage', in Benz, Wolfgang and Hermann Graml (eds), *Aspekte deutscher Außenpolitik im 20. Jahrhundert.* Stuttgart: Deutsche Verlags-Anstalt, 1976, 211–48.

Schlesinger, Arthur M. Jr. 'History's Impressario'. Keynote address to the International Churchill Society, Boston, 28 October 1995 [http://www.winstonchurchill.org/p94rschles.htm].

Schlie, Ulrich. *Kein Friede mit Deutschland: Die geheimen Gespräche im Zweiten Weltkrieg 1939–1941.* Munich: Langen Müller, 1994.

Schmidt, Gustav (ed.). *Grossbritannien und Europa – Grossbritannien in Europa.* Bochum: Brockmeyer, 1989.

Schmidt, Rainer F. 'Der Hess-Flug und das Kabinett Churchill. Hitlers Stellvertreter im Kalkül der britischen Kriegsdiplomatie Mai-Juni 1941'. *Vierteljahrshefte für Zeitgeschichte* 42/1 (1994), 1–38.

Schmidt, Rainer F. *Rudolf Hess. 'Botengang eines Toren?' Der Flug nach Grossbritannien vom 10. Mai 1941.* Düsseldorf: Econ, 1997.

Schneer, Jonathan. 'Hopes Deferred or Shattered: The British Labour Left and the Third Force Movement, 1945–59', *Journal of Modern History* 59/2 (1984), 197–226.

Schöllgen, Gregor. *Imperialismus und Gleichgewicht. Deutschland, England und die orientalische Frage 1871–1914.* Munich: R. Oldenbourg, 1984.

Schöttli, Thomas U. *USA und EVG. Truman, Eisenhower und die Europa-Armee.* Bern: Peter Lang, 1994.

Schrecker, Ellen. *Many Are the Crimes: McCarthyism in America.* Boston/London: Little, Brown, 1998.

Schröder, Hans-Jürgen. 'USA und westdeutscher Wiederaufstieg (1945–52)', in Larres, Klaus and Torsten Oppelland (eds), *Deutschland und die USA im 20. Jahrhundert. Geschichte der politischen Beziehungen.* Darmstadt: Wissenschaftliche Buchgesellschaft, 1997, 95–118.

Schulzinger Robert, D. *A Time for War: The United States and Vietnam, 1941–1975.* New York: Oxford University Press, 1997.

Schwabe, Klaus. 'Adenauer und England', in Kettenacker, Lothar, Manfred Schlenke and Hellmut Seier (eds). *Studien zur Geschichte Englands und der deutsch-britischen Beziehungen.* Festschrift für Paul Kluke. Munich: W. Fink, 1981, 353–74.

Schwabe, Klaus. '"Ein Akt konstruktiver Staatskunst" – die USA und die Anfänge des Schuman-Plans', in Schwabe, Klaus (ed.). *The Beginnings of the Schuman-Plan: Contributions to the Symposium in Aachen, May 28–30, 1986.* Baden-Baden: Nomos, 1988, 211–40.

Schwartz, Thomas Alan. *America's Germany: John J. Mccloy and the Federal Republic of Germany.* Cambridge, Mass.: Harvard University Press, 1991.

Schwarz, Bill. 'The Tide of History. The Reconstruction of Conservatism, 1945–51', in Tiratsoo, Nick (ed.), *The Attlee Years.* London/New York: Pinter Publishers, 1991, 147–66.

Schwarz, Hans-Peter. *Die Ära Adenauer: Gründerjahre der Republik 1949–1957.* Geschichte der Bundesrepublik Deutschland, Vol. 2. Wiesbaden: Deutsche Verlags-Anstalt & Brockhaus, 1981 (new edn, 1994).

Schwarz, Hans-Peter. *Adenauer. Der Aufstieg 1876–1952.* 2nd edn, Stuttgart: Deutsche Verlags-Anstalt, 1986.

Schwarz, Hans-Peter. *Adenauer. Der Staatsmann 1952–1967.* Stuttgart: Deutsche Verlags-Anstalt, 1992.

Schwarz, Hans-Peter. 'Churchill and Adenauer', in Parker, Robert A. C. (ed.) *Winston Churchill: Studies in Statesmanship.* London: Brassey's, 1995, 172–82.

Scott, Len V. *Macmillan, Kennedy and the Cuban Missile Crisis: Political, Military and Intelligence Aspects.* Basingstoke: Macmillan, 1999.

Seldon, Anthony. *Churchill's Indian Summer: The Conservative Government, 1951–55.* London: Hodder & Stoughton, 1981.

Seldon, Anthony. 'The Churchill Administration, 1951–55', in Hennessy, Peter and Anthony Seldon (eds), *Ruling Performance: British Governments from Attlee to Thatcher.* Oxford/New York: Basil Blackwell, 1989, 63–97.

Seldon, Anthony and Stuart Ball (eds). *Conservative Century: The Conservative Party since 1900.* Oxford/New York: Oxford University Press, 1994.

Sethe, Paul. *Öffnung nach Osten. Weltpolitische Realitäten zwischen Bonn, Paris und Moskau.* Frankfurt/M.: Scheffler, 1966.

Seymour, Charles. *The Intimate Papers of Colonel House Arranged as a Narrative, Vol. 1: Behind the Political Curtain, 1912–1915.* London: Ernest Benn, 1926.

Sfikas, Thanasias D. *The British Labour Government and the Greek Civil War, 1945–1949: The Imperialism of Non-Intervention.* Keele: Ryburn Publishing, 1994.

Sfikas, Thanasis D. 'War and Peace in the Strategy of the Communist Party of Greece, 1945–1949', *Journal of Cold War Studies* 3/3 (2001), 5–30.

Shennan, Andrew. *The Fall of France, 1940.* Harlow, Essex/New York: Longman (Pearson Education), 2000.

Sherwood, Robert E. *Roosevelt and Hopkins: An Intimate History.* New York: Harper & Brothers, 1948.

Shlaim, Avi. 'Prelude to Downfall: The British Offer of Union to France, June 1940', *Journal of Contemporary History* 9/3 (1974), 27–63.

Shlaim, Avi. *Britain and the Origins of European Unity 1940–1951.* Reading: Graduate School of Contemporary European Studies, University of Reading, 1978.

Shlaim, Avi. *The United States and the Berlin Blockade, 1948–1949: A Study in Crisis Decision-Making.* Berkeley, Calif.: University of California Press, 1983.

Short, Anthony. *The Origins of the Vietnam War.* London/New York: Longman, 1989.

Siebenmorgen, Peter. *Gezeitenwechsel: Aufbruch zur Entspannungspolitik.* Bonn: Bouvier, 1990.

Siebert, Ferdinand. *Aristide Briand, 1862–1932: Ein Staatsmann zwischen Frankreich und Europa.* Zurich/Stuttgart: Eugen Rentsch, 1973.

Sissons, Michael and Philip French (eds). *Age of Austerity.* London: Hodder & Stoughton, 1963.

Skidelsky, Robert Jacob Alexander. *John Maynard Keynes, Vol. 2: The Economist as Saviour.* London: Macmillan, 1992.

Skidelsky, Robert Jacob Alexander. *Keynes.* Past Masters. Oxford; New York: Oxford University Press, 1996.

Slessor, John Cotesworth. *What Price Coexistence?* London: Cassell, 1962.

Smith, Arthur L. *Churchill's German Army: Wartime Strategy and Cold War Politics, 1943–1947*. Beverly Hills/London: Sage Publications, 1977.

Smith, Bradley. 'Sharing ULTRA in World War II', *International Journal of Intelligence and Counter-intelligence* 2 (1988), 59–72.

Smith, Bradley F. *Sharing Secrets with Stalin: How the Allies Traded Intelligence, 1941–1945*. Lawrence, Kan.: University Press of Kansas, 1996.

Smith, E. D. *Victory of a Sort: The British in Greece, 1941–46*. London: Robert Hale, 1988.

Smith, Michael L. 'Introduction: European Unity and the Second World War', in Smith, Michael L. and Peter M.R. Stirk (eds), *Making the New Europe: European Unity and the Second World War*. London/New York: Pinter Publishers, 1990.

Smith, Raymond. 'Ernest Bevin, British Officials and British Soviet Policy, 1945–47', in Deighton, Anne (ed.), *Britain and the First Cold War*. Basingstoke: Macmillan, 1990, 32–52.

Smith, Raymond and Zametica, John. 'The Cold Warrior: Attlee Reconsidered, 1945–47', *International Affairs* 61 (1985), 237–52.

Snow, Charles Percy. *Variety of Men*. London: Macmillan, 1967. Paperback edn, Harmondsworth: Penguin, 1969.

Snyder, W. 'Walter Bedell Smith. Eisenhower's Chief of Staff', *Military Affairs* 48 (1984), 6–14.

Soames, Mary. *Clementine Churchill*. London: Cassell, 1979.

Soapes, Thomas F. 'A Cold Warrior Seeks Peace: Eisenhower's Strategy for Nuclear Disarmament', *Diplomatic History* 4 (1980), 57–71.

Somin, Ilya. *Stillborn Crusade: The Tragic Failure of Western Intervention in the Russian Civil War, 1918–1920*. New Brunswick, N.J.: Transaction Publishers, 1996.

Spencer, R. 'Alliance Perceptions of the Soviet Threat, 1950–1988', in Schweitzer, Carl Christoph. *The Changing Western Analysis of the Soviet Threat*. London: Pinter Publishers, 1990, 9–48.

Spierenburg, Dirk, and Raymond Poidevin. *The History of the High Authority of the European Coal and Steel Community: Supranationality in Operation*. London: Weidenfeld and Nicolson, 1994.

Spinelli, Altiero. 'The Growth of the European Movement since the Second World War' (1957), repr. in Hodges, Michael (ed.), *European Integration: Selected Readings*. Harmondsworth: Penguin Books, 1972, 43–68.

Spinosa, A. *Churchill: Il nemico degli italiani* (Milan, 2001).

Spittmann, Ilse and Karl Wilhelm Fricke (eds), *17. Juni 1953. Arbeiteraufstand in der DDR*, 2nd edn, Cologne: Edition Deutschland Archiv, 1988.

Stafford, David. *Churchill and Secret Service*. London: John Murray, 1997.

Stafford, David. *Roosevelt and Churchill: Men of Secrets*. London: Little, Brown, 1999.

Stansky, Peter and Philip Wainright. 'Winston Leonard Spencer Churchill', in Eccleshall, Robert R. and Graham Walker (eds). *Biographical Dictionary of British Prime Ministers*. London: Routledge, 1998, 295–305.

Staritz, Dietrich. *Geschichte der DDR 1949–90*, revd edn, Darmstadt: Wissenschaftliche Buchgesellschaft, 1997.

Steinberg, Jonathan. *Tirpitz and the Birth of the German Battle Fleet: Yesterday's Deterrent*. London: Macdonald, 1968. New edn, Aldershot: Gregg Revivals, 1992.

Steinberg, Jonathan. 'The German Background to Anglo-German relations, 1905–1914,' in Hinsley, F.H. (ed.), *British Foreign Policy under Sir Edward Grey*. Cambridge: Cambridge University Press, 1977, 193–215.

Steinberg, Jonathan. 'Diplomatie als Wille und Vorstellung. Die Berliner Mission Lord Haldanes im Februar 1912,' in Schottelius, Herbert and Wilhelm Deist (eds), *Marine und Marinepolitik im kaiserlichen Deutschland, 1871–1914*, 2nd edn. Düsseldorf: Droste, 1981, 268–9.

Steinberg, Mark D. and Vladimir M. Khrustalev. *The Fall of the Romanovs: Political Dreams and Personal Struggles in a Time of Revolution* (Russian documents trans. by E. Tucker). New Haven/London: Yale University Press, 1995.

Steiner, Zara S. *The Foreign Office and Foreign Policy, 1898–1914*. Cambridge: Cambridge University Press, 1969.

Steiner, Zara S. *Britain and the Origins of the First World War*. London: Macmillan, 1977.

Steininger, Rolf. 'Ein vereintes, unabhängiges Deutschland? Winston Churchill, der Kalte Krieg und die deutsche Frage im Jahre 1953,' *Militärgeschichtliche Mitteilungen* 34 (1984), 105–44.

Steininger, Rolf. 'Das Scheitern der EVG und der Beitritt der Bundesrepublik zur NATO', *Aus Politik und Zeitgeschichte* B17 (27 April 1985), 3–18.

Steininger, Rolf. *The German Question: The Stalin Note of 1952 and the Problem of Reunification* (transl. from the German by M. Cioc). New York: Columbia University Press, 1990.

Steininger, Rolf. 'Deutsche Frage und Berliner Konferenz 1954', in Venohr, Wolfgang (ed.), *Ein Deutschland wird es sein*. Erlangen: Straube, 1990, 39–88.

Steininger, Rolf. '1955: The Austrian State Treaty and the German Question', *Diplomacy & Statecraft* 3/3 (1992), 494–522.

Steininger, Rolf. *Deutsche Geschichte seit 1945. Darstellungen und Dokumente in vier Bänden*, Vol. 2: *1948–1955*. Frankfurt/M.: Fischer Taschenbuch Verlag, 1996.

Steininger, Rolf. *Der Mauerbau. Die Westmächte und Adenauer in der Berlinkrise 1958–1963*. Munich: Olzog, 2001.

Stent, Angela. *From Embargo to Ostpolitik: The Political Economy of West German-Soviet Relations, 1955–1980*. Cambridge: Cambridge University Press, 1981.

Stephanson, Anders. *Kennan and the Art of Foreign Policy*. Cambridge, Mass.: Harvard University Press, 1989.

Stern, Fritz. *Einstein's German World*. London: Allen Lane the Penguin Press, 1999.

Stevenson, David. *Armaments and the Coming of War: Europe, 1904–1914*. Oxford: Oxford University Press, 1996.

Stevenson, Richard W. *The Rise and Fall of Détente: Relaxations of Tension in US-Soviet Relations, 1953–84*. Urbana, Ill.: University of Illinois Press, 1985.

Stewart, Graham. *Burying Caesar: Churchill, Chamberlain and the Battle for the Tory Party*. London: Weidenfeld and Nicolson, 1999.

Stirk, Peter M.R. 'Authoritarian and Nationalist Socialist Conceptions of Nation, State and Europe', in Stirk, Peter M.R. (ed.), *European Unity in Context: The Interwar Period*. London/New York: Pinter Publishers, 1989, 125–48.

Stirk, Peter M. R. *A History of European Integration since 1914*. London: Pinter, 1996.

Stirk, Peter, M. R. and David Weigall (eds). *The Origins and Development of European Integration: A Reader and Commentary*. Leicester/New York: Leicester University Press, 1992.

Stoler, Mark A. *The Politics of the Second Front: American Military Planning and Diplomacy in Coalition Warfare, 1941–1943*. Westport, Conn./London: Greenwood Press, 1977.

Stoler, Mark S. *Allies and Adversaries: The Joint Chiefs of Staff, the Grand Alliance, and US Strategy in World War Two*. Chapel Hill, N.C.: University of North Carolina Press, 2001.

Stone, I. F. *The Haunted Fifties*. London: Merlin, 1964.

Stourzh, Gerald. *Um Einheit und Freiheit: Staatsvertrag, Neutralität und das Ende der Ost-West-Besetzung Österreichs 1945–1955*. Revd 4th edn, Vienna: Böhlau, 1998.

Straub, Eberhard. *Albert Ballin. Der Reeder des Kaisers*. Berlin: Siedler Verlag, 2001.

Stubmann, Peter Franz. *Ballin. Leben und Werk eines deutschen Reeders*. Revd 2nd edn, Berlin: Klemm, 1927; revd and extended new edn, Hamburg: Christians, 1960.

Stueck, William Whitney. *The Korean War: An International History*. Princeton, N.J.: Princeton University Press, 1995.

Sweet, D.W. 'Great Britain and Germany, 1905–1911,' in Hinsley, F.H. (ed.), *British Foreign Policy under Sir Edward Grey*. Cambridge: Cambridge University Press, 1977, 216–35.

Talbott, Strobe. *The Master of the Game: Paul Nitze and the Nuclear Peace*. New York: Knopf, 1988.

Taubman, William, Sergei Khrushchev and Abbott Gleason (eds), *Nikita Khrushchev*. New Haven/London: Yale University Press, 2000.

Taylor, A. J. P. 'The Statesman', in A.J.P. Taylor et al., *Churchill: Four Faces and the Man*. London: Allen Lane, 1969, 9–51.

Taylor, A.J.P. *The Struggle for Mastery in Europe, 1848–1918*. Oxford: Clarendon Press, 1954, 1971.

Taylor, A.J.P. *The War Lords*. London: Hamilton, 1976; Harmondsworth: Penguin, 1978.

Terchek, Ronald. *The Making of the Test Ban Treaty*. The Hague: Martinus Nijhoff, 1970.

Terry, Sarah M. *Poland's Place in Europe: General Sikorski and the Origin of the Oder-Neisse Line, 1939–43*. Princeton, N.J.: Princeton University Press, 1983.

Theoharis Athan, G. *Seeds of Repression: Harry S. Truman and the Origins of McCarthyism*. Chicago: Quadrangle Books, 1971.

Thompson Kenneth, W. *Winston Churchill's World View: Statesmanship and Power*. Baton Rouge, La.: Louisiana State University Press, 1983.

Thorne Christopher, G. *The Approach of War, 1938–1939*. London: Macmillan, 1967.

Thornton, Richard C. *Odd Man Out: Truman, Stalin, Mao, and the Origin of the Korean War*. Washington, D.C.: Brassey's, 2000.

Thorpe, D. R. *Selwyn Lloyd*. London: Cape, 1989.

Thoß, Bruno. 'Modellfall Österreich? Der österreichische Staatsvertrag und die deutsche Frage 1954/55', in Thoß, Bruno and Hans-Erich Volkmann (eds), *Zwischen Kaltem Krieg und Entspannung. Sicherheits- und Deutschlandpolitik der Bundesrepublik im Mächtesystem der Jahre 1953–1956*. Boppard: Boldt, 1988, 93–136.

Thoß, Bruno. 'Die Lösung der Saarfrage 1954/55', *Vierteljahrshefte für Zeitgeschichte* 38 (1990), 225–88.

Thoß, Bruno. 'Sicherheits- und deutschlandpolitische Komponenten der europäischen Integration zwischen EVG und EWG, 1954–1957', in Herbst, Ludolf, Werner Bührer and Hanno Sowade (eds), *Vom Marshallplan zur EWG: Die Eingliederung der Bundesrepublik Deutschland in die westliche Welt*. Munich: R. Oldenbourg, 1990, 475–500.

Thürk, Harry. *Dien Bien Phu. Die Schlacht, die einen Kolonialkrieg beendete*. 3rd edn, Berlin: Brandenburgisches Verlagshaus, 1994.

Tilford, R.B. (ed.). *The Ostpolitik and Political Change in Germany*. Farnborough, Hants: Saxon House, 1975.

Tinguy, Anne, de. *U.S.-Soviet Relations during the Détente*. New York: East European Monographs/ Columbia University Press, 1999.

Tiratsoo, Nick (ed.), *From Blitz to Blair: A New History of Britain since 1939*. Paperback edn, London: Phoenix, 1998.

Tomlinson, Jim. *Democratic Socialism and Economic Policy: The Attlee Years, 1945–1951*. Cambridge/New York: Cambridge University Press, 1997.

Tomlinson, Jim. 'Reconstructing Britain: Labour in Power, 1945–1951', in Tiratsoo, Nick (ed.), *From Blitz to Blair: A New History of Britain since 1939*. Paperback edn, London: Phoenix, 1998, 77–101.

Tomlinson, Jim. 'The Attlee Government and the Balance of Payments, 1945–51', *Twentieth Century British History* 2/1 (1999), 47–66.

Trachtenberg, Marc. *A Constructed Peace: The Making of the European Settlement, 1945–1963*. Princeton, N.J./Chichester: Princeton University Press, 1999.

Tratt, Jacqueline. *The Macmillan Government and Europe: A Study in the Process of Policy Development*. New York: St. Martin's Press, 1996.

Turner, John. *Macmillan*. London: Longman, 1994.

Turner, John. 'A Land Fit for Tories to Live in: The Political Ecology of the British Conservative Party, 1944–1994', *Contemporary European History* 4/2 (1995), 189–208.

Turner, John. 'The British Conservative Party in the Twentieth Century: From Beginning to End?' *Contemporary European History* 8/2 (1999), 275–87.

Tusa, Ann and John Tusa. *The Berlin Blockade*. Dunton Green: Hodder & Stoughton, 1988.

Tyrell, Albrecht. *Grossbritannien und die Deutschlandplanung der Alliierten, 1941–1945*. Frankfurt am Main: Metzner, 1987.

Ulam, Adam B. *The Rivals: America and Russia since World War II*. New York: Viking, 1971.

Ulam, Adam Bruno. *Expansion and Co-Existence: Soviet Foreign Policy, 1917–73*. New York: Praeger, 1974.

Ullman, Richard H. *Anglo-Soviet Relations, 1917–1921*, 3 vols. Princeton, N.J.: Princeton University Press, 1961–8.

Ullmann, Hans-Peter. *Das deutsche Kaiserreich, 1871–1918*. Darmstadt: Wissenschaftliche Buchgesellschaft, 1997.

Ullrich, Volker. *Die nervöse Großmacht 1871–1918. Aufstieg und Untergang des deutschen Kaiserreichs*. Frankfurt/M.: Propyläen, 1999.

Urwin, Derek W. *The Community of Europe: A History of European Integration since 1945*. 2nd edn, London/New York: Longman, 1995.

Uschner, Manfred. *Die Ostpolitik der SPD. Sieg und Niederlage einer Strategie*. Berlin: Dietz, 1991.

Vogelsang, Thilo. 'Großbritanniens Politik zwischen Mendès-France und Adenauer im August/September 1954', in Blumenwitz, Dieter et al (eds), *Konrad Adenauer und seine Zeit: Politik und Persönlichkeit des Ersten Bundeskanzlers*. Vol. 2: Beiträge der Wissenschaft. Stuttgart: Deutsche Verlags-Anstalt, 1976, 37–52.

Volkmann, Hans-Erich and Walter Schwengler (eds). *Die Europäische Verteidigungsgemeinschaft: Stand und Probleme der Forschung*. Boppard am Rhein: Boldt, 1985.

Volkogonov, Dimitrii A. *Stalin: Triumph and Tragedy* (trans. from the Russian by H. Shukman). London/New York: Weidenfeld and Nicolson, 1991.

Wacket, Markus. 'Wir sprechen zur Zone. Die politischen Sendungen des RIAS in der Vorgeschichte der Juni-Erhebung 1953', *Deutschland-Archiv* 26/9 (1993), 1035–48.

Waley, David. 'Lend-Lease', in McNeill William Hardy. *America, Britain and Russia: Their Cooperation and Conflict, 1941–1946* (Royal Institute of International Affairs. Survey of International Affairs, 1939–1946, Vol. 3). London: Oxford University Press, 1953 (repr., 1970), 772–89.

Walker, J.S. '"No More Cold War": American Foreign Policy and the 1948 Soviet Peace Offensive', *Diplomatic History* 5 (1981), 75–91.

Wall, Irwin M. *The United States and the Making of Postwar France 1945–1954*. Cambridge: Cambridge University Press, 1991.

Wallace, Henry. 'Churchill's Crusade', *New Republic* 116 (13 January 1947), 22–3.

Wallin, Jeffrey D. *By Ships Alone: Churchill and the Dardanelles*. Durham, N.C.: Carolina Academic Press, 1981.

Walton Richard, J. *Henry Wallace, Harry Truman, and the Cold War*. New York: Viking, 1976.

Wandycz, Piotr Stefan. *Czechoslovak-Polish Confederation and the Great Powers, 1940–43*. Bloomington: Indiana University Press, 1956 (repr., Westport, Colo.: Greenwood Press, 1979).

Ward, Patricia D. *The Threat of Peace: James F. Byrnes and the Council of Foreign Ministers, 1945–1946*. Kent, Ohio: Kent State University Press, 1979.

Warner, Geoffrey. 'Die britische Labour-Regierung und die Einheit Westeuropas', *Vierteljahrshefte für Zeitgeschichte* 28 (1980), 310ff.

Warner, Geoffrey. 'The Labour Governments and the Unity of Europe, 1945–51', in Ovendale, Ritchie (ed.), *The Foreign Policy of the British Labour Governments, 1945–51*. Leicester: Leicester University Press, 1984.

Warner, Geoffrey. 'Ernest Bevin and British Foreign Policy, 1945–51', in Craig, Gordon A. and Francis L. Loewenheim (eds), *The Diplomats, 1939–1979*. Princeton, N.J.: Princeton University Press, 1994, 103–34.

Warner, Geoffrey. 'From Ally to Enemy: Britain's Relations with the Soviet Union, 1941–48', in Dockrill, Michael L. and Brian J.C. McKercher (eds), *Diplomacy and World Power: Studies in British Foreign Policy, 1890–1950*. Cambridge/New York: Cambridge University Press, 1996, 221–43.

Watt, Donald Cameron. 'Großbritannien und Europa 1951–1959. Die Jahre Konservativer Regierung', *Vierteljahrshefte für Zeitgeschichte* 28 (1980), 389–409.

Watt, Donald Cameron. 'Churchill und der Kalte Krieg', *Schweizer Monatshefte* 61/11 (1981) [Sonderbeilage. Zurich: Schweizerische Winston Churchill Stiftung].

Watt Donald, Cameron. *Succeeding John Bull: America in Britain's Place 1900–1975: A Study of the Anglo-American Relationship and World Politics in the Context of British and American Foreign-Policy Making in the Twentieth Century*. The Wiles Lectures Given at the Queen's University of Belfast. Cambridge: Cambridge University Press, 1984.

Watt, Donald Cameron. 'Die Konservative Regierung und die EVG', in Volkmann, Hans-Erich and Walter Schwengler (eds), *Die Europäische Verteidigungsgemeinschaft: Stand und Probleme der Forschung*. Boppard am Rhein: Boldt, 1985, 81–99.

Watt, Donald Cameron. 'Britain and the Historiography of the Yalta Conference and the Cold War', *Diplomatic History* 13/1 (1989), 67–98.

Watt, Donald Cameron. *How War Came: The Immediate Origins of the Second World War, 1938–1939*. London: Heinemann. Paperback edn, Mandarin, 1990 (Pimlico, 2001).

Weber, Hermann. *Die DDR, 1945–1990*. Grundriß der Geschichte. 3rd revd edn, Munich: R. Oldenbourg, 2000.

Weber, Hermann. *Geschichte der DDR*. Munich: Deutscher Taschenbuch Verlag, 1985 (2nd revd edn, 2000).

Weigall, David. 'British Ideas of European Unity and Regional Confederation in the Context of Anglo-Soviet Relations, 1941–45', in Smith, Michael L. and Peter M.R. Stirk (eds), *Making the New Europe: European Unity and the Second World War*. London/New York: Pinter Publishers, 1990, 156ff.

Weiler, Peter. *Ernest Bevin*. Manchester/New York: Manchester University Press, 1993.

Weiler, Peter. 'Britain and the First Cold War: Revisionist Beginnings', *Twentieth Century British History* 9/1 (1998), 127–38.

Weinberg, Gerhard L. *A World at Arms: A Global History of World War II*. Cambridge: Cambridge University Press, 1994.

Weinroth, Howard. 'The British Radicals and the Balance of Power, 1902–1914', *Historical Journal* 13 (1970), 653–82.

Weinroth, Howard. 'Left-Wing Opposition to Naval Armaments in Britain before 1914', *Journal of Contemporary History* 6/4 (1971), 93–120.

Weldes, Jutta. *Constructing National Interests: The United States and the Cuban Missile Crisis*. Minneapolis, Minn.: University of Minnesota Press, 1999.

Wenger, Andreas. *Living with Peril: Eisenhower, Kennedy, and Nuclear Weapons*. Lanham, Md./Oxford: Rowman & Littlefield, 1997.

Wettig, Gerhard. *Entmilitarisierung und Wiederbewaffnung in Deutschland 1943–1955: Internationale Auseinandersetzungen um die Rolle der Deutschen in Europa*. Munich: R. Oldenbourg, 1967.

Wettig, Gerhard. 'Zum Stand der Forschung über Berijas Deutschland-Politik im Frühjahr 1953', *Deutschland-Archiv* 4/26 (1993), 674–82.

Wettig, Gerhard. 'Neue Erkenntnisse über Berijas Deutschland-Politik', *Deutschland-Archiv* 12/26 (1993), 1412–13.

Wettig, Gerhard. 'Stalin and German Reunification: Archival Evidence on Soviet Foreign Policy in Spring 1952', *Historical Journal* 37/2 (1994), 411–19.

Wettig, Gerhard. 'Die beginnende Umorientierung der sowjetischen Deutschland-Politik im Frühjahr und Sommer 1953', *Deutschland-Archiv* 28/5 (1995), 495–507.

Wettig, Gerhard. 'Berijas deutsche Pläne im Licht neuer Quellen', in Kleßmann, Christoph and Bernd Stöver (eds), *1953 – Krisenjahr des Kalten Krieges in Europa*. Cologne: Böhlau, 1999, 49–69.

Wettig, Gerhard. *Bereitschaft zur Einheit in Freiheit? Die sowjetische Deutschland-Politik 1945–1955.* Munich: Olzog, 1999.

Wheeler-Bennett, John Wheeler and Anthony Nicholls. *The Semblance of Peace: The Political Settlement after the Second World War.* New York/London: St. Martin's Press, 1972.

Whelan, Richard. *Drawing the Line: The Korean War, 1950–1953.* London: Faber and Faber, 1990.

White, Brian. *Britain, Détente, and Changing East-West Relations.* London: Routledge, 1992.

White, Mark J. *The Cuban Missile Crisis.* Basingstoke: Macmillan, 1996.

White, Ralph. 'The Europeanism of Coudenhove-Kalergi', in Stirk, Peter M. R. (ed.), *European Unity in Context: The Interwar Period.* London/New York: Pinter Publishers, 1989, 23–40.

Wiborg, Susanne. *Albert Ballin.* Hamburg: Ellert & Richter, 2000.

Wiggershaus, Norbert. 'Bedrohungsvorstellungen Bundeskanzler Adenauers nach Ausbruch des Korea-Krieges', *Militärgeschichtliche Mitteilungen* 25 (1979), 79–122.

Wiggershaus, Norbert. 'Aspekte westdeutscher Bedrohungsperzeptionen 1946–1959', in Rohwer, Jürgen (ed.), *Feindbilder und Militärstrategien seit 1945.* Bremen: Edition Temmen, 1992, 50–85.

Wilford, Richard A. 'The Federal Union Campaign', *European Studies Review* 10 (1980), 101–14.

Wilkens, Andreas. *Der Unstete Nachbar: Frankreich, die deutsche Ostpolitik und die Berliner Vier-Mächte-Verhandlungen 1969–1974.* Munich: R. Oldenbourg, 1990.

Willetts, David. *Modern Conservatism.* London: Penguin, 1992.

Williams, Charles. *Adenauer: The Father of the New Germany.* London: Little, Brown, 2000.

Williams, Joyce G. *Colonel House and Sir Edward Grey: A Study in Anglo-American Diplomacy.* Lanham, Md.: University Press of America, 1984.

Williamson, Samuel R. *The Politics of Grand Strategy: Britain and France Prepare for War, 1904–1914.* Cambridge, Mass.: Harvard University Press, 1969.

Wilson, Keith M. *The Policy of the Entente: Essays on the Determinants of British Foreign Policy 1904–1914.* Cambridge: Cambridge Unversity Press, 1985.

Wilson, Keith M. 'The Agadir Crisis, the Mansion House Speech, and the Double-Edgedness of Agreements', *Historical Journal* 15/3 (1972), 513–32.

Wilson, Peter. 'The New Europe Debate in Wartime Britain', in Murray, Philomena and Paul Rich (eds), *Visions of European Unity.* Boulder, Col.: Westview Press, 1996, 39–62.

Wilson, Theodore A. *The First Summit: Roosevelt and Churchill at Placentia Bay, 1941.* Boston, Mass.: Houghton-Mifflin, 1969 (revd edn, Lawrence, Kan.: University Press of Kansas, 1991).

Wilson, Thomas. *Churchill and the Prof.* London: Casssell, 1995.

Winand, Pascaline. *Eisenhower, Kennedy, and the United States of Europe.* London: Macmillan, 1993.

Winzen, P. *Bülows Weltmachtkonzept. Untersuchungen zur Frühphase seiner Außenpolitik, 1897–1901.* Boppard: Boldt, 1977.

Wittlin, Theodor. *Commissar: The Life and Death of Lavrenty Pavlovich Beria.* New York/London: Macmillan, 1972.

Wood, Ian S. *Churchill.* Basingstoke: Macmillan, 2000.

Woods, Frederick. *Young Winston's Wars: The Original Despatches of Winston S. Churchill, War Correspondent 1897–1900.* London: Leo Cooper, 1972.

Woods, Randall Bennett. *A Changing of the Guard: Anglo-American Relations, 1941–1946.* Chapel Hill, N.C./London: University of North Carolina Press, 1990.

Woodward, Llewellyn. *British Foreign Policy in the Second World War* [in one volume]. London: H.M.S.O., 1962.

Woodward, Llewellyn E. *Great Britain and the German Navy.* Oxford: Clarendon Press, 1935; London: Cass, 1965.

Woodward, Llewellyn. *British Foreign Policy in the Second World War.* History of the Second World War. 5 vols. London: H.M.S.O., 1976.

Wurm, Clemens (ed.). *Western Europe and Germany: The Beginning of European Integration.* Oxford: Berg, 1995.

Yergin, Daniel. *Shattered Peace: The Origins of the Cold War and the National Security State.* Boston: Houghton Mifflin, 1977.

Young, Hugo. *This Blessed Plot: Britain and Europe from Churchill to Blair.* London: Macmillan, 1998.

Young, John W. 'Churchill's "No" to Europe: The "Rejection" of European Union by Churchill's Postwar Government, 1951–52', *Historical Journal* 28 (1985), 923–37.

Young, John W. 'Churchill, the Russians and the Western Alliance: The Three-Power Conference at Bermuda, December 1953', *English Historical Review* 101 (1986), 889–912.

Young, John W. (ed.). *The Foreign Policy of Churchill's Peacetime Administration, 1951–1955.* Leicester: Leicester University Press, 1988.

Young, John W. 'Cold War and Détente with Moscow', in Young, John W. (ed.), *The Foreign Policy of Churchill's Peacetime Administration, 1951–1955.* Leicester: Leicester University Press, 1988, 55–80.

Young, John W. 'German Rearmament and the European Defence Community', in Young, John W. (ed.), *The Foreign Policy of Churchill's Peacetime Administration, 1951–1955.* Leicester: Leicester University Press, 1988, 81–107.

Young, John W. 'Churchill's Bid for Peace with Moscow, 1954', *History* 73 (1988), 425–48.

Young, John W. *France, the Cold War and the Western Alliance, 1944–49: French Foreign Policy and Post-War Europe.* Leicester: Leicester University Press, 1990.

Young, John W. *Winston Churchill's Last Campaign: Britain and the Cold War, 1951–5.* Oxford: Clarendon Press, 1996.

Young, John W. 'Winston Churchill's Peacetime Administration and the Relaxation of East–West Trade Controls, 1953–54', *Diplomacy & Statecraft* 7/1 (1996), 125–40.

Young, John W. *Britain and European Unity, 1945–1992.* Basingstoke: Macmillan, 1993 (new edn, 2000).

Young, John W. 'The Geneva Conference of Foreign Ministers, October–November 1955: The Acid Test of Détente', in Bischof, Günter and Saki Dockrill (eds), *Cold War Respite: The Geneva Summit of 1955.* Baton Rouge, La.: Louisiana State University Press, 2000, 271–91.

Young, John W. 'Churchill and East-West Détente', *Transactions of the Royal Historical Society,* 6th series, Vol. XI. Cambridge: Cambridge University Press, 2001, 373–92.

Yurechko, John Josef. 'The Day Stalin Died: American Plans for Exploiting the Soviet Succession Crisis of 1953', *Journal of Strategic Studies* 13/1 (1990), 44–73.

Zarusky, Jürgen (ed.). *Die Stalin-Note vom 10. März 1952. Neue Quellen und Analysen.* Munich: Oldenbourg Verlag, 2002.

Zeeman, Bert. 'Britain and the Cold War: An Alternative Approach. The Treaty of Dunkirk Example', *European History Quarterly* 16/3 (1986), 343–67.

Zeiler, Thomas W. 'Managing Protectionism: American Trade Policy in the Early Cold War', *Diplomatic History* 22/3 (1998), 337–60.

Zelikow, Philip and Condoleezza Rice. *Germany Unified and Europe Transformed: A Study in Statecraft.* Cambridge, Mass.: Harvard University Press, 1995.

Ziegler, Philip. 'Churchill and the Monarchy', in Blake, Robert and William Roger Louis (eds), *Churchill.* Oxford/New York: Oxford University Press, 1993, 187–98.

Zubok, Vladislav M. 'Soviet Intelligence and the Cold War: The "Small" Committee of Information, 1952–53', Working Paper, No.4. Washington: Cold War International History Project (CWIHP), 1992.

Zubok, Vladislav M. 'Soviet Intelligence and the Cold War: The "Small" Committee of Information, 1952–53', *Diplomatic History* 19/3 (1995), 453–72.

Zubok, Vladislav M., and Konstantin Pleshakov. *Inside the Kremlin's Cold War: From Stalin to Khrushchev.* Cambridge, Mass.: Harvard University Press, 1996.

Zubok, Vladislav. '"Unverfroren und grob in der Deutschlandfrage..." Berija, der Nachfolgestreit nach Stalins Tod und die Moskauer DDR-Debatte im April-Mai 1953', in Kleßmann, Christoph and Bernd Stöver (eds), *1953 – Krisenjahr des Kalten Krieges in Europa.* Cologne: Böhlau, 1999, 29–48.

Zubok, Vladislav M. 'Soviet Policy Aims at the Geneva Conference, 1955', in Bischof, Günter and Saki Dockrill (eds), *Cold War Respite: The Geneva Summit of 1955.* Baton Rouge, La.: Louisiana State University Press, 2000, 55–74.

Zubok, Vladislav M. 'The Case of a Divided Germany', in Taubman, William, Sergei Khrushchev and Abbott Gleason (eds), *Nikita Khrushchev.* New Haven/London: Yale University Press, 2000, 275–300.

Zurcher, Arnold John. *The Struggle to Unite Europe 1940–1958: An Historical Account of the Development of the Contemporary European Movement from Its Origin in the Pan-European Union to the Drafting of the Treaties for Euratom and the European Common Market.* Westport, Conn.: Greenwood Press, 1975 (first publ., New York University Press, 1958).

Zweiniger-Bargielowska, Ina. 'Rationing, Austerity and the Conservative Recovery after 1945', *Historical Journal* 37/1 (1994), 173–95.

Zweiniger-Bargielowska, Ina. *Austerity in Britain: Rationing, Controls, and Consumption, 1939–1955.* Oxford: Oxford University Press, 2000.

Index